Pat Keenan

*I understand, sir, there is no one else
ready to perform this business?*

Nathan Hale, Act II

PROSE
AND
POETRY
OF AMERICA

EDITED BY
H. WARD McGRAW, A.M

REVISED BY
JULIAN L. MALINE, S.J., Ph.D.
AND
WILLIAM J. McGUCKEN, S.J., Ph.D.

ILLUSTRATED BY
GUY BROWN WISER

THE · L · W · SINGER · COMPANY
SYRACUSE   CHICAGO   DALLAS

THE NEW PROSE AND POETRY SERIES

PROSE AND POETRY
FOR ENJOYMENT

PROSE AND POETRY
FOR APPRECIATION

PROSE AND POETRY
OF AMERICA

PROSE AND POETRY
OF ENGLAND

10–42

Printed in the United States of America
10232.5

CONTRIBUTING EDITORS

SARAH HEYWORTH BARBER, M.A.

Formerly Supervisor Speech Development
Public Schools, Omaha, Nebraska
Head of the English Department
High School, Peru, New York

HARRIET MARCELIA LUCAS, A.B.

English Department, South High School
Minneapolis, Minnesota

EUGENE F. MANGOLD, S.J., A.M.

English Department, St. Xavier High School
Cincinnati, Ohio

FLORETTE McNEESE, M.A.

Chairman, Oklahoma State Syllabus Committee on English
Director of English, Classen High School
Oklahoma City, Oklahoma

SARAH E. SIMONS, M.A.

Author, *American Literature through Illustrative Readings*
Head of the English Department, Junior-Senior
High Schools, Washington, D. C.

EMILY EVELETH SNYDER, A.B.

English Department, Little Falls High School
Little Falls, New York

DONALD MacLEAN TOWER, Ph.D.

Author, *Educational Dramatics*
Formerly Director of Curriculum, Public Schools
Binghamton, New York
Superintendent, Rye Neck Public Schools
Mamaroneck, New York

For helpful counsel and suggestions, thanks are extended to
Dora V. Smith, Ph.D., University of Minnesota,
Minneapolis, Minnesota, specialist in English of the
National Survey of Secondary Education

ACKNOWLEDGMENTS

For the courteous permission to use the following selections, grateful acknowledgment and thanks are extended to the following authors, publishers, and periodicals.

The America Press: selections from *An American Woman* by the Reverend Leonard Feeney, S.J.

D. Appleton-Century Company: "As One Finding Peace" from *Penelope*, by Sister Mary Madeleva, C.S.C.

Walter H. Baker Company: *Nathan Hale* by Clyde Fitch; copyright 1899 by Robert Howard Russell, copyright renewal 1927 by Richard W. Fitch, and reprinted by permission of and by special arrangement with Robert W. Fitch and Walter H. Baker Company.

The Bobbs-Merrill Company: "When the Frost Is on the Punkin" from *Neighborly Poems*, by James Whitcomb Riley, copyright 1891 and 1919; "A Parting Guest" from *Morning*, by James Whitcomb Riley, copyright 1907. Used by special permission of the publishers, The Bobbs-Merrill Company.

Brandt & Brandt: "God's World" from *Renascence*, published by Harper & Brothers, copyright 1917 by Edna St. Vincent Millay; "Travel" from *Second April*, published by Harper & Brothers, copyright 1921 by Edna St. Vincent Millay; "Portrait of a Boy" from *Ballads and Poems*, published by Doubleday, Doran & Company, copyright 1918, 1920, 1923, 1925, 1929, 1930, 1931, by Stephen Vincent Benét; "Mary Smith" from *The Fascinating Stranger and Other Stories*, by Booth Tarkington, copyright 1913 by Doubleday, Page & Company, reprinted by permission of the author.

The Bruce Publishing Company: "False Trails" from *Boscobel*, by the Reverend James J. Daly, S.J.; "Some Letters of Joyce Kilmer" from *A Cheerful Ascetic*, by the Reverend James J. Daly, S.J.; "True Liberty" from *Freedom under God*, by the Right Reverend Monsignor Fulton J. Sheen.

The Dial Press: "Willa Cather's Masterpiece" from *Catholicism and the Modern Mind*, by Michael Williams.

Dodd, Mead & Company, Inc.: "The People Next Door" from *Imaginary Obligations*, by Frank Moore Colby, copyright 1904, 1932, by Dodd, Mead & Company, Inc.; "A Vagabond Song" and "An April Morning" by Bliss Carman; "At the Crossroads" and "Sea Gypsy" by Richard Hovey.

Doubleday, Doran & Company, Inc.: "Leaves out of My Thrill-Book" from *Stickfuls*, by Irvin S. Cobb, copyright 1923 by Doubleday, Doran & Company, Inc.; "Christmas" from *Candles That Burn*, by Aline Kilmer, copyright 1919, by Doubleday, Doran & Company, Inc.; "As Winds That Blow against a Star," "Martin" and "Trees," from *Trees and Other Poems*, by Joyce Kilmer, copyright 1914, by Doubleday, Doran & Company, Inc.; "Blue Valentine" from *Main Street and Other Poems*, by Joyce Kilmer, copyright

iv

1917, by Doubleday, Doran & Company, Inc.; "Prayer of a Soldier in France" and "Rouge Bouquet" from *Poems, Essays, and Letters*, Vol. I, and "Holy Ireland" from *Poems, Essays, and Letters*, Vol. II, by Joyce Kilmer, copyright 1914, 1917, 1918, by Doubleday, Doran & Company, Inc.; "On Unanswering Letters" from *Mince Pie*, by Christopher Morley, copyright 1919, by Doubleday, Doran & Company, Inc.; "The Last Leaf" from *The Trimmed Lamp*, by O. Henry, copyright 1905, by Doubleday, Doran & Company, Inc.; "The Diary" from *Junípero Serra*, by Agnes Repplier, copyright 1933, reprinted by permission of Doubleday, Doran & Company, Inc.; selections from *Count Luckner, the Sea Devil*, by Lowell Thomas, copyright 1927, by Doubleday, Doran & Company, Inc.

E. P. Dutton & Co., Inc.: "Deserted" from *The Vale of Tempe*, by Madison Cawein.

Farrar & Rinehart, Inc.: "Old Saul" and "Tears" from *The Selected Poems* of Lizette Woodworth Reese, copyright 1926; "The Mountain Woman" from *Skylines and Horizons*, copyright by Dubose Heyward, author. Reprinted by permission of the publishers, Farrar & Rinehart, Inc.

Samuel French, Inc.: "Moonshine" by Arthur Hopkins.

Hamlin Garland: "The Return of a Private."

The Reverend James M. Gillis, C.S.P.: "The Discipline of the Secret" from *This Our Day*, reprinted by permission of The Paulist Press from *The Catholic World*.

Harcourt, Brace and Company, Inc.: "Da Younga 'Merican" from *Canzoni*, by T. A. Daly; "Factories" from *Factories and Other Poems*, by Margaret Widdemer; "The Fifty-First Dragon" from *Seeing Things at Night*, by Heywood Broun, copyright 1921. By permission of Harcourt, Brace and Company, Inc., publishers.

Harper & Brothers: "Hills" from *The Mirthful Lyre*, by Arthur Guiterman; "Jogues, an American Martyr" from *Saints among Savages*, by the Reverend Francis X. Talbot, S.J.; "The Canvasser's Tale" from *Tom Sawyer Abroad and Other Essays*, by Mark Twain; selections from *Life on the Mississippi*, by Mark Twain.

Esther La Rose Harris: "Mr. Rabbit Nibbles Up the Butter" by Joel Chandler Harris.

Henry Harrison: "Junípero Serra," by Annette McCarty from *California Poets*.

Henry Holt & Company: "Prayers of Steel" from *Cornhuskers*, by Carl Sandburg; "Mending Wall" from *North of Boston*, by Robert Frost; "Stopping by Woods on a Snowy Evening" and "The Runaway" from *New Hampshire*, by Robert Frost; "Birches" from *Mountain Interval*, by Robert Frost.

Houghton Mifflin Company: "Love on the Bon-Dieu" from *Bayou-Folk*, by Kate Chopin; "Nam Semen Est Verbum Dei" from *Happy Ending*, by Louise Imogen Guiney; "A Kitten" from *In the Dozy Hours*, by Agnes Repplier; the selections from John Burroughs, Amy Lowell, and Edward Rowland Sill, also used by permission of and by arrangement with Houghton Mifflin Company.

Sister Mary Jeremy, O.P.: "The Departure," reprinted from *Poetry*, a Magazine of Verse.

Sister Julie, O.P.: "Snow White" reprinted by permission of *The Ave Maria*.

Blanche Mary Kelly: "The Housewife's Prayer" from *The Valley of Vision*.

P. J. Kenedy & Sons: "Eulogy on George Washington" from *Eulogy on*

George Washington, by Archbishop John Carroll, with selections from the Foreword, by the Right Reverend Monsignor Peter Guilday; "The Conquered Banner" by the Reverend Abram J. Ryan.

Albert A. Knopf, Inc.: "Sea Lullaby" and "Atavism" from *Collected Poems,* by Elinor Wylie; "A Farmer Remembers Lincoln" by Witter Bynner. By permission of and special arrangement with Alfred A. Knopf, publishers.

Little, Brown & Company: "I Never Saw a Moor," "A Day," "The Railway Train," "A Book," and "I'm Nobody" from *The Poems of Emily Dickinson,* Centenary Edition, edited by Martha Dickinson Bianchi and Alfred Leete Hampson; "Furnace and I" from *The Comforts of Home,* by Ralph Bergengren, copyright 1918 by The Atlantic Monthly Press, Inc.; "Poor Aubrey" by George Kelly. Reprinted by permission of Little, Brown & Company.

Liveright Publishing Corporation: "He Whom a Dream Hath Possessed" by Shaemas O'Sheel.

Longmans, Green & Company: "Questionnaire" from *Rime of the Rood,* by the Reverend Charles L. O'Donnell, C.S.C.

The Macmillan Company: "The Congo" and "Abraham Lincoln Walks at Midnight" from *Collected Poems,* by Vachel Lindsay; "Laudate Pueri Dominum" from *Now There Is Beauty,* by Sister M. Thérèse, Sor. D.S.; "Woven of the Sky" from *Woven of the Sky,* by Sister Miriam, R.S.M.; "Barter" and "Night Song at Amalfi" from *Love Songs,* by Sara Teasdale; "A Chant Out-of-Doors" from *Bluestone,* by Marguerite Wilkinson.

Sister Mary Madeleva, C.S.C.: "Communion" from *A Question of Lovers.*

Edwin Markham: "The Man with the Hoe" and "Lincoln, the Man of the People."

Edgar Lee Masters: "Silence."

Mrs. Joaquin Miller: "Kit Carson's Ride" and "The Defense of the Alamo" by Joaquin Miller.

Schwartz, Kirwin & Fauss: "The Meaning of Literature" from *Religion and the Study of Literature,* by Brother Leo, F.S.C.

Sister Mary St. Virginia, B.V.M.: "To Catherine," from the *Commonweal.*

Charles Scribner's Sons: "Zenobia's Infidelity" from *Short Sixes,* by Henry Cuyler Bunner; "Jean-Ah Poquelin" from *Old Creole Days,* by George Washington Cable; "Echo o' the Morn" from *Gloucestermen,* by James B. Connolly; "Little Boy Blue" and "Seein' Things" by Eugene Field; "Ballad of Trees and the Master" and "Marshes of Glynn" by Sidney Lanier; "Miniver Cheevy," "An Old Story," and "Richard Cory" by Edwin Arlington Robinson; "I Have a Rendezvous with Death" by Alan Seeger.

Sister Maris Stella, C.S.J.: "For a Picture of Saint Catherine" from *Here Only a Dove,* by Sister Maris Stella, C.S.J.

Yale University Press: "The Falconer of God" by William Rose Benét.

Anzia Yezierska: "The Fat of the Land."

PREFACE

A New Approach to Literature Study

One of the tendencies in the so-called "new education" is a different approach to the study of literature. Traditionally, high school literature courses have emphasized the teaching of the classics, with a method of approach not very different from the translation of foreign masterpieces. The selection, whatever its type, was read slowly and painfully, was completely dissected, and practically paraphrased line by line. The objective evidently was the mastery of the factual material of the piece plus a mastery of analysis of the author's particular technique. More recently the objective seems to be first a genuine love of reading on the part of the pupil, and secondly, the broadening and enriching of his life through the experiences and thoughts of literary characters. The growing emphasis on reading as one of the natural activities for worthy use of leisure has made the change in approach necessary.

The Function of a Key Book

Advocates of both intensive and extensive reading programs have long clashed in their notions of relative values of the two general plans. A middle ground resulting in a less detailed reading of a few typical selections, followed by wide reading of similar pieces of the same type seems to be the preferred procedure. In order to carry out a literature program of this type, well-chosen selections for intensive study, or reading "in common," must be made available in convenient form. Carefully prepared, yet broad lists of suggestions for the follow-up extensive reading activities must also be accessible to the pupil in planning his own reading, and to the teacher in making suggestions.

The New PROSE AND POETRY series offers exactly this plan of organization. Type selections are included in each volume for intensive study. Carefully prepared background material and study suggestions are provided for the purpose of giving direction and assistance in the detailed analyses of the respective selections. Extensive lists of suggestions for outside reading follow each section.

Arrangement by Types

By the time the student has reached the senior high school level, his experience in exploratory reading of wide variety will have revealed to him that literature is divided naturally into types. His use of the library which has been encouraged throughout the earlier years of school, has acquainted him with library classification which is first of all by types. Hence, the type arrangement as followed in the PROSE AND POETRY books is the natural approach to literature study. It further provides a simple, direct organization not possible when all types of literature are intermingled, and an arrangement which lends itself readily to the unit system of teaching.

A further important advantage of type arrangement is that each type of literature receives its due emphasis, and none is neglected or overlooked. Hitherto, it has been the tendency in most anthologies to overemphasize one or two types, notably poetry and Shakespearean drama, and to underemphasize, or completely overlook, other important types. Biography, especially, has received little, if any, treatment in the past, and modern drama and the essay have also been neglected.

But even in the type arrangement it seems unwise to become too detailed in analysis and classification. Introductory work on types of literature is usually most effective if presented from the point of view of assisting students to master difficulties which they encounter in learning to read and enjoy the type in question, rather than from the point of view of literary classification and technique. Such a plan is followed in the PROSE AND POETRY books.

The History of Literature

The literary selections which the pupil will have read by the time he reaches senior high school cover a wide range in both time and type, but the student who has read only detached selections is not likely to have formed any idea of the continuity of literature nor to have seen much relationship between it and the development of the race. It is, therefore, the purpose of the literary history presented in the PROSE AND POETRY books to give the connected facts in the story and to show, as well as space permits, the influences which have been at work in the shaping of our literature.

In the past, the collegiate technique of teaching history of literature by chronological arrangement has been extended downward into the high school. The result has been a high school presentation which has been on the college level. Historical and political events have received more attention than the literature itself and the result has been to make literature study a task rather than a pleasure for the pupil.

The editors of the PROSE AND POETRY books believe that history of literature can be so presented to high school pupils that it becomes a fascinating story which reveals and interprets those influences which have produced great writing. In their presentation of the history of literature they have reduced political facts to a minimum and have given chief attention to showing the spirit and temper of the various literary periods and to interpreting literature in the light of daily living. The result is a narrative account, written from the point of view of high school students. The biographies of the authors have been written in interesting story form with emphasis on personality rather than on mere historical data.

When regional influences have markedly affected literature, as in various periods of American literature, recognition of these influences has been made. Regional treatment of the short story and of poetry emphasizes the influences that have been at work in the various sections such as the South, the West, and the East, and of the literature of these sections as the result of local conditions and environment.

Again, the arrangement by type is advantageous for it aids in the study of literary history. The history of each type of literature is developed naturally through each of the literary periods and the pupil is not confused by a study of all types within one period. Furthermore, the study of each successive type provides a form of review of the general characteristics of each literary period so that by the time the book has been completed the pupil has a very clear and definite picture of each of the periods and of the influences which have been at work in the shaping of our literature. Only a brief summary and review which may be given at the end of the year is necessary to place the whole story of literature in brief, concise form before the pupil.

Study Features

Just as the pupil has learned that literature falls naturally into types and that it reflects biographical incidents of authors, so also has he become aware of the fact that there is such a thing as technical skill. In the PROSE AND POETRY books are to be found carefully prepared study features which will aid the pupil in an appreciation of technical skill and of the reasons why the writers represented have achieved their places in the literary world.

Careful *Introductions* have been prepared to give the setting and background whenever such introductions are necessary for an understanding and appreciation of the selections. *Suggestions for Study* give direction and assistance in the detailed analyses of the respective pieces. Here, emphasis is rather upon questions which lead to appreciation rather than upon mere fact questions. *Creative Work* is provided for by suggestions for précis writing, for outlines, and for original stories, essays, and other compositions. *Vocabulary Study* emphasizes word history, the use of synonyms and antonyms, and pronunciation. Footnotes are used only in the case of difficult words or phrases which cannot be explained by dictionary definitions. All of the study features deliberately avoid the common fault of superfluous details and over-technicality of treatment.

Emphasis on Modern Material

The emphasis in this book has been placed on modern and contemporary literature. In this volume of PROSE AND POETRY 75% of the authors represented are contemporary writers of the twentieth century, and 80% are modern writers—the term "modern" being used here in the sense of belonging to the period of the last fifty years.

Catholic Edition

The publication of this Catholic Edition of the PROSE AND POETRY series is one more recognition of the manifest truth that textbooks designed primarily for use in the public schools cannot be wholly satisfactory for use in the Catholic schools of the country; the fundamental philosophies of the two school-systems are poles apart. Publishers of textbooks have long recognized this fact, and some of them have taken pains to eliminate material obviously offensive to Catholic sensibilities. Because the publisher of the PROSE AND POETRY series was particularly careful in this regard, this series has been widely used in Catholic high schools —for lack of something better. Now "the something better" is provided by the same publisher in this Catholic Edition of the PROSE AND POETRY series, a revision of the earlier general edition.

In the preparation of this Catholic Edition there could be no question of including the works of Catholic authors only, since English literature is as a matter of fact not dominantly Catholic. There was no question, either, of radically altering the general plan of the books, since experience had proven that plan generally satisfactory. The task of the editors of this Catholic Edition, therefore, was to incorporate appropriate selections from the wealth of Catholic literature to give representation to Catholic authors and to ensure a solidly Catholic tone to the revised works.

An examination of the table of contents will show that in this edition from one-fourth to one-third of the short stories, biographies, lyric poems, and essays are by Catholic authors and are for the most part frankly Catholic in spirit and content.

The study features in the Catholic Edition follow the pattern adopted in the general edition. In the extensive reading programs a limited number of titles have been supplanted by Catholic titles.

Conclusion

It is the hope of the editors that the Catholic Edition of the PROSE AND POETRY books will meet every need for the new program of teaching literature and will open wide the doors which lead to good reading as a worthy use of leisure. More than that, it is their hope that Catholic schools will find in this edition a valuable instrument for making Catholic secondary education what both its friends and critics say it should be—more truly Catholic.

JULIAN L. MALINE, S.J.

WILLIAM J. McGUCKEN, S.J.

EDITORS

CONTENTS

xi

PROSE
AND
POETRY
OF AMERICA

LITERARY PERIODS

THE PERIODS OF AMERICAN LITERATURE

The Historical Backgrounds of Literature

To understand and appreciate the literature of a people, it is necessary always to interpret it in the light of daily living. What people think, where they live, what their educational and cultural environments are, the problems with which they are faced, all influence the things they write. However, in the study of literary history, there is danger of over-emphasizing political backgrounds to the extent that the study becomes one of politics rather than of literature. In this book, an attempt has been made to emphasize not so much political events and dates in American history, as those social, economic and religious phases which bear a close relationship to American literature—in other words, to treat literature in the light of the daily lives of the people.

The number of literary periods to be considered is five. They are here briefly discussed in a general way in the light of their social and economic backgrounds. In connection with the study of each of the types of literature throughout the book, they will be discussed more in detail.

The Colonial Period (1607–1765)

The Colonial Period begins in 1607 with the establishment of the first permanent colony in Virginia and extends to 1765 which year saw the first manifestations of the political dissatisfaction and unrest which were to culminate in the Revolutionary War.

Even before the founding of Jamestown, Spanish colonists in Florida, New Mexico, and other portions of the Southwest were making their contributions to Spanish letters. This literature and that of the French colonies soon to spring up in Louisiana were wholly Catholic in spirit. But it was not these literatures that were to mould American thought.

The great influence in American literature was to come from the English colonies on the eastern seaboard, and theirs was a dominantly Protestant culture. The hard life of the pioneers merely accentuated the sombre Calvinism which most New Englanders professed. They were a hard-working and serious people, and their life was reflected in their literature. Of all the writings of the period, one-half is said to have been religious.

The books which were read were ones which had been printed in England. Few books were written and printed by the colonists them-

1

selves. There were two reasons for this. First, printing presses were few, and second, colonial writing and printing were discouraged by English censorship. Papers, almanacs, and books had to be licensed and it is little wonder, therefore, that the native literary output of the Colonial Period was small.

The Revolutionary Period (1765–1800)

This period begins in 1765 with the birth of the Revolutionary movement and extends to the end of the century. It covers the stormy decade before the War, the period of the War itself, and the years following in which the new government and Constitution were established.

Of necessity, the literature was largely political, consisting mainly of pamphlets and public addresses. Into the soberness and seriousness of colonial life had come the discords of Revolutionary disputes. The years immediately preceding the war witnessed disputes over legal and controversial questions and the whole history of this decade can be followed in the pamphlets of patriot and loyalist. Great men rose to meet a great crisis and by their pens and by their oratory made themselves useful to the Revolutionary cause. The colonial attitude of mind disappeared and was replaced by a new Americanism.

Although men of high literary abilities were compelled by the necessities of the times to turn their pens to political service, the Revolutionary Period did see the beginnings of poetry and of the novel—literary forms which were to burst into full fruition after the turn of the century.

The National Period (1800–1865)

The National Period begins with the establishment of American nationalism and ends with the close of the Civil War which tested and proved that nationalism.

The new century saw a new life and spirit on the American continent. The success of the Revolution gave people a feeling of self-sufficiency and national pride. The nation was enlarged by the purchase of Florida and the annexation of the Louisiana territory. The western migration which had begun during the Revolutionary Period was continued, the Northwest Territory was settled, and the Republic of Texas joined the Union. All of this enlarging of territory served to expand the feeling of nationalism. With the hardships of colonial days and the struggles of the Revolution in the background, the people were ready for enjoyment of the riches and resources of a new nation. They began to read for pleasure and pastime and there grew up a demand for an American literature.

The writings of the period reflect this expanding sentiment of national life. A change is to be noted from the serious and sober writings of the Colonial and Revolutionary Periods. We sense a new interest in life—a new joy in experience. The literature of the period is buoyantly romantic and expressive of a delight and joy in living.

This new interest in life was best expressed in fiction and in poetry, and these forms of literature enjoyed unparalleled development. In fiction, the novel took the commanding place but the short story made a brilliant beginning. Poetry was the most effective vehicle for the expression of delight in living and the group of American poets which this period produced will live forever in American literature. We note also the beginnings of the American essay and of interest in the drama. Of all periods in American literature, the National Period was perhaps the most fruitful and aggressive.

The Transition Period (1865–1900)

This period spans the years from the end of the Civil War to the twentieth century. It is one of "transition" from the literary style of the National Period to that of the present century.

With the issues of the Civil War settled, the nation was ready to concentrate on commercial and industrial expansion. The western boundary of the United States moved to the Pacific Ocean, transcontinental railroads were built, river and canal transportation was improved and electricity came into use. The movement from farm to city was under way. Population of eastern cities increased by leaps and bounds and great cities arose in the West. America was becoming a country of urban communities, and industry and commerce were becoming as important as agriculture.

These conditions brought about a new literature. New England was no longer the literary center of the country. Writers now appeared from every section. The South, which before the Civil War had been more or less cut off from the rest of the nation, now came into its own. The settlement of the West and Southwest provided a new point of view and injected a frontier spirit into literature. Industrial conditions also fostered the "local color" type of writing. In the desire to preserve local mannerisms, customs, and dialect before they were submerged by the rising capitalistic order, a great school of local color writers sprang up and this period is marked for its regional literature.

The literature of the National Period had been romantic—that is, it dealt with the imaginative and the ideal. The literature of the Transition Period became increasingly realistic, dealing with the true-to-life and the commonplace. In any period which tends toward the realistic there are always to be noted a decline in poetry and a corresponding increase in prose. This was true of the Transition Period. There were a few outstanding poets, but most of the writers expressed themselves in prose. The novel was important, but the short story was the leading literary form of the period. This type of writing provided a convenient form for the local colorists and the rapid growth of the newspaper and magazine fostered its popularity. There was some writing in the form of critical essays and the drama was attracting attention, but the period was definitely one of the novel and the short story.

The Twentieth Century (1900–   )

By the beginning of the twentieth century, America had become predominantly industrial. The frontier had passed forever and the population had concentrated in urban communities. Industrialism brought with it new problems—class struggles between capital and labor, exploitation of natural resources, and of course moral problems of a serious nature. Social injustice, widespread divorce, and the soulless ethics of unrestricted competition for profit were of grave concern to those interested in the preservation of a Christian culture in the United States. Too frequently self-appointed and well-meaning but incompetent reformers fell into errors as serious as the evils which they sought to correct. The social, economic, and religious conditions were further complicated by the flood of immigration into this country in the first years of the century.

All these problems affected both the subject matter and the spirit of the literature of the day.

The realism which had begun in the Transition Period now entirely dominated all literature. Even poetry, which had always been romantic, now became realistic. People assumed practical attitudes and distrusted the romantic point of view. This realistic tendency was encouraged and intensified by the scientific education in schools and colleges. Literature pictured the darker side of life and dealt with suffering and misery. It dealt with plain people in unpicturesque settings.

The period following the World War has seen on the part of many writers a still greater turning from idealism to bitter cynicism and disillusion. In pleasant contrast to this school, however, is another group of writers, who, affected differently by the War, have turned to a renewed nationalism and a study of the American past. The result has been a revival of romantic historical fiction and a new biography. This new biography tells the stories of famous people in a new way and is second only to fiction in present popularity.

Of the types of literature, the novel has perhaps been most important. Many brilliant writers have depicted the American scene in novels which will hold an enduring place in our literature. The short story at the beginning of the century suffered a decline from its high position of the preceding period but it is again attaining new heights in the hands of contemporary writers. The drama, particularly the one-act play, has seen unprecedented growth and the familiar essay is increasingly popular. In poetry, too, there has been a vigorous revival.

Only time can give contemporary writers their true places in American literature, but the present decades are seeing a new literature which is intensely American and it is safe to predict that much of it will survive for years to come.

THE SHORT STORY

THE SHORT STORY AS A TYPE OF LITERATURE

An American Contribution to Literature

The literary form known as the short story may be taken as a kind of symbol of American literary independence, for America has taken the lead in the development of it, a development which bears a close relationship to conditions of American life. The short story was called forth by the demand for something which could be read in the brief intervals of leisure snatched from a busy life and has been stimulated by the development of the magazine in America. In fact, most short stories owe their first publication to periodicals. There are thousands of people who read only newspapers and magazines and these readers want something short, sharp, and incisive. Indeed, it has been said that the American people have put such a premium on all things short that they have perfected beyond any other nation the short story, the familiar essay, and the one-act play.

What Is a Short Story?

In the first place, a short story is a story that is short. In addition, however, there are certain definite characteristics which distinguish it from other forms of literary art. Brander Matthews in 1885 used these words to characterize the short story: "A true short story differs from a novel chiefly in its essential unity of impression . . . A short story deals with a single character interest, a single event, a single emotion, or the series of emotions called forth by a single situation . . . Thus the short story has what the novel cannot have, the effect of 'totality' as Poe called it, the unity of impression." The novelist builds his characters and situations bit by bit, in a leisurely, sometimes laborious manner. He develops not only leading characters but also minor characters; not only plots but also sub-plots. The short story writer, on the other hand, must introduce his characters and set his scene briefly and vividly with no unnecessary details to mar the effect. He can relate only one important incident or closely related series of events, taking place usually in a short space of time, which must be acted out by a single chief character. Thus the short story is not a condensed novel, but a distinct literary form.

5

The Requirements of the Short Story

The essentials of a short story are plot, characters and setting. These essentials must be so organized as to produce a single "cameo-like" impression. According to Robert Louis Stevenson, this effect may be produced in one of three ways: "There are, so far as I know, three ways and three only of writing a story. You may take a plot and fit characters to it, or you may take a character and choose incidents and situations to develop it, or lastly, you may take a certain atmosphere and get actions and persons to express and realize it." If the single effect is produced by plot, the story is one of action in that the character accomplishes something. The setting is of secondary interest and the characters merely carry on the action of the plot. In the character story, the setting and plot must be subordinated to the character. Such a story depends upon the physical peculiarities or mental make-up of the leading character and may be one of physical action or of the type known as a "decision" story. If an author wishes to produce the single impression of setting, or "local color," the characters and plot must be so subordinated to the setting that the setting predominates. The setting cannot be changed without altering the development of the story. The characters are what they are, and the incidents happen as they do because of factors in the environment.

The Technique of the Short Story

Since the short story has become a distinct literary form, and, more particularly, since the teaching of short story writing has become a profession, an attempt has been made to formulate its technique. The plot has been compared to a skeleton. A skillful writer covers up the bones so that the reader is not conscious of the framework. The *introduction* of the story should give the locale and something about the leading characters, together with a suggestion, at least, of the theme or plot. All this information must be presented to the reader not as so many independent bits of information, but held together by the warp of interest. The main *body* of the story is made up of episodes each of which takes the story one step nearer the climax. Each episode has its own small climax and a carrying-over quality which connects it to the following episode. This carrying-over quality is often achieved by what is known to the writer as "planting." Something which is said or an article that seems trivial in one episode becomes the all important factor in the following one. An experienced writer does his "planting" in such a way that it is not obvious to the reader. The *climax* of the story is the most decisive episode—that summit toward which all the signposts in the other episodes have been pointing. A story may end with the climax, or a *dénouement* may follow which shows the result of the climax. The dénouement should be brief, for after the climax is reached, the fall of interest is rapid.

THE HISTORY OF THE AMERICAN SHORT STORY

THE NATIONAL PERIOD (1800–1865)

General Characteristics

It was not until after the Revolutionary War that the short story made its appearance as a part of American literature. But there were reasons for this comparatively late development. In the first place, a short story is fiction—the creation of the imagination. To be convincing it must of course be true to life, but nevertheless it is not based on actual fact. And when actual fact—life itself—is eventful and all-absorbing there is little inclination or time for the fictional and the imaginative. The prose literature of the Colonial and Revolutionary periods reflects the absorption and concentration of the colonists in settling the new country, their problems during the stormy period of party strife before the War, and the doubt and struggle over the Constitution and the new republic. Furthermore, the colonists were for the most part Calvinists, and the grim shadows of predestination stunted or killed all early attempts at fictitious writing. The first part of the nineteenth century, however, saw an awakening and expansion and a new enthusiasm for living which was to reflect itself in the beginnings of a great national literature. The new spirit and zest in life demanded poetry, romance, song, and thus this period saw the rise and growth of fiction and with it the beginning of the American short story.

Washington Irving (1783–1859)

In the development of the short story, Washington Irving is the first conspicuous pioneer. Born in New York City, the son of a leading merchant, he was prevented by illness from going to college and spent some time in his youth traveling in Europe. He was admitted to the bar, but never practiced, literature having had a greater fascination for him. In 1815 he went to England and during the following seventeen years lived abroad. It was while he was in London that *The Sketch Book*, by which he is best remembered today, was written and published. This was issued in numbers like a magazine and was varied in contents. It met with instant success. This type of writing which could be dashed off when the mood was upon him and stopped at will was the kind that appealed to Irving, for he was ever indolent

7

and he worked only by impulse. He was never to take the time to write a novel, and his books are rather collections of short pieces—stories and sketches. Thus he became the originator of the short story form, not because he deliberately chose the shortened form, but because he fell into it automatically on account of temperament and his dislike for long-continued efforts. The stories for which he is best remembered are *Rip Van Winkle* and *The Legend of Sleepy Hollow*, read by every American school child, and also *The Spectre Bridegroom, The Pride of the Village, Dolph Heyliger*, and *The Adventure of the Black Fisherman*. Although these stories differ from the modern short story in that they are diffuse and leisurely rather than compact and swift, they nevertheless have as strong an appeal today as they had a hundred years ago.

Irving's career is usually looked upon as ideal. Friends, influence, fame and wealth were his and he worked to the last. He completed what is perhaps his greatest work, *The Life of Washington*, on his seventy-sixth birthday and in November of the same year (1859) he died.

Nathaniel Hawthorne (1804–1864)

To understand and appreciate Hawthorne's writings we must consider him in the light of his background. Born in 1804, he lived a lonely, unnatural childhood. After the death of his father, his mother became a recluse. Every curtain was drawn, every shutter was closed and she lived in her own room. In this atmosphere the boy grew shy, sensitive and imaginative. His years at Bowdoin College furnished almost the first bright and natural spot in his life, but after his graduation he again went into seclusion. In 1837 he collected a number of short stories he had written, and, with their publication under the title of *Twice-Told Tales*, he became known as a writer. Thus he emerged into the world of affairs. His marriage was a happy one and his wife encouraged his writing. Besides his novels he produced more than a hundred short stories, some of the best known of which are *The Gray Champion, Mr. Higginbotham's Catastrophe, The Minister's Black Veil, David Swan, The Great Stone Face, Ethan Brand* and *The Birthmark*. For four years he served as United States Consul in Liverpool but then resigned to travel through France and Italy. His health began to fail shortly after his return to America. He died in 1864.

The circumstances of his life together with the sensitiveness of his nature and the influence of the stern Puritanism of his ancestors combined to produce in him an understanding and sympathy for the spiritual and idealistic rather than the real and commonplace. In most of his stories there is an allegorical significance or symbolism and many are adorned with a moral. Instead of writing about the ordinary details of life as did Irving, Hawthorne was interested in character and the eccentricities of conscience. If the short story began with Irving, it was Hawthorne who developed it from the rambling, leisurely tale with entertainment its only purpose and confined it to a single situation.

Edgar Allan Poe (1809–1849)

Poe was born in Boston of actor parents who died when he was very young. A rich merchant of Richmond, Virginia, by the name of John Allan adopted the boy and gave him all the advantages of a well-to-do home. He was a very handsome and precocious child. He was educated in private schools in this country and in England and studied for a while under private tutors. He excelled in everything he tried and delighted in the display of his powers. He promised much to his foster-parents, but they were to be bitterly disappointed. Shortly after entering college he repeatedly incurred gambling debts and, due to other faults of temperament and ways of living, he became estranged from them.

When he was twenty-six years old he won a $100 prize with the story, *A MS. Found in a Bottle.* This was the beginning of his popularity as a short story writer. In 1841 he published the first detective story ever written—*Murders in the Rue Morgue,* and two years later another story of the same type, *The Gold Bug.* In the meantime he was writing poetry and the publication of *The Raven* caused a sensation. But in spite of his brilliant success as a writer the years which followed were years of misfortune, poverty and ill health. His days were spent in a pitiful struggle for the bare necessities of life and his pen won him alternate fame and despair. Something perverse and fatalistic seemed to dog his whole life's footsteps. His untimely death occurred in 1849.

From the standpoint of foreign critics, Poe is the most gifted of all American writers. It was he, who, further than Hawthorne, emphasized the unity of the short story by selecting details to produce what he called totality of effect. His stories are brief and original and the subject matter deals with the unusual, the horrible and the supernatural. His stories do not give the impression of reality, for atmosphere takes the place of setting, but the details are cleverly selected and cunningly arranged to work out a single predetermined effect.

Minor Short Story Writers of the National Period

The names of Irving, Hawthorne, and Poe stand out as so important in the history of the early short story that the names of minor writers disappear almost into obscurity. There were a few, however, who deserve mention, namely James K. Paulding (1779–1860), author of a considerable number of pieces among which are *The Poet's Tale* and *Mine Uncle John;* Catherine M. Sedgwick (1789–1867), one of whose collections is entitled *Tales and Sketches;* Nathaniel Parker Willis (1806–1867), author of *Pedlar Karl* and *The Cherokee's Threat;* Donald Grant •Mitchell (1822–1908), some of whose stories appear in the collection *Seven Stories with Attic and Basement;* Herman Melville (1819–1891), better known as a novelist, but author of many short stories, some of which appear in *Piazza Tales;* and Fitz-James O'Brien (1828–1862), author of a large number of stories, best remembered of which are *The Diamond Lens* and *What Was It? A Mystery.*

Short Stories of the National Period

ADVENTURE OF THE BLACK FISHERMAN

WASHINGTON IRVING

By Way of Introduction: In the early days of our country, on a point of land which stretches out into Long Island Sound, there might have been found a rural inn which was the favorite resort of many of the old inhabitants of Manhattoes.* On the evening of this story, the habitual group was in session beside the fireplace. Wolfert Webber, a worthy Dutch burgher, was at his usual post, as were also the half-pay officer and his cronies. The landlord, according to his custom, hovered in the background. The place of honor, a huge leather-bottomed armchair, was occupied by Peechy Prauw, the story-teller, who could tell more stories in an evening than his hearers could digest in a month. A heavy thundergust had gathered and torrents of rain were falling which forbade all thoughts of setting off for home until the storm should subside. The men drew nearer together, therefore, and entreated the venerable Peechy Prauw to tell them a story. He readily complied, whispering, however, in a tone scarcely above his breath, and drowned occasionally by the rolling of the thunder. With frequent pauses, he related the following tale.

* MANHATTOES—An old name for Manhattan.

10

EVERYBODY knows Black Sam, the old negro fisherman, or, as he is commonly called, Mud Sam, who has fished about the Sound[1] for the last half century. It is now many years since Sam, who was then as active a young negro as any in the province, and worked on the farm of Killian Suydam on Long Island, having finished his day's work at an early hour, was fishing, one still summer evening, just about the neighborhood of Hell Gate.[2]

He was in a light skiff; and being well acquainted with the currents and eddies, had shifted his station according to the shifting of the tide, from the Hen and Chickens to the Hog's Back, from the Hog's Back to the Pot, and from the Pot to the Frying-Pan;[3] but in the eagerness of his sport he did not see that the tide was rapidly ebbing, until the roaring of the whirlpools and eddies warned him of his danger; and he had some difficulty in shooting his skiff from among the rocks and breakers, and getting to the point of Blackwell's Island. Here he cast anchor for some time, waiting the turn of the tide to enable him to return homewards. As the night set in, it grew blustering and gusty. Dark clouds came bundling up in the west; and now and then a growl of thunder or a flash of lightning told that a summer storm was at hand. Sam pulled over, therefore, under the lee of Manhattan Island, and coasting along, came to a snug nook, just under a steep beetling rock, where he fastened his skiff to the root of a tree that shot out from a cleft, and spread its broad branches like a canopy over the water. The gust came scouring along; the wind threw up the river in white surges; the rain rattled among the leaves; the thunder bellowed worse than that which is now bellowing; the lightning seemed to lick up the surges of the stream; but Sam, snugly sheltered under rock and tree, lay crouching in his skiff, rocking upon the billows until he fell asleep. When he awoke all was quiet. The gust had passed away, and only now and then a faint gleam of lightning in the east showed which way it had gone. The night was dark and moonless;

---

[1] SOUND—Long Island Sound.

[2] HELL GATE—The strait which is the north boundary of Manhattan Island and which separates it from the mainland to the north. It lies between the Hudson River and Long Island Sound.

[3] HEN AND CHICKENS, HOG'S BACK, POT, FRYING-PAN—Various positions along Hell Gate and at its mouth. The tide moving in Hell Gate causes very swift currents, hence the fisherman had to move from one position to another.

and from the state of the tide Sam concluded it was near midnight. He was on the point of making loose his skiff to return
homewards, when he saw a light gleaming along the water from
a distance, which seemed rapidly approaching. As it drew near
he perceived it came from a lantern in the bow of a boat gliding
along under shadow of the land. It pulled up in a small cove,
close to where he was. A man jumped on shore, and searching
about with the lantern, exclaimed, "This is the place—here's the
iron ring." The boat was then made fast, and the man, returning on board, assisted his comrades in conveying something
heavy on shore. As the light gleamed among them, Sam saw
that they were five stout desperate-looking fellows, in red
woollen caps, with a leader in a three-cornered hat, and that
some of them were armed with dirks, or long knives, and pistols.
They talked low to one another, and occasionally in some outlandish tongue which he could not understand.

On landing, they made their way among the bushes, taking
turns to relieve each other in lugging their burden up the
rocky bank. Sam's curiosity was now fully aroused; so leaving his skiff he clambered silently up a ridge that overlooked
their path. They had stopped to rest for a moment, and the
leader was looking about among the bushes with his lantern.
"Have you brought the spades?" said one. "They are here,"
replied another, who had them on his shoulder. "We must dig
deep, where there will be no risk of discovery," said a third.

A cold chill ran through Sam's veins. He fancied he saw before him a gang of murderers, about to bury their victim. His
knees smote together. In his agitation he shook the branch of
a tree with which he was supporting himself as he looked over
the edge of the cliff.

"What's that?" cried one of the gang.— "Some one stirs
among the bushes!"

The lantern was held up in the direction of the noise. One
of the red-caps cocked a pistol, and pointed it towards the
very place where Sam was standing. He stood motionless—
breathless; expecting the next moment to be his last. Fortunately his dingy complexion was in his favor, and made no
glare among the leaves.

" 'Tis no one," said the man with the lantern. "What a
plague! You would not fire off your pistol and alarm the
country!"

The pistol was uncocked; the burden was resumed, and the party slowly toiled along the bank. Sam watched them as they went; the light sending back fitful gleams through the dripping bushes, and it was not until they were fairly out of sight that he ventured to draw breath freely. He now thought of getting back to his boat, and making his escape out of the reach of such dangerous neighbors; but curiosity was all-powerful. He hesitated and lingered and listened. By and by he heard the strokes of spades.— "They are digging the grave!" said he to himself; and the cold sweat started upon his forehead. Every stroke of a spade, as it sounded through the silent groves, went to his heart; it was evident there was as little noise made as possible; everything had an air of terrible mystery and secrecy. Sam had a great relish for the horrible, —a tale of murder was a treat for him; and he was a constant attendant at executions. He could not resist an impulse, in spite of every danger, to steal nearer to the scene of mystery, and overlook the midnight fellows at their work. He crawled along cautiously, therefore, inch by inch; stepping with the utmost care among the dry leaves, lest their rustling should betray him. He came at length to where a steep rock intervened between him and the gang; for he saw the light of their lantern shining up against the branches of the trees on the other side. Sam slowly and silently clambered up the surface of the rock, and raising his head above its naked edge, beheld the villains immediately below him, and so near, that though he dreaded discovery, he dared not withdraw lest the least movement should be heard. In this way he remained, with his round black face peering above the edge of the rock, like the sun just emerging above the edge of the horizon, or the round-cheeked moon on the dial of a clock.

The red-caps had nearly finished their work; the grave was filled up, and they were carefully replacing the turf. This done, they scattered dry leaves over the place. "And now," said the leader, "I defy the devil himself to find it out."

"The murderers!" exclaimed Sam, involuntarily.

The whole gang started, and looking up, beheld the round black head of Sam just above them. His white eyes strained half out of their orbits; his white teeth chattering, and his whole visage shining with cold perspiration.

"We're discovered!" said one.

"Down with him!" cried another.

Sam heard the cocking of a pistol, but did not pause for the report. He scrambled over rock and stone, through brush and brier; rolled down banks like a hedge-hog; scrambled up others like a catamount. In every direction he heard some one or other of the gang hemming him in. At length he reached the rocky ridge along the river; one of the red-caps was hard behind him. A steep rock like a wall rose directly in his way; it seemed to cut off all retreat, when fortunately he espied the strong cord-like branch of a grape-vine reaching half-way down it. He sprang at it with the force of a desperate man, seized it with both hands, and being young and agile, succeeded in swinging himself to the summit of the cliff. Here he stood in full relief against the sky, when the red-cap cocked his pistol and fired. The ball whistled by Sam's head. With the lucky thought of a man in an emergency, he uttered a yell, fell to the ground, and detached at the same time a fragment of the rock, which tumbled with a loud splash into the river.

"I've done his business," said the red-cap to one or two of his comrades as they arrived panting. "He'll tell no tales, except to the fishes in the river."

His pursuers now turned to meet their companions. Sam, sliding silently down the surface of the rock, let himself quietly into his skiff, cast loose the fastening, and abandoned himself to the rapid current, which in that place runs like a mill-stream, and soon swept him off from the neighborhood. It was not, however, until he had drifted a great distance that he ventured to ply his oars, when he made his skiff dart like an arrow through the strait of Hell Gate, never heeding the danger of Pot, Frying-Pan, nor Hog's Back itself: nor did he feel himself thoroughly secure until safely nestled in bed in the cockloft of the ancient farm-house in the Suydams.

Here the worthy Peechy Prauw paused to take breath, and to take a sip of the gossip tankard that stood at his elbow. His auditors remained with open mouths and outstretched necks, gaping like a nest of swallows for an additional mouthful.

"And is that all?" exclaimed the half-pay officer.

"That's all that belongs to the story," said Peechy Prauw.

"And did Sam never find out what was buried by the red-caps?" said Wolfert, eagerly, whose mind was haunted by nothing but ingots and doubloons.

"Not that I know of," said Peechy; "he had no time to spare from his work, and, to tell the truth, he did not like to run the risk of another race among the rocks. Besides, how should he recollect the spot where the grave had been digged? Everything would look so different by daylight. And then, where was the use of looking for a dead body, when there was no chance of hanging the murderers?"

"Aye, but are you sure it was a dead body they buried?" said Wolfert.

"To be sure " cried Peechy Prauw, exultingly. "Does it not haunt in the neighborhood to this very day?"

"Haunts!" exclaimed several of the party, opening their eyes still wider, and edging their chairs still closer.

"Aye, haunts," repeated Peechy; "have none of you heard of father Red-cap, who haunts the old burnt farm-house in the woods, on the border of the Sound, near Hell Gate?"

"Oh, to be sure I've heard tell of something of the kind, but then I took it for some old wives' fable."

"Old wives' fable or not," said Peechy Prauw, "that farm-house stands hard by the very spot. It's been unoccupied time out of mind, and stands in a lonely part of the coast; but those who fish in the neighborhood have often heard strange noises there; and lights have been seen about the wood at night; and an old fellow in a red cap has been seen at the windows more than once, which people take to be the ghost of the body buried there. Once upon a time three soldiers took shelter in the building for the night, and rummaged it from top to bottom, when they found old father Red-cap astride of a cider-barrel in the cellar, with a jug in one hand and a goblet in the other. He offered them a drink out of his goblet, but just as one of the soldiers was putting it to his mouth—whew! —a flash of fire blazed through the cellar, blinded every mother's son of them for several minutes; when they recovered their eye-sight, jug, goblet, and Red-cap had vanished, and nothing but the empty cider-barrel remained."

"That's all fudge!" said the half-pay officer as Peechy finished his last story.

"Well, I don't vouch for the truth of it myself," said Peechy Prauw, "though all the world knows that there's something strange about that house and grounds; but as to the story of Mud Sam, I believe it just as well as if it had happened to myself."

The Type of Irving's Stories: With Irving began American literature in the shorter story form. He was for many years the model of later writers and his stories were excellent patterns to follow. In the first place, he realized that the short story had to show merit and strength in every paragraph of every page in contrast to the rambling narrative and the long-drawn-out novel. In the second place, he stripped his stories of moral teachings. He wrote entirely for entertainment. In the third place, his settings were definite localities, peopled by real individuals. And knowing human nature, he added humor to his characters and situations. His stories are full of descriptive material—scenery, people, manners, dress—but are lacking in plot, in movement, and in dialogue. Nevertheless, their power of entertainment is as strong today as it was a hundred years ago, and they are models of beautiful English prose.

For Appreciation: This story appeared in *Tales of a Traveller,* written in 1824. Irving had the ability to write clearly and to portray his settings and characters with distinctness. Give specific illustrations of this ability. Do you feel you know Mud Sam? This story is a tale. What characteristics of the story make it a tale? Irving was America's first humorist. What humor do you find in this story? Irving liked to use ghosts in his stories. What is the effect of ghosts in this story? What other stories by Irving do you know wherein ghosts are used? It is quite characteristic of Irving to end his stories with "explanations" as to the final disposition of his characters. What "explanations" are given here? Are they satisfactory to you as a reader? For what purpose do you think the story was written—to convey a moral, to record historical facts, to amuse, or to give local color setting of the Knickerbocker days?

For Further Study: What are the meanings of the following words and phrases: *light skiff; shifted his station; lee of Manhattan Island; beetling rock; white eyes; catamount; cockloft; ingots and doubloons; old wives' fable; time out of mind.*

What is the location of the story as to time and place? Why was Mud Sam detained out on the Sound? At what point is the reader's curiosity aroused? Does the story move rapidly or slowly from this point? Is the description of the mysterious characters clear? Give their description in your own words. Describe their movements. What clever bit of stratagem does Mud Sam employ to check the pursuit of the red-caps? What are the explanations of Peechy Prauw as to what the red-caps buried?

Exercises and Creative Work: Make a map of Manhattan Island and show Hell Gate, the Sound, Blackwell's Island, and the approximate spot where Mud Sam was fishing. Show where you think the farm of Killian Suydam was located, and also where you think the red-caps buried the chest.

Wolfert Webber was one of Peechy Prauw's auditors, and his mind was haunted by "ingots and doubloons." He decided to enlist Sam's help and locate the spot where the grave had been dug. Write a short story of his adventures, entitled *The Red-Cap Chest Discovered.*

DAVID SWAN

Nathaniel Hawthorne

WE CAN be but partially acquainted even with the events which actually influence our course through life, and our final destiny. There are innumerable other events, if such they may be called, which come close upon us, yet pass away without actual results, or even betraying their near approach by the reflection of any light or shadow across our minds. Could we know all the vicissitudes of our fortunes, life would be too full of hope and fear, exultation or disappointment, to afford us a single hour of true serenity. This idea may be illustrated by a page from the secret history of David Swan.

We have nothing to do with David until we find him, at the age of twenty, on the high road from his native place to the city of Boston, where his uncle, a small dealer in the grocery line, was to take him behind the counter. Be it enough to say that he was a native of New Hampshire, born of respectable parents, and had received an ordinary school education, with a classic finish by a year at Gilmanton Academy. After journeying on foot from sunrise till nearly noon of a summer's day, his weariness and the increasing heat determined him to sit down in the first convenient shade and await the coming up of the stagecoach. As if planted on purpose for him, there soon appeared a little tuft of maples, with a delightful recess in the midst, and such a fresh, bubbling spring that it seemed never to have sparkled for any wayfarer but David Swan. Virgin or not, he kissed it with his thirsty lips, and then flung himself along the brink, pillowing his head upon some shirts and a pair of pantaloons, tied up in a striped cotton handkerchief. The sunbeams could not reach him; the dust did not yet arise from the road after the heavy rain of yesterday; and his grassy lair suited the young man better than a bed of down. The spring murmured drowsily beside him; the branches waved dreamily across the blue sky overhead; and a deep sleep, perchance hiding dreams within its depths, fell upon David Swan. But we are to relate events of which he did not dream.

While he lay sound asleep in the shade, other people were wide awake, and passed to and fro, afoot, or horseback, and in all sorts of vehicles, along the sunny road by his bedchamber. Some looked neither to the right hand nor the left, and knew not that he was there; some merely glanced that way, without admitting the slumberer among their busy thoughts; some laughed to see how soundly he slept; and several whose hearts were brimming full of scorn ejected their venomous superfluity on David Swan. A middle-aged widow, when nobody else was near, thrust her head a little way into the recess, and vowed that the young fellow looked charming in his sleep. A temperance lecturer saw him, and wrought poor David into the texture of his evening's discourse as an awful instance of dead-drunkenness by the roadside. But censure, praise, merriment, scorn, and indifference were all one, or rather all nothing, to David Swan.

He had slept only a few moments when a brown carriage, drawn by a handsome pair of horses, bowled easily along, and was brought to a standstill nearly in front of David's resting place. A linch-pin [1] had fallen out, and permitted one of the wheels to slide off. The damage was slight, and occasioned merely a momentary alarm to an elderly merchant and his wife, who were returning to Boston in the carriage. While the coachman and a servant were replacing the wheel, the lady and gentleman sheltered themselves beneath the maple trees, and there espied the bubbling fountain, and David Swan asleep beside it. Impressed with the awe which the humblest sleeper usually sheds around him, the merchant trod as lightly as the gout would allow; and his spouse took heed lest David should start up all of a sudden.

"How soundly he sleeps!" whispered the old gentleman. "From what a depth he draws that easy breath! Such sleep as that, brought on without an opiate, would be worth more to me than half my income, for it would suppose health and an untroubled mind."

"And youth, besides," said the lady. "Healthy and quiet age does not sleep thus. Our slumber is no more like his than our wakefulness."

The longer they looked, the more did this elderly couple feel interested in the unknown youth, to whom the wayside and the maple shade were as a secret chamber, with the rich gloom of damask curtains brooding over him. Perceiving that a stray sunbeam glimmered down upon his face, the lady contrived to twist a branch aside, so as to intercept it. And having done this little act of kindness, she began to feel like a mother to him.

"Providence seems to have laid him here," whispered she to her husband, "and to have brought us hither to find him, after our disappointment in our cousin's son. Methinks I can see a likeness to our departed Henry. Shall we waken him?"

"To what purpose?" said the merchant, hesitating. "We know nothing of the youth's character."

"That open countenance!" replied his wife in the same hushed voice, yet earnestly. "This innocent sleep!"

While these whispers were passing, the sleeper's heart did not throb, nor his breath become agitated, nor his features betray the least token of interest. Yet Fortune was bending over him,

---

[1] LINCH-PIN—An iron pin that holds the wheel on the carriage.

just ready to let fall a burden of gold. The old merchant had lost his only son, and had no heir to his wealth except a distant relative, with whose conduct he was dissatisfied. In such cases people sometimes do stranger things than to act the magician, and awaken a young man to splendor who fell asleep in poverty.

"Shall we not awaken him?" repeated the lady persuasively.

"The coach is ready, sir," said the servant, behind.

The old couple started, reddened, and hurried away, mutually wondering that they should ever have dreamed of doing anything so very ridiculous. The merchant threw himself back in the carriage, and occupied his mind with the plan of a magnificent asylum for unfortunate men of business. Meanwhile, David Swan enjoyed his nap.

The carriage could not have gone above a mile or two when a pretty young girl came along with a tripping pace, which showed precisely how her little heart was dancing in her bosom. Perhaps it was this merry kind of motion that caused—is there any harm in saying it?—her garter to slip its knot. Conscious that the silken girth—if silk it were—was relaxing its hold, she turned aside into the shelter of the maple tree, and there found a young man asleep by the spring! Blushing as red as any rose that she should have intruded into a gentleman's bed-chamber, and for such a purpose, too, she was about to make her escape on tiptoe. But there was peril near the sleeper. A monster of a bee had been wandering overhead,—buzz, buzz, buzz,—now among the leaves, now flashing through the strips of sunshine, and now lost in the dark shade, till finally he appeared to be settling on the eyelid of David Swan. The sting of a bee is sometimes deadly. As free-hearted as she was innocent, the girl attacked the intruder with her handkerchief, brushed him soundly, and drove him from beneath the maple shade. How sweet a picture! This good deed accomplished, with quickened breath, and a deeper blush, she stole a glance at the youthful stranger, for whom she had been battling with a dragon in the air.

"He is handsome!" thought she, and blushed redder yet.

How could it be that no dream of bliss grew so strong within him, that, shattered by its very strength, it should part asunder, and allow him to perceive the girl among its phantoms? Why, at least, did no smile of welcome brighten upon his face? She had come, the maid whose soul, according to the old and beautiful idea, had been severed from his own, and whom, in all his vague but passionate desires, he yearned to meet. Her only could he love with a perfect love; him only could she receive into the depths of her heart; and now her image was faintly blushing in the fountain by his side; should it pass away, its happy luster would never gleam upon his life again.

"How sound he sleeps!" murmured the girl.

She departed, but did not trip along the road so lightly as when she came.

Now this girl's father was a thriving country merchant in the neighborhood, and happened, at that identical time, to be looking out for just such a young man as David Swan. Had David formed a wayside acquaintance with the daughter, he would have become the father's clerk, and all else in natural succession. So here, again, had good fortune—the best of fortunes—stolen so near that her garments brushed against him; and he knew nothing of the matter.

The girl was hardly out of sight when two men turned aside beneath the maple shade. Both had dark faces, set off by cloth caps, which were drawn down aslant over their brows. Their dresses were shabby, yet had a certain smartness. These were a couple of rascals who got their living by whatever the devil sent them, and now, in the interim of other business, had staked the joint profits of their next piece of villainy on a game of cards, which was to have been decided here under the trees. But, finding David asleep by the spring, one of the rogues whispered to his fellow, "Hist! Do you see that bundle under his head?"

The other villain nodded, winked, and leered.

"I'll bet you a horn of brandy," said the first, "that the chap has either a pocketbook, or a snug little hoard of small change, stowed away amongst his shirts. And if not there, we shall find it in his pantaloons pocket."

"But how if he wakes?" said the other.

His companion thrust aside his waistcoat, pointed to the handle of a dirk, and nodded.

"So be it!" muttered the second villain.

They approached the unconscious David, and while one pointed the dagger towards his heart the other began to search the bundle beneath his head. Their two faces, grim, wrinkled, and ghastly with guilt and fear, bent over their victim, looking horrible enough to be mistaken for fiends, should he suddenly awake. Nay, had the villains glanced aside into the spring, even they would hardly have known themselves as reflected there. But David Swan had never worn a more tranquil aspect, even when asleep on his mother's breast.

"I must take away the bundle," whispered one.

"If he stirs, I'll strike," muttered the other.

But, at this moment, a dog, scenting along the ground, came in beneath the maple trees, and gazed alternately at each of these wicked men, then at the quiet sleeper. He then lapped out of the fountain.

"Pshaw!" said one villain. "We can do nothing now. The dog's master must be close behind."

"Let's take a drink and be off," said the other.

The man with the dagger thrust back the weapon into his bosom, and drew forth a pocket pistol, but not of that kind which kills by a single discharge. It was a flask of liquor, with a block-tin tumbler screwed upon the mouth. Each drank a comfortable dram, and left the spot, with so many jests, and such laughter at their unaccomplished wickedness, that they might be said to have gone on their way rejoicing. In a few hours they had forgotten the whole affair, nor once imagined that the recording angel had written down the crime of murder against their souls, in letters as durable as eternity. As for David Swan, he still slept quietly, neither conscious of the shadow of death when it hung over him, nor of the glow of renewed life when that shadow was withdrawn.

He slept, but no longer so quietly as at first. An hour's repose had snatched from his elastic frame the weariness with which many hours of toil had burdened it. Now, he stirred—now, moved his lips, without a sound—now, talked, in an inward tone, to the noonday specters of his dream. But a noise of wheels came rattling louder and louder along the road, until it dashed through the dispersing mist of David's slumber—and there was the stagecoach. He started up with all his ideas about him: "Halloo, driver!—take a passenger?" shouted he.

"Room on top!" answered the driver.

Up mounted David, and bowled away merrily towards Boston, without so much as a parting glance at that fountain of dream-like vicissitude. He knew not that phantom of Wealth had thrown a golden hue upon its waters, nor that one of Love had sighed softly to their murmur, nor that one of Death had threatened to crimson them with his blood,—all in the brief hour since he lay down to sleep. Sleeping or waking, we hear not the airy footsteps of the strange things that almost happen. Does it not argue a superintending Providence that, while viewless and unexpected events thrust themselves continually athwart our path, there should still be regularity enough to mortal life to render foresight even partially available?

The Type of Hawthorne's Stories: Hawthorne's solitary life and the circumstances which made him introspective, moody, and reserved are reflected in his writings. He stood by and watched life pass; he did not enter as part of it. Unlike Irving who enjoyed life and its humorous aspects, Hawthorne was interested in the "inner man"—in conscience, soul, and character. He wrote upon a theme always with a moral or lesson attached, as a preacher does his sermon. This was a true reflection of his Puritanical background. He was highly serious and highly imaginative. He made the story the study of a single intense situation, built in terms of culminating action, each detail logically leading to the next. His stories are somber but never horrible or gruesome.

For Appreciation: This allegorical fantasy was published in *Token*, in 1837. Note the effectiveness of a single situation which is illustrated in this story. Is giving the life history of the leading character generally a good method for introducing a story? Is it important that the reader know anything about David's life before the particular day on which the story begins? What allegorical meaning do you perceive in the second episode? What allegories do you interpret in the third? Which of the following do you consider the theme of the story (a) that a protecting Providence, unseen but ever present, guides the unexpected events that come across one's path continually, or (b) that Providence should give one intimation sufficient to sense in some manner passing events even though they are not seen by the eye? Does this story illustrate Hawthorne's style of writing?

For Further Study: Give the meanings of the following words and phrases: *vicissitudes; venomous superfluity; bowled; opiate; open countenance; dirk.*

What is the purpose of the first paragraph? Do the three incidents used by Hawthorne as examples of his theme seem to repeat themselves? Is this effective? Are the incidents arranged in culminating order of intensity? Which one might have served the purpose of the author? In the first episode do details follow logically to the very climax and then drop abruptly into a conclusion? Is this good? What is the turning point of the first episode? Are events in the second logically arranged? Is the conclusion of the story short or long-drawn out? Does the author adhere to his text or theme throughout the story?

Exercises and Creative Work: Outline this story showing Introduction, Body and Conclusion, and the sub-headings under each. Draw conclusions as to the perfection of form.

Write an episode for the story which might be substituted for one of the three in the story.

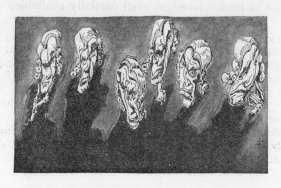

THE PIT AND THE PENDULUM

Edgar Allan Poe

I was sick—sick unto death with that long agony;[1] and when they at length unbound me, and I was permitted to sit, I felt that my senses were leaving me. The sentence—the dread sentence of death—was the last of distinct accentuation which reached my ears. After that, the sound of the inquisitorial voices seemed merged in one dreamy indeterminate hum. It conveyed to my soul the idea of *revolution,* perhaps from its association in fancy with the burr of a mill-wheel. This only for a brief period; for presently I heard no more. Yet, for a while, I saw; but with how terrible an exaggeration! I saw the lips of the black-robed judges. They appeared to me white, whiter than the sheet upon which I trace these words, and thin even to grotesqueness; thin with the intensity of their expres-

[1] Long agony—Torture.

sion of firmness—of immovable resolution, of stern contempt of human torture. I saw that the decrees of what to me was Fate were still issuing from those lips. I saw them writhe with a deadly locution. I saw them fashion the syllables of my name; and I shuddered because no sound succeeded. I saw, too, for a few moments of delirious horror, the soft and nearly imperceptible waving of the sable draperies which enwrapped the walls of the apartment. And then my vision fell upon the seven tall candles upon the table. At first they wore the aspect of charity, and seemed white, slender angels who would save me; but then, all at once there came a most deadly nausea over my spirit, and I felt every fiber in my frame thrill as if I had touched the wire of a galvanic battery,[2] while the angel forms became meaningless specters, with heads of flame, and I saw that from them there would be no help. And then there stole into my fancy, like a rich musical note, the thought of what sweet rest there must be in the grave. The thought came gently and stealthily, and it seemed long before it attained full appreciation; but just as my spirit came at length properly to feel and entertain it, the figures of the judges vanished, as if magically, from before me; the tall candles sank into nothingness; their flames went out utterly; the blackness of darkness supervened; all sensations appeared swallowed up in a mad rushing descent as of the soul into Hades. Then silence, and stillness, and night were the universe.

I had swooned; but still will not say that all of consciousness was lost. What of it there remained I will not attempt to define, or even to describe; yet all was not lost. In the deepest slumber—no! In delirium—no! In a swoon—no! In death —no! even in the grave all is not lost. Else there is no immortality for man. Arousing from the most profound of slumbers, we break the gossamer web of *some* dream. Yet in a second afterward (so frail may that web have been) we remember not that we have dreamed. In the return to life from the swoon there are two stages: first, that of the sense of mental or spiritual, secondly, that of the sense of physical, existence.

---

[2] GALVANIC BATTERY—At the time the story was written (1843), electric sparks and current were being produced for the first time by galvanic batteries. The electric sparks thus produced were still a mystery and hence the reference lends atmosphere to the story.

It seems probable that if, upon reaching the second stage, we could recall the impressions of the first, we should find these impressions eloquent in memories of the gulf beyond. And that gulf is—what? How at least shall we distinguish its shadows from those of the tomb? But if the impressions of what I have termed the first stage are not at will recalled, yet, after a long interval, do they not come unbidden, while we marvel whence they come? He who has never swooned is not he who finds strange palaces and wildly familiar faces in coals that glow; is not he who beholds floating in mid-air the sad visions that the many may not view; is not he who ponders over the perfume of some novel flower; is not he whose brain grows bewildered with the meaning of some musical cadence which has never before arrested his attention.

Amid frequent and thoughtful endeavors to remember, amid earnest struggles to regather some token of the state of seeming nothingness into which my soul had lapsed, there have been moments when I have dreamed of success; there have been brief, very brief periods when I have conjured up remembrances which the lucid reason of a later epoch assures me could have had reference only to that condition of seeming unconsciousness. These shadows of memory tell, indistinctly, of tall figures that lifted and bore me in silence down—down—still down—till a hideous dizziness oppressed me at the mere idea of the interminableness of the descent. They tell also of a vague horror at my heart, on account of that heart's unnatural stillness. Then comes a sense of sudden motionlessness throughout all things; as if those who bore me (a ghastly train!) had outrun in their descent the limits of the limitless, and paused from the wearisomeness of their toil. After this I call to mind flatness and dampness; and then all is *madness*—the madness of a memory which busies itself among forbidden things.

Very suddenly there came back to my soul motion and sound—the tumultuous motion of the heart, and, in my ears, the sound of its beating. Then a pause in which all is blank. Then again sound, and motion, and touch—a tingling sensation pervading my frame. Then the mere consciousness of existence, without thought—a condition which lasted long. Then, very suddenly, *thought,* and shuddering terror, and earnest endeavor to comprehend my true state. Then a strong desire

to lapse into insensibility.   Then a rushing revival of soul
and a successful effort to move.   And now a full memory of
the trial, of the judges, of the sable draperies, of the sentence,
of the sickness, of the swoon.   Then entire forgetfulness of all
that followed; of all that a later day and much earnestness of
endeavor have enabled me vaguely to recall.

So far, I had not opened my eyes.   I felt that I lay upon my
back unbound.   I reached out my hand, and it fell heavily upon
something damp and hard.   There I suffered it to remain for
many minutes, while I strove to imagine where and *what* I
could be.   I longed yet dared not to employ my vision.   I
dreaded the first glance at objects around me.   It was not that
I feared to look upon things horrible, but that I grew aghast
lest there should be *nothing* to see.   At length, with a wild
desperation at heart, I quickly unclosed my eyes.   My worst
thoughts, then, were confirmed.   The blackness of eternal night
encompassed me.   I struggled for breath.   The intensity of the
darkness seemed to oppress and stifle me.   The atmosphere was
intolerably close.   I still lay quietly, and made effort to exercise
my reason.   I brought to mind the inquisitorial proceedings,
and attempted from that point to deduce my real condition.
The sentence had passed; and it appeared to me that a very
long interval of time had since elapsed.   Yet not for a moment
did I suppose myself actually dead.   Such a supposition, notwithstanding what we read in fiction, is altogether inconsistent
with real existence—but where and in what state was I?   The
condemned to death, I knew, perished usually at the *autos-da-
fé*,[3] and one of these had been held on the very night of the
day of my trial.   Had I been remanded to my dungeon to await
the next sacrifice, which would not take place for many months?
This I at once saw could not be.   Victims had been in immediate demand.   Moreover, my dungeon, as well as all the
condemned cells at Toledo,[4] had stone floors, and light was not
altogether excluded.

A fearful idea now suddenly drove the blood in torrents upon
my heart, and for a brief period I once more relapsed into
insensibility.   Upon recovering, I at once started to my feet,

[3] *Autos-da-fé*—Sessions at which the court publicly sentenced prisoners.
[4] TOLEDO—In Spain.   The center of the Spanish Inquisition.

trembling convulsively in every fiber. I thrust my arms wildly above and around me in all directions. I felt nothing; yet dreaded to move a step, lest I should be impeded by the walls of a *tomb*. Perspiration burst from every pore, and stood in cold big beads upon my forehead. The agony of suspense grew at length intolerable, and I cautiously moved forward, with my arms extended, and my eyes straining from their sockets, in the hope of catching some faint ray of light. I proceeded for many paces; but still all was blackness and vacancy. I breathed more freely. It seemed evident that mine was not, at least, the most hideous of fates.

And, now, as I still continued to step cautiously onward, there came thronging upon my recollection a thousand vague rumors of the horrors of Toledo. Of the dungeons there had been strange things narrated—fables I had always deemed them —but yet strange, and too ghastly to repeat, save in a whisper. Was I left to perish of starvation in this subterranean world of darkness; or what fate, perhaps even more fearful, awaited me? That the result would be death, and a death of more than customary bitterness, I knew too well the character of my judges to doubt. The mode and the hour were all that occupied or distracted me.

My outstretched hands at length encountered some solid obstruction. It was a wall, seemingly of stone masonry—very smooth, slimy, and cold. I followed it up; stepping with all the careful distrust with which certain antique narratives had inspired me. This process, however, afforded me no means of ascertaining the dimensions of my dungeon; as I might make its circuit, and return to the point whence I set out, without being aware of the fact, so perfectly uniform seemed the wall. I therefore sought the knife which had been in my pocket when led into the inquisitorial chamber; but it was gone; my clothes had been exchanged for a wrapper of coarse serge. I had thought of forcing the blade in some minute crevice of the masonry, so as to identify my point of departure. The difficulty, nevertheless, was but trivial; although, in the disorder of my fancy, it seemed at first insuperable. I tore a part of the hem from the robe and placed the fragment at full length, and at right angles to the wall. In groping my way around the prison I could not fail to encounter this rag upon completing the circuit. So, at least, I thought; but I had not counted upon the extent of the dungeon, or upon my own weakness. The ground was moist and slippery. I staggered onward for some time, when I stumbled and fell. My excessive fatigue induced me to remain prostrate; and sleep soon overtook me as I lay.

Upon awaking, and stretching forth an arm, I found beside me a loaf and a pitcher with water. I was too much exhausted to reflect upon this circumstance, but ate and drank with avidity. Shortly afterward, I resumed my tour around the prison, and with much toil came at last upon the fragment of the serge. Up to the period when I fell, I had counted fifty-two paces, and, upon resuming my walk, I had counted forty-eight more—when I arrived at the rag. There were in all, then, a hundred paces; and, admitting two paces to the yard, I presumed the dungeon to be fifty yards in circuit. I had met, however, with many angles in the wall, and thus I could form no guess at the shape of the vault; for vault I could not help supposing it to be.

I had little object—certainly no hope—in these researches; but a vague curiosity prompted me to continue them. Quitting the wall, I resolved to cross the area of the enclosure. At first I proceeded with extreme caution, for the floor, although seemingly of solid material, was treacherous with slime. At length, however, I took courage, and did not hesitate to step firmly—endeavoring to cross in as direct a line as possible. I had advanced some ten or twelve paces in this manner, when the remnant of the torn hem of my robe became entangled between my legs. I stepped on it and fell violently on my face.

In the confusion attending my fall, I did not immediately apprehend a somewhat startling circumstance, which yet, in a few seconds afterward, and while I still lay prostrate, arrested my attention. It was this: my chin rested upon the floor of the prison, but my lips and the upper portion of my head, although seemingly at a less elevation than the chin, touched nothing. At the same time, my forehead seemed bathed in a clammy vapor, and the peculiar smell of decayed fungus arose to my nostrils. I put forward my arm, and shuddered to find that I had fallen at the very brink of a circular pit, whose extent, of course, I had no means of ascertaining at the moment. Groping about the masonry just below the margin, I succeeded in dislodging a small fragment, and let it fall into the abyss. For many seconds I hearkened to its reverberations as it dashed against the sides of the chasm in its descent; at length there was a sullen plunge into water, succeeded by loud echoes. At the same moment there came a sound resembling the quick opening and as rapid closing of a door overhead, while a faint gleam of light flashed suddenly through the gloom, and as suddenly faded away.

I saw clearly the doom which had been prepared for me, and congratulated myself upon the timely accident by which I had escaped. Another step before my fall, and the world had seen me no more. And the death just avoided was of that very character which I had regarded as fabulous and frivolous in the tales respecting the Inquisition. To the victims of its tyranny there was the choice of death with its direst physical agonies, or death with its most hideous moral horrors. I had been reserved for the latter. By long suffering my nerves had been unstrung, until I trembled at the sound of my own voice, and had become in every respect a fitting subject for the species of torture which awaited me.

Shaking in every limb, I groped my way back to the wall—resolving there to perish rather than risk the terrors of the wells, of which my imagination now pictured many in various positions about the dungeon. In other conditions of mind, I might have had courage to end my misery at once by a plunge into one of these abysses; but now I was the veriest of cowards. Neither could I forget what I had read of these pits—that the *sudden* extinction of life formed no part of their most horrible plan.

Agitation of spirit kept me awake for many long hours; but at length I again slumbered. Upon arousing, I found by my side, as before, a loaf and a pitcher of water. A burning thirst consumed me, and I emptied the vessel at a draught. It must have been drugged—for scarcely had I drunk, before I became irresistibly drowsy. A deep sleep fell upon me—a sleep like that of death. How long it lasted, of course, I know not; but, when once again I unclosed my eyes, the objects around me were visible. By a wild, sulphurous luster,[5] the origin of which

---

[5] SULPHUROUS LUSTER—Bluish light.

I could not at first determine, I was enabled to see the extent and aspect of the prison.

In its size I had been greatly mistaken. The whole circuit of its walls did not exceed twenty-five yards. For some minutes this fact occasioned me a world of vain trouble; vain indeed— for what could be of less importance, under the terrible circumstances which environed me, than the mere dimensions of my dungeon? But my soul took a wild interest in trifles, and I busied myself in endeavors to account for the error I had committed in my measurement. The truth at length flashed upon me. In my first attempt at exploration I had counted fifty-two paces, up to the period when I fell: I must then have been within a pace or two of the fragment of serge; in fact, I had nearly performed the circuit of the vault. I then slept— and, upon awaking, I must have returned upon my steps, thus supposing the circuit nearly double what it actually was. My confusion of mind prevented me from observing that I began my tour with the wall to the left, and ended it with the wall to the right.

I had been deceived, too, in respect to the shape of the enclosure. In feeling my way, I had found many angles, and thus deduced an idea of great irregularity; so potent is the effect of total darkness upon one arousing from lethargy or sleep! The angles were simply those of a few slight depressions, or niches, at odd intervals. The general shape of the prison was square. What I had taken for masonry seemed now to be iron, or some other metal, in huge plates, whose sutures or joints occasioned the depression. The entire surface of this metallic enclosure was rudely daubed in hideous and repulsive devices. The figures of fiends in aspects of menace, with skeleton forms, and other more really fearful images, overspread and disfigured the walls. I observed that the outlines of these monstrosities were sufficiently distinct, but that the colors seemed faded and blurred, as if from the effects of a damp atmosphere. I now noticed the floor, too, which was of stone. In the center yawned the circular pit from whose jaws I had escaped; but it was the only one in the dungeon.

All this I saw distinctly and by much effort, for my personal condition had been greatly changed during slumber. I now lay upon my back, and at full length, on a species of low framework of wood. To this I was securely bound by a long strap resembling a surcingle.[6] It passed in many convolutions about my limbs and body, leaving at liberty only my head, and my left arm to such extent that I could, by dint of much exertion, supply myself with food from an earthen dish which lay by my side on the floor. I saw, to my horror, that the pitcher had been removed. I say, to my horror—for I was consumed with intolerable thirst. This thirst it appeared to be the design of my persecutors to stimulate, for the food in the dish was meat pungently seasoned.

Looking upward, I surveyed the ceiling of my prison. It was some thirty or forty feet overhead, and constructed much as the side walls. In one of its panels a very singular figure riveted my whole attention. It was the painted figure of Time as he is commonly represented, save that, in lieu of a scythe, he held what, at a casual glance, I supposed to be the pictured image of a huge pendulum, such as we see on antique clocks. There was something, however, in the appearance of this machine which caused me to regard it more attentively. While I gazed directly upward at it (for its position was immediately over my own), I fancied that I saw it in motion. In an instant afterward the fancy was confirmed. Its sweep was brief, and of course slow. I watched it for some minutes, somewhat in fear, but more in wonder. Wearied at length with observing its dull movement, I turned my eyes upon the other objects in the cell.

A slight noise attracted my notice, and, looking to the floor, I saw several enormous rats traversing it. They had issued from the well, which lay just within view to my right. Even then, while I gazed, they came in troops, hurriedly, with ravenous eyes, allured by the scent of the meat. From this it required much effort and attention to scare them away.

It might have been half an hour, perhaps even an hour (for I could take but imperfect note of time), before I again cast my eyes upward. What I then saw, confounded and amazed me. The sweep of the pendulum had increased in extent by nearly a yard. As a natural consequence, its velocity was also much

---

[6] SURCINGLE—A girdle or belt, the leather of which is wound around and around.

*They came in troops, hurriedly,
with ravenous eyes . . .*

greater. But what mainly disturbed me, was the idea that it had perceptibly *descended*. I now observed—with what horror it is needless to say—that its nether extremity was formed of a crescent of glittering steel, about a foot in length from horn to horn; the horns upward, and the under edge evidently as keen as that of a razor. Like a razor, also, it seemed massy and heavy, tapering from the edge into a solid and broad structure. It was appended to a weighty rod of brass, and the whole *hissed* as it swung through the air.

I could no longer doubt the doom prepared for me by in-genuity in torture. My cognizance of the pit had become known to the inquisitorial agents—*the pit,* whose horrors had been destined for so bold a recusant as myself—*the pit,* typical of hell, and regarded by rumor as the Ultima Thule [7] of all their punishments. The plunge into this pit I had avoided by the merest of accidents, and I knew that surprise, or entrapment into torment, formed an important portion of all the gro-tesquerie of these dungeon deaths. Having failed to fall, it was no part of the demon plan to hurl me into the abyss; and thus (there being no alternative) a different and a milder destruction awaited me. Milder! I half smiled in my agony as I thought of such application of such a term.

What boots it to tell of the long, long hours of horror more than mortal, during which I counted the rushing oscillations of the steel! Inch by inch—line by line—with a descent only appreciable at intervals that seemed ages—down and still down it came! Days passed—it might have been that many days passed—ere it swept so closely over me as to fan me with its acrid breath. The odor of the sharp steel forced itself into my nostrils. I prayed—I wearied heaven with my prayer for its more speedy descent. I grew frantically mad, and struggled to force myself upward against the sweep of the fearful scimitar. And then I fell suddenly calm, and lay smiling at the glittering death, as a child at some rare bawble.

There was another interval of utter insensibility; it was brief; for, upon again lapsing into life, there had been no perceptible descent in the pendulum. But it might have been long; for

---

[7] ULTIMA THULE—The northernmost point on the ancient maps, hence, extremity or furthermost limit.

I knew there were demons who took note of my swoon, and who could have arrested the vibration at pleasure. Upon my recovery, too, I felt very—oh, inexpressibly—sick and weak, as if through long inanition. Even amid the agonies of the period the human nature craved food. With painful effort, I out-stretched my left arm as far as my bonds permitted, and took possession of the small remnant which had been spared me by the rats. As I put a portion of it within my lips, there rushed to my mind a half-formed thought of joy—of hope. Yet what business had I with hope? It was, as I say, a half-formed thought: man has many such, which are never completed. I felt that it was of joy—of hope; but I felt also that it had perished in its formation. In vain I struggled to perfect—to regain it. Long suffering had nearly annihilated all my ordinary powers of mind. I was an imbecile—an idiot.

The vibration of the pendulum was at right angles to my length. I saw that the crescent was designed to cross the region of the heart. It would fray the serge of my robe—it would return and repeat its operations—again—and again. Notwithstanding its terrifically wide sweep (some thirty feet or more), and the hissing vigor of its descent, sufficient to sunder these very walls of iron, still the fraying of my robe would be all that, for several minutes, it would accomplish. And at this thought I paused. I dared not go farther than this reflection. I dwelt upon it with a pertinacity of attention—as if, in so dwelling, I could arrest *here* the descent of the steel. I forced myself to ponder upon the sound of the crescent as it should pass across the garment—upon the peculiar thrilling sensation which the friction of cloth produces on the nerves. I pondered upon all this frivolity until my teeth were on edge.

Down—steadily down it crept. I took a frenzied pleasure in contrasting its downward with its lateral velocity. To the right —to the left—far and wide—with the shriek of a damned spirit! to my heart, with the stealthy pace of the tiger! I alternately laughed and howled, as the one or the other idea grew predominant.

Down—certainly, relentlessly down! It vibrated within three inches of my bosom! I struggled violently—furiously—to free my left arm. This was free only from the elbow to the hand. I could reach the latter from the platter beside me to my mouth, with great effort, but no farther. Could I have broken the fastenings above the elbow, I would have seized and attempted to arrest the pendulum. I might as well have attempted to arrest an avalanche!

Down—still unceasingly—still inevitably down! I gasped and struggled at each vibration. I shrunk convulsively at its every sweep. My eyes followed its outward or upward whirls with the eagerness of the most unmeaning despair; they closed themselves spasmodically at the descent, although death would have been a relief, oh, how unspeakable! Still I quivered in every nerve to think how slight a sinking of the machinery would precipitate that keen, glistening ax upon my bosom. It was *hope* that prompted the nerve to quiver—the frame to shrink. It was *hope*—the hope that triumphs on the rack [8]— that whispers to the death-condemned even in the dungeons of the Inquisition.

I saw that some ten or twelve vibrations would bring the steel in actual contact with my robe; and with this observation there suddenly came over my spirit all the keen, collected calmness of despair. For the first time during many hours— or perhaps days—I *thought*. It now occurred to me that the bandage, or surcingle, which enveloped me, was unique. It was tied by no separate cord. The first stroke of the razorlike crescent athwart any portion of the band would so detach it that it might be unwound from my person by means of my left hand. But how fearful, in that case, the proximity of the steel! The result of the slightest struggle, how deadly! Was it likely, moreover, that the minions of the torturer had not foreseen and provided for this possibility? Was it probable that the bandage crossed my bosom in the track of the pendulum? Dreading to find my faint, and, as it seemed, my last hope frustrated, I so far elevated my head as to obtain a distinct view of my breast. The surcingle enveloped my limbs and body close in all directions—*save in the path of the destroying crescent.*

Scarcely had I dropped my head back into its original position, when there flashed upon my mind what I cannot better describe than as the unformed half of that idea of deliverance

---

[8] RACK—A machine of torture.

to which I have previously alluded, and of which a moiety [9] only floated indeterminately through my brain when I raised food to my burning lips. The whole thought was now present —feeble, scarcely sane, scarcely definite—but still entire. I proceeded at once, with the nervous energy of despair, to attempt its execution.

For many hours the immediate vicinity of the low framework upon which I lay had been literally swarming with rats. They were wild, bold, ravenous—their red eyes glaring upon me as if they waited but for motionlessness on my part to make me their prey. "To what food," I thought, "have they been accustomed in the well?"

They had devoured, in spite of all my efforts to prevent them, all but a small remnant of the contents of the dish. I had fallen into an habitual seesaw, or wave of the hand about the platter; and, at length, the unconscious uniformity of the movement deprived it of effect. In their voracity the vermin frequently fastened their sharp fangs in my fingers. With the particles of the oily and spicy viand which now remained I thoroughly rubbed the bandage wherever I could reach it; then, raising my hand from the floor, I lay breathlessly still.

At first, the ravenous animals were startled and terrified at the change—at the cessation of movement. They shrank alarmedly back; many sought the well. But this was only for a moment. I had not counted in vain upon their voracity. Observing that I remained without motion, one or two of the boldest leaped upon the framework, and smelt at the surcingle. This seemed the signal for a general rush. Forth from the well they hurried in fresh troops. They clung to the wood— they overran it, and leaped in hundreds upon my person. The measured movement of the pendulum disturbed then not at all. Avoiding its strokes, they busied themselves with the anointed bandage. They pressed—they swarmed upon me in ever accumulating heaps. They writhed upon my throat; their cold lips sought my own; I was half stifled by their thronging pressure; disgust, for which the world has no name, swelled my bosom, and chilled, with a heavy clamminess, my heart. Yet one minute, and I felt that the struggle would be over. Plainly

---

[9] MOIETY—A part.

I perceived the loosening of the bandage. I knew that in more that one place it must be already severed. With a more than human resolution I lay *still*.

Nor had I erred in my calculations—nor had I endured in vain. I at length felt that I was *free*. The surcingle hung in ribbons from my body. But the stroke of the pendulum already pressed upon my bosom. It had divided the serge of the robe. It had cut through the linen beneath. Twice again it swung, and a sharp sense of pain shot through every nerve. But the moment of escape had arrived. At a wave of my hand my deliverers hurried tumultuously away. With a steady movement—cautious, sidelong, shrinking, and slow—I slid from the embrace of the bandage and beyond the reach of the scimitar. For the moment, at least, *I was free*.

Free! and in the grasp of the Inquisition! I had scarcely stepped from my wooden bed of horror upon the stone floor of the prison, when the motion of the hellish machine ceased, and I beheld it drawn up, by some invisible force, through the ceiling. This was a lesson which I took desperately to heart. My every motion was undoubtedly watched. Free!—I had but escaped death in one form of agony to be delivered unto worse than death in some other. With that thought I rolled my eyes nervously around on the barriers of iron that hemmed me in. Something unusual—some change which, at first, I could not appreciate distinctly—it was obvious, had taken place in the apartment. For many minutes of a dreamy and trembling abstraction I busied myself in vain, unconnected conjecture. During this period, I became aware, for the first time, of the origin of the sulphurous light which illumined the cell. It proceeded from a fissure,[10] about half an inch in width, extending entirely around the prison at the base of the walls, which thus appeared, and were, completely separated from the floor. I endeavored, but of course in vain, to look through the aperture.

As I arose from the attempt, the mystery of the alteration in the chamber broke at once upon my understanding. I have observed that, although the outlines of the figures upon the walls were sufficiently distinct, yet the colors seemed blurred

---

[10] FISSURE—A narrow opening.

and indefinite. These colors had now assumed, and were momentarily assuming, a startling and most intense brilliancy, and gave to the spectral and fiendish portraitures an aspect that might have thrilled even firmer nerves than my own. Demon eyes, of a wild and ghastly vivacity, glared upon me in a thousand directions, where none had been visible before, and gleamed with the lurid luster of a fire that I could not force my imagination to regard as unreal.

Unreal! Even while I breathed there came to my nostrils the breath of the vapor of heated iron! A suffocating odor pervaded the prison. A deeper glow settled each moment in the eyes that glared at my agonies! A richer tint of crimson diffused itself over the pictured horrors of blood. I panted! I gasped for breath! There could be no doubt of the design of my tormentors—oh, most unrelenting! Oh, most demoniac of men! I shrank from the glowing metal to the center of the cell. Amid the thought of the fiery destruction that impended, the idea of the coolness of the well came over my soul like balm. I rushed to its deadly brink. I threw my straining vision below. The glare from the enkindled roof illumined its inmost recesses. Yet, for a wild moment, did my spirit refuse to comprehend the meaning of what I saw. At length it forced —it wrestled its way into my soul—it burned itself upon my shuddering reason. Oh, for a voice to speak! Oh, horror! oh, any horror but this! With a shriek, I rushed from the margin, and buried my face in my hands—weeping bitterly.

The heat rapidly increased, and once again I looked up, shuddering as with a fit of the ague. There had been a second change in the cell—and now the change was obviously in the *form*. As before, it was in vain that I at first endeavored to appreciate or understand what was taking place. But not long was I left in doubt. The Inquisitorial vengeance had been hurried by my twofold escape, and there was to be no more dallying with the King of Terrors. The room had been square I saw that two of its iron angles were now acute—two, consequently, obtuse. The fearful difference quickly increased with a low, rumbling or moaning sound. In an instant the apartment had shifted its form into that of a lozenge.[11] But the altera-

---

[11] LOZENGE—A diamond-shaped figure.

tion stopped not here—I neither hoped nor desired it to stop. I could have clasped the red walls to my bosom as a garment of eternal peace. "Death," I said, "any death but that of the pit!" Fool! might I not have known that *into the pit* it was the object of the burning iron to urge me? Could I resist its glow? Or if even that, could I withstand its pressure? And now, flatter and flatter grew the lozenge, with a rapidity that left me no time for contemplation. Its center, and, of course, its greatest width, came just over the yawning gulf. I shrank back—but the closing walls pressed me resistlessly onward. At length for my seared and writhing body there was no longer an inch of foothold on the firm floor of the prison. I struggled no more, but the agony of my soul found vent in one loud, long, and final scream of despair. I felt that I tottered upon the brink—I averted my eyes——

There was a discordant hum of human voices. There was a loud blast as of many trumpets! There was a harsh grating as of a thousand thunders! The fiery walls rushed back! An out-stretched arm caught my own as I fell, fainting, into the abyss. It was that of General Lasalle.[10] The French army had entered Toledo. The Inquisition was in the hands of its enemies.

[10] GENERAL LASALLE—An officer in Napoleon's army. In 1808 he entered Toledo, thus taking Spain for Napoleon. This places the time of Poe's story at the beginning of the nineteenth century.

The Type of Poe's Stories: Like Hawthorne, Poe was interested in the supernatural and weird, but he was far less restrained. He reveled in horror, grimness, and terror which are never found in Hawthorne's stories. But he was answering a demand of his readers. Most of Poe's writings were done for magazines, and he was for many years himself a magazine editor. He studied the tastes of the magazine readers and gave them what they wanted. He wrote for effect only—to create an impression upon his readers for the brief moment that was his. He did not moralize, as did Hawthorne, nor were his events true to life. His characters are not real flesh and blood people and his stories are usually independent of time or place. He wanted atmosphere only, and cunningly selected and arranged his details to work out the single predetermined effect. The details lead to the moment of climax and leave nothing behind in the mind of the reader but a haunting memory and a depressing rather than elevating effect.

For Appreciation: *The Pit and the Pendulum* was published in *The Gift*, a magazine, in 1843. The single effect or single impression produced upon the reader is one of atmosphere. Time and place are unimportant. Even the character is subordinated. The feeling of horror or terror predominates from beginning to end. The effect is produced not by rapid movement but by variations upon the sensation of fear. Name in order the incidents which give you a thrill of fear, or a shudder. Do these seem to succeed each other in rapid succession? Are they arranged in order of climax? Did Poe control your feelings for the "few moments that were his"? In what respect was your feeling about this story like or different from the feeling about other stories you have read? Do you like Poe's method?

For Further Study: As applied to the story give the meanings of the following: *accentuation; locution; sable draperies; supervened; subterranean; insuperable; avidity; recusant; oscillations; frustrated; lozenge.* Make a list of words and expressions which add to the feeling of terror in the story.

When do you first have an interest in the story? Could the time be any time, the place be any place, and the character, anybody? What sentence was decreed by the black-robed judges? What impression was conveyed to the prisoner by the seven candles? Does it matter that you do not know the prisoner's name? What were some of the sensations the prisoner experienced as he recovered from the swoon? What effect did the blackness have upon him? Describe the tour of the prison and the escape from the pit. Why is a detailed description of the pit omitted? Does the sulphurous light lessen the prisoner's terrors? How was he bound to the floor? What effect does the appearance of the rats produce? Did the vibrating pendulum at first disturb the prisoner? How do the sounds heighten the effect? How does the author use the sense of smell to the same purpose? Explain how the surcingle was arranged to accommodate the vibrating pendulum. Do you think the main purpose of the pendulum was to kill the prisoner? What was the next torture? Was this greater than the pendulum torture? Where is the climax of the story? Is the conclusion satisfactory? Should it be longer?

Exercises and Creative Work: Write a paragraph on why you liked or did not like the story.

With three members chosen for each side, conduct a class debate on the following: Resolved: That horror and terror should be barred from stories and from moving pictures.

Give another title to Poe's story which you consider would be more attractive to catch magazine readers' attention.

Make a special report on the history of the Inquisition.

Let General Lasalle or another of the rescuing party tell in his own words the story of the rescue of the prisoner.

Develop a descriptive story creating a single effect such as horror, terror, pain, joy.

THE HISTORY OF THE AMERICAN SHORT STORY

THE TRANSITION PERIOD (1865–1900)

General Characteristics

This period was to see the development of the regional or local color story with its emphasis on setting. Two factors were instrumental in bringing about this new type of story. In the first place, the rapid territorial expansion of the country aroused interest in new localities and scenes and there was a corresponding demand for reading matter which would depict the life and people of these new and picturesque regions. Magazines greatly increased in number and the short story was the type of writing best adapted to fill them with interesting material. The second factor which was instrumental in popularizing the regional short story was the tendency toward realism in this period, and realism is always aided by a geographical setting peopled by characters native to the environment.

WRITERS OF THE WEST AND MIDDLE WEST

The local color story made its appearance in the West and from there spread to all other parts of the country. The Transition Period was the one which saw the final conquest of the West—it witnessed the last Indian fights, the picturesque mining towns, the slaughter of the buffalo herds and the passing of the last frontier. These scenes, so romantic and full of adventure, furnished new material for stories which were hailed with enthusiasm and applause by the admiring East.

Francis Bret Harte (1839–1902)

The local color story began with Bret Harte. He developed and made popular the story which is the logical and inevitable outcome of the environment.

His career was an interesting and varied one, beginning in Albany, New York, continuing in San Francisco, Germany and Scotland, and ending in London. To the boy, son of a poor schoolmaster, his childhood in Albany meant more or less privation. He left that city in 1854 to join his widowed mother who had gone to California the year before. His trip, made by way of Panama, was an adventure in itself. For three years he had a variety of experiences as express messenger, printer, teacher, drug clerk, miner, and editor. Finally he settled in San Francisco as a printer. In 1867 his first collection of poems was published and shortly after this he became editor of *The Overland Monthly*. He adopted a policy in connection with this magazine which quickly made him famous. He conceived the idea of making his magazine a mirror of the stirring events about him, and he depicted the romance and picturesqueness accompanying and following the California gold rush of 1849. *The Luck of Roaring Camp, The Outcasts of Poker Flat* and *Tennessee's Partner,* published in *The Overland* produced almost a sensation in the East. There followed in rapid succession a number of other stories, but the man who successfully pictured the days of early California was not to remain in the West. In 1871 Harte went East where for a time he was contributing editor to *The Atlantic Monthly.* Friends secured his appointment as United States Consul at Crefeld, Germany. In 1880 he was transferred to Glasgow where he remained for five years. He spent the remainder of his life in London where he died in 1901. By being the first to use the peculiarities of a single section of the country as the main interest in his stories, Harte made a distinct contribution to the art of short story writing.

Samuel L. Clemens (Mark Twain) (1835–1910)

Against the frontier background appears the figure of Mark Twain, the most representative American writer of this period. His place in American literature is unique. He was a voluminous writer, producing not only short stories, but also travel sketches, essays, biography, and novels. He is generally thought of as a humorist, but he was no mere clown. He is the embodiment of what we might call the American "Comic Spirit," for much of his humor proceeds from his good-natured ridicule of institutions, conventions, and manners which strangle humanity. His short stories are decidedly humorous, and if some of them are not in the strict sense of the word, "local color," they at least, like all of his writings, carry the sweep and vastness of the American frontier and portray its humor and democratic spirit.

Born in Missouri, he spent his boyhood on the banks of the Mississippi River. His early experiences as a pilot on the river were later to suggest to him his pen name, Mark Twain. "By the mark, twain," was the cry used by the man who sounded the depth of the water to tell the pilot it was two fathoms deep.

At the outbreak of the Civil War, navigation on the Mississippi ceased and Clemens' occupation was gone. In 1861 he went to Nevada where he was brought in touch with the gold fields of the West and where he caught the mining fever. He found only a very small amount of gold, however, and soon gave up mining in favor of newspaper work. His experiences in the West furnished the basis of some of his most popular stories, such as *The Celebrated Jumping Frog.* While on a trip to Europe, Egypt, and Palestine he wrote a series of letters for a San Francisco paper describing his trip. These letters were later published in book form under the name of *Innocents Abroad* and immediately attracted attention. From his early experiences on the Mississippi he drew his materials for *Life on the Mississippi, The Adventures of Tom Sawyer,* and *Huckleberry Finn.* The latter part of his life was spent in New England where he died in 1910.

Hamlin Garland (1860–1940)

Hamlin Garland was the chief interpreter of the region of the Middle West. He was born in Wisconsin, the son of a typical pioneer whose restless spirit with its visions and hopes of better soil and bigger crops farther west urged him continually to move on to new land. When Garland was still a small boy the family moved from Wisconsin to Minnesota, from Minnesota to Iowa, and from Iowa to Dakota. He attended school in winter and worked on the farm in summer. He attended the Cedar Valley Seminary in Osage, Iowa, for five winters and later became a country school teacher in Illinois. The call of the border was too strong to be resisted, however, and in 1883 he took up a claim in Dakota. This he sold in 1884 and went to Boston, the home of his ancestors, where he lived for several years, supporting and educating himself as best he could with the meager resources at his command. It was on a summer visit to his "Middle Border" home that he saw with new eyes the grinding toil and crushing burden of the border farmer. This visit started him upon a series of stories depicting farm life as he knew it and had lived it. This series, under the title of *Main-Travelled Roads*, was a group of realistic, almost grim, sketches of farm life picturing the overburdened, hard-worked farmer. It won instant recognition and was followed by other short stories and novels. After about nine years in Boston and New York, Garland surrendered his residence in the East and re-established his home in the West.

In later writings he turned to biographical and autobiographical material and here his style was less grim and harsh. His own life was written in *A Son of the Middle Border*, and the story of the girl who later became his wife was in *A Daughter of the Middle Border*. In all of his writings he depicted the life of the frontier farmers "in language which might do something to lift the desperate burdens of their condition."

Other Western and Mid-Western Writers

Other interpreters of the West and Mid-West are Maurice Thompson (1844–1901), author of *Hoosier Mosaics;* Alice French (1850–1934) who under the pen name of Octave Thanet wrote stories of the Arkansas canebrakes, some of which are collected under the title *Knitters in the Sun;* and Constance Fennimore Woolson (1840–1894), writer of Great Lake scenes in *Castle Nowhere: Lake-Country Sketches.*

The South was also to receive enthusiastic treatment at the hands of her short story writers.

George Washington Cable (1844–1925)

The first interpreter of the South was George Washington Cable, portrayer of life in early New Orleans. His characters were the Creoles, a population in Louisiana partly descended from the early Spaniards and partly from the French Acadians who had been transported from Nova Scotia.

Cable was born in New Orleans in 1844. His father was a Virginian and his mother a New Englander. When he was fourteen, his father died and the boy worked at odd jobs to support his mother and sisters. During the Civil War he enlisted in the 4th Mississippi Cavalry. His desire for learning was so great that even during his enlistment he studied Latin and the Bible. At the close of the war he helped survey along the Atchafalya River. Here he contracted malaria and for two years was unable to do physical work. He began to write at this time for newspapers. His column received such favorable attention that he was made a reporter. However, his religious convictions would not permit him to attend the theater and write up the press notices, so he was forced to leave the paper. These same religious convictions made him an active advocate for prison reforms and for justice for the negro. After his experience at newspaper work he became a clerk for a company dealing in cotton. Still his desire for learning was unsatisfied and even after his marriage and the birth of his children, he got up at four o'clock in the morning to study. When he had mastered French, he became extremely interested in the old records and archives of New Orleans. As Hawthorne had brooded over Puritan traditions, so did Cable brood over those of Louisiana, and at length put them in story form.

Cable's stories rank with Bret Harte's as local color stories. They are vivid pictures of a phase of life that has passed away. Cable was not a prolific writer, but he has won for himself a place of high honor in American literature.

Thomas Nelson Page (1853–1922)

Thomas Nelson Page chose Virginia for his settings. He used the negro dialect as a vehicle for telling his stories and portrays the plantation life of the southern aristocracy before the Civil War. His love for the South was passionate and intense, and in his stories there is expression of deep regret for the passing of the old times. His best stories are *Marse Chan* and *Meh Lady*.

Joel Chandler Harris (1849–1908)

What Cable did for Louisiana and Page for Virginia, Joel Chandler Harris accomplished for Georgia. He was born near Eatonton, Georgia, and after an elementary education acquired in rural schools and at the Eatonton Academy, he began his career as a printer's apprentice on a local weekly. He studied law and practiced for a time, but his special talent lay in journalism. For twenty years he edited *The Atlanta Constitution,* and it was during his connection with this paper that he created the famous character of Uncle Remus. Upon the retirement of a regular contributor of negro dialect stories, Harris, to supply the lack thus created in the paper, began the series of tales by which he was to achieve immortality. He had always been fascinated by the animal stories which he had heard old negroes tell, and he now put them on paper for a delighted reading public. He was not only a master of the art of writing dialect, but he knew the human heart. Although for years a Catholic in heart, he was received into the Church only two weeks before his death.

The first stories were collected and published in 1880 under the title *Uncle Remus, His Songs and His Sayings.* This volume was followed by *Nights with Uncle Remus, Uncle Remus and His Friends,* and *Told by Uncle Remus.* Harris wrote many stories of other kinds, but it is through "Uncle Remus" that he became known as one of America's most distinctively original writers, and it is for "Uncle Remus" that he will always be best remembered.

Kate O'Flaherty Chopin (1851–1904)

Another sympathetic interpreter of Southern life was Kate Chopin, who like Cable wrote of the Louisiana Creoles. Her best known works are *Bayou Folk* and *A Night in Acadie,* collections of sketches and stories of the people of Natchitoches Parish, whom she came to know and love during the years which she spent on her husband's plantation on the Red River.

Kate Chopin was born in St. Louis in 1851. Her father, a successful business man, died while she was but a child. Her formal schooling was received at the Sacred Heart Convent in St. Louis; a more influential part of her education she gathered in the attic of her home, whither she fled for uninterrupted reading of her favorite authors.

In 1870 she married a native of Louisiana, Oscar Chopin, and after a honeymoon in Europe the couple moved to New Orleans, where for the next ten years her husband engaged in the cotton trade. It was his decision to assume the personal management of his own plantation and his sister's on the Red River that brought his wife to the section of Louisiana which she was to portray so realistically in her stories. Devoted and busy mother of five children though she was, she found leisure in her new life to undertake writing for publication. In 1882 her husband died of swamp fever, and eventually she sold the plantation and returned to St. Louis. However, she never lost her affection for Natchitoches Parish and frequently revisited it.

Mrs. Chopin published two novels, *At Fault,* her earliest work, and *The Awakening,* her last; contributed children's stories to *The Youth's Companion* and other juvenile periodicals of her day; and to the *Century* and *Harpers* stories and sketches for more mature readers. But it is the masterful local-color stories of Natchitoches Parish in *Bayou Folk* and *A Night in Acadie* that won her distinction and assure the survival of her name in American letters.

WRITERS OF THE EAST

The task of gathering up and preserving the local manners and character and dialect of New England was to fall into the hands of men and women whose stories, while not exciting and adventurous, depict faithfully the New England mannerisms and ingrained peculiarities of conscience and mind.

Maurice Francis Egan (1852–1924)

Journalist, professor, diplomat, author, lecturer—in all these roles the genial character of Maurice Francis Egan was eminent. Born in Philadelphia in 1852, educated at home by a cultured mother, at La Salle College by the Christian Brothers, and at Georgetown University by the Jesuits, he spent ten years in New York journalism before going to Notre Dame University as professor of English. After eight years at Notre Dame and eleven years at the Catholic University, he was appointed Minister to Denmark by President Roosevelt, a post which he continued to hold under Presidents Taft and Wilson until his resignation because of ill health in 1918.

His contributions to the leading periodicals of his day were of a most diversified character. He wrote stories for boys and stories for girls, volumes of poetry, critical essays in abundance, studies in literature, memoirs of his diplomatic experiences, and recollections of his life. Through them all he invariably retained the amiable character that won him friends everywhere. A gentleman of the old school, courtesy and kindliness dominated his writing as they dominated his soul.

Mary E. Wilkins Freeman (1862–1930)

Many of Mrs. Freeman's characters are soul-embittered and somber. Among her best stories are *A Humble Romance, A New England Nun, A Village Singer,* and *The Revolt of Mother.*

Alice Brown (1857–   )

Alice Brown's stories are characterized by humor and by a delight in the open air. Her field is her native New Hampshire.

Contrasted to the local color writers of this period was a group of men, who, less affected by realism and the new tendencies in literature, were nevertheless to contribute important advances in the style, artistry, and technique of the short story.

Thomas Bailey Aldrich (1836–1907)

First and most important of this group was Thomas Bailey Aldrich, a native of Portsmouth, New Hampshire, whose early life is so delightfully described in his *Story of a Bad Boy*. From his youth he was interested in literature and he wrote poetry voluminously. His fame rests in his short story writing, however, and no story was ever received with more ovation by the public than his *Marjorie Daw*. His contributions to the short story were a perfect technique and an unexpected ending.

Henry Cuyler Bunner (1855–1896)

Also important in this group was Henry Cuyler Bunner, who was born in Oswego, New York. Circumstances made it necessary for him to give up plans for a college education, and after a brief period spent in an importing house, he entered the field of journalism. He became a reporter on the New York *World,* and later on the New York *Sun.* From the age of twenty-two until he died at forty-one he was editor of *Puck,* a humorous weekly, and almost all of his writing was done for the columns of this magazine. His stories are sparkling, lively and humorous, depending more upon style than upon character or setting. He emphasized brevity in the short story and, like Aldrich, delighted in the surprise element.

Frank R. Stockton (1834–1902)

Frank R. Stockton was born in Philadelphia, Pennsylvania. As a boy he was fond of making up children's stories and some of the best stories which he wrote in later years were for children. He had a rare sense of humor evidenced in such stories as *The Widow's Cruise* and *A Tale of Negative Gravity*. He delighted in the "trick" story and in treating impossible situations with absurd gravity. His *Lady or the Tiger* was the most talked-of short story of the period.

Other Writers

Two other writers of this group deserve mention. The first is Henry James (1843–1916), who gave the short story a psychological twist, and who is best remembered for *The Turn of the Screw* and *The Story in It.* The second is Ambrose Bierce (1842–1913) whose tales, though showing a mastery of the art of technique, are for the most part bitter anecdotes with horrible situations. Two of his best known stories are *A Horseman in the Sky* and *The Man and the Snake*.

Short Stories of the Transition Period
TENNESSEE'S PARTNER
Bret Harte

I DO not think that we ever knew his real name. Our ignorance of it certainly never gave us any social inconvenience, for at Sandy Bar in 1854 most men were christened anew. Sometimes these appellatives were derived from some distinctiveness of dress as in the case of "Dungaree Jack"; or from some peculiarity of habit, as shown in "Saleratus Bill," so called from an undue proportion of that chemical in his daily bread; or from some unlucky slip, as exhibited in "The Iron Pirate," a mild, inoffensive man, who earned that baleful title by his unfortunate mispronunciation of the term "iron pyrites." Perhaps this may have been the beginning of a rude heraldry; but I am constrained to think that it was because a man's real name in that day rested solely upon his own unsupported statement. "Call yourself Clifford, do you?" said Boston, addressing a timid newcomer with infinite scorn; "hell is full of such Cliffords!" He then introduced the unfortunate man, whose name happened to be really Clifford, as "Jaybird Charley,"—an unhallowed inspiration of the moment that clung to him ever after.

49

But to return to Tennessee's Partner, whom we never knew by any other than this relative title. That he had ever existed as a separate and distinct individuality we only learned later. It seems that in 1853 he left Poker Flat to go to San Francisco, ostensibly to procure a wife. He never got any farther than Stockton. At that place he was attracted by a young person who waited upon the table at the hotel where he took his meals. One morning he said something to her which caused her to smile not unkindly, to somewhat coquettishly break a plate of toast over his upturned, serious, simple face, and to retreat to the kitchen. He followed her, and emerged a few moments later, covered with more toast and victory. That day week they were married by a justice of the peace, and returned to Poker Flat. I am aware that something more might be made of this episode, but I prefer to tell it as it was current at Sandy Bar,—in the gulches and barrooms,—where all sentiment was modified by a strong sense of humor.

Of their married felicity but little is known, perhaps for the reason that Tennessee, then living with his partner, one day took occasion to say something to the bride on his own account, at which, it is said, she smiled not unkindly and chastely retreated,—this time as far as Marysville, where Tennessee followed her, and where they went to housekeeping without the aid of a justice of the peace. Tennessee's Partner took the loss of his wife simply and seriously, as was his fashion. But to everybody's surprise, when Tennessee one day returned from Marysville, without his partner's wife,—she having smiled and retreated with somebody else,—Tennessee's Partner was the first man to shake his hand and greet him with affection. The boys who had gathered in the cañon to see the shooting were naturally indignant. Their indignation might have found vent in sarcasm but for a certain look in Tennessee's Partner's eye that indicated a lack of humorous appreciation. In fact, he was a grave man, with a steady application to practical detail which was unpleasant in a difficulty.

Meanwhile a popular feeling against Tennessee had grown up on the Bar. He was known to be a gambler; he was suspected to be a thief. In these suspicions Tennessee's Partner was equally compromised; his continued intimacy with Tennessee after the affair above quoted could only be accounted for on the hypothesis of a copartnership of crime. At last Tennessee's guilt became flagrant. One day he overtook a stranger on his way to Red Dog. The stranger afterward related that Tennessee beguiled the time with interesting anecdote and reminiscence, but illogically concluded the interview in the following words: "And now, young man, I'll trouble you for your knife, your pistols, and your money. You see your weppings may get you into trouble at Red Dog, and your money's a temptation to the evilly disposed. I think you said your address was San Francisco. I shall endeavor to call." It may be stated here that Tennessee had a fine flow of humor, which no business preoccupation could wholly subdue.

This exploit was his last. Red Dog and Sandy Bar made common cause against the highwayman. Tennessee was hunted in very much the same fashion as his prototype, the grizzly. As the toils closed around him, he made a desperate rush through the Bar, emptying his revolver at the crowd before the Arcade Saloon, and so on up Grizzly Cañon; but at its farther extremity he was stopped by a small man on a gray horse. The men looked at each other a moment in silence. Both were fearless, both self-possessed and independent, and both types of a civilization that in the seventeenth century would have been called heroic, but in the nineteenth simply "reckless."

"What have you got there?—I call," said Tennessee quietly.

"Two bowers and an ace," said the stranger as quietly, showing two revolvers and a bowie-knife.

"That takes me," returned Tennessee; and, with this gambler's epigram, he threw away his useless pistol and rode back with his captor.

It was a warm night. The cool breeze which usually sprang up with the going down of the sun behind the chaparral-crested mountain was that evening withheld from Sandy Bar. The little cañon was stifling with heated resinous odors, and the decaying driftwood on the Bar sent forth faint sickening exhalations. The feverishness of day and its fierce passions still filled the camp. Lights moved restlessly along the bank of the river, striking no answering reflection from its tawny current. Against the blackness of the pines the windows of the old loft above the express-office stood out staringly bright; and through their curtainless panes the loungers below could see the forms of those who were even then deciding the fate of Tennessee. And above all this, etched on the dark firmament, rose the Sierra, remote and passionless, crowned with remoter passionless stars.

The trial of Tennessee was conducted as fairly as was consistent with a judge and jury who felt themselves to some extent obliged to justify, in their verdict, the previous irregularities of arrest and indictment. The law of Sandy Bar was implacable, but not vengeful. The excitement and personal feeling of the chase were over; with Tennessee safe in their hands, they were ready to listen patiently to any defense, which they were already satisfied was insufficient. There being no doubt in their own minds, they were willing to give the prisoner the benefit of any that might exist. Secure in the hypothesis that he ought to be hanged on general principles, they indulged him with more latitude of defense than his reckless hardihood seemed to ask. The Judge appeared to be more anxious than the prisoner, who, otherwise unconcerned, evidently took a grim pleasure in the responsibility he had created. "I don't take any hand in this yer game," had been his invariable but good-humored reply to all questions. The Judge—who was also his captor—for a moment vaguely regretted that he had not shot him "on sight" that morning, but presently dismissed his human weakness as unworthy of the judicial mind. Nevertheless, when there was a tap at the door, and it was said that Tennessee's Partner was there on behalf of the prisoner, he was admitted at once without question. Perhaps the younger members of the jury, to whom the proceedings were becoming irksomely thoughtful, hailed him as a relief.

For he was not, certainly, an imposing figure. Short and stout, with a square face, sunburned into a preternatural redness, clad in a loose duck "jumper" and trousers streaked and splashed with red soil, his aspect under any circumstances would have been quaint, and was now even ridiculous. As he stooped to deposit at his feet a heavy carpetbag he was carrying, it became obvious, from partially developed legends and inscriptions, that the material with which his trousers had been patched had been originally intended for a less ambitious covering. Yet he advanced with great gravity, and after shaking the hand of each person in the room with labored cordiality, he wiped his serious perplexed face on a red bandana handkerchief, a shade lighter than his complexion, laid his powerful hand upon the table to steady himself, and thus addressed the Judge:—

"I was passin' by," he began, by way of apology, "and I thought I'd just step in and see how things was gittin' on with Tennessee thar,—my pardner. It's a hot night. I disremember any sich weather before on the Bar."

He paused a moment, but nobody volunteering any other meteorological recollection, he again had recourse to his pocket handkerchief, and for some moments mopped his face diligently.

"Have you anything to say on behalf of the prisoner?" said the Judge finally.

"Thet's it," said Tennessee's Partner, in a tone of relief. "I come yar as Tennessee's pardner,—knowing him nigh on four year, off and on, wet and dry, in luck and out o' luck. His ways ain't allers my ways, but thar ain't any p'ints in that young man, thar ain't any liveliness as he's been up to, as I don't know. And you sez to me, sez you,—confidential-like, and between man and man,—sez you, 'Do you know anything in his behalf?' and I sez to you, sez I,—confidential-like, as between man and man, —'what should a man know of his pardner?'"

"Is this all you have to say?" asked the Judge impatiently, feeling, perhaps, that a dangerous sympathy of humor was beginning to humanize the court.

"Thet's so," continued Tennessee's Partner. "It ain't for me to say anything again' him. And now, what's the case? Here's Tennessee wants money, wants it bad, and don't like to ask it of his old pardner. Well, what does Tennessee do? He lays for a stranger, and he fetches that stranger; and you lays for *him*, and you fetches *him;* and the honors is easy. And I put it to you, bein' a fa'r-minded man, and to you, gentlemen all, as fa'r-minded men, ef this isn't so."

"Prisoner," said the Judge, interrupting, "have you any questions to ask this man?"

"No! no!" continued Tennessee's Partner hastily. "I play this yer hand alone. To come down to the bed-rock, it's just this: Tennessee, thar, has played it pretty rough and expensive-like on a stranger, and on this yer camp. And now, what's the fair thing? Some would say more, some would say less. Here's seventeen hundred dollars in coarse gold and a watch,—it's about all my pile,—and call it square!" And before a hand could be raised to prevent him, he had emptied the contents of the carpetbag upon the table.

For a moment his life was in jeopardy. One or two men sprang to their feet, several hands groped for hidden weapons, and a suggestion to "throw him from the window" was only overridden by a gesture from the Judge. Tennessee laughed. And apparently oblivious of the excitement, Tennessee's Partner improved the opportunity to mop his face again with his handkerchief.

When order was restored, and the man was made to understand, by the use of forcible figures and rhetoric, that Tennessee's offense could not be condoned by money, his face took a more serious and sanguinary hue, and those who were nearest to him noticed that his rough hand trembled slightly on the table. He hesitated a moment as he slowly returned the gold to the carpetbag, as if he had not yet entirely caught the elevated sense of justice which swayed the tribunal, and was perplexed with the belief that he had not offered enough. Then he turned to the Judge, and saying, "This yer is a lone hand, played alone, and without my pardner," he bowed to the jury and was about to withdraw, when the Judge called him back:—

"If you have anything to say to Tennessee, you had better say it now."

For the first time that evening the eyes of the prisoner and his strange advocate met. Tennessee smiled, showed his white teeth, and saying, "Euchred, old man!" held out his hand. Tennessee's Partner took it in his own, and saying, "I just dropped in as I was passin' to see how things was gettin' on," let the hand passively fall, and adding that "it was a warm night," again mopped his face with his handkerchief, and without another word withdrew.

The two men never again met each other alive. For the unparalleled insult of a bribe offered to Judge Lynch—who, whether bigoted, weak, or narrow, was at least incorruptible—firmly fixed in the mind of that mythical personage any wavering determination of Tennessee's fate; and at the break of day he was marched, closely guarded, to meet it at the top of Marley's Hill.

How he met it, how cool he was, how he refused to say anything, how perfect were the arrangements of the committee, were all duly reported, with the addition of a warning moral and example to all future evildoers, in the *Red Dog Clarion,* by its editor, who was present, and to whose vigorous English I cheerfully refer the reader. But the beauty of that midsummer morning, the blessed amity of earth and air and sky, the awakened life of the free woods and hills, the joyous renewal and promise of Nature, and above all, the infinite serenity that thrilled through each, was not reported, as not being a part of the social lesson. And yet, when the weak and foolish deed was done, and a life, with its possibilities and responsibilities, had passed out of the misshapen thing that dangled between earth and sky, the birds sang, the flowers bloomed, the sun shone, as cheerily as before; and possibly the *Red Dog Clarion* was right.

Tennessee's Partner was not in the group that surrounded the ominous tree. But as they turned to disperse, attention was drawn to the singular appearance of a motionless donkey cart halted at the side of the road. As they approached, they at once recognized the venerable "Jenny" and the two-wheeled cart as the property of Tennessee's Partner, used by him in carrying dirt from his claim; and a few paces distant the owner of the equipage himself, sitting under a buckeye tree, wiping the perspiration from his glowing face. In answer to an inquiry, he said he had come for the body of the "diseased," "if it was all the same to the committee." He didn't wish to "hurry anything"; he could "wait." He was not working that day; and when the gentlemen were done with the "diseased" he would take him. "Ef thar is any present," he added, in his simple, serious way, "as would care to jine in the fun'l, they kin come." Perhaps it was from a sense of humor, which I have already intimated was a feature of Sandy Bar,—perhaps it was from something even better than that, but two thirds of the loungers accepted the invitation at once.

It was noon when the body of Tennessee was delivered into the hands of his partner. As the cart drew up to the fatal tree, we noticed that it contained a rough oblong box,—apparently made from a section of sluicing,—and half filled with bark and the tassels of pine. The cart was further decorated with slips of willow and made fragrant with buckeye blossoms. When the body was deposited in the box, Tennessee's Partner drew over it a piece of tarred canvas, and gravely mounting the narrow seat in front, with his feet upon the shafts, urged the little donkey forward. The equipage moved slowly on, at that decorous pace which was habitual with Jenny even under less solemn circumstances. The men—half curiously, half jestingly, but all good-humoredly—strolled along beside the cart, some in advance, some a little in the rear of the homely catafalque. But whether from the narrowing of the road or some present sense of decorum, as the cart passed on, the company fell to the rear in couples, keeping step, and otherwise assuming the external show of a formal procession. Jack Folinsbee, who had at the outset played a funeral march in dumb show upon an imaginary trombone, desisted from a lack of sympathy and appreciation,—not having, perhaps, your true humorist's capacity to be content with the enjoyment of his own fun.

The way led through Grizzly Cañon, by this time clothed in funeral drapery and shadows. The redwoods, burying their moccasined feet in the red soil, stood in Indian file along the track, trailing an uncouth benediction from their bending boughs upon the passing bier. A hare, surprised into helpless inactivity, sat upright and pulsating in the ferns by the roadside as the cortège went by. Squirrels hastened to gain a secure outlook from higher boughs; and the bluejays, spreading their wings, fluttered before them like outriders, until the outskirts of Sandy Bar were reached, and the solitary cabin of Tennessee's Partner.

Viewed under more favorable circumstances, it would not have been a cheerful place. The unpicturesque site, the rude and unlovely outlines, the unsavory details, which distinguish the nest-building of the California miner, were all here with the dreariness of decay superadded. A few paces from the cabin there was a rough inclosure, which in the brief days of Tennessee's Partner's matrimonial felicity, had been used as a garden, but was now overgrown with fern. As we approached it, we were surprised to find that what we had taken for a recent attempt at cultivation was the broken soil about an open grave.

The cart was halted before the inclosure, and rejecting the offers of assistance with the same air of simple self-reliance he had displayed throughout, Tennessee's Partner lifted the rough coffin on his back, and deposited it unaided within the shallow

"And now, gentlemen," he added abruptly, "the fun'l's over."

grave. He then nailed down the board which served as a lid, and mounting a little mound of earth beside it, took off his hat and slowly mopped his face with his handkerchief. This the crowd felt was a preliminary to speech, and they disposed themselves variously on stumps and boulders, and sat expectant.

"When a man," began Tennessee's Partner, slowly, "has been running free all day, what's the natural thing for him to do? Why, to come home. And if he ain't in a condition to go home, what can his best friend do? Why, bring him home. And here's Tennessee has been running free, and we brings him home from his wandering." He paused and picked up a fragment of quartz, rubbed it thoughtfully on his sleeve, and went on: "It ain't the first time that I've packed him on my back, as you see'd me now. It ain't the first time that I brought him to this yer cabin when he couldn't help himself; it ain't the first time that I and Jinny have waited for him on yon hill, and picked him up and so fetched him home, when he couldn't speak and didn't know me. And now that it's the last time, why"—he paused and rubbed the quartz gently on his sleeve—"you see it's sort of rough on his pardner. And now, gentlemen," he added abruptly, picking up his long-handled shovel, "the fun'l's over; and my thanks, and Tennessee's thanks, to you for your trouble."

Resisting any proffers of assistance, he began to fill in the grave, turning his back upon the crowd, that after a few moments' hesitation gradually withdrew. As they crossed the little ridge that hid Sandy Bar from view, some, looking back, thought they could see Tennessee's Partner, his work done, sitting upon the grave, his shovel between his knees, and his face buried in his red bandana handkerchief. But it was argued by others that you couldn't tell his face from his handkerchief at that distance, and this point remained undecided.

In the reaction that followed the feverish excitement of that day, Tennessee's Partner was not forgotten. A secret investigation had cleared him of any complicity in Tennessee's guilt, and left only a suspicion of his general sanity. Sandy Bar made a point of calling on him, and proffering various uncouth but well-meant kindnesses. But from that day his rude health and great strength seemed visibly to decline; and when the rainy season fairly set in, and the tiny grass blades were beginning to peep from the rocky mound above Tennessee's grave, he took to his bed.

One night, when the pines beside the cabin were swaying in the storm and trailing their slender fingers over the roof, and the roar and rush of the swollen river were heard below, Tennessee's Partner lifted his head from the pillow, saying, "It is time to go to Tennessee; I must put Jinny to the cart;" and would have risen from his bed but for the restraint of his attendant. Struggling, he still pursued his singular fancy: "There, now, steady, Jinny,—steady, old girl. How dark it is! Look out for the ruts,—and look out for him, too, old gal. Sometimes, you know, when he's blind drunk, he drops right in the trail. Keep on straight up to the pine on the top of the hill. Thar! I told you so!—thar he is,—coming this way, too,—all by himself, sober, and his face a-shining. Tennessee! Pardner!"

And so they met.

The Type of Bret Harte's Stories: Bret Harte was the first writer to employ local color and dialect in his stories. His settings were the picturesque California mining camps, and his characters the motley crew which peopled the camps in the days following the California gold rush. In his stories, time and place predominate and character is the product of the environment. One of his favorite themes was the inherent goodness of every individual, no matter how black he might seem to be. His writing is theatrical and his purpose to create an impression.

For Appreciation: *Tennessee's Partner,* written in 1869, was one of three which sped Bret Harte to fame. What first gives the impression of local color? What is the effect of the humor in the first paragraph? Tennessee is the type of notorious gambler who was ever-present in the mining camps, and Tennessee's Partner embodies all of the rudeness, crudity, kind-heartedness, sympathy, and toil of the western miners. How do their descriptions and characterizations add to the effect of local color? How do the characters illustrate Harte's favorite theme of inherent good in every one? Whatever sentiment or pathos appears is immediately offset by humor. Point out two such instances. Is the humor kindly or otherwise? Give examples of description which create the impression of local color.

For Further Study: Give the meaning of each of the following words: *appellatives; iron pyrites; hypothesis; prototype; implacable; preternatural; meteorological; sanguinary; amity; catafalque; cortège.*

How did the miners usually get their names? Give a characterization of Tennessee. Tell of his capture. Was the method of his capture typical of the gold rush days of California? Describe the trial of Tennessee and the part his Partner played. Do you feel any sympathy for Tennessee? Did the proffer of money to the Judge seem like a bribe? Why was Tennessee's Partner absent from the scene of the hanging? Describe the funeral cortège. What makes the funeral plea so moving? Is the conclusion satisfactory?

Exercises and Creative Work: Write a local color story of your town, the street on which you live, or a place which you have visited.

Write an account of Tennessee's funeral as it might have appeared in the local news sheet.

THE CANVASSER'S TALE

Mark Twain

Poor, sad-eyed stranger! There was that about his humble mien, his tired look, his decayed-gentility clothes, that almost reached the mustard seed of charity that still remained, remote and lonely, in the empty vastness of my heart, notwithstanding I observed a portfolio under his arm, and said to myself, "Behold, Providence hath delivered his servant into the hands of another canvasser."

Well, these people always get one interested. Before I well knew how it came about, this one was telling me his history, and I was all attention and sympathy. He told it something like this:

My parents died, alas, when I was a little, sinless child. My uncle Ithuriel took me to his heart and reared me as his own. He was my only relative in the wide world; but he was good and rich and generous. He reared me in the lap of luxury. I knew no want that money could satisfy.

In the fullness of time I was graduated, and went with two of my servants—my chamberlain and my valet—to travel in foreign countries. During four years I flitted upon careless wing amid the beauteous gardens of the distant strand, if you will permit this form of speech in one whose tongue was ever attuned to poesy; and indeed I so speak with confidence, as one unto his kind, for I perceive by your eyes that you too, sir, are gifted with the divine inflation. In these far lands I revelled in the ambrosial food [1] that fructifies the soul, the mind, the heart. But of all things, that which most appealed to my inborn æsthetic taste was the prevailing custom there, among the rich, of making collections of elegant and costly rarities, dainty *objects de vertu*, [2] and in an evil hour I tried to uplift my uncle Ithuriel to a plane of sympathy with this exquisite employment.

I wrote and told him of one gentleman's vast collection of shells; another's noble collection of meerschaum pipes; another's elevating and refining collection of undecipherable autographs; another's priceless collection of old china; another's enchanting collection of postage stamps—and so forth and so on. Soon my letters yielded fruit. My uncle began to look about for something to make a collection of. You may know, perhaps, how fleetly a taste like this dilates. His soon became a raging fever, though I knew it not. He began to neglect his great pork business; presently he wholly retired and turned an elegant leisure into a rabid search for curious things. His wealth was vast, and he spared it not. First he tried cow-bells. He made a collection which filled five large *salons*, [3] and comprehended all the different sorts of cow-bells that ever had been contrived, save one. That one—an antique, and the only specimen extant—was possessed by another collector. My uncle offered enormous sums for it, but the gentleman would not sell. Doubtless you know what necessarily resulted. A true collector attaches no value to a collection that is not complete. His great heart breaks, he sells his hoard, he turns his mind to some field that seems unoccupied.

[1] AMBROSIAL FOOD—Food of the gods.
[2] *Objects de vertu*—Objects of decorative art, old and rare.
[3] *Salons*—Rooms.

Thus did my uncle. He next tried brickbats. After piling up a vast and interesting collection, the former difficulty supervened; his great heart broke again; he sold out his soul's idol to the retired brewer who possessed the missing brick. Then he tried flint hatchets and other implements of Primeval Man, but by and by discovered that the factory where they were made was supplying other collectors as well as himself. He tried Aztec inscriptions and stuffed whales—another failure, after incredible labor and expense. When his collection seemed at last perfect, a stuffed whale arrived from Greenland and an Aztec inscription from the Cundurango [4] regions of Central America that made all former specimens insignificant. My uncle hastened to secure these noble gems. He got the stuffed whale, but another collector got the inscription. A real Cundurango, as possibly you know, is a possession of such supreme value that, when once a collector gets it, he will rather part with his family than with it. So my uncle sold out, and saw his darlings go forth, never more to return; and his coal-black hair turned white as snow in a single night.

Now he waited, and thought. He knew another disappointment might kill him. He was resolved that he would choose things next time that no other man was collecting. He carefully made up his mind, and once more entered the field—this time to make a collection of echoes.

"Of what?" said I.

Echoes, sir. His first purchase was an echo in Georgia that repeated four times; his next was a six-repeater in Maryland; his next was a thirteen-repeater in Maine; his next was a nine-repeater in Kansas; his next was a twelve-repeater in Tennessee, which he got cheap, so to speak, because it was out of repair, a portion of the crag which reflected it having tumbled down. He believed he could repair it at a cost of a few thousand dollars, and, by increasing the elevation with masonry, treble the repeating capacity; but the architect who undertook the job had never built an echo before, and so he utterly spoiled this one. Before he meddled with it, it used to talk back like a mother-in-law, but now it was only fit for the deaf and dumb asylum. Well, next he bought a lot of cheap little double-barreled echoes, scattered around over various States and Terri-

[4] CUNDURANGO—A fictitious name.

tories; he got them at twenty per cent off by taking the lot. Next he bought a perfect Gatling-gun of an echo in Oregon, and it cost a fortune, I can tell you. You may know, sir, that in the echo market the scale of prices is cumulative, like the carat-scale in diamonds; in fact, the same phraseology is used. A single-carat echo is worth but ten dollars over and above the value of the land it is on; a two-carat or double-barreled echo is worth thirty dollars; a five-carat is worth nine hundred and fifty; a ten-carat is worth thirteen thousand. My uncle's Oregon echo which he called the Great Pitt Echo, was a twenty-two carat gem, and cost two hundred and sixteen thousand dollars— they threw the land in, for it was four hundred miles from a settlement.

Well, in the meantime my path was a path of roses. I was the accepted suitor of the only and lovely daughter of an English earl, and was beloved to distraction. In that dear presence I swam in seas of bliss. The family were content, for it was known that I was sole heir to an uncle held to be worth five millions of dollars. However, none of us knew that my uncle had become a collector, at least in anything more than a small way, for æsthetic amusement.

Now gathered the clouds above my unconscious head. That divine echo, since known throughout the world as the Great Koh-i-noor,[5] or Mountain of Repetitions, was discovered. It was a sixty-five-carat gem. You could utter a word and it would talk back at you for fifteen minutes, when the day was otherwise quiet. But behold, another fact came to light at the same time: another echo collector was in the field. The two rushed to make the peerless purchase. The property consisted of a couple of small hills with a shallow swale between, out yonder among the back settlements of New York State. Both men arrived on the ground at the same time, and neither knew the other was there.

The echo was not all owned by one man; a person by the name of Williamson Bolivar Jarvis owned the east hill, and a person by the name of Harbison J. Bledso owned the west hill; the swale between was the dividing line. So while my uncle was buying Jarvis's hill for three million two hundred and eighty-

[5] Koh-i-noor—A famous Indian diamond presented to Queen Victoria of England. It was reputed to bring ill luck to its owner.

five thousand dollars, the other party was buying Bledso's hill for a shade over three million.

Now, do you perceive the natural result? Why, the noblest collection of echoes on earth was forever and ever incomplete, since it possessed but the one-half of the king echo of the universe. Neither man was content with this divided ownership, yet neither would sell to the other. There were jawings, bickerings, heart-burnings. And at last that other collector, with a malignity which only a collector can ever feel toward a man and a brother, proceeded to cut down his hill!

You see, as long as he could not have the echo, he was resolved that nobody should have it. He would remove his hill, and then there would be nothing to reflect my uncle's echo. My uncle remonstrated with him but the man said, "I own one end of this echo; I choose to kill my end; you must take care of your own end yourself."

Well, my uncle got an injunction put on him. The other man appealed and fought it in a higher court. They carried it on up, clear to the Supreme Court of the United States. It made no end of trouble there. Two of the judges believed that an echo was personal property, because it was impalpable to sight and touch, and yet was purchaseable, salable, and consequently taxable; two others believed that an echo was real estate, because it was manifestly attached to the land, and was not removable from place to place; other of the judges contended that an echo was not property at all.

It was finally decided that the echo was property; that the hills were property; that the two men were separate and independent owners of the two hills, but tenants in common in the echo; therefore defendant was at full liberty to cut down his hill, since it belonged solely to him, but must give bonds in three million dollars as indemnity for damages which might result to my uncle's half of the echo. This decision also debarred my uncle from using defendant's hill to reflect his part of the echo, without defendant's consent; he must use only his own hill; if his part of the echo would not go, under these circumstances, it was sad, of course, but the court could find no remedy. The court also debarred defendant from using my uncle's hill to reflect *his* end of the echo, without consent. You see the grand result! Neither man would give consent, and so that astonishing and most noble echo had to cease from its great powers; and since that day that magnificent property is tied up and unsalable.

A week before my wedding day, while I was still swimming in bliss and the nobility were gathering from far and near to honor our espousal, came news of my uncle's death, and also a copy of his will, making me his sole heir. He was gone; alas, my dear benefactor was no more. The thought surcharges my heart even at this remote day. I handed the will to the earl; I could not read it for the blinding tears. The earl read it; then he sternly said, "Sir, do you call this wealth?—but doubtless you do in your inflated country. Sir, you are left sole heir to a vast collection of echoes—if a thing can be called a collection that is scattered far and wide over the huge length and breadth of the American continent; sir, this is not all; you are head and ears in debt; there is not an echo in the lot but has a mortgage on it; sir, I am not a hard man, but I must look to my child's interest; if you had but one echo which you could honestly call your own, if you had but one echo which was free from incumbrance, so that you could retire to it with my child, and by humble, painstaking industry, cultivate and improve it, and thus wrest from it a maintenance, I would not say you nay; but I cannot marry my child to a beggar. Leave his side, my darling; go, sir, take your mortgage-ridden echoes and quit my sight forever."

My noble Celestine clung to me in tears, with loving arms, and swore she would willingly, nay gladly, marry me, though I had not an echo in the world. But it could not be. We were torn asunder, she to pine and die within the twelvemonth, I to toil life's long journey sad and alone, praying daily, hourly, for that release which shall join us together again in that dear realm where the wicked cease from troubling and the weary are at rest. Now, sir, if you will be so kind as to look at these maps and plans in my portfolio, I am sure I can sell you an echo for less money than any man in the trade. Now this one, which cost my uncle ten dollars, thirty years ago, and is one of the sweetest things in Texas, I will let you have for——

"Let me interrupt you," I said. "My friend, I have not had a moment's respite from canvassers this day. I have bought a sewing-machine which I did not want; I have bought a map which is mistaken in all its details; I have bought a moth poison which the moths prefer to any other beverage; I have bought no end of useless inventions, and now I have had enough of this foolishness. I would not have one of your echoes if you were even to give it to me. I would not let it stay on the place. I always hate a man that tries to sell me echoes. You see this gun? Now take your collection and move on; let us not have bloodshed."

But he only smiled a sad, sweet smile, and got out some more diagrams. You know the result perfectly well, because you know that when you have once opened the door to a canvasser the trouble is done and you have got to suffer defeat.

I compromised with this man at the end of an intolerable hour. I bought two double-barreled echoes in good condition, and he threw in another, which he said was not salable because it only spoke German. He said, "She was a perfect polyglot once, but somehow her palate got down."

The Type of Mark Twain's Stories: Mark Twain has often been called "the man who kept the world laughing for a generation." Many of his stories abound in local color but his contribution to American literature was his humor. The world was his province. His cosmopolitanism was the result of his many experiences as printer, pilot, soldier, miner, reporter, editor, lecturer, correspondent, and publisher. His style is energetic and direct. His stories have humor in dialogue, characterization and situation.

For Appreciation: This story was written in 1878 and is typical of American humor. Discuss the effectiveness of the serious introduction. What is the first intimation of humor? Discuss the development of humor in the story. Do you think the author is poking fun at people who go to ridiculous extremes in making collections of various articles? Discuss the way the author builds up his story to a climax. Note that the story closes with a little follow-up laugh. What does this accomplish? How does this humorous story compare with others you have read? Account for Mark Twain's fame as a humorist.

For Further Study: Give the meaning of each of the following words and phrases: *mustard seed of charity; canvasser; æsthetic; injunction; tenants in common; polyglot; her palate got down.*

What in the canvasser's early life puts one in a good mood? Give instances to illustrate how the author develops the obsession or mania for collecting. Discuss the effect of bringing the echo case into the law courts. What can you say as to the use of proper names throughout the story? List some expressions which add humor to the story.

Exercises and Creative Work: Write of a modern sales experience. Write a humorous short story based on an insignificant object.

THE RETURN OF A PRIVATE

Hamlin Garland

Sunday comes in a Western wheat harvest with such sweet
and sudden relaxation to man and beast that it would be holy
for that reason, if for no other, and Sundays are usually fair
in harvest-time. As one goes out into the field in the hot morning sunshine, with no sound abroad save the crickets and the in-
describably pleasant silken rustling of the ripened grain, the
reaper and the very sheaves in the stubble seem to be resting,
dreaming.

Around the house, in the shade of the trees, the men sit, smoking, dozing, or reading the papers, while the women, never resting, move about at the housework. The men eat on Sundays
about the same as on other days, and breakfast is no sooner
over and out of the way than dinner begins.

But at the Smith farm there were no men dozing or reading. Mrs. Smith was alone with her three children, Mary, nine,
Tommy, six, and little Ted, just past four. Her farm, rented

67

to a neighbor, lay at the head of a coolly [1] or narrow gully, made at some far-off post-glacial period by the vast and angry floods of water which gullied these tremendous furrows in the level prairie—furrows so deep that undisturbed portions of the original level rose like hills on either side, rose to quite considerable mountains.

The chickens wakened her as usual that Sabbath morning from dreams of her absent husband, from whom she had not heard for weeks. The shadows drifted over the hills, down the slopes, across the wheat, and up the opposite wall in leisurely way, as if, being Sunday, they could take it easy also. The fowls clustered about the housewife as she went out into the yard. Fuzzy little chickens swarmed out from the coops, where their clucking and perpetually disgruntled mothers tramped about, petulantly thrusting their heads through the spaces between the slats.

A cow called in a deep, musical bass, and a calf answered from a little pen near by, and a pig scurried guiltily out of the cabbages. Seeing all this, seeing the pig in the cabbages, the tangle of grass in the garden, the broken fence which she had mended again and again—the little woman, hardly more than a girl, sat down and cried. The bright Sabbath morning was only a mockery without him!

A few years ago they had bought this farm, paying part, mortgaging the rest in the usual way. Edward Smith was a man of terrible energy. He worked "nights and Sundays," as the saying goes, to clear the farm of its brush and of its insatiate mortgage! In the midst of his Herculean struggle came the call for volunteers,[2] and with the grim and unselfish devotion to his country which made the Eagle Brigade able to "whip its weight in wildcats," he threw down his scythe and grub-axe, turned his cattle loose, and became a blue-coated cog in a vast machine for killing men, and not thistles. While the millionaire sent his money to England for safe-keeping, this man, with his girl-wife and three babies, left them on a mortgaged farm, and went away to fight for an idea. It was foolish, but it was sublime for all that.

That was three years before, and the young wife, sitting on

---

[1] COOLLY—Sometimes written "coule," a narrow gully between two low hills. It is a term used in western Wisconsin, Minnesota and Iowa.

[2] VOLUNTEERS—Volunteers were called for at the outbreak of the Civil War.

the well-curb on this bright Sabbath harvest morning, was right-eously rebellious. It seemed to her that she had borne her share of the country's sorrow. Two brothers had been killed, the renter in whose hands her husband had left the farm had proved a villain; one year the farm had been without crops, and now the over-ripe grain was waiting the tardy hand of the neighbor who had rented it, and who was cutting his own grain first.

About six weeks before, she had received a letter saying, "We'll be discharged in a little while." But no other word had come from him. She had seen by the papers that his army was being discharged, and from day to day other soldiers slowly percolated in blue streams back into the State and county, but still *her* hero did not return.

Each week she had told the children that he was coming, and she had watched the road so long that it had become uncon-scious; and as she stood at the well, or by the kitchen door, her eyes were fixed unthinkingly on the road that wound down the coolly.

Nothing wears on the human soul like waiting. If the stranded mariner, searching the sun-bright seas, could once give up hope of a ship, that horrible grinding on his brain would cease. It was this waiting, hoping, on the edge of despair, that gave Emma Smith no rest.

Neighbors said, with kind intentions: "He's sick, maybe, an' can't start north just yet. He'll come along one o' these days."

"Why don't he write?" was her question, which silenced them all. This Sunday morning it seemed to her as if she could not stand it longer. The house seemed intolerably lonely. So she dressed the little ones in their best calico dresses and home-made jackets, and, closing up the house, set off down the coolly to old Mother Gray's.

"Old Widder Gray" lived at the "mouth of the coolly." She was a widow woman with a large family of stalwart boys and laughing girls. She was the visible incarnation of hospitality and optimistic poverty. With Western open-heartedness she fed every mouth that asked food of her, and worked herself to death as cheerfully as her girls danced in the neighborhood harvest dances.

She waddled down the path to meet Mrs. Smith with a broad smile on her face.

"Oh, you little dears! Come right to your granny. Gimme a kiss! Come right in, Mis' Smith. How are yeh, anyway? Nice mornin', ain't it? Come in an' set down. Everything's in a clutter, but that won't scare you any."

She led the way into the best room, a sunny, square room, carpeted with a faded and patched rag carpet, and papered with white-and-green-striped wall-paper, where a few faded effigies of dead members of the family hung in variously sized oval walnut frames. The house resounded with singing, laughter, whistling, tramping of heavy boots, and riotous scufflings. Half-grown boys came to the door and crooked their fingers at the children, who ran out, and were soon in the midst of the fun.

"Don't s'pose you've heard from Ed?" Mrs. Smith shook her head. "He'll turn up some day, when you ain't lookin' for 'm." The good old soul had said that so many times that poor Mrs. Smith derived no comfort from it any longer.

"Liz heard from Al the other day. He's comin' some day this week. Anyhow, they expect him."

"Did he say anything of——"

"No, he didn't," Mrs. Gray admitted. "But then it was only a short letter, anyhow. Al ain't much for writin', anyhow.—— But come out and see my new cheese. I tell yeh, I don't believe I ever had better luck in my life. If Ed should come, I want you should take up a piece of this cheese."

It was beyond human nature to resist the influence of that noisy, hearty, loving household, and in the midst of the singing and laughing, the wife forgot her anxiety, for the time at least, and laughed and sang with the rest.

About eleven o'clock a wagon-load more drove up to the door, and Bill Gray, the widow's oldest son, and his whole family, from Sand Lake Coolly, piled out amid a good-natured uproar. Every one talked at once, except Bill, who sat in the wagon with his wrists on his knees, a straw in his mouth, and an amused twinkle in his blue eyes.

"Ain't heard nothin' o' Ed, I s'pose?" he asked in a kind of bellow. Mrs. Smith shook her head. Bill, with a delicacy very striking in such a great giant, rolled his quid in his mouth, and said:

"Didn't know but you had. I hear two or three of the Sand Lake boys are comin'. Left New Orleens some time this week.

Didn't write nothin' about Ed, but no news is good news in such cases, mother always says."

"Well, go put out yer team," said Mrs. Gray, "an' go'n bring me in some taters, an', Sim, you go see if you c'n find some corn. Sadie, you put on the water to bile. Come now, hustle yer boots, all o' yeh. If I feed this yer crowd, we've got to have some raw materials. If y' think I'm goin' to feed yeh on pie— you're jest mightily mistaken."

The children went off into the fields, the girls put dinner on to boil, and then went to change their dresses and fix their hair. "Somebody might come," they said.

"Land sakes, *I hope* not! I don't know where in time I'd set 'em, 'less they'd eat at the second table," Mrs. Gray laughed, in pretended dismay.

The two older boys, who had served their time in the army, lay out on the grass before the house, and whittled and talked desultorily about the war and the crops, and planned buying a threshing machine. The older girls and Mrs. Smith helped enlarge the table and put on the dishes, talking all the time in that cheery, incoherent, and meaningful way a group of such women have,—a conversation to be taken for its spirit rather than for its letter, though Mrs. Gray at last got the ear of them all and dissertated at length on girls.

"Girls in love ain't no use in the whole blessed week," she said. "Sundays they're a-lookin' down the road, expectin' he'll *come*. Sunday afternoons they can't think o' nothin' else, 'cause he's *here*. Monday mornin's they're sleepy and kind o' dreamy and slimpsy, and good f'r nothin' on Tuesday and Wednesday. Thursday they git absent-minded, an' begin to look off toward Sunday agin, an' mope aroun' and let the dishwater git cold, right under their noses. Friday they break dishes, an' go off in the best room an' snivel, an' look out o' the winder. Saturdays they have queer spurts o' workin' like all p'ssessed, an' spurts o' frizzin' their hair. An' Sunday they begin it all over agin."

The girls giggled and blushed, all through this tirade from their mother, their broad faces and powerful frames anything but suggestive of lackadaisical sentiment. But Mrs. Smith said:

"Now, Mrs. Gray, I hadn't ought to stay to dinner. You've got——"

"Now you set right down! If any of them girls' beaus comes, they'll have to take what's left, that's all. They ain't s'posed to have much appetite, nohow. No, you're goin' to stay if they starve, an' they ain't no danger o' that."

At one o'clock the long table was piled with boiled potatoes, cords of boiled corn on the cob, squash and pumpkin pies, hot biscuit, sweet pickles, bread and butter, and honey. Then one of the girls took down a conchshell from a nail, and going to the door, blew a long, fine, free blast, that showed there was no weakness of lungs in her ample chest.

Then the children came out of the forest of corn, out of the creek, out of the loft of the barn, and out of the garden.

"They come to their feed f'r all the world jest like the pigs when y' holler 'poo-ee!' See 'em scoot!" laughed Mrs. Gray, every wrinkle on her face shining with delight.

The men shut up their jack-knives, and surrounded the horse-trough to souse their faces in the cold, hard water, and in a few moments the table was filled with a merry crowd, and a row of wistful eyed youngsters circled the kitchen wall, where they stood first on one leg and then on the other, in impatient hunger.

"Now pitch in, Mrs. Smith," said Mrs. Gray, presiding over the table. "You know these men critters. They'll eat every grain of it, if yeh give 'em a chance. I swan, they're made o' India-rubber, their stomachs is, I know it."

"Haf to eat to work," said Bill, gnawing a cob with a swift, circular motion that rivalled a corn-sheller in results.

"More like workin' to eat," put in one of the girls, with a giggle. "More eat 'n work with you."

"*You* needn't say anything, Net. Any one that'll eat seven ears——"

"I didn't, no such thing. You piled your cobs on my plate."

"That'll do to tell Ed Varney. It won't go down here where we know yeh."

"Good land! Eat all you want! They's plenty more in the fiel's, but I can't afford to give you young uns tea. The tea is for us women-folks, and 'specially f'r Mis' Smith an' Bill's wife. We're a-goin' to tell fortunes by it."

One by one the men filled up and shoved back, and one by one the children slipped into their places, and by two o'clock the women alone remained around the débris-covered table, sipping their tea and telling fortunes.

As they got well down to the grounds in the cup, they shook them with a circular motion in the hand, and then turned them bottom-side-up quickly in the saucer, then twirled them three or four times one way, and three or four times the other, during a breathless pause. Then Mrs. Gray lifted the cup, and, gazing into it with profound gravity, pronounced the impending fate.

It must be admitted that, to a critical observer, she had abundant preparation for hitting close to the mark, as when she told the girls that "somebody was comin'." "It's a man," she went on gravely. "He is cross-eyed——"

"Oh, you hush!" cried Nettie.

"He has red hair, and is death on b'iled corn and hot biscuit." The others shrieked with delight.

"But he's goin' to get the mitten, that red-headed feller is, for I see another feller comin' up behind him."

"Oh, lemme see, lemme see!" cried Nettie.

"Keep off," said the priestess, with a lofty gesture. "His hair is black. He don't eat so much, and he works more."

The girls exploded in a shriek of laughter, and pounded their sister on the back.

At last came Mrs. Smith's turn, and she was trembling with excitement as Mrs. Gray again composed her jolly face to what she considered a proper solemnity of expression.

"Somebody is comin' to *you*," she said, after a long pause. "He's got a musket on his back. He's a soldier. He's almost here. See?"

She pointed at two little tea-stems, which really formed a faint suggestion of a man with a musket on his back. He had climbed nearly to the edge of the cup. Mrs. Smith grew pale with excitement. She trembled so she could hardly hold the cup in her hand as she gazed into it.

"It's Ed," cried the old woman. "He's on the way home. Heavens an' earth! There he is now!" She turned and waved her hand out toward the road. They rushed to the door to look where she pointed.

A man in a blue coat, with a musket on his back, was toiling slowly up the hill on the sun-bright, dusty road, toiling slowly, with bent head half hidden by a heavy knapsack. So tired it seemed that walking was indeed a process of falling. So eager to get home he would not stop, would not look aside, but plodded on, amid the cries of the locusts, the welcome of the crickets, and the rustle of the yellow wheat. Getting back to God's country, and his wife and babies!

Laughing, crying, trying to call him and the children at the same time, the little wife, almost hysterical, snatched her hat and ran out into the yard. But the soldier had disappeared over the hill into the hollow beyond, and, by the time she had found the children, he was too far away for her voice to reach him. And, besides, she was not sure it was her husband, for he had not turned his head at their shouts. This seemed so strange. Why didn't he stop to rest at his old neighbor's house? Tortured by hope and doubt, she hurried up the coolly as fast as she could push the baby wagon, the blue-coated figure just ahead pushing steadily, silently forward up the coolly.

When the excited, panting little group came in sight of the gate they saw the blue-coated figure standing, leaning upon the rough rail fence, his chin on his palms, gazing at the empty house. His knapsack, canteen, blankets, and musket lay upon the dusty grass at his feet.

He was like a man lost in a dream. His wide, hungry eyes devoured the scene. The rough lawn, the little unpainted house, the field of clear yellow wheat behind it, down across which streamed the sun, now almost ready to touch the high hill to the west, the crickets crying merrily, a cat on the fence near by, dreaming, unmindful of the stranger in blue——

How peaceful it all was. O God! How far removed from all camps, hospitals, battle lines. A little cabin in a Wisconsin coolly but it was majestic in its peace. How did he ever leave it for those years of tramping, thirsting, killing?

Trembling, weak with emotion, her eyes on the silent figure, Mrs. Smith hurried up to the fence. Her feet made no noise in the dust and grass, and they were close upon him before he knew of them. The oldest boy ran a little ahead. He will never forget that figure, that face. It will always remain as something epic, that return of the private. He fixed his eyes on the pale face covered with a ragged beard.

"Who *are* you, sir?" asked the wife, or, rather, started to ask, for he turned, stood a moment, and then cried:

"Emma!"

"Edward!"

The children stood in a curious row to see their mother kiss this bearded, strange man, the elder girl sobbing sympathetically with her mother. Illness had left the soldier partly deaf, and this added to the strangeness of his manner.

But the youngest child stood away, even after the girl had recognized her father and kissed him. The man turned then to the baby, and said in a curiously unpaternal tone:

"Come here, my little man; don't you know me?" But the baby backed away under the fence and stood peering at him critically.

"My little man!" What meaning in those words! This baby seemed like some other woman's child, and not the infant he had left in his wife's arms. The war had come between him and his baby—he was only a strange man to him, with big eyes; a soldier, with mother hanging to his arm, and talking in a loud voice.

"And this is Tom," the private said, drawing the oldest boy to him. "*He'll* come and see me. *He* knows his poor old pap when he comes home from the war."

The mother heard the pain and reproach in his voice and hastened to apologize.

"You've changed so, Ed. He can't know yeh. This is papa, Teddy; come and kiss him—Tom and Mary do. Come, won't you?" But Teddy still peered through the fence with solemn eyes, well out of reach. He resembled a half-wild kitten that hesitates, studying the tones of one's voice.

"I'll fix him," said the soldier, and sat down to undo his knapsack, out of which he drew three enormous and very red apples. After giving one to each of the older children, he said:

"*Now* I guess he'll come. Eh, my little man? Now come see your pap."

Teddy crept slowly under the fence, assisted by the over-zealous Tommy, and a moment later was kicking and squalling in his father's arms. Then they entered the house, into the sitting room, poor, bare, art-forsaken little room, too, with its rag carpet, its square clock, and its two or three chromos and pictures from *Harper's Weekly* pinned about.

"Emma, I'm all tired out," said Private Smith, as he flung himself down on the carpet as he used to do, while his wife brought a pillow to put under his head, and the children stood about munching their apples.

"Tommy, you run and get me a pan of chips, and Mary, you get the tea-kettle on, and I'll go and make some biscuit."

And the soldier talked. Question after question he poured forth about the crops, the cattle, the renter, the neighbors. He slipped his heavy government brogan shoes off his poor, tired, blistered feet, and lay out with utter, sweet relaxation. He was a free man again, no longer a soldier under command. At supper he stopped once, listened and smiled. "That's old Spot. I know her voice. I s'pose that's her calf out there in the pen. I can't milk her to-night, though. I'm too tired. But I tell you, I'd like a drink o' her milk. What's become of old Rove?"

"He died last winter. Poisoned, I guess." There was a moment of sadness for them all. It was some time before the husband spoke again, in a voice that trembled a little.

"Poor old feller! He'd 'a' known me half a mile away. I expected him to come down the hill to meet me. It 'ud 'a' been more like comin' home if I could 'a' seen him comin' down the road an' waggin' his tail, an' laughin' that way he has. I tell yeh, it kind o' took hold o' me to see the blinds down an' the house shut up."

"But, yeh see, we—we expected you'd write again 'fore you started. And then we thought we'd see you if you *did* come," she hastened to explain.

"Well, I ain't worth a cent on writin'. Besides, it's just as well yeh didn't know when I was comin'. I tell you, it sounds good to hear them chickens out there, an' turkeys, an' the crickets. Do you know they don't have just the same kind o' crickets down South? Who's Sam hired t' help cut yer grain?"

"The Ramsey boys."

"Looks like a good crop; but I'm afraid I won't do much gettin' it cut. This cussed fever an' ague has got me down pretty low. I don't know when I'll get rid of it. I'll bet I've took twenty-five pounds of quinine if I've taken a bit. Gimme another biscuit. I tell yeh, they taste good, Emma. I ain't had anything like it— Say, if you'd 'a' hear'd me braggin' to th' boys about your butter 'n' biscuits I'll bet your ears 'ud 'a' burnt."

The private's wife colored with pleasure. "Oh, you're always a-braggin' about your things. Everybody makes good butter."

"Yes; old lady Snyder, for instance."

"Oh, well, she ain't to be mentioned. She's Dutch."

"Or old Mis' Snively. One more cup o' tea, Mary. That's my girl! I'm feeling better already. I just b'lieve the matter with me is, I'm *starved*."

This was a delicious hour, one long to be remembered. They were like lovers again. But their tenderness, like that of a typical American family, found utterance in tones, rather than in words. He was praising her when praising her biscuit, and she knew it. They grew soberer when he showed where he had been struck, one ball burning the back of his hand, one cutting away a lock of hair from his temple, and one passing through the calf of his leg. The wife shuddered to think how near she had come to being a soldier's widow. Her waiting no longer seemed hard. This sweet, glorious hour effaced it all.

Then they rose, and all went into the garden and down to the barn. He stood beside her while she milked old Spot. They began to plan fields and crops for next year.

His farm was weedy and encumbered, a rascally renter had run away with his machinery (departing between two days), his children needed clothing, the years were coming upon him, he was sick and emaciated, but his heroic soul did not quail. With the same courage with which he had faced his Southern march he entered upon a still more hazardous future.

Oh, that mystic hour! The pale man with big eyes standing there by the well, with his young wife by his side. The vast moon swinging above the eastern peaks, the cattle winding down the pasture slopes with jangling bells, the crickets singing, the stars blooming out sweet and far and serene; the katydids rhythmically calling, the little turkeys crying querulously, as they settled to roost in the poplar tree near the open gate. The voices at the well drop lower, the little ones nestle in their father's arms at last, and Teddy falls asleep there.

The common soldier of the American volunteer army had returned. His war with the South was over, and his fight, his daily running fight with nature and against the injustice of his fellow-men, was begun again.

The Type of Garland's Stories: Hamlin Garland was born and brought up in the Middle West. He had himself endured the hardships and rigors of pioneer life, and knew whereof he wrote. His writings have a genuineness which few other writers can boast, and a freshness which comes only from a reproduction of the exact photographic situation. His characters, however, are usually composites—representatives of types, and not individuals. His stories picture farm and village life as he knew it and had lived it and he wrote with a full heart and deep earnestness. He depicts frankly the grinding toil and stern round of drudgery of the frontier farmer, but most of his stories end happily.

For Appreciation: *The Return of a Private* was written in 1890 and is one of six stories contained in *Main-Travelled Roads*. It is characteristic of Garland's style. It touches on the autobiographical for Garland's own father served in the Civil War and returned under conditions which must have been very similar to those experienced by Ed Smith of the story. The Smith family is representative of the Garland family and typical of any Wisconsin family of the coolly region. What effects are produced by these autobiographical elements? What are some of the features of the story which make it fall into the local color or regional class of short stories? What touches of humor do you find in the story? Compare the type of humor with that of Mark Twain.

For Further Study: Choose phrases in the opening paragraphs which describe country life. Are the descriptions true and faithful? Do you find anything artificial or added for effect? Are the hardships, loneliness, patience, and discouragements of Mrs. Smith well and faithfully portrayed? Sketch the character of "Widder Gray." Is she a definite, isolated individual, or composite of her type? Describe the preparation and eating of the dinner. Does the gaiety at Widder Gray's emphasize the loneliness of Mrs. Smith? What was the purpose of reading the tea grounds? Where does the element of suspense come into the story? The return of the private had a definite lasting effect on the oldest boy. Is there any significance in this? What thread runs through the joy of reunion and the subsequent conversation? Give instances in which the author shows his understanding of the frontier farmer. Is the ending of the story satisfactory?

Exercises and Creative Work: Write an account of a country gathering, a family reunion, or a dinner that you have personally enjoyed. Keep your story just as true to the actual happenings as possible.

The Return of a Private as printed in this book is Part II of the entire story as it appears in *Main-Travelled Roads*. Read Part I and then retell the story of Mr. Smith's arrival at LaCrosse by train and of his overland walk toward home. Do not neglect to tell of his expectation of seeing old Rove.

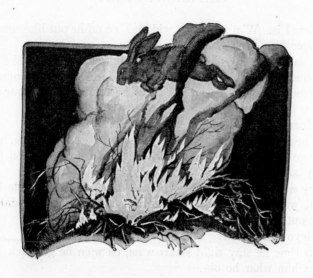

MR. RABBIT NIBBLES UP THE BUTTER

Joel Chandler Harris

"DE ANIMILS en de creeturs," said Uncle Remus, shaking his coffee around in the bottom of his tin-cup, in order to gather up all the sugar, "dey kep' on gittin' mo' en mo' familious wid wunner nudder, twel bimeby, 'twan't long 'fo' Brer Rabbit, en Brer Fox, en Brer Possum got ter sorter bunchin' der per-wishuns tergedder in de same shanty. Atter w'ile de roof sorter 'gun ter leak, en one day Brer Rabbit, en Brer Fox, en Brer Possum, 'semble fer ter see ef dey can't kinder patch her up. Dey had a big day's work in front un um, en dey fotch der dinner wid um. Dey lump de vittles up in one pile, en de butter w'at Brer Fox brung, dey goes en puts in de spring-'ouse fer ter keep cool, en den dey went ter wuk, en 'twan't long 'fo' Brer Rabbit stummuck 'gun ter sorter growl en pester 'im. Dat but-ter er Brer Fox sot heavy on his mine, en his mouf water eve'y time he 'member 'bout it. Present'y he say ter hisse'f dat he bleedzd ter have a nip at dat butter, en den he lay his plans, he did. Fus' news you know, w'ile dey wuz all wukkin' 'long, Brer Rabbit raise his head quick en fling his years forrerd en holler out:

" 'Here I is. W'at you want wid me?' en off he put like sump'n wuz atter 'im.

"He sallied 'roun', old Brer Rabbit did, en atter he make sho dat nobody ain't foller'n un 'im, inter de spring-'ouse he bounces, en dar he stays twel he git a bait er butter. Den he santer on back en go to wuk.

" 'Whar you bin?' sez Brer Fox, sezee.

" 'I hear my chilluns callin' me,' sez Brer Rabbit, sezee, 'en I hatter go see w'at dey want. My ole 'oman done gone en tuck mighty sick,' sezee.

"Dey wuk on twel bimeby de butter tas'e so good dat ole Brer Rabbit want some mo'. Den he raise up his head, he did, en holler out:

" 'Heyo! Hole on! I'm a comin'!' 'en off he put.

"Dis time he stay right smart w'ile, en w'en he git back Brer Fox ax him whar he bin.

" 'I been ter see my ole 'oman, en she's a sinkin',' sezee.

"Dreckly Brer Rabbit hear um callin' 'im ag'in en off he goes, en dis time, bless yo' soul, he gits de butter out so clean dat he kin see hisse'f in de bottom er de bucket. He scrape it clean en lick it dry, en den he go back ter wuk lookin' mo' samer dan a nigger w'at de patter-rollers bin had holt un.

" 'How's yo' ole 'oman dis time?' sez Brer Fox, sezee.

" 'I'm oblije ter you, Brer Fox,' sez Brer Rabbit, sezee, 'but I'm fear'd she's done gone by now,' en dat sorter make Brer Fox en Brer Possum feel in moanin' wid Brer Rabbit.

"Bimeby, w'en dinner-time come, dey all got out der vittles, but Brer Rabbit keep on lookin' lonesome, en Brer Fox en Brer Possum dey sorter rustle roun' fer ter see ef dey can't make Brer Rabbit feel sorter splimmy."

"What is that, Uncle Remus?" asked the little boy.

"Sorter splimmy-splammy, honey—sorter like he in a crowd— sorter like his ole 'oman ain't dead ez she mout be. You know how fokes duz w'en dey gits whar people's a moanin'."

The little boy didn't know, fortunately for him, and Uncle Remus went on:

"Brer Fox en Brer Possum rustle roun', dey did, gittin' out de vittles, en bimeby Brer Fox, he say, sezee:

" 'Brer Possum, you run down ter de spring en fetch de butter, en I'll sail 'roun' yer en set de table,' sezee.

"Brer Possum, he lope off atter de butter, en dreckly here he come lopin' back wid his years a tremblin' en his tongue a hangin' out. Brer Fox, he holler out:

" 'W'at de matter now, Brer Possum?' sezee.

" 'You all better run yer, fokes,' sez Brer Possum, sezee. 'De las' drap er dat butter done gone!'

" 'Whar she gone?' sez Brer Fox, sezee.

" 'Look like she dry up,' sez Brer Possum, sezee.

"Den Brer Rabbit, he look sorter sollum, he did, en he up'n say, sezee.

" 'I spect dat butter melt in somebody mouf,' sezee.

"Den dey went down ter de spring wid Brer Possum, en sho nuff de butter done gone. W'iles dey wuz sputin' over der wunderment, Brer Rabbit say he see tracks all 'roun' dar, en he p'int out dat ef dey'll all go ter sleep, he kin ketch de chap w'at stole de butter. Den dey all lie down en Brer Fox en Brer Possum dey soon drapt off ter sleep, but Brer Rabbit he stay 'wake, en w'en de time come he raise up easy and smear Brer Possum mouf wid de butter on his paws, en den he run off en nibble up de bes' er de dinner w'at dey lef' layin' out, en den he come back en wake up Brer Fox, en show 'im he butter on Brer Possum, en tell 'im 'bout it, but c'ose Brer Possum 'ny it ter de las'. Brer Fox, dough, he's a kinder lawyer, en he argafy dis way—dat Brer Possum wuz de fus one at de butter, en de fus one fer ter miss it, en mo'n dat, dar hang de signs on his mouf. Brer Possum see dat dey got 'im jammed up in a cornder, en den he up en say dat de way fer ter ketch de man w'at stole de butter is ter b'il' a big bresh-heap en set her afier, en all han's try ter jump over, en de one w'at fall in, den he de chap w'at stole de butter. Brer Rabbit en Brer Fox dey bofe 'gree, dey did, en dey whirl in en b'il' de bresh-heap, en dey b'il' her high en dey b'il' her wide, en den dey totch her off. W'en she got ter blazin' up good, Brer Rabbit, he tuck de fus turn. He sorter step back, en look 'roun' en giggle, en over he went mo' samer dan a bird flyin'. Den come Brer Fox. He got back little fudder, en spit on his han's, en lit out en made de jump, en he come so nigh gittin' in dat een' er his tail kotch afier. Ain't you never seen no fox, honey?" inquired Uncle Remus, in a tone that implied both conciliation and information.

The little boy thought probably he had, but he wouldn't commit himself.

"Well, den," continued the old man, "nex' time you see one un um, you look right close en see ef de een' er his tail ain't w'ite. Hit's des like I tell you. Dey b'ars de skyar er dat bresh-heap down ter dis day. Dey er marked—dat's w'at dey is—dey er marked."

"And what about Brother Possum?" asked the little boy.

"Ole Brer Possum, he tuck a runnin' start, he did, en he come lumberin' 'long, en he lit—kerblam!—right in de middle er de fier, en dat wuz de las' er ole Brer Possum."

"But, Uncle Remus, Brother Possum didn't steal the butter after all," said the little boy, who was not at all satisfied with such summary injustice.

"Dat w'at make I say w'at I duz, honey. In dis worril, lots er fokes is gotter suffer fer udder fokes sins. Look like hit's mighty onwrong; but hit's des dat away. Tribbalashun seem like she's a waitin' roun' de cornder fer ter ketch one en all un us, honey."

The Type of Harris's Stories: Joel Chandler Harris is best known today as the author of the Uncle Remus stories. In spite of the fact that they are now most often classified as humorous stories, Harris had a serious purpose in mind when he wrote them. The stories were written in order that the folk-lore of the negroes might be put in a permanent form. In the introduction to one of the editions of *Uncle Remus,* Harris writes, "Each legend has its variants, but in every instance I have retained that particular version which seemed to me to be the most characteristic, and have given it without embellishment and without exaggeration." In addition to preserving these legends for us, Harris accomplished other worthwhile objectives. He made Uncle Remus the "embodiment of all the negro has contributed to American culture." Also his reproduction in writing of the spoken dialect of the negro is excellent.

For Appreciation: *Mr. Rabbit Nibbles Up the Butter* appears in *Uncle Remus, His Songs and His Sayings* which was published in 1880. The characters in folk-tales are frequently animals that are endowed with human characteristics. In *Mr. Rabbit Nibbles Up the Butter,* the rabbit personifies greed. When the little boy is sorry for Brother Possum, what is Uncle Remus's philosophy? Is the story more or less amusing than if the characters had been humans?

For Further Study: List the excuses which Brer Rabbit gave for leaving the others. What evidence did Brer Rabbit use against Brer Possum? Why did Brer Possum want to use a fire to find out who was guilty?

JEAN-AH POQUELIN

GEORGE WASHINGTON CABLE

I

IN THE first decade of the present century,[1] when the newly established American Government was the most hateful thing in Louisiana—when the Creoles [2] were still kicking at such vile innovations as the trial by jury, American dances, anti-smuggling laws, and the printing of the Governor's proclamation in English—when the Anglo-American flood [3] that was presently to burst in a crevasse of immigration upon the delta had thus far been felt only as slippery seepage which made the Creole tremble for his footing—there stood, a short distance above what is now Canal Street,[4] and considerably back from the line of villas which fringed the river-bank on Tchoupitoulas Road, an old colonial plantation-house half in ruin.

[1] FIRST DECADE OF THE PRESENT CENTURY—1800–1810.
[2] CREOLES—A population in Louisiana, part French and part Spanish.
[3] ANGLO-AMERICAN FLOOD—As opposed to the Latin-American population.
[4] CANAL STREET—The main street in New Orleans.

It stood aloof from civilization, the tracts that had once been its indigo fields given over to their first noxious wildness, and grown up into one of the horridest marshes within a circuit of fifty miles.

The house was of heavy cypress, lifted up on pillars, grim, solid, and spiritless, its massive build a strong reminder of days still earlier, when every man had been his own peace officer and the insurrection of the blacks a daily contingency. Its dark, weather-beaten roof and sides were hoisted up above the jungly plain in a distracted way, like a gigantic ammunition-wagon stuck in the mud and abandoned by some retreating army. Around it was a dense growth of low water willows, with half a hundred sorts of thorny or fetid bushes, savage strangers alike to the "language of flowers" and to the botanist's Greek. They were hung with countless strands of discolored and prickly smilax, and the impassable mud below bristled with *chevaux de frise*[5] of the dwarf palmetto. Two lone forest-trees, dead cypresses, stood in the centre of the marsh, dotted with roosting vultures. The shallow strips of water were hid by myriads of aquatic plants, under whose coarse and spiritless flowers, could one have seen it, was a harbor of reptiles, great and small, to make one shudder to the end of his days.

The house was on a slightly raised spot, the levee of a draining canal. The waters of this canal did not run; they crawled, and were full of big, ravening fish and alligators, that held it against all comers.

Such was the home of old Jean Marie Poquelin, once an opulent indigo planter, standing high in the esteem of his small, proud circle of exclusively male acquaintances in the old city; now a hermit, alike shunned by and shunning all who had ever known him. "The last of his line," said the gossips. His father lies under the floor of the St. Louis Cathedral, with the wife of his youth on one side, and the wife of his old age on the other. Old Jean visits the spot daily. His half brother—alas! there was a mystery; no one knew what had become of the gentle, young half brother, more than thirty years his junior, whom once he seemed so fondly to love, but who, seven years ago, had disappeared suddenly and left no clew of his fate.

[5] *Chevaux de frise*—Obstructions in shallow water made by the roots, which projected in all directions, resembling a medieval defensive barrier of this name.

They had seemed to live so happily in each other's love. No father, mother, wife to either, no kindred upon earth. The elder a bold, frank, impetuous, chivalric adventurer; the younger a gentle, studious, book-loving recluse; they lived upon the ancestral estate like mated birds, one always on the wing, the other always in the nest.

There was no trait in Jean Marie Poquelin, said the old gossips, for which he was so well known among his few friends as his apparent fondness for his "little brother." "Jacques said this," and "Jacques was good," or "wise," or "just," or "far-sighted," as the nature of the case required; and "he should ask Jacques as soon as he got home," since Jacques was never elsewhere to be seen.

It was between the roving character of the elder brother, and the bookishness of the younger, that the estate fell into decay. Jean Marie, generous gentleman, gambled the slaves away one by one, until none was left, man or woman, but one old African mute.[6]

The indigo-fields and vats of Louisiana had been generally abandoned as unremunerative. Certain enterprising men had substituted the culture of sugar; but while the recluse was too apathetic to take so active a course, the other [7] saw larger, and, at that time, equally respectable profits, first in smuggling, and later in the African slave-trade. What harm could he see in it? The whole people said it was vitally necessary, and to minister to a vital public necessity,—good enough, certainly, and so he laid up many a doubloon,[8] that made him none the worse in the public regard.

One day old Jean Marie was about to start upon a voyage that was to be longer, much longer, than any he had yet made. Jacques had begged him hard for many days not to go, but he laughed him off, and finally said, kissing him:

"*Adieu, 'tit frère.*" [9]

"No," said Jacques, "I shall go with you."

They left the old hulk of a house in the sole care of the African mute, and went away to the Guinea coast together.

---

[6] MUTE—One who cannot speak.
[7] THE OTHER—The older brother.
[8] DOUBLOON—A Spanish coin worth about eight dollars.
[9] *Adieu, 'tit frère*—Good-by, little brother.

II

Two years after, old Poquelin came home without his vessel. He must have arrived at his house by night. No one saw him come. No one saw "his little brother"; rumor whispered that he, too, had returned, but he had never been seen again.

A dark suspicion fell upon the old slave-trader. No matter that the few kept the many reminded of the tenderness that had ever marked his bearing to the missing man. The many shook their heads. "You know he has a quick and fearful temper"; and "why does he cover his loss with mystery?" "Grief would out with the truth."

"But," said the charitable few, "look in his face; see that expression of true humanity." The many did look in his face, and, as he looked in theirs, he read the silent question: "Where is thy brother Abel?"[1] The few were silenced, his former friends died off, and the name of Jean Marie Poquelin became a symbol of witchery, devilish crime, and hideous nursery fictions.

The man and his house were alike shunned. The snipe and duck hunters forsook the marsh, and the woodcutters abandoned the canal. Sometimes the hardier boys who ventured out there snake-shooting heard a slow thumping of oar-locks on the canal. They would look at each other for a moment half in consternation, half in glee, then rush from their sport in wanton haste to assail with their gibes the unoffending, withered old man who, in rusty attire, sat in the stern of a skiff, rowed homeward by his white-headed African mute.

"O Jean-ah Poquelin! O Jean-ah! Jean-ah Poquelin!"

It was not necessary to utter more than that. No hint of wickedness, deformity, or any physical or moral demerit; merely the name and tone of mockery: "Oh, Jean-ah Poquelin!" and while they tumbled one over another in their needless haste to fly, he would rise carefully from his seat, while the aged mute, with downcast face, went on rowing, and rolling up his brown fist, and extending it toward the urchins, would pour forth such an unholy broadside of French imprecation and invective as would all but craze them with delight.

Among both blacks and whites the house was the object of a thousand superstitions. Every midnight, they affirmed, the *feu*

---

[1] ABEL—A Biblical reference to Abel who was slain by his brother Cain.

follet[2] came out of the marsh and ran in and out of the rooms, flashing from window to window. The story of some lads, whose words in ordinary statements were worthless, was generally credited, that the night they camped in the woods, rather than pass the place after dark, they saw, about sunset, every window blood-red, and on each of the four chimneys an owl sitting, which turned his head three times round, and moaned and laughed with a human voice. There was a bottomless well, everybody professed to know, beneath the sill of the big front door under the rotten veranda; whoever set his foot upon that threshold disappeared forever in the depth below.

What wonder the marsh grew as wild as Africa! Take all the Faubourg Ste Marie,[3] and half the ancient city, you would not find one graceless dare-devil reckless enough to pass within a hundred yards of the house after nightfall.

The alien races pouring into old New Orleans began to find the few streets named for the Bourbon princes[4] too strait for them. The wheel of fortune, beginning to whirl, threw them off beyond the ancient corporation lines, and sowed civilization and even trade upon the lands of the Graviers and Girods.[5] Fields became roads, roads streets. Everywhere the leveller[6] was peering through his glass, rodsmen were whacking their way through willow-brakes and rose-hedges, and the sweating Irishmen tossed the blue clay up with their long-handled shovels.

"Ha! that is all very well," quoth Jean-Baptistes, feeling the reproach of an enterprise that asked neither cooperation nor advice of them, "but wait till they come yonder to Jean Poquelin's marsh; ha! ha! ha!" The supposed predicament so delighted them, that they put on a mock terror and whirled about in an assumed stampede, then caught their clasped hands between their knees in excess of mirth, and laughed till the tears ran; for whether the street-makers mired in the marsh, or contrived to cut through old "Jean-ah's" property, either event would be joyful. Meantime a line of tiny rods, with bits of

---

[2] *Feu follet*—The phosphorescent light which comes from decaying vegetable matter.

[3] FAUBOURG STE MARIE—A suburb of New Orleans.

[4] BOURBON PRINCES—Princes of the famous Bourbon line of Spain.

[5] GRAVIERS AND GIRODS—Prominent families of New Orleans.

[6] LEVELLER—Surveyor.

white paper in their split tops, gradually extended its way straight through the haunted ground, and across the canal diagonally.

"We shall fill that ditch," said the men in mud-boots, and brushed close along the chained and pad-locked gate of the  haunted mansion. Ah, Jean-ah Poquelin, those were not Creole boys, to be stampeded with a little hard swearing.

He went to the Governor. That official scanned the odd figure with no slight interest. Jean Poquelin was of short, broad frame, with a bronzed, leonine face. His brow was ample and deeply furrowed. His eye, large and black, was bold and open like that of a war-horse, and his jaws shut together with the firmness of iron. He was dressed in a suit of Attakapas [7] cottonade, and his shirt unbuttoned and thrown back from the throat and bosom, sailor-wise, showed a herculean breast, hard and grizzled. There was no fierceness or defiance in his look, no harsh ungentleness, no symptom of his unlawful life or violent temper; but rather a peaceful and peaceable fearlessness. Across the whole face, not marked in one or another feature, but as it were laid softly upon the countenance like an almost imperceptible veil, was the imprint of some great grief. A careless eye might easily overlook it, but, once seen, there it hung—faint but unmistakable.

The Governor bowed.

"*Parlez-vous francais?*" [8] asked the figure.

"I would rather talk English, if you can do so," said the Governor.

"My name, Jean Poquelin."

"How can I serve you, Mr. Poquelin?"

"My 'ouse is yond'; *dans le marais là-bas.*" [9]

---

[7] ATTAKAPAS—A tribe of Indians inhabiting the southwestern part of Louisiana.

[8] *Parlez-vous francais?*—Do you speak French?

[9] *Dans le marais là-bas*—In the swamp yonder.

The Governor bowed.

"Dat *marais* billong to me."

"Yes, sir."

"To me; Jean Poquelin; I hown 'im meself."

"Well, sir?"

"He don't billong to you; I get him from me father."

"That is perfectly true, Mr. Poquelin, as far as I am aware."

"You want to make strit pass yond'?"

"I do not know, sir; it is quite probable; but the city will indemnify you for any loss you may suffer—you will get paid, you understand."

"Strit can't pass dare."

"You will have to see the municipal authorities about that, Mr. Poquelin."

A bitter smile came upon the old man's face:

"*Pardon, Monsieur,* you is not *le Gouverneur?*"

"Yes."

"*Mais,*[10] yes. You har *le Gouverneur*—yes. Veh—well, I come to you. I tell you strit can't pass at me 'ouse."

"But you will have to see——"

"I come to you. You is *le Gouverneur.* I know not the new laws. I ham a Fr-r-rench-a-man! Fr-r-rench-a-man have something *aller au contraire* [11]—he come at his *Gouverneur.* I come to you. If me had not been bought from me king like *bossals* [12] in the hold time, de king gof—France would-a-show *Monsieur le Gouverneur* to take care his men to make strit in right places. *Mais,* I know; we billong to *Monsieur le Président.* I want you do somesin for me, eh?"

"What is it?" asked the patient Governor.

"I want you tell *Monsieur le Président* strit—can't—pass—at me—'ouse."

"Have a chair, Mr. Poquelin"; but the old man did not stir. The Governor took a quill and wrote a line to a city official, introducing Mr. Poquelin, and asking for him every possible courtesy. He handed it to him, instructing him where to present it.

"Mr. Poquelin," he said with a conciliatory smile, "tell me,

[10] *Mais*—But.
[11] *Aller au contraire*—Go wrong.
[12] *Bossals*—Vassals.

is it your house that our Creole citizens tell such odd stories about?"

The old man glared sternly upon the speaker, and with immovable features said:

"You don't see me trade some Guinea nigga'?"

"Oh, no."

"You don't see me make some smugglin'?"

"No, sir; not at all."

"But, I am Jean Marie Poquelin. I mine me hown bizniss. Dat all right? *Adieu.*"

He put his hat on and withdrew. By and by he stood, letter in hand, before the person to whom it was addressed.

This person employed an interpreter.

"He says," said the interpreter to the officer, "he come to make you the fair warning how you muz not make the street pas' at his 'ouse."

The officer remarked that "such impudence was refreshing"; but the experienced interpreter translated freely.

"He says: 'Why don't want?'" said the interpreter.

The old slave-trader answered at some length.

"He says," said the interpreter, again turning to the officer, "the marass is a too unhealth' for peopl' to live."

"But we expect to drain his old marsh; it's not going to be a marsh."

"*Il dit* [13]—" The interpreter explained in French.

The old man answered tersely.

"He says the canal is private property," said the interpreter.

"Oh! *that* old ditch; that's to be filled up. Tell the old man we're going to fix him up nicely."

Translation being duly made, the man in power was amused to see a thunder-cloud gathering on the old man's face.

"Tell him," he added, "by the time we finish, there'll not be a ghost left in his shanty."

The interpreter began to translate, but——

"*J'comprehends,* [14] *j'comprehends,*" said the old man, with an impatient gesture, and burst forth, pouring curses upon the United States, the President, the Territory of Orleans, Congress, the Governor and all his subordinates, striding out of the apart-

[13] *Il dit*—He says.
[14] *J'comprehends*—I understand.

ment as he cursed, while the object of his maledictions roared with merriment and rammed the floor with his foot.

"Why, it will make his old place worth ten dollars to one," said the official to the interpreter.

" 'Tis not for de worse of de property," said the interpreter.

"I should guess not," said the other, whittling his chair,— "seems to me as if some of these old Creoles would liever live in a crawfish hole than to have a neighbor."

"You know what make old Jean Poquelin ack like that? I will tell you. You know——"

The interpreter was rolling a cigarette, and paused to light his tender; then, as the smoke poured in a thick double stream from his nostrils, he said, in a solemn whisper:

"He is a witch."

"Ho, ho, ho!" laughed the other.

"You don't believe it? What you want to bet?" cried the interpreter, jerking himself half up and thrusting out one arm while he bared it of his coat-sleeve with the hand of the other. "What you want to bet?"

"How do you know?" asked the official.

"Das what I goin' to tell you. You know, one evening I was shooting some *grosbec*.[15] I killed three; but I had trouble to find them, it was becoming so dark. When I have them I start' to come home; then I got to pas' at Jean Poquelin's house."

"Ho, ho, ho!" laughed the other, throwing his leg over the arm of the chair.

"Wait," said the interpreter. "I come along slow, not making some noises; still, still——"

"And scared," said the smiling one.

"*Mais*, wait. I get all pas' the 'ouse. 'Ah!' I say; 'all right!' Then I see two thing' before! Hah! I get as cold and humide, and shake like a leaf. You think it was nothing? There I see, so plain as can be (though it was making nearly dark) I see Jean-Marie-Po-que-lin walkin' right in front, and right there beside of him was something like a man—but not a man—white like paint!—I dropp' on the grass from scared—they pass'; so sure as I live 'twas the ghos' of Jacques Poquelin, his brother!"

"Pooh!" said the listener.

"I'll put my han' in the fire," said the interpreter.

---

[15] *Grosbec*—Grosbeak—a bird.

"But did you never think," asked the other, "that that might be Jack Poquelin, as you call him, alive and well, and for some cause hid away by his brother?"

"But there har' no cause!" said the other, and the entrance of third parties changed the subject.

III

SOME months passed and the street was opened. A canal was first dug through the marsh, the small one which passed so close to Jean Poquelin's house was filled, and the street, or rather a sunny road, just touched a corner of the old mansion's door-yard. The morass ran dry. Its venomous denizens slipped away through the bulrushes, the cattle roaming freely upon its hardened surface trampled the super-abundant undergrowth. The bellowing frogs croaked to westward. Lilies and the flower-de-luce sprang up in the place of reeds; smilax and poison-oak gave way to the purple-plumed iron-weed and pink spiderwort; the bindweeds ran everywhere blooming as they ran, and on one of the dead cypresses a giant creeper hung its green burden of foliage and lifted its scarlet trumpets. Sparrows and redbirds flitted through the bushes, and dewberries grew ripe beneath. Over all these came a sweet, dry smell of salubrity which the place had not known since the sediments of the Mississippi first lifted it from the sea.

But its owner did not build. Over the willow-brakes, and down the vista of the open street, bright new houses, some singly, some by ranks, were prying in on the old man's privacy. They even settled down toward his southern side. First a wood-cutter's hut or two, and all at once the faubourg [1] had flanked and half surrounded him and his dried-up marsh.

Ah! then the common people began to hate him. "The old tyrant!" "You don't mean an old *tyrant?*" "Well, then, why don't he build when the public need demands it? What does he live in that unneighborly way for?" "The old pirate!" "The old kidnapper!" How easily even the most ultra Louisianians put on the imported virtues of the North when they could be brought to bear against the hermit. "There he goes, with the boys after him! Ah! ha! ha! Jean-ah Poquelin!

[1] FAUBOURG—Suburb.

Ah! Jean-ah! Aha! aha! Jean-ah Marie! Jean-ah Poquelin! The old villain!" How merrily the swarming Américains echo the spirit of persecution! "The old fraud," they say—"pretends to live in a haunted house, does he? We'll tar and feather him some day. Guess we can fix him."

He cannot be rowed home along the old canal now; he walks. He has broken sadly of late, and the street urchins are ever at his heels. It is like the days when they cried: "Go up, thou bald-head," and the old man now and then turns and delivers ineffectual curses.

To the Creoles—to the incoming lower class of superstitious Germans, Irish, Silicians, and others—he became an omen and embodiment of public and private ill-fortune. Upon him all the vagaries of their superstitions gathered and grew. If a house caught fire, it was imputed to his machinations. Did a woman go off in a fit, he had bewitched her. Did a child stray off for an hour, the mother shivered with the apprehension that Jean Poquelin had offered him to strange gods. The house was the subject of every bad boy's invention who loved to contrive ghostly lies. "As long as that house stands we shall have bad luck. Do you not see our peas and beans dying, our cabbages and lettuce going to seed and our gardens turning to dust, while every day you can see it raining in the woods? The rain will never pass old Poquelin's house. He keeps a fetich.[2] He has conjured the whole Faubourg Ste Marie. And why, the old wretch? Simply because our playful and innocent children call after him as he passes."

A "Building and Improvement Company," which had not yet got its charter, "but was going to," and which had not, indeed, any tangible capital yet, but "was going to have some," joined the "Jean-ah Poquelin" war. The haunted property would be such a capital site for a market-house! They sent a deputation to the old mansion to ask its occupant to sell. The deputation never got beyond the chained gate and a very barren interview with the African mute. The President of the Board was then empowered (for he had studied French in Pennsylvania and was considered qualified) to call and persuade M. Poquelin to subscribe to the company's stock; but——

"Fact is, gentlemen," he said at the next meeting, "it would

[2] FETICH—A charm.

take us at least twelve months to make Mr. Pokaleen understand the original features of our system, and he wouldn't subscribe when we'd done; besides, the only way to see him is to
stop him on the street."

There was a great laugh from the Board; they couldn't help
it. "Better meet a bear robbed of her whelps," said one.

"You're mistaken as to that," said the President. "I did
meet him, and stopped him, and found him quite polite. But I
could get no satisfaction from him; the fellow wouldn't talk in
French, and when I spoke in English he hoisted his old shoulders
up, and gave the same answer to everything I said."

"And that was—?" asked one or two, impatient of the pause.

"That it 'don't worse w'ile.' " ·

One of the Board said: "Mr. President, this market-house
project, as I take it, is not altogether a selfish one; the community is to be benefited by it. We may feel that we are working in the public interest (the Board smiled knowingly), if we
employ all possible means to oust this old nuisance from among
us. You may know that at the time the street was cut through,
this old Poquelann did all he could to prevent it. It was owing
to a certain connection which I had with that affair that I heard
a ghost story (smiles, followed by a sudden dignified check)—
ghost story, which, of course, I am not going to relate; but I
may say that my profound conviction, arising from a prolonged
study of that story, is that this old villain, John Poquelann, has
his brother locked up in that old house. Now, if this is so, and
we can fix it on him, I merely *suggest* that we can make the matter highly useful. I don't know," he added, beginning to sit
down, "but that it is an action we owe to the community—
hem!"

"How do you propose to handle the subject?" asked the President.

"I was thinking," said the speaker, "that, as a Board of Directors, it would be unadvisable for us to authorize any action involving trespass; but if you, for instance, Mr. President, should,
as it were, for mere curiosity, *request* some one, as, for instance,
our excellent Secretary, simply as a personal favor, to look into
the matter—this is merely a suggestion."

The Secretary smiled sufficiently to be understood that, while
he certainly did not consider such preposterous service a part of

his duties as secretary, he might, notwithstanding, accede to the President's request; and the Board adjourned.

Little White, as the Secretary was called, was a mild, kind-hearted little man, who, nevertheless, had no fear of anything, unless it was the fear of being unkind.

"I tell you frankly," he privately said to the President, "I go into this purely for reasons of my own."

The next day, a little after nightfall, one might have descried this little man slipping along the rear fence of the Poquelin place, preparatory to vaulting over into the rank, grass-grown yard, and bearing himself altogether more after the manner of a collector of rare chickens than according to the usage of secretaries.

The picture presented to his eye was not calculated to enliven his mind. The old mansion stood out against the western sky, black and silent. One long, lurid pencil-stroke along a sky of slate was all that was left of daylight. No sign of life was apparent; no light at any window, unless it might have been on the side of the house hidden from view. No owls were on the chimneys, no dogs were in the yard.

He entered the place, and ventured up behind a small cabin which stood apart from the house. Through one of its many crannies he easily detected the African mute crouched before a flickering pine-knot, his head on his knees, fast asleep.

He concluded to enter the mansion, and, with that view, stood and scanned it. The broad rear steps of the veranda would not serve him; he might meet some one midway. He was measuring, with his eye, the proportions of one of the pillars which supported it, and estimating the practicability of climbing it, when he heard a footstep. Some one had dragged a chair out toward the railing, then seemed to change his mind and began to pace the veranda, his footfalls resounding on the dry boards with singular loudness. Little White drew a step backward, got the figure between himself and the sky, and at once recognized the short, broad-shouldered form of old Jean Poquelin.

He sat down upon a billet of wood, and, to escape the stings of a whining cloud of mosquitoes, shrouded his face and neck in his handkerchief, leaving his eyes uncovered.

He had sat there but a moment when he noticed a strange, sickening odor, faint, as if coming from a distance, but loathsome and horrid.

Whence could it come? Not from the cabin; not from the marsh, for it was as dry as powder. It was not in the air; it seemed to come from the ground.

Rising up, he noticed, for the first time, a few steps before him a narrow footpath leading toward the house. He glanced down it—ha! right there was some one coming—ghostly white!

Quick as thought, and as noiselessly, he lay down at full length against the cabin. It was bold strategy, and yet, there was no denying it, little White felt that he was frightened. "It is not a ghost," he said to himself. "I *know* it cannot be a ghost"; but the perspiration burst out at every pore, and the air seemed to thicken with heat. "It is a living man," he said in his thoughts. "I hear his footstep, and I hear old Poquelin's footsteps, too, separately, over on the veranda. I am not discovered; the thing has passed; there is that odor again; what a smell of death! Is it coming back? Yes. It stops at the door of the cabin. Is it peering in at the sleeping mute? It moves away. It is in the path again. Now it is gone." He shuddered. "Now, if I dare venture, the mystery is solved." He rose cautiously, close against the cabin, and peered along the path.

The figure of a man, a presence if not a body—but whether clad in some white stuff or naked the darkness would not allow him to determine—had turned, and now, with a seeming painful gait, moved slowly from him. "Great Heaven! Can it be that the dead do walk?" He withdrew again the hands which had gone to his eyes. The dreadful object passed between two pillars and under the house. He listened. There was a faint sound as of feet upon a staircase, then all was still except the measured tread of Jean Poquelin walking on the veranda, and the heavy respirations of the mute slumbering in the cabin.

The little Secretary was about to retreat; but as he looked once more toward the haunted house a dim light appeared in the crack of a closed window, and presently old Jean Poquelin came, dragging his chair, and sat down close against the shining cranny. He spoke in a low, tender tone in the French tongue, making some inquiry. An answer came from within. Was it the voice of a human? So unnatural was it—so hollow, so discordant, so unearthly—that the stealthy listener shuddered again from head to foot, and when something stirred in some bushes near by—though it may have been nothing more than a rat—and came scuttling through the grass, the little Secretary actually turned and fled. As he left the enclosure he moved with bolder leisure through the bushes; yet now and then he spoke aloud: "Oh, oh! I see, I understand!" and shut his eyes in his hands.

IV

How strange that henceforth little White was the champion of Jean Poquelin! In season and out of season—wherever a word was uttered against him—the Secretary, with a quiet, aggressive force that instantly arrested gossip, demanded upon what authority the statement or conjecture was made; but as he did not condescend to explain his own remarkable attitude, it was not long before the disrelish and suspicion which had followed Jean Poquelin so many years fell also upon him.

It was only the next evening but one after his adventure that he made himself a source of sullen amazement to one hundred and fifty boys, by ordering them to desist from their wanton hallooing. Old Jean Poquelin, standing and shaking his cane, rolling out his long-drawn maledictions, paused and stared, then gave the Secretary a courteous bow and started on. The boys, save one, from pure astonishment, ceased, but a ruffianly little Irish lad, more daring than any had yet been, threw a big hurtling clod, that struck old Poquelin between the shoulders and burst like a shell. The enraged old man wheeled with uplifted staff to give chase to the scampering vagabond; and—he may have tripped, or he may not, but he fell full length. Little White hastened to help him up, but he waved him off with a fierce imprecation and staggering to his feet resumed his way homeward. His lips were reddened with blood.

Little White was on his way to the meeting of the Board. He would have given all he dared spend to have staid away, for he felt both too fierce and too tremulous to brook the criticisms that were likely to be made.

"I can't help it, gentlemen; I can't help to make a case against the old man, and I'm not going to."

"We did not expect this disappointment, Mr. White."

"I can't help that, sir. No, sir; you had better not appoint any more investigations. Somebody'll investigate himself into trouble. No, sir; it isn't a threat, it is only my advice, but I warn you that whoever takes the task in hand will rue it to his dying day—which may be hastened, too."

The President expressed himself "surprised."

"I don't care a rush," answered little White, wildly and foolishly, "I don't care a rush if you are, sir. No, my nerves are not disordered; my head's as clear as a bell. No, I'm *not* excited."

A Director remarked that the Secretary looked as though he had waked from a nightmare.

"Well, sir, if you want to know the fact, I have; and if you choose to cultivate old Poquelin's society you can have one, too."

"White," called a facetious member, but White did not notice. "White," he called again.

"What?" demanded White, with a scowl.

"Did you see a ghost?"

"Yes, sir; I did," cried White, hitting the table, and handing the President a paper which brought the Board to other business.

The story got among the gossips that somebody (they were afraid to say little White) had been to the Poquelin mansion by night and beheld something appalling. The rumor was but a shadow of the truth, magnified and distorted as is the manner of shadows. He had seen skeletons walking, and had barely escaped the clutches of one by making the sign of the cross.

Some madcap boys with an appetite for the horrible plucked up courage to venture through the dried marsh by the cattle path, and come before the house at a spectral hour when the air was full of bats. Something which they but half saw—half a sight was enough—sent them tearing back through the willow-brakes and acacia bushes to their homes, where they fairly dropped down, and cried:

"Was it white?" "No—yes—nearly so—we can't tell—but we saw it." And one could hardly doubt, to look at their ashen faces, that they had, whatever it was.

"If that old rascal lived in the country we come from," said certain Américains, "he'd have been tarred and feathered before now, wouldn't he, Sanders?"

"Well, now he just would."

"And we'd have rid him on a rail, wouldn't we?"

"That's what I allow."

"Tell you what you *could* do." They were talking to some rollicking Creoles who had assumed an absolute necessity for doing *something*. "What is it you call this thing where an old man marries a young girl, and you come out with horns, and——"

"*Charivari?*"[1] asked the Creoles.

"Yes, that's it. Why don't you shivaree him?" Felicitous suggestion.

Little White, with his wife beside him, was sitting on their doorstep on the sidewalk, as Creole custom had taught them, looking toward the sunset. They had moved into the lately opened street. The view was not attractive on the score of beauty. The houses were small and scattered, and across the flat commons, spite of the lofty tangle of weeds and bushes, and spite of the thickets of acacia, they needs must see the dismal old Poquelin mansion, tilted awry and shutting out the declining sun. The moon, white and slender, was hanging the tip of its horn over one of the chimneys.

"And you say," said the Secretary, "the old black man has been going by here alone? Patty, suppose old Poquelin should be concocting some mischief; he don't lack provocation; the way that clod hit him the other day was enough to have killed him. Why, Patty, he dropped as quick as *that!* No wonder you haven't seen him. I wonder if they haven't heard something about him up at the drug-store. Suppose I go and see."

"Do," said his wife.

She sat alone for half an hour, watching that sudden going out of the day peculiar to the latitude.

"That moon is ghost enough for one house," she said, as her husband returned. "It has gone right down the chimney."

"Patty," said little White, "the drug clerk says the boys are going to shivaree old Poquelin to-night. I'm going to try to stop it."

"Why, White," said his wife, "you'd better not. You'll get hurt."

"No, I'll not."

"Yes, you will."

"I'm going to sit out here until they come along. They're compelled to pass right by here."

[1] *Charivari*—A bold burlesque serenade.

"Why, White, it may be midnight before they start; you're not going to sit out here till then."

"Yes, I am."

"Well, you're very foolish," said Mrs. White in an undertone, looking anxious, and tapping one of the steps with her foot.

They sat a very long time talking over little family matters.

"What's that?" at last said Mrs. White.

"That's the nine o'clock gun," said White, and they relapsed into a long-sustained, drowsy silence.

"Patty, you'd better go in and go to bed," said he at last.

"I'm not sleepy."

"Well, you're very foolish," quietly remarked little White, and again silence fell upon them.

"Patty, suppose I walk out to the old house and see if I can find out anything."

"Suppose," said she, "you don't do any such—listen!"

Down the street arose a great hubbub. Dogs and boys were howling and barking; men were laughing, shouting, groaning, and blowing horns, whooping, and clanking cow-bells, whinnying, and howling, and rattling pots and pans.

"They are coming this way," said little White. "You had better go in the house, Patty."

"So had you."

"No. I'm going to see if I can't stop them."

"Why, White!"

"I'll be back in a minute," said White, and went toward the noise.

In a few moments the little Secretary met the mob. The pen hesitates on the word, for there is a respectable difference, measurable only on the scale of the half century, between a mob and a *charivari*. Little White lifted his ineffectual voice. He faced the head of the disorderly column, and cast himself about as if he were made of wood and moved by the jerk of a string. He rushed to one who seemed, from the size and clatter of his tin pan, to be a leader. *"Stop these fellows, Bienvenu, stop them just a minute, till I tell them something."* Bienvenu turned and brandished his instruments of discord in an imploring way to the crowd. They slackened their pace, two or three hushed their horns and joined the prayer of little White and Bienvenu for silence. The throng halted. The hush was delicious.

"Bienvenu," said little White, "don't shivaree old Poquelin to-night; he's——"

"My fwang," said the swaying Bienvenu, "who tail you I goin' to chahivahi somebody, eh? You sink beckause I make a little playfool wiz zis tin pan zat I am *dhonk?*"

"Oh, no, Bienvenu, old fellow, you're all right. I was afraid you might not know that old Poquelin was sick, you know, but you're not going there, are you?"

"My fwang, I vay soy to tail you zat you ah dhonk as de dev'. I am *shem* of you. I ham ze servan' of ze *publique*. Zese *citoyens* goin' to wickwest Jean Poquelin to give to the Ursuline [2] two hondred fifty dolla'——"

"Hé quoi!" [3] cried a listener. *"Cinq cent piastres, oui!"*

"Oui!" said Bienvenu, "and if he wiffuse we make him some lit' *musique;* ta-ra ta!" He hoisted a merry hand and foot, then frowning, added: "Old Poquelin got no bizniz dhink s'much w'isky."

"But, gentlemen," said little White, around whom a circle had gathered, "the old man is very sick."

"My faith!" cried a tiny Creole, "we did not make him to be sick. W'en we have say we going make *le charivari,* do you want that we hall tell a lie? My faith! 'sfools!"

"But you can shivaree somebody else," said desperate little White.

"Oui!" cried Bienvenu, "et *chahivahi* Jean-ah Poquelin to-mo'w!"

"Let us go to Madame Schneider!" cried two or three, and amid huzzas and confused cries, among which was heard a stentorian Celtic call for drinks, the crowd again began to move.

"Cent piastres pour l'hôpital de charité!" [4]

---

[2] Ursuline—The order of Ursuline nuns.

[3] *Hé quoi*, etc.—O, what! Five hundred pesetas, yes!

[4] *Cent piastres*, etc.—One hundred pesetas for the Charity Hospital.

"Hurrah!"

"One hongred dolla' for Charity hospital!"

"Hurrah!"

"Whang!" went a tin pan, the crowd yelled, and Pandemonium gaped again. They were off at a right angle.

Nodding, Mrs. White looked at the mantel-clock.

"Well, if it isn't way after midnight."

The hideous noise down street was passing beyond earshot. She raised a sash and listened. For a moment there was silence. Some one came to the door.

"Is that you, White?"

"Yes." He entered. "I succeeded, Patty."

"Did you?" said Patty, joyfully.

"Yes. They've gone down to shivaree the old Dutch-woman who married her step-daughter's sweetheart. They say she has got to pay a hundred dollars to the hospital before they stop."

V

The couple retired, and Mrs. White slumbered. She was awakened by her husband snapping the lid of his watch.

"What time?" she asked.

"Half-past three. Patty, I haven't slept a wink. Those fellows are out yet. Don't you hear them?"

"Why, White, they're coming this way!"

"I know they are," said White, sliding out of bed and drawing on his clothes, "and they're coming fast. You'd better go away from that window, Patty. My! what a clatter."

"Here they are," said Mrs. White, but her husband was gone. Two or three hundred men and boys passed the place at a rapid walk straight down the broad, new street, toward the hated house of ghosts. The din was terrific. She saw little White at the head of the rabble brandishing his arms and trying in vain to make himself heard; but they only shook their heads laughing and hooting the louder, and so passed, bearing him on before them.

Swiftly they pass out from among the houses, away from the dim oil lamps of the street, out into the broad starlit commons, and enter the willowy jungles of the haunted ground. Some hearts fail and their owners lag behind and turn back, suddenly remembering how near morning it is. But the most part push on, tearing the air with their clamor.

Down ahead of them in the long, thicket-darkened way there is—singularly enough—a faint, dancing light. It must be very near the old house; it is. It has stopped now. It is a lantern, and is under a well-known sapling which has grown up on the wayside since the canal was filled. Now it swings mysteriously to and fro. A goodly number of the more ghost-fearing give up the sport; but a full hundred move onward at a run, doubling their devilish howling and banging.

Yes; it is a lantern, and there are two persons under the tree. The crowd draws near—drops into a walk; one of the two is the old African mute; he lifts the lantern up so that it shines on the other; the crowd recoils; there is a hush of all clangor, and all at once, with a cry of mingled fright and horror from every throat, the whole throng rushes back, dropping everything, sweeping past little White, and hurrying on, never stopping until the jungle is left behind, and then to find that not one in ten has seen the cause of the stampede, and not one of the tenth is certain what it was.

There is one huge fellow among them who looks capable of any villainy. He finds something to mount on, and, in the Creole *patois*,[1] calls a general halt. Bienvenu sinks down, and vainly trying to recline gracefully, resigns the leadership. The herd gather round the speaker; he assures them they have been outraged. Their right peaceably to traverse the public streets has been trampled upon. Shall such encroachments be endured? It is now daybreak. Let them go now by the open light of day and force a free passage of the public highway!

A scattering consent was the response, and the crowd, thinned now and drowsy, straggled quietly down toward the old house. Some drifted ahead, others sauntered behind, but every one, as he again neared the tree, came to a stand-still. Little White sat upon a bank of turf on the opposite side of the way looking very stern and sad. To each new-comer he put the same question:

"Did you come here to go to old Poquelin's?"

"Yes."

"He's dead." And if the shocked hearer started away he would say: "Don't go away."

---

[1] *Patois*—Dialect.

"Why not?"

"I want you to go to the funeral presently."

If some Louisianian, too loyal to dear France or Spain to understand English, looked bewildered, some one would interpret for him; and presently they went. Little White led the van, the crowd trooping after him down the middle of the way. The gate, that had never been seen before unchained, was open. Stern little White stopped a short distance from it; the rabble stopped behind him. Something was moving out from under the veranda. The many whisperers stretched upward to see. The African mute came very slowly toward the gate, leading by a cord in the nose a small brown bull, which was harnessed to a rude cart. On the flat body of the cart, under a black cloth, were seen the outlines of a long box.

"Hats off, gentlemen," said little White, as the box came in view, and the crowd silently uncovered.

"Gentlemen," said little White, "here come the last remains of Jean Marie Poquelin, a better man, I'm afraid, with all his sins,—yes a better—a kinder man to his blood—a man of more self-forgetful goodness—than all of you put together will ever dare to be."

There was a profound hush as the vehicle came creaking through the gate; but when it turned away from them toward the forest, those in front started suddenly. There was a backward rush, then all stood still again staring one way; for there, behind the bier, with eyes cast down and labored step, walked the living remains—all that was left—of little Jacques Poquelin, the long-hidden brother—a leper, as white as snow.

Dumb with horror, the cringing crowd gazed upon the walking death. They watched, in silent awe, the slow *cortège* [2] creep down the long, straight road and lessen on the view, until by and by it stopped where a wild, unfrequented path branched off into the undergrowth toward the rear of the ancient city.

"They are going to the *Terre aux Lépreux*," [3] said one in the crowd. The rest watched them in silence.

The little bull was set free; the mute, with strength of an ape, lifted the long box to his shoulder. For a moment more the mute and the leper stood in sight, while the former adjusted

[2] *Cortège*—Procession.
[3] *Terre aux Lépreux*—Land of the Lepers.

his burden; then, without one backward glance upon the unkind human world, turning their faces toward the ridge in the depths of the swamp known as the Leper's Land, they stepped into the jungle, disappeared, and were never seen again.

The Type of Cable's Stories: George Washington Cable was a pioneer in the writing of local color stories of the South. He had been born and reared in New Orleans and the mark of the French-Spanish-Creole city was upon him. He had pored over the early histories of the city and was steeped in its romantic background. Against the picturesque Louisiana background he wove romantic tales of a disappearing generation. But his settings are accurate, his characters are convincing. He aimed at producing a single effect, uniformity of tone and atmosphere, and in this way, his stories are comparable to those of Poe. His plots move slowly and deliberately, but none the less steadily, and he uses dialect to good advantage. He is a master of beautiful English, and his short stories are among the most perfect of all American short stories.

For Appreciation: *Jean-ah-Poquelin* is one of seven short stories which appear in *Old Creole Days* published in 1879. One reason why this story is worth studying is because of the skill with which the author acquaints the reader with a great deal of information—not as so many isolated facts, but as an integrated part of the story. For example, in the first paragraph, the reader learns of the attitude of the Creoles toward the government of the United States. When and from what country was Louisiana purchased? Can you explain this attitude of the Creoles? In the next few paragraphs the reader is told about some of the plant and animal life in the region. Find these passages. Also there are references to changes in the economic conditions in Louisiana. What had taken the place of the indigo industry? How is the feeling produced that there is something unnatural or weird about Jean Marie Poquelin and his house? The story is filled with superstitions. How do they increase the interest or suspense of the story? Select definite examples to illustrate this. Where does a suggestion of mystery first appear? What strengthens the feeling of mystery? When you first read the story did you detect any clues as to the outcome? Read the story again and see if you can now find more clues. What is your feeling at the end of the story? Note how the story develops through each part and the relation of each part to the whole. What would be the effect if any part were omitted? Give a definite illustration. What does this suggest to you in regard to short story technique?

For Further Study: Vocabulary study: Part I—*crevasse; delta; fetid; indigo fields; noxious; levee.* Part II—*dark suspicion; rusty attire; imprecation and invective; rodsmen; leonine; Attakapas cottonade.* Part

III—*venomous denizens; flower-de-luce; salubrity; most ultra Louisiani-* *ans; machinations; conjured; deputation; lurid.* Part IV—*arrested; hurtling; facetious; ineffectual.*

Part I—Make a list of phrases which tell the time of the story. Give a complete description of the old plantation house and its surroundings. Compare the brothers and describe their feeling for each other. In what business did the elder brother become engaged? What is the effect of the brief mention of the voyage to Guinea and the return?

Part II—How did Jean appear when he returned? How did the townspeople come to regard him? Do you share the feeling of the neighbors toward Jean? Why? How was civilization creeping upon the old house? Tell of Jean's going to the Governor. Describe the scene before the city official. Does the explanation of the interpreter after Jean's departure give any clue to the outcome of the story?

Part III—What changes were taking place around the old mansion? Show how the enmity of the people grows stronger and stronger. Do you join with the people in your feelings about Jean, or do you feel a bit of sympathy for him? What did the Board plan to do? Characterize little White. Describe his visit to the old mansion. Do you now have any clue as to the mysterious figure? Little White said "I understand." Does this have any significance?

Part IV—Whatever little White saw, he now is the champion of old Jean. Does this heighten the feeling of mystery and suspense? Do you think his attitude was assumed through fear or sympathy? What happened to old Jean? Describe a *charivari.* Tell how little White headed off the mob which had started for Jean's house.

Part V—The mob had not been stopped—it had only been delayed. Are little White's pleas effective this time? Is it possible to reason with a mob? What did the mob see when it reached Jean's house? Describe the funeral cortège. Tell what you know about leprosy. Trace back in the story and see if the details which little White observed at the old mansion are now explainable. What did little White mean when at the last he called Jean "a better man than all of you put together will ever dare to be"? Can you now explain little White's attitude in his former championing of old Jean?

Exercises and Creative Work: Collect some pictures to show scenes in Louisiana and New Orleans in the days of our story.

Write an account of the trip which Jean and Jacques made to the Guinea coast. Tell what happened and about the return.

Write a character sketch of Jean.

Write the conversation which might have taken place between Jean sitting on the veranda and Jacques in the house as they talked through the crack of the window at the time little White was watching them.

Write a story in a modern setting of a man's sacrifice for one he loves.

LOVE ON THE BON-DIEU

KATE CHOPIN

Upon the pleasant veranda of Père Antoine's cottage, that adjoined the church, a young girl had long been seated, awaiting his return. It was the eve of Easter Sunday, and since early afternoon the priest had been engaged in hearing the confessions of those who wished to make their Easters the following day. The girl did not seem impatient at his delay; on the contrary, it was very restful to her to lie back in the big chair she had found there, and peep through the thick curtain of vines at the people who occasionally passed along the village street.

She was slender, with a frailness that indicated lack of wholesome and plentiful nourishment. A pathetic, uneasy look was in her gray eyes, and even faintly stamped her features, which were fine and delicate. In lieu of a hat, a barège veil covered her light brown and abundant hair. She wore a coarse white cotton "josie," and a blue calico skirt that only half concealed her tattered shoes.

As she sat there, she held carefully in her lap a parcel of eggs securely fastened in a red bandana handkerchief.

Twice already a handsome, stalwart young man in quest of the priest had entered the yard, and penetrated to where she sat. At first they had exchanged the uncompromising "howdy" of strangers, and nothing more. The second time, finding the priest still absent, he hesitated to go at once. Instead, he stood upon the step, and narrowing his brown eyes, gazed beyond the river, off towards the west, where a murky streak of mist was spreading across the sun.

"It look like mo' rain," he remarked, slowly and carelessly.

"We done had 'bout 'nough," she replied, in much the same tone.

"It's no chance to thin out the cotton," he went on.

"An' the Bon-Dieu," she resumed, "it's on'y to-day you can cross him on foot."

"You live yonda on the Bon-Dieu, *donc?*" [1] he asked, looking at her for the first time since he had spoken.

"Yas, by Nid d'Hibout, m'sieur."

Instinctive courtesy held him from questioning her further.

[1] *Donc*—French expression, literally "then."

107

But he seated himself on the step, evidently determined to wait there for the priest. He said no more, but sat scanning critically the steps, the porch, and pillar beside him, from which he occasionally tore away little pieces of detached wood, where it was beginning to rot at its base.

A click at the side gate that communicated with the churchyard soon announced Père Antoine's return. He came hurriedly across the garden-path, between the tall, lusty rosebushes that lined either side of it, which were now fragrant with blossoms. His long, flapping cassock added something of height to his under-sized, middle-aged figure, as did the skullcap which rested securely back on his head. He saw only the young man at first, who rose at his approach.

"Well, Azenor," he called cheerily in French, extending his hand. "How is this? I expected you all the week."

"Yes, monsieur; but I knew well what you wanted with me, and I was finishing the doors for Gros-Léon's new house;" saying which, he drew back, and indicated by a motion and look that some one was present who had a prior claim upon Père Antoine's attention.

"Ah, Lalie!" the priest exclaimed, when he had mounted to the porch, and saw her there behind the vines. "Have you been waiting here since you confessed? Surely an hour ago!"

"Yes, monsieur."

"You should rather have made some visits in the village, child."

"I am not acquainted with any one in the village," she returned.

The priest, as he spoke, had drawn a chair, and seated himself beside her, with his hands comfortably clasping his knees. He wanted to know how things were out on the bayou.

"And how is the grandmother?" he asked. "As cross and crabbed as ever? And with that"—he added reflectively—"good for ten years yet! I said only yesterday to Butrand—you know Butrand, he works on Le Blôt's Bon-Dieu place—'And that Madame Zidore: how is it with her, Butrand? I believe God has forgotten her here on earth.' 'It isn't that, your reverence,' said Butrand, 'but it's neither God nor the Devil that wants her!'" And Père Antoine laughed with a jovial frankness that took all sting of ill-nature from his very pointed remarks.

Lalie did not reply when he spoke of her grandmother; she only pressed her lips firmly together, and picked at the red bandana.

"I have come to ask, Père Antoine," she began, lower than she needed to speak—for Azenor had withdrawn at once to the far end of the porch—"to ask if you will give me a little scrap of paper—a piece of writing for Monsieur Chartrand at the store over there. I want new shoes and stockings for Easter, and I have brought eggs to trade for them. He says he is willing, yes, if he was sure I would bring more every week till the shoes are paid for."

With good-natured indifference, Père Antoine wrote the order that the girl desired. He was too familiar with distress to feel keenly for a girl who was able to buy Easter shoes and pay for them with eggs.

She went immediately away then, after shaking hands with the priest, and sending a quick glance of her pathetic eyes towards Azenor, who had turned when he heard her rise, and nodded when he caught the look. Through the vines he watched her cross the village street.

"How is it that you do not know Lalie, Azenor? You surely must have seen her pass your house often. It lies on her way to the Bon-Dieu."

"No, I don't know her; I have never seen her," the young man replied, as he seated himself—after the priest—and kept his eyes absently fixed on the store across the road, where he had seen her enter.

"She is the granddaughter of that Madame Izidore"——

"What! Ma'ame Zidore whom they drove off the island last winter?"

"Yes, yes. Well, you know, they say the old woman stole wood and things,—I don't know how true it is,—and destroyed people's property out of pure malice."

"And she lives now on the Bon-Dieu?"

"Yes, on Le Blôt's place, in a perfect wreck of a cabin. You see, she gets it for nothing."

"Surely, it can't be that old abandoned hovel near the swamp, that Michon occupied ages ago?"

"That is the one, the very one."

"And the girl lives there with that old wretch?" the young man marveled.

"Old wretch to be sure, Azenor. But what can you expect from a woman who never crosses the threshold of God's house—who even tried to hinder the child's doing so as well? But I went to her. I said: 'See here, Madame Zidore,'—you know it's my way to handle such people without gloves,—'you may damn your soul if you choose,' I told her, 'that is a privilege which we all have; but none of us has a right to imperil the salvation of another. I want to see Lalie at mass hereafter on Sundays, or you will hear from me;' and I shook my stick under her nose. Since then the child has never missed a Sunday. But she is half starved, you can see that. You saw how shabby she is—how broken her shoes are? She is at Chartrand's now, trading for new ones with those eggs she brought, poor thing! There is no doubt of her being ill-treated. Butrand says he thinks Madame Zidore even beats the child. I don't know how true it is, for no power can make her utter a word against her grandmother."

Azenor, whose face was a kind and sensitive one, had paled with distress as the priest spoke; and now at these final words he quivered as though he felt the sting of a cruel blow upon his own flesh.

But no more was said of Lalie, for Père Antoine drew the young man's attention to the carpenter-work which he wished to intrust to him. When they had talked the matter over in all its lengthy details, Azenor mounted his horse and rode away.

A moment's gallop carried him outside the village. Then came a half-mile strip along the river to cover. Then the lane to enter, in which stood his dwelling midway, upon a low, pleasant knoll.

As Azenor turned into the lane, he saw the figure of Lalie far ahead of him. Somehow he had expected to find her there, and he watched her again as he had done through Père Antoine's vines. When she passed his house, he wondered if she would turn to look at it. But she did not. How could she know it was his? Upon reaching it himself, he did not enter the yard, but stood there motionless, his eyes always fastened upon the girl's figure. He could not see, away off there, how coarse her garments were. She seemed, through the distance that divided them, as slim and delicate as a flowerstalk. He stayed till she reached the turn of the lane and disappeared into the woods.

Mass had not yet begun when Azenor tiptoed into church on Easter morning. He did not take his place with the congregation, but stood close to the holy-water font, and watched the people who entered.

Almost every girl who passed him wore a white mull, a dotted swiss, or a fresh-starched muslin at least. They were bright with ribbons that hung from their persons, and flowers that bedecked their hats. Some carried fans and cambric handkerchiefs. Most of them wore gloves, and were odorous of *poudre de riz* [2] and nice toilet-waters; while all carried gay little baskets filled with Easter-eggs.

But there was one who came empty-handed, save for the worn prayer book which she bore. It was Lalie, the veil upon her head, and wearing the blue print and cotton bodice which she had worn the day before.

He dipped his hand into the holy water when she came, and held it out to her, though he had not thought of doing this for the others. She touched his fingers with the tips of her own, making a slight inclination as she did so; and after a deep genuflection before the Blessed Sacrament, passed on to the side. He was not sure if she had known him. He knew she had not looked into his eyes, for he would have felt it.

He was angered against other young women who passed him, because of their flowers and ribbons, when she wore none. He himself did not care, but he feared she might, and watched her narrowly to see if she did.

But it was plain that Lalie did not care. Her face, as she seated herself, settled into the same restful lines it had worn yesterday, when she sat in Père Antoine's big chair. It seemed good to her to be there. Sometimes she looked up at the little colored panes through which the Easter sun was streaming; then at the flaming candles, like stars; or at the embowered figures of Joseph and Mary, flanking the central tabernacle which shrouded the risen Christ. Yet she liked also to watch the young girls in their spring freshness, or to inhale the mingled odor of flowers and incense that filled the temple.

Lalie was among the last to quit the church. When she walked down the clean pathway that led from it to the road, she looked with pleased curiosity towards the groups of men and maidens who were gayly matching their Easter-eggs under the shade of the chinaberry trees.

[2] *Poudre de riz*—Rice powder.

Azenor was among them, and when he saw her coming solitary down the path, he approached her and, with a smile, extended his hat, whose crown was quite lined with the pretty colored eggs.

"You mus' of forgot to bring aiggs," he said. "Take some o' mine."

"Non, merci," she replied, flushing and drawing back.

But he urged them anew upon her. Much pleased, then, she bent her pretty head over the hat, and was evidently puzzled to make a selection among so many that were beautiful.

He picked out one for her,—a pink one, dotted with white clover-leaves.

"Yere," he said, handing it to her, "I think this is the pretties'; an' it look' strong too. I'm sho' it will break all of the res'." And he playfully held out another, half-hidden in his fist, for her to try its strength upon. But she refused to. She would not risk the ruin of her pretty egg. Then she walked away, without once having noticed that the girls, whom Azenor had left, were looking curiously at her.

When he rejoined them, he was hardly prepared for their greeting; it startled him.

"How come you talk to that girl? She's real *canaille*,[3] her," was what one of them said to him.

"Who say' so? Who say she's *canaille?* If it's a man, I'll smash 'is head!" he exclaimed, livid. They all laughed merrily at this.

"An' if it's a lady, Azenor? W'at you goin' to do 'bout it?" asked another, quizzingly.

"Tain' no lady. No lady would say that 'bout a po' girl, w'at she don't even know."

He turned away, and emptying all his eggs into the hat of a little urchin who stood near, walked out of the churchyard. He did not stop to exchange another word with any one; neither with the men who stood all *endimanchés*[4] before the stores, nor the women who were mounting upon horses and into vehicles, or walking in groups to their homes.

He took a short cut across the cotton-field that extended back of the town, and walking rapidly, soon reached his home. It was a pleasant house of few rooms and many windows, with fresh air blowing through from every side; his workshop was beside it. A

[3] *Canaille*—Epithet, here meaning bad by nature.
[4] *Endimanchés*—In Sunday array.

broad strip of greensward, studded here and there with trees, sloped down to the road.

Azenor entered the kitchen, where an amiable old black woman was chopping onion and sage at a table.

"Tranquiline," he said abruptly, "they's a young girl goin' to pass yere afta a w'ile. She's got a blue dress an' w'ite josie on, an' a veil on her head. W'en you see her, I want you to go to the road an' make her res' there on the bench, an' ask her if she don't want a cup o' coffee. I saw her go to communion, me; so she didn't eat any breakfas'. Eve'ybody else f'om out o' town, that went to communion, got invited somew'ere another. It's enough to make a person sick to see such meanness."

"An' you want me ter go down to de gate, jis' so, an' ax 'er pineblank ef she wants some coffee?" asked the bewildered Tranquiline.

"I don't care if you ask her poin' blank o' not; but you do like I say." Tranquiline was leaning over the gate when Lalie came along.

"Howdy," offered the woman.

"Howdy," the girl returned.

"Did you see a yalla calf wid black spots a t'arin' down de lane, missy?"

"*Non;* not yalla, an' not with black spot'. *Mais* [5] I see one li'le w'ite calf tie by a rope, yonda 'roun' the ben'."

"Dat warn't hit. Dis heah one was yalla. I hope he done flung hisse'f down de bank an' broke his nake. Sarve 'im right! But whar you come f'om, chile? You look plum wo' out. Set down dah on dat bench, an' le' me fotch you a cup o' coffee."

Azenor had already in his eagerness arranged a tray, upon which was a smoking cup of *café au lait.* [6] He had buttered and jellied generous slices of bread, and was searching wildly for something when Tranquiline reentered.

"W'at become o' that half of chicken-pie, Tranquiline, that was yere in the *garde manger* [7] yesterday?"

"W'at chicken-pie? W'at *garde manger?*" blustered the woman.

"Like we got mo' 'en one *garde manger* in the house, Tranquiline!"

"You jis' like ole Ma'ame Azenor use' to be, you is! You 'spec'

[5] *Mais*—But.
[6] *Café au lait*—Coffee with cream.
[7] *Garde manger*—Kitchen cupboard.

chicken-pie gwine las' etarnal? W'en somepin done sp'ilt, I flings it 'way. Dat's me—dat's Tranquiline!"

So Azenor resigned himself,—what else could he do?—and sent the tray, incomplete, as he fancied it, out to Lalie.

He trembled at thought of what he did; he, whose nerves were usually as steady as some piece of steel mechanism.

Would it anger her if she suspected? Would it please her if she knew? Would she say this or that to Tranquiline? And would Tranquiline tell him truly what she said—how she looked?

As it was Sunday, Azenor did not work that afternoon. Instead, he took a book out under the trees, as he often did, and sat reading it, from the first sound of the Vesper bell, that came faintly across the fields, till the Angelus. All that time! He turned many a page, yet in the end did not know what he had read. With his pencil he had traced "Lalie" upon every margin, and was saying it softly to himself.

．　　．　　．　　．　　．　　．

Another Sunday Azenor saw Lalie at mass—and again. Once he walked with her and showed her the short cut across the cotton-field. She was very glad that day, and told him she was going to work—her grandmother said she might. She was going to hoe, up in the fields with Monsieur Le Blôt's hands. He entreated her not to; and when she asked his reason, he could not tell her, but turned and tore shyly and savagely at the elder-blossoms that grew along the fence.

Then they stopped where she was going to cross the fence from the field into the lane. He wanted to tell her that was his house which they could see not far away; but he did not dare to, since he had fed her there on the morning she was hungry.

"An' you say yo' gran'ma's goin' to let you work? She keeps you f'om workin', *donc*?" He wanted to question her about her grandmother, and could think of no other way to begin.

"Po' ole grand'mère!" she answered. "I don' b'lieve she know mos' time w'at she's doin'. Sometime she say' I ain't no good, an' she fo'ce me to work. Then she say she know I'm goin' be one lady like *mamman,* an' she make me set down still, like she would want to kill me if I would move. Her, she on'y want' to be out in the wood', day an' night, day an' night. She ain' got her right head, po' grand'mère. I know she ain't."

Lalie had spoken low and in jerks, as if every word gave her pain. Azenor could feel her distress as plainly as he saw it. He wanted to say something to her—to do something for her. But her mere presence paralyzed him into inactivity—except his pulses, that beat like hammers when he was with her. Such a poor, shabby little thing as she was, too!

"I'm goin' to wait yere nex' Sunday fo' you, Lalie," he said, when the fence was between them. And he thought he had said something very daring.

But the next Sunday she did not come. She was neither at the appointed place of meeting in the lane, nor was she at mass. Her absence—so unexpected—affected Azenor like a calamity. Late in the afternoon, when he could stand the trouble and bewilderment of it no longer, he went and leaned over Père Antoine's fence. The priest was picking the slugs from his roses on the other side.

"That young girl from the Bon-Dieu," said Azenor—"she was not at mass to-day. I suppose her grandmother has forgotten your warning."

"No," answered the priest. "The child is ill, I hear. Butrand tells me she has been ill for several days from overwork in the fields. I shall go out to-morrow to see about her. I would go to-day, if I could."

"The child is ill," was all Azenor heard or understood of Père Antoine's words. He turned and walked resolutely away, like one who determines suddenly upon action after meaningless hesitation.

He walked towards his home and past it, as if it were a spot that did not concern him. He went on down the lane and into the wood where he had seen Lalie disappear that day.

Here all was shadow, for the sun had dipped too low in the west to send a single ray through the dense foliage of the forest.

Now that he found himself on the way to Lalie's home, he strove to understand why he had not gone there before. He often visited other girls in the village and neighborhood,—why not have gone to her, as well? The answer lay too deep in his heart for him to be more than half-conscious of it. Fear had kept him,—dread to see her desolate life face to face. He did not know how he could bear it.

But now he was going to her at last. She was ill. He would stand upon that dismantled porch that he could just remember. Doubtless Ma'ame Zidore would come out to know his will, and he would tell her that Père Antoine had sent to inquire how Mamzelle Lalie was. No! Why mention Père Antoine? He would simply stand boldly and say, "Ma'ame Zidore, I learn that Lalie is ill. I have come to know if it is true, and to see her, if I may."

When Azenor reached the cabin where Lalie dwelt, all sign of day had vanished. Dusk had fallen swiftly after the sunset. The moss that hung heavy from great live-oak branches was making fantastic silhouettes against the eastern sky that the big, round moon was beginning to light. Off in the swamp beyond the bayou, hundreds of dismal voices were droning a lullaby. Upon the hovel itself, a stillness like death rested.

Oftener than once Azenor tapped upon the door, which was closed as well as it could be, without obtaining a reply. He finally approached one of the small unglazed windows, in which coarse mosquito-netting had been fastened, and looked into the room.

By the moonlight slanting in he could see Lalie stretched upon a bed; but of Ma'ame Zidore there was no sign. "Lalie!" he called softly. "Lalie!"

The girl slightly moved her head upon the pillow. Then he boldly opened the door and entered.

Upon a wretched bed, under a cover of patched calico, Lalie lay, her frail body only half revealed by the moonlight that was upon it. One hand was plunged beneath her pillow; the other, which was free, he touched. It was as hot as flame; so was her head. He knelt sobbing upon the floor beside her, and called her his love and his soul. He begged her to speak a word to him,— to look at him. But she only muttered disjointedly that the cotton was all turning to ashes in the fields, and the blades of the corn were in flames.

If he was choked with love and grief to see her so, he was moved by anger as well; rage against himself, against the people upon the plantation and in the village, who had so abandoned a helpless creature to misery and maybe death. Because she had been silent—had not lifted her voice in complaint—they believed she suffered no more than she could bear.

But surely the people could not be utterly without heart. There must be one somewhere with the spirit of Christ. Père Antoine would tell him of such a one, and he would carry Lalie to her,—out of this atmosphere of death. He was in haste to be gone with her. He fancied every moment of delay was a fresh danger threatening her life.

He folded the rude bed-cover over Lalie's slight body, and

lifted her in his arms. She made no resistance. She seemed only loath to withdraw her hand from beneath the pillow. When she did, he saw that she held lightly but firmly clasped in her encircling fingers the pretty Easter-egg he had given her! He uttered a low cry of exultation as the full significance of this came over him. If she had hung for hours upon his neck telling him that she loved him, he could not have known it more surely than by this sign. Azenor felt as if some mysterious bond had all at once drawn them heart to heart and made them one.

No need now to go from door to door begging admittance for her. She was his. She belonged to him. He knew now where her place was, whose roof must shelter her, and whose arms protect her.

So Azenor, with his loved one in his arms, walked through the forest, surefooted as a panther. Once, as he walked, he could hear in the distance the weird chant which Ma'ame Zidore was crooning—to the moon, maybe—as she gathered her wood.

Once, where the water was trickling cool through rocks, he stopped to lave Lalie's hot cheeks and hands and forehead.

Then she knew him. She did not tell him so, but her stiffened fingers relaxed their tense hold upon the Easter bauble. It fell to the ground as she twined her arm around his neck; and he understood.

"Stay close by her, Tranquiline," said Azenor, when he had laid Lalie upon his own couch at home. "I'm goin' for the doctor an' for Père Antoine. Not because she is goin' to die," he added hastily, seeing the awe that crept into the woman's face at mention of the priest. "She is goin' to live! Do you think I would let my wife die, Tranquiline?"

The Type of Kate Chopin's Stories: Kate Chopin seems to have inherited from the Irish on her father's side, the story-teller's gift; from the French on her mother's side, a passion for artistry, cultivated by an assiduous study and translation of De Maupassant and other French masters. When she moved to her husband's Louisiana plantation on the Red River, her friends, charmed by her letters, urged her to put her writing talent to work. The plantation life gave leisure; she was a provocative and patient listener; the "bayou folk" had stories to tell. The result was happy, for "no more exquisite work may be found in the whole range of the local color school than in Kate Chopin's *Bayou Folk*."

For Appreciation: In what different ways is the local color introduced? What contribution to it is made by means of description of scene and characters? Is the language of the characters distinctive? Their very names and the names of the places mentioned have a distinctive charm.

For Further Study: Give the meaning of each of the following words and phrases: *in lieu of, a prior claim, josey, cambric, instinctive courtesy, livid, unglazed windows, bauble.*

The pathetic figure of Lalie is central in the story. Where is your sympathy for her first aroused? Scan the story for other factors which intensify your concern for this luckless child of the Bon-Dieu. The difficult nature of "po' ole grand'mère" made Lalie's existence a hard one. How does the author acquaint us with this important factor in the story? Why is it important? Where, early in the story, does the author prepare us for Azenor's hot resentment towards himself, the villagers, and all who had abandoned Lalie to her poor lot? What excuse is suggested for this general indifference? How does the figure of amiable Tranquiline heighten or interfere with the general mood of the story? Where is the climax of the story? Is the conclusion satisfactory?

Exercises and Creative Work: Discuss the various scenes and characters in "Love on the Bon-Dieu" in class, then write a brief composition on one of the following topics: *Père Antoine's Parish; Scenes on the Bon-Dieu; Creole Customs; A Day in the Deep South; Easter Eggs.*

ZENOBIA'S INFIDELITY

Henry Cuyler Bunner

Dr. Tibbitt stood on the porch of Mrs. Pennypepper's boarding house, and looked up and down the deserted Main Street of Sagawaug with a contented smile, the while he buttoned his driving gloves. The little doctor had good cause to be content with himself and with everything else—with his growing practice, with his comfortable boarding house, with his own good looks, with his neat attire, and with the world in general. He could not but be content with Sagawaug, for there never was a prettier country town. The doctor looked across the street and picked out the very house that he proposed to buy when the one remaining desire of his soul was gratified. It was a house with a hip roof and with a long garden running down to the river.

There was no one in the house today, but there was no one in any of the houses. Not even a pair of round bare arms were visible among the clothes that waved in the August breeze in every backyard. It was circus day in Sagawaug.

The doctor was climbing into his gig when a yell startled

him. A freckled boy with saucer eyes dashed around the corner.

"Doctor!" he gasped, "come quick! The circus got afire an' the trick elephant's most roasted!"

"Don't be silly, Johnny," said the doctor, reprovingly.

"Hope to die—honest Injun—cross my breast!" said the boy. The doctor knew the sacredness of this juvenile oath.

"Get in here with me," he said, "and if I find you're trying to be funny, I'll drop you in the river."

As they drove toward the outskirts of the town, Johnny told his tale.

"Now," he began, "the folks was all out of the tent after the show was over, and one of the circus men, he went to the oil barrel in the green wagon with Dan'l in the Lion's Den onto the outside of it, an' he took in a candle an' left it there, and fust thing the barrel busted, an' he wasn't hurted a bit, but the trick elephant she was burned awful, an' the ringtailed baboon, he was so scared he had a fit. Say, did you know baboons had fits?"

When they reached the circus grounds, they found a crowd around a small side-show tent. A strong odor of burnt leather confirmed Johnny's story. Dr. Tibbitt pushed his way through the throng, and gazed upon the huge beast, lying on her side on the grass, her broad shoulder charred and quivering. Her bulk expanded and contracted with spasms of agony, and from time to time she uttered a moaning sound. On her head was a structure of red cloth, about the size of a bushel basket, apparently intended to look like a British soldier's forage cap. This was secured by a strap that went under her chin—if an elephant has a chin. This scarlet cheese box every now and then slipped down over her eye, and the faithful animal patiently, in all her anguish, adjusted it with her prehensile trunk.

By her side stood her keeper and the proprietor of the show, a large man with a dyed mustache, a wrinkled face, and hair oiled and frizzed. These two bewailed their loss alternately.

"The boss elephant in the business!" cried the showman. "Barnum never had no trick elephant like Zenobia. And them lynes and Dan'l was painted in new before I took the road this season. Oh, there's been a hoodoo on me since I showed ag'inst the Sunday-school picnic!"

"That there elephant's been like my own child," groaned the keeper, "or my own wife, I may say."

The doctor had been carefully examining his patient.

"If there is any analogy—" he began.

"Neuralogy!" snorted the indignant showman; " 'tain't neuralogy, you jay pill box, she's *cooked!*"

"If there is any analogy," repeated Dr. Tibbitt, flushing a little, "between her case and that of a human being, I think I can save your elephant. Get me a barrel of linseed oil, and drive these people away."

The doctor's orders were obeyed with eager submission. He took off his coat and went to work. He had never doctored an elephant, and the job interested him. At the end of an hour, Zenobia's sufferings were somewhat alleviated. She lay on her side, chained tightly to the ground, and swaddled in bandages. Her groans had ceased.

"I'll call tomorrow at noon," said the doctor—"good gracious, what's that?" Zenobia's trunk was playing around his waistband.

"She wants to shake hands with you," her keeper explained. "She's a lady, she is, and she knows you done her good."

"I'd rather not have anything of the sort," said the doctor, decisively.

When Dr. Tibbitt called at twelve on the morrow, he found Zenobia's tent nearly roped in, an amphitheater of circus benches constructed around her, and this amphitheater packed with people.

"Got a quarter apiece from them jays," whispered the showman, "jest to see you dress them wounds." Subsequently the showman relieved his mind to a casual acquaintance. "He's got a heart like a gunflint, that doctor," he said, "made me turn out every one of them jays and give 'em their money back before he'd lay a hand on Zenobia."

But if the doctor suppressed the clinic, neither he nor the showman suffered. From dawn till dusk people came from miles around to stare a quarter's worth at the burnt elephant. Once in a while, as a rare treat, the keeper lifted a corner of her bandages, and revealed the seared flesh. The show went off in a day or two, leaving Zenobia to recover at leisure; and as it wandered westward, it did an increased business simply because it had had a burnt trick elephant. Such, dear friends, is the human mind.

The doctor fared even better. The fame of his new case spread far and wide. People seemed to think that if he could cure an elephant he could cure anything. He was called into consultation in neighboring towns. Women in robust health imagined ailments, so as to send for him and ask him shuddering questions about "that *wretched* animal." The trustees of the orphan asylum made him staff physician—in this case the doctor thought he could trace a connection of ideas, in which children and circus were naturally associated. And the local newspaper called him a *savant*.

He called every day upon Zenobia, who greeted him with trumpetings of joyful welcome. She also desired to shake hands with him, and her keeper had to sit on her head and hold her trunk to repress the familiarity. In two weeks she was cured, except for extensive and permanent scars, and she waited only for a favorable opportunity to rejoin the circus.

The doctor had got his fee in advance.

Upon a sunny afternoon in the last of August, Dr. Tibbitt jogged slowly toward Sagawaug in his neat little gig. He had been to Pelion, the next town, to call upon Miss Minetta Bunker, the young lady whom he desired to install in the house with the garden running down to the river. He had found her starting out for a drive in Tom Matson's dogcart. Now, the doctor feared no foe, in medicine or in love; but when a young woman is inscrutable as to the state of her affections, when the richest young man in the county is devoting himself to her, and when the young lady's mother is backing the rich man, a young country doctor may well feel perplexed and anxious over his chance of the prize.

The doctor was so troubled, indeed, that he paid no heed to a heavy, repeated thud behind him, on the macadamized road. His gentle little mare heard it, though, and began to curvet and prance. The doctor was pulling her in, and calming her with a "soo—soo—down, girl, down!" when he interrupted himself to shout,

"Great Caesar! get off me!"

Something like a yard of rubber hose had come in through

the side of the buggy, and was rubbing itself against his face. He looked around, and the cold sweat stood out on him as he saw Zenobia, her chain dragging from her hind foot, her red cap a-cock on her head, trotting along by the side of his vehicle, snorting with joy, and evidently bent on lavishing her pliant, serpentine, but leathery caresses upon his person.

His fear vanished in a moment. The animal's intentions were certainly pacific, to put it mildly. He reflected that if he could keep his horse ahead of her, he could toll her around the block and back toward her tent. He had hardly guessed, as yet, the depth of the impression which he had made upon Zenobia's heart, which must have been a large organ, if the size of her ears was any indication—according to the popular theory.

The doctor tolled his elephant around the block without further misadventure, and they started up the road toward Zenobia's tent, Zenobia caressing her benefactor while shudders of antipathy ran over his frame. In a few minutes the keeper hove in sight. Zenobia saw him first, blew a shrill blast on her trumpet, close to the doctor's ear, bolted through a snake fence, lumbered across a turnip field, and disappeared in a patch of woods, leaving the doctor to quiet his excited horse and to face the keeper, who advanced with rage in his eye.

"What do you mean, you cuss," he began, "weaning a man's elephant's affections away from him? You ain't got no more morals than a Turk, you ain't. That elephant an' me has been side partners for fourteen years, an' here you come between us."

"I don't want your confounded elephant," roared the doctor. "Why don't you keep it chained up?"

"She busted her chain to git after you," replied the keeper. "Oh, I seen you two lally-gaggin' all along the road. I knowed you wa'n't no good the first time I set eyes on yer, a-sayin' hoodoo words over the poor dumb beast."

The doctor resolved to banish "analogy" from his vocabulary.

The next morning, about four o'clock, Dr. Tibbitt awoke with a troubled mind. He had driven home after midnight from a late call, and he had had an uneasy fancy that he saw a great shadowy bulk ambling along in the mist-hid field by the roadside. He jumped out of bed and went to the window. Below him, completely covering Mrs. Pennypepper's nasturtium bed,

her prehensile trunk ravaging the early chrysanthemums, stood
Zenobia, swaying to and fro, the dew glistening on her seamed
sides beneath the early morning sunlight. The doctor hastily
dressed himself and slipped downstairs and out, to meet this
Frankenstein-monster [1] of affection.

There was but one thing to do. Zenobia would follow him
wherever he went—she rushed madly through Mrs. Pennypepper's roses to greet him—and his only course was to lead her
out of the town before people began to get up, and to detain
her in some remote meadow until he could get her keeper to
come for her and secure her by force or stratagem. He set off
by the least frequented streets, and he experienced a pang of
horror as he remembered that his way led him past the house
of his one professional rival in Sagawaug. Suppose Dr. Pettengill should be coming home or going out as he passed!

The doctor found a secluded pasture, near the woods that en-
circled the town, and there he sat him down, in the corner of a
snake fence, to wait until some farmer or market gardener
should pass by, to carry his message to the keeper. He had
another message to send, too. He had several cases that must
be attended to at once. Unless he could get away from his
pachydermatous familiar, Dr. Pettengill must care for his cases
that morning. It was hard—but what was he to do?

Zenobia stood by his side, dividing her attention between
the caresses she bestowed on him and the care she was obliged
to take of her red cap, which was not tightly strapped on,
and slipped in various directions at every movement of her
gigantic head. She was unmistakably happy. From time to
time she trumpeted cheerily. She plucked up tufts of grass, and
offered them to the doctor. He refused them, and she ate them
herself. Once he took a daisy from her, absent-mindedly, and
she was so greatly pleased that she smashed his hat in her
endeavors to pet him. The doctor was a kind-hearted man. He
had to admit that Zenobia meant well. He patted her trunk,
and made matters worse. Her elephantine ecstasy came near
being the death of him.

Still the farmer came not, nor the market gardener. Dr.

---

[1] FRANKENSTEIN-MONSTER—Frankenstein created a monster but was himself destroyed by it. The term is here synonymous for that which turns
against its benefactor.

*She rushed madly through Mrs.
Pennypepper's roses to greet him.*

Tibbitt began to believe that he had chosen a meadow that was *too* secluded. At last two boys appeared. After they had stared at him and at Zenobia for half an hour, one of them agreed to produce Dr. Pettengill and Zenobia's keeper for fifty cents. Dr. Pettengill was the first to arrive. He refused to come nearer than the farthest limit of the pasture.

"Hello, doctor," he called out, "hear you've been seeing elephants. Want me to take your cases? Guess I can. Got a half hour free. Brought some bromide down for you, if you'd like to try it."

To judge from his face, Zenobia was invisible. But his presence alarmed that sensitive animal. She crowded up close to the fence, and every time she flicked her skin to shake off the flies she endangered the equilibrium of the doctor, who was sitting on the top rail, for dignity's sake. He shouted his directions to his colleague, who shouted back professional criticisms.

"Salicylate of soda for that old woman? What's the matter with salicylate of cinchonidia? Don't want to kill her before you get out of this swamp, do you?"

Dr. Tibbitt was not a profane man, but at this moment he could not restrain himself. He burst forth with such vigor that the elephant gave a convulsive start. The doctor felt his seat depart from under him—he was going—going into space for a brief moment, and then he scrambled up out of the soft mud of the cow-wallow back of the fence on which he had been sitting. Zenobia had backed against the fence.

The keeper arrived soon after. He had only reached the meadow when Zenobia lifted her trunk in the air, emitted a mirthful toot, and struck out for the woods with the picturesque and cumbersome gallop of a mastodon pup.

"Dern *you*," said the keeper to Dr. Tibbitt, who was trying to fasten his collar, which had broken loose in his fall; "if the boys was here, and I hollered 'Hey, Rube!'—there wouldn't be enough left of yer to spread a plaster for a baby's bile!"

The doctor made himself look as decent as the situation allowed, and then he marched toward the town with the light of a firm resolve illuminating his face. The literature of his childhood had come to his aid. He remembered the unkind tailor who pricked the elephant's trunk. It seemed to him that the tailor was a rather good fellow.

"If that elephant's disease is gratitude," thought the doctor, "I'll give her an antidote."

He went to the drug store, and, as he went, he pulled out a blank pad and wrote down a prescription, from mere force of habit. It read thus:

PESSELS & MORTON,
DRUGGISTS,
Commercial Block, Main Street, Sagawaug.

☞ PRESCRIPTIONS CAREFULLY COMPOUNDED. ☜

℞   Calcium oxl   ℥ ij
     Calcis chl   ℥ xvj
     Capsicum pulv   ℥ j

     Ʀ et ft. Bol.
     Sig. Take at once.   Tibbitt

When the druggist looked at it, he was taken short of breath. "What's this?" he asked—"a bombshell?"

"Put it up," said the doctor, "and don't talk so much." He lingered nervously on the druggist's steps, looking up and down the street. He had sent a boy to order the stableman to harness his gig. By and by, the druggist put his head out of the door.

"I've got some asafetida pills," he said, "that are kind o' tired, and half a pound of whale-oil soap that's higher 'n Haman——"

"Put 'em in!" said the doctor, grimly, as he saw Zenobia coming in sight far down the street.

She came up while the doctor was waiting for the bolus. Twenty-three boys were watching them, although it was only seven o'clock in the morning.

"Down, Zenobia!" said the doctor, thoughtlessly, as he might have addressed a dog. He was talking with the druggist, and Zenobia was patting his ear with her trunk. Zenobia sank to her knees. The doctor did not notice her. She folded her trunk

about him, lifted him to her back, rose with a heave and a sway
to her feet, and started up the road. The boys cheered. The
doctor got off on the end of an elm-branch. His descent was
watched from nineteen second-story windows.

His gig came to meet him at last, and he entered it and drove
rapidly out of town, with Zenobia trotting contentedly behind
him. As soon as he had passed Deacon Burgee's house, he drew
rein, and Zenobia approached, while his perspiring mare stood
on her hind legs.

"Zenobia—pill!" said the doctor.

As she had often done in her late illness, Zenobia opened her
mouth at the word of command, and swallowed the infernal
bolus. Then they started up again, and the doctor headed for
Zenobia's tent.

But Zenobia's pace was sluggish. She had been dodging
about the woods for two nights, and she was tired. When the
doctor whipped up, she seized the buggy by any convenient projection, and held it back. This damaged the buggy and frightened the horse; but it accomplished Zenobia's end. It was eleven
o'clock before Jake Bumgardner's "Half-Way-House" loomed
up white, afar down the dusty road, and the doctor knew that
his roundabout way had at length brought him near to the field
where the circus tent had been pitched. He drove on with a
lighter heart in his bosom. He had not heard Zenobia behind
him for some time. He did not know what had become of her,
or what she was doing, but he learned later.

The doctor had compounded a pill well calculated to upset
Zenobia's stomach. That it would likewise give her a consuming thirst he had not considered. But chemistry was doing
its duty without regard to him. A thirst like a furnace burned
within Zenobia. Capsicum and chloride of lime were doing their
work. She gasped and groaned. She searched for water. She
filled her trunk at a wayside trough and poured the contents
into her mouth. Then she sucked up a puddle or two. Then
she came to Bumgardner's, where a dozen kegs of lager beer
and a keg of what passed at Bumgardner's for gin stood on
the sidewalk. Zenobia's circus experience had taught her what
a water barrel meant. She applied her knowledge. With her
forefoot she deftly staved in the head of one keg after another,
and with her trunk she drew up the beer and the gin, and de-

livered them to her stomach. If you think her taste at fault, remember the bolus.

Bumgardner rushed out and assailed her with a bung-starter. She turned upon him and squirted lager beer over him until he was covered with an iridescent lather of foam from head to foot. Then she finished the kegs and went on her way to overtake the doctor.

The doctor was speeding his mare merrily along, grateful for even a momentary relief from Zenobia's attentions, when, at one and the same time, he heard a heavy, uncertain thumping on the road behind him, and the quick patter of a trotter's hoofs on the road ahead of him. He glanced behind him first, and saw Zenobia. She swayed from side to side, more than was her wont. Her red cap was far down over her left eye. Her aspect was rakish, and her gait was unsteady. The doctor did not know it, but Zenobia was drunk.

Zenobia was sick, but intoxication dominated her sickness. Even sulphide of calcium withdrew courteously before the might of beer and gin. Rocking from side to side, reeling across the road and back, trumpeting in imbecile inexpressive tones, Zenobia advanced.

The doctor looked forward. Tom Matson sat in his dogcart, with Miss Bunker by his side. His horse had caught sight of Zenobia, and he was rearing high in air, and whinnying in terror. Before Tom could pull him down, he made a sudden break, overturned the dogcart, and flung Tom and Miss Minetta Bunker on a bank by the side of the road. It was a soft bank, well-grown with mint and stinging nettles, just above a creek. Tom had scarce landed before he was up and off, running hard across the fields.

Miss Minetta rose and looked at him with fire in her eyes.

"Well!" she said aloud, "I'd like mother to see you *now!*"

The doctor had jumped out of his gig and let his little mare go galloping up the road. He had his arm about Miss Minetta's waist when he turned to face his familiar demon—which may have accounted for the pluck in his face.

But Zenobia was a hundred yards down the road, and she was utterly incapable of getting any farther. She trumpeted once or twice, then she wavered like a reed in the wind; her legs weakened under her, and she sank on her side. Her red cap had slipped down, and she picked it up with her trunk, broke its band in a reckless swing that resembled the wave of jovial farewell, gave one titanic hiccup, and fell asleep by the roadside.

An hour later, Dr. Tibbitt was driving toward Pelion, with Miss Bunker by his side. His horse had been stopped at the tollgate. He was driving with one hand. Perhaps he needed the other to show how they could have a summer-house in the garden that ran down to the river.

But it was evening when Zenobia awoke to find her keeper sitting on her head. He jabbed a cotton hook firmly and decisively into her ear, and led her homeward down the road lit by the golden sunset. That was the end of Zenobia's infidelity.

The Type of Bunner's Stories: For twenty years Henry Cuyler Bunner was editor of the humorous weekly *Puck*. Since most of his writing was done for this magazine we would therefore expect his stories to be first of all humorous. Further requirements of the paper demanded brevity and vigor, and Bunner became a master of both. He had little interest in setting or character—his emphasis was rather on plot and movement. He constructed his plots very carefully and employed the surprise element in many of his stories.

For Appreciation: *Zenobia's Infidelity* was written in 1890 and appears in the volume entitled *Short Sixes*. It is somewhat longer than many of Bunner's stories, but true to his style, he carried sparkle and humor throughout the story. What gives you the first smile? Does the story seem to be about the doctor or about Zenobia? Show how the author builds up the humor from a smile at the beginning to a guffaw at the climax. What different kinds of humor does he employ? Give examples. How would you classify this story as to form?

For Further Study: Make a list of words by which the author indicates the size of Zenobia. Give the meaning of each of the following words: *hip roof; gig; prehensile; analogy; savant; curvet; tolled; bolus.*

What part does the freckled boy play? There is a humorous play on the word "analogy" in the first part of the story. Where is humor attached to this word again? Would you have had the story end sooner? If so, at what point? Or would you have added another episode? What was the author's purpose in writing this story? What is the significance of the title?

Exercises and Creative Work: Write an episode illustrating Zenobia's attachment to the doctor which might be substituted for one of the episodes in the story.

Write a humorous story about some animal.

THE HISTORY OF THE AMERICAN SHORT STORY

The Twentieth Century (1900–   )

General Characteristics

By 1900 the short story had become so popular that the production of it amounted to almost an industry. This popularity was greatly stimulated at the beginning of the century by the fifteen-cent magazine and the newspaper Sunday supplement. Magazine and newspaper offices became schools for short story writing where a new type, the journalistic short story, came into being. Local color or regional stories continued to be written about the romantic and unusual places, but different settings were creeping into other stories. Writers found that the environments of people in large cities and in certain restricted localities brought about and accentuated characteristics in the inhabitants. These writers attempted to portray life as they found it with its dirt, sorrow, poverty, fear, and bits of rough humor and by so doing earned for themselves the name of "realists." But realistic stories did not appeal to all readers because they did not take their minds from their own troubles. As a result, the market became flooded with the so-called "pulp" magazine. The stories in these magazines are not literature as the word is accepted by the critic, although they may have the structural foundations common with a literary type. They are written with the sole purpose of entertaining the reader, of making him forget the monotony and bareness of his own existence. Recently other writers, recognizing the desire on the part of the reader for the "escape" story, have begun in the more literary short story to swing again to romance and adventure. Historical backgrounds are being used in many cases as the settings for these stories.

It is not possible to evaluate the short story of today and say what will be its place in the permanent literature of America. Such judgment comes only with time. Nor is it possible to predict along what lines the short story will develop. The supply at present is so enormous and so diversified that any reader may find short stories, excellent, mediocre, or very poor, to suit his taste.

William Sydney Porter (O. Henry) (1862–1910)

Chief of the journalistic school was O. Henry, the most popular short story writer of his day. He was born in Greensboro, North Carolina. As a boy he was a great reader and among his favorite books were *The Arabian Nights*, *The Rubaiyat of Omar Khayyam*, and the works of Kipling, Tennyson, Conan Doyle and Byron. He enjoyed reproducing for the amusement of his schoolmates the stories he read, with his own humorous interpretations and additions. Because of failing health he went to Texas in 1884 and became for a time an amateur ranchman. While in Austin he became teller in a bank. From Austin he went to Houston as a reporter on the Houston *Post,* but while there he was summoned back to Austin to stand trial for a misappropriation of funds. He insisted that he was innocent and started for Austin, but on the way he changed his mind and boarded a fruiter for Honduras. He remained in South America, experimenting in banana culture, until he learned that his wife was very ill, when he returned to Austin, surrendered, and was sentenced to five years in the federal prison at Columbus, Ohio. No one in Austin believed him guilty and he would probably have been acquitted had he not run away. It was while he was in prison that he began writing stories and assumed the now famous pen name, O. Henry. Upon his release he went to New York where in 1903 he contracted with the New York *World* for a story a week at a hundred dollars a story. At first he wrote about scenes already familiar to him—scenes of the Southwest and of Central America, but he later turned to New York City scenes and life. His best work was done in the latter field. For two and a half years he produced his weekly stories and through them his fame quickly spread. He died in 1910. His short stories, like all of the journalistic type, have vigor and snap and a main purpose of entertainment. O. Henry was a master of the art of surprise and is quoted as saying of his own stories: "Be concise and familiar, and punch when your adversary is off guard. This stuns him, and you may then disappear."

James B. Connolly (1868–   )

James B. Connolly is familiar with all the seas, but his keenest interest is in the fishing fleets which have their home ports in New England. The sea in all its moods—its beauty and power, its placidity and rage, its servitude to man and its sudden cruelty to man—is the background of his stories. Connolly is wholly at home when writing of the sea. Well he may be, for his acquaintance with it began, he says, at the age of seven when he was washed out of a cabin bunk in a fishing schooner. He has fished in the Baltic, the North, and the Arctic Seas and has sailed on every type of sailing ship that floats in water. His favorite of all ships, however, is the deep-water fishing schooner.

Connolly was born in South Boston in 1868. In his colorful career he has been a member of the U. S. Engineering Corps, an Olympic champion at Athens in 1896, an infantryman in the Spanish-American War, a member of the U. S. Navy, a Progressive candidate for Congress, a news-correspondent on the Mexican Border and in the World War. Because he has lived so strenuously his stories are stories of action.

Booth Tarkington (1869–   )

Newton Booth Tarkington was born in Indianapolis, Indiana, in 1869. As a small boy he was frail, but in his early teens his health improved and he became an active fun-loving boy. Among his boyhood friends he was fortunate enough to have James Whitcomb Riley, with whom he frequently walked. After he began to write, Tarkington valued very highly Riley's opinion of his attempts. Tarkington attended Philip Exeter Academy, Purdue University, and Princeton. At Princeton he was very popular with his fellow students.

After finishing college, his ambition was to be an illustrator, but he became discouraged, when his drawings were not accepted, and turned to writing. He learned to write by imitating the style of literary masters "to find out how the thing was done." Nevertheless, success was slow in coming, for during the first eight years of writing he earned less than twenty-five dollars.

Tarkington spends the winters in Indianapolis and the summers in Kennebunkport, Maine. His summer home is commonly spoken of as "the house that Penrod built." He has twice been awarded the Pulitzer Prize for literature: in 1919 for *The Magnificent Ambersons* and in 1922 for *Alice Adams,* which is considered his most finished novel. He is probably best known as the creator of Penrod and Sam.

Jack London (1876–1916)

Jack London was born in San Francisco in January, 1876. After graduation from the grammar school in Oakland, California, he had little formal education. At an early age he was forced to earn his own living, which he did by delivering papers, working on an ice wagon and in a tannery, and by setting up pins in a bowling alley. In 1893 he joined the crew of a sealer. The next year he became a vagabond, sometimes traveling with workers' armies and sometimes alone. In the summer of 1897 he joined the Alaskan gold rush. All of this wandering gave him a rich background of experience when he determined to write. The popularity of his stories was and still is great.

He was a newspaper correspondent during the Russo-Japanese War and again during a war in Mexico in 1914. He spent a great deal of his later life in cruising. He died in November, 1916.

Anzia Yezierska (1885–   )

Problems arising from the urban life of the twentieth century industrialism as well as from the struggles of the foreign-born to adapt themselves to American life and customs are found in stories by such authors as Anzia Yezierska. Born in Russia, Miss Yezierska came to this country in 1901 when she was sixteen years old. She became a naturalized citizen in 1912. She worked in factories, sweat shops, and as servant in private families. In 1918 she began writing stories of East Side life in New York City and in 1919 her story, *The Fat of the Land,* was rated one of the best short stories of the year. Some of her other stories are *Hunger Hearts, Salome of the Tenements, Children of Loneliness* and *Bread Givers.*

Other Twentieth Century Short Story Writers

Short story writers of the twentieth century include Katherine Fullerton Gerould, author of *Vain Oblations* and *A Change of Air;* Ben Ames Williams, a local colorist, known for *They Grind Exceeding Small* and *Sheener;* Richard Harding Davis, a star reporter at twenty-four and later a war correspondent of international fame, best remembered for *Gallegher,* a newspaper story, and *The Bar Sinister,* one of the best dog stories ever written; Stephen Crane, whose best short story is *The Open Boat;* William Allen White, known for *The King of Boyville;* George Ade, famous for his *Fables in Slang;* Irvin S. Cobb, author of *Old Judge Priest* and *Local Color;* Stewart Edward White, many of whose stories portray picturesque scenes and adventurous life of the West and Southwest, best known for *The Blazed Trail* and *Arizona Nights;* Mary Austin, an interpreter of Indian life and customs in the desert regions of the Southwest, among whose best short stories are *Papago Kid* and *The Basket Woman;* Elsie Singmaster, who has written many stories of Pennsylvania life and the so-called "Pennsylvania Dutch," one of the best of which is *A Student of Languages;* Margaret Prescott Montague, whose stories such as *England to America* deal with patriotic themes; Wilbur Daniel Steele, author of *Footfalls* and *Ching, Ching, Chinaman,* whose stories, though brilliant, carry a hint of impending doom; Ruth Suckow, a number of whose stories are collected in *Iowa Interiors;* Sherwood Anderson, author of *I'm a Fool.*

Every novelist of consequence has also written short stories. Edith Wharton is known for *Xingu, The Mission of Jane* and *The Verdict;* Edna Ferber for *Shore Leave* and *The Gay Old Dog;* Owen Wister for *Philosophy 4;* Fannie Hurst for *Humoresque;* Joseph Hergesheimer for *Tol'able David* and *Lonely Valleys;* Zona Gale is author of *Friendship Village,* a collection of stories depicting life in a small Wisconsin town; Theodore Dreiser is known for *The Lost Phoebe;* Margaret Deland for *Old Chester Tales;* and Willa Cather for her interpretations of the Middle Western farming pioneers in such stories as *Neighbor Rosicky* and *The Sculptor's Funeral.*

Short Stories of the Twentieth Century

THE LAST LEAF

O. HENRY

In a little district west of Washington Square[1] the streets have run crazy and broken themselves into small strips called "places." These "places" make strange angles and curves. One street crosses itself a time or two. An artist once discovered a valuable possibility in this street. Suppose a collector with a bill for paints, paper and canvas should, in traversing this route, suddenly meet himself coming back, without a cent having been paid on account!

So, to quaint old Greenwich Village[2] the art people soon came prowling, hunting for north windows and eighteenth-century gables and Dutch attics and low rents. Then they imported some pewter mugs and a chafing dish or two from Sixth Avenue, and became a "colony."

At the top of a squatty, three-story brick Sue and Johnsy had their studio. "Johnsy" was familiar for Joanna. One was from Maine; the other from California. They had met at the *table d'hôte* of an Eighth Street "Delmonico's,"[3] and found

[1] WASHINGTON SQUARE—In lower New York City, at about 1st Street.
[2] GREENWICH VILLAGE—A vicinity in Washington Square.
[3] DELMONICO'S—In O. Henry's time Delmonico's was the most fashionable restaurant in the city. What would "Eighth Street 'Delmonico's'" mean?

their tastes in art, chicory salad and bishop sleeves so congenial that the joint studio resulted.

That was in May. In November a cold, unseen stranger,
whom the doctors called Pneumonia, stalked about the colony,
touching one here and there with his icy fingers. Over on the
east side this ravager strode boldly, smiting his victims by
scores, but his feet trod slowly through the maze of the narrow
and moss-grown "places."

Mr. Pneumonia was not what you would call a chivalric old
gentleman. A mite of a little woman with blood thinned by
California zephyrs was hardly fair game for the red-fisted,
short-breathed old duffer. But Johnsy he smote; and she lay,
scarcely moving, on her painted iron bedstead, looking through
the small Dutch window-panes at the blank side of the next
brick house.

One morning the busy doctor invited Sue into the hallway
with a shaggy, gray eyebrow.

"She has one chance in—let us say, ten," he said, as he shook
down the mercury in his clinical thermometer. "And that chance
is for her to want to live. This way people have of lining-up
on the side of the undertaker makes the entire pharmacopœia
look silly. Your little lady has made up her mind that she's
not going to get well. Has she anything on her mind?"

"She—she wanted to paint the Bay of Naples some day,"
said Sue.

"Paint?—bosh! Has she anything on her mind worth thinking about twice—a man, for instance?"

"A man?" said Sue, with a jew's-harp twang in her voice.
"Is a man worth—but, no, doctor; there is nothing of the
kind."

"Well, it is the weakness, then," said the doctor. "I will
do all that science, so far as it may filter through my efforts,
can accomplish. But whenever my patient begins to count the
carriages in her funeral procession I subtract fifty per cent
from the curative power of medicines. If you will get her to
ask one question about the new winter styles in cloak sleeves
I will promise you a one-in-five chance for her, instead of one
in ten."

After the doctor had gone Sue went into the workroom and
cried a Japanese napkin to a pulp. Then she swaggered into

Johnsy's room with her drawing board, whistling ragtime.

Johnsy lay, scarcely making a ripple under the bedclothes, with her face toward the window. Sue stopped whistling, thinking she was asleep.

She arranged her board and began a pen-and-ink drawing to illustrate a magazine story. Young artists must pave their way to Art by drawing pictures for magazine stories that young authors write to pave their way to Literature.

As Sue was sketching a pair of elegant horseshow riding trousers and a monocle on the figure of the hero, an Idaho cowboy, she heard a low sound, several times repeated. She went quickly to the bedside.

Johnsy's eyes were open wide. She was looking out the window and counting—counting backward.

"Twelve," she said, and a little later "eleven"; and then "ten," and "nine"; and then "eight" and "seven," almost together.

Sue looked solicitously out of the window. What was there to count? There was only a bare, dreary yard to be seen, and the blank side of the brick house twenty feet away. An old, old ivy vine, gnarled and decayed at the roots, climbed half way up the brick wall. The cold breath of autumn had stricken its leaves from the vine until its skeleton branches clung, almost bare, to the crumbling bricks.

"What is it, dear?" asked Sue.

"Six," said Johnsy, in almost a whisper. "They're falling faster now. Three days ago there were almost a hundred. It made my head ache to count them. But now it's easy. There goes another one. There are only five left now."

"Five what, dear. Tell your Sudie."

"Leaves. On the ivy vine. When the last one falls I must go, too. I've known that for three days. Didn't the doctor tell you?"

"Oh, I never heard of such nonsense," complained Sue, with magnificent scorn. "What have old ivy leaves to do with your getting well? And you used to love that vine, so, you naughty girl. Don't be a goosey. Why, the doctor told me this morning that your chances for getting well real soon were—let's see exactly what he said—he said the chances were ten to one! Why, that's almost as good a chance as we have in New York when we ride on the street cars or walk past a new building.

Try to take some broth now, and let Sudie go back to her drawing, so she can sell the editor man with it, and buy port wine for her sick child, and pork chops for her greedy self."

"You needn't get any more wine," said Johnsy, keeping her eyes fixed out the window. "There goes another. No, I don't want any broth. That leaves just four. I want to see the last one fall before it gets dark. Then I'll go, too."

"Johnsy, dear," said Sue, bending over her, "will you promise me to keep your eyes closed, and not look out the window until I am done working? I must hand those drawings in by to-morrow. I need the light, or I would draw the shade down."

"Couldn't you draw in the other room?" asked Johnsy, coldly.

"I'd rather be here by you," said Sue. "Besides, I don't want you to keep looking at those silly ivy leaves."

"Tell me as soon as you have finished," said Johnsy, closing her eyes, and lying white and still as a fallen statue, "because I want to see the last one fall. I'm tired of waiting. I'm tired of thinking. I want to turn loose my hold on everything, and go sailing down, down, just like one of those poor, tired leaves."

"Try to sleep," said Sue. "I must call Behrman up to be my model for the old hermit miner. I'll not be gone a minute. Don't try to move 'til I come back."

Old Behrman was a painter who lived on the ground floor beneath them. He was past sixty and had a Michael Angelo's Moses beard[4] curling down from the head of a satyr along the body of an imp. Behrman was a failure in art. Forty years he had wielded the brush without getting near enough to touch the hem of his Mistress's[5] robe. He had been always about to paint a masterpiece, but had never yet begun it. For several years he had painted nothing except now and then a daub in the line of commerce or advertising. He earned a little by serving as a model to those young artists in the colony who could not pay the price of a professional. He drank gin to excess, and still talked of his coming masterpiece. For the rest he was a fierce little old man, who scoffed terribly at softness in any one, and who regarded himself as especial mastiff-in-waiting to protect the two young artists in the studio above.

Sue found Behrman smelling strongly of juniper berries in his dimly lighted den below. In one corner was a black canvas

[4] MICHAEL ANGELO'S MOSES BEARD—A beard like those in Michael Angelo's famous paintings of Old Testament characters.
[5] MISTRESS—That is, art.

on an easel that had been waiting there for twenty-five years
to receive the first line of the masterpiece. She told him of
Johnsy's fancy, and how she feared she would, indeed, light
and fragile as a leaf herself, float away, when her slight hold
upon the world grew weaker.

Old Behrman, with his red eyes plainly streaming, shouted
his contempt and derision for such idiotic imaginings.

"Vass!" he cried. "Is dere people in de world mit der foolishness to die because leafs dey drop off from a confounded
vine? I haf not heard of such a thing. No, I will not bose
as a model for your fool hermit-dunderhead. Vy do you allow
dot silly pusiness to come in der prain of her? Ach, dot poor
leetle Miss Yohnsy."

"She is very ill and weak," said Sue, "and the fever has left
her mind morbid and full of strange fancies. Very well, Mr.
Behrman, if you do not care to pose for me, you needn't. But
I think you are a horrid old—old flibbertigibbet."

"You are just like a woman!" yelled Behrman. "Who said
I will not bose? Go on. I come mit you. For half an hour
I haf peen trying to say dot I am ready to bose. Gott! dis
is not any blace in which one so goot as Miss Yohnsy shall
lie sick. Some day I vill baint a masterpiece, and ve shall all
go away. Gott! Ves."

Johnsy was sleeping when they went upstairs. Sue pulled
the shade down to the window-sill, and motioned Behrman into
the other room. In there they peered out the window fearfully
at the ivy vine. Then they looked at each other for a moment without speaking. A persistent, cold rain was falling,
mingled with snow. Behrman, in his old blue shirt, took his
seat as the hermit-miner on an upturned kettle for a rock.

When Sue awoke from an hour's sleep the next morning she
found Johnsy with dull, wide-open eyes staring at the drawn
green shade.

"Pull it up; I want to see," she ordered, in a whisper.

Wearily Sue obeyed.

But, lo! after the beating rain and fierce gusts of wind that
had endured through the livelong night, there yet stood out
against the brick wall one ivy leaf. It was the last on the
vine. Still dark green near its stem, but with its serrated edges
tinted with the yellow of dissolution and decay, it hung bravely
from a branch some twenty feet above the ground.

"It is the last one," said Johnsy. "I thought it would surely fall during the night. I heard the wind. It will fall to-day, and I shall die at the same time."

"Dear, dear!" said Sue, leaning her worn face down to the pillow, "think of me, if you won't think of yourself. What would I do?"

But Johnsy did not answer. The lonesomest thing in all the world is a soul when it is making ready to go on its mysterious, far journey. The fancy seemed to possess her more strongly as one by one the ties that bound her to friendship and to earth were loosed.

The day wore away, and even through the twilight they could see the lone ivy leaf clinging to its stem against the wall. And then, with the coming of the night the north wind was again loosed, while the rain still beat against the windows and pattered down from the low Dutch eaves.

When it was light enough Johnsy, the merciless, commanded that the shade be raised.

The ivy leaf was still there.

Johnsy lay for a long time looking at it. And then she called to Sue, who was stirring her chicken broth over the gas stove.

"I've been a bad girl, Sudie," said Johnsy. "Something has made that last leaf stay there to show me how wicked I was. It is a sin to want to die. You may bring me a little broth now, and some milk with a little port in it, and—no; bring me a hand-mirror first, and then pack some pillows about me, and I will sit up and watch you cook."

An hour later she said.

"Sudie, some day I hope to paint the Bay of Naples."

The doctor came in the afternoon, and Sue had an excuse to go into the hallway as he left.

"Even chances," said the doctor, taking Sue's thin, shaking hand in his. "With good nursing you'll win. And now I must see another case I have downstairs. Behrman, his name is—some kind of an artist, I believe. Pneumonia, too. He is an old, weak man, and the attack is acute. There is no hope for him; but he goes to the hospital to-day to be made more comfortable."

The next day the doctor said to Sue: "She's out of danger. You've won. Nutrition and care now—that's all."

And that afternoon Sue came to the bed where Johnsy lay,

contentedly knitting a very blue and very useless woollen shoulder scarf, and put one arm around her, pillows and all.

"I have something to tell you, white mouse," she said. "Mr. Behrman died of pneumonia to-day in the hospital. He was ill only two days. The janitor found him on the morning of the first day in his room downstairs helpless with pain. His shoes and clothing were wet through and icy cold. They couldn't imagine where he had been on such a dreadful night. And then they found a lantern, still lighted, and a ladder that had been dragged from its place, and some scattered brushes, and a palette with green and yellow colors mixed on it, and—look out the window, dear, at the last ivy leaf on the wall. Didn't you wonder why it never fluttered or moved when the wind blew? Ah, darling, it's Behrman's masterpiece—he painted it there the night that the last leaf fell."

The Type of O. Henry's Stories: O. Henry met the demand of the magazines and periodicals for which he wrote. His stories were brief, original, and right to the point, with every word full of meaning and adroitly placed. He wrote for entertainment only and in his efforts to attract and hold the attention of his readers he became master of the surprise ending. No other writer before or since has approached his inimitable style. Although many of his phrases and words are "dated," that is, they no longer have the significance they had at the time of writing, his vocabulary is worthy of study.

For Appreciation: *The Last Leaf* was written in 1910. Notice with what few words the author describes the setting and characters. We say that O. Henry's style is "impressionistic." What does this mean? How is sympathy with the characters developed? How is a touch of humor introduced? What is its purpose? Did you anticipate the ending? What predominates in this story—character, plot, or setting? Had you been a reader of the New York Sunday *World* in 1910 would you have looked forward to next Sunday's paper for the O. Henry story?

For Further Study: Explain the meaning of each of the following words and phrases: *table d'hôte; chivalric, zephyrs; pharmacopœia; solicitously; serrated.*

Choose sentences which describe the city. Describe Sue and Johnsy as you think they look. Compare your description with O. Henry's. Do you like the doctor? Why is old Behrman made to seem rough and harsh? Is there significance to Behrman's statement, "Some day I vill baint a masterpiece"? Is this the key to the story? Who is the leading character? Do the rain and wind lend atmosphere to the story?

MARY SMITH *

Booth Tarkington

Henry Millick Chester, rising early from intermittent slumbers, found himself the first of the crowded Pullman to make a toilet in the men's smoke-and-wash-room, and so had the place to himself—an advantage of high dramatic value to a person of his age and temperament, on account of the mirrors which, set at various angles, afford a fine view of the profile. Henry Millick Chester, scouring cinders and stickiness from his eyes and rouging his ears with honest friction, enriched himself of this too unfamiliar opportunity. He smiled and was warmly interested in the results of his smile in reflection, particularly in some pleasant alterations it effected upon an outline of the cheek usually invisible to the bearer. He smiled graciously, then he smiled sardonically. Other smiles he offered —the tender smile, the forbidding smile, the austere and the seductive, the haughty and the pleading, the mordant and the compassionate, the tolerant but incredulous smile of a man of

* From *The Fascinating Stranger and Other Stories,* copyright, 1913, by Doubleday, Page and Company, reprinted by permission of the author.

the world, and the cold, ascetic smile that shows a woman that her shallow soul has been read all too easily—pastimes abandoned only with the purely decorative application of shaving lather to his girlish chin. However, as his unbeetling brow was left unobscured, he was able to pursue his physiognomical researches and to produce for his continued enlightenment a versatile repertory of frowns—the stern, the quizzical, the bitter, the treacherous, the bold, the agonized, the inquisitive, the ducal, and the frown of the husband who says: "I forgive you. Go!" A few minutes later Mr. Chester, abruptly pausing in the operation of fastening his collar, bent a sudden, passionate interest upon his right forearm, without apparent cause and with the air of never having seen it until that moment. He clenched his fingers tightly, producing a slight stringiness above the wrist, then crooked his elbow with intensity, noting this enormous effect in all the mirrors. Regretfully, he let his shirtsleeves fall and veil the rare but private beauties just discovered, rested his left hand negligently upon his hip, extended his right in a gesture of flawlessly aristocratic grace, and, with a slight inclination of his head, uttered aloud these simple but befitting words: "I thank ye, my good people." T' yoong Maister was greeting the loyal tenantry who acclaimed his return to Fielding Manor, a flowered progress thoroughly incomprehensible to the Pullman porter whose transfixed eye—glazed upon an old-gold face intruded through the narrow doorway—Mr. Chester encountered in the glass above the nickeled washbasins. The Libyan withdrew in a cloud of silence, and t' yoong Maister, flushing somewhat, resumed his toilet with annoyed precision and no more embroidery. He had yesterday completed his sophomore year; the brushes he applied to his now adult locks were those of a junior. And with a man's age had come a man's cares and responsibilities. Several long years had rolled away since for the last time he had made himself sick on a train in a club-car orgy of cubebs and sarsaparilla pop.

Zigzagging through shoe-bordered aisles of sleepers in morning dishevelment, he sought the dining car, where the steward escorted him to an end table for two. He would have assumed his seat with that air of negligent hauteur which was his chosen manner for public appearances, had not the train, taking a curve at high speed, heaved him into the undesirable embrace of an elderly man breakfasting across the aisle. "Keep your feet, sonny; keep your feet," said this barbarian, little witting that he addressed a member of the nineteen-something prom. committee. People at the next table laughed genially, and Mr. Chester, muttering a word of hostile apology, catapulted into his assigned place, his cheeks hot with the triple outrage.

He relieved himself a little by the icy repulsion with which he countered the cordial advances of the waiter, who took his order and wished him a good morning, hoped he had slept well, declared the weather delightful and, unanswered, yet preserved his beautiful courtesy unimpaired. When this humble ambassador had departed on his mission to the kitchen Henry Millick Chester, unwarrantably persuaded that all eyes were searching his every inch and angle—an impression not uncharacteristic of his years—gazed out of the window with an indifference which would have been obtrusive if any of the other breakfasters had happened to notice it. The chill exclusiveness of his expression was a rebuke to such prying members of the proletariat as might be striving to read his thoughts, and barred his fellow passengers from every privilege to his consideration. The intensely reserved gentleman was occupied with interests which were the perquisites of only his few existing peers in birth, position, and intelligence, none of whom, patently, was in that car.

He looked freezingly upon the abashed landscape, which fled in shame; nor was that wintry stare relaxed when the steward placed someone opposite him at the little table. Nay, our frosty scholar now intensified the bleakness of his isolation, retiring quite to the pole in reproval of this too close intrusion. He resolutely denied the existence of his vis-à-vis, refused consciousness of its humanity, even of its sex, and then inconsistently began to perspire with the horrible impression that it was glaring at him fixedly. It was a dreadful feeling. He felt himself growing red, and coughed vehemently to afford the public an explanation of his change of colour. At last, his suffering grown unendurable, he desperately turned his eyes full upon the newcomer. She was not looking at him at all, but down at the edge of the white cloth on her own side of the table; and she was the very prettiest girl he had ever seen in his life.

She was about his own age. Her prettiness was definitely

extreme, and its fair delicacy was complete and without any imperfection whatever. She was dressed in pleasant shades of tan and brown. A brown veil misted the rim of her hat, tan gloves were folded back from her wrists; and they, and all she wore, were fresh and trim and ungrimed by the dusty journey. She was charming. Henry Millick Chester's first gasping appraisal of her was perfectly accurate, for she *was* a peach—or a rose, or anything that is dewy and fresh and delectable. She was indeed some smooth. She was the smoothest thing in the world, and the world knows it!

She looked up.

Henry Millick Chester was lost.

At the same instant that the gone feeling came over him she dropped her eyes again to the edge of the table. Who can tell if she knew what she had done?

The conversation began with appalling formalities, which preluded the most convenient placing of a sugar bowl and the replenishing of an exhausted salt cellar. Then the weather, spurned as the placative offering of the gentle waiter, fell from the lips of the princess in words of diamonds and rubies and pearls. Our Henry took up the weather where she left it; he put it to its utmost; he went forward with it, prophesying weather; he went backward with it, recalling weather; he spun it out and out, while she agreed to all he said, until this overworked weather got so stringy that each obscurely felt it to be hideous. The thread broke; fragments wandered in the air for a few moments, but disappeared; a desperate propriety descended, and they fell into silence over their eggs.

Frantically Mr. Chester searched his mind for some means to pursue the celestial encounter. According to the rules, something ought to happen that would reveal her as Patricia Beekman, the sister of his roommate, Schuyler Beekman, and tonight he should be handing the imperturbable Dawkins a wire to send: "My dear Schuyler, I married your sister this afternoon." But it seemed unlikely, because his roommate's name was Jake Schmulze, and Jake lived in Cedar Rapids; and, besides, this train wasn't coming from or going to Palm Beach—it was going to St. Louis eventually, and now hustled earnestly across the placid and largely unbutlered plains of Ohio.

Often—as everyone knows—people have been lost to each

other forever through the lack of a word, and few have realized this more poignantly than our Henry, as he helplessly suffered the precious minutes to accumulate vacancy. True, he had thought of something to say, yet he abandoned it. Probably he was wiser to wait, as what he thought of saying was: "Will you be my wife?" It might seem premature, he feared.

The strain was relieved by a heavenly accident which saved the life of a romance near perishing at birth. That charming girl, relaxing slightly in her chair, made some small, indefinite, and entirely ladylike movement of restfulness that reached its gentle culmination upon the two feet of Mr. Chester which, obviously mistaken for structural adjuncts of the table, were thereby glorified and became beautiful on the mountains. He was not the man to criticise the remarkable ignorance of dining-car table architecture thus displayed, nor did he in any wise resent being mistaken up to the ankles for metal or wood. No. The light pressure of her small heels hardly indented the stout toes of his brown shoes; the soles of her slippers reposed upon his two insteps, and rapture shook his soul to its foundations, while the ineffable girl gazed lustrously out of the window, the clear serenity of her brilliant eyes making plain her complete unconsciousness of the nature of what added to her new comfort.

A terrific blush sizzled all over him, and to conceal its visible area he bent low to his coffee. She was unaware. He was transported, she—to his eyes—transfigured. Glamour diffused itself about her, sprayed about them both like showers of impalpable gold-dust, and filled the humble dining car—it filled the whole world. Transformed, seraphic waiters passed up and down the aisle in a sort of obscure radiance. A nimbus hovered faintly above the brown veil; a sacred luminosity was exhaled by the very tablecloth, where an angel's pointed fingers drummed absently.

It would be uncharitable to believe that a spirit of retaliation inspired the elderly and now replete man across the aisle, and yet, when he rose, he fell upon the neck of Henry as Henry had fallen upon his, and the shock of it jarred four shoes from the acute neighbourliness of their juxtaposition. The accursed graybeard, giggling in his senility, passed on; but that angel leaped backward in her chair while her beautiful eyes, wide open, stunned, her beautiful mouth, wide open, incredulous, gave proof that horror can look bewitching.

"Murder!" she gasped. "Were those your *feet?*"

And as he could compass no articulate reply, she grew pink as he, murmured inaudibly, and stared at him in wider and wilder amazement.

"It—it didn't hurt," he finally managed to stammer.

At this she covered her blushes with her two hands and began to gurgle and shake with laughter. She laughed and laughed and laughed. It became a paroxysm. He laughed, too, because she laughed. Other passengers looked at them and laughed. The waiters laughed; they approved—coloured waiters always approve of laughter—and a merry spirit went abroad in the car.

At last she controlled herself long enough to ask:

"But what did you think of me?"

"It—it didn't hurt," he repeated idiotically, to his own mortification, for he passionately aspired to say something airy and winsome; but, as he couldn't think of anything like that, he had to let it go. "Oh, not at all," he added feebly.

However, "though not so deep as a well," it served, 'twas enough, for she began to laugh again, and there loomed no further barrier in the way of acquaintance. Therefore it was pleasantly without constraint, and indeed as a matter of course, that he dropped into a chair beside her half an hour later, in the observation car; and something in the way she let the *Illustrated London News* slide into the vacant chair on the other side of her might have suggested that she expected him.

"I was still wondering what you must have thought of me."

This gave him an opportunity, because he had thought out a belated reply for the first time she had said it. Hence, quick as a flash, he made the dashing rejoinder:

"It wasn't so much what I thought of you, but what I thought of myself—I thought I was in heaven!"

She must have known what pretty sounds her laughter made. She laughed a great deal. She even had a way of laughing in the middle of some of her words, and it gave them a kind of ripple. There are girls who naturally laugh like that; others learn to, a few won't, and some can't. It isn't fair to the ones that can't.

"But you oughtn't to tell me that," she said.

It was in the middle of the "oughtn't" that she rippled. A pen cannot express it, neither can a typewriter, and no one has yet invented a way of writing with a flute; but the effect on Henry shows what a wonderful ripple it was. Henry trembled. From this moment she had only to ripple to make Henry tremble. Henry was more in love than he had been at breakfast. Henry was a Goner.

"Why oughtn't I to?" he demanded with white intensity. "If anything's true it's right to tell it, isn't it? I believe that everybody has a right to tell the truth, don't you?"

"Ye-es——"

"You take the case of a man that's in love," said this rather precipitate gentleman; "isn't it right for him to——"

"But suppose," she interrupted, becoming instantly serious with the introduction of the great topic— "Suppose he isn't *really* in love. Don't you think there are very few cases of people truly and deeply caring for each other?"

"There are men," he said firmly, "who know how to love truly and deeply, and could never in their lives care for anybody but the one woman they have picked out. I don't say all men feel that way; I don't think they do. But there are a few that are capable of it." The seats in an observation car are usually near neighbours, and it happened that the brown cuff of a tan sleeve, extended reposefully on the arm of her chair, just touched the back of his hand, which rested on the arm of his. This ethereally light contact continued. She had no apparent cognizance of it, but a vibrant thrill passed through him, and possibly quite a hearty little fire might have been built under him without his perceiving good cause for moving. He shook, gulped, and added: "I am!"

"But how could you be sure of that," she said thoughtfully, "until you tried?" And as he seemed about to answer, perhaps too impulsively, she checked him with a smiling, "At your age!"

"You don't know how old I am. I'm older than you!"

"How old are you?"

"Twenty-one next March."

"What day?"

"The seventh."

"That is singular!"

"Why?"

"Because," she began in a low tone and with full recognition of the solemn import of the revelation— "Because my birthday is only one day after yours. I was twenty years old the eighth of last March."

"By George!" The exclamation came from him, husky with awe.

There was a fateful silence.

"Yes, I was born on the eighth," she said slowly.

"And me on the seventh!" At such a time no man is a purist.

"It is strange," she said.

"Strange! I came into the world just one day before you did!"

They looked at each other curiously, deeply stirred. Coincidence could not account for these birthdays of theirs, nor chance for their meeting on a train "like this." Henry Millick Chester was breathless. The mysteries were glimpsed. No doubt was possible—he and the wondrous creature at his side were meant for each other, intended from the beginning of eternity.

She dropped her eyes slowly from his, but he was satisfied that she had felt the marvel precisely as he had felt it.

"Don't you think," she said gently, "that a girl has seen more of the world at twenty than a man?"

Mr. Chester well wished to linger upon the subject of birthdays; however, the line of original research suggested by her question was alluring also. "Yes—and no," he answered with admirable impartiality. "In some ways, yes. In some ways, no. For instance, you take the case of a man that's in love——"

"Well," interrupted the lady, "I think, for instance, that a girl understands men better at twenty than men do women."

"It may be," he admitted, nodding. "I like to think about the deeper things like this sometimes."

"So do I. I think they're interesting," she said with that perfect sympathy of understanding which he believed she was destined to extend to him always and in all things. "Life itself is interesting. Don't you think so?"

"I think it's the most interesting subject there can be. Real life, that is, though—not just on the surface. Now, for instance, you take the case of a man that's in——"

"Do you go in much for reading?" she asked.

"Sure. But as I was saying, you take——"

"I think reading gives us so many ideas, don't you?"

"Yes. I get a lot out of it. I——"

"I do, too. I try to read only the best things," she said. "I don't believe in reading everything, and there's so much to read nowadays that isn't really good."

"Who do you think," he inquired with deference, "is the best author now?"

It was not a question to be settled quite offhand; she delayed her answer slightly, then, with a gravity appropriate to the literary occasion, temporized: "Well, since Victor Hugo is dead, it's hard to say just who is the best."

"Yes, it is," he agreed. "We get that in the English course in college. There aren't any great authors any more. I expect probably Swinburne's the best."

She hesitated. "Yes, that's so. I expect he would be classed more as a poet."

He assented. "Yes, that's so. I expect he would be classed more as a poet. Come to think of it, I believe he's dead, too. I'm not sure, though; maybe it was Beerbohm Tree—somebody like that. I've forgotten; but, anyway, it doesn't matter. I didn't mean poetry; I meant who do you think writes the best books? Mrs. Humphry Ward?"

"Yes, she's good, and so's Henry James."

"I've never read anything by Henry James. I guess I'll read some of his this summer. What's the best one to begin on?"

The exquisite pink of her cheeks extended its area almost imperceptibly. "Oh, any one. They're all pretty good. Do you care for Nature?"

"Sure thing," he returned quickly. "Do you?"

"I love it!"

"So do I. I can't do much for mathematics, though."

"Br-r!" She shivered prettily. "I hate it!"

"So do I. I can't give astronomy a whole lot, either."

She turned a softly reproachful inquiry upon him. "Oh, don't you love to look at the stars?"

In horror lest the entrancing being think him a brute, he responded with breathless haste: "Oh, rath-er-r! To look at 'em, sure thing! I meant astronomy in college; that's mostly math, you know—just figures. But stars to look at—of course

that's different. Why, I look up at 'em for hours sometimes!"
He believed what he was saying. "I look up at 'em, and think
and think and think——"

"So do I." Her voice was low and hushed; there was something almost holy in the sound of it, and a delicate glow suffused
her lovely, upraised face—like that picture of Saint Cecilia,
he thought. "Oh, I love the stars! And music—and
flowers——"

"And birds," he added automatically in a tone that, could
it by some miracle have been heard at home, would have laid
his nine-year-old brother flat on the floor in a might-be mortal
swoon.

A sweet warmth centered in the upper part of his diaphragm
and softly filtered throughout him. The delicious future held
no doubts or shadows for him. It was assured. He and this
perfect woman had absolutely identical tastes; their abhorrences
and their enthusiasms marched together; they would never know
a difference in all their lives to come. Destiny unrolled before
him a shining pathway which they two would walk hand-in-
hand through the summer days to a calm and serene autumn,
respected and admired by the world, but finding ever their
greatest and most sacred joy in the light of each other's eyes—
that light none other than the other could evoke.

Could it be possible, he wondered, that he was the same
callow boy who but yesterday pranced and exulted in the "pee-
rade" of the new juniors! How absurd and purposeless that
old life seemed; how far away, how futile, and how childish!
Well, it was over, finished. By this time tomorrow he would
have begun his business career.

Back in the old life, he had expected to go through a law
school after graduating from college, subsequently to enter his
father's office. That meant five years before even beginning to
practice, an idea merely laughable now. There was a men's
furnishing store on a popular corner at home; it was an establishment which had always attracted him, and what pleasanter way to plow the road to success than through acres of
variously woven fabrics, richly coloured silks, delicate linens,
silver mountings and odorous leathers, in congenial association
with neckties, walking-sticks, hosiery, and stickpins? He would
be home in a few hours hence, and he would not delay. After

lunch he would go boldly to his father and say: "Father, I have reached a man's estate and I have put away childish things. I have made up my mind upon a certain matter and you will only waste time by any effort to alter this, my firm determination. Father, I here and now relinquish all legal ambitions, for the reason that a mercantile career is more suited to my inclinations and my abilities. Father, I have met the one and only woman I can ever care for, and I intend to make her my wife. Father, you have always dealt squarely with me; I will deal squarely with you. I ask you the simple question: Will you or will you not advance me the funds to purchase an interest in Paul H. Hoy & Company's Men Outfitting Establishment? If you will not, then I shall seek help elsewhere."

Waking dreams are as swift, sometimes, as the other kind—which, we hear, thread mazes so labyrinthine "between the opening and the closing of a door"; and a twenty-year-old fancy, fermenting in the inclosure of a six-and-seven-eighth plaid cap, effervesces with a power of sizzling and sparkling and popping.

"I believe I love music best of all," said the girl dreamily.

"Do you play?" he asked, and his tone and look were those of one who watches at the sick-bed of a valued child.

"Yes, a little."

"I love the piano." He was untroubled by any remorse for what he and some of his gang had done only two days since to a previously fine instrument in his dormitory entry. He had forgotten the dead past in his present vision, which was of a luxurious room in a spacious mansion, and a tired man of affairs coming quietly into that room—from a conference at which he had consolidated the haberdashery trade of the world —and sinking noiselessly upon a rich divan, while a beautiful woman in a dress of brown and tan, her hair slightly silvered, played to him through the twilight upon a grand piano, the only other sound in the great house being the softly murmurous voices of perfectly trained children being put to bed in a distant nursery upstairs.

"I like the stage, too," she said, "Don't you?"

"You know! Did you see The Tinkle-Dingle Girl?"

"Yes. I liked it."

"It's a peach of a show." He spoke with warranted authority. During the university term just finished he had gone eight times to New York, and had enriched his critical perceptions of music and the drama by ten visits to The Tinkle-Dingle Girl, two of his excursions having fallen on matinée days. "Those big birds that played the comedy parts were funny birds, weren't they?"

"The tramp and the brewer? Yes. Awfully funny."

"We'll go lots to the theatre!" He spoke eagerly and with superb simplicity, quite without consciousness that he was skipping much that would usually be thought necessarily intermediate. An enchanting vision engrossed his mind's eye. He saw himself night after night at The Tinkle-Dingle Girl, his lovely wife beside him—growing matronly, perhaps, but slenderly matronly—with a grace of years that only added to her beauty, and always wearing tan gloves and a brown veil.

The bewilderment of her expression was perhaps justified.

"What!"

At this he realized the import of what he had said and what, in a measure, it did assume. He became pinkish, then pink, then more pink; and so did she. Paralyzed, the blushing pair looked at each other throughout this duet in colour, something like a glint of alarm beginning to show through the wide astonishment in her eyes; and with the perception of this he was assailed by an acute perturbation. He had spoken thoughtlessly, even hastily, he feared; he should have given her more time. Would she rise now with chilling dignity and leave him, it might be forever? Was he to lose her just when he had found her? He shuddered at the ghastly abyss of loneliness disclosed by the possibility. But this was only the darkest moment before a radiance that shot heavenward like the flaming javelins of an equatorial sunrise.

Her eyes lowered slowly till the long, brown lashes shadowed the rose-coloured cheek and the fall of her glance came to rest upon the arms of their two chairs, where the edge of her coat sleeve just touched the knuckle of his little finger. Two people were passing in front of them; there was no one who could see; and with a lightning-swift impulse she turned her wrist and for a half second, while his heart stopped beating, touched all his fingers with her own, then as quickly withdrew her hand and turned as far away from him as the position of her chair permitted.

It was a caress of incredible brevity, and so fleeting, so airy, that it was a little more than a touch of light itself, like the faint quick light from a flying star one might just glimpse on one's hand as it passed. But in our pleasant world important things have resulted from touches as evanescent as that. Nature has its uses for the ineffable.

Blazing with glory, dumb with rapture, Henry Millick Chester felt his heart rebound to its work, while his withheld breath upheaved in a gulp that half suffocated him. Thus, blinded by the revelation of the stupefying beauty of life, he sat through a heaven-stricken interval, and time was of no moment. Gradually he began to perceive, in the midst of the effulgence which surrounded the next chair like a bright mist, the adorable contour of a shoulder in a tan coat and the ravishing outline of a rosy cheek that belonged to this divine girl who was his.

By and by he became dreamily aware of other objects beyond that cheek and that shoulder, of a fat man and his fat wife on the opposite side of the car near the end. Unmistakably they were man and wife, but it seemed to Henry that they had no reason to be—such people had no right to be married. They had no obvious right to exist at all; certainly they had no right whatever to exist in that car. Their relation to each other had become a sickening commonplace, the bleakness of it as hideously evident as their overfed convexity. It was visible that they looked upon each other as inevitable nuisances which had to be tolerated. They were horrible. Had love ever known these people? It was unthinkable! For lips such as theirs to have pronounced the name of the god would have been blasphemy; for those fat hands ever to have touched, desecration! Henry hated the despicable pair.

All at once his emotion changed: he did not hate them, he pitied them. From an immense height he looked down with compassion upon their wretched condition. He pitied everybody except himself and the roseate being beside him; they floated together upon a tiny golden cloud, alone in the vast sky at an immeasurable altitude above the squalid universe. A wave of pity for the rest of mankind flooded over him, but most of all he pitied that miserable sodden, befleshed old married couple.

He was dimly aware of a change that came over these fat

people, a strangeness; but he never did realize that at this crisis his eyes, fixed intently upon them and aided by his plastic countenance, had expressed his feelings and sentiments regarding them in the most lively and vivid way. For at the moment when the stout gentleman laid his paper down, preparatory to infuriated inquiry, both he and his wife were expunged from Henry's consciousness forever and were seen of him thenceforth no more than if they had been ether and not solid flesh. The exquisite girl had been pretending to pick a thread out of her left sleeve with her right hand—but now at last she leaned back in her chair and again turned her face partly toward Henry. Her under lip was caught in slightly beneath her upper teeth, as if she had been doing something that possibly she oughtn't to be doing, and though the pause in the conversation had been protracted—it is impossible to calculate how long— her charming features were still becomingly overspread with rose. She looked toward her rapt companion, not at him, and her eyes were preoccupied, tender, and faintly embarrassed.

The pause continued.

He leaned a little closer to her. And he looked at her and looked at her and looked at her. At intervals his lips moved as if he were speaking, and yet he was thinking wordlessly. Leaning thus toward her, his gaze and attitude had all the intensity of one who watches a ninth-inning tie in the deciding game of a championship series. And as he looked and looked and looked, the fat man and his wife, quite unaware of their impalpability, also looked and looked and looked in grateful fascination.

"Did you—" Henry Millick Chester finally spoke these words in a voice he had borrowed, evidently from a stranger, for it did not fit his throat and was so deep that it disappeared —it seemed to fall down a coal-hole and ended in a dusty choke, "Did you—" he began again, two octaves higher, and immediately squeaked out. He said, "Did you" five times before he subjugated the other two words.

"Did you—mean that?"

"What?" Her own voice was so low that he divined rather than heard what she said. He leaned even a little closer—and the fat man nudged his wife, who elbowed his thumb out of her side morbidly: she wasn't missing anything.

"Did you—did you mean that?"

"Mean what?"

"That!"

"I don't know what you mean."

"When you—when you—oh, you know!"

"No, I don't."

"When you—when you took my hand."

"I!"

With sudden, complete self-possession she turned quickly to face him, giving him a look of half-shocked, half-amused astonishment.

"When I took your hand?" she repeated incredulously. "What are you saying?"

"You—you know," he stammered. "A while ago when—when —you—you——"

"I didn't do anything of the kind!" Impending indignation began to cloud the delicate face ominously. "Why in the world should I?"

"But you——"

"I didn't!" She cut him off sharply. "I couldn't. Why, it wouldn't have been nice! What made you dream I would do a thing like that? How dare you imagine such things!"

At first dumfounded, then appalled, he took the long, swift, sickening descent from his golden cloud with his mouth open, but it snapped tight at the bump with which he struck the earth. He lay prone, dismayed, abject. The lovely witch could have made him believe anything; at least it is the fact that for a moment she made him believe he had imagined that angelic little caress; and perhaps it was the sight of his utter subjection that melted her. For she flashed upon him suddenly with a dazing smile, and then, blushing again but more deeply than before, her whole attitude admitting and yielding, she offered full and amazing confession, her delicious laugh rippling tremulously throughout every word of it.

"It must have been an accident—partly!"

"I love you!" he shouted.

The translucent fat man and his wife groped for each other feverishly, and a coloured porter touched Henry Millick Chester on the shoulder.

"Be in Richmon' less'n fi' minutes now," said the porter.

He tapped the youth's shoulder twice more; it is his office to awaken the rapt dreamer. "Richmon', In'iana, less'n fi' minutes now," he repeated more slowly.

Henry gave him a stunned and dishevelled "What?"

"You get off Richmon', don't you?"

"What of it? We haven't passed Dayton yet."

"Yessuh, long 'go. Pass' Dayton eight-fifty. Be in Richmon' mighty quick now."

The porter appeared to be a malicious liar. Henry appealed pitifully to the girl.

"But we haven't passed Dayton?"

"Yes, just after you sat down by me. We stopped several minutes."

"Yessuh. Train don't stop no minutes in Richmon' though," said the porter with a hard laugh, waving his little broom at some outlying freight cars they were passing. "Gittin' in now. I got you' bag on platfawm."

"I don't want to be brushed," Henry said, almost sobbing. "For heaven's sake, get out!"

Porters expect anything. This one went away solemnly without even lifting his eyebrows.

The brakes were going on.

One class of railway tragedies is never recorded, though it is the most numerous of all and fills the longest list of heart-breaks; statisticians ignore it, yet no train ever leaves its shed, or moved, that is not party to it. It is time and overtime that the safety-device inventors should turn their best attention to it, so that the happy day may come at last when we shall see our common carriers equipped with something to prevent these lovers' partings.

The train began to slow down.

Henry Millick Chester got waveringly to his feet; she rose at the same time and stood beside him.

"I am no boy," he began, hardly knowing what he said, but automatically quoting a fragment from his forthcoming address to his father. "I have reached a man's estate and I have met the only—" He stopped short with an exclamation of horror. "You—you haven't even told me your name!"

"My name?" the girl said, a little startled.

"Yes! And your address!"

"I'm not on my way home now," she said. "I've been visiting in New York and I'm going to St. Louis to make another visit."

"But your name!"

She gave him an odd glance of mockery, a little troubled.

"You mightn't like my name!"

"Oh, please, please!"

"Besides, do you think it's quite proper for me to——"

"Oh, please! To talk of that now! Please!" The train had stopped.

The glint of a sudden decision shone in the lovely eyes. "I'll write it for you so you won't forget."

She went quickly to the writing desk at the end of the compartment, he with her, the eyes of the fat man and his wife following them like two pairs of searchlights swung by the same mechanism.

"And where you live," urged Henry. "I shall write to you every day." He drew a long, deep breath and threw back his head. "Till the day—the day when I come for you."

"Don't look over my shoulder." She laughed shyly, wrote hurriedly upon a loose sheet, placed it in an envelope, sealed the envelope, and then, as he reached to take it, withheld it tantalizingly. "No. It's my name and where I live, but you can't have it. Not till you've promised not to open it until the train is clear out of the station."

Outside the window sounded the twice-repeated "Awl aboh-oh," and far ahead a fatal bell was clanging.

"I promise," he gulped.

"Then take it!"

With a strange, new-born masterfulness he made a sudden impetuous gesture and lifted both the precious envelope and the fingers that inclosed it to his lips. Then he turned and dashed to the forward end of the car where a porter remained untipped as Henry leaped from the already rapidly moving steps of the car to the ground. Instantly the wonderful girl was drawn past him, leaning and waving from the railed rear platform whither she had run for this farewell. And in the swift last look that they exchanged there was in her still-flushing, lovely face a light of tenderness and of laughter, of kindness and of something like a fleeting regret.

The train gained momentum, skimming onward and away, the end of the observation car dwindling and condensing into itself like a magician's disappearing card, while a white handkerchief, waving from the platform, quickly became an infinitesimal shred of white—and then there was nothing. The girl was gone.

Probably Henry Millick Chester owes his life to the fact that there are no gates between the station building and the tracks at Richmond. For gates and a ticket-clipping official might have delayed Henry's father in the barely successful dash he made to drag from the path of a backing local a boy wholly lost to the outward world in a state of helpless puzzlement, which already threatened to become permanent as he stared and stared at a sheet of railway notepaper whereon was written in a charming hand:

Mary Smith

Chicago

Ill.

The Type of Booth Tarkington's Stories: Although Booth Tarkington has written with deep feeling about life in industrial centers, his popularity has been greatly enhanced by his unique gift for presenting young characters. Penrod and Sam, for example, are boys everyone knows. Robert Cortes Holliday, in a discussion of Mr. Tarkington's work, uses a very apt figure of speech: "It is as if the author had a device in his head like the plumbing giving hot and cold water to a bath-tub, and as if he could at will turn off the stream of mature thinking and turn on boy thinking." Yet whether he is writing from the mature point of view, or about the strange things which are going on in the boy's mind, the reader feels that Mr. Tarkington is in sympathy with the boy. The reader may chuckle, as he turns the pages, but sooner or later, he will find his own sympathy with the boy is aroused. Mr. Tarkington does not seem to be particularly concerned about technique, and his plots are usually negligible. His interest is in character, and we enjoy his understanding of human nature.

For Appreciation: *Mary Smith* appears in *The Fascinating Stranger and Other Stories* published in 1923. By the time Henry is seated at the breakfast table you know quite a little about him. What are some of his characteristics? Has the story a forceful plot? Why does the story hold your interest? What purpose is served by having minor characters come into the observation car? Are you satisfied with the ending? Can you find a hint in the conversation of the girl which prepares you for the ending?

For Further Study: How many kinds of smiles did Henry have? How many frowns? Give the meaning of each of the following words: *sardonically; austere; mordant; incredulous; quizzical; catapulted; Libyan; ineffable; impalpable; juxtaposition; cognizance; blasphemy.*

Mr. Tarkington adds bit by bit to our understanding of Henry, but not by direct statements. Henry's nine-year-old brother is mentioned only once in the story; however, that is sufficient to give us an idea of the relation between them. What do you think the smaller boy thought of his brother? Why did the men's furnishing store appeal more to Henry than any other business? Why did the girl change the subject so quickly from books to Nature?

Exercises and Creative Work: Write an imaginary letter from Mary Smith to a school friend in which she tells of her experience with Henry.

Write a few paragraphs telling how Henry explained to his father why he did not notice the local train which nearly backed over him.

Suppose that Henry's small brother learns the details of Henry's episode with Mary Smith. In the boy's own words, write what you think he would tell his pal.

ECHO O' THE MORN

From *Gloucestermen*

JAMES B. CONNOLLY

It was right on the Nova Scotia coast that we were seining that summer. It's Billie and the *Echo o' the Morn,* I'm talking about now. Billie used to be a dog after mackerel those days. He'd get 'em, if there was any around to get. This was the height of the time when so many American vessels was being seized by the English cutters for fishing inside the three-mile limit. You know what hard feelings there used to be between the Canadians and our fellows about fishing inside the shore line. American fishermen were being fined right and left, the Gover'ment at Washington was doing little but make talk, and at home, in Gloucester, everybody was boiling over about it.

The Clayton brothers owned the *Echo.* They're out of business now, but some of you had dealings with 'em maybe. One was strong on religion—had Bibles fore and aft on every one of his vessels—and the other was, well, not the same kind of a man, and on account of their difference of opinion, they used to split on the names of the vessels. That's how there came the *Mutineer,* then the *Peace on Earth;* then the *Buccaneer,* and the *Three Shepherds.*

The *Avenger* and the *Good Will to Men* was launched the same week, and the *Roisterer* was chased off the stocks by the *Echo o' the Morn*. I mind well the launchin' of 'em both.

But if they split on the names, they had identical ideas 'bout skippers and crews. "Read the Bible, men," the old fellow would say, "and abide by what you find therein." We all found some pretty husky fighting men in that same Bible. The other brother's instructions to skippers was mostly, "Bring home the fish."

The *Echo* was just off the stocks, and a handsome vessel to look at, and I mind the curiosity of the Gover'ment sailing cutters down this way to try tracks with her. We went along for quite awhile without getting more than our share of official calls from the cutters—they were slow in the stays, most of 'em. We used to keep track of the cutters, read the battles in the old man's Bibles reg'lar, and keep a sharp watch for fish.

As the *Echo's* hull was beginning to get known along the coast, they begins to crowd us pretty close. And one day they ketched us at what they said was inside the three-mile limit, where, of course, we had no business to be—if we was inside. I don't know yet whether we was inside the line or not, and I wouldn't hold back the truth of it now, but anyway they said we was. They always gave themselves the benefit of any doubts, those lads, when they were dealing with American fishermen. There was two of 'em and a steam cutter. It was no disgrace, p'raps, it being a flat calm and they mounting two guns apiece, but they had the laugh on us, the two cutters, and they walked us into Barnsley between them, the sailing lad to wind'ard, where Billie said she'd never got by rights, and the steam fellow to loo'ard. Into the harbor of Barnsley they walked us, with two hundred barrels of salted mackerel in our hold.

They made the *Echo* fast to the dock, stripped the sails off her the first thing and put them in a sail-loft near by. Then they asked Billie to step up to the custom-house, where they asked him a lot of questions, which he didn't answer gen'rally, and when he did, they didn't put them down, Billie being a bit hot.

The crew was all turned loose, of course. It was the vessels they wanted, they used to say. They'd set a fine, they said, and they'd have no trouble getting it, for if the owners didn't settle, they'd sell the *Echo* at public auction and get it that way. There was a Gloucester vessel caught two weeks ahead of us and fined.

Things looked bad for the *Echo*. Billie telegraphed to the owners how it happened. I was there when he wrote the message. "Don't do anything 'till you hear further from me. Maybe we can settle to better advantage at this end," was the winding up of it. "Everybody in the place here will know what the message said inside of an hour," Billie said, coming out of the telegraph office. And they did. They was laughing at us and asking what soft kind of settlement we expected to make with the Provincial Gover'ment.

Next mornin' Billie just laid around and waited. In the afternoon he took a couple of us and a small boat and we sailed out to where the two cutters were anchored, three or four cablelengths off-shore. Billie had a talk with the Captain of the steam cutter, which was abreast the sailing lad, less than a cable's length between them, in a place where the harbor made a kind of a neck. "I tell you, Captain," says Billie, looking across the way, "a vessel that tried to sail out of here unbeknownst would have a bad time, wouldn't she—having to go between you two?"

"That's what she would," said the Captain. My, but he laughed just to think of it.

"It would be a good harbor, this one," says Billie again, taking a look around, "if 'twas only a mite wider up here."

"Well, it's wide enough below," says the Captain. "Deep water clear up to the shore. A blind man could pilot a vessel in and out here. He'd only have to keep her off the rocks." Then he takes Billie down below and tells him all about the steam gear. "Ready to move at half a minute's notice," he says, when he comes up on deck again. "You can't expect to get ahead of one of these machines with a sailing vessel," he says—"not when her machinery is in working order."

"I see," says Billie, "not when the steam gear's clear."

Then we gets inside the small boat again and sails around to have a look at the harbor, which was just about as they said it was—deep water to the shore. The last thing Billie said when he stepped out of the small boat was: "This time t'morrow morning the tide'll be 'bout like it is now." It was past three o'clock then, and the tide a fair ebb.

That night about ten o'clock it was pretty quiet in Barnsley. We warn't very much surprised when Billie passed the word, in a quiet way, to slip the boarding-house we were staying at, and meet him outside. Billie soon told us what the game was, and we started right away. Four of us dropped down to the sail-loft, caught the watchman, gagged him, and tied him up. He wouldn't tell us where the key was, and we broke in the door. We found the *Echo*'s sails done up in packages, sealed up fine with red wax—all official. We rolled the watchman up in some old sail, so he wouldn't ketch cold through the night, and then we hustled our packages down to the dock. We met a lad on the way who wanted to know what we was at. We tied him up, and took him along.

We found Billie had everything ready at the dock, with the vessel's two custom-house watchmen and the dock watchman all tied up nice, and laid near the dock shed. We set our man along-side the others, and they laid there in a row with not a sound out of them, they being all gagged.

We then started to bend on the sails. And let me tell you we druv things. Two of the crew stayed up to the street end of the dock to take care of any curious person that might happen to start to stroll down to take a look at the *Echo*. There was three of that kind, dark as it was. The three of them was captured, two of them policemen. Fitting on the sails, we couldn't find any main tops'l in the bunch. We must have left it behind, but we couldn't stop to go back after it to the sail-loft. We were driving you see, trying to get ready in time for the ebb tide, and out of the harbor before daylight. We was all strung up, of course, thinking of what we had ahead of us. We were pretty near done with the sails, only the head sails left to fit on, when somebody said: "Skipper, what about the steam cutter? Think we'll get by her?"

Billie studied awhile. "I've been thinking of her, and I guess we'd better tend to her now. Wesley, you, Hiram and Mike Feeney come with me. The rest of you'll have time to fit those jibs while we're gone."

Billie tells us to get up about twenty fathoms of small chain and a small anchor out of the hold and put them into the dory— the dory and seine-boat was astern the *Echo*. We then paddles over toward the steam cutter. Well, now you c'n believe we did some gentle rowin' toward that cutter—oars tied up in old rags, and the chain wrapped in blankets out of the bunks below, for the first three or four fathom.

Billie himself goes overboard when we were under the stern of the cutter. We paid the chain out to him, handing it out, link by link, as if we was handing out men's lives. Billie drops under and toggles the cutter's screws with the chain—takes two or three turns around each blade. Man, but he did a careful job! When he gets back in the dory again—a water rat wouldn't ha' made so little noise—we paid out the chain—careful—oh, careful —and paddles away. When we got the chain's length out, we lowered the little anchor to the bottom, easy as could be, with a small line. Then we worked back to the *Echo,* where they had everything ready to leave.

We warped her out of the dock—oh, first, Mike Feeney goes up and covers up our row of prisoners under the shed, gives 'em a drink of water all 'round, and left 'em. They were found there in the morning, I s'pose.

So we warped her clear of the dock—the sails had been hoisted afore we stirred at all, and you may be sure we had the masts and hoops pretty well slushed. We bore down on the two cutters. By their lights we knew they were laying broadside to each other, up and down stream just as they lay that afternoon. We knew we couldn't get outside either one, so Billy pointed the *Echo* up to go between. The wind was all right—not enough for fine work— but enough for the trick, and Billie had callated the tide 'bout right—it was with us.

We bore down. Of course, we was praying to get by without being seen. But it wasn't quite dark enough for that. Our sails must've showed, for we hadn't got between them at all, when there came a hail from the steam cutter—to port she was—"What vessel's that?" We stood on a little longer, and she hailed again, and the sailin' cutter—to wind'ard—she hailed too, and they both hailed as if they meant business—"What vessel's that?"

Billie standin' by the wheel, sings out: "We're the *Echo o' the Morn,* seiner, of Gloucester. Report me, will you, tomorrow? The harbor master was off duty, and the custom-house was closed when we left."

When he got that out we could hear the greatest racket on both cutters. They began to sing out—wind'ard and loo'ard both— "Put about or we'll fire," says one. "Go back or we'll sink you," hollers the other.

"Fire and sink who?" says Billie. "You'll only sink yourselves firin' across at each other." Which was right.

They was quiet for a few seconds. Then we heard the orders to make sail aboard one and the bells from the bridge on the other. "The sailin' lad won't bother us," says Billie. "She's a square-ended old tub, and till they get that collar and neck-tie off the propeller I don't think the steam boy'll do much either."

There certainly must've been some riotin' in the hold of that steam cutter. We heard the orders to slip the cable and we imagined we could hear the engine-room bells her Captain rung from the pilothouse. There was an awful flurry astern of her, and then such howls from above and below, from the bridge and the steam department. "I callate," says Billie, "our little toggle chain and anchor's gone into action." We were sliding by all the time.

They let to a couple of shot from their bow, but we were bowlin' along by then, all of us lying flat on deck, all but Billie. He stood to the wheel, back to 'em, contemptuous like. "They're firin' wide," he says, and out of the harbor he drives her.

We were barely outside when a big steamer passed outside of us and swung in for Barnsley.

"What do you make of that?" we asks Billie.

"A cruiser from Halifax, sure's fate, come to take the *Echo* in charge. I guess we'd better take to more private courses before daylight comes along!"

We put inside the islands along the coast soon's it got so's we could see at all. It was takin' chances going inside and driving her like we were, but we had to. If we stayed outside the cruiser'd get us on her way back. We kept two men to the mast-head all that day, pickin' out channels and passages ahead. There was times when we didn't know whether she'd go another mile or another length ahead, but, as Billie said, "We got to. Pile her up along here and there's a fighting chance for the owners to get insurance money, while if we go outside, it's all up, and the owners don't get so much as a dollar out of the hull or a single barrel of them mackerel in the hold. If they intended to fine us a couple of thousand dollars afore, they'll fine her all she's worth after this, not to speak of the partic'lar jail we'd fetch up in." So we druv her along inside the coast islands.

In the middle of the afternoon the lookouts to the masthead reported smoke to the east'ard and headed our way. We were well on toward Halifax, then—along Egg Island way, twenty odd miles east of here—and Billie says: "Might's well lay her up here for a while." So we picked out a cut behind a high island and we slid in there. Some of us went and made a landing in the seine-boat and climbed up the bluff of the island. It was our cruiser of the night before sure enough, and she was everlastin'ly poundin' along. We laid low among the broken rocks, and when she went by we could make out her tops full of lookouts. By and by comes two cutters steamin' along. One of them was our Barnsley cutter—the chain and anchor lad. They went on by, with more racket than so many fire-injuns ashore.

"There'll be a rondeevoo of Her Majesty's naval forces down Massachusetts Bay this time to-morrer," says Billie, "and all in honor of the *Echo o' the Morn*. But we'll beat 'em yet, we'll beat 'em yet. Can't you see the *Echo,* boys, runnin' the blockade? We'll run for Le Have Bank to-night boys, and we'll beat 'em yet."

When dark came, we put to the west'ard and south'ard, and all night long we druv her, everlastin'ly druv her till sun-up, when the log showed a hundred miles since sunset, and we were in among the haddockin' fleet off Le Have. We hunted around for one of the firm's vessels till we found the *Buccaneer*. Crump Taylor was skipper of her then. You all know Crump, of course, so I don't need to tell you about him. Crump hadn't been thinking of going home just then, but he takes all in and comes along when Billie tells him the story. The *Quickstep,* John McLeod, the John McLeod that they call Soudan, he was all filled up and ready to leave for home. He said he'd like mighty well to wait and run home along with the two of us, when Billie told him how things stood. "Might be of use, you can't tell, and we're most out of grub anyway," says Soudan.

Well, we first fits the *Buccaneer*'s main tops'l onto the *Echo,* then swaps the *Echo*'s seine-boat for the *Buccaneer*'s dories—piles the nest of 'em in our waist, making us look like any other haddocker, and the three of us wings it out to the west'ard afore as sweet and fair a breeze as ever fanned a vessel off Le Have.

That was long 'bout dusk. Night sailin' gen'rally is best in cases like that. The next afternoon we was in sight of Massachusetts Bay, Boston, I might say, when we notices the smoke of a steamer to the west'ard coming our way. The *Buccaneer* right away—that was Crump—he begins to drag behind and points off no'therly a little—as if she had a mind for a harbor on the Maine coast. And he hauls his seine-boat—the *Echo*'s seine-boat along-side, snug up, as if he wanted to hide it.

Of course they warn't letting any maneuvre of that kind get by them on the cruiser and they makes off after Crump. The *Buccaneer* and the *Echo,* mind, was as like as two number one mackerel. The only difference that day was the *Buccaneer* carried no main tops'l which, as I said, had been put onto the *Echo*.

The cruiser comes alongside and lets go a blank at Crump. He keeps right on. Then in a little while comes another blank, which Crump didn't pay much attention to. Then comes a solid shot, close enough, it looked to us. Crump seemed a bit slow yet, and they sent another solid shot—plump through her fores'l, this one. I guess that was close enough for Crump, and he jams the *Buccaneer* into the wind and waits. Crump told us all about the rest of it afterward, for we, of course, was making long legs of it to the west'ard.

The cruiser's gig comes roundin' to under the *Buccaneer*'s stern, where Crump hung a piece of old sail, as if he wanted to hide the name, by the way. They rows alongside. A petty officer— a petty officer, mind, as if that was good enough for a fisherman —he steps aboard by way of the seine-boat, which had her name —*Echo o' the Morn*—on her as plain's could be. The navy lad smiles, reads the name, and steps over the *Buccaneer*'s rail, looks up aloft, and says, for a starter: "There's a tops'l up in a Barnsley sail-loft that would come mighty nigh to fitting that main topm'st of yours."

He says that and smiles at Crump. Crump leans agin the main riggin' in that easy way of his, and looking up at the mast-head, he says—"It do look kind of bare, don't it?"

"Yes," says the navy boy, "and I s'pose you wish to know what we want?"

"I can't say's I do," says Crump.

"P'raps you would like to hear?"

"Oh, I dunno's I'll have any melancholy night-watches if I don't hear," says Crump, "but if it'll ease *you* any, why, drive her."

Well, the cruiser lad goes on with a long mess of stuff about the American schooner, the *Echo o' the Morn,* seized by Her Majesty's cutters—the *Calenso* and the *Seal*—for violation of the Inter-national Fishing Laws Treaty, and stolen from the custody of the Dominion Gover'ment's officers on the night of August the twenty-seventh, at Barnsley, Nova Scotia, and, further, there was charges of several assaults and batteries, not only to official persons, but to private persons, and so on. It took him nigh fifteen minutes to tell it all.

"Long live the Queen," says Crump, and spits over the rail— you know Crump's way—"that's all official, I s'pose?"

"Yes, sir—and be careful." The navy lad was pretty hot.

"Yes?" says Crump.

"Yes," fires back the navy lad.

"Well, you said it pretty nice, but what's it got to do with me?"

"What's it got—do you deny that you are the American fishing schooner, the *Echo o' the Morn?*"

"We're certainly a fisherman," answers Crump, "there's our gurry kids on deck under your nose, and a hundred thousand of fresh fish in the hold, if you want more proof, and we're certainly American—there's our flag to the peak for that—but it's most interestin' news to me that we're the *Echo o' the Morn,* though I'll admit we do look something like her, the two of them having been built off the same moulds and rigged to the same plans."

The navy lad only grins and looks over the side and points to the name on the seine-boat.

"Ho, ho," laughs Crump, as if he'd just caught on, "ho, ho." The Englishman smiles and Crump goes on. "You're the boys for cuteness, you navy lads. But gen'rally down our way, when we want to get at a vessel's name, we look at what it says astern of her or on the trailboard under her bow for'ard"; and, mind you, the canvas was hanging over the stern and the letters for'ard so chaffed that you couldn't have read 'em twenty feet away.

The Englishman smiles his everlastin' smile and sings out to his boat's crew to drop astern and look at the name. "We have to be certain," he says.

One of the men in the boat lifts the canvas and peeks underneath.

"What name?" sings out the petty officer, all ready to smile at Crump.

"Buccaneer, of Gloucester."

"What?" he screeches. He runs aft, pulls the canvas clear, leans way over and looks for himself. Then he runs for'ard, bends over the knightheads, and spells it out there. Back he comes, not quite so spry. "I've heard of such things as painting over names. Don't carry this thing too far," he bellows at Crump. "Yes," says Crump, "it do look like fresh paint, don't it?" "That will do," roars the navy lad. "Where are your papers?" Crump makes a great bluff to study some more. Fin'lly he says, turning to the crew: "Boys, let you all bear witness to this thing, for a claim for damages'll come out of it sure's I'm skipper of this vessel and my name's Henry Taylor. This man—bear witness to all I say, boys—this man is acting outside of his rights now, but it must never be said that Gloucester fishermen don't abide by the law." And he goes on for ten minutes or so in a patriotic way till the navy lad won't stand for any more of it. After that Crump uses up about twenty minutes finding his papers below. Of course the papers were all right. When the Englishman, after looking them all over, had handed them back, and as they were going up on deck again, Crump says, "Of course I might've shifted those papers, too, or made 'em myself or something like that. If you like you can step down to the fo'c's'le and see whether all the tin pans and cook's dishes is properly marked, or——"

"You could have exchanged outfits just the same. You could have met this vessel—" My, but he was hoppin' 'round, accordin' to Crump, and you oughter heard Crump tell it.

"Yes," goes on Crump, "maybe, and swapped suits of sails, too. In the leach of that fores'l that's handy to you there maybe you c'n make out where the word *Buccaneer* is stenciled on—not that I ain't saying it wouldn't be possible to swap sails, too—I've heard of such things as fitting on sails in a hurry. I've——"

"That will do. Where'd you get that seine-boat?"

"And of course," goes on Crump, paying no attention, "the *Echo o' the Morn*, being a mackerel catcher, would be likely to have gurry kids all over her deck, wouldn't she? And her hold full of fresh haddock and cod and the like. Lift the main hatch there, boys, and show the gentleman."

"Where did you get that seine-boat?" yelled the navy boy.

"On Le Have," yells back Crump. "Blowed aboard on Le Have at the same time we lost our dories and our tops'l. An awful blow. In all my experience——"

"A blow on Le Have? See here, there's been no blow off that way reported in Halifax lately."

"Maybe not—maybe—but there's lots of things happens on Le Have that ain't reported in Halifax."

The Englishman was fair boiling now, but at the same time he was beginning to come out of his dream. All of a sudden, Crump says, he puts his glasses onto the *Echo* and the *Quickstep* and then all at once he wakes up, jumps into the gig, and sings out, "Pull away, pull."

"Good-by," calls out Crump after him in his sociable way, "and next time you happen to be in Barnsley you might send me the tops'l you think would fit us so well. Mark it 'Henry C. Taylor, Master Schooner *Buccaneer*, Gloucester, Massachusetts, U. S. A.,' and I'll be sure to get it. Good-by," hollers Crump again, "and I'll pay the freight," but he says he didn't get any answer.

Well the cruiser was pretty near hull down to us on the *Echo* when she came 'round on her heel again, thanks to Crump, and it was getting pretty late in the afternoon. We could see by the way smoke was coming out of her that they were driving her. But the wind holding, we knew she couldn't get us short of two hours, and that gave us time to do something, with the night coming on.

The last thing we did on the *Echo* for the cruiser's partic'lar benefit was to rig up our side-lights on the blades of two long seiner's oars and lash 'em straight up in a dory. That raised them up about as high as side-lights ought to be, y' see. The dory was lowered over the side and I dropped into her. Billie heaves a splitting-knife after me, and says, "You'll need that." There was an everlastin' long painter—a forty-fathom line—coiled in her bow. Billie hails Soudan and tells him what to do. Soudan throws the *Quickstep* up and waits for us. The *Echo* hauls across the *Quickstep*'s bow and Billie casts me off. I heaves the long painter to the *Quickstep* and they takes it and drops me astern. The *Echo* goes winging off with nary a light up at all, and me in the dory, and the dory like any vessel with her lights up proper, being towed along in the wake of the *Quickstep,* and she hauling away for Minot's Light as if she was crazy to get to Boston.

When the cruiser overhauled us—I could hear her screws long before she got to us—she ranges up to starboard and sings out for us to heave to. "Both of you," hollers the voice. I couldn't see her clear, except for her lights, but I could hear her plain enough, for she lets go a blank at the same time that makes me feel like curling up in the dory. "Bless me," thinks I, "if they ever send one of those six-inch boys aboard o' this dory, where'll I be?" I was praying that Soudan wouldn't try any of Crump's tricks and be too slow to come to.

But Soudan throws her up pretty prompt and waits. Then I heard the cruiser's falls makin' ready to lower away a boat and it was my move. I outs with my splitting-knife and cuts down the red light to get that out of the way. That being to port, of course they couldn't see it, and I puts it out and heaves it overboard. Then I cuts away the starboard oar below, slashes the lashin's from the light—the green light, toward them—opens the slide, blows out the light and heaves that over—all this jumpin', mind you. Then I cuts the dory's painter free, jumps overboard with the bight of the painter, and hits out for the *Quickstep*. Let me tell you I was drivin'.

I hadn't got fair started, hauling myself along by the painter and under water most of the time, when I hears:

"Aboard the le'ward schooner, there! Put up your side-lights again, or we'll fire."

Of course I didn't say anything to that, but keeps on.

They hollers again, gets no answer, and then—boom! Man! And boom!—another one. "Bless me!" thinks I, "if one of them goes astray and gets me in the small of the back—" But all the time I was putting in big strokes for the *Quickstep*, my hair fair curlin' up with thinking of one of those shells jibing to wind'ard and ketching me.

Anyway, I got aboard. It was Soudan helped me over the stern of the *Quickstep*.

"Are you all right?" he says.

"All right," says I, "but I guess the dory's shook up some."

"Yes," he says. "They've spoiled her carryin' capacity by this time, I guess. There's number eight—they'll be giving her a broadside soon." Boom!—Boom!—Boom!—they went. 'Bout this time they must have figured out they'd blown the *Echo* out the water, so they stopped shootin'. Then we could hear their boats rowin' our way and soon we made out one of them heading for us. There was a petty officer in charge of the one coming to board us—the same lad that boarded the *Buccaneer*, we found out, when we swapped stories with Crump afterward.

"I say," this lad sings out, "she didn't get away that time, did she?" And he steps over the rail.

"No," says Soudan. "I guess you fixed her that time."

Pretty soon the second boat comes alongside. This one had a sure-enough officer, a lootenant, in charge. He was sorter worked up. "Captain," he says to Soudan, "I'm sorry for those men. Here's all we found, an oar and some pieces of a dory, apparently, and some lines with hooks in a half-barrel—trawls, you call them?"

"A tub of trawls, I guess," says Soudan. "Fetch a torch, boys." He looks and goes on: "Yes, that's one of their tubs of trawls, sure enough."

"We could find nothing else. Isn't it queer?" says the officer.

"The tides hereaway are queer," says Soudan, without so much as a wink. "We are now over a most peculiar place, on one edge of Middle Bank, in Massachusetts Bay, and there's queerer spots here than was ever in the Bay of Fundy or on the Grand Banks."

"Really?" says the officer.

"Yes," says Soudan, "for queer tides and eddies this is the spot. There's been some mysterious disappearances traced to here. But, letting that go, this is a bad business, Lootenant, blowing up the *Echo*."

"Yes, it certainly is bad—horrible. But they should not have put their lights out as they did. What were they thinking of—she directly under our guns!"

"Yes," says Soudan, "Billie oughter had more respect for a real man-o'-war. Maybe he thought you was only a cutter in the dark?"

"Thought? Didn't he see us just before dark, when we boarded the other ship, the *Buccaneer?*"

"Yes," says Soudan, "he did. He must have. I saw you and he must have. But it's liable to lead to big things, to international complications—in-ter-nation-al compli-ca-tions"—he rolls it out like an election orator—"it may ter-min-ate in bloody war," says Soudan.

"War?" says the officer, studying, "war?"

"Or eye-dem-ity," says Soudan, swellin' out with happiness to think of so fine a word just then.

"Possibly—very likely—yes, yes, most likely," says the officer. Then he takes down Soudan's full name, name of vessel, name of vessel's owner, gets all the figures he can about the *Echo*—Soudan raising the builder's price a few thousand—gets Billie's name, and names of crew and all that. Then he puts off, goes back to the cruiser, the petty officer with him, and they steams off—her course about east by south, which would clear Cape Sable and put her on her way to Halifax, where I s'pose she got in next night with her bearings all hot and a great deal to tell.

Next morning, when we came into Gloucester in the *Quickstep,* there was the *Echo* lying in the stream and her colors all set, the sassiest-looking vessel in the whole North Atlantic. The city was just getting warmed up to the thing when we arrived. The newspapers had been full of the seizure down East. England, they said, was trying to crowd us on the fishery laws and the United States was a little slow picking it up, and so the country was boiling over when they heard about the *Echo*'s escape. It was speeches, mass meetings and editorials and lots of people got a chance to blow off steam. When the *Echo* was reported escaped, there warn't many ever really thought she'd get by the cutters and the cruiser that was known to be after her. Then there was the three days or so when they didn't know where she was. So all Gloucester came running down to the docks when the word was passed that she was home. "The *Echo*'s in—the *Echo*'s in," was ringing all over Gloucester like a fire alarm. The *Quickstep* and *Buccaneer* coming in four or five hours afterward had cannons fired for 'em as they sailed up the harbor, but that was only the overflow—it was the *Echo*'s crew that got it. People came from everywhere to look at the *Echo* and shake hands with Billie and us. It was Captain William Simms and the darin' crew of the *Echo o' the Morn.* Yes, sir. They wrote songs about it—and City Hall was lit up and there was bonfires in the middle of Main Street. And there was parades with red and blue and green lights and all kinds of queer fireworks. One showed the *Echo* running through a fleet of men-o'-war, every blessed one of 'em blazing broadsides at her and she never losing a spar. For a few days lots of people didn't do a tap of work—just stood on the curb-stones and talked about the *Echo.* Whenever one of us showed up there'd be a rush and we'd have to tell how it happened all over again. We was given the freedom of the city. There was a purse made up and we got a hundred and fifty dollars apiece out of that, besides a good share from the two hundred barrels in her hold, which fetched patriotic prices, everybody wantin' to get hold of some of the *Echo*'s mackerel. It beat reg'lar fishin' all out. Billie got a big solid silver punch-bowl, and there was smaller bowls for the rest of us, and they gave me a monstrous big meersh'm pipe, gold mounted, with my name in gold letters on the case. That was for standing by the lights in the dory, they said. And—what you say? Ever smoke that pipe? H-m-m—no more than I'm smoking this one now—I wonder how long it's been out?

The Type of James B. Connolly's Stories: So wholly has James B. Connolly limited his writing to sea stories that the very mention of his name seems to carry with it the tang of salt water. Other writers may surpass him in the wider scope of their talents; few equal him in the ability to create the atmosphere which is half the telling of a sea story; in the ability to portray the characters of sailors and fishermen so truly that even a landlubber knows they cannot be otherwise; or in the ability to spin a yarn in the manner which is the seadog's salty secret.

For Appreciation: "Echo o' the Morn" appears in *Gloucestermen,* published in 1930, Mr. Connolly's own selection from his celebrated stories of the Gloucester Fishing Fleet. How did Billie show a bit of humor in addition to his originality? Why did the English cruiser mistake the *Buccaneer* for the *Echo?* Why were the people of Gloucester so jubilant over the *Echo's* escape?

For Further Study: By using nautical terms of everyday speech, even when no sailor is speaking, the author helps create the atmosphere he wants. Find instances in which this device is used, and by substituting landsmen's language see how colorful is this use of nautical language.

A short story always presents a problem to be solved; the plot development consists in the solving. What is the problem in "Echo o' the Morn"? At what point in the story do you first recognize it? The writer arouses curiosity and interest by hinting now and then at an element in the solution of the problem. Can you find such a hint early in the story?

Give the meaning of the following words and phrases: *cutter; three-mile limit; fore and aft; ebb; tops'l; mast-head; in the stays; dory.*

Exercise and Creative Work: Draw a map and chart the course followed by the *Echo* in its escape.

Sailors are not the only people who apply the language of their calling or major interest to other fields of activity. Retell an incident—it need not be original—in the language of an ardent fisherman, golf fiend, garage man, baseball fan, beauty-shop operator; for that matter, choose any type of person you prefer.

Choose sides and debate, using the following statement as resolution: Resolved: That the conduct of the crew of the *Echo* in effecting their escape was justifiable.

THE FAT OF THE LAND

Anzia Yezierska

I

In an air-shaft so narrow that you could touch the next wall with your bare hands, Hanneh Breineh leaned out and knocked on her neighbor's window.

"Can you loan me your wash-boiler for the clothes?" she said.

Mrs. Pelz threw up the sash.

"The boiler? What's the matter with yours again? Didn't you tell me you had it fixed already last week?"

"A black year on him, the robber, the way he fixed it! If you have no luck in this world, then it's better not to live. There I spent out fifteen cents to stop up one hole, and it runs out another. How I ate out my gall bargaining with him he should let it down to fifteen cents! He wanted yet a quarter, the swindler. Gottuniu! my bitter heart on him for every penny he took from me for nothing!"

"You got to watch all those swindlers, or they'll steal the whites out of your eyes," admonished Mrs. Pelz. "You should have tried out your boiler before you paid him. Wait a minute till I empty out my dirty clothes in a pillow-case; then I'll hand it to you."

174

Mrs. Pelz returned with the boiler and tried to hand it across to Hanneh Breineh, but the soap-box refrigerator on the window-sill was in the way.

"You got to come in for the boiler yourself," said Mrs. Pelz.

"Wait only till I tie my Sammy on to the high-chair he shouldn't fall on me again. He's so wild that ropes won't hold him."

Hanneh Breineh tied the child in the chair, stuck a pacifier in his mouth, and went in to her neighbor. As she took the boiler Mrs. Pelz said:

"Do you know Mrs. Melker ordered fifty pounds of chicken for her daughter's wedding? And such grand chickens! Shining like gold! My heart melted in me just looking at the flowing fatness of those chickens."

Hanneh Breineh smacked her thin, dry lips, a hungry gleam in her sunken eyes.

"Fifty pounds!" she gasped. "It ain't possible. How do you know?"

"I heard her with my own ears. I saw them with my own eyes. And she said she will chop up the chicken livers with onions and eggs for an appetizer, and then she will buy twenty-five pounds of fish, and cook it sweet and sour with raisins, and she said she will bake all her strudels on pure chicken fat."

"Some people work themselves up in the world," sighed Hanneh Breineh. "For them is America flowing with milk and honey. In Savel Mrs. Melker used to get shriveled up from hunger. She and her children used to live on potato-peelings and crusts of dry bread picked out from the barrels; and in America she lives to eat chicken, and apple strudels soaking in fat."

"The world is a wheel always turning," philosophized Mrs. Pelz. "Those who were high go down low, and those who've been low go up higher. Who will believe me here in America that in Poland I was a cook in a banker's house? I handled ducks and geese every day. I used to bake coffee-cake with cream so thick you could cut it with a knife."

"And do you think I was a nobody in Poland?" broke in Hanneh Breineh, tears welling in her eyes as the memories of her past rushed over her. "But what's the use of talking? In

America money is everything. Who cares who my father or grandfather was in Poland? Without money I'm a living dead one. My head dries out worrying how to get for the children the eating a penny cheaper."

Mrs. Pelz wagged her head, a gnawing envy contracting her features.

"Mrs. Melker had it good from the day she came," she said begrudgingly. "Right away she sent all her children to the factory, and she began to cook meat for dinner every day. She and her children have eggs and buttered rolls for breakfast each morning like millionaires."

A sudden fall and a baby's scream, and the boiler dropped from Hanneh Breineh's hands as she rushed into her kitchen, Mrs. Pelz after her. They found the high-chair turned on top of the baby.

"Gevalt! Save me! Run for a doctor!" cried Hanneh Breineh as she dragged the child from under the high-chair. "He's killed! He's killed! My only child! My precious lamb!" she shrieked as she ran back and forth with the screaming infant.

Mrs. Pelz snatched little Ṣammy from the mother's hands.

"Mushugneh! What are you running around like a crazy, frightening the child? Let me see. Let me tend to him. He ain't killed yet." She hastened to the sink to wash the child's face, and discovered a swelling lump on his forehead. "Have you a quarter in your house?" she asked.

"Yes, I got one," replied Hanneh Breineh, climbing on a chair. "I got to keep it on a high shelf where the children can't get it."

Mrs. Pelz seized the quarter Hanneh Breineh handed down to her.

"Now pull your left eyelid three times while I'm pressing the quarter, and you'll see the swelling go down."

Hanneh Breineh took the child again in her arms, shaking and cooing over it and caressing it.

"Ah-ah-ah, Sammy! Ah-ah-ah-ah, little lamb! Ah-ah-ah, little bird. Ah-ah-ah-ah, precious heart! Oh, you saved my life; I thought he was killed," gasped Hanneh Breineh, turning to Mrs. Pelz. "Oi-i!" she sighed, "a mother's heart! Always in fear over her children. The minute anything happens to them all life goes out of me. I lose my head and I don't know where I am any more."

"No wonder the child fell," admonished Mrs. Pelz. "You should have a red ribbon or red beads on his neck to keep away the evil eye. Wait. I got something in my machine-drawer."

Mrs. Pelz returned, bringing the boiler and a red string, which she tied about the child's neck while the mother proceeded to fill the boiler.

A little later Hanneh Breineh again came into Mrs. Pelz's kitchen, holding Sammy in one arm and in the other an apron full of potatoes. Putting the child down on the floor, she seated herself on the unmade kitchen-bed and began to peel the potatoes in her apron.

"Woe to me!" sobbed Hanneh Breineh. "To my bitter luck there ain't no end. With all my other troubles, the stove got broke'. I lighted the fire to boil the clothes, and it's to get choked with smoke. I paid rent only a week ago, and the agent don't want to fix it. A thunder should strike him! He only comes for the rent, and if anything has to be fixed, then he don't want to hear nothing.

"Why comes it to me so hard?" went on Hanneh Breineh, the tears streaming down her cheeks. "I can't stand it no more. I came into you for a minute to run away from my troubles. It's only when I sit myself down to peel potatoes or nurse the baby that I take time to draw a breath, and beg only for death."

Mrs. Pelz, accustomed to Hanneh Breineh's bitter outbursts, continued her scrubbing.

"Ut!" exclaimed Hanneh Breineh, irritated at her neighbor's silence, "what are you tearing up the world with your cleaning? What's the use to clean up when everything only gets dirty again?"

"I got to shine up my house for the holidays."

"You've got it so good nothing lays on your mind but to clean your house. Look on this little blood-sucker," said Hanneh Breineh, pointing to the wizened child, made prematurely solemn from starvation and neglect. "Could anybody keep that brat clean? I wash him one minute, and he is dirty the minute after." Little Sammy grew frightened and began to cry. "Shut up!" ordered the mother, picking up the child to nurse it again. "Can't you see me take a rest for a minute?"

The hungry child began to cry at the top of its weakened lungs.

"Na, na, you glutton." Hanneh Breineh took out a dirty pacifier from her pocket and stuffed it into the baby's mouth. The grave, pasty-faced infant shrank into a panic of fear, and chewed the nipple nervously, clinging to it with both his thin little hands.

"For what did I need yet the sixth one?" groaned Hanneh Breineh, turning to Mrs. Pelz. "Wasn't it enough five mouths to feed? If I didn't have this child on my neck, I could turn myself around and earn a few cents." She rang her hands in a passion of despair. "Gottuniu! the earth should only take it before it grows up!"

"Pshaw! pshaw!" reproved Mrs. Pelz. "Pity yourself on the child. Let it grow up already so long as it is here. See how frightened it looks on you." Mrs. Pelz took the child in her arms and petted it. "The poor little lamb! What did it done you should hate it so?"

Hanneh Breineh pushed Mrs. Pelz away from her.

"To whom can I open the wounds of my heart?" she moaned. "Nobody has pity on me. You don't believe me, nobody believes me until I'll fall down like a horse in the middle of the street. Oi weh! mine life is so black for my eyes. Some mothers got luck. A child gets run over by a car, some fall from a window, some burn themselves up with a match, some get choked with diphtheria; but no death takes mine away."

"God from the world! stop cursing!" admonished Mrs. Pelz. "What do you want from the poor children? Is it their fault that their father makes small wages? Why do you let it all out on them?" Mrs. Pelz sat down beside Hanneh Breineh. "Wait only till your children get old enough to go to the shop and earn money," she consoled. "Push only through those few years while they are yet small; your sun will begin to shine, you will live on the fat of the land, when they begin to bring you in the wages each week."

Hanneh Breineh refused to be comforted.

"Till they are old enough to go to the shop and earn money they'll eat the head off my bones," she wailed. "If you only knew the fights I got by each meal. Maybe I gave Abe a bigger piece of bread than Fanny. Maybe Fanny got a little more soup in her plate than Jake. Eating is dearer than diamonds. Potatoes went up a cent on a pound, and milk is only for millionaires. And once a week, when I buy a little meat for the Sabbath, the butcher weighs it for me like gold, with all the bones in it. When I come to lay the meat out on a plate and divide it up, there ain't nothing to it but bones. Before, he used to throw me in a piece of fat extra or a piece of lung, but now you got to pay for everything, even for a bone to the soup."

"Never mind; you'll yet come out from all your troubles. Just as soon as your children get old enough to get their working papers [1] the more children you got, the more money you'll have."

"Why should I fool myself with the false shine of hope? Don't I know it's already my black luck not to have it good in this world? Do you think American children will right away give everything they earn to their mother?"

"I know what is with you the matter," said Mrs. Pelz. "You didn't eat yet to-day. When it is empty in the stomach, the whole world looks black. Come, only let me give you something good to taste in the mouth; that will freshen you up." Mrs. Pelz went to the cupboard and brought out the saucepan of gefulte fish that she had cooked for dinner and placed it on the table in front of Hanneh Breineh. "Give a taste my fish," she said, taking one slice on a spoon, and handing it to Hanneh Breineh with a piece of bread. "I wouldn't give it to you on a plate because I just cleaned up my house, and I don't want to dirty up more dishes."

"What, am I a stranger you should have to serve me on a plate yet!" cried Hanneh Breineh, snatching the fish in her trembling fingers.

"Oi weh! How it melts through all the bones!" she exclaimed, brightening as she ate. "May it be for good luck to us all!" she exulted, waving aloft the last precious bite.

Mrs. Pelz was so flattered that she even ladled up a spoonful of gravy.

---

[1] WORKING PAPERS—State permits to allow children in New York State to stop school and begin working at the age of sixteen.

"There is a bit of onion and carrot in it," she said as she handed it to her neighbor.

Hanneh Breineh sipped the gravy drop by drop, like a connoisseur sipping wine.

"Ah-h-h! A taste of that gravy lifts me up to heaven!" As she disposed leisurely of the slice of onion and carrot she relaxed and expanded and even grew jovial. "Let us wish all our troubles on the Russian Czar! Let him burst with our worries for rent! Let him get shriveled with our hunger for bread! Let his eyes dry out of his head looking for work!

"Pshaw! I'm forgetting from everything," she exclaimed, jumping up. "It must be eleven or soon twelve, and my children will be right away out of school and fall on me like a pack of wild wolves. I better quick run to the market and see what cheaper I can get for a quarter."

Because of the lateness of her coming, the stale bread at the nearest bakeshop was sold out, and Hanneh Breineh had to trudge from shop to shop in search of the usual bargain, and spent nearly an hour to save two cents.

In the meantime the children returned from school, and, finding the door locked, climbed through the fire escape, and entered the house through the window. Seeing nothing on the table, they rushed to the stove. Abe pulled a steaming potato out of the boiling pot, and so scalded his fingers that the potato fell to the floor; whereupon the three others pounced on it.

"It was my potato," cried Abe, blowing his burned fingers, while with the other hand and his foot he cuffed and kicked the three who were struggling on the floor. A wild fight ensued, and the potato was smashed under Abe's foot amid shouts and screams. Hanneh Breineh, on the stairs, heard the noise of her famished brood, and topped their cries with curses and invectives.

"They are here already, the savages! They are here already to shorten my life! They heard you all over the hall, in all the houses around!"

The children, disregarding her words, pounced on her market-basket, shouting ravenously: "Mama, I'm hungry! What more do you got to eat?"

They tore the bread and herring out of Hanneh Breineh's basket and devoured it in starved savagery, clamoring for more.

"Murderers!" screamed Hanneh Breineh, goaded beyond endurance. "What are you tearing from me my flesh? From where should I steal to give you more? Here I had already a pot of potatoes and a whole loaf of bread and two herrings, and you swallowed it down in the wink of an eye. I have to have Rockefeller's millions to fill your stomachs."

All at once Hanneh Breineh became aware that Benny was missing. "Oi weh!" she burst out, wringing her hands in a new wave of woe, "Where is Benny? Didn't he come home yet from school?"

She ran out into the hall, opened the grime-coated window, and looked up and down the street; but Benny was nowhere in sight.

"Abe, Jake, Fanny, quick, find Benny!" entreated Hanneh Breineh as she rushed back into the kitchen. But the children, anxious to snatch a few minutes' play before the school-call, dodged past her and hurried out.

With the baby on her arm, Hanneh Breineh hastened to the kindergarten.

"Why are you keeping Benny here so long?" she shouted at the teacher as she flung open the door. "If you had my bitter heart, you would send him home long ago and not wait till I got to come for him."

The teacher turned calmly and consulted her record-cards. "Benny Safron? He wasn't present this morning."

"Not here?" shrieked Hanneh Breineh. "I pushed him out myself he should go. The children didn't want to take him, and I had no time. Woe is me! Where is my child?" She began pulling her hair and beating her breast as she ran into the street.

Mrs. Pelz was busy at a push-cart, picking over some spotted apples, when she heard the clamor of an approaching crowd. A block off she recognized Hanneh Breineh, her hair disheveled, her clothes awry, running toward her with her yelling baby in her arms, the crowd following.

"Friend mine," cried Hanneh Breineh, falling on Mrs. Pelz's neck, "I lost my Benny, the best child of all my children." Tears streamed down her red, swollen eyes as she sobbed. "Benny! Mine heart, mine life! Oi-i-i!"

Mrs. Pelz took the frightened baby out of the mother's arms.

"Still yourself a little! See how you're frightening your child."

"Woe to me! Where is my Benny? Maybe he's killed already by a car. Maybe he fainted away from hunger. He didn't eat nothing all day long. Gottuniu! Pity yourself on me!"

She lifted her hands full of tragic entreaty.

"People, my child! Get me my child! I'll go crazy out of my head! Get me my child, or I'll take poison before your eyes!"

"Still yourself a little!" pleaded Mrs. Pelz.

"Talk not to me!" cried Hanneh Breineh, wringing her hands. "You're having all your children. I lost mine. Every good luck comes to other people. But I didn't live yet to see a good day in my life. Mine only joy, mine Benny, is lost away from me."

The crowd followed Hanneh Breineh as she wailed through the streets, leaning on Mrs. Pelz. By the time she returned to her house the children were back from school; but seeing that Benny was not there, she chased them out in the street, crying:

"Out of here, you robbers, gluttons! Go find Benny!" Hanneh Breineh crumpled into a chair in utter prostration. "Oi weh! He's lost! Mine life; my little bird; mine only joy! How many nights I spent nursing him when he had the measles! And all that I suffered for weeks and months when he had the whooping-cough! How the eyes went out of my head till I learned him how to walk, till I learned him how to talk! And such a smart child! If I lost all the others, it wouldn't tear me so by the heart."

She worked herself up into such a hysteria, crying, and tearing her hair, and hitting her head with her knuckles, that at last she fell into a faint. It took some time before Mrs. Pelz, with the aid of neighbors, revived her.

"Benny, mine angel!" she moaned as she opened her eyes.

Just then a policeman came in with the lost Benny.

"Na, na, here you got him already!" said Mrs. Pelz. "Why did you carry on so for nothing? Why did you tear up the world like a crazy?"

The child's face was streaked with tears as he cowered, frightened and forlorn. Hanneh Breineh sprang toward him, slapping his cheeks, boxing his ears, before the neighbors could rescue him from her.

"Woe on your head!" cried the mother. "Where did you lost yourself? Ain't I got enough worries on my head than to go around looking for you? I didn't have yet a minute's peace from that child since he was born."

"See a crazy mother!" remonstrated Mrs. Pelz, rescuing Benny from another beating. "Such a mouth! With one breath she blesses him when he is lost, and with the other breath she curses him when he is found."

Hanneh Breineh took from the window-sill a piece of herring covered with swarming flies, and putting it on a slice of dry bread, she filled a cup of tea that had been stewing all day, and dragged Benny over to the table to eat.

But the child, choking with tears, was unable to touch the food.

"Go eat!" commanded Hanneh Breineh. "Eat and choke yourself eating!"

II

"MAYBE she won't remember me no more. Maybe the servant won't let me in," thought Mrs. Pelz as she walked by the brownstone house on Eighty-fourth Street where she had been told Hanneh Breineh now lived. At last she summoned up enough courage to climb the steps. She was all out of breath as she rang the bell with trembling fingers. "Oi weh! Even the outside smells riches and plenty! Such curtains! And shades on all windows like by millionaires! Twenty years ago she used to eat from the pot to the hand, and now she lives in such a palace."

A whiff of steam-heated warmth swept over Mrs. Pelz as the door opened, and she saw her old friend of the tenements dressed in silk and diamonds like a being from another world.

"Mrs. Pelz, is it you!" cried Hanneh Breineh, overjoyed at the sight of her former neighbor. "Come right in. Since when are you back in New York?"

"We came last week," mumbled Mrs. Pelz as she was led into a richly carpeted reception-room.

"Make yourself comfortable. Take off your shawl," urged Hanneh Breineh.

"See a crazy mother!" remonstrated Mrs. Pelz.

But Mrs. Pelz only drew her shawl more tightly around her, a keen sense of her poverty gripping her as she gazed, abashed by the luxurious wealth that shone from every corner.

"This shawl covers up my rags," she said, trying to hide her shabby sweater.

"I'll tell you what; come right into the kitchen," suggested Hanneh Breineh. "The servant is away for this afternoon, and we can feel more comfortable there. I can breathe like a free person in my kitchen when the girl has her day out."

Mrs. Pelz glanced about her in an excited daze. Never in her life had she seen anything so wonderful as a white tiled kitchen, with its glistening porcelain sink and the aluminum pots and pans that shone like silver.

"Where are you staying now?" asked Hanneh Breineh as she pinned an apron over her silk dress.

"I moved back to Delancey Street, where we used to live," replied Mrs. Pelz as she seated herself cautiously in a white enameled chair.

"Oi weh! What grand times we had in that old house when we were neighbors!" sighed Hanneh Breineh, looking at her old friend with misty eyes.

"You still think on Delancey Street? Haven't you more high-class neighbors up-town here?"

"A good neighbor is not to be found every day," deplored Hanneh Breineh. "Up-town here, where each lives in his own house, nobody cares if the person next door is dying or going crazy from loneliness. It ain't anything like we used to have it in Delancey Street, when we could walk into one another's rooms without knocking, and borrow a pinch of salt or a pot to cook in."

Hanneh Breineh went over to the pantry-shelf.

"We are going to have a bite right here on the kitchen-table like on Delancey Street. So long there's no servant to watch us we can eat what we please."

"Oi! How it waters my mouth with appetite, the smell the herring and onion!" chuckles Mrs. Pelz, sniffling the welcome odors with greedy pleasure.

Hanneh Breineh pulled a dish-towel from the rack and threw one end of it to Mrs. Pelz.

"So long there's no servant around, we can use it together for a napkin. It's dirty, anyhow. How it freshens up my heart to see you!" she rejoiced as she poured out her tea into a saucer. "If you would only know how I used to beg my daughter to write for me a letter to you; but these American children, what is to them a mother's feelings?"

"What are you talking!" cried Mrs. Pelz. "The whole world rings with you and your children. Everybody is envying you. Tell me how began your luck?"

"You heard how my husband died with consumption," replied Hanneh Breineh. "The five-hundred-dollars lodge money gave me the first lift in life, and I opened a little grocery store. Then my son Abe married himself to a girl with a thousand dollars. That started him in business, and now he has the biggest shirt-waist factory on West Twenty-ninth Street."

"Yes, I heard your son had a factory." Mrs. Pelz hesitated and stammered; "I'll tell you the truth. What I came to ask you—I thought maybe you would beg your son Abe if he would give my husband a job."

"Why not?" said Hanneh Breineh. "He keeps more than five hundred hands. I'll ask him he should take in Mr. Pelz."

"Long years on you, Hanneh Breineh! You'll save my life if you could only help my husband get work."

"Of course my son will help him. All my children like to do good. My daughter Fanny is a milliner on Fifth Avenue, and she takes in the poorest girls in her shop and even pays them sometimes while they learn the trade." Hanneh Breineh's face lit up, and her chest filled with pride as she enumerated the successes of her children. "And my son Benny he wrote a play on Broadway and he gave away more than a hundred free tickets for the first night."

"Benny? The one who used to get lost from home all the time? You always did love that child more than all the rest. And what is Sammy your baby doing?"

"He ain't a baby no longer. He goes to college and quarterbacks the football team. They can't get along without him.

"And my son Jake, I nearly forgot him. He began collecting rent in Delancey Street, and now he is boss of renting the swellest apartment-houses on Riverside Drive."

"What did I tell you? In America children are like money

in the bank," purred Mrs. Pelz as she pinched and patted Hanneh Breineh's silk sleeve. "Oi weh! How it shines from you! You ought to kiss the air and dance for joy and happiness. It is such a bitter frost outside; a pail of coal is so dear, and you got it so warm with steam-heat. I had to pawn my feather-bed to have enough for the rent, and you are rolling in money."

"Yes, I got it good in some ways, but money ain't everything," sighed Hanneh Breineh.

"You ain't yet satisfied?"

"But here I got no friends," complained Hanneh Breineh.

"Friends?" queried Mrs. Pelz. "What greater friend is there on earth than the dollar?"

"Oi! Mrs. Pelz, if you could only look into my heart! I'm so choked up! You know they say, a cow has a long tongue, but can't talk." Hanneh Breineh shook her head wistfully, and her eyes filmed with inward brooding. "My children give me everything from the best. When I was sick, they got me a nurse by day and one by night. They bought me the best wine. If I asked for dove's milk, they would buy it for me; but— but—I can't talk myself out in their language. They want to make me over for an American lady, and I'm different." Tears cut their way under her eyelids with a pricking pain as she went on: "When I was poor, I was free, and could holler and do what I like in my own house. Here I got to lie still like a mouse under a broom."

The door-bell rang, and Hanneh Breineh jumped up with a start.

"Oi weh! It must be the servant back already!" she exclaimed as she tore off her apron. "Oi weh! Let's quickly put the dishes together in a dish-pan. If she sees I eat on the kitchen table, she will look on me like the dirt under her feet."

Mrs. Pelz seized her shawl in haste.

"I better run home quick in my rags before your servant sees me."

"I'll speak to Abe about the job," said Hanneh Breineh as she pushed a bill into the hand of Mrs. Pelz, who edged out as the servant entered.

III

"I'm having fried potato lotkes special for you, Benny," said Hanneh Breineh as the children gathered about the table for the family dinner given in honor of Benny's success with his new play. "Do you remember how you used to lick the fingers from them?"

"O, Mother!" reproved Fanny. "Anyone hearing you would think we were still in the push-cart district."

"Stop your nagging, Sis, and let ma alone," commanded Benny, patting his mother's arm affectionately. "I'm home only once a month. Let her feed me what she pleases. My stomach is bomb-proof."

"Do I hear that the President is coming to your play?" said Abe as he stuffed a napkin over his diamond-studded shirt-front.

"Why shouldn't he come?" returned Benny. "The critics say it's the greatest antidote for the race hatred created by the war. If you want to know, he is coming to-night; and what's more, our box is next to the President's."

"Nu, Mammeh," sallied Jake, "did you ever dream in Delancey Street that we should rub sleeves with the President?"

"I always said that Benny had more head than the rest of you," replied the mother.

As the laughter died away, Jake went on:

"Honor you are getting plenty; but how much mezummen[1] does this play bring you? Can I invest any of it in real estate for you?"

"I'm getting ten per cent royalties of the gross receipts," replied the youthful playwright.

"How much is that?" queried Hanneh Breineh.

"Enough to buy up all your fishmarkets in Delancey Street," laughed Abe in good-natured raillery at his mother.

Her son's jest cut like a knife-thrust in her heart. She felt her heart ache with the pain that she was shut out from their successes. Each added triumph only widened the gulf. And when she tried to bridge this gulf by asking questions, they only thrust her back upon herself.

"Your fame has even helped me get my hat trade solid with

[1] Mezummen—Money.

the Four Hundred," put in Fanny. "You bet I let Mrs. Van Suyden know that our box is next to the President's. She said she would drop in to meet you. Of course she let on to me that she hadn't seen the play yet, though my designer said she saw her there on the opening night."

"Oh, Gosh! The toadies!" sneered Benny. "Nothing so sickens you with success as the way people who once shoved you off the sidewalk come crawling to you on their stomachs begging you to dine with them."

"Say, that leading man of yours he's some class," cried Fanny. "That's the man I'm looking for. Will you invite him to supper after the theater?"

The playwright turned to his mother.

"Say, Ma," he said laughingly, "how would you like a real actor for a son-in-law?"

"She should worry," mocked Sam. "She'll be discussing with him the future of the Greek drama. Too bad it doesn't happen to be Warfield,[2] or mother could give him tips on the *Auctioneer*."

Jake turned to his mother with a covert grin.

"I guess you'd have no objection if Fanny got next to Benny's leading man. He makes at least fifteen hundred a week. That wouldn't be such a bad addition to the family, would it?"

Again the bantering tone stabbed Hanneh Breineh. Everything in her began to tremble and break loose.

"Why do you ask me?" she cried throwing her napkin into her plate. "Do I count for a person in this house? If I'll say something, will you even listen to me? What is to me the grandest man that my daughter could pick out? Another enemy in my house! Another person to shame himself from me!" She swept in her children in one glance of despairing anguish as she rose from the table. "What worth is an old mother to American children? The President is coming to-night to the theater, and none of you asked me to go." Unable to check the rising tears, she fled toward the kitchen and banged the door.

They all looked at one another guiltily.

"Say, Sis," Benny called out sharply, "what sort of frame-up

[2] WARFIELD—David Warfield, a famous actor. His first great success was in the *Auctioneer* which was played 1400 times.

is this? Haven't you told mother that she was to go with us to-night?"

"Yes—I—" Fanny bit her lips as she fumbled evasively for words. "I asked her if she wouldn't mind my taking her some other time."

"Now you have made a mess of it!" fumed Benny. "Mother'll be too hurt to go now."

"Well, I don't care," snapped Fanny. "I can't appear with mother in a box at the theater. Can I introduce her to Mrs. Van Suyden? And suppose your leading man should ask to meet me?"

"Take your time, Sis. He hasn't asked yet," scoffed Benny.

"The more reason I shouldn't spoil my chances. You know mother. She'll spill the beans that we come from Delancey Street the minute we introduce her anywhere. Must I always have the black shadow of my past trailing after me?"

"But have you no feelings for mother?" admonished Abe.

"I've tried harder than all of you to do my duty. I've lived with her." She turned angrily upon them. "I've borne the shame of mother while you bought her off with a present and a treat here and there. God knows how hard I tried to civilize her so as not to have to blush with shame when I take her anywhere. I dressed her in the most stylish Paris models, but Delancey Street sticks out from every inch of her. Whenever she opens her mouth, I'm done for. You fellows had your chance to rise in the world because a man is free to go up as high as he can reach up to; but I, with all my style and pep, can't get a man my equal because a girl is always judged by her mother."

They were silenced by her vehemence, and unconsciously turned to Benny.

"I guess we all tried to do our best for mother," said Benny thoughtfully. "But wherever there is growth, there is pain and heartbreak. The trouble with us is that the Ghetto of the Middle Ages and the children of the twentieth century have to live under one roof, and——"

A sound of crashing dishes came from the kitchen, and the voice of Hanneh Breineh resounded through the dining-room as she wreaked her pent-up fury on the helpless servant.

"Oh, my nerves! I can't stand it any more! There will be no girl again for another week," cried Fanny.

"Oh, let up on the old lady," protested Abe. "Since she can't take it out on us any more, what harm is it if she takes it out on the servants?"

"If you fellows had to chase around employment agencies, you wouldn't see anything funny about it. Why can't we move into a hotel that will do away with the need of servants altogether?"

"I got it better," said Jake, consulting a note-book from his pocket. "I have on my list an apartment on Riverside Drive where there's only a small kitchenette; but we can do away with the cooking, for there is a dining service in the building."

IV

The new Riverside apartment to which Hanneh Breineh was removed by her socially ambitious children was for the habitually active mother an empty desert of enforced idleness. Deprived of her kitchen, Hanneh Breineh felt robbed of the last reason of her existence. Cooking and marketing and puttering busily with pots and pans gave her an excuse for living and struggling and bearing up with her children. The lonely idleness of Riverside Drive stunned all her senses and arrested all her thoughts. It gave her that choked sense of being cut off from air, from life, from everything warm and human. The cold indifference, the each-for-himself look in the eyes of the people about her were like stinging slaps in the face. Even the children had nothing real or human in them. They were starched and stiff miniatures of their elders.

But the most unendurable part of the stifling life on Riverside Drive was being forced to eat in the public dining-room. No matter how hard she tried to learn polite table manners, she always found people staring at her, and her daughter rebuking her for eating with the wrong fork or guzzling the soup or staining the cloth.

In a fit of rebellion Hanneh Breineh resolved never to go down to the public dining-room again, but to make use of the gas-stove in the kitchenette to cook her own meals. That very day she rode down to Delancey Street and purchased a new market-basket. For some time she walked among the haggling push-cart venders, relaxing and swimming in the warm waves of her old familiar past.

A fish-peddler held up a large carp in his black, hairy hand and waved it dramatically:

"Women! Women! Fourteen cents a pound!"

He ceased his raucous shouting as he saw Hanneh Breineh in her rich attire approach his cart.

"How much?" she asked, pointing to the fattest carp.

"Fifteen cents, lady," said the peddler, smirking as he raised his price.

"Swindler! Didn't I hear you call fourteen cents?" shrieked Hanneh Breineh, exultingly, the spirit of the penny chase surging in her blood. Diplomatically, Hanneh Breineh turned as if to go, and the fishman seized her basket in frantic fear.

"I should live; I'm losing money on the fish, lady," whined the peddler. "I'll let it down to thirteen cents for you only."

"Two pounds for a quarter, and not a penny more," said Hanneh Breineh, thrilling again with the rare sport of bargaining, which had been her chief joy in the good old days of poverty.

"Nu, I want to make the first sale for good luck." The peddler threw the fish on the scale.

As he wrapped up the fish, Hanneh Breineh saw the driven look of worry in his haggard eyes, and when he counted out for her the change from her dollar, she waved it aside.

"Keep it for your luck," she said, and hurried off to strike a new bargain at a push-cart of onions.

Hanneh Breineh returned triumphantly with her purchases. The basket under her arm gave forth the old, homelike odors of herring and garlic, while the scaly tail of a four-pound carp protruded from its newspaper wrapping. A gilded placard on the door of the apartment-house proclaimed that all merchandise must be delivered through the trade entrance in the rear; but Hanneh Breineh with her basket strode proudly through the marble-paneled hall and rang nonchalantly for the elevator.

The uniformed hall-man, erect, expressionless, frigid with dignity, stepped forward:

"Just a minute, Madam, I'll call a boy to take up your basket for you."

Hanneh Breineh, glaring at him, jerked the basket savagely from his hands.

"Mind your own business," she returned. "I'll take it up myself. Do you think you're a Russian policeman to boss me in my own house?"

Angry lines appeared on the countenance of the representative of social decorum.

"It is against the rules, Madam," he said stiffly.

"You should sink into the earth with all your rules and brass buttons. Ain't this America? Ain't this a free country? Can't I take up in my own house what I buy with my own money?" cried Hanneh Breineh, reveling in the opportunity to shower forth the volley of invectives that had been suppressed in her for the weeks of deadly dignity of Riverside Drive.

In the midst of this uproar Fanny came in with Mrs. Van Suyden. Hanneh Breineh rushed over to her, crying:

"This bossy policeman won't let me take up my basket in the elevator."

The daughter, unnerved with shame and confusion, took the basket in her white-gloved hand and ordered the hallboy to take it around to the regular delivery entrance.

Hanneh Breineh was so hurt by her daughter's apparent defense of the hallman's rules that she utterly ignored Mrs. Van Suyden's greeting and walked up the seven flights of stairs out of sheer spite.

"You see the tragedy of my life?" broke out Fanny, turning to Mrs. Van Suyden.

"You poor child! You go right up to your dear, old lady mother, and I'll come some other time."

Instantly Fanny regretted her words. Mrs. Van Suyden's pity only roused her wrath the more against her mother.

Breathless from climbing the stairs, Hanneh Breineh entered the apartment just as Fanny tore the faultless millinery creation from her head and threw it on the floor in a rage.

"Mother, you are the ruination of my life! You have driven away Mrs. Van Suyden, as you have driven away all my best friends. What do you think we got this apartment for but to get rid of your fish smells and your brawls with the servants? And here you come with a basket on your arm as if you just landed from steerage! And this afternoon, of all times, when

Benny is bringing his leading man to tea. When will you ever stop disgracing us?"

"When I'm dead," said Hanneh Breineh, grimly. "When the earth will cover me up, then you'll be free to go your American way. I'm not going to make myself over for a lady on Riverside Drive.[1] I hate you and all your swell friends. I'll not let myself be choked up here by you or by that hall-boss-policeman that is higher in your eyes than your own mother."

"So that's your thanks for all we've done for you?" cried the daughter.

"All you've done for me?" shouted Hanneh Breineh. "What have you done for me? You hold me like a dog on a chain. It stands in the Talmud;[2] some children give their mothers dry bread and water and go to heaven for it, and some give their mother roast duck and go to Gehenna[3] because it's not given with love."

"You want me to love you yet?" raged the daughter. "You knocked every bit of love out of me when I was yet a kid. All the memories of childhood I have is your everlasting cursing and yelling that we were gluttons."

The bell rang sharply, and Hanneh Breineh flung open the door.

"Your groceries, ma'am," said the boy.

Hanneh Breineh seized the basket from him, and with a vicious fling sent it rolling across the room, strewing its contents over the Persian rugs and inlaid floor. Then seizing her hat and coat, she stormed out of the apartment and down the stairs.

[1] RIVERSIDE DRIVE—A fashionable residential street in New York City.
[2] TALMUD—The book of Jewish civil and canonical law.
[3] GEHENNA—A place of abomination; hell.

V

MR. AND MRS. PELZ sat crouched and shivering over their meager supper when the door opened, and Hanneh Breineh in fur coat and plumed hat charged into the room.

"I come to cry out to you my bitter heart," she sobbed. "Woe is me! It is so black for my eyes!"

"What is the matter with you, Hanneh Breineh?" cried Mrs. Pelz in bewildered alarm.

"I am turned out of my own house by the brass-buttoned policeman that bosses the elevator. Oi-i-i-i! Weh-h-h-h! What have I from my life? The whole world rings with my son's play. Even the President came to see it, and I, his mother, have not seen it yet. My heart is dying in me like in a prison," she went on wailing. "I am starved out for a piece of real eating. In that swell restaurant is nothing but napkins and forks and lettuce-leaves. There are a dozen plates to every bite of food. And it looks so fancy on the plate, but it's nothing but straw in the mouth. I'm starving, but I can't swallow down their American eating."

"Hanneh Breineh," said Mrs. Pelz, "you are sinning before God. Look on your fur coat; it alone would feed a whole family for a year. I never had yet a piece of fur trimming on a coat, and you are in fur from the neck to the feet. I never had yet a piece of feather on a hat, and your hat is all feathers."

"What are you envying me?" protested Hanneh Breineh. "What have I from all my fine furs and feathers when my children are strangers to me? All the fur coats in the world can't warm up the loneliness inside my heart. All the grandest feathers can't hide the bitter shame in my face that my children shame themselves from me."

Hanneh Brieneh suddenly loomed over them like some ancient, heroic figure of the Bible condemning unrighteousness.

"Why should my children shame themselves from me? From where did they get the stuff to work themselves up in the world? Did they get it from the air? How did they get all their smartness to rise over the people around them? Why don't the children of born American mothers write my Benny's plays? It is I, who never had a chance to be a person, who gave him the fire in his head. If I would have had a chance to go to school and learn the language, what couldn't I have been? It is I and my mother and my mother's mother and my father and father's father who had such a black life in Poland; it is our choked thoughts and feelings that are flaming up in my children and making them great in America. And yet they shame themselves from me!"

For a moment Mr. and Mrs. Pelz were hypnotized by the sweep of her words. Then Hanneh Breineh sank into a chair in utter exhaustion. She began to weep bitterly, her body shaking with sobs.

"Woe is me! For what did I suffer and hope on my children? A bitter old age—my end. I'm so lonely!"

All the dramatic fire seemed to have left her. The spell was broken. They saw the Hanneh Breineh of old, ever discontented, ever complaining even in the midst of riches and plenty.

"Hanneh Breineh," said Mrs. Pelz, "the only trouble with you is that you got it too good. People will tear the eyes out of your head because you're complaining yet. If I only had your fur coat! If I only had your diamonds! I have nothing. You have everything. You are living on the fat of the land. You go right back home and thank God that you don't have my bitter lot."

"You got to let me stay here with you," insisted Hanneh Breineh. "I'll not go back to my children except when they bury me. When they will see my dead face, they will understand how they killed me."

Mrs. Pelz glanced nervously at her husband. They barely had enough covering for their one bed; how could they possibly lodge a visitor?

"I don't want to take up your bed," said Hanneh Breineh. "I don't care if I have to sleep on the floor or on the chairs, but I'll stay here for the night."

Seeing that she was bent on staying, Mr. Pelz prepared to sleep by putting a few chairs next to the trunk, and Hanneh Breineh was invited to share the rickety bed with Mrs. Pelz.

The mattress was full of lumps and hollows. Hanneh Breineh lay cramped and miserable, unable to stretch out her limbs. For years she had been accustomed to hair mattresses and ample woolen blankets, so that though she covered herself with her fur coat, she was too cold to sleep. But worse than the cold were the creeping things on the wall. And as the lights were turned low, the mice came through the broken plaster and raced across the floor. The foul odors of the kitchen-sink added to the night of horrors.

"Are you going back home?" asked Mrs. Pelz as Hanneh Breineh put on her hat and coat the next morning.

"I don't know where I'm going," she replied as she put a bill into Mrs. Pelz's hand.

For hours Hanneh Breineh walked through the crowded Ghetto streets. She realized that she no longer could endure the sordid ugliness of her past, and yet she could not go home to her children. She only felt that she must go on and on.

In the afternoon a cold, drizzling rain set in. She was worn out from the sleepless night and hours of tramping. With a piercing pain in her heart she at last turned back and boarded the subway for Riverside Drive. She had fled from the marble sepulcher of the Riverside apartment to her old home in the Ghetto; but now she knew that she could not live there again. She had outgrown her past by the habits of years of physical comforts, and these material comforts that she could no longer do without choked and crushed the life within her.

A cold shudder went through Hanneh Breineh as she approached the apartment house. Peering through the plate glass of the door she saw the face of the uniformed hall-man. For a hesitating moment she remained standing in the drizzling rain, unable to enter and yet knowing full well that she would have to enter.

Then suddenly Hanneh Breineh began to laugh. She realized that it was the first time she had laughed since her children had become rich. But it was the hard laugh of bitter sorrow. Tears streamed down her furrowed cheeks as she walked slowly up the granite steps.

"The fat of the land!" muttered Hanneh Breineh, with a choking sob as the hall-man with immobile face deferentially swung open the door—"the fat of the land!"

The Type of Anzia Yezierska's Stories: It seems hardly possible that an immigrant could come to our shores, knowing not a word of English, and in a few short years become an American writer. But such is the case of Anzia Yezierska. Her biography is interesting as is also the type of stories she developed. She writes of the immigrants to America and of life in the crowded tenements of East Side New York. Her stories are not mere pictures of life, but life itself—life with its poverty, privations, ambitions, opportunities, sorrows. It is life as she herself had known and shared it.

For Appreciation: Miss Yezierska began writing in 1918 and the next year *The Fat of the Land* was chosen as one of the best short stories of the year. The setting is real, the characters are real. What happens is typical of what has often happened in the families of immigrants to our shores. Feeling and emotion run deep, and interest is focused on the mother who cannot adapt herself to the changes which a new life has forced upon her. Do you find traces of humor?

Give examples. What is the effect of the dialect in the story? How would you classify this story as to form—does character, plot, or setting predominate?

For Further Study: Make a list of expressions and words which lend atmosphere to the story.

Part I—Choose phrases and sentences which describe the crowded tenement life. Is the dialogue convincing? What is meant by "The world is a wheel always turning"? Discuss Hanneh Breineh's statement that "In America money is everything." Do you think Hanneh Breineh cares as little for her children as she would have Mrs. Pelz believe? How did she act when she believed Benny to be lost? What does Mrs. Pelz mean when she says, "Your sun will begin to shine, you will live on the fat of the land"?

Part II—In Part I the excitement runs high. In Part II there is a new setting, a feeling of quietness. Is this a relief? Are the successes which come to the children quite typical of those which come to many immigrant families? Can you give instances, either from cases you know about personally or from those you have read? Does the mother show pride in her children's achievements? Illustrate. Why is she not entirely satisfied with her present situation?

Part III—Characterize each of the children. Which do you think best understands the mother's feelings? Does your sympathy for Mrs. Breineh increase? Why? What does Benny mean when he says, "Wherever there is growth, there is pain and heartbreak"? Why do the children decide to move to another apartment?

Part IV—Why does the mother now feel that she has been "robbed of the last reason of her existence"? What is the purpose of the scene with the fish-peddler? Describe the scene in the hall of the apartment house. Are your sympathies with the mother or the daughter? What can you say of the ensuing scene in the apartment?

Part V—Why does the author send the mother back to Delancey Street to spend the night? Does Mrs. Pelz think that her old friend is to be pitied? Is the conclusion satisfactory?

Exercises and Creative Work: Write the next chapter for the story.

Write a paragraph on either Benny's play or Fanny's success.

Write a short story which has for its theme some problem of Americanization.

Read the chapters in Mary Antin's *Promised Land* which have to do with the author's difficulties after her family first come to this country. Write a short report on these chapters to be read in class.

EXTENSIVE READING PROGRAM—THE SHORT STORY

THE NATIONAL PERIOD (1800–1865)

Washington Irving
The Specter Bridegroom
The Pride of the Village
Dolph Heyliger
The Bold Dragoon
The Devil and Tom Walker

Nathaniel Hawthorne
Mr. Higginbotham's Catastrophe
The Gray Champion
The Ambitious Guest
The Prophetic Pictures
The Great Carbuncle
The Birthmark
Ethan Brand
The Minister's Black Veil

Edgar Allan Poe
MS. Found in a Bottle
The Fall of the House of Usher
Murders in the Rue Morgue
The Tell-Tale Heart
The Black Cat

James K. Paulding
Mine Uncle John

Catherine M. Sedgwick
The Country Cousin

Nathaniel Parker Willis
The Lunatic's Skate

Fitz-James O'Brien
The Diamond Lens
What Was It? A Mystery

THE TRANSITION PERIOD (1865–1900)

Francis Bret Harte
The Luck of Roaring Camp
The Outcasts of Poker Flat
A Ghost of the Sierras
Left Out on Lone Star Mountain
Brown of Calaveras

Samuel L. Clemens (Mark Twain)
The Celebrated Jumping Frog
A Curious Dream
Baker's Blue Jay Yarn
A Double-Barreled Detective Story
The $30,000 Bequest

Hamlin Garland
Mrs. Ripley's Trip
Under the Lion's Paw
Among the Corn Rows
Up the Coolly

Maurice Thompson
A Dusky Genius
A Pair of Old Boys

Alice French (Octave Thanet)
Otto the Knight
Trusty No. 49

George Washington Cable
'Sieur George
Posson Jone'
Madame Delphine
Grande Pointe

Thomas Nelson Page
Marse Chan
Meh Lady
Old 'Stracted

Joel Chandler Harris
*Free Joe and the Rest of the
World*
Mingo
Trouble on Lost Mountain

Mary N. Murfree (Charles Egbert
Craddock)
The Star in the Valley
Drifting Down Lost Creek

James Lane Allen
The White Cowl
A Kentucky Cardinal

Kate Chopin
A No-Account Creole
Beyond the Bayou

Sarah Orne Jewett
The Dulham Ladies
A White Heron
The Courting of Sister Wisby

Mary E. Wilkins Freeman
A Humble Romance
The Twelfth Guest

Rebecca Harding Davis
Life in the Iron Mills

Alice Brown
Farmer Eli's Vacation
A Day Off

Thomas Bailey Aldrich
A Rivermouth Romance
Marjorie Daw

Henry Cuyler Bunner
The Tenor
A Successful Failure
Our Aromatic Uncle

Frank R. Stockton
The Lady or the Tiger
The Widow's Cruise

Henry James
The Turn of the Screw
The Story in It

Ambrose Bierce
A Horseman in the Sky
The Eyes of the Panther

Rose Terry Cooke
Turkey Tracks

The Twentieth Century (1900–　　　)

William Sidney Porter (O.
Henry)
The Furnished Room
A Municipal Report
Romance of a Busy Broker
Shoes

Richard Harding Davis
Gallegher
The Bar Sinister

Stephen Crane
The Little Regiment
The Open Boat
A Dark-Brown Dog

William Allen White
The King of Boyville
A Victory for the People

George Ade
Effie Whittlesy
To Make a Hoosier Holiday

Irvin S. Cobb
The Belled Buzzard
Boys Will Be Boys

Stewart Edward White
The Riverman
The Two Cartridges
The River Boss

Kathleen Norris
The Hour of Ida Moran
Sinners

James B. Connolly
Dan Magee: White Hope
Strategy and Seamanship
Beyond the Horizon

Mary Hunter Austin
The Last Antelope
Readjustment
The House of Offense

Jack London
The Sun-Dog Trail
To Build a Fire
A Son of the Sun
To the Man on Trail

Ben Ames Williams
The Nurse
The Field of Honor
Sheener

Anzia Yezierska
Hunger
Salome of the Tenements
Children of Loneliness
Bread Givers

Katherine Fullerton Gerould
A Change of Air
The Poppies in the Wheat

Margaret Prescott Montague
England to America
Of Water and the Spirit
No. 10 Blank Street

Maxwell Struthers Burt
The Water-Hole

Charles Finger
The Shame of Gold
My Friend Julio

Edith Wharton
The Pelican
Xingu
The Rembrandt

Edna Ferber
Roast Beef Medium
The Gay Old Dog

Owen Wister
Little Big Horn Medicine
How Lin McLean Went East

Fanny Hurst
The Sob Sister
Humoresque

Joseph Hergesheimer
Tol'able David

Wilbur Daniel Steele
The Yellow Cat
Ching, Ching, Chinamen
Footfalls

Doran Hurley
Heart to Heart Speaks
Least Said, Soonest Mended
*Daughters of Eve, But Children
of Mary*

Zona Gale
White Bread
Friendship Village Stories

Margaret Deland
Mr. Tommy Dove

Booth Tarkington
Monsieur Beaucaire
Cherry
Little Cousin Sarah

Willa Cather
The Profile
The Bohemian Girl
The Sculptor's Funeral

Dorothy Canfield Fisher
A Thread Without a Knot
The Heyday of the Blood
Old Man Warner

Vera Marie Tracy
It Was a Drama
The Shining Quest
Christmas Comes

John Gibbons
The Court Was Poorly Attended
The Village Where God Was Dead

English

The following English short story writers should be known to every pupil: L. Andres Beck, Arnold Bennett, John Davys Beresford, Algernon Blackwood, John Buchan, G. K. Chesterton, Enid Dinnis, Percival Gibbon, Sir Philip Gibbs, Cecily Hallack, Cosmo Hamilton, E. Phillips Oppenheim, Eden Philpotts, Frank Swinnerton, Hugh Walpole, Pelham Grenville Wodehouse, Joseph Conrad, Edgar Wallace, Katherine Mansfield, John Galsworthy, and Cecil Roberts.

BIOGRAPHY

BIOGRAPHY AS A TYPE OF LITERATURE

What Is Biography

A *biography* is the life of a person written by another. An *autobiography* is the life of a person written by himself.

Biography is in one sense a form of history which is applied to one individual rather than to a group of individuals. In fact, it is only within modern times that biography has been considered distinct from history and independent as a branch of literature. The quality which makes a biography literature instead of history is a literary one which causes it to give pleasure and enjoyment to generations of readers. Although biographies have always been written, comparatively few of them have stood this literary test and therefore survived as literature. Perhaps the main reason why most early biographies did not meet literary standards was because they did not depict life as it was lived. In early days the purpose of writing a biography was to teach a moral lesson. Human weaknesses were glossed over and only virtues were stressed. Consequently, there were few faithful and unprejudiced studies.

The New Biography

The new biography shows the great man as a human being capable of doing wrong as well as right. He is not placed on a pedestal to be worshipped but is introduced to us as an acquaintance or friend to be entertained in our schools or in our homes or wheresoever we may get together for a pleasant chat. The new biography does not merely recount historical events in the life of a person from birth till death. It shows the effect of the age on the man and of the man on his age. It is a study in character development.

Biography, because it gives the true tale of a man who lived and moved and had his being on this earth, even as you and I, has a double charm. Our imagination can make us live with the characters in a story; in a biography we get the added thrill of knowing that the story is true. The double appeal of interest and truth in a biography makes the book very much worth while. Reading of the mistakes and triumphs of a real person causes a sympathetic response in our own lives. We, too, have made similar mistakes. We, too, may have similar triumphs.

THE HISTORY OF AMERICAN BIOGRAPHY

The Colonial and Revolutionary Periods (1607–1800)

General Characteristics

Of all the types of literature, biography yields itself least readily to historical treatment. In the first place, biography apart from history was late in developing. In the second place, we are usually more interested in the person about whom the biography is written than in the author and his historical placement. In this volume biographies are located in time according to subject matter, not according to authorship.

During the Colonial and Revolutionary Periods people were too much occupied with settling the country and waging war to do much writing of any kind. Especially were they disinclined to write of the lives of the dead when their own lives were so eventful and all-absorbing.

Biographies of the Period

A glance backward reveals that before the nineteenth century the most important piece of biographical writing in America was Benjamin Franklin's *Autobiography*. Among other writings of the period which might be classed as biographical are the sketches of contemporaries which appeared in *The Jesuit Relations* and similar chronicles prepared by Franciscan, Dominican, and other missionaries, detailed reports, that is, sent to their superiors in the homeland. From these rich source materials were to come the biographies we now have of men like Junípero Serra, of the North American Martyrs, and of Kateri Tekakwitha.

The National Period (1800–1865)

General Characteristics

The National Period saw the romantic movement in American literature—the birth of a new interest in life and the flowering of romantic fiction and poetry. The pendulum swung far from the factual, historical writing of the Colonial and Revolutionary days—so far, in fact, that even the biography of the period did not adhere to facts. Much of it was inaccurate; much was exaggerated. In many cases it served as the vehicle for fawning flattery; in others for expressing bitter personal grudges. Only a few biographies of the period have survived.

Biographies of the Period

Perhaps the best biography of the period is Washington Irving's *The Life of Washington*. This was Irving's last work, completed just before his death. Ralph Waldo Emerson, James Russell Lowell, and Oliver Wendell Holmes all turned to biographical writings in their later years. Holmes wrote a notable biography of Emerson, as did also Lowell.

THE TRANSITION PERIOD (1865–1900)

General Characteristics

The tendency toward realism in the Transition Period saw the beginnings of a new biography which grew in public favor and which was to reach full development in the twentieth century. This period also saw a sectional or "local color" style of biography. From the South came biographies of war heroes and other notables; from the West came biographies of pioneers and frontiersmen.

Biographies of the Period

Of the "local color" biographies, perhaps the most notable is Mark Twain's *Life on the Mississippi*. This is exceedingly interesting and readable and, as its title suggests, it depicts early scenes on the Mississippi. The "family" biography, written of some notable by a member of his own family, became popular. Such biographies were written of Harriet Beecher Stowe, Julia Ward Howe, and Nathaniel Hawthorne. The "campaign" biography written to exalt the political candidate also came into being, one of the notable examples being William Dean Howells' biography of Lincoln.

THE TWENTIETH CENTURY (1900–   )

General Characteristics

The twentieth century has given us a new biography, so fascinating that it is nearly as widely read as fiction. Many universities are establishing chairs of biography, the first one having been founded as early as 1919 at Carlton College, Northfield, Minnesota.

Unfortunately, however, not all biographies of the twentieth century have high literary merit. In an over-zealous attempt to be chatty and personal, many biographers lost their sense of proportion. They over-emphasized weakness and failings, they exposed all kinds of family skeletons, they seemed to delight in dragging notable names in the mud. Truth was sacrificed for sensation and realism degenerated into muck-raking. Of recent years, however, public opinion has revolted against this type of biography. Just as the reader of the early biography revolted against an exaggeration of virtues, so now does the reader of the present-day biography revolt against an exaggeration of weaknesses. The present demand is creating a biography which is not only vastly entertaining but which is fair and unprejudiced. Indeed, the striking feature of American literature today is the triumph of biography as *the* literary form of the hour.

Biographies of the Period

The list of excellent biographies by contemporary writers is a long one. A number which are especially worth while are listed at the end of this section under the *Extensive Reading Program*.

A Biography of the Colonial Period

AN AMERICAN MARTYR

From *Saint among Savages*

FRANCIS X. TALBOT

By Way of Introduction: Over three hundred years ago, on April 8, 1636, Father Isaac Jogues and seven other Jesuit Blackrobes sailed from the France of Richelieu for the New France across the seas. They sought neither riches nor adventure, only the spiritual welfare of the Indians. Yet adventures they had, adventures which culminated for two of that band of eight, Fathers Jogues and Garnier, in cruel martyrdom.

After sharing for six years the crude life of the natives, Jogues and a little band of his fellow laborers were ambushed and captured by the fierce Mohawks. A year of torture and enslavement followed for Jogues before he, the only one of the captives to survive, made his escape with the help of Dutch officials at New Amsterdam and returned to France.

There, to his great discomfort, he was hailed by all as a hero from the Front; his gaunt body and mangled hands were his medals of distinction. These honors weighed heavily on him; he was eager for nothing but to return to New France and his Indians. Before his return could he perhaps obtain permission to offer the Holy Sacrifice of the Mass in spite of the loss of his left thumb and the crippled condition of other fingers? The Holy Father's answer to his petition is celebrated: *"Indignum esset Christi martyrem Christi non bibere sanguinem."* "It would be a shame not to allow a martyr of Christ to drink the blood of Christ."

In this chapter from Father Talbot's *Saint among Savages* we find Father Jogues, less than a year after his escape, at Three Rivers, south of Quebec, preparing to return to the treacherous Mohawks who but lately had treated him with the utmost barbarism.

A COLD dawn spread over Three Rivers on Monday, September twenty-fourth. It was a blue lingering of the night rather than a flushed break of the day. Father Jogues gave communion to young Jean de la Lande and finished his Mass in the Chapel de la Conception. They gulped down their breakfast hurriedly, and, accompanied by one or two of the Fathers who then happened to be at the residence, walked briskly down the road along the hillside to the strand of the river. Scarcely any of the French were about. Governor Montmagny, Father Lalemant, and all the important personages had departed a few days previously for Quebec. Sieur de la Poterie, the Commandant, had not yet emerged from his residence. Most of the people still slept, or were occupied in beginning the week's work. A knot of Hurons stood and haunched about the canoes.

All was hushed and silent, save the lapping of the waters and the muted voices which sounded hollow in the mist. The Hurons were ready to start. Jogues bundled his black cassock up about his waist, cleaned the sand and mire from his feet, and climbed into the canoe. Jean de la Lande raised himself carefully over the rim and took his place. Otrihouré and another Huron jumped in skilfully, and the Hurons in the other canoe settled themselves and held the paddles poised for the stroke. A third canoe was filled with Mohawks who were returning home for the winter. The Hurons standing about the shore uttered their guttural farewells. The Fathers raised their arms in benediction. The canoes glided into the fog.

On the second evening, Father Jogues' band turned the lip of land that banked the Richelieu River. They ascended the hill and encamped near the ruins of Fort Richelieu. The garrison had been withdrawn that summer, both because in wartime the fort had been ineffective as a barrier to the Iroquois and because peace with the Iroquois was now a certainty. The fort always had been regarded with especial hate by the Mohawks, and on its abandonment they had reduced it to a charred mound.

That night, among the ruins of the old fort, Jogues and the Hurons talked tensely. He realized fully how precarious was the situation. On the one side, the peace seemed to be firmly pledged. The Mohawk nation professed to be dealing honestly; it had faithfully fulfilled all the requirements of the code of statecraft sacred among the natives. As far as he could see, there was no ground for suspicion, no cause for alarm. And yet, there was some subtle, some intangible something that was disturbing and unsettling. As for himself and de la Lande, they were resolved to go forward and to dare what might be.

Not so with the Huron ambassadors. Neither they nor their chiefs had put such implicit trust in the Mohawk promises and fair words. They wanted peace, and they were willing to work for the peace under the moral suasion of the French; but their instincts told them to beware. Now, in the camp at Richelieu, when they were about to paddle down to and be swallowed up in the Mohawk territory, the Huron envoys were seized with dread. Their observations, which could not be expressed in words,— their intuitions, warned them against continuing the journey. They were convinced that somehow, somewhere, was a trap which would close in and destroy them.

Ondessonk [1] argued with them and tried to quiet their trepidation. Otrihouré also strove to hearten them. But their courage was gone. The Huron ambassadors decided they would postpone their journey to the Mohawk villages. Pointing their canoe across the St. Lawrence, they wildly scurried back to their own people. Otrihouré, who had a special, personal claim of protection from the Mohawks, was alone resolute enough to continue with Jogues and de la Lande. About this time there was an added cause for suspicion. The Mohawks deserted and drove their canoe off on a scouting expedition.

The three voyageurs struck out the next morning against the rippling flow of the Richelieu River. They were in the vast wilderness of the narrow river which cut its way between the close banks of the forests. They paddled for hours in the utter stillness, clambered over the rocks along the rapids and trudged across the portages. Their progress was slow, their labors were exhausting. After several days of struggle they reached the Lake of Champlain. They had expected, before this, to be meeting with stray bands of Mohawks. But not a living soul was passing up or down along the route, not a sound of anything human was anywhere heard. The quiet was strange and forbidding.

September had now turned into October. Autumn cooled the summer heats and sapped the green from the leaves and the grass. The hillsides along Lake Champlain were faded into brown and russet, and many of the trees showed their naked branches. The far elevations of the mountains were dull and depressing. All the land seemed to be desolated and so rugged as to be menacing. An ominous quiet seemed to be brooding over all the earth and the waters. Ceaselessly the three travelers pulled the canoes through the heavy calm, past the slow succession of banks until, about the middle of the second week of October, they twisted up the little stream to the rapids that poured the Lake of the Blessed Sacrament [2] into Lake Champlain.

[1] ONDESSONK—The Indian name, "Bird of Prey," given to Father Jogues by the Hurons.

[2] LAKE OF THE BLESSED SACRAMENT—Now Lake George, situated directly west of Lake Champlain in the state of New York.

They climbed the trail through the woods, with the canoe over their heads, and debouched on the smaller lake. Even yet they encountered no Mohawks. They found no signs of parties who had recently passed along the way. There was nothing but the impenetrable mystery of the forests and lakes. A few days of paddling through the stupendous heights that hemmed in the Lake of the Blessed Sacrament brought them to the circular inclosure of Andiatarocté. It was about the twentieth day since they had left Three Rivers. They had journeyed safely along the water route; there remained but three or four days along the trail through the mountains. Then they would be arriving at Ossernenon.[3]

The three of them were worn out by now, and their store of food was sparse. Young Jean de la Lande had proved himself to be a lad of worth and mettle. He was more agile than René Goupil,[4] more experienced in the ways of the wilderness, and far more venturesome. He had, too, the dogged fidelity of René and much of his simple faith. He had not been molded in the savage life, as had Guillaume Coûture,[4] but he had the sharpness and intelligence of Guillaume. All through the laborious days he had borne up strongly under the physical and mental strain, and his courage still flamed. He had listened eagerly to Father Isaac's instructions as to how he must comport himself among the Mohawks. He was prepared for any emergency. He prayed in unison with Father Isaac, and often expressed his spiritual joy that he should have been chosen for this service of God in the Mission of the Martyrs. His young eyes glowed and his heart expanded under the inspired words that *mon père* spoke to him. Again and again, he protested that he was ready for life or death, through love of God.

It was October the fourteenth when they defiled along the leaf-strewn trail that led to Ossernenon. They were burdened down, all three of them, with the baggage of clothes and blankets and presents. They grew more apprehensive than ever when they were shrouded by the tree trunks and the overhanging branches. They mounted the rise of the path over the ridge of hills and dug

[3] OSSERNENON—A Mohawk village on the Mohawk River, which flows into the Hudson above Albany, New York.

[4] RENÉ GOUPIL AND GUILLAUME COÛTURE—Young men who like Jean de la Lande had come to New France in search of adventure, had attached themselves to the Fathers, and served them as guides, interpreters, catechists, and servants. Captured with Jogues the year before, Goupil had been martyred at Ossernenon; Coûture, like Jogues, had been enslaved.

their heels into it as they descended to the depression caused by
the juncture of the Oiogué and Sacandaga rapids. A few days
more and they would have the first welcome, friendly or hostile,
at Ossernenon. It might be only a few hours, for most certainly
there would be Mohawks along these well-traveled trails.

Father Jogues was exalted in spirit, now that he was coming
back to the village he had dedicated to the Holy Trinity. He was
at the ending of the journey that he had prayed for so insistently,
that he had longed for amid such desolation. He was back with
the beloved Mohawks, he would sit at their fires in their cabins
and talk to them of God and the mysteries of the Faith. He
would try to convert his "aunt"[5] and Honatteniate and other
friendly ones; he would make these the corner stones for the
Church, as he had helped for six years despite all the assaults of
the devil to build the Church among the Hurons. He hurried his
steps along the trail, so that de la Lande and Otrihouré could
scarcely keep pace with him. He was never so happy, never so
expectant in all his life. He had the thought that he was coming
to his own home. When he had traveled this trail before, in the
first journey, his steps had lagged and he had begged Goupil and
Coûture to escape, to die of starvation in the woods rather than
face the tortures. Now he was encouraging young Jean to hurry
along faster with him, and Jean, panting breathlessly, beamed
with the ardor of an apostle.

A file of savages came toward them along the trail. Jogues
halted, and called out a greeting. The savages melted away out
of sight. He sharpened his eyes and peered anxiously through the
trees. Again he shouted his welcome and announced that he was
Ondessonk. The Mohawks emerged from the trees on all sides
and closed in with blood-curdling warwhoops. Jogues stood
fastened to the earth, shocked and amazed; Jean de la Lande
froze beside him; Otrihouré was terrified. The Mohawks were
streaked with crimson war paint. They swung their muskets before them, and held gleaming knives in their right hands. They
howled and shrieked wildly, danced about Father Jogues menacingly, as if they were about to fall on him and tear him to pieces.

Father Jogues could not comprehend. He thought perhaps this
was play-acting. He spoke to them in a friendly way and smiled

---

[5] FATHER JOGUES' "AUNT"—Sister of the chief who owned Father Jogues during his captivity, and on more than one occasion, the one who saved his life.

but they drowned out his words with their screeches and glared
at him fiercely. All of an instant the warriors leaped on him and
de la Lande, bore them to the ground, pounded and rolled them
around, and with violent rage tore off the black robe and under-
clothes of Father Jogues, and stripped him naked. They ripped
off the garments of Jean de la Lande, meanwhile beating him
furiously.

Appalled, Jogues understood. This was a war party. The
Mohawks had repudiated the peace. These warriors were taking
the trail to the St. Lawrence, to surprise the Algonquins and
Hurons, to take the French unawares. His soul sickened at the
terror of the thought. All was ended. There was war again. He
began to understand the howls of the savages. They hated the
French. They were going to massacre all the French. They
hated him. He was an evil sorcerer. He had plotted their ruin
and death. They intended to cut him to pieces, to burn him at the
stake, to split open his head, to eat his flesh.

Meanwhile, they were dragging him and de la Lande and
Otrihouré along the path with them, triumphantly, to their village.
They held their archenemy, Ondessonk. They would revenge
themselves on him. This time he would not escape them. Run-
ners sped along the path as fast as their legs could carry them to
announce that Ondessonk was captured and was being led into the
village.

Father Jogues groaned in the abyss of his soul. He had dared
death and he did not fear it. He was heartbroken for young Jean
whom he had led with him; he would secure the release of the lad
if he possibly could. He feared the havoc that would be wrought
along the St. Lawrence; hundreds of Algonquins would be caught
during the autumn and winter hunts; miserably the Hurons would
perish. He was in terror when he thought of possible sudden,
ruthless onslaughts on Montreal, even on Three Rivers. There
would be no warning given. There was no help, now, save in the
good God.

Driven madly along, he was prodded up the series of hills till
he reached the ridge above the valley and river of the Mohawks.
He padded down the incline with his persecutors to the flats by
the bank of the river and the ford where he had first been
caressed by the villagers. They mobbed about the place in a
terrifying turmoil. They were struggling with one another, Jogues

could see, arguing among themselves, threatening and impre-
cating. He and de la Lande were hurled into the midst of the
throng. Some threatened him and lifted their arms as if to strike
him. Others warded off the blows and pressed in to guard him.
It was an angry, aroused crowd that rioted about him and split
his ears with their cries. He and Jean, finally, were extricated,
were hurried up the roadway to the summit of the hill, dragged
through the gate of the stockade, and pushed violently into a
cabin.

For the time being they were safe. They had been rescued by
the Wolf and Turtle clans from the old enemies, the Bears. They
were in the Wolf's lodge, and no one of the Mohawks, however
lawless, would dare to invade this sanctuary. Father Jogues'
"aunt," her grandson Honatteniate and some few friendly persons
sat them on the mat and put food in their hands. They explained
what had happened to change the minds of the people since his
last visit. Part of the story was well known to him. Kiotseaeton,
supported by the Wolf and Turtle and some less powerful clans,
had advocated the peace with the French and their allies in good
faith and with all sincerity. They had overcome the resistance of
the strong union of the Bear families who raged violently, in and
out of the national councils, against carrying on any peace ne-
gotiations. The Bears had aroused their kinsmen among the
Upper Iroquois, the Oneidas, the Onondagas, the Senecas, the
Cayugas,[6] to support them, while the Mohawk Wolfs could not
persuade their clansmen among these nations to follow their
leadership. And so, after their temporary victory in pledging the
Mohawks to the peace, the Wolfs were being worsted. That had
been the state of affairs since June when Ondessonk had visited
them as ambassador.

Not many weeks after he had left them, the friendly Wolfs
related, a few of the people had fallen sick. They were not
disturbed much. But then others had contracted the disease. It
had spread from cabin to cabin. It had appeared in Andagaron,
then in Tionontoguen. They had invoked the sorcerers, they had
watched their dreams, they had fulfilled the commands of their
okis, they had offered sacrifices to the demons, and made feasts;
they had danced and chanted and played games; they had held
sweats; but to no avail. The sickness had become more prevalent

[6] UPPER IROQUOIS . . . CAYUGAS—All tribes of the Iroquois nation.

during August. Many of the warriors and squaws and children had died. By the beginning of September, the people had been frantic. It looked as though they were being ruined by another epidemic.

There had been some adopted Hurons who offered an explanation. They remembered how six or seven years before, their peoples had been similarly afflicted; they had blamed the disease on Ondessonk and the Blackrobes, and had been on the point of murdering them time and time again. These Blackrobes were evil sorcerers, and Ondessonk was the worst of them. He and Echon[7] and the other Blackrobes wrought frightful witchery. They wished to destroy all the native peoples so that they would have the land to themselves. They brought disease and pestilence and destruction wherever they went. They and the French were not truly seeking for peace; they were trying to annihilate the Iroquois. The sickness had been brought on by Ondessonk, they asserted. Many of the Mohawks had accepted their words.

In September, the corn in the fields down by the river had begun to wither, just when it should have been fattening for the harvest. The stalks shriveled, and the ears of corn were destroyed by worms. There would be no corn for the winter, and without corn there would be starvation. Under this new affliction, the Mohawks had grown more frenzied. Some demon was persecuting them. Again they had consulted their sorcerers and wizards. Pitifully they had employed their superstitions. But again to no avail. The crop had been ruined.

Then they had remembered the chest which Ondessonk had left in the cabin of his "aunt." The sorcerers had pronounced their infallible judgment. Ondessonk had left an evil spirit locked up in this black box. They had accused him of this before he left, but he had denied it. True, he had opened the box in their presence and had shown them the articles inclosed in it. But he had fastened it in such a manner that no one of them could open it without smashing it. Why had he done this if he did not wish to conceal something from them? Ondessonk was a wicked magician, he was in league with the devil. He had left his demon, over which he had control, in this firmly fastened box. It was this demon which was killing the people and destroying the corn.

[7] ECHON—The Indian name for Jean de Brébeuf, given to him by the Hurons.

The suspicion had not taken long to become a firm conviction in the minds of many of the Mohawks. Ondessonk had preached a strange doctrine when he was among them. He had told them of a Deity who would punish them for their wrongdoings, of a place where they would burn forever after they died; he had reprimanded them for certain of their actions and habits; he had always sought out those who were sick and dying, and made queer motions over them, pouring water on their heads and saying some words of a charm; he had made the sign which the Dutch told them was an abomination and for which they had killed the other Frenchman who came with Ondessonk. As an ambassador of the French, he had not worn his black robe, nor had he spoken openly to them of his beliefs, as he had done on his first visit. It was clear that he meant to deceive them and take them off their guard. He did not wish peace with them. He planned only to exterminate them. For that reason he had locked up the evil demon in the chest.

They must destroy that chest left by Ondessonk. They had come to the cabin where it was stored and demanded it. They would not listen to any assurances that the chest contained no evil spirit. They had asserted they had proved conclusively that there was a demon in the box. They dared not smash it open, nor pry the bands apart. For then the demon would escape and would find some other place where it could lurk and continue to do them harm. Some of the more courageous among the sorcerers, those with powerful demons of their own who would protect them, had taken up the box left by Ondessonk and fearfully carried it out of the village and down the trail to the river. Some distance below, where the water was deep, they had lifted it carefully out of their canoe and let it sink down into the water. The demon was now trapped and could not escape, but would perish. However, Ondessonk still lived. He had plotted to kill and ruin them. They had destroyed his demon. They had only to capture and murder him. Then they would be free of their curse.

At the time when the chest of Father Jogues was being destroyed, about the middle of September, the Mohawks had held a council for the reopening of the discussions about peace. The Bear clan was stronger now, with the suspicion against Ondessonk and the French so clearly confirmed. Their orators pleaded with the assembly to remain loyal to the traditions of their nation and the doctrine of their ancestors. They pointed out the danger of the Mohawks' alienating themselves from the alliances which their forefathers had established with the other Iroquois nations, and of their breaking all the bonds of blood and marriage with these nations which were their brothers and their children. With vivid recitals they recalled the murder of the Mohawks perpetrated by their ancient enemies, the Algonquin nations and by the Huron nation which they had sworn to subjugate.

The Bear chiefs swayed the minds of the people, now already unbalanced by the spread of the epidemic and the plague on the corn, and now quite firmly convinced that the French were contriving evil through witchcraft and the power of the evil spirit. Kiotseaeton and the peace advocates were repudiated. The council resolved to send presents and envoys to the Oneidas, the Onondagas, the Cayugas and the Senecas in order to reaffirm and consolidate the alliance and kinship of the Mohawks with them, and in order to indicate their willingness to join with them in their war expeditions against the French, the Hurons, and the Algonquins.

Father Jogues listened and understood. This was the end of all the peace efforts. The Mohawks had raised the bloody hatchet. They had raised it treacherously and were giving no warning that they were once more taking up the warpath. As for his own fate and that of de la Lande, he knew nothing. His friends told him that messengers had been sent through all the cabins and villages, announcing that a great council would be held the next night in Tionontoguen. The chiefs and the elders would then decide upon their fate.

It was on Wednesday evening, October seventeenth, 1646, that Father Isaac Jogues and Jean de la Lande were brought captive into the village of Oneougiouré, formerly called Ossernenon. All that night their ears rang with threats and maledictions. "You will die tomorrow. Do not be surprised," one of the braves shrieked into Ondessonk's ear. Another, gloating, told him: "We will not torture you or burn you. Keep up your courage. We will strike you over the head with a hatchet. We will set your head on the points of the stockade, so that when we bring some of your brothers here as captives, they may still see you." Still another made as if to slash him with a knife, saying: "Let us see if this white flesh is the flesh of a manitou or demon." Jogues answered calmly: "No, I am nothing more than a man like you. And understand, I have no fear either of your torments or of death. I do not know why you threaten to kill me. I have come into your country to help you to preserve the peace, and to level the earth, and to show you the road to heaven. And you treat me like a dog. God governs the French and the Iroquois; He knows well how to punish you."

All through that night Oneougiouré was noisy with disputes. The clans of the Wolf and the Bear were in violent altercation, the one demanding safety for Ondessonk and the Frenchman, the other swearing to kill the two of them. The chiefs were powerless to quell the rioting. They feared that the young braves, lusting for revenge and notoriety, under the impulse of dreams or their demons, would commit a deed that would be regretted. Both factions ranged through the cabin where Ondessonk lodged, and beset the doorways, some to tomahawk him if he emerged, others to obey their chiefs and guard him faithfully.

October eighteenth dawned. Emotions had quieted with the morning. Ondessonk and Jean were now accepted as public hostages. They were not to be troubled until the council was held and the elders had pronounced sentence. Jogues was warned by his friends that he must be most cautious, for there were many ready, on the slightest provocation, to strike him down. He was forbidden absolutely to venture out of the gates or to go beyond the stockade, unless with a strong guard about him. He was given back some of his clothes, so that he could appear in public without shame. He felt quite secure. The storm had played itself out, as usual, in the first violent gusts. Now the Mohawks would consider his presence more calmly, and with some logic reason out what had best be done. The moment of greatest peril was safely past.

During the morning he made opportunity to talk to the chiefs, not as the docile, silent slave of four years ago, but with the air and the dignity of the ambassador he had been in June, though he did not pretend to hold that same office now. He professed boldly that he had come to them this third time as a Blackrobe, to teach them the trail to heaven, to instruct them in true thoughts, to reveal to them the knowledge of God. Facing them defiantly, he accused them of the basest treachery in violating the peace without warning, and he threatened them with the terrible wrath of Onontio [8] and the French.

In regard to the little black box which he had left with them, he recalled how he opened it in their presence, how he showed them all the contents, how he had tried to make them see that no demon was shut up in it. He ridiculed their superstitions, and swore to them that he had had absolutely nothing to do with bringing the sickness and the blight on the corn. While he professed his sorrow for these afflictions, he begged them to rid themselves of their fancies and absurdities, to listen to the things he would tell them, to believe as he believed in the great God who ruled all men. They listened. Some approved while others flared out at him anew for being a sorcerer and a dealer in death.

That afternoon, the chiefs of all degrees, the elders of the families, all the responsible people of Ossernenon trailed out of the village and along the river path to Tionontoguen. They knew the arguments that would be presented on both sides. Kiotseaeton and the Wolfs would harangue for peace with the French and their allies. They would, failing in this, scarify those who were bringing dishonor on the nation by breaking out into war without signifying that resolution to Onontio. If they decided for war, let them release Ondessonk and his comrade, and send them back to their people to announce that the Mohawks had changed their mind and no longer were in favor of peace. Let them not commit an act of treachery that would disgrace them among all the nations, so that no one ever after would put faith in the word of a Mohawk.

The Bear orators would brush aside the thoughts of peace. They would appeal to the bonds of blood and alliances with the other Iroquois nations. They would point out that there was no need to truckle to the French for their trade, since they had the Dutch near by who would continue to supply them with guns and powder. They would point out the immemorial enmity with the Algonquins and cry for their extermination. They would demand that the Huron nations should be subdued and thus forced to form one people with them, as had been in the days of their fathers. The Mohawks had no need to placate Onontio, nor to

[8] ONONTIO—Indian name given to Charles Huault de Montmagny, Governor-General of New France.

give him warning of their change of policy, save by a sudden attack.

As for Ondessonk, he must be killed. He had wandered among them of his own free will, not as an envoy whose person must be protected. He was a Blackrobe in the employ of evil demons. Already he had committed hideous wrong by hiding his demon in his black box, by sending the disease, by destroying the corn. He would always practise his prayers and incantations and gestures. Arrogantly, he preached to them about his God; he was an offense to the gods and demons of the Mohawks. He must be sacrificed in order to placate Areskoui and their other friendly spirits.

Thus the orators would debate. Neither they nor any of the people could estimate the effect that their words would have. The nation was divided in opinion, as it had been for years. It had veered from war to peace, from peace to war. The people would listen to the speeches of the chiefs. In family groups they would weigh the arguments. In clans they would compare their findings. In the general council they would declare their decisions. Then only would the will of the nation be made manifest.

Oneougiouré was deserted and strangely quiet that Thursday afternoon. Jogues and de la Lande were in no way molested. Father Isaac spent these hours of peace in prayer with Jean, in raising the thoughts of the lad to God, in exhorting him to courage and confidence in the Providence of God. He explained the situation fully. It was possible that the council would condemn them to death, that they would both be murdered. It might be that he alone would be struck down, but that Jean would be held as a prisoner. Or else, both of them might be allowed to live but be forced to return to Three Rivers. This last, Jogues said, would probably happen. However, he instructed Jean what he should do in all emergencies.

About sundown, when the shadows were lengthening over the village, there came a young brave to the cabin. He sought out Ondessonk and invited him to visit another lodge where there were people who wished to eat and talk with him. Jogues recognized the man as belonging to the Bear clan, a man who had been somewhat hostile. To refuse this brave would be interpreted as an act of great discourtesy and would betray a suspicion that might breed greater ill-feeling. Spurning an invitation to eat in a cabin was an insult not easily forgiven. Besides, Jogues thought, to show fear of this brave would be cowardly.

He consulted with his "aunt" and the friends of his family. They were of two minds, as to whether it would be safe for him to venture out into the village or whether it would be more prudent to offer the proper excuses. Jogues was eager to make friends with the young brave and the Bears who had invited him. His "aunt" feared treachery. Nevertheless, she agreed that he should go. She sent Honatteniate, her grandson and the sworn brother of Ondessonk, to guard him. Jean was left in the lodge.

The smoky half-light of the October evening lingered over the cabins and the tang of autumn was cool in the air as Jogues emerged into the open. He and Honatteniate followed their guide silently through the subdued paths of the village till they arrived before the long house where their guide turned to pause. Jogues could discern in the dimness the rough carvings of the Bear signs on the doorpost. He looked quizzically at his guide, but the young brave gave back a stolid and expressionless stare. Jogues did not hesitate for long. Suspicion or fear, either one would give the Mohawk an advantage over him. Casually, then, he placed his hand against the stiff skin which hung down from the lintel and pushed it inward so that he might enter. Honatteniate followed closely after him. A blast of warm, smelly air assailed him. Through the heavy gloom and smoke he glimpsed the fires gleaming down the center of the long, narrow room, and saw the people dimly shadowed about them. He shoved with his shoulder against the shaggy skin and bent his head under the low doorway. He saw and knew no more.

Behind the doorpost a warrior stood, with a tomahawk poised ready to strike. The bowed head of Ondessonk came forward around the edge of the skin curtain. Honatteniate leaped into the entry, thrusting out his arm to ward off the blow he saw crashing down. The tomahawk slashed his forearm and thudded upon the head of Ondessonk. The guide sent Honatteniate reeling into a corner and with another blow the murderer smashed the skull of Ondessonk. Father Jogues lay as he fell, crumpled at the doorway of the lodge. The moment was still. No one spoke. The braves leaned over the bleeding head and the prostrate form. They whispered in awed tones that Ondessonk was dead.

Honatteniate roared curses on the murderers and rushed out of the cabin, shouting wildly. Aroused, the village came flocking to the cabin. The murderers and their friends dragged the body of Ondessonk out into the street. They set up a frenzied dance and chant of triumph. They had saved the nation. They had destroyed the great sorcerer, the Blackrobe Ondessonk. They had revenged themselves for all the evil he had brought on them. They had drowned his demon. They had split his head. They were free from his spells and charms. Into the mob, Ondessonk's "aunt" fought her way. She confronted the murderers. She raged against them: "You kill me!" she screamed shrilly in the darkness. "It is I myself whom you kill! He was my kinsman! He belonged to my family! You must pay the penalty! What will the two other villages say? You have not consulted them! You have not waited for the decision of the council! What will the others say about this murder, so unexpectedly, so rashly perpetrated?"

The people of the Bear pushed her aside. The braves bent over Ondessonk, scalped him, and with their long knives cut the head from the neck. They held it up, streaming with blood, and started down in procession through the dark lanes between the cabins, toward the corner of the stockade that faced to the north and the east. While some held flaring torches, others clambered up on the latticed scaffolding along the inner side of the palisades. They lifted up the head of Ondessonk. One of them jammed it down on the sharpened point of a pole at the angle of the walls. The face of Father Jogues looked across the valley of the Mohawks, over toward the trail which descended from the hills beyond, northward toward the St. Lawrence. With boasts and imprecations the Mohawks shrieked their defiance against the French and warned that all French palefaces would be slaughtered. Look at Ondessonk!

Another Frenchman still lived. He was concealed in the village. He must be found and killed. The mob spread out from the corner of the stockade and streamed through the lanes. Everywhere they searched for the young paleface named Jean. He was in the cabin of the Wolfs. He was under their protection. The leaders of the crowd would not dare to invade that cabin, for it would be a grievous offense to the families who lodged there and to all their kinsmen throughout the five Iroquois nations. They must force the Wolf family to surrender the Frenchman to them, or they must trick the Frenchman out into the open night.

Braves stood about the cabin, and in the darkness bellowed their threats and curses. They had killed Ondessonk. They would kill his brother. This other Frenchman was also a sorcerer. He talked to himself, when no one was listening; he lifted his head and eyes to the sky; he bent his knees on the earth and held himself upright; he made the hateful sign on his forehead and shoulders and breast; he had little beads tied together and flat pieces of iron with marks on them; he wove incantations with Ondessonk and invited deadly demons to descend on the Mohawks and destroy them off the face of the earth. He was an evil witch. He must be destroyed out of their midst, that very night, before he could do any more harm. If he were allowed to live, he would wreak a terrible revenge and call on his gods to punish them for murdering Ondessonk.

Young Jean de la Lande remained quietly sitting by the fire of Father Isaac's "aunt." The old squaw, after she had raged against the killers of her "nephew," hurried back to protect the other Frenchman from his assailants. She related to Jean what had happened, and warned him to beware. He must not move one step from the circle of the fire, she told him. She and Honatteniate, whose arm was deeply gashed by the blow of the tomahawk, and others of her young men haunched about Jean, guarding him closely. Beyond the doors and the bark walls, the village was in tumult. The raucous cries and excited voices sounded menacingly.

Jean waited. Father Isaac was dead. His body was cast somewhere on the streets, his head was pinned on the palisades. Jean prayed. He was doomed to death. Nothing could save him. He felt the tremor pass through him. He was feverish. He looked into the burning embers of the fire and watched the weird shadows that flickered through the cabin and across the posts and walls. Father Isaac was dead. He alone remained, the only white man in all the Mohawk villages. He prayed to God for courage. He examined his conscience. That day he had confessed his sins and Father Isaac had spoken the words of absolution. He was ready to die, for he knew he was in the state of grace, that he should not dread meeting God. He had pledged himself to follow Father Isaac, in life and death, for God's greater glory and service. He had known from the beginning that he might be murdered. Father Jogues had told him often that he must be prepared.

While Jean prayed and waited in meditation, the turmoil of the village softened into silence. The crowds were no longer shouting about the cabin and pressing against the walls. The savages were evidently gone off to their huts to sleep. Those of the cabin felt reassured. Nothing more would happen that night, so they wrapped themselves in their blankets and skins and laid themselves on their beds of twigs about the warmth of the fires. The silence of night brooded over Ossernenon. The fires crackled, the soft winds ruffled the bark walls, the people breathed heavily and snored. Jean stretched himself on the earth, in the darkness. Father Isaac was beyond this silence, beyond this world. He was with God, a martyr of Christ. He had hoped for so much. He was so certain that God would soften the hearts of the Iroquois. He was so brave. He had known he might die, and yet he was not afraid. He was not afraid of anything. He was a saint.

Jean remembered the story Father Isaac had told him about René Goupil; of how they had murdered René and thrown his body in the ravine; of how he had sought for the body, everywhere, since René was a martyr and his bones sacred. Father Isaac had escaped then. He was not killed. He was kept a slave and then he managed to free himself. Guillaume Coûture had lived four years among the Mohawks. He was adopted by them, and became well liked and respected. Father Isaac's "aunt" was friendly and her family was powerful. They would probably protect him against the Bear clan. As he thought, he inclined to believe that he would not be put to death. At least, now that the village was quiet as the grave, he had nothing much to fear for the rest of the night. In the morning, the Mohawks of Ossernenon would be calmer and the chiefs holding council at Tionontoguen would make known their decision. The fires burned low. All were soundly asleep.

He grieved for his dear Father. Into his mind came the instructions Father Isaac had given him in case he survived. He must be faithful, he must have courage. The body of Father Isaac was outside, he believed, abandoned on the path not far from the cabin. Jean longed to see his Father. He wanted to recover some articles which Father Isaac carried with him. If he waited till the morning, he would not be allowed to venture out. Besides, the savages would have carried the body off and thrown it over the side of the ravine, as they had done to the corpse of René. Now was the chance. It was dark, past midnight, and all the cabin and all the village was asleep. This was the time. He had a duty. He must slip out before the dawn and find Father Isaac. He would save the relics and bring them back to Three Rivers, if he were released or if he escaped. He listened intently. There was no sound.

Stealthily, Jean lifted himself to his feet and stepped slowly and carefully toward the door. It was so dark that he could scarcely see. He strained his eyes to discover the posts and the cracks of the door. He crept forward on his toes and safely reached the doorway. Cautiously, lest the skin barring the outer door creak, he pushed it aside, and felt the tingle of the night air on his face and neck. The night was clear and fresh. He could see more clearly now. The yellow paths were light, the dark cabins were heavy against the deep-blue sky. The winds sighed faintly as they rustled the dried leaves of the trees and there sounded the whir of the night creatures. No dark figures or shadows moved. He thought he knew where the body of Father Isaac lay. He would steal from the dark shelter of cabin to cabin.

More noiseless than Jean, blacker than the shadows of the trees and cabins, were the savages who lay motionless by the wall of his cabin. They were on guard through the stillness of the night. They rose like specters out of the earth, and before he could utter a cry crashed down the tomahawk upon his head. The blow felled him. Another blow, and another cracked his skull. They had the Frenchman, the brother of Ondessonk, the other sorcerer. He and Ondessonk had come together, they had prayed together, they had only one mind, to ask their God to bring ruin on the Mohawk nation. The braves did not rouse the village, but they laughed and rejoiced quietly among themselves. Expertly, they cut off his scalplock, and with the strong strokes

of their knives they severed the head from the trunk. They left
the body where it was, in the roadway. The head they carried
over to the angle of the palisades, and there they placed it on
the point of a pole, next to the head of Ondessonk.

The night passed quietly in Oneougiouré. The villagers stirred.
The old squaw and Honatteniate and their families looked about
for their Frenchman. They found his dead body a few steps from
their door. The cabins were awake, the buzz of voices rose to
a roar. In the first gleams of the morning sun the people rushed
to see with their own eyes the heads of the two Frenchmen
perched on the poles of the palisades. All of the Bear clan exulted and chanted and danced in triumph. Those of the Wolf and
Turtle families burst with anger and threats and curses. They
demanded revenge. Almost they were tempted to strike down
the jeering Bears. They knew that all was over now. They were
powerless.

Scarcely had the sun risen over the hills above the valley
when messengers raced up the trail from the river flats and burst
through the west gate of the stockade. They came from Tionontoguen, bearing the decisions of the council that had been debating through the night. They spoke to no one, nor listened to anyone, as was their custom, until they had reached the cabin where
the Frenchmen lodged and had eaten of the food placed before
them. Then they announced their message. The great chiefs
and the ancients of the Mohawks had ordained: Ondessonk and
his French brother were free; no harm must be done to them;
they were ordered out of the Mohawk village and were to be escorted back to Three Rivers.

At first in silence, and then in an uproar, the villagers heard
the judgment of the chiefs. It had happened as the Bear clan had
feared. Slyly they rejoiced in that they had circumvented the
Wolf, who had sought the release of the French. They had clam-
ored for the death of Ondessonk four years before, but the Wolf
and Turtle had always obstructed them. They had tried to prove
from the beginning that he was an evil genius, a malicious sorcerer, a Blackrobe who preached an unheard-of doctrine, who
prayed and made signs hateful in their eyes, who was in league
with enemy demons. They feared him always, even when he
pretended to be a harmless slave. He had escaped from them

through the treachery of the Dutch, just when they were surely
going to murder him. He had deceived the people when he came
back dressed like other Frenchmen, calling himself an ambassador. But then he came back dressed in his black robe, after
he had begun their ruin through the demon locked up in his black
box. When they killed his demon by drowning it in the river,
he was in their power. He was no longer protected. Still, as
they had feared, the council even then sought to let him live,
foolishly, since he was an enemy who would keep on striving to
destroy them. Now they had destroyed him outright, and they
had destroyed his brother. There was nothing more for the
council to debate.

The messengers who had come to Oneougiouré ordering the
release of Ondessonk, immediately turned back along the trail to
announce his murder. The chiefs and sachems, still assembled
at Tionontoguen, heard of the murders with amazement and
consternation. Hurriedly they assembled in a new council. In
a public session they all agreed in condemnation of the act.
Even the chiefs of the Bear clan expressed regret and blamed the
deed on the senseless, rash, unscrupulous young men of their
tribe. The Wolf and the Turtle orators vehemently denounced
the murderers and their accomplices. They cried woe on this
treachery that would forever shame and humiliate the Mohawks
before all nations.

Above all others, the lordly Kiotseaeton bewailed the death of
his brother, Ondessonk. Untold evils would descend upon the
Mohawks, he prophesied, because of this mutinous, rebellious
deed carried out by the young men of the Bears. Now there
was no alternative but war. This war, he foretold as one seeing
a vision, was to bring ruin upon his people. The more that the
hatchets and the arms of the Iroquois were raised for war, so
much the worse it would be for the nation, so much the greater
would be the calamities that would befall his people.

No punishment could legally be inflicted upon the murderers
of Ondessonk and the young French paleface. Nevertheless,
Kiotseaeton and his colleagues still hoped to preserve good relations with Onontio and the French. They were jealous of the
honor and faith of their nation, as they were sincerely outraged
by the perfidy of their own warriors. They therefore commis-

sioned the Huron, Otrihouré, who had been the comrade of Ondessonk, to assure Onontio that the Mohawks had no intention of
breaking the peace and waging war against the French, that they
were hostile only to the Algonquins. Furthermore, Otrihouré
was instructed to announce to Onontio that the Mohawks would
refrain from warlike acts until they had clearly announced their
intention to repudiate the peace with the Algonquins. Finally,
they commissioned the Huron to carry back presents which would
speak to Onontio, saying that the Mohawks apologized for the
killing of Ondessonk and his white brother, that Kiotseaeton and
the chiefs were so indignant that they had difficulty in restraining
their arms against the murderers, that they would like to kill
and exterminate all the proud, uncontrollable madmen in their
midst. But Otrihouré was also killed before ever he reached
Three Rivers.

So grieved and humiliated were the chiefs that they counseled
all the people to keep secret the vile deeds. Nevertheless, the
news leaked from the mouths of some of them down at the Dutch
village of Rensselaerswyck.[9] Arendt Van Corlaer, Dominie Megapolensis, Jean Labatie and the other burghers were horrified.
They were fond of Isaac, priest and Jesuit though he was. They
made diligent inquiries as to the cause and the details of his
death. They could learn but little, since the Mohawks were
secretive. No one would admit that he witnessed the affair.
Each one solemnly swore that he was not in Oneougiouré that
night. All that they would admit they knew was that Ondessonk
was struck down by young braves belonging to the Bear clan,
and that their act was in disobedience to the desires of their
elders.

Jean Labatie, the interpreter of the Dutch, collected the scant
bits of information he could pry out of the savages and forwarded an account to New Amsterdam,[10] to his friend, Johannes
La Montagne, a French Huguenot. In due time, Father Jogues'
"aunt" came down to Rensselaerswyck and gave to Dominie
Megapolensis all the goods of Ondessonk that she had been able
to save from the rapacious hands of the Iroquois. His possessions were few, a pair of pantaloons, a small missal, a breviary,
a ritual and a few trinkets.

[9] RENSSELAERSWYCK—Now Albany, New York.
[10] NEW AMSTERDAM—New York City.

Long since, his body and that of John de la Lande had been dragged down the hill under the stockade and across the flats to the Mohawk River, where they were carried off by the current. Through October, through November, through the bleak winter, on the point of the palisades overlooking the valley, remained impaled the withered heads of John de la Lande and Isaac Jogues.

The Biographer—The Reverend Francis X. Talbot, S.J. (1889–): The author of *Saint among Savages,* from which this selection is taken, is Father Francis X. Talbot, like Jogues a Jesuit. He was born in Philadelphia in 1889 and received his A.B. from St. Joseph's College in that city in 1909. Literary editor of *America* from 1922 to 1936, he became editor-in-chief of that journal in 1936. Father Talbot is widely known for his work in the field of Catholic journalism and for his active promotion of the Catholic Book Club and the Spiritual Book Associates. Of his published works the best known are his *Saint among Savages* and *Shining in Darkness,* the latter work a series of religious dramas of the Nativity and the Resurrection.

Suggestions for Study: Why was Jogues returning to the Mohawks? What made him rather confident of a good reception? Why did the Huron ambassadors desert him on the way? Who were faithful to him to the end? How was he actually received by the Mohawks? What provoked such a reception? What treachery brought about the death of Jogues? Why did the Indians not attack Jean openly instead of stealthily lying in wait for him? What became of Otrihouré? Why was it difficult to learn the truth about Saint Isaac Jogues' martyrdom?

Prove that the Indians were superstitious. Enumerate the reasons for which Jogues was murdered; for which de la Lande was killed. Were they both truly martyrs?

Exercises and Creative Work: Choose one of the following topics for essay writing or for class discussion: "The Missionary and the Trader," showing the contrast of motives, the dependence of one on the other, the adventures of each, the contributions of each toward the development of the frontier; "The Martyrdom of St. Isaac Jogues," a condensed and graphic narrative in your most vivid style, which you will then compare with the foregoing account; "Jogues the Man," an analysis of his character as portrayed in "An American Martyr"; "The Laws of the Mohawks," as revealed in this selection.

Report as you imagine they were the direct words of the debaters in the council of the Wolfs and Bears at Tionontoguen.

If you are interested in early American history, compile a series of short sketches of the lives of other famous missionaries.

A Biography of the Revolutionary Period

JUNÍPERO SERRA, APOSTLE OF CALIFORNIA

From *Junípero Serra, Pioneer Colonist of California*

AGNES REPPLIER

By Way of Introduction: In the Capitol at Washington stands a statue of Fray Junípero Serra in his Franciscan habit, holding a cross in his right hand and a model of a mission church in his left—California's tribute to "The Apostle of California." With other monuments of bronze and stone California honors the greatest of her pioneers and keeps his memory fresh, as well it should. But no memorial, we may be sure, gives greater pleasure to the apostolic soul of Fray Junípero Serra than the preservation of the blessed and melodious names with which he baptized the missions which he founded up and down the Pacific Coast from San Diego to San Francisco. For Junípero Serra was first and last the missionary in quest of souls, and it was to win Heaven's benediction on his missions that he named them in honor of the saints. The practice was not new with him. In adopting it he was but following the lead of Spanish explorers and missionaries from the days of Columbus on. These Christian men gave their new settlements the names of saints because they were confident that the heavenly patrons, with a proper sense of responsibility, would take a celestial interest in their terrestrial namesakes.

The story of the apostle of California is, indeed, but the climax of a long story which has its origin back in the days of Cortés, who entered Mexico City as conqueror in 1521, a good two centuries before Serra set foot on the shore of what is now San Diego, and almost a century before the first English settlement was made in America in 1607. It was a group of Spanish soldiers sent by Cortés in 1533 that first explored Lower California. Three years later Cortés himself set foot on the peninsula. Seven years later Juan Rodríguez Cabrillo, dispatched by Cortés on a tour of exploration up the coast, reached the site of San Diego, the first European to land on what is now California.

Apparently Spain found itself for a time too much occupied in colonizing Mexico to be concerned with exploiting its explorations to the north. At least, it was not until sixty years later, in 1602, that Sebastian Vizcaino took up the trail of Cabrillo, and after definitely settling the position of San Diego harbor, pushed on to the site of Monterey. At Monterey it was that the Holy Sacrifice of the Mass was first offered on Californian soil. Although Vizcaino reported that (Upper) California, in marked contrast to Lower California, was a veritable land of promise, the Spanish authorities had not, at the time, the money to profit by this voyage of discovery. The most it could do then, in 1697, was to allow two Jesuit missionaries, Padre Salvatierra and Padre Eusebio Kino, to try their hand again at establishing missions in Lower California, where the Jesuits themselves had already been compelled to give up once and where the Franciscans before them had found it impossible to remain. But the missionaries would have to finance the enterprise themselves; the government had no money for the purpose. Perhaps both government and Jesuits were hoping that by degrees the missions would be extended up the peninsula until they finally reached the promised land of which Vizcaino had so glowingly written.

At any rate, for seventy years the Padres toiled on in Lower California, persevering in the face of almost insuperable obstacles. The soil was barren and water was scarce. There was small hope of making many of the missions self-supporting. The spiritual soil was, if anything, more barren, for the natives were a depraved lot, given to polygamy, sorcery, and the vilest habits. Their utter indifference to religious ideas was disheartening in the extreme to missionaries more interested in their souls than in their bodies. Frequent epidemics of sickness and almost continual wars among the several tribes of Indians often destroyed overnight missions that had cost years of labor to build. At least two of the missionaries were murdered by hostile Indians; others barely escaped with their lives. In spite of these drawbacks and the lack of almost every convenience of life, the missionaries held on doggedly and even succeeded in extending their line of missions far up the peninsula. They were, in fact, not far distant from the boundary line between Lower and (Upper) California, when, in 1767, like a lightning stroke came the edict of Charles the Third banishing the Jesuits from Spain and all the Spanish colonies.

What was to happen to these missions established and maintained at the cost of so much self-sacrificing toil, in the face of such discouraging odds? Who would carry on the work? The Viceroy in Mexico answered those questions by asking the Franciscans of the Apostolic Missionary College of San Fernando in Mexico City to replace the banished Jesuits.

Although a dearth of subjects made compliance with this request difficult, the Friars showed their readiness to resume this most trying of enterprises, by sending to Lower California fifteen volunteers, with Fray Junípero Serra at their head. The little band reached the chief mission station at Loreto on Good Friday, April 1, 1768, were distributed at once through the several mission posts, and set to work with a will to repair as well as they could the damage done by one year of secular control. They continued the mission march toward the north. But the Franciscans were not to remain in Lower California for long.

As early as 1768 the Dominicans had sought the King's permission to found missions in Lower California. Deeming the territory too sparsely populated for two missionary bands, the Franciscans volunteered to cede the territory to the sons of St. Dominic, and in 1772 an agreement to that effect was finally signed by both parties and approved by the viceroy. Like their predecessors, the Dominicans worked on in spite of almost insuperable obstacles, and like them pushed even farther north toward San Diego. Their valiant work and the work of all who had gone before them was finally undone when the Mexican government secularized the missions of Lower California in 1834. The result was inevitable—the gradual decay of the mission stations and the almost complete disappearance of the Indians; in 1856 a government report gave the total Indian population of the peninsula as only 1938 souls.

One happy result of the transfer of Lower California from Franciscans to Dominicans was that it left Fray Junípero Serra free to cultivate other fields; free, that is, to undertake the lifework for which Providence had prepared him—the evangelization of (Upper) California. Of a truth, his career was now to begin. Before we follow him on his northward march, however, let us have a glance at the story of his earlier life.

Miguel José Serra was born at Petra on the Island of Majorca in 1713. He took the name of Junípero, after the gay-tempered disciple of St. Francis of Assisi, at the time of his profession in the Franciscan Order at Palma. Although he longed from the beginning of his religious life for a post on the missions, he showed such talent as a student and professor of philosophy that he was kept at Palma until 1749, when his heart's desire was finally realized. With twenty other Franciscans and six Dominicans he reached Vera Cruz in Mexico on New Year's day of 1750. Following the letter as well as the spirit of the Franciscan rule he walked the hundred miles to Mexico City. He was never to forget that hundred mile jaunt, for on the way he was bitten by a snake and received a wound which left him lame for the rest of his days.

After a successful three years of labor among the Pame Indians of the Sierra Gorda, he was recalled to the Apostolic College of San Fernando in the capital to prepare himself for the evangelization of the more difficult and more warlike Apaches of the Rio Sabá, who but recently had murdered two missionaries and several soldiers. The prospect pleased Junípero, but, to his disappointment, the Apaches were forgotten and he was called upon to devote his powers as a preacher to the reformation of the Spaniards in Mexico City. In spite of his impassioned excoriation of their luxurious and self-indulgent living, all classes flocked to hear him, and held him in the highest esteem; they liked a man who did not spare them and did not spare himself, either. Legends began to grow up around his name. Seven years of this separation from his dear Indians Fray Junípero had to endure before he finally received the assignment for which Providence had been preparing him—the evangelization and colonization of Upper California.

By 1768, more than two hundred years after Cabrillo's discovery of the harbor of San Diego, Spain had finally become aware of the fact that if she did not colonize Upper California, other nations would. Further delay was out of the question. Accordingly, the viceroy, Carlos Francisco de Croix and the inspector general, José de Gálvez, planned a "Sacred Expedition" to settle Monterey, which Sebastian Vizcaino had located beyond dispute in 1602. To Junípero Serra was to be confided the presidency of the missions to be settled there and elsewhere along the coast.

The party bound for Monterey was to travel in four divisions, two by water and two by land. Serra was to join the second land division commanded by Gaspar de Portolá. The first objective of the land parties was to be the harbor of San Diego; from there they would push northward to their ultimate destination. Their route of travel took them north through Lower California from the mission of Loreto to Guadalupe, thence to Santa Maria, and from Santa Maria to Velicatá, where one Friar was left to found a mission which might serve as a link between the old colonies and the new. The diary which Fray Junípero kept during his journey from San Loreto to San Diego, has provided the material for the following excerpt from the life of *Junípero Serra, Pioneer Colonist of California*, by Agnes Repplier.

ON HIS journey from Loreto to San Diego, Fray Serra kept a diary, the only personal record, save letters, of his long and arduous life. This was in accordance with the eighteenth century from which he seems so curiously remote. It was a diary-keeping period, and travelers were especially wont to record their experiences, because everybody did not then travel. Serra, entering a new and unknown land, felt that all he encountered was of interest, and perhaps importance, to the friars who stayed at home. The diary, which begins on the twenty-eighth of March and ends on the thirtieth of June, 1769, is now in the Ramirez Collection in Chicago. It fills thirty-four closely written folio pages, the letters so small and so crowded as to be almost imperceptible. Paper must have been a scarce commodity on that adventurous trip.

Serra, always lame, was lamer than ever when the time came to start. He had worked ceaselessly to forward the expedition. He had sung the last Mass on board the *San Carlos* before it "set forth joyfully on its voyage," and the last Mass on board the *San Antonio* when it followed. He had aroused the enthusiasm of soldiers and sailors, and had put fresh life into the hearts of all who were to travel by sea or land. Now when the fourth division (his division) was ready to go, he had so grievous an ulcer on his leg that Palou [1] besought Gálvez to leave him at San Francisco

---

[1] PALOU—Francisco Palou, a Franciscan Friar, was the lifelong intimate friend of Fray Junípero, and later his biographer.

Xavier,[2] and to accept himself (Palou) as a substitute. But Gálvez did not select his men with so much care in order to change
them for others. Substitutes formed no part of his plan. He
wrote characteristically to Palou: "I am glad that the Reverend
Padre Junípero insists on accompanying the expedition. I commend his faith, and his confidence that he will improve in health,
and that God will permit him to reach San Diego. I firmly believe
he will get there."

Which, being interpreted, meant that Serra was expected to go,
lame or otherwise. An order he gladly obeyed.

Portolá, being in command of the expedition, was perhaps less
pleased when the invalid joined it. He said plainly enough that
the lame friar might be unable to either walk or ride, and that to
carry him on a litter would be a difficult and burdensome piece of
work. But he could not oppose both Gálvez and Serra, and they
proved eventually to be right. A muleteer, whose name, Juan
Antonio Coronel, has been preserved for us, was summoned to give
help. He had made an ointment of suet and herbs which he used
for his galled mules, and Serra bade him apply it to the ulcerated
leg. It worked wonders, easing the pain, lessening the swelling,
and enabling the patient to ride with some degree of comfort.
The friars of San Francisco Xavier fitted him out with the simple
requirements for his journey, doing all they could to meet the
inevitable fatigue and suffering. Serra accepted these services
with the naive delight of one unaccustomed to any self-indulgence.
"For my sins I do not cease to be fond of my conveniences," he
wrote with a pleasant mixture of penitence and contentment.

At the mission of Guadalupe he fared better still; for there
Fray Juan Sancho, once a Spanish scholar of parts, Master of Arts
and Doctor of Philosophy, and now a lonely missionary in an
isolated post, gave him an Indian boy of fifteen as acolyte and
attendant. "The lad can speak Spanish, and has been taught to
serve Mass," wrote Serra in his diary. "Fray Juan clothed him
new for me, with leather jacket and boots, and gave him a saddle
mule with which he was well content. His parents were also
highly gratified by his good fortune."

Before the final departure from Velicatá it was decided to found
there a mission which might serve as a link between the old colo-

[2] San Francisco Xavier—A mission near Loreto, at this time still manned
by the Franciscans.

nies and the new. The proceeding, as described by Serra, seems incredibly casual. A rude hut had been erected by the first land division. In it Mass was said, the soldiers discharging their muskets at the Consecration. Fray Miguel de la Campa was chosen as the victim to be abandoned in this lonely spot, while his companions went on their way. We are told that he accepted his fate "very joyfully," which may have been true, though it sounds improbable. He was given a fair share of provisions, including soap and chocolate, a pair of saddle mules and some cattle. Two soldiers remained with him to guard the post. There were many Indians in the neighborhood, and Serra had hoped that they would be tempted by curiosity to approach the white men; but he considered sensibly that perhaps the musketry had frightened them off. "So much thunder," he said, "was not likely to make them feel at ease."

It was not until the expedition had broken camp and was leaving Velicatá that the first "Gentiles" made their hesitating appearance. They were twelve in number, ten men and two young boys. Serra hastened to meet them. The missionary, knowing by experience what Indians always wanted, lost no time in supplying his visitors with dried figs and raisins, which they devoured with avidity. In return they made an offering of fish, very rotten and ill-smelling. Serra then explained to them that Fray Miguel would be their friend, that they should come to him if they were in need —a rash invitation—and that they must never, *never* be guilty of stealing livestock from the mission. The savages, petrified with astonishment, listened so attentively to this harangue that the friar wound up his account of the incident with the confident hope that they would "soon be caught in the apostolic net."

By the middle of May the travelers had reached "green pastures and running waters." Many a night they slept under the brilliant stars, and woke to hear the snarling cry of the mountain lion as it prowled about the camp. Many a day they saw the pretty little cottontail rabbits scurrying from their forms, and rejoiced to find the land grow "smiling and gladsome." After a time they observed herds of deer feeding serenely, and giving no indications of fright. Nothing that happened *en route* is omitted from the diary. Once a Genoese cook, bad-tempered, committed "burricide," running his long knife through a she-ass because it blocked his path. Portolá sentenced this malefactor to pay four times the

value of the beast, which could ill be spared, and to walk the rest
of the way, a punishment well fitted to the crime. On the same
day which saw the murder of the ass, the *comandante*'s finest mare
gave birth to a beautiful little mule. The poor infant, being unable to follow its mother, was killed, to the distress of the Spaniards and to the satisfaction of the Indians, "who ate it joyfully."

A sharp lookout was kept for savages, and whenever a party of
them ventured within reach of the expedition they were promptly
invited, or compelled, to present themselves for inspection and
interrogation. One young hunter, more courageous or more desperately frightened than his comrades, fought so fiercely that his
captors were compelled to bind him with leather thongs, and drag
him, struggling and kicking, into camp. "Even after I had loosened his bonds, and assured him that no harm should come to
him," wrote Serra, "he was greatly disturbed. He carried a bow
and arrows, and his long hair, disheveled from his exertions, was
bound with a cord of bright blue wool, very well made. I tried to
find out how he came by it, and failed. He said his name was
Axajui. We gave him dried meat, tortillas, and figs. He ate
moderately, and with evident discomposure."

On the twenty-eighth of May Father Serra encountered two
squaws, one old and one young, who came through the woods,
"talking rapidly and vivaciously as is the custom of the sex, and
so respectably dressed that I could but wish that Christian ladies
were as modest." It is curious to hear this Spanish friar echo the
words of the French missionaries in Canada. "Modesty is natural
to the Indian women," wrote one of them, Père Cauchetière. "I
doubt if the most pious of French ladies are so irreproachably
modest in their dress."

Serra's first impression of the California Indians was modified
as time went on, though he retained a fair share of his early enthusiasm. "Their grace, vigor, friendliness, and gayety are charming," he wrote with confidence. "They have given us fish and
mussels, and have danced for our entertainment. Our mules ter-
rify them, and nothing will induce them to approach one."

This was in the beginning. . After a time these attractive savages
grew more curious and more familiar. They ceased to be frightened by the mules, and found out how easy it was for them to
alarm the poor beasts. The discovery delighted them beyond
measure, and woke the latent mischief in their hearts. To charge

with piercing yells on the little caravan, and see the heavily burdened animals plunge and scatter was their conception of a joke; and only a few musket shots fired in the air put an end to the diversion. "It was a necessary measure," sighed Serra, "but I could not but feel that this demonstration of our power left them in doubt of our affection."

In good truth, the childishness of adults quickly loses its charm. These children of nature were in their own fashion friendly to the strangers; but if they lacked the malignancy of the Mohawks and Onondagans, they lacked also their dignity of demeanor. It is always from missionaries that we get the most tolerant account of natives; but the breadth of the friar's sympathy in no wise dimmed the clearness of his vision. Portolá's attitude toward the Indians was one of disciplined endurance (he had been bidden to conciliate), Serra's one of understanding and compassion. "They have stolen my heart from me," he wrote simply, though well aware that they would, if they could, have stolen all his more portable possessions.

They were the most shameless and insistent of beggars. They wanted everything they saw, and they asked for everything they wanted. Though it was the custom of the men to go without clothes, they importuned the poor Franciscan to give them his brown robe, clutching it with eager covetous fingers. They had the audacity to beg Portolá's leather jerkin and his boots. They affected an innocent curiosity concerning Serra's spectacles, and when he rashly took them off his nose, he found to his consternation that they had vanished. "God only knows what it cost me to recover them," he wrote. "They had been passed from hand to hand, and it was only after a thousand difficulties that I got them back from some women who had fancied them as a decoration."

In trading, the Indians were fairly honest, though their keenness at a bargain was vastly amusing to the Spanish soldiers, who had not expected to find such competent merchants in the wilderness. They had nothing to sell but fish and occasional game; and what they wanted in return was any odd bit of cloth, or silk, or metal, which could be used as an ornament. Handkerchiefs, though their purpose was unknown, were in great demand. Sometimes the fish was not fresh. On one occasion Portolá tasted it and shook his head disapprovingly; whereupon the Indians offered him a grass basket filled with a dark-colored, pleasant-smelling powder. They intimated that he must sprinkle it on the doubtful fish, and true enough it imparted a spicy flavor which made the food palatable if not wholesome. These simple savages had discovered at least one of the devices of civilization.

Every day of the long journey helped to convince Serra that there was no Strait of Anian.[3] Had it existed, he said, it must inevitably have crossed their path and blocked their progress. They could not have evaded it if they had wanted to. The travelers gave a name, usually that of a saint, to every site at which they stopped. One pleasant spot, which they were loath to leave, they adroitly dedicated to *Nuestra Senora la Peregrina* (Our Lady the Pilgrim), "so as to bring the Holy Virgin into the enterprise, and have her as a member of the expedition." On the thirteenth of June there is a fervent entry in the diary: "The feast of my beloved San Antonio de Padua. We rose so early that Mass was said before daybreak. At six we started, having sent men ahead to search for running water, or, if need be, open water holes. The road lasted but a league or two. Our beasts drank all the water in the two holes. There was none left for cooking, and we found it almost impossible to push on. In memory of these troubles—or favors—sent by Heaven, we wished to call the place *San Antonio de los trabajos*" (of the hardships); "but the most miraculous Saint desired to temper our trials with consolations. Word was brought by our explorers that tomorrow we should reach two good watering places, one of them three leagues, and the other five leagues, away. Both have clear running streams with pasture for the beasts. Blessed be God."

Three days later the expedition reached a spot so beautiful and so fertile that Serra declared it was worthy, not of a mission, but of a city; a city within sight of the hills and within sound of the sea; and that it should be dedicated to the "miraculous Saint," to make amends for their lack of confidence.[4]

The greenness of the land, which became fairer day by day, rejoiced the friar's beauty-loving heart. The flowers were his especial delight, and he failed to reproach himself for the pleasure he took in them because they grew wild by the watercourses, God's gift to the lowly. There were vines heavy with unripe grapes, and

[3] STRAIT OF ANIAN—A mythical water route believed by early explorers to connect the Atlantic and the Pacific oceans somewhere north of Mexico.

[4] LACK OF CONFIDENCE—In 1771 Fray Junípero did dedicate a mission to San Antonio de Padua, but its location was much farther up the coast.

fields of poppies, and above and beyond all else roses—roses that would have thrilled an Andalusian with their sweet abundance. Early in June we find Serra writing in a sort of ecstasy: "Today we have seen the queen of all flowers, the rose of Castile. I have before me now a branch with three perfect blossoms, others half-blown, and six as yet unpetaled. I would I were a chemist, and could distil and preserve their fragrance."

The kind of "favors" which we ungodly ones call troubles were not yet over. If there were spreading trees under which the pilgrims found grateful shelter, there were also fleas and ticks to harass them. If they had plenty of water one day, it was scarce and brackish the next. If there were pleasant marches over grassy plains, there were also hills to be laboriously climbed and perilously descended, "the earth sliding beneath our feet." Sometimes these hills were so precipitous that no one dared to ride. "Half walking, half creeping, stumbling and scrambling to our feet only to fall again, we made our toilsome way into the valley." If Portolá's control over his soldiers was so absolute that they never relaxed their vigilance or disregarded a command, the Indians who had accompanied the expedition from the start were less reliable. No sooner had the forbidding desert been replaced by a smiling and verdant country than they began to grow restless and to slip away, perhaps to seek a less laborious life, perhaps to join the nearest tribe. An entry in the diary records this lamentable fact:

"Today, after we had eaten our noonday meal, nine Indians deserted the camp. Search was made for them, but they had disappeared utterly. Their comrades declared they did not know where or why they had gone. They had always been well fed and well treated, and had appeared content. God bless them, as well for the service they have given, as for the loss they have inflicted upon us."

A typically Franciscan sentiment.

Happily the long journey was drawing to an end, and it is a pleasing circumstance that the travelers were made aware of this fact by seeing in the distance two "Gentiles" one of whom wore a blue cotton tunic. They made sure that this garment must have been given him at San Diego by one of the earlier expeditions. Gálvez, it was remembered, had been determined that the Indians should be clad. It was to his mind the first step toward civilization. It chanced that at the time he was visiting Lower California,

six French Academicians, accompanied by several officers of the
Spanish marine, came to the peninsula to observe the transit of
Venus. The mere thought that these distinguished foreigners
might perchance see subjects of the King of Spain wandering un-
clad over the land so humiliated Gálvez that he confiscated several
bales of cotton cloth, and gave stern orders that all who could be
reached should be covered. It was his express desire that this
rule should be followed in the Franciscan, as it had been always
followed in the Jesuit, missions. Therefore when Portolá and
Serra beheld the blue tunic they felt sure that their countrymen
were at hand.

And they were right. The approaching Indians brought them
the good tidings that San Diego was but a two-days' journey even
for Portolá's tired men and still more tired beasts. They said
that both ships were in port, that the first land expedition had
arrived long since, and that there were many friars on the spot.
Cheered and heartened, the company pushed on over a country so
broken and rock-strewn that Serra—always a truth-teller—feared
his heart would stop beating from sheer fright. The next day they
were met by ten soldiers whom the *comandante,* Rivera y Mon-
cada, had sent to escort them to their destination. Under their
guidance they encamped for the last night on level ground by
running water, and in the morning, July first, 1769, they reached a
gentle eminence from which they could see the ships riding at
anchor, and the Spanish flag flying in the breeze. Portolá's soldiers fired a salute which was answered joyously from land and
sea. The Sacred Expedition of Gálvez had entered the promised
land. The colonization of California had begun.

The Biographer—Agnes Repplier: The life story of this author
appears elsewhere in this book. See the index.

Suggestions for Study: Why did travellers like Fray Junípero Serra
keep diaries of their journeys? How did his party treat the Indians whom
they met? How did Serra's attitude toward the Indians differ from that
of Portolá? Why are missionaries' accounts of the savages always more
tolerant than those of other explorers? Why do you suppose the Indians
were terrified at their first sight of the Spaniards' mules? Why did the
party give a saint's name to every site where they encamped? Miss
Repplier thinks that Fray Junípero lacked a sense of humor. After your
reading of the excerpts from his diary do you agree or disagree with her?
What did Fray Junípero's beloved San Antonio de Padua find for the

party? What were some other things, besides Indians, which delighted Junípero on his journey? And what were some of the major hardships and troubles which his party had to endure? By what token did the party know that they were nearing San Diego?

Exercises and Creative Work: Even today some people, and not all of them are travellers, keep diaries. Why do they do it? What do they record in their diaries? If Chesterton was right in saying that "nothing is, or can be uninteresting," plenty of things happen to you to furnish material for a worth-while diary, provided you are interested. Try keeping one for a week. It may not become a precious document like the diary of Fray Junípero Serra, but it should help you in many ways. What ways?

Junípero Serra and the missionaries of his time had few of the conveniences which surround you today. Make a list of some of the conveniences they lacked, and discuss whether their coming has made for better living or only for more comfortable living.

Make a litany of the Spanish names of saints given to cities in Lower and Upper California, and report on the life of the saint whose name most appeals to you, or who you think is a most fitting patron for a city in California.

For Further Reading: By all means read the rest of Miss Repplier's biography of Junípero Serra, or at least, the chapter entitled "The Land of Promise," in which you will see how Serra's magnetic force won the easy-going Indians of Monterey to the Faith; how he "cut out bright-colored cotton clothes for the children, and taught the delighted mothers how to make them up." Read how he taught the Indians, as their first lesson in Spanish, to say "Amar a Dios," (Love God), so that it became the universal greeting in that land. You will surely enjoy, too, "The Challenge to Saint Francis," the chapter which recounts the discovery of the great Bay of San Francisco.

Some other titles for reading about Fray Junípero Serra and the California missions are:

Helen Hunt Jackson	*Father Junípero Serra and the Mission Indians of California*
Charles Warren Stoddard	*In the Footprints of the Padres*
Zephyrin Engelhardt	*The Missions and Missionaries of California*

A Biography of the National Period

MOTHER SETON

From *An American Woman*

LEONARD FEENEY

By Way of Introduction: Born two years before the outbreak of the Revolutionary War; granddaughter of the rector of St. Andrew's Episcopal Church, Richmond, Staten Island; motherless at the age of three; married at nineteen and mother of two sons and three daughters; founder of the first charitable organization in New York and probably in the United States; widow at the age of twenty-nine and practically penniless at thirty-three—who would have dreamed that this Elizabeth Ann Bayley Seton was to become the foundress of the first native religious community of Catholic nuns and the "patroness of the parochial school system" in the United States? The story of Mother Seton's life is indeed that of "An American Woman"; it is also that of the "valiant woman" held up for our admiration in the Holy Scriptures.

IN THE hope of having soon on the calendar of our saints a name to rank in equal brilliance with such spiritual heroes as Teresa of Avila, Thérèse of Lisieux, Catherine of Genoa, Rose of Lima, Joan of Arc, Jane Frances of Dijon, Bernadette of Lourdes, let us review, in brief outline, some of the facts in the career of our own Elizabeth Ann Seton, "Elizabeth of New York," an achievement of holiness of the New World; an American Woman!

The facts about Elizabeth Seton are most impressive. To begin, she was the mother of five children, the grandmother and aunt of two Archbishops. She was the spiritual mother of 8,911 nuns now alive (not to speak of the hundreds of others who have died under the aegis of her inspiration). If there are in America today (1937) —and there are— 8 Colleges, 160 High Schools and Academies, 447 Parochial Schools, 91 Hospitals, 69 Schools for Nursing, 6 Orphanages, 18 Day Nurseries, 21 Infant Asylums, 3 Technical Schools, 6 Retreats for Nervous Diseases, 5 Homes for Working Girls, 1 Leper Home, 8 Schools and Asylums, 2 Schools for Deaf Mutes, 20 Commercial Schools, and 3 Normal Schools under the direction of her "Daughters of Charity," there is no other reason to explain it except the courage and spiritual inspiration of one little American girl. For from her, whether in the white coronettes of the French peasant, or in the black caps of the Italian widow, or in other styles, stem directly or indirectly all the Sisters of Charity in the United States of America.

During Elizabeth Bayley's childhood the American Revolutionary War was fought. But what is the use of commemorating the details of a war waged when one was a baby? Do you remember, if any, the wars that were fought when you were booing and cooing in the cradle? Wars pass over an infant's head like vapors in the night. And if, as it is asserted, a child does not reach the full use of reason until about the age of seven, it may be said of the Revolutionary War that it occurred wholly within Elizabeth's lifetime, but that it had as much importance to her as something that happened in the pre-historic age.

Except, perhaps, she might have remembered (for she was then six) the miseries of the winter of 1780, when New York was under siege, and between cold and starvation the inhabitants barely managed to survive until peace was restored. The city harbored many Royalists, of whom Elizabeth's father was one, but despite their allegiance to the crown of England, even these were under suspicion,[1] and anything that resembled or could be taken for an American soldier was quickly either shot by a Redcoat or else tomahawked by an Indian.

The fact that Richard Bayley's sympathies in the war were with England can be explained by the fact that he was a surgeon in the British army, and was loath to be accused of disloyalty to his duty as a soldier. But such were the qualities of his character and learning that when the American Independence was established he was warmly received by the citizens of the new Republic and was given posts of honor in the community. The war cost him no serious reversal of fortune, and the days of Elizabeth's girlhood were passed in extreme comfort. Her education was genteel, and she was able, in her time as a belle, to achieve rank in the most exclusive New York society of the day.

Elizabeth's mother, it should be said, died when the child was three years old, and soon afterwards her father married again.

---

[1] THESE WERE UNDER SUSPICION—By the English, who were then holding New York City.

Elizabeth came to love and respect her stepmother as much as is possible in such cases, but her father became for her henceforth pretty much of mother and father combined. Nor did he cease to make her the chief object of his affection and interest even when other children came to him in the second marriage.

Elizabeth was brought up in an age when a girl was given a distinctly feminine education, one that coincided in practically nothing with the training given a boy. She did not undertake the heavy studies like science, business, and accounting, and never dreamed of being prepared for one of the professions. Music, drawing, French, literature, sewing, dancing, housewifery, and similar studies were in the curriculum allotted to her. In Elizabeth's case there was especial opportunity for developing her mind because of her father's library. She grew into books naturally; was, and was encouraged to be, an inveterate reader, and came to be acquainted extensively with religious literature, history, and most of the greater poets. She even shied away from French and music, but at her father's command (she could truly say in later life that she never once disobeyed him) she resumed them and became proficient in both.

To Richard Bayley's credit be it said that his daughter was his daughter, not his son. And his moral training of her was flawless. Everything that was fine in the way of natural virtue he strove to inculcate, even to curbing excessive exuberance of spirits, which, in an affectionate nature, is a necessary astringent. Under his discipline, reasonably lenient, judiciously severe, there developed in Elizabeth's character, as Madame De Barberey [2] has remarked, that happy combination of vivacity and restraint that makes a girl so delightful.

What was lacking in Richard Bayley was a belief consonant with his disciplinary regime. The discipline was Christian,— the dogma indefinite. She needed to be told, by way of heartening her in her penances, that a little girl just like herself once became the Mother of God. She needed to know that the Incarnation was not merely an opinion but a fact, and that the Body of Christ, wounded on the Cross for love of us, has become, not merely commemoratively, but in substance and truth, our Food. There is, however, a lesson for Catholic parents to learn from this type of

[2] MADAME DE BARBEREY—Author of the biography, *Elizabeth Seton.*

righteous, though faint-believing Christian father. If his tendency was to emphasize the moral training of his daughter by way of compensating for what he could not teach her in the way of Christian dogma, shall it be theirs, in face of what they know of the justice of God through the Incarnation and death of Christ, to teach their children all Catechism and no moral precept and practice? The "righteous" non-Catholic may drive his child to despair. But the "pious" Catholic may let his children go to the dogs.

Furthermore, in Dr. Bayley's case, his love of God was deeper then he knew. Granted that God had seemed to mean no more to him than an abstract being, without light or warmth, there were times when the sheer goodness of his nature seemed to ally itself to Grace to effect a most touching display of Christ-like charity.

There is the story told of him, how, when he was seated one evening in the living room of his home in the Battery, then the fashionable section of New York City, a surgeon from Staten Island came to ask his advice concerning a critical operation. Though anxious to oblige, Dr. Bayley felt unequal to going to see the patient. It was late at night, the distance was great; he was exhausted from his absorbing engagements during the day. It was very dark too, in the ill-illuminated New York of those days. And if there is one thing more than another that requires the most heroic self-conquest, it is to put one's shoes on again after one has settled into one's slippers for the night.

Doctor Bayley's fellow surgeon was disappointed. "How your refusal will grieve those needy persons who are so anxious to see you!" he said. "It will pain me very much to impart this news to them. They are already so unfortunate, and they are so poor!"

"They are poor?" exclaimed Dr. Bayley, jumping to his feet. "They are poor? Well, why didn't you tell me that before? Let us go to them!"

God makes strange alliances in the order of charity. Dr. Richard Bayley lost his life through ministering to poor, plague-ridden Irish immigrants, marooned in Quarantine in New York's port. He had caught the infection of these poor immigrants, who had yellow fever. Had he also caught the infection of their Faith? We do not know, except for this description of his death, seven days later, written by his most loved daughter, who had rushed immediately to his side. It is dated September 5, 1801.

"No remedy could give him a moment's relief, nor could he ever lie still without holding my hand. 'All the horrors are coming, my child, I feel them all': this and other expressions and the charge he gave me of his keys convinced me that he knew the worst from the beginning. No remedy produced any change for the better, and the third day he looked earnestly into my face and said: 'The hand of God is in all this: nothing more can be done,' and repeatedly called, 'My Christ Jesus, have mercy on me!' He was in extreme pain until about half-past two on Monday afternoon, the seventeenth, when he became perfectly easy, put his hand in mine and breathed the last of life."

This was not the only time in the life of Elizabeth Seton that a loved one would die with a hand in hers, and in succumbing, mention for the first time the holy name of Jesus. It seems to have been her lot throughout life, both after her conversion to the Catholic Faith and even in the years when she was groping about for it, to have been almost miraculously effective at the deathbeds of those she loved. Her presence seemed always destined to be a benediction to the souls of her dear ones.

Richard Bayley was, as we can see, just the father Elizabeth needed. He had spirit, he had courage, he had charity seeking an outlet into the realm of the Divine. What was deficient in him his daughter, his Betty, more than fulfilled for him vicariously in her own good time. In the high place he holds with her now in Heaven, and in the much hoped-for day of her canonization, a day well-celebrated in the next world as in this, Richard Bayley may be proud to have been such a father to such a daughter, and in the last breath of life to have held her hand.

Be it also said of him that for all the intensity of his love for his favorite daughter, he was not a possessive father. No one welcomed more than he the advent into her life of romance and a husband in young William Seton.

It cannot be denied that William Seton was honorable, loyal, charming, and easy to love. But the flaming spirit in that union was Elizabeth, the little girl with the oval face and the large dark eyes whom he came eventually to prize more than all the donnas of Italy and demoiselles of France. He was an adequate, but indifferent, Christian. But her spirit worked in his, and her holiness set him on fire even to bursting into a beautiful invocation of the name of Jesus on his deathbed, just as her father had done under the influence of her prayers. This was her way, to inflame all she met with the contagion of her sanctity. The social people of New York, seeing her going out in the early morning with her little basket of medicines and food for the poor, could find no other name for her but Protestant "Sister of Charity."

Indeed it can be said that in the first years of Elizabeth's life (other than a very mild concern for William's health) there was not a single dark cloud. She describes her quiet Sunday, with a good coal fire in the evening and a volume of Blair's sermons for spiritual reflection. She tells her friend Mrs. Sadler, sojourning in Paris, that "as for your Boulevards, I dare say they are very inferior to the pure air of the Battery," and can describe to the same lady the much-praised beauty of her first child, Anna Maria, by saying, "Respecting a certain pair of eyes, they are much nearer black than any other color, which with a very small nose and mouth, dimpled cheeks and chin, rosy face and never-ceasing animation, form an object rather too interesting for my pen. Her grandfather Bayley will tell you that he sees more sense, intelligence and inquiry in that little face than in any other in the world, that he can converse more with her than with any woman in New York. In short, she is her mother's own daughter, and you may be sure, her father's pride."

Elizabeth had a remarkable ability at literary expression, a keen relish for and judgment of books, could dance, played the piano beautifully, and in the circle of intimates in her own parlor could sing with a certain appeal. There was in her correspondence of affection with relatives or friends no forced religiosity, and God was not dragged in for others to witness in public display. All of the qualities of the good old-fashioned girl that would have delighted the hearts of our Victorian ancestors were present in Elizabeth. As a model letter of such a type, we can quote a passage from this to her father, which was written five years after her marriage:

"Should you be, in your retirement, unoccupied by the cares and solicitudes that generally accompany you, a letter from your daughter will be very acceptable; if otherwise, it will be read in haste, and the idea, 'Bett is a goose,' will cross your mind. I send it to take its chance, hoping, as the children say, it may find you well, as I am the same. It is currently reported that you are gone to New London to inquire into the origin of the fever, and that you are to proceed to Boston to see your children. But I hope you will very soon return, and convince the ladies who chatter on the subject that the origin is not the object of your pursuit, but the remedy."

And again: "My dear Mr. Monitor (her father): That you are in the enjoyment of health in the midst of dangers, toil, and death, is a subject of high exultation to me; and if the prayers of a good, quiet, little female are supposed to be of any avail, it will be long continued to you, with the hope that the visual rays of our fellow-citizens will in time be brightened by your labors. If you would sometimes direct Helen's (her step-sister's) pen to Bloomingdale, it would be a most grateful substitute for your own."

And again, after the mention of the coal fire and the volume of sermons on a Sunday evening, quoted above:

"But avast! I am an American savage, I suppose, and should not mention such dull insipidities to a lady in the largest metropolis in the world, who can go and see blond perukes [3] on Sunday eve and dance among the gayest. After all I think the first point of religion is cheerfulness and harmony. They who have these in view are certainly right."

All this surface gaiety might be skimmed from the heart of Elizabeth Seton without one's ever realizing the thunder, the urge, the stress,—in a word, the Grace, that was forever beating at the core of it. The conflict in her life, from the very beginning, was religious. Otherwise, how is it that, at this very period, in the atmosphere of loving friends, happy children, admiring relatives, and an adoring husband,—with no worries, physical or financial, to harass her, we find her constantly retreating to her little study to write in her private journal of devotions such intense prayers as this:

"Almighty Giver of all mercies! Father of all, who knowest my heart and pitiest its weakness and errors, thou knowest the desire of my soul; it struggles to wing its flight to thee, its Creator, and sinks again in sorrow for that imperfection which draws it back again to earth. How long shall I contend with sin and mortality? When will that hour arrive which will free the

[3] PERUKES—Wigs or periwigs worn by men.

troubled spirit from its prison, and change the shadow of this life for immortality and endless happiness? I bow to thee, my God! in cheerful hope that, confiding in thy infinite mercy and assisted by thy powerful grace, I shall soon arrive to that hour of unspeakable joy. But if it is thy will the spirit shall yet contend with its dust, assist me to conduct myself through this life as not to render it an enemy, but a conductor to that happy state where all mortal contentions are done away, and where thy eternal presence will bestow eternal felicity."

Of these and similar passages, Elizabeth was to write, upon reading them after her conversion, "Oh, how different now. Oh, praise and eternal gratitude!" Yet who shall have scorn for a spirit achieving as much as it was capable of in the days in which this diary was penned? God's arm is not shortened because the chosen one of His heart is confined, for the moment, in the dismal twilight of heresy. Upon the soul of Elizabeth Seton He had set His seal.

It may suffice to end this part of our story with some excerpts from the letters she wrote to her own children, chiefly to Anna Maria, her oldest. The following are subjoined as specimens of her soul's greatness:

"My Dear Anna Maria:

This is your birthday, the day I first held you in my arms. May God Almighty bless you, my child, and make you His child forever. Your mother's soul prays to Him to lead you through this world, so that we may come to His Heavenly kingdom in peace, through the merits of our blessed Saviour."

Again:

"My dearest Anna must remember that our blessed Lord gave us the parable of the wise and foolish virgins to make us careful to choose our part with the wise ones, and to keep in readiness for His coming, which will be in an hour we know not of; and should He find us, dear child, out of the road of our duty, like sheep gone astray from their shepherd, where shall we hide from His presence who can see through the darkest shades and bring us from the farthest ends of the world? If we would please Him, and be found among His children, we must learn what our duty is, pray to Him for grace to do it, and then set our whole heart and soul to perform it. And what is your duty, my dear child? You know it, and I pray God to keep you in it, that, in that blessed day when He shall come to call us to our heavenly home, we may see our dear Anna in the number of those dear children to whom He shall say, 'Come, ye blessed of My Father.'

. . . Your own dear mother"

During the winter of 1803 Elizabeth Seton lost her husband. She had gone with him, taking their daughter Anna and leaving the other children with friends in New York, to Italy. From the beginning of his illness William had longed to be with some noble Italian friends of his earlier years, the Filicchis, and it was thought that the climate of Italy might do him good. The journey was one of almost unbelievable hardship. The little brig, "The Shepherdess," finally made the crossing from New York to Leghorn in fifty-six days. The unfortunate family was refused permission to proceed at once to the home of the Filicchis, for fear of contagion. Elizabeth, her eight-year-old daughter, and her helpless husband, were confined in an unhealthy lazaretto for forty endless days and nights before they were allowed to go to the home of the friends who awaited them anxiously. Eight days later William died, secure in his wife's belief that his soul would be saved.

In this time of trial the Filicchi family sustained and comforted Elizabeth. Her health was delicate, and she had endured ninety-six days of the strictest confinement, under the most trying conditions. The faith of the Filicchis gave them the power of comforting the lonely widow, and she saw the power, as well as the beauty of that faith, in their daily lives. More and more was the conviction borne in upon her that she should surrender her life to the Catholic Church. She was not unduly influenced, as is evidenced by the fact that she did not at this time definitely decide the issue, but returned to her children in New York with the problem unsolved. The charity of the Filicchis continued to sustain her. Throughout her lifetime Elizabeth was free to use any and all of the resources of the wealthy Italian family. This was most necessary at this time, because William's long illness had exhausted the resources of the little family, and the growing children must be cared for.

Eventually Elizabeth made her great decision. She must, for the sake of her own soul and the souls of her children, enter the Catholic Church. Her friends might, and did, desert her; the city which had been the loved home of her childhood might, and did, become unbearable to her so that she should flee from it in willing exile, but she had no choice. In the spring of 1805 Elizabeth entered the communion of the Church.

Her courage in making this decision is difficult for us to appreciate in this day when Catholic teachers are honored and respected by the general public. She had been teaching in various private schools, gradually approaching nearer and nearer to that financial independence which her self-respect demanded. But the parents of her students would not allow their children to be taught by a "Roman Catholic." When she entered the Church she lost her means of livelihood.

It chanced that a visitor to New York, Father Du Bourg of Baltimore, heard of her plight from her parish priest. He was informed of her great desire to conduct a school for Catholic girls, thus to secure the necessities of life for herself and her children, and at the same time to perform the service she felt herself most able to do for the Church. The idea seemed to him to be very good, but the prospects were very poor in New York. When he returned to his home city Father Du Bourg wrote to Elizabeth in New York:

"Come to us, Mrs. Seton; we will help you to form a plan of life that will save your children from the dangers of ridicule and persecution that threaten them. You will find here at Baltimore more of the consolations of your faith than you have yet tasted. There need be no building. You can rent a house."

Nothing but an Homeric recital of details could satisfactorily describe the incidents that followed from Elizabeth's arrival at Baltimore until the hour of her death. It is impossible to give here an exact dissertation as to how a religious community is founded, with what canonical permissions, and with what regulations. Nor is it possible to embark on a treatise as to the precise difference between the Sisters of Charity who eventually went under the French rule, and adopted those big-winged hats, and those who stayed under the American rule and still retain the little black bonnets with a ribbon and a bow. It is sufficient to say that had it not been for Elizabeth Seton, Divine Providence would have had to find some other way of supplying us with our Sisters of Charity and our Parochial Schools. However, it may be necessary to explain just what a nun is.

A nun is a little lady *all* consecrated to God. She arises at five in the morning and goes to bed about nine at night. Before she has breakfast she has at least two hours of prayer, including Holy Mass. Every moment of the day in which she is not occupied with some necessary task she is bettering her soul by way of spiritual reading, examination of conscience, and the like. She has no worldly ambitions, seeks no romance,—asks no reward offered on this earth. She is poor, chaste, obedient; anxious to be always the maximum of service to her sisters and to her neighbors, and the minimum of annoyance. She has the loveliest manners existent in this world, is modest, soft-voiced, invariably gay. Laughter comes to her as easily as sunlight. She is most tender in her affections, but chastity gives her a strength that is almost masculine. Perhaps I should better call her "boyish." Indeed, I feel that is her right epithet. She talks easily and freely because the practice of contemplation has taught her what is valuable to speak. She holds more fondness for her parents in a single thought than all their married daughters do in a thousand. She retains her girlishness longest, and at forty, fifty, or even sixty, it is hard to guess her age. Yet she is never coy or "feminine." She is as much at home discussing a new furnace for the cellar with the janitor as she is discussing the virtues of Saint Catherine of Genoa with her sisters at recreation. She wears a dress that clearly distinguishes her from the world, yet has her little precisions as to how it should be arranged in an attractive manner. She is most responsive to affection, but will not allow herself to be spoiled. Compliments please her, but she banishes them with a gesture, and prefers to shine in one's eyes in simple innocence and sober black. She feels safest and most at home in the chapel, and will spend hours kneeling there, unmindful of any physical distress, before the Blessed Sacrament. She calls Our Lady "Her Mother" and Our Lord "Her Spouse," and she has little secrecies with them that no one dare inquire about or conjecture. She is beautiful in sickness, and capable of bearing pain more silently than any creature of this earth. She is modest and undramatic in her death, asking only to be laid in the grave-yard of her community as "one of the sisters," with a tombstone distinguishable only by the name, from any other. In death she rejoices most in those hours of her life that were lived through pure faith, in which she took Christ's revelation literally, and did not question or doubt. It usually costs no more than ten or twelve dollars to bury her. And there are no flowers. . . .

This is the Catholic nun as her people know her. And of her kind there were only a few scattered handfuls here in America until Elizabeth Seton arrived on the scene. . . .

Father Du Bourg rented a house for Elizabeth in Paca Street, Baltimore, not far from Saint Mary's Seminary. It was two stories in height, not counting a little attic, and Elizabeth and the children adored it. So happy was she in her new surroundings that she immediately wrote to a member of the Filicchi family: "If I ever dared ask God for anything touching our temporal future, it would most assuredly be that we might never be forced to return to New York." When summer came on and the boys were released for vacation from Georgetown College, to which the Filicchi family had sent them, Father Du Bourg took them in at his seminary, sparing her the added expense of keeping them at home.

In the little house rented for her in Paca Street Elizabeth opened her school for girls. The Catholics of Baltimore were numerous and fervent, and so many children came at once that the house was filled. The summer passed hopefully and happily.

A great event occurred in the autumn of 1808. Not only did plenty of children return for instruction at Elizabeth's school, but something much more interesting arrived. It seems there was in Philadelphia a very beautiful and spiritual young girl named Cecilia O'Conway who wanted to become a nun; felt she had an imperative vocation to become one. But we had precious few con-vents at that time, and the most natural place for her to go was to Europe to find admission to one of the Orders there.

Fortunately it happened that Father Babade, from Saint Mary's Seminary in Baltimore, who had been acting for some time as chaplain to Elizabeth's little establishment, (indeed, had become her confessor)—was visiting in Philadelphia and he met the father of the O'Conway girl. He told him that there was something in the nature of a convent in Baltimore, in charge of a holy little widow, "the admiration of all who knew her," not yet a nun, but who was in the way of becoming one, and who could at least offer his daughter all she desired in the way of retirement, sacrifice, and good works.

Miss O'Conway immediately communicated with Elizabeth, and a few weeks later arrived in Baltimore as her first postulant.

Next, Mr. Samuel Sutherland Cooper, a wealthy convert studying for the priesthood at Saint Mary's, undertook to dispose of some of his fortune, and bought Elizabeth a piece of property with a house of sorts upon it, in Emmitsburg, fifty miles west of Baltimore, feeling that the country was the best place to start the mother-house of a religious community, which project everyone saw was soon to come.

The year went on happily, with some hardships, but still with great promises ahead for the future, especially when the group should go to Emmitsburg.

In the spring of 1809 another little postulant arrived, again from Philadelphia, a Miss Maria Murphy. And a month later two more, Mary Ann Butler and Susan Clossy of New York. Many young Baltimore girls became interested, began reading spiritual books, examining their consciences, scrapping their beaux, and taking counsel with their confessors.

With five aspiring nuns under one roof, Bishop Carroll and Father Du Bourg held conferences and made plans for uniting them as a religious community. The first procedure was to let Elizabeth and the young ladies take simple vows to bind for a year. This they did, and Elizabeth was appointed their directress. They had as yet no permanent rule or any permanent name. They called themselves for the time being The Sisters of Saint Joseph. They put their heads together and chose a form of religious dress. The choice fell for almost the identical costume Elizabeth had worn since the beginning of her widowhood, a black dress with a short cape. The only difference was that they also added a small white muslin cap, with a fluted border, and a black band holding it on, and fastened under the chin. It was similar to a costume Elizabeth had seen on some nuns in Italy, and admired.

It was in June, 1809, on the Feast of Corpus Christi, that this little band of five sisters appeared for the first time in public, in Saint Mary's Chapel, at Mass. The place was crowded. That they felt strange both to themselves and others cannot be denied. And yet a little proud, too, for there is a certain indefinable and subtle pleasure in being uniformed, as the young seminarian will tell you when he puts on his cassock for the first time, the letter-carrier when he puts on his first light-blue uniform, the policeman his first dark-blue one, and most naturally, the young Catholic girl when she is displayed in public the first time, accoutred as the Bride of Christ.

The school continued to run at full quota. In no time two more postulants arrived to join the community. The seventh arrival was the most astounding of all. It was none other than Cecilia Seton, Elizabeth's sister-in-law from New York, determined, despite the precarious state of her health, to live always with Elizabeth, and become a nun.

From the time Mother Seton (for that is her name to the Catholics of America since the time in her life of which we are speaking), was appointed the temporary directress of the first little religious community of nuns in America, every month, every week, every day, was an incessant march on to her death. True, there were nearly twelve years to intervene until that time, but it was to be strict soldiering all the way to her last breath. One must only strive to do what one can with what little strength one has at one's command, until the last summons is sent and one goes to the Judgment of God to find out how valuable one has been in the way of Grace and character. But there must be no looking back, and in Mother Seton's case there was none.

Mother Seton soon became dissatisfied with her establishment at Paca Street. Paca Street would never be large enough or suitable to accommodate the number of young girls who were already clamoring for entrance into her community, and who needed, if they were to be correctly trained, a place that could properly be called a "mother-house," the technical name for probation places in the nomenclature of all nuns.

Emmitsburg was the site where Mr. Cooper had bought them the property. It had the added advantage of being only two miles from a new establishment started on the mountain of Emmitsburg, called Mount Saint Mary's Seminary, by a very

devout priest named Father Dubois, later to become a Sulpician.
This seminary survives as both a seminary and a college until
this day, and its alumni pride themselves on being called "Mountaineers," the title by which all Mount Saint Mary's men are
known both among themselves and among others. The nearness
of the seminary and the priests would assure the Sisters of a
daily Mass, counsel, confessors, and spiritual instruction when
they required it.

Mother Seton, accompanied by her sisters-in-law, Cecilia and
Harriet, her daughter Anna, and Sister Maria Murphy, set out in
June of 1809 as the first vanguard for Emmitsburg, to discover
what sort of mother-house Mr. Cooper had provided for them
and into what sort of place they could transform it.

The little party traveled in a covered wagon, drawn by lazy
horses, who walked most of the journey, and were competed with
by the travelers themselves, who walked most of the way. For
there is an irresistable urge to get out of a wagon and walk when
you can walk faster than the horse. Inside, wrapped in a blanket,
the ailing Cecilia rode alone. The distance was fifty miles, but
the journey required several days. "The dogs and pigs came out
to meet us, and the geese stretched out their necks in mute demand to know if we were any of their company, to which we
gave assent," writes Mother Seton, commenting on the journey.
The natives stood in their door-ways, astonished. Never had they
seen such funny-looking creatures as Mother Seton and Sister
Maria, garbed in the costumes of nuns. Little did the natives
realize that this convoy, traveling to remote parts for the glory
of God and the Catholic Church, carried some of the most sought-
for belles of social New York. Harriet Seton was conceded to
be the most beautiful girl in New York in her time. She had
not come to Baltimore to become a nun, nor to join the Church.[4]
She was engaged to be married to a young man she loved very
dearly, and she carried his picture in a locket which she wore
around her neck until her death. She lived only until December
of the same year. She did, however, become a devout Catholic,
giving up all contact with her previous life. Her betrothed, wherever he may now be in eternity, can be proud of her. She became

[4] Harriet Seton had come because she had found the spiritual needs of her
nature incapable of being satisfied apart from her adored Cecilia and Elizabeth.

a Catholic, but not a nun, and never parted with the locket he had given her.

What trials had to be endured when the little group reached Emmitsburg! It was true that Mr. Cooper had bought them property, but the house in which they were to live was not nearly completed when they arrived. So hard were their straits that Father Du Bourg undertook to give them his own house, and went to live at the Seminary. But the house he gave them—he was a hardy pioneer, and little likely to know the needs of delicate women—had only two rooms! Outdoors the prospect was very satisfactory. The climate, at least during the summer and autumn months, was good.

When things were settled at Emmitsburg, ten nuns were housed in the infant "mother-house." They were all sorts of girls, with all sorts of origins and all sorts of cultures and attainments. Those who were not strong in intellectual pursuits could cook, wash, scrub. Those who were not good at these observances, could qualify as "scribes," "secretaries," and other workers. But one and all were given to charity and prayer.

In autumn of the same year Archbishop Carroll came to visit his new community of nuns. He was, as is well known, a member of the famous Maryland Carrolls, one of whom was a signer of the Declaration of Independence, and had no inferiority complexes about the Faith—as no noblemen have, once they receive it—and was a great comfort to his first little band of Sisters by reason of his benevolence, his authority, and his charm.

The first winter of the little Emmitsburg community was most distressing. The house promised them had not as yet materialized, despite slow progress. The strictest economies had to be practiced in view of dwindling finances. There could be no such expensive beverages as tea and coffee. Fresh meat was forbidden. Butter and milk were also among the prohibitions. They did not even have enough clothing-material to supply them their ordinary religious dress, and some of the nuns (this an humiliation beyond compare) were obliged to go in lay attire. The shack in which they were quartered had no glass in the places for the window-panes. And so fortified against the winter, the nuns saw the first snowstorm arrive. In blew the snow through the open windows, and the nuns had to shovel it out again. In the face of extreme undernourishment, they had to fight against disease. Scarcely anyone withstood the emergency, and the little farmhouse was reduced to a hospital in which the less unwell nursed those who were unable to hold up their heads. Yet their spirits flamed in the midst of these hardships. "All hearts," Mother Seton wrote, "applied themselves to mortification with such good will that they found the carrot coffee, the buttermilk soup, and the stale lard too delicate food." This was the condition of these Catholic nuns during their first winter in America.

In February the new house destined for the Sisters was "completed." That is to say, it was physically possible for the Sisters to move into it. And move in the nuns did with all ceremony and gaiety, making much of the procession of the Blessed Sacrament when It was being tabernacled for the first time in their new home. For decorations in His new altar-home God was supplied with a small pair of silver candlesticks and a few vases filled with mountain laurel and some paper flowers. When the school opened—a most unpropitious time, right in the middle of winter —on George Washington's Birthday, a splendid enrollment of pupils was realized.

Not only that, but as the winter went on, despite the fact that to one and all Mother Seton explained the hardships of their condition, persistent applications began to arrive from young girls who wanted to become nuns and to be enrolled in the new community.

In March a most astounding postulant arrived,—a young girl named Elizabeth Boyle, who, though of an Irish name, was of an English family and was a convert from Episcopalianism. A well-born lady, as Mother Seton was, she came to be Mother's closest confidante and most treasured disciple. After Mother's death she became the first Superioress of the New York Community of the Sisters of Charity, the branch that still survives in the identical dress, save for a change of color in the bonnet, which Mother Seton bequeathed to her daughters. It is recorded of Miss Boyle that she welcomed the most menial tasks. Of her quality, Mother Seton was later to remark that she believed Elizabeth Boyle had never lost her Baptismal innocence in a single detail. This was high praise from one who knew her every thought. She was an expert horsewoman, and when a postulant came to Emmitsburg bringing a horse as part of her dowry, Sister Elizabeth Boyle was given the horse to ride every Saturday when she went to the churches (two of them) entrusted to the Sisters' charge, to supply fresh linens for the altar and make general preparations for the Sunday Mass. She must have been quite an impressive, if not a spectral figure galloping down the roads of Maryland with her large black cloak wrapped about her and the little white muslin cap bobbing on her head. The farmers working in their fields, or housewives pumping at their wells, must have greatly wondered what strange sort of women had been planted in their midst in the name of religion.

Today America knows what sort of women they were, and honors them and their foundress, Mother Seton. She was a brave woman, a wise leader, a tender mother, a devout Catholic, and a holy servant of God. We may be proud and happy to add the significant statement that she was An American Woman!

The Biographer—The Reverend Leonard Feeney, S.J. (1897–   ): Father Feeney was born in Lynn, Massachusetts, in 1897; he entered the Society of Jesus in 1914. Best known for his several books of poetry, he has also written two volumes of sketches and essays, *Fish on Friday* and *You'd Better Come Quietly*. *An American Woman* is his first venture into the field of biography. Since 1936 he has been literary editor of *America*.

Suggestions for Study: Compare the education, particularly the moral education, which Elizabeth Bayley received with that which you are receiving, and draw your own conclusions. Can you trace in her subsequent career the results of her father's influence on her education? What is your opinion of her statement that "after all the first point of religion is cheerfulness and harmony"? Does the spirit of the prayer quoted from her private journal correspond to the principle enunciated? Do you find the quotations from her letters entertaining or dull? Why?

Why may her trying days in Italy be considered a turning point in her life? The lot of a prominent convert to Catholicism in Mother Seton's day was difficult. If it is easier today, why may she be justly credited with at least partial credit for the change? Why was Baltimore a better place in which to open a school for Catholic girls and to inaugurate a religious congregation than New York?

How do you account for the cheerfulness and courage of the little Emmitsburg community during the difficult times that marked their taking possession of their new mother-house? Does Father Feeney's description of the life of a nun give a clue? What do you think of that description?

Look up the meaning of each of the following words and phrases that is unfamiliar to you: *coronettes, genteel, inveterate, astringent, consonant with, dogma, vicariously, a possessive father, religiosity, lazaretto, postulant, nomenclature, spectral.*

Exercises and Creative Work: From her earliest days Elizabeth Bayley was devoted to the poor. Discover if you can what organizations of social service operate in your neighborhood, and write a plea for the participation of your classmates in the work of one of these organizations.

If many orders of nuns are represented in your community, plan a class symposium on the history and activities of the several orders.

Show how Mother Seton's "remarkable literary expression" must have aided her in the successive phases of her varied career; or show how such a power would be valuable to you in the career which you have tentatively chosen for yourself.

For Further Reading: If you wish to extend your acquaintance with the first nuns of North America, read *Great American Foundresses,* by Joseph B. Code, who introduces his readers to sixteen of the "truly great women of pioneer days." The following list gives only a sampling of the many full-length biographies of the great nuns who have left a strong impress upon our country:

Marjory Erskine	*Mother Philippine Duchesne*
Katherine Burton	*Sorrow Built a Bridge, a Daughter of Hawthorne*
Sister Helen Louise	*Sister Louise, American Foundress of the Sisters of Notre Dame de Namur*
Sister Mary Theodosia	*Journal and Letters of Mother Theodore Guerin*
Agnes Repplier	*Mère Marie of the Ursulines*

An Autobiography of the Transition Period

SCENES ON THE MISSISSIPPI

From *Life on the Mississippi*

MARK TWAIN

By Way of Introduction: Samuel Langhorne Clemens, or Mark Twain as we better know him, was born in Florida, Missouri. When he was four years old the family moved to Hannibal, Missouri, which is on the Mississippi River. Most of his boyhood was spent in Hannibal and it is of his early days on the river that he now tells . . .

EARLY AMBITION

WHEN I was a boy, there was but one permanent ambition among my comrades in our village on the west bank of the Mississippi River. That was, to be a steamboatman. We had transient ambitions of other sorts, but they were only transient. When a circus came and went, it left us all burning to become clowns; the first negro minstrel show that ever came to our section left us all suffering to try that kind of life; now and then we had a hope that, if we lived and were good, God would permit us to be pirates. These ambitions faded out, each in its turn; but the ambition to be a steamboatman always remained.

Once a day a cheap, gaudy packet arrived upward from St.

Louis, and another downward from Keokuk.[1] Before these events, the day was glorious with expectancy; after them, the day was a dead and empty thing. Not only the boys, but the whole village, felt this. After all these years I can picture that old time to myself now, just as it was then: the white town drowsing in the sunshine of a summer's morning; the streets empty, or pretty nearly so; one or two clerks sitting in front of the Water Street stores, with their splint-bottomed chairs tilted back against the walls, chins on breasts, hats slouched over their faces, asleep—with shingle-shavings enough around to show what broke them down; a sow and a litter of pigs loafing along the sidewalk, doing a good business in watermelon rinds and seeds; two or three lonely little freight piles scattered about the "levee"; a pile of "skids" on the slope of the stone-paved wharf, and the fragrant town drunkard asleep in the shadow of them; two or three wood flats at the head of the wharf, but nobody to listen to the peaceful lapping of the wavelets against them; the great Mississippi, the majestic, the magnificent Mississippi, rolling its mile-wide tide along, shining in the sun; the dense forest away on the other side; the "point" above the town, and the "point" below, bounding the river-glimpse and turning it into a sort of sea, and withal a very still and brilliant and lonely one.

Presently a film of dark smoke appears above one of those remote "points"; instantly a negro drayman, famous for his quick eye and prodigious voice, lifts up the cry, "S-t-e-a-m-boat a-comin'!" and the scene changes! The town drunkard stirs, the clerks wake up, a furious clatter of drays follows, every house and store pours out a human contribution, and all in a twinkling the dead town is alive and moving. Drays, carts, men, boys, all go hurrying from many quarters to a common center, the wharf. Assembled there, the people fasten their eyes upon the coming boat as upon a wonder they are seeing for the first time. And the boat *is* rather a handsome sight, too. She is long and sharp and trim and pretty; she has two tall, fancy-topped chimneys, with a gilded device of some kind swung between them; a fanciful pilot-house, all glass and "gingerbread," perched on top of the "texas" deck behind them; the paddle-boxes are gorgeous with a picture or with gilded rays above the

[1] KEOKUK—Keokuk, Iowa, sixty miles above Hannibal on the Mississippi.

boat's name; the boiler-deck, the hurricane-deck, and the texas deck are fenced and ornamented with clean white railings; there is a flag gallantly flying from the jack-staff; the furnace doors are open and the fires glaring bravely; the upper decks are black with passengers; the captain stands by the big bell, calm, imposing, the envy of all; great volumes of the blackest smoke are rolling and tumbling out of the chimneys—a husbanded grandeur created with a bit of pitch-pine just before arriving at a town; the crew are grouped on the forecastle; the broad stage is run far out over the port bow, and an envied deck-hand stands picturesquely on the end of it with a coil of rope in his hand; the pent steam is screaming through the gauge-cocks; the captain lifts his hand, a bell rings, the wheels stop; then they turn back, churning the water to foam, and the steamer is at rest. Then such a scramble as there is to get aboard, and to get ashore, and to take in freight and to discharge freight, all at one and the same time; and such a yelling and cursing as the mates facilitate it all with! Ten minutes later the steamer is under way again, with no flag on the jack-staff and no black smoke issuing from the chimneys. After ten more minutes the town is dead again, and the town drunkard asleep by the skids once more.

My father was a justice of the peace, and I supposed he possessed the power of life and death over all men, and could hang anybody that offended him. This was distinction enough for me as a general thing; but the desire to be a steamboatman kept intruding, nevertheless. I first wanted to be a cabin-boy, so that I could come out with a white apron on and shake a table-cloth over the side, where all my old comrades could see me; later I thought I would rather be the deck-hand who stood on the end of the stage-plank with the coil of rope in his hand, because he was particularly conspicuous. But these were only day-dreams—they were too heavenly to be contemplated as real possibilities.

By and by one of our boys went away. He was not heard of for a long time. At last he turned up as apprentice engineer or "striker" on a steamboat. This thing shook the bottom out of all my Sunday-school teachings. That boy had been notoriously worldly, and I just the reverse; yet he was exalted to this eminence, and I left in obscurity and misery. There was nothing generous about this fellow in his greatness. He would always manage to have a rusty bolt to scrub while his boat tarried at our town, and he would sit on the inside guard and scrub it, where we all could see him and envy him and loathe him. And whenever his boat was laid up he would come home and swell around the town in his blackest and greasiest clothes, so that nobody could help remembering that he was a steamboatman; and he used all sorts of steamboat technicalities in his talk, as if he were so used to them that he forgot common people could not understand them. He would speak of the "labboard" side of a horse in an easy, natural way that would make one wish he was dead. And he was always talking about "St. Looy" like an old citizen; he would refer casually to occasions when he was "coming down Fourth Street," or when he was "passing by the Planter's House," or when there was a fire and he took a turn on the brakes of "the old Big Missouri"; and then he would go on and lie about how many towns the size of ours were burned down there that day. Two or three of the boys had long been persons of consideration among us because they had been to St. Louis once and had a vague general knowledge of its wonders, but the day of their glory was over now. They lapsed into a humble silence, and learned to disappear when the ruthless "cub"-engineer approached. This fellow had money, too, and hair-oil. Also an ignorant silver watch and a showy brass watch-chain. He wore a leather belt and used no suspenders. If ever a youth was cordially admired and hated by his comrades, this one was. No girl could withstand his charms. He "cut out" every boy in the village. When his boat blew up at last, it diffused a tranquil contentment among us such as we had not known for months. But when he came home the next week, alive, renowned, and appeared in church all battered up and bandaged, a shining hero, stared at and wondered over by everybody, it seemed to us that the partiality of Providence for an undeserving reptile had reached a point where it was open to criticism.

This creature's career could produce but one result, and it speedily followed. Boy after boy managed to get on the river. The minister's son became an engineer. The doctor's and the postmaster's sons became "mud clerks"; the wholesale liquor dealer's son became a barkeeper on a boat; four sons of the chief merchant, and two sons of the county judge, became pilots. Pilot was the grandest position of all. The pilot, even in those days of trivial wages, had a princely salary—from a hundred and fifty to two hundred and fifty dollars a month, and no board to pay. Two months of his wages would pay a preacher's salary for a year. Now some of us were left disconsolate. We could not get on the river—at least our parents would not let us.

So, by and by, I ran away. I said I would never come home again till I was a pilot and could come in glory. But somehow I could not manage it. I went meekly aboard a few of the boats that lay packed together like sardines at the long St. Louis wharf, and humbly inquired for the pilots, but got only a cold shoulder and short words from mates and clerks. I had to make the best of this sort of treatment for the time being, but I had comforting day-dreams of a future when I should be a great and honored pilot, with plenty of money, and could kill some of these mates and clerks and pay for them.

I TAKE A FEW EXTRA LESSONS

DURING the two or two and a half years of my apprenticeship I served under many pilots, and had experience of many kinds of steamboatmen and many varieties of steamboats; for it was not always convenient for Mr. Bixby [1] to have me with him, and in such cases he sent me with somebody else. I am to this day profiting somewhat by that experience; for in that brief, sharp schooling, I got personally and familiarly acquainted with about all the different types of human nature that are to be found in fiction, biography, or history. The fact is daily borne in upon me that the average shore-employment requires as much as forty years to equip a man with this sort of an education. When I say I am still profiting by this thing, I do not mean that it has constituted me a judge of men—no, it has not done that, for judges of men are born, not made. My profit is various in kind and degree, but the feature of it which I value most is the zest which that early experience has given to my later reading. When I find a well-drawn character in fiction or biography I generally take a warm personal interest in him, for

[1] MR. BIXBY—Horace Bixby, the pilot who has taken Samuel as a cub and who is teaching him to be a pilot.

the reason that I have known him before—met him on the river.

The figure that comes before me oftenest, out of the shadows of that vanished time, is that of Brown, of the steamer *Pennsylvania*. He was a middle-aged, long, slim, bony, smooth-shaven, horse-faced, ignorant, stingy, malicious, snarling, fault-hunting, mote-magnifying tyrant. I early got the habit of coming on watch with dread at my heart. No matter how good a time I might have been having with the off-watch below, and no matter how high my spirits might be when I started aloft, my soul became lead in my body the moment I approached the pilot-house.

I still remember the first time I ever entered the presence of that man. The boat had backed out from St. Louis and was "straightening down." I ascended to the pilot-house in high feather, and very proud to be semi-officially a member of the executive family of so fast and famous a boat. Brown was at the wheel. I paused in the middle of the room, all fixed to make my bow, but Brown did not look around. I thought he took a furtive glance at me out of the corner of his eye, but as not even this notice was repeated, I judged I had been mistaken. By this time he was picking his way among some dangerous "breaks" abreast the woodyards; therefore it would not be proper to interrupt him; so I stepped softly to the high bench and took a seat.

There was silence for ten minutes; then my new boss turned and inspected me deliberately and painstakingly from head to heel for about—as it seemed to me—a quarter of an hour. After which he removed his countenance and I saw it no more for some seconds; then it came around once more, and this question greeted me:

"Are you Horace Bixby's cub?"

"Yes, sir."

After this there was a pause and another inspection. Then:

"What's your name?"

I told him. He repeated it after me. It was probably the only thing he ever forgot; for although I was with him many months he never addressed himself to me in any other way than "Here!" and then his command followed.

"Where was you born?"

"In Florida, Missouri."

A pause. Then:

"Dern sight better stayed there!"

By means of a dozen or so pretty direct questions, he pumped my family history out of me.

The leads were going now in the first crossing. This interrupted the inquest. When the leads had been laid in he resumed:

"How long you been on the river?"

I told him. After a pause:

"Where'd you get them shoes?"

I gave him the information.

"Hold up your foot!"

I did so. He stepped back, examined the shoe minutely and contemptuously, scratching his head thoughtfully, tilting his high sugar-loaf hat well forward to facilitate the operation, then ejaculated, "Well, I'll be dod derned!" and returned to his wheel.

What occasion there was to be dod derned about it is a thing which is still as much of a mystery to me now as it was then. It must have been all of fifteen minutes—fifteen minutes of dull, homesick silence—before that long horse-face swung around upon me again—and then what a change! It was as red as fire, and every muscle in it was working. Now came this shriek:

"Here! You going to set there all day?"

I lit in the middle of the floor, shot there by the electric suddenness of the surprise. As soon as I could get my voice I said apologetically: "I have had no orders, sir."

"You've had no *orders!* My, what a fine bird we are! We must have *orders!* Our father was a *gentleman*—owned slaves —and *we've* been to *school*. Yes, *we* are a gentleman, *too,* and got to have *orders!* Orders, is it? ORDERS is what you want! Dod dern my skin, *I'll* learn you to swell yourself up and blow around *here* about your dod-derned *orders!* G'way from the wheel!" (I had approached it without knowing it.)

I moved back a step or two and stood as in a dream, all my senses stupefied by this frantic assault.

"What you standing there for? Take that ice-pitcher down to the texas-tender! Come, move along, and don't you be all day about it!"

The moment I got back to the pilot-house Brown said:

"Here! What was you doing down there all this time?"

"I couldn't find the texas-tender; I had to go all the way to the pantry."

"Derned likely story! Fill up the stove."

I proceeded to do so. He watched me like a cat. Presently he shouted:

"Put down that shovel! Derndest numskull I ever saw—ain't even got sense enough to load up a stove."

All through the watch this sort of thing went on. Yes, and the subsequent watches were much like it during a stretch of months. As I have said, I soon got the habit of coming on duty with dread. The moment I was in the presence, even in the darkest night, I could feel those yellow eyes upon me, and knew their owner was watching for a pretext to spit out some venom on me. Preliminarily he would say:

"Here! Take the wheel."

Two minutes later:

"*Where* in the nation you going to? Pull her down! Pull her down!"

After another moment:

"Say! You going to hold her all day? Let her go—meet her! meet her!"

Then he would jump from the bench, snatch the wheel from me, and meet her himself, pouring out wrath upon me all the time.

George Ritchie was the other pilot's cub. He was having good times now; for his boss, George Ealer, was as kind-hearted as Brown wasn't. Ritchie had steered for Brown the season before; consequently, he knew exactly how to entertain himself and plague me, all by the one operation. Whenever I took the wheel for a moment on Ealer's watch, Ritchie would sit back on the bench and play Brown, with continual ejaculations of "Snatch her! Snatch her! Derndest mud-cat I ever saw!" "Here! Where are you going *now?* Going to run over that snag?" "Pull her *down!* Don't you hear me? Pull her *down!*" "There she goes! *Just* as I expected! I *told* you not to cramp that reef. G'way from the wheel!"

So I always had a rough time of it, no matter whose watch it was; and sometimes it seemed to me that Ritchie's good-natured badgering was pretty nearly as aggravating as Brown's dead-earnest nagging.

I often wanted to kill Brown, but this would not answer. A cub had to take everything his boss gave, in the way of vigorous comment and criticism; and we all believed that there was a United States law making it a penitentiary offense to strike or threaten a pilot who was on duty. However, I could *imagine* myself killing Brown; there was no law against that; and that was the thing I used always to do the moment I was abed. Instead of going over my river in my mind, as was my duty, I threw business aside for pleasure, and killed Brown. I killed Brown every night for months; not in old, stale, commonplace ways, but in new and picturesque ones—ways that were sometimes surprising for freshness of design and ghastliness of situation and environment.

Brown was *always* watching for a pretext to find fault; and if he could find no plausible pretext, he would invent one. He would scold you for shaving a shore, and for not shaving it; for hugging a bar, and for not hugging it; for "pulling down" when not invited, and for *not* pulling down when not invited; for firing up without orders, and for waiting *for* orders. In a word, it was his invariable rule to find fault with *everything* you did; and another invariable rule of his was to throw all his remarks to you into the form of an insult.

One day we were approaching New Madrid, bound down and heavily laden. Brown was at one side of the wheel, steering; I was at the other, standing by to "pull down" or "shove up." He cast a furtive glance at me every now and then. I had long ago learned what that meant; viz., he was trying to invent a trap for me. I wondered what shape it was going to take. By and by he stepped back from the wheel and said in his usual snarly way:

"Here! See if you've got gumption enough to round her to."

This was simply *bound* to be a success; nothing could prevent it; for he had never allowed me to round the boat to before; consequently, no matter how I might do the thing, he could find free fault with it. He stood back there with his greedy eye on me, and the result was what might have been foreseen: I lost my head in a quarter of a minute, and didn't know what I was about; I started too early to bring the boat around, but detected a green gleam of joy in Brown's eye, and corrected my mistake. I started around once more while too high up, but corrected myself again in time. I made other false moves, and still managed to save myself; but at last I grew so confused and anxious that I tumbled into the very worst blunder of all —I got too far *down* before beginning to fetch the boat around. Brown's chance was come.

His face turned red with passion; he made one bound, hurled me across the house with a sweep of his arm, spun the wheel down, and began to pour out a stream of vituperation upon me which lasted till he was out of breath. In the course of this speech he called me all the different kinds of hard names he could think of, and once or twice I thought he was even going to swear—but he had never done that, and he didn't this time. "Dod dern" was the nearest he ventured to the luxury of swearing, for he had been brought up with a wholesome respect for future fire and brimstone.

That was an uncomfortable hour; for there was a big audience on the hurricane-deck. When I went to bed that night, I killed Brown in seventeen different ways—all of them new.

BROWN AND I EXCHANGE COMPLIMENTS

Two TRIPS later I got into serious trouble. Brown was steering; I was "pulling down." My younger brother appeared on the hurricane-deck, and shouted to Brown to stop at some landing or other, a mile or so below. Brown gave no intimation that he had heard anything. But that was his way: he never condescended to take notice of an under-clerk. The wind was blowing; Brown was deaf (although he always pretended he wasn't), and I very much doubted if he had heard the order. If I had had two heads, I would have spoken; but as I had only one, it seemed judicious to take care of it; so I kept still.

Presently, sure enough, we went sailing by that plantation. Captain Klinefelter appeared on the deck, and said:

"Let her come around, sir, let her come around. Didn't Henry tell you to land here?"

"*No,* sir!"

"I sent him up to do it."

"He *did* come up; and that's all the good it done, the dod-derned fool. He never said anything."

"Didn't *you* hear him?" asked the captain of me.

Of course I didn't want to be mixed up in this business, but there was no way to avoid it; so I said:

"Yes, sir."

I knew what Brown's next remark would be, before he uttered it. It was:

"Shut your mouth! You never heard anything of the kind."

I closed my mouth, according to instructions. An hour later Henry entered the pilot-house, unaware of what had been going on. He was a thoroughly inoffensive boy, and I was sorry to see him come, for I knew Brown would have no pity on him. Brown began, straightway:

"Here! Why didn't you tell me we'd got to land at that plantation?"

"I did tell you, Mr. Brown."

"It's a lie!"

I said:

"You lie, yourself. He did tell you."

Brown glared at me in unaffected surprise; and for as much as a moment he was entirely speechless; then he shouted to me: "I'll attend to your case in a half a minute!" then to Henry, "And you leave the pilot-house; out with you!"

It was a pilot law, and must be obeyed. The boy started out, and even had his foot on the upper step outside the door, when Brown, with a sudden access of fury, picked up a ten-pound lump of coal and sprang after him; but I was between, with a heavy stool, and I hit Brown a good honest blow which stretched him out.

I had committed the crime of crimes—I had lifted my hand against a pilot on duty! I supposed I was booked for the penitentiary sure, and couldn't be booked any surer if I went on and squared my long account with this person while I had the chance; consequently I stuck to him and pounded him with my fists a considerable time. I do not know how long, the pleasure of it probably made it seem longer than it really was; but in the end he struggled free and jumped up and sprang to the wheel: a very natural solicitude, for, all this time, here was this steamboat tearing down the river at the rate of fifteen miles an hour and nobody at the helm! However, Eagle Bend was two miles wide at this bank-full stage, and correspondingly long and deep: and the boat was steering herself straight down the middle and taking no chances. Still, that was only luck—a body *might* have found her charging into the woods.

Perceiving at a glance that the *Pennsylvania* was in no danger, Brown gathered up the big spy-glass, war-club fashion, and ordered me out of the pilot-house with more than Comanche bluster. But I was not afraid of him now; so, instead of going, I tarried, and criticized his grammar. I reformed his ferocious speeches for him, and put them into good English, calling his attention to the advantage of pure English over the bastard dialect of the Pennsylvania collieries whence he was extracted. He could have done his part to admiration in a cross-fire of mere vituperation, of course; but he was not equipped for this species of controversy; so he presently laid aside his glass and took the wheel, muttering and shaking his head; and I retired to the bench. The racket had brought everybody to the hurricane-deck, and I trembled when I saw the old captain looking up from amid the crowd. I said to myself, "Now I *am* done for!" for although, as a rule, he was so fatherly and indulgent toward the boat's family, and so patient of minor shortcomings, he could be stern enough when the fault was worth it.

I tried to imagine what he *would* do to a cub pilot who had been guilty of such a crime as mine, committed on a boat guard-deep with costly freight and alive with passengers. Our watch was nearly ended. I thought I would go and hide somewhere till I got a chance to slide ashore. So I slipped out of the pilot-house, and down the steps, and around to the texas-door, and was in the act of gliding within, when the captain confronted me! I dropped my head, and he stood over me in silence a moment or two, then said impressively:

"Follow me."

I dropped into his wake; he led the way to his parlor in the forward end of the texas. We were alone, now. He closed the after door; then moved slowly to the forward one and closed that. He sat down; I stood before him. He looked at me some little time, then said:

"So you have been fighting Mr. Brown?"

I answered meekly:

"Yes, sir."

"Do you know that that is a very serious matter?"

"Yes, sir."

"Are you aware that this boat was plowing down the river fully five minutes with no one at the wheel?"

"Yes, sir."

"Did you strike him first?"

"Yes, sir."

"What with?"

"A stool, sir."

"Hard?"

"Middling, sir."

"Did it knock him down?"

"He—he fell, sir."

"Did you follow it up? Did you do anything further?"

"Yes, sir."

"What did you do?"

"Pounded him, sir."

"Pounded him?"

"Yes, sir."

"Did you pound him much? that is, severely?"

"One might call it that, sir, maybe."

"I'm deuced glad of it! Hark ye, never mention that I said that. You have been guilty of a great crime; and don't you ever be guilty of it again, on this boat. *But*—lay for him ashore! Give him a good sound thrashing, do you hear? I'll pay the expenses. Now go—and mind you, not a word of this to anybody. Clear out with you! You've been guilty of a great crime, you whelp!"

I slid out, happy with the sense of a close shave and a mighty deliverance; and I heard him laughing to himself and slapping his fat thighs after I had closed his door.

When Brown came off watch he went straight to the captain, who was talking with some passengers on the boiler-deck, and demanded that I be put ashore in New Orleans—and added:

"I'll never turn a wheel on this boat again while that cub stays."

The captain said:

"But he needn't come round when you are on watch, Mr. Brown."

"I won't even stay on the same boat with him. *One* of us has got to go ashore."

"Very well," said captain, "let it be yourself," and resumed his talk with the passengers.

During the brief remainder of the trip I knew how an emancipated slave feels, for I was an emancipated slave myself.

A SECTION IN MY BIOGRAPHY

IN DUE course I got my license. I was a pilot now, full-fledged. I dropped into casual employments; no misfortunes resulting, intermittent work gave place to steady and protracted engagements. Time drifted smoothly and prosperously on, and I supposed—and hoped—that I was going to follow the river the rest of my days, and die at the wheel when my mission was ended. But by and by the war came, commerce was suspended, my occupation was gone.

I had to seek another livelihood. So I became a silver-miner in Nevada; next, a newspaper reporter; next, a gold-miner in California; next, a reporter in San Francisco; next, a special correspondent in the Sandwich Islands; next, a roving correspondent in Europe and the East; next, an instructional torch-bearer on the lecture platform; and, finally, I became a scribbler of books, and an immovable fixture among the other rocks of New England.

In so few words have I disposed of the twenty-one slow-drifting years that have come and gone since I last looked from the windows of a pilot-house.

Let us resume, now.

I RETURN TO MY MUTTONS

AFTER twenty-one years' absence I felt a very strong desire to see the river again, and the steamboats, and such of the boys as might be left; so I resolved to go out there. I enlisted a poet for company, and a stenographer to "take him down," and started westward about the middle of April.

As I proposed to make notes, with a view to printing, I took some thoughts as to methods of procedure. I reflected that if I were recognized, on the river, I should not be as free to go and come, talk, inquire, and spy around, as I should be if unknown; I remembered that it was the custom of steamboatmen in the old times to load up the confiding stranger with the most picturesque and admirable lies, and put the sophisticated friend off with few dull and ineffectual facts: so I concluded that, from a business point of view, it would be an advantage to disguise our party with fictitious names. The idea was certainly good, but it bred infinite bother; for although Smith, Jones, and Johnson are easy names to remember when there is no occasion to remember them, it is next to impossible to recollect them when they are wanted. How do criminals manage to keep a brand-new *alias* in mind? This is a great mystery. I was innocent; and yet was seldom able to lay my hand on my new name when it was needed; and it seemed to me that if I had had a crime on my conscience to further confuse me, I could never have kept the name by me at all.

TRAVELING INCOGNITO

A VICKSBURG packet, the *Gold Dust,* was to leave at 5 P.M. We took passage in her for Memphis, and gave up the idea of stopping off here and there, as being impracticable. She was neat, clean, and comfortable. We camped on the boiler-deck, and bought some cheap literature to kill time with.

At eight o'clock, promptly, we backed out and—crossed the river. As we crept toward the shore, in the thick darkness, a blinding glory of white electric light burst suddenly from our forecastle, and lit up the water and the warehouses as with a noonday glare. Another big change, this—no more flickering, smoky, pitch-dripping, ineffectual torch-baskets, now: their day is past. Next, instead of calling out a score of hands to man the stage, a couple of men and a hatful of steam lowered it from the derrick where it was suspended, launched it, deposited it in just the right spot, and the whole thing was over and done with before a mate in the olden time could have got his profanity-mill adjusted to begin the preparatory services. Why this new and simple method of handling the stages was not thought of when the first steamboat was built is a mystery which helps one to realize what a dull-witted slug the average human being is.

We finally got away at two in the morning, and when I turned out at six we were rounding to at a rocky point where there was an old stone warehouse—at any rate, the ruins of it; two or three decayed dwelling-houses were near by in the shelter of the leafy hills, but there were no evidences of human or other animal life to be seen. I wondered if I had forgotten the river, for I had no recollection whatever of this place; the shape of the river, too, was unfamiliar; there was nothing in sight anywhere that I could remember ever having seen before. I was surprised, disappointed, and annoyed.

Presently I ascended to the hurricane-deck and cast a longing glance toward the pilot-house.

MY INCOGNITO IS EXPLODED

AFTER a close study of the face of the pilot on watch, I was satisfied that I had never seen him before, so I went up there. The pilot inspected me; I reinspected the pilot. These customary preliminaries over, I sat down on the high bench, and he faced about and went on with his work. Every detail of the pilot-house was familiar to me, with one exception—a large-mouthed tube under the breast-board. I puzzled over that thing a considerable time; then gave up and asked what it was for.

"To hear the engine-bells through."

It was another good contrivance which ought to have been invented half a century sooner. So I was thinking when the pilot asked:

"Do you know what this rope is for?"

I managed to get around this question without committing myself.

"Is this the first time you were ever in a pilot-house?"

I crept under that one.

"Where are you from?"

"New England."

"First time you have ever been West?"

I climbed over this one.

"If you take an interest in such things, I can tell you what all these things are for."

I said I should like it.

"This," putting his hand on a backing-bell rope, "is to sound the fire-alarm; this," putting his hand on a go-ahead bell, "is to call the texas-tender; this one," indicating the whistle-lever, "is to call the captain"—and so he went on, touching one object after another and reeling off his tranquil spool of lies.

I had never felt so like a passenger before. I thanked him,

with emotion, for each new fact, and wrote it down in my note-book. The pilot warmed to his opportunity, and proceeded to load me up in the good old-fashioned way. At times I was afraid he was going to rupture his invention; but it always stood the strain, and he pulled through all right. He drifted, by easy stages, into revealments of the river's marvelous eccentricities of one sort and another, and backed them up with some pretty gigantic illustrations. For instance:

"Do you see that little boulder sticking out of the water yonder? Well, when I first came on the river, that was a solid ridge of rock, over sixty feet high and two miles long. All washed away but that." [This with a sigh.]

I had a mighty impulse to destroy him, but it seemed to me that killing, in any ordinary way, would be too good for him.

Once, when an odd-looking craft, with a vast coal scuttle slanting aloft on the end of a beam, was steaming by in the distance, he indifferently drew attention to it, as one might to an object grown wearisome through familiarity, and observed that it was an "alligator-boat."

"An alligator-boat? What's it for?"

"To dredge out alligators with."

"Are they so thick as to be troublesome?"

"Well, not now, because the government keeps them down. But they used to be. Not everywhere; but in favorite places, here and there, where the river is wide and shoal—like Plum Point, and Stack Island, and so on—places they call alligator-beds."

"Did they actually impede navigation?"

"Years ago, yes, in very low water; there was hardly a trip, then, that we didn't get aground on alligators."

It seemed to me that I should certainly have to get out my tomahawk. However, I restrained myself and said:

"It must have been dreadful."

"Yes, it was one of the main difficulties about piloting. It was so hard to tell anything about the water; the darned things shift around so—never lie still five minutes at a time. You can tell a wind-reef, straight off, by the look of it; you can tell a break; you can tell a sand-reef—that's all easy; but an alligator-reef doesn't show up, worth anything. Nine times in ten you can't tell where the water is; and when you *do* see where it is, like as not it ain't there when *you* get there, the devils have swapped around so, meantime. Of course there were some few pilots that could judge of alligator-water nearly as well as they could of any other kind, but they had to have natural talent for it; it wasn't a thing a body could *learn*, you had to be born with it. Let me see: There was Ben Thornburg, and Beck Jolly, and Squire Bell, and Horace Bixby, and Major Downing, and John Stevenson, and Billy Gordon, and Jim Brady, and George Ealer, and Billy Youngblood—all A-1 alligator-pilots. *They* could tell alligator-water as far as another Christian could tell whisky. Read it? Ah, *couldn't* they, though! I only wish I had as many dollars as they could read alligator-water a mile and a half off. Yes, and it paid them to do it, too. A good alligator-pilot could always get fifteen hundred dollars a month. Nights, other people had to lay up for alligators, but those fellows never laid up for alligators; they never laid up for anything but fog. They could *smell* the best alligator-water —so it was said. I don't know whether it was so or not, and I think a body's got his hands full enough if he sticks to just what he knows himself, without going around backing up other people's say-so's, though there's a plenty that ain't backward about doing it, as long as they can roust out something wonderful to tell. Which is not the style of Robert Styles, by as much as three fathom—maybe quarter-*less*."

[My! Was this Rob Styles? This mustached and stately figure? A slim enough cub, in my time. How he has improved in comeliness in five-and-twenty years—and in the noble art of inflating his facts.] After these musings, I said aloud:

"I should think that dredging out the alligators wouldn't have done much good, because they could come back again right away."

"If you had had as much experience of alligators as I have, you wouldn't talk like that. You dredge an alligator once and he's *convinced*. It's the last you hear of *him*. He wouldn't come back for pie. If there's one thing that an alligator is more down on than another, it's being dredged. Besides, they were not simply shoved out of the way; the most of the scoopful were scooped aboard; they emptied them into the hold; and when they had got a trip, they took them to Orleans to the government works."

"What for?"

"Why, to make soldier-shoes out of their hides. All the government shoes are made of alligator-hide. It makes the best shoes in the world. They last five years, and they won't absorb water. The alligator fishery is a government monopoly. All the alligators are government property—just like the live-oaks. You cut down a live-oak, and government fines you fifty dollars; you kill an alligator, and up you go for misprision of treason [1]—lucky duck if they don't hang you, too. And they will, if you're a Democrat. The buzzard is the sacred bird of the South, and you can't touch him; the alligator is the sacred bird of the government, and you've got to let him alone."

"Do you ever get aground on the alligators now?"

"Oh, no! It hasn't happened for years."

"Well, then, why do they still keep the alligator-boats in service?"

"Just for police duty—nothing more. They merely go up and down now and then. The present generation of alligators know them as easy as a burglar knows a roundsman; when they see one coming, they break camp and go for the woods."

After rounding out and finishing up and polishing off the alligator business, he dropped easily and comfortably into the historical vein, and told of some tremendous feats of half a dozen old-time steamboats of his acquaintance, dwelling at special length upon a certain extraordinary performance of his chief favorite among this distinguished fleet—and then adding:

"That boat was the *Cyclone*—last trip she ever made—she sunk, that very trip; captain was Tom Ballou, the most immortal liar that ever I struck. He couldn't ever seem to tell the truth, in *any* kind of weather. Why, he would make you fairly shudder. He *was* the most scandalous liar! I left him, finally; I couldn't stand it. The proverb says, 'like master, like man'; and if you stay with that kind of a man, you'll come under suspicion by and by, just as sure as you live. He paid first-class wages; but said I, 'What's wages when your reputation's in danger?' So I let the wages go, and froze to my reputation. And I've never regretted it. Reputation's worth everything, ain't it? That's the way I look at it. He had more selfish

[1] MISPRISION OF TREASON—Concealment of, or omission to give notice of treason or felony.

organs than any seven men in the world—all packed in the stern-sheets of his skull, of course, where they belonged. They weighed down the back of his head so that it made his nose tilt up in the air. People thought it was vanity, but it wasn't, it was malice. If you only saw his foot, you'd take him to be nineteen feet high, but he wasn't; it was because his foot was out of drawing. He was intended to be nineteen feet high, no doubt, if his foot was made first, but he didn't get there; he was only five feet ten. That's what he was, and that's what he is. You take the lies out of him, and he'll shrink to the size of your hat; you take the malice out of him, and he'll disappear. That *Cyclone* was a rattler to go, and the sweetest thing to steer that ever walked the waters. Set her amidships, in a big river, and just let her go; it was all you had to do. She would hold herself on a star all night, if you let her alone. You couldn't ever feel her rudder. It wasn't any more labor to steer her than it is to count the Republican vote in a South Carolina election. One morning, just at daybreak, the last trip she ever made, they took her rudder aboard to mend it; I didn't know anything about it; I backed her out from the wood-yard and went a-weaving down the river all serene. When I had gone about twenty-three miles, and made four horribly crooked crossings——"

"Without any rudder?"

"Yes—old Captain Tom appeared on the roof and began to find fault with me for running such a dark night——"

"Such a *dark night?* Why, you said——"

"Never mind what I said—'twas as dark as Egypt *now*, though pretty soon the moon began to rise, and——"

"You mean the *sun*—because you started out just at break of—look here! Was this *before* you quitted the captain on account of his lying, or——"

"It was before—oh, a long time before. And as I was saying, he——"

"But was this the trip she sunk, or was——"

"Oh, no! months afterward. And so the old man, he——"

"Then she made *two* last trips, because you said——"

He stepped back from the wheel, swabbing away his perspiration, and said:

"Here!" Calling me by name. "*You* take her and lie awhile

—you're handier at it than I am; trying to play yourself for a stranger and an innocent! Why, I knew you before you had spoken seven words; and I made up my mind to find out what was your little game. It was to *draw me out*. Well, I let you, didn't I? Now take the wheel and finish the watch; and next time play .fair, and you won't have to work your passage."

Thus ended the fictitious-name business. And not six hours out from St. Louis! but I had gained a privilege, anyway, for I had been itching to get my hands on the wheel, from the beginning. I seemed to have forgotten the river, but I hadn't forgotten how to steer a steamboat, nor how to enjoy it, either.

Suggestions for Study: What was the master ambition of Mark Twain's youth? Describe the peaceful Missouri town in which his boyhood was spent. Describe the effect of the arrival and departure of the steamboats on the townspeople. Describe the typical Mississippi riverboat. Explain: "This shook the bottom out of my Sunday-school teachings." Describe the boy who became "striker" on the boat.

Of what peculiar value in later life was Mark Twain's apprenticeship of two and a half years in learning to be a pilot? Describe and characterize Brown. Tell of the first meeting with Brown. How did Brown trap Samuel in rounding the boat into New Madrid? Tell about the encounter with Brown in defense of Henry. Give an account of the interview with the Captain and the result. What interrupted Samuel's career as a pilot? What other vocations did he try?

Give an account of his return to the river after twenty-one years. What was his purpose in returning? What ruse did he adopt? What difficulty did he find? Tell of his interview with the pilot—the alligator stories, the discovery of his identity, the result—at the wheel again.

Exercises and Creative Work: Mark Twain is considered one of America's greatest humorists. Substantiate this statement by citing humorous passages from *Scenes on the Mississippi*.

Make a bibliography of Mark Twain's writings; also a bibliography of writings about Mark Twain.

Prepare a nautical dictionary by defining the nautical words and phrases used in *Scenes on the Mississippi*.

For Further Reading: You will want to read the entire book, *Life on the Mississippi*. You will find it extremely entertaining as you can see from the illustration given. The following books about Mark Twain are also recommended:

Clara Clemens	*My Father, Mark Twain*
William Dean Howells	*My Mark Twain*
Albert B. Paine	*Boys' Life of Mark Twain*
Mark Twain	*Autobiography*

A Biography of the Twentieth Century

SHIPWRECKED IN SOUTHERN SEAS

From *Count Luckner, the Sea Devil*

LOWELL THOMAS

By Way of Introduction: One of the most romantic stories of the World War is that of the German raider, the *Seeadler,* and her daring commander, Count Felix von Luckner. The *Seeadler* was originally an American ship belonging to the Boston Lumber Company. In August of 1915 she was captured by a German U-boat and sent into Bremen. There she was fitted with oil engines and in December 1916 slipped through the British blockade under command of Count von Luckner and a crew of sixty-four men. Then began a period of buccaneering during which Von Luckner earned "the unique and enviable reputation of disrupting Allied shipping without having taken a human life or so much as drowning a ship's cat." He captured and destroyed thirteen vessels in the Atlantic, rounded the Horn and sank three more in the Pacific. It is on the Pacific that we now find the ship and its crew . . .

WE amused ourselves by playing with the sharks. The landlubber can scarcely imagine the hatred the sailor feels for those bloodthirsty monsters. We had a particular grievance against them. A swim now and then would have provided us with needed baths and would have been a pleasant and vigorous diversion from the endless monotony of cabin and deck, our wooden prison. Many a time I looked down into the cool, refreshing element, and a shark would idle beneath my gaze, as though waiting for me there. The sailors passed the time by angling for the voracious monsters. They would catch a couple, tie their tails together and throw them back into the water. The sharks, unable to agree on the direction of their mutual movement, would have a great tug of war. The sailors thought the plight of their loathed enemies quite comical.

Or they would take a large shark, tie an empty and watertight barrel to his tail, and heave him over. The fish would dart downward, but the barrel would stay relentless at the surface. Now would ensue a desperate struggle which we could follow by watching the gyrations of the barrel. The sharks displayed an excellent eye for chunks of bacon with hand grenades in them. When the bomb went off in the creature's stomach, pieces of shark would go flying in all directions.

We had been in the Pacific for five months now, and had sailed 35,000 miles. With our stale water and the lack of fresh food, scurvy was breaking out among our men, and then beriberi, which "turns the blood to water." Limbs and joints were swelling. We imperatively needed fresh water and food and a rest on shore. But where could we go? All the islands of the Pacific were in the hands of the French, British, and Japanese. We certainly felt it keenly, now that the whole world was against us. There was no inhabited place that would welcome us. It made us feel very lonely.

"Well," I said to my boys, "we will pick out some nice deserted island where there will be no hand raised against us and no wireless to call the cruisers, and we will get water and some kind of vegetables and maybe shoot some game and have a fine shore leave. Then, after we have rested up, what ho, boys, and away for more adventure."

Buccaneering in the Pacific, with only three ships sunk in five months, seemed much too unprofitable. I planned that, after a brief sojourn on some peaceful South Sea Isle, we would sail for the Antipodes. Then we would destroy the English whaling station and oil tanks at South Georgia, sink a few ships, capture one on which to ship our prisoners, and, if we got away safely, continue our cruise in the prosperous waters of the Atlantic.

Our first plan was to sail direct to one of the larger Cook Islands. But we gave that up for fear of finding a wireless station there that might give us away. We did not want to move east of our present longitude, for that would have taken us against the trade wind and compelled us to use our motor. It was necessary to save the engine as much as possible and not have it wear out on us. We hoped we would need it for further captures and escapes. Mopelia, one of the Society Islands (some geographies include it in the Scilly Isles), seemed about right for our purpose. It was a French possession, and, so far as we knew, uninhabited. It was one of those isles of the South Seas so fantastically beautiful and so awkward for the sailor to approach. Only seldom does he find one with a decent anchorage, and nowhere in the world are the winds and currents more treacherous.

On the morning of July 29th, we sighted Mopelia, and steered toward it. Words fail me when I try to describe its beauties. From the blue ocean rises a mass of green palms. The sunlight glows in the green. It somehow even seems to turn the sunlight green. Against the dark blue of the sea and the light blue of the sky, the sunlight seems to be drawing the green island out of the water, and the soft south wind carried the scent of flowers far out to sea. It is the greeting of the island, and we inhale it deeply.

Here was a typical coral atoll—the kind you dream about. A circular reef studded with waving palms and within the reef a lovely, placid lagoon. The coral shore was snow white, and, with the sun's rays reflecting from it, it looked like a sparkling jewel set in an alabaster ring, like emeralds set in ivory. There were coral terraces below the water. The shallower ones were white or pale green, and as you peered deeper into the water you saw every conceivable tint of green and blue, sea green, emerald green, blue green, azure blue, sapphire blue, navy blue, violet.

As we sailed nearer and nearer that alluring coral shore, we saw flowers among the palms, flowers of all colours, and immense numbers of orchids. The hues of the flowers were reflected in the water over the white coral that deepened and turned green. Within the circular reef the lagoon seemed fully as deep as the sea outside, only at perfect peace and smooth like a mirror. It would have made a perfect anchorage for us, save that it had one entrance so narrow that only a small boat could pass through it.

A strong current ran through the opening. We cast our anchor on the coral and tethered our ship to it with a long cable. The pull of the current kept her far enough offshore. I was afraid, for a while, that a shift of the wind might blow her on the reef, but we saw, after a while, that she had dragged anchor. If the current were strong enough for that, why surely it would be strong enough to keep her from blowing ashore. Leaving several men aboard as a watch, we went on land for a glorious shore leave, sailors, officers, prisoners, and all.

What would we find? We wanted water and fresh food. When we got inside of the lagoon, we found to our astonishment that it was a breeding place for turtles. There were hundreds of them in the water and on the shore, huge fellows weighing two or three hundred pounds. The water was full of beautiful fish. I recognized the moray, a fish like the eel, which is a great delicacy and will provide you with a substantial meal, too. It weighs from fifteen to twenty pounds. They say the Romans used to feed their slaves to this fish. There were big lobsters without claws that promised to be the best of food. The atoll was alive with birds, hundreds of thousands of them, with nests and eggs everywhere. They were so tame that one of my boys whom I sent to collect enough eggs for an omelette returned, saying:

"I didn't get an egg. The birds were so tame and trusting that I hadn't the heart to disturb them and take their eggs."

Nor was the island without human inhabitants. We found three Kanakas, Polynesians who had been left there by a French firm to catch turtles. They were greatly frightened when they found that we were Germans. The French had told them frightful tales about the *Boches*. We, however, quickly made friends with them. They were much relieved when they found that we did not intend to injure them and when we made amicable overtures, they were only too glad to respond.

First, my boys ran hither and thither to satisfy their curiosity about this strange island. Then they quickly settled down to useful occupations. Some set about catching fish and lobsters. Others gathered birds' eggs. A few brought armfuls of cocoanuts. Three boys turned a big turtle on its back and pulled it along with a rope. There were wild pigs on the island. We shot a couple. Soon the boat put out to the ship loaded deeply with a huge collection of epicurean delicacies. That night the mess was fit for the table of a royal palace—turtle soup with turtle eggs, broiled lobster, omelettes of gull's eggs, roast pork, and, for dessert, fresh cocoanut.

For days we lived a delightful poetic life, dining in a way that millionaires could not afford. We smoked quantities of fish and pork and stowed it away. We found fresh water on the island and refilled our tanks. Our traces of scurvy and beri-beri disappeared, and we were rapidly getting ready to continue our cruise and work of havoc in Australian waters.

On the second of August, we made ready to leave the ship for another day ashore. At nine-thirty I noticed a strange bulge on the eastern rim of the sea. I called my officers' attention to it. At first we thought it a mirage. But it kept growing larger. It came toward us. Then we recognized it—a tidal wave such as is caused by submarine earthquake and volcanic disturbances. The danger was only too clear. We lay between the island and the wave.

"Cut the anchor cable. Clear the motor. All hands on deck."

We dared not raise sail, for then the wind would drive us on the reef. So our only hope of getting clear of the island was our motor. The huge swell of the tidal wave was rushing toward us with breakneck speed.

The motor didn't stir. The mechanics were working frantically. They pumped compressed air into the engine. We waited in vain for the sound of the ignition. Now, right at the critical moment, our motor had failed us, just as it had so often failed us before. By this time, the tidal wave was only a few hundred yards away. We were lost. To our frightened eyes it looked like a whole mountain range of water. It must have been thirty or forty feet high. It came rushing with a roar that drowned out our voices.

A gigantic, violent hand seemed to grasp the ship. The wave swung her on high and threw her forward. It flung us crashing on the coral reef. Our masts and rigging went over, broken like matchsticks. The shattering impact of the ship smashed the coral, and pieces flew in all directions like shrapnel from an exploding shell. The swirling water seized great pieces of coral and whipped them around, beating them against the ship. The *Seeadler* had heeled over until her deck was almost perpendicular. The water swept over the deck, and the swirling eddies bombarded us with chunks of coral. I clung to an iron post near the lower rail. The rail saved me from the tons of shattered coral that were hurled up by the blow of the falling ship. In a moment, the wave had ebbed away, leaving us high and dry. It had passed over the circling reef and the lagoon, though not over the main part of the island. And on its way it had swept hundreds of thousands of birds' nests into the lagoon.

I arose, scarcely knowing whether I was alive or dead, and stood alone with one foot on my slanting deck and the other on the rail. For a moment, I thought I was the only one saved.

"Boys, where are you?" I shouted weakly.

"Here," came the reply, "still standing like an oak."

My men and the prisoners had taken refuge in the bow, and had been sheltered by the rail, as I had been. Not a one was injured. For that at least we could be thankful. For that and not much else. The *Seeadler* was a total wreck. The jagged coral was rammed deep into our hull.

We stand like an oak! I adopted the reply of my sailors as our motto henceforth. We were castaways on this coral atoll in one of the loneliest and least-visited reaches of the South Pacific. Everything lost, but "we stand like an oak."

CASTAWAYS ON A CORAL ATOLL

THE last German colony! We founded it on this beautiful, isolated coral atoll in the middle of the Pacific. The Imperial German flag of war flew from the top of the tallest palm. I was the viceroy, by chance and not by desire, of course, and my sailors and our prisoners were my subjects. The only visiting nationals from elsewhere were the three Kanakas, the turtle catchers. "The White King of the Society Isle of Mopelia," my mate facetiously called me. One of the Yankee captains put it differently. He called me "the Sea Devil King of the South Seas." And he caustically described our lovely isle as "a poisoned paradise." Everybody was good-humoured, despite our hard luck.

But our little South Sea colony passed its first nights uneasily. For sleeping places, we slung hammocks between the palms. At intervals, a cocoanut would fall from a height of fifty or sixty feet and go whizzing close by a man's head. While our fellow countrymen back in the cities along the Rhine were complaining about the night raids of the French and British bombing squadrons, we had our bombing problem also. It didn't make much difference whether you were bumped off with a falling cocoanut or a falling bomb. The result was all the same. After one whizzed by your ear, you would very likely go down to the open beach to quiet your nerves. Then if you tried to sleep there, the land crabs would soon convince you that the beach was no place for a weary war veteran either. Patrols of fighting marine crabs would raid that beach every night. After being chased out by the crabs, you would go back to your hammock and lie awake wondering when the next aërial cocoanut bombardment would commence. So life during those first days on our tropic isle was not all skittles and beer or orchids and cocoanut milk. You can bet we worked hard getting up the huts! Luckily, there were no casualties from either crabs or cocoanuts. We cleared a large space for our village, and built huts out of timbers, sailcloth, and palm leaves. The first one up was a queer-looking thing, but our architecture improved with practice. Our prisoners, who were all Americans, helped us a great deal. They understood the art of pitching tents. They built a special town for themselves, and gave the streets such names as Broadway, State Street, Pennsylvania Avenue, and the Bowery. In time we contrived to arrange quite decent dwelling places. We had plenty of furnishings. From the wrecked *Seeadler*, which remained perched forlornly on the coral reef, we took everything we could carry. We even built a chapel, took the Bible from the *Seeadler*, and from parts of the wreck we built a fine altar and crucifix. Of course, we also installed our wireless set ashore in order to keep in touch with passing ships and events happening out on this side of the world. Nor did we neglect to take ashore a heavy arsenal of arms and ammunition, including rifles, Luger pistols, hand grenades, and dynamite. In short, we had a perfect little town with everything except a calaboose. Some of our men who had romantic tendencies constructed "country homes" for themselves a few hundred yards away in the jungle. Then we named the place Seeadlerburg, Sea Eagle Town.

There were gull's eggs everywhere along the shore, but the

birds were brooding now, and most of the eggs we collected had half-formed little gulls in them. We got around this by clearing a large section of beach and throwing the old eggs into the lagoon. Then the gulls flocked back and laid more eggs, and thus a supply of fresh eggs was assured.

Our American prisoners were nearly all cheery fellows. Some of them fitted in with the new life better than my men. They seemed to know all about the art of fishing, and taught us Germans things we had never dreamed of. They were accustomed to what in the States, along the Gulf of Mexico, is called spearing eels. They fastened iron barbs to shafts of wood and with these speared big fish in the coral lagoon. They also showed us a clever way of catching fish on a grand scale. They took some forty men and boys and, just as high tide was turning, formed in a line about fifty yards offshore. Then the line came splashing in, driving the fish before it toward shore, just as the natives round up tigers for a rajah in India. Many of the fish floundered into shallow water, and a few minutes later were left stranded by the receding tide. You see, the water, as it backed offshore, left large pools on top of the irregular coral reef, and there the fish were trapped. Sometimes we caught five or six hundred pounds a day, and it was exciting sport.

One night, while we were sitting around our fire, we heard a scratching sound. It seemed to come from everywhere. We looked and found a lot of crabs with big claws. They were hermit crabs. We caught several and put them in boiling water to cook. Meanwhile, the crab invasion continued, and more from behind kept pushing the rest forward. We tried the ones we had cooked, and they were delicious. They were as good as the best lobster.

"By Joe," I said, "boys, let's get busy."

We spread out a large sail and filled it up with crabs, like a sack. We must have had several thousand of them. For days we lived on them, until most of us couldn't look a crab in the face. We had 'em boiled, broiled, and in soup. Then that invasion of these hermits passed as mysteriously as it had come, and we never saw them again. But the turtles were always with us. We caught a number of them and kept them in a coral basin at one end of the lagoon.

The wild pigs on the island provided us with more fun and

more food. They fed on cocoanuts, which is the best kind of fodder to make good pork. These animals were said to be the descendants of swine brought to the South Seas by early explorers long ago. They are found on many islands, and New Zealand is a regular paradise for them and for the hunter who likes to chase wild pigs. After generations of living on cocoanuts, they had changed a lot and had developed a special kind of tusk and jaw.

There were snipe on our island, too, and we hunted them with great success, thereby varying our sea food and pork diet. Using cocoanut shells for fuel, we smoked what flesh and fish we could.

By way of vegetables, we had cocoanuts, and bread made of cocoanut flour, which the Kanakas taught us to prepare, and hearts of palms. This latter is one of the rarest of delicacies, and outside the tropics only multimillionaires can afford it. The price, when you get palm hearts in Europe, is higher than that of Russian caviar. For the most part, it is reserved for castaway sailors and buccaneers like ourselves. It is the core taken from the very tip of the cocoanut palm, right where the new leaves form. For each heart, weighing about ten pounds, a noble palm has to be sacrificed. The taste is between that of hazel nuts and asparagus, only finer and sweeter than either.

But I must tell you more about that invasion of hermit crabs. It caused the first and only fatality in the course of all our adventures. My dog Schnaeuzchen had all of the prying, curious nature of the dachshund. The island, with its teeming life, was endless source of wonder to her. She investigated everything, forever had her nose sniffing somewhere or other. The swarming hermit crabs, which covered the ground almost like a carpet, sent her into a perfect spasm of astonishment. She jumped and barked and yelped. She cocked one eye and studied the strange creatures, and quite obviously did not like their looks. They crawled on all sides of her, and she was filled with bewilderment and fright. She was furious with them, but kept nimbly out of their way. Finally, however, the pugnacity of her dachs nature got the better of her, and she felt she must attack something. A particularly large and villainous-looking crab excited her ire. She leaped upon it to devour it. The crab raised its great, ferocious claws to strike at her. Schnaeuzchen gave a strange yelp of fright, and rolled over in a spasm. She kicked convulsively for a few moments, and then was still— dead. Poor little Schnaeuzchen! The exotic life of the South Seas had been too much for her. She was only two years old, and on the island she had for the first time found an opportunity to give vent to her passion for hunting. We gave her a fine grave, and planted a cocoa palm on it. Her comrade, Piperle, looked around disconsolately for her and was sad for a long time.

Piperle had an adventure with the birds. He undertook one day to invade one of the densely populated rookeries. Somehow or other, he contrived to antagonize the birds. I suppose he tried to raid a nest. The angry gulls swarmed above him. One seized one ear. Another seized the other. Several struck at his eyes. One hung on to his tail. Piperle howled and struggled. It was at this point that one of our men saw him execute an intelligent bit of strategy. There was a clump of underbrush near by. He struggled toward it, taking the birds with him. He dragged himself into the brush and thereby shook off the birds. He returned to camp a sadly mishandled dog, and never went near any of the rookeries again. From then on he confined his courage and daring to chasing the wild pigs at night, which he did with a prodigious barking and yelping. The pet opossum that our prisoners had carefully rescued from the wreck picked up an excellent living on the island, and came into the messroom every night, asking for water.

If our new home teemed with useful, edible creatures, it was not lacking in pestilential forms of life, either, these both of native origin and imported from ships. A thousand kinds of insects were everywhere. If you awakened thirsty at night and reached for your glass of water, you were likely to find that it contained more cockroaches than water. You had to reconcile yourself to getting up in the morning and finding your toothbrush alive with ants. The ants were particularly pervasive. We could only guard against them by putting the legs of tables, chairs, and other articles of furniture in cups of water. We slept at night to the ceaseless shuffle of rats, huge insolent fellows, running about on the tops of our tents. Piperle waged war against them, but the odds were too great. It would have taken a whole regiment of terriers to end that plague.

Flashing birds of paradise flew from palm to palm. Gorgeous

humming birds with green and yellow breasts darted among the branches. With every flower there seemed to be a great butterfly. The whole island was aglow with butterflies. They floated on wide, beating wings of greens, violets, and reds.

Once, in the middle of the night, I was awakened by a small, sharp, repeated sound—knick, knick, knack. It was the opening of tropical flowers. I went outside and there I saw the lovely Queen of Night, which blossoms by the light of the tropical stars. It is a great, gorgeous bloom, eight or ten inches across. There were thousands of them. Scores of glowworms, far brighter than any we know, hovered above each, eager to catch the magnificent perfume that the opening Queen of Night gives forth. In the darkness I could see the flowers only by the light of the glowworms. On every side were these eerie nocturnal lights, a dancing lamp of gathered glowworms illuminating each flower. In that unearthly gleaming, like a kind of moonlight only stranger, the odorous petals shone with the ghostly nuances of their naturally flaming colours, white, crimson, sapphire blue, violet blue. In the South Seas, the flowers have little scent by day, while the sun shines on them. At night, when the dew falls, perfume awakens. It is truly a perfumed night. And the nostrils of man are excited by the rich and almost oppressive blending of odours. The Queen of Night gives off the perfume of vanilla. Mingled with it comes the scent of hyacinth, orchid, mayflower, and heliotrope. Sweet-smelling breezes blow, and above is the tropical sky with its clustered flashing stars and gorgeous Milky Way. Hanging above the horizon is the far-famed Southern Cross.

The Rest of the Story: After three weeks the monotony of the island existence began to get on the men's nerves. Consequently the best one of the life boats was conditioned and Von Luckner and five of his men set off for the Cook Islands. Later in the Fiji Islands their identity was discovered and they were imprisoned. The men who had been left on the island were more fortunate, however. They captured a small French schooner that visited the island, and leaving its crew behind they set off for another buccaneering expedition. The schooner was wrecked, however, off the coast of Chile and the men had to swim for shore. In Chile they lived as guests of German colonists to the end of the war. Von Luckner and his companions were taken after a time to an island off the coast of New Zealand. An attempted escape met with failure and they were kept prisoners until after the Armistice was signed.

The Biographer—Lowell Thomas (1892–   ): The author of the fascinating book from which these extracts are taken is Lowell Thomas, the well-known newspaper man whom you often hear over the radio, giving news of the world. He himself has led an interesting, adventurous life. After graduation from college he was connected with various newspapers as reporter. At the time of the World War he was sent to Europe by President Wilson as chief of a civilian commission to prepare an historical record of the war. In Europe he was attached in turn to Belgian, French, Italian, Serbian, American, British, and Arabian armies. In 1919 he made his début as a lecturer. In between his lecture tours he has had many experiences among which have been a trip around the world; a tour of India with the Prince of Wales; explorations in Malay, India and Central Asia; and a 25,000 mile airplane trip over twenty-one countries of Europe, Asia and North Africa. He is author of a number of books among which are *With Lawrence in Arabia, The First World Flight,* and *Count Luckner, the Sea Devil,* an extract from which you have just read. None of the Germans, Thomas tells us, "had a tale to tell like Count Felix von Luckner. . . . I pass it on to you in the words of the Sea Devil, and, I hope, with something of the tang of the sea."

Suggestions for Study: Give an account of the pranks of the sailors with the sharks. Describe Mopelia. Tell about the life of the crew on the island. Tell about the first sight of the tidal wave, its approach, and the miraculous escape of Von Luckner and his men. Describe the building of Sea Eagle town.

Describe the plants on the island; describe the animals. Relate the experience of the dog, Schnaeuzchen, with the hermit crabs. Relate the adventure of the other dog, Piperle, with the birds. Describe the insects of the atoll; also the flowers, especially the Queen of Night.

Examine the vocabulary. Is it that of those "who go down to the sea in ships"? Has it the tang of the sea? Give illustrations to prove your points. Is the selection biography or autobiography?

Exercises and Creative Work: On a map determine the location of Mopelia, the Cook Islands, the Fiji Islands, New Zealand.

Bring pictures to class of coral, of tropical flowers, insects, birds, or other plant or animal life to be found on an island such as Mopelia.

Write an imaginary chapter in the life of the shipwrecked sailors.

For Further Reading: After such a fascinating glimpse, you will, of course, want to read the entire book, *Count Luckner, the Sea Devil.* You cannot fail to be interested in the romantic story of such a romantic character.

The Desert Island Adventure Book contains "good tales and true" of castaways of the last three hundred years who were in search of adventure. The tales are told by the castaways themselves and give the lover of sea stories real thrills.

EXTENSIVE READING PROGRAM—BIOGRAPHY

Biography as a Matter of Individual Interest

The reading of biography is perhaps more entirely a matter of individual interest than the reading of any other form of literature. An extensive reading program has therefore been prepared for you which offers a wide choice of interesting biographies from which you may choose along the lines of your own personal interests.

Reports of Biographies Read

Since your reading of biography will be done largely outside the classroom, you will want to make a report on each biography you read. The following questions will help you to prepare such reports.

1. Which of the biographies or autobiographies that you have read did you like best? Why? Because of the subject matter or because of the biographer?
2. Is there such a vivid re-creation of the times that you see, feel, and live in them? How does the author accomplish this?
3. Does the book seem long-drawn out or is it firmly organized and well developed?
4. What qualities of the writer does the book reveal?
5. Does the biographer intrude his own personality in a way that makes or mars the book?
6. Give instances of leadership, service, human sympathy, in the biographies you have read.
7. Examine the vocabulary used. Is it commonplace? unique? picturesque? Give examples.
8. Summarize the character of one of the men or women about whom you have read, illustrating your points by concrete instances.
9. Are personal details, habits, mannerisms made to seem important? Are they over-emphasized?
10. Has the author a sense of humor? Give instances.
11. Has the author charm? Illustrate.
12. Is there a sympathetic understanding between the biographer and the subject? Cite a case or two.
13. Have you discovered in your reading that background influences character development? Illustrate.
14. Choose one author and show how his way of writing a biography differs from that of other authors.
15. Is the autobiography you have read a revelation of the real person?

Exercises and Creative Work

What is the Pulitzer Prize? Nominate a biography you have read for consideration for such a prize.

Let a group of four or five pupils choose a biography from the list, read it, and then select scenes for dramatization by the group. Such scenes might be:

1. A scene in a country store in which young Abe Lincoln is talking to a group of townsmen about a book he has just read. (See Sandburg's *Abraham Lincoln: The Prairie Years*.)
2. A scene back stage at a rehearsal of *Rip Van Winkle*. (See Joseph Jefferson's *Autobiography*.)
3. A scene advertising Barnum's circus. (See Werner's *Barnum*.)

A semester project—*Who's Who in the Classroom*. (See *The English Journal*, April, 1933.) This will suggest working up individual biographies by class members, classmates being the subjects for this experiment.

Another semester project—*Famous American Writers*. Throughout this volume of PROSE AND POETRY are interesting "biographies of personality" of writers of American literature. Choose the ones which you think should go in a collection entitled *Famous American Writers*. Other collective biographies can be made under such titles as *American Poets, Writers of the National Period, The Short Story Writers in American Literature, The Writers of American Essays, Who's Who in American Literature*.

American Biographies

Among the biographies and autobiographies listed below, you will surely be able to find several that are peculiarly attractive because of their appeal to your own tastes. They are conveniently grouped so that you may the more readily make your selection.

ADVENTURE

Herbert Eugene Bolton   *The Padre on Horseback*
A sketch of the life of Padre Kino, by the greatest authority on Kino.

W. F. Cody   *Autobiography of Buffalo Bill*
Here is a thrilling tale of the West in the days of Indians, cowboys, and buffaloes. Buffalo Bill became popular by re-enacting his western adventures for eastern audiences in Wild West shows and on the stage.

C. A. Eastman   *Indian Boyhood*
This is an amusing story of boyhood life among the Indians. The author was a Sioux Indian and lived with the tribe during his early years. His education in forest lore and tribal conventions contains many points worthy of adoption. You will also want to read *From the Deep Woods to Civilization* by this author.

Hamlin Garland   *A Son of the Middle Border*
This is a classic. It is considered not merely one of the finest autobiographies in the English language, but is also outstanding among world auto-

biographies. In it the author tells the story of his family in winning the West—Wisconsin, Iowa and Dakota. The pioneer life depicted is thrilling and realistic, in startling contrast to the school life of the city boy today with his movies, radios, automobiles—everything to make life easy. But do not we in the city miss something vital and character-forming in the rough outdoor life here described? Another autobiographical book of Hamlin Garland which you will enjoy is *Companions on the Trail.*

Joseph Gurn   *Commodore John Barry*

The life of "Saucy Jack" Barry, Irish-born Father of the American Navy; a story of action.

Marion Habig   *Heroes of the Cross*

A collective biography of the Franciscan Friars who gave their lives as martyrs in North America in the years between 1541 and 1908.

The Conquest of Nature

Mitchell V. Charnley   *The Boys' Life of the Wright Brothers*

An appreciative and interesting story of the development of an idea which was realized, a realization which gave man dominion over air as well as over earth and sea.

G. J. Cohen and W. Scarlet *George W. Goethals* (In *Modern Pioneers*)

The builder of the Panama Canal. His Dutch name, *Goethals,* means "good neck." One of his ancestors, when commended for brave deeds by his king replied, "Sire, I break before I bend." The tradition was carried on in the family, and the builder of the Panama Canal exemplifies it.

G. J. Cohen and W. Scarlet   *Luther Burbank* (In *Modern Pioneers*)

A veritable plant magician, Burbank, on his farm in Santa Rosa, California, actually created new forms. He developed seedless grapes, white blackberries, and made almond trees bear prunes. He was buried in the garden where he worked, beneath a tree he planted.

Burton J. Hendrick   *Gorgas: His Life and Work*

Gorgas worked at Panama and Havana for the conquest of yellow fever by applying Walter Reed's theory that the mosquito was the carrier of the disease. An interesting story of the man who made the tropical world a safe place to live in, and made the building of the Panama Canal by Goethals a possibility.

Dallas Lore Sharp   *The Boys' Life of John Burroughs*

A delightfully written book. The author is a kindred soul of the great nature lover and fine writer, John Burroughs. Your interest will be held from the first word to the last.

Famous People in Literature, Music, and Drama

M. D. Bianchi   *Life and Letters of Emily Dickinson*

The story of one of the most unique figures in American literature whose poems, with one or two exceptions, were published only after her death. The story is a sympathetic treatment by her niece.

Francis J. Finn   *Father Finn, S.J.*
The story of his life, told by himself, "for his friends young and old," as edited by Daniel A. Lord, S.J.

Hildegarde Hawthorne   *The Romantic Rebel*
A sympathetic, intimate, and authentic life of Nathaniel Hawthorne written by his granddaughter. It reads like a novel and shows through incidents and illustrations from old letters and diaries the kindly nature of Hawthorne. Another biography of Hawthorne is entitled *The Rebellious Puritan* written by Lloyd Morris.

William Dean Howells   *My Mark Twain*
The story of the long friendship of two of America's leading writers. Sympathetic and altogether delightful is the treatment of Mark Twain by Howells. It makes fascinating reading. Another biography of Mark Twain has been written by his daughter, Clara Clemens, and is entitled *My Father, Mark Twain*.

Joseph Jefferson   *Autobiography*
The story of a great actor and a lovable human being. Interesting reminiscences of the stage and of his friends before and beyond the footlights. To him life was the stage and the stage was life.

Elizabeth Jordan   *Three Rousing Cheers*
The refreshing autobiography of one who, through a long career as reporter, editor, dramatic critic, novelist, and short-story writer, has kept her view of life wholesomely Catholic.

Theodore Maynard   *The World I Saw*
An outspoken and absorbing autobiography of a poet, biographer, literary critic, and teacher. He was born in India, where his parents were officers in the Salvation Army; he was educated in England, where he entered the Church; he has lived and labored in the United States for over twenty years.

Lewis Mumford   *Herman Melville*
This story of Melville's life published in 1929 has done much to increase the popularity of *Moby Dick* and *Typee*. These tales were not widely read at the time they were written, but today their real literary and artistic worth are appreciated by critics and the reading public alike. The persistence of Melville in clinging to his ideals and pursuing them against great odds until he succeeded must give us all pause today. Mumford draws a stirring picture of his struggles.

Mary Roberts Rinehart   *My Story*
You will enjoy reading the life story of this popular author. *The Circular Staircase* and many of her other stories have given audiences much enjoyment on both stage and screen.

Otis Skinner   *Footlights and Spotlights*
A sprightly account of the struggles and achievements of a famous American actor. The story of his friendship with Barnum, Barrett, Booth and other famous men of the time makes interesting reading.

Edward H. Sothern   *The Melancholy Tale of Me*
Interesting, lively, anecdotal, whimsical. Intimate stories of the stage and its great personalities of the nineteenth and twentieth centuries. Good reading for leisure hours.

Genevieve Taggard   *The Life and Mind of Emily Dickinson*

This is considered the most authentic life of the poet. Letters, poems, and anecdotes make this book most interesting.

Mark Twain   *Autobiography*

Original in method, as might be expected. Abounds in anecdotes and experiences told in characteristic manner. "Finally in Florence," he says in 1904, "I hit upon the right way to do an autobiography; start at no particular time of your life; wander at your free will all over your life; talk only about the thing which interests you for the moment; drop it the moment its interest threatens to pale, and turn your talk upon the new and more interesting thing that has intruded itself into your mind meantime."

Notable Figures in Our National Development

James Truslow Adams   *The Adams Family*

For four generations the Adams family has made notable contributions "by public service in the highest of offices or by intellectual contributions" to American civilization—to our public life, two presidents and several cabinet officers; to our intellectual life, really great historical writing by the last representatives of the family, Henry and Brooks. The author, although bearing the same name, does not belong to the family.

Gamaliel Bradford   *Lee, The American*

This is perhaps Bradford's masterpiece. In his preface, Mr. Bradford says the book is not a biography, but rather a psychography, the story of a human soul. And this is what it is, a fascinating study of the development of a great character. "Here," says Bradford, "is a man who remains great although he fails."

Joseph Gurn   *Charles Carroll of Carrollton*

Catholics will be interested in this life story of the one Catholic signer of the Declaration of Independence.

Burton J. Hendrick   *Life and Letters of Walter H. Page*

Walter Hines Page was ambassador to Great Britain during the World War. He was a close friend and devoted admirer of Woodrow Wilson and one of the first to recognize his presidential possibilities. Page's letters are considered models. Read them and form your own opinion. This biography of Page won the Pulitzer Prize for biography in 1923.

Francis Clement Kelly   *The Bishop Jots It Down*

This autobiography of the Bishop of Oklahoma City and founder of the Church Extension Society tells the story of his full and absorbing life from his birth on Prince Edward Island to his appointment to the see of Oklahoma City.

Carl Sandburg   *Abraham Lincoln: The Prairie Years*

An intimate story of Lincoln's daily life. Lincoln understood the big things, the real things of life and nature, and so does his biographer. There is a bond between them which makes this biography of Lincoln the most human, the most understanding of all Lincoln biographies. Not only does Sandburg bring this understanding to his task, but he also brings the perception and skill of the artist. His *Abraham Lincoln* is a great literary achievement.

Overcoming Handicaps

Edward W. Bok *The Americanization of Edward Bok*

This book which was awarded the Pulitzer Prize in 1921 as "the best American biography teaching patriotic and unselfish service to the nation, and at the same time illustrating an eminent example," tells how Bok "left the world a little better than he found it," as instructed to do by his grandparents.

Andrew Carnegie *The Autobiography of Andrew Carnegie*

The story of the rise of a poor Scotch boy from a cotton weaver's assistant to lord of the steel industry in the United States. The "Carnegie Library," a gift from the philanthropist, is a feature of many cities in our country.

William T. Kane *A Memoir of William A. Stanton, S.J.*

The life story of a young Jesuit who; with the choice of fame as a scientist or obscurity as a missionary before him, chose the bush of Central America, and became famous anyway.

Michael Pupin *From Immigrant to Inventor*

A lively description of the author's school days and summer work in the fields guiding and guarding oxen in his native village in Hungary. His long summer nights spent in the open turned his thoughts towards the wonders of light and sound and were, perhaps, responsible for his future scientific study of these phenomena. This book won the Pulitzer Prize in 1924.

Jacob Riis *The Making of an American*

This interesting tale of triumph over hard conditions is the early life of the man who became a prominent civic and social leader of the community in which he lived.

Daniel Sargent *Catherine Tekakwitha*

Sargent provides the background against which the brief life-story of this saintly Indian girl, who is now a candidate for the honors of the altar, is told splendidly and sympathetically.

Eduard A. Steiner *From Alien to Citizen*

The story of the struggle of a young man from Austria to make good in this country. He overcame difficulties and finally reached his goal—American citizenship. The native-born may learn much from this foreigner's attitude towards the privilege and responsibility of American citizenship.

Booker T. Washington *Up from Slavery*

The story of the overcoming of the almost insuperable difficulties of a freed slave in his pursuit of education. Washington founded Tuskegee Institute for the education of his race and has rendered inestimable service to his people.

Miscellaneous

Harriet C. Brown *Grandmother Brown's Hundred Years*

The homely story of the active domestic life of a woman who lived through one hundred years of devoted service to her large family. Remarkable mainly in its span (1827–1927) and in the fact that on her one hundredth birthday she was still an interesting, intelligent, and really beautiful woman, judging by the photograph taken on that occasion.

Katherine Burton   *Sorrow Built a Bridge*

After the death of her husband, Rose Hawthorne, youngest child of
Nathaniel Hawthorne, became a Dominican nun and devoted the remaining
twenty-five years of her life to the destitute, incurable cancer sufferers of
New York City. The story of a beautiful life is beautifully told by one who
is herself a convert to Catholicism. Miss Burton also has published a life
of Mother Seton, *His Dear Persuasion.*

Dorothy Day   *From Union Square to Rome*

Once a Communist herself, the author, now originator and leader of the
Catholic Worker movement, addresses this brave apologia to her Com-
munist brother and to all who may ask: "How could you become a
Catholic?"

Francis A. MacNutt   *A Papal Chamberlain*

Ever so graciously does this "gentleman from Indiana" introduce his readers
to the great in diplomatic, ecclesiastical, and literary circles, whom he met
throughout his life in many lands.

John Moody   *The Long Road Home*

The head of a well known investment service tells a winning story of his
travels through various religions on his way home to the Catholic Church.

M. R. Werner   *Barnum*

A lively and correct story of the life of America's great circus man. It
gives interesting facts about Jenny Lind, whose first American tour he
managed, and Tom Thumb, the dwarf, who traveled with him. The episode
of the elephant trained to plough the fields as an advertisement of the show
is amusing.

ADDITIONAL BIOGRAPHIES OF INTEREST

Jane Addams
Twenty Years at Hull House

Mrs. Thomas Bailey Aldrich
Crowding Memories

W. T. Grenfell
A Labrador Doctor

Eva Le Gallienne
At 33

Severin and Stephen Lamping
Through Hundred Gates

G. H. Palmer
Life of Alice Freeman Palmer

Mrs. C. S. Parker
An American Idyll

Agnes Repplier
Mère Marie of the Ursulines

Laura E. Richards
Stepping Westward

Lincoln Steffens
Autobiography

Mrs. E. G. L. Stein
My Mother and I

Stanley Vestal
Kit Carson

Edith Wharton
A Backward Glance

Michael Williams
Book of High Romance

POETRY

POETRY AS A TYPE OF LITERATURE

How to Read Poetry

In order to enjoy poetry, one must know how to read it and what to look for in it. To begin with, poetry should be read aloud. You never can get the full flavor of a poem by reading it silently. The reason for this is easily understood if you think of the sound of poetry as music. You do not so much enjoy looking at a sheet of music as you do hearing the sound when it is played. When you hear it, your feelings are moved—you are happy and excited or you feel downcast and sad—your imagination begins to work and you often picture yourself doing great things—you do not know why, other than that the sound thus affects your feelings. The movement of a poem or its rhythm is its music, and to sense this you must hear the poem read aloud.

What to Look for in Poetry

Many people think only of the meaning of the words when they read a poem, as if the purpose of a poem were the same as that of a history book—to give information. But this is not the purpose of poetry, not even of poetry which tells a story. It is not the meaning of a poem which makes good poetry. Telling the most heroic of deeds, or voicing the noblest of thoughts in verse does not make the verse a great poem. The test of poetry is not so much what the writer says, as how he says it. We all know persons who have a manner of describing a feeling or a sight in a way to make us feel or see vividly ourselves. This is the gift which the true poet has in abundance. In a line or two he flashes before us a picture, or a mood, or a feeling, or drives home to us the realization of some truth.

Besides being able to express himself so that he appeals to us, the poet is more sensitive to the beauty, or the hidden meaning of things about him than we are. He sees beauty where we never thought it was, and points it out to us. He sees injustice where we never saw it and makes us see it too. He senses a great truth and states it so that we feel it. He tells us how we feel on a spring morning, and after we read the poem we realize that we have felt like that many times but couldn't express it.

Narrative and Lyric Poetry

There are two main divisions of poetry—narrative and lyric poetry. In narrative poetry, the poet describes or relates events. In lyric poetry, he expresses his thoughts and feelings on a subject and tries to make us feel as he does. Bryant, for example, in *The Waterfowl*, does not tell a story about the bird nor does he give a description of it. He is merely trying to make us feel as he felt when he saw the bird against the sunset.

How to Appreciate Poetry

To fully appreciate poetry, one must get the author's mood. To do this, one must imagine oneself in the same emotional setting that the author presumably was in when he wrote the poem. It is not possible to visualize exactly as some one else does, but nearly every one has had experiences in life similar to those of other people, and can approximate some kind of emotion akin to that about which he is reading. Poetry is a matter of feeling and of visual picturing. Each poem appeals directly to the senses and should build up in the mind of the reader the visual pictures which the author endeavors to create. If the author expresses sadness, one needs to recall a time in his life when he felt very sad, and then to read the poem holding this mood throughout the reading. Surely each of us has had the emotions of joy, sorrow, love, patriotism, loneliness, in varying degrees of intensity. If we let the poet's mood and the pictures he paints become a part of our mental content by associating them with similar moods and feelings of our own, we can learn to read poetry with appreciation and understanding.

Poetry is the open door to new experiences. It helps us to understand other people better, and to understand ourselves better. It gives us different views of things and of people, and different feelings about them from those we had before. After spending an hour or two with the best poets, we have finer mental attitudes and a greater appreciation of truth and beauty.

FIGURES OF SPEECH

Figures of speech are used in all types of writing but they appear most often in poetry. Following are some of the common figures. The examples are taken, for the most part, from poems included in this book.

Simile: A simile is an expressed comparison between two objects of unlike nature. *Like* and *as* are the signs of the simile.

> Helen, thy beauty is to me
> Like those Nicean barks of yore.
> EDGAR ALLAN POE, *To Helen*

> And when he fell in whirlwind, he went down
> As when a lordly cedar, green with boughs,
> Goes down with a great shout upon the hills.
> EDWIN MARKHAM, *Lincoln, The Man of the People*

Metaphor: A metaphor is an implied comparison. *Like* and *as* are not used.

> My Vigor is a new-minted penny.
> AMY LOWELL, *A Lady*

> My heart a dewdrop is.
> JOHN BANNISTER TABB, *To Sidney Lanier*

Allegory: An allegory is an extended metaphor. A short allegory is a fable.

> The best examples of allegory are to be found in prose. Excellent examples are *The Pilgrim's Progress* and Aesop's *Fables*.

Personification: Personification gives the attributes of life to inanimate objects.

> Bid Time and Nature gently spare
> The shaft we raise to them and thee.
> RALPH WALDO EMERSON, *The Concord Hymn*

> My apple trees will never get across
> And eat the cones under his pines.
> ROBERT FROST, *Mending Wall*

Apostrophe: Apostrophe is directly addressing the inanimate object as if it were present.

> Darest thou now, O Soul.
> WALT WHITMAN, *Darest Thou Now, O Soul*

> O World, I cannot hold thee close enough.
> EDNA ST. VINCENT MILLAY, *God's World*

Metonymy: Metonymy is the substituton of one word for another which is associated with it or is suggested by it.

(Locality for inhabitants) To the glory that was Greece.
> EDGAR ALLAN POE, *To Helen*

(The author for his books) Read from some humbler poet.
> HENRY WADSWORTH LONGFELLOW, *The Day Is Done*

(Container for the contents) By every cup of sorrow that you had.
> LIZETTE WOODWORTH REESE, *Tears*

Synecdoche: Synecdoche is a substitution of a part for a whole, a whole for a part, the material for the thing made, etc. It is a form of metonymy but is so frequently used that it is given a special name.

> None couldn't quicker pitch a ton.
> JAMES RUSSELL LOWELL, *The Courtin'*

> The world is growing green.
> BLISS CARMAN, *An April Morning*

Alliteration: Alliteration consists of a repetition of successive words having the same beginning consonant.

> A tapering turret overtops the work.
> RALPH WALDO EMERSON, *The Snow Storm*

> By midnight moons, o'er moistening dews.
> PHILIP FRENEAU, *The Indian Burying Ground*

> I have known the silence of the stars, and of the sea.
> EDGAR LEE MASTERS, *Silence*

Hyperbole: Hyperbole is an extravagance of utterance. It is an exaggeration of expression in which more is said than could possibly be true.

> How many million Aprils came.
> SARA TEASDALE, *Blue Squills*

> He ate and drank the precious words.
> EMILY DICKINSON, *A Book*

Onomatopoeia: Onomatopoeia is the use of words in which the sound suggests the sense.

> From the jingling and the tinkling of the bells.
> EDGAR ALLAN POE, *The Bells*

> Boomlay, boomlay, boomlay, boom.
> VACHEL LINDSAY, *The Congo*

Antithesis: Antithesis is an opposition or contrast of words and ideas. Words are contrasted or balanced against each other to make the meaning more emphatic.

> Character is what we think we are; reputation is what men think we are.

Vision: Vision is the treatment of an event of the past or the future as if it were present. It is particularly effective in describing a race or a game.

> The horses are coming under the wire. The judge signals a start. They are off.

Irony: Irony is an utterance, in the form of humor or light sarcasm, in which the opposite of what is said is meant. The following is one of the finest examples of irony in literature.

> He hath brought many captives home to Rome,
> Whose ransoms did the general coffers fill;
> Did this in Caesar seem ambitious?
> When that the poor have cried, Caesar hath wept.
> Ambition should be made of sterner stuff:
> Yet Brutus says he was ambitious,
> *And Brutus is an honorable man.*
> WILLIAM SHAKESPEARE, *Julius Caesar*

THE HISTORY OF AMERICAN POETRY

THE COLONIAL PERIOD (1607–1765)

General Characteristics

We are told by literary historians that the early colonists had no soul for poetry, but this is not true of them. They had love for rhythm and love for beauty, and these are the foundations for poetic expression. Their love for rhythm is clearly shown in their singing, for they were a singing people. The *Bay Psalm Book* (1640) was the first book of verse published in America. This was a translation of the Psalms into verses which were sung in the churches, or meeting houses as they were called in those days. The book has little poetic value, it is true, but it marks the beginning of poetic effort. The colonists' love of beauty is indicated by the flower gardens which the women cultivated, even in the wilderness, and many old letters speak of the geraniums and plants which the Colonial women kept in the windows. Surely there could be no firmer proof of their love of beauty, and while they were not able to express this love of beauty and rhythm, the medium of expression, which is poetry, was only slumbering and waiting for the time when it could spring into being. Nor is it surprising that the colonists were unable to express themselves in poetry, for their time was almost wholly occupied with facing the stern realities of life, and with wresting a living from the earth and fighting the dangers which constantly menaced them on all sides.

Anne Dudley Bradstreet (1612–1672)

The first author of a book of poetry was Anne Dudley Bradstreet, a cultivated English girl. She married at the age of sixteen and left her comfortable home in England to come to a cabin in the American wilderness. It is hard for American boys and girls of to-day to picture what this coming to America meant for that cultured English girl. Even the evening sounds about her rude home in the clearing were different from the peaceful, soothing sounds she had heard in her English home at twilight. Yet she wrote poems, and besides brought up eight children and helped take care of the stock. She wrote of nature and the following lines from her poem *Contemplations* are free and natural.

> I heard the merry grasshopper then sing,
>   The black-clad cricket bear a second part;
> They kept one tune, and played on the same string,
>   Seeming to glory in their little art.
> Shall creatures abject, thus their voices raise,
> And in their kind resound their maker's praise,
> Whilst I, as mute, can warble forth no higher lays?

303

Michael Wigglesworth (1631–1705)

Michael Wigglesworth was the next colonial poet who is worthy of mention. His poem, *The Day of Doom; or, A Poetical Description of the Great and Last Judgment,* was very popular in early New England. Its title indicates the subject matter and it reflects the spirit of the times, for the early colonists were greatly concerned with happenings of the other world and death and judgment. Here again we see a struggling for poetic expression even through such a serious topic. Had Wigglesworth lived in a different environment, he no doubt would have created a living, pulsating poem, for there is worth in his *Day of Doom.* However, we can think of him only as one of the builders who laid the foundation of better work to follow.

Thomas Godfrey (1736–1763)

Thomas Godfrey was a young lad whose poems showed great promise. He was the first to break away from the theme of death and judgment and to start a new spirit in poetry. He wrote love songs, odes, and pastorals and was the forerunner of poetry as depicting noble emotions. He was interested in many things, for he saw beauty all about him. He died at the age of twenty-seven, and it was not until after his death that his poems were published in a volume entitled *Juvenile Poems; with The Prince of Parthia, a Tragedy.*

THE REVOLUTIONARY PERIOD (1765–1800)

General Characteristics

We are told that the literature of a country reflects a real picture of the times. This is undoubtedly true, for during war we have war poems, during a period of social unrest we have poems of injustice, and during times of peace we have poems dealing more with nature, sentiment, and topics of tranquillity.

With the rapid increase of trade and wealth, with more widespread education, with the growth from lonely isolated log cabins to villages having newspapers, schools, and churches, the ideas of the colonists changed from their earlier morbid concentration upon the thought of predestination, to opportunity and success. Following quickly upon this social and economic growth came the desire for recognition of their rights as colonists and the War for Independence.

With these changes we note also a great change in the poetry of the country. No longer was the theme death or unworldliness as portrayed by Wigglesworth in his *Day of Doom.* There was no time now to dwell on death. On the contrary, the colonists were more concerned with living in the present and with the chance to enjoy themselves and to succeed and progress.

The development of the ballad and the poetry of Philip Freneau were the two noteworthy poetic creations of the Revolutionary Period.

The Ballad

A ballad is a story told in song. When the early settlers came to America, they brought old English ballads with them, but it was not long before native American ballads came into being. The period of the Revolution was productive of more than a thousand songs and ballads. Every hamlet had its ballad maker, and every important event was celebrated in song. Every company in the army had its poet who beguiled the weariness of the march or the encampment by his songs. Many of these ballads have been lost, but some have been preserved. Among them *Yankee Doodle* is probably best known. It was sung to the delight of citizens and soldiers during the Revolutionary War and still retains its hold on the public. Another popular ballad of the day was *The Dance*, which delighted in the discomfiture of General Cornwallis, and a third, *The Battle of the Kegs*, was a satirical ballad on the British troops during Howe's occupation of Philadelphia.

Philip Freneau (1752–1832)

The two political parties of the period were the Whigs and the Tories. Freneau threw his talents whole-heartedly to the side of the Whigs and denounced the Tories in bitter satire and scathing verse. His versatile life and varied experiences had given him plenty of background to do this effectively. After his graduation from Princeton he had taught school, tried his hand at law and also traveled extensively. His poetry cheered the patriot, railed at the English and exulted in the American victories. He fitted out a vessel which he himself commanded but he was captured and thrown into a British prison ship. After the tumult of the Revolution was over, however, and peace established, the type of Freneau's writing changed. He no longer railed in satire or jeered the English, but instead he reflected the condition of the country and wrote simple, true poems of nature and humanity. It is for these later poems that we best remember him. He was the first genuine American poet and is often called "the poet of the Revolution."

Other Poets of the Revolutionary Period

Other than the songs and ballads inspired by the War and the romantic verse of Freneau, there was little poetry of note in this period except that of the so-called "Hartford (or Connecticut) Wits." The "Hartford Wits" were a group of ten or twelve young college men, mostly from Yale, who especially delighted in writing long political satires. Three of this group were very popular in their day. They were John Trumbull (1750–1831), whose masterpiece *M'Fingal* was directed against an imaginary Tory squire; Joel Barlow (1754–1812), author of *The Columbiad*, and also a humorous poem dedicated to Martha Washington entitled *The Hasty Pudding;* and Timothy Dwight (1752–1817), later president of Yale College, from whose pen came two long poems, *Greenfield Hill* and *The Conquest of Canaan*.

Poems of the Revolutionary Period

THE WILD HONEYSUCKLE

PHILIP FRENEAU

Poem Interest: Freneau probably received his inspiration for *The Wild Honeysuckle* from seeing this white flower somewhere in a secluded spot in the woods. Picture yourself in some woodland spot that you know; feel the quietness; hear the rippling sound of the brook, and let the atmosphere of the place steal over you. Shut your eyes to intensify the picture.

FAIR flower, that dost so comely grow,
    Hid in this silent, dull retreat,
Untouched thy honied blossoms blow,
    Unseen thy little branches greet:
5   No roving foot shall crush thee here,
       No busy hand provoke a tear.

By nature's self in white arrayed,
    She bade thee shun the vulgar eye,
And planted here the guardian shade,
10   And sent soft waters murmuring by;
       Thus quietly thy summer goes,
       Thy days declining to repose.

Smit with those charms, that must decay,
    I grieve to see your future doom;
15   They died—nor were those flowers more gay,
       The flowers that did in Eden bloom;
       Unpitying frosts and Autumn's power,
       Shall leave no vestige of this flower.

From morning suns and evening dews
20   At first thy little being came;
If nothing once, you nothing lose,
    For when you die you are the same;
       The space between is but an hour,
       The frail duration of a flower.

Poem Development: This poem is said to have been the first American poem written about a native wild flower. What a vivid picture Freneau gives of this shy, retiring blossom! He sees not only the whole life of the flower, but also a comparison to the life of man. What line gives evidence that he made this comparison? What words does the poet use to express "from beginning to end"? What is the theme of the poem? Give its central thought.

Interpretations: Comely; honied blossoms; no roving foot; vulgar eye; guardian shade; Autumn's power; frail duration of a flower.

Significant Expressions: Quote two lines describing the flower; quote two lines showing extent of time; quote one line giving a feeling of quietness.

THE INDIAN BURYING GROUND

PHILIP FRENEAU

Poem Interest: It was the custom of the North American Indians to bury their dead in a sitting position. In the grave were also placed the bow, arrows, pottery, and trinkets which were thought necessary for the journey into the "Happy Hunting Ground." Suppose you have accompanied the poet to an Indian burying ground, and as you stand with him he says—

IN SPITE of all the learned have said,
  I still my old opinion keep;
The posture that we give the dead
  Points out the soul's eternal sleep.

5 Not so the ancients of these lands;—
  The Indian, when from life released,
Again is seated with his friends,
  And shares again the joyous feast.

His imaged birds, and painted bowl,
10 And venison, for a journey dressed,
Bespeak the nature of the soul,
  Activity, that wants no rest.

His bow for action ready bent,
  And arrows with a head of stone,
15 Can only mean that life is spent,
  And not the old ideas are gone.

Thou, stranger, that shalt come this way,
 No fraud upon the dead commit,—
Observe the swelling turf, and say,
20 They do not lie, but here they sit.

Here still a lofty rock remains,
 On which a curious eye may trace
(Now wasted half by wearing rains)
 The fancies of a ruder race.

25 Here still an aged elm aspires,
 Beneath whose far-projecting shade
(And which the shepherd still admires)
 The children of the forest played.

There oft a restless Indian queen
30 (Pale Shebah with her braided hair)
And many a barbarous form is seen
 To chide the man that lingers here.

By midnight moons, o'er moistening dews,
 In habit for the chase arrayed,
35 The hunter still the deer pursues,
  The hunter and the deer—a shade!

And long shall timorous Fancy see
 The painted chief, and pointed spear,
And Reason's self shall bow the knee
40 To shadows and delusions here.

30. SHEBAH—Sheba was a queen of ancient times.

Poem Development: Compare the burying posture of the Indian with that of the white man. What would each signify? What is the "nature of the (Indian) soul"? What is the Indian idea of the hereafter? What is the theme? What is the central thought of the poem?

Interpretations: The learned; ancients of these lands; line 18; swelling turf; fancies of a ruder race; children of the forest; to chide; lines 31–32; in habit for the chase; a shade.

Significant Expressions: Quote three expressions from the poem meaning the Indian race. Quote the line showing the time when the Indian started out on the hunt. Point out two personifications.

THE HISTORY OF AMERICAN POETRY

General Characteristics

It seems strange that the early gloomy psalm singing and moralizing about death could ever evolve into the great school of poetry to which Bryant, Emerson, Lanier, Poe, and Whittier belong. Yet such is the case. After the toils of the early pioneering life were over and men no longer had to struggle night and day to keep alive, and the wealth and opportunities of America began to give them some leisure, we find an awakening of a true poetic spirit. With the end of the Revolutionary War came a period of expansion. A national road was built from the Chesapeake to the Ohio, Fulton's steamboat appeared, railroads were built, and a new national unity was born. It was an age of nation-making. Towns sprang up as if by magic, factories were busy, and money began to circulate freely. The only cloud on an otherwise clear sky was that of slavery—a cloud, at first very small, but growing in size and constantly becoming more menacing.

The end of the Revolutionary War, with the gaining of independence, seems to have given the poets of the day a feeling that they too could be independent in thought and expression. Up to this time poetry had followed the patterns of the English masters and had been flowery, stilted, and elaborate in expression. Beginning with Bryant we note a change—the old yoke was discarded, and the poets wrote with simple expression and pictured what they felt and saw.

During this period there were three outstanding characteristics of the nation, and the poetry of the period falls naturally into the same grouping. Americans were nature lovers, home lovers, and lovers of country.

The colonists had been so surrounded by large unsettled tracts of land and had lived so close to nature and all its beauties that they naturally wrote of the material all about them. With the exception of Poe, the poets all wrote of nature. "Bryant," we are told, "loved nature for her own sake," and Whittier "regarded nature as a background for life." Emerson's conception of nature is as a symbol of God's power, and he is perhaps the most skillful writer of them all. The rivers, trees, birds, bees, the sea, and the flowers were all a part of their lives, and the true poet writes of what he knows.

The second great characteristic of the American people during the Period of Nationalism was their intense love of home. Longfellow typifies this more vividly than do the others and has been called "the household poet" because he wrote almost entirely of home life. However, both Lowell and Whittier wrote poems of the home and both gave delightful pictures of fireside groups. We must remember that social life in those days revolved about the home, for there were no movies nor automobiles, nor other outside attractions. The center of interest was the home and in choosing this subject to write about, the poets chose one that was near and dear to the hearts of the American people.

The third characteristic was the feeling of patriotism which the American people had to such a marked degree. Many poems were written to the flag, among them *The Star-Spangled Banner*. When the black cloud of slavery had reached its full size, all of this group of poets, with the exception of Poe, wrote poems favoring the side which they believed to be right. The Southern poets, Lanier, Hayne, Ryan, and Timrod, all fought on the side of slavery. Lanier lost his health in the Civil War. Whittier, because of his intense participation in the North in the anti-slavery campaigns, was unable to obtain a position and at one time could not get a magazine to publish his articles. However, there appeared many patriotic poems other than those dealing with slavery, among them such favorites as the *Concord Hymn, Old Ironsides*, and *Paul Revere's Ride*.

Besides these three characteristics, the high moral tone of all the poetry of this period should be noted. In nearly every instance there is a lesson to be learned from each poem, a central thought which predominates and which is inspiring and helpful. The reader seems to be lifted to a higher intellectual level and to finish the reading with a feeling of inspiration to accomplish more and better things, and with a greater appreciation of the beautiful and noble in life.

In these early days, literature definitely reflected the life and problems characteristic of various sections of the country, so the poetry of the period falls into two main groups—that of the New England poets, and that of the Southern writers.

THE NEW ENGLAND POETS

William Cullen Bryant, Ralph Waldo Emerson, Henry Wadsworth Longfellow, John Greenleaf Whittier, Oliver Wendell Holmes, and James Russell Lowell all belong to the group of poets known as the New England poets. They were descended from Puritan ancestors, and their writings show plainly this inheritance. The stern, unrelenting pioneers had planted so firmly the seeds of moral courage and faith in God that the generations between them and this New England group did little to eradicate any of their teachings. "Faith in work, faith in God, faith in country" was written by Lowell of his Puritan ancestors, and he could as well have applied it to his own group.

Their writings reflect the three general characteristics of the period, for their poems are those about the home, those dealing with nature subjects, and those of patriotism. The nature poems were written mostly of the rugged country about New England—"the stern and rock bound coast," the "rock ribbed hills," "Indian summer" and the birds and flowers of the New England section. Bryant was the most nationally inclined of this group, but on the whole these poets stayed well within the boundaries of their own beloved section. When the slavery cloud appeared on the horizon, all threw their efforts to the side of the North. Whittier was called "the Poet of the Civil War." Lowell was greatly concerned with the politics of the section and in his writings expressed his ideas on questions of the day. Longfellow, Whittier, and Lowell all wrote of the home. The pictures they give are all those of the northern home. They have been well named the New England group.

William Cullen Bryant (1794–1878)

Bryant was born and grew to manhood in the Berkshire Hills of New England. His parents were Puritans, and he was brought up in the rigid religious atmosphere of the time. His father, a physician of some note locally, took unusual interest in the education of his children. As a boy Bryant was not physically strong, and he turned eagerly to the experiences of books. "I well remember the delight," he wrote, "with which we welcomed the translation of the *Iliad.* . . . My brother and myself, in emulation of the ancient heroes, made for ourselves wooden shields, swords, and spears, and fashioned old hats in the shape of helmets with plumes of tow; and in the barn when nobody observed us, we fought the battles of the Greeks and Trojans over again." He began to write poetry before he was nine. Some of it was plain "nonsense," but his father encouraged him to keep at it.

He was prepared for college by the local preacher, and in his sixteenth year entered Williams College in the sophomore class. After two terms he had to leave, for his father had no money to give him. He was heart-broken, and while grieving over this wrote *Thanatopsis*. He wanted to devote his time to poetry, but he knew that poetry would earn him no living. He had an ambition to become an editor, but editorial openings were few. He turned to the study of law, but his heart was not in it. However, he had to earn his living, so he persisted in his studies and was admitted to the bar when he was twenty-one. He continued his law practice for a time and then became connected with the New York *Evening Post* which he edited for forty-nine years. Bryant took a great deal of interest in the affairs of the day. His home life was wonderfully happy. He knew Poe, Longfellow, and Whittier.

Four-fifths of his poetry deals with death or nature, both subjects coming naturally from the stern, unrelenting environment of the Puritans, from which his early training never let him entirely escape. The Puritans had always looked upon death with great interest. Two of the books which they read were *Paradise Lost* and *Pilgrim's Progress*, both of which are concerned with life hereafter. It is not so surprising, therefore, that Bryant's thoughts turned to the theme of death. Then, too, a very much beloved sister died during his boyhood and this had its effect on his thoughts.

Bryant was our first great nature poet, and he wrote of nature as he knew it in his own New England. We recognize his pictures as accurate word-paintings of the things in nature with which we are familiar, and we sense in his poems that he felt toward the birds of the air and the flowers of the field much as we ourselves feel. He rarely touches the lighter, more joyous moods in poems, although in *Robert of Lincoln* and *The Gladness of Nature,* he does give us two poems in a lighter key. He was of a deeply religious nature, and his poems show an unfaltering trust in God. Most of his poems reflect serious thoughtfulness and have the deep, full tones of dignified, solemn music.

Ralph Waldo Emerson (1803–1882)

Emerson, a descendant from a long line of clergymen, was born in Boston, Massachusetts. His ancestors were Puritans who had helped build the nation, who had cleared the forests, and fought for their independence. Perhaps the last accounts for Emerson's own independence of thought, for after he had graduated from Harvard and was preaching in a Boston church, he resigned his position and told his congregation that he could not believe some of the things which, as pastor, he was obliged to profess. He retired to Concord and spent the rest of his life lecturing and writing.

Although we must respect Emerson for retiring from the pastorate in a church in which he could no longer believe, at the same time we must regret that he employed his power over language and men to attack the whole of the Christian revelation as outmoded and ill-fitted to modern times. He had tried Protestantism and found it empty. He simply took it for granted without investigation, an early companion of his tells us, that Catholicism could offer nothing better. As a substitute for revealed religion he took refuge in a vague transcendentalism and pantheism and in a hearty confidence in the saving value of self-reliance.

Indeed, his own large share of that worthy natural virtue tended to make him dogmatic and oracular in his utterances. And yet he could write frankly to a former colleague in the ministry: "I could not possibly give you one of the arguments on which any doctrine of mine stands. . . . I delight in telling what I think; but if you ask me how I dare say so, or why it is so, I am the most helpless of mortals." By his own admission, then, we need not echo the oft-repeated plaudits paid the "Sage of Concord," as a profound thinker. But, on the other hand, to deny him the title of philosopher is certainly not to challenge his worth as a poet when he sings whereof he knows, as in the famous "Concord Hymn."

Henry Wadsworth Longfellow (1807-1882)

Longfellow was born in Maine and received his education in his home state. He has been called "the household poet," but we could with truth call him "the universal poet," for he writes of nature, love, home, children, of various emotions, of historical incidents; and not content with writing the legends of his own country, he appropriates literary gems from Europe and writes about them.

He came of an old New England family which traced itself to John Alden of the *Mayflower*. He was well educated both by schooling and by travel abroad. He was opposed by

his father in his desire to be a poet, and for a time studied law in his father's office. However, when Bowdoin College offered him a professorship in modern languages, he left the law office with alacrity and thankfulness. The best and happiest years of his life were spent at Bowdoin and later at Harvard as professor of literature. He was a man of culture and refinement whose interests were largely in books. Sorrow he knew, but never hardship. He was of a calm and gentle nature. It is difficult to imagine him as ever in bitter mood, or in violent passion. Certainly his poetry never reveals him in such light. In fact, though it is invariably graceful, it is generally lacking in the intensity of feeling which is to be sensed in the poems of Whittier. He had wonderful ability to tell a story in verse, an ability equaled by few men in literature. Some of his best known story-poems are *The Courtship of Miles Standish, Hiawatha, Evangeline, Paul Revere's Ride,* and *The Birds of Killingworth.*

Longfellow was happily married and was blessed with children. He was a man of simple tastes, of high ideals, and nobility of thought. Children loved him and flocked to his Cambridge home to see and talk with him. Massachusetts has declared his birthday a holiday, and England has placed his bust in the Poet's Corner of Westminster Abbey, an honor which has been accorded to only one American poet. Longfellow is said to have created the love for poetry in the hearts of a practical money-making people. As long as there is a home left in America, the poems of the beloved "household poet" will be read again and again.

John Greenleaf Whittier (1807-1892)

Whittier was born near Haverhill, Massachusetts, on the same farm which his great-great-grandfather had cleared in the wilderness in 1647, and in the same house which that sturdy pioneer had built in 1688. Unlike the other New England poets of whom you have read, he had few opportunities for education, nor were the surroundings of his home such as to encourage a boy's liking for books as they were in the home of Bryant. Whittier's parents were devout Quakers; and his father, a stern, austere man, was neither sympathetic toward literature, nor perhaps able to buy many books. The boy never went beyond two terms at the Haverhill Academy, and for those two terms he paid his own way by making and selling slippers. He had to be up early and work late on the farm, but instead of being disconsolate at his lot, he found plenty of joy in the life he led. He manifested an early delight in poetry and entertained hopes of himself becoming a poet. At night after the chores were done, he wrote rhymes on his slate, and read his favorites. His father objected to his writing poetry, partly on religious grounds, and partly for the good practical reason that it "would not give him bread." It is said that Whittier's first poems were secretly sent to a local newspaper by his sister.

While yet a young man, he threw himself with religious zeal into the Abolitionist movement. At this time, about 1830, the Abolitionists were looked upon by most people as agitators and trouble-makers. They were

not infrequently mobbed even in Boston. By nature Whittier was a quiet man, a "hater of din and riot"; and withal a man of practical sense. There is more than a possibility that he might have been elected to Congress in 1832, and that he might have enjoyed a successful career in politics. It is said he fully realized that in joining the Abolitionists he would sacrifice his chances for political success, and that he might become an object of popular dislike and contempt.

Whittier lived to see the cause he championed finally become victorious, and as soon as the Civil War was over, he turned with relief to the writing of poems of simpler themes, of home and nature. More than any of his contemporaries, Whittier was the poet of New England. His poems have the smack and tang of elemental things—they root deep in New England soil. His *Snow-Bound* is a faithful and accurate picture of rural life in his day and has been considered America's greatest pastoral poem. Although he loved his own New England, he did not limit his writings to its boundaries. The *Song of the Kansas Emigrants* takes us far from the New England shores. So does *The Barefoot Boy*, who could come from any section. The ballads which Whittier wrote form a large section of his productions and fortunate it is for the American people that these old stories have been preserved for us through poems. Whittier wrote many poems which may be classed as idyls. These are simple, descriptive poems depicting country scenes and rural people. Each one teaches a definite lesson. Of this group perhaps the best known is *Maud Muller.* Whittier was always a lover of nature. The long hours of work on the farm enabled him to store in his mind many beautiful pictures which he could call forth at will. His descriptions of nature are beautiful word pictures, always in a perfect setting. Some of his poems are religious and reflect a simple true faith, and appeal to the deeper, finer emotions of the human heart. *My Soul and I* and *Trust* give us an insight into this unwavering faith. Whittier was essentially American. His spirit was one of service and he speaks in a language we all understand. The word pictures he paints are simple and true, and the lessons to be drawn from them altruistic and clear.

Oliver Wendell Holmes (1809–1894)

Holmes was born in Cambridge, Massachusetts. He was a descendant of the Puritans on both his father's and mother's side, and was related to Anne Dudley Bradstreet, our first Colonial poet. By profession he was a physician, and an eminent one in his day, rather than a man of letters. It cannot be said that he took the business of writing seriously, as did Longfellow; it was his amusement rather than his vocation, yet he possessed genuine literary ability in no small measure. He is particularly remembered for his genial, pleasant humor. It is useless to wonder what he might have done had he devoted himself wholly to writing. Perhaps, had he taken himself too seriously, he would not have given us the playful and delightfully humorous things in both prose and verse which came from his pen. We think of him as looking out upon the world with a twinkle in his eye, yet he was a shrewd observer of men. He was no merely funny man, however, who raised empty laughter; whatever he wrote, though it causes us to laugh heartily as it frequently does, appeals to us on second thought for its common sense or its genuine pathos.

Holmes was always a great favorite among his associates. He was a member of a Boston society called The Saturday Club, of which Longfellow and Lowell were fellow members, and it is said he was the wittiest talker in the club. He gave the name *Atlantic Monthly* to the magazine when it was first published in Boston, and contributed a series of delightful essays to it. Lowell was then its editor-in-chief. Holmes could have been called the "reunion poet," for he was repeatedly called upon for poetry to celebrate class reunions. Each year for forty years he wrote a poem for the annual reunion of his Harvard class. *The Boys* reflects vividly the whimsical spirit of these kindly poems. *The Chambered Nautilus* is probably Holmes' best serious poem. He had a genial kindly spirit which endeared him to all his friends and which is reflected in his writings. He alone in our literature has the gift of mingling humor and pathos.

James Russell Lowell (1819–1891)

Lowell was born in Cambridge, Massachusetts, ten years after Oliver Wendell Holmes. They were always the greatest of friends. Lowell came from an old New England family distinguished through generations for the number of able men which it had produced. As in his ancestry, so in the outward facts of his life he resembles many another famous son of New England. His father was a clergyman of note. He was brought up in a home where learning was valued, where books were known and appreciated, and where literary aspirations were encouraged. He was given a good education begun at a dame school, and continued at a Cambridge day school and Harvard, which he entered at the age of fifteen. Like Holmes he studied law, and even opened an office; but he soon gave it up for literature.

After Longfellow resigned his professorship in Harvard, Lowell was called upon to take his place. He was at this time also editor of the *Atlantic Monthly*. When he was nearly fifty, he was appointed American minister to Spain, and three years later he was sent as minister to England. Lowell had an intense interest in politics. We see this in his *Biglow Papers*, which were a series of political tracts. Besides his interest in politics Lowell loved nature. His nature writings are not as spontaneous as Whittier's, but some of them are appealing and beautiful. His best known poem is perhaps *The Vision of Sir Launfal*. Lowell also has given us many patriotic poems, for he lived during the Civil War period and was heartily against slavery. All of his poetry plainly shows the careful thinking of a trained mind. To his mother he was much indebted for his ability as a poet. There existed a close sympathy and rare understanding between the two. The boy was somewhat of a dreamer; the mother was a woman of imaginative temperament, possessed of a keen appreciation for poetry and music. Lowell was many-sided and contributed to several fields of literature. He was essayist, poet, political reformer, diplomat, and statesman.

THE SOUTHERN POETS

Edgar Allan Poe, Henry Timrod, Paul Hamilton Hayne, Sidney Lanier, and Father Abram Joseph Ryan comprise the Southern group of the National Period poets. One must necessarily consider Edgar Allan Poe as a man apart from the others. His themes had nothing to do with any special section of the country. He gave no evidence of any special interest in any one region. He is one among the group but not one of them. Poe stood alone. Lanier, Hayne, Timrod, and Father Ryan were all ardent Southern men, ready at any time to live or die for the South. All gave themselves to the Southern cause, and all returned from the

War broken in health. Lanier wrote no poems which favored either side during the Civil War, but the others threw themselves heartily into the Southern cause and contributed many patriotic poems intended to stir people to action. In their nature lyrics, however, these men seem to reflect the beauty and sunshine of the South. They write about their own section of the country, about the birds and flowers found there—the mocking birds, pine trees, marshes, the sea. Their poems are bright bits of color and harmony. They have none of the finely drawn lessons which are found in the poems of the New England group. Their notes are high and musical. We know these Southern writers best for these nature lyrics which seem to reflect the sunshine, culture, and sweetness of the Southern people.

Edgar Allan Poe (1809–1849)

Although Poe was born in Boston, he belongs to the South both because of his Southern ancestors and because he received his schooling in the South and spent most of his life there. His parents died when he was very young, and he was adopted by a wealthy family in Richmond, Virginia. He was always a lonely child, distinctly of the genius type, and because few could understand him, he was left alone. He made acquaintances but few real friends. The death of a schoolmate's mother, to whom he was devoted, caused him the deepest despair. Deprived of a mother's love he had turned to her for sympathy and understanding, and when she died he was broken-hearted. He seems to have been always a ship without a rudder.

Perhaps his later years would have been filled with satisfactory attainments if his parents had lived. His foster parents were over-indulgent, and the boy had no restraining influence in the early years when he most needed it. He studied abroad, had tutors in Richmond, and when he was seventeen, entered the University of Virginia. He stayed in the University only one year. In some studies he showed remarkable ability but he gambled and drank, and ran deeply into debt. Mr. Allan, his foster-father, refused to pay his gambling debts and took him from the University. He was placed in a counting room in Richmond, but finding the work most distasteful, he soon broke away and went to Boston. The next few years were spent in wandering from place to place and in attempting newspaper work. Finally he obtained a position as assistant editor of the *Southern Literary Messenger*, a magazine published in Richmond. He married his young cousin, Virginia Clemm, whom he idolized, and since his writings were beginning to attract attention, the future seemed bright. He was at this time twenty-six years old. For a few years Poe was very happy. Virginia's mother and Virginia herself were devoted to him, and he thrived in an atmosphere of love. He seemed to have two personalities, one which he showed to those whom he loved, and one which he kept for the world.

His best traits were brought out in his associations with these two beloved women of his household, for with them he was patient, chivalrous, and devoted.

The following years of his life are best passed over hurriedly. His temperament quite unfitted him for making a practical success. He was brilliant, clever, and not without genius; he worked hard over his

writings, and he set for himself a high standard, yet he could not get along with others. He had good opportunities; men offered him friendship and more substantial help. But he was proud and over-sensitive, and the last thirteen years of his life were years of opportunities wasted. He slipped back into his old habits of drinking and gambling and lost his position. Poverty and want stalked hand in hand with him. Virginia developed tuberculosis and even though Mrs. Clemm kept boarders to help eke out an existence, things went from bad to worse. Virginia died in abject poverty without even food or fuel to keep the house warm. Poe was heart-broken. Two years later he, too, died.

One wishes Poe had had more moral fiber. He always succumbed to situations, never became the master of them. When we consider his poetry, we do, however, forget the man. His theme was frequently death and a gloom and melancholy overshadow all his poems, but nevertheless his verse is of great beauty. He stands alone in the characteristics of his writings. Other poets reflected their environment, their inheritance, the social tendencies of the hour, and the spirit of the times, but Poe did not. Most of his writings were really about some phase of himself. They should be read not to be wholly understood, for that is impossible, but for the beauty they express and the melodious tones of their lines. England considers him our greatest poet.

Henry Timrod (1829–1867)

Henry Timrod was born in Charleston, on December 8, 1829. As a boy he was very active in outdoor sports and games. At seventeen he entered the University of Georgia, but he was not able to complete his course due to lack of finances. He returned to his home in Charleston, and entered a law office to take up that profession, but it was distasteful to him and he turned to teaching.

Timrod early showed ability for writing. In college he was fond of the classics, and did some verse writing at that time. In later life, he contributed to *Russell's Magazine* and *The Southern Literary Messenger*. Then when the Civil War broke out, since he was not physically strong enough to bear arms, he entered the war as a war correspondent for the

Charleston Mercury. His verse and songs at this time won him a place as a foremost Southern poet.

After the War, his fortune gone, his health broken and tuberculosis fastened upon him, he faced a hopeless battle. Just before his death he wrote the *Ode to the Confederate Dead* which is his finest poem. This is said to be perfect in tone and workmanship. Timrod was a man of simple tastes, sincere and true. His poetry reflects the charm and culture of the Southerner. His was lyrical poetry of great sweetness and pathos.

Paul Hamilton Hayne (1830–1886)

Hayne was born in Charleston, South Carolina. He graduated from the College of Charleston and started to practice law. He cared very little for this profession, however, and soon gave it up for literary work. He became editor of *Russell's Magazine,* a periodical to which the literary group of Charleston and the South contributed. It corresponded in the South to the *Atlantic Monthly* published in Boston, which contained the contributions of the New England group. Hayne was happily married, financially comfortable, and his future seemed to bear great promise. Then came the years of the Civil War. Hayne's home in Charleston was burned, and his splendid collection of books was consumed in the flames. He enlisted in the Southern army and served until the close of the War, but his health was broken. With no means of support, for the War had used up his fortune, he lived in poverty and ill health for twenty years, with only the meager earnings of his pen to keep him from starvation.

His poetry consists largely of nature and patriotic lyrics. He shows the same delicate touch in his nature poems that we find in the writings of the other Southern poets, the same idealism, unselfishness, and purity of thought. His verse seems to radiate the warmth of sunshine, and if there are shadows in the pictures, they only serve to accentuate the brightness of the sunshine. *MacDonald's Raid* is perhaps the best of his patriotic lyrics. Here we see vivid pictures of an incident in the Revolutionary War when one of Marion's men, MacDonald, with four comrades, raided the Redcoats. It is a thrilling incident, skillfully related, and every picture stands out clearly in the mind as one reads the poem. Simplicity of expression and vividness of portrayal are characteristic of Hayne's poetry. His wife's untiring devotion was the one bright ray in his last years. He has given us an idea of his great love for her in the poem *A Little While I Fain Would Linger Yet.* Hayne died when he was only fifty-six.

Sidney Lanier (1842–1881)

Lanier, born at Macon, Georgia, came from an ancestry distinguished for its musicians. He himself early showed an extraordinary musical talent, being able to play without instruction the violin and flute, and other instruments. In fact, he has been said to have been America's greatest flute player. Lanier believed that he was intended for a musician, but his father, a lawyer, opposed him in this desire and wished him to pursue the legal profession. He entered Oglethorpe College as a sophomore when he was fourteen years old. When he was only nineteen, however, all plans for his future were interrupted, for the Civil War had broken out. He enlisted in the Confederate Army and served until he was captured in 1864. His confinement in the war prison broke his health which was never rugged, and brought on tuberculosis against which he fought manfully until his death. His life after the War was so sorrowful that a biographer's pen hesitates to depict such sadness. Impoverished by the War, and torn between the desires to study and the necessity to support his family and to live, Lanier's short life was an agonizing heart throb. His first poem to win recognition was *The Symphony,* written in 1867. He was offered a position in Johns Hopkins University which he accepted, but his health almost immediately became worse. He traveled from place to place in search of a more healthful climate, but it availed nothing. He died when he was only thirty-nine years old.

Lanier has been considered the most important poet and man of letters that the South has produced. The beauty of his poetry can be appreciated most when the poem is read aloud. It is like the song of a bird, the murmur of the brook, the whisper of trees. No other poet has caught so well the tones of exquisite melody in nature. Bryant had a realizing sense of this melody, too, but never reached the joyous tones that did Lanier. The delicate sweetness of the melody of *Life and Song, Song of the Chattahoochee,* and *Ballad of Trees and the Master* is like the music of Israfel's lute. Lanier's poems cannot be analyzed, but who wants to analyze sheer beauty of expression! Emerson said, "Beauty is its own excuse for being." Read Lanier's poems for the music in them. Let them make you happy as he meant them to. Let the harmony and melody bring the message of truth Lanier wished to instill in the human heart.

The Reverend Abram Joseph Ryan (1839–1886)

Ryan was a Virginian. His youth was spent in preparing for the Roman Catholic priesthood. A few years before the Civil War broke out he was ordained, and when the conflict came between the North and the South, he entered the Southern ranks as a chaplain. During this time he wrote patriotic poems under the *nom de plume* of Moina. After the War he continued his writing of poetry, and it was during this period that he produced the poems which endeared him to the hearts of the Southerners. We are told that he preferred that his writings be called "verses," not "poems." The War had a great influence on Father Ryan and produced a note of sadness in his poetry. *The Sword of Lee, The Deathless Dead,* and *The Conquered Banner* are his best known poems. These poems are all lyrics, and although in them we are conscious of a mood almost of despair, we also sense a strong religious faith. He felt deeply the injustice he thought had been done the South, and he expressed this in his patriotic poems. However, when the yellow fever epidemic raged in 1878, and the northern people responded so nobly with immediate aid, he changed his attitude toward the North and did his best to unite the two sections. Father Ryan was a gifted Southern singer. His poems reveal the deep effect of the War upon him. They are sad but have a touch of the spiritual about them which makes them different from the other Southern writings.

OTHER POETS OF THE NATIONAL PERIOD

In the Northern group should be included Joseph Rodman Drake (1795–1820) and Fitz-Greene Halleck (1790–1867). These two men, intimate friends, wrote much verse together, and were associated in many literary ventures. The former is best known for his poem *The American Flag* and the latter for *Marco Bozzaris.* In this group also belongs Charles Fenno Hoffman (1806–1844), editor of the *Knickerbocker Magazine* which numbered among its contributors such men as Washington Irving and William Cullen Bryant. He is best remembered for his poem *Monterey.* Bayard Taylor (1825–1878), although better known as a writer of travel prose, was also a poet who will be remembered for his *Bedouin Song* and *A Song of the Camp.* The following also deserve mention: George Pope Morris (1802–1864) whose chief poem is *Woodman, Spare That Tree;* and Thomas Buchanan Reed (1822–1872), best known for *Sheridan's Ride.*

To the Southern group belong a number of poets now chiefly remembered for one or more poems. Among these are Francis O. Ticknor (1822–1874) who wrote the stirring ballad *Little Giffen;* Richard Henry Wilde (1789–1847), author of *My Life Is Like a Summer Rose;* William Gilmore Simms (1806–1870), better known as a novelist, but also a poet of considerable ability as shown in *The Lost Pleiad;* Theodore O'Hara (1820–1867), remembered for *The Bivouac of the Dead;* and John R. Thompson (1823–1873), author of *Music in Camp.*

This period was also productive of a large number of songs, most of them patriotic. Chief among these are *America,* written in 1832 by Samuel Francis Smith; and *The Star Spangled Banner,* written by Francis Scott Key in 1814. The Civil War was the inspiration of such songs as *Dixie; Maryland, My Maryland; Tenting To-night; Carolina; John Brown's Body; Battle Hymn of the Republic;* and *The Battle Cry of Freedom.* Of the songs not inspired by the War, the best remembered are *Home Sweet Home, The Old Oaken Bucket, A Life on the Ocean Wave, Ben Bolt,* and *My Old Kentucky Home.*

Poems of the National Period

TO THE FRINGED GENTIAN

William Cullen Bryant

Poem Interest: Bryant was a poet of nature, particularly of nature as he knew it in his own New England. He was always a "delighted observer" of it, and never missed the least detail in his portrayals. He wrote of the things he saw, and in such a way that others may see these beauties of nature also.

Thou blossom bright with autumn dew,
And colored with the heaven's own blue,
That openest, when the quiet light
Succeeds the keen and frosty night;

5   Thou comest not when violets lean
O'er wandering brooks and springs unseen,
Or columbines, in purple dressed,
Nod o'er the ground bird's hidden nest.

Thou waitest late, and com'st alone,
10   When woods are bare and birds are flown,
And frosts and shortening days portend
The aged year is near his end.

Then doth thy sweet and quiet eye
Look through its fringes to the sky,
15   Blue—blue—as if that sky let fall
A flower from its cerulean wall.

I would that thus, when I shall see
The hour of death draw near to me,
Hope, blossoming within my heart,
20   May look to heaven as I depart.

16. Cerulean (sē-rụ′lē-an)—Azure, blue.

Poem Development: How is Bryant's intense love of nature shown in this poem? What are some of the details which make the picture vivid and lasting? Why did Bryant choose a flower which was the last of the season? In many of Bryant's poems there occurs, following the picture, a kind of afterthought, in which he makes the thing described the bearer of a lesson. Do you find such a lesson in this poem? What is the keynote or theme? Do you think Bryant chose the flower for his poem and then worked out the theme, or vice versa?

Interpretations: The quiet light; portend; aged year; cerulean wall.

Significant Expressions: Quote two lines to show the time of year. Quote the last stanza and give its meaning.

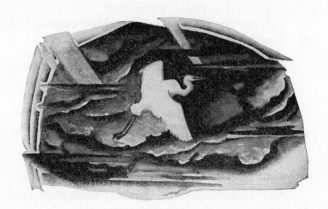

TO A WATERFOWL

William Cullen Bryant

Poem Interest: Because of the lack of finances, Bryant had not been able to continue his studies at Yale and had turned to the study of law. His heart was not in it, however, for his interests lay in poetry. On a December evening in 1815, feeling forlorn and desolate with respect to his future, he set out on foot to go from Cummington to Plainfield where he was to begin the practice of law. It was during this walk that he saw against the evening sky the lone waterfowl which was the inspiration of this poem.

> Whither, midst falling dew,
> While glow the heavens with the last steps of day,
> Far, through their rosy depths, dost thou pursue
> Thy solitary way?

5 Vainly the fowler's eye
Might mark thy distant flight to do thee wrong,
As, darkly seen against the crimson sky,
 Thy figure floats along.

 Seek'st thou the plashy brink
10 Of weedy lake, or marge of river wide,
Or where the rocking billows rise and sink
 On the chafed ocean-side?

 There is a Power whose care
Teaches thy way along that pathless coast—
15 The desert and illimitable air—
 Lone wandering, but not lost.

 All day thy wings have fanned,
At that far height, the cold thin atmosphere,
Yet stoop not, weary, to the welcome land,
20 Though the dark night is near.

 And soon that toil shall end;
Soon shalt thou find a summer home, and rest,
And scream among thy fellows; reeds shall bend
 Soon, o'er thy sheltered nest.

25 Thou'rt gone, the abyss of heaven
Hath swallowed up thy form; yet, on my heart
Deeply has sunk the lesson thou hast given
 And shall not soon depart.

 He who, from zone to zone,
30 Guides through the boundless sky thy certain flight,
In the long way that I must tread alone,
 Will lead my steps aright.

Poem Development: What color predominates in this poem? Is the description vivid? Bryant felt that he too was "lone wandering." What effect did the sight of this bird, separated from the flock, yet evidently sure of its way, have on him? What lines express this? What is the theme of the poem? What is the central thought?

Interpretations: Thy solitary way; fowler's eye; darkly seen; plashy brink; marge of river; lone wandering; abyss of heaven; from zone to zone.

Significant Expressions: Quote a description of evening. Quote the lines which show the poet's belief in a divine power. Quote the last verse and interpret it in your own words.

THE CONCORD HYMN

RALPH WALDO EMERSON

Poem Interest: Renowned for its part in the first battle of the Revolution, Concord Bridge still stands, a small wooden structure spanning the gap between two small hills. Today the scene is peaceful—trees grow thickly overhead, birds are singing, beauty borders the shady paths—yet the very quietness recalls the memory of the men who gathered there in strife to give their lives to the cause of American independence.

On April 19, 1836, sixty years after the battle, the Concord Monument was dedicated. *The Concord Hymn* was written for this dedication.

> By THE rude bridge that arched the flood,
>   Their flag to April's breeze unfurled,
> Here once the embattled farmers stood,
>   And fired the shot heard round the world.
>
> 5   The foe long since in silence slept;
>   Alike the conqueror silent sleeps;
> And Time the ruined bridge has swept
>   Down the dark stream which seaward creeps.
>
> On this green bank, by this soft stream,
> 10   We set to-day a votive stone;
> That memory may their deed redeem,
>   When, like our sires, our sons are gone.
>
> Spirit, that made those heroes dare
>   To die, and leave their children free,
> 15   Bid Time and Nature gently spare
>   The shaft we raise to them and thee.

10. VOTIVE—Consecrated by a vow.

Poem Development: Discuss the value of memorials like the Concord Monument. On July 4, 1876, one hundred years after the battle, a memorial to the Minute Men was erected near the Concord Monument. *The Concord Hymn* was sung at the dedication, and the first verse of the poem appears on the base of this statue. What is the theme of the poem? What is the central thought?

Interpretations: April's breeze; embattled farmers; votive stone; their deed; leave their children free.

Significant Expressions: Quote the line that shows the importance of the first battle of the Revolution.

THE HUMBLE BEE

Ralph Waldo Emerson

Poem Interest: It is a drowsy summer day. The air is heavy and warm; there is no sound but the buzz of a big bee which flits from flower to flower in the sunshine. "Burly, dozing humble-bee!" What does a poet think of you?

> Burley, dozing humble-bee,
> Where thou art is clime for me.
> Let them sail for Porto Rique,
> Far-off heats through seas to seek;
> 5 I will follow thee alone,
> Thou animated torrid zone!
> Zigzag steerer, desert cheerer,
> Let me chase thy waving lines;
> Keep me nearer, me thy hearer,
> 10 Singing over shrubs and vines.
>
> Insect lover of the sun,
> Joy of thy dominion!
> Sailor of the atmosphere;
> Swimmer through the waves of air;
> 15 Voyager of light and noon;
> Epicurean of June;
> Wait, I prithee, till I come
> Within earshot of thy hum,—
> All without is martyrdom.
>
> 20 When the south wind, in May days,
> With a net of shining haze

16. Epicurean—One who, devoted to luxurious enjoyment of food, is nevertheless choice and dainty.

Silvers the horizon wall,
And with softness touching all,
Tints the human countenance
25 With the color of romance,
And infusing subtle heats,
Turns the sod to violets,
Thou, in sunny solitudes,
Rover of the underwoods,
30 The green silence dost displace
With thy mellow, breezy bass.

Hot midsummer's petted crone,
Sweet to me thy drowsy tone
Tells of countless sunny hours,
35 Long days, and solid banks of flowers,
Of gulfs of sweetness without bound
In Indian wildernesses found;
Of Syrian peace, immortal leisure,
Firmest cheer, and birdlike pleasure.

40 Aught unsavory or unclean
Hath my insect never seen;
But violets and bilberry bells,
Maple-sap and daffodels,
Grass with green flag half-mast high,
45 Succory to match the sky,
Columbine with horn of honey,
Scented fern and agrimony,
Clover, catchfly, adder's tongue
And brier roses, dwelt among;
50 All beside was unknown waste,
All was picture as he passed.

Wiser far than human seer,
Yellow-breeched philosopher
Seeing only what is fair,
55 Sipping only what is sweet,

43. DAFFODELS—Note the spelling to rhyme with bells.
45. SUCCORY—Chicory; a common plant with blue flowers.
47. AGRIMONY—A yellow-flowered herb.

Thou dost mock at fate and care,
Leave the chaff and take the wheat.
When the fierce northwestern blast
Cools sea and land so far and fast,
60   Thou already slumberest deep;
Woe and want thou canst outsleep;
Want and woe, which torture us,
Thy sleep makes ridiculous.

Poem Development: An entry in Emerson's Journal under the date of May 9, 1837, reads as follows: "Yesterday in the woods I followed the fine humble-bee with rhymes and fancies fine." Is this poem a true description of the habits of a bee? Do you like the rhyme and rhythm of the lines? What sounds do you find which are like those of a bee? What similes are made with reference to the sea? What "poetic license" do you find in lines 3 and 43? What lines show the bee to be carefree? What lines or phrases suggest the drowsiness of summer? Is this poem representative of the poet's works? Did he write on what was familiar to him? What is the central thought of the poem.

Interpretations: Clime; Epicurean; silvers; thy mellow breezy bass; aught unsavory; succory to match the sky; with horn of honey; yellow-breeched; line 57.

Significant Expressions: Quote what you consider the most descriptive line about the bee. Quote a line or two which gives the sounds of a bee. Which line shows that the bee takes only the best and is therefore wiser than man?

THE SNOW STORM

RALPH WALDO EMERSON

Poem Interest: From an entry made in his journal, November 27, 1832, we learn how Emerson came to write *The Snow Storm.* "Instead of lectures on architecture, I will make a lecture on God's architecture, one of his beautiful works, a Day. I will draw a sketch of a winter day. . . ."

ANNOUNCED by all the trumpets of the sky,
Arrives the snow, and, driving o'er the fields,
Seems nowhere to alight: the whited air
Hides hills and woods, the river, and the heaven,
5   And veils the farm-house at the garden's end.
The sled and traveller stopped, the courier's feet

Delayed, all friends shut out, the housemates sit
Around the radiant fireplace, enclosed
In a tumultuous privacy of storm.

10   Come see the north wind's masonry.
Out of an unseen quarry evermore
Furnished with tile, the fierce artificer
Curves his white bastions with projected roof
Round every windward stake, or tree, or door.
15   Speeding, the myriad-handed, his wild work
So fanciful, so savage, nought cares he
For number or proportion.   Mockingly
On coop or kennel he hangs Parian wreaths;
A swan-like form invests the hidden thorn;
20   Fills up the farmer's lane from wall to wall,
Maugre the farmer's sighs; and at the gate
A tapering turret overtops the work.
And when his hours are numbered, and the world
Is all his own, retiring, as he were not,
25   Leaves, when the sun appears, astonished Art
To mimic in slow structures, stone by stone,
Built in an age, the mad wind's night-work,
The frolic architecture of the snow.

13. BASTIONS—Projecting parts of a fort.
18. PARIAN—A marble which comes from Paros, an island in the Ægean Sea, is noted for its whiteness.
21. MAUGRE—Notwithstanding.

Poem Development: Do you think Emerson succeeded in drawing "a sketch of a winter's day"? Have you ever watched the coming of a storm? Describe your experience. Would Emerson's poem describe the same snow storm? How has the poet carried out his idea of making a lecture on God's "architecture"? Give examples. What is the theme of the poem? What is the central thought?

Interpretations: Trumpets of the sky; whited air; courier's feet delayed; tumultuous privacy; fierce artificer; tapering turret; Parian wreaths; frolic architecture of the snow.

Significant Expressions: Quote the line or lines which produce for you the most vivid picture of the storm.

Picture orally or describe in writing, "frolic architecture" you have seen the snow create.

Tell some of the ways in which human artists copy nature.

HYMN TO THE NIGHT

HENRY WADSWORTH LONGFELLOW

Poem Interest: The soothing fingers of the night bless many hearts with peace and repose. In the midst of sorrow, the kindly Longfellow felt their touch, and rejoiced. His tribute is expressed in rich beauty in the following poem—truly called a "hymn," for it is both song and reverence.

> I HEARD the trailing garments of the Night
> Sweep through her marble halls!
> I saw her sable skirts all fringed with light
> From the celestial walls!
>
> 5 I felt her presence, by its spell of might,
> Stoop o'er me from above;
> The calm, majestic presence of the Night,
> As of the one I love.
>
> I heard the sounds of sorrow and delight,
> 10 The manifold, soft chimes
> That fill the haunted chambers of the Night,
> Like some old poet's rhymes.
>
> From the cool cisterns of the midnight air
> My spirit drank repose;
> 15 The fountain of perpetual peace flows there—
> From those deep cisterns flows.
>
> O holy Night! from thee I learn to bear
> What man has borne before!
> Thou layest thy finger on the lips of Care,
> 20 And they complain no more.

Peace! Peace! Orestes-like I breathe this prayer!
Descend with broad-winged flight,
The welcome, the thrice-prayed for, the most fair,
The best-beloved Night!

21. ORESTES—A Greek youth who was punished by the Furies for the murder of his own mother.

Poem Development: The line "trailing garments of the Night" carries out the feeling of quietness after the surcease of daily cares. The whole poem is one of rest. To what two senses does the poet appeal? Why should night be more restful than day? In line 9, were the sounds he heard real or imaginary? Why did Orestes desire peace? This poem was written not long after the death of Longfellow's first wife. Can you find lines which might indicate that he was thinking of her? Do you think he found consolation? What is the theme? What is the central thought?

Interpretations: Trailing garments; sable skirts; majestic presence; lips of Care; Orestes-like.

Significant Expressions: Quote phrases to show the personification of Night. Quote the verse which shows that the poet bears a great sorrow without complaint.

THE ARSENAL AT SPRINGFIELD

HENRY WADSWORTH LONGFELLOW

Poem Interest: At one time when the Longfellows were visiting the Arsenal at Springfield, Massachusetts, Mrs. Longfellow was struck with the idea that the many guns stacked row on row, were like the pipes of an organ. She spoke the thought to her husband, who wove it into this poem:——

THIS is the Arsenal. From floor to ceiling,
　　Like a huge organ, rise the burnished arms;
But from their silent pipes no anthem pealing
　　Startles the villages with strange alarms.

5　Ah! what a sound will rise, how wild and dreary,
　　When the death-angel touches those swift keys!
What loud lament and dismal Miserere
　　Will mingle with their awful symphonies!

7. MISERERE—Psalm for mercy.

I hear even now the infinite fierce chorus,
10   The cries of agony, the endless groan,
Which, through the ages that have gone before us,
    In long reverberations reach our own.

On helm and harness rings the Saxon hammer,
    Through Cimbric forest roars the Norseman's song,
15 And loud, amid the universal clamor,
    O'er distant deserts sounds the Tartar gong.

I hear the Florentine, who from his palace
    Wheels out his battle-bell with dreadful din,
And Aztec priests upon their teocallis
20   Beat the wild war-drums made of serpent's skin;

The tumult of each sacked and burning village;
    The shout that every prayer for mercy drowns;
The soldiers' revels in the midst of pillage;
    The wail of famine in beleaguered towns;

25 The bursting shell, the gateway wrenched asunder,
    The rattling musketry, the clashing blade;
And ever and anon, in tones of thunder,
    The diapason of the cannonade.

Is it, O man, with such discordant noises,
30   With such accursed instruments as these,
Thou drownest Nature's sweet and kindly voices,
    And jarrest the celestial harmonies?

13. HELM AND HARNESS—Steel helmet and coat of mail or steel armor.
13. SAXON HAMMER—Battle-ax of the Saxons. The Saxons were the early conquerors of England.
14. CIMBRIC—The Cimbri were an ancient tribe of Norsemen inhabiting northern Germany.
16. TARTAR—A member of one of the numerous Mongolian and Turkic hordes inhabiting central and eastern Asia.
17. FLORENTINE—A native of Florence, Italy.
19. AZTEC—The native Indian of Mexico.
19. TEOCALLIS—The teocalli was the Aztec temple of worship.
24. BELEAGURED—Surrounded by the enemy.
28. DIAPASON—Entire compass of notes.

Were half the power that fills the world with terror,
   Were half the wealth bestowed on camps and courts,
35   Given to redeem the human mind from error,
   There were no need of arsenals and forts:

The warrior's name would be a name abhorrèd!
   And every nation, that should lift again
Its hand against a brother, on its forehead
40   Would wear forevermore the curse of Cain!

Down the dark future, through long generations,
   The echoing sounds grow fainter and then cease;
And like a bell, with solemn, sweet vibrations,
   I hear once more the voice of Christ say, "Peace!"

45   Peace! and no longer from its brazen portals
   The blast of War's great organ shakes the skies!
But beautiful as songs of the immortals,
   The holy melodies of love arise.

40. CURSE OF CAIN—The curse on Cain who slew his brother, Abel.

Poem Development: This poem is one of sound images rather than of visual images. Mrs. Longfellow was reminded of the pipes of an organ; Mr. Longfellow carried the picture from the visual to the auditory images. He heard sounds rather than saw the pipes of the organ. What was the battle music in the days of the Saxons which he heard? How did the Norsemen advance to battle? How were the Tartars called to battle? How did the Florentines and the Aztec priests call their men to battle? Longfellow even recalls the sounds of a whole battle which he says runs the entire compass of notes. This poem was written before the Civil War, and therefore our country has seen two great conflicts since Longfellow made this plea for peace. Does this poem carry the message for us that it did for the people of a hundred years ago? Give the thought in lines 33–36. What is the theme? What is the central thought of the poem?

Interpretations: Death-angel; dismal Miserere; cries of agony; Saxon hammer; Cimbric forest; Florentine; teocallis; beleaguered towns; diapason of the cannonade; curse of Cain; melodies of love.

Significant Expressions: Quote lines to show the horrors of war. In what lines does Longfellow prophesy that all nations will cast war aside and will show the spirit of brotherly love?

THE DAY IS DONE

HENRY WADSWORTH LONGFELLOW

Poem Interest: Late afternoon is the saddest time of day. Then the worker is tired from the daily toil, and his mind, taken from attention to work, dwells on his own cares and troubles. Sometimes a walk will counterbalance this loneliness of spirit; sometimes a talk with a friend; oftentimes the companionship found in a good book will banish the disquieting thoughts. Longfellow felt this sadness steal over him, but his remedy for it was none of those already mentioned. Read what he found would soothe his restlessness, and drive away his cares.

THE day is done, and the darkness
　　Falls from the wings of Night,
As a feather is wafted downward
　　From an eagle in his flight.

5　I see the lights of the village
　　Gleam through the rain and the mist,
And a feeling of sadness comes o'er me,
　　That my soul cannot resist;

A feeling of sadness and longing
10　　That is not akin to pain,
And resembles sorrow only
　　As the mist resembles the rain.

Come, read to me some poem,
　　Some simple and heartfelt lay,
15　That shall soothe this restless feeling,
　　And banish the thoughts of day.

· 334 ·

Not from the grand old masters,
Not from the bards sublime,
Whose distant footsteps echo
20   Through the corridors of Time.

For, like strains of martial music,
Their mighty thoughts suggest
Life's endless toil and endeavor;
And to-night I long for rest.

25   Read from some humbler poet,
Whose songs gushed from his heart,
As showers from the clouds of summer,
Or tears from the eyelids start;

Who, through long days of labor,
30   And nights devoid of ease,
Still heard in his soul the music
Of wonderful melodies.

Such songs have power to quiet
The restless pulse of care,
35   And come like the benediction
That follows after prayer.

Then read from the treasured volume
The poem of thy choice,
And lend to the rhyme of the poet
40   The beauty of thy voice.

And the night shall be filled with music,
And the cares that infest the day,
Shall fold their tents, like the Arabs,
And as silently steal away.

Poem Development: The mood of the poem is one of sadness. The picture Longfellow paints of the coming night is very beautiful, and one can feel the enveloping darkness surround him. What adds to the feeling of sadness besides the time of day? What is his remedy for the feeling of sadness? Why does he object to the works of the old masters? Why does he prefer a humbler poet? Longfellow recognizes the value of the voice in reading poems. It is an art to be able to read a poem well, but you can do a great deal toward an acceptable reading if you can feel the poet's mood and picture the images as he paints them. What will become of his cares? What is the theme? What is the central thought?

Interpretations: Wings of Night; heartfelt lay; grand old masters; bards sublime; martial music; fold their tents like Arabs.

Significant Expressions: Quote the verse that tells how night comes on. Repeat the verse that tells how weariness and cares fade away. What is this figure of speech called which the poet uses in the first stanza? What is the figure of speech in the second stanza?

THE BRIDGE

Henry Wadsworth Longfellow

Poem Interest: Standing on a bridge which spans a moving tide, one is irresistibly drawn to a contemplation of the waters. Such an experience was that of Longfellow as he stood on the bridge which spanned the Charles River between Cambridge and Boston. He saw reflected in the waters not only the unfulfilled desires of his own youth, but the procession of countless others who had also dreamed and gone on.

I stood on the bridge at midnight,
    As the clocks were striking the hour,
And the moon rose o'er the city,
    Behind the dark church tower.

5   I saw her bright reflection
    In the waters under me,
Like a golden goblet falling
    And sinking into the sea.

And far in the hazy distance
10   Of that lovely night in June,
The blaze of the flaming furnace
    Gleamed redder than the moon.

Among the long, black rafters
    The wavering shadows lay,
15 And the current that came from the ocean
    Seemed to lift and bear them away;

As, sweeping and eddying through them,
    Rose the belated tide,
And, streaming into the moonlight,
20   The seaweed floated wide.

And like those waters rushing
    Among the wooden piers,
A flood of thoughts came o'er me
    That filled my eyes with tears.

25 How often, oh, how often,
    In the days that had gone by,
I had stood on that bridge at midnight
    And gazed on that wave and sky!

How often, oh, how often,
30   I had wished that the ebbing tide
Would bear me away on its bosom
    O'er the ocean wild and wide.

For my heart was hot and restless,
    And my life was full of care,
35 And the burden laid upon me
    Seemed greater than I could bear.

But now it has fallen from me,
    It is buried in the sea;
And only the sorrow of others
40   Throws its shadow over me.

Yet whenever I cross the river
    On its bridge with wooden piers,
Like the odor of brine from the ocean
    Comes the thought of other years.

45 And I think how many thousands
    Of care-encumbered men,
Each bearing his burden of sorrow,
    Have crossed the bridge since then!

I see the long procession
50   Still passing to and fro,
The young heart hot and restless,
      And the old subdued and slow.

And forever and forever,
      As long as the river flows,
55 As long as the heart has passions,
      As long as life has woes;

The moon and its broken reflection
      And its shadows shall appear,
As the symbol of love in heaven,
60   And its wavering image here.

Poem Development: What line gives you the idea that the poet is in the later years of life? Compare the thoughts that Longfellow had when he first crossed the bridge with the thoughts of later years. Why should "love in heaven" be symbolized as a wavering image on earth? What is the theme? What is the central thought?

Interpretations: Hazy distance; current that came from the sea; ebbing tide; life was full of care; care-encumbered men.

Significant Expressions: In which lines does the poet seem discouraged? In which lines does he show sympathy for his fellow men?

MAUD MULLER

JOHN GREENLEAF WHITTIER

Poem Interest: While driving through the country one sunny day, Whittier was delighted at the sight of a lovely girl raking hay in a field. So pleasing was the scene that he wove it into this charming verse.

MAUD MULLER, on a summer's day
Raked the meadow sweet with hay.

Beneath her torn hat glowed the wealth
Of simple beauty and rustic health.

5 Singing, she wrought, and her merry glee
The mock-bird echoed from his tree.

But when she glanced to the far-off town,
White from its hill-slope looking down,

The sweet song died, and a vague unrest
10 And a nameless longing filled her breast,—

A wish, that she hardly dared to own,
For something better than she had known.

The Judge rode slowly down the lane,
Smoothing his horse's chestnut mane.

15 He drew his bridle in the shade
Of the apple-tree to greet the maid,

And ask a draught from the spring that flowed
Through the meadow across the road.

She stooped where the cool spring bubbled up
20 And filled for him her small tin cup,

And blushed as she gave it, looking down
On her feet so bare, and her tattered gown.

"Thanks!" said the Judge; "a sweeter draught
From a fairer hand was never quaffed."

25 He spoke of the grass and flowers and trees,
Of the singing birds and the humming bees;

Then talked of the haying, and wondered whether
The cloud in the west would bring foul weather.

And Maud forgot her brier-torn gown,
30 And her graceful ankles bare and brown;

And listened, while a pleased surprise
Looked from her long-lashed hazel eyes.

At last, like one who for delay
Seeks a vain excuse, he rode away.

35   Maud Muller looked and sighed: "Ah me!
That I the Judge's bride might be!

"He would dress me up in silks so fine,
And praise and toast me at his wine.

"My father should wear a broadcloth coat;
40   My brother should sail a painted boat.

"I'd dress my mother so grand and gay,
And the baby should have a new toy each day.

"And I'd feed the hungry and clothe the poor,
And all should bless me who left our door."

45   The Judge looked back as he climbed the hill,
And saw Maud Muller standing still.

"A form more fair, a face more sweet,
Ne'er hath it been my lot to meet.

"And her modest answer and graceful air
50   Show her wise and good as she is fair.

"Would she were mine, and I to-day,
Like her, a harvester of hay:

"No doubtful balance of rights and wrongs,
Nor weary lawyers with endless tongues,

55   "But low of cattle and song of birds,
And health and quiet and loving words."

But he thought of his sisters proud and cold,
And his mother vain of her rank and gold.

So, closing his heart, the Judge rode on,
60   And Maud was left in the field alone.

But the lawyers smiled that afternoon,
When he hummed in court an old love-tune;

And the young girl mused beside the well,
Till the rain on the unraked clover fell.

65 He wedded a wife of richest dower,
Who lived for fashion, as he for power.

Yet oft, in his marble hearth's bright glow,
He watched a picture come and go;

And sweet Maud Muller's hazel eyes
70 Looked out in their innocent surprise.

Oft, when the wine in his glass was red,
He longed for the wayside well instead;

And closed his eyes on his garnished rooms,
To dream of meadows and clover-blooms.

75 And the proud man sighed, with a secret pain,
"Ah, that I were free again!

"Free as when I rode that day,
Where the barefoot maiden raked her hay."

She wedded a man unlearned and poor,
80 And many children played round her door.

But care, and sorrow, and childbirth pain,
Left their traces on heart and brain.

And oft, when the summer sun shone hot,
On the new-mown hay in the meadow lot,

85 And she heard the little spring brook fall
Over the roadside, through the wall,

In the shade of the apple-tree again
She saw a rider draw his rein.

And, gazing down with timid grace,
90 She felt his pleased eyes read her face.

Sometimes her narrow kitchen walls
Stretched away into stately halls;

The weary wheel to a spinnet turned,
The tallow candle an astral burned,

95   And for him who sat by the chimney lug,
Dozing and grumbling o'er pipe and mug,

A manly form at her side she saw,
And joy was duty and love was law.

Then she took up her burden of life again,
100   Saying only, "It might have been."

Alas for maiden, alas for Judge,
For rich repiner and household drudge!

God pity them both! and pity us all,
Who vainly the dreams of youth recall.

105   For of all sad words of tongue or pen,
The saddest are these: "It might have been!"

Ah, well! for us all some sweet hope lies
Deeply buried from human eyes;

And in the hereafter, angels may
110   Roll the stone from its grave away!

93. SPINNET—A very small, old-fashioned piano.
94. ASTRAL—A tall, old-fashioned lamp.
95. LUG—A crane on which kettles were hung in the fireplace.

Poem Development: Do you think that if the judge had had a strong enough character to oppose the ideas of his proud mother and sisters and had married Maud Muller, he would have been happy? Do you think he deserved the unhappiness that he received when he married a fashionable, haughty wife? Maud Muller seems to be the one who stirs our pity. The picture of her husband in line 96 is not a very attractive one. Could Maud Muller have taken the position of the judge's wife? Give the central thought.

Interpretations: Toast me at his wine; lawyers with endless tongues; garnished rooms; rich repiner.

Significant Expressions: Quote the two lines applicable to situations that might have been otherwise than they are.

TELLING THE BEES

John Greenleaf Whittier

Poem Interest: In the old days in England there was a custom of draping the beehives in black when a member of the family died, and telling the bees to stay at home. This custom was brought to New England. Whittier enjoyed searching out such old stories of colonial life and putting the legends into poetry.

HERE is the place; right over the hill
    Runs the path I took;
You can see the gap in the old wall still,
    And the stepping stones in the shallow brook.

5 There is the house, with the gate red-barred,
    And the poplars tall;
And the barn's brown length, and the cattle yard,
    And the white horns tossing above the wall.

There are the beehives ranged in the sun;
10   And down by the brink
Of the brook are her poor flowers, weed-o'errun,
    Pansy and daffodil, rose and pink.

A year has gone, as the tortoise goes,
    Heavy and slow;
15 And the same rose blows, and the same sun glows,
    And the same brook sings of a year ago.

There's the same sweet clover smell in the breeze;
    And the June sun warm
Tangles his wings of fire in the trees,
20   Setting, as then, over Fernside farm.

I mind me how, with a lover's care,
    From my Sunday coat
I brushed off the burrs, and smoothed my hair,
    And cooled at the brookside my brow and throat.

25 Since we parted, a month had passed,—
 To love, a year;
Down through the beeches I looked at last
 On the little red gate and the well-sweep near.

I can see it all now,—the slantwise rain
30 Of light through the leaves,
The sundown's blaze on her window-pane,
 The bloom of her roses under the eaves.

Just the same as a month before,—
 The house and the trees,
35 The barn's brown gable, the vine by the door,—
 Nothing changed but the hives of bees.

Before them, under the garden wall,
 Forward and back,
Went, drearily singing, the chore girl small,
40 Draping each hive with a shred of black.

Trembling, I listened; the summer sun
 Had the chill of snow;
For I knew she was telling the bees of one
 Gone on the journey we all must go!

45 Then I said to myself, "My Mary weeps
 For the dead to-day;
Haply her blind old grandsire sleeps
 The fret and the pain of his age away."

But her dog whined low; on the doorway sill,
50 With his cane to his chin,
The old man sat; and the chore girl still
 Sang to the bees stealing out and in.

And the song she was singing ever since
 In my ear sounds on:
55 "Stay at home, pretty bees, fly not hence!
 Mistress Mary is dead and gone!"

Poem Development: The details of description in this poem are very beautiful. How many visual images do you get from the first stanza? In the second stanza, what stands out the most vividly in your mind as you read? What picture first gives you the idea that someone may be dead? Evidently the person who is telling the story was in love with the dead girl. It would seem, as he writes of the time, that a year has passed since the events of the story. What was the chore girl doing? What is the theme? What is the central thought?

Interpretations: Barn's brown length; horns tossing above the wall; as the tortoise goes; lines 43-44; fret and pain of his age.

Significant Expressions: Quote two lines that tell how slowly time may pass.

THE CHAMBERED NAUTILUS

OLIVER WENDELL HOLMES

Poem Interest: Among all the animals of the sea, none is more interesting than the chambered nautilus. The little animal outgrows his home from time to time, but he patiently builds himself a new one by adding a new chamber to the old. Then he moves into his new home, builds a wall across the old, and lives in the new until he outgrows that. He repeats this performance until he has reached the end of his growth. Too, the nautilus is the only sea animal able to sail on the ocean. He extends himself out of his shell like a sail, using the shell as a boat. Holmes has written what many consider his best poem in this one about the chambered nautilus.

THIS is the ship of pearl, which, poets feign,
Sails the unshadowed main,—
The venturous bark that flings
On the sweet summer wind its purpled wings,
5   In gulfs enchanted, where the Siren sings,
And coral reefs lie bare,
Where the cold sea-maids rise to sun their streaming hair.

2. UNSHADOWED MAIN—The ocean.
5. SIREN—A beautiful sea nymph who sang so beautifully that sailors were lured to their deaths.

Its webs of living gauze no more unfurl;
Wrecked is the ship of pearl!
10 And every chambered cell,
Where its dim dreaming life was wont to dwell,
As the frail tenant shaped his growing shell,
Before thee lies revealed,—
Its irised ceiling rent, its sunless crypt unsealed!

15 Year after year beheld the silent toil
That spread his lustrous coil;
Still, as the spiral grew,
He left the past year's dwelling for the new,
Stole with soft step its shining archway through,
20 Built up its idle door,
Stretched in his last-found home, and knew the old no more.

Thanks for the heavenly message brought by thee,
Child of the wandering sea,
Cast from her lap, forlorn!
25 From thy dead lips a clearer note is born
Then ever Triton blew from wreathèd horn!
While on mine ear it rings,
Through the deep caves of thought I hear a voice that sings:

Build thee more stately mansions, O my soul,
30 As the swift seasons roll!
Leave thy low-vaulted past!
Let each new temple, nobler than the last,
Shut thee from heaven with a dome more vast,
Till thou at length art free,
35 Leaving thine outgrown shell by life's unresting sea!

14. IRISED—Iris was the goddess of the rainbow.
14. CRYPT—An enclosed place like a cell or vault.
26. TRITON—Neptune was the god of the sea. Triton was his son.
32-33. LET EACH NEW TEMPLE, etc.—Dome is used here as meaning the limit line of our lives. Thus the finer lives we live and the more good we can do, the nearer heaven we come. Each season of life should be so lived that its limits will be too narrow to contain the activities of the next season.

Poem Development: Where can the nautilus be found? What is meant by the "ship of pearl"? Why does the poet say "purpled wings"? The first stanza refers to the shell as it is when the animal is alive. In

the second stanza the poet evidently sees the shell broken open on the
seashore, and the little animal dead. What would you judge the color
of the shell to be? What precept for life can be made from the life
of the nautilus? What is the central thought of the poem?

Interpretations: Poets feign; unshadowed main; Siren; frail tenant;
irised ceiling; line 23; wreathèd horn; life's unresting sea.

Significant Expressions: Repeat the lines of the last stanza and
give their meaning.

MY AUNT

Oliver Wendell Holmes

Poem Interest: In the colonial days girls were sent to what were then
called "finishing schools." There they were taught manners and social
deportment. Little was given them of practical knowledge, for it was
not intended that they should work to earn a living. Holmes had an aunt
of the finishing school type. His humorous poem about her will delight
you.

> My aunt! my dear unmarried aunt!
>   Long years have o'er her flown;
> Yet still she strains the aching clasp
>   That binds her virgin zone;
> 5 I know it hurts her,—though she looks
>   As cheerful as she can;
> Her waist is ampler than her life,
>   For life is but a span.
>
> My aunt! my poor deluded aunt!
> 10   Her hair is almost gray;
> Why will she train that winter curl
>   In such a spring-like way?
> How can she lay her glasses down,
>   And say she reads as well,
> 15 When through a double convex lens
>   She just makes out to spell?
>
> Her father—grandpapa! forgive
>   This erring lip its smiles—
> Vowed she should make the finest girl
> 20   Within a hundred miles;

He sent her to a stylish school;
'Twas in her thirteenth June;
And with her, as the rules required,
"Two towels and a spoon."

25   They braced my aunt against a board,
       To make her straight and tall;
     They laced her up, they starved her down,
       To make her light and small;
     They pinched her feet, they singed her hair,
30   They screwed it up with pins;
     Oh, never mortal suffered more
       In penance for her sins.

     So, when my precious aunt was done,
       My grandsire brought her back
35   (By daylight, lest some rabid youth
       Might follow on the track);
     "Ah!" said my grandsire, as he shook
       Some powder in his pan,
     "What could this lovely creature do
40   Against a desperate man!"

     Alas! nor chariot, nor barouche,
       Nor bandit cavalcade,
     Tore from the trembling father's arms
       His all-accomplished maid.
45   For her how happy had it been!
       And Heaven had spared to me
     To see one sad, ungathered rose
       On my ancestral tree.

Poem Development: Holmes gives us a ridiculous picture of age trying to be youthful. What are two silly things that the aunt does? The human touch in the third stanza is very appealing. Most fond parents think their own children are perfect. What does Holmes say about the aunt's father in this respect? What is the central thought?

Interpretations: Winter curl; spring-like way; double convex lens; stylish school; nor chariot, nor barouche; bandit cavalcade; ungathered rose; ancestral tree.

Significant Expressions: What is the figure of speech in line 12? Quote lines telling what was done at the school.

THE LAST LEAF

Oliver Wendell Holmes

Poem Interest: This poem was suggested by the sight of a figure well known to Bostonians, that of Major Thomas Melville, "the last of the cocked hats," as he was sometimes called. The Major had been a very handsome young man and was one of the "Indians" of the famous Boston Tea Party in 1774. As you read the poem, watch your feelings.

I saw him once before,
As he passed by the door,
   And again
The pavement stones resound,
5   As he totters o'er the ground
   With his cane.

They say that in his prime,
Ere the pruning-knife of Time
   Cut him down,
10   Not a better man was found
   By the Crier on his round
   Through the town.

349

But now he walks the streets,
And he looks at all he meets
15   Sad and wan,
And he shakes his feeble head,
That it seems as if he said,
    "They are gone!"

The mossy marbles rest
20   On the lips that he has pressed
      In their bloom,
And the names he loved to hear
Have been carved for many a year
      On the tomb.

25   My grandmamma has said—
Poor old lady, she is dead
      Long ago—
That he had a Roman nose,
And his cheek was like a rose
30   In the snow;

But now his nose is thin,
And it rests upon his chin
      Like a staff,
And a crook is in his back,
35   And a melancholy crack
      In his laugh.

I know it is a sin
For me to sit and grin
      At him here;
40   But the old three-cornered hat,
And the breeches, and all that,
      Are so queer!

And if I should live to be
The last leaf upon the tree

---

19. Mossy marbles—Refers to slabs of marble laid over their graves.

44. The last leaf, etc.—The old man reminded Holmes of a "withered leaf, which had held to its stem through the storms of autumn and winter, and finds itself still clinging to its boughs while the new growths of spring are bursting their buds all around it."

45   In the spring,
Let them smile, as I do now,
At the old forsaken bough
Where I cling.

Poem Development: What were your feelings as you read? Were you at first inclined to laugh? Abraham Lincoln called the poem "inexpressibly touching" and knew it by heart. In the last stanza the poet says to let them laugh at him when he is old if they want to. Do you think, from what you know of his history, he would care? Would this be true of everyone? Strangely enough Holmes lived to the age of eighty-five—"long enough" in his own words, "to serve as an illustration of my own poem." Would you call this a humorous poem? What is the theme? What is the central thought?

Interpretations: Pruning-knife of Time; Crier; mossy marbles; melancholy crack; last leaf upon the tree in the spring.

Significant Expressions: Quote lines which tell that the Major had been a very handsome young man. Would you find this poem difficult to memorize? Why?

THE BOYS

Oliver Wendell Holmes

Poem Interest: Each year for forty years Holmes wrote a poem for the annual reunion of his Harvard class. *The Boys* was his contribution to the celebration of their thirtieth anniversary in 1829.

Has there any old fellow got mixed with the boys?
If there has, take him out, without making a noise.
Hang the Almanac's cheat and the Catalogue's spite!
Old Time is a liar! We're twenty to-night!

5   We're twenty! We're twenty! Who says we are more?
He's tipsy,—young jackanapes!—show him the door!
"Gray temples at twenty?"—Yes! *white* if we please!
Where the snowflakes fall thickest there's nothing can
     freeze!

Was it snowing I spoke of? Excuse the mistake!
10   Look close,—you will not see a sign of a flake!
We want some new garlands for those we have shed,—
And these are white roses in place of the red.

We've a trick, we young fellows, you may have been told,
Of talking (in public) as if we were old:—
15　That boy we call "Doctor," this we call "Judge";
It's a neat little fiction,—of course it's all fudge.

That fellow's the "Speaker,"—the one on the right;
"Mr. Mayor," my young one, how are you to-night?
That's our "Member of Congress," we say when we chaff;
20　There's the "Reverend" what's his name?—don't make me
　　　laugh!

That boy with the grave mathematical look
Made believe he had written a wonderful book,
And the Royal Society thought it was *true!*
So they chose him right in; a good joke it was, too!

25　There's a boy, we pretend, with a three-decker brain,
That could harness a team with a logical chain;
When he spoke for our manhood in syllabled fire,
We called him "The Justice," but now he's "The Squire."

And there's a nice youngster of excellent pith,—
30　Fate tried to conceal him by naming him Smith;
But he shouted a song for the brave and the free,—
Just read on his medal, "My country," "of thee!"

You hear that boy laughing?—you think he's all fun;
But the angels laugh, too, at the good he has done;
35　The children laugh loud as they troop to his call,
And the poor man that knows him laughs loudest of all!

Yes, we're boys,—always playing with tongue or with pen,—
And I sometime have asked,—Shall we ever be men?
Shall we always be youthful, and laughing, and gay,
40　Till the last dear companion drops smiling away?

Then here's to our boyhood, its gold and its gray!
The stars of its winter, the dews of its May!
And when we have done with our life-lasting toys,
Dear Father, take care of thy children, THE BOYS!

Poem Development: Do you think that Holmes read or recited this poem himself? Would the manner of reading add anything to the listeners' enjoyment? Would you say that the group was a distinguished one? Why? Who was the man referred to in lines 29–32? How does the last stanza affect you? What is the theme? What is the central thought?

Interpretations: Almanac's cheat; Catalogue's spite; line 8; grave mathematical look; Royal Society; three-decker brain; excellent pith; playing with tongue or with pen.

Significant Expressions: Quote phrases or lines describing three different "boys."

THE COURTIN'

JAMES RUSSELL LOWELL

Poem Interest: In a farmhouse of the early days, the life of the family centered in the kitchen, and there was no pleasanter place on earth. Let us take a look into such a room. The floor is spotless, scrubbed until it is almost white. From the ceiling, hang in long loops, strings of drying apples. The spinning wheel is pushed back against the wall; bright-colored rugs cover a part of the floor; the table is set with a red and white tablecloth, and in front of the fireplace the crane holds a kettle of water bubbling merrily and waiting for the cornmeal to be poured in for the "mush" for supper. In front of the windows, with their tiny panes of glass, are bright pink and red geraniums. A few dishes of "Old Mulberry" ware are ranged at the back of the fireplace shelf, and the kettles of copper and brass shine like the sun as the firelight dances on them. Now we are ready for the poem:

> God makes sech nights, all white an' still
> Fur's you can look or listen,
> Moonshine an' snow on field an' hill,
> All silence an' all glisten.
>
> 5 Zekle crep' up quite unbeknown
> An' peeked in thru' the winder,
> An' there sot Huldy all alone,
> 'Ith no one nigh to hender.

1. SECH—Such.
5. ZEKLE—Ezekiel.
8. 'ITH—With.

2. FUR'S—As far as.
7. HULDY—Hildah.
8. To HENDER—To hinder, or bother.

A fireplace filled the room's one side
10   With half a cord o' wood in—
There warn't no stoves (tell comfort died)
      To bake ye to a puddin'.

The wa'nut logs shot sparkles out
      Towards the pootiest, bless her,
15   An' leetle flames danced all about
      The chiny on the dresser.

Agin the chimbley crook-necks hung,
      An' in amongst 'em rusted
The ole queen's-arm thet gran'ther Young
20   Fetched back f'om Concord busted.

The very room, coz she was in,
      Seemed warm f'om floor to ceilin',
An' she looked full ez rosy agin
      Ez the apples she was peelin'.

25   'T was kin' o' kingdom-come to look
      On sech a blessed cretur,
A dogrose blushin' to a brook
      Ain't modester nor sweeter.

He was six foot o' man, A 1,
30   Clear grit an' human natur',
None couldn't quicker pitch a ton
      Nor dror a furrer straighter.

11. Tell—Until. In the words "tell comfort died" the speaker implies that
the old fireplace was more comfortable than the new-fangled stove, which
was so hot it baked one to a puddin'.

14. Pootiest—Prettiest, refers to Huldy.

16. Chiny on the Dresser—China dishes arranged on the buffet or side-
board.

17. Crook-necks—Crookneck gourds. They were hung by the chimney to
dry, later to be used in making dippers.

19. Queen's-arm—A musket bearing the stamp of Queen Anne.

19. Gran'ther—Grandfather.

32. Dror—Draw.   32. Furrer—Furrow.

He'd sparked it with full twenty gals,
　　He'd squired 'em, danced 'em, druv 'em,
35　Fust this one, an' then thet, by spells—
　　All is, he couldn't love 'em.

But long o' her his veins 'ould run
　　All crinkly like a curled maple,
The side she breshed felt full o' sun
40　　Ez a south slope in Ap'il.

She thought no v'ice hed sech a swing
　　Ez hisn in the choir;
My! when he made Ole Hundred ring,
　　She *knowed* the Lord was nigher.

45　An' she'd blush scarlit, right in prayer,
　　When her new meetin'-bonnet
Felt somehow thru' its crown a pair
　　O' blue eyes sot upun it.

Thet night, I tell ye, she looked *some!*
50　　She seemed to 've gut a new soul,
For she felt sartin-sure he'd come,
　　Down to her very shoe-sole.

She heerd a foot, an' knowed it tu,
　　A-raspin' on the scraper,—
55　All ways to once her feelin's flew
　　Like sparks in burnt-up paper.

He kin' o' l'itered on the mat,
　　Some doubtfle o' the sekle,
His heart kep' goin' pity-pat,
60　　But hern went pity Zekle.

34. SQUIRED—Escorted.
36. ALL IS—A colloquial expression meaning the fact, or truth, is.
37. LONG O' HER—Beside her, or at her side.
37. 'OULD—Would.
43. OLE HUNDRED—A favorite old hymn.
44. NIGHER—Nearer.
54. SCRAPER—Foot scraper for cleaning mud off.
55. ALL WAYS—In every direction.
57. L'ITERED—Loitered.
58. SEKLE—Sequel, i.e., he was somewhat doubtful as to how things would turn out.

An' yit she gin her cheer a jerk
Ez though she wished him furder,
An' on her apples kep' to work,
Parin' away like murder.

65   "You want to see my Pa, I s'pose?"
       "Wal . . . no . . . I come dasignin' "—
       "To see my Ma? She's sprinklin' clo'es
       Agin to-morrer's i'nin'."

       To say why girls act so or so,
70   Or don't, 'ould be persumin';
       Mebby to mean *yes* an' say *no*
       Comes nateral to women.

       He stood a spell on one foot fust
       Then stood a spell on t' other,
75   An' on which one he felt the wust
       He could n't ha' told ye nuther.

61. GIN—Gave. CHEER—Chair.
65. Hilda speaks this line.
66. Ezekiel replies in this line.
66. DASIGNIN'—Designing, intending.
68. I'NIN'—Ironing.
70. PERSUMIN'—Presuming to know something about them.
73. FUST—First.

Says he, "I'd better call agin;"
   Says she, "Think likely, Mister:"
Thet last word pricked him like a pin,
80   An' . . . Wal, he up an' kist her.

When Ma bimeby upon 'em slips,
   Huldy sot pale ez ashes,
All kin' o' smily roun' the lips
   An' teary roun' the lashes.

85   For she was jes' the quiet kind
    Whose naturs never vary,
Like streams that keep a summer mind
    Snowhid in Jenooary.

The blood clost roun' her heart felt glued
90   Too tight for all expressin',
Tell mother see how metters stood,
   An' gin 'em both her blessin'.

Then her red come back like the tide
   Down to the Bay o' Fundy,
95   An' all I know is they was cried
   In meetin' come nex' Sunday.

88. JENOOARY—January.
94. BAY O' FUNDY—The tides come rapidly into the Bay of Fundy.
95. WAS CRIED—Their "bans," or betrothal, was announced in the church.

Poem Development: It is said that Washington's cook refused to use the stove that was installed at Mount Vernon, for he said he could not get dinner over "that thing," but if he were allowed to use the old fireplace, he could serve forty in no time. Lines 11 and 12 of the poem express something of this same idea about the stove. Describe Huldy in your own terms. What would be some excellent qualifications for a man in those days? Give a word picture of Huldy's reception of Zekle. This poem can be dramatized in pantomime by a boy and a girl, while some other student reads the poem. What is the theme? What is the central thought?

Interpretations: Lines 5–8; line 20; lines 33–36; lines 57–60; lines 69–72; lines 95–96.

Significant Expressions: Quote lines to describe a New England fireplace; quote lines to show Zekle loved Huldy; other lines to show Huldy's feelings toward Zekle.

WHAT MR. ROBINSON THINKS

James Russell Lowell

Poem Interest: Written just before the Mexican War, this poem
was one of the *Biglow Papers,* a series of satires in which Lowell expressed his views on political situations through the lips of Hosea Biglow,
a Yankee farmer. This explains the dialect. Governor B. was George
Nixon Briggs, Whig governor of Massachusetts in 1844. The candidate
against him in 1847 was Caleb Cushing, who was then in Mexico and
who had been given the rank of brigadier-general by President Polk.
John P. Robinson was a lawyer in Lowell, Massachusetts.

GUVENER B. is a sensible man;
  He stays to his home an' looks arter his folks;
He draws his furrer ez straight ez he can,
    An' into nobody's tater-patch pokes;—
5   But John P.
        Robinson he
  Sez he wunt vote fer Guvener B.

My! aint it terrible? Wut shall we du?
  We can't never choose him o' course—thet's flat;
10 Guess we shall hev to come round, (don't you?)
    An' go in fer thunder an' guns, an' all that;
      But John P.
        Robinson he
  Sez he wunt vote fer Guvener B.

15 Gineral C. is a dreffle smart man:
  He's ben on all sides thet give places or pelf;
But consistency still wuz a part of his plan—
    He's been true to *one* party—an' that is himself;—
      So John P.
20   Robinson he
  Sez he shall vote fer Gineral C.

Gineral C. he goes in fer the war;
  He don't vally principle more 'n an old cud;

2. ARTER—After.   3. FURRER—Furrow.   4. TATER—Potato.
7. WUNT—Won't.   15. DREFFLE—Dreadful.   23. VALLY—Value.

Wut did God make us raytional creeturs fer,
25   But glory an' gunpowder, plunder an' blood?
     So John P.
     Robinson he
     Sez he shall vote fer Gineral C.

We were gittin' on nicely up here to our village,
30   With good old idees o' wut's right an' wut aint,
We kind o' thought Christ went agin war an' pillage,
     An' thet eppyletts worn't the best mark of a saint,
     But John P.
     Robinson he
35   Sez this kind o' thing's an exploded idee.

The side of our country must ollers be took,
     An' Presidunt Polk, you know, *he* is our country.
An' the angel thet writes all our sins in a book
     Puts the *debit* to him, an' to us the *per contry;*
40   An' John P.
     Robinson he
     Sez this is his view o' the thing to a T.

Parson Wilbur he calls all these argimunts lies;
     Sez they're nothin' on airth but jest *fee, faw, fum:*
45 An' thet all this big talk of our destinies
     Is half on it ign'ance, an' t' other half rum,
     But John P.
     Robinson he
     Sez it aint no sech thing; an', of course, so must we.

50 Parson Wilbur sez *he* never heerd in his life
     Thet th' Apostles rigged out in their swaller-tail coats,
An' marched round in front of a drum an' a fife,
     To git some on 'em office, an' some on 'em votes,
     But John P.
55   Robinson he
     Sez they didn't know ever'thin' down in Judee.

---

32. Eppyletts—Epaulets.   36. Ollers—Always.
39. *Per contry—Per contra,* Latin for on the contrary, or the opposite.

Wal, it's a marcy we've gut folks to tell us
  The rights an' the wrongs o' these matters, I vow—
God sends country lawyers, an' other wise fellers,
60   To start the world's team wen it gits in a slough;
          Fer John P.
          Robinson he
      Sez the world 'll go right, ef he hollers out Gee!

Poem Development: What are the characteristics of Governor B. which make you think he would have made a good governor? Did Governor B. want to have war with Mexico? What is the character of General C.? Was Lowell in favor of Polk's policy? Which stanza tells you of Lowell's choice for governor? Does John P. Robinson give any arguments? Point out the satire in the poem. What is the thought of the poem?

Interpretations: Lines 1–4; line 11; lines 22–25; lines 31–32; lines 50–53; lines 59–60.

Significant Expressions: Quote lines to show what principles Lowell himself regarded as best for the country. Lowell later became active in political life and was ambassador to Spain and later to England. What kind of a representative do you judge he was from reading this poem?

SHE CAME AND WENT

James Russell Lowell

Poem Interest: Lowell wrote this poem in memory of his first child, Blanche, who lived only fourteen months. Lowell never recovered from this loss, although he later had three other children. The little shoes of the first baby hung over the corner of a picture frame in his study as long as he lived.

As A twig trembles, which a bird
  Lights on to sing, then leaves unbent,
So is my memory thrilled and stirred;
  I only know she came and went.

5   As clasps some lake, by gusts unriven,
  The blue dome's measureless content,
So my soul held that moment's heaven;
  I only know she came and went.

As, at one bound, our swift spring heaps
10   The orchards full of bloom and scent,
So clove her May my wintry sleeps;
    I only know she came and went.

An angel stood and met my gaze,
    Through the low doorway of my tent;
15   The tent is struck, the vision stays;
    I only know she came and went.

Oh, when the room grows slowly dim,
    And life's last oil is nearly spent,
One gush of light these eyes will brim,
20   Only to think she came and went.

Poem Development: How is the feeling of sadness intensified throughout the poem? In what ways does the poet indicate the brevity of life of his little daughter? In what metaphor does Lowell tell how death came? What is the theme? What is the central thought?

Interpretations: Twig trembles; by gusts unriven; measureless content; moment's heaven; line 11; life's last oil.

Significant Expressions: Which line shows the poet was happy for a brief time? What lines show that the poet never recovered from his loss?

AUF WIEDERSEHEN

JAMES RUSSELL LOWELL

Poem Interest: Soon after Lowell graduated from Harvard, he met a charming young lady, Miss Maria White, who after a few years' courtship became his wife. Their life together was very happy but was not destined to last long, for Mrs. Lowell lived only about nine years. This poem was written the year after her death and is tenderly reminiscent of the courtship days.

THE little gate was reached at last,
    Half hid in lilacs down the lane;
She pushed it wide, and, as she passed,
A wistful look she backward cast,
5   And said,—*"Auf wiedersehen!"*

5. *Auf wiedersehen*—German, meaning "till we meet again."

With hand on latch, a vision white
  Lingered reluctant, and again
Half doubting if she did aright,
Soft as the dews that fell that night,
10   She said,—*"Auf wiedersehen!"*

The lamp's clear gleam flits up the stair;
  I linger in delicious pain;
Ah, in that chamber, whose rich air
To breathe in thought I scarcely dare,
15   Thinks she,—*"Auf wiedersehen!"*

'Tis thirteen years; once more I press
  The turf that silences the lane;
I hear the rustle of her dress,
I smell the lilacs, and—ah, yes,
20   I hear,—*"Auf wiedersehen!"*

Sweet piece of bashful maiden art!
  The English words had seemed too fain,
But these—they drew us heart to heart,
Yet held us tenderly apart;
25   She said,—*"Auf wiedersehen!"*

Poem Development: What is the significance of the words "Auf Wiedersehen"? In their use do you think the poet was recalling only a scene of courtship days? Why? What is the meaning of line 22? What impression do you get of Maria White from the poem? What is the theme? What is the central thought?

Interpretations: Wistful look; vision white; lamp's clear gleam; delicious pain; I press the turf; the English words had seemed too fain.

Significant Expressions: Quote phrases to describe Maria White; quote what to you is the most beautiful passage.

TO HELEN

EDGAR ALLAN POE

Poem Interest: When Poe was a young, motherless lad, he often visited the home of one of his classmates. There his friend's mother was so very sympathetic toward the disconsolate and lonely boy that he grew devotedly attached to her. This woman was Mrs. Jane Stanard, and the poem *To Helen* is written to her.

HELEN, thy beauty is to me
    Like those Nicean barks of yore,
That gently, o'er a perfumed sea,
    The weary, way-worn wanderer bore
5   To his own native shore.

On desperate seas long wont to roam,
    Thy hyacinth hair, thy classic face,
Thy naiad airs have brought me home
    To the glory that was Greece,
10   And the grandeur that was Rome.

Lo! in yon brilliant window niche
    How statue-like I see thee stand,
    The agate lamp within thy hand!
Ah, Psyche, from the regions which
15   Are Holy Land!

2. NICEAN BARKS, etc.—Nicæa was an ancient seaport of Asia Minor. If in line 4 by "weary . . . wanderer" Poe had in mind Odysseus, he should have used Phæacian instead of Nicean, for it was the Phæacian king who sent Odysseus safely home. Perhaps he substituted for the sake of rhythm.

7. HYACINTH HAIR—Curling hair, such as demanded by the Greek fashion.

8. NAIAD—The naiads were water nymphs, inexpressibly fair.

14. PSYCHE—Symbolizes the soul. Probably with the lamp, the idea is the light of knowledge.

Poem Development: What beautiful woman of history does the first stanza suggest? In each stanza we find the indications of the strong influence which Mrs. Stanard had on the young poet. How could she have brought home to him "the glory that was Greece and the grandeur that was Rome"? What is the central thought?

Interpretations: Nicean barks of yore; perfumed sea; weary, way-worn wanderer; desperate seas; classic face; agate lamp.

Significant Expressions: What two lines are often quoted? Quote the lines which show the influence his friend's mother had on the poet.

THE BELLS

EDGAR ALLAN POE

Poem Interest: Bells play an important part in the sound world. Joy, sadness, alarm, and peace can be expressed through their tones. It remained for Poe to bring the music of the bells into poetry. Few would have thought of writing a poem to bring out the different emotions expressed by the music of bells, but this Poe has done with marvelous skill. Each kind of bell creates a different sound image in the mind. This poem should be read aloud.

HEAR the sledges with the bells—
  Silver bells!
What a world of merriment their melody foretells!
  How they tinkle, tinkle, tinkle,
5   In the icy air of night!
  While the stars that oversprinkle
  All the heavens, seem to twinkle
   With a crystalline delight;
  Keeping time, time, time,
10   In a sort of Runic rhyme,
To the tintinnabulation that so musically wells
  From the bells, bells, bells, bells,
   Bells, bells, bells—
From the jingling and the tinkling of the bells.

15 Hear the mellow wedding bells—
   Golden bells!
What a world of happiness their harmony foretells!
  Through the balmy air of night
  How they ring out their delight!—
20   From the molten-golden notes,
   And all in tune,
   What a liquid ditty floats
To the turtle-dove that listens, while she gloats
   On the moon!
25 Oh, from out the sounding cells,
What a gush of euphony voluminously wells!
   How it swells!
   How it dwells
  On the Future!—how it tells
30 Of the rapture that impels
  To the swinging and the ringing
   Of the bells, bells, bells—

1. SLEDGES—Sleighs.
10. RUNIC—Secret or mysterious.
11. TINTINNABULATION—A word which Poe coined. Is it expressive?
26. EUPHONY—Sweet sound.

Of the bells, bells, bells, bells,
    Bells, bells, bells—
35   To the rhyming and the chiming of the bells!

    Hear the loud alarum bells—
      Brazen bells!
What a tale of terror now their turbulency tells!
    In the startled ear of night
40   How they scream out their affright!
      Too much horrified to speak,
      They can only shriek, shriek,
        Out of tune.
In a clamorous appealing to the mercy of the fire,
45   In a mad expostulation with the deaf and frantic fire,
      Leaping higher, higher, higher,
      With a desperate desire,
    And a resolute endeavor
    Now—now to sit, or never,
50   By the side of the pale-faced moon.
      Oh, the bells, bells, bells!
      What a tale their terror tells
        Of Despair!
    How they clang, and clash, and roar!
55   What a horror they outpour
On the bosom of the palpitating air!
      Yet the ear, it fully knows,
        By the twanging,
        And the clanging,
60   How the danger ebbs and flows;
     Yet the ear distinctly tells;
        In the jangling,
        And the wrangling,
    How the danger sinks and swells,
65   By the sinking or the swelling in the anger of the bells—
      Of the bells—
    Of the bells, bells, bells, bells,
      Bells, bells, bells—
In the clamor and the clanging of the bells!

70   Hear the tolling of the bells—
              Iron bells!
      What a world of solemn thought their monody compels!
              In the silence of the night
              How we shiver with affright
75   At the melancholy menace of their tone!
              For every sound that floats
              From the rust within their throats
                  Is a groan.
          And the people—ah, the people—
80   They that dwell up in the steeple,
              All alone,
          And who, tolling, tolling, tolling,
              In that muffled monotone
          Feel a glory in so rolling
85   On the human heart a stone—
          They are neither man nor woman,—
          They are neither brute nor human—
                  They are Ghouls:—
          And their king it is who tolls:—
90   And he rolls, rolls, rolls,
                  Rolls
              A pæan from the bells!
          And his merry bosom swells
              With the pæan of the bells!
95   And he dances, and he yells;
          Keeping time, time, time,
          In a sort of Runic rhyme,
              To the pæan of the bells:—
                  Of the bells:
100   Keeping time, time, time,
          In a sort of Runic rhyme,
              To the throbbing of the bells—
          Of the bells, bells, bells—
              To the sobbing of the bells:—
105   Keeping time, time, time,
              As he knells, knells, knells,
          In a happy Runic rhyme,

72. Monody—Funeral song.

*In the silence of the night
How we shiver with affright.*

> To the rolling of the bells—
> Of the bells, bells, bells:—
110   To the tolling of the bells—
> Of the bells, bells, bells, bells,
> Bells, bells, bells—
> To the moaning and the groaning of the bells.

Poem Development: Notice the alliteration used throughout the poem to create a more musical sound. Poe creates sound images. In this poem we hear, not see. In most other poems we have studied we have had visual instead of auditory images. Note the short, rather tinkling syllables used all through the first stanza which give the sound of sleigh bells. In the next stanza notice the use of the long sounds of the vowels—ō, ōō, ū. Words with these sounds give a much more smooth, mellow tone when read. Practice on such words as molten, golden, moon, and note the deep, mellow tones you can get. Then when the poet wished to express alarm, notice that he used the harsh, sibilant sounds, the consonants which are breathy— t, c, d, f, sh, p. Find the words using these sounds and notice how they crash on the ear, just as the bells they are picturing crash and clang. In the last sound unit, Poe combines what two types of sounds to obtain the effect of solemness and the quietness of death? Who rings the tolling bells? What is the central thought?

Interpretations: What is the picture laid around the silver bells? the golden bells? the brazen bells? the iron bells? Might these represent four stages of man's life? Explain.

Significant Expressions: Quote a line showing merriment; another showing happiness; another showing terror and fright; another solemness or death. Do the sounds help in giving interpretation?

ISRAFEL

Edgar Allan Poe

Poem Interest: Israfel is the angel of music and is said to have the "most melodious voice of all God's creatures." Poetry is word music and of all our poets, Poe and Lanier have given us our most musical stanzas. A life of Poe has been written and entitled Israfel because he has given us such exquisite musical verse.

"And the angel Israfel, whose heart-strings are a lute, and who has the sweetest voice of all God's creatures."—Koran.

In Heaven a spirit doth dwell,
  "Whose heart-strings are a lute."
None sing so wildly well
As the angel Israfel,
5 And the giddy stars (so legends tell)
Ceasing their hymns, attend the spell
  Of his voice, all mute.

Tottering above,
  In her highest noon,
10 The enamoured moon
Blushes with love,
  While, to listen, the red levin
  (With the rapid Pleiads, even,
  Which were seven)
15 Pauses in Heaven.

And they say (the starry choir
  And the other listening things)
That Israfel's fire
Is owing to that lyre
20 By which he sits and sings,—
The trembling living wire
  Of those unusual strings.

But the skies that angel trod,
  Where deep thoughts are a duty—
25 Where Love's a grownup God—
Where the Houri glances are
  Embued with all the beauty
Which we worship in a star.

Therefore, thou art not wrong,
30 Israfel, who despisest
An unimpassioned song;

12. Levin—Lightning.
13. Pleiads—The stars of the constellation Pleiades. According to mythology the Pleiades were the seven daughters of Atlas who were transformed
into a group of stars.
26. Houri—A nymph of the Mohammedan paradise, gifted with great
beauty and everlasting youth.

> To thee the laurels belong,
> Best bard, because the wisest!
> Merrily live, and long!
>
> 35 The ecstasies above
> With thy burning measures suit—
> Thy grief, thy joy, thy hate, thy love,
> With the fervor of thy lute—
> Well may the stars be mute!
>
> 40 Yes, Heaven is thine; but this
> Is a world of sweets and sours;
> Our flowers are merely—flowers,
> And the shadow of thy perfect bliss
> Is the sunshine of ours.
>
> 45 If I could dwell
> Where Israfel
> Hath dwelt, and he where I,
> He might not sing so wildly well
> A mortal melody,
> 50 While a bolder note than this might swell
> From my lyre within the sky.

Poem Development: Poe has taken the line "whose heart-strings are a lute" as the reason for the beauty of Israfel's voice. Israfel sings so sweetly that even the stars cease their hymn singing in the heavens. What heavenly bodies besides the stars stop to listen? What is the significance of "laurels" in line 32? What is meant by the last stanza? What is the central thought?

Interpretations: Giddy stars; enamoured moon; red levin; an unimpassioned song; world of sweets and sours.

Significant Expressions: Quote the line that tells why Israfel is such a sweet singer. Quote three lines as a toast to Israfel.

ELDORADO

EDGAR ALLAN POE

Poem Interest: Eldorado means city of gold. In the early days of the Spanish conquest of South America there was a legend that in the interior of the country was to be found a city of gold. The Spanish adventurers, their imaginations fired by the prospect of untold wealth, set out to find it. The natives were afraid of the Spaniards and to be rid of them insisted that Eldorado was a little farther on. The result was that the Spanish, led by their dreams of wealth, pushed on and on, only to perish in the wilderness.

GAYLY bedight,
A gallant knight,
In sunshine and in shadow,
Had journeyed long,
5   Singing a song,
In search of Eldorado.

But he grew old—
This knight so bold—
And o'er his heart a shadow
10   Fell as he found
No spot of ground
That looked like Eldorado.

And as his strength
Failed him at length
15   He met a pilgrim shadow—
"Shadow," said he,
"Where can it be—
This land of Eldorado?"

"Over the Mountains
20   Of the Moon,
Down the Valley of the Shadow,
Ride, boldly ride,"
The shade replied,—
"If you seek for Eldorado."

Poem Development: If you think of Poe as the gallant knight setting out in quest of success and literary fame—his Eldorado—and dying at the age of forty, disappointed and unhappy, you will see how the poem is linked with his own sad experience in life. In the first stanza, what symbolizes the beginning of life work? What is the mood of the poem? What is particularly discouraging about the ending? What is the theme? What is the central thought?

Interpretations: Gayly bedight; pilgrim shadow; Mountains of the Moon; Valley of the Shadow; shade.

Significant Expressions: Quote the lines showing Eldorado to be only a mythical city.

A LITTLE WHILE I FAIN WOULD LINGER YET

Paul Hamilton Hayne

Poem Interest: Hayne addressed this poem to his wife who by her deep understanding and sympathy, her help and hopefulness, made endurable the disappointments and griefs of his life. She was a woman of wonderful character, completely unselfish and untiring in her devotion to her husband. Hayne was dying of tuberculosis when he wrote the poem.

A LITTLE while (my life is almost set!)
    I fain would pause along the downward way,
    Musing an hour in this sad sunset ray,
While, Sweet! our eyes with tender tears are wet:
5   A little hour I fain would linger yet.

A little while I fain would linger yet,
    All for love's sake, for love that cannot tire;
    Though fervid youth be dead, with youth's desire,
And hope has faded to a vague regret,
10   A little while I fain would linger yet.

A little while I fain would linger here:
    Behold! who knows what strange, mysterious bars
    'Twixt souls that love may rise in other stars?
Nor can love deem the face of death is fair:
15   A little while I still would linger here.

A little while I yearn to hold thee fast,
    Hand locked in hand, and loyal heart to heart;
    (O pitying Christ! those woeful words, "We part!")
So ere the darkness fall, the light be past,
20   A little while I fain would hold thee fast.

A little while, when light and twilight meet,—
    Behind, our broken years; before, the deep
    Weird wonder of the last unfathomed sleep,—
A little while I still would clasp thee, Sweet,
25   A little while, when night and twilight meet.

A little while I fain would linger here;
  Behold! who knows what soul-dividing bars
  Earth's faithful loves may part in other stars?
Nor can love deem the face of death is fair:
30   A little while I still would linger here.

Poem Development: Through the poem one feels the great love Hayne had for his wife. What reason does he give in the second stanza for wanting to stay on earth longer? In the third stanza he mentions two more reasons. What are they? In which stanza do we find the greatest grief expressed at the coming parting? What is the central thought?

Interpretations: Fain; downward way; sad sunset ray; Sweet; vague regret; line 14; ere the darkness fall; when light and twilight meet; last unfathomed sleep.

ASPECTS OF THE PINES

PAUL HAMILTON HAYNE

Poem Interest: The changing aspects of nature are a source of never ending joy. Probably no better example can be given of changing lights and shadows, changing colors and forms, than the Grand Canyon in Colorado. As one watches this wonderful creation of nature, it changes minute by minute. Colors run the whole range of the spectrum. It is as if an enormous picture were passing before the eyes. Hayne saw changes in the pine trees as he watched them through the day. Read the poem carefully for the delicate changes in color and form which his skillful pen depicts.

TALL, somber, grim, against the morning sky
  They rise, scarce touched by melancholy airs,
Which stir the fadeless foliage dreamfully,
  As if from realms of mystical despairs.

5   Tall, somber, grim, they stand with dusky gleams
  Brightening to gold within the woodland's core,
Beneath the gracious noontide's tranquil beams—
  But the weird winds of morning sigh no more.

A stillness, strange, divine, ineffable,
10   Broods round and o'er them in the wind's surcease,
And on each tinted copse and shimmering dell
  Rests the mute rapture of deep-hearted peace.

Last, sunset comes—the solemn joy and might
 Borne from the West when cloudless day declines—
15 Low, flutelike breezes sweep the waves of light,
 And lifting dark green tresses of the pines,

Till every lock is luminous—gently float,
 Fraught with hale odors up the heaves afar
To faint when twilight on her virginal throat
20 Wears for a gem the tremulous vesper star.

Poem Development: What impression of the pines is given in the first line? Does the sighing of the wind add to the mysticism of the early morning? What is the mood of the first stanza? In the second stanza what is the meaning of the second line? What is the mood of the stanza? Have you ever lived in a pine country and felt the deep-hearted peace suggested in the third stanza? How does the aspect of the pines in the late afternoon differ from that in the morning? How is it similar? What is the theme? What is the central thought?

Interpretations: Fadeless foliage; noontide's tranquil beams; ineffable; wind's surcease; tinted copse; flutelike breezes; vesper star.

Significant Expressions: Give three words that describe the pines. Quote three phrases which indicate the three periods of the day.

CHARLESTON

Henry Timrod

Poem Interest: In all of Timrod's poems we see reflected his great love for the South. His home was in Charleston, and he married a Charleston girl. His beloved city was early in the War, for the surrender of Fort Sumter was the call to arms and a siege was laid on Charleston. As Timrod wandered about the blockaded city, wondering as each inhabitant must have done, when the city would be in the midst of battle, his poetic mind found expression in the following lines. In times of peace it is difficult to picture the sad conditions which must have existed when this poem was written.

Calm as that second summer which precedes
 The first fall of the snow,
In the broad sunlight of heroic deeds,
 The city bides the foe.

5 As yet, behind their ramparts, stern and proud,
    Her bolted thunders sleep,—
  Dark Sumter, like a battlemented cloud,
    Looms o'er the solemn deep.

  No Calpe frowns from lofty cliff or scaur
10   To guard the holy strand;
  But Moultrie holds in leash her dogs of war
    Above the level sand.

  And down the dunes a thousand guns lie couched,
    Unseen, beside the flood,—
15 Like tigers in some Orient jungle crouched,
    That wait and watch for blood.

  Meanwhile, through streets still echoing with trade,
    Walk grave and thoughtful men,
  Whose hands may one day wield the patriot's blade
20   As lightly as the pen.

  And maidens, with such eyes as would grow dim
    Over a bleeding hound,
  Seem each one to have caught the strength of him
    Whose sword she sadly bound.

25 Thus girt without and garrisoned at home,
    Day patient following day,
  Old Charleston looks from roof and spire and dome,
    Across her tranquil bay.

  Ships, through a hundred foes, from Saxon lands
30   And spicy Indian ports,
  Bring Saxon steel and iron to her hands,
    And summer to her courts.

  But still, along yon dim Atlantic line,
    The only hostile smoke
35 Creeps like a harmless mist above the brine,
    From some frail floating oak.

7. Sumter—Fort Sumter on Charleston harbor which was in the hands of the Southern forces.
9. Calpe—An ancient word meaning Gibraltar.
11. Moultrie—Fort Moultrie, also held by the Southerners.

Shall the spring dawn, and she, still clad in smiles,
    And with an unscathed brow,
Rest in the strong arms of her palm-crowned isles,
40   As fair and free as now?

We know not; in the temple of the Fates
    God has inscribed her doom;
And, all untroubled in her faith, she waits
    The triumph or the tomb.

29. SHIPS . . . FROM SAXON LANDS—Ships from England which ran the blockade.

Poem Development: Can you visualize the images as Timrod creates them for you? Do you get the feeling of the "dread waiting" in the first stanza? Why were the men grave and thoughtful? Charleston was the literary center of the South. Does this explain the significance of lines 19 and 20? Does the poet give you the impression that Charleston is troubled at the outcome? What is the central thought?

Interpretations: Second summer; line 4; bolted thunders; Calpe; scaur; holds in leash her dogs of war; lines 17–20; girt without; a hundred foes; the triumph or the tomb.

Significant Expressions: Quote lines to show how Charleston was protected. Quote lines to show how the city waits its fate.

AT MAGNOLIA CEMETERY

HENRY TIMROD

Poem Interest: This poem, with its strain of sweet music, is sometimes called *Ode to the Confederate Dead*, an ode being a song addressed to some noble character. It is one of the many beautiful tributes written to commemorate the bravery of the Southern soldiers.

SLEEP sweetly in your humble graves,
    Sleep, martyrs of a fallen cause;
Though yet no marble column craves
    The pilgrim here to pause.

5   In seeds of laurel in the earth
    The blossom of your fame is blown,
And somewhere, waiting for its birth,
    The shaft is in the stone!

Meanwhile, behalf the tardy years
10   Which keep in trust your storied tombs,
Behold! your sisters bring their tears,
    And these memorial blooms.

Small tributes! but your shades will smile
    More proudly on these wreaths to-day,
15   Than when some cannon-moulded pile
    Shall overlook this bay.

Stoop, angels, hither from the skies!
    There is no holier spot of ground
Than where defeated valor lies,
20   By mourning beauty crowned.

15. CANNON-MOULDED PILE—This could mean either an impressive monument, moulded to represent a cannon, or a monument moulded from the metal of the cannon used in the war.

Poem Development: In no other group of poets do we find the sweetness of expression, the delicate touch of refinement, that we find flowing from the pens of the Southern writers. The sincerity of this poem rings as true as the tones of a beautiful bell. What did the poet mean in lines 3 and 4? There was no monument to the Confederate soldiers in Magnolia Cemetery when this poem was written. Since then, however, a stone has been erected. Explain line 8. Why did the poet say "tardy" years in line 9? What is the theme? Give the central thought.

Interpretations: Martyrs of a fallen cause; marble column; laurel; line 6; tardy years; storied tombs; shades; cannon-moulded pile; defeated valor.

Significant Expressions: Quote the last three lines of the poem and give their meaning.

THE CONQUERED BANNER

ABRAM J. RYAN

Poem Interest: After the Civil War many beautiful poems were written of the conflict. The unspeakable disappointments, the heartaches, the broken families, the irreparable losses, all bore with crushing weight upon the Southern heart. The poems of the period give us some understanding of this, but through them all the high ideal and fine culture and refinement of the South are nevertheless predominant. The beloved flag under which the Southerners had fought so valiantly was

sorrowfully laid aside, for only one flag now waved over North and
South. Father Ryan fought for and loved that Southern banner. How
dearly he loved it is shown in the following lines:

FURL that Banner, for 'tis weary;
Round its staff 'tis drooping dreary:
    Furl it, fold it—it is best;
For there's not a man to wave it,
5   And there's not a sword to save it,
And there's not one left to lave it
In the blood which heroes gave it,
And its foes now scorn and brave it:
    Furl it, hide it—let it rest!

10   Take that Banner down! 'tis tattered;
Broken is its staff and shattered;
And the valiant hosts are scattered,
    Over whom it floated high.
Oh, 'tis hard for us to fold it,
15   Hard to think there's none to hold it,
Hard that those who once unrolled it
    Now must furl it with a sigh!

Furl that Banner—furl it sadly!
Once ten thousands hailed it gladly,
20   And ten thousands wildly, madly,
    Swore it should forever wave;
Swore that foeman's sword should never
Hearts like theirs entwined dissever,
Till that flag should float forever
25   O'er their freedom or their grave!

Furl it! for the hands that grasped it,
And the hearts that fondly clasped it,
    Cold and dead are lying low;
And that Banner—it is trailing,
30   While around it sounds the wailing
    Of its people in their woe.

For, though conquered, they adore it—
Love the cold, dead hands that bore it,
Weep for those who fell before it,

35 Pardon those who trailed and tore it;
And oh, wildly they deplore it,
  Now to furl and fold it so!

Furl that Banner! True, 'tis gory,
Yet 'tis wreathed around with glory,
40 And 'twill live in song and story
  Though its folds are in the dust!
For its fame on brightest pages,
Penned by poets and by sages,
Shall go sounding down the ages—
45   Furl its folds though now we must.

Furl that Banner, softly, slowly!
Treat it gently—it is holy,
  For it droops above the dead.
Touch it not—unfold it never;
50 Let it droop there, furled forever—
  For its people's hopes are fled!

Poem Development: What is the meaning of "furl"? What were the poet's reasons for putting the flag away? Throughout the poem there is great sadness—one almost hears a despairing sob. What line do you consider the saddest of all? What is the central thought?

Interpretations: Furl that Banner; valiant hosts; foeman's sword; lines 30–31; 'tis gory; line 51.

Significant Expressions: Quote a line to show love for the flag; a line to show sadness for those who fell fighting for it; a line to show forgiveness for those who fought against it.

SONG OF THE MYSTIC

Abram J. Ryan

Poem Interest: A mystic, in Father Ryan's use of the word, is one who keenly appreciates the spiritual meaning of life, and lives in intimate union with God. The mystic singer of this poem learned from his disappointment in the false promises of the world that only in a Perfect Being is satisfaction to be found. He discovered God. Since making that discovery he has lived in recollection of spirit, in the "Valley of Silence," close to God. The Valley is glorious; but enduring penitence and prayer are, he has discovered, the only roads that lead to it, over "the dark mount of Sorrow and . . . the bright mountain of Prayer."

I WALK down the Valley of Silence—
    Down the dim, voiceless valley—alone!
And I hear not the fall of a footstep
    Around me, save God's and my own;
5   And the hush of my heart is as holy
    As hovers where angels have flown!

Long ago was I weary of voices
    Whose music my heart could not win;
Long ago was I weary of noises
10   That fretted my soul with their din;
Long ago was I weary of places
    Where I met but the human—and sin.

I walked in the world with the worldly;
    I craved what the world never gave;
15 And I said: "In the world each Ideal,
    That shines like a star on life's wave,
Is wrecked on the shores of the Real,
    And sleeps like a dream in a grave."

And still did I pine for the Perfect,
20   And still found the False with the True;
I sought 'mid the Human for Heaven,
    But caught a mere glimpse of its Blue:
And I wept when the clouds of the Mortal
    Veiled even that glimpse from my view.

25 And I toiled on, heart-tired of the Human,
    And I moaned 'mid the mazes of men,
Till I knelt, long ago, at an altar
    And I heard a voice call me. Since then
I walk down the Valley of Silence
30   That lies far beyond mortal ken.

Do you ask what I found in the Valley?
    'Tis my Trysting Place with the Divine.

1. VALLEY OF SILENCE—The spirit of recollection, essential for union with God.
6. HOVERS—Hover: a shelter or retreat.
23. CLOUDS OF THE MORTAL—Creatures may reveal God; they may also hide God from us.

And I fell at the feet of the Holy,
    And above me a voice said: "Be Mine."
35   And there arose from the depths of my spirit
    An echo—"My heart shall be Thine."

Do you ask how I live in the Valley?
    I weep—and I dream—and I pray.
But my tears are as sweet as the dew-drops
40   That fall on the roses in May;
And my prayer, like a perfume from censers,
    Ascendeth to God night and day.

In the hush of the Valley of Silence
    I dream all the songs that I sing;
45   And the music floats down the dim Valley,
    Till each finds a word for a wing,
That to hearts, like the Dove of the Deluge,
    A message of Peace they may bring.

But far on the deep there are billows
50   That never shall break on the beach;
And I have heard songs in the Silence
    That never shall float into speech;
And I have had dreams in the Valley
    Too lofty for language to reach.

55   And I have seen Thoughts in the Valley—
    Ah me! how my spirit was stirred!
And they wear holy veils on their faces,
    Their footsteps can scarcely be heard;
They pass through the Valley like Virgins,
60   Too pure for the touch of a word!

Do you ask me the place of the Valley,
    Ye hearts that are harrowed by Care?
It lieth afar between mountains,
    And God and His angels are there:
65   And one is the dark mount of Sorrow,
    And one the bright mountain of Prayer.

57. HOLY VEILS—In meditation the mystic has glimpsed divine mysteries which he would not even try to express in words.

Poem Development: There is a single introductory stanza and a single concluding stanza. The eight intervening stanzas are divided into two groups. Indicate the divisions and show how the first group enriches the meaning of the second group. What is the theme of the poem? What did the mystic crave which "the world never gave"? How may the mystic have caught a glimpse of Heaven's blue, of God, " 'mid the Human"? Remembering that the mystic is also a poet, explain the meaning of the eighth stanza. Explain the concluding stanza in straightforward prose. Why is the mount of Sorrow dark; the mountain of Prayer bright? In barest outline, what is the basic picture which the poet uses to convey his message? Can we and should we all try to be mystics in the poet's meaning of the word?

Interpretations: Lines 15–18; Trysting Place with the Divine; Dove of the Deluge; lines 55–60.

Significant Expressions: In stanzas 3, 4, and 5 find the verbs which most vividly express the mystic's longing for the object of his soul's desire. What figure of speech is found in lines 7, 9, and 11? In line 16?

A BALLAD OF TREES AND THE MASTER

SIDNEY LANIER

Poem Interest: About to be betrayed by one apostle, denied by another, deserted by the rest, crucified by His Chosen People, apparently forsaken even by His Heavenly Father, our Lord finds strength, this ballad tells us, in the kindness of Gethsemane's trees.

> INTO the woods my Master went,
> Clean forspent, forspent.
> Into the woods my Master came,
> Forspent with love and shame.
> 5 But the olives they were not blind to Him,
> The little gray leaves were kind to him:
> The thorn-tree had a mind to Him
> When into the woods He came.
>
> Out of the woods my Master went,
> 10 And He was well content.
> Out of the woods my Master came,
> Content with death and shame.
> When Death and Shame would woo Him last,
> From under the trees they drew Him last:
> 15 'Twas on a tree they slew Him—last
> When out of the woods He came.

Poem Development: The poet seems to have striven to recapture the simplicity of the old folk ballad, with its naive repetition of words and phrases, its plain, almost archaic vocabulary, and its economy of detail. Do you think he has succeeded? Is this simplicity in keeping with the poet's theme and with the mood he wishes to create? What is the dominant mood? Does the little word "my" which modifies "Master" each time Jesus is mentioned provide a clue to the mood of the poem? What is the irony of the last two lines of the poem?

Interpretations: Clean forspent. Why are Death and Shame capitalized when they occur the second time, in the fourth from the last line?

Significant Expressions: Quote the line you like best in each of the two stanzas. Point out three examples of personification.

THE MARSHES OF GLYNN

SIDNEY LANIER

Poem Interest: For many years Lanier moved from one locality to another in the hope of recovering from the tuberculosis which had fastened upon him during his Civil War prison confinement. However, when he finally realized that his fight was a losing one, his mood was one of quiet resignation, and in this mood he wrote the following poem.

I

GLOOMS of the live-oaks, beautiful-braided and woven
With intricate shades of the vines that myriad-cloven
Clamber the forks of the multiform boughs,—
    Emerald twilights,—
5   Virginal shy lights,
Wrought of the leaves to allure to the whisper of vows,
When lovers pace timidly down through the green colon-
    nades
Of the dim sweet woods, of the dear dark woods,
    Of the heavenly woods and glades,
10   That run to the radiant marginal sand-beach within
    The wide sea-marshes of Glynn;—

MARSHES OF GLYNN—Glynn is a seacoast county in Georgia. Along the coast, between the sea and the strip of sand shore, are wide stretches of marsh grass which stand waist high and wave gently in the fanning breezes.

1. GLOOMS OF THE LIVE-OAKS—The narrow strip of sand shore is bordered on the landward side by beautiful live-oaks, hung with gray Spanish moss. The moss is often so heavy and hangs so low from the gnarled and crooked branches that light beams enter with difficulty and a twilight pervades the whole.

II

Beautiful glooms, soft dusks in the noonday fire,—
Wildwood privacies, closets of lone desire,
Chamber from chamber parted with wavering arras of
　　leaves,—
15　Cells for the passionate pleasure of prayer for the soul
　　that grieves,
Pure with a sense of the passing of saints through the
　　wood,
Cool for the dutiful weighing of ill with good;—

III

O braided dusks of the oak and woven shades of the vine,
While the riotous noonday sun of the June-day long did
　　shine
20　Ye held me fast in your heart and I held you fast in mine;
But now when the noon is no more, and riot is rest,
And the sun is await at the ponderous gate of the West,
And the slant yellow beam down the wood-aisle doth seem
Like a lane into heaven that leads from a dream,—
25　Ay, now, when my soul all day hath drunken the soul of
　　the oak,
And my heart is at ease from men, and the wearisome
　　sound of the stroke
　Of the scythe of time, and the trowel of trade is low,
　And belief overmasters doubt, and I know that I know,
　And my spirit is grown to a lordly great compass within,
30　That the length and the breadth and the sweep of the
　　marshes of Glynn
Will work me no fear like the fear they have wrought
　　me of yore
When length was fatigue, and when breadth was but
　　bitterness sore,
And when terror and shrinking and dreary unnameable
　　pain
Drew over me out of the merciless miles of the plain,—

IV

35　Oh, now, unafraid, I am fain to face
　　The vast sweet visage of space.

To the edge of the wood I am drawn, I am drawn,
Where the gray beach glimmering runs, as a belt of the
    dawn,
    For a mete and a mark
40   To the forest-dark :—
         So :
Affable live-oak, bending low,—
Thus—with your favor—soft, with a reverent hand,
(Not lightly touching your person, Lord of the land!)
45 Bending your beauty aside, with a step I stand
On the firm-packed sand,
        Free
By a world of marsh that borders a world of sea.

V

    Sinuous southward and sinuous northward the shimmer-
      ing band
50   Of the sand-beach fastens the fringe of the marsh
      to the folds of the land.
Inward and outward to northward and southward the
    beach-lines linger and curl
As a silver-wrought garment that clings to and follows
    the firm sweet limbs of a girl.
Vanishing, swerving, evermore curving again into sight,
Softly the sand-beach wavers away to a dim gray looping
    of light.
55 And what if behind me to westward the wall of the
    woods stands high?
The world lies east : how ample, the marsh and the sea
    and the sky!
A league and a league of marsh-grass, waist-high, broad
    in the blade,
Green, and all of a height, and unflecked with a light or
    a shade,
Stretch leisurely off, in a pleasant plain,
60 To the terminal blue of the main.

VI

Oh, what is abroad in the marsh and the terminal sea?
    Somehow my soul seems suddenly free

From the weighing of fate and the sad discussion of sin,
By the length and the breadth and the sweep of the
     marshes of Glynn.

VII

65   Ye marshes, how candid and simple and nothing-
     withholding and free
Ye publish yourselves to the sky and offer yourselves
     to the sea!
Tolerant plains, that suffer the sea and the rains and
     the sun,
Ye spread and span like the catholic man who hath
     mightily won
God out of knowledge and good out of infinite pain
70   And sight out of blindness and purity out of a stain.
As the marsh-hen secretly builds on the watery sod,
Behold I will build me a nest on the greatness of God:
I will fly in the greatness of God as the marsh-hen flies
In the freedom that fills all the space 'twixt the marsh
     and the skies.
75   By so many roots as the marsh-grass sends in the sod
I will heartily lay me a-hold on the greatness of God:
Oh, like to the greatness of God is the greatness within
The range of the marshes, the liberal marshes of Glynn.

VIII

And the sea lends large, as the marsh: lo, out of his
     plenty the sea
80   Pours fast: full soon the time of the flood-tide must be:
Look how the grace of the sea doth go
About and about through the intricate channels that flow
       Here and there,
          Everywhere,
85   Till his waters have flooded the uttermost creeks and the
     low-lying lanes
And the marsh is meshed with a million veins,
That like as with rosy and silvery essences flow
     In the rose-and-silver evening glow.
       Farewell, my lord Sun!
90   The creeks overflow; a thousand rivulets run

---

86. THE MARSH IS MESHED, etc.—At high tide the water rises through the
marsh grass and has the appearance of a million rosy and silvery veins.

'Twixt the roots of the sod; the blades of the marsh-
  grass stir;
Passeth a hurrying sound of wings that westward whirr;
Passeth, and all is still; and the currents cease to run;
And the sea and the marsh are one.
95 Hot still the plains of the waters be!
The tide is in his ecstasy;
The tide is at his highest height;
  And it is night.

IX

And now from the Vast of the Lord will the waters of sleep
100 Roll in on the souls of men,
But who will reveal to our waking ken
The forms that swim and the shapes that creep
  Under the waters of sleep?
And I would I could know what swimmeth below when
  the tide comes in
105 On the length and the breadth of the marvellous marshes
  of Glynn.

Poem Development: There is no authority for considering that this poem was written by Lanier of himself, but the lines can well be interpreted in this way. Throughout the poem is the musical note which predominates in all of Lanier's poems. It is somber here and with an element of pain which ends in almost exultation as he accepts the will of God.

In the last three stanzas the poet seems to be expressing thanks to the marshes and the plains for helping him to acquiesce to God's will. Find the line that sums this up. With the fullness of the tide a sound of wings whirring westward is heard. What does this mean? What is the theme? What lesson has the poet learned from the marshes? What is the central thought?

Interpretations: Stanza I—live-oaks; beautiful-braided . . . vines. Stanza II—soft dusks; closets of lone desire; cells; line 17. Stanza III —noon is no more; I know that I know. Stanza IV—line 37; lines 45–48. Stanza V—Sinuous; lines 49–50; dim gray looping of light; the world lies east; line 60. Stanza VI—abroad; weighing of fate; sad discussion of sin. Stanza VII—offer yourselves to the sea; lines 69–70; lay me a-hold; liberal. Stanza VIII—time of the flood-tide; rose-and-silver evening glow; line 92; currents cease to run; line 98. Stanza IX—Vast of the Lord; waking ken; lines 101–105.

Significant Expressions: Quote a line that describes the time of youth. Quote a phrase to indicate middle life. Quote two lines to represent the last years of one's life.

THE HISTORY OF AMERICAN POETRY

The Transition Period (1865–1900)

General Characteristics

The year which saw the end of the Civil War may be taken as marking the beginning of a new period in our literature. The great issues which had agitated the country before the War were now settled and attention was turned to new problems. There followed a period of expansion in which America moved steadily westward across the Mississippi River and the Rocky Mountains. Not only was the western boundary of the United States moved to the Pacific Ocean, and California and Oregon settled, but a transcontinental railroad was built and cable laid across the Atlantic.

This period also saw an economic revolution. Hundreds of factories were built and thousands of patents were issued during the years following the Civil War. Industries increased and the nation experienced a tremendous growth. With these changes came a great change in the literature also. Just as the poets of the National Period had thrown off the yoke of the writers before them and branched out into a new type of poetry in form and content, so the Transition poets discarded the type of writing of the National Period and developed a new, frank, rugged type of writing characteristic of the age. This has been the way of each successive period of literature. As the economic and social conditions change, literary productions of the period change also. There now came upon the scene a great number of writers, most of whom, born before the Civil War, were to live into the twentieth century. In various ways they reflect the changes which were taking place in American life.

THE EASTERN POETS

Walt Whitman and Emily Dickinson are the two outstanding poets of the Transition Period. They were both born and lived in the East, but while Emily Dickinson limited her poetry to stanzas dealing mostly with subjects close about her and to quaint bits of philosophy based on daily incidents, Whitman knew no boundary limitations in his writings. The whole country was his, and all its interests were vital to him. His breadth of vision included North, South, East, and West and he loved equally every section.

These two poets differed in so many ways that it seems strange they could have belonged to the same period. Emily Dickinson was as shy as Whitman was courageous. While he challenged, she retired to solitude. When he pictured the greatness of America and wrote of its struggles and accomplishments, promoted brotherhood and featured fervidly the importance of the individual, she saw the simple beauty of some unimportant object about her and wrote vivid word pictures about it. Whitman traveled the United States over to know his own country; Emily Dickinson rarely left her own home.

They had one characteristic in common, however, and that was an interest in a new form of poetic expression. Both Whitman and Emily Dickinson pioneered in writing of the commonplace, and they mark a new age in American poetry. The poets following them caught much of the spirit and followed the lead in independence of poetic form which these two pioneers started.

Walt Whitman (1819–1892)

Walt Whitman was born on Long Island. He was the first writer to recognize the need of a new type of poetic expression and really belonged to the National Period of writers, for the dates of his birth and death nearly coincide with those of Lowell. He had, however, advanced in his ideas of poetical expression beyond the men of the period in which he was born. Bryant, Longfellow, and Lowell, as well as Emerson, Holmes, and Whittier, were still alive, but they had withdrawn from participation in active events and were living in the past, contenting themselves with writing of old subjects and revising old themes. Not so with Whitman. He, on the contrary, came out into the sunlight of progress and stayed there. He led in a new movement, glorifying the commonplace happenings of life, and throwing off in his writings the old ideas of form, meter, and rhyme. He entered into the realm of the real, and discarded the romantic. Occasionally he did write with a set form of rhyme and meter, as in *O Captain, My Captain,* but in most instances he paid no attention to either.  Poetry to him meant an expression of the feelings and emotions which were aroused by everyday happenings. A ride on the ferry, the impressions given him in the thick of battle, a child's question, or a day spent in a hospital all inspired him to write his interpretations of what they meant to him. Wherever life throbbed Whitman found inspiration. His first volume, *Leaves of Grass,* published in 1855, was an attempt to put America and its turbulent democracy "freely, fully, and truly on record." Nothing like *Leaves of Grass* had ever been seen in America, or anywhere else for that matter. It was wholly new in form, and in content it was still more astonishing—even shocking to Whitman's generation. In it he announced himself as the poet of democracy and of America. His inspiration was not in literature but in life itself, and here was intense life, tremendous imaginative power, and powerful vigor. The influence of Whitman at home and abroad has been tremendous. It has been said that England considers him, with the exception of Poe, our greatest American poet. If he is not the greatest of American poets, he is at all events the most American. We are indebted to him for throwing off the shackles of the former writers and for leaving the over-moralizing and the elaborate phrases behind. Whitman wrote in simple language of commonplace events. The democracy of the country had its effect on him in that it enabled him to write as he chose without regard for the criticism which he brought upon himself.

Whitman had very little schooling. We are told that he stopped school when he was twelve years old. He was interested in everything in which people were involved, and whatever he did and wherever he went, he made himself a part of the life and events of that place. He never tired of making new acquaintances and friends during his wanderings. He gave himself unstintingly to the care of the sick in the hospitals in Washington, and it is said that he personally attended over fifty thousand soldiers during the War. His unselfishness and sympathy were unlimited.

The form of Whitman's poetry is unusual. He rejected the old smooth rhyming forms as unsuited to the expression of what he had to say. If in reading him, you read aloud, and let yourself be guided by your ear rather than by your eye, you will become sensible to the strong rhythm of his verse. It is rough, but it is strong and full of force. Not infrequently does he show his contempt for the rules of grammar and the dictionary. He uses language as he wills to make his expression vigorous and imaginative.

Emily Dickinson (1830–1886)

Emily Dickinson was born in Massachusetts, and although she lived and wrote during the generation which knew Whitman, little was heard of her in her own day. The reason for this is that she lived a retired, almost hermit-like existence, shunning publicity, and writing her poems merely to give outlet to her own thoughts and feelings.

Her father was a Puritan of the old type, and she seems from girlhood to have been out of sympathy with his religion and with that of the family. Instead of breaking out in open rebellion against it, she remained in the family but not of it, and lived in and with her own thoughts. Then, too, when she was about twenty she fell in love with a man who was already married. They were deeply, sincerely attracted to each other, but she was highly honorable and refused to ever see him again, and she never did. This event forced her still deeper into seclusion and she rarely left her home.

She never tried to put her poems before the public. When writing letters to one or two of her friends, she often inclosed verses written on any sort of scrap paper, but it was not until forty years after her death that her poems were collected and published. They instantly became popular. It seems a pity that she could not have enjoyed the friends she might have made through her poetry.

One would not expect to find issuing from such a life poetry such as came from Walt Whitman's many-sided experience with life. Emily Dickinson's poetry is the result of her communing with herself. Like its author, it is quiet, even delicate; yet she wrote with surprising clearness and one marvels at the brilliant images left in the mind after reading her stanzas. She wrote her own thoughts freely and painted beautiful word pictures as vividly as the dew sparkles in the early morning sunlight. It is said of Emily Dickinson that she could say more in fewer words than any poet we have ever had.

THE SOUTHERN POETS

Of the southern poets of this period, Father John B. Tabb and Madison Cawein are the best known. They both show an exquisite musical note in their verses. In fact, all of the southern poets, whether they were greater or lesser lights in the field, have written poems of a high note, reflecting the bright sunshine and warmth of the southern climate. Many poems were of course written about the War, but more were written of the beauty of nature to be seen in the surrounding country. These nature lyrics are musical and have the delicate touch of writers who were particularly sensitive to beauty.

The Reverend John Bannister Tabb (1845-1909)

John Bannister Tabb was better known as Father Tabb. He was a Virginian and during the Civil War both he and Sidney Lanier were confined in the same prison. Both of them loved music and poetry, and they became firm friends. This friendship, which started in the prison when Tabb heard Lanier's flute and finally after a great deal of difficulty managed to get to him, lasted for many years. Tabb studied music and taught English literature. He was ordained to the priesthood in 1884. He is said to be next to Emily Dickinson in being able to say a great deal in a few words. Most of his verses are short and contain, closely packed in the lines, a tremendous amount of meaning. He shows a "rare love of nature," an unfaltering faith in God, and a great appreciation of beauty.

Madison Julius Cawein (1865-1914)

Madison Cawein was a Kentuckian and spent most of his life in his own state. His works can be classed under two headings: those dealing with nature, and those dealing with the feuds, lynchings, and man hunts of the older life of Kentucky. These last were probably the outcome of the years which Cawein spent as cashier in a gambling house in Kentucky. Some of his nature poems when read aloud have a musical lilt that carries the reader along like the music of a song.

THE MIDWESTERN POETS

The three leading poets who comprise this group are James Whitcomb Riley, Richard Hovey, and Bliss Carman. Their poetry falls naturally into two classes—that depicting scenes of home and childhood and that reflecting the spirit of "vagabondia." Riley was the home lover, and his childhood poems are so tenderly reminiscent of youthful days and of scenes and incidents so lovingly cherished by old and young alike that he made for himself an established place in the hearts of the American people. From his own locality he drew material for his Hoosier poems, writing of the characters about him in a masterly way. The keen shrewdness of the "hoss trader," the realness of the "old swimmin' hole," the homely sincerity of the "raggedy man," all had a universal appeal, for they depicted scenes and people, not necessarily identical, but similar in all localities. On the other hand, Hovey and Carmen drew their pictures from nature as they saw it in their wanderings about the country. The friendship of the midwestern section seems a part of their poems—good fellowship radiates in every line. The Midwest had not been so long settled that it had lost the elements of comradeship and friendliness which Hovey and Carmen portrayed in their verse.

James Whitcomb Riley (1849–1916)

James Whitcomb Riley was the beloved poet of Indiana and is known as "the Hoosier poet." Most of his poems are reminiscent of childhood. They appeal to the young because they depict the scenes through which they are passing, and to the old because they recall the memories and emotions which have been lulled by the passage of years but which are nevertheless dear to the heart. Riley had marvelous ability in the writing of simple things which have a universal appeal and could incite the reader to tears or laughter as he willed. His early life gave him unusual opportunity to understand people. His father was a lawyer and a speaker of ability. Riley often accompanied him to the courthouse where he came in contact with country people and came to know their manner of speech, their feelings, and their ways of looking at things. His father wanted him to study law, but Riley found it hard to settle down to an ordered life. For a time he wandered about the country doing any odd job he could find to earn his living. He painted signs, acted as an extra man for a party of traveling players, and finally joined a traveling medicine troup where he played the banjo for the entertainment of the patrons of the show. This mingling with people gave him the understanding and human interest which, when put into poetry, endeared him to the hearts of his readers. He wrote most successfully in dialect. He was very popular as an entertainer, and people flocked to hear him recite his own poems. He was a good actor and mimic which added to the entertainment of his readings. October seventh is Riley

Day in Indiana, the day on which the school children celebrate the birthday of "the Hoosier poet."

Richard Hovey (1864–1900)

Richard Hovey was a native of Illinois. He first studied for the ministry, but gave that up to become a journalist, then a professor of English, and finally a poet and dramatist. Of a poet, he wrote, "It is not his mission to write elegant canzonettas for the delectation of the dilettanti, but to comfort the sorrowful and hearten the despairing, to champion the oppressed and declare to humanity its inalienable rights, to lay open to the world the heart of man—all its heights and depths, all its glooms and glories, to reveal the beauty in things, and to breathe into his fellows a love of it." He followed the requirements which he himself laid down for poets, for he dispels gloom in his rollicking stanzas; he comforts his fellow-beings by putting them into a jolly mood and is altogether happy-go-lucky and boisterously gay in his verses. His is the verse of a joyous American youth who loves adventure and action.

Bliss Carman (1861–1929)

Although Bliss Carman lived well into the twentieth century, it is for the poems which he wrote in the nineties in collaboration with Richard Hovey that we best remember him. He was born in Canada but spent most of his life in the United States. He was a relative of Ralph Waldo Emerson. His plans were to become a teacher, but before he had completed his course of training at Harvard University, he met Richard Hovey and the two became close friends. Carman then gave up the idea of teaching, and together he and Hovey wrote poetry. From their pens came *The Songs of Vagabondia, More Songs from Vagabondia,* and *Last Songs from Vagabondia.* Carman held several positions on the editorial staffs of various magazines, and contributed largely to the best newspapers in the country. His writings are very similar to those of Hovey. Both captivate the reader with their exuberance, their jollity, and high spirits.

THE WESTERN POETS

The western movement brought a new note into poetry. The themes based on western life during the days of pioneering and homesteading and of the gold rush in California were far different from those of Puritan background expressed by the New England poets. The romance of the covered wagons, the motley society of the mining camps, the struggles with the Indians, the hardships of the frontier, as well as the vastness and splendor of the newly opened country, were new themes which had powerful appeal for the eastern readers. Such interpreters of this frontier life as Bret Harte and Joaquin Miller now came into prominence. They chose their subjects from the life about them and their verse abounds with picturesque descriptions of the country itself and vibrates with thrilling stories of the times and the men and women who made the country. They truly reflect the western movement.

Francis Bret Harte (1839–1902)

Bret Harte spent his childhood in the East, but when he was only fifteen, he went to California. This was only five years after the great gold rush of 1849 which peopled California with mining camps and picturesque characters. Harte found work as a typesetter and later became editor of various newspapers and magazines in San Francisco. He came to public notice quite by accident. When he was editor of *The Overland Monthly,* to fill up a blank page he printed the poem *Plain Language from Truthful James.* He had written it some time before, but he did not consider it worth much as literature. However, the public, its imagination fired by tales of the mining camps, liked it; and it brought Harte to general notice. He was surrounded by Mexicans, Indians, miners, Chinamen, outcasts, and nondescript characters of all sorts, both bad and good. They were the subjects of his stories and poems. His favorite theme was the depicting of bad characters who had some splendid streak of good in them.

Joaquin Miller (1841–1913)

Joaquin Miller was born, quite appropriately, in a "covered wagon, pointed west" somewhere near the Indiana-Ohio line. When he was twelve years old, the family made a 3,000 mile trek overland to Oregon, and Miller's recollections of this trip were very vivid. It took them seven months and five days to make the journey, which was a constant struggle with cholera, tornadoes, and Indians. Much of the traveling was over such difficult roads that only a short distance was made each day—so short a distance sometimes that the remains of yesterday's camp fire could still be seen at nightfall. Before he was fifteen, "he began a roving life of adventure which led him into half a dozen Indian campaigns and struggles with mountain flood, prairie fire, desert thirst, and buffalo stampede." Later he attended a mission college in Oregon, and was in turn express messenger, editor, lawyer, and judge. His whole life was one of adventure, which we see clearly reflected in his poems. He gives us vivid, local color in his writings, and we thrill to the adventurous spirit and sweep and rush of his poetry.

Edward Rowland Sill (1841–1887)

Of the West, but productive of another kind of poetry, was Edward Rowland Sill. Instead of being a painter of frontier scenes, he was a questioner of beliefs. Rather than being the frank outward expression of what he saw and heard, his poetry reflects the inward questioning attitude which governed his thoughts. Although born in Connecticut, Sill spent most of his life in California, where he had gone for his health. After spending some years in California he returned to the East to attend the Harvard School of Divinity, but being unable to confine himself to any one belief, he gave up the idea of entering the ministry. He eventually returned to California where he spent the rest of his life. He was a man of few certainties, and his poems reflect his deep, questioning attitude.

Eugene Field (1850–1895)

Eugene Field was born in Missouri. He was educated in the East, but he always loved his West and preferred to live there. He is known chiefly as a poet of childhood, but is also known for a book of western verse which has been very popular with the American public. This is written in western dialect and sparkles with wit and humor. Like Riley, he writes of common experiences which have a deep appeal to the emotions. *Little Boy Blue,* a poem which is said to have been about his own little son, has become almost a classic. Field will always be deeply enshrined in the hearts of the American people, for he is a poet of the home, and Americans will forever keep a warm place in their hearts for any poet who writes of childhood and of home.

OTHER POETS OF THE TRANSITION PERIOD

This period gave us the names of many writers who contributed poems which will always be remembered. In the East were Lucy Larcom (1826–1893), whose employment in a Massachusetts textile mill furnished the background for *Hannah Binding Shoes;* Thomas Bailey Aldrich (1836–1907), whose *Pessimist and Optimist* would be enjoyed and appreciated by any high school student; John Burroughs (1837–1921), the nature writer, whose fame as a poet rests upon the beautiful stanzas of *Waiting;* Celia Thaxter (1836–1894), author of delightful nature verse of which *The Sandpiper* is best known; John Townsend Trowbridge (1827–1916), a humorist, who, in *Darius Green and His Flying Machine,* wrote delightfully of flying machines at a time when such things were only visions; Edmund Clarence Stedman (1833–1908), known for his poems about Lincoln; Francis Miles Finch (1827–1907), who wrote *The Blue and the Gray;* and Stephen Crane (1871–1900), better known as a novelist but also a writer of poems among which are *War Is Kind* and *A Man Said to the Universe.*

The South gave us Irwin Russell (1853–1879) and Joel Chandler Harris (1848–1908), both writers of negro dialect verse. The former is rememebered for *De Fust Banjo* and the latter for *Revival Hymn.* Paul Lawrence Dunbar (1872–1906), although born in the North, is also remembered for his negro dialect poems, among which *When Malindy Sings* has been very popular.

In the West were John Hay (1863–1905), widely known for his *Pike County Ballads* which portray the rough frontier life of the early days in the West; and William Vaughn Moody (1869–1919), dramatist and poet, remembered for his poem *On A Soldier Fallen in the Philippines.*

Poems of the Transition Period

WHEN I HEARD THE LEARN'D ASTRONOMER

WALT WHITMAN

Poem Interest: Whitman had very little schooling. His education came not from books and the discussions of learned professors, but from nature and everyday experiences. He regarded learning highly, but for him nature held more lessons than did textbooks.

> WHEN I heard the learn'd astronomer;
> When the proofs, the figures, were ranged in columns
>   before me;
> When I was shown the charts and the diagrams, to add,
>   divide, and measure them;
> When I, sitting, heard the astronomer, where he lectured
>   with much applause in the lecture-room,
> 5   How soon, unaccountable, I became tired and sick;
> Till rising and gliding out, I wander'd off by myself,
> In the mystical moist night-air, and from time to time,
> Look'd up in perfect silence at the stars.

Poem Development: What is the meaning of lines 2 and 3? What makes you think the lecture may have been a good one? What opinion do you think Whitman held regarding the learning of the astronomers? Give the thought of the poem in your own words.

Interpretations: Astronomer; mystical.

Significant Expressions: What is the figure of speech in line 7? Quote the lines which show the poet's love of nature.

A NOISELESS PATIENT SPIDER

WALT WHITMAN

Poem Interest: Thinkers for ages have tried to fathom the mystery of life and the hereafter. They have written their thoughts in prose and poetry. Almost everything in nature has been to them at one time or another an incentive to write their thoughts on the whys and wherefores of life. Emerson wrote a poem in answer to the query "Whence is the flower"? Holmes saw the wonder of creation in the sea shell. To Whitman also, a humble bit of nature is symbolic of life's mystery.

A NOISELESS patient spider,
I mark'd where on a little promontory it stood isolated,
Mark'd how to explore the vacant vast surrounding,
It launch'd forth filament, filament, filament, out of itself,
5   Ever unreeling them, ever tirelessly speeding them.

And you, O my soul, where you stand,
Surrounded, detached, in measureless oceans of space,
Ceaseless musing, venturing, throwing, seeking the spheres
   to connect them,
Till the bridge you will need be form'd, till the ductile
   anchor hold,
10   Till the gossamer thread you fling catch somewhere, O
   my soul.

Poem Development: Whitman sees the gropings of the soul in the toiling of the patient spider. In line 8, to what does "them" refer? Did Whitman find an answer to his seeking? What is the theme? What is the central thought?

Interpretations: Promontory; vacant vast surrounding; measureless oceans of space; ductile anchor; gossamer thread.

Significant Expressions: Quote the lines describing the spider. Quote the line telling what the soul seems to be trying to do.

I HEAR AMERICA SINGING

WALT WHITMAN

Poem Interest: Wherever life throbbed Whitman found inspiration.

I HEAR America singing, the varied carols I hear;
Those of mechanics—each one singing his, as it should
    be, blithe and strong;
The carpenter singing his, as he measures his plank or
    beam,
The mason singing his, as he makes ready for work, or
    leaves off work;
5 The boatman singing what belongs to him in his boat—the
    deckhand singing on the steamboat deck;
The shoemaker singing as he sits on his bench—the hatter
    singing as he stands;
The woodcutter's song—the ploughboy's, on his way in the
    morning, or at the noon intermission, or at sundown;
The delicious singing of the mother—or of the young wife
    at work—or of the girl sewing or washing—each sing-
    ing what belongs to her, and to none else;
The day what belongs to the day—at night, the party of
    young fellows, robust, friendly,
10 Singing, with open mouths, their strong melodious songs.

Poem Development: Whitman is known as the poet of the people.
How would this poem substantiate such a statement? What is the theme
of the poem?
   Interpretations: Varied carols; the day what belongs to the day.
   Significant Expressions: Quote the line you like best.

MIRACLES

WALT WHITMAN

Poem Interest: It is the poet who sees beauty and mystery in the
commonplace things of life. His are the eyes open to the miracles which
surround our lives.

WHY! who makes much of a miracle?
As to me, I know of nothing else but miracles,

Whether I walk the streets of Manhattan,

Or dart my sight over the roofs of houses toward the sky,

5   Or wade with naked feet along the beach, just in the edge
    of the water,

Or stand under trees in the woods,

Or talk by day with any one I love—or sleep in the bed
    at night with any one I love,

Or sit at table at dinner with my mother,

Or look at strangers opposite me riding in the car,

10   Or watch honeybees busy around the hive, of a summer
    forenoon,

Or animals feeding in the fields,

Or birds—or the wonderfulness of insects in the air,

Or the wonderfulness of the sundown—or of stars shining
    so quiet and bright,

Or the exquisite, delicate, thin curve of the new moon in
    spring;

15   Or whether I go among those I like best, and that like
    me best—mechanics, boatmen, farmers,

Or among the savants—or to the soirée—or to the opera,

Or stand a long while looking at the movements of
    machinery,

Or behold children at their sports,

Or the admirable sight of the perfect old man, or the
    perfect old woman,

20   Or the sick in hospitals, or the dead carried to burial,

Or my own eyes and figure in the glass;

These, with the rest, one and all, are to me miracles,

The whole referring—yet each distinct, and in its place.

To me, every hour of the light and dark is a miracle,

25   Every cubic inch of space is a miracle,

Every square yard of the surface of the earth is spread
    with the same,

Every foot of the interior swarms with the same;

Every spear of grass—the frames, limbs, organs, of men
    and women, and all that concerns them,

All these to me are unspeakably perfect miracles.

30   To me the sea is a continual miracle;
The fishes that swim—the rocks—the motion of the waves
    —the ships, with men in them,
What stranger miracles are there?

Poem Development: Has Whitman opened your eyes to the beauty of the commonplace? Can you add to his list of miracles?
Interpretations: Miracle; savants; soirée; line 23.
Significant Expressions: Quote the miracle you like best.

BEAT! BEAT! DRUMS!

WALT WHITMAN

Poem Interest: We all know the effect of music on the emotions. Think of how you feel at the sound of a stirring march played by a good band. You can't keep your feet from keeping step to the music, and you want to march right along with the band. During times of war, the rousing notes of the fife and stirring sound of the drum fill men with patriotism and inspire them to action.

Beat! beat! drums!—Blow! bugles! blow!
Through the windows—through doors—burst like a
    ruthless force,
Into the solemn church, and scatter the congregation;
Into the school were the scholar is studying;
5   Leave not the bridegroom quiet—no happiness must he
    have now with his bride;
Nor the peaceful farmer any peace, plowing his field
    or gathering his grain;
So fierce you whirr and pound, you drums—so shrill you
    bugles blow.

Beat! beat! drums!—Blow! bugles! blow!
Over the traffic of cities—over the rumble of wheels in
    the streets:
10   Are beds prepared for sleepers at night in the houses? No
    sleepers must sleep in those beds;
No bargainers' bargains by day—no brokers or speculators
    —would they continue?
Would the talkers be talking? would the singer attempt
    to sing?

Would the lawyer rise in the court to state his case
    before the judge?
Then rattle quicker, heavier drums—you bugles wilder
    blow.

15 Beat! beat! drums!—Blow! bugles! blow!
Make no parley—stop for no expostulation;
Mind not the timid—mind not the weeper or prayer;
Mind not the old man beseeching the young man;
Let not the child's voice be heard, nor the mother's
    entreaties;
20 Make even the trestles to shake the dead, where they lie
    awaiting the hearses,
So strong you thump, O terrible drums—so loud you
    bugles blow.

20. TRESTLES—Braced frames upon which coffins could be placed.

Poem Development: Whitman was very intense in his patriotic feelings at the opening of the Civil War. This poem was one of his strongest war poems. Who are the various people he wishes to have the drums arouse? Would he leave any men at home? How would he drown out all protest against entering the War? What is the theme? What is the central thought?

Interpretations: Make no parley; expostulation; prayer.

Significant Expressions: What is the figure of speech in line 2? Quote the line which appeals to your sympathy.

COME UP FROM THE FIELDS, FATHER

WALT WHITMAN

Poem Interest: During the Civil War, there were few homes which had not sent a loved one to the front. Here is a peaceful Ohio farmhouse, from which the only son has long been gone. How anxiously does the family await each message from the front! How eagerly does the sister receive the latest letter, and how happily does she call . . .

COME up from the fields, father, here's a letter from our
    Pete;
And come to the front door, mother—here's a letter from
    thy dear son.

Lo, 'tis autumn;
Lo, where the trees, deeper green, yellower and redder,
5 Cool and sweeten Ohio's villages, with leaves fluttering in
         the moderate wind;
Where apples ripe in the orchards hang, and grapes on
         the trellis'd vines;
(Smell you the smell of the grapes on the vines?
Smell you the buckwheat, where the bees were lately
buzzing?)

Above all, lo, the sky, so calm, so transparent after the
         rain, and with wondrous clouds;
10 Below, too, all calm, all vital and beautiful—and the
         farm prospers well.

Down in the fields all prospers well;
But now from the fields come, father—come at the
         daughter's call;
And come to the entry, mother—to the front door
         come, right away.

Fast as she can she hurries—something ominous—her
         steps trembling;
15 She does not tarry to smoothe her hair, nor adjust her cap.

Open the envelope quickly;
Oh, this is not our son's writing, yet his name is sign'd;
Oh, a strange hand writes for our dear son—O stricken
         mother's soul!
All swims before her eyes—flashes with black—she
         catches the main words only;
20 Sentences broken—*gunshot wound in the breast, cavalry
         skirmish, taken to hospital,
At present low, but will soon be better.*

Ah, now, the single figure to me,
Amid all teeming and wealthy Ohio, with all its cities
         and farms,
Sickly white in the face, and dull in the head, very faint,
25 By the jamb of a door leans.

Grieve not so, dear mother (the just-grown daughter speaks
    through her sobs;
The little sisters huddle around, speechless and dismay'd);
See, dearest mother, the letter says Pete will soon be better.

Alas, poor boy, he will never be better (nor maybe needs
    to be better, that brave and simple soul);
30   While they stand at home at the door, he is dead already;
The only son is dead.

But the mother needs to be better;
She, with thin form, presently drest in black,
By day her meals untouch'd—then at night fitfully sleep-
    ing, often waking,
35   In the midnight waking, weeping, longing with one deep
    longing,
O that she might withdraw unnoticed—silent from life,
    escape and withdraw,
To follow, to seek, to be with her dear dead son.

Poem Development: Notice how quickly the daughter calls out.
There would have been no delay in the actual happening, so Whitman
permits none in the poem. Why does the poet create pictures of a calm,
prosperous farm? What lines give the most vivid picture of the mother?

I NEVER SAW A MOOR

EMILY DICKINSON

Poem Interest: Actual travel is not necessary for an appreciation
and enjoyment of other lands. Emily Dickinson tells you how in the same
manner she believes in the existence of God and Heaven.

I NEVER saw a moor,
    I never saw the sea;
Yet know I how the heather looks,
    And what a wave must be.

5   I never spoke with God,
    Nor visited in heaven;
Yet certain am I of the spot
    As if the chart were given.

Poem Development: How does the idea in this poem of faith in God compare with the expressions of faith found in the poems of the National Period? What is the theme? What is the central thought?

Interpretations: What is a moor? What is heather? What is a chart?

Significant Expressions: The whole poem is significant and is worthy of committing to memory.

A DAY

EMILY DICKINSON

Poem Interest: How does a day begin and how end? Emily Dickinson says:

> I'll tell you how the sun rose,—
> A ribbon at a time.
> The steeples swam in amethyst,
> The news like squirrels ran.
>
> 5   The hills untied their bonnets,
> The bobolinks begun.
> Then I said softly to myself,
> "That must have been the sun!"
>
> But how he set, I know not.
> 10   There seemed a purple stile
> Which little yellow boys and girls
> Were climbing all the while
>
> Till when they reached the other side,
> A dominie in gray
> 15   Put gently up the evening bars
> And led the flock away.

Poem Development: The poet appeals to our feeling for colors. Is the word "amethyst" well chosen? What colors predominate at the close of day? What is the theme? What is the central thought?

Interpretations: A ribbon at a time; line 3; untied their bonnets; purple stile; little yellow boys and girls; dominie in gray.

Significant Expressions: Quote a line to show the color of morning; one to show the color of evening.

THE RAILWAY TRAIN

Emily Dickinson

Poem Interest: We must read Emily Dickinson purely for the enjoyment we can have in re-creating the mental images she pictures. There is rarely a moral or a lesson to be drawn, but just a delightful, brilliantly painted word picture for us to see. How many of us have watched a boat sail over the water and thought of its being almost alive! Or an automobile racing along the highway as if it were human! Here is another inanimate object that seems to live.

> I LIKE to see it lap the miles,
> And lick the valleys up,
> And stop to feed itself at tanks;
> And then, prodigious, step
>
> 5   Around a pile of mountains,
> And, supercilious, peer
> In shanties by the sides of roads;
> And then a quarry pare
>
> To fit its sides, and crawl between,
> 10   Complaining all the while
> In horrid, hooting stanza;
> Then chase itself down hill
>
> And neigh like Boanerges;
> Then, punctual as a star,
> 15   Stop—docile and omnipotent—
> At its own stable door.

13. BOANERGES—Sons of thunder.

Poem Development: In the first stanza what animal do you think the poet has in mind? The pictures are so vivid one follows right along with the train. Does it seem to you as you watch it to "step around a pile of mountains" and "peer in shanties"? How does it "pare a quarry"? Has the poet painted a true picture in using the word "complaining" in line 10? In the last stanza we know what animal the locomotive represents in the poet's mind. Is there any discrepancy between this and the picture of the first stanza? What is the theme? What is the central thought?

Interpretations: Lap; lick; prodigious; supercilious; quarry; horrid, hooting stanza; docile; omnipotent.

Significant Expressions: Quote the lines which give you the most vivid picture of the train.

I'M NOBODY

EMILY DICKINSON

Poem Interest: There are many to whom title, wealth, prestige mean everything. There are others to whom these things mean nothing.

> I'M NOBODY! Who are you?
> Are you nobody too?
> Then there's a pair of us—don't tell!
> They'd banish us, you know.
>
> How dreary to be somebody!
> How public like a frog
> To tell your name the livelong day
> To an admiring bog!

Poem Development: In the first stanza there is a seeking for the understanding of another human being. Which line expresses this? What is the meaning of line 4? Explain the thought in the last four lines. Give the central thought of the poem.

Significant Expressions: Find a figure of speech in the poem.

A BOOK

EMILY DICKINSON

Poem Interest: One writer has said that books are windows through which we may see the panorama of events—past, present, future. Emily Dickinson also has an interesting idea about them . . .

HE ATE and drank the precious words,
　　His spirit grew robust;
He knew no more that he was poor,
　　Nor that his frame was dust.

5　He glanced along the dingy days,
　　And this bequest of wings
Was but a book. What liberty
　　A loosened spirit brings!

Poem Development: Books are our best friends, and we can spend many pleasant and absorbing hours in their company. We can read them and forget our cares. What was the effect of a book on the reader of the poem? How could a book be considered "wings"? What is the theme? What is the central thought?

Interpretations: Robust; line 4; bequest; loosened spirit.

Significant Expressions: Quote the lines which give the thought of the poem.

TO SIDNEY LANIER

JOHN BANNISTER TABB

Poem Interest: You will remember that Father Tabb and Sidney Lanier became firm friends through an acquaintance which began in the prison in which they were both confined as war prisoners. Lanier died in 1884 and Father Tabb wrote the following poem to him:

THE dewdrop holds the heaven above
　　Wherein a lark, unseen,
Outpours a rhapsody of love
　　That fills the space between.

5　My heart a dewdrop is, and thou,
　　Dawn spirit, far away,
Fillest the void between us now
　　With an immortal lay.

Poem Development: Why did Father Tabb use a lark to compare with Sidney Lanier? Who is the "dawn spirit"? Explain "immortal lay." What is the theme? What is the central thought?

Interpretations: Rhapsody; the space between; void.

Significant Expressions: Quote the lines which refer directly to Sidney Lanier.

FAME

John Bannister Tabb

Poem Interest: Although the stars are in the sky at noon just as at night, you cannot see them for the brilliance of the sun is stronger than their light. Read the following poem and note the keenness of thought in the subtle comparison the poet has drawn.

> THEIR noonday never knows
> What names immortal are:
> 'Tis night alone that shows
> How star surpasseth star.

Poem Development: Few artists have ever enjoyed fame in their own day. The judgment of time has had to pass upon their productions, and this judgment has usually come too late for the artists to enjoy their own successes. What is meant by "noonday"? What is the comparison in the poem? What is the theme? What is the central thought?

Significant Expressions: The poem is so short and yet so full of meaning that it would be worth while to memorize it.

EVOLUTION

John Bannister Tabb

Poem Interest: The poem is a concise description of three surprising transformations, or in a loose sense, evolutions. The first is inanimate creation (1–2), then animate creation (3–4), human creation (5) and original sin (6). These creations are climaxed by the Resurrection and Incarnation (7–8) which create man anew.

> OUT of the dusk a shadow,
>   Then, a spark;
> Out of the cloud a silence,
>   Then, a lark;
> 5   Out of the heart a rapture,
>   Then, a pain;
> Out of the dead, cold ashes,
>   Life again.

Poem Development: Which of the first three transformations best illustrates the fourth? How does the third differ from the first two? Point out in each of the four pairs of lines the two words which stand in strongest contrast. Can you suggest another appropriate title for the poem?

FATHER DAMIEN

JOHN BANNISTER TABB

Poem Interest: Father Damien, a Belgian priest, went as a missionary to the Hawaiian Islands in 1864, and in 1873, at his own request, was made resident chaplain to 600 lepers on the island of Molokai. After twelve years of devoted service he contracted the deadly disease and died three years later.

O God, the cleanest offering
Of tainted earth below,
Unblushing to Thy feet we bring—
"A leper white as snow!"

4. *"A leper white as snow!"*—The quotation is from the Fourth *Book of Kings,* V, 27. Naaman, a Syrian general was cured of leprosy through the prayers of the prophet Eliseus, who would not accept any recompense from Naaman. But his avaricious servant Giezi overtook Naaman and in the name of his master Eliseus asked for and received money and garments from the Syrian. In punishment for the deceit, "the leprosy of Naaman," Eliseus tells Giezi, "shall also stick to thee, and to thy seed forever. And he went out from him *a leper as white as snow,"* white, that is, with the scales of leprosy.

Poem Development: Once you understand the story of Father Damien, the poem is crystal clear. Note the sharp contrast between "cleanest" and "tainted." How significant is the dash at the end of the third line? The meaning given by Father Tabb to the quotation with which he closes is very different from that of the scriptural verse. What is the difference?

Interpretations: What is earth's "cleanest offering"? With what is earth "tainted"?

Read the story of "the leprosy of Naaman" in the Fourth *Book of Kings,* in order that you may appreciate Father Tabb's use of the quotation in the fourth line of this short poem. Only thus will you be enabled to "interpret" this poem as the poet intended you should.

Significant Expressions: It would be a violation of this poem's unity to emphasize unduly the value of its component phrases. Memorize the whole.

GOD

John Bannister Tabb

Poem Interest: "What," one is tempted to ask, "can a poet say in a mere three-line verse? And his theme is God!" It is better to ask the question, "How well do the three lines speak of God?" One reads and is answered.

I see Thee in the distant blue;
But in the violet's dell of dew,
Behold, I *breathe* and *touch* Thee too.

Poem Development: In what sense is it true to say that I see God in the distant blue? Do all men see Him there? Which better suggests the nearness of an object,—to see it, or to breathe and touch it? Why are "breathe" and "touch" italicized?

Interpretations: Explain "the violet's dell of dew." Did you notice that only one word in each line is a polysyllable?

Significant Expressions: Memorize this whole poem.

DESERTED

Madison Cawein

Poem Interest: An old deserted house is as desolate a picture as can be found. Joyce Kilmer says, "A house with nobody in it is a house with a broken heart."

The old house leans upon a tree
　　Like some old man upon a staff:
The night wind in its ancient porch
　　Sounds like a hollow laugh.

5　The heaven is wrapped in flying clouds
　　As grandeur cloaks itself in gray:
The starlight flitting in and out,
　　Glints like a lanthorn ray.

The dark is full of whispers. Now
10　　A foxhound howls: and through the night,
Like some old ghost from out its grave,
　　The moon comes misty white.

8. Lanthorn—Lantern.

Poem Development: The picture in the first two lines is very vivid. Cawein was adept at creating clear pictures. In the next two lines what sense does the poet appeal to? Give the picture of the second stanza in your own words. What is the feeling in the last stanza? What is the mood of the poem? What is the theme? What is the central thought?

Interpretations: Staff; hollow laugh; grandeur cloaks itself; lanthorn ray; the dark is full of whispers.

Significant Expressions: Quote three lines illustrating personification; one illustrating simile; one illustrating onomatopœia.

WHEN THE FROST IS ON THE PUNKIN *

JAMES WHITCOMB RILEY

Poem Interest: Of all seasons of the year, none is more satisfying to the farmer than the autumn. Yonder are his apple trees laden with fruit all ready to be picked. There in the fence corner is a pile of yellow pumpkins, which will soon be made into luscious pies. Here are crates of vegetables ready to be stored in the cellar. And in the whole picture is the gorgeous coloring which Nature has given the trees and plants—the reds, the yellows and the greens. The autumn seems to satisfy the senses —one sees the marvelous colorings; feels the crispness of the air; hears the sound of activity and the bustle of the harvesting. Riley, too, sensed the peaceful plenty of this season in the following poem . . .

When the frost is on the punkin and the fodder's in the shock,
And you hear the kyouck and gobble of the struttin' turkey-cock,
And the clackin' of the guineys, and the cluckin' of the hens,
And the rooster's hallylooer as he tiptoes on the fence;
5 O, it's then's the times a feller is a-feelin' at his best,
With the risin' sun to greet him from a night of peaceful rest,
As he leaves the house, bareheaded, and goes out to feed the stock,
When the frost is on the punkin and the fodder's in the shock.

They's something kindo' harty-like about the atmusfere
10   When the heat of summer's over and the coolin' fall is
          here—
     Of course we miss the flowers, and the blossums on the
          trees,
     And the mumble of the himmin'-birds and buzzin' of the
          bees;
     But the air's so appetizin'; and the landscape through the
          haze
     Of a crisp and sunny morning of the airly autumn days
15   Is a pictur' that no painter has the colorin' to mock—
     When the frost is on the punkin and the fodder's in the
          shock.

     The husky, rusty russel of the tossels of the corn,
     And the raspin' of the tangled leaves, as golden as the
          morn;
     The stubble in the furries—kindo' lonesomelike, but still
20   A-preachin' sermuns to us of the barns they growed to fill;
     The strawstack in the medder, and the reaper in the shed;
     The hosses in theyr stalls below—the clover overhead!—
     O, it sets my hart a-clickin' like the tickin' of a clock,
     When the frost is on the punkin and the fodder's in the
          shock!

25   Then your apples all is gethered, and the ones a feller keeps
     Is poured around the celler-floor in red and yeller heaps;
     And your cider-makin's over, and your wimmern-folks is
          through
     With their mince and apple-butter, and theyr souse and
          sausage, too! . . .
     I don't know how to tell it—but ef sich a thing could be
30   As the Angels wantin' boardin', and they'd call around on
          me—
     I'd want to 'commodate 'em—all the whole-indurin' flock—
     When the frost is on the punkin and the fodder's in the
          shock!

Poem Development: Can you read in this poem the love the farmer
has for his farm? Note the homeliness of his philosophy, with the stubble

"a-preachin' sermuns," and the "Angels wantin' board." What sermons could the stubble preach? Notice the thought in the last stanza. Is this a natural and fitting climax to a "song of plenty"? Give the theme of the poem, and its central thought.

Meanings and Interpretations: Fodder; shock; kyouck; hallylooyer; airly; furries; souse; whole-indurin'.

Significant Expressions: Paint a word picture of your own of each of the four stanzas. Which of the four do you like best, and why?

A PARTING GUEST *

James Whitcomb Riley

Poem Interest: Nothing was of more interest to Riley than the fact that he was alive and had friends.

What delightful hosts are they—
    Life and Love!
Lingeringly I turn away,
    This late hour, yet glad enough
5   They have not withheld from me
    Their high hospitality.
So, with face lit with delight
    And all gratitude, I stay
Yet to press their hands and say,
10 "Thanks.—So fine a time!   Good night."

Poem Development: This poem could be a final tribute to Riley himself. It expresses his own idea of life very beautifully. What is the theme? What is the central thought?

Interpretations: Delightful hosts; this late hour; high hospitality; all gratitude.

Significant Expressions: Which line shows who the hosts are? Quote the line to show the poet is getting into old age; quote the line which shows the poet has enjoyed his span of life.

*From *Morning,* by James Whitcomb Riley, copyright 1907. Used by special permission of the publishers, The Bobbs-Merrill Company.

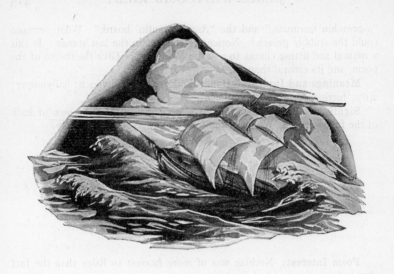

THE SEA GYPSY

Richard Hovey

Poem Interest: We all feel at times that the world we know is hum-
drum and that we'd like to get away. In Hovey this "wander-thirst" was
particularly strong.

> I AM fevered with the sunset,
>   I am fretful with the bay,
> For the wander-thirst is on me
>   And my soul is in Cathay.
>
> 5   There's a schooner in the offing,
>   With her topsails shot with fire,
> And my heart has gone aboard her
>   For the islands of Desire.

4. CATHAY—An old name for China.
5. OFFING—The open sea.

I must forth again to-morrow!
10   With the sunset I must be
Hull down on the trail of rapture
In the wonder of the Sea.

11. HULL DOWN—So far out at sea that the hull cannot be seen.

Poem Development: This poem may express the call of life and romance rather than the call of the sea. With such an interpretation, the word "Sea" in the last line might mean "life." There is a call in the lilt of the lines. Is it true that when one wants to get away, nothing seems right about his present surroundings? What expresses this in the poem? What would you think were some of the characteristics of a man who wrote such a poem? What is the theme? What is the central thought?

Interpretations: I am fevered; wander-thirst; line 5; islands of Desire; line 11.

Significant Expressions: Which line gives the strongest feeling of unrest?

AT THE CROSSROADS

RICHARD HOVEY

Poem Interest: As a rule, the people who say good-bye with a happy wave and a smile are the ones who do the most to keep the world in a genial frame of mind.

> Laugh and the world laughs with you,
>   Weep and you weep alone,
> For the sad old earth has need of your mirth,
>   It has tears enough of its own.

So wish your friend good luck as Hovey does, and leave him in a pleasant frame of mind.

You to the left and I to the right,
    For the ways of men must sever—
And it well may be for a day and a night,
    And it well may be forever.
5   But whether we meet or whether we part
    (For our ways are past our knowing),
A pledge from the heart to its fellow heart
    On the ways we all are going!
Here's luck!
10   For we know not where we are going.

3. WELL—Perhaps.

Whether we win or whether we lose
  With the hands that life is dealing,
It is not we nor the ways we choose
  But the fall of the cards that's sealing.
15 There's a fate in love and a fate in fight,
  And the best of us all go under—
And whether we're wrong or whether we're right,
  We win, sometimes, to our wonder.
Here's luck!
20 That we may not yet go under!

With a steady swing and an open brow
  We have tramped the ways together,
But we're clasping hands at the crossroads now
  In the Fiend's own night for weather;
25 And whether we bleed or whether we smile
  In the leagues that lie before us
The ways of life are many a mile
  And the dark of Fate is o'er us.
Here's luck!
30 And a cheer for the dark before us!

You to the left and I to the right,
  For the ways of men must sever,
And it well may be for a day and a night
  And it well may be forever!
35 But whether we live or whether we die
  (For the end is past our knowing),
Here's two frank hearts and the open sky,
  Be a fair or an ill wind blowing!
Here's luck!
40 In the teeth of all winds blowing.

Poem Development: This poem has such an animated spirit of good fellowship that we are happier for having read it. Hovey's creed was to create good fellowship and to promote friendship. He believed that we should "keep our fellow feeling for one another alive and fresh." Give the picture of the first stanza as the poet makes you see it. What is the meaning of lines 11–14? Do you feel after reading the poem a friendlier feeling toward your associates? What is the theme? What is the central thought?

Interpretations: Ways of men; line 7; line 12; steady swing; open brow; leagues; lines 39–40.

Significant Expressions: Quote the lines of the first stanza which are repeated in the last stanza.

AN APRIL MORNING

Bliss Carman

Poem Interest: April has been the inspiration of nature lyrics the world over. The beginning of growth, the coming of birds, the softness of the air call forth poetic expression.

> Once more in misted April
> The world is growing green,
> Along the winding river
> The plumey willows lean.
>
> 5 Beyond the sweeping meadows
> The looming mountains rise,
> Like battlements of dreamland
> Against the brooding skies.
>
> In every wooden valley
> 10 The buds are breaking through,
> As though the heart of all things
> No languor ever knew.
>
> The golden-wings and bluebirds
> Call to their heavenly choirs.
> 15 The pines are blue and drifted
> With smoke of brushwood fires.
>
> And in my sister's garden
> Where little breezes run,
> The golden daffodillies
> 20 Are blowing in the sun.

Poem Development: Paint the picture of the first four stanzas in your own words. Why does Carman say "wooden valley"? What are the "golden-wings"? What is the theme? What is the central thought?

Interpretations: Misted April; plumey willows; languor; heavenly choirs.

Significant Expressions: Quote a line to describe spring. Quote a simile and also a metaphor from the poem.

A VAGABOND SONG

Bliss Carman

Poem Interest: If any time of year more than another calls the spirit of wanderlust within us, it is October. The season has a strangely gripping fascination—we want to hold fast to the delights of summer which will soon be gone. Bliss Carman has put this feeling into words . . .

THERE is something in the Autumn that is native to my
  blood—
Touch of manner, hint of mood;
And my heart is like a rhyme,
With the yellow and the purple and the crimson keeping
  time.

5 The scarlet of the maples can shake me like a cry
Of bugles going by.
And my lonely spirit thrills
To see the frosty asters like smoke upon the hills.

There is something in October sets the gypsy blood astir;
10 We must rise and follow her,
When from every hill of flame
She calls and calls each vagabond by name.

Poem Development: The rhythm of the first verse seems like a quick, lively tune as you read it aloud. In which line do you find a musical rhythm almost like a joyous skip? The poet includes the sound of bugles in the picture he creates. What is the significance of this? What is the theme? What is the central thought?

Interpretations: Native to my blood; hint of mood; scarlet of the maples, line 8; gypsy blood; hill of flame.

Significant Expressions: Quote phrases which give color pictures.

JIM

BRET HARTE

Poem Interest: The good fellowship that springs up between men of the open plains is one of the finest kinds of friendship. Neither time nor space—nor life itself—holds restrictions when the need of one calls for the support of the other. Jim was one of such a partnership.

SAY there! P'r'aps
Some on you chaps
   Might know Jim Wild?
Well,—no offense:
5   Thar ain't no sense
   In gittin' riled!

Jim was my chum
   Up on the Bar:
That's why I come
10   Down from up yar,
Lookin' for Jim.
Thank ye, sir! *You*
Ain't of that crew,—
   Blest if you are!

15   Money? Not much:
   That ain't my kind;
I ain't no such.
   Rum? I don't mind,
Seein' it's you.

20   Well, this yer Jim,—
Did you know him?
Jes' 'bout your size;
Same kind of eyes;—
Well, that is strange:
25   Why, it's two year
   Since he came here,
Sick, for a change.

Well, here's to us:
Eh?
30   What's that you say?
Dead?
That little cuss?

What makes you star',
You over thar?
35   Can't a man drop
'S glass in yer shop
But you must r'ar?
It wouldn't take
Very much to break
40   You and your bar.

Dead!
Poor—little—Jim!
Why, thar was me,
Jones, and Bob Lee,
45   Harry and Ben,—
No-account men:
Then to take *him!*

Well, thar—Good-by—
No more, sir—I—
50   Eh?
What's that you say?
Why, dern it!—sho!—
No? Yes! By Joe!
Sold!

55   Sold! Why, you limb,
You ornery,
Derned old
Long-legged Jim.

Poem Development: Describe in your own words the moving picture of this poem, following Jim's pal through each stanza. Note his special characteristics. Give the central thought of the poem.

Meanings and Interpretations: Riled; ain't no such; r'ar; sold; limb; ornery.

Significant Expressions: Quote lines describing Jim. Give also lines in support of the characteristics you noted in Jim's pal.

PLAIN LANGUAGE FROM TRUTHFUL JAMES

BRET HARTE

Poem Interest: Fascinating tales are told of the card sharpers of the early days when the West was in the making. It remained for Bret Harte to put one of these stories into poetry.

WHICH I wish to remark,—
    And my language is plain,
That for ways that are dark,
    And for tricks that are vain,
5 The heathen Chinee is peculiar,—
    Which the same I would rise to explain.

Ah Sin was his name.
    And I shall not deny
In regard to the same
10   What that name might imply;
But his smile it was pensive and childlike,
    As I frequent remarked to Bill Nye.

It was August the third;
    And quite soft was the skies:
15 Which it might be inferred
    That Ah Sin was likewise;
Yet he played it that day upon William
    And me in a way I despise.

4. VAIN—Underhanded.
12. BILL NYE—A popular humorist of Bret Harte's day.

421

Which we had a small game,
20   And Ah Sin took a hand:
It was euchre. The same
    He did not understand;
But he smiled as he sat at the table,
    With the smile that was childlike and bland.

25   Yet the cards they were stacked
    In a way that I grieve.
And my feelings were shocked
    At the state of Nye's sleeve:
Which was stuffed full of aces and bowers,
30   And the same with intent to deceive.

But the hands that were played
    By that heathen Chinee,
And the points that he made,
    Were quite frightful to see.—
35   Till at last he put down a right bower,
    Which the same Nye had dealt unto me.

Then I looked up at Nye,
    And he gazed upon me;
And he rose with a sigh,
40   And said, "Can this be?
We are ruined by Chinese cheap labor";
    And he went for that heathen Chinee.

In the scene that ensued
    I did not take a hand;
45   But the floor it was strewed
    Like the leaves on the strand
With the cards that Ah Sin had been hiding,
    In the game "he did not understand."

29. BOWERS—In the game of euchre the "bowers" are important cards.
41. CHINESE CHEAP LABOR—The Chinese would work for less than the white man, and "ruined" white labor.

In his sleeves which were long,
50 He had twenty-four packs,—
Which was coming it strong,
Yet I state but the facts;
And we found on his nails, which were taper,
What is frequent in tapers,—that's wax.

55 Which is my remark,
And my language is plain,
That for ways that are dark,
And for tricks that are vain,
The heathen Chinee is peculiar,—
60 Which the same I am free to maintain.

Poem Development: This poem is said to have been based upon an incident which happened at Table Mountain Gold Camp in 1870. What lines make you think the miners thought it would be easy to cheat Ah Sin? Is this poem real poetry? What is the value of the poem? What is the theme? What is the central thought?

Interpretations: Ways that are dark; tricks that are vain; small game; bland; stacked.

KIT CARSON'S RIDE

Joaquin Miller

Poem Interest: Kit Carson, famous trapper and scout, lived a picturesque and romantic life in the West and the Southwest. There are many stories of his deeds and daring. While it is not known if the incident related in the poem is based on fact, the scene itself was one of the most spectacular, yet dreaded, sights that occurred in the early days of the western frontier.

Room! room to turn round in, to breathe and be free,
To grow to be giant, to sail as at sea
With the speed of the wind on a steed with his mane
To the wind, without pathway or route or a rein.
5 Room! room to be free where the white border'd sea
Blows a kiss to a brother as boundless as he;
Where the buffalo come like a cloud on the plain,
Pouring on like the tide of a storm-driven main,
And the lodge of the hunter to friend or to foe

10   *Offers rest; and unquestion'd you come or you go.*
      My plains of America! Seas of wild lands!
      From a land in the seas in a raiment of foam,
      That has reached to a stranger the welcome of home,
      I turn to you, lean to you, lift you my hands.

15   "Run? Run? See this flank, sir, and I do love him so!
      But he's blind, badger blind. Whoa, Pache, boy, whoa,
      No, you wouldn't believe it to look at his eyes,
      But he's blind, badger blind, and it happen'd this wise:

      "We lay in the grass and the sunburnt clover
20   That spread on the ground like a great brown cover
      Northward and southward, and west and away
      To the Brazos, where our lodges lay,
      One broad and unbroken level of brown.
      We were waiting the curtains of night to come down
25   To cover us trio and conceal our flight
      With my brown bride, won from an Indian town
      That lay in the rear the full ride of a night.

      "We lounged in the grass—her eyes were in mine,
      And her hands on my knee, and her hair was as wine
30   In its wealth and its flood, pouring on and all over
      Her bosom wine red, and press'd never by one.
      Her touch was as warm as the tinge of the clover
      Burnt brown as it reach'd to the kiss of the sun.
      Her words they were low as the lute-throated dove,
35   And as laden with love as the heart when it beats
      In its hot, eager answer to earliest love,
      Or the bee hurried home by its burthen of sweets.

      "We lay low in the grass on the broad plain levels,
      Old Revels and I, and my stolen brown bride;
40   'Forty full miles if a foot, and the devils

15. FLANK—Side of the horse.
16. BADGER BLIND—The badger, a burrowing animal, sees better at night than in the daytime. Its difficulty in seeing in daylight has given rise to the impression that the badger is blind.
16. PACHE—The name of the horse, probably from the Indian name Apache.
22. BRAZOS—A river in southern Texas.
39. OLD REVELS—A fellow scout.

Of red Comanches are hot on the track
When once they strike it. Let the sun go down
Soon, very soon,' muttered bearded old Revels
As he peer'd at the sun, lying low on his back,
45   Holding fast to his lasso. Then he jerk'd at his steed
And he sprang to his feet, and glanced swiftly around,
And then dropp'd, as if shot, with an ear to the ground;
Then again to his feet, and to me, to my bride,
While his eyes were like flame, his face like a shroud,
50   His form like a king, and his beard like a cloud,
And his voice loud and shrill, as both trumpet and reed,—
'Pull, pull in your lassoes, and bridle to steed,
And speed you if ever for life you would speed.
Aye, ride for your lives, for your lives you must ride!
55   For the plain is aflame, the prairie on fire,
And the feet of wild horses hard flying before
I heard like a sea breaking high on the shore,
While the buffalo come like a surge of the sea,
Driven far by the flame, driving fast on the three
60   As a hurricane comes, crushing palms in his ire.'

"We drew in the lassoes, seized the saddle and rein,
Threw them on, cinched them on, cinched them over again,
And again drew the girth; and spring we to horse,
With head to Brazos, with a sound in the air
65   Like the surge of a sea, with a flash in the eye,
From that red wall of flame reaching up to the sky;
A red wall of flame and a black rolling sea
Rushing fast upon us, as the wind sweeping free
And afar from the desert blown hollow and hoarse.

70   "Not a word, not a wail from a lip was let fall,
We broke not a whisper, we breathed not a prayer,
There was work to be done, there was death in the air,
And the chance was as one to a thousand for all.

"Twenty miles! . . . thirty miles! . . . a dim distant
   speck . . .
75   Then a long reaching line, and the Brazos in sight!
And I rose in my seat with a shout of delight.

41. COMANCHES—The Indians of northern Texas and Oklahoma.

I stood in my stirrup, and look'd to my right—
But Revels was gone; I glanced by my shoulder
And saw his horse stagger; I saw his head drooping
80   Hard down on his breast, and his naked breast stooping
Low down to the mane, as so swifter and bolder
Ran reaching out for us the red-footed fire.
He rode neck to neck with a buffalo bull,
That made the earth shake where he came in his course, ·
85   The monarch of millions, with shaggy mane full
Of smoke and of dust, and it shook with desire
Of battle, with rage and with bellowings hoarse.
His keen, crooked horns, through the storm of his mane,
Like black lances lifted and lifted again;
90   And I looked but this once, for the fire licked through,
And Revels was gone, as we rode two and two.

"I look'd to my left then—and nose, neck, and shoulder
Sank slowly, sank surely, till back to my thighs,
And up through the black blowing veil of her hair
95   Did beam full in mine her two marvelous eyes,
With a longing and love yet a look of despair
And of pity for me, as she felt the smoke fold her,
And flames leaping far for her glorious hair.
Her sinking horse falter'd, plunged, fell and was gone
100   As I reach'd through the flame and I bore her still on.
On! into the Brazos, she, Pache, and I—
Poor, burnt, blinded Pache. I love him . . .
That's why."

Poem Development: What is the purpose of the first fourteen lines?
Does it give you a feeling of the wild and free western life? How does
the poet show his great love for that country? Who speaks in the
opening stanza? Explain this stanza. Describe the bride. Does the
tenderness of the description presage ill to come? Give lines 42–60
in your own words. Tell how wild horses and buffalo act in cases of
prairie fire. Why did they head for the Brazos? Read the stanza which
intensifies the suspense of the action. Relate the ride of old Revels.
Then relate what happened to the bride. Who is the hero of the poem?
Would a longer conclusion be more desirable? What is the theme?
What is the central thought?

Interpretations: Seas of wild lands, (l. 11); see this flank, sir
(l. 15); won from an Indian town (l. 26); his face like a shroud (l.

49); hard flying before (l. 56); surge of the sea (l. 58); crushing palms in his ire (l. 60); red wall of flame (l. 66); black rolling sea (l. 67); red-footed fire (l. 82); monarch of millions (l. 85); storm of his mane (l. 88); I love him . . . that's why (l. 102–103).

Significant Expressions: Quote four lines which show the poet's love for his western prairies. Quote lines which to you give the two most vivid pictures of the poem. Quote lines which show fast movement. Is the figure of speech, onomatopœia, shown here? Quote the line of climax.

THE DEFENSE OF THE ALAMO

Joaquin Miller

Poem Interest: In the war for Texan independence against Mexico, the Mexican army surrounded a small force of Texans in a Franciscan mission, called the Alamo, at San Antonio. One of the men escaped; those who remained died to the last man. To Joaquin Miller, there was true inspiration in that indomitable courage which knew no surrender.

SANTA ANA came storming, as a storm might come;
    There was rumble of cannon; there was rattle of blade;
There was cavalry, infantry, bugle and drum—
    Full seven thousand in pomp and parade.
5   The chivalry, flower of Mexico;
And a gaunt two hundred in the Alamo!

And thirty lay sick, and some were shot through
    For the siege had been bitter, and bloody, and long.
"Surrender, or die!"—"Men, what will you do?"
10   And Travis, great Travis, drew sword, quick and strong;
Drew a line at his feet . . . "Will you come? Will you go?
I die with my wounded, in the Alamo."

Then Bowie gasped, "Lead me over that line!"
    Then Crockett, one hand to the sick, one hand to his gun,
15   Crossed with him; then never a word or a sign
    Till all, sick or well, all, all save but one,
One man. Then a woman stepped, praying, and slow
Across; to die at her post in the Alamo.

1. SANTA ANA—Commander of the Mexican forces.
10. TRAVIS—Leader of the Texan forces.
13. BOWIE—Col. James Bowie, the pioneer who invented the bowie knife.
17. ONE MAN—One man escaped.

Then that one coward fled, in the night, in that night
20   When all men silently prayed and thought
Of home; of to-morrow; of God and the right,
    Till dawn; and with dawn came Travis's cannon-shot,
In answer to insolent Mexico,
From the old bell-tower of the Alamo.

25   Then came Santa Ana; a crescent of flame!
    Then the red escalade; then the fight hand to hand;
Such an unequal fight as never had name
    Since the Persian hordes butchered that doomed Spartan
        band.
All day—all day and all night; and the morning? so slow,
30   Through the battle smoke mantling the Alamo.

Now silence! Such silence! Two thousand lay dead
    In a crescent outside! And within? Not a breath
Save the gasp of a woman, with gory gashed head,
    All alone, all alone there, waiting for death;
35   And she but a nurse. Yet when shall we know
Another like this of the Alamo?

Shout "Victory, victory, victory ho!"
    I say 'tis not always to the hosts that win!
I say that the victory, high or low,
40   Is given the hero who grapples with sin,
Or legion or single; just asking to know
When duty fronts death in his Alamo.

26. ESCALADE—The scaling of the walls by the Mexican troops.
28. The reference is to Thermopylæ where a handful of Spartans withstood
the great Persian army in a narrow pass until they were betrayed.

Poem Development: This poem gives us a splendid picture of the
pioneers whose courage in the face of overwhelming odds has made
their names live forever in glorious history. Relate some of the
striking incidents of the fight as given in the poem. Look up an historical account of the defense of the Alamo and make a class report on
it. What is the theme of the poem? Give the central thought.

Interpretations: Chivalry; gaunt; insolent Mexico; crescent; or
legion or single; fronts death.

Significant Expressions: Give the figure of speech in line 1. Quote
lines which stir you most.

SEEIN' THINGS

Eugene Field

Poem Interest: *Seein' Things* is a life-sized portrait of a little boy. Can you guess how old he is?

I AIN'T afraid uv snakes or toads, or bugs or worms or mice,
An' things 'at girls are skeered uv I think are awful nice!
I'm pretty brave I guess; an' yet I hate to go to bed,
For, when I'm tucked up warm an' snug an' when my
    prayers are said,
5 Mother tells me "Happy Dreams" an' takes away the light,
An' leaves me lyin' all alone an' seein' things at night!

Sometimes they're in the corner, sometimes they're by
    the door,
Sometimes they're all a-standin' in the middle uv the floor;
Sometimes they are a-sittin' down, sometimes they're
    walkin' round
10 So softly and so creepy-like they never make a sound!
Sometimes they are as black as ink, an' other times they're
    white—
But color ain't no difference when you see things at night!

Once, when I licked a feller 'at had just moved on our
        street,
An' father sent me up to bed without a bite to eat,
15   I woke up in the dark an' saw things standin' in a row,
A-lookin' at me cross-eyed an' p'intin' at me—*so!*
Oh, my! I wuz so skeered 'at times I never slep' a mite—
It's almost alluz when I'm bad I see things at night!

Lucky thing I ain't a girl or I'd be skeered to death!
20   Bein' I'm a boy, I duck my head an' hold my breath.
An' I am, oh *so* sorry I'm a naughty boy, an' then
I promise to be better an' I say my prayers again!
Gran'ma tells me that's the only way to make it right
When a feller has been wicked an' sees things at night!

25   An' so when other naughty boys would coax me into sin,
I try to skwush the Tempter's voice 'at urges me within;
An' when they's pie for supper, or cakes 'at's big an' nice,
I want to—but I do not pass my plate f'r them things
        twice!
No, ruther let Starvation wipe me slowly out o' sight
30   Then I should keep a-livin' on an' seein' things at night!

Poem Development: List the things which best characterize a little
boy of the age you have imagined this one to be. What are the theme
and central thought of the poem?

LITTLE BOY BLUE

Eugene Field

Poem Interest: "Little Boy Blue" with his faithful toy soldier and
little toy dog will live down through the years, in song and poem, for
those who understand and love children and childhood's spirit.

THE little toy dog is covered with dust,
    But sturdy and staunch he stands;
The little toy soldier is red with rust,
    And his musket molds in his hands.
5   Time was when the little toy dog was new,
    And the soldier was passing fair;
And that was the time when our Little Boy Blue
    Kissed them and put them there.

"Now don't you go till I come," he said,
10   "And don't you make any noise!"
So, toddling off to his trundle bed,
    He dreamt of the pretty toys;
And, as he was dreaming, an angel song
    Awakened our Little Boy Blue—
15   Oh! the years are many, the years are long,
    But the little toy friends are true!

Ay, faithful to Little Boy Blue they stand,
    Each in the same old place,
Awaiting the touch of a little hand,
20   The smile of a little face;
And they wonder, as waiting the long years through
    In the dust of that little chair,
What has become of our Little Boy Blue,
    Since he kissed them and put them there.

Poem Development: Eugene Field was very fond of children, and he has caught in his verses a true picture of childhood. It is said that he wrote this poem after his own little son died. For sheer beauty of expression and thought, note lines 13 and 14. What is the change in mood in lines 15 and 16? Can you feel the throb of sorrow all through the selection? What is the theme? What is the central thought?

OPPORTUNITY

Edward Rowland Sill

Poem Interest: The ability to make the best of whatever comes may be observed in varying degrees in every group of people, young or old, the old world over. The more use that one can make of the things at hand, the more successful he will be. The following poem illustrates how such ability won a great battle.

This I beheld, or dreamed it in a dream:—
There spread a cloud of dust along a plain;
And underneath the cloud, or in it, raged
A furious battle, and men yelled, and swords
5   Shocked upon swords and shields. A prince's banner
Wavered, then staggered backward, hemmed by foes.
A craven hung along the battle's edge,

And thought, "Had I a sword of keener steel—
That blue blade that the king's son bears, but this
10   Blunt thing!" he snapt and flung it from his hand,
And lowering crept away and left the field.
Then came the king's son, wounded, sore bestead,
And weaponless, and saw the broken sword,
Hilt-buried in the dry and trodden sand,
15   And ran and snatched it, and with battle-shout
Lifted afresh he hewed his enemy down,
And saved a great cause that heroic day.

Poem Development: So many times we hear people wishing for something that someone else has. Are these people usually successful in the things they try to do? For what did the craven wish? How did the king's son act when he saw the broken sword? Contrast the two characters. What is the theme? What is the central thought?

THE FOOL'S PRAYER

Edward Rowland Sill

Poem Interest: In many plays and stories, clowns or fools, instead of being simple, stupid characters, often prove themselves the opposite. In their mouths are put rare words of wisdom.

THE royal feast was done; the King
  Sought some new sport to banish care,
And to his jester cried: "Sir Fool,
  Kneel now, and make for us a prayer!"

5   The jester doffed his cap and bells,
  And stood the mocking court before;
They could not see the bitter smile
  Behind the painted grin he wore.

He bowed his head, and bent his knee
10   Upon the monarch's silken stool;
His pleading voice arose: "O Lord,
  Be merciful to me, a fool!

"No pity, Lord, could change the heart
From red with wrong to white as wool:
15   The rod must heal the sin; but, Lord,
Be merciful to me, a fool!

" 'T is not by guilt the onward sweep
Of truth and right, O Lord, we stay;
'T is by our follies that so long
20   We hold the earth from heaven away.

"These clumsy feet, still in the mire,
Go crushing blossoms without end;
These hard, well-meaning hands we thrust
Among the heartstrings of a friend.

25 "The ill-timed truth we might have kept—
Who knows how sharp it pierced and stung!
The word we had not sense to say—
Who knows how grandly it had rung!

"Our faults no tenderness should ask,
30   The chastening stripes must cleanse them all;
But for our blunders—oh, in shame
Before the eyes of heaven we fall.

"Earth bears no balsam for mistakes;
Men crown the knave, and scourge the tool
35   That did his will; but Thou, O Lord,
Be merciful to me, a fool!"

The room was hushed; in silence rose
The King, and sought his gardens cool,
And walked apart, and murmured low,
40   "Be merciful to me, a fool!"

Poem Development: During the Middle Ages the court fool or jester played an important part in the life of the court. Give in your own words lines 17-32. How did the king accept the rebuke? Is the word "fool" used in more than one sense? Illustrate. What is the theme? What is the central thought?

THE HISTORY OF AMERICAN POETRY

THE TWENTIETH CENTURY (1900-   )

General Characteristics

For the first decade of the twentieth century, poetry writing seemed at a standstill. Then suddenly the name of Edwin Markham "flashed across the continent." His *The Man with the Hoe* has been called "the battle cry of the next thousand years," and it was a reflection of the economic conditions with which the country was faced. America had become an industrial nation,—producing, manufacturing. Factories, mills, and mines were working ceaselessly, and armies of men and women were employed to keep the machinery moving. For the most part workers were poorly paid and had little or no happiness in their lives. Social unrest was the result, with strikes and panics. The social and economic conditions were further complicated by the immense numbers of immigrants which came to this country during the first years of the century. It was natural, therefore, that poetic expression should reflect the times, and much of the poetry of this period deals with industrial and social topics.

The World War period witnessed the appearance of a large number of war poems, some of which have endured beyond the War years. Nature is still a favorite and important subject, and a number of the new poets have produced nature lyrics of great beauty. Commonplace characters and scenes furnish new themes for another group of poets. But whatever the theme, the new poetry throws aside the generalities of the older poetry and shows evidence of having gone to life itself for its inspiration and material.

In form and diction also, the new poetry differs from that of Longfellow's day. The newer poets have insisted that the older conventional, metrical forms are unsuited to the expression of newer moods and have experimented with different rhythms, and especially with free verse. The newer school insists upon the language of common speech, upon rhythms to suit the mood of the poem, and upon hard, clear imagery. Classic references are dropped and the poets deal with the commonplace with frankness and dignity. Some of the new school have gone to bizarre extremes and there has been a great deal of experimentation which has produced poetry of little merit, but the effect of the whole movement has been to produce a rebirth of genuine poetry.

NEW POETS OF THE EAST

Poetry of the National Period definitely divided itself into the New England and the Southern groups. In the Transition Period we found that in addition to the Eastern and Southern groups, poets appeared to depict scenes in the Mid-West and Far West as the western boundary of the country moved to the Pacific. When we come to the twentieth century, however, we find that all boundaries seem to melt away and the poets of the whole country seem to meet on a common ground of subject material. True it is that occasionally we find a poet who writes of a definite locality, but for the most part all of America belongs to all of the poets. The sectional arrangement in this period has therefore little real significance, but is employed merely as a convenient way of grouping the writers.

Edwin Markham (1852–1940)

Although he was born in Oregon and spent the early years of his life in California, Edwin Markham lived in the East after 1901. He knew hardship and hard work as a growing boy—farming, blacksmithing, and working on a ranch. He read what books he could find, attended such schools as the country afforded, and after graduation from the San Jose Normal School became a teacher in the California schools. He was principal of a school in Oakland when he published *The Man with the Hoe*—the poem which brought him widespread recognition.

Markham was a new voice in our literature. Not the least of the new social problems was that involving the rights of labor, and Markham's sympathies were wholly on the side of the great masses who earn their living by the sweat of their brow. He believed that they are entitled not merely to a living wage and the material comforts of life, but to a full share in the things which beautify and ennoble life, and develop the spiritual side of man. He wanted the soul of man to be recognized, and he saw little justice or conscience in a social order which does not look upon men as any different from beasts of burden, to be worked as long as they can make a profit for their employers, and then to be turned adrift. He wanted to see a social order in which man should be given an opportunity to grow to the "heroism and loftiness" of which Walt Whitman dreamed, and his poems gave expression to his feeling.

Louise Imogen Guiney (1861–1920)

Louise Imogen Guiney was born in Boston, the daughter of Major General Patrick R. Guiney, a hero of the Civil War and a brave man even in death. One day in March, when Louise was but sixteen, her father feeling death coming upon him, knelt down in the street, made the sign of the cross, and gave up his soul to God, leaving his daughter the example of a noble and loyal soul.

Miss Guiney was educated at Elmhurst, the convent school of the Religious of the Sacred Heart in Providence, Rhode Island. Although she early made a name for herself in Boston literary circles, she still had to earn a livelihood for herself and mother, and for three years was postmistress at Auburndale, Massachusetts. Later she was employed in the Boston Public Library. But two visits to England had made her yearn to live and labor there. In 1901 the opportunity came, and thereafter she made her home at Oxford, where she devoted the rest of her life to writing and research.

The best of her poetry she published in a slight volume entitled *Happy Ending*. The most ambitious of her scholarly work is *Recusant Poets,* an anthology of Catholic poets from Sir Thomas More to Alexander Pope, of which only one volume has thus far (1940) been published.

Edwin Arlington Robinson (1869–1935)

Edwin Arlington Robinson was born in Maine. After his graduation from Harvard he lived in New York City for a number of years, working at various occupations to make a living. During this period he persistently kept at his writing although he was seriously handicapped by lack of funds. Theodore Roosevelt became interested in the poet and wrote in terms of high praise of his poetry in the *Outlook* magazine. This recognition helped to make Robinson better known, and after a few more years he was able to devote his entire time to writing. Robinson does not concern himself with social problems. On the contrary, he portrays characters with which he came in contact during his years of poverty—many of them men who were failures. He seems more interested in the failures than in the successes. He tries to find out the reason for the failure and goes upon the assumption that when one knows the underlying reasons for apparent failure, one understands and thinks more kindly of the character portrayed. Many readers prefer Robinson's poetry to that of any other present-day author because he is interested in the real individual back of the outward appearance of his characters. Furthermore, his character studies are not dependent for their interest upon "local color." They are such as might have been made in almost any community, for while the characters are distinct individuals, they are likewise universal. Robinson had the unusual ability to use language in so simple, clear and direct a way as to make it seem that it is no trick at all to write such poems—yet this is the very thing which is most difficult.

Amy Lowell (1874–1925)

Amy Lowell was born in Massachusetts and maintained her residence in that state throughout her life. She was a member of the distinguished Lowell family of New England. James Russell Lowell was a cousin of her grandfather, and Lawrence Lowell, President of Harvard University, her brother. She traveled extensively and this, together with an education obtained from private schools and from a very cultured mother, gave her an excellent background for literary work.

She had wealth, social position and every advantage that culture and travel could give. This assuredness of position is reflected in her life and works. She was afraid of no criticism or opposition and threw her unlimited energy into battling for the supremacy of the new poetry. She was indefatigable in her interest in technique and declared that "a poet must learn his trade in the same manner and with the same painstaking care as a cabinet maker." She is the best known, and the best, of the so-called "Imagist" poets, who contend that poetry should present an image in clear, definite tones, without dealing in vague generalities. Her choice of subjects is varied and colorful. Her poetry seems to be intellectual rather than emotional, although this is not true in every instance, for *Madonna of the Evening Flowers* shows a rare bit of emotional sense appreciation. Miss Lowell stands out as a distinct personality and a most important contributor to the field of poetry.

Robert Lee Frost (1875–   )

Frost's ancestors for nine generations were New Englanders and lived in Lowell, Massachusetts. Frost had a rather meager education for he never seemed to want to stay in school. He attended Dartmouth for a few months, but college was not to his liking and he left it to work as bobbin boy in a cotton mill. After his marriage he attended Harvard for two years, but he still found college uncongenial and left without a degree to earn a living for his growing family. In 1900 his grandfather bought him a farm in New Hampshire from which he wrested a living, supplemented by teaching, for twelve years. From the standpoint of his poetry, this is no doubt an important period in his development, for he is distinctly and almost exclusively the poet of the New England countryside and country people. Of all the Eastern poets he is the most distinctly "local color" in his writing. He is a realist for he gives us faithful pictures of things as they are, and keeps his writing in plain, simple language. He has been twice winner of the Pulitzer Prize for poetry and in 1931 won the first $1,000 award of the National Institute of Arts and Letters in America. Mr. Frost now lives in South Shaftsbury, Vermont.

Blanche Mary Kelly

Miss Kelly was born in Troy, New York, and educated at the Sacred Heart Convent in Albany, New York. She served on the staff of the *Catholic Encyclopedia* and of the *Catholic Dictionary*. A frequent contributor of both prose and poetry to Catholic periodicals in the United States and England, she is perhaps best known for her volume of poetry,

The Valley of Vision, from which "The Housewife's Prayer" is taken. Her most recent work, *The Well of English,* is a critical study of the influence of the Catholic tradition on English literature. For several years Miss Kelly has been on the faculty of Mount St. Vincent College, New York City.

William Rose Benét (1886–   )

Benét was born in New York City. He graduated from Yale and became a corresponding editor of the *Century* magazine. During the World War he received a commission as second lieutenant in the air service. After the War he worked for an advertising agency and finally became one of the founders of *The Saturday Review of Literature.* An oriental strain runs through some of his poems giving them riotous colors and a gorgeous splendor of colorful pictures. In his *Merchants from Cathay* there is also a swinging rhythm which "vibrates with a vigorous music." He occasionally writes in a quieter vein, but his most characteristic poems are those in which his rich imaginative abilities are given full sway.

Sister Miriam, R.S.M.

Sister Miriam, professor of English and librarian at College Misericordia, Dallas, Pennsylvania, has long been fashioning not only poems, but poets as well. First her work was done as high-school teacher in various schools conducted by her Congregation, and, since 1927, as a college teacher of English at College Misericordia. Born in Hazleton, Pennsylvania, she joined the Sisters of Mercy of the Union in 1903. As an author Sister Miriam has contributed both poetry and prose to such periodicals as *Ave Maria, Catholic World, Commonweal,* and *Good Housekeeping;* and has published *Richard Le Gallienne, Painter of Shadows,* and more recently a volume of poetry, *Woven of the Sky.*

Shaemas O'Sheel (1886–   )

Shaemas O'Sheel was born in New York City and received his education there. After leaving Columbia University he established, in 1908, a magazine named *Moods*—some of Joyce Kilmer's first poems appeared in it—but the venture collapsed. Undismayed, O'Sheel continued to write, and has several volumes of poetry to his credit. His admirers, however, complain that he does not write as much as he used to and should. He answers this complaint in some interesting verses entitled "Replying to the Many Kind Friends Who Ask Me If I No Longer Write Poetry."

Elinor Wylie (1887–1928)

Elinor Wylie, in private life Mrs. William Rose Benét, was born in New Jersey. Her father was Solicitor-General in Theodore Roosevelt's administration, and she spent most of her girlhood in Washington. She completed her education at Holton Arms School in Washington and after a period of travel began her literary career in New York City. In 1923 she married William Rose Benét. It is said of Miss Wylie that she always took the side of the unfortunate and that she was generous in an unusual degree. Her tragic and untimely death in 1928 ended the career of a poet whose work shows unusual grace and beauty.

Edna St. Vincent Millay (1892–   )

Miss Millay was born in Maine. She was graduated from Vassar and when only nineteen wrote the poem *Renascence* which made her famous. She was awarded the Columbia poetry prize in 1921 and the Pulitzer Prize in 1922. Her verse is lyrical and full of melody and music. She chooses her themes from nature, especially from the sea, and she writes of love and death. She is particularly pleasing in her sonnets and it is in this form that she prefers to write. She holds an undisputed place among the present-day women poets.

Stephen Vincent Benét (1898–   )

Stephen Vincent Benét is the younger brother of William Rose Benét. The name Benét is of Spanish origin and is pronounced Benay. The family originally came from the island of Minorca and settled in St. Augustine, Florida. Benét's paternal ancestors, including his father, were army officers, and transfers from post to post meant a continual change of scene for the Benét children. Stephen graduated from Yale, and early began writing. His poetry, like that of his brother, abounds in pictures of the bizarre and whimsical, and his imagination creates pictures of vivid coloring. His long poem, *John Brown's Body*, won the Pulitzer Prize in 1928.

NEW POETS OF THE MID-WEST

Although all of the poets of this group have written on a variety of subjects, in a few instances there seems to be a more definite relationship between the poems and the region from which the poets come than is noticeable in the Eastern group. Sandburg writes definitely of his Chicago and its industrial activities, Masters portrays clearly the characteristics of a small Mid-West town, and in many poems Neihardt portrays realistically the Indians among whom he lived.

Edgar Lee Masters (1869–   )

Edgar Lee Masters was born in Kansas and became a successful attorney in Chicago. Early in life he showed a tendency to write and he did publish a number of poems but these attracted little or no attention. It was when an interested friend suggested that for style he read the Greek *Anthology,* a collection of brief poetic sketches, and for material he draw upon the things surrounding him that he began his *Spoon River Anthology* which was to make his name famous. The sketches which comprise this *Anthology* are the confessions of some two hundred men and women from a small Mid-West town who tell their inmost thoughts in the first person. They tell only the truth, for they are dead. Masters represents them as coming from the grave to tell their stories to the world. Masters has written other poetry since, but his *Spoon River Anthology* is considered a remarkable contribution to literature and his finest work.

The Reverend James J. Daly, S.J. (1872–   )

Father Daly was born in Chicago in 1872, received his college training at St. Ignatius College in that city, entered the Society of Jesus at Florissant, Missouri, in 1890, and was ordained to the priesthood in 1905. He has taught English in several Jesuit colleges in the Middle West, and has been literary editor of three Catholic periodicals, *America,* the *Queen's Work,* and *Thought*.

The volume of Father Daly's published works is relatively slight— one book of poetry, two of essays, and one of biography. But the passion for perfection which has thus restricted the quantity of his works has given them the flawless perfection which he seeks and a charm of style which is inescapable. His genius, said Louise Imogen Guiney, "is nothing short of genius of the sympathetic and interpretative kind."

Nicholas Vachel Lindsay (1879–1931)

Lindsay ranks as one of the outstanding poets of our day, and one of the most singular. Springfield, Illinois, where Abraham Lincoln lived and

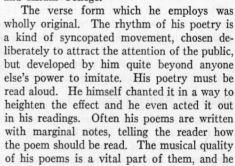

lies buried, was his birthplace and lifelong home and it was there he died in 1931. He was educated at the Springfield High School and Hiram College.

The verse form which he employs was wholly original. The rhythm of his poetry is a kind of syncopated movement, chosen deliberately to attract the attention of the public, but developed by him quite beyond anyone else's power to imitate. His poetry must be read aloud. He himself chanted it in a way to heighten the effect and he even acted it out in his readings. Often his poems are written with marginal notes, telling the reader how the poem should be read. The musical quality of his poems is a vital part of them, and he himself said that he had endeavored to carry out the idea of the half-chanted lyric of old Greek times. Lindsay is at his best when writing poetry expressive of religious experience, particularly where the religious experience is highly emotional as it is among the negroes.

Carl Sandburg (1878–)

Carl Sandburg was born in Illinois. His rise in the field of literature shows the remarkable progress America has made in her sympathetic relations with the immigrants. Both of Sandburg's parents were Swedish and came to this country with practically no education. Sandburg himself worked at any odd job he could find to earn a living. He was a driver of a milk wagon, porter in a barber shop, and truck operator at a brick kiln before he was seventeen. Then he rode "blind baggage" and went west where he washed dishes in hotels and sold stove polish. He had left school at thirteen, but after the Spanish-American War, when he volunteered his services, he went to Lombard College with the little money he had saved from his soldier's pay. Here he worked his way as bell ringer and janitor and it was here that under the influence of an inspiring teacher he first felt the impulse to write. After he finished college he got into newspaper work and finally became editorial writer of the Chicago *Daily News*.

All of these early experiences gave Sandburg the background for his poems. He had made contacts with all sorts of people in all kinds of places. He is the poet of industrial America. He uses slang and the language of the street, but he writes true to the conditions as they exist. More than any other poet, he is the poet of the worker. He has intense vigor but he is also capable of great tenderness.

Sara Teasdale (1884–1933)

Sara Teasdale was born in Missouri but her poems have none of the local color of the Mid-Western region. Her poetry is intensely feminine in its tone. It has none of the vigor of Sandburg or the crudeness of Lindsay. It has charming simplicity and sincere beauty of expression, and voices the poet's moods in clear musical lines. There is a tenderness in some of the poems which is very beautiful. Many of Miss Teasdale's poems have been set to music.

The Reverend Charles L. O'Donnell, C.S.C. (1884–1934)

Father O'Donnell was born in Greenfield, Indiana; entered the Holy Cross Seminary at Notre Dame in 1899; and was graduated from the University in 1906. In the year 1910, that of his ordination to the priesthood, he received the degree of Doctor of Philosophy at the Catholic University in Washington. After a biennium of teaching in the English department of Notre Dame University he became associate editor of *Ave Maria*. Father O'Donnell was a chaplain with the A. E. F. first in France, and then in Italy. The war over, after filling various executive positions in the Holy Cross Order, he became president of the University of Notre Dame in 1928. He died June 4, 1934. An extraordinary thing about Father O'Donnell's life is that in spite of such varied and engrossing occupations he produced three volumes of poetry which placed him in the front rank of American Catholic poets.

OTHER POETS OF THE TWENTIETH CENTURY

In addition to the outstanding Eastern and Mid-Western poets who have received mention, there are a number of other poets of the present day whose poems deserve place in any collection of contemporary poetry. They come from all sections of the country and write on a variety of themes.

Lizette Woodworth Reese (1856–1936)

Lizette Woodworth Reese, born in Baltimore, Maryland, received her education in private schools in that city, and for many years taught English in a Baltimore high school. It has been said of Miss Reese's poetry that it is more English than American in its tone, but this is explained by the facts of her inheritance and environment. Her parents were of English and German stock, and the country around Baltimore was settled by English. Furthermore, it closely resembles English land. Miss Reese knew this section thoroughly. Many of her nature poems were inspired by the flowers, shrubs, and scenes of the surrounding country. She wrote delightfully of simple topics and painted charming pictures in an exceedingly colorful way.

Thomas Augustine Daly (1871–   )

Daly, a native of Pennsylvania, received his education at Villanova College and Fordham University. At the end of his sophomore year he left Fordham to enter newspaper work, and he has been a newspaper man ever since. He has written much humorous verse, but he has been particularly successful in dialect poems of Irish and Italian immigrants. These poems are successful not merely because they are humorous, or in dialect, but because they bring home to us the fact that our immigrants are not a strange species, but human beings with human hearts.

Arthur Guiterman (1871–   )

Arthur Guiterman was born in Vienna, Austria, of American parents. He was educated in the College of the City of New York and later succeeded Joyce Kilmer as lecturer in the New York School of Journalism. He has contributed many humorous verses to *Life,* and has been on the editorial staff of the *Literary Digest* and the *Woman's Home Companion.* He is the author of several volumes of poetry and is at his best in skillful and melodious light verse.

Margaret Widdemer (1880–   )

Margaret Widdemer (Mrs. Robert Haven Schauffler) is a native of Pennsylvania. She graduated from Drexel Institute Library School in Philadelphia and became a magazine writer of short stories, poetry, and essays. In 1918 her *The Old Road to Paradise* shared the Pulitzer Prize with Carl Sandburg's *Corn Huskers.* Miss Widdemer shares with Markham, Sandburg, and Neihardt a sense of the injustice done the underpaid laborer. Her writing expresses deep sympathy for the worker and has attracted widespread attention.

Witter Bynner (1881–   )

Witter Bynner was born in New York City. He was educated at Harvard, graduating in 1902, and since that time has been on the editorial staff of a number of different publications, has been instructor in English at the University of California, and has lectured widely on poetry. He is essentially a lyric poet and has published several volumes of verse.

Marguerite Wilkinson (1883–1928)

Miss Wilkinson was born in Halifax, Nova Scotia, but was educated in Evanston, Illinois, and graduated from Northwestern University. She was a writer of plays, essays, and lyrics and lectured extensively on contemporary poetry.

Dubose Heyward (1885–1940)

Dubose Heyward was born in South Carolina of an aristocratic family. When he was an infant, his father died, leaving the family in financial straits. At nine years of age he helped support the family by selling newspapers and at fourteen he left high school and worked in a hardware store. He became ill from too much hard work and was unable to do much for several years. This period was spent in reading, and in this way he educated himself. Then he went to work on the wharves in Charleston and was thrown into contact with the negroes. Later he moved to North Carolina and devoted his time to writing. His studies are the negroes and the hardy mountaineers.

Joyce Kilmer (1886–1918)

Joyce Kilmer was born in New Jersey. He graduated from Columbia University and for three years was editorial assistant on a new edition of the Standard Dictionary. He also did book reviews for the New York *Times*. He held positions with *The Churchman* and *The Review of Reviews* and lectured on English literature at the University of the South at Sewanee, Tennessee. In 1913 he and his wife, Aline Kilmer, entered the Catholic Church. Three weeks after America entered the World War, he enlisted and was killed in action, July, 1918, at the age of thirty-two. In his death America lost a poet of rare accomplishment and great promise. It is a man deeply tender at heart who speaks to us in lyrics of great beauty.

Aline Kilmer (1888–   )

Aline Kilmer was born at Norfolk, Virginia, and educated at Rutgers Preparatory School, Brunswick, New Jersey, and at the Vail-Deane

School, Elizabeth, New Jersey. She was married to Joyce Kilmer in 1908, and with him embraced Catholicism in 1913. A poet and essayist in her own right and author of several volumes of poems and essays, she has, since her husband's death, also lectured much on poetry and kindred subjects throughout the United States.

Alan Seeger (1888–1916)

Alan Seeger was born in New York City. He graduated from Harvard and was one of the editors of the Harvard *Monthly*. He enlisted in the Foreign Legion when the World War broke out, was wounded in action, and died shortly after in July, 1916. We know him for the one poem *I Have a Rendezvous with Death*. Had he lived he would no doubt have contributed many beautiful selections to the field of poetry.

Sister Maris Stella, C.S.J.

Sister Maris Stella is a native of Iowa, and her poems about children have Des Moines and Okoboji as a background. At sixteen she entered the preparatory school of the College of St. Catherine in St. Paul. At twenty she entered the novitiate of the Sisters of St. Joseph. She teaches literature and creative writing at St. Catherine's, and has published a volume of her poetry, "Here Only A Dove," 1939.

Sister Maris Stella is particularly adept at the sonnet form. Her sonnets are graceful, delicate, rhythmic and vivid with imagery, very often symbolic.

Sister Mary Madeleva, C.S.C.

Sister Madeleva, in the words of Katherine Brégy, "the Lady Abbess of our singing sisterhoods today," was born in Cumberland, Wisconsin. She received her Bachelor of Arts degree in 1909 from St. Mary's College, Notre Dame, Indiana. For her Doctor of Philosophy degree (1925) she moved westward to the University of California; and was president of St. Mary-of-the-Wasatch College in Salt Lake City, Utah, from 1926 to 1933. In 1934 she returned to St. Mary's College, Notre Dame, to become its president.

Like her neighbor and fellow-poet, Father O'Donnell of Notre Dame University, Sister Madeleva has devoted much of her time in the Congregation of the Holy Cross to administrative work. Like him, through it all, she has maintained her poet's soul intact and inspired. Indeed, one who reads and rereads her several volumes of poetry will scarcely charge with exaggeration the critic who crowns her "the laureate of Catholic spirituality in the United States."

Sister M. Thérèse, Sor.D.S.

Sister M. Thérèse is particularly well qualified to write of "God's organ," for even before receiving her Bachelor's degree from Marquette

University in 1933, and her Master's degree in 1937, she had received the Diploma in Piano from the Wisconsin Conservatory of Music, in 1928. She was born in Oconto Falls, Wisconsin, in 1902, and entered the Congregation of the Sisters of the Divine Savior in 1923. She was director of music at the Sisters' Training School of St. Mary's Convent, Milwaukee, from 1928 to 1938, and since 1933 has taught English there. In 1933 she was appointed Poet Laureate of Marquette University. Besides contributing to numerous reviews Sister M. Thérèse has published two volumes of poetry, *Vox Jubilantium* and *Now There Is Beauty*.

Sister Mary St. Virginia, B.V.M.

If it takes a craftsman to teach a craft, Sister Mary St. Virginia's pupils at the Immaculata High School, Chicago, where she has been teaching English since 1935, are fortunate, for she has proven her skill in what she calls "the wondercraft" by winning first prize in the national Poem-for-Our-Lady contest conducted by *America* in 1936 and second prize in a Marian poetry contest conducted by *The Far East* in the same year. Other poems by her have been published in *Columbia, Commonweal, The Literary Digest,* and *The Queen's Work*. Born in Iowa, and a graduate of Saint Mary's College, Prairie du Chien, Wisconsin (now Mount Mary College, Milwaukee), she entered the novitiate of the Sisters of Charity of the Blessed Virgin Mary three years later, in 1932.

Sister Mary Jeremy, O.P.

Sister Mary Jeremy was born in Chicago and educated at Saint Thomas the Apostle High School, and the University of Chicago. At the last named institution she received the John Billings Fiske award for poetry. After taking her master's degree at the University of Chicago she entered the congregation of the Dominican Sisters at Saint Clara Convent, Sinsinawa, Wisconsin, where for several years she taught in Saint Clara Academy. In 1939 she entered the graduate school of Yale University.

Other Poets of the Twentieth Century

Other poets, selections from whom must be omitted for lack of space, but whose work nevertheless is deserving of mention include Katharine Lee Bates, author of *America, the Beautiful* and *The Debt;* Max Eastman, best known for *At the Aquarium;* Nathalia Crane and Hilda Conkling, two child poets of the period who began writing before the age of ten, the former author of *The Janitor's Boy* and the latter known for *Poems by a Little Girl;* Dana Burnet, known for *Roses in the Subway;* and Henry van Dyke, author of *The Glory of Ships*.

Poems of the Twentieth Century

THE MAN WITH THE HOE

EDWIN MARKHAM

Poem Interest: In this poem the author gives a vivid and moving description of the French peasant of the days before the French Revolution, as he saw him pictured by the painter Millet. After you read the poem once, reread it slowly, comparing the description with the picture. The thought conveyed by the poem is that a man made into a brute by brutal labor, and seeing nothing in life to make him better than a beast, cannot be expected to develop splendid and beautiful qualities or to be other than a beast. This poem has been repeatedly called "The Supreme Poem of the Century."

God made man in his own image
In the image of God He made him.—Genesis.

BOWED by the weight of centuries he leans
Upon his hoe and gazes on the ground,
The emptiness of ages in his face,
And on his back the burden of the world.
5   Who made him dead to rapture and despair,

    1. BOWED, etc.—His form is bent because his ancestors for centuries have had their backs bent in toil.
    3. THE EMPTINESS, etc.—His face reveals no delight in life, as the faces of his toiling ancestors have never shone with the gladness of life.
    4. BURDEN OF THE WORLD—The work of the world upon which the world's progress depends.
    5. DESPAIR—He does not despair for he has never known better things.

446

A thing that grieves not and that never hopes,
Stolid and stunned, a brother to the ox?
Who loosened and let down this brutal jaw?
Whose was the hand that slanted back this brow?
10   Whose breath blew out the light within this brain?

Is this the Thing the Lord God made and gave
To have dominion over sea and land;
To trace the stars and search the heavens for power;
To feel the passion of Eternity?
15   Is this the dream He dreamed who shaped the suns
And markt their ways upon the ancient deep?
Down all the caverns of Hell to their last gulf
There is no shape more terrible than this—
More tongued with cries against the world's blind greed—
20   More filled with signs and portents for the soul—
More packt with danger to the universe.

What gulfs between him and the seraphim!
Slave of the wheel of labor, what to him
Are Plato and the swing of Pleiades?
25   What the long reaches of the peaks of song,
The rift of dawn, the reddening of the rose?
Thru this dread shape the suffering ages look;
Time's tragedy is in that aching stoop;
Thru this dread shape humanity betrayed,
30   Plundered, profaned and disinherited,
Cries protest to the Powers that made the world,
A protest that is also prophecy.
O masters, lords and rulers in all lands,
Is this the handiwork you give to God,
35   This monstrous thing distorted and soul-quencht?
How will you ever straighten up this shape;
Touch it again with immortality;
Give back the upward looking and the light;
Rebuild in it the music and the dream;
40   Make right the immemorial infamies,
Perfidious wrongs, immedicable woes?

19. TONGUED WITH CRIES—Testifying against.
24. PLATO—A Greek philosopher.
24. PLEIADES—A constellation of stars.
35. SOUL-QUENCHT—His soul killed.

O masters, lords and rulers in all lands,
How will the future reckon with this Man?
How answer his brute question in that hour
45   When whirlwinds of rebellion shake all shores?
How will it be with kingdoms and with kings—
With those who shaped him to the thing he is—
When this dumb Terror shall rise to judge the world,
After the silence of the centuries?

Poem Development: Study the picture and note the characteristics of the peasant. He is a mere wreck of a man, toiler of the soil, bent from hard physical work, showing no hope, no show of intelligence— downtrodden, desecrated, typical of France before the Revolution. Keep this man in mind as you read every line of the poem. Notice how the first lines start out descriptive of the man. As you read each line, look back at the picture and see if the line is full of meaning for the peasant. Is the first line true? the second line? the third line, etc.? What is the full meaning of "a thing," line 6? Can you, from your knowledge of French history, answer the question in line 9? From what is line 12 quoted? Does line 24 refer to education? To what do lines 25–26 refer? Simplify the question asked in lines 36–41. To what extent has the prophecy about duration of kings and kingdoms in line 46 come true? Why do you consider this a strong poem? What is the theme of the poem, and its central thought?

Interpretations: Line 3; line 6; line 9; line 10; line 13; line 21; line 22; time's tragedy; line 35; line 38; lines 44–45.

Significant Expressions: Write phrases or lines descriptive of the peasant's appearance. What line or lines show he is uneducated? Give lines to show upon whom the blame for this condition rests. Quote a line showing a prophecy in the poem. Quote lines to show hope for the oppressed peoples of the world.

LINCOLN, THE MAN OF THE PEOPLE

Edwin Markham

Poem Interest: It is said that for every crisis in the history of America, a man has come forth to carry the country through the strenuous period. Washington and Lincoln are examples. With the thought of the great need for such a man as Lincoln during the Civil War period, read the following poem.

WHEN the Norn Mother saw the Whirlwind Hour
Greatening and darkening as it hurried on,
She left the Heaven of Heroes and came down
To make a man to meet the mortal need.
5   She took the tried clay of the common road—
Clay warm yet with the genial heat of Earth,
Dasht through it all a strain of prophecy,
Tempered the heap with thrill of human tears
Then mixt a laughter with the serious stuff.
10 Into the shape she breathed a flame to light
That tender, tragic, ever-changing face;
And laid on him a sense of the Mystic Powers,
Moving—all husht—behind the mortal veil.
Here was a man to hold against the world,
15 A man to match the mountains and the sea.

The color of the ground was in him, the red earth,
The smack and tang of elemental things:
The rectitude and patience of the cliff,
The good-will of the rain that loves all leaves,
20 The friendly welcome of the wayside well,
The courage of the bird that dares the sea,
The gladness of the wind that shakes the corn,
The pity of the snow that hides all scars,
The secrecy of streams that make their way
25 Under the mountain to the rifted rock,
The tolerance and equity of light
That gives as freely to the shrinking flower
As to the great oak flaring to the wind—
To the grave's low hill as to the Matterhorn
30 That shoulders out the sky. Sprung from the West,
He drank the valorous youth of a new world.
The strength of virgin forests braced his mind,
The hush of spacious prairies stilled his soul.

Up from log cabin to the Capitol,
35 One fire was on his spirit, one resolve—

---

1. NORN MOTHER—In Scandinavian mythology, a divine giantess who presides over the fates of men.

1. WHIRLWIND HOUR—The approaching Civil War.

To send the keen ax to the root of wrong,
Clearing a free way for the feet of God,
The eyes of conscience testing every stroke,
To make his deed the measure of a man.
40 He built the rail-pile as he built the State,
Pouring his splendid strength through every blow:
The grip that swung the ax in Illinois
Was on the pen that set a people free.

So came the Captain with the mighty heart;
45 And when the judgment thunders split the house,
Wrenching the rafters from their ancient rest,
He held the ridgepole up, and spikt again
The rafters of the Home. He held his place—
Held the long purpose like a growing tree—
50 Held on through blame and faltered not at praise—
Towering in calm rough-hewn sublimity.
And when he fell in whirlwind, he went down
As when a lordly cedar, green with boughs,
Goes down with a great shout upon the hills,
55 And leaves a lonesome place against the sky.

Poem Development: Give the mythical story of the creation of this great man. What was the need for this creation? Make a list of his characteristics as you read them from the poem. What was his one resolve? How did he build the rail-pile? Give the meanings of lines 42–43. Why is he called "Captain"? What were the "judgment thunders" that "split the house"? Tell how he died.

Interpretations: Norn Mother; Whirlwind Hour; line 2; line 4; thrill of human tears; line 9; mystic powers; lines 14–15; line 17; line 23; Matterhorn; line 31; strength of virgin forests; hush of spacious prairies; his words were oaks in acorns; granite truth; line 34; line 36; line 38; line 40; lines 42–43; Captain; lines 45–48; lines 52–55.

Significant Expressions: Give the figure of speech in the following lines: 9; 20; 49; 52–54. Quote the line or lines which show what you believe to be Lincoln's strongest characteristic. Quote the line or lines to show the characteristic which you liked best about Lincoln. Quote the two lines telling about Lincoln's words and thoughts. Quote the line which shows his rise from poverty to fame. Quote the line which gives Lincoln's high purpose in life, the measurement of all his acts. Quote the lines which refer to the Civil War. What line is the most tender in sentiment? Quote five to eight lines that you have memorized from the poem.

NAM SEMEN EST VERBUM DEI

Louise Imogen Guiney

Poem Interest: Do you recall our Lord's parable of the sower, and His explanation of it to the Apostles: "The seed is the word of God"? Read the whole passage in St. Luke, chapter eight, verses 4–15. In this sonnet the poet applies the parable to a congregation listening to the priest's sermon. The priest at the altar rail is the sower; the souls of his hearers are the soil in which he sows the word of God.

> SPRINGTIDE of spirits, at the Altar rail:
> A mystic Sowing, in the morning light
> A gentleness of Love that yet can smite
> As on the granary floor the threshing-flail.
> 5 O happy soil! O terror beyond wail,
> If never sheaf the Sowing should requite,
> And time between were busied but to blight
> Good will, which only can make God avail!
>
> Till souls be corn and vintage of His feast,
> 10 As He was aye of ours, how grave and slow
> Like any weary husbandman, a Priest
> Fills the long furrow, treading to and fro!
> And there my clod of earth, the last, the least,
> Vows that pure Seed some harvest, ere the snow.

Poem Development: At what season of the year is sowing usually done? Does the love of God the Sower express itself through His priest gently or sternly? How stern can it be? What does it matter whether the soil stifles the seed or makes it fruitful? Once the word of God is sown, what else is needed to promote its growth? In the sestet our attention is turned to the results of the sowing: the harvest is gathered not for its own sake, but that the product may grace the table of the Sower. When did the word of God the Father fully fructify in Christ's soul? And when was He ground like wheat, and pressed like grapes that we might feast? How long must God, through His priest, go on sowing the word of God in our souls?

Interpretations: Mystic sowing; happy soil; time between; the long furrow; my clod of earth; ere the snow.

Significant Expressions: Quote the lines that best reveal the humility of the poet. After making sure what a threshing-flail looks like, and how and for what it is used, memorize at least the first four lines.

MINIVER CHEEVY

EDWIN ARLINGTON ROBINSON

Poem Interest: Among the many types of people upon the path of life, you will always find a Miniver Cheevy. He is indistinguishably marked by constant reference to the past—"The good old days for me," says he. Edwin Arlington Robinson has given us here the portrait of just such a man.

> MINIVER CHEEVY, child of scorn,
> 　　Grew lean while he assailed the seasons;
> He wept that he was ever born,
> 　　And he had reasons.
>
> 5　Miniver loved the days of old
> 　　When swords were bright and steeds were prancing;
> The vision of the warrior bold
> 　　Would set him dancing.
>
> Miniver sighed for what was not,
> 10　　And dreamed, and rested from his labors;
> He dreamed of Thebes and Camelot,
> 　　And Priam's neighbors.
>
> Miniver mourned the ripe renown
> 　　That made so many a name so fragrant;
> 15　He mourned Romance, now on the town,
> 　　And Art, a vagrant.
>
> Miniver loved the Medici,
> 　　Albeit he had never seen one;
> He would have sinned incessantly
> 20　　Could he have been one.
>
> Miniver cursed the commonplace,
> 　　And eyed a khaki suit with loathing;

11. THEBES—An ancient Greek city famous for its heroes.
11. CAMELOT—Where King Arthur held his court.
12. PRIAM'S NEIGHBORS—Priam was King of Troy. His neighbors were the famous Greek heroes of *The Iliad* and *Odyssey*.
17. MEDICI—An Italian family of the Middle Ages, famous for the unscrupulous use of its power.

He missed the medieval grace
  Of iron clothing.

25   Miniver scorned the gold he sought,
      But sore annoyed was he without it;
    Miniver thought, and thought, and thought,
      And thought about it.

    Miniver Cheevy, born too late,
30   Scratched his head and kept on thinking;
    Miniver coughed, and called it fate,
      And kept on drinking.

Poem Development: Miniver Cheevy was forever bemoaning the better times of ages past. Name some of the bygone days he praises so much. For what did Miniver sigh? For what good in the world would such a man be? Does the poem give you a feeling that you would like to live in a dream world of the past? Discuss the opportunities about you for knightly deeds. Is romanticism a thing of the past? This form of writing is satire, which was much employed by Edwin Arlington Robinson. Does it appeal to you?

Interpretations: Lines 2; 5; 10; Thebes; Camelot; Priam; ripe renown; lines 15--16; the Medici; lines 21--24; sore annoyed; born too late.

Significant Expressions: Quote a line to show Miniver's bad disposition. Quote another to show that he was lazy.

AN OLD STORY

Edwin Arlington Robinson

Poem Interest: Too often, in self-pride, we miss the vision beautiful of those about us. The poet tells us of that sad trait of humankind which realizes true worth only after its loss.

    Strange that I did not know him then,
      That friend of mine!
    I did not even show him then
      One friendly sign;

5   But cursed him for the ways he had
      To make me see
    My envy of the praise he had
      For praising me.

I would have rid the earth of him
10   Once, in my pride!
I never knew the worth of him
Until he died.

Poem Development: Great men are seldom appreciated until after their death. Great authors, poets, artists, are given praise for their masterpieces, not while they are living but sometimes centuries after their lifetime. Sometimes one does not appreciate his immediate, personal friend until after that friend has met death. Read the poem having in mind such a personal friend.

Significant Expressions: Quote the first two and last two lines as if composing one stanza.

RICHARD CORY

Edwin Arlington Robinson

Poem Interest: Recently in a small city a man who had been the envy of the community killed himself. Apparently he had everything for which to live—money, family, and friends—but after his death it was found that he had no money and was heavily in debt. Robinson is at his best in writing of such unfortunates. Notice how truly he paints a picture which we have had continually before us during the years 1930 to 1934.

Whenever Richard Cory went down town,
We people on the pavement looked at him:
He was a gentleman from sole to crown,
Clean favored, and imperially slim.

5   And he was always quietly arrayed,
And he was always human when he talked;
But still he fluttered pulses when he said,
"Good-morning," and he glittered when he walked.

And he was rich—yes, richer than a king—
10   And admirably schooled in every grace:
In fine, we thought that he was everything
To make us wish that we were in his place.

So on we worked, and waited for the light,
And went without the meat, and cursed the bread;

15   And Richard Cory, one calm summer night,
      Went home and put a bullet through his head.

Poem Development: Robinson writes of the failures in life more
than of the successes. There is a tremendous lesson in this poem. One
wonders why Richard Cory committed suicide and also what could have
been done to prevent such a happening. Too, one cannot but wonder
where his neighbors failed in thinking all was so well with him when
tragedy was so near. What is your impression of Richard Cory in the
first three stanzas? Describe his appearance. In the second stanza,
what two indications are there that all was not well with Richard
Cory? What lesson, regarding your attitude toward other people, can
you learn from this poem? Is the poem satisfactory without a reason
for his suicide? What is the theme? What is the central thought?

Interpretations: From sole to crown; clean favored; imperially;
quietly arrayed; fluttered pulses; glittered; admirably schooled; waited
for the light; line 14.

Significant Expressions: List phrases descriptive of Richard Cory.
Quote the line that gives Richard Cory's greatest asset.

MEETING-HOUSE HILL

Amy Lowell

Poem Interest: There is poetry in everything about us. It needs
only a master touch to bring out the beauty through poetic expression.
The most commonplace objects around us, objects we have seen every
day of our lives, can be made alive and beautiful if an artist paints the
word pictures for us to see. Amy Lowell writes a glowingly clear image
of a simple object of everyday observance—a white church on a hill.

      I must be mad, or very tired,
      When the curve of a blue bay beyond a railroad track
      Is shrill and sweet to me like the sudden springing of a
            tune,
      And the sight of a white church above thin trees in a city
            square
5   Amazes my eyes as though it were the Parthenon.
      Clear, reticent, superbly final,
      With the pillars of its portico refined to a cautious elegance,
      It dominates the weak trees,
      And the shot of its spire
10   Is cool and candid,

Rising into an unresisting sky.
Strange meeting-house
Pausing a moment upon a squalid hill-top.
I watch the spire sweeping the sky,

15   I am dizzy with the movement of the sky;
       I might be watching a mast
       With its royals set full
       Straining before a two-reef breeze.
       I might be sighting a sea-clipper,
20   Tacking into the blue bay,
       Just back from Canton
       With her hold full of green and blue porcelain
       And a Chinese coolie leaning over the rail
       Gazing at the white spire
25   With dull, sea-spent eyes.

Poem Development: The poet seems to recognize in the first lines that her ordinary topic is an unusual selection. What two pictures do you get in the first five lines? Then the poet takes up one picture in detail. Describe it in your words. The moving sky seems like a rolling sea. And then what does the church seem like? From where does the poet imagine the ship to have come, and with what is it laden? Do you like this wandering of the imagination? What is the theme of the poem? What is its central thought?

Interpretations: Blue bay; thin trees; Parthenon; reticent; superbly final; portico; cautious elegance; weak trees; shot of its spire;

unresisting sky; squalid hill-top; royals; two-reef breeze; tacking; Canton; hold; coolie; sea-spent.

Significant Expressions: What two figures of speech are found in line 3? Quote the lines describing the white church. What two metaphors are given for the white church? What is the metaphor in lines 9–11?

A LADY

AMY LOWELL

Poem Interest: There is something very beautiful in the kindly expression and lines of sympathetic understanding which are shown in the faces of old people. John McCormick sings *Mother McCree* with so much feeling that we too love the face that is wrinkled with care. Whistler painted his masterpiece, *Mother*, and we love the beautiful lady there. Amy Lowell accomplishes the same result with her poem.

> You are beautiful and faded
> Like an old opera tune
> Played upon a harpsichord;
> Or like the sun-flooded silks
> 5 Of an eighteenth-century boudoir.
> In your eyes
> Smolder the fallen roses of out-lived minutes,
> And the perfume of your soul
> Is vague and suffusing,
> 10 With the pungence of sealed spice-jars.
> Your half-tones delight me,
> And I grow mad with gazing
> At your blent colors.
> My Vigor is a new-minted penny,
> 15 Which I cast at your feet.
> Gather it up from the dust,
> That its sparkle may amuse you.

Poem Development: The poet talks to a lovely old lady when she addresses the first word of her poem to "you." The "old opera tune on the harpsichord" takes us back a couple of centuries and gives an atmosphere of colonial days. This is reflected and strengthened with the "sun-flooded silks." How does the perfume embellish the picture? To what two sense perceptions is the appeal made in this poem? What

is the meaning of the last four lines? What is the whole theme and
central thought of the poem?

Interpretations: Harpsichord; sun-flooded silks; eighteenth-century
boudoir; line 7; line 9; half-tones; your blent colors; new-minted penny.

Significant Expressions: Quote two similes from the poem. What
figure of speech is given in line 10? line 14?

BIRCHES *

ROBERT FROST

Poem Interest: An outstanding characteristic of a grove of birch
trees is the fact that many of the trees are bent over. Do you know
why they are bent? Robert Frost does.

WHEN I see birches bend to left and right
Across the line of straighter darker trees,
I like to think some boy's been swinging them.
But swinging doesn't bend them down to stay.
5 Ice-storms do that. Often you must have seen them
Loaded with ice a sunny winter morning
After a rain. They click upon themselves
As the breeze rises, and turn many-colored
As the stir cracks and crazes their enamel.
10 Soon the sun's warmth makes them shed crystal shells
Shattering and avalanching on the snow-crust—
Such heaps of broken glass to sweep away
You'd think the inner dome of heaven had fallen.
They are dragged to the withered bracken by the load,
15 And they seem not to break; though once they are bowed
So low for long, they never right themselves:
You may see their trunks arching in the woods
Years afterwards, trailing their leaves on the ground
Like girls on hands and knees that throw their hair
20 Before them over their heads to dry in the sun.
But I was going to say when truth broke in
With all her matter-of-fact about the ice-storm
I should prefer to have some boy bend them
As he went out and in to fetch the cows—
25 Some boy too far from town to learn baseball,

*From *Mountain Interval* by Robert Frost. Reprinted by permission of
Henry Holt and Company, publishers.

Whose only play was what he found himself,
Summer or winter, and could play alone.
One by one he subdued his father's trees
By riding them down over and over again
30 Until he took the stiffness out of them,
And not one but hung limp, not one was left
For him to conquer. He learned all there was
To learn about not launching out too soon
And so not carrying the tree away
35 Clear to the ground. He always kept his poise
To the top branches, climbing carefully
With the same pains you use to fill a cup
Up to the brim, and even above the brim.
Then he flung outward, feet first, with a swish,
40 Kicking his way down through the air to the ground.

So I was once myself a swinger of birches;
And so I dream of going back to be.
It's when I'm weary of considerations,
And life is too much like a pathless wood
45 Where your face burns and tickles with the cobwebs
Broken across it, and one eye is weeping
From a twig's having lashed across it open.
I'd like to get away from earth awhile
And then come back to it and begin over.

50 May no fate wilfully misunderstand me
And half grant what I wish and snatch me away
Not to return. Earth's the right place for love:
I don't know where it's likely to go better.
I'd like to go by climbing a birch tree,
55 And climb black branches up a snow-white trunk
Toward heaven, till the tree could bear no more,
But dipped its top and set me down again.
That would be good both going and coming back.
One could do worse than be a swinger of birches.

Poem Development: When the poet sees birches bent over, what
does he like to think? Describe the picture of the trees with ice upon
their branches. Why do they never right themselves? Give the simile
to which the poet likens the trees. Again, what theory did the poet say
he wished to believe about their bending? Tell how a boy swings on

the trees. What symbolism is there in climbing a birch? What is the theme of the poem, and its central thought?

   Interpretations: Straighter darker trees; line 4; they click upon themselves; crazes their enamel; crystal shells; line 13; withered bracken; line 24; too far from town; line 26; not launching out too soon; not carrying the tree away clear to the ground; with a swish; weary of considerations; line 44; lines 45–47; line 51; lines 52–53; black branches; snow-white trunk; line 58.

   Significant Expressions: Find two similes in the poem. Quote the two or three lines you like best.

MENDING WALL *

ROBERT FROST

   Poem Interest: In New England, stone walls are very common on the farms. The line fence between two farms must be kept up by both owners, half of the responsibility belonging to each one. Hence it is customary in the spring for neighbors to "walk the line" and repair the fence between them. But these neighbors may have entirely different attitudes about the work as shown in the following poem.

SOMETHING there is that doesn't love a wall,
That sends the frozen-ground-swell under it,
And spills the upper boulders in the sun;
And makes gaps even two can pass abreast.

5   The work of hunters is another thing:
I have come after them and made repair
Where they have left not one stone on a stone,
But they would have the rabbit out of hiding,
To please the yelping dogs. The gaps I mean,

10 No one has seen them made or heard them made,
But at spring mending-time we find them there.
I let my neighbor know beyond the hill;
And on a day we meet to walk the line
And set the wall between us once again.

15 We keep the wall between us as we go.
To each the boulders that have fallen to each.
And some are loaves and some so nearly balls
We have to use a spell to make them balance:
"Stay where you are until our backs are turned!"

*From *North of Boston* by Robert Frost. Reprinted by permission of Henry Holt and Company, publishers.

20   We wear our fingers rough with handling them,
Oh, just another kind of out-door game,
One on a side. It comes to little more:
There where it is we do not need the wall:
He is all pine and I am apple orchard.
25   My apple trees will never get across
And eat the cones under his pines, I tell him.
He only says, "Good fences make good neighbors."
Spring is the mischief in me, and I wonder
If I could put a notion in his head:
30   *"Why* do they make good neighbors? Isn't it
Where there are cows? But here there are no cows.
Before I built a wall I'd ask to know
What I was walling in or walling out,
And to whom I was like to give offence.
35   Something there is that doesn't love a wall,
That wants it down." I could say "Elves" to him,
But it's not elves exactly, and I'd rather
He said it for himself. I see him there
Bringing a stone grasped firmly by the top
40   In each hand, like an old-stone savage armed.
He moves in darkness as it seems to me,
Not of woods only and the shade of trees.
He will not go behind his father's saying,
And he likes having thought of it so well
45   He says again, "Good fences make good neighbors."

Poem Development: What tears the fence down? How do the two men repair the fence? How is this work like a game? What line tells you of the poet's opinion of the fence? Give a character sketch of each of the two men. Which do you think has the more education, and why? What is meant by "good fences make good neighbors"? Is this true to any degree? Why didn't he say "elves" to his neighbor? What line gives the best clue to the character of the "neighbor beyond the hill"? What is the theme of the poem? The central thought?

Interpretations: Line 1; line 5; use a spell; to make them balance; line 19; line 24; spring is the mischief in me; isn't it where there are cows; walling in or walling out; line 34; old-stone savage armed; line 41.

Significant Expressions: Give the figure of speech in line 17; line 28. Quote the author's reasons for not wanting the wall, and his arguments to that effect. Give also a line showing why the neighbor clung to his idea of retaining the wall.

THE RUNAWAY *

Robert Frost

Poem Interest: When driving through the country, have you ever seen a lively young colt dash across the fields, and then swing back to the fence to stand and look at you? Recalling such a picture, you will be interested in the antics of the spirited young Morgan in this poem.

Once when the snow of the year was beginning to fall,
We stopped by a mountain pasture to say, "Whose colt?"
A little Morgan had one forefoot on the wall,
The other curled at his breast. He dipped his head
5   And snorted at us. And then he had to bolt.
We heard the miniature thunder where he fled,
And we saw him, or thought we saw him, dim and grey,
Like a shadow against the curtain of falling flakes.
"I think the little fellow's afraid of the snow.
10   He isn't winter broken. It isn't play
With the little fellow at all. He's running away.
I doubt if even his mother could tell him, 'Sakes,
It's only weather.' He'd think she didn't know!
Where is his mother? He can't be out alone."
15   And now he comes again with clatter of stone,
And mounts the wall again with whited eyes
And all his tail that isn't hair up straight.
He shudders his coat as if to throw off flies.
"Whoever it is that leaves him out so late,
20   When other creatures have gone to stall and bin,
Ought to be told to come and take him in."

Poem Development: A Morgan is one of the best breed of horses, and a beautiful creature. Describe him as the poet pictures him. Would this be a subject for a beautiful oil painting? What background would you have in the picture? What effect does the snow have upon the colt? Would it add to the oil painting? What makes you think one of the watchers understands horses? Why do you think the colt came back? Why did he "shudder his coat"? Do you agree with the last two lines? Comment on the following as the theme of the poem: The *Runaway* gives a delightful, realistic picture of a colt

*From *New Hampshire* by Robert Frost. Reprinted by permission of Henry Holt and Company, publishers.

frightened by falling snow, and the plain matter-of-fact comment of two country people.

Interpretations: Curled at his breast; bolt; miniature thunder; winter broken; sakes; whited eyes; gone to stall and bin.

Significant Expressions: Quote a line containing a simile. Quote a line describing the colt. Quote an imaginary saying of the colt's mother. Quote the lines which tell what should have been done with the colt.

STOPPING BY WOODS ON A SNOWY EVENING *

Robert Frost

Poem Interest: This poem is a study in black and white—an etching that will keep presenting itself before you in unexpected moments. Read it slowly, as if each word were one of its drifting snowflakes.

> Whose woods these are I think I know.
> His house is in the village though;
> He will not see me stopping here
> To watch his woods fill up with snow.
>
> 5 My little horse must think it queer
> To stop without a farmhouse near
> Between the woods and frozen lake
> The darkest evening of the year.
> He gives his harness bells a shake
> 10 To ask if there is some mistake.
> The only other sound's the sweep
> Of easy wind and downy flake.
>
> The woods are lovely, dark and deep,
> But I have promises to keep,
> 15 And miles to go before I sleep,
> And miles to go before I sleep.

Poem Development: Is this winter experience real to you? Write down your own description of the scene. Explain the last stanza, commenting on the effect of lines 15–16.

Significant Expressions: Quote the lines you consider most effective. Give reasons for your choice.

*From *New Hampshire* by Robert Frost. Reprinted by permission of Henry Holt and Company, publishers.

C-AM

THE HOUSEWIFE'S PRAYER

Blanche Mary Kelly

Poem Interest: Plain but sensible soul that she is, the housewife knows that the home no less than the church is a proper place for prayer, that Mary and her Son are as concerned about the rising of the bread as about the rising of the sun.

Lady, who with tender word
Didst keep the house of Christ the Lord,
Who didst set forth the bread and wine
Before the Living Wheat and Vine,
5 Reverently didst make the bed
Whereon was laid the Holy Head
That such a cruel pillow prest
For our behoof, on Calvary's crest;
Be beside me while I go
10 About my labors to and fro.
Speed the wheel and speed the loom,
Guide the needle and the broom,
Make my bread rise sweet and light,
Make my cheese come foamy white,
15 Yellow may my butter be
As cowslips blowing on the lea.
Homely though my tasks and small,
Be beside me at them all.
Then when I shall stand to face
20 Jesu in the judgment place,
To me thy gracious help afford,
Who art the Handmaid of the Lord.

Poem Development: How are the first eight lines related to the remainder of the poem? Why would they find Mary a ready listener? Why is the housewife so interested in her household tasks? Why does she feel a special claim on Mary's aid? Are there any insignificant duties in which she could dispense with Mary's help?

Interpretations: Tender word; Living Wheat and Vine; cruel pillow; behoof; line 11; homely tasks.

Significant Expressions: Which lines are most suggestive of the "Hail Mary"? What figure of speech is used in line 4? in lines 15–16? Which lines seem to you most homely and housewifely?

WOVEN OF THE SKY

Sister Miriam

Poem Interest: The immensity and intimacy of God and the strength which He shares with those who have audience with Him are revealed by one who knows them, not by hearsay, but by loving experience.

When dusk is neither grey nor blue but gold,
    Into a spacious tent I slip away
From griefs that all the heavier lie untold,
    From tasks that bind both hands and heart all day.

5   This tent that is the thought of You is wide
    And high as heaven is high, yet fearlessly
I wander up and down, alone, inside
    This canvas woven of the sky for me.

When I emerge into the alien air
10   With quiet hands and still more quiet eyes,
The chariot of the stars is waiting there
    To bear me on, by love made strong and wise:
So strong that now at last I can be brave;
So wise, all briefer loves must find a grave.

Poem Development: Briefly summarize the thought of the two quatrains and of the sestet. What is the tent into which the poet slips away at dusk? From what is she slipping away? What makes her walk fearlessly within the spacious tent? What is the dominant mood of the poem?

Interpretations: Griefs that all the heavier lie untold; wide and high as heaven is high; this canvas woven of the sky for me; line 9; the chariot of the stars; line 14.

Significant Expressions: Quote lines that tell of the effectiveness of this evening stroll within the spacious tent. Also, quote the line which gives the ultimate source of the strength thus won.

THE FALCONER OF GOD

William Rose Benét

Poem Interest: The olive branch is the symbol of peace; the ring of eternity; the laurel of victory; the willow of sorrow. Of what has Benét made the falcon the symbol in the following poem?

I FLUNG my soul to the air like a falcon flying.
I said, "Wait on, wait on, while I ride below!
   I shall start a heron soon
   In the marsh beneath the moon—
5   A strange white heron rising with silver on its wings,
      Rising and crying
    Wordless, wondrous things;
The secret of the stars, of the world's heart-strings
    The answer to their woe.
10 Then stoop thou upon him, and grip him and hold him so!"

My wild soul waited on as falcons hover.
I beat the reedy fens as I trampled past.
   I heard the mournful loon
   In the marsh beneath the moon.
15 And then with feathery thunder—the bird of my desire
     Broke from the cover
    Flashing silver fire.
High up among the stars I saw his pinions spire.
    The pale clouds gazed aghast
20 As my falcon stooped upon him, and gripped and held him
    fast.

My soul dropped through the air—with heavenly plunder?—
Gripping the dazzling bird my dreaming knew?
   Nay! but a piteous freight,
   A dark and heavy weight
25 Despoiled of silver plumage, its voice forever stilled,—
     All of the wonder
    Gone that ever filled
Its guise with glory. Oh, bird that I have killed,
    How brilliantly you flew
30 Across my rapturous vision when first I dreamed of you!

   Yet I fling my soul on high with new endeavor,
   And I ride the world below with a joyful mind.
   I shall start a heron soon
   In the marsh beneath the moon—

35   *A wondrous silver heron its inner darkness pledges!*
        I beat forever
      The fens and the sedges.
      The pledge is still the same—for all disastrous pledges,
        All hopes resigned!
40   My soul still flies above me for the quarry it shall find.

Poem Development: This poem is one of symbolism. In the first stanza, the poet paints a picture of great charm. You can see the falcon flying high in the air—the soul of man, or the human spirit, flying on high while the solitary hunter below rides beneath the moon seeking ideal beauty. This Beauty is symbolized by the white heron with the silver wings. What is the meaning of the poet's desire to have the falcon swoop and seize the heron? Do you like the way the poet used the refrain? Give the theme of the poem, and its central thought.

Interpretations: I flung my soul; I ride below; start a heron; in the marsh; secret of the stars; hold him so; reedy fens.

Significant Expressions: Quote the lines to show how dazzling and brilliant was Beauty—the symbolic heron.

HE WHOM A DREAM HATH POSSESSED

Shaemas O'Sheel

Poem Interest: In the world there are vacillating souls, blown hither and yon by every veering breath of opinion; souls without anchorage in a fixed vision of their goal; sorrowful souls, therefore, mindful of woes that are gone, fearful of woes that may come. If only they were possessed by vision, by a high and absorbing dream, they would be secure, would stand fast, would know joy, and would flash through the world, God's battle-field, confident, courageous, and gay.

He whom a dream hath possessed knoweth no more of
      doubting,
    For mist and the blowing of winds and the mouthing of
      words he scorns;
Not the sinuous speech of schools he hears, but a knightly
      shouting,
    And never comes darkness down, yet he greeteth a million
      morns.

5   He whom a dream hath possessed knoweth no more of roam-
      ing;
    All roads and the flowing of waves and the speediest flight
      he knows,

But wherever his feet are set, his soul is forever homing,
　　And going he comes, and coming he heareth a call and goes.

He whom a dream hath possessed knoweth no more of
　　sorrow,
10　　At death and the dropping of leaves and the fading of suns
　　　he smiles,
　　For a dream remembers no past and scorns the desire of a
　　　morrow,
　　And a dream in a sea of doom sets surely the ultimate isles.

He whom a dream hath possessed treads the impalpable
　　marches,
　　From the dust of the day's long road he leaps to a laughing
　　　star,
15　And the ruin of worlds that fall he views from eternal arches,
　　　And rides God's battlefield in a flashing and golden car.

Poem Development: What does it mean "to be possessed" by an idea, a vision, a dream? From what three woes is he saved whom a dream hath possessed? What has scorn of mist to do with freedom from doubt? How do the sinuous speech of schools and a knightly shouting stand in contrast to one another? Explain how the soul of the dream-possessed is forever homing. How comes it that he is immune to sorrow? What spirit in the dream-possessed does his flashing and golden car suggest?

Interpretations: Blowing of winds and mouthing of words; line 4; flowing of waves; line 8; line 12; impalpable marches.

Significant Expressions: Quote the stanza you like best; if asked to do so, tell why you prefer it to the others.

SEA LULLABY

Elinor Wylie

Poem Interest: This poem presents a most unusual picture of the sea.

THE old moon is tarnished
With smoke of the flood,

The dead leaves are varnished
With color like blood,

5   A treacherous smiler
With teeth white as milk,
A savage beguiler
In sheathings of silk,

The sea creeps to pillage,
10   She leaps on her prey;
A child of the village
Was murdered today.

She came up to meet him
In a smooth golden cloak,
15   She choked him and beat him
To death, for a joke.

Her bright locks were tangled,
She shouted for joy,
With one hand she strangled
20   A strong little boy.

Now in silence she lingers
Beside him all night
To wash her long fingers
In silvery light.

Poem Development: What is the mood of the opening stanza? In the second stanza, what is the poet describing? Could one paint a picture of the sea from the description? What is forewarned by the word "treacherous" in line 5? How is this carried out in the third stanza? Did you ever before think of the "white caps" of the waves as teeth? Or of the sea dressed in green silk? The "smooth golden cloak" with which the sea beguiled the little boy was the golden sand in which he was playing—then a huge wave swept over him and the undertow carried him out to sea. Was the boy's body recovered from the sea? What villainy is displayed in the last stanza? Interpret lines 23–24. Do you think the title appropriate for the poem? What are the theme and central thought of the poem?

Interpretations: Tarnished; smoke of flood; varnished; color like blood; teeth white as milk; sheathings of silk; smooth golden cloak; choked him; lines 21–22; in silvery light.

Significant Expressions: In what line do you find the following figures of speech; simile; personification; alliteration. How many metaphors can you find in the poem? Quote a line showing how the sea looked; how it acted.

ATAVISM

Elinor Wylie

Poem Interest: To those who fear, fear lurks in many things. It is the unseen form behind tree stumps, in dark corners, at the bottom of ponds, or just behind one—and when one turns, the form turns also and always keeps behind. This state of mind predominates in primitive people, and when a civilized person reverts to the primitive type, it is called atavism.

I always was afraid of Somes's Pond:
Not the little pond, by which the willow stands,
Where laughing boys catch alewives in their hands
In brown, bright shallows; but the one beyond.
5   There, when the frost makes all the birches burn
Yellow as cow-lilies, and the pale sky shines
Like a polished shell between black spruce and pines,
Some strange thing tracks us, turning where we turn.

You'll say I dream it, being the true daughter
10   Of those who in old times endured this dread.
Look! Where the lily-stems are showing red
A silent paddle moves below the water.
A sliding shape has stirred them like a breath;
Tall plumes surmount a painted mask of Death.

Poem Development: Contrast the two ponds. What line suggests horror to you? What is the meaning of "those who in the old times endured this dread"? What picture is given in the last four lines? What is the thought of the poem?

Interpretations: Alewives; brown, bright shallows; cow-lilies; pale sky; like a polished shell; line 8; lily-stems; sliding shape; line 14.

Significant Expressions: Quote a line which shows the pleasantness of one pond, and another which shows the sinister aspect of the other. What is the figure of speech in line 7? Quote a line which gives you a feeling of dread. What is the figure of speech in line 13?

GOD'S WORLD *

EDNA ST. VINCENT MILLAY

Poem Interest: From depths of soul is this glorious prayer of perfect, passionate love for beauty. It is filled with loveliness, and overflowing with an ecstasy of joy.

O WORLD, I cannot hold thee close enough!
　　Thy winds, thy wide grey skies!
　　Thy mists that roll and rise!
Thy woods, this autumn day, that ache and sag
5　And all but cry with colour! That gaunt crag
To crush! To lift the lean of that black bluff!
World, World, I cannot get thee close enough!

Long have I known a glory in it all,
　　But never knew I this;
10　　Here such a passion is
As stretcheth me apart. Lord, I do fear
Thou'st made the world too beautiful this year.
My soul is all but out of me,—let fall
No burning leaf; prithee, let no bird call.

Poem Development: Have you seen such an autumn as the poet describes, with winds and mists and autumn woods that "all but cry with color"? Interpret the descriptive phrase in lines 4–5. Explain Miss Millay's reaction to its beauty. What is the meaning of the last of line 11 and the first of line 12? What can you say of the desire for silence in lines 13–14? Give the central thought of the poem. What would you say is the primary appeal of the poem as a whole?

Interpretations: Gaunt crag; black bluff; burning leaf; prithee.

Significant Expressions: Quote the lines showing deepest feeling; greatest color; those most descriptive.

*From *Renascence,* published by Harper & Brothers. Copyright, 1917, by Edna St. Vincent Millay.

TRAVEL *

Edna St. Vincent Millay

Poem Interest: It is hardly to be wondered at that, in a universe so vast and ever-moving, in a world so packed with interesting things, the pressure to be up and off should be forever in our hearts. Edna St. Vincent Millay felt this alertness keenly.

THE railroad track is miles away,
    And the day is loud with voices speaking,
Yet there isn't a train goes by all day
    But I hear its whistle shrieking.

5   All night there isn't a train goes by,
    Though the night is still for sleep and dreaming,
But I see its cinders red on the sky,
    And hear its engine steaming.

My heart is warm with the friends I make,
10   And better friends I'll not be knowing,
Yet there isn't a train I wouldn't take,
    No matter where it's going.

Poem Development: The human mind has a most interesting faculty for shutting out, at any given time, all but a desired experience. In what way does the thought in the first two stanzas illustrate this? Interpret line 2. Explain the meaning of the last stanza. What central thought do you find in this poem?

Significant Expressions: Quote the lines you liked best from the poem, and tell why you liked them. What makes the poem so effective?

A PORTRAIT OF A BOY †

Stephen Vincent Benét

Poem Interest: The fantasy of the poet carries us magically afar, into the realm of a little boy's desire . . .

AFTER the whipping, he crawled into bed;
Accepting the harsh fact with no great weeping.

How funny uncle's hat had looked striped red!
He chuckled silently. The moon came, sweeping
5   A black frayed rag of tattered cloud before
In scorning; very pure and pale she seemed,
Flooding his bed with radiance. On the floor
Fat motes danced. He sobbed; closed his eyes and
       dreamed.
Warm sand flowed round him. Blurts of crimson light
10 Splashed the white grains like blood. Past the cave's
       mouth
Shone with a large fierce splendor, wildly bright,
The crooked constellations of the South;
Here the Cross swung; and there, affronting Mars,
The Centaur stormed aside a froth of stars.
15 Within, great casks like wattled aldermen
Sighed of enormous feasts, and cloth of gold
Glowed on the walls like hot desire. Again,
Beside webbed purples from some galleon's hold,
A black chest bore the skull and bones in white
20 Above a scrawled "Gunpowder!" By the flames,
Decked out in crimson, gemmed with syenite,
Hailing their fellows by outrageous names
The pirates sat and diced. Their eyes were moons.
"Doubloons!" they said. The words crashed gold
25   "Doubloons!"

13. Cross—The Southern Cross—a constellation in the southern skies, four
bright stars forming a cross.
13. Mars—One of the planets, name of the Roman god of war.
14. Centaur—A constellation of stars in the general shape of a centaur, a
mythological creature half horse, half man.

Poem Development: For what reason was the boy punished? What
significance can you give for "the black frayed rag of tattered cloud"?
What colors did you notice through the poem? The whipping seemed
to have troubled the boy little enough—his head was filled with pirates,
and he was soon off with them beneath the deep blue, star-studded tropic
skies. The heavens, the rich velvets from some galleon's hold, the white
skull and cross-bones, the flames flashing their faces crimson, the bright or-
ange-yellow ringing Spanish gold are as vivid to us as to the dreaming boy.

Interpretations: No great weeping; line 3; very pure and pale she
seemed; fat motes danced; line 12; the Cross; Centaur; froth of stars.

Significant Expressions: Quote a line showing how the boy accepted the whipping. What figure of speech do you find in line 10?

SILENCE

Edgar Lee Masters

Poem Interest: Out of the great silence of a whirling world we come, thrown from the heart of the infinite, to fill a place on earth. When this one span of life is done, we are returned again to the silent company of the stars. In the stillness, then, we find the answer and connecting link to all that has been, is, and ever will be.

I have known the silence of the stars and of the sea,
And the silence of the city when it pauses,
And the silence of a man and a maid,
And the silence for which music alone finds the word,
5 And the silence of the woods before the winds of spring
     begin,
And the silence of the sick
When their eyes roam about the room.
And I ask: For the depths
Of what use is language?
10 A beast of the field moans a few times
When death takes its young.
And we are voiceless in the presence of realities—
We cannot speak.

A curious boy asks an old soldier
15 Sitting in front of the grocery store,
"How did you lose your leg?"
And the old soldier is struck with silence,
Or his mind flies away
Because he cannot concentrate it on Gettysburg.
20 It comes back jocosely
And he says, "A bear bit it off."
And the boy wonders, while the old soldier
Dumbly, feebly lives over
The flashes of guns, the thunder of cannon,
25 The shrieks of the slain,
And himself lying on the ground,
And the hospital surgeons, the knives,
And the long days in bed.

But if he could describe it all

30 He would be an artist.
But if he were an artist there would be deeper wounds
Which he could not describe.

There is the silence of a great hatred,
And the silence of a great love,

35 And the silence of a deep peace of mind,
And the silence of an embittered friendship,
There is the silence of a spiritual crisis,
Through which your soul, exquisitely tortured,
Comes with visions not to be uttered

40 Into a realm of higher life,
And the silence of the gods who understand each other
    without speech.
There is the silence of defeat.
There is the silence of those unjustly punished;
And the silence of the dying whose hand

45 Suddenly grips yours.
There is the silence between father and son,
When the father cannot explain his life,
Even though he be misunderstood for it.

There is the silence that comes between husband and wife;

50 There is the silence of those who have failed;
And the vast silence that covers
Broken nations and vanquished leaders.
There is the silence of Lincoln,
Thinking of the poverty of his youth.

55 And the silence of Napoleon
After Waterloo.
And the silence of Jeanne d'Arc
Saying amid the flames, "Blessèd Jesus"——
Revealing in two words all sorrow, all hope.

60 And there is the silence of age,
Too full of wisdom for the tongue to utter it
In words intelligible to those who have not lived
The great range of life.
And there is the silence of the dead.

65 If we who are in life cannot speak

Of profound experiences,
Why do you marvel that the dead
Do not tell you of death?
Their silence shall be interpreted
70 As we approach them.

Poem Development: Read again slowly the mystical lines of the poem, to get their fullest meaning. Give a general definition of silence, and the poet's specific illustrations which appeal to you. Explain lines 12–13. Are these lines significant in relation to the rest of the poem? Give your interpretation of lines 29–32. Which lines give you the central thought? What are the theme and central thought?

Interpretations: When it pauses; realities; jocosely.

Significant Expressions: Memorize at least four lines which you like best.

FALSE TRAILS

James J. Daly

Poem Interest: An old, old story tells of a youth who wandered far and wide in search of a treasure, buried all the while in his own farm. St. Augustine wandered thus and in the light of his own experience warns us: "Go not abroad; return upon thyself; truth dwells within man's soul." Father Daly develops the warning into this daring sonnet.

Noli foras ire, in teipsum redi: in interiori
homine habitat veritas.—St. Augustine.

I KICKED the earth from under, and swung up
    From star to star through alien days and nights;
I turned on end adventure's heady cup,
    And scorned the cowardice of safer flights.
5 My quest, I said, was God; God was my goal.
    And so I clambered up until I trod
The topmost star of all, a vagrant soul
    On the last lookout, scanning voids for God.

In secret pride I wept upon the peak
10   Of time and space. Then through the boundary wall
    Of silences a Voice crashed like a dart
Of thundering flame: "Yourself, not Me, you seek!
    Like some poor suitor, I have chafed in all
    The overcrowded porches of your heart."

Poem Development: In breath-taking language the octave describes the false trails followed by the soul; the sestet, the soul's disillusionment. In view of the object of the soul's quest, how appropriate are the figures of speech describing that quest? Do you perceive a crescendo in the thought of the octave? a decrescendo in the sestet? Where should the explorer have looked for God? Why did he not notice Him there? What is the force of the modest "I said" in the fifth line? In the same line what is the effect of the repetition of the word "God"? In what regard is "False Trails" similar to Father Ryan's "Song of the Mystic"?

Interpretations: Alien days and nights; adventure's heady cup; vagrant soul; last lookout; boundary wall of silences; thundering flame.

Significant Expressions: Quote the two most vigorous lines; the lines containing the most daring figures of speech.

ABRAHAM LINCOLN WALKS AT MIDNIGHT *

VACHEL LINDSAY

Poem Interest: This poem, *Abraham Lincoln Walks at Midnight*, was written when the World War broke out in Europe in 1914. To Lindsay the war was an insane thing—a sacrifice to the greed of war lords. He imagined that the folly and injustice of it aroused from the grave the great, kindly Lincoln to pace the streets until the wrong was made right.

It is portentous, and a thing of state
That here at midnight, in our little town,
A mourning figure walks, and will not rest,
Near the old court house pacing up and down.

5 Or by his homestead, or in shadowed yards
He lingers where his children used to play,
Or through the market, on the well-worn stones
He stalks until the dawn-stars burn away.

A bronzed, lank man! His suit of ancient black,
10 A famous high top-hat and plain worn shawl
Make him the quaint great figure that men love,
The prairie-lawyer, master of us all.

* From *Collected Poems* by Vachel Lindsay. Reprinted by permission of The Macmillan Company, publishers.

2. OUR LITTLE TOWN—Springfield, Lindsay's home town; also Lincoln's former home.

He cannot sleep upon his hillside now.
He is among us:—as in times before!
15 And we who toss and lie awake for long,
Breathe deep, and start, to see him pass the door.

His head is bowed. He thinks of men and kings.
Yea, when the sick world cries, how can he sleep?
Too many peasants fight, they know not why;
20 Too many homesteads in black terror weep.

The sins of all the war-lords burn his heart.
He sees the dreadnaughts scouring every main.
He carries on his shawl-wrapped shoulders now
The bitterness, the folly and the pain.

25 He cannot rest until a spirit-dawn
Shall come;—the shining hope of Europe free:
The league of sober folk, the Workers' Earth,
Bringing long peace to Cornland, Alp, Sea.

It breaks his heart that kings must murder still,
30 That all his hours of travail here for men
Seem yet in vain. And who will bring white peace
That he may sleep upon his hill again?

23. SHAWL-WRAPPED—Lincoln often wore a shawl or cape according to custom in dress at his time.

Poem Development: Lindsay took America's greatest man, who was the leading exponent of freedom for all people, and imagined him returning to earth because the world turmoil would not allow him to rest in his grave. In what place does Lindsay have his "mourning figure" return? Is this appropriate? Is Lindsay's portraiture of Lincoln true to the man? Explain fully the worries mentioned in the poem which would be carried on "his shawl-wrapped shoulders." What is the challenge in the very last sentence of the poem? Give the theme of the poem, and its central thought.

Interpretations: Portentous; our little town; mourning figure; the well-worn stones; the prairie-lawyer; when the sick world cries; sins of all the war-lords; a spirit-dawn; Cornland; Alp; Sea; his hours of travail; white peace.

Significant Expressions: List the lines through the poem which describe Lincoln. Quote the lines showing where the figure walks.

THE CONGO *

VACHEL LINDSAY

Poem Interest: In each race, special characteristics show themselves early in history, and evolve higher in their expression as time moves on. Wildly blended in the negro race are the spirit of revelry, vivid fantasy, and simple religious depth which *The Congo* depicts with richness of color and sound.

A Study of the Negro

I THEIR BASIC SAVAGERY

Fat black bucks in a wine-barrel room,
Barrel-house kings, with feet unstable,
Sagged and reeled and pounded on the table,   A deep
                                                     rolling bass.
Pounded on the table,
5   Beat an empty barrel with the handle of a
        broom,
Hard as they were able,
Boom, boom, BOOM,

*From *Collected Poems* by Vachel Lindsay. Reprinted by permission of The Macmillan Company, publishers.

With a silk umbrella and the handle of a
   broom,
Boomlay, boomlay, boomlay, BOOM.

10 THEN I had religion, THEN I had a vision.
I could not turn from their revel in derision.
THEN I SAW THE CONGO, CREEPING THROUGH   *More deliberate. Solemnly chanted.*
   THE BLACK,
CUTTING THROUGH THE JUNGLE WITH A GOLDEN
   TRACK.
Then along the riverbank
15 A thousand miles
Tattooed cannibals danced in files;
Then I heard the boom of the blood-lust song
And a thigh-bone beating on a tin-pan gong.   *A rapidly piling climax of speed and racket.*
And "BLOOD" screamed the whistles and the
   fifes of the warriors,
20 "BLOOD" screamed the skull-faced, lean witch-
   doctors,
"Whirl ye the deadly voodoo rattle,
Harry the uplands,
Steal all the cattle,
Rattle-rattle, rattle-rattle,
25 Bing!
Boomlay, boomlay, boomlay, BOOM,"

A roaring, epic, rag-time tune   *With a philosophic pause.*
From the mouth of the Congo
To the Mountains of the Moon.
30 Death is an Elephant,
Torch-eyed and horrible,   *Shrilly and with a heavily accented meter.*
Foam-flanked and terrible.
BOOM, steal the pygmies,
BOOM, kill the Arabs,
35 BOOM, kill the white men,
Hoo, HOO, HOO.   *Like the wind in the chimney.*
Listen to the yell of Leopold's ghost
Burning in Hell for his hand-maimed host.
Hear how the demons chuckle and yell.
40 Cutting his hands off, down in Hell.

Listen to the creepy proclamation,
Blown through the lairs of the forest-nation,
Blown past the white-ants' hill of clay,
Blown past the marsh where the butterflies
    play:—
45   "Be careful what you do,
Or Mumbo-Jumbo, God of the Congo,
And all of the other
Gods of the Congo,
Mumbo-Jumbo will hoo-doo you,
50   Mumbo-Jumbo will hoo-doo you,
Mumbo-Jumbo will hoo-doo you."

All the O sounds very golden.
Heavy accents very heavy.
Light accents very light.
Last line whispered.

II   THEIR IRREPRESSIBLE HIGH SPIRITS

Wild crap-shooters with a whoop and a call
Danced the juba in their gambling-hall
And laughed fit to kill, and shook the town,
55   And guyed the policeman and laughed them
        down
With a boomlay, boomlay, boomlay, BOOM . . .
THEN I SAW THE CONGO, CREEPING THROUGH
        THE BLACK,
CUTTING THROUGH THE JUNGLE WITH A GOLDEN
        TRACK.

Rather shrill and high.

Read exactly as in first section.

A negro fairyland swung into view,
60   A minstrel river
Where dreams come true.
The ebony palace soared on high
Through the blossoming trees to the evening
        sky.
The inlaid porches and casement shone
65   With gold and ivory the elephant-bone.
And the black crowd laughed till their sides
        were sore
At the baboon butler in the agate door,
And the well-known tunes of the parrot band
That thrilled on the bushes of that magic land.

Lay emphasis on the delicate ideas.
Keep as light-footed as possible.

70 A troupe of skull-faced witch-men came
    Through the agate doorway in suits of flame,
    Yea, long-tailed coats with a gold-leaf crust
    And hats that were covered with diamond-
        dust.
    And the crowd in the court gave a whoop and
        a call
75 And danced the juba from wall to wall.
    But the witch-men suddenly stilled the throng
    With a stern cold glare, and a stern old
        song:—
    "Mumbo-Jumbo will hoo-doo you." . . .
    Just then from the doorway, as fat as shotes,
80 Came the cake-walk princes in their long red
        coats,
    Shoes with a patent leather shine,
    And tall silk hats that were red as wine.
    And they pranced with their butterfly partners
        there,
    Coal-black maidens with pearls in their hair,
85 Knee-skirts trimmed with the jessamine sweet,
    And bells on their ankles and little black feet.
    And the couples railed at the chant and the
        frown
    Of the witch-men lean, and laughed them down.
    (O rare was the revel and well worth while
90 That made those glowering witch-men smile.)

    The cake-walk royalty then began
    To walk for a cake that was tall as a man
    To the tune of "Boomlay, boomlay, BOOM,"
    While the witch-men laughed with a sinister air,
95 And sang with the scalawags prancing there:—
    "Walk with care, walk with care,
    Or Mumbo-Jumbo, God of the Congo,
    And all of the other
    Gods of the Congo,
100 Mumbo-Jumbo will hoo-doo you.
    Beware, beware, walk with care,
    Boomlay, boomlay, boomlay, boom.

Side notes:

With pomposity.

With a great deliberation and ghostliness.

With overwhelming assurance, good cheer, and pomp.

With growing speed and sharply marked dance-rhythm.

With a touch of negro dialect and as rapidly as possible toward the end.

Boomlay, boomlay, boomlay, boom.
Boomlay, boomlay, boomlay,
105   Boom."
Oh, rare was the revel, and well worth while   Slow philo-
That made those glowering witch-men smile.   sophic calm.

Poem Development: Interpret the scene in stanza 1. What reaction did it awaken in the poet? Carefully consider lines 12–13, and
give their meaning. Follow the poet's vision through lines 14–26; and
also relate his thought on this first picture as explained in lines 27–36;
37–51. Give a brief description of voodoo as you see and hear it from
the poem. The pageantry in lines 52–107 is a step forward from the
savagery of the first part. Give the significance of lines 87–90; 106–107.

Interpretations: Black bucks; barrel-house kings; in files; skull-
faced; witch-doctors; voodoo; harry; pygmies; Leopold's ghost; hand-
maimed host; Mumbo-Jumbo; hoo-doo; juba; guyed; minstrel river;
baboon butler; agate door; parrot band; gold-leaf crust; cake-walk
princes.

Significant Expressions: Quote lines which illustrate the original
savagery of the negro people; lines which illustrate their high spirits.
Also choose lines you liked best, and tell why.

PRAYERS OF STEEL *

CARL SANDBURG

Poem Interest: Each thing in the universe has its place and purpose in the plan of life, moving ever onward, upward, Godward through
uprooting of the worn-out old, and acceptance of the worthy new. In
this poem, Carl Sandburg has voiced the silent service of steel—its part
in the world's work.

LAY me on an anvil, O God.
Beat me and hammer me into a crowbar.
Let me pry loose old walls;
Let me lift and loosen old foundations.

Lay me on an anvil, O God.
Beat me and hammer me into a steel spike.
Drive me into the girders that hold a skyscraper together.
Take red-hot rivets and fasten me into the central girders.
Let me be the great nail holding a skyscraper through
    blue nights into white stars.

*From *Cornhuskers* by Carl Sandburg. Reprinted by permission of Henry
Holt and Company, publishers.

Poem Development: Into what does the unshaped steel in the first stanza wish to be made? Then what does it wish to do? In the second stanza, what does the steel wish to become? What is the ultimate wish of the big nail?

Interpretations: Anvil; crowbar; pry loose old walls; girder.

Significant Expressions: What is the figure of speech in line 4? Can you find this same figure of speech in another line?

BARTER *

Sara Teasdale

Poem Interest: What beauty there is in the world about us!

<blockquote>

Life has loveliness to sell—
All beautiful and splendid things,
Blue waves whitened on a cliff,
Climbing fire that sways and sings,
5　And children's faces looking up
Holding wonder like a cup.

Life has loveliness to sell—
Music like a curve of gold,
Scent of pine trees in the rain,
10　Eyes that love you, arms that hold,
And for your spirit's still delight,
Holy thoughts that star the night.

Spend all you have for loveliness,
Buy it and never count the cost;
15　For one white singing hour of peace
Count many a year of strife well lost,
And for a breath of ecstasy
Give all you have been or could be.

</blockquote>

Poem Development: What are some of the things Life has to sell? List them as you find them in the poem. What should we offer in barter?

Interpretations: Whitened; sways and sings; holding wonder; curve of gold; scent of pine trees; line 12; line 15; breath of ecstasy.

Significant Expressions: Quote a line with a complete picture. Sketch or draw the picture. What figure of speech is there in line 8?

*From *Love Songs* by Sara Teasdale. Reprinted by permission of The Macmillan Company, publishers.

NIGHT SONG AT AMALFI *

SARA TEASDALE

Poem Interest: "Reflection" might well be another title for *Night Song at Amalfi*. See what thoughts the "heaven of stars" and "darkened sea" will bring to you.

> I ASKED the heaven of stars
>   What I should give my love—
> It answered me with silence,
>   Silence above.
>
> 5 I asked the darkened sea
>   Down where the fishermen go—
> It answered me with silence,
>   Silence below.
>
> Oh, I could give him weeping,
> 10   Or I could give him song—
> But how can I give silence
>   My whole life long?

Poem Development: Where is Amalfi? Explain the situation in the first stanza; the second stanza. How do you interpret the last four lines? Weave these conclusions into a complete word picture or story.

QUESTIONNAIRE

CHARLES L. O'DONNELL

Poem Interest: A questionnaire is, generally speaking, a bothersome device used to obtain much information from many people in a short time. But when a Father O'Donnell is inspired to ply Mary with questions you have long wanted answered and to record her perfect answers too, then a questionnaire is no longer a questionnaire—it is a poem.

> WHAT did you think of, Mary,
>   As He looked up from your breast?
> I saw His eyes like stars
>   In the early evening west.
>
> 5 And when you bathed His limbs
>   In waters warm and sweet?
> I loved Him, adorable, perfect
>   From head to perfect feet.

What waking vision stirred you
10   As He slept, small and weak?
For hours and hours I watched
    The little curve of His cheek.

And when the first words came
    At length from His learning lips?
15   I could feel my blood listening
    Down to my finger-tips.

On that amazing day
    Along the temple hall
He taught the Scribes, you thought?—
20   My Boy grows straight and tall.

At Cana when your words
    Hurried His coming hour,
You saw?—I saw His hands,
    Beautiful, with power.

25   Oh, and when at the last
    He was slain by the crowd?
Never of my dear Son
    Was I so fond, so proud.

Then, when His cheek to yours
30   Lay lifeless and cold?
I thought how never now
    Would my Son grow old.

But, ah, on Easter morn
    You had your heart's desire!
35   He came to me at dawn
    And helped me with the fire.

Did you know that He was God?
    From Gabriel's word, of course,
Alpha, Omega, of all
40   The End and the Source.

But, women of all the world
That ever children bore,
Remember, He is my Son,
And human, forevermore.

Poem Development: Most people dislike questionnaires. Do you
think Mary would mind? Does the poem help you to understand Mary
better? Do the answers ring true to Mary as you know her? What do
they reveal of her that escaped you before, or what impression of her do
they deepen in you? Are the questions arranged in any particular order?
Does Mary appear to answer promptly, as if she had the answers at the
tip of her tongue, or does she seem hesitant about her answers? Is not
the last question, in stanza ten, a stupid one for anyone to ask Mary?
Which is emphasized in the poem—the Divinity or the Humanity of
our Lord?

Interpretations: I saw . . . evening west; waking vision; Cana;
coming hour; Gabriel's word; Alpha, Omega.

Significant Expressions: Quote the answer which most surprised
you; the answer which most pleased you; the stanza which best shows
Christ's love for His Mother.

OLD SAUL

Lizette Woodworth Reese

Poem Interest: In a yard near an old colonial farmhouse grew a
cedar tree which had gnarled branches and uneven limbs. A young man
pleaded with his grandfather to be allowed to cut the old thing down.
"It spoils the looks of the lawn," the boy said. "Son," replied the old
man, "I watched my father set out that tree, and I want to see it there
while I live. I think it will last as long as I do." The old grandfather
died the next spring, and when the tree was cut down, it was found
to be hollow and would never have lived another year. In the following poem note how Old Saul had a similar idea to the grandfather's.

I CANNOT think of any word
To make it plain to you,
How white a thing the hawthorn bush
That delicately blew

5   Within a crook of Tinges Lane;
Each May Day there it stood;
And lit a flame of loveliness
For the small neighborhood.

So fragile-white a thing it was,
10   I cannot make it plain,
Or the sweet fumbling of the bees,
Like the break in a rain.

Old Saul lived near. And this his life:—
To cobble for his bread;
15   To mourn a tall son lost at sea;
A daughter worse than dead.

And so, in place of all his lack,
He set the hawthorn-tree;
Made it his wealth, his mirth, his god
20   His Zion to touch and see.

Born English he. Down Tinges Lane
His lad's years came and went,
He saw out there behind his thorn,
A hundred thorns of Kent.

25   At lovers slipping through the dusk,
He shook a lover's head;
Grudged them each flower. It was too white
For any but the dead.

Once on a blurred, wet, silver day,
30   He said to two or three:
"Folks, when I go, pluck yonder bloom,
That I may take with me."

But it was winter when he went,
The road wind-wrenched and torn,
35   They laid upon his coffin lid
A wreath made all of thorn.

Poem Development: Describe the blooming of the hawthorn bush.
In what country is the scene of this poem? For what were the flowers
used? What is the full significance of "silver day"? Explain the last
line of the poem and its symbolism.

Interpretations: Delicately blew; a crook of Tinges Lane; flame of
loveliness; line 14; in place of all his lack; his Zion; lines 23–24; lines
25–26; wind-wrenched; lines 35–36.

TEARS

LIZETTE WOODWORTH REESE

Poem Interest: The poem *Tears* has been said to be "one of the most famous sonnets written by an American." It has been placed upon a bronze tablet which was presented by the pupils, teachers, and alumni in the school in Baltimore where Miss Reese taught for many years. We hear many older people say that life is altogether too brief. Miss Reese says this too, but adds some helpful and sympathetic ideas which are both instructive and comforting.

WHEN I consider Life and its few years—
A wisp of fog betwixt us and the sun;
A call to battle, and the battle done
Ere the last echo dies within our ears;
5   A rose choked in the grass; an hour of fears;
The gusts that past a darkening shore do beat;
The burst of music down an unlistening street—
I wonder at the idleness of tears.
Ye old, old dead, and ye of yesternight,
10 Chieftains, and bards, and keepers of the sheep,
By every cup of sorrow that you had,
Loose me from tears, and make me see aright
How each hath back what once he stayed to weep;
Homer his sight, David his little lad!

Poem Development: Name the things to which the poet compares life. What idea of time do they contain? What feeling or meaning, in relation to Life, do these 8 lines convey to you? What is the poet's idea of tears? How does the poet hope to be made "to see aright"? What was the story of Homer? Tell about David and his little lad. How many lines has a sonnet? Is this poem a sonnet? What is the theme? What is the central thought?

Interpretations: A call to battle; the battle done; an hour of fears; ye old, old dead; ye of yesternight; chieftains; bards; keepers of the sheep; cup of sorrow.

Significant Expressions: What figure of speech do you find in line 1; line 2; line 7? Find three or more metaphors for Life given in the poem. What figure of speech is "cup of sorrow"? Quote a line describing Life. Quote a line showing the shortness of our span of life. Quote a line which shows the afflictions two men endured.

DA YOUNGA 'MERICAN

Thomas Augustine Daly

Poem Interest: For all parents, in all walks of life, there is something mystical in watching their children, flesh of their flesh, grow and evolve, succeeding where the older folk have failed, preparing for places in the world of tomorrow. The self-styled "ole Dago man" of the poem was moved by this inward pride and yearning as he saw "Da Younga 'Merican" fit into the magic new America to which he himself could never fully belong.

I, MYSAL', I feela strange
 Een dees countra. I can no
Mak' mysal' agen an' change
 Eento 'Merican, an' so
5 I am w'at you calla me,
  Justa "dumb ole Dago man."
Alla same my boy ees be
 Smarta younga 'Merican.
Twalv' year ole! but alla same
10 He ees learna soocha lot
He can read an' write hees name—
  Smarta keed? I tal you w'at!

He no talk Italian;
He says: "Dat's for Dagoes speak,
15 I am younga 'Merican,
Dago langwadge mak' me seeck."
Eef you gona tal heem, too,
He ees "leeta Dago," my!
He ees gat so mad weeth you
20 He gon' ponch you een da eye.
Mebbe so you gona mak'
Fool weeth heem—an' mebbe not.
Queeck as flash he sass you back;
Smarta keed? I tal you w'at!

25 He ees moocha " 'shame" for be
Meexa weeth Italian;
He ees moocha 'shame of me—
I am dumb ole Dago man.
Evra time w'en I go out
30 Weetha heem I no can speak
To som'body. "Shut your mout',"
He weell tal me pretta queeck,
"You weell geeve yoursal' away
Talkin' Dago lika dat;
35 Try be 'Merican," he say—
Smarta keed? I tal you w'at!

I am w'at you calla me,
Justa "dumb ole Dago man":
Alla same my boy ees be
40 Smarta younga 'Merican.

Poem Development: Explain the situation in the first stanza. What is the meaning of "I tal you w'at!"? Tell some of the characteristics of Da Younga 'Merican. Is the boy true to life? Interpret the last four lines. What is the central thought of the poem?

Interpretations: Mak' mysal' agen; dumb ole Dago man; smarta younga 'Merican; fool weeth heem.

Significant Expressions: Quote lines which picturize for you the father in this poem-story. Quote lines which express the central thought.

HILLS

Arthur Guiterman

Poem Interest: Hills have a fascination all their own—a challenge to strength—an inspiration to achieve. And oftentimes they symbolize man's loftiest ideals. Keep this in mind while you read the poem.

I never loved your plains,
    Your gentle valleys,
Your drowsy country lanes
    And pleachèd alleys.

5   I want my hills!—the trail
    That scorns the hollow—
Up, up the ragged shale
    Where few will follow.

Up, over wooded crest,
10   And mossy boulder,
With strong thigh, heaving chest,
    And swinging shoulder.

So let me hold my way,
    By nothing halted,
15 Until, at close of day,
    I stand, exalted,

High on my hills of dream—
    Dear hills that know me!
And then how fair will seem
20   The lands below me!

How pure, at vesper-time,
    The far bells chiming!
God, give me hills to climb,
    And strength for climbing!

4. Pleachèd—Alleys through overhanging branches of trees.

Poem Development: The poet starts out with his dislike of the valleys and country lanes, and gives his reasons for not liking them.

What are they? What type of man would say "I want my hills—
where few will follow"? What is the meaning of "by nothing halted"?
What is the comparison in this poem to life? What supplication or
prayer is given in the poem? What are the theme and central thought?

Significant Expressions: Quote lines to describe the trail. Find
two figures of speech. Quote the lines of supplication for living.

THE FACTORIES

Margaret Widdemer

Poem Interest: Vitally important to world welfare of today and
tomorrow is the protest of this poem. When men and women realize
the proper proportion between the lives of human beings and the production of things, then and only then will a new social and economic
structure do away with "the starving of life" which Margaret Widdemer
portrays so well.

I HAVE shut my little sister in from life and light
    (For a rose, for a ribbon, for a wreath across my hair),
I have made her restless feet still until the night,
    Locked from sweets of summer and from wild spring air,
5   I who ranged the meadowlands, free from sun to sun,
    Free to sing and pull the buds and watch the far wings
       fly,
I have bound my little sister till her playing time was
     done—
    Oh, my little sister, was it I? Was it I?

I have robbed my sister of her day of maidenhood
10   (For a robe, for a feather, for a trinket's restlessness),
Shut from Love till dusk shall fall, how shall she know good,
    How shall she go scatheless through the sin-lit dark?
I who could be innocent, I who could be gay,
    I could have love and mirth before the light went by,
15 I have put my sister in her mating-time away—
    Sister, my young sister, was it I? Was it I?

I have robbed my sister of the lips against her breast,
    (For a coin, for the weaving of my children's lace and
      lawn),

Feet that pace beside the loom, hands that cannot rest—
20   How can she know motherhood, whose strength is gone?
I who took no heed of her, starved and labor worn,
    I, against whose placid heart my sleepy gold-heads lie,
Round my path they cry to me, little souls unborn—
    God of Life! Creator! It was I! It was I!

Poem Development: To whom does the poet refer when she writes "I"? What is the picture in line 3? Margaret Widdemer writes against social injustice and especially against child and woman labor. Whom does she mean by "little sister"? What are the things the child misses? What is the stage of life represented in the second stanza? What is the "little sister" denied during this time of life? What stage of life is represented in the third stanza? What is denied the working woman? The poet sees the things denied to her "little sisters" who must work in factories, ironically enough, making beautiful things for other women who can afford to buy them—under a social and industrial system which permits child labor and woman labor. What is the theme of the poem, and its central thought?

Interpretations: Little sister; from life and light; rose, ribbon, wreath; line 3; sweets of summer; wild spring air; free from sun to sun; her playing time; robe, feather, trinket.

Significant Expressions: Quote a line containing a metaphor. Quote three lines of irony.

A FARMER REMEMBERS LINCOLN

Witter Bynner

Poem Interest: Lincoln was most democratic, and there was "none too poor to do him reverence." You may set this scene where you will. Perhaps it is Memorial Day and the place a crossroads grocery store. Someone asks an old war veteran if he ever saw Lincoln. "Lincoln?" he asks . . .

"Lincoln?—
Well, I was in the old Second Maine,
The first regiment in Washington from the Pine Tree State.
Of course I didn't get the *butt* of the clip;
5   We was there for guardin' Washington—
We was all green.

"I ain't never ben to but one theater in my life—
I didn't know how to behave

I ain't never ben since.

10 I can see as plain as my hat the box where he sat in
When he was shot.
I can tell you, sir, there was a panic
When we found our President was in the shape he was in!
Never saw a soldier in the world but what liked him.

15 "Yes, sir. His looks was kind o' hard to forget.
He was a spare man,
An old farmer.
Everything was all right, you know,
But he wasn't a smooth-appearin' man in no ways;
20 Thin faced, long-necked,
And a swellin' kind of a thick lip like.

"And he was a jolly old fellow—always cheerful;
He wan't so high but the boys could talk to him their own
ways.
While I was servin' at the Hospital
25 He'd come in and say, 'You look nice in here,'
Praise us up, you know.
And he'd bend over and talk to the boys—
And he'd talk so good to 'em—so close—
That's why I call him a farmer.
30 I don't mean that everything about him wan't all right, you
understand,
It's just—well, I was a farmer—
And he was my neighbor, anybody's neighbor.

"I guess even you young folks would'a' liked him."

Poem Development: Picture the old farmer. You need little else
than the dialect he uses for a clue to his looks. What does he tell
about himself? Tell about his theater-going. Describe Lincoln as this
farmer pictures him to you. What does he say endeared Lincoln to the
people? What makes these stanzas poetry? What is the theme of the
poem, and the central thought?

Interpretations: Old Second Maine; Pine Tree State; butt of the
clip; line 6; plain as my hat; the box; there was a panic; line 16;
smooth-appearin'; he wan't so high; line 32.

Significant Expressions: Quote lines to describe Lincoln's death. Quote lines to describe Lincoln himself.

A CHANT OUT-OF-DOORS *

MARGUERITE WILKINSON

Poem Interest: It was four o'clock in the morning when two comrades who had been sleeping on the top of a mountain arose to see the great red dawn come up in the eastern sky. The air was brisk and sharp, the dew still heavy on the balsams, the air laden with the freshness of the early morning. On such an occasion could the following lines be chanted with the full mood and feeling which only the out-of-doors can give.

> GOD of grave nights,
> God of brave mornings,
> God of silent noon,
> Hear my salutation!

> 5 For where the rapids rage white and scornful,
> I have passed safely, filled with wonder;
> Where the sweet pools dream under willows,
> I have been swimming, filled with life.

> God of round hills,
> 10 God of green valleys,
> God of clear springs,
> Hear my salutation!

> For where the moose feeds, I have eaten berries;
> Where the moose drinks, I have drunk deep.

Poem Development: To whom does the poet address her lines? What part of life does line 5 symbolize? line 7? What stanza indicates a god of time? a god of places? What can you say of the inspiration which prompted the writing of such a poem? What is the meaning of the whole poem? Do you interpret the whole poem as one of joy, or merely the acquiescence of life?

Significant Expressions: Quote the phrases symbolic of time of one's life. Give the figure of speech in line 5; line 7.

* From *Bluestone* by Marguerite Wilkinson. Reprinted by permission of The Macmillan Company, publishers.

THE MOUNTAIN WOMAN

DuBose Heyward

Poem Interest: It is difficult for those of us who are accustomed to the comforts and benefits of pleasant homes to picture a life among barren mountains—a life almost apart from civilization—a life of grinding toil—a life which permits not even one bit of beauty—a life such as is pictured by the poet.

Among the sullen peaks she stood at bay
And paid life's hard account from her small store.
Knowing the code of mountain wives, she bore
The burden of the days without a sigh;
5   And, sharp against the somber winter sky,
I saw her drive her steers afield that day.

Hers was the hand that sunk the furrows deep
Across the rocky, grudging souther slope.
At first youth left her face, and later hope;
10 Yet through each mocking spring and barren fall,
She reared her lusty brood, and gave them all
That gladder wives and mothers love to keep.

497

And when the sheriff shot her eldest son
Beside his still, so well she knew her part,
15   She gave no healing tears to ease her heart;
But took the blow upstanding, with her eyes
As drear and bitter as the winter skies.
Seeing her then, I thought that she had won.

But yesterday her man returned too soon
20   And found her tending, with reverent touch,
One scarlet bloom; and, having drunk too much,
He snatched its flame and quenched it in the dirt.
Then, like a creature with a mortal hurt,
She fell, and wept away the afternoon.

Poem Development: This poem is written of mountain life in the Great Smokies of western North Carolina. It is very typical of the mountaineers, of whom the poet, Dubose Heyward, wrote a great deal. What was the code of the Mountain Woman? Was there any pleasure in her life? What changes came to her, as expressed in the ninth line? Describe her reactions to the shooting of her son. What does the poet mean by "I thought that she had won"? What was one thing that brought a little happiness to her? Paint a word picture of lines 19–24. Was she capable of tenderness, in spite of the harshness of her life? What does the one scarlet bloom symbolize? What is the theme? What is the central thought?

Interpretations: Line 1; life's hard account; her small store; code of mountain wives; line 5; grudging; souther slope; mocking spring; barren fall; her lusty brood; beside his still; healing tears; took the blow upstanding; her man; mortal hurt.

Significant Expressions: Quote lines to show the life of the Mountain Woman. Quote lines to show her character. Quote a line which tells how she accepted her life. Give the figure of speech in line 8; line 11; line 17; line 22; line 23. Quote a line to show the tenderness in her heart. Quote lines to show her bitter grief.

MARTIN

Joyce Kilmer

Poem Interest: What a kindly impression some people convey! Little traits of personality make them charming. These may be only a cheerful way of greeting, a meticulous way of dressing, a kindly, courteous manner, but the characteristics are so prominent that any thought of the individual always recalls to mind a picture of his special traits. Such was the case with Martin.

WHEN I am tired of earnest men,
Intense and keen and sharp and clever,
Pursuing fame with brush or pen,
Or counting metal disks forever,
5   Then from the halls of Shadowland,
Beyond the trackless purple sea,
Old Martin's ghost comes back to stand
Beside my desk and talk to me.

Still on his delicate pale face
10   A quizzical thin smile is showing,
His cheeks are wrinkled like fine lace,
His kind blue eyes are gay and glowing.
He wears a brilliant-hued cravat,
A suit to match his soft grey hair,
15   A rakish stick, a knowing hat,
A manner blithe and debonair.

How good that he who always knew
That being lovely was a duty,
Should have gold halls to wander through
20   And should himself inhabit beauty.
How like his old unselfish way
To leave those halls of splendid mirth
And comfort those condemned to stay
Upon the dull and sombre earth.

25   Some people ask: "What cruel chance
Made Martin's life so sad a story?"
Martin? Why, he exhaled romance,
And wore an overcoat of glory.
A fleck of sunlight in the street,
30   A horse, a book, a girl who smiled,
Such visions made each moment sweet
For this receptive ancient child.

Because it was old Martin's lot
To be, not make, a decoration,
35   Shall we then scorn him, having not
His genius of appreciation?

Rich joy and love he got and gave;
His heart was merry as his dress;
Pile laurel wreaths upon his grave
40   Who did not gain, but was, success!

Poem Development: The first stanza is introductory to the story of this kindly old gentleman. Is it a good introduction? Describe the "busy world" from which the poet seeks rest. How tranquilly the ghost of Old Martin slips in! Do you like this contrast? Outline the description of Martin, following the same order of details which the poet employs. Is this a logical manner of description? Would this order of details be commendable for a student to follow in writing? Explain lines 17–20. Is the last stanza a good conclusion, both as to form and subject matter? Why did the poet choose laurel wreaths instead of some other flower? What is the whole theme of the poem, and its central thought?

Interpretations: Earnest men; line 2; line 3; metal disks; trackless purple sea; quizzical; thin; like fine lace; rakish stick; knowing hat; line 16; gold halls; inhabit beauty; halls of splendid mirth; he exhaled romance; line 28; ancient child; line 34; genius of appreciation; line 38; laurel wreaths; line 40.

Significant Expressions: Quote two lines to show two types of "earnest men" of this world. Quote the lines telling from whence came Martin's ghost. Quote two lines, either consecutive or separated, which you like best in the poem.

ROUGE BOUQUET

Joyce Kilmer

Poem Interest: In *Rouge Bouquet*, our World War poet, Joyce Kilmer, pays splendid tribute to his comrades who fought and died. Note especially the interesting use of meter.

In a wood they call the Rouge Bouquet
There is a new-made grave today,
Built by never a spade nor pick
Yet covered with earth ten metres thick.
5   There lie many fighting men,
         Dead in their youthful prime,
Never to laugh nor love again
         Nor taste the Summertime.
For Death came flying through the air
10   And stopped his flight at the dugout stair,

Touched his prey and left them there,
   Clay to clay.
He hid their bodies stealthily
In the soil of the land they fought to free
15   And fled away.
Now over the grave abrupt and clear
   Three volleys ring;
And perhaps their brave young spirits hear
   The bugle sing:
20   "Go to sleep!
Go to sleep!
Slumber well where the shell screamed and fell.
Let your rifles rest on the muddy floor,
You will not need them any more.
25   Danger's past;
Now at last,
Go to sleep!"

There is on earth no worthier grave
To hold the bodies of the brave
30   Than this place of pain and pride
Where they nobly fought and nobly died.
Never fear but in the skies
   Saints and angels stand
Smiling with their holy eyes
35   On this new-come band.
St. Michael's sword darts through the air
And touches the aureole on his hair
As he sees them stand saluting there,
   His stalwart sons:
40   And Patrick, Brigid, Columkill
Rejoice that in veins of warriors still
   The Gael's blood runs.
And up to Heaven's doorway floats,
   From the wood called Rouge Bouquet,
45   A delicate cloud of bugle notes
   That softly say:

36. The archangel Michael is represented as a military commander in the
heavenly war against Satan.
40. PATRICK, BRIGID, COLUMKILL—Patron saints of Ireland.
42. GAEL'S BLOOD—Irish blood.

"Farewell! Farewell.
Comrades true, born anew, peace to you!
Your souls shall be where the heroes are

50   And your memory shine like the morning-star.
Brave and dear,
Shield us here.
Farewell!"

Poem Development: The poem tells of the death of many brave men, and how their graves were made on the battle fields of Europe. Death, in the form of enemy shells, is personified in its coming to the dugouts where the soldiers were concealed. Note how taps were played for the dead. Tell of the eulogy which the poet gives for the dead soldiers.

Interpretations: New-made grave; today (when?); line 3; youthful prime; dugout stair; touched his prey; clay to clay; line 14; three volleys ring; muddy floor; place of pain and pride; new-come band; St. Michael's sword; aureole on his hair; Gael.

Significant Expressions: Give the figures of speech in the following: line 8; line 9; line 10; line 22; line 30; line 48; line 50.

TREES

Joyce Kilmer

Poem Interest: Majestically they stand against the earth and sky— have you ever paused to wonder at the loveliness of trees? Joyce Kilmer did, and this is what he thought.

I think that I shall never see
A poem lovely as a tree.

A tree whose hungry mouth is prest
Against the earth's sweet flowing breast;

5   A tree that looks at God all day
And lifts her leafy arms to pray;

A tree that may in summer wear
A nest of robins in her hair;

Upon whose bosom snow has lain;
10   Who intimately lives with rain.

Poems are made by fools like me,
But only God can make a tree.

Poem Development: Is it true that no poem could ever be as lovely as a tree? The picture created by lines 5 and 6 seems a particularly beautiful one. Name the various human attributes the poet gives the tree. What do you think was the poet's mood when he wrote the last two lines? What is the theme? What is the central thought?

Interpretations: Hungry mouth; line 5; leafy arms; in her hair; intimately lives.

Significant Expressions: Quote lines about the tree in summer; in winter. Give the figure of speech in line 2; line 6; line 8.

PRAYER OF A SOLDIER IN FRANCE

JOYCE KILMER

Poem Interest: During the World War, every private in France endured the physical and mental pains of soldiering. But it took a sensitive Catholic soul like Kilmer's to transform them into a prayer and to see in them, with St. Paul, an opportunity to "fill up those things that are wanting of the sufferings of Christ." (*Col.* I, 24.)

> My SHOULDERS ache beneath my pack
> (Lie easier, Cross, upon His back).
>
> I march with feet that burn and smart
> (Tread Holy Feet, upon my heart).
>
> 5   Men shout at me who may not speak
> (They scourged Thy back and smote Thy cheek).
>
> I may not lift a hand to clear
> My eyes of salty drops that sear.
>
> (Then shall my fickle soul forget
> 10   Thy Agony of Bloody Sweat?)
>
> My rifle hand is stiff and numb
> (From Thy pierced palm red rivers come).
>
> Lord, Thou didst suffer more for me
> Than all the hosts of land and sea.
>
> 15   So let me render back again
> This millionth of Thy gift. Amen.

Poem Development: Joyce Kilmer ended one of his last letters thus: "Pray for me, dear Father, that I may love God more and that I may be unceasingly conscious of Him—that is the greatest desire I have." What evidence is there in this poem that he was realizing his "greatest desire"?

Significant Expressions: Quote the lines that are the heart of the prayer. Quote the couplet which you consider most military in tone.

AS WINDS THAT BLOW AGAINST A STAR

(For Aline)

JOYCE KILMER

Poem Interest: When Joyce Kilmer dedicated his poem, "Thanksgiving," to his friend and fellow-poet, John Bunker, he did not mean to address the words of that poem to him. But when he inscribed the present poem to his wife, Aline, he was also, if we may trust those who know her well, addressing her as one in whom he knew its truth was verified.

> Now by what whim of wanton chance
> Do radiant eyes know sombre days?
> And feet that shod in light should dance
> Walk weary and laborious ways?
>
> 5 But rays from Heaven, white and whole,
> May penetrate the gloom of earth;
> And tears but nourish, in your soul,
> The glory of celestial mirth.
>
> The darts of toil and sorrow, sent
> 10 Against your peaceful beauty, are
> As foolish and as impotent
> As winds that blow against a star.

Poem Development: The first stanza raises a general question. Tell briefly what the question is. The second stanza gives a possible answer. What is it? The third finds another answer in a specific example. Tell how tears may nourish the glory of celestial mirth in a soul.

Interpretations: Wanton chance; feet shod in light; rays white and whole; celestial mirth; peaceful beauty.

Significant Expressions: Which stanza do you consider most quotable? Why did the poet choose to make the last line the title of his poem?

A BLUE VALENTINE

(For Aline)

JOYCE KILMER

Poem Interest: Joyce Kilmer had little use for free verse—you will find no other example of it in his poetry—and wrote this poem, we are told, as a literary lark. He was much surprised at its popularity; but popular it certainly became. "The beautiful lady" is, of course, his wife, Aline.

MONSIGNORE,
Right Reverend Bishop Valentinus,
Sometime of Interamna, which is called Ferni,
Now of the delightful Court of Heaven,
5   I respectfully salute you,
I genuflect
And I kiss your episcopal ring.

It is not, Monsignore,
The fragrant memory of your holy life,
10   Nor that of your shining and joyous martyrdom,
Which causes me now to address you.
But since this is your august festival, Monsignore,
It seems appropriate to me to state
According to a venerable and agreeable custom,
15   That I love a beautiful lady.
Her eyes, Monsignore,
Are so blue that they put lovely little blue reflections
On everything that she looks at,
Such as a wall
20   Or the moon
Or my heart.
It is like the light coming through blue stained glass,
Yet not quite like it,
For the blueness is not transparent,
25   Only translucent.
Her soul's light shines through,
But her soul cannot be seen.

It is something elusive, whimsical, tender, wanton,
    infantile, wise
And noble.
30 She wears, Monsignore, a blue garment,
Made in the manner of the Japanese.
It is very blue—
I think that her eyes have made it more blue,
Sweetly staining it
35 As the pressure of her body has graciously given it
    form.
Loving her, Monsignore,
I love all her attributes;
But I believe
That even if I did not love her
40 I would love the blueness of her eyes,
And her blue garment, made in the manner of the
    Japanese.

Monsignore,
I have never before troubled you with a request.
The saints whose ears I chiefly worry with my pleas
    are the most exquisite and maternal Brigid,
45 Gallant Saint Stephen, who puts fire in my blood,
And your brother bishop, my patron,
The generous and jovial Saint Nicholas of Bari.
But, of your courtesy, Monsignore,
Do me this favour:
50 When you this morning make your way
To the Ivory Throne that bursts into bloom with
    roses because of her who sits upon it,
When you come to pay your devoir to our Lady,
I beg you, say to her:
"Madame, a poor poet, one of your singing servants
    yet on earth,
55 Has asked me to say that at this moment he is
    especially grateful to you
For wearing a blue gown."

Poem Development: Richard Le Gallienne speaks of this poem as
"that masterpiece of playful reverence." How well does his designation

fit? Do you like the poet's favorite saints: Brigid, Stephen, and Nicholas? Does the object of the poet's gratitude described in the last line surprise you? Why? Why was he especially grateful to our Lady for wearing a blue gown?

Interpretations: Fragrant memory; venerable custom; not transparent, only translucent; line 28; pay your devoir.

Significant Expressions: What effect is produced by the frequent repetition of the word "Monsignore" throughout the poem?

CHRISTMAS

ALINE KILMER

Poem Interest: Sometimes upon the gayety of Christmas, home-feast of the year, there intrude sobering thoughts of the missing members of the family circle, those who are dead or absent. When Mrs. Kilmer wrote this poem, her husband was in France; her daughter Rose was dead.

"AND shall you have a tree," they say,
"Now one is dead and one away?"

Oh, I shall have a Christmas tree!
Brighter than ever it shall be;
5   Dressed out with coloured lights to make
The room all glorious for your sake.

And under the Tree a Child shall sleep
Near shepherds watching their wooden sheep.
Threads of silver and nets of gold,
10   Scarlet bubbles the Tree shall hold,
And little glass bells that tinkle clear.
I shall trim it alone but feel you near.

And when Christmas Day is almost done,
When they all grow sleepy one by one,
15   When Kenton's books have all been read,
When Deborah's climbing the stairs to bed,

I shall sit alone by the fire and see
Ghosts of you both come close to me.
For the dead and the absent always stay
20   With the one they love on Christmas Day.

Poem Development: What would make this poem a most welcome Christmas gift to Joyce Kilmer in far-away France? To whom is the poem addressed? How does the poet show her understanding of the true meaning of Christmas?

Interpretations: Why is the Christmas tree to be "brighter than ever" this year? What sense is there in making the "room all glorious" for the sake of one who will not see it? What is the meaning of "under the Tree a Child shall sleep"?

Significant Expressions: Which are the gayest lines? The most sombre? The most musical? The most offhand?

I HAVE A RENDEZVOUS WITH DEATH

Alan Seeger

Poem Interest: Alan Seeger was at the front in the World War. Just before going into battle—the battle in which he was killed—he wrote the following poem.

I HAVE a rendezvous with Death
At some disputed barricade,
When Spring comes back with rustling shade
And apple-blossoms fill the air—
5   I have a rendezvous with Death
When Spring brings back blue days and fair.

It may be he shall take my hand
And lead me into his dark land
And close my eyes and quench my breath—
10   It may be I shall pass him still.

I have a rendezvous with Death
On some scarred slope of battered hill,
When Spring comes round again this year
And the first meadow-flowers appear.

15 God knows 'twere better to be deep
Pillowed in silk and scented down,
Where Love throbs out in blissful sleep,
Pulse nigh to pulse and breath to breath,
Where hushed awakenings are dear. . . .
20 But I've a rendezvous with Death
At midnight in some flaming town,
When Spring trips north again this year,
And I to my pledged word am true,
I shall not fail that rendezvous.

Poem Development: The first two lines state the prophecy. The third and fourth lines are memories of home, then his thoughts are snatched back to the impending fate. In the second stanza, the poet says that he may die, but in line 10 he tells of a slight hope of evading the grim reaper. Again in the third stanza, the thought of his home comes back until he turns to the fateful rendezvous. What characteristic of the poet is seen in line 23? What theme runs through the whole poem?

Interpretations: Rendezvous; disputed barricade; blue days and fair; dark land; quench my breath; line 10; scarred slope; battered hill; line 16; lines 17–19; flaming town; trips north again.

Significant Expressions: Quote all the lines in the poem where the poet's thoughts wander back home. His home was in New York. How is this indicated in the poem? Which is the saddest line of the poem?

FOR A PICTURE OF SAINT CATHERINE

Sister Maris Stella

Poem Interest: According to legends grown up around her name, St. Catherine of Alexandria vanquished and converted fifty Greek philosophers appointed by the Emperor Maxentius to refute her in a public argument. Persisting in her refusal to become the wife of the pagan Emperor, she was whipped and imprisoned. Later a wheel set with razors, on which she was placed for execution, is said to have broken, the razors flying about and hacking the throats of the bystanders. Finally she was beheaded, and angels carried off her body to Mount Sinai. Catherine is venerated as the patroness of jurists, philosophers, students, millers, wheelmakers, and teachers.

In the picture which evoked this poem, painted by a student at the College of St. Catherine in St. Paul, the saint is represented with remarkable eyes. In these eyes the poet reads the mighty soul of the heavenly patron of philosophers, who pursued wisdom, sanctity, and suffering with never-faltering step.

So ARE their eyes who seek infinity,
who stand, cloud-girt and bound with shining stars,
upon the high white hilltops by that sea
whose waters wash eternal Heaven's bars.
5 So are their eyes who burn with deep desire
for truth and righteousness and heights unknown;
with yearning, high, swift-wingèd, strong as fire
they tread the thorny mountain paths alone.
So are their eyes who gaze upon the sun
10 like mighty eagles suns may never blind,
guarding of all fair treasures only one—
the fierce and fragile burden of the mind.
So are their eyes who count it endless gain
to wear for beauty coronals of pain.

Poem Development: The soul of Catherine, the poet lets us know, is in her eyes. Can you think of anything that better reveals the soul of a man than his eyes? With what great souls is Catherine compared? What qualities are revealed by the fourfold comparison? Which comparison stirs your soul most?

Interpretations: Who seek infinity; strong as fire; the fierce and fragile burden of the mind; coronals of pain.

Significant Expressions: Quote lines that express the loftiness of St. Catherine's godly ambition. Whither do the thorny mountain paths lead? What emotion is aroused by the lines "Who gaze upon the sun like mighty eagles suns may never blind"? How did St. Catherine look on the pain which most men flee? Which lines would most commend themselves to philosophers, of whom she is the heavenly patroness?

COMMUNION

Sister M. Madeleva

Poem Interest: Whiteness, the cold physicist tells us, contains all colors. Whiteness, the soulful poet shows us, contains much more meaning than that, when the whiteness of Holy Communion is our theme.

HAVING held you
I have held whiteness intense and austere as the snows that rest
On that far, lone mountain, against my breast.
I have held whiteness more shining and splendid than clouds that start
5 In still skies of summer, upon my heart.
I have held whiteness more wistful and dear than a child's alarms,
Than a flower upfolded, within my arms.
I have held whiteness that burns like a flame, that broods like a dove
In my soul forever,—I have held love.

Poem Development: What images does the poet use to show the richness of the whiteness of which she speaks? What are the differences between these qualities of whiteness? What feeling is associated with each? If the poem reaches a climax, where is it?

Interpretations: Intense; austere, shining and splendid; still skies; wistful; child's alarms; upfolded; broods.

Significant Expressions: Which kind of whiteness most appeals to you? Why? Quote examples of alliteration.

AS ONE FINDING PEACE

Sister M. Madeleva

Poem Interest: A maid, just now come to womanhood, is ecstatically surprised by God's overpowering love of her. Fearful of losing Him, she prays that this strong love may compass her like a sea. For, unlike human love, this love surrendered to brings peace—even though it does mean that she must be like a strong wall and door barring entrance to all save Him. The first fine rapturous peace finally gives way to the even more rapturous but profounder peace that comes of being His silent captive, silent in the company of His sure love.

THE secret of the King possesses me
Unutterably.
I am a child to sudden woman grown
Who never yet has known
5   Invasion so imperious, so complete,
Blindly and madly sweet.
I am a bud to sudden blossom blown,
Intoxicate, replete
With fragrance most divinely not its own.
10   I am dew thirstily drunk up
Out of dawn's lifted cup
I am my own impotent, daring self, plunged in a sea
Ecstatically!

O God, encompass me!
15   Be infinitely mine to hold, to bound me;
Absorb, consume, encompass and confound me;
Be in me and beneath me and above me;
O Father, love me, love me!
Tremendously be,
20   Strong God, my sea.

In ultimate joy upon this Lover's breast
I come to rest.
Peace, like a song,
Envelopes me:
25   Peace, like the night,
Folds me in conscious, beautiful delight.
Never has human love held me in tranquil thrall,
For not to human love does peace belong.
What if I be for the Lord God a wall,
30   Beauteous as cedar and as cedar strong;
What if I be a door, and sealed to all save Him,
Cunningly joined, guarded by flashing cherubim?
I am a door, a wall, a tower of passionate strength
Around which multitudinously throng
35   Wild ecstasies, wild joys, unending blisses,
A God's caresses and a Father's kisses.

Presently let this rapture in profounder rapture cease;
A silver bulwark of wrought silence be,
My Father, since that I am come at length,
40 Captive and free,
Into Your presence as one finding peace.

Poem Development: Who is the King, and what is His secret which so unutterably possesses the maiden? By what figures of speech does she express the suddenness of her realization of the bliss that is hers? In the second stanza is her attitude more that of possessiveness or of surrender? Why does she pray the Strong God to be her sea?

Interpretations: Invasion so imperious; line 11; to hold, to bound me; confound me; lines 24–25; lines 32–33; a silver bulwark of wrought silence.

Significant Expressions: Select the lines which best express the particular mood of each stanza. Study the poet's very effective use of adverbs: unutterably, thirstily, and the like. Quote the simile which you find most striking. What is the most powerful metaphor in the poem?

LAUDATE PUERI DOMINUM*

Sister M. Thérèse

Poem Interest: Praising the Lord is not only the duty of adults, but of children too. We are indebted to Sister M. Thérèse for letting us see how a child at an organ can praise the Lord and set all Heaven listening.

Today God's organ shall have holiday
From ritual mode and Palestrinian air
Wedded to cloistered voices sweet in prayer—
For Rita Alice climbs the loft to play . . .
5 Strong in her blithe seven years, and seeming gay
For such bold venture. Tunes from a gypsy-fair
Ripple the reverent dusk, and debonair
Snatches of childish dance and roundelay.

Saints marble-gowned, and carven seraphim
10 Start from their ancient niches, as such hymn
Mellows the hush with magical lingerings—
Where little cherubs smile behind their wings.
One looks through tears—His parted lips abreath—
Remembering songs and games at Nazareth.

* Laudate pueri dominum—Praise the Lord, ye children. *Psalm* 112.

Poem Development: What new turn of thought does the sonnet take in the sestet? What marked difference do you observe between the closing couplet and the other lines in the sestet? Why is the title of the poem given in Latin rather than in English? In what type of chapel is the organ which Rita Alice plays? What kind of music is usually heard there? What makes the little cherubs smile?

Interpretations: Ritual mode; Palestrinian air; cloistered voices; debonair snatches of childish dance; magical lingerings.

Significant Expressions: Quote lines to describe the organist. Quote lines to describe the music which she plays.

TO CATHERINE

Sister Mary St. Virginia

Poem Interest: It would be a privilege to know the Catherine who merits the beautifully sincere tribute of these lines. Perhaps they will suggest to you a "Catherine" of your acquaintance whom the verses fit equally well.

You are the little room in Nazareth
Wherein He dreamed;
You are the tomb that held Him close in death
Till morning gleamed.

5   You are the beauty passionate and sweet
Of Magdalen
Crushed into nard, poured out upon His feet
Away from men.

You are the word He held upon His tongue,
10   Yet never said;
You are the shining sword He never swung
Unscabbarded.

You are the music in the lute afar
No hand has swept;
15   You are the burning undiscovered star
The night has kept.

Poem Development: The poet resorts to seven distinct metaphors to express her message. What common element binds all seven into a

unity? Show how each metaphor makes its peculiar contribution to the
general theme of the poem. What sort of person must she be to whom
this poem was written? Is she of the Mary or Martha type? Would
she love the public life or the hidden life more?

Interpretations: Till morning gleamed; crushed into nard; away
from men; the lute afar.

Significant Expressions: Quote the lines that express the most intense feeling. Quote the lines that you find most musical.

THE DEPARTURE

SISTER MARY JEREMY

Poem Interest: Sometimes after the departure of a friend one feels
the separation more keenly than at the very moment of leave-taking.
Perhaps it was so with the poet, who after the last farewell was past began
to realize not only the sorrows of the departing one but also the comfort
and peace that her presence had given to her friends.

> WHAT you took with you no one knew.
> The night was cold for setting forth;
> The wet leaves stirred without a sound
> Till the wind wheeled and galloped north.
> 5   We listened, but the rain came on
> And no one knew when you had gone.
>
> Between our pity and our grief
> That would not break itself in words
> What holiest of signs should pass?
> 10   The sea of swords, the hill of glass
> That every questing princess knows
> Were waiting in the dark for you.
> You would remember what to do.
>
> But meanwhile lonely clamors rose
> 15   Chilling the heart with prophecy
> Till your remembered silences
> Allured them to tranquility

As if a star should leave a wake
Of peace above some stricken land,
20   Saying beyond a ravaged hill,
"This world small-spinning in God's hand
Is His dear jewel still."

Poem Development: Farewells are commonly painful. What sort of departure is referred to in the poem that it should be more than commonly sorrowful? How do the circumstances of the departure make it very somber? Why do you suppose the grief of those who remained behind "would not break itself in words"? Do you remember the fairy stories of the sea of swords through which the princess must pass unscathed and the hill of glass which she must successfully climb to reach her beloved prince? What do the sea of swords and hill of glass symbolize here? What prince was this princess seeking? Is it true that *every* princess knows the sea of swords, the hill of glass? How could the poet be so sure that the departed one would remember what to do? With what sort of prophecy would lonely rumors be chilling the hearts of those left behind? In days before her final setting forth how must the departed one have sometimes quieted the worried souls who came in distress to her? What must have been the constant refrain in her words of reassurance? In the last stanza, with what does the poet compare the departed one? With what, the troubled souls of those bereft of her presence? What is the dominant mood of the poem?

Interpretations: Line 1; line 9; the dark; a wake of peace; this world small-spinning.

Significant Expressions: Quote a simile from the poem. Cite the lines that best reveal the character of the departed. What line best expresses the poet's esteem for the departed? Find in the last stanza an example of personification.

JUNÍPERO SERRA

Annette McCarty

Poem Interest: Padre Junípero, as you must realize if you have read the chapter from his biography by Agnes Repplier which appears in this book, would have been pleased with this poem. The poet shows a sympathetic understanding of the goal of all Father Junípero's journeyings, the motivation of all his labors; and echoes the prayer that was often on his lips and always in his heart.

ALONG the King's Highway we see you pass,
   Brown-robed, with dusty sandals on your feet;
     But Castile's roses scent the air for you,
     And mocking birds sing in the heaven's blue,
5   And all the weary, lonely miles are sweet
      With high resolves to fill the desert ways,
     With busy peoples happy in His praise.

And who are we that we should pity you
   Tired of body—we, the sick of soul?
10   Oh, Father Serra, let your mission bell
     Ring in our hearts to tell us all is well!
Help us to make your California whole!
   Let every lovely, purple mountain peak
   Proclaim your Saviour whom your children seek.

Poem Development: What marked differences in the character of the first and second stanzas can you discover? What is the more musical Spanish name for the King's Highway? What made Padre Serra's travels from mission to mission along that highway painful? What solace in his weariness did nature offer him? What hopes buoyed up his soul as he plodded on? Why does the poet feel that Fray Junípero deserves less pity than we? How would the ringing of the mission bell tell us that all is well? What does the poet imply is needed to make California whole?

Interpretations: Castile's roses; lonely miles; high resolves; sick of soul; ring in our hearts; purple mountain peak.

Significant Expressions: What lines best suggest California's beauties? What short phrase evokes a whole picture of the California missions? What line tells us where the poet resides? What figure of speech do you find in the last two lines?

EXTENSIVE READING PROGRAM—POETRY

THE COLONIAL PERIOD (1607–1765)

Anne Dudley Bradstreet
Contemplations
The Flesh and the Spirit
Longing for Heaven

Michael Wigglesworth
The Day of Doom
Thomas Godfrey
Juvenile Poems

THE REVOLUTIONARY PERIOD (1765–1800)

Ballads
Nathan Hale
Yankee Doodle
The Battle of the Kegs
Derry-Down
Philip Freneau
Captain Barney's Victory
The British Prison Ship
To a Honey Bee
To a Caty-Did

John Trumbull
M'Fingal
Timothy Dwight
Greenfield Hill
The Conquest of Canaan
Joel Barlow
The Columbiad
The Hasty Pudding
Joseph Hopkinson
Hail, Columbia

THE NATIONAL PERIOD (1800–1865)

THE NEW ENGLAND POETS

William Cullen Bryant
A Forest Hymn
Song of Marion's Men
The Death of the Flowers
The Prairies
Robert of Lincoln
The Battlefield
June
The Past
The Death of Lincoln
Ralph Waldo Emerson
Good-Bye
Give All to Love
Days
A Fable
Threnody
Terminus
Compensation
Thought
Forbearance
The Apology

Henry Wadsworth Longfellow
The Building of the Ship
The Skeleton in Armor
The Bells of San Blas
Mad River
The Birds of Killingworth
The Saga of King Olaf
A Psalm of Life
The Old Clock on the Stairs
Loss and Gain
Ladder of St. Augustine
John Greenleaf Whittier
Snowbound
Skipper Ireson's Ride
The Barefoot Boy
In School Days
The Trailing Arbutus
Barclay of Ury
Conductor Bradley
The Wishing Bridge
The Corn Song

Oliver Wendell Holmes
  The Deacon's Masterpiece
  Old Ironsides
  The Height of the Ridiculous
  Contentment
  To an Insect
  Dorothy Q
  Hymn of Trust
  The Frost Spirit
  Bill and Joe

James Russell Lowell
  The Vision of Sir Launfal
  Commemoration Ode
  Aladdin
  The Heritage
  The Singing Leaves
  The Finding of the Lyre
  For an Autograph
  O Beautiful! My Country
  Beaver Brook

THE SOUTHERN POETS

Edgar Allan Poe
  Annabel Lee
  The City in the Sea
  The Valley of Unrest
  Ulalume
  The Lake
  Romanc
  Lenore

Henry Timrod
  Carolina
  The Cotton Boll
  Spring

Paul Hamilton Hayne
  MacDonald's Raid
  The Mocking Bird

  Midsummer in the South
  In Harbor

Abram Joseph Ryan
  The Sword of Lee
  The Deathless Dead
  Life of the Immaculate Conception
  Feast of the Sacred Heart

Sidney Lanier
  The Symphony
  Tampa Robins
  Life and Song
  The Mocking Bird
  The Power of Prayer

OTHER POETS OF THE NATIONAL PERIOD

Richard Henry Wilde
  My Life Is Like the Summer Rose

Fitz-Greene Halleck (1790–1867)
  Marco Bozzaris

Joseph Rodman Drake
  The American Flag

George P. Morris (1802–1864)
  Woodman, Spare That Tree

William Gilmore Simms
  The Swamp Fox
  The Slain Eagle

Charles Fenno Hoffman
  Monterey

Alexander Beaufort Meek
  Land of the South
  The Mocking Bird

John G. Saxe
  The Blind Men and the Elephant
  Pyramus and Thisbe

Josiah Gilbert Holland
  Bitter-Sweet
  Gradatim

Theodore O'Hara
  The Bivouac of the Dead

Francis O. Ticknor
  Little Giffen

Thomas Buchanan Reed
  Sheridan's Ride

John Reuben Thompson
  Music in the Camp

Bayard Taylor
  A Song of the Camp
  Bedouin Song

The Transition Period (1865–1900)

THE EASTERN AND SOUTHERN POETS

Walt Whitman
Mannahatta
Give Me the Splendid Silent Sun
O Captain! My Captain!
When Lilacs Last in the Door-
yard Bloom'd
John Bannister Tabb
The Stranger
Goldenrod
Nekros
The Postulant

The Sacrament
The Agony
Emily Dickinson
A Snowflake
To Fight Aloud Is Very Brave
Indian Summer
The Little Stone
Exultation
Madison Julius Cawein
To a Wind-Flower
The Man Hunt

THE MIDWESTERN AND WESTERN POETS

James Whitcomb Riley
The Old Swimmin' Hole
The Raggedy Man
Out to Old Aunt Mary's
Knee-Deep in June
An Old Sweetheart of Mine
Francis Bret Harte
Grizzly
The Reveille
Joaquin Miller
Westward Ho!
Crossing the Plains
For Those Who Fail

Richard Hovey
The Wander Lovers
Unmanifest Destiny
Bliss Carman
Daisies
Joys of the Road
Edward Rowland Sill
Solitude
Dare You
Eugene Field
Jest 'Fore Christmas
Ashes on the Slide
In the Firelight

OTHER POETS OF THE TRANSITION PERIOD

Lucy Larcom
The Brown Thrush
Calling the Violet
John Townsend Trowbridge
Darius Green and His Flying
Machine
Francis Miles Finch
The Blue and the Gray
Thomas Bailey Aldrich
Memory
A Snowflake
Edmund Clarence Stedman
The Hand of Lincoln
Honest Abe

Celia Thaxter
The Sandpiper
The Scarecrow
Charles Warren Stoddard
The Bells of San Gabriel
Joel Chandler Harris
Revival Hymn
Irwin Russell
The Song of the Banjo
Nebuchadnezzar
Samuel Minturn Peck
The Grapevine Swing
Aunt Jemima's Quilt
John Hay
Jim Bludso

Walter Malone
Opportunity
William Vaughn Moody
Gloucester Moors

Crane, Stephen
War Is Kind
A Man Said to the Universe

THE TWENTIETH CENTURY (1900–   )

NEW POETS OF THE EAST

Edwin Markham
Preparedness
The Great Guest Comes
Memory of Good Deeds
Our Israfel
William Rose Benét
How to Catch Unicorns
Night
The Horse Thief
Moons of Grandeur
Amy Lowell
Patterns
Solitaire
Wind and Silver
Night Clouds
Robert Frost
Mowing
The Road Not Taken
Brown's Descent
The Death of the Hired Man
The Cow in Apple Time

Edwin Arlington Robinson
Two Men
The Master
John Evereldown
The House on the Hill
Flammonde
Mr. Flood's Party
Calvary
Stephen Vincent Benét
The Mountain Whippoorwill
John Brown's Body
Elinor Wylie
Escape
Velvet Shoes
Nonsense Rhyme
Nets to Catch the Wind
Edna St. Vincent Millay
Renascence
Euclid
Lament
The Pear Tree
Ballad of the Harp Weaver

NEW POETS OF THE MID-WEST

Edgar Lee Masters
Slip Shoe Lovey
Jacob Goodpasture
Hosea Chambers
Old Fiddler Jones
Emily Sparks
Vachel Lindsay
The Santa Fé Trail
The Eagle That Is Forgotten
Simon Legree
*General William Booth Enters
  Into Heaven*

Carl Sandburg
Cool Tombs
Skyscrapers
Washington Monument by Night
Good Morning, America
John G. Neihardt
Cry of the People
Song of Hugh Glass
Song of Three Friends
Sara Teasdale
Spring Night
Swallow Flight

OTHER POETS OF THE TWENTIETH CENTURY

Lizette Woodworth Reese
Spicewood
Ellen Hanging Clothes
A Little Song of Life
A Girl's Mood

Thomas Augustine Daly
Mia Carlotta
Between Two Loves

Fannie Stearns Davis
Up a Hill and a Hill

Sister M. Madeleva
A Question of Lovers
You Ask My Age
Concerning Certain Matters of Dress
Candle-Light

Arthur Guiterman
In the Hospital
Pussy-Willows

Margaret Widdemer
Whistle-Fantasy
Old Books

Joyce Kilmer
Easter
Roofs

Katherine Lee Bates
America, The Beautiful
Love Planted a Rose

Max Eastman
At the Aquarium

Nathalia Crane
The Reading Boy
The Janitor's Boy
The Flathouse Roof

Witter Bynner
A Mocking Bird
Ghosts of Indians

Marguerite Wilkinson
In Vivid Gardens
Bluestone

Hilda Conkling
Water
Hay-Cock
I Keep Wondering

Dana Burnet
Roses in the Subway
The Bread Line
The Riddle

Henry van Dyke
God of the Open Air
The Maryland Yellow-Throat

Alfred Barrett
Cyrano of the Saints
Her Sewing Room
Linen

Aline Kilmer
If I Had Loved You More
Olim Meminisse Juvabit
Candles That Burn
A Wind in the Night

Leonard Feeney
The Teacher
A Saint for Sunday Morning
That Family Overhead
Ruins

Louise Imogen Guiney
The Squall
The Knight Errant
Cobwebs
The Precept of Peace

Charles L. O'Donnell
In the Upper Room
Song

Thomas Walsh
Ad Astra
Jungle Dance
Egidio of Coimbra

Mary Blanche Kelly
Swallow Song
Silentium Altum
Horizons

Theodore Maynard
The World's Miser
O Felix Culpa

Thomas B. Feeney
Favorites
The Secret
Dialogue

THE ESSAY

THE ESSAY AS A TYPE OF LITERATURE

The Nature of an Essay

The reading of a group of essays, such as are included in this volume, is in effect an informal meeting with a company of distinguished persons who know how to talk. Their lives may have the hairbreadth quality of adventures in far countries, or be bounded in the nutshell of home, kindred, office, and community. The really significant thing about them is that they like to play with their minds, to romp with ideas, to explore the world of fact, fancy and opinion. Hence they write essays.

An essay is, then, an attempt to put on paper some meditations on a chosen subject which interest the author, and for which he solicits the interest of the reader. It may be written as a letter, a public address, an editorial, a magazine article, or a book review. The form is little; the spirit everything. All that we require of the essayist is that he follow a train of thought to something like a conclusion, and that along the way he point out to us some new ideas. He may lead us by a devious and rambling path, but, if he keep the mood which attracted us to him, we shall vote him delightful company, and part from him with regret.

The Essay Reveals Personality

Consequently, the essay is, more than any other form of literature—with the possible exception of lyric poetry—the full revelation of the personality of the author. He may speak to us in the first person or the third; he may address us directly or be seemingly unconscious of our presence. He may air his personal prejudices, or sift some of ours. He may treat of habits, tendencies, movements, or morals. But before he has finished, he has, consciously or unconsciously, told us something of himself. From this cross-section of his mind, we are able, in some sense at least, to reconstruct the whole man. But Michel de Montaigne, father of the modern essay, summed it all up in the Preface to his *Essais,* first published in 1580, when he said, "It is myselfe I pourtray."

It is equally true that the essays of a nation are self-revealing. To read a representative group of essays from any country is like listening in on a cross-section—if conversation can be sectioned—of that country's polite conversation. When we read the essays of America, we are really listening to ourselves talk. And in so doing, many are the things we learn about ourselves. Histories and acts of Congress record the business of national growth. Literature discloses the humanness behind all that. The essays which follow unfold the personality of a great people. A sort of composite American emerges in friendly detail. There is his energy, his love of fun, his high idealism, his delight in the out-of-doors, his sense of fair-play, his liking for people, his simple forthright nature. These are American traits, and nowhere are they more truly mirrored than in the American essay.

THE HISTORY OF THE AMERICAN ESSAY

The Colonial and Revolutionary Periods (1607–1800)

General Characteristics

During the Colonial and Revolutionary Periods the essay was unknown. Prose there was in abundance—journals, diaries, histories, letters, sermons, orations—but not the pleasant familiar essay. When the country was young, there was little time for small talk. There were forests to clear, Indians to fight, an oppressive mother country to combat, and a nation to set up. Out of such stirring activity grew the sober writings of a number of men who deserve brief mention here.

John Woolman (1720–1772)

One book of our early Colonial Period which is sure of a permanent place in our literature is the *Journal* of John Woolman. Woolman was a New Jersey tailor and a Quaker. His *Journal* is a record of his journeys to various places in the colonies, interspersed with his comment on slavery, war, and other evils, and here and there revealing his mind turned inward in self-examination. The book is written in a simple, clear, unaffected style.

Samuel Sewall (1652–1730)

Sewall was a Harvard graduate and at one time Chief Justice of the Supreme Court of Massachusetts. In this latter capacity he was one of those who sat at the trial of the Salem witches. He afterwards confessed that some of his rulings in this trial were wrong and for the last thirty-nine years of his life he spent one day a year in fasting and prayer by way of penance. He was one of the first men in New England to raise his voice against slavery, publishing a tract against it in 1700. The most interesting thing which came from his pen, however, is his diary.

Hector St. John de Crèvecœur (1731–1813)

Born of a noble family in Normandy, De Crèvecœur was educated in England and moved to America when he was twenty-three. Here he engaged in farming, first in New England and then in Pennsylvania.

He is remembered for his *Letters from an American Farmer* which give a pleasing portrayal of rural life and scenes in America.

Historians of the Period

Among the historians of the period, the first writer of prominence was Captain John Smith, founder of the first colony in Virginia. His pamphlet entitled *A True Relation of Some Occurrences and Accidents of Noate as Hath Hapned Since the First Planting of the Colony* contains an account of the first year in the life of the Virginia colony and is usually regarded as the first book in American literature. Another southern writer who deserves mention is Colonel William Byrd (1674–1744), author of *The Westover MSS, or The History of the Dividing Line Run in 1728.* Two historians of the northern colonies were Governor William Bradford (1590–1657), author of the *History of the Plymouth Plantation* and Governor John Winthrop (1588–1649), remembered for his *History of New England.*

THE NATIONAL PERIOD (1800–1885)

General Characteristics

The story of the American essay is briefly told. There was no long, slow development. Rather the emergence was like the flowering of those magic oriental posies which lie folded within a shell until someone drops them into water, whereupon they burst into instant and perfect bloom. So suddenly did the essay appear in American literature.

After the turn into the nineteenth century, the new nation paused to draw breath. Her government established, almost at once she prospered. With prosperity came leisure, and with leisure—the essay.

Washington Irving began it. The comfortable circumstances of his family paralleled the growing wealth and ease of the nation. Not bound too strictly by the need of making a living, he found time to read, to browse, to travel, and to write. He made his writing an art and a diversion, two certain marks of the essayist.

While Irving was still busy writing, other essayists began to appear, and by the middle of the century there was a sort of literary circle centered about Concord, Massachusetts, and the nurture of the American essay was in its hands. This Concord group was a literary aristocracy. Men were admitted to it if they had wealth of ideas. Money mattered not at all. Henry David Thoreau who could and did live for six months on twenty-five dollars was no less welcome than Longfellow or Lowell. The circle included poets, lecturers, scientists, journalists. All lived in or near Concord. Most of them were closely attached to Harvard as alumni or instructors. All were idealists interested in philosophy and culture. Other writers of the day felt their influence, and there is a sober undertone to most of the nineteenth century essays. The lives of these writers help to explain their works.

Washington Irving (1783–1859)

Irving's years span the interesting period between the presidency of Washington (for whom he was named) and the election of Lincoln. He was born in New York City in April, 1783, the eleventh and youngest child of well-to-do parents. His schooling was mostly private and somewhat intermittent. In his twenty-first year he was threatened with consumption and was sent abroad for his health. In two years' time he returned cured, to spend his next twelve years in America. It was during this period that he undertook the publication of the *Salmagundi Papers* with his brother William as one of the co-editors and that he brought out the rollicking Knickerbocker history.

In 1815 he sailed for England where at first he traveled at will, making friends with many writers—among them, Sir Walter Scott. In 1819, his brothers' business failed, and Irving began to write in earnest. *The Sketch Book of Geoffrey Crayon, Gent.* was the first book to appear. When it proved successful in England as well as in America, his literary career was assured. Thereafter, Irving produced with his pen a fortune for himself and his family. He remained abroad for seventeen years, but the last years of his life were spent at "Sunnyside," his home at Tarrytown on the Hudson River. There in November of 1859 he died, and there in Sleepy Hollow Cemetery he is buried.

Three scenes form the background for most of Irving's works— New York, England, and Spain. The works that endeared him to the American public—*Rip Van Winkle, The Legend of Sleepy Hollow, The Knickerbocker History of New York*—these have their setting in picturesque old New York and mirror the quaintness of its Dutch settlers. The essays from the *Sketch Book* and *Bracebridge Hall* which won him his first international fame, have an English scene and flavor drawn from his long residence in the British Isles. His more serious historical studies such as *The Life of Columbus* and *The Conquest of Granada* are the result of an equally long residence in Spain. Irving's style is reflective of his day and of his cosmopolitan life. His sentences are long and elaborate; his vocabulary is enormous. Many of his essays are wordy and sentimental. But for his gracious old world manner, his quaint charm, and his sly humor he is still read with appreciation.

Ralph Waldo Emerson (1803–1882)

"The great man is he who in a crowd keeps with perfect sweetness, the independence of solitude." This sentence from *Self-Reliance* almost reflects Emerson's life. We see him, a tall, erect figure moving about the streets of Concord—honored, beloved by all—yet somehow alone. That it is a spiritual aloneness, he himself confesses: "I have no social talent; most of the persons whom I see, I see across a gulf. I can not go to them, nor they come to me." But the perfect sweetness was there. An unusually self-sufficient man, Emerson bore no ill-will to the meanest, weakest person living. He was in manner gentle and kind. His thoughts were on a different plane—on the importance of the immaterial elements of life.

Emerson's philosophy explains his life better than his life explains his philosophy—for Emerson did not choose the easiest way. After a boyhood of hardship and self-sacrifice, young Ralph found himself established as pastor of the Old North Church of Boston. Here life might have fallen into easy, pleasant ways, for he was an eloquent speaker and his pastorate enjoyed him. However, he was troubled by doctrinal doubts. The creed of his church he could not fully accept. A persistent inner voice said, "Trust thyself. Speak thy latent conviction." Emerson obeyed the voice. He resigned his position and renounced the ministry.

He had married the daughter of a merchant. Mrs. Emerson received a share in her father's estate, and even after her tragically early death, this small income continued to provide Emerson with means for a living. To eke out his living, he did occasional preaching and lecturing. The lectures became extremely popular; and the years between 1834 and 1870 were a busy, productive period. During this period appeared such essays as *Nature, Representative Men* and *Society and Solitude.*

Emerson was the inspiration of all the Concord group. He was an idealist and poet as well as a philosopher. His favorite theme was the importance of the individual and the need for faith in oneself. He rebelled against the complexity of civilization. He pleaded for less hurry and more inspiration, more meditation and communion with nature. This doctrine colors the writings of his associates.

After his second marriage, he made his home in the historic "Old Manse." Here his children were born. Here in 1882 he died, mourned not only by his Concord neighbors but by the whole English-speaking world. Indeed, very far-reaching had been the influence of the gentle "sage of Concord."

Oliver Wendell Holmes (1809–1894)

Can you picture a twinkling-eyed physician who preferred making puns to writing out prescriptions? Or a Harvard professor who would rather scribble verses than lecture to his students? Or an authority on anatomy who proved to be the most delightedly-read magazine writer of his day? Such was Oliver Wendell Holmes. For nearly forty years he was professor of anatomy at Harvard—a favorite instructor, by the way—yet for over sixty years he delighted readers in America and England with his verses and essays.

Born in 1809 and educated in the traditional Harvard manner, he became nationally known at twenty-one through his history-making poem *Old Ironsides*. Almost at the same time his reputation as a humorist began to be noised about.

It was not, however, until Holmes was nearly fifty that his genius as an essayist was discovered. In 1857, Lowell was concerned with establishing a new literary magazine and he turned to Holmes for assistance. The Doctor—so all Cambridge knew the professor-physician—responded by furnishing the name, the *Atlantic Monthly*, and by promising to become a regular contributor. In casting about for something to write, Holmes was reminded of two articles he had written twenty-five years before for the *New England Magazine* and decided to go on with the series. Thus *The Autocrat of the Breakfast Table* became a feature of the *Atlantic*. So successful was this whimsical series of essays done as a monologue that other series followed: *The Poet at the Breakfast Table*, *The Professor at the Breakfast Table*, and *Over the Teacups*. The papers are chatty and personal in style. Without doubt if Holmes were living today, he would be a newspaper columnist of the higher order.

Fate must have taken the closing stanza of Holmes' youthful poem *The Last Leaf* as a challenge; for the Doctor did live to be the last leaf of his generation, dying in 1894 at the age of eighty-five years. He gave to the world an illustrious son, bearing the same name, who for three decades served as associate justice of the United States Supreme Court.

Lesser Known Early Essayists

There were, of course, other prose writers in this period. Some of them were very popular in their day and many were gifted writers. They too found the magazine their medium of expression. Several were publishers or journalists. A discussion of the American essay would not be complete without mention of Edgar Allan Poe (1809–1849), who, though known chiefly as a poet and story-teller, produced some interesting critical essays. Particularly significant are *The Philosophy of Composition* and *The Poetic Principle*, expressing as they do the ideas after which he fashioned his own writings and the bases of his ruthless criticisms of such contemporaries as Longfellow and Whittier. Eminent among the publicists was George William Curtis (1824–1892), who was associated with the New York *Tribune* and *Harper's Magazine*.

Essays of the National Period

WOUTER VAN TWILLER

From *The Knickerbocker History of New York*

WASHINGTON IRVING

By Way of Introduction: Believe it or not—once the city of New York fell for a joke. It was way back in 1809, but even then New York was a sophisticated town. Most of its leading inhabitants were of Dutch descent and very proud of the aristocratic *Van's* in their names. For two months there had been rumors and notices of a comprehensive history of New York about to be published. That it would glorify the Dutch ancestors of the present townsfolk was indicated by its title *A History of New York from the Beginning of the World to the End of the Dutch Dynasty*. It appeared, as the notices of the press had promised, on December 6, 1809, in two handsome volumes. The Stuyvesants, the Vanderbilts, the Van Rensselaers hastened to buy.

Imagine yourself one Walter Van Twiller. You hurry home from the bookstore with your two volumes; you feverishly scan the index for the name of your great-great-grandfather who had been a governor of old New York. Yes, there it is, Book III, Chapter I, "In Which is Recorded the Golden Reign of Wouter Van Twiller." You thumb back the pages. You read—

THE renowned Wouter (or Walter) Van[1] Twiller was descended from a long line of Dutch burgomasters, who had successively dozed away their lives and grown fat upon the bench of magistracy in Rotterdam, and who had comported themselves with such singular wisdom and propriety that they were never either heard or talked of—which, next to being universally applauded, should be the object of ambition of all magistrates and rulers. There are two opposite ways by which some men make a figure in the world: one, by talking faster than they think, and the other by holding their tongues and not thinking at all. By the first, many a smatterer acquires the reputation of a man of quick parts; by the other, many a dunderpate, like the owl, the stupidest of birds, comes to be considered the very type of wisdom. This, by the way, is a casual remark, which I would not for the universe have it thought I apply to Governor Van Twiller. It is true he was a man shut up within himself, like an oyster, and rarely spoke except in monosyllables; but then it was allowed he seldom said a foolish thing. So invincible was his gravity that he was never known to laugh or even to smile through the whole course of a long and prosperous life. Nay, if a joke were uttered in his presence that set light-minded hearers in a roar, it was observed to throw him into a state of perplexity. Sometimes he would deign to inquire into the matter, and when, after much explanation, the joke was made as plain as a pike-staff, he would continue to smoke his pipe in silence, and at length, knocking out the ashes, would exclaim: "Well! I see nothing in all that to laugh about."

With all his reflective habits, he never made up his mind on a subject. His adherents accounted for this by the astonishing magnitude of his ideas. He conceived every subject on so grand a scale that he had not room in his head to turn it over and examine both sides of it. Certain it is, that, if any matter were propounded to him on which ordinary mortals would rashly determine at first glance, he would put on a vague, mysterious look, shake his capacious head, smoke some time in profound silence, and at length observe that he "had his doubts about the matter"; which gained him the reputation of a man slow of be-

[1] VAN—Like the *Von* in German names and *De* in French, meaning "of" or "from." The name that followed denoted the family or estate from which a man came; hence it indicated a person of prominence. These prepositions are properly spelled without the capital: Thomas de Quincey.

lief and not easily imposed upon. What is more, it gained him a lasting name, for to this habit of mind has been attributed his surname of Twiller, which is said to be a corruption of [2] the original Twijfler, or, in plain English, *Doubter*.

The person of this illustrious old gentleman was formed and proportioned, as though it had been molded by the hands of some cunning Dutch statuary, as a model of majesty and lordly grandeur. He was exactly five feet six inches in height and six feet five inches in circumference. His head was a perfect sphere, and of such stupendous dimensions that Dame Nature, with all her sex's ingenuity, would have been puzzled to construct a neck capable of supporting it; wherefore she wisely declined the attempt, and settled it firmly on the top of his backbone, just between the shoulders. His body was oblong and particularly capacious at bottom; which was wisely ordered by Providence, seeing that he was a man of sedentary habits and very averse to the idle labor of walking. His legs were short, but sturdy in proportion to the weight they had to sustain, so that when erect he had not a little the appearance of a beer-barrel on skids. His face, that infallible index of the mind, presented a vast expanse, unfurrowed by any of those lines and angles which disfigure the human countenance with what is termed expression. Two small gray eyes twinkled feebly in the midst, like two stars of lesser magnitude in a hazy firmament, and his full-fed cheeks, which seemed to have taken toll of everything that went into his mouth, were curiously mottled and streaked with dusky red, like a spitzenberg apple.

His habits were as regular as his person. He daily took his four stated meals, appropriating exactly an hour to each; he smoked and doubted eight hours, and he slept the remaining twelve of the four-and-twenty. Such was the renowned Wouter Van Twiller—a true philosopher, for his mind was either elevated above, or tranquilly settled below, the cares and perplexities of this world. He had lived in it for years without feeling the least curiosity to know whether the sun revolved round it or it round the sun; and he had watched for at least half a century the smoke curling from his pipe to the ceiling, without troubling his head with any of those numerous theories by which a philos-

---

[2] CORRUPTION OF—A less accurate form of.

opher would have perplexed his brain in accounting for its rising above the surrounding atmosphere.

In his council he presided with great state and solemnity. He sat in a huge chair of solid oak, hewn in the celebrated forest of the Hague, fabricated by an experienced timmerman [3] of Amsterdam, and curiously carved about the arms and feet into exact imitations of gigantic eagle's claws. Instead of a sceptre he swayed a long Turkish pipe, wrought with jasmin and amber, which had been presented to a stadtholder of Holland at the conclusion of a treaty with one of the petty Barbary powers. In this stately chair would he sit and this magnificent pipe would he smoke, shaking his right knee with a constant motion, and fixing his eye for hours together upon a little print of Amsterdam which hung in a black frame against the opposite wall of the council chamber. Nay, it has ever been said that when any deliberation [4] of extraordinary length and intricacy was on the carpet,[5] the renowned Wouter would shut his eyes for full two hours at a time, that he might not be disturbed by external objects; and at such times the internal commotion of his mind was evinced by certain regular guttural sounds, which his admirers declared were merely the noise of conflict made by his contending doubts and opinions.

[3] TIMMERMAN—A carpenter or cabinetmaker. Compare with the German *Zimmermann.*
[4] DELIBERATION—Matter for consideration.
[5] ON THE CARPET—A figurative expression meaning "brought before a magistrate to be decided."

Vocabulary Study: If you are not familiar with the meanings of any of the following words, look them up in a dictionary: *comported; casual; invincible; gravity; deign; reflective; adherents; ingenuity; sedentary; infallible; toll; appropriating; philosopher* (two different meanings); *fabricated; stadtholder; Barbary; intricacy; evinced; guttural; contending.*

Give the shades of meaning of these synonyms: *deign, condescend, vouchsafe.* Give antonyms of: *casual; invincible; sedentary.*

A Postscript to the Introduction: How did New York receive this burlesque history whose very author, Diedrich Knickerbocker, proved to be a myth? Irving himself has told us: "The main object of my work had been to embody the traditions of our city in an amusing form. At the first, its drift and aim were misapprehended by some descendants of the Dutch worthies. But when I find after a lapse of nearly forty years this haphazard production of my youth still cherished among them; when I find its very name become a household word; and when I find New Yorkers of Dutch descent priding themselves upon being 'genuine Knickerbockers,' I please myself with the persuasion that I have struck the right chord."

By Way of Appreciation: It is sometimes interesting to see just why a selection is funny. What brings the chuckles as we read of the renowned Van Twiller? Of course, in the first place, the passage is ironic; but irony—the art of saying one thing and meaning the opposite —is not always funny. Clumsily handled, it is childish and crude. The fun in this irony lies in its subtlety. Irving does not blurt out, "Van Twiller was a wise guy, oh yeah!" He remarks blandly, "By holding his tongue and not talking at all, many a dunderpate comes to be considered the very type of wisdom—a casual remark by the way, which I would not for the world have it thought that I apply to Governor Van Twiller." It is interesting to note that Irving never needs to resort to italics, exclamation points, or parenthetical question marks to label his satire. With him, irony is a gentle art.

A second source of fun in this essay lies in the clever use of simile. (A simile, you may recall, is an expressed comparison between two essentially different objects which have some common characteristic.) Irving's similes are classics. We recall the Baron of Katzenellenbogen "buzzing about, as restless and importunate as a blue-bottle fly on a hot summer's day," or Ichabod Crane's "small head with a long snipe nose that looked like a weathercock perched on his neck to show which way the wind blew."

Finally, as in most burlesques, there is obvious exaggeration (hyperbole). Though we can scarcely visualize a man of the proportions Irving ascribes to Van Twiller, the very turn of the phrases is delightful. In fact, Irving's fall of phrases always pleases our fancy. There is artistry in even his broadest humor.

Suggestions for Study: What is the first hint that the essay is not from a serious history of New York? Select two ironic sentences besides the one quoted above. The essay contains at least seven similes. Can you find them all? Find two examples of obvious exaggeration.

Write a paragraph, free from figures of speech and free from irony, in which you describe Wouter Van Twiller as he appears to you.

Choose the passage which you consider the best example of Irving's humorous style and read it aloud to someone who would enjoy it. Remember that Irving is read with just a sly twinkle in the eye.

Exercises and Creative Work: Write a précis of the essay.

You meet in your life a number of odd and eccentric characters. Make a list of people of this type about whom you would be interested to write. From this list develop a character study with a touch of ironic humor, or choose one of the following titles: *The Beggar on Main Street; An Old Resident; The Blind Fiddler; Only a Newsboy.*

ALBUM VERSES

From The Autocrat of the Breakfast Table

OLIVER WENDELL HOLMES

By Way of Introduction: There is a pleasure in the give and take of conversation, but probably the best talking we do no one else ever hears. You see it takes place in our own imaginations. Then we are always brilliant; then no one else can outshine us; the first as well as the last word is ours.

Once upon a time Oliver Wendell Holmes got the idea that it would be fun to write down just such a conversational day-dream. He created an imaginary audience—the round-table of a genteel boarding house—and made of himself an imaginary character—a precise bachelor with literary leanings. Then he proceeded to shine. Let us listen in to a bit of the breakfast-table conversation lorded over by the self-appointed autocrat.

——WHAT if, instead of talking this morning, I should read you a copy of verses, with critical remarks by the author? Any of the company can retire that like.

> When Eve had led her lord away,
>   And Cain had killed his brother,
> The stars and flowers, the poets say,
>   Agreed with one another
>
> To cheat the cunning tempter's art,
>   And teach the race its duty,
> By keeping on its wicked heart
>   Their eyes of light and beauty.
>
> A million sleepless lids, they say,
>   Will be at least a warning;
> And so the flowers would watch by day,
>   The stars from eve to morning.
>
> On hill and prairie, field and lawn,
>   Their dewy eyes upturning,
> The flowers still watch from reddening dawn
>   Till western skies are burning.
>
> Alas! each hour of daylight tells
>   A tale of shame so crushing,
> That some turn white as sea-bleached shells,
>   And some are always blushing.

But when the patient stars look down
    On all their light discovers,
The traitor's smile, the murderer's frown,
    The lips of lying lovers,

They try to shut their saddening eyes,
    And in the vain endeavour
We see them twinkling in the skies
    And so they wink forever.

What do *you* think of these verses my friends?— Is that
piece an impromptu? said my landlady's daughter. (AEt.[1] 19+.
Tender-eyed blonde. Long ringlets. Cameo pin. Gold pencil-
case on a chain. Locket. Bracelet. Album. Autograph
book. Accordeon. Reads Byron, Tupper, and Sylvanus
Cobb, junior,[2] while her mother makes the puddings. Says
"Yes?" when you tell her anything.)—*Oui et non, ma petite,*—
Yes, and no, my child. Five of the seven verses were written
off-hand; the other two took a week,—that is, were hanging
round the desk in a ragged, forlorn, unrhymed condition as long
as that. All poets will tell you just such stories. *C'est le* DER-
NIER *pas qui coute.*[3] Don't you know how hard it is for some
people to get out of a room after their visit is really over?
They want to be off, and you want to have them off, but they
don't know how to manage it. One would think they had been
built in your parlor or study, and were waiting to be launched.
I have contrived a sort of ceremonial inclined plane [4] for such
visitors, which being lubricated with certain smooth phrases, I
back them down, metaphorically speaking, stern-foremost, into
their "native element," the great ocean of outdoors. Well, now,
there are poems as hard to get rid of as these rural visitors.
They come in glibly, use up all the serviceable rhymes, *day,
ray, beauty, duty, skies, eyes, other, brother, mountain, foun-*

---

[1] AET.—Abbreviation for the Latin *aetatis*, "of the age," or "aged."

[2] BYRON, TUPPER AND SYLVANUS COBB, JUNIOR—Byron was a romantic
English poet (1788–1824) whose works were frowned upon by the more conservative critics. Tupper was an English poet (1810–1889), now almost forgotten. His *Proberbial Philosophy* was enormously popular with the unthink-
ing multitude in nineteenth-century America, but critics made it the chief
butt of their ridicule. It is altogether commonplace. Cobb was a popular
novelist and prolific story writer (1823–1887).

[3] *C'est* . . . *coute*—"It's the last step that hurts (costs)."

[4] CEREMONIAL INCLINED PLANE—Holmes is continuing the figure of speech
begun with the word "launched."

tain, and the like; and so they go on until you think it is time for the wind-up, and the wind-up won't come on any terms. So they lie about until you get sick of the sight of them, and end by thrusting some cold scrap of a final couplet upon them, and turning them out of doors. I suspect a good many "impromptus" could tell just such a story as the above.—Here turning to our landlady, I used an illustration which pleased the company much at the time, and has since been highly commended. "Madam," I said, "you can pour three gills and three quarters of honey from that pint jug, if it is full, in less than one minute; but, Madam, you could not empty that last quarter of a gill, though you were turned into a marble Hebe,[5] and held the vessel upside down for a thousand years."

One gets tired to death of the old, old rhymes, such as you see in that copy of verses,—which I don't mean to abuse, or to praise either. I always feel as if I were a cobbler, putting new top-leathers to an old pair of boot-soles and bodies, when I am fitting sentiments to these venerable jingles.

.	.	.	.	.	youth
.	.	.	.	.	morning
.	.	.	.	.	truth
.	.	.	.	.	warning

Nine tenths of the "Juvenile Poems" written spring out of the above musical and suggestive coincidences.

"Yes?" said our landlady's daughter.

I did not address the following remark to her, and I trust, from her limited range of reading, she will never see it; I said it softly to my next neighbor.

When a young female wears a flat circular side-curl, gummed on each temple,—when she walks with a male, not arm in arm, but his arm against the back of hers,—and when she says "Yes?" with the note of interrogation, you are generally safe in asking her what wages she gets, and who the "feller" was you saw her with.

"What were you whispering?" said the daughter of the house, moistening her lips, as she spoke, in a very engaging manner.

"I was only laying down a principle of social diagnosis."

"Yes?"

---

[5] HEBE—Goddess of youth, once cup-bearer on Mount Olympus.

Helps for Reading: For clearness, the author made use of these devices: A long dash at the beginning of a paragraph indicated the introduction of a new topic, perhaps of a new day and the opening of a fresh conversation. Words in parenthesis are addressed to Holmes' invisible companion, the reader. Words in brackets are in the nature of stage-directions. There was no occasion to use brackets in the talk about his *Album Verses,* but if you are going to read more of *The Autocrat,* you should be familiar with the device.

Vocabulary Study: Since Holmes is merely jotting down a one-sided boarding-house conversation, his style is free and his vocabulary easy. The reader, however, should be sure of the meanings of the following words: *autocrat; impromptu; lubricated; metaphorically; sternforemost; couplet; venerable; diagnosis; wages.*

What is the difference in the meaning of the following synonyms: *wages, hire, salary, pay, emolument?* What is an antonym of *impromptu?*

By Way of Appreciation: As the "autocrat" of the breakfast table, Holmes makes himself a bit pompous and a bit pedantic. Though we understand that it is just a pose, we realize also that the opinions of the autocrat are the opinions of Holmes. We learn from the present essay, for example, that Holmes did not admire such a girl as the landlady's daughter and that he disapproved of Byron.

The present selection illustrates also the gently ironic humor which is characteristic of the *Autocrat.* It gives just a glimpse of the pleasant philosophy in which the work abounds. Holmes was a genial person who enjoyed living. Let this essay serve as an introduction to the breakfast-table series which will in turn reveal to you the charm of a whimsical, kindly companion.

Suggestions for Study: How would you answer the author's question, "What do *you* think of these verses, my friends?" What, do you suppose, were some of the "smooth phrases" with which Holmes assisted awkward visitors in their leave-taking? What is the meaning of the sentence, "Nine tenths of the 'Juvenile Poems' written spring out of the above musical and suggestive coincidences"? Does the dictionary give you any clue to Holmes' scornful use of the word "wage"? Are we accustomed to making class distinctions between wage-earners and salary-earners to-day? To bring the characterization of the landlady's daughter up to date what word would you use instead of "feller" and what stock comeback would the girl use instead of "Yes?" Think of a single adjective that sums up the young lady.

Exercises and Creative Work: Write a précis of the poem which appears in the essay.

Try to think of a modern miss of the same type as the landlady's daughter; then rewrite the description substituting up-to-the-minute details in the way of hair-dress, jewelry, reading matter and so on.

THE HISTORY OF THE AMERICAN ESSAY

THE TRANSITION PERIOD (1865–1900)

General Characteristics

There is no real history of the development of the essay such as we find in poetry and the short story. Because the essay is so very much a personal thing, the essayist is less affected by changing times and conditions than the writer of any other form of literature. Unlike the novelist, the short story writer, or the poet, he feels no urge to reflect the external conditions with which he is surrounded, but rather gives us a glimpse of that which is within himself.

Neither are the literary periods so sharply defined. Many of the great writers of the National Period were to continue their prose writings well after the Civil War. This was particularly true of Lowell. Likewise we find a number of writers, who although they began their work before 1900, we consider among the twentieth century essayists because much of their writing was done after the turn of the century. However, there are a few essayists who are definite links between the Concord writers of the National Period and the twentieth century group, and who therefore belong in the Transition Period.

Samuel Langhorne Clemens (Mark Twain) (1835–1910)

First and foremost of this group is Samuel Langhorne Clemens, or Mark Twain, as we better know him.

The general background of Mark Twain's growing up was the happy-go-lucky environment of a Missouri river town. His mother, a good woman, was a wholesome influence, but the family was poor. When the father died, Samuel's regular schooling stopped. He was apprenticed to a printer, and before long was a wage-earner in the family. This apprenticeship he later termed his "high school course"; and a subsequent four-year period as apprentice and pilot on the river, his "university career."

Both training schools did effectually prepare him for his real calling. The boyhood years in the printing office prepared him for the newspaper work which carried him on to his success as a writer; the years of early manhood on the Mississippi furnished him with material for some of his most entertaining books as well as with his pseudonym, "Mark Twain."

Samuel might have remained a river pilot had not the Civil War stopped navigation on the lower river. Uncertain days followed, but eventually he went with his brother, who had a secretarial position, to the territory of Nevada. Experiences in the far West furnished material for his first sketches; and with the publication of a series of humorous letters which were the result of a tour of Europe as a newspaper correspondent, he knew success as a journalist, humorist, and lecturer.

When he was sixty, the failure of a printing firm in which he had invested heavily swept away what money he had accumulated. Courageously, he continued writing and speaking to win back a competence for his family. His last years were spent in the New England states, and even in that conservative stronghold he commanded respect and admiration. On his seventieth birthday he was honored by a testimonial dinner. When he visited England two years later, Oxford conferred upon him an honorary degree—an unusual tribute to one who had left school at the end of his twelfth year! Twenty-five volumes of his collected writings appeared in 1910, the year of his death.

A natural shrewdness, an eye for characterization, and an easy flow of language are apparent in his works. Like most humorists, he saw life soberly and had a fine sense of values. Sometimes he is serious in his appreciation, as when he writes of Joan of Arc. Sometimes his fun sugar-coats a serious purpose, as in the *Connecticut Yankee*. He could tell uproariously funny stories with a lugubrious face; and he could, in an instant, shift from the ridiculous to the momentous. He was a vivid American personality.

Lafcadio Hearn (1850–1904)

Born of Irish and Greek parents under the blue sky of an island in the Ægean Sea, educated in France and England, living for brief periods in Cincinnati and New Orleans where he poured into the local newspapers his astonishingly vivid sketches, finally becoming a citizen of Japan, even to adopting its dress, manners and religion—these are the high points in the life of Lafcadio Hearn. No more fantastic or mysterious figure can be found in American literature—or, for that matter, in the literature of any country.

His father, member of an ancient Irish family, had accompanied his regiment as surgeon-major to Corfu. Becoming infatuated with a beautiful Grecian girl, Rosa Cerigote, he married her. They named their first son for the island where he was born, his mother's home, Leucadia, in modern Greek Lefcadia.

The facts of Hearn's life are very imperfectly known. His mother spent some time in Ireland and then, when Lafcadio was only seven, she went away to Smyrna, never to return. Now the boy stayed for a time with an aunt in Ireland, and then spent some time in school in France and England. It was while in school that by means of an accident at play he was almost completely blinded for the rest of his life.

For a vague period he lived in the slums of London, hungry and sick, restless and ambitious. At nineteen he was in New York, reading omnivorously, despite his feeble vision, in the public library. He drifted to Cincinnati where his intensely vivid account of a murder made the city gasp with horror and won him a place on the *Enquirer*. His wanderings brought him to New Orleans where for the first time in his life he found congenial surroundings, where his knowledge of French was of genuine service to him, and where he could support himself by reporting for the *Times-Democrat*. His imagination fed upon the French past of this romantic and colorful city, he wandered among the ancient buildings, and devoured its legends and chronicles.

After several years, armed with a commission from *Harper's Magazine*, he went to Japan. Here he promptly forgot his commission in his delight over this new world of sensation. His later writings, beginning with *Glimpses of Unfamiliar Japan*, published in 1894, are attempts to interpret the country of his adoption, vivid impressions of a romantic country which he saw with equally romantic eyes.

Other Essayists of the Transition Period

Charles Dudley Warner (1829–1900) is an important link between the Concord writers and the twentieth century group. First a lawyer, and then editor and writer, he shared the New England background of the former group. His essays, however, have a lighter touch. His *Back-Log Studies* pick up the vein of tolerant satire used by Irving. His point of view is practical, modern; his expression, flavored with wit. *The Hunting of the Deer* and *Camping Out* are good examples of his art.

Another popular writer of this period was Donald Grant Mitchell (1822–1902), who was known to his public as "Ik Marvel." *Reveries of a Bachelor* and *My Farm at Edgewood* are typical volumes of his essays.

Essays of the Transition Period

HOW TO TELL A STORY

Mark Twain

By Way of Introduction: There is modesty in the opening sentence of *How to Tell a Story;* but men of Mark Twain's day tell us that the writer was himself the master of all expert story-tellers. If you would see Mark Twain as he used to tell the story of "The Golden Arm," you must picture a ruddy-faced man with a shock of white hair, a man with a face dejected and with the drooping, shambling set-up of the southern negro—dejected, that is, until the moment he electrifies himself and his audience with the "catch" of the story.

I do not claim that I can tell a story as it ought to be told. I only claim to know how a story ought to be told, for I have been almost daily in the company of the most expert story-tellers for many years.

There are several kinds of stories, but only one difficult kind —the humorous. I will talk mainly about that one. The humorous story is American, the comic story is English, the witty story is French. The humorous story depends for its effect upon the manner of the telling; the comic story and the witty story upon the matter.

The humorous story may be spun out to great length, and may wander around as much as it pleases, and arrive nowhere in particular; but the comic and witty stories must be brief and end with a point. The humorous story bubbles gently along, the others burst.

The humorous story is strictly a work of art—high and delicate art—and only an artist can tell it; but no art is necessary in telling the comic and the witty story; anybody can do it. The art of telling a humorous story—understand, I mean by word of mouth, not print—was created in America, and has remained at home.

The humorous story is told gravely; the teller does his best to conceal the fact that he even dimly suspects that there is anything funny about it; but the teller of the comic story tells you beforehand that it is one of the funniest things he has ever heard, then tells it with eager delight, and is the first person to laugh when he gets through. And sometimes, if he has had good success, he is so glad and happy that he will repeat the "nub" of it and glance around from face to face, collecting applause, and then repeat it again. It is a pathetic thing to see.

Very often, of course, the rambling and disjointed humorous story finishes with a nub, point, snapper, or whatever you like to call it. Then the listener must be alert, for in many cases the teller will divert attention from that nub by dropping it in a carefully casual and indifferent way, with the pretence that he does not know it is a nub.

Artemus Ward [1] used that trick a good deal; then when the belated audience presently caught the joke he would look up with innocent surprise, as if wondering what they had found to laugh at. Dan Setchell used it before him. Nye and Riley [2] and others use it to-day.

But the teller of the comic story does not slur the nub; he shouts it at you—every time. And when he prints it, in England, France, Germany, and Italy, he italicizes it, puts some whooping exclamation-points after it, and sometimes explains it

---

[1] ARTEMUS WARD—Pseudonym of Charles Farrar Brown (1834–1867), an American humorist, lecturer and writer.

[2] NYE AND RILEY—Edgar Wilson Nye (1850–1896), known as "Bill Nye," American humorist, and James Whitcomb Riley (1854–1916), American poet and humorist.

in a parenthesis. All of which is very depressing, and makes one want to renounce joking and lead a better life.

Let me set down an instance of the comic method, using an anecdote which has been popular all over the world for twelve or fifteen hundred years. The teller tells it in this way:

THE WOUNDED SOLDIER

In the course of a certain battle a soldier whose leg had been shot off appealed to another soldier who was hurrying by to carry him to the rear, informing him at the same time of the loss which he had sustained: whereupon the generous son of Mars,[3] shouldering the unfortunate, proceeded to carry out his desire. The bullets and cannon-balls were flying in all directions, and presently one of the latter took the wounded man's head off—without, however, his deliverer being aware of it. In no long time he was hailed by an officer, who said:

"Where are you going with that carcass?"

"To the rear, sir—he's lost his leg!"

"His leg, forsooth?" responded the astonished officer; "you mean his head, you booby."

Whereupon the soldier dispossessed himself [4] of his burden, and stood looking down upon it in great perplexity. At length he said:

"It is true, sir, just as you have said." Then after a pause he added, "But he TOLD me IT WAS HIS LEG! ! ! ! !"

Here the narrator bursts into explosion after explosion of thunderous horse-laughter, repeating that nub from time to time through his gaspings and shriekings and suffocatings.

It takes only a minute and a half to tell that in its comic-story form; and isn't worth the telling, after all. Put into the humorous-story form it takes ten minutes, and is about the funniest thing I have ever listened to—as James Whitcomb Riley tells it.

He tells it in the character of a dull-witted old farmer who has just heard it for the first time, thinks it is unspeakably funny, and is trying to repeat it to a neighbor. But he can't remember it; so he gets all mixed up and wanders helplessly round and round, putting in tedious details that don't belong in the tale and only retard it; taking them out conscientiously and

[3] MARS—The Roman god of war.

[4] DISPOSSESSED HIMSELF—Got rid of, put down.

putting in others that are just as useless; making minor mistakes now and then and stopping to correct them and explain how he came to make them; remembering things which he forgot to put in their proper place and going back to put them in there; stopping his narrative a good while in order to try to recall the name of the soldier that was hurt, and finally remembering that the soldier's name was not mentioned, and remarking placidly that the name is of no real importance, anyway—better, of course, if one knew it, but not essential, after all—and so on, and so on, and so on.

The teller is innocent and happy and pleased with himself, and has to stop every little while to hold himself in and keep from laughing outright; and does hold in, but his body quakes in a jelly-like way with interior chuckles; and at the end of the ten minutes the audience have laughed until they are exhausted, and the tears are running down their faces.

The simplicity and innocence and sincerity and unconsciousness of the old farmer are perfectly simulated, and the result is a performance which is thoroughly charming and delicious. This is art—and fine and beautiful, and only a master can compass it; but a machine could tell the other story.

To string incongruities and absurdities together in a wandering and sometimes purposeless way, and seem innocently unaware that they are absurdities, is the basis of the American art, if my position is correct. Another feature is the slurring of the point. A third is the dropping of a studied remark apparently without knowing it, as if one were thinking aloud. The fourth and last is the pause.

Artemus Ward dealt in numbers three and four a good deal. He would begin to tell with great animation something which he seemed to think was wonderful; then lose confidence, and after an apparently absent-minded pause add an incongruous remark in a soliloquizing way; and that was the remark intended to explode the mine—and it did.

For instance, he would say eagerly, excitely, "I once knew a man in New Zealand who hadn't a tooth in his head"—here his animation would die out; a silent, reflective pause would follow, then he would say dreamily, and as if to himself, "and yet that man could beat a drum better than any man I ever saw."

The pause is an exceedingly important feature in any kind of story, and a frequently recurring feature, too. It is a dainty thing, and delicate, and also uncertain and treacherous; for it must be exactly the right length—no more and no less—or it fails of its purpose and makes trouble. If the pause is too long the impressive point is passed, and the audience have had time to divine that a surprise is intended—and then you can't surprise them, of course.

On the platform I used to tell a negro ghost story that had a pause in front of the snapper on the end, and that pause was the most important thing in the whole story. If I got it the right length precisely, I could spring the finishing ejaculation with effect enough to make some impressible girl deliver a startled little yelp and jump out of her seat—and that was what I was after. This story was called "The Golden Arm," and was told in this fashion. You can practise with it yourself—and mind you look out for the pause and get it right.

THE GOLDEN ARM

Once 'pon a time dey wuz a monsus [5] mean man, en he live 'way out in de prairie all 'lone by hisself, 'cep'n he had a wife. En bimeby she died, en he tuck en toted [6] her way out dah in de prairie en buried her. Well, she had a golden arm—all solid gold, fum de shoulder down. He wuz pow'ful mean—pow'ful; en dat night he couldn't sleep, caze he want dat golden arm so bad.

When it come midnight he couldn't stan' it no mo'; so he git up; he did, en tuck his lantern en shoved out thoo de storm en dug her up en got de golden arm; en he bent his head down 'gin de win', en plowed en plowed en plowed thoo de snow. Den all on a sudden he stop (*make a considerable pause here, and look startled, and take a listening attitude*) en say: "My lan', what's dat!"

En he listen—en listen—en de win' say (*set your teeth together and imitate the wailing and wheezing singsong of the wind*), "Bzzz-z-zzz"—en den, way back yonder whah de grave is, he hear a voice! —he hear a voice all mix' up in de win'—can't hardly tell 'em 'part — "Bzzz-zzz—W-h-o—g-o-t—m-y—g-o-l-d-e-n—arm?—zzz—zzz —W-h-o—g-o-t—m-y—g-o-l-d-e-n—arm?" (*You must begin to shiver violently now.*)

En he begin to shiver en shake, en say, "Oh, my! Oh, my lan'!" en de win' blow de lantern out, en de snow en sleet blow

[5] Monsus—Monstrous.
[6] Toted—Carried.

in his face en mos' choke him, en he start a-plowin' knee-dee}
towards home mos' dead, he so sk'yerd [7]—en pooty soon he hear
de voice agin, en (*pause*) it 'us comin' after him! "Bzzz—zzz—
zzz—W-h-o—g-o-t—m-y—g-o-l-d-e-n—arm?"

When he git to de pasture he hear it again—closter now, en
a-comin'!—a-comin' back dah in de dark en de storm—(*repeat the
wind and the voice*). When he git to de house he rush up-stairs
en jump in de bed en kiver up, head and years, en lay dah shiverin'
en shakin'—en den way out dah he hear it agin!—en a-comin'! En
bimeby he hear (*pause—awed, listening attitude*)—pat—pat—pat—
hit's a-comin' up-stairs. Den he hear de latch, en he know it's in
de room!

Den, pooty soon he know it's a-stanin' by de bed! (*Pause.*)
Den—he know it's a-bendin' down over him—en he can't skasely [8]
git his breath! Den—den—he seem to feel someth'n c-o-l-d, right
down 'most agin his head! (*Pause.*)

Den de voice say, right at his year—"W-h-o—g-o-t—m-y—
g-o-l-d-e-n—arm?" (*You must wail it out very plaintively and ac-
cusingly; then you stare steadily and impressively into the face of
the farthest-gone auditor—a girl, preferably—and let that awe-
inspiring pause begin to build itself in the deep hush. When it has
reached exactly the right length, jump suddenly at the girl and yell:
"YOU'VE GOT IT!"*)

If you've got the pause right, she'll fetch a dear little yelp
and spring right out of her shoes. But you must get the pause
right; and you will find it the most troublesome and aggravating and uncertain thing you ever undertook.

[7] SK'YERD—Scared.
[8] SKASELY—Scarcely.

Vocabulary Study: *Divert; belated; slur; anecdote; tedious; retard;
simulated; compass* (verb); *incongruities; plaintively; animation; soliloquizing; divine* (verb); *comedy; wit; humor.*
Give the difference between the synonyms *anecdote* and *story; wit*
and *humor; amuse, entertain, divert.* Give an antonym for *tedious.*

By Way of Appreciation: *How To Tell a Story* is an essay that
needs little interpretation—it speaks so clearly for itself. Notice that
the author draws for us a distinction between comedy and humor. The
ways of the humorist as here described are the ways that made Mark
Twain famous. Notice how the fun of the essay is heightened if it is
read aloud by someone with a deep, mournful voice. The only occasion
for the reader to laugh is during the recital of the Wounded Soldier
story. There he imitates the guffaws of the low comedian. Mark Twain
himself rarely laughed. One who knew him well, in his later days, has

said that he could not remember ever having seen the humorist smile!

Suggestions for Study: How do the dictionary distinctions between *comedy* and *humor* tally with the author's distinctions as presented in the essay? Is it a compliment to us that he calls the humorous story American? Explain. From your acquaintances among English writers, can you name any who share the American gift for telling a humorous story? (There are some.) Can you illustrate the difference between the *comic* and the *humorous* by finding at least one cartoon of each type? by naming two motion picture stars who play comedy rôles and two who often play humorous rôles? by naming two comic radio stars and two humorous radio stars (or programs)?

What speakers have you heard who seem to have the same sort of technique in telling a story as did Artemus Ward and James Whitcomb Riley? Do you agree that the humorous story is the hardest kind of story to tell or write? Why or why not? Mark Twain's *A Connecticut Yankee in King Arthur's Court* is an illustration of humor achieved by "stringing incongruities and absurdities together, apparently unaware that they are absurdities." Can you name five other examples of this distinctly "American art"? The examples may be humorous stories, or speeches, or plays, or cartoons, or essays.

Exercises and Creative Work: Briefly put in your own words the content of the first part of the essay up to the story of the wounded soldier.

One of the following may be used as the title for an essay of your own: *The Story Telling Bore; Another Story; When Do We Laugh; Good Listeners; Now I Have a Good Story: Have You Heard This One?; Among Best Sellers; Old Favorites Among the Stories.* First make an outline of your essay in order to give it coherence.

SUNRISE IN LOUISIANA

Lafcadio Hearn

By Way of Introduction: "For me, words have color, form, character: they have faces, ports, manners, gesticulations; they have moods, humors, eccentricities; they have tints, tones, personalities . . . I have never yet made, and never expect to make any money. . . . I write for beloved friends who can see color in words, can smell the perfume of syllables in blossom, can be shocked by the fine elfish electricity of words." It is Lafcadio Hearn that is speaking.

His books bear him out. They are fragmentary—bits of gorgeous description written with intense imagination and feeling for beauty. His method was to take a single incident, or a single feature of a landscape, and by a few intensely vivid strokes, suggest the entire picture to our imaginations. Like a painting in its colorful beauty is *Sunrise in Louisiana.*

I once thought, when sailing up the Ohio one bright Northern summer, that the world held nothing more beautiful than the scenery of the Beautiful River—those voluptuous [1] hills with their sweet feminine curves, the elfin gold of that summer haze, and the pale emerald of the river's verdure-reflecting breast. But even the loveliness of the Ohio seemed faded, and the Northern sky-blue palely cold, like the tint of iceberg pinnacles, when I beheld for the first time the splendor of the Mississippi.

"You must come on deck early to-morrow," said the kind Captain of the *Thompson Dean;* "we are entering the Sugar Country."

So I saw the sun rise in Louisiana.

It rose with a splendor that recalled the manner of its setting at Memphis, but of another color; an auroral flush of pale gold and pale green bloomed over the long fringe of cottonwood and cypress trees, and broadened and lengthened halfway round the brightening world. The glow seemed tropical, with the deep green of the trees sharply cutting against it; and one naturally looked for the feathery crests of cocoanut palms. Then the day broke gently and slowly—a day too vast for a rapid dawn—a day that seemed deep as Space. I thought our Northern sky narrow and cramped as a vaulted church roof beside that sky—

[1] Voluptuous—Appealing to the sense of beauty.

a sky so softly beautiful, so purely clear in its immensity, that it made one dream of the tenderness of a woman's eyes made infinite.

And the giant river broadened to a mile—smooth as a mirror, still and profound as a mountain lake. Between the vastness of the sky and the vastness of the stream, we seemed moving suspended in the midst of day, with only a long, narrow tongue of land on either side breaking the brightness. Yet the horizon never became wholly blue. The green-golden glow lived there all through the day; it was brightest in the South. It was so tropical, that glow; it seemed of the Pacific, a glow that forms a background to the sight of lagoons and coral reefs and "lands where it is always afternoon."

Below this glow gleamed another golden green, the glory of the waving cane fields beyond the trees. Huge sugar mills were breathing white and black clouds into the sky, as they masticated their mighty meal; and the smell of saccharine sweetness floated to us from either shore. Then we glided by miles of cotton fields with their fluttering white balls; and by the mouths of broad bayous; past swamps dark with cypress gloom, where the gray alligator dwells, and the gray Spanish moss hangs in elfish festoons from ancient trees; past orange trees and live oaks, pecans and cottonwoods and broad-leaved bananas; while the green of the landscape ever varied, from a green so dark that it seemed tinged with blue to an emerald so bright that it seemed shot through with gold. The magnificent old mansions of the Southern planters, built after a generous fashion unknown in the North, with broad verandas and deliciously cool porches, and all painted white or perhaps a pale yellow, looked out grandly across the water from the hearts of shadowy groves; and, like villages of a hundred cottages, the negro quarters dotted the verdant face of the plantation with far-gleaming points of snowy whiteness.

And still that wondrous glow brightened in the south, like a far-off reflection of sunlight on the Spanish Main.

"But it does not look now as it used to in the old slave days," said the pilot, as he turned the great wheel. "The swamps were drained, and the plantations were not overgrown with cottonwood; and somehow or other the banks usen't to cave in then as they do now."

I saw indeed signs of sad ruin on the face of the great plantations; there were splendid houses crumbling to decay, and
whole towns of tenantless cabins; estates of immense extent
were lying almost untilled, or with only a few acres under cultivation; and the vigorous cottonwood trees had shot up in whole
forests over fields once made fertile by the labor of ten thousand
slaves.   The scene was not without its melancholy; it seemed
tinged by the reflection of a glory passed away—the glory of
wealth, and the magnificence of wealth; of riches and the luxury
of riches.

O fair paradise of the South, if still so lovely in thy ruin,
what must thou have been in the great day of thy greatest
glory!

White steamboats, heavily panting under their loads of cotton, came toiling by, and called out to us wild greetings long
and shrill, until the pilot opened the lips of our giant boat, and
her mighty challenge awoke a thousand phantom voices along
the winding shore.   Red sank the sun in a sea of fire, and
bronze-hued clouds piled up against the light, like fairy islands
in a sea of glory, such as were seen, perhaps, by the Adelantado [2] of the Seven Cities. [3]

"Those are not real clouds," said the pilot, turning to the
west, his face aglow with the yellow light.   "Those are only
smoke clouds rising from the sugar mills of Louisiana, and drifting with the evening wind."

The daylight died away and the stars came out, but that
warm glow in the southern horizon only paled, so that it seemed
a little farther off.   The river broadened till it looked with
the tropical verdure of its banks like the Ganges, until at last
there loomed up a vast line of shadows, dotted with points of
light, and through a forest of masts and a host of phantom-
white river boats and a wilderness of chimneys the *Thompson
Dean,* singing her cheery challenge, steamed up to the mighty
levee of New Orleans.

[2] ADELANTADO—The governor of a province in Spain.
[3] SEVEN CITIES—In the fourteenth and fifteenth centuries there was supposed to exist in the Atlantic, west of Europe, the Island of the Seven Cities.
It was said to have been peopled by seven bishops who, with their followers,
had been driven out of Spain by the Moors.

Vocabulary Study: Look up the correct pronunciation of Louisiana in a fairly recent dictionary. You should also know the following words: *auroral; immensity; vastness; infinite; masticated; saccharine; bayous; verdure; Ganges.*

What shades of meaning are shown by the synonymous terms: *enormous, immense, huge, vast?* What is an antonym of *infinite?*

By Way of Appreciation: It is human nature to value most highly the things that are denied us, or that are at least nearly out of reach. Helen Keller says, "Only the deaf appreciate hearing; only the blind realize the manifold blessings that lie in sight." Perhaps it is because Lafcadio Hearn had only a fraction of normal vision that he was so unusually sensitive to loveliness of color and form. But Hearn was sensitive to beauty of sound as well; hence his words have a musical cadence. He chooses his syllables with a poet's regard for rhythm and melody. *Sunrise in Louisiana* might be called a word-painting with a musical setting.

Suggestions for Study: Reread the quotation from Hearn in the introduction to the essay. Make a list of at least ten words from the essay that have color. List ten more that have form (like "curves"). Do you find any words or phrases here that are suggestive of mood?

Alliteration—the use within a line of several words beginning with the same consonant—is a favorite device of poets. There are several striking examples of alliteration in sentences of this essay. See how many you can find.

Certain words are popular with poets because they sound musical. For instance, "golden" is more pleasing to the ear than "yellow"; and "rose" sounds prettier than "pink." Find from six to ten examples of words which Hearn chose for their melody.

What details suggest a "tropical" setting? With what poetic figures does the author soften such prosaic details as sugar mills and city wharves?

Exercises and Creative Work: When you next have an opportunity to watch a sunset, a sunrise, or a moonlit landscape, look for colors and forms and movement. Then as quickly as possible jot down your impressions so that when you have leisure you may work them into a descriptive essay of your own.

Read another colorful essay by Lafcadio Hearn. Write a précis of it to be read in class.

THE HISTORY OF THE AMERICAN ESSAY

General Characteristics

The essay of the twentieth century presents a bewildering range of writers and types. Since its inception, the American essay has walked side by side with the American magazine. Our most successful essayists have been editors or regular contributors to such magazines as the *Atlantic Monthly, Harper's* and the *Century.* Today the chief medium of circulation of the essay is the literary magazine and the better-class popular magazine. Besides the featured articles of established essayists, delightful familiar essays appear monthly in such departments as "The Contributors' Club" and the "Lion's Mouth." It will require the judgment of time to determine which of these scores of writers shall be called "great." Today we at least enjoy scores of essayists, several of whom are represented here.

Types of the Modern Essay

People are unquestionably the most interesting of all things in an interesting world, and much of the fascination that some folks have for other folks lies in their difference. No two persons are exactly alike. No one person is always the same. Personalities are delightfully varied and delightfully variable. Now any work that is as personal as the essay must share this infinite variety, as indeed it does. There are almost as many different kinds of essays as there are different kinds of people and kinds of moods. It is thus rather difficult to separate them into hard and fast classifications of type and form, but the authors' reasons for writing the essays makes a good basis of division.

Here we are considering particularly the informal essay, the purpose of which is to entertain. But people find entertainment in different ways. Some like to go camping; some like to visit; some like to daydream; and some like to joke. All these forms of entertainment—and many more—are reflected in our writings. Because Americans are so fond of life in the open, it is not surprising that the group of "Essays of the Out-of-Doors" is very large. And the range is broad. There are such different sorts as the wild-life studies of Burroughs, the camping-out experiences of Van Dyke or Eaton, the scientific journeyings of Beebe or Byrd. Another writer takes his flights with his imagination, and the "Essay of Fancy" sweeps us along as stowaways. Occasionally the light essay hides a serious purpose beneath its gayer cloak and we have "The Essay for Reflection." The American is reputedly unemotional, but he is not without sentiment. On the contrary, he feels deeply; and his finest literature voices his real pleasure in people or in places or in beauty of nature and art. Thus it is that his "Essays of Appreciation" are most delightful. And then the true American has a lively sense of humor. Often he writes an essay just "For Fun." Yes, the American essay has a many-sided appeal. Let us study some of the groups more closely.

ESSAYS OF THE OUT-OF-DOORS

One need only to glance at the titles of a bookcaseful of essays to note the great number of out-of-door volumes. If, lured by their captions, he pauses to read, a wealth of pleasure and adventure is his. He may make camp in the wilds of Canada or on the slopes of the Sierras. He may share the joys of jungle days and jungle nights. He may trail the wild bee to its honey tree. Manifestly the American sportsman is an honest sportsman, for he gives his reader both sides of the picture. It is no earthly paradise which one visits but an outdoor world of reality. There are sun and wind and rain and flies. Sometimes mud, sometimes snow slows the march. Often the biggest fish gets away. But the zest for the trail is there. One forgets the 5,000-foot climb in the breathtaking beauty of the view from the mountain-top. And when the smudge has been built and the mosquito-net dropped, there is sleep on a balsam bed, to an undertone of soft night noises of the woods. Who are the men that lead into such pleasant trails? Where did they learn their outdoor lore?

John Burroughs (1837–1921)

John Burroughs is a pleasant link between the essayists of the nineteenth and twentieth centuries. Born on a farm in the Catskills in 1837, his early manhood knew Irving, Emerson, Holmes, and Lowell—all in their prime. His period of greatest activity immediately followed the Civil War. By 1873, he was ready to retire and take his ease at "Riverby" on the banks of the Hudson; yet there was left to him nearly half a century of living and writing. His death in 1921 allows him to be ranked with the "moderns" in American literature.

Like Thoreau, Burroughs knew the secrets that nature will unfold to him who waits and watches on her doorstep; yet for all his delight in nature study, he was not a recluse. Burroughs knew and liked men. He was a successful business man. He was forceful and active, and counted among his friends such leaders as Theodore Roosevelt and John Muir. In one of his essays Burroughs says that the student of nature

"has only to stay at home and see the procession pass." More consistent
than many another writer, for over forty years he did just that. Most
of his observations on bees and birds and plants were made in his orchards
at Riverby; in his rustic retreat, "Slabsides"; or on the farm of his birth
near Roxbury.

John Burroughs began his writings as a child. At fourteen he wrote
his first essays, and at nineteen he had had his first acceptance from
the *Atlantic Monthly*. His best known works, however, appeared in the
last forty years of his life. Volume after volume flowed from his pen
—mostly wood-lore with such revealing titles as *Birds and Poets, Locusts
and Wild Honey, Afoot and Afloat,* and *The Summit of the Years.* So
full of interests and simple pleasures was his life that he could, in all
sincerity, write in his closing years, "Serene I fold my hands and wait."
And serenely it was that he died in the home that he loved, at the
age of eighty-four.

Other Writers of the Out-of-Doors

To give in a short space a complete list of American essayists who
find—or found—their inspiration in the out-of-doors would be impossible. Among those who have reached the widest circles of readers one
remembers John Muir, Scotch-born, American-bred naturalist who helped
to secure many of our western national parks and who wrote entranc-
ingly of his adventures in the Sierras and in Alaska. Enos Mills is
another writer who has voiced the lure of the West, as his *Spell of the
Rockies* testifies. Nor must we forget Theodore Roosevelt whose joy
in the out-of-doors is preserved for us in such volumes as *Hunting Adventures in the West.* Then there are men of today—men like Akeley
and Byrd and Ditmars, as well as Charles William Beebe, and Stewart
Edward White, who bring the far corners of the earth near to us in
popular volumes.

We must remember that the magazines of America are still the chief
outlet for the American essay. The well-known literary magazines, the
better-class popular magazines, and such specialized publications as *The
National Geographic* and *Travel* present usually the first accounts of
adventures at home and abroad. Moreover, the outdoor magazines such
as *American Forests, Field and Stream, Nature Magazine, Open Road
for Boys,* and *Outdoor Life* are filled with interesting articles, many of
which will eventually find their way into volumes for the essay book-
shelves.

ESSAYS OF FANCY

It is not only young folks who love to wander in the "Land of Let's
Pretend." *Alice in Wonderland* offers as rare entertainment to the
grown-up as to the child for whom it was written—sometimes, one
suspects, more. Few folks ever outgrow their delight in fairy tales.
Probably as many good "yarns" are spun for the fun of spinning as for

the fun of the listeners. Certainly most writers like to take a mental holiday once in a while and let fancy have a fling. Ancient mythology pictured poetry as a winged horse, Pegasus, who mounted into the clouds with the writer astride him. Sometimes prose seems to borrow a sister steed and wing her way aloft. In these flights, however, the imaginary steed is not quite successful in shaking off the restraining reins. The essay of fancy, more often than not, hints at an underlying meaning and so distinguishes itself from the essay written just for fun.

Heywood Broun (1888–1939)

Heywood Broun was a newspaper man by vocation and by avocation. After his graduation from Harvard in 1910, he held many journalistic jobs, progressing from reporter to correspondent, to critic, to columnist and feature writer. From 1928 to 1939 he was employed by the Scripps-Howard papers. He transferred to the *New York Post* only two weeks before his death. "It Seems to Me" was his popular column. He was also a lecturer on the drama and dramatic critic for *Vanity Fair*. The humorous, imaginative quirk so necessary to the columnist flavors the essays which he wrote between assignments. To hear the titles is to want to sample them. Besides *Seeing Things at Night,* there are *Pieces of Hate, The Boy Grew Older,* and *Gandle Follows His Nose.*

Because of his prominence as a columnist and because of his long association with radical movements, his conversion to the Catholic Church in May, 1939, created a sensation. You will find the absorbing story of his conversion and will gain a clear insight into the "Broun nobody knew" by reading the sermon preached by Monsignor Fulton Sheen at Broun's funeral in St. Patrick's Cathedral, New York City, December 20, 1939.

Other Writers of Essays of Fancy

Almost every writer of the familiar essay at one time or another finds himself in a mood for an imaginative theme; hence one may surprise bits of fancy tucked away in volumes where he would least expect to find them. Even Samuel McChord Crothers whom we associate with rather sedate ideas, one day turned a convention of librarians topsy-turvy and gave us instead a *Convention of Books* in which the books discuss their readers. Among the few volumes which are characteristically fanciful is *Penguin Persons and Peppermints* which was written by Walter Prichard Eaton for his little sister.

ESSAYS FOR REFLECTION

Occasionally the essay wishes to instruct or persuade rather than merely to entertain. In this case it will usually be more formal in tone, more orderly in development, more rigid in structure. The essay for reflection or appreciation is often cast in this more formal mold. It may present a theory about getting on in the world, about understanding oneself

or the other fellow, about smoothing the difficulties—real and imaginary
—that trouble us all. At any rate, it calls for reflection and well repays
in new ideas the time one takes to ponder it.

Agnes Repplier (1858–   )

Turning to writing as a career because she had to earn a living and
writing was the only thing she could do, Miss Repplier began with short
stories. When the editor of the *Catholic World* told her that she would
never be a story writer and should try her hand at essays, she acted on his
suggestion, to become, as a matter of fact, one of the ablest of American
essayists. Wit, imagination, an intimate acquaintance with the best literature, and a keen, searching mind are the equipment which enable Miss
Repplier to transform often unpromising topics into exquisite essays
perfect in form and delightfully informal in manner. She might well be
called the Essayist Laureate of cats. Besides devoting to them one entire
book, *The Fireside Sphinx,* and single essays in other volumes, she published *The Cat,* an anthology of verse and prose about cats.

Miss Repplier was born of French parentage in Philadelphia in April,
1858. Her early education was received at the Sacred Heart Convent,
Torresdale, Pennsylvania. Honorary degrees have been conferred upon
her by the University of Pennsylvania, Columbia, and Yale, and in 1911
she was awarded the Laetare Medal by the University of Notre Dame.

The Reverend James M. Gillis, C.S.P. (1876–   )

Father Gillis was born in Boston in 1876. After graduation from the
Boston Latin School he continued his education at St. Charles College,
Catonsville, Maryland, St. John's Seminary, Brighton, Massachusetts, and
the Catholic University, Washington. He joined the Paulist Fathers in
1900, and was ordained priest in 1901. Since 1922 he has been editor of
the *Catholic World.*

As editor, lecturer, and radio speaker Father Gillis has established a
national reputation in Catholic circles. Because he has "a lawyer's instinct
for basic principles," and a style that is pointed, graphic, and vigorous,
Father Gillis' editorials, like his sermons and lectures, have more than
the ephemeral value which usually attaches to these forms of writing. In
fact, most of his books, collections of such writing, have been published in
answer to popular demand. Thousands who have not read his books have
learned to regard him highly for his several series of radio lectures on the
Catholic Hour.

Other Writers of Essays for Reflection

In the essay for reflection the writer offers to his readers his ideas
and thoughts on questions concerning life. Usually the reflective essay
has an abstract theme, such as faith, the behavior of crowds, or the delight
with which one studies a favorite subject. A popular writer of reflective
essays is Father Leonard Feeney, author of *Fish on Friday,* and

You'd Better Come Quietly. Henry van Dyke's essays are often reflective such as *Fair Play and Democracy* and *Is the World Growing Better*.

ESSAYS OF APPRECIATION

One of the charms of the light essay is the subtle way in which it opens the eyes of the reader to values hitherto unnoticed or neglected. The writer has paused to record his own appreciation of a happy moment, a favorite book, a helpful friend; and in so doing he stirs the reader to appreciation of experiences or persons or places near to himself. The essay of appreciation sometimes leads us to admire, even to love, those whom we had never known. In a sense, any essay which helps one to discover or rediscover truth and beauty in the world and joy in human relationships is an essay of appreciation.

Brother Leo, F.S.C. (1881–   )

Asked by an interviewer from *The Queen's Work* what advice on their reading he could give to Catholic young men and women, Brother Leo replied: "Tell them to concentrate on the worthwhile things. . . . Their only salvation is acquaintance with what Matthew Arnold called 'the best thought in the world.'" He added, "An educated person should make a choice of two or three of the following and get to know them thoroughly. First of all there is the Bible, taken merely as a masterpiece of literature. Then Homer, Dante, Virgil, the Greek dramatists, Goethe, Shakespeare. I'm almost tempted to add Horace. If a man is immersed in two or three of these, he can never be wholly common or unclean from a literary standpoint." For fear that such a list might seem to represent the belief that all great books belong to the past, he hastened to add that "age and time have nothing to do with the excellence of a book. Time merely proves that a book has stood the test. Time canonizes really good books." This message from a man of Brother Leo's literary stature is not only precious advice for the young (and old), but also an indication of the ideals held by him through a long life of literary activity—"the worthwhile things."

Like that other outstanding Catholic literary critic of an earlier day, Brother Azarias, Brother Leo is a member of the Congregation of the Brothers of the Christian Schools; he entered that order in 1897. Besides holding the Bachelor's and Master's degrees from St. Mary's College, Oakland, California, he has a Doctor's degree from the Catholic University and an honorary degree of Doctor of Laws from Santa Clara College. He began his career as a teacher of English in the Sacred Heart High School, San Francisco, in 1903. Since 1908 he has taught English at his Alma Mater, St. Mary's College. Since 1931 he has also been a member of the summer-school faculty at the University of California.

The varied types of books which he has published indicate his versatility. Besides a textbook in *English Literature*, a book for teachers on *Religion and the Study of Literature*, and a life of *St. John Baptist de La Salle*, founder of the Christian Brothers, he has published two novels, *False Gods*, and *The Tree of Kerioth*, two dramas, *Dante the Wingbearer*, and *Ecce Homo*, and a learned study called *Contrast in Shakespeare's Historical Plays*. Ever since 1906 he has been a feature writer for the *San Francisco Monitor*, and for long his column of *Book Chat* has been a valued feature in several Catholic magazines. How he finds time, in addition to all this and his regular teaching assignment, to give frequent lectures on Dante and Shakespeare is his own secret.

Michael Williams (1877–   )

The reader of Michael Williams' spiritual autobiography, *The Book of the High Romance*, published in 1918, will readily understand why he was well qualified to write ten years later a volume entitled *Catholicism and the Modern Mind*, the book from which a selection is included in this volume. For thirty years Williams had struggled along as one of the very "modern minds," in quest of an answer to a long, long question—to find it finally in Catholicism.

Michael Williams was born in Halifax, Nova Scotia, in 1877, the son of a sea captain; was only fourteen when his father died at sea and left the family penniless. From that day on his life was a struggle to realize his ambition to discover the true meaning of life and to interpret that discovery to the world worthily. Even as a boy he longed to become a literary artist. During dreary hours of work in a drygoods warehouse in Halifax he stole time for reading and writing, even for editing a literary magazine, which died after the third issue—and lost his job.

When the family moved to Boston to improve its fortunes, he slaved in the dank sub-cellar of a five-and-ten-cent store by day and wrote by night. Tuberculosis drove him South for a cure. Between sieges of that dread scourge he was a newspaper reporter and free-lance writer in Boston, New York, and San Francisco; was lucky enough to be city editor of the San Francisco *Daily News* at the time of the earthquake and fire in 1906; resigned, and joined Upton Sinclair's Socialist colony at Helicon Hall in New York; and collaborated with Sinclair in the writing of *Good Health and How We Won It*. He had not won it. He returned to California, to rebuild his health at Carmel-by-the-Sea. The reading of the autobiography of St. Teresa of Lisieux, a meeting with Archbishop Hanna, a call at the Carmelite convent in San Francisco, and what appears to have been the direct intervention of "The Little Flower," brought him back in 1912 to the Church which he had deserted at the age of fourteen, before he had really known it. He had found the answer to his quest.

Since then Catholic journalism has engaged his energies. As editor of the *Commonweal* and as author of several books, he worthily interprets Catholicism to the modern mind; the modern mind to Catholicism.

Sister Julie, O.P.

Sister Julie was born in Washington, D. C. After graduation from Notre Dame Academy in that city she received her Bachelor's degree from Trinity College and spent a year at the Catholic University. After profession in the Dominican Congregation of the Most Holy Rosary at Sinsinawa, Wisconsin, Sister Julie became a member of the English faculty of St. Clara College, Sinsinawa, later transferred to River Forest, Illinois, under the name of Rosary College. She received her Master of Arts degree from Notre Dame University. After two years of study in the Honor School of English Language and Literature at Oxford University, England, she received the M. A. (Oxon.). Sister Julie has published poems and essays in *Commonweal, Ave Maria, Orate Fratres,* and the *Journal of Adult Education.*

Other Writers of Appreciative Essays

Much larger in numbers than any other type of essay are the essays of appreciation. To be a poet or an essayist one must be possessed of the seeing eye and the understanding heart. Naturally then, the poet and essayist help their readers to see and understand. It is impossible to name all such sympathetic essayists, but there follows a partial list of the better-known writers.

Harry Esty Dounce is a young newspaper man who helps to increase our enjoyment of current literature through his comments and reviews, but he is probably best known for his little paper, *Some Nonsense about a Dog.* William Lyon Phelps is a popular college professor who writes about books and authors, and appreciates sports. Woodrow Wilson discussed keenly personalities and philosophies as well as economics and politics.

ESSAYS FOR FUN

Love may make the world go round, but fun eases the strain. A bit of well-placed humor is like a lubricant in the machinery of living. If, as Emerson says, man's ability to appreciate beauty is sufficient excuse for the existence of all things lovely, then his ability to laugh must be reason enough for having fun. Even serious writers like to play once in a while. Some essays have not a grain of sense. They were written for fun. Such works fall into two general classes—the occasional diversions of writers who are paid to be serious, and the regular output of the men who are paid to be funny.

Most humorous prose is short, and much of it carries an undercurrent of homely philosophy.

Christopher Morley (1890–   )

Books and people—these two interests lie at the heart of Christopher Morley's life and works. Whether we listen to him from the lecture

platform or from the pages of his books, we are impressed with his
knowledge of writers old and new and with his reverence for the volumes
which preserve their works.   Morley comes naturally enough by his love
of books, for his father has been for years a college professor and his
mother is a musician and poet.   Thus young Christopher grew up in a
cultured, scholarly atmosphere.   After graduating from Haverford College at the age of twenty, he was appointed Rhodes Scholar from the
state of Maryland to Oxford University.   His three years at the English
school deepened and broadened his love for English literature.   Loosely
quoted, his advice today to young people who aspire to write is this:
"Read the classics.   Read the prose of Lamb and De Quincey and Hazlitt
and Coleridge.   Read all the English literature you can get your hands on."

Frank Moore Colby (1865–1925)

A shy, reserved man with a vast store of information and a ready
wit—that was Frank Moore Colby.   To the world he was known as an
editor of encyclopedias.   To a small circle of friends he showed himself
a warmly human individual.   He was brilliant and scholarly, so it seems
natural that after finishing his schooling at Columbia University, in 1888,
he became a college professor and lecturer, specializing in the field of
history and economics.   He began writing for encyclopedias as a side
line, but it eventually replaced teaching as his life work.   From 1900 to
1925 most of his working hours were devoted to writing for and editing
the *International Encyclopedia* and the *New International Encyclopedia.*

If you are at all familiar with books of general reference, you know
that they are not the dull, dry books they are reputed to be.   Yet they
do deal with facts and they do demand accuracy.   As a sort of diversion
from the exactness of his profession, Mr. Colby began writing sketches,
humorous essays, all sorts of lighter miscellany in his leisure.   These
contributions found eager reception with such periodicals as the *Bookman,
Harper's Weekly, Vanity Fair* and *Harper's Magazine.*   From time to
time collections of the essays appeared under titles like *Imaginary Obligations, Constrained Attitudes* and *The Margin of Hesitation.*   Mr. Colby
had become, at the time of his death in 1925, one of the most popular
writers of the light essay.   Of him the *Bookman* said, "He had both feet
planted firmly on the ground and his head grazed the stars."

Ralph Bergengren (1871–   )

Ralph Bergengren (his middle names are Wilhelm Alexis) has been
a writer and artist by profession since his graduation from Harvard in
1893.   His jobs have ranged from cartoonist to art critic and from
dramatic critic to editor and independent author.   Born in Gloucester,
Massachusetts, he has done most of his work in Boston.   "The Contributor's Club" of the *Atlantic Monthly* has introduced many of his
essays to the reader.   He writes, besides, feature articles and fiction
for a number of magazines.   The most pleasing of his essays have been

published in volumes like *In Case of Need, The Comforts of Home, The Seven Ages of Man,* and *Gentlemen All and Merry Companions.*

Other American Humorists

Humor is a broad and crowded field. Which of the last generation will survive to rank with the great American wits, we can only guess. It is safe to say that Will Rogers and Irvin S. Cobb will be assured of a place. There are others that seem to stand out among the crowd, and the newspaper has been in almost every case the means of introducing them to the world. The "column," the popular feature of the American paper, has paved the way to recognition for many a humorist. It takes wit and originality plus an interest in people to make a successful column-ist, and the reporter with the right combination eventually gets his chance. If his chatter hits just right, his name is made, thanks to the "by-line" and the syndicates. Some of the earlier humorists who followed this road to success were George Ade, Abe Martin, and Ring Lardner. Two of today's journalists who have branched from column-conducting to successful independent writing are Donald Ogden Stewart and Don Marquis.

Essays of the Out-of-Doors

THE PASTORAL BEES

From *Locusts and Wild Honey*

JOHN BURROUGHS

By Way of Introduction: The life story of a hive of bees or a colony of ants is as thrilling as any movie serial ever shown. Besides, it is a true story. The price of admission to the show is reckoned in time and patience rather than in money. If you have keen senses and an alert interest, and if you are willing to wait and watch, you may see an amazing drama, with love, jealousy, rebellion, murder, majority rule, order—all in turn directing the action. John Burroughs had the necessary patience and saw the show again and again. Scores of papers on bees give his intimate reports on the dramas. The following selection shows the insects in a prosaic mood—at work gathering bread and honey. Even so, it is good entertainment.

THE honey-bee goes forth from the hive in spring like the dove from Noah's ark, and it is not till after many days that she brings back the olive leaf, which in this case is a pellet of golden pollen upon each hip, usually obtained from the alder or the swamp willow. In a country where maple sugar is made the bees get their first taste of sweet from the sap as it flows from the spiles, or as it dries and is condensed upon the sides of the buckets. They will sometimes, in their eagerness, come about the boiling-place and be overwhelmed by the steam and the smoke. But bees appear to be more eager for bread in the spring than for honey: their supply of this article, perhaps, does not keep as well as their stores of the latter; hence fresh bread, in the shape of new pollen, is diligently sought for. My bees get their first supplies from the catkins of the willows. How quickly they find them out! If but one catkin opens anywhere within range, a bee is on hand that very hour to rifle it, and it is a most pleasing experience to stand near the hive some mild April day and see them come pouring in with their little baskets packed with this first fruitage of the spring. They will have new bread now; they have been to mill in good earnest; see their dusty coats, and the golden grist they bring home with them.

When a bee brings pollen into the hive he advances to the cell in which it is to be deposited and kicks it off, as one might his overalls or rubber boots, making one foot help the other; then he walks off without ever looking behind him; another bee, one of the indoor hands, comes along and rams it down with his head and packs it into the cell, as the dairymaid packs butter into a firkin with a ladle.

The first spring wild-flowers, whose shy faces among the dry leaves and rocks are so welcome, are rarely frequented by the bee. The anemone,[1] the hepatica, the arbutus,[2] the numerous violets, the spring beauty, the corydalis,[3] woo all lovers of nature, but seldom woo the honey-loving bee. The arbutus, lying low and keeping green all winter, attains to perfume and honey, but only once have I seen it frequented by bees.

The first honey is perhaps obtained from the flowers of the red maple and the golden willow. The latter sends forth a wild, delicious perfume. The sugar maple blooms a little later, and from its silken tassels a rich nectar is gathered. My bees will not label these different varieties for me, as I really wish

---

[1] ANEMONE—The anemone, like the hepatica and bloodroot, is a delicate, nearly odorless, spring flower, growing low among the grasses.

[2] ARBUTUS—The trailing arbutus has exquisitely fragrant, tiny, wax-like flowers of pink and white.

[3] CORYDALIS—The co-ryd′a-lis is a showy but scentless flower belonging to the family of fume-worts.

they would. Honey from the maple, a tree so clean and whole-some, and full of such virtues every way, would be something to put one's tongue to. Or that from the blossoms of the apple, the peach, the cherry, the quince, the currant,—one would like a card [4] of each of these varieties to note their peculiar qualities. The apple-blossom is very important to the bees. A single swarm has been known to gain twenty pounds in weight during its continuance. Bees love the ripened fruit, too, and in August and September will suck themselves tipsy upon varieties such as the sops-of-wine.

The interval between the blooming of the fruit trees and that of the clover and the raspberry is bridged over in many locali-ties by the honey locust. What a delightful summer murmur these trees send forth at this season! I know nothing about the quality of the honey, but it ought to keep well. But when the red raspberry blooms, the fountains of plenty are unsealed indeed; what a commotion about the hives then, especially in localities where it is extensively cultivated, as in places along the Hudson! The delicate white clover, which begins to bloom about the same time, is neglected; even honey [5] itself is passed by for this modest, colorless, all but odorless flower. A field of these berries in June sends forth a continuous murmur like that of an enormous hive. The honey is not so white as that obtained from clover, but it is easier gathered; it is in shallow cups, while that of the clover is in deep tubes. The bees are up and at it before sunrise, and it takes a brisk shower to drive them in. But the clover blooms later and blooms every-where, and is the staple source of supply of the finest quality of honey. The red clover yields up its stores only to the longer proboscis of the bumblebee, else the bee pasturage [6] of our agricultural districts would be unequaled.

The rose, with all its beauty and perfume, yields no honey to the bee, unless the wild species be sought by the bumblebee.

Among the humbler plants let me not forget the dandelion that so early dots the sunny slopes, and upon which the bee languidly grazes, wallowing to his knees in the golden but not

---

[4] CARD—A sheet or layer of honeycomb.

[5] EVEN HONEY, ETC.—Bees are very fond of their own honey, and it is often used as bait by those who are trying to capture wild bees.

[6] PASTURAGE—Here used in the general sense of feeding-ground or food-source.

over-succulent pasturage. From the blooming rye and wheat the bee gathers pollen, also from the obscure blossoms of Indian corn. Among weeds, catnip is the great favorite. It lasts nearly the whole season and yields richly. It could no doubt be profitably cultivated in some localities, and catnip honey would be a novelty in the market. It would probably partake of the aromatic properties of the plant from which it was derived.

Among your stores of honey gathered before midsummer you may chance upon a card, or mayhap only a square inch or two of comb, in which the liquid is as transparent as water, of a delicious quality, with a slight flavor of mint. This is the product of the linden or basswood, of all the trees in our forest the one most beloved by the bees. Melissa, the goddess of honey, has placed her seal upon this tree. The wild swarms in the woods frequently reap a choice harvest from it. I have seen a mountain-side thickly studded with it, its straight, tall, smooth, light gray shaft carrying its deep green crown far aloft, like the tulip-tree or the maple.

In some of the northwestern states there are large forests of it, and the amount of honey reported stored by strong swarms in this section during the time the tree is in bloom is quite incredible. As a shade and ornamental tree the linden is fully equal to the maple, and, if it were as extensively planted and cared for, our supplies of virgin honey would be greatly increased.

It is a homely old stanza current among bee folk that

> A swarm of bees in May
> Is worth a load of hay;
> A swarm of bees in June
> Is worth a silver spoon;
> But a swarm in July
> Is not worth a fly.

A swarm in May is indeed a treasure; it is, like an April baby,[7] sure to thrive, and will very likely itself send out a swarm a month or two later: but a swarm in July is not to be despised; it will store no clover or linden honey but plenty of the sun-

[7] APRIL BABY—Before scientific care and modern sanitation became general, the death-rate of infants was unbelievably high. A baby born in the spring of the year had the best chances of surviving because natural conditions were most favorable.

tanned product of the plebeian buckwheat. Buckwheat honey [8]
is the black sheep in this white flock, but there is spirit and
character in it. It lays hold of the taste in no equivocal manner,
especially when at a winter breakfast it meets its fellow, the
russet buckwheat cake. Bread and honey to cover it from the
same stalk is double good fortune. It is not black, either, but
nut-brown. How the bees love it, and they bring the delicious
odor of the blooming plant to the hive with them, so that in
the moist warm twilight the apiary is redolent with the perfume
of buckwheat.

Yet evidently it is not the perfume of any flower that attracts the bee; they pay no attention to the sweet-scented
lilac, or to heliotrope, but work upon sumach, silkweed, and the
hateful snapdragon. In September they are hard pressed, and
do well if they pick up enough sweet to pay the running expenses of their establishment. The purple asters and the goldenrod are about all that remain to them.

Bees will go three or four miles in quest of honey, but it is a
great advantage to move the hive near the good pasturage, as
has been the custom from the earliest times in the Old World.
Some enterprising person, taking a hint perhaps from the ancient
Egyptians, who had floating apiaries on the Nile, has tried the
experiment of floating several hundred colonies [9] north on the
Mississippi, starting from New Orleans and following the opening season up, thus realizing a sort of perpetual May or June,
the chief attraction being the blossoms of the river willow,
which yield honey of rare excellence. Some of the bees were
no doubt left behind, but the amount of virgin honey secured
must have been very great. In September they should have
begun the return trip, following the retreating summer south.

It is the making of wax that costs with the bee. As with
the poet, the form, the receptacle, gives him more trouble than
the sweet that fills it, though, to be sure, there is always more
or less empty comb in both cases. The honey he can have for
the gathering, but the wax he must make himself,—must evolve
from his own inner consciousness. When wax is to be made,
the wax-makers fill themselves with honey and retire into their

[8] BUCKWHEAT HONEY—Honey gathered from the flowers of the buckwheat
is darker in color and more strongly flavored than other varieties.
[9] COLONIES—Of bees.

chamber for private meditation; it is like some solemn religious rite: they take hold of hands, or hook themselves together in long lines that hang in festoons from the top of the hive, and wait for the miracle to transpire. After about twenty-four hours their patience is rewarded, the honey is turned into wax, minute scales of which are secreted from between the rings of the abdomen of each bee; this is taken off and from it the comb is built up. It is calculated that about twenty-five pounds of honey are used in elaborating one pound of comb, to say nothing of the time that is lost. Hence the importance, in an economical point of view, of a recent device by which the honey is extracted and the comb returned intact to the bees. But honey without the comb is the perfume without the rose,—it is sweet merely, and soon degenerates into candy. Half the delectableness is in breaking down these frail and exquisite walls yourself, and tasting the nectar before it has lost its freshness by contact with the air. Then the comb is a sort of shield or foil that prevents the tongue from being overwhelmed by the first shock of the sweet.

Honey was a much more important article of food with the ancients than it is with us. As they appear to have been unacquainted with sugar, honey, no doubt, stood them instead. It is too rank [10] and pungent for the modern taste; it soon cloys upon the palate. It demands the appetite of youth, and the strong, robust digestion of people who live much in the open air. It is a more wholesome food than sugar, and modern confectionery is poison beside it. Besides grape sugar, honey contains manna,[11] mucilage, pollen, acid, and other vegetable odoriferous substances and juices. It is a sugar with a kind of wild natural bread added. The manna of itself is both food and medicine, and the pungent vegetable extracts have rare virtues.

Hence it is not without reason that with the ancients a land flowing with milk and honey should mean a land abounding in all good things; and the queen in the nursery rhyme, who lingered in the kitchen to eat "bread and honey" while the "king was in the parlor counting out his money," was doing a very sensible thing.

[10] RANK—Here, merely "strong."
[11] MANNA—A sweet fluid with medicinal properties which seeps out of cuts made in the stems of certain varieties of the ash tree. Look in an encyclopedia under *Fraxinus* (the family name for *ash*) for further information.

The best honey is the product of the milder parts of the temperate zone. There are too many rank and poisonous plants in the tropics. But honey is honey the world over; and the bee is the bee still. "Men may degenerate," says an old traveler, "may forget the arts by which they acquired renown; manufacturers may fail, and commodities be debased; but the sweets of the wild-flowers of the wilderness, the industry and natural mechanics of the bee, will continue without change or derogation."

Vocabulary Study: *Pellets; pollen; spiles; rifle* (verb); *grist; firkin; proboscis; succulent; obscure; aromatic; incredible; plebeian; equivocal; apiary; redolent; transpire; intact; delectableness; foil; cloys; mucilage; odoriferous; derogation.*

Give the difference between *dark, opaque, obscure.* From the following list choose two synonyms for *obscure: obtain, want, dark, light, opaque, bright, hidden.* What is an antonym of *plebeian?*

By Way of Appreciation: The charm of John Burroughs' essays lies in the simplicity and directness of his manner. He just sits down and talks to us about the things he has learned. His writings are remarkably free from scientific terms—perhaps because he studied nature from life rather than from books. Notice in this particular essay his easy familiarity not only with the ways of the bees but also with all sorts of flowering plants. Others of his works prove him an equally interesting authority on birds, animals, the weather, fruits, gardening—in fact, on any outdoor subject.

Suggestions for Study: If there is anyone in the class qualified to talk on bee culture and the production of honey, an oral report would provide an interesting introduction to the study of the essay.

Explain the metaphor of the olive leaf and the pollen in the first sentence. (See the story of Noah in Genesis, vi–viii.) What is meant, by "bread and honey from the same stalk"? Can you explain the second sentence in the paragraph beginning, "It is the making of wax that costs with the bee"? Why is there "always more or less empty comb in both cases"? Most commercial honey is now strained from the comb and sold in glasses or jars. Do you agree with Mr. Burroughs that "honey without the comb is perfume without the rose"? If not, give reasons for your preference of strained honey. Most of the trees and flowers mentioned in the essay are common in the temperate zone. Test your nature lore by listing those that you know and can recognize upon sight. Who in the class can produce the longest list?

Exercises and Creative Work: Write a précis of the paragraph beginning, "It is the making of wax that costs with the bee."

Draft an out-of-door essay by making an outline on one of the following topics: *Community Ants; Hornets; Wild Geese; Muskrats Are Industrious Fellows; Our House Wren.*

Essays of Fancy

THE FIFTY-FIRST DRAGON

From *Seeing Things at Night*

HEYWOOD BROUN

By Way of Introduction: "Take one high school boy—athlete pre-ferred—and one good measure of *Ivanhoe* or *Idylls of the King;* add two bowls of pop-corn, one apple, and one large mince pie; mix well before retiring and let simmer until beautifully done"—so might run the recipe for *The Fifty-First Dragon.* Whether or not Mr. Broun followed the directions literally, he produced the dragon—beautifully done.

OF ALL the pupils at the knight school Gawaine le Coeur-Hardy [1] was among the least promising. He was tall and sturdy, but his instructors soon discovered that he lacked spirit. He would hide in the woods when the jousting class was called, al-though his companions and members of the faculty sought to appeal to his better nature by shouting to him to come out and break his neck like a man. Even when they told him that the lances were padded, the horses no more than ponies, and the field unusually soft for late autumn, Gawaine refused to grow en-thusiastic. The Headmaster and the Assistant Professor of Pleas-aunce [2] were discussing the case one spring afternoon, and the Assistant Professor could see no remedy but expulsion.

"No," said the Headmaster, as he looked out at the purple hills which ringed the school, "I think I'll train him to slay dragons."

"He might be killed," objected the Assistant Professor.

"So he might," replied the Headmaster, brightly; but he added, more soberly, "we must consider the greater good. We are responsible for the formation of this lad's character."

"Are the dragons particularly bad this year?" interrupted the Assistant Professor. This was characteristic. He always seemed restive when the head of the school began to talk ethics and the ideals of the institution.

"I've never known them worse," replied the Headmaster. "Up in the hills to the south last week they killed a number of peas-ants, two cows, and a prize pig. And if this dry spell holds

---

[1] GAWAINE LE COEUR-HARDY—Gawaine the Stout-Hearted.
[2] PLEASAUNCE—Literally, "that which pleases"; here probably "sports."

there's no telling when they may start a forest fire simply by breathing around indiscriminately."

"Would any refund on the tuition fee be necessary in case of an accident to young Coeur-Hardy?"

"No," the principal answered judicially; "that's all covered in the contract. But as a matter of fact he won't be killed. Before I send him up in the hills I'm going to give him a magic word."

"That's a good idea," said the Professor. "Sometimes they work wonders."

From that day on Gawaine specialized in dragons. His course included both theory and practice. In the morning there were long lectures on the history, anatomy, manners, and customs of dragons. Gawaine did not distinguish himself in these studies. He had a marvelously versatile gift for forgetting things. In the afternoon he showed to better advantage, for then he would go down to the South Meadow and practice with a battle-axe. In this exercise he was truly impressive, for he had enormous strength as well as speed and grace. He even developed a deceptive display of ferocity. Old alumni say that it was a thrilling sight to see Gawaine charging across the field toward the dummy paper dragon which had been set up for his practice. As he ran he would brandish his axe and shout "A murrain on thee!"[3] or some other vivid bit of campus slang. It never took him more than one stroke to behead the dummy dragon.

Gradually his task was made more difficult. Paper gave way to papier-mâché and finally to wood, but even the toughest of these dummy dragons had no terrors for Gawaine. One sweep of the axe always did the business. There were those who said that when the practice was protracted until dusk and the dragons threw long, fantastic shadows across the meadow, Gawaine did not charge so impetuously nor shout so loudly. It is possible there was malice in this charge. At any rate, the Headmaster decided by the end of June that it was time for the test. Only the night before, a dragon had come close to the school grounds and had eaten some of the lettuce from the garden. The faculty decided that Gawaine was ready. They gave him a diploma and a new battle-axe, and the Headmaster summoned him to a private conference.

[3] A MURRAIN ON THEE!—"A plague on thee," a reputed war-cry of the knights of old.

The faculty now decided that Gawaine was ready.

"Sit down," said the Headmaster. "Have a cigarette." Gawaine hesitated.

"Oh, I know it's against the rules," said the Headmaster; "but, after all, you have received your preliminary degree. You are no longer a boy. You are a man. Tomorrow you will go out into the world—the great world of achievement."

Gawaine took a cigarette. The Headmaster offered him a match, but he produced one of his own and began to puff away with a dexterity which quite amazed the principal.

"Here you have learned the theories of life," continued the Headmaster, resuming the thread of his discourse; "but, after all, life is not a matter of theories. Life is a matter of facts. It calls on the young and the old alike to face these facts, even though they are hard and sometimes unpleasant. Your problem, for example, is to slay dragons."

"They say that those dragons down in the south wood are five hundred feet long," ventured Gawaine, timorously.

"Stuff and nonsense!" said the Headmaster. "The curate saw one last week from the top of Arthur's Hill. The dragon was sunning himself down in the valley. The curate didn't have an opportunity to look at him very long because he felt it was his duty to hurry back to make a report to me. He said the monster —or shall I say, the big lizard?—wasn't an inch over two hundred feet. But the size has nothing at all to do with it. You'll find the big ones even easier than the little ones. They're far slower on their feet and less aggressive, I'm told. Besides, before you go I'm going to equip you in such fashion that you need have no fear of all the dragons in the world."

"I'd like an enchanted cap," said Gawaine.

"What's that?" answered the Headmaster, testily.

"A cap to make me disappear," explained Gawaine.

The Headmaster laughed indulgently. "You mustn't believe all those old wives' stories," he said. "There isn't any such thing. A cap to make you disappear, indeed! What would you do with it? You haven't even appeared yet. Why, my boy, you could walk from here to London, and nobody would so much as look at you. You're nobody. You couldn't be more invisible than that."

Gawaine seemed dangerously close to a relapse into his old habit of whimpering. The Headmaster reassured him: "Don't worry; I'll give you something much better than an enchanted cap. I'm going to give you a magic word. All you have to do is to repeat this magic charm once and no dragon can possibly harm a hair of your head. You can cut off his head at your leisure."

He took a heavy book from the shelf behind his desk and began to run through it. "Sometimes," he said, "the charm is a whole phrase or even a sentence. I might, for instance, give you 'To make the—' No, that might not do. I think a single word would be best for dragons."

"A short word," suggested Gawaine.

"It can't be too short or it wouldn't be potent. There isn't so much hurry as all that. Here's a splendid magic word: 'Rumplesnitz.' Do you think you can learn that?"

Gawaine tried and in an hour or so he seemed to have the word well in hand. Again and again he interrupted the lesson to inquire, "And if I say 'Rumplesnitz' the dragon can't possibly hurt me?" And always the Headmaster replied, "If you only say 'Rumplesnitz,' you are perfectly safe."

Toward morning Gawaine seemed resigned to his career. At daybreak the Headmaster saw him to the edge of the forest and pointed him to the direction in which he should proceed. About a mile away to the southwest a cloud of steam hovered over an open meadow in the woods, and the Headmaster assured Gawaine that under the steam he would find a dragon. Gawaine went forward slowly. He wondered whether it would be best to approach the dragon on the run, as he did in his practice in the South Meadow, or to walk toward him, shouting "Rumplesnitz" all the way.

The problem was decided for him. No sooner had he come to the fringe of the meadow than the dragon spied him and began to charge. It was a large dragon, and yet it seemed decidedly aggressive in spite of the Headmaster's statement to the contrary. As the dragon charged, it released huge clouds of hissing steam through its nostrils. It was almost as if a gigantic teapot had gone mad. The dragon came forward so fast, and Gawaine was so frightened, that he had time to say "Rumplesnitz" only once. As he said it he swung his battle-axe, and off popped the head of the dragon. Gawaine had to admit that it was even easier to kill a real dragon than a wooden one, if only you said "Rumplesnitz."

Gawaine brought the ears home and a small section of the tail. His schoolmates and the faculty made much of him and the Headmaster wisely kept him from being spoiled by insisting that he go on with his work. Every clear day Gawaine rose at dawn and went out to kill dragons. The Headmaster kept him at home when it rained, because he said the woods were damp and unhealthy at such times, and he didn't want the boy to run needless risks. Few good days passed in which Gawaine failed to get a dragon. On one particularly fortunate day he killed three, a husband and wife and a visiting relative. Gradually he developed a technique. Pupils who sometimes watched him from the hilltops a long way off said that he often allowed the dragon to come within a few feet before he said "Rumplesnitz." He came to say it with a mocking sneer. Occasionally he did stunts. Once when an excursion party from London was watching him he went into action with his right hand tied behind his back. The dragon's head came off just as easily.

As Gawaine's record of killings mounted higher, the Headmaster found it impossible to keep him completely in hand. He fell into the habit of stealing out at night and engaging in long drinking bouts at the village tavern. It was after such a debauch that he rose a little before dawn one fine August morning and started out after his fiftieth dragon. His head was heavy and his mind sluggish. He was heavy in other respects as well, for he had adopted the somewhat vulgar practice of wearing his medals, ribbons and all, when he went out dragon-hunting. The decorations began on his chest and ran all the way down to his abdomen. They must have weighed at least eight pounds.

Gawaine found a dragon in the same meadow where he had killed the first one. It was a fair-sized dragon but evidently an old one. Its face was wrinkled and Gawaine thought he had never seen so hideous a countenance. Much to the lad's disgust the monster refused to charge, and Gawaine was obliged to walk toward him. He whistled as he went. The dragon regarded him hopelessly but craftily. Of course it had heard of Gawaine. Even when the lad raised his battle-axe, the dragon made no move. It knew that there was no salvation in the quickest thrust of the head, for it had been informed that this hunter was protected by an enchantment. It merely waited, hoping something would turn up. Gawaine raised the battle-axe and suddenly lowered it again. He had grown very pale, and he trembled violently. The dragon suspected a trick. "What's the matter?" it asked, with false solicitude.

"I've forgotten the magic word," stammered Gawaine.

"What a pity!" said the dragon. "So that was the secret. It doesn't seem quite sporting to me, all this magic stuff, you know. Not cricket,[4] as we used to say when I was a little dragon; but, after all, that's a matter of opinion."

Gawaine was so helpless with terror that the dragon's confidence rose immeasurably and it could not resist the temptation to show off a bit.

"Could I possibly be of any assistance?" it asked. "What's the first letter of the magic word?"

"It begins with an 'R'," said Gawaine, weakly.

"Let's see," mused the dragon, "that doesn't tell us much, does it? What sort of a word is this? Is it an epithet,[5] do you think?"

Gawaine could do no more than nod.

"Why, of course," exclaimed the dragon, "reactionary Republican."

Gawaine shook his head.

"Well, then," said the dragon, "we'd better get down to business. Will you surrender?"

With the suggestion of a compromise Gawaine mustered up enough courage to speak.

"What will you do if I surrender?" he asked.

"Why, I'll eat you," said the dragon.

"And if I don't surrender?"

"I'll eat you just the same."

"Then it doesn't make any difference, does it?" moaned Gawaine.

"It does to me," said the dragon, with a smile. "I'd rather you didn't surrender. You'd taste much better if you didn't."

The dragon waited for a long time for Gawaine to ask

[4] CRICKET—English expression for "sportsmanlike."

[5] EPITHET—A name (sometimes uncomplimentary), or a descriptive phrase.

"Why?" but the boy was too frightened to speak. At last the dragon had to give the explanation without his cue line. "You see," he said, "if you don't surrender, you'll taste better because you'll die game."

This was an old and ancient trick of the dragons. By means of some such quip [6] he was accustomed to paralyze his victims with laughter and then to destroy them. Gawaine was sufficiently paralyzed as it was, but laughter had no part in his helplessness. With the last word of the joke the dragon drew back and struck. In that second there flashed into the mind of Gawaine the magic word "Rumplesnitz" but there was no time to say it. There was time only to strike, and without a word Gawaine met the onrush of the dragon with a full swing. He put all his back and shoulders into it. The impact was terrific, and the head of the dragon flew away almost a hundred yards and landed in a thicket.

Gawaine did not remain frightened very long after the death of the dragon. His mood was one of wonder. He was enormously puzzled. He cut off the ears of the monster almost in a trance. Again and again he thought to himself, "I didn't say 'Rumplesnitz!'" He was sure of that, and yet there was no question that he had killed the dragon. In fact, he had never killed one so utterly. Never before had he driven a head for anything like the same distance. Twenty-five yards was perhaps his best previous record. All the way back to the knight school he kept rumbling about in his mind, seeking an explanation for what had occurred. He went to the Headmaster immediately and, after closing the door, told him what had happened. "I didn't say 'Rumplesnitz,'" he explained with great earnestness.

The Headmaster laughed. "I'm glad you've found out," he said. "It makes you ever so much more of a hero. Don't you see that? Now you know that it was you who killed all these dragons, and not that foolish little word 'Rumplesnitz.'"

Gawaine frowned. "Then it wasn't a magic word, after all?" he asked.

"Of course not," said the Headmaster; "you ought to be too old for such foolishness. There isn't any such thing as a magic word."

[6] QUIP—Here used in the sense of pun or jest.

"But you told me it was magic," protested Gawaine. "You said it was magic, and now you say it isn't."

"It wasn't magic in a literal sense," answered the Headmaster, "but it was much more wonderful than that. The word gave you confidence. It took away your fears. If I hadn't told you that, you might have been killed the very first time. It was your battle-axe did the trick."

Gawaine surprised the Headmaster by his attitude. He was obviously distressed by the explanation. He interrupted a long philosophic and ethical discourse by the Headmaster with, "If I hadn't of hit 'em all mighty hard and fast any one of 'em might have crushed me like a, like a—" He fumbled for a word.

"Eggshell," suggested the Headmaster.

"Like a eggshell," assented Gawaine and he said it many times. All through the evening meal people who sat near him heard him muttering, "Like a eggshell, like a eggshell."

The next day was clear, but Gawaine did not get up at dawn. Indeed, it was almost noon when the Headmaster found him cowering in bed, with the clothes pulled over his head. The principal called the Assistant Professor of Pleasaunce, and together they dragged the boy toward the forest.

"He'll be all right as soon as he gets a couple more dragons under his belt," explained the Headmaster.

The Assistant Professor of Pleasaunce agreed. "It would be a shame to stop such a fine run," he said. "Why, counting that one yesterday, he's killed fifty dragons."

They pushed the boy into a thicket above which hung a meager cloud of steam. It was obviously quite a small dragon. But Gawaine did not come back that night or the next. In fact, he never came back. Some weeks afterward, brave spirits from the school explored the thicket but they could find nothing to remind them of Gawaine except the metal parts of his medals. Even the ribbons had been devoured.

The Headmaster and the Assistant Professor of Pleasaunce agreed that it would be just as well not to tell the school how Gawaine had achieved his record, and still less how he came to die. They held that it might have a bad effect on school spirit. Accordingly Gawaine has lived in the memory of the school as its greatest hero. No visitor succeeds in leaving the building today without seeing a great shield which hangs on the wall of the dining hall. Fifty pairs of dragons' ears are mounted upon the shield, and underneath in gilt letters is "Gawaine le Coeur-Hardy," followed by the simple inscription, "He killed fifty dragons." The record has never been equaled.

Vocabulary Study: *Jousting* (note pronunciation); *restive; ethics; indiscriminately; versatile; papier-mâché* (note pronunciation); *preliminary; curate; aggressive; testily; potent; technique; solicitude; quip; literal.* Discuss Broun's use of appropriate words.

Give the word origin of *papier-mâché* and its meaning. What is the difference between the synonyms *powerful* and *potent?* Give an antonym for *versatile.*

By Way of Appreciation: If you have a sense of humor, you cannot help appreciating *The Fifty-First Dragon.* Whether you find a moral in it or not, it is worth reading for pure enjoyment.

Technically, the source of fun here is the same as in Mark Twain's *Connecticut Yankee*—anachronism skillfully used. According to the dictionary, an anachronism is "something represented as occurring out of its proper time." In clever hands it is a sure-fire fun-maker.

The careful reader, however, suspects that there is more than a chuckle or two concealed in the lines of *The Fifty-First Dragon.* A keen sarcasm cuts through from time to time. In another essay, *Dying for Dear Old* ——, Mr. Broun reveals his disapproval of the enshrinement of college football upon its present pedestal. Is it possible that there is here a similar thought disguised in the trappings of chivalry? It would be interesting for you to read the essay on football for the sake of comparison; besides, it presents some telling arguments against a popularly accepted institution. Like many another humorist, Mr. Broun knows how to provoke thought as well as laughter.

Suggestions for Study: Check the "chuckle-points" in the essay and be ready to read the best ones to the class. Double-check the passages which seem edged with sarcasm and prepare to discuss them in class. Do you discover any respects in which Gawaine resembles the popular conception of a football hero? Do you see any respects in which the administration of the knight school resembles the administration of real schools? Do you see any significance—quite apart from schools and sports—in Gawaine's use of the magic word and his failure when he lost faith in it?

Exercises and Creative Work: Make an outline of the essay, using either the sentence or topical form.

Write an essay, if possible based on your personal experience, using one of the following topics, or a similar one of your own choosing: *Getting the Best of My Giant; Possible Use for a Magic Word; Turning Out a Hero; Overcoming Obstacles; I Couldn't Go On; Handicaps; A Camp Tenderfoot.*

HOLY IRELAND

Joyce Kilmer

By Way of Introduction: Less than three weeks after the United States entered the World War, Joyce Kilmer enlisted and was soon a member of the "Fighting Sixty-Ninth," with Father Duffy as Regimental Chaplain. Within a year, in July, 1918, he was killed in action while locating enemy machine guns which were delaying the advance of his battalion. In the preceding January Kilmer had written to the Reverend Edward F. Garesche, S.J., "I am surprised, I acknowledge, by the passionate Catholicity of the [French] people. Even 'Holy Ireland' can scarcely be more Catholic than rural France."

We had hiked seventeen miles that stormy December day—the third of a four days' journey. The snow was piled high on our packs, our rifles were crusted with ice, the leather of our hobnailed boots was frozen stiff over our lamed feet. The weary lieutenant led us to the door of a little house in a side street.

"Next twelve men," he said. A dozen of us dropped out of the ranks and dragged ourselves over the threshold. We tracked snow and mud over a spotless stone floor. Before an open fire stood Madame and the three children—a girl of eight years, a boy of five, a boy of three. They stared with round frightened eyes at *les soldats Americains*, the first they had ever seen. We were too tired to stare back. We at once climbed to the chill attic, our billet, our lodging for the night. First we lifted the packs from one another's aching shoulders; then, without spreading our blankets, we lay down on the bare boards.

For ten minutes there was silence, broken by an occasional groan, or the striking of a match. Cigarettes glowed like fireflies in a forest. Then a voice came from the corner.

"Where is Sergeant Reilly?" it said. We lazily searched. There was no Sergeant Reilly to be found.

"I'll bet the old bum has gone out," said the voice. And with the curiosity of the American and the enthusiasm of the Irish we lumbered downstairs in quest of Sergeant Reilly.

He was sitting on a low bench by the fire. His shoes were off and his bruised feet were in a pail of cold water. He was too good a soldier to expose them to heat at once. The little girl was on

579

his lap and the little boys stood by and envied him. And in a voice that twenty years of soldiering had failed to rob of its Celtic sweetness, he was softly singing "Ireland isn't Ireland any more." We listened respectfully.

"They cheer the King and then salute him," said Sergeant Reilly.

"A regular Irishman would shoot him," and we all joined in the chorus, "Ireland isn't Ireland any more."

"Ooh, la, la," exclaimed Madame, and she and all the children began to talk at the top of their voices. What they said nobody knows, but the tones were friendly, even admiring.

"Gentlemen," said Sergeant Reilly from his post of honor, "the lady who runs this billet is a very nice lady indeed. She says yez can all take off your shoes and dry your socks by the fire. But take turns and don't crowd or I'll trun yez all upstairs."

Now Madame, a woman of some forty years, was a true *bourgeoise*,[1] with all the thrift of her class. And by the terms of her agreement with the authorities she was required to let the soldiers have for one night the attic of her house to sleep in— nothing more; no light, no heat. Also, wood is very expensive in France—for reasons that are engraven in letters of blood on the pages of history. Nevertheless——

"*Asseyez-vous, s'il vous plait*,"[2] said Madame. And she brought nearer to the fire all the chairs the establishment possessed and some chests and boxes to be used as seats. And she and the little girl, whose name was Solange, went out into the snow and came back with heaping armfuls of small logs. The fire blazed merrily—more merrily than it had blazed since August, 1914, perhaps. We surrounded it, and soon the air was thick with steam from our drying socks.

Meanwhile Madame and the Sergeant had generously admitted all eleven of us to their conversation. A spirited conversation it was, too, in spite of the fact that she knew no English and the extent of his French was "du pain," "du vin," "cognac" and "bon jour."[3] Those of us who knew a little more of the language of the country acted as interpreters for the others. We learned

---

[1] *Bourgeoise*—A member of the commercial middle class.

[2] *Asseyez-vous, s'il vous plait*—Sit down, please.

[3] *Du pain . . . du vin . . . cognac . . . bon jour*—Bread . . . wine . . . brandy . . . Good day.

the names of the children and their ages. We learned that our hostess was a widow. Her husband had fallen in battle just one month before our arrival in her home. She showed us with simple pride and affection and restrained grief his picture. Then she showed us those of her two brothers—one now fighting at Salonica,[4] the other a prisoner of war—of her mother and father, of herself dressed for First Communion.

This last picture she showed somewhat shyly, as if doubting that we would understand it. But when one of us asked in halting French if Solange, her little daughter, had yet made her First Communion, then Madame's face cleared.

"*Mais oui!*" she exclaimed. "*Et vous, ma foi, vous êtes Catholiques, n'est-ce pas?*"[5]

At once rosaries were flourished to prove our right to answer this question affirmatively. Tattered prayer-books and somewhat dingy scapulars were brought to light. Madame and the children chattered their surprise and delight to each other, and every exhibit called for a new outburst.

"*Ah, la bon S. Benoît! Ah, voila, la Conception Immaculée! Ooh la la, le Sacré Coeur!*"[6] (which last exclamation sounded in no wise as irreverent as it looks in print).

Now other treasures, too, were shown—treasures chiefly photographic. There were family groups, there were Coney Island snapshots. And Madame and the children were a gratifyingly appreciative audience. They admired and sympathized; they exclaimed appropriately at the beauty of every girl's face, the tenderness of every pictured mother. We had become the intimates of Madame. She had admitted us into her family and we her into ours.

Soldiers—American soldiers of Irish descent—have souls and hearts. These organs (if the soul may be so termed) had been satisfied. But our stomachs remained—and that they yearned was evident to us. We had made our hike on a meal of hardtack and "corned willy." Mess call would sound soon. Should we force our wet shoes on again and plod through the snowy streets

---

[4] SALONICA—A Greek city which served the Allies as the base of the Salonica campaigns of 1915–1918.
[5] *Mais oui! . . . Catholiques, n'est-ce pas?*—"Of course," she exclaimed. "And you are Catholics, aren't you?"
[6] *Ah, le bon S. Benoît! . . . Sacré Coeur!*—"Ah, it's St. Benedict! Look! The Immaculate Conception! Oh, the Sacred Heart!"

to the temporary mess-shack? We knew our supply wagons had not succeeded in climbing the last hill into town, and that therefore bread and unsweetened coffee would be our portion. A great depression settled upon us.

But Sergeant Reilly rose to the occasion.

"Boys," he said, "this here lady has a good fire going, and I'll bet she can cook. What do you say we get her to fix us up a meal?"

The proposal was received joyously at first. Then someone said:

"But I haven't got any money." "Neither have I—not a *sou!*" said another. And again the spiritual temperature of the room fell.

Again Sergeant Reilly spoke:

"I haven't any money to speak of, meself," he said. "But let's have a show-down. I guess we've got enough to buy somethin' to eat."

It was long after pay-day, and we were not hopeful of the results of the search. But the wealthy (that is, those who had two *francs*) made up for the poor (that is, those who had two *sous*). And among the coins on the table I noticed an American dime, an English half-crown and a Chinese piece with a square hole in the center. In negotiable tender the money came in all to eight *francs*.

It takes more money than that to feed twelve hungry soldiers these days in France. But there was no harm in trying. So an ex-seminarian, an ex-bookkeeper and an ex-street-car conductor aided Sergeant Reilly in explaining in French that had both a brogue and a Yankee twang that we were hungry, that this was all the money we had in the world, and that we wanted her to cook us something to eat.

Now Madame was what they call in New England a "capable" woman. In a jiffy she had the money in Solange's hand and had that admirable child cloaked and wooden-shod for the street, and fully informed as to what she was to buy. What Madame and her children had intended to have for supper I do not know, for there was nothing in the kitchen but the fire, the stove, the table, some shelves of dishes and an enormous bed. Nothing in the way of a food cupboard could be seen. And the only other room in the house was the bare attic.

When Solange came back she carried in a basket bigger than herself these articles: 1, two loaves of war-bread; 2, five bottles of red wine; 3, three cheeses; 4, numerous potatoes; 5, a lump of fat; 6, a bag of coffee. The whole represented, as was afterwards demonstrated, exactly the sum of ten *francs,* fifty *centimes.*

Well, we all set to work peeling potatoes. Then with a veritable French trench-knife Madame cut the potatoes into long strips. Meanwhile Solange had put the lump of fat into the big black pot that hung by a chain over the fire. In the boiling grease the potatoes were placed, Madame standing by with a big ladle punched full of holes (I regret that I do not know the technical name for this instrument) and keeping the potato-strips swimming, zealously frustrating any attempt on their part to lie lazily at the bottom of the pot.

We forgot all about the hike as we sat at supper that evening. The only absentees were the two little boys, Michel and Paul. And they were really absent only from our board—they were in the room, in the great built-in bed that later was to hold also Madame and Solange. Their little bodies were covered by the three-foot thick mattress-like red silk quilt, but their tousled heads protruded and they watched us unblinkingly all the evening.

But just before we sat down, before Sergeant Reilly began his task of dishing out the potatoes and starting the bread on its way, Madame stopped her chattering and looked at Solange. And Solange stopped her chattering and looked at Madame. And they both looked rather searchingly at us. We didn't know what was the matter, but we felt rather embarrassed.

Then Madame began to talk, slowly and loudly, as one talks to make foreigners understand. And the gist of her remarks was that she was surprised to see that American Catholics did not say grace before eating like French Catholics.

We sprang to our feet at once. But it was not Sergeant Reilly who saved the situation. Instead, the ex-seminarian (he is only temporarily an ex-seminarian, he'll be preaching missions and giving retreats yet if a bit of shrapnel doesn't hasten his journey to Heaven) said, after we had blessed ourselves: *"Benedic, Domine, nos et haec tua dona quae de tua largitate sumus sumpturi, per Christum Dominum nostrum.* Amen." [7]

[7] *Benedic . . . Amen*—The Latin version of the familiar grace before meals.

Madame and Solange, obviously relieved, joined us in the Amen, and we sat down again to eat.

It was a memorable feast. There was not much conversation—except on the part of Madame and Solange—but there was plenty of good cheer. Also there was enough cheese and bread and wine and potatoes for all of us—half starved as we were when we sat down. Even big Considine, who drains a can of condensed milk at a gulp and has been known to eat an apple pie without stopping to take breath, was satisfied. There were toasts, also, all proposed by Sergeant Reilly—toasts to Madame, and to the children, and to France, and to the United States, and to the Old Grey Mare (this last toast having an esoteric significance apparent only to *illuminati* of Sergeant Reilly's circle).

The table cleared and the *"agimus tibi gratias"* [8] duly said, we sat before the fire, most of us on the floor. We were warm and happy and full of good food and good wine. I spied a slip of paper on the floor by Solange's foot and unashamedly read it. It was an accounting for the evening's expenditures—totaling exactly ten *francs* and fifty *centimes*.

Now when soldiers are unhappy—during a long, hard hike, for instance—they sing to keep up their spirits. And when they are happy, as on the evening now under consideration, they sing to express their satisfaction with life. We sang "Sweet Rosie O'Grady." We shook the kitchen-bedroom with the echoes of "Take Me Back to New York Town." We informed Madame, Solange, Paul, Michel, in fact, the whole village, that we had never been a wanderer and that we longed for our Indiana home. We grew sentimental over "Mother Machree." And Sergeant Reilly obliged with a reel—in his socks—to an accompaniment of whistling and hand-clapping.

Now, it was our hostess's turn to entertain. We intimated as much. She responded, first by much talk, much consultation with Solange, and finally by going to one of the shelves that held the pans and taking down some paper-covered books.

There was more consultation, whispered this time, and much turning of pages. Then, after some preliminary coughing and humming, the music began—the woman's rich alto blending with

---

[8] *Agimus tibi gratias*—"We give Thee thanks," the opening words of grace after meals.

the child's shrill but sweet notes. And what they sang was *"Tantum ergo Sacramentum."*

Why she should have thought that an appropriate song to offer this company of rough soldiers from a distant land I do not know. And why we found it appropriate it is harder still to say. But it did seem appropriate to all of us—to Sergeant Reilly, to Jim (who used to drive a truck), to Larry (who sold cigars), to Frank (who tended a store on Fourteenth Street). It seemed for some reason eminently fitting. Not one of us then or later expressed any surprise that this hymn, familiar to most of us since our mothers first led us to the parish church down the pavements of New York or across the Irish hills, should be sung to us in this strange land.

Since the gracious Latin of the Church was in order and since the season was appropriate, one of us suggested the *"Adeste Fideles"* for the next item on the evening's program. Madame and Solange and our ex-seminarian knew all the words and the rest of us came in strong with *"Venite, adoremus Dominum."*

Then, as if to show that piety and mirth may live together, the ladies obliged with *"Au Clair de la Lune"* and other simple ballads of old France. After taps had sounded in the street outside our door, and there was yawning, and wrist-watches were being scanned, the evening's entertainment ended, by general consent, with patriotic selections. We sang—as best we could—the *Star Spangled Banner,* Solange and her mother humming the air and applauding at the conclusion. Then we attempted *La Marseillaise.* Of course we did not know the words. Solange came to our rescue with two little pamphlets containing the song, so we looked over each other's shoulders and got to work in earnest. Madame sang with us, and Solange. But during the final stanza Madame did not sing. She leaned against the great family bedstead and looked at us. She had taken one of the babies from under the red comforter and held him to her breast. One of the red and toil-scarred hands half covered his fat little back. There was a gentle dignity about that plain, hard-working woman, that soldier's widow—we all felt it. And some of us saw the tears in her eyes.

There are mists, faint and beautiful and unchanging, that hang over the green slopes of some mountains I know. I have seen them on the Irish hills and I have seen them on the hills of France. I think that they are made of the tears of good brave women.

Before I went to sleep that night I exchanged a few words with Sergeant Reilly. We lay side by side on the floor, now piled with straw. Blankets, shelter-halves, slickers and overcoats insured warm sleep. Sergeant Reilly's hard old face was wrapped round with his muffler. The final cigarette of the day burned lazily in a corner of his mouth.

"That was a pretty good evening, Sarge," I said. "We sure were in luck when we struck this billet."

He grunted affirmatively, then puffed in silence for a few minutes. Then he deftly spat the cigarette into a strawless portion of the floor, where it glowed for a few seconds before it went out.

"You said it," he remarked. "We were in luck is right. What do you know about that lady, anyway?"

"Why," I answered, "I thought she treated us pretty white."

"Joe," said Sergeant Reilly, "do you realize how much trouble that woman took to make this bunch of roughnecks comfortable? She didn't make a cent on that feed, you know. The kid spent all the money we give her. And she's out about six *francs* for firewood, too—I wish I had the money to pay her. I'll bet she'll go cold for a week now, and hungry, too.

"And that ain't all," he continued, after a pause broken only by an occasional snore from our blissful neighbors. "Look at the way she cooked them *pommes de terres* [9] and fixed things up for us and let us sit down there with her like we was her family. And look at the way she and the little Sallie there sung for us.

"I tell you, Joe, it makes me think of old times to hear a woman sing them Church hymns to me that way. It's forty years since I heard a hymn sung in a kitchen, and it was my mother, God rest her, that sang them. I sort of realize what we're fighting for now, and I never did before. It's for women like that and their kids.

"It gave me a turn to see her a-sitting there singing them hymns. I remembered when I was a boy in Shangolden. I wonder if there's many women like that in France now—telling their beads and singing the old hymns and treating poor traveling men the way she's just after treating us. There used to be lots of women like that in the Old Country. And I think that's why it was called 'Holy Ireland.' "

[9] *Pommes de terres*—Potatoes.

Vocabulary Study: *Billet, shrapnel, trench knives, negotiable, eso-teric, intimated, tousled, alto, illuminati.*

What is the difference between a *dialect,* a *brogue,* and a *twang?*

By Way of Appreciation: This echo of the A. E. F. reveals much of Joyce Kilmer: his sincere and noble devotion to God and country; his deep Catholic faith; his tender sympathy. Among these American soldiers of Irish descent he was at home, just as they were at home in the Catholic atmosphere of Madame's house. For religion, poetry, sympathy, tenderness, loyalty, sincerity, qualities usually associated with the Irish character, were also the fibre of Kilmer's life, as he reveals in some measure in this essay.

Suggestions for Study: Whence does the essay get its title? Is Madame or the Sergeant the dominant character? The reader is given the impression that the soldiers were weary. In what different ways does Kilmer drive home that impression? What bond of union made these American soldiers and this little French family at home together in spite of language barriers? What made the singing of the *Adeste Fideles* appropriate? How did the evening's entertainment change Sergeant Reilly's attitude toward the war?

Exercises and Creative Work: Imagine yourself the lone representative of your school at a Sodality Convention. Things are bleak until a chance remark of another delegate reveals your common admiration for a teacher who was transferred this year from his school to yours. Invent some other topic of common interest if you care to. Then the essay!

Or, you have a minor automobile accident, and the Good Samaritan who comes to your aid turns out to be—your next door neighbor, whom you had thought utterly aloof. Now the essay!

On the basis of the information provided in "Holy Ireland" write a character sketch of the Sergeant or of Madame.

Essays for Reflection

A KITTEN

From *In the Dozy Hours*

AGNES REPPLIER

By Way of Introduction: Household pets are every bit as interesting as hobbies; indeed, they are a kind of hobby. Just as one is eager to grasp the lapel of his fellowman and regale him with stories about his hobby, so the animal lover seizes every opportunity to acquaint the world with the antics, the extraordinary intelligence of his pet. When the enthusiast is an essayist, it is only natural that his pet should become the subject of his pen. And when the essayist is as gifted as Agnes Repplier, we are treated to just such a delightful sketch as the following.

ι   IF

"The child is father of the man," [1]

why is not the kitten father of the cat? If in the little boy there lurks the infant likeness of all that manhood will complete, why does not the kitten betray some of the attributes common to the adult puss? A puppy is but a dog, plus high spirits, and minus common sense. We never hear our friends say they love puppies, but cannot bear dogs. A kitten is a thing apart; and many people who lack the discriminating enthusiasm for cats, who regard these beautiful beasts with aversion and mistrust, are won over easily, and cajoled out of their prejudices by the deceitful wiles of kittenhood.

The little actor cons another part, [2]

and is the most irresistible comedian in the world. Its wide-open eyes gleam with wonder and mirth. It darts madly at nothing at all, and then, as though suddenly checked in the pursuit, prances sideways on its hind legs with ridiculous agility and zeal. It makes a vast pretense of climbing the rounds of a chair, and swings by the curtain like an acrobat. It scrambles up a table leg, and is seized with comic horror at finding itself full two feet

---

[1] THE CHILD IS FATHER OF THE MAN—A line from Wordsworth's poem, "My Heart Leaps Up when I Behold."

[2] THE LITTLE ACTOR CONS ANOTHER PART—From Wordsworth's "Ode on Immortality."

from the floor. If you hasten to its rescue, it clutches you nervously, its little heart thumping against its furry sides, while its soft paws expand and contract with agitation and relief;

> And all their harmless claws disclose,
> Like prickles of an early rose.

Yet the instant it is back on the carpet it feigns to be suspicious of your interference, peers at you out of "the tail o' its ee," [3] and scampers for protection under the sofa, from which asylum it presently emerges with cautious trailing steps, as though encompassed by fearful dangers and alarms. Its baby innocence is yet unseared. The evil knowledge of uncanny things which is the dark inheritance of cathood has not yet shadowed its round infant eyes. Where did witches find the mysterious beasts that sat motionless by their fires, and watched unblinkingly the waxen manikins dwindling in the flame? They never reared these companions of their solitude, for no witch could have endured to see a kitten gamboling on her hearthstone. A witch's kitten! That one preposterous thought proves how wide, how unfathomed, is the gap between feline infancy and age.

2   So it happens that the kitten is loved and cherished and caressed as long as it preserves the beguiling mirthfulness of youth. Richelieu,[4] we know, was wont to keep a family of kittens in his cabinet, that their grace and gayety might divert him from the cares of state, and from black moods of melancholy. Yet, with short-sighted selfishness, he banished these little friends when but a few months old, and gave their places to younger pets. The first faint dawn of reason, the first indication of soberness and worldly wisdom, the first charming and coquettish pretenses to maturity, were followed by immediate dismissal. Richelieu desired to be amused. He had no conception of the finer joy which springs from mutual companionship and esteem. Even humbler and more sincere admirers, like Joanna Baillie,[5] in whom we wish to believe Puss found a friend and champion, appear to take it for granted that the kitten should be the spoiled darling of the household, and the cat a social outcast, degraded into usefulness,

[3] Ee—Scotch for eye.
[4] RICHELIEU—Famous cardinal and statesman, minister of Louis XIII (1585–1642).
[5] JOANNA BAILLIE—Scotch dramatist and authoress, admired friend of Sir Walter Scott (1762–1851).

and expected to work for her living. What else can be understood
from such lines as these?

> Ah! many a lightly sportive child,
> Who hath, like thee, our wits beguiled,
> To dull and sober manhood grown,
> With strange recoil our hearts disown.
> Even so, poor Kit! must thou endure,
> When thou becomest a cat demure,
> Full many a cuff and angry word,
> Chid roughly from the tempting board.
> And yet, for that thou hast, I ween,
> So oft our favored playmate been,
> Soft be the change which thou shalt prove,
> *When time hath spoiled thee of our love;*
> Still be thou deemed, by housewife fat,
> A comely, careful, mousing cat,
> Whose dish is, for the public good,
> Replenished oft with savory food.

Here is a plain exposition of the utilitarian theory which Shakespeare is supposed to have countenanced because Shylock speaks
of the "harmless, necessary cat." Shylock, forsooth! As if he,
of all men in Christendom or Jewry, knew anything about cats!
Small wonder that he was outwitted by Portia and Jessica, when
an adroit little animal could so easily beguile him. But Joanna
Baillie should never have been guilty of those snug commonplaces
concerning the

> "comely, careful, mousing cat,"

remembering her own valiant Tabby who won Scott's respectful
admiration by worrying and killing a dog. It ill became the
possessor of an Amazonian cat, distinguished by Sir Walter's
regard, to speak with such patronizing kindness of the race.

3   We can make no more stupid blunder than to look upon our
pets from the standpoint of utility. Puss, as a rule, is another
Nimrod,[6] eager for the chase, and unwearyingly patient in pursuit
of her prey. But she hunts for her own pleasure, not for our
convenience; and when a life of luxury has relaxed her zeal, she
often declines to hunt at all. I knew intimately two Maryland

[6] NIMROD—Called in the Book of Genesis, chapter 10, "a stout hunter before
the Lord."

cats, well born and of great personal attractions. The sleek, black Tom was named Onyx, and his snow-white companion Lilian. Both were idle, urbane, fastidious, and self-indulgent as Lucullus.[7] Now, into the house honored, but not served, by these charming creatures came a rat, which secured permanent lodgings in the kitchen, and speedily evicted the maid servants. A reign of terror followed, and after a few days of hopeless anarchy it occurred to the cook that the cats might be brought from their comfortable cushions upstairs and shut in at night with their hereditary foe. This was done, and the next morning, on opening the kitchen door, a tableau rivaling the peaceful scenes of Eden was presented to the view. On one side of the hearth lay Onyx, on the other, Lilian; and ten feet away, upright upon the kitchen table, sat the rat, contemplating them both with tranquil humor and content. It was apparent to him, as well as to the rest of the household, that he was an object of absolute, contemptuous indifference to those two lordly cats.

4. There is none of this superb unconcern in the joyous eagerness of infancy. A kitten will dart in pursuit of everything that is small enough to be chased with safety. Not a fly on the windowpane, not a moth in the air, not a tiny crawling insect on the carpet, escapes its unwelcome attentions. It begins to "take notice" as soon as its eyes are open, and its vivacity, outstripping its dawning intelligence, leads it into infantile perils and wrong doing. I own that when Agrippina[8] brought her first-born son— aged two days—and established him in my bedroom closet, the plan struck me at the start as inconvenient. I had prepared another nursery for the little Claudius Nero, and I endeavored for a while to convince his mother that my arrangements were best. But Agrippina was inflexible. The closet suited her in every respect; and, with charming and irresistible flattery, she gave me to understand, in the mute language I knew so well, that she wished her baby boy to be under my immediate protection. "I bring him to you because I trust you," she said as plainly as looks can speak. "Downstairs they handle him all the time, and it is not good for kittens to be handled. Here he is safe from harm, and here he shall remain." After a few weak remonstrances, the

---

[7] LUCULLUS—Ancient Roman commander who lived in extravagant luxury.

[8] AGRIPPINA—Named after the mother of the Roman emperor, Claudius Nero. Miss Repplier devotes another essay to Agrippina—the cat, not the Roman.

futility of which I too clearly understood, her persistence carried the day. I removed my clothing from the closet, spread a shawl upon the floor, had the door taken from its hinges, and resigned myself, for the first time in my life, to the daily and hourly companionship of an infant.

5   I was amply rewarded. People who require the household cat to rear her offspring in some remote attic, or dark corner of the cellar, have no idea of all the diversion and pleasure that they lose. It is delightful to watch the little blind, sprawling, feeble, helpless things develop swiftly into the grace and agility of kittenhood. It is delightful to see the mingled pride and anxiety of the mother, whose parental love increases with every hour of care, and who exhibits her young family as if they were infant Gracchi,[9] the hope of all their race. During Nero's extreme youth, there were times, I admit, when Agrippina wearied both of his companionship and of her own maternal duties. Once or twice she abandoned him at night for the greater luxury of my bed, where she slept tranquilly by my side, unmindful of the little wailing cries with which Nero lamented her desertion. Once or twice the heat of early summer tempted her to spend the evening on the porch roof which lay beneath my windows, and I have passed some anxious hours awaiting her return, and wondering what would happen if she never came back, and I were left to bring up the baby by hand.

6   But as the days sped on, and Nero grew rapidly in beauty and intelligence, Agrippina's affection for him knew no bounds. She could hardly bear to leave him even for a little while, and always came hurrying back to him with a loud frightened mew, as if fearing he might have been stolen in her absence. At night she purred over him for hours, or made little gurgling noises expressive of ineffable content. She resented the careless curiosity of strangers, and was a trifle supercilious when the cook stole softly in to give vent to her fervent admiration. But from first to last she shared with me her pride and pleasure; and the joy in her beautiful eyes, as she raised them to mine, was frankly confiding and sympathetic. When the infant Claudius rolled for the first time over the ledge of the closet, and lay sprawling on the bedroom floor, it would have been hard to say which of us was

---

[9] GRACCHI—A famous Roman family. The mother, Cornelia, called her children her jewels.

the more elated at his prowess. A narrow pink ribbon of honor was at once tied around the small adventurer's neck, and he was pronounced the most daring and agile of kittens. From that day his brief career was a series of brilliant triumphs. He was a kitten of parts. Like one of Miss Austen's heroes,[10] he had air and countenance. Less beautiful than his mother, whom he closely resembled, he easily eclipsed her in vivacity and the specious arts of fascination. Never were mother and son more unlike in character and disposition, and the inevitable contrast between kittenhood and cathood was enhanced in this case by a strong natural dissimilarity which no length of years could have utterly effaced.

7   Agrippina had always been a cat of manifest reserves. She was only six weeks old when she came to me, and had already acquired that gravity of demeanor, that air of gentle disdain, that dignified and somewhat supercilious composure, which won the respectful admiration of those whom she permitted to enjoy her acquaintance. Even in moments of self-forgetfulness and mirth her recreations resembled those of the little Spanish Infanta,[11] who, not being permitted to play with her inferiors, and having no equals, diverted herself as best she could with sedate and solitary sport. Always chary of her favors, Agrippina cared little for the admiration of her chosen circle; and, with a single exception, she made no friends beyond it.

8   Claudius Nero, on the contrary, thirsted for applause. Affable, debonair, and democratic to the core, the caresses and commendations of a chance visitor or of a housemaid were as valuable to him as were my own. I never looked at him "showing off," as children say,—jumping from chair to chair, balancing himself on the bedpost, or scrambling rapturously up the forbidden curtains,—without thinking of the young Emperor who contended in the amphitheatre for the worthless plaudits of the crowd. He was impulsive and affectionate,—so, I believe was the Emperor for a time,—and as masterful as if born to the purple. His mother struggled hard to maintain her rightful authority, but it was in vain. He woke her from her sweetest naps; he darted at her tail, and leaped down on her from sofas and tables with the grace of

[10] MISS AUSTEN—Jane Austen, noted English novelist, wrote *Pride and Prejudice* and other novels (1775–1817).
[11] SPANISH INFANTA—Daughter of the King and Queen of Spain.

a diminutive panther. Every time she attempted to punish him for these misdemeanors he cried piteously for help, and was promptly and unwisely rescued by some kind-hearted member of the family. After a while Agrippina took to sitting on her tail, in order to keep it out of his reach, and I have seen her many times carefully tucking it out of sight. She had never been a cat of active habits or of showy accomplishments, and the daring agility of the little Nero amazed and bewildered her. "A Spaniard," observes that pleasant gossip, James Howell,[12] "walks as if he marched, and seldom looks upon the ground, as if he contemned it. I was told of a Spaniard who, having got a fall by a stumble, and broke his nose, rose up, and in a disdainful manner said, 'This comes of walking on the earth.'"

9   Now Nero seldom walked on the earth. At least, he never, if he could help it, walked on the floor; but traversed a room in a series of flying leaps from chair to table, from table to lounge, from lounge to desk, with an occasional dash at the mantelpiece, just to show what he could do. It was curious to watch Agrippina during the performance of these acrobatic feats. Pride, pleasure, the anxiety of a mother, and the faint resentment of conscious inferiority struggled for mastership in her little breast. Sometimes, when Nero's radiant self-satisfaction grew almost insufferable, I have seen her eyelids narrow sullenly, and have wondered whether the Roman Empress ever looked in that way at her brilliant and beautiful son, when maternal love was withering slowly under the shadow of coming evil. Sometimes, when Nero had been prancing and paddling about with absurd and irresistible glee, attracting and compelling the attention of everybody in the room, Agrippina would jump up on my lap, and look in my face with an expression I thought I understood. She had never before valued my affection in all her little petted, pampered life. She had been sufficient for herself, and had merely tolerated me as a devoted and useful companion. But now that another had usurped so many of her privileges, I fancied there were moments when it pleased her to know that one subject, at least, was not to be beguiled from allegiance; that to one friend, at least, she always was and always would be the dearest cat in the world.

10   I am glad to remember that love triumphed over jealousy, and that Agrippina's devotion to Nero increased with every day of

[12] JAMES HOWELL—Author of *Epistolae Ho-Elianae,* or *Familiar Letters.*

his short life. The altruism of a cat seldom reaches beyond her kittens; but she is capable of heroic unselfishness where they are concerned. I knew of a London beast, a homeless, forlorn vagrant, who constituted herself an out-door pensioner at the house of a friendly man of letters. This cat had a kitten, whose youthful vivacity won the hearts of a neighboring family. They adopted it willingly, but refused to harbor the mother, who still came for her daily dole to her only benefactor. Whenever a bit of fish or some other especial dainty was given her, this poor mendicant scaled the wall, and watched her chance to share it with her kitten, her little wealthy, greedy son, who gobbled it up as remorselessly as if he were not living on the fat of the land.

11   Agrippina would have been swift to follow such an example of devotion. At dinner time she always yielded the precedence to Nero, and it became one of our daily tasks to compel the little lad to respect his mother's privileges. He scorned his saucer of milk, and from tenderest infancy aspired to adult food, making predatory incursions upon Agrippina's plate, and obliging us finally to feed them in separate apartments. I have seen him, when a very young kitten, rear himself upon his baby legs, and with his soft and wicked little paw strike his mother in the face until she dropped the piece of meat she had been eating, when he tranquilly devoured it. It was to prevent the recurrence of such scandalous scenes that two dining-rooms became a necessity in the family. Yet he was so loving and so lovable, poor little Claudius Nero! Why do I dwell on his faults, remembering, as I do, his winning sweetness and affability? Day after day, in the narrow city garden, the two cats played together, happy in each other's society, and never a yard apart. Night after night they retired at the same time, and slept upon the same cushion, curled up inextricably into one soft, furry ball. Many times I have knelt by their chair to bid them both goodnight; and always, when I did so, Agrippina would lift her charming head, purr drowsily for a few seconds, and then nestle closer still to her first-born, with sighs of supreme satisfaction. The zenith of her life had been reached. Her cup of contentment was full.

12   It is a rude world, even for little cats, and evil chances lie in wait for the petted creatures we strive to shield from harm. Remembering the pangs of separation, the possibilities of unkindness or neglect, the troubles that hide in ambush on every un-

turned page, I am sometimes glad that the same cruel and selfish blow struck both mother and son, and that they lie together, safe from hurt or hazard, sleeping tranquilly and always, under the shadow of the friendly pines.

Vocabulary Study: *Discriminating, aversion, cajoled, manikins, feline, preposterous, beguiling, utilitarian, adroit, Amazonian, fastidious, supercilious, anarchy, plaudits, altruism, vagrant, dole, mendicant, predatory.*

Note the specific character of the verbs Miss Repplier uses. Make a list of at least ten specific verbs, like *dart* and *prance,* used to describe the antics of the kitten.

By Way of Appreciation: The familiar essay has been well styled the butterfly of literature; like the butterfly it is beautiful in itself, and like the butterfly it brings with it fragrant memories of the flowers among which it has wandered. Miss Repplier's essay has both these beauties: beauty of style and beauty of allusion. The excellence of her style is due in part to her acute word sense, her flair for the exact word, and also to the charm of her exquisitely rounded sentences. Although they are frequently rambling, her sentences have a unity and coherence that is faultless. There is logic too in her writing, and a sanity that has earned for her the title of "The Apostle of Common Sense."

In addition to exquisite word carving and delightful rhythm her writing is rich with the wealth which allusion provides. The romance of far-off places, the charm of olden times, and the fragrance of imperishable beauty are the result of her tasteful use of allusion. Her own formula is revealing: "It is the hour of rapturous reading and the power of secret thinking which make for personal distinction."

Suggestions for Study: What is the theme that lends unity to this essay? How are descriptive narration, reminiscence, allusion, and comment used to illustrate this theme? Why is the comparison of a child with a kitten a good introduction to the essay? Are the two similar? Can the same be said for a grown person and a cat? Discuss the value of the use of classical names in the essay. Can you suggest other appropriate names for Agrippina and Nero? Explain two passages which seem to throw light on the character of the writer of the essay. Compare this essay with "Agrippina," by the same author or with "The Character of Dogs," by R. L. Stevenson.

Exercises and Creative Work: Outline an essay on Agrippina and Nero to be written by one who dislikes both cats and kittens.

If you have a household pet at home, study its character closely and, after observing the details of its conduct, describe it in terms of its detailed behavior, as Miss Repplier has done for Nero.

Write what you think Richelieu might have written in answer to Miss Repplier's charges against him.

THE DISCIPLINE OF THE SECRET

From *This Our Day*

JAMES M. GILLIS

By Way of Introduction: Since 1922 Father Gillis, of the Paulist Fathers, has been editor of *The Catholic World,* the veteran literary monthly which celebrated its seventy-fifth birthday in 1940. "The Discipline of the Secret" first appeared under a different title, in that representative journal, in August of 1926, immediately after the International Eucharistic Congress in Chicago. In 1933 this editorial was reprinted in *This Our Day,* a collection of Father Gillis' vigorous editorials selected by his admiring friends for preservation in more permanent form.

Any editorial may be classified as an essay of opinion expressing the views of the editorial staff on topics of concern to their readers. In it the writer analyzes significant movements, suggests solutions of current problems, or interprets events of the day in terms of the journal's accepted code of principles. To comment, illuminate, and clarify is the task of the editorial writer. In the very first paragraph of this editorial we see Father Gillis, after attending the Eucharistic Congress, searching for a new viewpoint from which to observe one of the oldest Catholic institutions,—the Holy Eucharist.

1   EVERY man who sat in the press-box in Chicago, on those forever memorable days and nights of the Eucharistic Congress [1] had thoughts of his own, not shared by the writing men at his elbow. So it happens that, though I have read reams upon reams of description of the services, I have not discovered that any of the men who were so industriously scribbling, or pounding the keys of a typewriter, or clicking a telegraph key, all around me, had their mind and imagination stirred in precisely the same way as my own. We all saw the same sights and heard the same sounds, but not all of us experienced the same mental and spiritual reaction.

2   Perhaps my principal and most frequently recurring thought as I witnessed the Sacred Mysteries celebrated on an altar one hundred feet high under the open sky, in the midst of a huge modern city was, "What an appalling violation of the *Disciplina Arcani!*" [2] Appalling, but, by a paradox, immensely gratifying.

---

[1] EUCHARISTIC CONGRESS—The International Eucharistic Congress of 1926.
[2] *Disciplina Arcani*—The Discipline of the Secret.

All who are familiar with the history of the Blessed Eucharist, will remember that in the earliest Christian centuries the Catholic people seldom, if ever, expressed in public the full truth concerning the Blessed Sacrament. Prospective converts to the faith, catechumens, were not told of the Real Presence until they had been under instruction for a long time. Even when the days of persecution were over, and there was, presumably, little danger from spies in the Christian assembly, reticence about the real meaning of the Blessed Sacrament was still observed.

3   To this day, in the ritual of the Eastern Churches, neophytes, the "uninitiated," are bidden to leave before the consecration. We have a relic of the custom in our *Ite Missa Est,* which is, of course, misplaced in the Roman Mass of to-day. It means *not* "Go, for the Mass is over"; but "Go, for now comes the Mass." In ancient sermons on the Eucharist the preacher would frequently say mysteriously, "The initiated will know what I mean." And, in general, there was a strict discipline forbidding the telling of the full truth about the Mass to anyone not actually a member of the Church.

4   There is, of course, no such discipline in vogue to-day. Yet, I think I correctly express the mind of Catholics when I say that we still feel a certain reluctance and diffidence about bruiting abroad the truth concerning our Sacredest Mystery. One feels as if the sudden revelation of the truth to a people unprepared to receive it, were, in a way, indecent.

5   But at Chicago, the truth of the Blessed Eucharist was preached aloud, sung, printed, and broadcast with absolute freedom. Millions of people were hearing or reading about the "True Body and Blood of Jesus in the Blessed Sacrament," as they might read or hear the report of a presidential election, or the score of a baseball game, or some other quite profane matter.

6   Time was when Catholics were a hunted people, a *gens luci-fuga.*[3] We fled the light, not because we "loved the darkness rather than the light," but because we were not allowed by law to appear in the day. *"Non licet esse vos,"* [4] said Nero, and that edict has been, in substance, repeated again and again in our history. "Sufferance is the badge of all our tribe," says Shylock, of the Jews. Sufferance and suppression is the badge of all the Catholic tribe. In the beginning we were driven underground,

---

[3] *Gens lucifuga*—A people that flees the light.
[4] *"Non licet esse vos"*—"You may not exist."

into the catacombs. Sooner or later we have been proscribed in almost every country, and we have been outlawed, somewhere, almost continuously. In Ireland we were driven to worship behind the hedges or on the hillside, with watchers ever ready to give the alarm. In England, to this day, you may see the evidences of our being a hunted people, not only in the hidden chapels of old country houses, but even in the location of some of our churches. The Jesuit church in Farm Street, for example, was tolerated only because it was out of the way among the stables. Here in America, we were for centuries scarcely tolerated, and even when tolerated, despised, because we had "not many wise, not many mighty, not many noble."

7   At Chicago we came,—so to speak,—out of our holes and corners, out of our catacombs into a blinding light. We became the cynosure of the eyes of America, and of the world, and even according to the judgment of our most exacting critics, we conducted ourselves as those "to the manner born."

8   Day after day, as the services continued and every gathering seemed more vast than those that had preceded it, there kept recurring to my mind, phrases about multitudes, not only from the Scriptures, "Devout men [5] from every nation under heaven"; "A great multitude [6] which no man could number, of all nations, and tribes and peoples, and tongues, standing before the throne, and in sight of the Lamb," but from non-Biblical writings: for example the *ingens multitudo* [7] of Pliny, reporting from Bithynia, to the Emperor Trajan, that the Christians in those outlandish parts had become a "great multitude." Above all, there ran constantly in my brain the familiar *hesterni sumus,* of Tertullian: [8] "We are but of yesterday, and yet we fill all places among you, the camp, the forum, the market place, cities, towns, islands. We are even in the emperor's palace—we leave you only the temples of your gods."

9   We Catholics in the United States are of yesterday. As late as thirteen years after the Declaration of Independence we had but one bishop,[9] and he governed only thirty priests and twenty-five thousand people. But to-day we are an *ingens multitudo,* in

[5] "Devout men," etc.—From *The Acts of the Apostles,* II, 5.

[6] "Great multitude," etc.—From *The Apocalypse of St. John,* VII, 9.

[7] *Ingens multitudo*—A great multitude.

[8] Tertullian—A prolific Christian writer in the second and third centuries. Unfortunately he left the Church in 211 or 212.

[9] One bishop—Bishop John Carroll of Baltimore. See his "Eulogy on George Washington" in this volume.

comparison with which Pliny's "multitude" must have been only a handful. And we fill all places, not in the imagination of the perfervid and perhaps over-rhetorical Tertullian, but in sober truth. As Secretary Davis,[10] speaking in the place of President Coolidge, said in the Coliseum on the night of the civic opening of the Congress, "Many of the leading citizens of our country are of your faith. They are graduates of our universities; they are to be found in editorial chairs; they are leaders in art and science; many are illustrious men of letters; they have taken eminent rank in the professions and in business. Catholics are found in our halls of legislation, and upon the bench; two of their number have been chief justices of the Supreme Court of the United States."

10   And yet all this evidence of our growth in numbers and prestige is relatively unimportant. Numbers, of themselves, mean nothing. On the day I write, 50,000 are gathering in Brooklyn to see a prize fight. There are 500,000 people at Coney Island on a hot Sunday. There were a million, or perhaps two million in the battle of the Marne. The Eucharistic Congress was not unique as a gathering of human beings. It was not intended to be a demonstration of the size of the Catholic population.

11   You may have stood on Michigan Avenue and watched the uncountable multitudes pushing on for hours upon hours, like the endless stream of *Poilus,* and Tommies and Doughboys moving up to battle; debouching into that incredibly capacious Stadium; you may have swept with your field glasses the entire amphitheater, and observed those swarming men and women filling and overflowing the 200,000 seats, jamming the porches, choking the stairways and hanging from jutting balconies, like the crowds in the ancient Coliseum upon the occasion of a Roman Triumph, or those in the Circus at Antioch during a Chariot Race; and yet you did not fully sense the radical dissimilarity between all other great gatherings and that of the Eucharistic Congress, unless you were present when the trumpets announced the Elevation in the Mass, and the hush of religious awe came over the throng, and the very atmosphere seemed to sense the Presence of God. That was incomparable; unique, overwhelming.

12   Crowds gathered for sport,—especially for bloody sport,—are riotously noisy, but here were a quarter of a million men and women hushed into utter stillness. Those were the supreme

[10] SECRETARY DAVIS—United States Secretary of War under Coolidge.

moments of the Congress. Not the cheering of thousands as the "red-train" pulled in; not the murmur as of swarming bees while the crowds were assembling; not the chorus of 62,000 children singing the Mass; but the awful silence of several hundred thousand persons, when the celebrant spoke the divinely potent words that summoned Christ to His altar of sacrifice,—that moment revealed the Power that had drawn the multitudes over sea and land, from the ends of the earth: "I, if I be lifted up, will draw all hearts to Me." Only believers can understand this mystical fact. "The initiated know."

13   We frequently say that the Mass is the oldest extant form of Christian worship. And surely it is ancient. Imbedded in the liturgy of the Mass are evidences that it was composed when the language of the civilized world was still Greek—before Latin had thoroughly "arrived." Indeed, in the words of the Canon of the Mass there are reminiscences of the time when virtually all Christians were converts from Judaism,—prior to the time when the pagans commenced to come in. Naturally, therefore, there may be some persons who think of the Mass as merely a rite, hoary with antiquity, archaic and obsolescent. But at Chicago, it became possible for all men to see that the Mass comports quite well with all things strictly modern—radios, telephones, telegraph instruments. Even the aeroplane was summoned to service. Over the Stadium and over the grounds at Mundelein, men in ships of the air, half a mile high, were taking panoramic photographs of the scene. Then the films were brought to earth, and the pictures were sent *by telephone* to Rome. And the amplifying devices! Not only the choir of three score thousands of children, not only the stentorian chorus of 200,000 men, but the solo chant of the Preface and of the *Pater Noster* by the celebrant, indeed even those words of the Canon which the rubrics require shall be spoken in a low voice, were heard in San Francisco and in New York,—perhaps even in London and Paris. The ancient and the modern met, and the modern was the servant of the ancient. Words spoken by Jesus in the supper-room at Jerusalem, and repeated, after all these centuries, by the priest at the open-air altar in the central city of the New World, were caught up by cunning modern instruments, amplified, and broadcast to the north and south poles, not to say to the earth's companion planets.

14   These facts, stunning as they are to the imagination, help to

corroborate our faith. Modern science has made us see that the universe is one huge mystery. And the Mass is mystery. Transubstantiation is incomprehensible. But so is radio. Nothing is too stupendous to be true. The modern mind is predisposed to believe any miracle, if only it be big enough. *"Credo quia impossible"* [11] is a maxim that science has brought into good repute once more. And the end of miracles is not yet. The day is coming when we shall not only *hear* from one end of the earth to the other, we shall *see* in New York what is happening in Nijni Novgorod or Timbuctoo. When that day comes, the Pope will say Mass in St. Peter's or at his private altar in the Vatican, and 500 million Catholics from Shanghai to Chicago, and from Punta Arenas to Spitzbergen will see and hear him. Yes, the Mass is out of the Catacombs. The ancient rite is performed under ultra-modern conditions. We are already living in eternity. Time is not. And space is not. When the minds of men catch up with the new revelations of science, they will see that all that is true is mystery, and that the only true religion is the one that is steeped and saturated in mystery. The Mass is mystery *par excellence.* The Mass is the worship of the future,—as of the past.

15   It cannot be too often repeated that the Eucharistic Congress had no ulterior purpose beyond the worship of the Son of God in the Blessed Sacrament. But, incidentally, and inevitably, it was many other things,—for example, a Peace Congress. One could not help thinking, when the Apostolic delegate from the center of Christendom saluted prelates and people with the gracious words —*"Pax Domini sit semper vobiscum,"* "May the Peace of the Lord be forever with you," that here was the note lacking at Versailles, and the lack of which has produced only "confusion worse confounded."

16   Also, as I heard the celebrant of the Mass, on each day of the Congress chant in the presence of that international assembly, *"Dimitte nobis debita nostra,"* "Forgive us our trespasses, as we forgive those who trespass against us," I thought—"if we could only stop up the flood of crimination and recrimination, the books and treatises that have appeared almost every day since the World War began, written with the absurd purpose of locating the blame!" We are all to blame, America included.

[11] *"Credo quia impossibile"*—"I believe the impossible."

17   Be that as it may, here were delegates from England and Ireland, from France and Germany and Austria and Hungary, from Poland, Lithuania, Italy, Czecho-Slovakia, Jugo-Slavia, Switzerland, Australia, China, Japan, Mexico, all the countries of South America, East Indians and American Indians, Haitians and travelers from New Zealand. And, as if by a moral miracle, amongst all these members of traditionally hostile nationalities, there was no dissension, no jealousy, no racial prejudice, no commercial rivalry, no subterranean political machinations, but peace and harmony and brotherly love. Here the German and the Frenchman, the Italian and the Austrian, the Belgian and the Hungarian, the Englishman and the Irishman, met and greeted one another with the kiss of peace. To any dispassionate observer, this must have seemed a truly supernatural phenomenon. If the League of Nations could only succeed in thus bringing together inhabitants of all the world, and diffusing amongst them that spirit of peace, I believe that we should all feel ourselves bound in conscience to advocate and to prosper the League of Nations. If some one asks why the Catholic Church, having this power to assemble and to harmonize conflicting populations, does not succeed in effecting universal and permanent peace, the only reply is that whenever the Catholic Church has attempted to function as a peacemaker in modern society, the politicians and the diplomats have grown jealous and suspicious that the Church was actuated by political ambition. The pope offered himself as an assistant in the work that was to be done at Versailles after the World War, but his services were not accepted. The Catholic Church has not failed to produce peace. She has not been given the chance to try to produce peace.

18   In spite of all the "pomp" at the Congress, there was no pomposity. The most democratic individuals we have seen in many a day were those red-robed princes of the Church. On the platform at the Coliseum, on the opening night (or to speak more precisely, the night preliminary to the opening), cardinals and clergy and laity were hobnobbing as informally as if they were a crowd of college boys at a "frat" meeting, or graduates at a reunion. It seemed as if anybody might touch elbows with a cardinal. I am sure that some people quite unknown to the papal legate, asked him, with the usual loud American geniality, "How do you like our city? And have you seen the stockyards?" And I sus-

pect that some country pastors buttonholed the dignitaries, and asked them to come and open a church bazaar in Scoharie Junction or Hickville Center. Such was the atmosphere of *bonhomie*.[12] The cardinals were treated like Brother Elks or Rotarians and they seemed to enjoy it.

19   And during the procession, as the prelates from San Francisco, or from Hartford, or St. Louis, or New Orleans, or from any other See, passed along, there were glad shouts from pilgrims in the crowd, *"My* archbishop!" *"Our* cardinal!" *"Our* bishop!" It was all delightfully democratic.

[12] *Bonhomie*—Good-fellowship.

Vocabulary Study: "That," writes Father Gillis, "was *incomparable, unique, overwhelming.*" Explain the exact meaning of each of the italicized words. What are the shades of meaning expressed by *"hoary* with antiquity, *archaic,* and *obsolescent"?* What is the difference between *pomp* and *pomposity?* Between *geniality* and *bonhomie?*

Be sure you know the meaning of the following words and phrases: *appalling, paradox, reticence, neophytes, bruit abroad, proscribe, cynosure, outlandish, perfervid, corroborate, ultra-modern, par excellence.*

By Way of Appreciation: According to the old saw there is nothing new under the sun. Certainly to the Catholic there is nothing novel about the Holy Eucharist, and in our day a Eucharistic Congress is certainly not an innovation. To write freshly, then, about the old,—to give new meaning to the familiar, was the task Father Gillis set himself. Like the industrious camera-man searching for a new angle from which to "shoot" St. Peter's in Rome, photographed a million times before, the editor studied his own reactions to the ancient ritual. How he came upon his interpretation we do not know, but as we read we do see that his focusing on the Eucharistic Congress in Chicago as "an appalling violation of the *Disciplina Arcani"* compels our interest.

Suggestions for Study: We have stressed the significance of the point of view adopted by Father Gillis. Does he maintain it consistently throughout the article?

What explanation of the term *"Disciplina Arcani"* does he give? (The footnote is merely a literal translation.) Compare the author's explanation with that given in the *Catholic Encyclopedia,* under *disciplina arcani,* and tell why you prefer one of these explanations to the other.

Editorials, as comments on passing events in the news, ordinarily have but little permanent value as literature. What is there about this editorial which gives it more than ephemeral value? What was the prime purpose of the Eucharistic Congress? What incidental purposes did it also serve?

Select a paragraph which you think is well developed by means of contrasting ideas or pictures, and point out the contrasting elements. Select another paragraph in which the language is predominantly concrete and graphic, and test the effectiveness of such language by substituting abstract and general terms to express the same ideas. In general, does Father Gillis show a preference for long or short sentences? Compare the effect of paragraph 11 with that of paragraph 10, in which short sentences are used.

Exercises and Creative Work: At midnight an emergency case of acute appendicitis is brought to the hospital; an immediate operation is imperative. Word goes out to all concerned: surgeon, internes, nurses, chaplain, relatives, and patient. In four or five paragraphs relate, always in the first person, the reactions of four or five of the people concerned, each of whom regards the approaching operation from a different point of view.

Find an interesting editorial in your favorite Catholic periodical and be prepared to read and discuss it before the class.

The closing ceremony of the Chicago Eucharistic Congress, which took place at Mundelein, ended in a pouring rain. Write letters home for two of the pilgrims, one of whom was sorely disgruntled because of the damage done to her clothes; the other of whom thought it glorious fun to have suffered something for her Eucharistic Lord.

SOME LETTERS OF JOYCE KILMER

From *A Cheerful Ascetic and Other Essays*

JAMES J. DALY

By Way of Introduction: When a gifted and admiring writer pens an essay in appreciation of an admiring friend who is also a gifted writer, the result should be a feast for the gods. That is what we have in the following sketch, in which Father Daly, writing for the Catholic reading public of England, lets us know Joyce Kilmer, at least in part, as he knew him through their years of mutually devoted friendship.

1   *The Month*[1] for May, 1917, contains a glowing, yet judicious, appreciation of the poetry of Joyce Kilmer by Mr. Hugh Anthony Allen. The bright little essay ends on a note of prophecy: "Over the shoulders of this green old world is rising the dawn of better things in literature and life. And Kilmer is the blithe herald of their coming." These are brave words. In July of the following year Joyce Kilmer, acting as observer for the leading battalion of his regiment, was killed in action near the Ourcq.

[1] *The Month*—A Catholic monthly magazine published by the English Jesuits since 1864. "Some Letters of Joyce Kilmer" first appeared in this magazine.

2   Joyce Kilmer was the most distinguished American soldier to fall in the World War. Two volumes, containing a selection from his poems, essays, and letters, together with a brilliantly written memoir by Mr. Robert Cortes Holliday, appeared a few months after his death, and were among the best-selling books of the season. It was not a flash in the pan. Kilmer was so wholly and so intensely Catholic that his religion showed through nearly everything that he wrote. It is not surprising, therefore, that he is still a popular author among American Catholics, especially, I am glad to say, in our schools and colleges. One might suppose that what commends him to Catholic readers would injure him elsewhere. I do not know whether it is a triumph of his personality or his art, or of both together, that, with what may be described as a flaunting and triumphant Catholicism, Kilmer has always been able to attract the general reader. That the American public had not grown tired of him six years after his death was disclosed in a poll to determine the best ten books published since 1900, conducted in 1924 by the *International Book Review*, of New York. Ballots were cast for 1,201 authors and 2,164 different books. The prevalent type among the voters may be conjectured from the fact that Mr. Wells' *Outline of History* stood highest in the poll. A list of the next 167 titles was published, the last in the column being Woodrow Wilson's *A History of the American People*. Francis Thompson's *Poems*, I am sorry to say, ranked only 158 in the list; while such popular writers as Mr. W. L. George, and Mr. Frank Swinnerton failed to come within the first hundred. Joyce Kilmer's name was fifty-fourth.

3   It is needless, perhaps, to state that I attach no conclusive significance to the value of this evidence in testimony of literary worth. But I think it records a remarkable phenomenon. It would seem to indicate that, after six years two volumes of poems, essays, and letters, of a strongly Catholic tone, were still popular in the English language.

4   This may be surprising information to English Catholic readers. When the news of Kilmer's death appeared, it was probably Mr. Gilbert K. Chesterton who wrote in the *New Witness*: "Multitudes of friends on both sides of the Atlantic, as well as many who have never seen his face, will learn with very real and poignant grief of the death in battle of Joyce Kilmer. Of his remarkable power as a poet we have no need to remind our readers." I should like to believe that Joyce Kilmer is known to multitudes

on the Irish and English side of the Atlantic. It would mean that a very salutary leaven was working in the mass of contemporary reading matter. And, especially, it would mean that young Catholic writers had a gracious example to inspire them in the cultivation of the dangerous arts of beauty.

5   The union of piety and artistic preoccupations is as happy as it is rare. In the belief that it is a kind of concurrence which, as the world goes, attracts attention, and is of special interest to Catholics, I venture to give some extracts from his letters which throw light upon the spirit pervading Joyce Kilmer's life and work. Most of these extracts do not appear in the two volumes prepared by Mr. Holliday.

6   The letters, from which I quote, cover about six years. They were busy years. Kilmer was only a little over thirty when he was killed. He had married in 1906, the year of his graduation from Columbia University, on little more than a brave confidence in his future. He taught Latin in Morristown for a year and then went to New York where he was one of the editors of Funk and Wagnall's *Standard Dictionary* for three years.

> Since I wrote to you last, I have left the employ of Funk and Wagnall's. . . . My present occupation is that of asisstant editor of *The Churchman,* an Anglican weekly paper. It is a church newspaper, with some literary features. I am glad to say that we hope to print some of Miss Guiney's poems this winter. . . . Your remarks, in your last letter, on the fact that many of our most famous writers today are anti-Christian, are certainly justified. Still, do you not think that a reaction is coming? Already we have Chesterton, and Belloc, and Bazin, and Miss Guiney, and Father Vincent McNabb, and a number of other brilliant writers who, not as theologians but purely as literary artists, express a fine and wholesome faith. People are beginning to tire of cheap eroticism and "realism" and similar absurdities. But the flood of putrid literature still pours from the presses. Here on my desk as I write lies *The* ——, by one X. He is a vulgarian and a liar; his book is written in wretched English; it is full of grotesque and obvious falsities—and it is in its third edition. I have read the book through, and I am so sick of the fellow's cheap blasphemies that I cannot quiet myself enough to review it in printable words. I understand now thoroughly the custom of having books burned by the common hangman. It was not necessarily because the books were dangerous, or likely to lead people astray—it was just because they were essentially evil, things to be put out of the way. Well, we can't have *The* —— burned, but you must pray for me to get words fiery enough to consume the book utterly when I review it.

7   Kilmer after some months left the staff of *The Churchman* and plunged into the journalism of Broadway. He began to lead a very active life, filling three or four positions on newspapers and weeklies, writing poems and articles—he had already published a volume of poems which was well received by critics—often using for his work the greater part of the nights after "commuting" to the little outlying town where he had established his home. One of his children was stricken with infantile paralysis. Months of anxiety were passed by the busy wage earner and his wife. Then the news came of their entrance into the Church. I may mention that his wife, Aline Kilmer, is widely known as a poet of fine and delicate distinction. Shortly after his conversion he writes:

> The Church refuses to live up to its reputation. In the first place, no one ever tried to proselytize me. I hung on the edge, but my Catholic friends would not push. I had to jump. And now that I am in, the Church still refuses to live up to its reputation. I was warned that I would be shocked by the begging of the parish clergy. I wish I could find a real begging priest. My pastor begs not half enough. Seriously, I think the Church is slandered more by educated Catholic laymen than by Protestants. Even when I was a Protestant, I was pained by some things that Catholics of my acquaintance said about the Church. Surely there should be reticence about family scandals.
>
> Of course you understand my conversion. I am beginning to understand it. I believed in the Catholic position, the Catholic view of ethics and aesthetics, for a long time. But I wanted something not intellectual, some conviction not mental—in fact, I wanted faith. Just off Broadway, on the way from the Hudson Tube Station to the *Times* Building, there is a church, called the Church of the Holy Innocents. Since it is in the heart of the Tenderloin, this name is strangely appropriate—for there surely is need of youth and innocence. Well, every morning for months I stopped on my way to the office and prayed in this church for faith. When faith did come, it came, I think, by way of my little paralyzed daughter. Her lifeless hands led me; I think her tiny still feet know beautiful paths. You understand this, and it gives me a selfish pleasure to write it down.

8   In another letter about this time:

> My wife and I are very comfortable now that we are Catholics. I think we rather disappointed the priest who received us by not showing any emotion during the ceremony. But our chief sensation is simply comfort—we feel that we are where we belong, and it's a very pleasant feeling.

9 And a little later on:

> I need some stricter discipline, I think, and it's hard to get it. I enjoy my confessor's direction very much; he is a fine old Irishman with no nonsense about him. But I need to be called a fool. I need to have some of the conceit and sophistication knocked out of me. I suppose you think this is "enthusiasm"—that much-heralded danger of converts. Perhaps it is, but I don't think so. I know I'm glad I live two miles from the church, because it's excellent for a lazy person like myself to be made to exert himself for religion. And I wish I had a stern medieval confessor—the sort one reads about in anti-Catholic books—who would inflict real penances. The saying of Hail Marys and Our Fathers is no penance, it's a delight.

10 After this letter the discerning reader will not have to be informed that Kilmer had a conscience peculiarly delicate without being unduly scrupulous. I had frequent occasions of surprise over the sensitiveness of conscience which he preserved in occupations popularly supposed to destroy spiritual refinements. He was a daily communicant. One evening during a visit he told me that he had been reading that day an article which appeared on the first page of a reputable newspaper. He began to realize that he should not continue reading, and he cast the paper aside; but he was not sure whether he had acted promptly enough, and might he receive in the morning? Although very substantial and cheerful in appearance, he impressed everyone with a sense of purity and spirituality. Mr. Richard Le Gallienne noted this fact in an article shortly after Kilmer's death: he ends a long description of his first meeting with Kilmer with these words: "I must not omit from my impression the feeling of an unaccustomed contact with vigorous purity, again masculine, not feminine, purity."

11 To go back to letters.

> Did I tell you my confessor sent me to Msgr. Mooney (Vicar-General of the Diocese) to get permission to read anti-religious books and magazines? I am obliged to read them in my work, you know. Msgr. Mooney told me to go ahead and read them if I had to.

12 A schoolroom essay on his poems sent to him from a convent drew the following acknowledgment:

> Your generous and well-phrased appreciation has made me happy, and I am grateful. I hope and pray that I may never write anything unworthy to be read by you.

13   Joyce Kilmer found genuine pleasure, I think, in giving readings and lectures. The popular demand for them grew every year,
and he found in them recreation and a welcome means of eking out
an income for an increasing family. He enjoyed Catholic audiences; but, in starting out as a Catholic lecturer, certain reluc-
tances had to be overcome.

> I'll probably lecture before Catholic organizations as well as secu-
> lar ones, but I don't want to for reasons you will understand. In the
> first place, I don't want in any way to make money out of my religion,
> to seem to be a "professional Catholic." In the second place, I have
> delight chiefly in talking veiled Catholicism to non-Catholics, in
> humbly endeavoring to be an apostle to Bohemia. For instance, I'd
> rather smash an evil book by X. in *The Times* than praise a good book
> in *America.* I have no real message for Catholics; I have Catholo-
> cism's message to modern pagans. So I want to lecture chiefly to
> pagans.

14   In the summer of 1916 he met with an accident on the railway
at the little country station near his home:

> It may interest you to know that I had received the Blessed Sacra-
> ment half an hour before the train struck me, and that to this fact I
> attribute my escape from death—since at the place where I was
> struck several men have been killed, being thrown forward and under
> the wheels, instead of (as I was) to one side.

15   His practice of daily Communion made it necessary to go into
New York without his breakfast and to have his morning coffee at
a restaurant. He was living in Mahwah, New Jersey, two hours
by rail from New York. He wore his piety without heroics:

> Terribly pious, I am. You won't know me when you see me.
> Probably I'll sit around and lecture you all the time. Daily commu-
> nicant and all that sort of thing. And I find all other daily communi-
> cants are funny old women with disreputable bonnets and two clank-
> ing rosaries apiece. They clatter up to the rail leaning on canes and
> pray audibly.

16   He was always ready to improve the frequent opportunities
which came to him of urging the claims of Catholic literary merit.

> By the way, it may interest you to know of an experience I had
> recently with Warner's Library of the World's Best Literature. This

is, as you undoubtedly are aware, a monumental work founded by the late Charles Dudley Warner. It is supposed to represent adequately all the world's greatest writers, and the biographical and critical articles are supposed to be authoritative. The list of editors is most imposing, and when I was asked to contribute to the revised edition articles on Cawein, Masefield, and Moody, I was much pleased. Out of curiosity, I asked the editor who was writing the article on Francis Thompson. To my amazement I found he had not thought of including Thompson! I am glad to say that I succeeded in persuading him to include an article on Thompson. I am writing it and selecting four or five pages of extracts from Thompson to accompany it. Do you think that some of Thompson's prose should be included, or only his verse?

17   In a letter, dated May 19th, 1917, he writes:

> I resigned from the Officers' Reserve Training Corps and enlisted in the Seventh Regiment, National Guard, New York, as a private.

18   Joyce Kilmer has been the object of some disapproval for taking this step. He had a wife and five children depending upon him for their support, and there was no urgency for a sacrifice which involved others as well as himself. And, as afterward transpired, once in the army and at the front he deliberately sought the most perilous employments. My own explanation, which space will not permit amplifying, is that Joyce Kilmer acted at this time from spiritual motives at least as much as from patriotic motives. As for his family, he had received what seemed to be the most reliable assurances that they would be provided for in the event of his death. If misunderstanding on this score developed afterward, he could not possibly have foreseen it.

19   In the letter announcing his enlistment, after telling about certain courtesies he had received, he proceeds:

> On the whole I'm too well treated—it's likely to turn my head. That's why it's good for me to be a private and be bossed around by a young snip of an officer I wouldn't hire as an office boy. Every drill night I have about 300 exercises in humility—every time the sergeant says, "Get your belly in!" "Hold up your head!" "Say, that's a gun you're carrying, not a hod!"

20   He seldom thereafter referred in his letters to the hardships of his soldier life. He obtained a transfer from the Seventh to the Sixty-Ninth, the Irish Regiment of New York, principally because

it had a Catholic chaplain and was predominantly Catholic and Irish, a combination which always attracted him. His regiment was a part of the Rainbow Division which was one of the earliest to go overseas. On the eve of its departure, his favorite child, the crippled Rose, died, and another child was born. It was a difficult time. He refers to the "eight hours a day of violent physical exercise (most deadening to the brain, a useful anodyne to me, coming as it did after my grief)," and that is all one hears of the sordid horrors of war, bad enough during the regiment's first winter in France. His letters were for the most part full of good humor and high spirits. The last lines of a short poem sent home from the front tell us much:

> Lord, Thou didst suffer more for me
> Than all the hosts of land and sea.
> So let me render back again
> This millionth of Thy gift. Amen.

21 Even if it be granted that the radiant presence of Joyce Kilmer is still a vivid memory, influencing those who knew him to set too high a value upon his literary work, it is nevertheless true that his writings disclose an extraordinary personality in which amiable human qualities, literary activity and ambition, and high natural virtues, were fused with a scrupulously exact Catholic and supernatural life and faith. This alone should keep him from dropping into oblivion among Catholics. It is not often that the febrile pursuits of journalism and literature produce a popular writer who can be cited as an example and an inspiration in the great and the small Catholic fidelities. These words, written in one of his last letters to his wife and appearing in the two-volume work to which reference has been made, might well be framed and hung on the wall wherever writing talent is laboring for mastery in the art of expression:

> If what you write does not clearly praise the Lord and His saints and angels, let it praise such types of heaven as we know in our life —God knows they are numerous enough. I can honestly offer *Trees* and *Main Street* [the titles of the two volumes of poems which he published after he had become a Catholic] to Our Lady, and ask her to present them, as the faithful work of her poor and unskilled craftsman, to her Son. I hope to be able to do it with everything I write hereafter—and to be able to do this is to be a good poet.

Vocabulary Study: Father Daly is almost meticulous in his choice of words. Although this essay reveals such care less manifestly than any other essay in the volume from which it is taken, you will do well to observe the precision with which the key word is chosen for the following phrases, and to make sure of the precise meaning of each: *flaunting Catholicism, salutary leaven, artistic preoccupations, eking out an income, without heroics, as afterwards transpired, the radiant presence, the febrile pursuits of journalism, the great and small Catholic fidelities.*

By Way of Appreciation: Like other high-school students many a time you have heard your teacher of English say: "Take pains with your letters. A man reveals himself in his letters." The statement is so often repeated that it is safe to assume that it is fundamentally true. It must be confessed, however, that sometimes what is revealed is, to say the least, scarcely significant. It may be that the letter-writer has little personality to reveal; or that he lacks the command of language requisite for a measure of self-expression; or, finally, that the character of the recipient of the letter calls for reticence rather than self-revelation on the part of the writer. But when a Joyce Kilmer writes to his close friend, the Reverend James J. Daly, all the requisites are present for letter writing at its best. When, further, that intimate friend weaves those letters into an essay of appreciation, as Father Daly has done here, then truly is a man—and a man well worth knowing—revealed in his letters.

Suggestions for Study: In this essay Father Daly is more matter of fact and less lyrical than in other essays appearing in the same volume. Can you see any good reason for this difference of treatment? Has the fact that the essay was originally written for an English periodical influenced the writer's treatment of his subject? Should it influence him? What purpose is served by the quotation in the first paragraph?

What qualities do you find in Joyce Kilmer, as pictured in this essay, likely to inspire "young Catholic writers"? What is Father Daly's purpose in publishing these extracts? The title of the essay implies that the author has not included all the letters which he received from Kilmer. What would guide him in making his selection?

Why, do you suppose, does the author consider the cultivation of the arts of beauty "dangerous"? And why is "the union of piety and artistic preoccupations" rare? What is the point of Kilmer's remark that he would "rather smash an evil book in *The Times* than praise a good one in *America*"?

Exercises and Creative Work: A newspaper columnist is normally more guarded in his daily contributions to the newspaper than he is in his familiar correspondence. Still he does in the course of time reveal to his reading public much of his real character. Clip your favorite column daily over a period of two weeks to a month, and then, by judicious selection and pertinent comment compose an essay about your columnist similar to Father Daly's essay on Joyce Kilmer.

Essays of Appreciation

SNOW WHITE

By Way of Introduction: "A quick ear and eye," writes Alexander Smith, the author of *Dreamthorp*, "an ability to discern the infinite suggestiveness of common things, a brooding meditative spirit, are all that the essayist requires to start business with." To a Dominican nun the meditative spirit is habitual; living long years as a member of a white-robed community, she very understandably has an affection for white; the suggestiveness of common and uncommon things she sees and plays upon so effectively that, whatever your earlier opinion of color may have been, you read "Snow White" and are won to white.

1   THERE is something compellingly attractive about color; but white is lovelier. The pageantry of October with its lavish gold and bronze, here and there a burning bush of red maple among yellow oaks and poplars, can restore the glamour of the most frayed personality. Flags and uniforms and parades, Elizabethan costumes, mediaeval illuminations, the crimson sweaters, orange scarves, blue and yellow peasant kerchiefs of youth, the red berets of Spanish soldiers—all these things stir and excite us. We think at times that no relief is so gracious as the relief of color after drabness or whiteness.

2   But white is lovelier. "It is the low sun that brings forth the color," murmured hapless Guinevere; and though the heart thrills with delight when blossoms of lovely color flower from the golden bowl of the sun, yet Guinevere's recognition of the highest beauty, the beauty of whiteness, comes to all of us, sometime.

3   White is mysterious and subtle and capable of a variety of effects. It is a mystic symbol of a reality rare and precious. Something of its potency may be felt, perhaps, in the mediaeval heroines whose names express their personalities, like Blanchefleur, beloved by Galahad, or Isolde of the White Hands, whose meek gentleness won Tristram in spite of himself.

4   Something of this potency, this symbolism, is felt in nature's use of white. Is it the rarity of white that gives it charm? There is the whiteness of the lily, rising queen-like from its wrappings of green, stately and radiant, aloof, enchantingly lovely; and the

whiteness of the lily-of-the-valley, fragile as gossamer, with its tiny perfect white bells, silent as peace, like a procession of First Communicants, the white bells of their veils in flower-like rows as they march demurely up the aisle.

5   There is the swift surprise whiteness of dogwood, among other frail heralds of spring like the luminous bloodroot and the pale anemone, dainty as a tiny girl. There is the startling smooth whiteness of birch-bark, innocent and bride-like among the rough dark trunks of the forest trees. There is edelweiss growing high on the Alps, with furry white stem, foliage, and petals, the ghost of a flower, or perhaps a flower in a white woolen snow suit, dressed for the altitude, tiny memento in the cold grandeur of the snowcapped heights of the gracious beauty of the valleys. A nostalgia for beauty less dazzling must pierce the heart at sight of its gallant blossoming.

6   Other whites in nature are potent to suggest its mystery. There is the whiteness of clouds, stately, full-sailed galleons skimming the blue ocean of sky. There is the whiteness of swans, especially the swans of the Thames. No wonder Spenser drew from their majestic beauty the imagery that builds on the refrain "Sweete Thames run softly till I end my song," that lovely castle of music. Even the swans in the moat around the Bishop's Palace in Wells (the only moated castle extant in England) impress us first with the beauty of their accomplishments. For these swans are not only beautiful; they are highly intelligent and practical. For hundreds of years, the swans of this particular moat have sailed majestically upstream, lovely snowy ships, towards a window in the gatehouse from which depends a rope, which generations of swans have pulled to notify the porter that they would be grateful if he would bestir himself and provide them with their daily rations. There is something deliciously incongruous in the royal elegance of the swans and the practical measure of ringing the dinner bell. They have the bland manner of a well-groomed matron; and they are but food-hunters after all. But even a hungry swan makes a beautiful picture because he (or she) is garbed in snowy white.

7   The peculiar satisfaction that emanates from white, whether because of its rarity or its perfection, nothing in nature conveys more powerfully than snow. It falls silently during the night and in the morning we look upon a strange new world. Its beauty is literally astonishing. Under the shining raiment of new-fallen snow all unseemliness is hidden and the meanest objects, a squat bucket for

instance, or a sagging woodshed, are transformed into things of beauty. The kindness of snow is like the tenderness of Mary, blessed among women, who, compassionating the most refractory souls, wins them to virtue. Of her immaculateness it is a symbol. A landscape robed in its soft loveliness has the beauty of nature enhanced by the perfection and the poignancy of art. Its quality of rare loveliness reminds us of Sidney's description of poetry: "Nature never set forth the earth in so rich tapestry as diverse poets have done, neither with so pleasant rivers, fruitful trees, sweet-smelling flowers, nor whatsoever else may make the too much loved earth more lovely; her world is brazen; the poets only deliver a golden." Nature transformed by snow seems art. "Poetry is the complex sense of past delights," says Abbe Dimnet. In the exquisite perfection of a landscape glorified by snow, there is the complex sense not only of past but of future delights; for we feel instinctively that the beauty of snow holds the promise of the ideal, of a better life, a more beautiful world, whose splendor will dazzle the eyes and pierce the mind with the glory of the fulness of truth.

8   Just here, perhaps, with an unexpected tact, we have touched upon the explanation of the mystery of white. It appeals universally because it reminds us of the ideal. It is the unforgettable, unmistakable emblem of purity.

9   The symbolism is emphasized in its liturgical usage. Pure white linens are the vesture of the altar, symbol of Christ. The fulness of joy at Eastertide, central feast of the ecclesiastical year, is expressed by white vestments. Joyous white is worn for Feasts of our Lord and of His Blessed Mother; it celebrates also the victory of Confessors and Doctors, the purity of Virgins, and the innocence of Holy Women. There is, perhaps, nothing more poignantly joyful than the white vestments used in the Burial Mass of children.

10   In the white vesture of the Holy Father, Vicar of the Prince of Peace, we have a most significant use of the symbolism of white. Nothing befits him, Christ-on-earth, like white, so harmonious with his character and with the nature of his mission; white, symbol of joy, of purity, of peace, pledge to the stained world of the white radiance of eternity.

Vocabulary Study: Learn the precise meaning of the following words and phrases as used in the essay: *pageantry; frayed; drabness; hapless;*

subtle; potency; fragile as gossamer; memento; nostalgia; incongruous; galleons; bland manner; squat bucket; refractory souls; poignantly joyful.

By Way of Appreciation: Although chemist, physicist, and psychologist may all write of whiteness, each in his own way, no cold scientist can endow it with the lyric charm which Sister Julie gives it. Poet-like she broods over her subject with the warmth that is wholly human until it glows with the vitality of her own personality.

Suggestions for Study: What is there about the opening sentence that challenges your attention? State in one sentence the thesis, or unifying idea, of the essay. Choose any five paragraphs and show by what method of development each one is expanded in support of the general theme. What quality of whiteness do you find most appealing? What peculiar value have the literary allusions in a familiar essay of this type? Make a sentence outline of the essay, and discover, if you can, the author's reason for developing the topics in the particular order which she follows.

Exercises and Creative Work: After rereading "Snow White" several times to capture the easy spirit in which the essayist plays with her subject, try your hand at developing an essay on a similar topic such as: *Blue, Scarlet, Black;* or try something like *Sounds at Night, Soothing Sounds,* or *Stirring Sounds.*

WILLA CATHER'S MASTERPIECE

From *Catholicism and the Modern Mind*

MICHAEL WILLIAMS

By Way of Introduction: The Catholic Church has played a large part in the development of our country. Great self-sacrificing souls, their ideals and achievements, their moral and physical courage in conflict form a treasury of historical lore that has scarcely been drawn upon in our literature. Willa Cather, though not a Catholic, has discovered the art value in the Catholic traditions of the French and Spanish sections of our country and has created lasting literature in her recital of these discoveries. In the following review of *Death Comes to the Archbishop* an outstanding Catholic journalist, Michael Williams, expresses his appreciation of Willa Cather's abilities and his gratitude for her choice of subject matter.

I   WHEN Walt Whitman cried out on some page or other of "Leaves of Grass," that who touched that book really touched a man, he said something that was true in its special sense not only of his book but of all true books. They are living things. They have in them not only the life, or something of the life, of their writers, but also they have a life of their own: individual, separate, unique. Like men, they are composed of body and soul. As in the case of man, we can recognize the palpable fact of their living quality, but we experience the same difficulty in any attempt precisely to define that quality as we experience in trying to define any man or any woman. "All things find their end in mystery," wrote some Schoolman long ago. Even the most convinced materialist, one to whom what we call the soul is merely the product or effect of mechanical processes of the blood, and nerves, and glands, when asked for his explanation of how matter itself began, can only say that all things, matter included, certainly begin in a mystery, however they may end. He may believe, or try to believe, that some day he will know it all; will be able to explain the beginning and foresee the end; but here and now he must admit the mystery.

2   All works of human art contain or partially express the ambient mystery of life, of which death itself is only an element. Among these works of art: temples, cathedrals, symphonies, peasant songs, sculpture, paintings, dramas, roads and bridges, ships (whether of the air or of the sea), books,—true books, living books—are especially steeped in mystery. Criticism may usefully attempt to deal with such books for the sake of the value of incidental discoveries, helpful minor interpretations, though criticism never understands creation. But at least it may do it reverence. It may be its missionary, hunting out and bringing to the shrine of art all those who may be seeking beauty but who do not know where it is to be found.

3   It seems to me that it is the duty of criticism so to call attention to Willa Cather's book, *Death Comes to the Archbishop,* that all readers competent to appreciate a great work of literary art may have their opportunity to enjoy it. When I say "all readers competent to appreciate a great work of literary art," I have no intention of being supercilious; I do not address myself to any coterie of highbrows; I have no thought of those superior persons of Mallarmé's dictum,[1] the inbred aristocrats of the mind, to whom only are the inner secrets of art revealed. For readers who delight in what is vaguely called "style," to whom the rhythms and the verbal coloring of "fine writing" are delight-giving things in themselves, there are indeed many wonderful pages in this book. For those who seek in prose fiction not only the attraction of in-

[1] Stéphane Mallarmé—French poet and theorist (1842–1898).

teresting characters, places, events, adventures, but also the more subtle but no less real attraction of philosophy—which, broadly speaking, is surely the effort of the human intellect to examine deeply, and, if possible, to understand, the universe in which and through which the pageant of human life proceeds—there also is much and worth-while stuff. And at the same time the simplest and most humble of readers may and surely will find this book acceptable and more than acceptable. I know few book. so deep, even so profound, in subject matter, which are expressed in so simple a vocabulary.

4   The stylistic beauty of Willa Cather's book: beauty of the rarest, truest kind, is in her pages as perfume mingled with incense breathes from flowers on some altar: as color appears in those flowers, or in the sky at sunrise or sunset, or in a rainbow, or in the eyes, the lips, the cheeks of living men and women. In order to write this book, she has read a great deal in other books, she has studied books; she has observed the desert country of the American Southwest morning, noon, and night, through all four seasons of the year; she has lived among and with its people; and she has thought very deeply, very long, about all those things, and about life itself; moreover, she has brooded; she has been affected by movements of her soul, by intuitions and inspirations coming from beyond the frontiers of thought. Thus her spirit became mysteriously maternal; and this book was born, not made. Her words and phrases, simple, and nearly always words of common use, are so vivified by their association with her marvelous inner processes that they shine with their real meanings, which are so blurred and defaced in the hands of hasty or dishonest writers; they mix and mingle in rare combinations of color and music. A child could read this book without effort; artists, philosophers, and priests may, and will, ponder it profoundly.

5   Is it a novel? I do not know. All depends upon what one's definition of a novel may happen to be. Is it history, or biography; rewritten, or rather, recreated? Historical characters, like Kit Carson; historical events, like the Gadsden purchase of Arizona,[2] or the building up of the Archdiocese of Santa Fé, are dealt

---

[2] JAMES GADSDEN—American soldier and diplomatist who negotiated the purchase of what is now Arizona and New Mexico from Mexico in 1854 for $10,000,000 (1788–1858).

with in such a way that the book throws more light upon the southwestward sweep of the United States than many volumes of professed history. Yet the book decidedly is not—or certainly is not only—an exercise in the present-day habit or fad of "novelizing" history or biography. There is no "love interest" in its pages—at least, not of the kind that one ordinarily associates with novels, and perhaps even more with the new order of fictionized biographies. The love that glows in Willa Cather's book can never be put into the movies because it is the love that moves the universe and all its stars, the love of God for man, of man for God. It is one of the serenest, most mellow, most peaceful books ever written; but the peace, the serenity, the mellowness are not shallow, not superficial. They are there as a starlit sky and a calm sea combine upon some perfect night of beauty; but the unimaginable depths and distances of space, the power and dread of the sea, are unforgotten.

6   One would have to be able to write as well as Miss Cather, and on the same subjects, and that is a highly improbable thing, adequately to pay tribute to one high merit of her wonderful book; namely its description of the colors, the sounds, the scents, the aspects of the Southwestern desert. But "description" is a misleading word. Willa Cather does not really describe the desert; she magically evokes it. Perhaps only those who know it by personal experience can fully appreciate her wizardry; but surely no reader can be insensitive to the enchantment of her crystalline prose; crystalline and limpid, yet at the right moments shot through and scintillant with colors, and ghosts of colors, and tones of color, and super-tones. Not even Mary Austin[3] can bring the desert country into language with more success; and that is the highest praise, in terms of comparison, that I can give. I know that country; I have lived in it, many months at a time; I can remember; but I do more than remember, I live it again, in this book.

7   It tells the story of one Jean Marie Latour, a Catholic missionary priest who, when a young man, is sent to New Mexico as the Bishop of Santa Fé, after that portion of the country comes into the possession of the United States. With him is his friend from youth, Father Joseph Vaillant, now his vicar, and destined also to become a bishop in the turbulent gold fields of Colorado.

[3] MARY AUSTIN—An American novelist and essayist whose chief interest was the interpretation of the American Indian and his contribution to American culture (1868–1934).

Vaillant is the son of a peasant. Latour comes of an aristocratic family that in past centuries gave cathedral-building bishops to France; he is one who, without a vocation to the priesthood, might have been a typical man of the world, a somewhat delicate-minded, courteous, virile yet gentle person. But the vocation makes all the difference. It brings him to New Mexico, cuts him off from the sophisticated European culture and refinement of life which he so appreciates, to labor a long lifetime amid Indians and semi-barbarous white folk, living crudely, hardly, dangerously, and at last dying in exile. Vaillant, however, you cannot think of save as a priest, and a missionary priest.

8   The first comers of the American conquest are swarming into Santa Fé, meeting the scanty and static Mexican population, and the older aboriginal life of the Indians, the Pueblo people, the Navajos, and other tribes. The two priests ride hundreds, sometimes thousands of miles, on horse- or mule-back; they sleep, on those journeys, on the ground, in sandstorms or snowstorms, in the dry, torrid heat of the deserts, or in the dry, knife-edged cold of the hills; they are almost murdered by a degenerate American renegade; they glimpse strange things of the primitive religious secrets of the Indians; they meet curious Mexican priests who defy the power of Rome and set up schisms of their own; they gather the legends of the Spanish pioneers, the Franciscan martyrs to whom the hardships, very real ones indeed, of the French priests of this transition period of American life, are even mild. And always, everywhere, they give all their powers, their endurance, their courage, their strength, their culture, their riches of European experience, to the task that has brought them to this oldest, this newest of regions: the task of extending the Catholic Church, the Faith; the task of saving souls.

9   It is in her treatment of this central motive of the life of Archbishop Latour and his companion, Father Vaillant, that Willa Cather succeeds most surely. Her book is a wonderful proof of the power of the true artist to penetrate and understand and to express things not part of the equipment of the artist as a person. Miss Cather is not a Catholic, yet certainly no Catholic American writer that I know of has ever written so many pages steeped in spiritual knowledge and understanding of Catholic motives and so sympathetically illustrative of the wonder and beauty of Catholic mysteries, as she has done in this book.

10   There is one short chapter, or section, for example, entitled

December Night, which contains the quintessence of the meaning, the power, the consolation, the charm, the beauty of Catholic
devotion to the Blessed Virgin. "Bishop Latour had been going
through one of those periods of coldness and doubt which, from
his boyhood, had occasionally settled down upon his spirit and
made him feel an alien, wherever he was." One night, nearing
Christmas, lying in bed, depressed with a sense of failure, he
wants to pray but cannot pray. By and by he realizes that in
his mind is a desire to leave bed and go to his church, there to
find, if he may, near the tabernacle on the altar, the contagion of
that spiritual warmth and force which he craves; and also he
realizes that he dreads leaving bed and facing the cold. Once
seizing the truth, the Bishop acts as always he acts. He gets
up and goes to the church. He finds an old Mexican woman, a
slave of an American family, crouched in the snow against the
sacristy door, weeping. Her owners, being bigots, would not permit her to go to the Catholic Church or to receive a priest.
Scantily clothed, she had escaped from the house hoping to steal
into the church and pray. The bishop lights a candle and looks
at her. "It seemed to him that he had never seen pure goodness
shine out of a human countenance as it did from hers." He
covers her with his warm cloak, he takes her to the altar of the
Virgin; and the aristocratic ecclesiastic and the Mexican slave
woman pray together. Then the courtly archbishop learns from
the old slave woman secrets of the joy and the truth of religion
such as he has not glimpsed since the days of his pure and ardent
youth.

Kneeling beside the much-enduring bondwoman, he experienced
those holy mysteries as he had done in his young manhood. He
seemed able to feel all it meant to her to know that there was a
Kind Woman in Heaven, though there were such cruel ones on earth.
Old people, who have felt blows and toil and known the world's
hard hand, need, even more than children do, a woman's tenderness.
Only a woman, divine, could know all that a woman can suffer. Not
often, indeed, had Jean Marie Latour come so near to the Fountain
of all Pity as in the Lady Chapel that night; the pity that no man
born of woman could ever utterly cut himself off from; that was for
the murderer on the scaffold, as it was for the dying soldier or the
martyr on the rack. The beautiful concept of Mary pierced the
priest's heart like a sword.

11   I should like to quote the entire section, for the sheer pleasure of slowly savoring a most beautiful piece of prose; and for me also it is like repeating a most efficacious prayer. Well indeed did Miss Cather write on her title page, *"Auspice Maria."* [4]

12   My colleague George Shuster has written one or two big books and lectured up and down the country trying to get people to understand the rich soil and background that American art, in literature, music, painting, sculpture, possesses in the shape of its Catholic element—the works and ways of the Spanish, Portuguese, French, and English explorers who came companioned by the men of the Cross, men of the same stuff as Willa Cather's Jean Marie Latour and Joseph Vaillant. It is not, in this connection, a matter of the truth, whether final and absolute, or provisional and relative, of the Catholic faith; it is a matter of the rich heritage of heroism, of authentic deeds and fascinating folklore, and of the solid, substantial contributions flowing from the work of the early Catholics for the enrichment and strengthening and beautifying of American life and culture. If the Spaniard came as a swordsman, with him also came the man of the Cross. The swordsman died losing to others the lands and power he had fought for; but from the blood-dewed paths of the missionary flowered the things that last—agriculture, the vine, arts, letters, lessons of the highest deeds of the human spirit.

13   Willa Cather is one of the few American artists who has perceived the great treasures lying in wait for art in the Catholic tradition of the United States. One of her books is called "O Pioneers!" She, too, is a pioneer. She will lead others to that treasure-trove. Let us hope that among them may be a few Catholics. American Catholics sorely lack, and even more sorely need, authentic artists. Producing rich men and politicians, a scattering of judges and a host of lawyers, isn't quite the proof that the nation needs of the civilizing influence of the Faith. The Church in the United States has never failed in its succession of splendid priests and even more splendid nuns. But the laity has not as yet flowered to any notable extent in the production of the finer works of culture and of life. Books like Willa Cather's may and should help to remedy the matter. At any rate, I consider it the duty of Catholics to buy and read and spread Willa Cather's masterpiece.

[4] *Auspice Maria*—"With Mary's Blessing."

C-AM

Vocabulary Study: The journalist, writing for a vast and varied reading public, seldom indulges in unusual words. Make sure, however, that you know the meaning of the following words and can use them correctly in your writing: *palpable, unique, ambient, supercilious, coterie, crystalline, limpid, scintillant, courteous, virile, savor, scanty, static, aboriginal, torrid, renegade, quintessence.*

By Way of Appreciation: The more extended our acquaintance with the persons, places, events, and institutions described in our reading, the more deeply can we penetrate the message which a writer has for us. As we grow in age and experience, the more meaningful do significant books become to us, and the more capable do we become of judging the merits of what we read. Michael Williams, therefore, a journalist of years, forever travelling up and down the United States in the interests of his Church and his country, is well equipped to be the literary critic of things American and Catholic. Because he is familiar with the scenes of Willa Cather's novel, he appreciates the more the magic by which she recreates them. Because he loves the Faith which motivates the characters of her novel, he appreciates the fidelity of their portrayal. Speaking out of the fullness of this experience, he puts it down as "the duty of Catholics to buy and read and spread Willa Cather's masterpiece." You will find the duty a pleasant one to satisfy.

Suggestions for Study: In what sense is it a fact that all true books "have a life of their own"? What does Michael Williams consider the purposes of literary criticism? Would you say that he achieves these purposes? Explain his assertion: "This book was born, not made." Do you agree with him when he says, "The love that glows in Willa Cather's book can never be put into the movies"? Miss Cather is not a Catholic, yet has caught the spirit of Catholicism and written what may rightly be called a Catholic novel. Why is this a remarkable achievement?

Exercises and Creative Work: A good book review does two things: it gives a summary of the contents of the book reviewed; and it evaluates the worth of the book in the light of the interests and needs of those who will read the review. Judged by these criteria is Michael Williams' essay a good book review?

The average man's first-hand experience is limited in range. The readiest way to compensate for this limitation is by the vicarious experience which reading gives. Recount a valuable experience which you have thus lived through in your reading.

If the Church has made signal contributions to the development of your community, write an essay about a significant detail of those contributions.

THE MEANING OF LITERATURE

From *Religion and the Study of Literature*

Brother Leo

By Way of Introduction: Unquestionably a man may enjoy good reading and develop good literary taste without ever having framed a formal definition of literature. Asked what is good literature, such a man might well answer, "I don't know, and what is more, with the author of the *Imitation of Christ,* I should rather feel compunction than be able to define it." Neatly said, we should have to concede, if a choice must be made. But if, without impairing his enjoyment and without injury to his taste, he can himself evolve or in some other way come by a good explanation of the meaning of literature, he will be shortsighted indeed not to avail himself of a piece of good fortune. For, given the natural craving of the human mind to get to the heart of things, to see "what makes the wheels go around," the man who not only knows good literature and enjoys it but also understands what it is that makes it literature and not mere writing, is bound to be better satisfied himself and better able to satisfy those doubters who sooner or later will put the inevitable question, "But what makes it literature?" than is the man who relies solely on his intuitive judgment of things.

We are fortunate, then, in having so lucid and suggestive an analysis of the meaning of literature as that found in the following selection from Brother Leo. In it he answers a question that has tried the best minds down the ages, and answers it, we venture to say, in an essay that itself merits the name of literature. But perhaps it will be better to leave the reader free to judge for himself after he has read "The Meaning of Literature."

1   PERHAPS we can get most readily to the heart of our subject if we assume as valid a definition of literature which, though conceivably lacking in logical precision, has worth by reason of its suggestiveness: *Literature is a verbal portrait of life.*

OF LIFE

2   THAT Alexander Pope was a great poet is a debatable point, but there is no doubt whatever that he was wellnigh matchless as a coiner of epigrams and aphorisms envisaging essential truths. And one of the finest and most penetrating of his epigrams, one that has passed by reason of its appositeness into the proverbs of the English tongue, one that is recognized as a truism, even, so

obvious and withal so significant is its kernel of sound sense, is this: "The proper study of mankind is man." That epigram is a foundation principle, a seed thought, a point of departure, for the musician, for the painter, for the sculptor, for the philosopher, for the historian; but especially does it shape the aims and control the methods of the litterateur. For, in the last analysis, human life is the stuff out of which great books are made. Every maker of literature and every student of literature might appropriately take as his motto that distillation of Popean wisdom; that, or else that similarly searching utterance of the Latin dramatist, Terence: "I am a man; and nothing that is human can be foreign to me."

3   This *vital* element in literature—the essential truth of the great book to the life of man and of men—is an unfailing and indispensable characteristic of all literary masterpieces, no matter what philosophy of life looms as their background or what ideal of life animates their inspiration. It is as true of the Homeric poems, which embody a naïve, a boyish, outlook on life, as it is true of the novels of George Meredith or of Mr. Joseph Conrad, which embody an outlook on life immeasurably more complicated and sophisticated; it holds good for the rude and vigorous religious plays which mark the beginnings of the English drama not less than for the highly technical and painfully polished dramatic contributions of a later day; . . . it is present in the Psalms as in Sappho, in Theocritus as in Mr. Alfred Noyes or in Mr. Walter de la Mare. Literature springs from the heart of a man who knows much about life and who sympathizes deeply with life; and its educational, its cultural value springs from the fact that the reading of literature produces a corresponding growth of human knowledge and human sympathy in the heart of the student.

A PORTRAIT

4   YET, not every book that concerns itself with human life is literature, not every man who writes with a fullness of human knowledge and a store of human sympathy is a literary artist. A treatise on moral theology is undeniably a very human—conceivably, even a very humane—sort of book; yet it is not literature. This morning's newspaper veritably bristles with facts about men and women, about human conditions and human aspirations; yet it is not literature. The love letters exchanged

between a rustic Darby and a suburban Joan are, to say the least, astonishingly sympathetic missives; yet they are not literature. How comes it that Hawthorne's "The Scarlet Letter" is literature, and the treatise on moral theology—with which that novel has so much in common—is not? That Shakespeare's historical plays are literature, and the morning newspaper is not? That Mrs. Browning's love letters, the "Sonnets from the Portuguese," are literature, and Joan's love letters are not? What is the difference?

5   It is the difference between the snapshot and the portrait. We are all familiar with the devotee of the folding camera who peremptorily stands us against a blank wall, admonishes us to look pleasant, and photographs us even while our mouths widen in unavailing protest. If we are of a philosophic turn of mind, the resulting picture ordinarily gives us abundant food for speculation. We can, on the one hand, establish by a strictly scientific line of reasoning that the print does really represent us and no other human being; and yet, on the other hand, we are absolutely certain—and in this all of our friends, except the amateur photographer, will agree—that this counterfeit presentment is not our likeness at all. Our garments do not hang upon our frame in that unseemly fashion; our hands and our ears are manifestly not so large and prominent; we hold the mirror up to nature and assure ourselves that our poor faces are innocent of so many marring lines and shadows. And, like a good many philosophers, when confronted with all the evidence, we seek refuge in an eminently human form of dualism, and to the momentous query, "Is this your likeness?" we equivocally reply, "Extrinsically, yes; intrinsically, no!"

6   And now let us suppose that to salve our vanity and conserve our self-respect, we arrange for sittings with a celebrated portrait painter. We shall probably find the process lengthy, even to the point of fatigue. The artist makes us come to his studio day after day, and he paints very little and talks very much. He makes us talk, too. He probes our mind, he sounds our soul; he familiarizes himself with our likes and our dislikes, with our political and religious beliefs, with our theories of art and life, with our sorrows and our joys, our ideals and our ambitions. And, again if we are of a philosophical turn of mind, we presently say to ourselves, "This man is painting my likeness from the inside." Eventually, the portrait is completed and exhibited to the scru-

tiny of a few discreet friends and true. They look at the painting, and then at us; and when we ask them, "Is this my likeness?" they, too, take refuge in the convenient dualistic formula and impressively reply: "Intrinsically, yes; extrinsically, no!"

7   What is the difference between the snapshot and the portrait? It is the difference between *fact* and *truth*. And that, bereft of accidental distinctions, is likewise the difference between "The Scarlet Letter" and the treatise on moral theology, between Shakespeare and the newspaper, between the love letters of Mrs. Browning and the love letters of suburban Joan. The portrait has an aesthetic appeal, as have Hawthorne and Shakespeare and the "Sonnets from the Portuguese"; and that *aesthetic* element in the real book is an unfailing characteristic of real literature.

8   Somebody has said that literature immortalizes the best moments of the best minds, and that view is felicitous; for while human life is truly the substance of literature, not everything in human life, or every moment or every manifestation of human life, is fit literary material. Art, after all, is largely selection, and selection of what is typical, significant. That is the essence of the art of portraiture; and it is the essence likewise of the art of writing. Art is not the mere presentation of human life in the raw, in the rough; rather is it, as Michelangelo said, the purgation of superfluities. Like the portrait painter, the literary artist depicts human life from the inside; and in so doing he concentrates on essential truth and makes his work a thing of beauty. Literature deals not with facts, but with truth; that is why Shakespeare's plays constitute a work of art, and that is why the morning newspaper does not.

A VERBAL PORTRAIT

9   PORTRAITURE of life is, so to say, the genus of literature; language is its specific difference. The painter, the musician, the poet, all three aim in general at interpreting and manifesting human life in terms of beauty; that is the general aim of all art. But each uses distinct materials. The painter sings in lines and colors; the musician paints in concourse of sweet sounds; but the poet's brush is human speech and his music a symphony of words. Literature, therefore, is a verbal portrait; and when we recognize that obvious fact we recognize the *formal* element in literature.

10   Since the literary artist records in words the breath and finer spirit of his knowledge of human life, the quintessence of his interpretation of life, since his masterpiece is a portrait of life produced by the pigments of human speech selected in accord with the flair of his mood and personality, it follows that literature is a human document at once general and particular. The great book is a world in little, for the life of all humanity throbs in its pages; and the great book is at the same time something specific and unique, for it enshrines likewise the reactions to human experience of an individual mind and heart unusually keen and responsive. The classical writer—that is, the writer whose work is recognized as a faithful portrait of human experience, as an object of intrinsic and surpassing beauty and as an original contribution to the philosophy of living—is necessarily endowed in a high degree with the faculty of expression. He probably knows life better than we do and sympathizes with it more keenly; but his distinctive trait is that he is articulate, that he is able to tell what he knows and to record what he feels. He transmits a significant message "along the slender wires of speech." The ordinary man may know life profoundly and may feel keenly its tragedy, its comedy, its sublimity, its beauty; but he lacks the ability to express his intellectual and emotional reactions in words fraught with conviction and aesthetic appeal. To revert to our earlier illustration, the lovelorn Joan may experience a very deep and genuine affection for the Darby of her heart; but when she seeks to record her emotions she evolves a screed positively grotesque in its clumsiness and inadequacy; but Mrs. Browning, moved and stirred by a similarly profound and authentic passion, is able to make her mood manifest and contagious in the delicate and touching sonnets that throb from her pen. For Mrs. Browning not only has something important to say about a given aspect of life, but likewise knows how to say it in words that delight us by reason of their beauty and convince us by reason of their essential truth.

11   The rôle of literature in life and the procedure of the literary artist may be hinted at in allegory. Five men were present at the creation of the world: the philosopher, the scientist, the business man, the saint and the poet. And when God said, "Let there be light," and all things were made, each of the five men thought within himself. And the philosopher said, *"Why* has this thing

been done?" And the scientist said, "*How* has this thing been done?" And the business man said, "Let me have it." And the saint said, "Lo, I will strive to unite myself for ever and ever with Him Who has done these things, for He is the Infinite Goodness and the ultimate consolation of my heart." But the poet pondered deeply and said low to himself, "These things are exceedingly beautiful"; and then going forth he made worlds of his own. And he fashioned his creations in living words, and he ceased not to sing, for a mighty impulse urged him ever on. And after many years the poems of his making were scattered even to the four corners of the earth. And the philosopher found some of the poet's songs, and he said, "These songs help me to see why the world was made." And the scientist found some of the poet's songs, and he said, "These songs are of a truth most skilfully constructed." And the business man found some of the poet's songs, and he said, "These songs I can sell to my fellow men and thereby make much money." And the saint found some of the poet's songs, and he said, "These songs are truly beautiful things, for the soul of them is the Infinite Beauty after Whom my spirit yearns." And the poet's songs echoed in the ears of many men as the singer wandered down the byways of the world. And lovers heard them, and they loved the more; and haters heard them, and they hated less; and falling upon the hearts of the joyous, those songs multiplied the joy; and upon the hearts of the sorrowing, and their sorrow was not without hope. And after many years the poet ceased to sing; but the children of men said unto themselves: "Verily, his songs shall endure forever, for they are true and beautiful, and they tell us that which we ourselves do know."

Vocabulary Study: What is the difference between *epigram, aphorism, proverb*, and *truism?* Between *naive* and *sophisticated?* Between *human* and *humane?* Between *letters* and *missives?* Between *extrinsically* and *intrinsically?* Between *genus* and *specific difference?*

Make sure of the meanings of these words and phrases: *appositeness; stuff; peremptorily; equivocally; discreet; bereft of; aesthetic appeal; quintessence; flair; screed; grotesque; allegory.*

By Way of Appreciation: Brother Leo's study of the meaning of literature is particularly well suited to the mentality of the high-school student. The very brevity of the definition makes it easy to remember. If you do remember and understand it, you will be in possession of a reliable norm to guide you in the evaluation of your future reading. To be sure, you should test the validity of the definition by applying it to a course of wide reading in the best of literature, for only thus will it become a ready and effective tool of judgment, and only thus will your canons of literary taste be securely established. But just as surely will you find this exposition of the meaning of literature a guide and directive in the cultivation of your taste and critical thinking.

Brother Leo handles a difficult subject with admirable clarity. At the very outset he gives a definition of literature, which serves as his proposition from which he never deviates. The division of his exposition into three distinct sections could scarcely be clearer. By illustrating every point that he makes, with examples drawn from a world more or less familiar to all of us, he keeps his language concrete and appealingly human. And it would be hard to think of a better way of reenforcing his message than his use of the simple but crystal-clear allegory with which he closes his discussion of the meaning of literature.

Suggestions for Study: Quote exactly the definition of literature given in the opening paragraph. Memorize it. In elaborating this definition what term does the author first develop? What one sentence well summarizes the central thought of the first paragraph in this section? Cite at least five examples which the author uses in the second paragraph of this section to establish the point made in the preceding paragraph.

In the second section of the essay, how does Brother Leo show that not every book that concerns itself with human life is literature? What are some of the differences between a snapshot and a portrait emphasized by the author? Can you suggest others? How does he make use of these differences to clarify his definition of literature?

What is the general aim of all art? What is the specific tool, or medium, of the literary artist? What is needed beyond a keen knowledge of life and sympathy with it, to produce literature?

How does literature differ from philosophy, from science, from commerce, from sanctity? If the songs of the poet "tell us that which we ourselves do know," why do men read poetry?

Exercises and Creative Work: Write a sentence outline of the essay. Apply Brother Leo's definition of literature to his own essay and try to decide whether or not it qualifies as literature.

The ambitious will find it interesting and valuable to compare Brother Leo's definition of literature with one or several of those given on page 81 of *Literature, A Lecture by John Henry Cardinal Newman,* edited by Gilbert J. Garraghan, S.J.

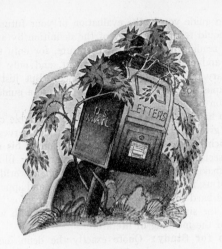

Essays for Fun

ON UNANSWERING LETTERS

From *Mince Pie*

CHRISTOPHER MORLEY

By Way of Introduction: There is one form of amusement reserved for the writer—playing with an idea. First find the idea—the crazier it seems the better—then proceed to make it plausible. It is surprising to see what logical reasons can be thought up for the most unreasonable procedures. In such a playful mood, Christopher Morley sat down one day to enlarge upon the thought of "unanswering letters."

THERE are a great many people who really believe in answering letters the day they are received, just as there are people who go to the movies at nine o'clock in the morning; but these people are stunted and queer.

It is a great mistake. Such crass and breathless promptness takes away a great deal of the pleasure of correspondence.

The psychological didoes [1] involved in receiving letters and making up one's mind to answer them are very complex. If the tangled process could be clearly analyzed and its component involutions [2] isolated for inspection we might reach a clearer

[1] DIDOES—Tricks; capers.
[2] INVOLUTIONS—Complications; entanglements.

632

comprehension of that curious bag of tricks, the efficient Masculine Mind.

Take Bill F., for instance, a man so delightful that even to contemplate his existence puts us in good humor and makes us think well of a world that can exhibit an individual equally comely in mind, body and estate. Every now and then we get a letter from Bill, and immediately we pass into a kind of trance, in which our mind rapidly enunciates the ideas, thoughts, surmises and contradictions that we would like to write to him in reply. We think what fun it would be to sit right down and churn the inkwell, spreading speculation and cynicism over a number of sheets of foolscap to be wafted Billward.

Sternly we repress the impulse for we know that the shock to Bill of getting so immediate a retort would surely unhinge the well-fitted panels of his intellect.

We add his letter to the large delta of unanswered mail on our desk, taking occasion to turn the mass over once or twice and run through it in a brisk, smiling mood, thinking of all the jolly letters we shall write some day.

After Bill's letter has lain on the pile for a fortnight or so it has been gently silted over by about twenty other pleasantly postponed manuscripts. Coming upon it by chance, we reflect that any specific problems raised by Bill in that manifesto will by this time have settled themselves. And his random speculations upon household management and human destiny will probably have taken a new slant by now, so that to answer his letter in its own tune will not be congruent with his present fevers. We had better bide a wee until we really have something of circumstance to impart.

We wait a week.

By this time a certain sense of shame has begun to invade the privacy of our brain. We feel that to answer that letter now would be an indelicacy. Better to pretend that we never got it. By and by Bill will write again and then we will answer promptly. We put the letter back in the middle of the heap and think what a fine chap Bill is. But he knows we love him, so it doesn't really matter whether we write or not.

Another week passes by, and no further communication from Bill. We wonder whether he does love us as much as we thought. Still—we are too proud to write and ask.

A few days later a new thought strikes us. Perhaps Bill thinks we have died and he is annoyed because he wasn't invited to the funeral. Ought we to wire him? No, because after all we are not dead, and even if he thinks we are, his subsequent relief at hearing the good news of our survival will outweigh his bitterness during the interval. One of these days we will write him a letter that will really express our heart, filled with all the grindings and gear work of our mind, rich in affection and fallacy. But we had better let it ripen and mellow for a while. Letters, like wines, accumulate bright fumes and bubblings if kept under cork.

Presently we turn over that pile of letters again. We find in the lees of the heap two or three that have gone for six months and can safely be destroyed. Bill is still on our mind, but in a pleasant, dreamy kind of way. He does not ache or twinge us as he did a month ago. It is fine to have old friends like that and keep in touch with them. We wonder how he is and whether he has two children or three. Splendid old Bill!

By this time we have written Bill several letters in imagination and enjoyed doing so, but the matter of sending him an actual letter has begun to pall. The thought no longer has the savor and vivid sparkle it had once. When one feels like that it is unwise to write. Letters should be spontaneous outpourings: they should never be undertaken merely from a sense of duty. We know that Bill wouldn't want to get a letter that was dictated by a feeling of obligation.

Another fortnight or so elapsing, it occurs to us that we have entirely forgotten what Bill said to us in that letter. We take it out and con it over. Delightful fellow! It is full of his own felicitous kinks of whim, though some of it sounds a little old-fashioned by now. It seems a bit stale, has lost some of its freshness and surprise. Better not answer it just yet, for Christmas will soon be here and we shall have to write then anyway. We wonder, can Bill hold out until Christmas without a letter?

We have been rereading some of those imaginary letters to Bill that have been dancing in our head. They are full of all sorts of fine stuff. If Bill ever gets them he will know how we love him. To use O. Henry's immortal joke, we have days of Damon and Knights of Pythias [3] writing those uninked letters

---

[3] PYTHIAS—A pun upon Damon and Pythias, the classic exemplars of perfect friendship.

to Bill. A curious thought has come to us. Perhaps it would be better if we never saw Bill again. It is very difficult to talk to a man when you like him so much. It is much easier to write in the sweet fantastic strain. We are so inarticulate when face to face. If Bill comes to town we will leave word that we have gone away. Good old Bill! He will always be a precious memory.

A few days later a sudden frenzy sweeps over us, and though we have many pressing matters on hand, we mobilize pen and paper and literary shock troops and prepare to hurl several battalions at Bill. But, strangely enough, our utterance seems stilted and stiff. We have nothing to say. *My dear Bill,* we begin, *it seems a long time since we heard from you. Why don't you write? We still love you, in spite of all your shortcomings.*

That doesn't seem very cordial. We muse over the pen and nothing comes. Bursting with affection, we are unable to say a word.

Just then the phone rings. "Hello?" we say.

It is Bill, come to town unexpectedly.

"Good old fish!" we cry, ecstatic. "Meet you at the corner of Tenth and Chestnut in five minutes."

We tear up the unfinished letter. Bill will never know how much we love him. Perhaps it is just as well. It is very embarrassing to have your friends know how you feel about them. When we meet him we will be a little bit on our guard. It would not be well to be betrayed into any extravagance of cordiality.

And perhaps a not altogether false little story could be written about a man who never visited those most dear to him, because it panged him to say good-by when he had to leave.

Vocabulary Study: Although Morley's style in the present essay is not "bookish," he has the vocabulary of the widely-read individual. Some words you may need to get acquainted with, such as: *crass; psychological; component; silted; manifesto; congruent; fallacy; lees; pall* (note pronunciation); *savor; spontaneous; con; felicitous; mobilize; panged* (a coined word—look up *pang*).

By Way of Appreciation: Humor, no matter how far fetched, always springs from reaiity. A caricature may be ridiculously exaggerated and distorted, but it must bear a resemblance to its subject or the very essence of its fun is lost. In humorous writings, the same principle holds. Be the development ever so funny, it must be based upon certain elemental truths which lend plausibility to the fabrication. For instance, we recognize *Unanswering Letters* as a bit of refreshing nonsense; yet as we read, we are struck again and again by familiar excuses, evasions, and moods. We would not for the world agree seriously that letters should not be answered, but we have all allowed letters to go unanswered and we are therefore familiar with the accompanying "psychological didoes"—plausible self-excuse, guilty evasion, chagrin, resolution, exasperation, and the like. Now Morley has merely taken those common feelings, distorted them here, exaggerated them there, and behold—a whimsical essay that is heaps of fun to read!

Suggestions for Study: Have you any unanswered letters on your conscience right now? If so, can you jot down the various states of mind you have passed through with any one of them? Explain the figure of speech in the sentence, "We add his letter to the large delta of unanswered mail on our desk." What word in the next paragraph continues that figure? Morley's manner of expression is always piquant. Can you find five other interesting figures of speech in the essay? Which paragraphs in the essay show the most ridiculous exaggeration? Is there any modicum of truth in the idea that it is sometimes difficult to talk or write to a person because we like him so much? Why not answer one of those letters?

Exercises and Creative Work: Outline an essay of your own, giving personal observations, on one of the following topics: *Letters That Answer Themselves; Concerning an Odious Promptness in Answering Letters; The Perfect Correspondence.*

THE PEOPLE NEXT DOOR

From *Imaginary Obligations*

Frank Moore Colby

By Way of Introduction: Roughly speaking our neighbors are divided into two classes—those we know and those we don't. "The People Next Door" are the ones we don't. They are the folks who have just moved in or the ones who have not warmed to our friendship; anyhow, they are not "Joe and Vi" to us yet. It is their impersonality that keeps them "the people next door," and it is their impersonality that makes them the victims of our superiority complex. If we must work off the holier-than-thou fever once in a while, what safer target can we pick for our carping than the nameless neighbors next door?

OUTWARDLY you may be on friendly terms with the people next door, but, if the truth were known, you do not think much of them. Their ways may be well enough, but they are not your ways. It is not hatred, far less envy; neither is it contempt exactly. Only do you not understand why they live as they do. You account for some things by the differences in social traditions. They were not brought up as you were—not that they are to blame for that, but certain advantages that you had were denied them. Rude noises come from that house next door that you would not expect from people in their station. There is nothing that so reveals the breeding of the inmates as the noises that come from a house. Laughter late at night, when you want to sleep—how coarse it sounds! That is what the strong writer probably means by ribald laughter. Then there is that young woman who sings. What voices the people next door always have, and what a repertoire of songs! Why do they never try a new one? There must be new songs from time to time within the means of any one, but you never hear them next door. Years after a song is forgotten elsewhere it goes on next door. A popular song never dies. The people next door rescue it after it is hounded off the street and warm it into eternal life. Girls begin on it in their teens and worry it away on into womanhood. Even after they are married off they do not get over it, and when they come home to visit you hear it again—"Eyes so balloo and tender," or whatever it may be. Fancy the kind of people that would let a young woman sing "Eyes so balloo and tender" all through life, even if she wanted to. It must injure her mind.

And so it goes. Everything they do shows just what sort of people they are. Look at the things they hang out in their back yard—and is there ever a day when some of their old traps are not hanging out or standing around there? If your things looked like that you would at least keep them indoors. It is not that they are so old, though for the matter of that you should think they would be afraid of germs, but they were chosen with such monstrously bad taste in the first place. What in the world do people want to furnish a house with things like that for? They must have cost enough, too, and for that amount of money they could have bought—but what is the use of talking? There are distinctions that you never can make people feel.

That cook of theirs you would not have in your house five minutes. It must surely be unsafe to eat what a person like that would cook. A certain degree of neatness is indispensable, and people who were used to things would insist upon it. That is the trouble with the people next door—they are not used to things. It is easy enough to put a stop to certain matters if you take them in hand, such, for instance, as those awful Irish whoops that issue every evening from their kitchen windows. But the people next door do not mind—that is the sum of it—they simply do not mind things that would drive you stark mad. They can sleep through their own hideous noise, eat their own ill-prepared food, put up with anything, just because it is theirs. Content is a good thing and family affection is laudable but in this particular case each goes too far. It annoys you to think of the narrow basis on which it subsists. What can the wife see in the husband or the husband in the wife, or either of them in those young ones?

Yesterday a correspondent wrote to a newspaper complaining of the carpet beating that went on next door. Hitherto he had thought those people were gentlefolk. He doubts it now. The people next door are always doing things that enable you to "size them up." You size them up ten or fifteen times a day. The women in your family size them up much oftener. That doubt of next-door gentility is universal. It is no accident that brings that kind of people next door to you. It is the working of a mighty social law. You are charitable in the matter. You admit their virtues—that is, the big ones, which nobody uses more than once a year. They are respectable people and well-intentioned. But they always lack one indefinable thing which you have whatever may be your faults. It is very important. The social plane always slants downward to the people next door. One should not be snobbish about it, but the slant is there, nevertheless, and you cannot help knowing it. If we created a nobility over here the people next door could never get in. If you ever mention these things you do so with the utmost delicacy and you explain over and over again that you do not mean anything against the people. You would not for the world let them know you felt as you do. This is all wasted. This is the land of subjective aristocracy.

Vocabulary Study: *Ribald* (note pronunciation); *repertoire* (note pronunciation); *laudable; aristocracy; carp* (verb); *subjective* (note the discussion of the difference in meaning between *subjective* and *objective*). Give the word history of *repertoire*.

By Way of Appreciation: There is a kind of writing which holds up to ridicule the faults and follies of humanity. Sometimes the mood is bitter and the attack personal, in which case the composition drops from the ranks of polite literature. Sometimes, though, it is an amusing lampooning of traits more or less common to mankind and the result is a social satire.

The People Next Door borders upon this second type of writing, but Mr. Colby's touch is so light that one hesitates to call it satire. There is ironic intent, it cannot be denied, but it is irony of the most subtle sort. Notice, for instance, that it is not the people next door who are being ridiculed. No indeed! The satire is aimed at the tendency of human beings to find fault with one another. Do you recognize in the essay echoes of comments you have made about the folks who have just moved in across the street? If you had been invited in to spend the evening would you have found the laughter "ribald"? Isn't much of the fun derived from the fact that you know in six months you and the family next door will be old friends and will be exchanging similar remarks about the queer-looking family that has just rented the house across the street?

Yes, it is ourselves that we are laughing at—ourselves and the traces of snobbery that give even America a "subjective aristocracy." Whenever we laugh at ourselves and *with,* not *at,* the rest of the world, satire loses its sting and becomes just good fun.

Suggestions for Study: How many points of criticism do you recognize as ones that you and your family have made about people in your neighborhood? Which of the comments have a distinctly feminine flavor as if Mr. Colby were quoting the women of the household?

A world of difference is made by a shift in point of view. For instance, there is a difference in what you think about laughter late at night when you want to sleep and laughter when you are in the center of the party and it is the folks next door who want to sleep. Can you give any other specific illustrations of this point from suggestions in the essay? An interesting companion essay might be written on what the people next door are probably saying about you. Explain the significance of the three sentences in the last paragraph beginning with "That doubt of next-door gentility is universal." Explain also "The social plane always slants downward to the people next door." What does the author mean by a "land of subjective aristocracy"?

Exercises and Creative Work: Write a précis of the first paragraph of the essay.

If Mr. Colby's essay inspires you, write an essay of your own on some experience in your neighborhood, such as: *The Kid Across the Street; Our Neighbor's Cat; The Ball Team in the Corner Lot.*

FURNACE AND I

From *The Comforts of Home*

Ralph Bergengren

By Way of Introduction: Have you a little furnace in your home? Or a great big greedy one? Has it been your job to put it to bed at night, or give it breakfast in the morning? Do you know what it is to waken to those heart-sinking words, "The furnace is out"? If you have, your enjoyment of *Furnace and I* is assured; for true it is, misery loves—well, to commiserate. But if your days slip by in the easy temperate zone of an apartment or in lands of the South that know not the contraption, take Mr. Bergengren's word for it—the furnace may be a nightmarish octopus "all the more horrible because it has no face."

Summer is the favorite time to advertise furnaces, for, although a pacifist might argue that being prepared for cold weather encourages frost, the practical persons who make and sell heating plants are firm believers in preparedness. They produce diagrams showing how *their* furnace bisects the coal bill and pictures showing how easily a pretty child can run it from the front hall. But my furnace is different. I defy the prettiest child imaginable to run it. Indeed, in a strict sense, I defy anybody to run it, for this furnace has a mind of its own and an ambition to behave like a thermometer. On a warm day it goes up, on a cold day it goes down; in zero weather it takes all the time of a determined man to head it off from becoming a large, inconvenient refrigerator. As for bisecting coal bills, the creature *likes* coal. I have even thought it made strange, self-congratulatory, happy noises whenever there occurred a rise in the price of its favorite edible. Before meeting this furnace I had lived in apartments, and my mental conception of a ton of coal had been as of something enormous, sufficient to heat the average house a month. A furnace was to me a remote mystery operated by a high priest called "janitor," whom I vaguely connected with the lines of Smollett [1]—

> Th' Hesperian [2] dragon not more fierce and fell;
> Nor the gaunt, growling janitor of Hell.

I took my heat as a matter of course. If I wanted more of it, I spoke warmly to the janitor through a speaking tube and— after a while—there was more heat. If I wanted less I spoke to him coldly, in the same distant, godlike way—and, after a while, there was less heat. In neither case, I discovered, did an ordinary tone of voice get any result whatever; and, although a fat man himself, he sometimes growled back through the tube very much like the gaunt specimen mentioned by Smollett. But I gave little thought to him. I had what is called an "intelligent idea" that to produce more heat he opened a "draft," and to reduce heat he closed it, the effect of a draft on a furnace being just the opposite to its effect on a janitor. At night he "shook the furnace down" and in the morning he "shook the furnace up." One gathers such knowledge casually, picks it up here and there without conscious effort or realization. I had in fact no more curiosity about the furnace than about the sun, for I seemed as unlikely ever to run one heater as the other.

Then, like many another man who has lived in apartments, I turned suburbanite. I had a furnace, and I had to run it myself. How well I remember that autumn day when I started my first furnace fire!

There sat the monster on the floor of the cellar, impassive

[1] SMOLLETT—Tobias Smollett (1721–1771), a Scotchman, novelist and miscellaneous writer.
[2] HESPERIAN—In the west.

as Buddha [3] and apparently holding up the house with as many arms as an octopus, hollow arms through which presently would flow the genial heat. I peeked cautiously through a little door into his stomach, and marveled at its hollow immensity. I reached in till my arm arched—and my hand dangled in empty space. But my intelligence told me that there must be a bottom. Crumpling a newspaper into a great wad, I dropped it down, down into the monster's gullet, where it vanished forever; I crumpled and dropped another; I continued until at last—oh, triumph of mind and industry over incalculable depth!—I *saw newspaper*, and had something tangible on which to erect a pyre of kindlings. Where I could reach I laid them crosswise, and where I couldn't I tossed them in at varying angles, gaining skill with practice.

"It is like a great wooden nest!" I cried in astonishment. "*Now* I know why the coal I have bought for my furnace is called 'egg'."

I lit the fire and made a grand smoke.

It rose through the kindlings; it piled out through the little door; it hung like great cobwebs to the roof of the cellar. With great presence of mind I hastily closed the little door and ran lightly up the cellar stairs. The smoke had preceded me; it got there first through the convenient registers; and more was coming. I met a woman.

"*Is* the house afire?" she asked excitedly.

"It is *not*," I replied quietly, in a matter-of-course way. "When you start your fire for the winter it always smokes a little."

We opened the windows. We went outside and looked at the house. It leaked smoke at every crevice except, curiously enough, at the chimney. Ah-h-h-h-h! I saw what had happened. I groped my way to the cellar and opened the back damper. Now the smoke went gladly up the chimney and the view through the little door was at once beautiful and awful; it was like looking into the heart of an angry volcano.

Evidently it was time to lay the eggs on the nest.

I shoveled the abyss full of coal, and the volcano became extinct. Presently, instead of a furnace full of fire I had a

[3] BUDDHA—A deity worshiped in northern Hindustan, and central and southern Asia. His images are devoid of expression.

furnace full of egg coal. I began taking it out, egg by egg, at first with my fingers and then with the tongs from the dining-room fireplace. And when the woman idly questioned me as to what I was going to do down cellar with the tongs, I bit my lip. . . .

To the man who runs it (an absurd term as applied to a thing that has no legs and weighs several tons) the furnace is his first thought in the morning and his last thought at night. His calendar has but two seasons—winter, when the furnace is going; and summer when the furnace is out. But in summer his thoughts are naturally more philosophical. He sees how profoundly this recent invention (which he is not at the time running) has changed man's attitude toward nature. Why, he asks himself, have past generations of men regarded autumn as continuously melancholy, which it isn't, and spring as continuously cheerful, which it isn't either? Because they had no furnaces. They couldn't warm their houses in winter. They suffered. Autumn was melancholy because it led to winter, and spring was cheerful because it preceded summer when nobody needed a furnace. It is unfortunate, he realizes whimsically, that a man often forgets what a blessing his furnace is at the time he is running it; but even so there is a kind of discipline, a strengthening of the moral nature——

I am, of course, not referring to those furnaces which are endowed with more than the average human intelligence; those Superfurnaces met with in the advertisements, which shake themselves down, shovel their own coal, carry and sift their own ashes, regulate their own drafts, and, if they do not actually order and pay for their own coal, at least consume it as carefully as if they did. Such furnaces—so long as nobody gives me one—seem positively weakening. There is no struggle, no opposition of wills, no variety of experience, no exercise of those noble characteristics, faith, hope, and charity. For the man with a Superfurnace life is too easy.

"Toddlekins," he says to his little daughter, "press the button."

"Yes, papa," says Toddlekins. She puts down her doll, skips merrily into the front hall, presses the button—and that is all there is to it.

But with a furnace like mine a man experiences all the emotions of which he is capable. He loves, he hates, he admires, he despises, he grieves, he exults. There have been times when I have felt like patting my furnace; and again times when I have slammed his little door and spoken words to him far, far hotter than the fire that smouldered and refused to burn in his bowels. I judge from what I have read that taming a wild animal must be a good deal like taming a furnace, with one important exception. The wild-animal-tamer never loses his temper or the beast would kill him; but a furnace, fortunately for suburban mortality, cannot kill its tamer.

When his furnace happens to be good-natured, however, a man will often find the bedtime hour with it pleasant and even enjoyable. He descends, humming or whistling, to the cellar; and the subsequent shaking and shoveling is, after all, no more than a healthy exercise which he would not otherwise take and which will make him sleep better. He is friendly with this rotund, coal-eating giant; he regards it almost like a big baby which he is putting to bed—or at least he *might* so regard it if putting a baby to bed was one of his recognized pleasures. In such a mood he may even nod back gayly over his shoulder as he goes up the cellar stairs, and find himself saying "Good night, Old Furnace." Or, if he has lately been reading one of our more popular authors, "Good night, Old Top."

But oh, what a difference in the morning! He awakes in the dark, startled perhaps from some pleasant dream by the wild alarm-m-m-m-m-m of a clock under his pillow; and outside the snug island of warmth on which he lies, the Universe stretches away in every direction, above, below, and on every side of him, cold, dreary, and unfit for human habitation, to and beyond the remotest star. In that cold Universe how small he is! How warm and how weak! Instantly he thinks of the furnace, and the remotest star seems near by comparison. The thought of getting up and going down cellar seems as unreal as the thought of getting up and going to meet the sun at that pale streak, which, through his easterly window heralds the reluctant coming of another day. Yet he knows that he MUST and that eventually he WILL get up. In vain he tells himself how splendid, how invigorating will be the plunge *from his warm bed* right into the fresh, brisk, hygienic morning air.

The fresh, brisk, hygienic morning air does not appeal to him. Unwillingly he recalls a line in the Superfurnace advertisement—"Get up warm and cozy"—and helplessly wishes that *he* had such a furnace. "Like Andrew Carnegie!"[4] he adds bitterly. At that moment he would anarchistically assassinate Andrew provided he could do it without getting up. Nevertheless—he gets up! He puts on—"Curse it, *where* is that sleeve?" —the bathrobe and slippers that have been all night cooling for him, and starts on his lonely journey through the tomblike silence. Now, if ever, is the time to hum, but there is not a hum in him: down, down, down he goes to the cellar and peeks with dull hope through the familiar little door. "Good morning, Fire." He shakes, he shovels, he opens drafts and manipulates dampers. And the Furnace, impassive, like a Buddha, holding up the house with as many arms as an octopus, seems to be watching him with a grave yet idle interest. Which is all the more horrible because it has no face.

[4] ANDREW CARNEGIE—American millionaire and philanthropist who made his fortune in steel and iron.

Vocabulary Study: *Bisects; fell* (adjective); *casually; suburbanite; impassive; octopus; tangible; pyre; abyss; extinct; mortality; anarchistically assassinate.*

By Way of Appreciation: Little need be said by way of appreciation for *Furnace and I.* It is the sort of essay that one reads, laughs over, and lays aside. But ever afterward when one goes into the cellar to minister to his own furnace, it is with a reminiscent smile. Mr. Bergengren illustrates the truth that if "poetry is emotion recollected in tranquillity," humor may be discomfort recollected when it's all over. There is nothing funny about trying to start a fire in a frigid house; but the harder job you have of it, the jollier story there is to tell when the house is ruddy with the warmth of your success.

Suggestions for Study: Reread the notes on appreciation of Irving's *Wouter Van Twiller.* Does this modern essay on the furnace employ any of the humorous devices used in the earlier selection? Illustrate your reply by definite examples. One definition of the word "picturesque" reads "abounding in striking or original expression or imagery." Select what seem to you the ten most picturesque words or word-combinations in the essay. What guess do you make as to the identity of the woman mentioned in the essay? Why the impersonal tone of the reference? Is the "Superfurnace," that runs itself, more nearly a reality today than it was at the time this essay was written, over fifteen years ago? Explain your answer.

Exercises and Creative Work: What other common objects of home or school or office might serve as subjects for essays of a somewhat similar nature? Follow one of them out with an original essay.

EXTENSIVE READING PROGRAM—THE ESSAY

THE NATIONAL PERIOD (1800–1865)

Washington Irving
John Bull
English Writers on America
London Antiques
Literary Life
The Bermudas
Sleepy Hollow
The Author's Account of Himself
The Sketch Book *
Tales of a Traveller *
Wolfert's Roost *

Ralph Waldo Emerson
Compensation
Friendship
Works and Days
Success

George William Curtis
From the Easy Chair *

Edwin Percy Whipple
Recollections of Eminent Men *

Edgar Allan Poe
The Philosophy of Composition
The Poetic Principle

Henry David Thoreau
Economy
The Ponds
The Pond in Winter
Brute Neighbors
Walden *

James Russell Lowell
New England Two Centuries Ago
My Garden Acquaintance
Among My Books *
My Study Windows *

Oliver Wendell Holmes
The Autocrat of the Breakfast Table *
The Professor at the Breakfast Table *
The Poet at the Breakfast Table *
Over the Teacups *

THE TRANSITION PERIOD (1865–1900)

Donald Grant Mitchell
Reveries of a Bachelor *
My Farm at Edgewood *

Charles Dudley Warner
Backlog Studies *
My Summer in a Garden *
Calvin, a Study of Character
Camping Out
How I Killed a Bear
The Hunting of the Deer
Being a Boy *

Samuel Langhorne Clemens
(Mark Twain)
The Private History of the "Jumping Frog" Story
Travelling with a Reformer

Lafcadio Hearn
My First Day in the Orient
In a Japanese Garden
Gulf Winds
Valentine Vagaries

Charles Warren Stoddard
Pearl Hunting in the Pomotons
The Chapel of the Palms

* If the title is that of a collection instead of a single essay, it is indicated by a star.

646

THE TWENTIETH CENTURY (1900–   )

ESSAYS OF THE OUT-OF-DOORS

John Burroughs
Birds and Bees *
Locusts and Wild Honey *
Signs and Seasons *
An Idyll of the Honey Bee
Afoot and Afloat *
Henry van Dyke
Days Off *
Little Rivers
A Leaf of Spearmint
The Thrilling Moment
A Fatal Success
Camp Fires and Guide Posts *
Walter Prichard Eaton
The Harvest of Wild Places
The Bluest Lake in the World
Dallas Lore Sharp
A Watcher in the Woods *
The Marsh
The Edge of Night
A January Summer
The Whole Year Through *

Stewart Edward White
The Cabin *
The Mountains *
The Forest *
Charles William Beebe
Hammock Nights
A Chain of Jungle Life
The Arcturus Adventure *
The Edge of the Jungle *
Jungle Peace *
John Muir
Travels in Alaska *
Our National Parks *
Steep Trails *
Theodore Roosevelt
Getting Christmas Dinner on a Ranch
Enos Mills
Spell of the Rockies *
Snow-Blinded on the Summit
A Day with a Nature Guide
Trees at Timberline

ESSAYS OF VARIOUS TYPES

Samuel McChord Crothers
The Convention of Books
An Interview with an Educator
Among Friends *
The Cheerful Giver *
The Gentle Reader *
Agnes Repplier
Agrippina
The Grocer's Cat
Points of Friction *
Essays in Miniature *
Theodore Roosevelt
American Ideals
Morality and Efficiency
The American Boy

Edwin Emery Slosson
Creative Chemistry *
William Lyon Phelps
The Great American Game
Mark Twain
Essays on Modern Novelists *
Frank Moore Colby
Our Refinement
Thomas L. Masson
Wanted: A Secretary of Athletics
Surrender Books
William Allen White
To an Anxious Friend
Cheer Up, America

* If the title is that of a collection instead of a single essay, it is indicated by a star.

David Grayson
  Adventures in Contentment *
  Adventures in Friendship *
  The Friendly Road *
  Great Possessions *
Ralph Bergengren
  The Comforts of Home *
Woodrow Wilson
  Abraham Lincoln
  When a Man Comes to Himself
Harry Esty Dounce
  Some Nonsense About a Dog
Robert M. Gay
  The Flavor of Things
  Tympano
Walter Prichard Eaton
  The Bubble Reputation
  Spring in the Garden
  A Confession in Prose
  On Giving Up Golf Forever
Frances Lester Warner
  Retrieving the Airedale
  Endicott and I Conduct an Orchestra
  Surprising the Family *
Charles Stephens Brooks
  Like Summer's Cloud
  To Be Read Only By Serious Stupid Persons
  On Going to a Party
  On Hanging a Stocking at Christmas
  On Going Afoot
  Tunes for Spring
Heywood Broun
  Dying for Dear Old——
  Buying a Farm
  Holding a Baby
  Pieces of Hate *
Christopher Morley
  Time to Light the Furnace
  Letting Out the Furnace

Sister Mary Eleanore
  The Promise of Young America
  Hospitals for the Hopelessly Healthy
Leonard Feeney
  You'd Better Come Quietly *
James M. Gillis
  George Bernard Shaw
  Conan Doyle
  Mark Twain
Louise Imogen Guiney
  On a Pleasing Encounter with a Pickpocket
  The Under Dog
  Irish
Aline Kilmer
  Hunting a Hair Shirt
Joyce Kilmer
  A Bouquet for Jenny
  The Gentle Art of Christmas Giving
Agnes Repplier
  In Our Convent Days *
  In the Dozy Hours *
Joseph J. Reilly
  Dear Prue's Husband
Maurice Francis Egan
  Confessions of a Book Lover *
Katherine Brégy
  Poets and Pilgrims *
  The Poets' Chantry *
James J. Daly
  A Cheerful Ascetic and Other Essays *
  The Road to Peace *
Francis P. Donnelly
  Leave It to the Donkey
  Am I Like That?
  Fuming and Fretting
  Stooping to Conquer
  If I Were You
Michael Earls
  Literary Vaudevillians
  The Service of the Voice

* If the title is that of a collection instead of a single essay, it is indicated by a star.

MAGAZINES AND NEWSPAPERS

AMERICAN LITERATURE AS INFLUENCED BY JOURNALISM AND THE MAGAZINE

The Importance of Printing

Literature in relationship to the written word has no such ancient riddle as whether the hen or the egg came first. In song and folk tale, literature had matured before the first writing on stone tablets. There is merely no means of knowing how much of it was lost before it could be recorded. By way of compensation for late arrival, writing and its sturdy child, printing, hold no uncertain place in the preservation and development of every form of literature. From the ancient manuscripts that retain for modern scrutiny the testaments of the past, to the manifold presses that turn out the world's news and entertainment, the presenting medium has served as a stimulus to authorship and, incidentally, as a means of the writer's livelihood. Although we think of literature in terms of books, these owe their vogue in no small degree to the less permanent forms of transferring creative thought from author to reader, the magazine and the newspaper.

It is not a coincidence that in a comparatively young country like the United States authorship and book publication have increased in direct ratio to the growth in the number of these periodicals and to the size of their circulation. With mounting census figures, a larger number of persons turn each year to writing, numbers encouraged and for that matter developed by an educational system which introduces the youth of the nation to and interests it in good reading, the parent of good writing. Performance would lag without encouragement. This exists in the printed medium at hand to reward ability. It is present in both the American newspaper and magazine, though the type of writing utilized by the two differs. There is a relationship between them, however, which in practice is well defined.

THE AMERICAN NEWSPAPER

Historical Development

The newspaper appeared before the magazine. Several newspapers now published date back either in retained identity or by direct lineage to journals born in the colonies. By the time of the Revolution, many newspapers had become profitable enterprises. Despite comparative success then and later, however, the golden age of American journalism did not arrive until after the Civil War. The post-1870 era with its metropolitan development created the extraordinary financial success for the press not only in large centers but even in medium-sized and small towns.

If *Publick Occurrences,* printed by Richard Pierce for Benjamin Harris in Boston in September, 1690, and immediately suppressed by the government, is excepted, the first American newspaper was the *Boston News-Letter* with a first issue dated April 20, 1704. In the remaining seventy-two years before the Declaration of Independence, the newspaper rapidly became a conspicuous factor in American life. Between 1755 and 1783, the colonial journals can be discerned sharpening the public intellect and giving it a means of expression, an impetus to political and religious liberty responsible in large degree for the American Revolution.

Writing in 1872, when the *New York Herald,* the *London Times* and the *Paris Journal des Debats* had achieved the then astounding circulation of a quarter of a million daily, Frederic Hudson recognized in them, in spite of their advantages in steam, electricity, and photographic development, the lineal descendants in molding opinion of the newspapers of 1700 which with two thousand copies reached ten thousand readers. Another half century has carried journalistic invention and circulation beyond Hudson's well-informed view, but the great metropolitan dailies now are possibly no stronger influences on public sentiment than the leading newspapers of the colonial and revolutionary eras, the *Boston Gazette,* the *Philadelphia Mercury,* the *New York Gazette,* the *New England Journal,* the *Rhode Island Gazette,* Benjamin Franklin's *Pennsylvania Gazette,* Samuel Adams' *Independent Advertiser,* the *New York Mercury* and the *Freeman's Journal* of Philadelphia.

The Field of Journalism as an Occupation

It remains a debatable question whether the influence of the daily newspaper on literature was greater in the days of small circulation and next to no return for literary contributors or in the past three decades when newspaper publishing has become a major industry. The final conclusion may well be that the type of influence exerted in these different eras has differed, too. Since 1900, successful American journalism may be said accurately to have fostered two types of writers foreign to the first hundred years of its existence when it had a more personal relationship with the native author.

The increasing demands of local reporting and of correspondence both for daily papers and the highly developed world-covering news services have opened up a field to young writers little available prior to 1900. In it they find at once an actual livelihood, daily contact with life, and impetus to create. In consequence, most American writers to-day, men and women, have obtained their start in or serve now American journalism as a gainful occupation. In addition, the stress placed by circulation managers on a newspaper by-product which is classed as entertainment rather than strict news has created a secondary market for the output of recognized authorship. The magazine section of large newspapers swings open for the established figures in the world of letters not only in original articles but in the reprint of novels and short stories once used. The institution keeps author royalties flow-ing in for a period that would have astonished the writers of the 80's. Nor is the device confined to great metropolitan centers. Syndi-cated services spread the same material to smaller cities.

In necessary terseness of news presentation and employment of accurately expressed English, the training supplied to the American pub-lic by its newspapers is invaluable to the writer of tomorrow. Now-adays, progressive papers employ nearly every widely published author not only to write articles on special subjects but even to "cover" im-portant news event fixtures, party conventions or even sports competi-tions. It is not unusual today to find on a single page the straight report of a hard-working athletic specialist and the same event as dis-cussed by two of the nation's leading humorists and a serious novelist.

Journalism and the American Author

Newspaper employment of the American author by way of launching him on his career is well-nigh as old as the country's journalism. Philip Freneau, the poet of the Revolution, was a newspaper editor for most of his picturesque life. Bret Harte and Mark Twain served on daily and weekly papers. Even Noah Webster, the lexicographer, was in-duced in 1793 to desert his legal vocation to edit the Federal *Minerva*. Benjamin Franklin was an editor and publisher. Joseph Rodman Drake established his literary reputation with the humorous "Croaker Pieces" published in the *New York Evening Post* in 1819, and it was Fitz-Greene Halleck's partnership in their creation that evoked from him in his column "The Recorder" in the same paper when Drake died at twenty-six, the tender elegy:

> Green be the turf above thee,
> Friend of my better days,
> None knew thee but to love thee,
> None named thee but to praise.

In 1826, William Cullen Bryant was chief editor of the *Post*. John Greenleaf Whittier edited a Boston newspaper of small circulation in 1829 and a year later was associated with George D. Prentice and Gideon Welles in editorial management of the *New England Review*. Still later, his strong abolition sentiment made him editor of *The Free-man*, a Philadelphia organ of that cause. Much of Whittier's verse found newspaper publication in the *National Era,* and it was not until after its death that he turned to the more agreeable magazine field.

No history of American letters omits the great controversialists, Wendell Phillips, Horace Greeley, and Henry Ward Beecher, and all three are better known as editors of secular or public press than in literature.

The Catholic Newspaper

It is easy to see why Catholic journalism would be slow in getting under way; in the early days of our country Catholics were few and generally poor. The first Catholic journal published in the United States made only one appearance, on August 31, 1809. It was the *Michigan Essay or Impartial Observer,* an enterprise of Father Gabriel Richard, of Detroit, Michigan, one of the founders of the University of Michigan. The next to appear, Bishop England's *United States Miscellany,* a weekly, ran from 1822 to 1861, when the Civil War forced it to suspend publication. Of all the other Catholic newspapers born in the first half of the last century the only ones surviving today are the *Catholic Telegraph,* of Cincinnati (1831); the *Pilot,* of Boston (1837); the *Freeman's Journal,* of New York (1840); and the *Catholic,* of Pittsburgh (1846). Today there are upwards of seventy Catholic weekly newspapers published in the English language in the United States.

The American Penny Press

The American penny press dates from 1833 and introduced commercial newspaper rivalry. It is responsible for one of the best known incidents in disguised fun, the "Moon Hoax." This was the publication by Richard Adams Locke in the *New York Sun,* apparently in all seriousness, of a series of articles purporting to be the Cape of Good Hope discoveries on the moon by Sir John Herschel. The hoax could not last long but its imprint survives as it furnished the inspiration for Edgar Allan Poe's *Trip to the Moon.* Poe's is a strange figure intimately connected with the newspaper and magazine history of the United States just prior to 1850. Both sheltered for a time his tempestuous career.

The penny press has had its centennial. It has been the most significant development in American journalism.

Contemporary Writers for Newspapers

In the rôle of critic, the present-day newspaper writer is stimulating the book trade. The book page of the daily newspaper is itself making a material contribution to the story of letters.

Then there is the diurnal "columnist" controlling a department through which the aspiring amateur finds his way into print. In the hands of an F.P.A., a Christopher Morley, a Don Marquis, the succession of anonymous "Edward Hopes" and their contemporaries, a high standard is set for admission even into unpaid print, one that has a marked effect in raising the level of amateur writing and eventually improving it. It is not surprising that the column has proved the entering wedge to successful achievement for such humorists as Dorothy Parker and Newman Levy and even a novelist and playwright, Laurence Stallings.

One other contribution of the newspaper to the fosterage of letters remains to be mentioned. The limits of magazine publication for the small army of verse writers are narrow. Newspapers the country over, even in small towns, have widened an opportunity for the poets by finding space for original contributions and paying for these.

THE AMERICAN MAGAZINE

Magazines of the Colonial Period

The magazine was later in birth than the newspaper and began a long period of tribulation which continued until comparatively recent years. Within three days of each other appeared the two first American magazines in 1741. Only three numbers were published of Andrew Bradford's *American or a Monthly View,* six of Benjamin Franklin's *General Magazine or Historical Chronicle.* These were the first interments in a cemetery that has since been plentifully populated by publication aspirants for leadership in letters, most of which have never attained maturity. The funeral cortège still winds its way to the last resting place and even today the survivors can look back on a startling list of decade obituaries. The oldest magazine in the country dates back only to 1844, having recently celebrated the ninetieth anniversary of its founding by E. Littell.

Because the newspaper is essentially a record, not a literary depository, its effect on the course of American letters is not as marked as has been that of the magazine. Between the short-lived publications of Bradford and Franklin and the first successful American periodical, fifty-nine years were to elapse, but the predecessors of the *New York Magazine* (1790) played their part in the shaping of indigenous literature. Primarily this was in affording opportunity for publication. Few of the contributors were paid. But lack of return has never discouraged art, though it may have starved it to death. Philip Freneau's first published work, a metrical translation of a Psalm, appeared anonymously in the *United States Magazine.* Charles Brockden Brown, an important figure in the account of early American letters, found publication in the *Weekly Magazine* (Philadelphia) long before he himself initiated the *New York Monthly.*

Though few survived long in the effort, the eighteenth century magazines made a splendid effort to transplant to the shores of the United States the literary culture of England and the continent and deserve credit for awakening American interest in the development of its native literature. Mathew Carey's *Columbian Magazine or Monthly Miscel-*

lany and the *Massachusetts Magazine* which endured from 1789 to 1796 contributed to this cause.

Magazines of the National Period

Following the pioneer period and up to 1865, American magazine publication is represented by a few outstanding names, though several born prior to that year and more significant later, had already achieved a decided standing when it arrived. So it is really difficult to assign some to a definite period. Beside the *Review* and the *Living Age*, the formative years saw the "three Philadelphia graces," *Graham's, Godey's,* and *Sartain's,* New York's *Knickerbocker,* and later the little group, rising in the 60's and 70's and destined to endure to today. The South had its *Southern Literary Messenger,* which failed to rally gallantly after the Civil War. Around these comparatively long-lived periodicals, there were occasional magazines, born but to die, which invaded this field when prosperity depended on circulation and advertising was an unknown means of support. Even at this time, publishers had begun to pay well, comparatively speaking, for American writing in strange contrast with earlier years when mere appearance in print was sufficient reward for the author.

The North American Review

At the turn of the century, the appearance of the *Boston Anthology,* which at the end of its tenth volume would be merged in the *North American Review,* marks the definite arrival of the magazine in American life. For the next half century, this publication was to house some of the best American writing and memorable in its early inclusion, before it abandoned its poetry department, was Bryant's *Thanatopsis.* William Tudor, the first editor, found a growing American literature. In his *Miscellanies,* he noted that the success of the magazine was due to "the considerable stock of literature already accumulated in the country," where earlier he had deplored American dependence on England in this regard. The *Review* from the start placed its destiny in the hands of letters, for, after Tudor, Jared Sparks went from tutoring at Harvard to conduct it, and the list of its editors later included Edward Everett, James Russell Lowell, and Charles Eliot Norton. But even more important in its effect on American literature was the opportunity it afforded the writers. There remains Longfellow's unforgettable remark on looking over Cushing's index: "It is like walking through a graveyard and reading the inscriptions on the graves. So many familiar names. So many old associations!" The files reveal that here is a larger contribution to worth-while American letters than can be claimed by any other magazine, even today. To the *Review* went the first articles of Edward Everett Hale, fresh out of college. In 1876, Henry Adams and Henry Cabot Lodge were resigning as its editors over a difference of opinion as to policy with the owners. Their names are significant of the trends in a magazine whose transfer from Boston to New York was a shock to all New England. The atmosphere of American writing from 1830 to beyond 1900 is itself staid and stately and the *Review* must be credited or charged as its influence was keenly felt.

Graham's Magazine

The real debt which American literature owes to George Graham cannot be overestimated. He established his memorable magazine by merging with the *Gentleman's Magazine,* which he purchased from William E. Burton, his own small 1500 subscriber *Casket.* By 1843, his third year, he was paying $25 for stories and $10 for poems, and Park Benjamin was writing an offer to obtain Longfellow's poems for $20 for Graham, although the poet was asking others $25. Graham early established a reputation for strict payment which made his magazine more popular than New York's already veteran *Knickerbocker* which offered higher rates but did not always settle.

Graham's was an important sponsor for Edgar Allan Poe. Poe had first contributed to and then become editor for Burton who recommended him to Graham, when the latter found it impossible to conduct both the editing and business end of his magazine. Poe's own claims as to his responsibility for the success of *Graham's* were undoubtedly extravagant but even after his break with the wild genius, the publisher declared that Poe was an admirable editor. *Graham's* and other magazines kept Poe alive long enough for him to do the work which makes him an enduring figure in letters. For these various publications, Poe too established his place, too often ignored, as one of the first and ablest of American critics. Some of his best short stories were written for *Graham's,* including *Descent into the Maelstrom, Mystery of Marie Roget* and *Murders in the Rue Morgue.* Poe was probably wrong in ascribing the quick rise in Graham's circulation figures to his editorship, but his actual writing certainly played a part with a discerning public. The latter, however, stayed with the ably managed periodical which went on to new triumphs while Poe failed miserably with his own *Broadway Journal.*

Washington Irving was the only important American writer of the day who did not contribute to *Graham's.* His entire output had been contracted for by *Knickerbocker's.*

George Graham was the pioneer in bidding for recognized talent and found it a device that paid. The first names of the 40's and 50's were constantly in his pages. One number alone included Longfellow, Cooper, Bryant, R. H. Dana, Sr., Tuckerman, Hoffman and Osgood. In this respect, *Graham's* was the forerunner of the modern practice of building up circulation by contracting for the stories and articles of those who have already "arrived." Even in Graham's time, this was recognized as justifiable commercialism. P. G. Cooke wrote to Griswold, the biographer of Poe: "Longfellow's worst poem, however a chance effort of mine might excel it, would be vastly more valuable to Graham than anything I can send him."

Graham's finally expired in 1855. It had outlived by eight years the fantastic Poe who had given it but three years to survive his resignation. Along with *Godey's*, *Graham's* is preserved to immortality in Hawthorne's *House of the Seven Gables*.

Godey's, Salmagundi, Knickerbocker's, The Dial

With *Graham's* gone, *Godey's* seemed only to take a new lease on life. Begun in 1830 and uniting seven years later with the *Ladies' Magazine* of Boston, *Godey's Lady's Book* flourished as the fashion plate of its time and the literary ægis of several decades. It set a style in combination of publishing interest that is still profitably followed. Godey, too, bolstered Poe's failing fortunes by hiring him to do the series of savage criticisms which the gentle Lowell described as written in prussic acid.

In New York, *Salmagundi*, forever associated with Irving, had arisen and lasted from 1807 to 1822. *Knickerbocker's*, which came along in the middle 20's, was far more enduring, outlasting though only with difficulty, the war between the states. Founded by Charles Fenno Hoffman, it was carried on by Lewis Gaylord Clark and in its time rivalled its Philadelphia contemporaries. During this period, other magazines and the writers depending on them were having a precarious existence. From 1815 to the beginning of the *Knickerbocker*, says Tassin, there were at least thirty New York magazines, not one of which even for a short while flourished. One rival which *"Knick"* found in the New York field was the *Mirror* of which Samuel Woodworth, who wrote the *Old Oaken Bucket*, was the first editor and which lasted twenty years.

No account of the period is complete without mention of *The Dial*, edited first by Margaret Fuller, which appeared in 1840 and continued for four years, the last two under the direction of Ralph Waldo Emerson, one of its moving spirits. Almost all of Emerson's poems appeared in *The Dial* and through it his style was diffused in immediate New England.

The Atlantic and Putnam's

The *Atlantic* made its appearance in 1857, declaring itself on the cover "a magazine of literature, art, and politics." James Russell Lowell was the editor at a salary of $2500 and a page rate of $6 for his own contributions. At the start, the little coterie of significant contributors included Cabot, Motley, Longfellow, Lowell, Holmes, and Harriet Beecher Stowe. Thirty-three years later, Lowell wrote to his successor and biographer, Scudder, that by then (1890) "twenty people could write English where in 1857 one could." Certainly the *Atlantic* had contributed to the situation. Its presence was responsible for Howells' declaring that in 1860 the center of American literature was in Boston. In New York at that time, *Putnam's* had ended, *Knickerbocker's* was ailing, and the newcomers had not raised their flags. Probably no magazine begun in the period set out so definitely to impress itself on the American home and succeeded so thoroughly in setting the style for two generations of our writing. Holmes' revival of *The Autocrat* for its pages might alone have made it memorable, for Tassin says of him that "no American author has ever been more a part of a magazine than Holmes was of the *Atlantic.*" And Mrs. Stowe was only one of the galaxy of contributing women to whom this periodical lent encouragement, the list including Harriet Prescott Spofford, Gail Hamilton, Helen Hunt, and Rebecca Harding Davis.

Putnam's first issue appeared in New York in 1853. Two years later the little group of *Dial* literati were all writing for it and under George William Curtis (Holmes' "accomplished and delightful writer") it achieved marked success. The new magazine did not, like *Graham's,* pursue only the established reputation. In its first year alone, it culled the best from 489 contributions, mostly by unknown writers. Later, however, it followed after "names" in the stress of competition and after its reëstablishment had at one time on its staff Bayard Taylor, Edmund Clarence Stedman, and Richard Henry Stoddard. In its pages can be found Irving, Bryant, Emerson, Longfellow, Lowell, Hawthorne, Thoreau, Ripley, Miss Sedgwick, Mrs. Kirkland, J. P. Kennedy, Fred Cozzens, Richard Grant White, Melville, Stoddard, Read, and Maria Lowell.

Magazines of the Transition Period

The close of the Civil War saw the beginning of a new period in American magazine publication which extended to the new century. The rise of the *Round Table* and *The Nation,* independent and forceful speaking publications, gave an opportunity for writers in tune with the spirit of revolt. Holmes had poked fun at an irritating custom of earlier editors of revising accepted copy at will. Authors had justifiably resented that autocratic rule, unless, like Mrs. Stowe, they expected editorial molding to better form of outpoured thought. From 1875 on, the author began to be captain of his own soul. It was the period of liberalism, never better illustrated than in the decision of one magazine to cultivate southern literature. In 1873, *Scribner's* sent a special train through the South to secure a series of articles on the reorganization of the section's social life. The importance of this move in healing the wounds of war cannot be overestimated. It threw a life line to needy Southern writers who had watched their own magazines struggle unsuccessfully, and it may have rescued from oblivion the young Southerners whom the doomed Baltimore *Southern* could not save—Margaret

Preston, Malcolm Johnston, Sidney Lanier, Paul Hamilton Hayne, Maurice Thompson, and Professors Gildersleeve and Price. It discovered George W. Cable and Frances Hodgson Burnett. The appearance in northern pages of John Esten Cooke, Thomas Nelson Page and Joel Chandler Harris established for American readers the splendid tradition of the old South.

To this period belongs the little group of magazines, some still existent and sharing with new contemporaries the same purpose, which were made house organs for the large publishing firms. These magazines then and now serve to introduce new writers, to exploit the old and to further the primary business of the publisher, putting books into the hands of more readers.

Although the first half of the nineteenth century saw the launching of several Catholic periodicals—the *Metropolitan, or Catholic Monthly Magazine,* published in Baltimore in 1830, was the first,—it was not until after the Civil War that any really became thriving. In the period of one year, 1865–1866, however, were established three different journals which are still prospering: the pioneer of them all, the *Catholic World,* founded by the Paulist, Father Hecker; the *Ave Maria,* soul-child of the celebrated Father Sorin, C.S.C., founder of Notre Dame University; and the *Messenger of the Sacred Heart,* established by the Jesuit, Father B. Sestini.

The *Rosary Magazine,* organ of the Dominicans; the *Magnificat,* edited by the Sisters of Mercy; the *America,* offshoot of the earlier *Messenger;* the *Sign,* published by the Passionists; the *Extension Magazine,* publication of the Church Extension Society; and the *Commonweal,* the only Catholic periodical directed by a board of laymen, are a few of the more than 150 monthlies, bimonthlies, quarterlies, and weeklies which today carry the message of Catholic culture to millions of Catholics in the United States. The contribution of these periodicals to the life of Catholic American letters has been of inestimable value.

At least one magazine of the period, *Harper's Magazine,* still published today, was founded to offer to American consumption the best of European writing for which, under the loose copyright laws, no payment was to be made. The intention was to show the loose working of the law itself. Contemporary writers overlooked the crusade in resentment against their own unprofitable exclusion from an American outlet. Certainly within a few years, the policy was completely altered, and for over a decade the mainstays of the publication were G. P. Morris, Epes Sargent, the two Abbotts and B. J. Lossing. But it was long in overcoming the prejudice against its original plan.

Magazines of the Twentieth Century

Looking back from the decade of the 1940's to the new phase of American magazine publication which began in the late 90's and has continued with small change except in the advance of the mechanics of production and the increase of available material, it is worth noting that the historical, political, and biographical aspect of present-day publication was begun before the century was actually turned. The running of such a serial as Sloan's *Life of Napoleon* was widely advertised and brought energetic rivals to print counter attractions. Before 1900, the American magazine had achieved a political slant and had created a semi-journalistic status retained to the present by many of its exemplars. The complete revolution in life insurance practice in the United States was achieved by a series of magazine articles. For nearly thirty years now the magazine has welcomed the services of the political research student with a lance couched against the *status quo*.

It is in this period, amplifying the experience of the first half century of tentative experiment, that the magazine has well established its position as not only the unquestioned home of the short story which is unlikely to see the light unless placed in a periodical, but the accepted medium for the long novel broken into serial installments. "This book has not been serially published" is encountered occasionally on a new novel, apparently placed there in defensive attitude. Publishing experience finds that accepted serial publication stimulates instead of retards later book sales.

Today there are literally hundreds of magazines. A few survive from the last century, not always under the same ownership or preserving the same policies. But no magazine publisher overlooks the one continued essential creed that there must be reader interest. From 1880 on, advertising had replaced circulation as the main support of publications but the necessity of having wide reader fields to hold the advertiser persists and has increased both the opportunity and the reward for successful magazine writing.

The plethora of magazines is not an unmixed blessing in its effect on American writing. There are scores of excellent periodicals with general appeal or devoted to such specialties as technical and scientific subjects, politics, literature, art, and travel. But the book stalls do not confine their trade to these and side by side with them appears a horde of badly written and cheaply produced magazines with every variety of objectionable lure from the thriller to saccharine and prurient romance.

Up to 1915, if the old type of thriller for the worldly young is excepted, the influence of the American magazine on writing style was distinctly only for good. The constant example of ably written stories and articles they held before the public encouraged emulation. The ventures of Frank Munsey, Frank Leslie, and others in the low priced field were not exceptions. Today the wheat must be winnowed from the chaff. The predominance of excellent periodicals does not minimize the competition for the attention of the undiscerning with the trash which clutters every store and which contributes neither to good reading nor encourages good writing.

The condition does not dim the unquestioned service of the first-class magazine to American letters. A consistent policy of encouragement to young and unknown writers whose work is carefully read in every leading magazine office and of liberal return for accepted work has made the American magazine outstanding. As late as 1910 the British and Continental periodicals could criticize justly and harshly their American contemporaries and much of American letters, but the pendulum has swung in the other direction. Foreign authors find a more liberal market here than abroad but must face keen competition from American writing. Even in its popular phases, the latter from the magazine viewpoint is setting an increasingly high standard. If in 1890 twenty people could write readable English for one in 1857, there are hundreds now for every score then. The American school system must be given the first credit for that but it has been partly supplied and made further possible by the reading and writing incentive given a now literate people by the American magazine and newspaper.

ORATORY

THE ORATION AS A TYPE OF LITERATURE

Definition

An oration is a public discourse in which truth is presented in a way to convince the hearer and to persuade him to action. The orator wants his audience to perform some particular act, adopt some policy, carry out some program, or follow habitually some principle. The truth presented must be one that touches the personal interests and ideals of the hearers, so that they may be led to act in accordance with it. They must be intellectually convinced of the truth and of its bearing on their own lives and on the action which the orator wishes them to perform. But this alone is not sufficient; they must also be moved through an appeal to their emotions so that they want to perform this action. The orator convinces by proving the truth with arguments and by presenting strong motives for action; he persuades by clothing these arguments and motives with feeling and emotional appeal.

The Development of Oratory

The rudiments of oratory are used constantly in the daily life of man. There is scarcely an hour of waking life when one is not trying directly or indirectly to persuade others to follow a line of conduct which he has decided is the proper one. The baby pleads with voice and gesture for his desires. The child begs his parents for whatever he sees as desirable, adding tears and gesticulations to win his point. The youth is never at a loss for arguments as a means of persuading others to follow his desires. This is the beginning of oratory.

As life becomes more complex and as the number of people who must live together increases, the need of common lines of action becomes imperative. All governments are formed for the purpose of securing this unanimity of action. The monarchy secures it by the domination of a single man. Democracy is built on the will of the majority. If then, the majority is to rule, there must be a comparatively large group with similar ideas of what needs to be done. Here is the orator's field, and the reason why oratory reaches its greatest perfection under a republican form of government. If we read orations with the thought in mind that the speaker has decided upon the proper course of action to pursue under the given circumstances and that he is trying to persuade others to follow the same course, we will have more appreciation for his art.

Essentials of an Oration

According to Daniel Webster, himself an orator, there are three essentials for an oration—the man, the subject, and the occasion. In judging an oration, then, these three should be studied together. One can readily understand that the man who would move others must have certain qualities in greater degree than the average man. He must have an active, versatile mind, must be sensitive in judging reactions in others and quick to modify his words to fit the reaction of his audience. He must have a knowledge of human nature, must understand the motives from which people act, and must have the ability to use this knowledge. The orator must have a mastery of words. Upon his choice of words alone will often depend his success or failure. He needs a strong sense of rhythm in language, an unerring sense of fitness in figures of speech, and a fund of apt illustrations. Most of all he must have a strong emotional nature; he must *feel*. The emotion may be carefully curbed, perfectly controlled, but it must be there. No man has ever been able to sway the emotions of others unless he felt the emotion himself. He must, however, be able to direct both his own feelings and those of his audience. Oratory does not have as its main purpose the arousing of emotions. It is primarily for the purpose of arousing to action of some kind, the emotional appeal being a necessary step in putting the hearers into a proper frame of mind for action. The orator must be able to produce a feeling of trust in his audience. He must at least seem honest, and for great oratory, he must be honest. Tact, sagacity, leadership, a controlled sense of humor, these go to making a great orator. Emerson in his essay on *Eloquence* thus pictures the orator:

"Him we call an artist, who shall play on an assembly of men as a master on the keys of a piano,—who, seeing the people furious, shall soften and compose them, shall draw them, when he will, to laughter and to tears. Bring him to his audience, and, be they who they may,—coarse or refined, pleased or displeased, sulky or savage, with their opinions in the keeping of a confessor, or with their opinions in their bank-safes,—he will have them pleased or humored as he chooses; and they shall carry and execute that which he bids them.—This is a power of many degrees, and requiring in the orator a great range of faculty and experience, requiring a large composite man, such as nature rarely organizes."

The Subject and Occasion of an Oration

What of the subject? What topics lend themselves to oratory? These questions have been partially answered already. The subject must be one in which people are interested and about which they have, or are capable of having, strong feelings. Argument is directed toward the intellect; oratory toward the emotion. But the intellect must be satisfied as well as the emotions if people are roused to act. The whole sphere of human interests and duties. social, religious, and political conduct, appreciative and cultural aims—whatever touches the emotional life of man is the field of persuasion. It is a fact that the best-known American orations deal with political subjects because in a republic there must be conviction on the part of the majority before any action or change of policy can be had. So the subject most used will be some phase of political life.

The occasion likewise is usually some social or political crisis when decisions must be made. The declaration of war, the election of a candidate, the passage of laws—these are occasions upon which men arise to state their views and to win others to their way of thinking. A crisis in government is a challenge to the orator. Another favorite occasion is the commemoration of some person or event known to all the people. At such a time the orator's object is to recall the thought and feelings that once attached to the person or event thus honored, and to direct the emotions thus aroused into some definite channel of thought or action for the future.

Styles in Oratory

Styles in oratory change with the times. Early American oratory was often artificial and stilted, ornamented with flowery figures of speech which tickled the ears of the hearers but lacked force and directness. Later these devices were discarded and their place was taken by anecdotes and witticisms to illustrate a point or to gain the attention of the crowd. Contemporary speakers of the highest type do neither. They never pose. They try to state the things they have to say in a simple, direct, conversational manner, without ornamentation other than that any man uses when he wishes to illustrate a point or press it home. They use in their public addresses the language of everyday speech. Naturally, men of culture will have a more pleasing manner of speech than uneducated people, so that modern oratory is more nearly a gauge of the man than the carefully prepared, ornate speeches of an older generation.

Modern and Contemporary Oratory

The recent development of the radio has revived the public's interest in oral communication. People are becoming tone conscious. They are learning to take in ideas through the ear again after years of visual education. The results of President Roosevelt's radio talks have proved anew the power of the spoken word; and the future is likely to see a new era of awakened interest in national affairs through the use of the radio and the talking pictures in bringing national problems directly to the masses of people. There is no lack of evidence that audiences still respond to the living voice and compelling personality of the genuine orator. Orations may change but not oratory. To-day we place a lower value on mere rhetorical devices, but the orator who has a noble theme and can present it nobly will not lack for hearers.

A very good proof that public speaking still looms large in the consciousness of our people is the national interest that has been taken in oratorical contests of late years. High school boys and girls have written and delivered hundreds of speeches which are of consequence, not for the intrinsic value of the speeches, but because they are keeping alive the love of beautiful, effective platform speaking. The occasions for public speeches to-day are innumerable, and each occasion calls for a fitting type of speech. As never before, it behooves the young student of to-day to acquaint himself with the effective oratory of the past and prepare himself for effective delivery of thoughts and feelings on the platform, in the newspaper, and over the radio.

What to Look for in an Oration

In reading an oration it is well to remember constantly that it was composed for oral delivery and not primarily for reading. It will then be understood that the speaker has frequently to repeat a thought which he wishes his hearers to grasp. Since it is impossible for them to turn back to a previous page to review what he has already said and thus understand its bearing upon what he is now saying, it is necessary for the orator to employ this emphasis of repetition. He will not, of course, say the same thing in the same words—that would lead to mere monotony—but will clothe his thought anew, examine it from different angles, furnish it with illustration and example, enforce it with contrast or comparison, and finally come back to a repetition of the thought so that his hearers will be certain to have grasped his meaning.

Then, too, it must be kept in mind that an oration appeals primarily to the emotions, rather than to the intellect. Its purpose is not to inform, instruct, or explain, but to move—to induce in its hearers a state of feeling which may or may not have consequences in action. Thus the reader will try to put himself in the mental attitude of the listener. He will try to reconstruct the scene, to hear again the voice of the orator, to feel with the throng its emotional reaction to the occasion.

The reader, however, has some slight advantage over the hearer, for the former can study, if he will, some of the means which the orator employs to make his effects. Thus the sentence structure in an oration is likely to be balanced, each part corresponding to the other. Sharp contrasts, or antitheses, are often employed to heighten the effect. Repetition is deliberately encouraged. Phrases will be arranged in the order of increasing emphasis. Short sentences will succeed long ones in order to furnish a contrast of manner, and to arrest and hold the attention of the hearers.

And because emotion is exhausting, the orator will not attempt to keep his hearers in its grip for long. Quiet passages succeed those in which there has been a definite appeal to sympathy, sorrow, patriotism, anger, or any other consuming passion. This is not alone necessary for both the orator and his hearers, but furnishes the contrast which heightens the emotional passages.

THE HISTORY OF AMERICAN ORATORY

The Colonial Period (1607–1765)

General Characteristics

Whenever ideas become involved with emotions, oratory is likely to result. Thoughts about the deep subjects of life, or religion, or of government, when brought home to people by actual events which illustrate them or which are closely connected with them, occasion oratory. Our nation was formed at a time when theories were rapidly developing into facts. The early colonists came to America during the Elizabethan Age. During that age England's development had been marvelous. Hardy adventurers sailed around a new-found world, avid for new experiences, new knowledge. The people at home were busy perfecting and making use of that gift of the Renaissance, the printing press; or taking excursions into the realm of thought opened by Copernicus, or the older realms of the Greeks, now revealed again to them. Everywhere people were thinking. However, there was no room in Elizabeth's realm for religious freedom, so many people left England to live elsewhere, some of them emigrating in groups. Indeed the northern settlers came to America to be free to think, and to be free to worship God as their consciences dictated.

That the early oratory was religious is to be expected. Both debate and oratory come from excursions into the realm of thoughts and ideas, but a certain amount of freedom is required before such excursions are possible. The early Puritans took great freedom in discussing religious principles and tenets. They reveled in the process of thinking out and expressing to others their own, sometimes narrow and misguided, interpretations of Biblical truths and philosophical reasonings about the facts of life about them. Hence, pulpit oratory flourished.

In New England the ministers were the leaders for various reasons. They were usually the best educated men in the colony. Together with the lawyers they made up the intellectual aristocracy. Moreover, they were not merely preachers—they were men of strong intellect, courage, and personality. Besides supplying their congregation with spiritual food, they took the place of newspapers, lecturers, and entertainers. The ministers kept in touch with friends in England through correspondence and the English newspapers. The Puritan went to church as a religious duty, but he went also to hear the latest news from England or from the other scattered colonies, and to find out what side the preacher was taking in local controversies. So the world's happenings were discussed from the pulpit, and, as always, the oratory of the period dealt with the problems of the period.

Among the most eloquent of the religious leaders were Roger Williams, Cotton Mather, and Jonathan Edwards.

Roger Williams (1607–1684)

Roger Williams seems to have had an unusual personality. He had in a great degree one essential element of the orator—earnestness. While a minister at Salem, he preached so zealously in favor of religious liberty that he was forced to leave Massachusetts and, after a winter spent with friendly Indians, founded Providence, Rhode Island, where others of his belief were given refuge.

Cotton Mather (1663–1728)

Mather was stern and fanatical in his intense devotion to what he thought right. As a preacher he thundered denunciations against sinners with such force that his listeners trembled with fear. But when a small-pox epidemic struck Boston, he encouraged one of the physicians to try inoculation, and although his life was threatened, he continued advocating this new method of fighting disease until he convinced others, by example as well as argument, that lives could be saved by inoculation. He is remembered in history for his part in the Salem witchcraft affair.

Jonathan Edwards (1703–1758)

Jonathan Edwards, of the generation following Cotton Mather, was the greatest of all colonial preachers and the first American philosopher of any note. He seems to have been a many-sided man. He was dominated by his awe of the majesty, and the power of God, and he possessed a convincing power of utterance. A good illustration of his clear and powerful prose is to be seen in his famous sermon, *Sinners in the Hands of an Angry God,* preached at Enfield, Connecticut, in 1741, in which he declared, "The God that holds you over the pit of hell, much as one holds a spider, or some loathsome insect, over the fire, abhors you, and is dreadfully provoked; his wrath towards you burns like fire; he looks upon you as worthy of nothing else, but to be cast into the fire; he is of purer eyes than to bear to have you in his sight." This sermon is considered one of the most powerful ever uttered, the effect on the audience being intense. His *Treatise on the Freedom of the Will* gained him a reputation as a philosophic thinker. Despite the rigor of his doctrine, Edwards, unlike Mather, was a man of gentle nature. Many of his writings are quite poetic and gentle in their beauty of thought, of spirit, and of expression. He died in 1758, president of Princeton University.

The Revolutionary Period (1765–1800)

General Characteristics

Jonathan Edwards was the last of the famed colonial preachers. Not long after his death, the attention of the colonists was turned toward political affairs by the attempt of the king, James II, to take away the charters of some of the colonies and unite them more closely under his arbitrary rule. From that time until after the Revolutionary War, political problems connected with English rule in America absorbed the intellect and the passions of the colonists. As the colonies grew in size and population, they grew in a feeling of self-sufficiency. This made them resent England's supervisory attitude toward their affairs, and when a stupid king, with the assistance of a group of short-sighted advisers, tried the temper of the colonists too far, open war resulted.

In building up the resistance of the colonies to the English king and Parliament, the orators were important. Among them, Patrick Henry and George Washington were perhaps the most outstanding. Patrick Henry was a real orator, who drew inspiration from an audience and was at his best in extempore speaking on a subject about which he felt deeply. George Washington, on the other hand, was more of an essayist, thinking out and writing down his speeches before he presented them to his public. Each in his own way strongly influenced his age.

Patrick Henry (1736–1799)

Patrick Henry was born in Hanover County, Virginia, of Scotch and Welsh descent. After a somewhat irregular schooling he tried unsuccessfully to make a living as a farmer and again as a storekeeper. Finally he decided to study law, and he was licensed in 1760. At last he had found his work. His natural fire and eloquence made him almost immediately successful in spite of the fact that his knowledge of law was meager compared with that of most of the Virginia lawyers.

In 1765 he became a member of the House of Burgesses. Insignificant and unknown, he created a furor by offering a resolution declaring that the Burgesses and the Governor had the exclusive right to impose taxes in Virginia, and that all attempts of the British Parliament to tax the colonies were unconstitutional. In the stormy debate that followed he scandalized even his friends when he cried, "Cæsar had his Brutus, Charles the First his Cromwell, and George the Third—(here he was stopped by cries of "Treason! treason!", but calmly proceeded)—may profit by their example. If this be treason, make the most of it." His resolution was adopted, and Patrick Henry was recognized as a power in the colony.

Thereafter he took an active part in all the discussions, continuing a member of the House of Burgesses until it was dissolved. He was elected a delegate to the First Continental Congress at Philadelphia in 1774. The following words from a speech made there show how far he had gone in anticipating nationalism. "Fleets and armies and the present state of things show that the government is dissolved. Where are your landmarks—your boundaries of colonies? All distinctions are thrown down; all America is thrown into one mass. The distinctions between Virginians, Pennsylvanians, New Yorkers, and New Englanders are no more. I am not a Virginian, but an American."

For the rest of his life Patrick Henry continued active in governmental matters. Washington offered him the position of Secretary of State, which he declined. Other similar offers were likewise declined. He died June 6, 1799.

George Washington (1732–1799)

It would seem that the tradition which pictures Washington as growing up in aristocratic ease and affluence on a broad Virginia plantation is somewhat in need of revision. It is true that he came of an old family and that his father was a man of substance, but the latter's property seems to have gone to the children of his first wife—George's half-brothers. The death of his father occurred when George was eleven. The mother removed to Fredericksburg where she lived apparently in modest, if not in somewhat straitened, circumstances.

At Fredericksburg he attended the school of the Rev. James Mayre. Washington's master was one who firmly believed that "manners maketh man." Part of the education which Washington received was in *Rules of Civility and Decent Behaviour*—a hundred and ten of them which he copied carefully in an even, well-written, legible hand. Owen Wister says, "It is a misfortune for all American boys in our schools to-day, that they should be told the untrue and foolish story of the hatchet and cherry tree, and denied the immense benefit of instruction from George Washington's authentic copybook." The first of the rules is as follows: "Every Action done in Company, ought to be with Some Sign of Respect to those that are Present." Wister believes that from consideration of these "flowed his power of address—the consideration and the sympathy —which won for him—the esteem and devotion of those who could help him." To the present age when such a thing as personal dignity seems to have been forgotten, when men and 'women of prominence and sometimes of social consequence sell their names to all kinds of advertisers for a page of cheap publicity, Washington's rules may seem somewhat stilted, but they engendered in him a respect not only for others, but for himself—a respect which in any age is one of the foundation stones of character.

When he was about sixteen, his schooling ended. Now began a period of about five years during which he surveyed the vast holdings of Lord Fairfax and gained, especially in the ways of the frontier, a valuable experience. From this time on the facts of his life are well known. Few men of Revolutionary fame are better "documented." His diary, kept with care during the years he was in Fairfax's employ and the reports, state papers, and letters of subsequent years fill fourteen large volumes. The knowledge of the frontier which came to him as a surveyor as well as the qualities of personality and character which he displayed led to his being chosen by Governor Dinwiddie for the mission to the French fort on the Ohio with which the forty-five years of public service which he mentions in his Farewell Address may be said to begin.

The Most Reverend Bishop John Carroll (1735–1815)

John Carroll, descendant of the Maryland Calverts and cousin of Charles Carroll of Carrollton, the only Catholic to sign the Declaration of Independence, was the first bishop and archbishop in the United States.

He was born in Upper Marlborough, Maryland, three years after George Washington; he survived him by sixteen years. His elementary education he received at home. When twelve years of age he attended the Jesuit school at Bohemia Manor, and in the following year, in company with his cousin Charles, went across the sea to continue his schooling at St. Omer's in France. At the age of eighteen he entered the Jesuit novitiate at Watten, near St. Omer's, and after a period of sixteen years was ordained to the priesthood.

Shortly after the suppression of the Society of Jesus in 1773 Father Carroll returned to Maryland. Though an ardent patriot, he occupied himself exclusively with priestly work in and about the manorial home of his widowed mother until 1776. He then accompanied a Congressional Committee of Three (Benjamin Franklin, Charles Carroll, and Samuel Chase) to Canada in the futile hope of bringing the French Canadians to side with the Revolution.

Two months after the signing of the treaty of peace between the United States and England in 1783, Carroll and four other American priests petitioned Rome to allow them to select a superior with limited episcopal powers. Rome listened to the petition kindly, and in the following year Carroll himself was named Prefect-Apostolic. In 1789 he became Bishop of Baltimore. Although sagacious and energetic in the execution of all his episcopal duties, his particular concern was the establishment of worthy educational institutions; and Georgetown College, the Visitation Convent in Washington, and St. Mary's Seminary in Baltimore, to mention only a few, owe very much to his initiative and foresight.

The Church grew slowly in those difficult days; yet Bishop Carroll's immense see was in 1808 raised to the status of an archdiocese with four suffragan sees, the dioceses of Boston, New York, Philadelphia, and Bardstown, Kentucky. Until his death in 1815 he continued to be the guiding spirit of the struggling Church in the new United States. This great soul was chosen by Providence to be the father of the Catholic hierarchy in this country as George Washington, object of Bishop Carroll's glowing admiration, was chosen by that same Providence to be the father of the nation's political government. Both deserved and won the highest praise from their contemporaries. Time has justified and swelled the volume of that praise.

Other Writers of Patriotic Prose

Other men whose patriotic writings stand out from the great mass are Thomas Jefferson (1743–1826), Alexander Hamilton (1757–1804), and James Madison (1751–1836). John Dickinson (1732–1808), and Thomas Paine (1737–1809) were also very influential.

Orations of the Revolutionary Period

SPEECH IN THE VIRGINIA CONVENTION

Patrick Henry

Historical Background: The Virginia House of Burgesses had been dissolved by order of the royal governor, but in March, 1775, a Provincial Convention met in the "Old Church" at Richmond, Virginia. Patrick Henry was present, and believing that nothing could prevent armed conflict with Great Britain, he offered the following resolution:

1. Resolved: That a well-regulated militia, composed of gentlemen and yeomen, is the natural strength and only security of a free government; and that such a militia in this colony would forever render it unnecessary for the mother country to keep among us, for the purpose of our defense, any standing army or mercenary forces, always subversive of the quiet and dangerous to the liberties of the people, and would obviate the pretext of taxing us for their support.

2. That such a militia is at this time especially necessary to protect our rights and liberties, which have been rendered insecure by the remissness of government in calling our Legislature together.

3. That this colony be immediately put into a posture of defense.

There was considerable opposition to taking such drastic measures at that time, and Colonel Richard Bland, Colonel Benjamin Harrison, Robert Carter Nichols and Edmund Pendleton spoke against the resolution. The scene which followed is thus recorded in Tyler's *Life of Patrick Henry*: "Henry rose with an unearthly fire burning in his eye. He commenced somewhat calmly, but the smothered excitement began more and more to play upon his features and thrill in the tones of his voice. The tendons of his neck stood out white and rigid like whipcords. His voice rose louder and louder, until the walls of the building, and all within them, seemed to shake and rock in its tremendous vibrations. Finally his pale face and glaring eyes became terrible to look upon. Men leaned forward and their eyes glared like the speaker's. His last exclamation, 'Give me liberty or give me death!' was like the shout of the leader which turns back the rout of battle."

MR. PRESIDENT:

No man thinks more highly than I do of the patriotism, as well as abilities, of the very worthy gentlemen [1] who have just addressed the house. But different men often see the same subject in different lights; and, therefore, I hope it will not be thought disrespectful to those gentlemen, if, entertaining as I do opinions of a character very opposite to theirs, I shall speak forth my sentiments freely, and without reserve. This is no time for ceremony. The question before the house is one of awful moment [2] to this country. For my own part, I consider it as nothing less than a question of freedom or slavery. And in proportion to the magnitude of the subject ought to be the freedom of the debate. It is only in this way that we can hope to arrive at truth, and fulfill the great responsibility which we hold to God and our country. Should I keep back my opinions at such a time, through fear of giving offense, I should consider myself as guilty of treason toward my country, and of an act of disloyalty toward the Majesty of Heaven, which I revere above all earthly kings.

Mr. President, it is natural to man to indulge in the illusions of hope. We are apt to shut our eyes against a painful truth, and listen to the song of that siren [3] till she transforms us into beasts. Is this the part of wise men, engaged in a great and arduous struggle for liberty? Are we disposed to be of the number of those who having eyes see not, and having ears hear

[1] WORTHY GENTLEMEN—The gentlemen who had opposed Henry's resolution.

[2] AWFUL MOMENT—The speaker thought, with others, that war could not be averted.

[3] SONG OF THAT SIREN, etc.—The Sirens were monsters with faces of beautiful women who lured sailors to their island by their singing and then devoured them. It was Circe, an enchantress, who transformed men into beasts. Ulysses tells of both Circe and the Sirens in the *Odyssey*. Patrick Henry may have confused the two, although the term "siren" is often used in a general way to mean any enchantress.

not, the things which so nearly concern their temporal salvation? For my part, whatever anguish of spirit it may cost, I am willing to know the whole truth; to know the worst and to provide for it.

I have but one lamp by which my feet are guided, and that is the lamp of experience. I know of no way of judging of the future but by the past. And judging by the past, I wish to know what there has been in the conduct of the British ministry for the last ten years, to justify those hopes with which gentlemen have been pleased to solace themselves and the house? Is it that insidious smile [4] with which our petition has been lately received? Trust it not, sir: it will prove a snare to your feet. Suffer not yourselves to be betrayed with a kiss.[5] Ask yourselves how this gracious reception of our petition comports with those warlike preparations [6] which cover our waters and darken our land. Are fleets and armies necessary to a work of love and reconciliation? Have we shown ourselves so unwilling to be reconciled that force must be called in to win back our love? Let us not deceive ourselves, sir. These are the implements of war and subjugation—the last arguments to which kings resort. I ask, sir, What means this martial array, if its purpose be not to force us to submission? Can gentlemen assign any other possible motive for it? Has Great Britain any enemy in this quarter of the world, to call for all this accumulation of navies and armies? Not, sir, she has none. They are meant for us: they can be meant for no other. They are sent over to bind and rivet upon us those chains which the British ministry have been so long forging. And what have we to oppose to them? Shall we try argument? Sir, we have been trying that for the last ten years.[7] Have we anything new to offer upon the subject? Noth-

[4] INSIDIOUS SMILE—Characterized by treachery and deceit.

[5] BETRAYED WITH A KISS—Judas betrayed Christ with a kiss. This is a metaphor signifying the worst kind of treachery.

[6] WARLIKE PREPARATIONS—After the French and Indian Wars, British troops remained in the colonies, much against the wishes of the colonists. (See note 1.) In 1768 the fifty-gun frigate *Romney* had been sent to Boston Harbor. Later, two regiments of soldiers were quartered in Boston.

[7] FOR THE LAST TEN YEARS—The French and Indian Wars ended with the Treaty of Paris in 1763. As early as 1660 England had begun to regulate the commerce of the colonies to her own advantage by a series of Navigation Acts whereby she forbade the colonists to trade with any other nation. As years passed, these acts became more and more detrimental to the colonists and were increasingly resented. Smuggling increased to escape the restrictions of the Navigation Acts. In 1763, George Grenville, prime minister to George

ing. We have held the subject up in every light of which it is capable; but it has been all in vain. Shall we resort to entreaty and humble supplication? What terms shall we find which have not been already exhausted? Let us not, I beseech you, sir, deceive ourselves longer.

Sir, we have done everything that could be done to avert the storm which is now coming on. We have petitioned; we have remonstrated; we have supplicated; we have prostrated ourselves before the throne, and have implored its interposition to arrest the tyrannical hands of the ministry and Parliament. Our petitions have been slighted; our remonstrances have produced additional violence and insult; our supplications have been disregarded; and we have been spurned with contempt from the foot of the throne! [8] In vain, after these things, may we indulge the fond hope of peace and reconciliation. There is no longer any room for hope. If we wish to be free, if we mean to preserve inviolate those inestimable privileges for which we have been so long contending, if we mean not basely to abandon the noble struggle in which we have been so long engaged, and which we have pledged ourselves never to abandon until the glorious object of our contest shall be obtained—we must fight! I repeat it, sir, we must fight! An appeal to arms and to the God of Hosts is all that is left us!

They tell us, sir, that we are weak—unable to cope with so formidable an adversary.[9] But when shall we be stronger? Will it be the next week, or the next year? Will it be when we are totally disarmed, and when a British guard shall be stationed in every house? Shall we gather strength by irresolution and

III, attempted to enforce these laws more vigorously. Writs of Assistance were issued, which permitted officers to search the homes of the colonists for smuggled goods. This enforcement of the Navigation Acts, together with the maintenance of a standing army of English soldiers in the colonies, and the taxes introduced by Grenville, were the causes of the Revolutionary War. During this whole time the colonists had tried by petition and by argument to gain the freedom of action they desired.

[8] SPURNED . . . FROM THE FOOT OF THE THRONE—The speaker here refers to the various petitions sent to the king by the colonies. For example, Samuel Adams petitioned the king for the Massachusetts Assembly in a sincere and humble letter which the king received with silent contempt. The First Continental Congress sent the king a humble petition begging him to redress their wrongs.

[9] FORMIDABLE AN ADVERSARY—Even Benjamin Franklin, who was representing Pennsylvania at this time in England, counseled submission because of the difference in numbers.

inaction? Shall we acquire the means of effectual resistance by lying supinely on our backs, and hugging the delusive phantom of hope until our enemies shall have bound us hand and foot? Sir, we are not weak, if we make a proper use of those means which the God of nature hath placed in our power. Three millions of people, armed in the holy cause of liberty, and in such a country as that which we possess, are invincible by any force which our enemy can send against us. Besides, sir, we shall not fight our battles alone. There is a just God who presides over the destinies of nations, and who will raise up friends to fight our battles for us.[10] The battle, sir, is not to the strong alone; it is to the vigilant, the active, the brave. Besides, sir, we have no election.[11] If we were base enough to desire it, it is now too late to retire from the contest. There is no retreat but in submission and slavery! Our chains are forged! their clanking may be heard on the plains of Boston![12] The war is inevitable—and let it come! I repeat it, sir, let it come!

It is in vain, sir, to extenuate[13] the matters. Gentlemen may cry, Peace, Peace—but there is no peace. The war is actually begun! The next gale that sweeps from the north will bring to our ears the clash of resounding arms![14] Our brethren are already in the field! Why stand we here idle? What is it that gentlemen wish? What would they have? Is life so dear, or peace so sweet, as to be purchased at the price of chains and slavery? Forbid it, Almighty God! I know not what course others may take; but as for me, give me liberty or give me death!

[10] FRIENDS TO FIGHT OUR BATTLES FOR US—France did join the colonies against England. [11] ELECTION—Choice.

[12] ON THE PLAINS OF BOSTON—This speech was delivered in March, 1775. In April, the battles of Lexington and Concord were fought, and in June the Battle of Bunker Hill. [13] EXTENUATE—Underrate.

[14] THE NEXT GALE . . . RESOUNDING ARMS—See note 12.

By Way of Appreciation: This oration like all of Patrick Henry's speeches, was delivered *extempore*. It was never given as it stands to-day. The speech as we have it was reconstructed from notes and from memory, years after it was delivered, by William Wirt, who wrote a life of Patrick Henry.

Notice that it has the characteristics of the oratory of that time—eloquence, intense feeling, singleness of aim, and effectiveness of language. Notice the balanced sentences, the classical allusions, the metaphors, the repetition, and the rhetorical questions. Note also that it gives the author's reaction toward the great problem of that day, the relation between the colonies and England. It was given for the purpose of making others think as he did about this question and of persuading them to vote for his resolution.

Suggestions for Study: Would you have been swayed by this speech? What argument does Henry make for his resolutions? Do you think he is talking directly about his resolutions, or about his belief in the inevitability of war with England? Is he trying to persuade the audience intellectually or to move them emotionally? Do you think it required courage to make such a speech at that time?

FAREWELL ADDRESS

TO THE PEOPLE OF THE UNITED STATES

George Washington

Historical Background: In his *Farewell Address* Washington gives expression to what he called "the disinterested warnings of a parting friend." The *Address* came straight from his heart, born of his solicitude for the young republic. Eight years as its president had acquainted him with the dangers, external and internal, which threatened its welfare; phrase after phrase of the *Address* reflects some incident or condition of affairs which had occupied Washington's attention or aroused his apprehensions in the course of his two terms. An outstanding characteristic of the paper is its foundation in practicality; it is in no wise a theoretical treatise on government; it is throughout based squarely on fact and experience.

Washington had gone into the presidency with the idea of conducting a nonpartisan government. He called into his Cabinet men conspicuous for their attachment to the new Constitution and for their past services to the new nation. Among these were Hamilton and Jefferson, his Secretaries of the Treasury and of State respectively. He apparently was confident that all men would work together for the common good, keeping themselves above party and personal differences, and thinking only of the national welfare.

This whole-hearted coöperation which he had looked for, however, was not forthcoming, either on the part of individuals or communities. He counted perhaps too much on the singleness of attachment to the new government and expected too much of human nature. He found himself perplexed from the outset by personal jealousies and party differences which split his Cabinet and at length forced him into the arms of the Federalists. Nor was party warfare the worst of his problems. Treaties with Spain and England, mainly in regard to boundary disputes, set up cries of sectional favoritism, and the passionate attachment of the Republicans to France during the French Revolution was not without grave consequences in domestic affairs.

The letters of Washington during the years of his presidency reflect the growing concern which all these sectional and party jealousies gave him. His experience was sufficient to convince him of the baneful effects of party, for he had had abundant opportunity to see its consequences in domestic and foreign affairs. Having, as he did, only the welfare of his country at heart and knowing from experience how difficult a task it was to guide the destinies of the Republic, it was with a genuine solicitude that he offered his *Farewell Address* to the people. Washington did not deliver this address. It was printed in Claypoole's *American Daily Advertiser* for September 19, 1796, at Philadelphia, in accordance with Washington's wishes.

FRIENDS AND FELLOW CITIZENS: The period for a new election [1] of a citizen, to administer the executive government of the United States, being not far distant, and the time actually arrived when your thoughts must be employed in designating the person who is to be clothed with that important trust, it appears to me proper, especially as it may conduce [2] to a more distinct expression of the public voice, that I should now apprise you of the resolution I have formed, to decline being considered

[1] A NEW ELECTION—The election of the chief executive then took place not by direct vote of the people as at present but according to the method laid down originally in Article II, Section I of the Constitution. "Washington asked Hamilton when the document ought to appear, and the latter said that it ought to come about two months before the meeting of the electoral college. It was issued three months before that event."—Bassett, *Federalist System*, p. 146. [2] CONDUCE—Lead.

among the number of those out of whom a choice is to be made.

I beg you, at the same time, to do me the justice to be assured, that this resolution has not been taken without a strict regard to all the considerations appertaining to the relation which binds a dutiful citizen to his country; and that, in withdrawing the tender [3] of service, which silence in my situation might imply, I am influenced by no diminution of zeal for your future interest; no deficiency of grateful respect for your past kindness; but am supported by a full conviction that the step is compatible with both.

The acceptance of, and continuance hitherto in, the office to which your suffrages [4] have twice called me, have been a uniform sacrifice of inclination [5] to the opinion of duty, and to a deference for what appeared to be your desire. I constantly hoped that it would have been much earlier in my power, consistently with motives which I was not at liberty to disregard, to return to that retirement from which I had been reluctantly drawn. The strength of my inclination to do this, previous to the last election, had even led to the preparation of an address [6] to declare it to you; but mature reflection on the then perplexed and critical posture of our affairs with foreign nations,[7] and the unanimous advice of persons entitled to my confidence,[8] impelled me to abandon the idea.

I rejoice that the state of your concerns, external as well as internal, no longer renders the pursuit of inclination incompatible with the sentiment of duty or propriety; and am persuaded, whatever partiality may be retained for my services, that, in the

---

[3] TENDER—Offer. [4] SUFFRAGES—Votes.

[5] SACRIFICE OF INCLINATION—"Washington hesitated before he made up his mind to accept the presidency. He had a genuine love of retirement . . . and he had been so active in securing the adoption of the Constitution that he feared that people would say, if he now became president, that he had been seeking his own advancement."—Bassett, *Federalist System*.

[6] PREPARATION OF AN ADDRESS—Washington hoped in 1792 that he might retire from the Presidency, and he began at that time, with the help of Madison, a farewell address from which the first two paragraphs of this *Address* came with some change.

[7] POSTURE OF OUR AFFAIRS WITH FOREIGN NATIONS—Washington here refers to boundary difficulties with England in the Northwest, and to the refusal of England to make a treaty of commerce; to Spanish intrigues in the Southwest; and to the affair of Citizen Genet.

[8] PERSONS ENTITLED TO MY CONFIDENCE—Washington here refers to Randolph, Hamilton, Jefferson, Madison, and Knox, all of whom urged him to accept a second term.

present circumstances [9] of our country, you will not disapprove my determination to retire.

The impressions with which I first undertook the arduous trust were explained on the proper occasion.[10]   In the discharge of this trust I will only say that I have with good intentions contributed toward the organization and administration of the government the best exertions of which a very fallible [11] judgment was capable.   Not unconscious in the outset of the inferiority of my qualifications,[12] experience in my own eyes, perhaps still more in the eyes of others,[13] has strengthened the

[9] PRESENT CIRCUMSTANCES—By 1796, "external as well as internal" affairs had somewhat improved.   For example, treaties had been concluded with England and with Spain, Hamilton's financial system had restored the national credit, the collapse of the Whiskey Rebellion had strengthened the hand of the federal government, and while party animosity was still bitter there was, nevertheless, discernible a stronger national spirit.

[10] PROPER OCCASION—Washington here alludes to his *First Inaugural Address:* "Among the vicissitudes incident to life, no event could have filled me with greater anxieties, than that of which the notification was transmitted by your order, and received on the 14th day of the present month [April, 1789].   On the one hand, I was summoned by my country, whose voice I can never hear but with veneration and love, from a retreat which I had chosen with the fondest predilection. . . .   On the other hand, the magnitude and difficulty of the trust, to which the voice of my country called me, being sufficient to awaken in the wisest and most experienced of her citizens a distrustful scrutiny into his qualifications, could not but overwhelm with despondence one, who, inheriting inferior endowments from nature, and unpractised in the duties of civil administration, ought to be peculiarly conscious of his own deficiencies.   In this conflict of emotions, all I dare aver is, that it has been my faithful study to collect my duty from a just appreciation of every circumstance by which it might be affected.   All I dare hope is, that, if in executing this task, I have been too much swayed by a grateful remembrance of former instances, or by an affectionate sensibility of this transcendent proof of the confidence of my fellow-citizens; and have thence too little consulted my incapacity as well as disinclination for the weighty and untried cares before me; my error will be palliated by the motives which misled me, and its consequences be judged by my country with some share of the partiality in which they originated.   Such being the impressions under which I have, in obedience to the public summons, repaired to the present station."

[11] FALLIBLE—Liable to error.

[12] INFERIORITY OF MY QUALIFICATIONS—See the note above, the sentence beginning: "On the other hand, the magnitude . . ."

[13] IN THE EYES OF OTHERS—Bassett says, "Washington's action had been taken, not so much because he sought retirement in his old age as because he was disgusted with the abuse of the Republicans. . . . Among those who refused to give Washington the compliment of a last God-speed were Andrew Jackson, Edward Livingston, Nathaniel Macon, and W. B. Giles, men long afterwards noted for their unyielding Republicanism.   Giles probably expressed the feeling of this group when he said in the debate on the reply: 'I must acknowledge that I am one of those who do not think as much of the President as others do.' "

motives to diffidence [14] of myself; and every day the increasing
weight of years admonishes me more and more that the shades
of retirement is as necessary to me as it will be welcome. Satisfied that, if any circumstances have given peculiar value to my
services, they were temporary, I have the consolation to believe
that, while choice and prudence invite me to quit the political
scene, patriotism does not forbid it.

In looking forward to the moment which is intended to termi-
nate the career of my public life, my feelings do not permit me
to suspend the deep acknowledgment of that debt of gratitude
which I owe to my beloved country for the many honors it has
conferred upon me; still more for the steadfast confidence with
which it has supported me; and for the opportunities I have
thence enjoyed of manifesting my inviolable [15] attachment by
services faithful and persevering, though in usefulness unequal
to my zeal. If benefits have resulted to our country from these
services, let it always be remembered to your praise, and as
an instructive example in our annals, that under circumstances
in which the passions, agitated in every direction, were liable
to mislead, amidst appearances sometimes dubious, vicissitudes
of fortune often discouraging, in situations in which not unfre-
quently want of success has countenanced the spirit of criticism, [16] the constancy of your support [17] was the essential prop
of the efforts, and a guaranty of the plans by which they were
effected. Profoundly penetrated with this idea, I shall carry it
with me to my grave, as a strong incitement to unceasing vows
that Heaven may continue to you the choicest tokens of its
beneficence; that your union and brotherly affection may be perpetual; that the free constitution, which is the work of your
hands, may be sacredly maintained; that its administration in
every department may be stamped with wisdom and virtue; that,

[14] DIFFIDENCE—Distrust of self.

[15] INVIOLABLE—That is, one that he could not violate.

[16] UNDER CIRCUMSTANCES . . . SPIRIT OF CRITICISM—Each phrase here might
be illustrated by some incident or circumstance from the history of Washington's eight years in the presidency.

[17] CONSTANCY OF YOUR SUPPORT—For example, in 1792 when Washington
consulted with his friends on the advisability of refusing a second election,
"Jefferson, divided between his political views and his friendship for his
chief, hesitated to give an answer, probably intending to get the counsel
of his friends; but he soon realized the extent of the demand for Washington,
and he added his opinion to that of the other leaders, that the president
should accept another term."—Bassett, *Federalist System*, p. 54.

in fine, the happiness of the people of these States, under the auspices of liberty, may be made complete, by so careful a preservation and so prudent a use of this blessing, as will acquire to them the glory of recommending it to the applause, the affection, and adoption of every nation which is yet a stranger to it.

II

HERE, perhaps, I ought to stop. But a solicitude for your welfare, which cannot end but with my life, and the apprehension of danger natural to that solicitude, urge me, on an occasion like the present, to offer to your solemn contemplation, and to recommend to your frequent review, some sentiments, which are the result of much reflection, of no inconsiderable observation, and which appear to me all-important to the permanency of your felicity[1] as a people. These will be offered to you with the more freedom, as you can only see in them the disinterested warnings of a parting friend, who can possibly have no personal motive to bias[2] his counsel. Nor can I forget, as an encouragement to it, your indulgent reception of my sentiments on a former and not dissimilar occasion.[3]

Interwoven as is the love of liberty with every ligament[4] of your hearts, no recommendation of mine is necessary to fortify or confirm the attachment.

The unity of government, which constitutes you one people, is also dear to you.[5] It is justly so; for it is a main pillar in the edifice of your real independence, the support of your tranquillity at home, your peace abroad; of your safety; of your prosperity; of that very liberty which you so highly prize. But

---

[1] FELICITY—Happiness.

[2] BIAS—Influence or prejudice.

[3] FORMER AND NOT DISSIMILAR OCCASION—An allusion to Washington's resignation of his commission at the close of the War at Annapolis, December 23, 1783, when he said: "I resign with satisfaction the appointment I accepted with diffidence . . . and the assistance I received from my Countrymen, increases with every review of the momentous contest."

[4] LIGAMENT—Tie. Compare the expression "heart strings."

[5] UNITY . . . ALSO DEAR TO YOU—In 1792 Jefferson wrote Washington: "The confidence of the whole Union is centered in you. Your being at the helm will be more than an answer to every argument, which can be used to alarm and lead the people in any quarter into violence or secession. North and South will hang together, if they have you to hang on." By 1796 the strong feeling of local patriotism which had threatened the complete adoption of the Constitution had considerably diminished.

as it is easy to foresee that from different causes and from different quarters much pains will be taken, many artifices [6] employed, to weaken in your minds the conviction of this truth; as this is the point in your political fortress against which the batteries of internal and external enemies will be most constantly and actively (though often covertly and insidiously [7]) directed, it is of infinite moment [8] that you should properly estimate the immense value of your national union to your collective and individual happiness; that you should cherish a cordial, habitual, and immovable attachment to it; accustoming yourselves to think and speak of it as of the palladium [9] of your political safety and prosperity; watching for its preservation with jealous anxiety; discountenancing whatever may suggest even a suspicion that it can in any event be abandoned; and indignantly frowning upon the first dawning of every attempt to alienate any portion of our country from the rest, or to enfeeble the sacred ties which now link together the various parts.

For this you have every inducement of sympathy and interest. Citizens, by birth or choice, of a common country, that country has a right to concentrate your affections.[10] The name of America, which belongs to you, in your national capacity, must always exalt the just pride of patriotism, more than any appellation [11] derived from local discriminations. With slight shades of difference, you have the same religion, manners, habits, and political principles. You have in a common cause fought and triumphed together; the independence and liberty you possess are the work of joint counsels and joint efforts, of common dangers, sufferings and successes.

But these considerations, however powerfully they address themselves to your sensibility,[12] are greatly outweighed by those which apply more immediately to your interest. Here every

---

[6] ARTIFICES—Devices, stratagems, wiles.

[7] INSIDIOUSLY—By a stealthy treachery.

[8] MOMENT—Consequence, importance.

[9] PALLADIUM—Safeguard. In classical mythology, the palladium was a statute of Pallas Athene in the citadel of ancient Troy. It was believed that the safety of Troy depended upon this statute.

[10] TO CONCENTRATE YOUR AFFECTIONS—That is, to demand that your affections be centered upon it.

[11] APPELLATION—Name. Washington alludes to the pride which some of his contemporaries took in being called Virginians or New Yorkers.

[12] SENSIBILITY—Feelings, sentiment.

portion of our country finds the most commanding motives for carefully guarding and preserving the union of the whole.

The North, in an unrestrained intercourse with the South, protected by the equal laws of a common government, finds in the productions of the latter great additional resources of maritime and commercial enterprise and precious materials of manufacturing industry. The South in the same intercourse, benefiting by the agency of the North, sees its agriculture grow and its commerce expand. Turning partly into its own channels the seamen of the North, it finds its particular navigation invigorated; and, while it contributes in different ways to nourish and increase the general mass of the national navigation, it looks forward to the protection of a maritime strength, to which itself is unequally adapted. The East, in a like intercourse with the West, already finds, and in the progressive improvement of interior communications [13] by land and water will more and more find, a valuable vent for the commodities which it brings from abroad, or manufactures at home. The West derives from the East supplies requisite to its growth and comfort, and, what is perhaps of still greater consequence, it must of necessity owe the secure enjoyment of indispensable outlets for its own productions to the weight, influence, and the future maritime strength of the Atlantic side of the Union, directed by an indissoluble community of interest as one nation. Any other tenure [14] by which the West can hold this essential advantage, whether derived from its own separate strength or from an apostate and unnatural connection [15] with any foreign power, must be intrinsically precarious.[16]

While, then, every part of our country thus feels an immedi-

[13] INTERIOR COMMUNICATION—Roads and canals. It is said that the first man who really saw the future of canal communication was Washington. The idea of a canal between the Chesapeake and Ohio Rivers seems to have originated with him. What seems to be the first canal in the United States was built around the rapids of the Connecticut River at South Hadley, Massachusetts, in 1793.

[14] TENURE—Terms.

[15] APOSTATE . . . CONNECTION—A connection made by forsaking previous associations. Washington alludes here to attempts on the part of Spain to induce the territories of Kentucky and Tennessee to forsake the United States and transfer their allegiance to Spain, offering as an inducement an outlet for their produce at New Orleans. He also seems to have had in mind the agitation in the southwest territories to set up an independent government which could treat with Spain for commercial privileges.

[16] PRECARIOUS—Insecure.

ate and particular interest in union, all the parts combined cannot fail to find in the united mass of means and efforts greater strength, greater resource, proportionably greater security from external danger, a less frequent interruption of their peace by foreign nations, and, what is of inestimable value, they must derive from union an exemption from those broils and wars between themselves, which so frequently afflict neighboring countries not tied together by the same governments, which their own rivalships alone would be sufficient to produce, but which opposite foreign alliances, attachments, and intrigues would stimulate and embitter. Hence, likewise, they will avoid the necessity of those overgrown military establishments which, under any form of government, are inauspicious to liberty, and which are to be regarded as particularly hostile to republican liberty. In this sense it is that your union ought to be considered as a main prop of your liberty, and that the love of the one ought to endear to you the preservation of the other.

These considerations speak a persuasive language to every reflecting and virtuous mind, and exhibit the continuance of the Union as a primary object of patriotic desire. Is there a doubt whether a common government can embrace so large a sphere?[17] Let experience solve it. To listen to mere speculation[18] in such a case were criminal. We are authorized to hope that a proper organization of the whole, with the auxiliary agency of governments for the respective subdivisions, will afford a happy issue to the experiment. It is well worth a fair and full experiment. With such powerful and obvious motives to union, affecting all parts of our country, while experience shall not have demonstrated its impracticability, there will always be reason to distrust the patriotism of those who in any quarter may endeavor to weaken its bands.

In contemplating the causes which may disturb our Union, it occurs as a matter of serious concern, that any ground should have been furnished for characterizing parties by geographical discriminations Northern and Southern, Atlantic and Western; whence designing men may endeavor to excite a belief that there

[17] EMBRACE SO LARGE A SPHERE—Washington alludes here to the doubt expressed by many in his day that a republican form of government could be made to work over so great a territory as that which lay between the Mississippi and the Atlantic Ocean.
[18] MERE SPECULATION—Mere theorizing.

is a real difference of local interests and views. One of the expedients of party to acquire influence, within particular districts, is to misrepresent the opinions and aims of other districts. You cannot shield yourselves too much against the jealousies and heart-burnings which spring from these misrepresentations; they tend to render alien to each other those who ought to be bound together by fraternal affection.

[Here Washington further warns against parties based on geographical divisions; enlarges on the necessity of union; urges respect for existing laws; declares that any attempt to act contrary to existing laws is destructive of government; and pleads against the "spirit of innovation."]

III

I HAVE already intimated to you the danger of parties in the State, with particular reference to the founding of them on geographical discrimination. Let me now take a more comprehensive view, and warn you in the most solemn manner against the baneful effects of the spirit of party,[1] generally.

This spirit, unfortunately, is inseparable from our nature, having its root in the strongest passions of the human mind. It exists under different shapes in all governments, more or less stifled, controlled, or repressed; but in those of the popular form it is seen in its greatest rankness, and is truly their worst enemy.

The alternate domination of one faction over another, sharpened by the spirit of revenge, natural to party dissension, which in different ages and countries has perpetrated the most horrid enormities,[2] is itself a frightful despotism. But this leads at length to a more formal and permanent despotism. The disorders and miseries which result, gradually incline the minds of

---

[1] BANEFUL EFFECTS OF THE SPIRIT OF PARTY—Washington himself suffered much from what he called the "baneful effects of party." According to Bassett, he was charged by the Republicans with "betraying the pledge given to France, and taking more salary than was allotted to him. His mail was even tampered with, in the hope of finding political matters of advantage to his opponents, and a most shameful forgery of letters in 1777 was searched out and reprinted as genuine. He was sensitively devoted to official integrity, and all these attacks cut him to the quick."

[2] MOST HORRID ENORMITIES—Washington had in mind very likely the excesses to which party rivalry led in the French Revolution, and also the proscriptions in Rome under Marius and Sulla.

men to seek security and repose in the absolute power of an individual;[3] and sooner or later the chief of some prevailing faction, more able or more fortunate than his competitors, turns this disposition to the purposes of his own elevation, on the ruins of public liberty.

Without looking forward to an extremity of this kind (which nevertheless ought not to be entirely out of sight), the common and continued mischiefs of the spirit of party are sufficient to make it the interest and duty of a wise people to discourage and restrain it.

It serves always to distract the public councils, and enfeeble the public administration. It agitates the community with ill-founded jealousies and false alarms; kindles the animosity of one part against another, foments occasionally riot and insurrection. It opens the doors to foreign influence and corruption, which find a facilitated access to the government itself through the channels of party passions. Thus the policy and the will of one country are subjected to the policy and will of another.

There is an opinion, that parties in free countries are useful checks upon the administration of the government, and serve to keep alive the spirit of liberty. This within certain limits is probably true, and in governments of a monarchical cast, patriotism may look with indulgence, if not with favor, upon the spirit of party. But in those of the popular character, in governments purely elective, it is a spirit not to be encouraged. From their natural tendency, it is certain there will always be enough of that spirit for every salutary purpose. And there being constant danger of excess, the effort ought to be, by force of public opinon to mitigate and assuage it. A fire not to be quenched, it demands a uniform vigilance to prevent its bursting into a flame, lest, instead of warming, it should consume.

[3] THE DISORDERS . . . INDIVIDUAL—The rise of Napoleon is a good illustration of this statement, but it is to be questioned if Washington had Napoleon in mind. It is more likely that he was thinking of such men as Marius, Sulla, and Julius Cæsar.

IV

IT IS important, likewise, that the habits of thinking in a free country should inspire caution, in those intrusted with its administration, to confine themselves within their respective constitutional spheres, avoiding in the exercise of the powers of one department to encroach upon another.[1] The spirit of encroachment tends to consolidate the powers of all the departments in one, and thus to create, whatever the form of government, a real despotism. A just estimate of that love of power, and proneness to abuse it, which predominates in the human heart, is sufficient to satisfy us of the truth of this position. The necessity of reciprocal checks[2] in the exercise of political power, by dividing and distributing it into different depositories and constituting each the guardian of the public weal against invasions by the others, has been evinced by experiments ancient and modern, some of them in our country and under our own eyes.[3] To preserve them must be as necessary as to institute them. If, in the opinion of the people, the distribution or modification of the constitutional powers be in any particular wrong, let it be corrected by an amendment in the way which the Constitution designates. But let there be no change by usurpation; for, though this, in one instance, may be the instrument of good, it is the customary weapon by which free governments are destroyed. The precedent must always greatly overbalance in permanent evil any partial or transient benefit which the use can at any time yield.

[1] TO CONFINE . . . ENCROACH UPON ANOTHER—Washington here alludes, of course, to the danger which would follow upon permitting one department of the government, say for example, the executive, to usurp the powers of the legislative and judicial branches. In the course of our history Congress has shown itself very jealous of its privileges. Possibly Washington himself had in mind a resolution of the House of Representatives passed in March, 1796, requesting him to lay before the House "a copy of the instructions to the minister of the United States, who negotiated the treaty with the King of Great Britain, together with the correspondence and other documents relative to that treaty."

[2] RECIPROCAL CHECKS—Washington here refers to such constitutional checks as the following: (1) the President may make no appointments to office without the advice and consent of the Senate; (2) the laws made by Congress may be declared unconstitutional by the Supreme Court; (3) the President is given the power of veto. Can you give other illustrations of the division of power under our government?

[3] IN OUR OWN COUNTRY AND UNDER OUR OWN EYES—As a matter of fact, those things in our Constitution which have worked well had been in operation in various colonial governments before the separation from England.

V

OF ALL the dispositions and habits which lead to political prosperity, religion and morality are indispensable supports. In vain would that man claim the tribute of patriotism, who should labor to subvert these great pillars of human happiness, these firmest props of the duties of men and citizens. The mere politician equally with the pious man ought to respect and to cherish them. A volume could not trace all their connections with private and public felicity. Let it simply be asked, Where is the security for property, for reputation, for life, if the sense of religious obligation desert the oaths, which are the instruments of investigation in courts of justice? And let us with caution indulge the supposition, that morality can be maintained without religion. Whatever may be conceded to the influence of refined education on minds of peculiar structure, reason and experience [1] both forbid us to expect, that national morality can prevail in exclusion of religious principle.

It is substantially true that virtue or morality is a necessary spring of popular government. The rule, indeed, extends with more or less force to every species of free government. Who, that is a sincere friend to it, can look with indifference upon attempts to shake the foundation of the fabric?

Promote, then, as an object of primary importance, institutions for the general diffusion of knowledge.[2] In proportion as the structure of a government gives force to public opinion, it is essential that public opinion should be enlightened.

As a very important source of strength and security, cherish public credit. One method of preserving it is, to use it as sparingly as possible; avoiding occasions of expense by cultivating peace, but remembering also that timely disbursements to prepare for danger frequently prevent much greater disbursements to repel it; avoiding likewise the accumulation of debt, not only by shunning occasions of expense, but by vigorous exertion in time of peace to discharge the debts, which unavoidable wars may have occasioned, not ungenerously throwing upon

[1] EXPERIENCE—Washington no doubt had in mind the attempt made by the French Revolutionists to abolish both God and religion and to set up a rule of reason. We have seen a similar thing attempted in our day in revolutionary Russia.

[2] DIFFUSION OF KNOWLEDGE—Washington once wrote "It has always been a source of serious reflection and sincere regret with me, that the youth of the United States should be sent to foreign countries for purposes of education." When he was preparing his *Farewell Address*, he wrote Hamilton asking him to introduce into the *Address* a section expressive of his sentiments on education. See *The Authorship of the Address*.

posterity the burden which we ourselves ought to bear. The execution of these maxims belongs to your representatives, but it is necessary that public opinion should coöperate. To facilitate to them the performance of their duty it is essential that you should practically bear in mind, that towards the payment of debts there must be revenue; that to have revenue there must be taxes; that no taxes can be devised which are not more or less inconvenient and unpleasant; that the intrinsic embarrassment, inseparable from the selection of the proper objects (which is always a choice of difficulties), ought to be a decisive motive for a candid construction of the conduct of the government in making it, and for a spirit of acquiescence in the measures for obtaining revenue which the public exigencies may at any time dictate.

VI

OBSERVE good faith and justice towards all nations; cultivate peace and harmony with all. Religion and morality enjoin this conduct; and can it be, that good policy does not equally enjoin it? It will be worthy of a free, enlightened, and at no distant period a great nation, to give to mankind the magnanimous and too novel example of a people always guided by an exalted justice and benevolence. Who can doubt that in the course of time and things, the fruits of such a plan would richly repay any temporary advantages, which might be lost by a steady adherence to it? Can it be that Providence has not connected the permanent felicity of a nation with its virtue? The experiment, at least, is recommended by every sentiment which ennobles human nature. Alas! is it rendered impossible by its vices?

In the execution of such a plan, nothing is more essential than that permanent, inveterate antipathies against particular nations, and passionate attachments[1] for others, should be excluded; and that, in place of them, just and amicable feelings towards all should be cultivated. The nation which indulges

---

[1] ANTIPATHIES . . . ATTACHMENTS—Washington here alludes to the pro-British sympathies of the Federalists and the pro-French sympathies of the Republicans which had heightened the bitter party strife of his two administrations.

towards another an habitual hatred, or an habitual fondness, is in some degree a slave. It is a slave to its animosity or to its affection, either of which is sufficient to lead it astray from its duty and its interest. Antipathy in one nation against another disposes each more readily to offer insult and injury, to lay hold of slight causes of umbrage, and to be haughty and intractable when accidental or trifling occasions of dispute occur. Hence, frequent collisions, obstinate, envenomed, and bloody contests. The nation, prompted by ill-will[2] and resentment, sometimes impels to war the government, contrary to the best calculations of policy. The government sometimes participates in the national propensity, and adopts through passion what reason would reject; at other times, it makes the animosity of the nation subservient to projects of hostility instigated by pride, ambition, and other sinister and pernicious motives. The peace often, sometimes perhaps the liberty, of nations has been the victim.

So likewise, a passionate attachment of one nation for another produces a variety of evils. Sympathy for the favorite nation, facilitating the illusion of an imaginary common interest in cases where no real common interest exists, and infusing into one the enmities of the other, betrays the former, into a participation in the quarrels and wars of the latter, without adequate inducement or justification. It leads also to concessions to the favorite nation of privileges denied to others, which is apt doubly to injure the nation making the concessions, by unnecessarily parting with what ought to have been retained, and by exciting jealousy, ill-will, and a disposition to retaliate, in the parties from whom equal privileges are withheld. And it gives to ambitious, corrupted, or deluded citizens (who devote themselves to the favorite nation), facility to betray or sacrifice the interests of their own country, without odium, sometimes even with popularity; gilding with the appearances of a virtuous sense of obligation, a commendable deference for public opinion, or a laudable zeal for public good, the base or foolish compliances of ambition, corruption, or infatuation.

---

[2] THE NATION, PROMPTED BY ILL-WILL—In this and the following paragraph Washington is making allusions, no doubt, to the party strife which made it so difficult for our government to maintain neutrality in the war between England and France.

As avenues to foreign influence in innumerable ways such attachments are particularly alarming to the truly enlightened and independent patriot. How many opportunities do they afford to tamper with domestic factions, to practice the arts of seduction, to mislead public opinion, to influence or awe the public councils! Such an attachment of a small or weak, towards a great and powerful nation, dooms the former to be the satellite of the latter.

Against the insidious wiles of foreign influence (I conjure you to believe me, fellow citizens), the jealousy of a free people ought to be constantly awake, since history and experience prove that foreign influence is one of the most baneful foes of republican government. But that jealousy, to be useful, must be impartial; else it becomes the instrument of the very influence to be avoided, instead of a defense against it. Excessive partiality for one foreign nation, and excessive dislike for another, cause those whom they actuate [3] to see danger only on one side, and serve to veil and even second the arts of influence on the other. Real patriots, who may resist the intrigues of the favorite, are liable to become suspected and odious; while its tools and dupes usurp the applause and confidence of the people, to surrender their interests.

The great rule of conduct for us, in regard to foreign nations, is, in extending our commercial relations, to have with them as little political connection as possible. So far as we have already formed engagements, let them be fulfilled with perfect good faith. Here let us stop.

Europe has a set of primary interests, which to us have none, or a very remote relation. Hence she must be engaged in frequent controversies, the causes of which are essentially foreign to our concerns. Hence, therefore, it must be unwise in us to implicate ourselves, by artificial ties, in the ordinary vicissitudes of her politics, or the ordinary combinations and collisions of her friendships or enmities.

Our detached and distant situation invites and enables us to pursue a different course. If we remain one people, under an efficient government, the period is not far off when we may defy material injury from external annoyance; when we may take

[3] ACTUATE—Influence.

such an attitude as will cause the neutrality, we may at any time resolve upon, to be scrupulously respected; when belligerent nations, under the impossibility of making acquisitions upon us, will not lightly hazard the giving us provocation; when we may choose peace or war, as our interest, guided by justice, shall counsel.

Why forego the advantages of so peculiar a situation? Why quit our own to stand upon foreign ground? Why, by interweaving our destiny with that of any part of Europe, entangle our peace and prosperity in the toils of European ambition, rivalship, interest, humor, or caprice?

It is our true policy to steer clear of permanent alliances with any portion of the foreign world; so far, I mean, as we are now at liberty to do it; for let me not be understood as capable of patronizing infidelity to existing engagements. I hold the maxim no less applicable to public than to private affairs, that honesty is always the best policy. I repeat it, therefore, let those engagements be observed in their genuine sense. But, in my opinion, it is unnecessary and would be unwise to extend them.

Taking care always to keep ourselves, by suitable establishments, on a respectable defensive posture, we may safely trust to temporary alliances for extraordinary emergencies.

Harmony, liberal intercourse with all nations, are recommended by policy, humanity, and interest. But even our commercial policy should hold an equal and impartial hand; neither seeking nor granting exclusive favors or preferences; consulting the natural course of things; diffusing and diversifying by gentle means the streams of commerce, but forcing nothing; establishing with powers so disposed, in order to give trade a stable course, to define the rights of our merchants, and to enable the government to support them, conventional rules of intercourse, the best that present circumstances and mutual opinion will permit, but temporary, and liable to be from time to time abandoned or varied, as experience and circumstances shall dictate; constantly keeping in view, that it is folly in one nation to look for disinterested favors from another; that it must pay with a portion of its independence for whatever it may accept under that character; that, by such acceptance, it may place itself in the condition of having given equivalents for nominal favors, and yet of being reproached with ingratitude for not giving more. There can be no greater error than to expect or calculate upon real favors from nation to nation. It is an illusion, which experience must cure, which a just pride ought to discard.

VII

IN OFFERING to you, my countrymen, these counsels of an old and affectionate friend, I dare not hope they will make the strong and lasting impression I could wish; that they will control the usual current of the passions, or prevent our nation from running the course which has hitherto marked the destiny of nations. But, if I may even flatter myself that they may be productive of some partial benefit, some occasional good; that they may now and then recur to moderate the fury of party spirit, to warn against the mischiefs of foreign intrigue, to guard against the impostures of pretended patriotism; this hope will be a full recompense for the solicitude for your welfare, by which they have been dictated.

How far in the discharge of my official duties I have been guided by the principles which have been delineated,[1] the public records and other evidences of my conduct must witness to you and to the world. To myself, the assurance of my own conscience is, that I have at least believed myself to be guided by them.

In relation to the still subsisting war in Europe,[2] my proclamation of the 22d of April, 1793, is the index of my plan. Sanctioned by your approving voice, and by that of your Representatives in both Houses of Congress, the spirit of that measure has continually governed me, uninfluenced by any attempts to deter or divert me from it.

After deliberate examination, with the aid of the best lights I could obtain, I was well satisfied that our country, under all

---

[1] DELINEATED—Set forth.

[2] STILL SUBSISTING WAR IN EUROPE—The war between France on one hand, and Great Britain and her allies on the other. Washington alludes here to his proclamation of neutrality of April 22, 1793, in the preamble of which he said, "The duty and interest of the United States require, that they should with sincerity and good faith adopt and pursue a conduct friendly and impartial towards the belligerent powers."

the circumstances of the case, had a right to take, and was bound in duty and interest to take, a neutral position. Having taken it, I determined, as far as should depend upon me, to maintain it, with moderation, perseverance and firmness.

The considerations which respect the right to hold this conduct, it is not necessary on this occasion to detail. I will only observe, that, according to my understanding of the matter, that right, so far from being denied by any of the belligerent powers, has been virtually admitted by all.

The duty of holding a neutral conduct may be inferred, without anything more, from the obligation which justice and humanity impose on every nation, in cases in which it is free to act, to maintain inviolate the relations of peace and amity towards other nations.

The inducements of interest for observing that conduct will best be referred to your own reflections and experience. With me a predominant motive has been to endeavor to gain time to our country to settle and mature its yet recent institutions, and to progress without interruption to that degree of strength and consistency which is necessary to give it, humanly speaking, the command of its own fortunes.

Though, in reviewing the incidents of my administration, I am unconscious of intentional error, I am nevertheless too sensible of my defects not to think it probable that I may have committed many errors. Whatever they may be, I fervently beseech the Almighty to avert or mitigate the evils to which they may tend. I shall also carry with me the hope that my country will never cease to view them with indulgence; and that, after forty-five years of my life dedicated to its service with an upright zeal, the faults of incompetent abilities will be consigned to oblivion, as myself must soon be to the mansions of rest.

Relying on its kindness in this as in other things, and actuated by that fervent love towards it, which is so natural to a man who views in it the native soil of himself and his progenitors [3] for several generations, I anticipate with pleasing expectation that retreat, in which I promise myself to realize, without alloy,[4] the

[3] PROGENITORS—Forefathers. John Washington, the great-grandfather of the President, emigrated to Virginia and settled in Westmoreland County in 1658.

[4] WITHOUT ALLOY—That is, wholly.

sweet enjoyment of partaking, in the midst of my fellow citizens, the benign influence of good laws under a free government, the ever favorite object of my heart, and the happy reward, as I trust, of our mutual cares, labors, and dangers.

G Washington

The Origin and Authorship of the *Address:* In the preparation of the *Farewell Address*, Washington had the assistance of both Madison and Hamilton. It is clear, however, that what both of these men did was really no more than what might be intrusted to a competent secretary. In May, 1792, when Washington contemplated retiring from the Presidency, he wrote Madison asking him to prepare a Valedictory Address "expressing in plain and modest terms, that, having been honored with the Presidential chair, and to the best of my abilities contributed to the organization and administration of the government, that having arrived at a period of life when the private walks of it in the shades of retirement become necessary, . . . I take leave of them as a public man." Madison prepared a draft of such an address but of course it was not used. It was quite characteristic of Washington that he should save this unused address. In May, 1796, he had some conversation with Hamilton about the preparation of the address which he finally gave to the public and Hamilton prepared a first draft. Washington gave to Hamilton, Madison's draft and also a paper entitled "Hints and Heads of Topics" which was to be a kind of outline for Hamilton. After several letters on the matter in the course of which Washington made a number of suggestions and corrections, a draft of the *Farewell Address* as it now stands was produced.

To say that Hamilton wrote an address for Washington to deliver is no more true than to say that a stenographer who takes a letter is the author of it. The opening paragraphs of the *Address* owe something to Madison. It was Washington, however, who carefully revised and criticized what Hamilton wrote. Washington who was really a most diffident person was well aware that his grammar and his spelling were his weak points. It would be interesting to know to what extent this diffidence was responsible for his asking Madison and Hamilton to do the actual phrasing of the *Address*.

On the question: Was Washington the author of his *Farewell Address*, see the *Forum*, Volume 27, pages 145–155.

Suggestions for Study: *Part I:* Does Washington feel that he is neglecting his country by refusing to be a candidate for a third term? Has his example established a powerful tradition in American public life? Compare his declination with that of the late President Coolidge. Are there any other evidences than his present declaration which prove that he was "reluctantly drawn" from retirement? Why does he feel that he is entitled to withdraw at this time? Was Washington supported by the "steadfast confidence" of the nation? What personal characteristics does he exhibit in the first part of the *Address?* What are his wishes for the country which called him "father"?

Part II: Had Washington any reason to suppose that his counsels would be given a hearing by his countrymen? Had the unity of government, which he considers so essential, always been "dear" to them? Why does Washington emphasize the importance of national unity? Have Americans to-day "the same religion, manners, habits, and political principles"? What are some of the causes which have produced these changed conditions? Are common dangers the only forces adequate to unite peoples? Has Washington any reason for mentioning the various sections of the country by name, and for pointing out to them the advantages of a "Union of the whole"? In warning against an "unnatural connection" has he any particular "foreign power" in mind?

List the advantages of union which Washington sets forth. Can you add to them? Was there at the time doubt "whether a common government can embrace so large a sphere"? Is there to-day? Washington terms the American Union an "experiment." Has it emerged from that state, or is it still an experiment? Is there still "reason to distrust the patriotism of those who in any quarter may endeavor to weaken its bands"?

Part III: Are Washington's words to be here interpreted as a warning against political parties? What was the political situation at this time? What was Washington's attitude toward political parties? What is the present attitude? Contrast the party situation in the United States with that in certain European countries. Which is better? Why? Does the United States need a new alignment of political parties? Why? Is this, in your judgment, likely to take place within the near future? Is it now taking place by slow evolution? Does party feeling run as high as it used to? Does it run high enough?

Part IV: Is the love of power universal, as Washington suggests? And do those who exercise it tend to abuse it? Is political power the only kind which is exercised to-day? Have the checks upon the abuse of power devised by the makers of the Constitution always operated in the manner they intended? Has the power of the executive grown disproportionately great? Has the judicial branch arrogated to itself any powers not contemplated in the Constitution? Is there, in general, to-day a tendency toward strong, central governments—possibly dictatorships— or toward the diffusion of powers and direct popular government? Cite examples from our own history, and that of other nations.

Part V: What is the American doctrine of the relation of the church and the state? Are we always consistent in our application of this doctrine? Has history any examples of nations which have been hostile to religion? With what results? Is there to-day any state which has adopted an attitude toward religion which is radically different from most? What, in your judgment, will be the outcome of this attitude? Would Washington approve of the agencies of popular education which we have to-day? Have we followed his advice with regard to public credit? Is there a tendency ungenerously to "throw upon posterity the burden which we ourselves ought to bear"? How may this be done?

Part VI: Are religion and morality the only forces which to-day are making for peace? Does war pay? Was the late President Wilson echoing Washington's words when he said—prior to America's entrance into the World War—that a nation might be "too proud to fight"? Are we, as a people, prone to any special antipathies or attachments? Have these colored our official actions? Have we seen in our own time any examples of "the insidious wiles of foreign influence"? Summarize Washington's rule for dealing with foreign nations. Have we always followed his counsel in this respect? Have our relations with Europe changed since 1796? Trace this development and its causes. Is it still true that "Europe has a set of primary interests which to us have none, or a very remote, relation"? Is our situation as "distant and detached" as when Washington uttered these words? What has brought about the change? Is Washington's counsel an argument for or against our joining the League of Nations? Would it be fair to quote it in a debate on that subject? Despite its failure to join the League, is the United States interesting itself in Europe in any way? How?

Part VII: Trace Washington's career as a public servant during the forty-five years which he says he has dedicated to public life. Did he commit "many errors" during his two administrations? Summarize the chief events of his presidency. Is he right in saying that he has served his country with an "upright zeal"? What is the verdict of history upon his public career?

The Address as a Whole: Allowing for differences in the manner of writing between our own and Washington's time, what is the general tone of the *Address?* From the reading of it do you get a portrait of Washington, both as a man and as a public servant? Referring to definite portions of the *Address,* point out the characteristics of Washington which they reveal. Have the counsels of the *Address* proved wise in the light of history? What influence did the publication of the *Address* have upon American policies, either domestic or foreign? Compare the sentence structure in Washington's address with that in Patrick Henry's speech. Explain the difference.

Exercises and Creative Work: Compare or contrast the United States of Washington's day with the same country to-day, touching, among others, upon the following points:

1. The character and extent of the territory now comprising the United States.
2. The increase in population and its changed character.
3. The changed character of the South and West since 1796.
4. Reasons for the very rapid growth in territory and increase in population.
5. The attitude of the people toward the Federal government.
6. The spirit in which the Constitution is regarded.
7. The power of the executive.
8. Political parties then and now.
9. The United States in its relations to Europe.

If Washington were living to-day, what do you think his attitude would be toward the following? Give reasons for your beliefs, referring, where possible, to definite passages in the *Address:*

1. The League of Nations and the World Court.
2. Legislation in behalf of the farmers of the Middle West.
3. The development of aviation.
4. A Federal department of education.
5. A third term for the president.
6. The army and navy.
7. The entry of the United States into the World War.
8. The development of the merchant marine.
9. Government control of business and industry.

Choose an important national topic of to-day, and paraphrase a part of Washington's address to meet the topic.

Do you agree with the following statements made by Washington in the *Farewell Address?* Give your reasons for endorsing or opposing these views:

1. "Foreign influence is one of the most baneful foes of republican government."
2. "Let me now . . . warn you in the most solemn manner against the baneful effects of the spirit of party."
3. "Europe has a set of primary interests which to us have none, or a very remote, relation."
4. "It is our true policy to steer clear of any permanent alliances with any part of the foreign world."
5. "Citizens by birth or choice of a common country, that country has a right to concentrate your affections."
6. "Timely disbursements to prepare for danger frequently prevent much greater disbursements to repel it."

Write the Farewell Address which Washington would now compose if he were retiring from the Presidency to-day. (This may be divided among a number of individuals, or assigned to committees.)

EULOGY ON GEORGE WASHINGTON

John Carroll

Historical Background: [1] By a singular felicity that has more than a passing significance to the Catholic heart, the two founders and fathers of our political government and of our established hierarchical jurisdiction—George Washington, first President of the United States, and John Carroll, first Bishop of the Catholic Church in the American Republic—were not only contemporaries but to a remarkable extent men of the same constructive statesmanship.

The lives of both Carroll and Washington ran along smoothly enough up to 1773, when to each there came what may be called the most serious crisis in his career. Washington's honest loyalty to the motherland was being brought gradually to the breaking-point owing to the accumulation of grievances caused by the political and commercial attitude of the English Parliament towards the American colonists. The end of the year found him, together with the leading citizens of Virginia and Massachusetts, face to face with the imperative duty of deciding upon separation from England. A crisis not dissimilar in its nature had come to John Carroll, then a teacher in the English Jesuit College at Bruges. Three months after the papal decree *Dominus ac Redemptor noster* was promulgated (August 16, 1773) suppressing the Society of Jesus, occurred the first direct act of rebellion in the American colonies—the Boston Tea Party of December sixteenth. Delegates to the First Continental Congress were being chosen by the colonies during the summer of 1774, when John Carroll, "a care-worn man of forty, destitute of fortune, and disappointed in the hopes he had formed for the triumph of religion, to be achieved by the Society to which he had pledged his faith forever," set sail for the land of his birth. During the rest of the year after his arrival (June 26, 1774) in Maryland, up to the Declaration of Independence, John Carroll followed with growing anxiety the illiberal attitude towards the Catholic Church as expressed in the earliest state papers issued by the Continental Congress; but he was buoyed up at the same time with the hope that the presence of his kinsman, Charles Carroll of Carrollton, who was chosen to represent Maryland on July 4, 1776, in the Congress, would gradually alleviate the religious anxieties of the Fathers of the Republic.

It is needless to say that from the moment George Washington took supreme command of the American forces (June 15, 1775), he was the heart-centre of the rebellion. Every Catholic heart in the colonies must have taken courage when on November 5, 1775, Washington destroyed for

---

[1] The material for this historical background is taken, with the kind permission of the publishers, from the excellent foreword written by the Reverend Peter Guilday, Ph.D., for an edition of Bishop Carroll's "Eulogy on Washington," published by P. J. Kenedy & Sons in 1931.

all time "that ridiculous and childish custom of burning the effigy of the Pope" by issuing an order which characterized the annual Guy Fawkes celebration as a monstrous insult to the Catholics of the rebelling colonies and of Canada.

No one in the colonies rejoiced more over the alliance with France which followed upon the victory of Saratoga on October 17, 1777, than John Carroll and his brethren in the Catholic priesthood who had spent many years in France as students and educators. News travelled slowly in those days owing to the war upon the sea, and it may have been long after independence had been won that Carroll and his fellow-priests learned of the magnificent generosity of the French clergy who voted unanimously on May 29, 1780, the sum of thirty million *livres* to the royal treasury, in order that the government of Louis XVI might not be financially hampered in its cooperation with the American rebellion. That generosity can never be disassociated from the glorious conclusion of the war the following October at Yorktown; for undoubtedly the Catholic subsidy of 1780 made possible Count De Grasse's victory over the British fleet off the Virginian Capes on September 5, 1781, and made equally possible the presence of over nine thousand French soldiers among the land forces surrounding Cornwallis.

There were ninety Catholic chaplains on the twenty-four ships of Admiral De Grasse's fleet, and some of these priests who decided to remain in the United States later came under John Carroll's jurisdiction.

Washington's allies and friends were so predominantly Catholic that even Yorktown with its French fleet, Catholic chaplains, and French soldiers who outnumbered the loyal Americans, is no surprise. Nor was it a surprise to Catholics of that day, when six years later Washington took his place as presiding officer of the Constitutional Convention, to find written into the immortal document which made us a more perfect union those basic principles of Christian equality which had been denied to their forefathers in all English-speaking lands from the days of Elizabeth.

On April 29, 1789, Washington took the oath of office as first President of the United States. On November 6, 1789, Pope Pius VI named John Carroll first Bishop of Baltimore with spiritual jurisdiction over all the Catholics in the new Republic. During the five years of his Prefectship (1784–1789) John Carroll succeeded in creating a compact ecclesiastical organization of his flock, scattered from Maine to the Middle West, at a time when we were passing through a political crisis far more perilous than the war itself.

The cordial relations existing between Washington and John Carroll are clearly revealed in an address (included in Doctor Guilday's foreword, but too long to quote here) presented to the newly elected President by a group of prominent Catholics under the leadership of Bishop Carroll. Washington had already received letters from many representatives of the religious bodies in the new Republic, and he had replied in Christian sentiments to all these formal addresses. There is, however, in his reply to the American Catholics a note which is quite different. The letter was indeed addressed to them; but the lesson of the message was addressed to the larger audience of the entire nation:

"As Mankind becomes more liberal, they will be more apt to allow, that all those who conduct themselves worthy members of the Community, are equally entitled to the protection of Civil Government. I hope ever to see America among the foremost Nations in examples of Justice and Liberality. And I presume that your fellow-citizens will not forget the patriotic part, which you took in the accomplishment of their Revolution, and the establishment of their Government—or the important assistance which they received from a Nation, in which the Roman Catholic Faith is professed." [2]

George Washington's second term ended in March, 1797, and he returned to Mount Vernon to spend his remaining days in the peace and quiet he craved so much. Two years later, after a short illness, on December 14, 1799, he passed away.

On December 29, 1799, Bishop Carroll issued to his clergy a circular letter, requesting their cooperation with Congress in holding February 22, 1800, as a day of national mourning for the great leader. On that day he himself delivered the eulogy which is reprinted here, in St. Peter's Church, then the pro-Cathedral of Baltimore.

[The spelling and punctuation used in this volume is that of Doctor Guilday's edition, published by P. J. Kenedy & Sons, 1931, except that in Doctor Guilday's version the archaic form of the letter s (f) was retained. (Editor's Note)]

1   WHEN the death of men distinguished by superior talents, high endowments, and eminent services to their country, demands the expression of public mourning and grief; their loss is accompanied generally with this mitigation, that, however grievous and painful, it is not irreparable; and that the void, caused by their mortality, will perhaps be filled up by others, uniting equal abilities with the same zeal and watchfulness for the general welfare. Hope then wipes off the tears, with which sorrow bedews the grave of departed worth. But on the present occasion, no such consolation can be administered; for he, whose expectations are most sanguine, dares not promise again to his country the union of so many splendid and useful virtues, as adorned that illustrious Man, whose memory excites our grateful and tender sensibility, and to whose tomb the homage of his country is to be solemnly offered on this day. Whether we consult our own experience, by bringing into

[2] NATION—France.

comparison with Washington, any of our contemporaries, most eminent for their talents, virtues and services; or whether we search through the pages of history, to discover in them a character of equal fame; justice and truth will acknowledge, that he stands supereminent and unrivalled in the annals of mankind; and that no one before him, acting in such a variety of new and arduous situations, bore with him to the grave a reputation as clear from lawless ambition, and as undefiled by injustice or oppression; a reputation, neither depressed by indolence, nor weakened by irresolution, nor shadowed by those imperfections, which seemed to be the essential appendages of human nature, till providence exhibited in Washington this extraordinary phenomenon.

2   What language can be equal to the excellence of such a character? what proportion can exist between eloquence, and the tribute of praise, due to so much virtue? Nevertheless, my fellow citizens, I read in the eagerness of your attention, your desire to offer this tribute: Methinks I hear your filial piety, your tender reverence for your best friend, the Father of his country, calling on me to bear for you, at least a feeble testimony of your unextinguishable gratitude for his services, your immortal remembrance of, and veneration for his virtues. In your name therefore, I presume to add some grains of incense to the homage, which throughout the United States every friend to their happiness now presents at the shrine of Washington. Pardon, O departed spirit of the first of Heroes! if with the cold accents of an exhausted imagination, I likewise dare attempt to celebrate thy name, whilst so many sons of genius, ardent in youthful vigour, delineate in glowing colours the vivid features of thy mind, and the glorious deeds of thy virtuous life. With unequal steps I venture on the same career, not seeking to add lustre to the fame of Washington, or perpetuate his memory to future times; for he is already enshrined in the records of immortality: but humbly hoping, that a recital of his services will open to our countrymen the road to true honour, and kindle in their breasts the warmth of generous emulation, and real patriotism. To contribute in this manner to the best interests of his beloved country, will be to him the most gratifying commendation, if in the regions of immortality, human affairs still claim a share of his solicitude.

3   The language uniformly held by Washington, the maxim invariably inculcated and repeated by him in almost every manifestation

of his sentiments, was the acknowledgment of a superintending
providence, preparing, regulating and governing all human events
for the accomplishment of its eternal purposes, and predisposing
the instruments, by which they are to be effected. Religion and
observation had taught him, that God's provident wisdom "reach-
eth from end to end mightily, and disposeth all things sweetly." [3]
He contemplated with Christian piety, and the philosophy of a
Sage, the most remarkable revolutions and occurrencies of former,
as well as his own times; and learned therefrom to refer every
human event to the moral government of a supreme intelligent
Being. This became the polar star, by which he was guided in
his progress through life, and in all his anxious solicitude for
maintaining the liberty, perfecting the policy, preserving the
peace, insuring the stability of his country on the foundations of
order and morality, and guarding it against the turbulence of faction, licentiousness, foreign hostility and artifice.

4   This virtuous maxim of religious, moral, and political wisdom,
which so deeply impressed him, never perhaps was more illustrated, than by the course of providence in preparing and
adapting his body and mind to suit the destinies of his life. He
was to be himself a most luminous proof of that truth which was
so rooted in his soul.

5   That infinite knowledge, which in its comprehensive range
through the whole extent of creation, embraces the future, no less
distinctly, than past and present contingencies, beheld the period
approaching, when this vast portion of America, now constituting
the U. States; this country spread through so many climates;
so diversified in its productions; so abundant in natural resources;
so benefited by land and water; so admirably calculated for the
employment of industry, and for affording subsistance for millions
and millions, was to break the bonds of its antient connection
with G. Britain, and, emancipated from vassalage, elevate itself to
the station of a great, powerful and independent Empire!

6   A convulsion so violent in the political system of Europe and
America, involved the demolition of deeply rooted habits and
opinions. The associations arising out of consanguinity, habitual
intercourse, unity of government, identity of laws, language and
religion were to be melted down, before that wonderful revolution
could be compleated. A new people, unconscious before of their

---

[3] Quotation from *The Book of Wisdom,* chapter 8.

own strength, were to feel in their physical and moral energies the ripeness of manhood. Accustomed to respect the nation, with which they would have to contend, as irresistible in arms, and inexhaustible in resources, they must dare nevertheless to make the vigorous effort, and conceive a reliance on their own native strength. Powerful interests, the necessary effects of long established government, would naturally counteract every tendency toward its downfall; but these interests were to be resisted by force, and borne down by the enthusiastic ardor of patriotism.

7   To superintend the movements, and operations of such a revolution; to controul, during its progress, jealousies, enmities, suspicions, and other conflicting passions; and from their collision, to educe national and individual prosperity, peace, order, liberty and regular government; required the discernment and masterly contrivance of that Supreme Director and Artist, who unites together the links, and holds in his hands the chain of all human events. Contemplating, as much as is allowed to feeble mortals, his divine agency in preparing the means and conducting the progress of the American revolution, we may presume to say, that heaven impressed a character on the life of Washington, and a temper on his soul, which eminently qualified him to bear the most conspicuous part, and be its principal instrument in accomplishing this stupendous work.

8   We trace as far back, as to his early youth, the evidences of this providential interposition. Born in times, and circumstances, unfavourable to the spirit and exertions of bold enterprise, he however soon devoted himself to useful and active exercises. He disdained the inglorious ease, and ignoble pursuits, which fettered, or perverted the talents of his young countrymen; unactive, not thro' choice, but wanting objects and encouragement. To deliver Washington from the danger of contracting similar habits, he was inspired to embrace the hardy discipline of difficult and perilous labours, which added vigour to his constitution, and a robustness to his nerves, that never after shrunk from danger. Following the instinct of his towering genius, he had not reached the years of manhood, when he was engaged in exercises pregnant with terror, and presenting to his view objects of a most formidable aspect. He did not however enter on them with thoughtless temerity. At that early period he began, what he persisted in thro' life, to associate motives of public utility with magnanimous

undertakings. The usual occupations of his young countrymen were not a sufficient employment for his active mind: he therefore turned his views toward that vast Western region, now so familiar to our ears and acquaintance, but then known only by the terrors it inspired, and the cruelties practiced by the savage Indians, lurking in its forests and recesses. He left the endearments of society to explore the courses of rivers, to traverse plains and mountains far beyond the then inhabited frontiers; hoping to discover sources, whence future opulence might flow to his country; to examine the productions, and estimate the fertility of immense tracts, capable of rewarding the industry of thousands, pining in want and oppression in foreign lands; whose descendants might people the wilderness, beautify it by cultivation, and multiply the resources of his native province. In these achievements the heroic youth was to inure himself to hunger and thirst; to lie on the damp earth without any covering, but the spreading branches of the oak, and the canopy of the heavens; to accustom himself to the vicissitudes of seasons, the parching heat, and chilling frost; to herd with the beasts of the forest; to be exposed to the tomahawk and scalping knife; to be surrounded by difficulties, yet never to be disheartened; to meet at every step the image of death, without ever being appalled, or admitting a momentary sentiment of despair.

9   Imagine not my fellow citizens, that this is an ideal and fanciful representation of Washington's youthful years. No; it is faintly, but truely copied from real scenes of his life. Who, on the wing of imagination, has followed him, clambering over the lofty Western mountains, fording unfathomed and rapid rivers, exposing his invaluable life to innumerable accidents of treachery and hostility, without shuddering for his existence, and admiring his cool, collected courage, in conquering obstacles and surmounting danger? Such was the training and education, by which Providence prepared him for the fulfillment of his future destinies.

10   . Far different were the motives, which urged the youth of Sparta and Rome to encounter toils of danger and opposition. They obeyed the institutions of their country; they were stimulated by the goad of aspiring ambition, and a desire of acquiring that false glory, which, in the erroneous opinions of their cotemporaries, attached itself to the men, who carried devastation and carnage into the bowels of neighboring nations. With better views, and

superior courage, Washington penetrated into the inhospitable confines of the savage Indians; that he might render them the abodes of peace, and introduce into their bosom the improvements of civilization. So successfully the guardian angel of this chosen Youth, ministring to the designs of Providence, had infused already into his soul the sweet spirit of benevolence, together with heroical fortitude.

11   For him it was decreed, in the progression of his life, to defend, and ultimately to establish, by just and necessary warfare, the liberties of his country. Providence therefore permitted a train of occurrences to ensue, which served to furnish his mind with the first rudiments of military science, and discipline him to the vigilance and profession of a soldier. At that time, two powerful European nations held North America in their subjection: their territories bordered on each other, and each claimed rights, disallowed by its rival power. One of them, France, sent out a military force and her Indian allies, to occupy posts, deemed to be within the territory of Virginia, and contiguous to the stations, selected by Washington, as best adapted to the protection of his native land: for his intrepidity and local knowledge had already placed him at the head of a small body of his countrymen, collected together to stop the progress of the Invaders. With those he covered the inhabitants from hostile encroachment; he won the confidence of the savage Indian; and conducted a dangerous and intricate negotiation for the suspension of hostilities.

12   But the durable preservation of peace depended not on the counsels of America. England and France[4] transported their enmity to her shores, and covered our country with hostile array. England, confident of her prowess and the discipline of her armies, would not commit the defense of her interests to raw Provincials. Washington's ardent soul suffered him not to remain behind in safety, while the security of his country was at stake. The hand of Providence led him forward, that he might add to his experience and native fortitude. He fought under Braddock;[5] and that ill-fated commander having paid by his death the tribute of his rashness; his army dispirited by defeat, and flying before an enemy flushed with victory; Washington in

---

[4] ENGLAND AND FRANCE—The French and Indian War, 1756–1763.
[5] BRADDOCK—In 1755, before the formal opening of the French and Indian War.

that perilous moment, gathered round him his first companions in arms, and rescued out of the jaws of death the remains of the vanquished battallions. He did more; he stood in the front of danger, and everywhere opposing himself to the merciless savages, ready to burst as a dark cloud, fraught with the thunderbolts of heaven, on a terrified land, he averted the storm, and restored to his trembling country the serenity of hope, and peace.

13   The theatre of war was transported afterwards to distant provinces of America. Then the same all-wise Providence, which had inured him to danger, prepared him for the toils of government, and the important duty of superintending, in his riper years, the political administration of a great and widely extended people. His services in the field had won the confidence of his fellow citizens; they committed to his vigilance and integrity their highest interests in their legislative assembly. In this school he perfected himself in the knowledge of mankind; he observed the contentions of parties, the artifices and conflicts of human passions; he saw the necessity of curbing them by salutary restraints; he studied the complicated science of legislation; he learned to venerate the sanctity of laws, to esteem them as the palladium of civil society, and deeply imbibed this maxim, so important for the Soldier and the Statesman, and which he ever after made the rule of his conduct, that the armed defenders of their country would break up the foundations of social order and happiness, if they availed themselves of the turbulence of war, to violate the rights of private property, and personal liberty.

14   Thus Washington, during the interval of peace, stored his mind with the treasures of political wisdom. The time was approaching for him to expend those treasures on his country's welfare.

15   I need not recapitulate the origin of the discontents between G. Britain, and her American dependencies. Suffice it to say, that America viewed the claims of the parent country, as incompatible with her freedom and happiness. The great soul of Washington revolted at the idea of national degradation; but tempering his ardor with deliberate wisdom, he associated with other Sages of his country, to meditate on her new and critical situation.

16   Here let us pause, fellow citizens, to contemplate this exalted man, revolving in his breast the natural and social rights of human kind; comparing these with actual and impending grievances, and with the obligations of an allegiance due to a long

established government. Had lawless ambition reigned in his breast, he would have decided the public voice for immediate hostility. But in this point also, Providence destined him to leave a memorable and salutary example. He was not dazzled by the prospect of being elevated to the chief command of the military force of America. In his opinion, nothing could justify a recurrence to the sword, and a revolt from established authority, but extreme necessity. All reasonable means of redress should be tried, before a good citizen will dissolve the fabric of government, and expose a people to the convulsive shocks of a revolution, the explosions of which no considerate man can promise himself to regulate, or foresee their termination.

17   A reflection here forces itself upon my mind, which I ought not to withold from my respectable auditors. Would to God, that the principal authors and leaders of the many revolutions, through which unhappy France has passed in the course of a few years, would to God, that they had been influenced by a morality as pure and enlightened, as that of Washington, and his associates in the first Congress! What scenes of carnage and cruelty! what private woes and public calamity would have been spared to that ill-fated country? and how sacred and venerable would have still remained to it the sanctuary of religion?

18   Washington and his colleagues obeying at the same time the dictates of patriotism, and the duty of allegiance, represented their wrongs to their Sovereign, and claimed their rights. On the event of their remonstrance, depended the redress of their grievances; or, if no redress followed, their justification for standing on their defense. Britain would not relent, and all, that remained to America, was submission, or resistance. The election was soon made; every one prepared himself for the awful contest, and all eyes and hopes were turned toward Washington. With universal approbation he was summoned to place himself in the front of danger, and assume supreme military command. The possession of such a citizen, at a moment so critical, was an invaluable treasure, and an animating presage of the favourable issue of the great contest.

19   But far other thoughts absorbed his attention. Modest, as he was eminent in valour and wisdom, he contemplated with mingled emotions of self-diffidence, and generous resolution, the important stake placed in his hands; the subjection or independence; the

vassalage or freedom of an immense territory, destined to be the habitation of countless millions. When therefore, in obedience to the voice of his country, he placed himself at the head of her army, the expressions of his dependence on Providence should never be forgotten. Claiming no personal merit, apprehensive of injuring the public interest through some misconduct; yet trusting to the justice of his cause, and conscious of the purity of his motives, he called upon his fellow citizens to remember, that he depended for success, not upon his own military skill, but on the God of battles, to whom he made his solemn appeal.

20   Washington, now at a period of his highest elevation, drew on him the attention, not only of this Western Continent; but of every European nation. O fellow citizens! what days and years of anxious disquietude revolved over us, whilst we gazed on this splendid luminary, uncertain whether it would shed on its country the effulgence of victory and peace, crowned by liberty; or whether its brightness would be shadowed by the cloud of disaster and defeat?

21   Here language fails: I cannot, I dare not follow the heroic Washington in the career of his military glory. To baffle the stratagems of the ablest Generals, to repel the onset of the bravest, and best disciplined armies, what had America to place in his hands? neither soldiers trained to arms, or accustomed to subjection; nor the implements of war, nor the treasures to purchase them. But the genius of the commander finally supplied every deficiency. He introduced order and discipline; inspired love and confidence; and with these auxiliaries, he kept together uncloathed and unpaid armies, which, under other generals, would perhaps have demanded justice at the point of their bayonets. Always vigilant to foil hostile attempts, he exhausted the resources of the enemy, without suffering them to force him to action. Tender of the blood of his fellow soldiers, and never exposing their lives without cause, or prospect of advantage, humanity was as dear to him, as victory; as his enemies, that fell into his power, always experienced. When a decree of retaliation became necessary to restrain their licentious excesses, with what delicacy, without the least abatement of fortitude, did he save the life of the victim, devoted to atone for the cruelty, that had been committed on an American officer? not however until he had compelled the opposing General to restrain and disavow outrages, that aggravate so much the necessary evils of war. How sacred was his respect to

the civil authority; how effectual his protection of the property
of his fellow citizens? When the generous feelings of the virtuous
and beneficent Lewis,[6] whose deplorable fate should draw tears
of blood from every American heart, sent out his Nobles, and
legions, to combat by his side, the dignity of his manners and
his unassuming merit won their entire confidence: His integrity
and conciliating spirit united, as a band of Brothers, nations before unknown to each other, and totally different in manners,
habits and religion. Their union, of which he was the soul, was
a new omen of victory, and gained for America the prize, for
which she bled and contended; honourable peace and Independence.

22 What but unfading laurels remained now for Washington, after
satisfying his honest ambition, and steering the vessel of the
American republic, through so many storms, into the safe harbour
of liberty and tranquillity? It remained for him to leave this
important lesson to the chiefs of armies, vested with great commands; that magnanimity and true glory consist in laying down
their swords at their country's feet, when the object is attained,
for which alone it was permitted to draw them. It remained for
him, after abdicating public employments, to exhibit in the shade
of retirement those private virtues, which are the true foundations
of national prosperity. Dutiful to this moral principle, Washington, before he left his army, stipulated for no personal reward,
and even refused all that could be offered: Unmindful of himself, he was only sollicitous to obtain for his faithful legions a
generous and liberal acknowledgment of their constancy and
valour. This being effected, as far as it depended on him, he
resigned the insignia of his command to those, from whom he
had received it, and resumed the rank of a private citizen, carrying with him into his domestic retreat, the esteem, respect and
veneration of an admiring world.[7]

23 Here the curtain drops, and seems to close for ever from the
public eye and public duty this wonderful man. His country has
no more right to disturb his calm repose: He has paid super-
abundantly her claim to his services. But the views of providence
over him are not yet compleated: Peace and independence are

[6] THE BENEFICENT LEWIS—King Louis XVI of France, beheaded by the
French Revolutionaries, January, 1793.

[7] On Christmas Eve, 1783, Washington wrote to a friend, "I feel now, however, as I conceive a wearied traveller must do, who, after treading many a painful step with a heavy burthen on his shoulders, is eased of the latter . . ."

obtained; but to preserve them, experience soon made it manifest, that to invigorate with one spirit the vast mass of population throughout the U. States one general superintending government was essentially requisite, which saving the rights of all, should likewise be competent to command the services of all for the public weal; to maintain order within, and repel aggression from abroad; inforce the demands of justice, and infuse over important national acts, dignity, energy, unity of design and execution. Washington's penetration soon discovered the want of such a government, and in a paternal, affectionate address to his countrymen, had bequeathed to them, as a legacy, his earnest recommendation for its establishment.

24   Various causes delayed the execution of this necessary work, till the edifice of American independence, unsupported by its necessary pillars, was crumbling into ruin. Then every friend to his country remembered Washington's fatherly advice; every patriotic hand was ready to prop up the tottering fabric. Wisdom and experience combined to blend in a republican form of government all the advantages, of which other forms are productive, without many of their evils. Our illustrious Deliverer presided at the deliberations, which produced it: The American people besought him once more to quit his beloved retreat, and perfect a work, of which he had been the first founder and a principal architect. The earnestness of their request overpowered his reluctant mind; he could not resist their unanimous wishes, nor could any personal dangers stand in competition with the advancement of general happiness. Yet how immense were his sacrifices! how perilous his hazards! Sacrifices known only to them, who having spent their best years in transactions, that kept every nerve on the stretch, are permitted in the evening of their days to taste of the calm repose of rural felicity, and the solace of domestic endearments. Disheartening was the prospect in venturing again on the agitated ocean of national responsibility. There existed not in the world a name so bright as his: no character stood on such lofty preeminence. Shall he expose these to the capricious fluctuations of popular opinion? Shall he embark, the treasure of a reputation purchased by so many services, on a sea, sown thick with rocks of envy, pride and disappointment? These were sufficient to appall a heart less sublime, and less inflamed with genuine patriotism. But such considerations had no ef-

fect on him, and he took into his hands the helm of the state.

25   What were the effects of his administration? are we not deceived by magical delusion? or is the transformation, which our senses witness, really effected? Have the U. States risen from a lethargic, impoverished, degraded condition to activity, opulence and respect? Does the farmer receive a generous retribution for his industry? does the merchant cover the seas with his ships, conveying to every clime the productions of our native soil? does the public creditor obtain security and payment for his generous reliance on national faith? does justice dispense her equitable awards to every suitor approaching her sanctuary? do distant nations respect the counsels, and solicit the friendship of the U. States? are the natives of every land wafted to our shores, as to a refuge of peace, the residence of true liberty? Yes, fellow citizens, this is not delusion. These are the real effects and monuments of Washington's administration. Yet it was thwarted and embarrassed by internal opposition, and foreign intrigue. Scarce had we tasted of the sweets of peace, enlivened by industry and commerce, when attempts were made to ravish from us these inestimable blessings, and plunge us into the horrors of war: not only of war, but of a war of that kind,[8] which connecting our interests and fate with that of a country, delivered up to anarchy, and a prey to frantic, outrageous passions, would have tended to extinguish amongst us the principles of morality; inflame us with the rage of innovation; intoxicate us with delusive, ruinous theories of government; and most probably, would have substituted them to that excellent constitution, which is, and may it long continue to be! our pride and happiness. But, thanks to thy immortal spirit, O ever dear and venerable Father of thy country! thy wisdom discerned the approaching storm, and thy firmness baffled its violence. Our peace and constitution remain to us, unimpaired. No foreign influence dictated to the counsels of America. She increased in vigour; she rose in character; and by self-government, by keeping herself disentangled from the strifes of contending nations, she evinced herself worthy of her independence.

26   After settling his country in this desirable state, Washington had fulfilled the destinies of that providence, which formed him

[8] A WAR OF THAT KIND—Reference is to the war between France and England, declared in 1793. Washington declared the neutrality of the United States.

for the exalted purpose of diffusing the choicest blessings over millions of men, and preparing the same for millions yet unborn. His wish to bury himself again in the shades of retirement returned to him with redoubled force; to hide, if possible, his greatness from the world; and in the sweet repose of domestic life, diversified however by useful and honourable occupations, to forget his past glory. The last act of his supreme magistracy was to inculcate in most impressive language on his countrymen, or rather on his dearest children, this, his deliberate and solemn advice; to bear incessantly in their minds, that nations and individuals are under the moral government of an infinitely wide and just providence; that the foundations of their happiness are morality and religion; and their union amongst themselves their rock of safety: that to venerate their constitution and its laws is to insure their liberty. Then he took his tender farewell of public employments, devoting the remainder of his precious life to a commendable self-review of it, through all its vicissitudes and agitations; a review, for which every wise man, knowing his accountability to a sovereign Judge, should allot time and make opportunity.

27 After endeavouring thus far to satisfy our common duty to our illustrious Deliverer, before I conclude, I am earnest, my fellow citizens, to leave impressed on you, in strong characters, some principal features of his mind, and furnish you with short memorials of his most remarkable actions, hoping thereby to perpetuate your gratitude, and incite you to emulate his virtues. Happily, to supply my inability, I find this talk executed, as it would seem, by the spirit of prophecy, and in the language of inspiration, in the eighth chapter of *The Book of Wisdom;* where the author's expressions need no comment to appropriate them to Washington. So striking the resemblance! so true is the picture! Here are the words of the inspired writer:

> I purposed, says he, to take wisdom with me to live with me, knowing that she will communicate with me of her good things, and will be a comfort in my care—for her sake I shall have glory among the multitude, and honour with the antient, though I am young; and—I shall be admired in the sight of the mighty, and the faces of princes shall wonder at me.—By the means of her, I shall have immortality, and shall leave behind me an everlasting memory to them, that come after me. I shall set the people in order, and nations shall be subject to me. Terrible kings hearing shall be afraid of me; among the multitude I shall be found good and valiant in war. When I go into my

house, I shall repose myself with her; for her conversation hath no bitterness, nor her company any tediousness, but joy and gladness. Thinking these things with myself, and pondering them in my heart, that to be allied to wisdom, is immortality.—I went about seeking, that I might take her to myself.

28   In this picture, every stroke of the pencil exhibits traits of Washington. The early maturity of his judgment was the fruit of his youthful conferences with wisdom. She initiated him into her counsels, and procured for him love, respect, honour, confidence, authority and command: She enabled him to "set the people in order" by good government, and an impartial, disinterested administration of it; and when, all public duties fulfilled, he "went to his house" to repose himself, "no tediousness" or "bitterness" mingled themselves in their conversation, but "joy and gladness," serenity of mind, and the pleasing prospect of conscious integrity.

29   Providence having preserved and lengthened his days, that he might rear up his country in the infancy of her independence, suffered him now to withdraw himself from the disquietudes of government. He had infused the spirit of his administration into all its departments. His excellent Successor [9] inherited, not only the mantle of his office, but his wisdom, firmness, and love of peace, subordinate only to a determination of never purchasing it, at the price of national dishonour.

30   Washington beheld from his retirement, as the Jewish legislator from the summit of Mount Phasga,[10] the flourishing prosperity of his country. Health sweetened his repose and rural occupations; his body and mind retained their usual vigour. We flattered ourselves with the expectation of his continuing long to retain them: Joy beamed in our hearts, when on every annual revolution, we gratefully hailed this, his auspicious birthday. But, alas! how dark is the cloud, that now overshadows it? The songs of festivity converted into the throbs of mourning! The prayers of thanksgiving for his health and life changed into lamentations for his death! Who feels not for him, as for his dearest friend, his protector and his Father? Whilst he lived, we seemed to

---

[9] SUCCESSOR—John Adams succeeded Washington in the Presidency, his term of office lasting from 1797 to 1801. President Adams was in office at the time Bishop Carroll was speaking.

[10] MOUNT PHASGA—Mount Pisgah, from which Moses viewed the promised land of Canaan.

stand on loftier ground, for breathing the same air, inhabiting the same country, and enjoying the same constitution and laws, as the sublime and magnanimous Washington. He was invested with a glory, that shed a lustre on all around him. For his country's safety, he often had braved death, when clad in her most terrific form; he had familiarised himself with her aspect; at her approaching to cut the thread of his life, he beheld her with constancy and serenity; and with his last breath, as we may believe from knowing the ruling passion of his soul, he called to heaven to save his country, and recommended it to the continual protection of that Providence, which he so reverently adored. May his prayer have been heard! May these United States flourish in pure and undefiled religion, in morality, peace, union, liberty and the enjoyment of their excellent Constitution, as long as respect, honour, and veneration shall gather round the name of Washington; that is, whilst there shall be any surviving record of human events.

By Way of Appreciation: In *The Life and Times of John Carroll* Doctor Guilday calls this eulogy of George Washington "the best specimen of Carroll's eloquence." Certainly two of Webster's essentials for an oration were present: the subject was the Father of the American Republic (a French visitor in America in 1783 says "The Americans, that cool and sedate people . . . are roused, animated, and inflamed at the very mention of his name"); the occasion was the gathering of a large and distinguished audience on "a day appointed by the State of Maryland as a day of general mourning for the death of General Washington and for a solemn tribute of respect to his memory." Would the *man* be equal to the subject and to the occasion? That, no doubt, was the question in the minds of many of those waiting in St. Peter's Church, Baltimore, for Bishop John Carroll to mount the pulpit. Those who knew Bishop Carroll, however, did not doubt for a minute that he would be worthy of the occasion; they had heard his eloquence before; they knew his unbounded admiration for Washington; they knew that his sincere devotion to Washington's memory would fire his words with unusual persuasiveness. They were not disappointed. Neither will you be disappointed if, making due allowances for the somewhat flamboyant style of oratory then popular, you will put yourself in the position of an expectant auditor in that old pro-Cathedral in Baltimore almost a hundred and fifty years ago, listening to one who knew Washington well, eulogize his career and trace throughout that career the guiding hand of a benevolent Providence.

Suggestions for Study: *The Address as a Whole:* Has the reading of this address in any way changed your appreciation of Washington? In what way? Unless the eulogy of a great man's career has a single theme binding together the several parts of his life story, it does not satisfy. What is the unifying theme in this eulogy of Washington? Why is it the kind of theme you would expect from one in Bishop Carroll's position? Where in the address does it first appear? Where is it referred to for the last time? Point out at least five other references to it in the body of the speech.

Find examples of periodic sentences which give power and sweep to Carroll's language. Let each member of the class select what he considers the most powerful paragraph in the speech, analyze it, and defend his choice. Styles in oratory change with the times. Does Bishop Carroll employ any oratorical devices which would not appeal to a present-day audience?

The Address in More Detail: By what method of paragraph development does Bishop Carroll, at the very opening of his address, pay Washington superlative praise? What makes him diffident about assuming the role of eulogist of Washington? What does he declare to be the purpose of his eulogy?

What virtuous maxim did Washington almost invariably inculcate in his public utterances? What striking example is brought forward in support of Washington's strong belief in the rule of Providence? What bearing on the general theme have the paragraphs which describe the richness of our country and the violence involved in the political upheaval of the Revolution?

How did Washington's youth prepare him for his future role as Commander-in-Chief of the Revolutionary Army? What motives led him to penetrate "the inhospitable confines of the savage Indian"? To what purpose are Sparta and Rome introduced in the address? How did respite from war after the defeat of the French by the English contribute, in its turn, to the making of the future Washington?

How is Washington's freedom from lawless ambition proved? In what did his attitude toward the American Revolution differ from that of the French leaders toward the French Revolution? How popular was Washington's appointment as military commander of the Revolutionary forces? What made him confident of success in the struggle against Great Britain? Where does Carroll suggest that Washington's countrymen may not have shared his optimism? In what way did his genius as a commander go far beyond mere military strategy? What was his attitude toward prisoners of war? At the close of the Revolutionary War how did Washington show his noble disinterestedness?

What sacrifices had he to make and what risks to run on accepting the presidency of the United States? How does Bishop Carroll prove the beneficial character of Washington's administration? Does his summary of Washington's Farewell Address do it justice? How successful do you find his application of the selection from the Book of Wisdom to the character and career of Washington?

THE HISTORY OF AMERICAN ORATORY

The National Period (1800-1865)

General Characteristics

Since the conflict between ideals which touch our emotions closely and events in the world about us is the great source of oratory, it is plain that any era when deep principles of life are being attacked will bring forth orators. And no speakers ever had themes which appealed more to the emotions—slavery, democracy, states' rights versus nationalism—than the speakers of the National Period.

Many of the speeches of this period seem over-ornate and declamatory to our practical, unimaginative age, but they fit the time. It was a time of vision, of glory in a new world, of excursions into new fields of thought, of inventions which opened endless vistas of possibilities of human advancement. The great leaders of this age were not merely jugglers of words. They were men who were trying to find words to express intense feelings. American thinking has always tended toward practical results. In dealing with the questions that arose in a new nation trying out a new form of government, national leaders must interpret political philosophy and apply it to the real and vital problems of the day. This the orators tried to do. Many of the speeches of this period have little interest for present-day readers—the occasion which brought them forth is gone; gone, too, is much of the emotional reaction which made them so effective. Others continue to hold their vital interest. All are a priceless heritage of our nation.

John Caldwell Calhoun (1782-1850)

Calhoun was one of the most important orators of the early National Period. A native of South Carolina, he was educated at Yale, studied law, became interested in politics and in 1811 entered Congress. Here he was a leader among the younger men and was known as a nationalist. But as sentiment grew at home for state sovereignty, he became a champion for this doctrine, in defense of which his greatest speeches were made.

Henry Clay (1777-1852)

Henry Clay, the "silver-tongued orator," was born in Hanover County, Virginia, became a lawyer, and settled in Kentucky where he lived for the rest of his life. He was the most popular orator of his time, which says much for his personality and ability as a speaker, since his speeches, as we read them to-day, do not move us as do those of less popular orators. He was a constant advocate of American nationalism, never losing an opportunity to appeal to the people for the preservation of the Union. Interesting speeches are *Defense of the American System, Compromise of 1850,* and *Farewell to the Senate.*

Daniel Webster (1782–1852)

Daniel Webster is without doubt America's greatest orator and one of the world's greatest. He was born in Salisbury, New Hampshire, was educated at Dartmouth College, studied law, and entered the House of Representatives from Massachusetts in 1813. Few lawyers have been so able that their speeches to a jury live after the case has been decided. Yet Webster's speech in the White murder case is still read and declaimed, and passages from the *Dartmouth College Case* speech, made before the Supreme Court, are still quoted. His *First Bunker Hill Oration, Second Bunker Hill Oration, Reply to Hayne, Seventh of March Speech*—all show his unusual ability, and these are read to-day with interest and appreciation.

In appearance he was stately, with a leonine head and marvelous eyes. His voice was an instrument capable of expressing every shade of feeling. "It was low and musical in conversation, in debate it was high but full, ringing out in moments of excitement like a clarion, and then sinking to deep notes with the solemn richness of organ-tones, while the words were accompanied by a manner in which grace and dignity mingled in complete accord." His contemporaries all attest the profound spell he cast upon his audience. But almost as great is the spell his words cast over us as we read them to-day. He had a natural gift for words, an unerring feel for the rhythm of sentences, and a discriminating intellect which made his figures of speech vivid and effective.

Abraham Lincoln (1809–1865)

Abraham Lincoln, born February 12, 1809, near Hodgenville, Kentucky, stands to-day one of the great men, not only of the nation but of the world. The story of his humble birth, his struggle with poverty, his intellectual curiosity that could not be satisfied, his slow rise to political power with its culmination in the highest office in the United States—these are facts known to every American; yet each retelling seems but to burnish more brightly the fame of this unusual man. When Lincoln was eight years of age, his father moved from Kentucky to Indiana, where the family lived until Lincoln was twenty-one. He then moved with his father to Illinois, with which state he was ever after associated.

A trip down the Mississippi River to New Orleans in 1831 gave Lincoln a glimpse of slavery and fixed in him a deep and endless hatred of the institution. The next year he began to study law and in 1834 was elected to the Illinois legislature.

The slavery question had become involved with nearly every phase of politics. Slave and anti-slave states fought over admission of territories, over the tariff; suspicion grew, and peace was constantly menaced. The Missouri Compromise of 1820, fixing the line between slave and free states at 36° 30′ north latitude, did more to waken in the two sections a consciousness of the growing differences between them than to settle the question of the spread or destruction of slavery. Holding the balance of power between the two sections took all the juggler tricks the statesmen and politicians could master. In 1858 Lincoln said in a speech accepting the Republican nomination for United States senator, "A house divided against itself cannot endure permanently half slave and half free. I do not expect the Union to be dissolved, I do not expect the house to fall, but I do expect it will cease to be divided."

In the Lincoln-Douglas debates during the campaign that followed, Lincoln had many opportunities to put before the public his ideas of Union and of slavery. Defeated by Douglas for the senatorship, he had nevertheless made himself so popular that he was nominated for president by the Republican party in its National Convention at Chicago two years later. The facts of his life from this time on are a part of history, and are too well known to be rehearsed here. We know him as the American who, not even Washington excepted, is closest to the nation's heart and love.

The Most Reverend Bishop John England (1786–1842)

John England came from Ireland in 1820 to assume the bishopric of Charleston, South Carolina. His influence in Ireland had been second only to that of Daniel O'Connell, and in America he quickly earned recognition as a great orator. His audiences included the educated and refined; the leisured class and the working man; the Negroes, slave and free. He gloried in being the first priest to address the House of Representatives in the presence of the President, Senators, and a large gallery. His style was clear and graceful, but his greatest asset was his vigorous sincerity and his winning personality. His work as a promoter of education earned him the title of "restorer of classical learning in South Carolina." In 1822 he founded the *United States Catholic Miscellany,* the first distinctly Catholic journal in this country.

The Most Reverend Bishop John Joseph Hughes (1797–1864)

John Hughes, first archbishop of New York, played a prominent part in establishing the Catholic Church in this country on a sound basis and in defending it against bitter attacks. His services to Catholic education were outstanding; he may be said to be the founder of the parochial school system. His chief literary works include sermons, lectures, and controversial writings. It was at the request of J. Q. Adams, Calhoun, Benton, Douglas, and others that on December 12, 1847, he preached before Congress on "Christianity the only Source of Moral, Social, and Political Regeneration." As a speaker he was clear, forceful, and direct.

Other Orators of the National Period

Besides the political orators, there were in this period several speakers who gave orations and lectures on subjects other than politics.

Edward Everett (1794–1865), lectured on literary subjects and delivered orations of an occasional nature. He was a polished, cultured speaker, sometimes too polished, as he seems to have refined his language until the life of the sentences is rubbed out and no feeling is left. He is best remembered for his speech, *George Washington*.

Henry Ward Beecher (1813–1887) was a minister and an orator, depending on an audience for inspiration. He lacked the literary purity of Webster, but even yet his speeches show his charming, wholesome personality. In 1863 he traveled in England delivering almost impromptu speeches to English audiences on the subject of the American Civil War. Even when the audiences became violent in their antagonism, Beecher won them. His English speeches were a strong factor in disposing England to be neutral during the Civil War. Besides his volumes of sermons, readers still find pleasure in his *Lectures to Young Men, Star Papers,* and *Lecture Room Talks*. His *Effect of the Death of Lincoln* shows his rather ornate but agreeable style.

Wendell Phillips (1811–1886) was a reformer. Before the war he was an abolitionist. After the slavery question had been decided, he gave his attention to woman suffrage, prohibition, and labor reforms. He also spoke on popular themes, two of the best known of his speeches being his lectures on *Toussaint l'Overture* and *The Lost Arts*.

Horace Greeley (1811-1872) was much sought after during his lifetime as a popular lecturer. He was shrewd, had an unusual fund of common sense, and was not afraid to say what he believed. He wrote *Essays in Political Economy, What I Know of Farming,* and *Recollections of a Busy Life,* besides many occasional essays and lectures.

SECOND INAUGURAL ADDRESS
ABRAHAM LINCOLN

Historical Background: Between Lincoln's first and second inaugurals stretch four fateful years—four years of war.

FELLOW-COUNTRYMEN:

At this second appearing to take the oath of the presidential office,[1] there is less occasion for an extended address than there was at first. Then a statement, somewhat in detail, of a course to be pursued, seemed fitting and proper. Now, at the expiration of four years, during which public declarations have been constantly called forth on every point and phase of the great contest which still absorbs the attention and engrosses the energies of the nation, little that is new could be presented. The progress of our arms, upon which all else chiefly depends, is as well known to the public as to myself; and it is, I trust, reasonably satisfactory and encouraging to all.[2] With high hopes for the future, no prediction in regard to it is ventured.

On the occasion corresponding to this four years ago, all thoughts were anxiously directed to an impending civil war. All dreaded it—all sought to avoid it. While the inaugural address

---

[1] AT THIS SECOND APPEARING, etc.—This speech was given on March 4, 1865.

[2] THE PROGRESS OF OUR ARMS, etc.—In August, 1864, Admiral Farragut had taken Mobile. In September, Sherman had reached Atlanta and started on his march to the sea, which ended with the capture of Savannah in December. The North was winning on every front. Just after this speech was made the army of the Potomac began a new drive on Richmond. April 3, 1865, the Union forces entered the city. Lee surrendered April 9, 1865.

was being delivered from this place, devoted altogether to saving the Union without war, insurgent agents were in the city seeking to destroy it without war—seeking to dissolve the Union, and divide effects, by negotiation.[3] Both parties deprecated war; but one of them would make war rather than let the nation survive; and the other would accept war rather than let it perish. And the war came.

One-eighth of the whole population were colored slaves, not distributed generally over the Union, but localized in the southern part of it. These slaves constituted a peculiar and powerful interest. All knew that this interest was the object for which the insurgents would rend the Union, even by war; while the government claimed no right to do more than to restrict the territorial enlargement of it.[4]

Neither party expected for the war the magnitude or the duration which it has already attained. Neither anticipated that the cause of the conflict[5] might cease with, or even before, the conflict itself should cease. Each looked for an easier triumph and a result less fundamental and astounding. Both read the same Bible, and pray to the same God; and each invokes His aid against the other. It may seem strange that any men should dare to ask a just God's assistance in wringing their bread from the sweat of other men's faces; but let us judge not, that we be not judged. The prayers of both could not be answered—that of neither has been answered fully.

The Almighty has his own purposes. "Woe unto the world because of offenses! for it must needs be that offenses come; but woe to that man by whom the offense cometh."[6] If we shall suppose that American slavery is one of those offenses which in the providence of God, must needs come, but which, having continued through his appointed time, He now wills to remove, and that He gives to both North and South this terrible

---

[3] INSURGENT AGENTS WERE IN THE CITY, etc.—"Three agents of the confederate government were in Washington to negotiate for the recognition of independence, the surrender of the forts, and an adjustment of monetary losses to the federal government through the surrender of federal property in the South." Bassett, *Short History of the United States.*

[4] THE GOVERNMENT CLAIMED NO RIGHT, etc.—See Lincoln's *First Inaugural Address.* He reiterates his belief that he has no right "to interfere with the institution of slavery in the states where it exists."

[5] CAUSE OF THE CONFLICT—Slavery was the real cause. The Emancipation Proclamation was January 1, 1863.

[6] WOE UNTO THE WORLD, etc.—See *Matthew,* xviii:7.

war, as the woe due to those by whom the offense came, shall we discern therein any departure from those divine attributes which the believers in a living God always ascribe to Him? Fondly do we hope—fervently do we pray—that this mighty scourge of war may speedily pass away. Yet, if God wills that it continue until all the wealth piled by the bondman's two hundred and fifty years of unrequited toil shall be sunk, and until every drop of blood drawn with the lash shall be paid by another drawn with the sword, as was said three thousand years ago, still it must be said, "The judgments of the Lord are true and righteous altogether." [7]

With malice toward none; with charity for all; with firmness in the right, as God gives us to see the right, let us strive on to finish the work we are in; to bind up the nation's wounds; to care for him who shall have borne the battle, and for his widow and his orphan—to do all which may achieve and cherish a just and lasting peace among ourselves, and with all nations.

[7] THE JUDGMENTS OF THE LORD, etc.—See *Psalms* xix:9. In 1862 Lincoln had written in his personal papers for his own comfort: "The will of God prevails. In great contests each party claims to act in accordance with the will of God. Both may be, and one must be wrong. God can not be for and against the same thing at the same time. In the present civil war it is quite possible that God's purpose is something different from the purpose of either party; and yet the human instrumentalities, working just as they do, are of the best adaptation to effect His purpose. I am almost ready to say that this is probably true; that God wills this contest, and wills that it shall not end yet. By his mere great power on the minds of the now contestants, He could have either saved or destroyed the Union without a human contest. Yet the contest began. And, having begun, He could give the final victory to either side any day. Yet the contest proceeds."

By Way of Appreciation: In this speech we see the perfection of Lincoln's style, the simplicity which is the highest art, the unerring feeling for rhythm, the wealth of emotional appeal. Perhaps it was worth the years of suffering to have given the world such orations as this one and his *Gettysburg Address*.

Suggestions for Study: Why is this speech so short? Is the tone of this second Inaugural Address fearful or confident? Are the expression and thought mean or noble? Does this speech show evidence that Lincoln has lived and suffered since he became president? Do you see any evidence of doubt in the right of the course he had taken? What problems does he mention that are problems of any war? Notice the rhythm of the sentences. Such rhythm comes only when thought, emotion, and words are perfectly blended. Pick out sentences which seem to you to express more than they say on the surface.

GETTYSBURG ADDRESS

Abraham Lincoln

Historical Background: The battle of Gettysburg, July, 1863, is regarded as one of the decisive battles of the Civil War. The loss of life on both sides was very large. After the battle Lee retreated south with Meade in close pursuit. The burial of the dead was thus necessarily left to authorities of the state of Pennsylvania. The idea was conceived of setting aside a part of the battlefield as a cemetery, and accordingly a ceremony was planned for the dedication. Edward Everett was chosen to give the address, and the President was requested to "formally set aside these grounds to their sacred use by a few appropriate remarks." Everett made his customary eloquent oration which lasted for two hours and won the applause of the multitude. Then Lincoln arose to make his "few remarks," in one of the few flawless works of literary art in the world's history.

FOUR SCORE and seven years ago our fathers brought forth on this continent a new nation, conceived in liberty, and dedicated to the proposition that all men are created equal.

Now we are engaged in a great civil war, testing whether that nation, or any nation so conceived and so dedicated, can long endure. We are met on a great battlefield of that war. We have come to dedicate a portion of that field as a final resting-place for those who here gave their lives that that nation might live. It is altogether fitting and proper that we should do this.

But in a larger sense we cannot dedicate, we cannot consecrate, we cannot hallow this ground. The brave men, living and dead, who struggled here have consecrated it, far above our poor power to add or detract. The world will little note nor long remember what we say here, but it can never forget what they did here. It is for us, the living, rather, to be dedicated here to the unfinished work which they who fought here have thus far so nobly advanced. It is rather for us to be here dedicated to the great task remaining before us—that from these honored dead we take increased devotion to that cause for which they gave the last full measure of devotion; that we here highly resolve that these dead shall not have died in vain; that this nation, under God, shall have a new birth of freedom; and that government of the people, by the people, and for the people, shall not perish from the earth.

THE TRANSITION PERIOD (1865–1900)

General Characteristics

After the Civil War had been won by the North and an assassin's hand had closed the earthly career of Abraham Lincoln, the great problem was the healing of the breach between the North and the South. Had Lincoln lived, the disgraceful events of the reconstruction period would never have occurred. Immediately after his second inauguration Lincoln had begun to plan what he could do for both the North and the South as soon as the war came to a close. Among other plans was one to appropriate four hundred millon dollars to compensate the southern slaveowner for his loss of slaves and to furnish material for a new start in agriculture and business. With the death of Lincoln, all hopes for sane plans were gone. There were many wise and generous men on both sides who tried to stem the tide of bitterness and retaliation which swept across the country in the wake of war. But it took time. When Rutherford B. Hayes was elected president in 1876, he felt that his chief duty was to reconcile the South. He invited a former Confederate general, D. M. Kee of Tennessee, to become a member of his cabinet, and he withdrew all federal troops that had been quartered in the southern states. With this encouragement, the better class of citizens rallied to drive out "carpetbaggers" and "scalawags," and gradually order and safety took the place of disorder and fear.

In the banishment of sectional animosity two Southerners were important—Henry Woodfin Grady and Henry Watterson.

Henry Woodfin Grady (1850–1889)

Growing up during the period of reconstruction, Henry Woodfin Grady understood conditions thoroughly. Born in Athens, Georgia, he was educated at the Universities of Georgia and Virginia. His father, a much-loved Confederate officer, was killed in the war. Naturally of a happy, cheerful disposition, Grady did not allow defeat to embitter him. After failing in an attempt to make a living by journalism in Atlanta, he went to New York where his ability secured him a position as southern correspondent almost at once. In a few years he bought an interest in the *Atlanta Constitution* and returned home to spend the rest of his life in working to build up the South into a new economic prosperity. He was known and loved in both North and in South.

Henry Watterson (1840–1921)

Born in Washington, D. C., Watterson became a reporter, served in the Confederate Army, and in 1868 founded the Louisville (Kentucky) *Courier-Journal*, of which he was the editor for years. A brilliant speaker and writer, he soon became a leader in the Democratic party.

Other Orators of the Transition Period

This period was comparatively unproductive of great orations. However, the political speeches of Grover Cleveland (1837–1908) and Ulysses S. Grant (1828–1885) are worthy of mention. Chauncey M. Depew (1834–1928), Thomas Nelson Page (1853–1922), Edward Everett Hale (1822–1909), and Phillips Brooks (1835–1893) attained prominence as lecturers and masters of the occasional oration. Patrick John Ryan (1831–1911), Archbishop of Philadelphia, was perhaps the greatest Catholic preacher of his day. He commanded large and distinguished audiences, Protestant as well as Catholic. He was also much in demand as an occasional speaker and lecturer. Martin John Spalding (1810–1872), Archbishop of Baltimore, was a noted journalist, author, controversialist, and lecturer. James Cardinal Gibbons (1854–1921) was one of the greatest prelates America has produced. His famous works, *The Faith of Our Fathers* and *Our Christian Heritage,* are still widely read. His oratorical ability was on a par with his literary talents.

An Oration of the Transition Period

THE NEW SOUTH

Henry Woodfin Grady

Historical Background: The eighty-first anniversary celebration of the New England Society in New York City took the form of a large banquet on the night of December 22, 1886. The company assembled was composed of distinguished lawyers, noted bankers, prominent politicians, wealthy merchants, and other eminent people. After the dinner, several speakers were called upon, among whom was Dr. Talmage, a man well known for his brilliant lectures. Then Mr. Grady was introduced—a young man unknown to most of the assemblage and with a reputation as an orator still to be made. His speech on this occasion made his reputation. Before he had closed his second sentence he had caught the exclusive attention of his large audience, and before he had spoken five minutes he had entirely captured his listeners.

MR. PRESIDENT AND GENTLEMEN:—"There was a South of slavery and secession—that South is dead. There is a South of union and freedom—that South, thank God, is living, breathing, growing every hour." These words, delivered from the immortal lips of Benjamin H. Hill,[1] at Tammany Hall in 1866, true then, and truer now, I shall make my text to-night.

Let me express to you my appreciation of the kindness by which I am permitted to address you. I make this abrupt acknowledgment advisedly, for I feel that if, when I raise my provincial[2] voice in this ancient and august presence, I could find courage for no more than the opening sentence, it would be well if, in that sentence, I had met in a rough sense my obligation as a guest, and had perished, so to speak, with courtesy on my lips and grace in my heart. Permitted through your kindness to catch my second wind, let me say that I appreciate the significance of being the first Southerner to speak at this board, which bears the substance, if it surpasses the semblance, of original New England hospitality, and honors a sentiment that in turn honors you, but in which my personality is lost, and the compliment to my people[3] made plain.

I bespeak the utmost stretch of your courtesy to-night. I am not troubled about those from whom I come. You remember the man whose wife sent him to a neighbor with a pitcher of milk, and who, tripping on the top step, fell, with such casual interruptions as the landing afforded, into the basement; and while picking himself up had the pleasure of hearing his wife call out: "John, did you break the pitcher?" "No, I didn't," said John, "but I be dinged if I don't!"

So, while those who call to me from behind may inspire me with energy if not with courage, I ask an indulgent hearing from you. I beg that you will bring your full faith in American fairness and frankness to judgment upon what I shall say. There

---

[1] BENJAMIN H. HILL—A statesman from Georgia who spoke at Tammany Hall on the occasion mentioned.

[2] PROVINCIAL—Characteristic of a distant or outlying district.

[3] COMPLIMENT TO MY PEOPLE—Grady was honest in saying this. His feeling for his native state and for the South in general was so strong that his own individuality was submerged in his love for his country. He preferred to think he had been invited because he represented the South, rather than because of any personal qualities.

was an old preacher once who told some boys of the Bible lesson he was going to read in the morning. The boys, finding the placed, glued together the connecting pages. The next morning he read on the bottom of one page: "When Noah was one hundred and twenty years old he took unto himself a wife, who was" —then turning the page—"one hundred and forty cubits long, forty cubits wide, built of gopher-wood, and covered with pitch inside and out." He was naturally puzzled at this. He read it again, verified it, and then said: "My friends, this is the first time I ever met this in the Bible, but I accept it as an evidence of the assertion that we are fearfully and wonderfully made." If I could get you to hold such faith to-night, I could proceed cheerfully to the task I otherwise approach with a sense of consecration.

Pardon me one word, Mr. President, spoken for the sole purpose of getting into the volumes that go out annually freighted with the rich eloquence of your speakers—the fact that the Cavalier as well as the Puritan[4] was on the continent in its early days, and that he was "up and able to be about." I have read your books carefully, and I find no mention of that fact, which seems to me an important one for preserving a sort of historical equilibrium if for nothing else. Let me remind you that the Virginia Cavalier first challenged France on this continent —that Cavalier John Smith gave New England its very name, and was so pleased with the job that he has been handing his own name around ever since.

But having incorporated the Cavalier as a fact in your charming little books, I shall let him work out his own salvation, as he has always done with engaging gallantry, and we will hold no controversy as to his merits. Why should we? Neither Puritan nor Cavalier long survived as such. The virtues and traditions of both happily still live for the inspiration of their sons and the saving of the old fashion. But both Puritan and Cavalier were lost in the storm of the first Revolution; and the American citizen, supplanting both and stronger than either, took possession of the Republic bought by their common blood and fashioned to wisdom, and charged himself with teaching men government and establishing the voice of the people as the voice of God.

[4] CAVALIER, PURITAN—The former, a term for a colonial Virginian, meaning here Southerner; the latter, a New England colonist, here meaning Northerner.

My friend, Dr. Talmage,[5] has told you that the typical American has yet to come. Let me tell you that he has already come. Great types like valuable plants are slow to flower and fruit. But from the union of these colonist Puritans and Cavaliers, from the straightening of their purposes and the crossing of their blood, slow perfecting through a century, came he who stands as the first typical American, the first who comprehended within himself all the strength and gentleness, all the majesty and grace of this Republic—Abraham Lincoln. He was the son of Puritan and Cavalier, for in his ardent nature were fused the virtues of both, and in the depths of his great soul the faults of both were lost. He was greater than Puritan, greater than Cavalier, in that he was American, and that in his homely form were first gathered the vast and thrilling forces of his ideal government— charging it with such tremendous meaning and so elevating it above human suffering that martyrdom, though infamously aimed, came as a fitting crown to a life consecrated from the cradle to human liberty. Let us, each cherishing the traditions and honoring his fathers, build with reverent hands to the type of this simple but sublime life, in which all types are honored; and in our common glory as Americans there will be plenty and to spare for your forefathers and for mine.

In speaking to the toast with which you have honored me, I accept the term, "The New South,"[6] as in no sense disparaging to the Old. Dear to me, sir, are the home of my childhood and the traditions of my people. I would not, if I could, dim the glory they won in peace and war, or by word or deed take aught from the splendor and grace of their civilization—never equaled and, perhaps, never to be equaled in its chivalric strength and grace. There is a New South, not through protest against the Old, but because of new conditions, new adjustments and, if you please, new ideas and aspirations. It is to this that I address myself, and to the consideration of which I hasten lest it become the Old South before I get to it. Age does not endow all things with strength and virtue, nor are all new things to be despised.

[5] DR. TALMAGE—The orator who had preceded Grady. Talmage was a noted speaker and lecturer from New Jersey and had given his address in florid style on the achievements of the victorious Northern armies, drawing a touching picture of the soldier's return to his home. Note how Grady answers him.

[6] THE NEW SOUTH—Benjamin H. Hill, mentioned at the beginning, was the first to use this term.

The shoemaker who put over his door "John Smith's shop. Founded 1760," was more than matched by his young rival across the street who hung out this sign: "Bill Jones. Established 1886. No old stock kept in this shop."

Dr. Talmage has drawn for you, with a master's hand, the picture of your returning armies.[7] He has told you how, in the pomp and circumstances of war, they came back to you, marching with proud and victorious tread, reading their glory in a nation's eyes! Will you bear with me while I tell you of another army that sought its home at the close of the late war—an army that marched home in defeat and not in victory—in pathos and not in splendor, but in glory that equaled yours, and to hearts as loving as ever welcomed heroes home. Let me picture to you the footsore Confederate soldier, as, buttoning up in his faded gray jacket the parole which was to bear testimony to his children of his fidelity and faith, he turned his face southward from Appomattox[8] in April, 1865. Think of him as ragged, half-starved, heavy-hearted, enfeebled by want and wounds; having fought to exhaustion, he surrenders his gun, wrings the hands of his comrades in silence, and lifting his tear-stained and pallid face for the last time to the graves that dot the old Virginia hills, pulls his gray cap over his brow and begins the slow and painful journey. What does he find—let me ask you who went to your homes eager to find in the welcome you had justly earned, full payment for four years' sacrifice—what does he find when, having followed the battle-stained cross[9] against overwhelming odds, dreading death not half so much as surrender, he reaches the home he left so prosperous and beautiful? He finds his house in ruins, his farm devastated, his slaves free, his stock killed, his barns empty, his trade destroyed, his money worthless; his social system, feudal in its magnificence, swept away; his people without law or legal status, his comrades slain, and the burdens of others heavy on his shoulders. Crushed by defeat, his very traditions are gone; without money, credit, employment, material or training; and besides all this, con-

[7] RETURNING ARMIES—See note 5.
[8] APPOMATTOX—General Lee surrendered to General Grant at Appomattox Court House, Virginia, and thus ended the war.
[9] BATTLE-STAINED CROSS—The Confederate flag had white stars on narrow bands of blue which formed an X against a red background. It was known as the "Southern Cross."

fronted with the gravest problem that ever met human intelligence—the establishing of a status for the vast body of his liberated slaves.

What does he do—this hero in gray with a heart of gold? Does he sit down in sullenness and despair? Not for a day. Surely God, who had stripped him of his prosperity, inspired him in his adversity. As ruin was never before so overwhelming, never was restoration swifter. The soldier stepped from the trenches into the furrow; horses that had charged Federal guns marched before the plow, and fields that ran red with human blood in April were green with the harvest in June; women reared in luxury cut up their dresses and made breeches for their husbands, and, with a patience and heroism that fit women always as a garment, gave their hands to work. There was little bitterness in all this. Cheerfulness and frankness prevailed. "Bill Arp" [10] struck the keynote when he said: "Well, I killed as many of them as they did of me, and now I am going to work." Or the soldier returning home after defeat and roasting some corn on the roadside, who made the remark to his comrades: "You may leave the South if you want to, but I am going to Sandersville, kiss my wife and raise a crop, and if the Yankees fool with me any more I will whip 'em again." I want to say to General Sherman [11]—who is considered an able man in our parts, though some people think he is a kind of careless man about fire—that from the ashes he left us in 1864 we have raised a brave and beautiful city; that somehow or other we have caught the sunshine in the bricks and mortar of our homes, and have builded therein not one ignoble prejudice or memory.

But in all this what have we accomplished? What is the sum of our work? We have found out that in the general summary the free negro counts more than he did as a slave. We have planted the schoolhouse on the hilltop and made it free to white and black. We have sowed towns and cities in the place of theories and put business above politics. We have challenged your spinners in Massachusetts and your ironworkers in Penn-

---

[10] BILL ARP—The pen name of Major Charles H. Smith of Georgia, an author and humorist.

[11] GENERAL SHERMAN—The Northern general, who with 100,000 men marched from Chattanooga, Tennessee, to Atlanta, Georgia, burned the latter city, and then across Georgia to Savannah, laying waste all the country along his march. It has been estimated that property worth eighty millions of dollars was destroyed on this march.

sylvania. We have learned that the $400,000,000 annually received from our cotton crop will make us rich, when the supplies that make it are home-raised. We have reduced the commercial rate of interest from twenty-four to six per cent, and are floating four per cent bonds. We have learned that one Northern immigrant is worth fifty foreigners, and have smoothed the path to southward, wiped out the place where Mason and Dixon's line used to be, and hung our latchstring out to you and yours. We have reached the point that marks perfect harmony in every household, when the husband confesses that the pies which his wife cooks are as good as those his mother used to bake; and we admit that the sun shines as brightly and the moon as softly as it did "before the war." We have established thrift in city and country. We have fallen in love with work. We have restored comfort to homes from which culture and elegance never departed. We have let economy take root and spread among us as rank as the crab grass [12] which sprung from Sherman's cavalry camps, until we are ready to lay odds on the Georgia Yankee, as he manufactures relics of the battlefield in a one-story shanty and squeezes pure olive oil out of his cotton seed, against any down-easter [13] that ever swapped wooden nutmegs for flannel sausages in the valleys of Vermont. Above all, we know that we have achieved in these "piping times of peace" a fuller independence for the South than that which our fathers sought to win in the forum by their eloquence or compel on the field by their swords.

It is a rare privilege, sir, to have had part, however humble, in this work. Never was nobler duty confided to human hands than the uplifting and upbuilding of the prostrate and bleeding South, misguided, perhaps, but beautiful in her suffering, and honest, brave, and generous always. In the record of her social, industrial, and political illustrations we await with confidence.

But what of the negro? Have we solved the problem he presents or progressed in honor and equity toward the solution? Let the record speak to the point. No section shows a more prosperous laboring population than the negroes of the South; none in fuller sympathy with the employing and landowning

---

[12] CRAB GRASS—A reference to the areas laid waste by Sherman's army. Crab grass will grow only on barren ground.

[13] ANY DOWN-EASTER, etc.—The Yankee of New England had the reputation of being a shrewd trader and not over-scrupulous in business dealings.

class. He shares our school fund, has the fullest protection of our laws, and the friendship of our people. Self-interest, as well as honor, demand that he should have this. Our future, our very existence depend upon our working out this problem in full and exact justice. We understand that when Lincoln signed the Emancipation Proclamation, your victory was assured; for he then committed you to the cause of human liberty, against which the arms of man cannot prevail; while those of our statesmen who trusted to make slavery the cornerstone of the Confederacy doomed us to defeat as far as they could, committing us to a cause that reason could not defend or the sword maintain in the sight of advancing civilization. Had Mr. Toombs [14] said, which he did not say, that he would call the roll of his slaves at the foot of Bunker Hill, he would have been foolish, for he might have known that whenever slavery became entangled in war it must perish, and that the chattel in human flesh ended forever in New England when your fathers—not to be blamed for parting with what didn't pay—sold their slaves to our fathers —not to be praised for knowing a paying thing when they saw it.

The relations of the Southern people with the negro are close and cordial. We remember with what fidelity for four years he guarded our defenseless women and children, whose husbands and fathers were fighting against his freedom. To his eternal credit be it said that whenever he struck a blow for his own liberty he fought in open battle, and when at last he raised his black and humble hands that the shackles might be struck off, those hands were innocent of wrong against his helpless charges, and worthy to be taken in loving grasp by every man who honors loyalty and devotion. Ruffians have maltreated him, rascals have misled him, philanthropists [15] established a bank for him, but the South, with the North, protests against injustice to this simple and sincere people. To liberty and enfranchisement is as far as law can carry the negro. The rest must be left to conscience and common sense. It should be left to those among whom his lot is cast, with whom he is indissolubly connected and

---

[14] Mr. Toombs—A brilliant statesman and orator from Georgia who is remembered chiefly as an ardent southern partisan. He refused to take the oath of allegiance after the war.

[15] Philanthropists—A "Freedman's Bureau" was created to look after the affairs of the negro. Well-meaning men from the North went to rather ridiculous extremes in trying to help the freed slaves.

whose prosperity depends upon their possessing his intelligent sympathy and confidence. Faith has been kept with him in spite of calumnious assertions to the contrary by those who assume to speak for us [16] or by frank opponents. Faith will be kept with him in the future, if the South holds her reason and integrity.

But have we kept faith with you? In the fullest sense, yes. When Lee surrendered—I don't say when Johnston [17] surrendered, because I understand he still alludes to the time when he met General Sherman last as the time when he "determined to abandon any further prosecution of the struggle"—when Lee surrendered, I say, and Johnston quit, the South became, and has since been, loyal to this Union. We fought hard enough to know that we were whipped, and in perfect frankness accepted as final the arbitrament of the sword to which we had appealed. The South found her jewel in the toad's head of defeat. [18] The shackles that had held her in narrow limitations fell forever when the shackles of the negro slave were broken. Under the old régime the negroes were slaves to the South, the South was a slave to the system. The old plantation, with its simple police regulation and its feudal habit, was the only type possible under slavery. Thus we gathered in the hands of a splendid and chivalric oligarchy the substance that should have been diffused among the people, as the rich blood, under certain artificial conditions, is gathered at the heart, filling that with affluent rapture, but leaving the body chill and colorless.

The Old South rested everything on slavery and agriculture, unconscious that these could neither give nor maintain healthy growth. The New South presents a perfect democracy, the oligarchs leading in the popular movement—a social system compact and closely knitted, less splendid on the surface but stronger at the core—a hundred farms for every plantation, fifty homes for every palace, and a diversified industry that meets the complex needs of this complex age.

[16] THOSE WHO ASSUME TO SPEAK FOR US—Grady later said that he referred here to writers whom he considered had misrepresented the South.

[17] JOHNSTON—Joseph E. Johnston, a Confederate officer. He had surrendered to General Sherman but President Lincoln would not accept the terms. Johnston was an able officer, and greatly admired in the South.

[18] JEWEL, etc.—"Sweet are the uses of adversity,
  Which, like the toad, ugly and venomous,
  Wears yet a precious jewel in his head."
                                —Shakespeare, *As You Like It*.

The New South is enamored of her new work. Her soul is stirred with the breath of a new life. The light of a grander day is falling fair on her face. She is thrilling with the consciousness of growing power and prosperity. As she stands upright, full-statured and equal among the people of the earth, breathing the keen air and looking out upon the expanding horizon, she understands that her emancipation came because in the inscrutable wisdom of God her honest purpose was crossed and her brave armies were beaten.

This is said in no spirit of time-serving or apology. The South has nothing for which to apologize. She believes that the late struggle between the States was war and not rebellion, revolution and not conspiracy, and that her convictions were as honest as yours. I should be unjust to the dauntless spirit of the South and to my own convictions if I did not make this plain in this presence. The South has nothing to take back. In my native town of Athens is a monument that crowns its central hills—a plain, white shaft. Deep cut into its shining side is a name dear to me above the names of men, that of a brave and simple man who died in brave and simple faith. Not for all the glories of New England—from Plymouth Rock all the way—would I exchange the heritage he left me in his soldier's death. To the foot of that shaft I shall send my children's children to reverence him who ennobled their name with his heroic blood. But, sir, speaking from the shadow of that memory, which I honor as I do nothing else on earth, I say that the cause in which he suffered and for which he gave his life was adjudged by higher and fuller wisdom than his or mine, and I am glad that the omniscient God held the balance on the battle in his Almighty hand, and that human slavery was swept forever from American soil —the American Union saved from the wreck of war.

This message, Mr. President, comes to you from consecrated ground. Every foot of the soil about the city in which I live is sacred as a battle ground of the Republic. Every hill that invests it is hallowed to you by the blood of your brothers, who died for your victory, and doubly hallowed to us by the blood of those who died hopeless, but undaunted, in defeat—sacred soil to all of us, rich with memories that make us purer and stronger and better, silent but stanch witnesses in its red desolation of the matchless valor of American hearts and the deathless glory of American arms—speaking an eloquent witness in its white peace and prosperity to the indissoluble union of American States and the imperishable brotherhood of the American people.

Now, what answer has New England to this message? Will she permit the prejudices of war to remain in the hearts of the conquerors, when it has died in the hearts of the conquered? Will she transmit this prejudice to the next generation, that in their hearts, which never felt the generous ardor of conflict, it may perpetuate itself? Will she withhold, save in strained courtesy, the hand which straight from his soldier's heart Grant offered to Lee [19] at Appomattox? Will she make the vision of a restored and happy people, which gathered above the couch of your dying captain,[20] filling his heart with grace, touching his lips with praise and glorifying his path to the grave; will she make this vision, on which the last sight of his expiring soul breathed a benediction, a cheat and delusion? If she does, the South, never abject in asking for comradeship, must accept with dignity its refusal; but if she does not; if she accepts in frankness and sincerity this message of good will and friendship, then will the prophecy of Webster, delivered in this very Society forty years ago amid tremendous applause, be verified in its fullest and final sense, when he said: "Standing hand to hand and clasping hands, we should remain united as we have been for sixty years, citizens of the same country, members of the same government, united, all united now and united forever. There have been difficulties, contentions, and controversies, but I tell you that in my judgment

> Those opposed eyes,
> Which like the meteors of a troubled heaven,
> All of one nature, of one substance bred,
> Did lately meet in th' intestine shock,
> Shall now, in mutual well-beseeming ranks,
> March all one way."

[19] THE HAND WHICH . . . GRANT OFFERED TO LEE—When Lee surrendered, Grant spared him every humiliation possible, especially permitting officers to retain their swords, permitting the soldiers to keep their horses, and stopping the celebration of victory among the Union forces.

[20] DYING CAPTAIN—Lincoln. Lee surrendered on April 9th. Two days later Lincoln read a message (his last public address) to a large crowd that had gathered before the White House to congratulate him. Nowhere are his common sense, his broad-mindedness, and his loving sympathy more evident than in this address.

By Way of Appreciation: Grady's speech was a tremendous success. As soon as he had taken his seat, he was overwhelmed with congratulations. The New York *Times* pronounced it the greatest oration ever delivered in New York by a Southerner. It is an excellent example of an after-dinner speech. Notice how the speaker wins his audience by flattery, puts them in a good humor with a few stories, and assumes an air of humility and awe in the presence of such great people to create the atmosphere he desires. His tribute to Lincoln came from deep admiration for the great leader. Grady carefully balances the grave and the gay. When he seems to be getting too serious, he drops in a bit of humor. But he makes his audience realize the depth of his feelings, and the latter part of his speech is most sincere, intense, and touching.

Suggestions for Study: Do you think the feeling of timidity in speaking to this group that Grady expresses is genuine or assumed? Does he seem eager to put the case of the South before his audience as honestly as he can? Are his stories appropriate? What is the purpose of the humor?

Why does he bring in a discussion of the Puritan and the Cavalier? What parallel between the Puritan and the Cavalier in the Revolutionary War and the North and the South in the Civil War does he draw? How does this lead to his eulogy of Lincoln?

From his references to Dr. Talmage, do you conclude that he agreed with him, or do you feel a little antagonism? Show how Grady skillfully mingles seriousness and humor in his description of the South. Is this more or less effective than if he had omitted humor? Would he necessarily be less serious here than if he were trying to secure the passage of some law in Congress? Why? Do you like the concluding paragraph of Part III? What does it show of the speaker?

Rehearse what the South did for the negro after freeing him from slavery. Was this in keeping with the rights of humanity? Do you think the relations of the Southern people with the negro were close and cordial? Explain. In opposition to this, what had misguided Northerners done for the negro? Give Grady's argument as to why the abolition of slavery was the best thing for the South.

Why has Grady omitted humor in the last part of the speech? Was he right in assuming that the North retained the bitterness of war when the South had forgotten it? Was this the keynote of his speech? Does the poem at the conclusion strengthen or weaken the speech?

The Speech as a Whole: Compare this speech with Patrick Henry's in tone, sentence structure, figures of speech, logical argument, and effect sought. Explain in each case the difference you find. Compare Grady's style with Webster's, pointing out likenesses or differences.

Discuss the value of humor in a public address. Would humor have been effective in Patrick Henry's speech, or becoming to either Webster or Lincoln? In what type of address is humor most effective? In what type would it be offensive?

THE HISTORY OF AMERICAN ORATORY

THE TWENTIETH CENTURY (1900–   )

General Characteristics

The late nineteenth and the early twentieth centuries saw tremendous progress in the United States. Improved means of communication and transportation enabled people to come closer together and to learn more about each other than they had ever done before. The Spanish-American War showed that the nation had become united—that it was more a unity than it had ever been before the Civil War. Newspapers and magazines had usurped the place of the spoken word in disseminating political and social ideas. Telephone and telegraph had assisted in spreading information all over the world. Yet there were still occasions on which only the spoken word from the lips of the orator seemed adequate, and the public address still swayed audiences as before.

With the country's progress, however, there arose new problems for solution. Building up the ruins left by the Civil War had taken time and was not accomplished without conflict. A new industrial age opened with differences of opinion about how control should be administered. Trusts rose and fell and rose again. The war with Spain brought new responsibilities. The Hague Conference drew us into European affairs, as the "Open Door" and the Boxer Rebellion increased our interest and responsibility in China and brought us into contact with Japan. Woman suffrage, election reforms, socialism, labor and capital, tariff, progressivism—all found exponents and enemies who fought their battles in the press and on the platform. Then came the World War with a host of problems that challenged men then and are not yet solved. The second European War has its peculiar problems, too, which are being discussed in the press and on the rostrum, but more than ever over the radio and through the medium of the talking pictures.

William Jennings Bryan (1860–1925)

Political campaigns were occasions for bringing to bear upon the voters all the candidate's eloquence and personality. The powerful effect of oratory has never been better illustrated than in the case of William Jennings Bryan whose famous *Cross of Gold* speech, made when he was practically unknown, won him the nomination for president at the Democratic National Convention in 1896. Of this speech Mark Sullivan says: "That speech, in which Bryan won his nomination and burst flaming upon the country, is one of the great orations of American history,—great, that is, in the light of its purpose and its superb adaptation to that purpose. . . . The *Cross of Gold* speech was oratory wholly, and oratory of the highest order." Such an incident shows that oratory is not dead.

Theodore Roosevelt (1858-1919)

Theodore Roosevelt was born in New York City of Dutch descent. As a child he was frail, but through careful husbanding of his strength and grim determination he was able to graduate from Harvard in 1880. Immediately he began his political career, being elected to the New York State legislature the same year he left college. At once he showed the qualities that were to distinguish him all his life and the trend his political views were to take.

In 1884 he became aware that if he wished to continue in strenuous political life he must build himself physically. With this in mind he spent two years on a ranch in North Dakota, where the wild outdoor life fascinated him and where he found health and strength. The years spent here forever identified Roosevelt with the West, for here he gained an appreciation for that part of the country and an understanding of its problems and beliefs which colored his later career.

During McKinley's first term as president, Roosevelt held the position of Assistant Secretary of the Navy. When war with Spain seemed inevitable, he organized the Rough Riders, a regiment of volunteer cavalry from the West, with whom he went to Cuba as Lieutenant-Colonel. He returned from the war to serve as governor of New York, and when McKinley was reëlected to the presidency, Roosevelt was elected Vice-President. This position seems to have been forced upon him by his enemies who hoped thus to remove him from the political picture. But the assassination of President McKinley in the summer of 1901 placed Roosevelt in the president's chair. His career as president was a constant fight against the abuses of organized business, especially the trusts. His popularity with the people, gained by his direct appeals to them through press and platform and his vigorous denunciation of those whom they had long felt to be their enemies, won him the election of 1904 and what was practically a second term as president.

Probably no man of modern times has more profoundly influenced American ideals. Again and again we come back to his vigorous phrasing of American principles, and we have come to think of him as one of the great Americans.

Woodrow Wilson (1856-1924)

Woodrow Wilson was born at Staunton, Virginia, December 28, 1856. After graduating from Princeton in 1879 he studied law at the University of Virginia and began his practice in Atlanta, Georgia. But law did not satisfy him, so he entered Johns Hopkins University to study history and political science, winning his doctor's degree with a thesis on Congressional Government. After holding several teaching positions he was elected president of Princeton University in 1902, having served the institution as professor of jurisprudence and political economy for twelve years. He continued to hold the position of president until 1910 when he entered politics and was elected governor of New Jersey. Two years later he was elected President of the United States.

These few facts contrast strongly with the varied career of Roosevelt. But the smoothness of Wilson's life is only seeming. Wilson came to the presidency at a time when many difficulties confronted him. He encountered opposition to his desire for progressive legislation both in the leaders of his own party and in Congress, and found difficulty in developing the "consciousness of democracy" in the people, which Roosevelt had preached and in which Wilson believed. His first term was beset with the difficulties of maintaining strict neutrality in the great war that had broken out in Europe in 1914. His second term was beset with the problems of the war itself. The part which he played during the World War, his "fourteen points" on which he believed peace could be made, his activity at the Peace Conference, his failure to bring the United States into the League of Nations—these are all too well known to be retold. Broken by the war and blamed for business conditions by the people he had led, President Wilson came to the end of his term. He died in 1924, but his idealism lives.

The Right Reverend Monsignor Fulton J. Sheen (1895–   )

A happy marriage between eloquence and scholarship is rare. A successful union of the emotional warmth essential to true eloquence and of the impersonal objectivity indispensable for true scholarship is difficult to achieve. Either the heart runs away with the head, or the head chills the heart. Because Monsignor Fulton Sheen represents the accomplishment of this difficult combination he is one of the outstanding Catholic orators in the United States today. No other Catholic has been called upon so often to deliver radio addresses on the Catholic Hour; no other is in such demand for important occasions that call for the best in public addresses.

Monsignor Sheen was born in El Paso, Illinois, in 1895. After receiving the Bachelor of Arts degree from Saint Viator's College, he pursued philosophical and theological studies at the Saint Paul Seminary, the Catholic University of America, and the University of Louvain. He was made an *Agregé en Philosophie* by Louvain in 1925; a Doctor of Divinity in Rome in 1924. Since 1926 he has been on the faculty of the Catholic University of America.

His first and very notable book, *God and Intelligence*, appeared in 1925. Others have followed at fairly regular intervals of approximately a year.

Other Speakers and Writers on National Problems

Among the distinguished leaders in American thought there are many whose speeches and writings can be read with pleasure and profit. They represent every phase of life and thought and endeavor, showing the richness of our civilization. Charles W. Eliot, David Starr Jordan, Henry van Dyke, Edward Bok, Susan B. Anthony, Elihu Root, Shailer Mathews, Edward Phelps—these are a few names known for their lectures,

after-dinner speeches, and occasional orations. Political orators are
Theodore Roosevelt, Woodrow Wilson, Franklin K. Lane, William Mc-
Kinley, William Jennings Bryan, William Howard Taft, Oliver Wendell
Holmes, Robert LaFollette, Albert J. Beveridge, and many others. The
names of many contemporary speakers, those of politicians, clergymen,
statesmen, are well known to radio listeners.

An Oration of the Twentieth Century

TRUE LIBERTY

Fulton J. Sheen

Historical Introduction: Freedom is dear to Americans. What
American is not everlastingly jealous of the freedom of religion, speech,
press, and assembly guaranteed him by the Bill of Rights? Ask him, if
need be, to undergo other privations; do not ask him to surrender his
cherished liberty. With enthusiasm he repeats Patrick Henry's "Give me
liberty or give me death!"

All too frequently, however, his understanding of the meaning of
liberty is hazy, if not erroneous. Because they lack a clear conception of
liberty many mistake its caricature, license, for the original article, and
in the sacred name of liberty demand toleration of conduct which would
in time, if borne with, mean the end of true liberty.

Monsignor Sheen's discourse on the nature of true liberty, therefore,
is offered here not only as an example of an address in the modern radio
manner, but also as a valuable contribution toward a correct understanding of true liberty and therefore of true Americanism. Clear and direct,
typical of his best radio addresses, it was delivered on the nationwide
Catholic Hour, produced by the National Council of Catholic Men, in
cooperation with the National Broadcasting Company. This address, delivered on January 15, 1939, was the third of a series of seven on the subject of social freedom.

1   Last Sunday we spoke of the two false concepts of liberty:
the liberty of indifference and the liberty of necessity—one the
freedom of decaying liberalism, the other the freedom of enslaving
dictatorships.

2   Liberty of indifference forgets the purpose of freedom, and
ignores the common good. Liberty of necessity places liberty in
the collectivity, the mass, and the class, and ignores the personal
freedom of the man. Both views are wrong. Liberty is not the

right to do whatever I please; nor is liberty the necessity of doing whatever I must, whatever the dictator dictates; rather liberty is the right to do what I ought. In these three words, "please" "must" and "ought" are given the choices facing the modern world. Of the three, we choose "ought."

3   That little word "ought" implies that man is free. Fire must be hot, ice must be cold, but a man ought to be good. "Ought" is the beginning of morality for it distinguishes man as moral power from a physical power like a steam engine. Freedom is not the power to do anything you please, so often expressed by modern youth as: "I can do it if I want to, can't I? Who will stop me?" Certainly you can do anything you please or want to. You can rob your neighbor, you can beat your wife, you can stuff mattresses with old razor blades, and you can shoot your neighbor's chickens with a machine gun, but you ought not do these things because "ought" implies morality: rights and duties. Freedom then is a moral power rather than a physical power; an "ought" instead of a "can."

4   Furthermore, "ought" is intrinsically related to purpose. When I say "I ought to eat my dinner," I have reference to the unmistakable relation between eating and health; that is, the purpose of eating is to conserve my health. When I say: "I ought to study," the word "ought" involves the purpose of study, namely, the acquisition of knowledge. There are thousands of little "oughts" in every life, each one of which is inseparable from a goal or an end or a purpose, as, for example, "I ought to pay my bills"; "I ought to be kind." Reason is constantly setting up little targets of "oughts" or purposes, and the will like an arrow tries to hit the mark. Underlying all the little "oughts" of life, there is one supreme "ought," namely, I ought to attain the end for which I was made. Behind all purposes is one great purpose, which is given in answer to the question, "Why do I exist?"

5   That is a question very few ever ask themselves. They would not have a ten cent gadget in their homes for five minutes without knowing its purpose, but they will go through life without knowing why they are living. Modern education is very skillful in telling students the purposes of electricity, dynamos, and Diesel engines, but it ignores entirely the real purpose of education, namely, to give the purpose of living. Until we answer that question there

is no question worth answering; and the way we answer it determines our character in this world and our destiny in the next.

6   What then is the purpose of life? The one great supreme purpose of human existence is the perfection of our personality by the attainment of perfect life, truth, and love.

7   Man does not want life for only the next thirty-two minutes, but always; he does not want merely to know the truths of geography, but all Truth; he does not want merely a love that dies, but an eternal, beautiful, ecstatic love. Hence the ridiculousness of modern marriages with their divorces. "I will love you for two years and six months," is a pretty sickly substitute for "until death do us part." Earth does not give lasting happiness, for when man has raised his family he hates to leave it, when he has piled up his dollars he wants a larger pile, and when he has become educated he begins to feel proud of what he knows and thus lapses into the most abysmal ignorance. Since the happiness of eternal life, truth, and love, cannot be realized here below, it follows that their attainment is beyond this life, for if there were no food there would be no stomach, if there were no things to see there would be no eyes, and if there were no Perfect Life, Truth, and Love there would be no mind or will or heart craving and striving for them.

8   Reason thus suggests the purpose of man, which is identical with the answer of Revelation. The best way of finding out why a thing was made is to go to its maker. The Catechism puts the question: "Why did God make you?" and The Maker gives the answer, "God made me to know Him, to love Him, to serve Him in this world, and to be eternally happy with Him in the next."

9   To summarize our steps thus far: "ought" is inseparable from purpose; and the supreme purpose of life is the perfection of our personality in the Life and Truth and Love which is God. That brings us to the next question: When is man more free, when he does what he ought, or when he does what he pleases? Certainly doing what we ought is a higher kind of freedom than doing what we please, because the former develops man in his higher reaches while the latter enslaves. The mistake the modern world makes is thinking liberty means independence of law and that breaking the commandments of God is a form of "self-expression."

10   What we must get into our heads as citizens is that freedom

does not mean lawlessness. On the contrary, freedom is conditioned upon free obedience to law. There is no such thing as freedom from law; there is only freedom within law, whether that law be scientific, natural, human, or divine. For example, an aviator is free to fly only on condition that he obey the law of gravitation; that is, he must act within the law, and not outside it. Just try to be self-expressive and jump off the Empire State Building, and you will find that within a minute you have lost all freedom—even the freedom to live. Try and be broadminded and draw a triangle with four sides as a proof that you can do anything you please, and you will discover that you are no longer free to draw a triangle. Forget the purpose of a razor and use it for opening tomato cans, and you destroy the razor because you forgot its purpose. Be a broadminded artist ignoring the nature of things and draw a giraffe with a short neck, and you find you are not free to draw a giraffe.

11   So it is with the moral law; we are most free when we obey the purpose or the law for which we were made, namely, the unfolding and development of our personality by eternal happiness with God. O yes, we are free to ignore the moral law, to drink, to steal, to be adulterous, to shake our fists in violent hate, just as we are free to ignore the law of gravitation; but each time we ignore it we either diminish or destroy our liberty. Real freedom is attained not by acting outside the law, but inside it. As long as I obey traffic laws I am free to drive, but when I say liberty means the right to do what I please, and I drive through red traffic lights, I soon discover that I am no longer free to drive. So it is with the moral law. God has implanted in conscience and in His Church, those laws which enable us to realize the purpose of life and attain the highest goal of our personality. These laws are not like dams impeding progress, they are like levees, preventing the waters of selfishness and unlawful desire from flooding the countryside. If I obey, or do what I ought, I am free. If I disobey them, or do what I please, I am acting against the best interests of my nature. Every time I sin, I am to that extent less a man, just as an engine used in violation of the maker's instructions is, or soon becomes, less an engine. Sinning, which is a contempt of purpose and the law of life, is not the proof of freedom—it is the beginning of slavery; for as Our

Lord has put it "whosoever committeth sin, is the servant of sin."
It should be evident that freedom is not merely a constitutional
right, or a state grant; it is above all things else a spiritual right,
inseparable from the purpose of man and the supreme "ought" of
his life.

12   One of the reasons why democracy finds it so difficult to set
any limits upon what man may say or do or think, is because it
frequently forgets the purpose of man. Classical Liberalism, as
distinguished from the Progressivism which is now commonly
called Liberalism, and Dictatorship, must each realize its error.
Our Liberal freedom had created monstrous economic injustices;
our Dictatorship freedom has re-created slavery. Each loved
liberty in his own sphere: the Liberal in his own selfish ego and
the Dictatorship in its collective ego. Liberalism was not the
birth of liberty; dictatorship is not its discovery. Freedom had
its roots in man's spiritual nature before there was a Liberal, a
Democrat, a Fascist, or a Communist. Freedom did not arise out
of any social organization, or any constitution, or any party, but
out of the soul of man. Nazis, Fascists, and Communists flatter
themselves that they are restoring liberty to man by handing him
over to the collectivity. Liberals flatter themselves that they are
preserving liberty because they give greater satisfaction to material appetites. How confused and muddled is the world's thinking is proved by the fact that Stalin can justify a purge of the
innocent, and a Union Square orator can justify overthrow of the
American Government, both in the name of Liberty.

13   It is about time the Liberals and Dictators stopped talking
about giving liberty to man, and realized that man gives them
their liberty. Then let man in his turn realize that the roots of
his freedom are in his purpose as a creature made to the image
and likeness of God. We have gone on the assumption too long
that if we were free, we would discover the truth. Our Blessed
Lord has put it the other way around: "The truth shall make you
free." This means that real liberation comes from the knowledge
of the purpose and destiny of man. Our indifference to truth
has resulted in our loss of the passion for truth. The result is
that today there are very few ideals for which a man would die,
or even suffer sacrifice. Our false broadmindedness, if we only
knew it, is born of our loss of faith and certitude. As we forget

the purpose of life, we lose the dynamism to attain it; as we lose
the basic certainties of life we also lose the energy to strive for
them. Because we have lost our passion for Truth, Justice, and
Righteousness, a lethargy and an apathy have so seized our civilization that we find it difficult to defend even the ordinary loyalties
of life. We have no strong passion for great causes, no great
hatred of evil, but only half-drawn swords and one-fisted battles.
We have thrown away our maps of life and know not which way
to turn. It is horrible to contemplate, but there is probably not
enough love of truth in the world to start a crusade.

14   This loss of enthusiasm for the good has had the sorry consequences of permitting evil and irreligion to spread like a pestilence. Many men love truth less than others hate it. This is a
grave danger for democracy. Hatred is rapidly becoming a
stronger force than Love, or Truth, or Justice, or Righteousness.
There is, for example, a greater hatred of capitalism by certain
groups in our country than there is among those very groups a
love of social justice. There is a greater hatred of labor unions
among certain groups in our country than there is love for a downtrodden fellow man. This growth of hatred is dangerous for
any civilization. It has now reached such a point that in order to
spread it, hypocrisy ceases to be a sin and becomes a virtue. Because we have forgotten the reason for living, there are those who
say that "Only a class has a right to live." Because we have forgotten truth there are those who say that "Only error shall be
spread." Because we have forgotten justice there are those who
say that "Only violence shall rule." Because we have forgotten
man there are those who say that "Only the State shall endure."
The ideologies of Fascism, Nazism, and Communism seek to confine the purpose of man within the phenomenal limits of blood or
a party. By forcing man to surrender to their final authority they
cut man off absolutely from the very ends to which he had already
become indifferent through irreligion. The world-man as a result
has thrown dust in his own eyes and then had his eyes plucked
out so that he can no longer find the gate which leads back home.
He was told religion was an opium and eternal purpose only
theological folklore, and that if he dispossessed himself of its
obligations and worries, he could make a paradise of this world.
Foolishly man did this, but instead of finding his material life

enriched, he discovers that it becomes more precarious each day without the consolation of any hope beyond the grave. Having lost the purpose of life he now has left only purposes which are so many loose ends he never can piece together.

15   There is no way to stop this betrayal of liberty other than by Christianity's preaching the purpose of man, namely the social, economic, and political unfolding of his personality in this world and his spiritual efflorescence in the next.

16   God could save us from our chaos and our slavery by force, but that would be the destruction of Liberty. God awaits man's free and unforced response to His call; that is why His last farewell to the world was from the powerlessness of the Cross where only His eyes could summon us to the sweet purpose of life. He even bore with the greatest wrongdoers for the sake of freedom. Such freedom is not a freedom which is indifferent to truth, nor tolerant to untruth, but a freedom which believes truth so sacred that it is worth a death on a cross and therefore is always a freedom strong enough to enforce freedom. Faith in the Truth of Calvary is faith in the freedom of man. Only under that Cross does man realize that freedom is not in liberation from truth, not in violent subjection to it, but in the loving embrace of a soul that has realized its purpose and cries out from the depths of a heart aflame with truth: "I am Thine O God! Help me whom Thou hast made."

By Way of Appreciation: In Monsignor Sheen the philosopher and poet combine to form the ideal orator. The philosopher in him penetrates to the heart of vital problems and with superb clarity satisfies his listeners' appetite for substantial food for thought. The poet in him warms his message with a great sympathy learned in the school of Christ, and brings his listeners to share his own great fellow-feeling for mankind in all its moods and vagaries. The directness of his language, the aptness of his illustrations, and something of a Chestertonian fondness for paradoxes make his addresses as entertaining as they are illuminating and instructive.

Monsignor Sheen's addresses are notable among modern radio orations because of the orator's fine enthusiasm and his intellectual sincerity. Nowhere in literature is there found more of the passion for truth, broader understanding of human emotions and problems, and keener perception of the problems of the times than in the great Catholic orators, of whom Monsignor Sheen, in this century, is surely one, as was Bishop Carroll in the eighteenth century.

Suggestions for Study: Since this address was one of a series on social freedom, very properly Monsignor Sheen opens with some reference to the preceding address. Observe how in two short paragraphs he graphically sums up what he said in the previous lecture and glides smoothly into his present subject.

How does he demolish the fallacy that true liberty is the right to do whatever I please? By examples show that "ought" is inseparable from purpose. What is the supreme "ought" which underlies all the little "oughts" of life? How does reason show that the ultimate purpose of life can be realized only in eternity? According to Monsignor Sheen, what is the best way of finding out the purpose of any object? Why is doing what we ought a higher kind of freedom than doing what we please? How does he demonstrate that true freedom is to be found only *within* the law? To what does he attribute democracy's difficulty in setting limits upon what a man may say or do or think? What are some of the sorry results of man's forgetting the truth that the roots of his freedom are in his purpose as a creature made to the image and likeness of God? By what means may the betrayal of true liberty be halted?

Find particular passages in which the use of concrete language or homely examples or a *reductio ad absurdum* make this discussion of a rather abstract subject eminently readable and convincing. Which paragraph of the address do you find most emotional? Why should it be so?

EXTENSIVE READING PROGRAM—THE ORATION

THE COLONIAL PERIOD (1607–1765)

Cotton Mather
*The Ecclesiastical History of
New England
Wonders of the Invisible World*

Jonathan Edwards
*Freedom of the Will
Treatise Concerning the Religious Affections*

THE REVOLUTIONARY PERIOD (1765–1800)

James Otis
Against the Writs of Assistance

Patrick Henry
On Arming the Colony of Virginia

Samuel Adams
American Independence

George Washington
*Address Delivered upon Surrendering to Congress His
Commission as Commander-in-Chief of the Revolutionary
Army*

Alexander Hamilton
*The Federalist Papers
The Farmer Refuted*

John Carroll
*An Address to the Roman Catholics of the United States of
America*

Thomas Paine
*The Crisis
Common Sense
The Rights of Man*

Richard Henry Lee
*Address to the People of British
America*

Thomas Jefferson
*The Declaration of Independence
A Summary View of the Rights
of America
First Inaugural Address* (1801)

John Dickinson
*Letters of a Pennsylvania Farmer
to the Inhabitants of the British Colonies*

THE NATIONAL PERIOD (1800–1865)

John C. Calhoun
Last Speech—Slavery

Henry Clay
*Emancipation of the South
On the Compromise of 1850*

Daniel Webster
*Supposed Speech of John Adams
The Constitution and the Union
Reply to Hayne*

Robert Y. Hayne
Doctrine of State Rights

Stephen A. Douglas (1813–1860)
Lincoln-Douglas Debates

Edward Everett
*The History of Liberty
Speech at Gettysburg*

John England
*Classical Education
American Citizenship*

Abraham Lincoln
Central Ideas of the Republic
Cooper Union Speech
Farewell Address at Springfield
House Divided
Last Public Address
Jefferson Davis
*On the Withdrawal from the
Union*

Wendell Phillips
John Brown and the Spirit of '59
Toussaint l' Overture
Henry W. Beecher
The Glory of New England
*Raising the Flag over Fort
Sumter*
John J. Hughes
The Civil War in America

THE TRANSITION PERIOD (1865–1900)

Henry W. Grady
The Race Problem
Speech at Dallas, Texas
Henry Watterson
Abraham Lincoln
The Puritan and the Cavalier
Grover Cleveland
Good Citizenship
Chauncey M. Depew
The Columbian Oration
John Ireland
*The Duty and Value of Patriot-
ism*
The Church and the Age

Thomas Nelson Page
The Torch of Civilization
Edward Everett Hale
The Mission of Culture
Boston
Ulysses S. Grant
The Adopted Citizen
Phillips Brooks
*The Character of Abraham
Lincoln*
John Lancaster Spalding
Opportunity
Catholic Charity

THE TWENTIETH CENTURY (1900–   )

Charles W. Eliot
Arming of the Nations
Durable Satisfactions of Life
David Starr Jordan
Higher Education for Women
Henry van Dyke
Books, Literature, and People
The Typical Dutchman
Edward W. Bok
The Keys to Success
Susan B. Anthony
Woman's Right to Suffrage
Elihu Root
American Ideals
Business and Politics
A Plea for the League of Nations

Franklin K. Lane
Makers of the Flag
The Message of the West
The American Pioneer
William Jennings Bryan
America's Mission
The Cross of Gold
The Prince of Peace
William H. Taft
America and England
The Law's Delays
William E. Borah
The League of Nations
Brander Matthews
American Character
Edwin Booth

THE DRAMA

THE DRAMA AS A TYPE OF LITERATURE

A Distinct Literary Form

Although plays are thought of by many people as fiction, it is quite plain that they differ from novels, short stories, and narrative poems. Because of this variation, plays have a special classification all their own—*drama*. The original significance of the word was a literary piece to be played, or, in the strict Greek sense of the word, to be "done." The dramatic instinct is strong in peoples of every nation, and plays, however crude, are preserved in tribal rites, in folklore, or in the written literature of every racial group. Among English speaking people, plays were at first merely "done," but early found their way into manuscript or printed record. Today, successful plays appear on the stage, in motion pictures and in print almost simultaneously. At one stage in the development of English literature, careful distinction was made between plays to be staged and plays to be read. Now, however, the form of printed and acted plays is identical.

Many definitions of the drama have been formulated, but all seem to agree that the term should be applied to that type of literature which seeks to present a picture of actual life or a section of actual life in brief, vivid form. It is dependent for expression on actors or characters who use voice, gesture, action and reaction. The purpose is to convey an idea of emotions and events to an audience or reader and to arouse emotions of sympathy, understanding, anger, disgust, and the like in those who read or see.

The Elements of Drama

Drama differs from other types of literature in so many ways that it is difficult to list all. In the first place, it is written for interpretation by several *characters* or actors, each of whom must be true to the type of character he represents. Then it must be brief and move swiftly to its conclusion. This means that every character, every speech and every action must count. Long descriptive passages, except in the stage directions or in an occasional dramatic speech of one of the characters, must be omitted. Characterization must be developed rapidly. Since the play may be produced on the stage, carefully planned, detailed and

C-AM

explicit directions must be included. Hints for interpretation must frequently accompany speeches assigned to various characters. These and the stage directions are usually given in italics. Again because of the necessity for brevity, drama must be limited to a single theme and to very few objects or aims.

In addition to characters which carry the action of the play forward, there must be a *plot*—an outline or general plan of the action of the story. The plot includes brief inserted *introductory* material concerning the characters, the setting, the period, and sufficient review of incidents preceding the time of the play itself to make it understandable; a continuous thread of story *(rising action)* leading to the big dramatic moment or scene of the play called the *climax;* and what is technically known as *falling action*—a thread of story leading from the climax to the *conclusion.* Especially in modern plays, it is not always possible to analyze a plot into these parts, for much of the material making up the plot is given in stage directions, in parenthetical notes, and in speeches by the various characters.

A third element of plays is known as the *setting.* Its purpose is to give the locale of the story (country, city, town, house, office, a forest, etc.) and the time (century, season, hour of the day, etc.).

Given characters, plot, and setting, the supreme test of the drama is that it must "act." The playwright who is its author must be a master of his craft. He must know how to handle his story, how to organize it, and how to present it on the stage of the theatre. "Actability," therefore, may be said to be the most important element of all great drama.

Types of the Drama

The general type of literature classified as drama is sub-divided into several special types. If we think of the action or story of a play as a conflict between two opposing forces, such as man and his environment or man and some personal weakness or personal enemy, the outcome of the conflict determines the sub-classification of the play. If in the struggle, man is victorious, the play is a *comedy;* if he is overcome by the opposing force the play is a *tragedy.* It is necessary for the student to understand that a comedy is not necessarily "funny," and that a tragedy does not always end in bloodshed and death. The real test is the outcome of the plot.

A few years ago, *melodrama* was a very popular stage production, and the modern motion picture makes frequent use of this type. It is characterized by very rapid action, overly sentimental scenes or incidents, and many thrilling situations. The sudden arrival of the hero, just in time to rescue the threatened heroine, is a typical feature of this type of play. Because of the sudden and usually unexplained or unexpected solution of the difficulty, it is often considered a not-too-good type of drama. Pure comedy or tragedy in which events take their natural course is felt to be a more literary type of drama.

THE HISTORY OF AMERICAN DRAMA

General Characteristics

Owing to the fact that the colonists were busy clearing forests and establishing homes, this period of American history was not very productive of literature. Rigid religious and moral principles led to the feeling that the theatre and things theatrical were particularly objectionable. As a result, drama flourished least, perhaps, of all the literary arts. The influence of the mother country shows itself strongly in the few specimens that have survived. Many of the plays of the period reflect the strong anti-British sentiment of pre-Revolutionary and the war days. Others suggest the intense local patriotism and early nationalism of the period.

George Cockings' *The Siege of Quebec* and Thomas Godfrey's *The Prince of Parthia* are the only two American-written plays known to have been produced in this country previous to the Revolutionary War. Representative plays of the years of the war and the close of the century were *Ponteach, or the Savages of America* by Robert Rogers; *The Blockheads* and *The Group* by Mercy Warren; *The Battle of Bunker's Hill* by Hugh Brackenridge; *The Fall of British Tyranny* by John Leacock; *André* by William Dunlap; and *The Contrast* by Royall Tyler.

The two authors mentioned last are deserving of special mention. They are often called by historians and critics the "fathers of American drama."

William Dunlap (1766–1839)

With the background of a portrait painter, Dunlap brought to drama writing real artistic skill and a genuine insight into character depiction. Born in New Jersey, he received much of his education in England. Loving all of the arts, he was particularly fond of the drama. His *History of the American Theatre* was a standard reference for many years after its publication in 1832. His tragedy *André,* based on the life and death of historic Major André was an outstanding play of the early period. Other plays written by him were *Leicester* and *The Father.*

Royall Tyler (1757–1826)

After graduation from Harvard in 1776 Tyler had interesting and varied experiences as a law student with John Adams, as military aide during the Revolutionary War, as practicing lawyer, and as judge of the Vermont Supreme Court. Supplementing his military and legal interests he wrote several plays and came to be one of the earliest successful American playwrights. Three noteworthy dramas by Tyler were *The Contrast, May Day,* and *The Georgia Spec.*

The National Period (1800–1865)

General Characteristics

With the major part of the problem of establishing homes in a new country taken care of, and with political freedom from England guaranteed after the Revolutionary War, there seemed to be more freedom for the development of the arts, including the drama. Lessening of the Puritan influence also gave a freedom to the theatre which served as an impetus to play writing. British influence was still strong, however, and much of the work was purely imitative.

During the first quarter of the new century appeared such titles as *The Indian Princess* by James Nelson Barker, *Charles the Second* and *The Fall of Tarquin* by John Howard Payne, and *The Triumph of Platts-burg* by Richard Smith. Barker's play was to become the forerunner of many plays and musical sketches based on the Pocahontas theme. Playwrights increased in number and importance from 1825 to the Civil War and a few plays of this period are still known to American, and even to foreign audiences. Two are *Uncle Tom's Cabin* (Aiken's dramatization of Harriet Beecher Stowe's novel by the same name) and Joseph Jefferson's adaptation of Washington Irving's *Rip Van Winkle*.

Three dramatists stand out in this period—Mrs. Mowatt, Nathaniel Parker Willis, and Steele Mackaye.

Anna Cora Ogden Mowatt (1819–1870)

Mrs. Mowatt, although of French birth and a favorite actress in both France and England, won most of her fame as an American writer of plays. She wrote under the pen names of "Ogden" and "Isabella" and "Helen Berkeley." She is particularly noteworthy as the author of *Fashion*, probably the first American comedy of manners. This play was produced with tremendous success in 1845 and was one of the first American plays to merit European production. Although the style shows the influence of British dramatists, *Fashion* is considered one of the best literary works of early American art.

Nathaniel Parker Willis (1806–1867)

During Willis' undergraduate days at Yale he wrote verse so excellent that it was published by New England magazines. Soon after graduation he established a monthly magazine and acted in an editorial capacity with several publishing houses. Most of his writings were prose —sketches, biographies, and travel. In addition to one novel and a volume of poems, he is known chiefly in dramatic literature for *Bianca Visconti; The Kentucky Heiress; Fortesa, the Usurer;* and *Two Ways of Dying for a Husband*.

Steele Mackaye (1842–1894)

Although Steele Mackaye belongs to two distinct periods of literature as followed in this book, his influence was so strongly felt in the later years of the National Period that he should be noted here. He was a native of Buffalo, New York, and a great patron of the arts. He was a painter of some reputation and an actor who won great favor both in Europe and in America. He wrote some thirty plays, two of which are still known today—*Hazel Kirke* and *Money Mad*. But it was not for his drama alone that he was so important in this phase of American literature. His greatest contribution was probably in the field of stage production. He it was who first introduced large theatres, moving stages, folding theatre chairs and many beautiful scenic and lighting effects. His revolutionizing of theatrical devices made possible the many varied and broadening effects found in the plays of the next period of literary development.

THE TRANSITION PERIOD (1865–1900)

General Characteristics

In the biographical note on Steele Mackaye, cognizance was taken of the fact that his inventions in the field of theatrical mechanics made possible variations in the dramatic writings of the period which followed. Perhaps the greatest single characteristic of the Transition Period was the trend toward the realistic, although a love of the romantic and whimsical influenced a number of the playwrights. During the last decade of the century the realism became much more intense, culminating in the starkness of many of the dramas of our own day. Throughout the period, foreign influence was felt, but it should be noted that it was during the Transition Period that American drama really came into its own as a recognized body of literature.

Many of the people who made valuable contributions to the dramatic literature of the period really did their best work in the first part of the Twentieth Century. For that reason, they are treated as belonging to that period although their lives more properly seem to belong in the Transition Period. What is called by some authorities the renaissance in American drama seemed to begin about 1890, the last decade of the Transition Period, and seems to be still in process in the 1930's. A few outstanding names, however, belong primarily to the Transition Period.

James A. Herne (James Aherne) (1840–1901)

Mr. Herne, as he was known in dramatic circles, was born in Troy, New York, and received his education there. He was always interested in literature and in amateur dramatics. From long association with the theatre he learned many "tricks of trade" which contributed greatly to his playwriting ability. He is chiefly known for three successful plays, *Hearts of Oak, Shore Acres,* and *Sag Harbor.* The second is still a favorite with readers, stock companies, and amateurs.

Bronson Howard (1842–1908)

Howard arrived at the vocation of playwright by way of years of experience in journalism, a route not uncommon in literary fields. Two of his plays insured him fame, *Saratoga* and *Shenandoah*.

William Gillette (1855–   )

Perhaps no name has had a closer connection with the theatre than that of William Gillette. As an actor, producer and an author he has made an outstanding contribution to the American stage. In youth he was a personal friend of Mark Twain who had much to do with Gillette's career as an actor and writer. While most of his training was gained through practical experience in stock companies, he did do special study at Harvard, New York University, and Massachusetts Institute of Technology. *Held by the Enemy* is his best known play.

Other Dramatists of the Transition Period

Two names deserving brief mention in the list of notable dramatists of the Transition Period are Langdon Mitchell and Dion Boucicalt (Bōō′sē kō). Mitchell, using the pen name "John Philip Varley," wrote two particularly successful plays, *Becky Sharp* and *The New York Idea*. Boucicalt was not American born, but Irish. After an enviable career in London, however, he came to America to act as a theatrical adviser and became an outstanding feature in national drama between 1876 and 1890. Besides making valuable contributions in producing technique, he brought to New York an American version of one of the great plays of the period, *The Octoroon*. He was also author of *Foul Play* and of a superior dramatization of *Rip Van Winkle*.

The Twentieth Century (1900–   )

General Characteristics

Many of the best plays of authors listed in the preceding period were either written or first produced in the early 1900's. Their influence shows to a certain extent in the works of their contemporaries and successors.

It is almost impossible to ascribe any one characteristic or set of characteristics to modern plays. Were that to be done, probably absolute freedom concerning subject, theme, and treatment would come closest to being accurate. Complete frankness, brutal realism, concern over social problems of all sorts—these are type qualities of the plays of the century, relieved here and there by romances, whimsical plays, historical plays, "plays with music," fantasies, and pageants. Translations from the foreign are common. Successful novels are frequently dramatized. Not only do successful stage productions find their way into motion pictures, but also there is strong evidence of the influence of motion picture technique in the writing and producing of drama. Tremendous innovations in stage and lighting equipment alone have made possible the inclusion in modern play scripts of practically any type of treatment. In general, the Twentieth Century thus far has been a period of experiment, of daring, of stupendous stage effects, all resulting in much that is little better than trash, but also in some plays that will in all probability stand the test of time and literary survival.

The Little Theatre Movement

No attempted treatment of the modern period, however brief, would be complete without mention of the happy influence of the great interest in playwriting shown by schools and colleges since the turn of the century, and the fine work undertaken in countless amateur theatrical groups throughout the country. Many of the finest literary gems have come from so-called "Little Theatre" groups or directly from school and college courses in playwriting and stage production.

The One-Act Play

The activity just mentioned leads to special comment on the *one-act play* as a type. Plays of earlier periods were commonly longer plays of from two to six acts. Even as early as Shakespeare's time, little dramatic sketches, called "curtain raisers," were used to open longer plays or to fill in time between acts. Today, one-act plays are a favorite type with both playwrights and producers, especially of Little Theatre groups. The one-act play is never just a short form of a longer play. It is a distinct form and a complete unit in itself. It treats a single dramatic moment out of life, but treats it completely. In its relationship to the longer play, it parallels the short story in its relationship to the full-length novel. It has all of the literary characteristics of the longer play except sustained treatment of a series of related incidents.

David Belasco (1859–1929)

A conspicuously great name in the American theatre is that of David Belasco. Both as a writer and as a producer he achieved an enviable place. Possibly no one man has done more to modernize the theatre and to revolutionize stage lighting and scenery. His inventions are almost countless. Early in boyhood he worked about the theatre and can be said to have devoted his whole life to it. Four plays were written by him during the latter part of the Transition Period: *The Wife, Lord Chumly, The Girl I Left Behind Me,* and *The Heart of Maryland.* Among his best works of the new century, *The Return of Peter Grimm,* written especially for his dearest friend, the famous actor David Warfield, was perhaps the greatest favorite. Two other successes, however, made very favorable impressions, *The Rose of the Rancho* and *The Girl of the Golden West*. Belasco built his own theatre, casted and directed his own plays, and is conceded the greatest advocate of the "star system" of featuring one actor or actress in a series of plays.

Augustus Thomas (1857–1919)

Another of the great personages of American drama, making notable contributions in both periods, was Augustus Thomas. His work won such general favor he came to be considered an authority on dramatic questions and to occupy a position practically of dramatic dictator. He too worked his way to literary greatness by the journalistic route. His earliest plays included *The Burglar, A Man of the World,* and *Arizona.* His first play in the new century was *Oliver Goldsmith.* A comedy, *Mrs. Leffingwell's Boots,* was received very favorably, but genuine acclaim was given to *The Witching Hour.* This was one of the first psychological studies in drama form and is still a favorite. Perhaps the climax of his dramatic technique was *The Copperhead.*

Clyde Fitch (1865–1909)

Born in Elmira, New York, and educated at Amherst, Fitch became one of the most prolific writers of our dramatic literary history. His original plays and adaptations and translations from the foreign total more than sixty. Equal variety is noticeable in the subject matter of the plays—historical, fanciful, and modern social problem material. Time will probably show his greatest claim to literary fame to be *Beau Brummell.* Among his other plays of fame and quality are *The Climbers, The Girl with the Green Eyes,* and *The Truth.* The latter particularly is deserving both of study and modern production. Fitch's play *Nathan Hale,* an excellent example of historical drama, is included in this volume.

Booth Tarkington (1869–)

A native of Indiana, trained in Exeter and at Princeton, Booth Tarkington ranks high as an American literary man. His novels are among the best loved and his plays, both one-act and longer, give him an enviable place among dramatists. While some of his plays have been done in collaboration with E. G. Sutherland and Harry Leon Wilson, his original works are, perhaps, his best. Chief among these is *Monsieur Beaucaire.* Others of his plays are *The Man from Home, Clarence, The Country Cousin,* and *Your Humble Servant.*

Percy Mackaye (1875–)

Reference has already been made to the debt of American drama to Steele Mackaye. As a novelist, poet, biographer and playwright, his son, Percy, a native of Rochester, New York, is carrying on his father's example. His special claim to greatness in the field of drama lies in the play, *The Scarecrow*. Besides several masques and special program plays for Christmas and other holidays, he has also written *Jeanne d' Arc, Tomorrow,* and *A Thousand Years Ago*.

Eugene O'Neill (1888–)

Undoubtedly America's surest claim to literary greatness, and certainly one of the greatest of modern writers, O'Neill is an example of the realistic movement of the twentieth century. His realism is frank, sometimes brutal, stark, and usually tragic. Therein lies his peculiar strength. Realism which handled by anyone else might be only revolting, rises to genuine literary excellence with his deft treatment. O'Neill is the son of an actor. He attended Princeton, Harvard, and received an honorary degree from Yale. He lived in South America at one time, and has travelled widely, spending much time on the sea. From 1919 to the present he has had an unbelievably long series of successes, both commercially and from a literary standpoint. He writes one-act plays and full-length plays equally well. He has done many interesting experiments in dramaturgy, each of which in his hands seems to have proved valuable. Among his plays are *The Moon of the Carribees, Beyond the Horizon, Ile, Emperor Jones, Anna Christie, Where the Cross Is Made, Lazarus Laughed,* and *Strange Interlude*.

Other Important Playwrights of the Twentieth Century

Because they are all important in the field of twentieth century drama, the following writers deserve more than the brief mention which can be given them here. George M. Cohan (1878–) should be mentioned as a writer of light comedies which seem to win favor with the American public, important among which are *The Tavern, The Talk of New York,* and *The Song and Dance Man*. Better known for his clever *Fables in Slang*, George Ade (1866–) deserves special mention as a writer of light comedies through three plays, *The County Chairman, The College Widow,* and *Father and the Boys*. Both while a student and as a teacher of English at Harvard, William Vaughan Moody (1869–1910) showed distinct promise of a literary career, and two of his plays, *The Great Divide* and *The Faith Healer*, have given him a place in the literary hall of fame. Three plays, forerunners of plays of the social problem variety, were written by Eugene Walter (1874–), *Paid in Full, The Easiest Way,* and *Fine Feathers*. Three plays of Edward Knoblock (1874–) called him to the attention of the American literary and theatre public, *Kismet, Milestones* (written in collaboration with Arnold Bennett), and his play based on a novel of the same name by Vicki Baum, *Grand Hotel*. Best known for his huge stage success, *Romance*, interpreted so ably by Doris Keane, Edward Sheldon (1886–   ) has written two other notable plays, *The Nigger* and *Song of Songs*. The best work of Charles Klein (1867–1915) is to be found in *The Lion and the Mouse*, *The Auctioneer*, and *The Music Master*, the latter two of which, staged by David Belasco and acted by David Warfield, gave the American theatre-going public two exceptionally fine dramatic treats.

Four Women Playwrights

Among the many women writing plays during the past twenty years, four seem to be especially successful: Edna Ferber, writing both independently and in collaboration with George S. Kaufman, who wrote *Our Mrs. McChesney*, *Cimarron*, *Show Boat*, and *Dinner at Eight*; Zona Gale, who holds three college degrees and who has acted as a member of the Board of Regents of the University of Wisconsin, author of *Miss Lulu Bett*, the 1921 Pulitzer Prize play, and of *Mister Pitt*; Clare Kummer, known for *Be Calm, Camille!, Good Gracious, Annabelle!*, and *A Successful Calamity*; and Rachel Crothers, who has a long list of both literary and stage successes, and who always acts as director of the productions of her own plays, among the best of which are *The Three of Us, Nice People, Mary the Third*, and *Let Us Be Gay*.

Other Promising Playwrights of the Twentieth Century

George S. Kaufman and Marc Connelly, writing sometimes independently and sometimes in collaboration, have given the stage some successful plays, among which are *Merton of the Movies, Dulcy*, and *Beggar on Horseback*; George Kelly is a promising young writer who is notable chiefly for *The Torchbearers, The Show-Off, Craig's Wife*, and *Philip Goes Forth*; Maxwell Anderson as co-author with Lawrence Stallings of *What Price Glory* won a place in American drama, and his plays, *White Desert, Saturday's Child* and *Elizabeth the Queen* have seemed to bear out the prediction that he will give native drama some fine contributions; Elmer Rice, a law school graduate, has demonstrated that he has a genuine gift for dramatic writing in such plays as *On Trial, The Iron Cross, Street Scene*, and *Counsellor at Law*; Paul Green as a professor in the University of North Carolina has made several noteworthy contributions to American drama and two remarkable plays, *In Abraham's Bosom* and *The House of Connelly*, have resulted from his interest in folk-ways and in preserving them for the nation in dramatic form; Philip Barry, having prepared for his chosen vocation as a playwright under Professor Baker's guidance in the famous Harvard "47-Workshop," showed unusual promise of fine literary ability in his first play *You and I*, and this ability has developed rapidly in a succession of plays among which are *The Youngest, Holiday, Tomorrow and Tomorrow,* and *The Animal Kingdom.*

Writers of One-Act Plays

A list of the writers of worth-while contemporary one-act plays could become almost endless. A few are given here: Rachel Lyman Field, Alexander Dean, Louise Driscoll, Kenneth Sawyer Goodman, Doris F. Halman, Constance D'Arcy Mackay, George Middleton, Oscar M. Wolff, Zona Gale, Eugene O'Neill, Percival Wilde, Oliphant Down, Clare Kummer, George Kelly, Lewis Beach, Walter Prichard Eaton, Glenn Hughes, Clarence Stratton, John Golden, Theresa Hilburn, Beulah Marie Dix, Alice Gerstenberg, Rita Wellman, Booth Tarkington, Louise Saunders, George M. Savage, Ida Benjamin Burroughs, Babette Hughes, George Kelly, and Arthur Hopkins. The last two are represented in this book and are deserving of special mention.

George Kelly (1887–   )

George Edward Kelly was born and educated in Philadelphia. When twenty-four years of age he followed the example of an elder brother and went on the stage. After five years in theatrical companies playing up and down the United States, he spent another five on the vaudeville stage, carrying the lead in one-act sketches written by himself. *Poor Aubry* was one of these.

His first full-length production, *The Torchbearers,* was not an unqualified success, but his second, *The Show-Off,* was a hit. It had a phenomenal run in New York and almost won Kelly the Pulitzer Prize in 1924. The Prize was awarded him the following year for *Craig's Wife. The Flattering Word, The Weak Spot,* and *Finders-Keepers* are other one-act plays by Kelly. Among his full-length plays are *Daisy Mayme, Behold the Bridegroom, Maggie the Magnificent,* and *Philip Goes Forth.*

Arthur Hopkins (1878–   )

When *The Poor Little Rich Girl,* that delightful and yet pathetic glimpse into the mind of a child, was first presented to the audiences of New York, Philadelphia, and Boston, it was noted that it was produced by Arthur Hopkins. Hitherto unknown, Mr. Hopkins made his début as a producer under most auspicious circumstances. He has continued to present some of the most interesting plays of our time, and has given them such a richness of background and such intelligent and skillful direction as to mark him as one of the foremost of producing managers. He is also author of *Burlesque,* a play of back stage life, which was filmed under the title of *The Dance of Life.* Of his one-act plays, *Moonshine* is perhaps the best known.

Dramas of the Twentieth Century

NATHAN HALE *

Clyde Fitch

The Historical Background of the Play: One of the favorite stories of the period of the Revolutionary War is that of the brave American hero, Nathan Hale. Is there anyone who does not thrill at the famous words, "I only regret that I have but one life to give for my country"? The incident of Hale's original statement, together with some of the historical events leading up to it, was used by the author, Clyde Fitch, as the background of the play. Fictitious characters and happenings are of course used in the development of the plot.

Records disagree concerning the date of Hale's birth, but all are agreed that his birthplace was Coventry, Connecticut, and the year either 1755 or 1756. He was educated at Yale, training especially for the ministry. There seems to be no record of his having preached. Soon after finishing college he became a teacher in one of the Latin grammar schools common in New England at that time, in New London,

Connecticut. Tradition has it that young Hale was always intensely patriotic and frequently unwisely bitter in his remarks against British officials in this country. As soon as the war broke out he joined a Connecticut regiment, earning promotion to the rank of captain in 1776.

Hale's war record shows service in the siege of Boston and the Battle of Long Island. Tradition again enters the picture with the story that he was one of a small and venturesome band of men who made a daring capture of a small boat loaded with provisions directly under the guns of an enemy man-of-war. Washington, after his disastrous defeat at Long Island, withdrew to Harlem Heights, just outside New York. Desperately needing confidential plans of the enemy's maneuvers he called for a volunteer to go into the enemy camp as spy. Hale offered to go.

Disguised as a Dutch schoolmaster, Hale successfully entered the enemy lines and secured the desired information. He was caught, the papers were found on his person, and without even the formality of a trial he was ordered hanged as a spy by General Howe. The execution took place at dawn on September 22, 1776. Hale's name has always been considered that of a great, self-sacrificing hero, and many statues have been erected in his memory in different American cities. One of the most famous is in City Hall Park, New York City.

CHARACTERS

NATHAN HALE (*Yale, 1773*)
GUY FITZROY
LIEUT. COL. KNOWLTON
CAPT. ADAMS
CUNNINGHAM
EBENEZER LEBANON
TOM ADAMS
WILLIAM HULL (*Yale, 1773*)
THE JEFFERSON BOY
THE TALBOT BOY
JASPER
SENTINEL
THREE SOLDIERS
ALICE ADAMS
MISTRESS KNOWLTON
ANGELICA KNOWLTON
THE WIDOW CHICHESTER

Schoolboys, Schoolgirls, Soldiers, Townsmen and Townswomen.

ACT I

SCENE: *The Union Grammar Schoolhouse, New London, Connecticut, in 1775. It is a simple room with a door on the left side. At the back are two smallish windows through which are seen trees and the blue sky; between them is a big blackboard. At the right of the room is a small, slightly raised platform on which is the teacher's desk; on the latter are papers, quill pens, an old ink-well, pamphlets, and books. A large globe of the world stands beside the platform. On the wall behind hangs a "birch." In front of the platform, and to one side, is a three-legged dunce's stool, unoccupied for the present. Two long, low benches for the classes are placed beneath the blackboard, and the desks and benches for the scholars are placed on the left, facing the teacher's platform. It is toward noon of a sunny day, and the music of "Yankee Doodle" is in the air. As the curtain rises a very badly drawn, absurd picture is seen on the blackboard, representing the boys on the ice pond of Boston Common, with their thumbs to their noses, driving away the British army! ALICE ADAMS is by the blackboard finishing this drawing. MISS ADAMS is one of the older pupils, somewhat of a hoyden, already a little of a woman, lovely to look upon, and altogether a charming, natural girl full of high spirits. All the scholars are half out of their places and they are laughing, shouting, talking, and gesticulating. Above the din, a* BOY'S *voice is heard.*

Talbot Boy. [*In warning.*] Quick, Alice! Teacher!
[*There is a wild scramble for their places, and just as* LEBANON *enters sudden silence reigns. All pretend to be absorbed in their books, but keep one eye on* LEBANON *and the blackboard, till he, following their glances, discovers the drawing.*]
Lebanon. [*A prim and youthful assistant teacher, with a pompous manner, intended to deceive his pupils.*] Who drew that picture? [*There is silence.*] Who drew this picture? [*No one replies, and only a few suppressed giggles are heard.*] I will keep you all after hours till the boy confesses.
Alice. [*Interrupts mischievously.*] Perhaps it was a *girl*, sir. [*The children giggle and snicker.*]

Lebanon. No interruptions! I will keep you all in till the boy confesses. [LEBANON *looks about expectantly; nobody speaks.*] I am in earnest.

Talbot Boy. It wasn't a boy, it was Alice Adams. [*The scholars hiss and cry "Shame! Shame!"*]

Lebanon. Miss Alice Adams, stand up. [ALICE *rises.*] Is that true?

Alice. [*Biting her lips to keep from laughing.*] Yes, sir.

Lebanon. [*To* ALICE.] Sit down. [*She does so, very leisurely. —To the Boy.*] Well, Master Talbot, you deserve to be punished more than Miss Adams, for telling on a fellow pupil, and on a girl, too. I shall report you both to Mr. Hale.

Tom Adams (ALICE'S *younger brother*). Please tell him I did it, sir, instead of my sister. Mr. Hale's always punishing Alice.

Alice. No, Mr. Lebanon, that wouldn't be fair, sir. Besides, I want Mr. Hale to know how well I can draw. [*Smiling mischievously. All the scholars laugh.*]

Lebanon. [*Raps on the table.*] Silence! That is enough. We will now begin the session in the usual manner by singing "God Save the King." [*A knock on the door. All the scholars are excited and curious.*] Master Adams, please open the door. [TOM *goes to the door and opens it; all the children looking over the tops of their books curiously.*] Everybody's eyes on their books. [*Each one holds his book up before his face between him or her and* LEBANON.]

[MRS. KNOWLTON *and* ANGELICA *enter.* MRS. KNOWLTON *is a handsome, but rather voluble and nervous lady, an undeterminated trifle past middle age. Her daughter,* ANGELICA, *is a pretty, quaint little creature, with a sentimental bearing; she is dressed in the top of the fashion.* LEBANON *rises and* TOM *returns to his place.*]

Alice. [*Half rising in surprise, and sitting again immediately.*] Well! Angelica Knowlton! What are you doing here?

Lebanon. [*Raps on his desk with his ruler.*] Miss Adams! [ANGELICA *throws* ALICE *a kiss.*]

Mrs. Knowlton. Is this Mr. Hale?

[ALICE *gives a little explosion of laughter, which is at once followed by giggles from all the children.* LEBANON *raps again sharply.*]

Lebanon. No, madam, I am Mr. Lebanon, Mr. Hale's assistant.

[ALICE *coughs very importantly.*]

Mrs. Knowlton. I wrote Mr. Hale I would visit his schoolhouse to-day with my daughter, Angelica, to arrange for her becoming a pupil. [*Bringing* ANGELICA *slightly forward with one hand;* ANGELICA *is embarrassed, and plays nervously with her parasol.*] Her cousin, Miss Adams, is already a scholar, and it will be well for the girls to be together. Angelica, dear, stop fiddling with your parasol, you make my nerves quite jumpy!

Lebanon. Mr. Hale will be here in one moment, madam. Won't you be seated, meanwhile?

Mrs. Knowlton. Thank you, yes. Be careful of your dress, when you sit, Angelica—don't make any more creases than are absolutely necessary. [*They sit carefully in chairs placed for them by* LEBANON *beside the desk.*]

Lebanon. Your daughter is a most intelligent appearing young lady, madam. I look forward with pleasure to instructing her.

Mrs. Knowlton. Thank you, sir, but it's only fair to tell you her appearances are deceitful. She is painfully backward in everything but spelling, and her spelling's a disgrace to the family. Angelica, dear, untie your bonnet strings; you'll get a double chin in no time if you're not more careful!

[ALICE ADAMS *lifts her hand.*]

Lebanon. What is it, Miss Adams?

Alice. Please may I go and kiss my aunt and cousin how d' you do?

[*The scholars giggle softly.*]

Mrs. Knowlton. That will not be at all necessary, Mr. Lebanon.

Lebanon. You must wait until recess, Miss Adams. Now, attention, please!

[*The scholars all shut their books, which they have made a
    pretence of studying, and rise without noise.*]

Mrs. Knowlton. [*To* ANGELICA.] Do you like this teacher, my darling?

Angelica. I think he is beautiful, mother.

Mrs. Knowlton. Well, that is scarcely the adjective I should use; *harmless* would be better I think. Cross your feet, my dear, it looks much more ladylike.

Lebanon. [*Rising.*] Ready! [*He strikes a tuning fork on the desk, motions three times with his finger, and at the third stroke all begin to sing "God Save the King."* MRS. KNOWLTON *and* ANGELICA *rise and sing. All sing except* TOM ADAMS. *After the first line,* LEBANON *stops them.*] Stop! Thomas Adams is not singing. Now, *everyone,* mind, and Thomas, if you don't sing, it will be five raps on the knuckles. [*All sing except* TOM, *two lines;* LEBANON *again stops them.*] Thomas Adams, come forward! [TOM *comes slowly forward.*] I am ashamed of you, being disobedient in this manner, before your esteemed relative, too. What do you mean, sir?

Tom. I won't sing "God Save the King."

Lebanon. And why not?

Tom. Because I hate him and his red coats. Hip! Hip! I say, for the Boston Indians, and Hooray for their tea-party! [*There is a low suppressed murmur of approval from the scholars, and a loud "Oh!" of astonishment from* ANGELICA.]

Lebanon. We'll see if we can't *make* you sing. Hold out your hand. [TOM *holds out his hand, and* LEBANON *takes up his ruler.*]

Angelica. Oh— [*She cries out and rises involuntarily.*] Oh, please, Mr. Teacher——

Lebanon. [*After a moment's hesitation.*] I cannot be deaf to the voice of beauty. [*Bowing to* ANGELICA, *he lays down the ruler.*]

Mrs. Knowlton. Child, compose your nerves; watch your mother!

Tom. Oh, you can whack me if you want. But when Mr. Hale's here, he don't punish me for not singing.

Lebanon. He doesn't? How's that?

Tom. No, sir. He said he didn't blame me!

Lebanon. Mr. Hale said that?

Tom. Yes, sir, and he said he had half a mind not to sing it himself any longer.

Lebanon. That's treason! We'll see about that when Mr. Hale arrives.

[TOM *goes back to his seat.*]

Mrs. Knowlton. Does Mr. Hale never come to the schoolhouse till toward noon?—Angelica! [*She motions aside to* Angelica *to pull down her skirts,—that her ankles are showing.*]

Lebanon. No, madam. Only there was a rumor to-day that there had been bloodshed between the British and Americans at Concord, and Mr. Hale is at the Post waiting for news.

The Talbot Boy. [*With his eyes turned toward one of the windows.*] Please, sir, here comes Mr. Hale now.

Lebanon. Very well. You will all please begin again and sing, whether Master Adams sings or not.

Tom. [*Who has been straining to see out.*] Mr. Hale is out of breath, and he's wondrous excited!

[Lebanon *raps for them to sing, and strikes tuning fork. The children sing—all except* Tom—*through three lines, when* Hale *enters, excited.*]

Hale. [*Lifting his hand.*] Stop that singing! [*The children stop.*]

Lebanon. Why is that, Mr. Hale?

Hale. I won't have my school sing any more anthems to that tyrant!

Lebanon. We will be punished for treason. Will you kindly notice the drawing on the board?

Hale. Hello! Hello! [*Laughing.*] What is it?

The Jefferson Boy. It's our boys, sir, in Boston, driving the red coats off the Common.

Lebanon. I have left the punishment for *you* to fix on, sir.

Hale. Punishment! Punishment! Not a bit of it! Give the boy who did it a prize. Listen to me, boys and girls—how many of you are Whigs? Say "Aye." [*All but the* Talbot Boy *raise their right hands and shout "Aye!"*] Who's a Tory?

Talbot Boy. Aye! [*Raising his right hand, but he takes it down quickly as all the others hiss him.*]

Hale. I make all the boys here "Sons of Liberty."[1] And all the *girls* too! Listen to me, boys and girls! Two days ago, eight hundred Britishers left Boston for Concord to capture our military stores there!——

All the Scholars. Boo! [*Groans.*]

Hale. But the Yankees were too smart for them! I want you to give three cheers for Paul Revere,—Ready!

---

[1] Sons of Liberty—A famous club of the day.

All. Hip, hip, hip, hooray!

Tom. [*Excitedly.*] What did he do, sir?

Hale. He rode like mad to Lexington and warned the people there, and all the farmers on the way, and other men rode in other directions, and when the Britishers came back to Lexington from Concord—[*Stops for breath.*]

All the School. [*Excited, and rising in disorder.*] Yes—yes——

Hale. [*Continues in crescendo.*] They found Minute Men by every fence, inside each house, behind every rock and tree! and the Americans chased those Regulars clean back to Boston, —at least what was left of them, for the British lost two hundred and seventy-three men, and we only eighty-eight! [*The whole school breaks loose in shouting,—whistles, catcalls, cries, applause, jumping up on their chairs and desks, etc.* LEBANON *tries in vain to quell the tumult; finally* HALE *comes to his rescue and silences the scholars; he turns to* LEBANON *questioningly.*]

Lebanon. Excuse me, Mr. Hale, there are visitors present; Mrs. Knowlton, the lady who wrote you yesterday.

Hale. Madam. [*Bows.*]

Mrs. Knowlton. [*Who has risen, curtseys.*] Sir! Angelica, rise and curtsey. [*To* HALE.] My daughter, of whom I wrote you, sir. [HALE *bows and* ANGELICA *curtseys.*] Angelica— what a curtsey! Who'd ever think you'd been taught all the fashionable attainments [2] at a guinea a quarter? [3]

Hale. I'm afraid you find us rather upside down this morning, madam. But I assure you it's nothing compared to what's going on in Boston, where the public schools were closed several days last week.

Mrs. Knowlton. So I heard, sir, which was one of my reasons for selecting New London. Sit down, Angelica. [ANGELICA *sits.*]

Hale. Excuse me one moment, madam. [*To* LEBANON.] Take Miss——

Angelica. Angelica, sir.

Hale. Miss Angelica to one side, and inquire about her studies.

---

[2] ATTAINMENTS—Accomplishments.

[3] A GUINEA A QUARTER—The sum of a guinea each three months (quarter of a year). A guinea was an English coin worth approximately $5 in present money, but valued considerably higher at the time of the play.

Lebanon. This way, Miss. [*They go beside the window up the stage.*]

Hale. Miss Alice Adams, please come forward. [ALICE *rises and comes to* HALE *in front of desk; she assumes an air of innocence, but with a mischievous and conscious twinkle in her eye when she looks at* HALE.] It will be a great pleasure for you, I am sure, to have your cousin with you.

Alice. [*Sweetly and conventionally.*] Yes, Mr. Hale. [*She looks into his face, and deliberately winks mischievously at him, biting back a smile.*]

Hale. [*Coming nearer her and whispers.*] Can I keep you in at recess? Have you done something I may punish you for?

Alice. Yes, sir. *I* drew the picture.

Hale. [*Delighted.*] Good!

Alice. But I'm afraid you've spoiled it all by not disapproving.

Hale. Not a bit of it! As *you've* done it, I'll disapprove mightily! [*Smiles lovingly at her, and adds, as he goes back to his desk,*] Very well—that is all, Miss Adams. I will give you an opportunity to talk with your aunt and cousin during recess.

Alice. [*About to go, turns back disappointedly, and speaks to him aside.*] What—aren't you going to punish me?

Hale. [*Aside to her.*] Certainly, that is only to blind the others. You know I'm obliged to change my mind rather suddenly about this picture. [ALICE *goes back to her seat.*] Mr. Lebanon! [LEBANON *joins* HALE *and they talk together aside.*]

Angelica. [*Joining her mother.*] Oh, mother, he is really beautiful! He says I know a great deal. [*She stands by her mother, with one arm about* MRS. KNOWLTON.]

Mrs. Knowlton. Humph! He must be a fool. One of your mitts[4] is off, child! Why is that?

Angelica. [*Drawing her hand away.*] He wanted to kiss my hand.

Mrs. Knowlton. Put on your mitt, this minute—and remember this, my dear: you are not here to learn coquetry, but arithmetic,—the French *language* if you like, but not French *manners!*

Hale. In honor of the day, we will omit the first recitation, and recess will begin at once. [*A general movement and suppressed murmur of pleasure from all the scholars.*] One mo-

---

[4] MITTS—A mitt was a kind of glove fashionable at the time.

ment, however; on second thoughts, I have decided this picture
—ahem—is, after all, very reprehensible. The perpetrator must
suffer. Who is the culprit—she—he— [*Correcting himself
quickly*] must be punished.

Tom. [*Before any one else can speak, rises.*] I did it, sir.

Alice. [*Rising.*] No, sir, it was I!

Hale. Miss Adams, I am *surprised!* And deeply as it pains
me, I must keep you in during recess.

Tom. It's a shame! [*Turns to school.*] He's always doing it!

Hale. Silence, Master Adams! Ten minutes' recess.

[*All the scholars rise, get their hats and caps from pegs on the
wall, and go out talking and laughing gaily, except* TOM,
who goes out slowly, angry; and ALICE, *who remains behind.*]

Mrs. Knowlton. [*To* ANGELICA, *as the scholars are leaving.*]
I think he is rather strict with your cousin. You'll have to
mind your P's and Q's, my dear.

Angelica. I don't like him one-half as much as Mr. Lebanon.

Mrs. Knowlton. [*Snapping her fingers on* ANGELICA'S *shoulder.*] Tut, my bird! Enough of that person.

Hale. [*Rising and turning to* MRS. KNOWLTON.] Madam,
if you will allow Mr. Lebanon, he will escort you and your
daughter about the play-grounds.

Mrs. Knowlton. [*Rising.*] Thank you! Can my daughter
remain to-day, sir? Angelica, straighten your fichu [5] strings.
You do give me the fidgets!

Hale. Certainly, madam. Mr. Lebanon——

[LEBANON *offers his arm to* MRS. KNOWLTON, *who takes it
after a curtsey to* MR. HALE.]

Mrs. Knowlton. Come, Angelica, and don't drop your mantilla! [6]

[ANGELICA, *after a curtsey, takes* MRS. KNOWLTON'S *hand and
they go out—all three.* HALE *and* ALICE *watch them closely
till they are off and the door closes behind them, then both
give a sigh of relief, and smile,* ALICE *rising and* HALE *going
to her.*]

Hale. [*Very happy.*] Well? [*Takes her two hands in his.*]

---

[5] FICHU—A light three-cornered ornamental kerchief worn over the shoulders and about the neck.

[6] MANTILLA—A light cape or cloak.

Alice. [*Also very happy.*] Well? [HALE *sits on desk before her,* ALICE *back in her seat.*]

Hale. I'm afraid your brother is becoming unruly. I'll not be able to keep you in at recess much longer. You see you're not half bad enough. [*Smiling.*] I ought *not* to punish you, and all the scholars will soon be perceiving that.

Alice. I try my best to think of something really bad to do, but my very wickedest things are always failures, and turn out so namby-pamby and half-way good,—I'm ashamed.

Hale. [*Impulsively.*] You darling!

Alice. [*Laughing; delighted, but drawing back in mock fear, and holding her arithmetic open between them.*] Mr. Hale!

Hale. [*Seriously, passionately, taking the book from her unconsciously and throwing it aside.*] Alice, did a young man ever tell you that he loved you?

Alice. Yes, sir,— [*Taking up her geography.*] Several have. [*Looking down into the book.*]

Hale. What!

Alice. [*Looks up at him coyly, then down again into her book.*] And one of them three times.

Hale. [*Closing the book in her hands and holding it closed so she will look at him.*] I'll keep you in three recesses in succession—one for each time.

Alice. [*Looks straight into his eyes.*] Then I wish he'd asked me twice as often.

Hale. Alice!

Alice. It was my cousin Fitzroy! He says he will persist till he wins, and mother says he will.

Hale. And you—do you like this cousin Fitzroy?

Alice. If I say I like him, will you keep me in another recess?

Hale. [*Moodily.*] I'll keep you in a dozen.

Alice. Then I *love* him!

Hale. [*Forgetting everything but her words, and leaving her.*] Alice—Alice—go, join the others. I'll never keep you in again.

Alice. No—no—you *must!* [*She throws away the geography.*] You promised if I would say I liked my cousin Fitzroy, you'd keep me in a dozen recesses. [HALE *goes back to her.*] It isn't treating me fair.

Hale. Do you know what I wish? I wish life were one long recess and I could keep you in with me forever.

Alice. [*Shyly looking down, speaks softly, naïvely.*]   Well—why—don't—you—sir?

Hale. [*Eagerly, delighted.*]   May I?

Alice. As if you didn't *know* you could.   Only there is one thing——

Hale. [*Tenderly.*]   What is it?

Alice. When we're married, I think it's only fair that *I* should turn the tables, and sometimes *keep you in!*

Hale. Agreed!   I'll tell you what——

Alice. [*Interrupting.*]   Oh!   I have an idea.

Hale. So have I. . . .   I wonder if they're not the same?

Alice. I'll try again to do something really naughty!

Hale. And I will keep you after school.

Alice. [*Rises.*]   *My* idea—and then you will walk home with me——

Hale. *My* idea, too!   And I will ask your father to-day!

Alice. [*With a half-mocking curtsey.*]   And if he won't give me to you, you will kindly take me all the same, sir.

[*The school-bell rings outside.*]

Hale. Here come the scholars!   You love me, Alice?

Alice. Yes.

Hale. Half as much as I love you?

Alice. No, *twice* as much!

Hale. That couldn't be.   My love for you is full of all the flowers that ever bloomed! of all the songs the birds have ever sung! of all the kisses the stars have given the sky since night was made.   [*He kisses her.*]

[*The door opens and the scholars enter.* HALE *goes quickly to his desk.* ALICE *buries her face in a book.* ANGELICA *and* LEBANON *enter together, after the scholars.*]

Lebanon. Mr. Hale, I think I had best point out to Miss Knowlton what her lessons will be,—and shall she sit next to Miss Adams, sir?

Hale. Yes.   And the first class in grammar will now come forward.

[*Seven scholars come forward and take their places on the forms in front of* HALE, *and while they are doing so* LEBANON *has arranged* ANGELICA *at a desk in front of* ALICE.]

Lebanon. This will be your desk, Miss Angelica.

Angelica. Thank you, sir.   Can I see you from here?

Lebanon. Yes, I always occupy Mr. Hale's chair. But you mustn't look at me *all* the time, young lady.

Angelica. I'll try not to, sir. [*She sighs.* HALE *begins to hear his class.* LEBANON *bends over* ANGELICA, *opening several books, marking places in them for her, etc. He is showing her where her lessons are to be.*]

Hale. Master Tom Adams.

Tom. [*Rising.*] Yes, sir.

Hale. The positive, comparative and superlative of good?

Tom. Good, better, best.

Hale. Yes. I wish you'd try and act on one or two of those in school. [TOM *sits, grinning.*] Master Talbot! [TALBOT BOY *rises.*] Positive, comparative and superlative of sick?

Talbot Boy (*who lisps*). Thick——?

Hale. Well? [*Pause.*] Why, any boy half as old as you could answer that. There's our little visitor, Master Jefferson there, I'll wager he knows it. Master Jefferson! [THE JEFFERSON BOY *comes forward.*] Positive, comparative and superlative of sick?

The Jefferson Boy. Sick— [*Pause.*] Worse— [*Longer pause.*] Dead! [*The school laughs.*]

Hale. [*Laughing.*] That's a good answer for the son of a doctor to make. [*He nods to the boy to sit, and he does so.*] What is it? [*He looks about and sees* ANGELICA *and* LEBANON *engrossed in each other behind a grammar book.*] Miss Angelica— [ANGELICA *and* LEBANON *start.*] Can *you* give it to us?

Angelica. [*Timidly, rising.*] I love—you love—he or she loves. [*The school giggles.*]

Hale. That was hardly my question, Miss Angelica. [*She sits, embarrassed. A slight commotion is heard outside.*] What I asked was— [*The door bursts open and* FITZROY *enters. He is a young handsome fellow of about twenty-five, in the uniform of a British officer; he is excited, and somewhat loud and noisy.*]

Fitzroy. Is this the Union Grammar School?

Hale. [*Rising.*] Yes!

Fitzroy. I have been sent here by General Gage, who is in Boston, to hold a meeting of your townspeople who are loyal to King George.

Hale. What for?

Fitzroy. Boston is in a state of siege. The rebels who chased

the Regulars through Lexington have been joined by other colonists around, and have cut the town completely off from all
communication, except by sea. This state of affairs is nothing
else than war, and Great Britain calls upon her loyal children!

Hale.   And my schoolhouse?

Fitzroy.   Is where the meeting is to be held, at once.

Hale.   [*Coming down from platform.*]   A *Tory* meeting!
Here! Have you been properly empowered?

Fitzroy.   [*Flourishing a paper.*]   Yes, here is my permit. A
crier is going about the town now, calling the men to meet within
the hour.

Hale.   A Tory meeting here!   [*He turns to the school.*]   Then
we'll get out, eh, boys?

All the School.   Yes—yes!

Fitzroy.   What—are you all *rebels* here?   [*Looking over the
school.*]

Tom.   No! We're "Sons of Liberty!"

Fitzroy.   You fool!   [HALE *interrupts him with a gesture, motioning to the girls on their side of the room.* FITZROY *takes off
his bearskin hat and bows gracefully.*]   I'll warrant the young
ladies favor the British— What, Alice,—you here? You will
allow me, sir?   [HALE *bows assent, but not too pleased, and*
FITZROY *goes to* ALICE.]

Hale.   What do you say now, Mr. Lebanon? Are *you* going
to stay for this meeting?

Lebanon.   No, sir-ee. I am going out to buy a gun.

Angelica.   [*Gives an unconscious cry, and forgetting herself
and her surroundings, rises frightened, crying,*]   Oh, no, Mr.
Lebanon, oh, no, no, no!

Hale.   Don't be alarmed, Miss Knowlton! I doubt if he ever
uses it.

Angelica.   Make him promise me, sir, he'll never carry it
loaded!

Hale.   [*After a jealous look at* ALICE *and* FITZROY, *who are
talking together at one side, turns to the school.*]   Boys! I have
a proposition to make. What do you say to joining a small
volunteer company with me at your head? Every boy over
fifteen eligible.

Boys.   Yes—yes!

The Jefferson Boy.   Please, Mr. Hale, make it boys over
'leven.

Hale. We'll make you drummer-boy, Master Jefferson. Come —all boys who want to join, sign this paper. [*They all crowd around the desk and sign, the constant murmur of their voices being heard through the following scene.* FITZROY *and* ALICE *come down stage together,* ALICE *leading,* FITZROY *following.*]

Alice. Please do not ask me that again. I tell you, you can *never* persuade me. Nor can my mother influence me the least in this. Twenty mothers couldn't make my heart beat for you, if you can't make it beat yourself. And even if I did love you— [*She adds quickly,*] which I *don't*—I'd let my heart *break* before I'd marry a man who is willing to take up arms against his own country!

Fitzroy. That's a girl's reasoning. England is too great a power to be defeated by an upstart little government like the American, and when she wins, those of us who have stood by her will be rewarded! These poor rebel fools will have their every penny confiscated, while I have a grant of land, promotion in the army—who knows, perhaps a *title.* Don't refuse me again too quickly!

Alice. Too quickly! There are no words short enough for me to use. You may *sell* your country for money and power, if you like, but you can't buy *me* with it, also. And that's the last word I'll ever say to you, Guy Fitzroy.

Fitzroy. Huh! You'll change your mind some day! I mean to *have* you,—do you hear me? If I can't beg or buy you, then I'll steal. You know what I'm like when I'm in my cups![7] Some day when I've made up my mind I can't wait any longer, I'll drink myself mad for you, and then beware of me. You remember that evening two months ago, after your mother's punch, when I dragged you behind the window curtain and kissed you against your will on your arms and neck and lips till you called for help? Remember that, and don't think you can refuse me carelessly, and have it done with. No, watch for me. [*She stands facing him haughtily, showing her disgust for him. There is a moment's pause in which he gazes passionately and determinedly at her.* FITZROY *by a gesture and a toss of his head, as much as to say, "We'll see, I am sure to win," breaks the pause and the feeling of the scene, looking at his watch and speaking as boys go back in single file to their places, having signed the*

---

[7] IN MY CUPS—Drunk.

volunteer roll-call.] It only lacks fifteen minutes of noon; I must be off. I will be back, Mr. Hale, for the meeting at twelve. How many of you boys wish to stay and rally round King George's flag? [*He waits for some sign from the boys. There is only silence*.] You little fools! [*He turns to* HALE.] Is this *your* teaching?

Hale. Not altogether, though I've done my best, sir. There is a gentleman in the Virginia Assembly who said "Cæsar"— [*He looks at boys with a look and nod of invitation to join him, and they all finish with him heartily*.] "Cæsar had his Brutus, Charles the First his Cromwell, and George III"— [TOM *throws up his cap*.]

Fitzroy. [*Loudly*.] Treason—this is treason!

Hale. "George III may profit by their example." That's what Patrick Henry said.

Fitzroy. Fortunate for him he went no farther!

Hale. Oh, he is still moving! I think he will go far enough before he stops.

Fitzroy. He may go up! [*With a motion across the throat, of hanging*.] See that the house is ready for us. [HALE *nods*. FITZROY *looks hard at* ALICE, *then says*,] Good day to you all! [*and goes out*.]

Hale. The school will assemble to-morrow as usual. Of course, if there's really any fighting to be done I shall go, and the boys who are too young to go with me——

The Jefferson Boy. None of us are, sir.

All the Boys. None of us! none of us!

Hale. Ah, I'm *proud* of you! Proud of you all! But your parents have something to say; and for the girls and the younger boys we must find another teacher.

Lebanon. I will stay, Mr. Hale. I feel it's my duty.

Hale. [*Amused*.] Ahem! Very well—that is settled then. For to-day the school is now dismissed, except Miss Alice Adams, who must remain behind.

Tom. [*Rises, angrily*.] What for? She hasn't done anything —she hasn't had a chance to do anything. You kept her in all recess, and you shan't keep her in again! [ALICE *and* HALE *are secretly amused. The school looks on surprised and excited*.]

Hale. Look here, Master Adams, what right have you to say as to what shall or shall not be done in this school?

Tom. She's my sister, and you're always punishing her, and I won't have it!

Hale. [*Amused.*] Oh, won't you?

Tom. No, sir, I won't! She never does anything worth being punished for. You've got a grudge against her; all the boys have seen it! Haven't you, boys? Go on, speak out,—haven't you seen it? [*Turning to the boys, who murmur, rather timidly,*] Yes.

Hale. Really— May I ask who is master here? School is dismissed, except Miss Alice Adams,—she remains behind.

Tom. [*Excited, coming out from his seat to in front of the benches.*] I say she shan't!

Hale. And I say it's none of your business, sir, and she shall.

Tom. [*Off his head with excitement.*] She shan't! [*Beginning to take off his coat.*] Will you fight it out with me? Come on—a fair fight!

Alice. Tom!

[*The school rise and go out slowly with* LEBANON, *but casting curious looks behind them as they go.* ALICE, HALE, *and* TOM *are left behind.*]

Hale. I will leave it with Miss Adams herself whether she does as I say, or not.

Tom. Come on, Alice, come on with me.

Alice. No, I prefer to stay.

Tom. Bah—just like a girl! Very well, then *I* shall stay, too. [HALE *and* ALICE *look surprised and disappointed, yet secretly amused.*] Every time you punish my sister, you'll have to punish me now. If she stays behind, I stay too, to keep her company. [*Behind* TOM'S *back* ALICE *and* HALE *exchange amused and puzzled looks and affectionate signals. Finally* HALE *has an idea.*]

Hale. Tom, come here,—go to the blackboard. [TOM *goes sullenly to the board.*] I think we'll have a little Latin out of you. Write the present tense of the Latin word to love. [TOM *sneers, but with a piece of chalk writes,*

"Amo, *I love,*
Amas, *Thou lovest,*
Amat, *He—*"

is interrupted.] Never mind the "he or she"; just make it "she." [TOM *puts an "s" in front of the "he," making it "she," and adds "loves."* Tom *looks sullen and rather foolish, not understanding.* Hale *goes to board and taking a piece of chalk adds after first line* "Alice," *and also to end of second line* "Alice;" *he adds to third line* "me," *and signs it* "Nathan Hale." *The blackboard then reads:*

> "Amo, *I love* Alice,
> Amas, *Thou lovest* Alice,
> Amat, *She loves*—me.
>   Nathan Hale."]

Tom. [*Embarrassed, surprised, not altogether pleased.*] What—I don't believe it—it isn't true!

Alice. [*Rising and coming forward.*] Yes, it is, Tom.

Tom. Well, I'll be blowed!— [*He stops short, crimson in the face, and rushes from the room.* Hale *goes toward* Alice *with his arms outstretched to embrace her;* Alice *goes into his arms—a long embrace and kiss; a loud tattoo on a drum outside startles them.*]

Hale. The Tory meeting!

Alice. Fitzroy will be back. I don't want to see him!

Hale. Quick—we'll go by the window! [*Putting a chair under the window, he jumps onto chair and out; then leans in the window and holds out his hands to* Alice, *who is on the chair.*] And if to-morrow another drum makes me a soldier——?

Alice. It will make me a soldier's sweetheart!

Hale. Come. [*She gets out of the window with his help, and with loud drum tattoo and bugle call, the Stage is left empty, and the Curtain Falls.*]

ACT II

Scene: *September, 1776. At* Colonel Knowlton's *house on Harlem Heights.*[1] *A large, general room with white walls and columns. The furniture of the room is heavy mahogany upholstered in crimson brocade, this latter material also hanging in curtains at the windows. Life-sized portraits by Copley and Stuart,*[2] *of* Colonel *and* Mrs. Knowlton *at the time of their marriage, hang on each side of the room. A broad window at back shows the brick wall of the garden,*

---

[1] Harlem Heights—The heights on upper Manhattan Island, now part of New York City.

[2] Copley and Stuart—Famous portrait painters of the day.

She gets out of the window with his help.

and through a tall, ornamental, iron gate is caught a glimpse of the river.[3] MRS. KNOWLTON *is nervously looking out of the window. She comes from the window, pulls the bell-rope, and returns agitatedly to window. A happy old colored servant in a light blue and silver livery enters in answer.*

Servant. Yaas, m'm?

Mrs. Knowlton. Oh, Jasper, how long since Miss Angelica went out?

Servant. I dunno, m'm.

Mrs. Knowlton. It isn't safe for her to go out alone, Jasper.

Servant. No, m'm.

Mrs. Knowlton. [*Looking again out of window.*] And I've expressly forbidden her.

Servant. Yaas, m'm.

Mrs. Knowlton. [*Turning and coming back excitedly on her toes.*] And you don't know?

Servant. Dunno nothing, m'm.

Mrs. Knowlton. And the other servants?

Servant. None of the servants in this hyah house, m'm, dunno nothing whatsomever what ole Jasper dunno.

[COLONEL KNOWLTON *enters hurriedly. He is a tall, striking-looking man, aquiline features, and iron-gray hair. He is strong in character, brave in spirit, and affectionate in heart. He is dressed in the blue and buff uniform of a Revolutionary Colonel.*]

Colonel Knowlton. [*Speaks as he enters.*] Ah, Martha, that's good I've found you!

Servant. [*Eagerly.*] Beg pardon, sah, but am thar any news, Colonel?

Colonel Knowlton. Yes, Jasper. You servants must turn all our rooms into bedchambers by to-night. [*Sits heavily on the sofa as if he were tired.*]

Mrs. Knowlton. What! [*Going to him and sitting beside him on the sofa.*]

[JASPER *leaves the room, taking the Colonel's sword and hat.*]

Colonel Knowlton. The army has abandoned the city, under Washington's orders, to take a position here, on Harlem Heights.

[3] RIVER—The Hudson River.

Washington is making his own headquarters at the house of Robert Murray, on Murray Hill, and we must take in all the staff officers we can.

Mrs. Knowlton. [*Brushing the dust off his shoulders, and holding his arm affectionately.*] Well, I'm glad of a chance to be of some sort of use, even if it's only to turn the house into a tavern! Have we abandoned the city entirely?

Colonel Knowlton. No, General Putnam is there with four thousand men. But every one who can is leaving. The sick have been sent over to Paulus Hook.[4] I told Captain Adams he should stay with us, and he brings Alice with him.

Mrs. Knowlton. That's most desirable for Angelica. This Lebanon person proposed for her again to me this morning! He doesn't seem to understand the meaning of the word "No." The next time *you'd* better say it and see if he *will* understand.

Colonel Knowlton. What is there against Mr. Lebanon?— Where is Angelica?

Mrs. Knowlton. I don't know, and I'm that worried. [*Rises and goes again to the window.*] She's been gone two hours, and she didn't wear her pattens.[5]

Jasper. [*Enters, announcing,*] Captain Adams, sah, and Missy. [COLONEL KNOWLTON *rises as* CAPTAIN ADAMS *and* ALICE *come in.* ALICE *looks much more of a young lady than in the first act, and very charming in a full blue and white dress, big hat, and black silk pelisse*[6] *for traveling. Her father,* CAPTAIN ADAMS, *is a portly, dignified, good-hearted man, older than* COLONEL KNOWLTON, *and like him in colonial uniform.* CAPTAIN ADAMS *kisses* MRS. KNOWLTON, *then goes to* KNOWLTON, *while* ALICE *kisses* MRS. KNOWLTON.]

Mrs. Knowlton. I'm so glad you came, too, Alice. Angelica is worrying me terribly. [*Helping* ALICE *off with her pelisse. The two women go up the stage together.*]

Captain Adams. I've been seeing about the public stores which are being taken to Dobb's Ferry. General Washington tells me he has asked you to hold a conference here to-day.

Colonel Knowlton. Yes. [*Turning to* MRS. KNOWLTON.] We must prepare this room, Martha.

---

[4] PAULUS HOOK—Now Jersey City.
[5] PATTENS—A kind of overshoe.
[6] PELISSE—A long outer-garment.

Mrs. Knowlton. What is the conference for?

Colonel Knowlton. We must discover, in some way, what the enemy's plans are.

Captain Adams. Yes, what are these British going to do? We *must* know. The army is becoming more and more demoralized every day.

Alice. Only to think! We've heard our soldiers are actually in need of the barest necessities of clothing, and there are practically no blankets. [*During* ALICE'S *speech,* MRS. KNOWLTON *goes to the door at left, opens it and listens for* ANGELICA. *Closes it and comes back.*]

Mrs. Knowlton. No blankets—and the winter coming! Well! I was married with six pairs, and mother was married with six, and Angelica shan't be married at all—at least not till this war's over! So there's three times six,—eighteen pairs for the Continental soldiers—bless their hearts! Alice, how about young Fitzroy? It's rumored again you're going to marry him. [*Crossing to* ALICE *as she speaks her name. At the same time the two men go a few steps up the stage and talk together confidentially.*]

Alice. Oh, that rumor spreads every time I refuse him; and I did again by post, yesterday.

Mrs. Knowlton. I'm glad of it! He's nothing like Captain Hale's equal. People aren't through talking yet of *his* gallant capture of the British sloop in the East River!

Colonel Knowlton. Hale's done a hundred brave things since then! The eyes of the whole army are upon him.

Alice. [*Very happy and proud.*] I know something very few are aware of. Not long ago the men of his company, whose term of service had expired, determined to leave the ranks, and he offered to give them his pay if they would only remain a certain time longer. [*The two men come forward.*]

Captain Adams. Good heavens! What my daughter doesn't know about Captain Hale!——

Alice. [*Beseeching.*] Father!

Captain Adams. [*Smiling.*] If you allow Alice, she will spend the day discanting on Captain Hale's merits. As for Fitzroy, he's a blackguard. They say he would like to join the Americans now, but don't dare, because he killed one of his old friends in a drunken brawl, and he's afraid he'd get strung for it.

C-AM

Colonel Knowlton. And just at present, Martha, Captain Adams would probably be pleased to go to his room.

Mrs. Knowlton. By all means. This way, Captain. Alice, I will return for you in a moment. You must share with Angelica, now the house is to be turned into a barracks.

Colonel Knowlton. Be careful you girls don't do any wounding on your own account. We've no men to spare. [ALICE *laughs.* MRS. KNOWLTON *and* CAPTAIN ADAMS *go out by the door, left.* ALICE *stops* COLONEL KNOWLTON, *as he is about to follow. She pantomimes him to come back, pushes him down onto the sofa—she is behind it—and with her arms about his neck, speaks cajolingly.*]

Alice. Uncle Knowlton?

Colonel Knowlton. Yes, my dear.

Alice. Have you any news of Captain Hale?

Colonel Knowlton. How long is it since you have seen him?

Alice. Much too long, and I've made up my mind not to have it any more.

Colonel Knowlton. That's right, don't trust him. In Connecticut, where he's been, the girls are far too pretty. [*Insinuatingly, bending his head back and looking up at her humorously.*]

Alice. [*Jealously.*] You've heard some stories of him?

Colonel Knowlton. [*Teasing her.*] Ahem! Far be it from me to expose a fellow soldier.

Alice. Uncle Knowlton, I'm ashamed of you! An old man like you!

Colonel Knowlton. Oh, not so old!

Alice. *What* do you know?

Colonel Knowlton. [*Rising.*] Nothing, my dear. I was only jesting. [*Starting to go.*]

Alice. I'm not so sure of that. Wait a minute! [*Coming from behind the sofa to him, she seizes hold of him by a button on the breast of his coat, taking a pair of scissors from the table —the house bell is heard.*]

Colonel Knowlton. What are you doing?

Alice. Getting a soldier's button to make Captain Hale jealous with! He shan't think he is the only one to flirt.

[JASPER *enters from the hall in answer to the house bell and crosses the room to the door which leads to upstairs.*]

Colonel Knowlton. We soldiers don't *give* buttons away—we sell them!

Alice. Oh, I'm going to kiss you! You're quite old enough for that, [*She kisses him.*] but, when I tell Nathan about it, I shall pretend you were somebody else, and young, and good looking!

[JASPER, *who has watched them by the doorway, right, chuckles and goes out.*]

Colonel Knowlton. Well, you can tell him to-day if you like!— [*For a second* ALICE *cannot speak for surprise and joy; then she catches her breath and cries,*]

Alice. He's coming here!

Colonel Knowlton. Yes. [*Nods his head violently.*]

Alice. Oh! [*She cries out for very happiness, and running across the room throws herself in an ecstasy of joy upon the sofa; then quickly jumps up and runs back to* COLONEL KNOWLTON.] I'll kiss you again for that good news. [*Starts to kiss him; changes her mind.*] No, I won't, either!

Colonel Knowlton. No, you must save all the rest of your kisses for Captain Hale!

Alice. Oh, dear no! Yours weren't at all the kind I give him. You know there are two kinds of visits,—those we make because we want to see people, and those we make on strangers, or after a party, whether we want to or not. The latter are called *duty visits!* Well?—Do you understand?

Colonel Knowlton. No, not in the least.

Alice. Stupid! Your *kiss* was a *duty visit.* [*With a low mocking curtsey.*] What hour is he coming?

Colonel Knowlton. I won't tell you, Miss! I won't give you another party, all for that one little duty visit. [*And he starts to go out by the door, left.*]

Mrs. Knowlton. [*Off the stage, left, calls,*] Thomas!

Colonel Knowlton. Coming, Martha! [*He closes the door behind him.*]

Alice. [*Dances half-way around the room, singing,*]
        "Nathan is coming, to-day, to-day!
        Nathan is coming to-day, to-day!" etc., etc.

[*Till she reaches the mirror on the wall at the left. She examines herself critically in the glass, still singing, takes a rose from a vase and puts it in her hair, retouches her toilet where she can, and pinches her cheeks to make them red.*] Oh, dear, I wish I were prettier! I wonder what those Connecticut girls are like!—[ANGELICA *appears outside the window, and thrusts her head in.*]

Angelica. [*Whispers.*] Alice!

Alice. [*Startled.*] Oh! Angelica!

Angelica. Sh! . . . don't look—turn your head the other way.

Alice. What in the world——!

Angelica. Sh—Go on—Please. . . . [ALICE *turns her back to the window.* ANGELICA *beckons, off left, and runs past the window, followed by* LEBANON, *quickly. The front door is heard to slam.* ANGELICA *puts her head in at the doorway, right.*]

Alice. What's the matter?

Angelica. Alice! Matter! Matter enough! I'm married!!

Alice. [*Loudly.*] What!!

Angelica. [*Frightened.*] Sh! Where is mother?

Alice. Upstairs.

Angelica. Very well. [*Speaks over her shoulder.*] Come along, darling! [*She enters, followed by* LEBANON, *dressed in Continental uniform. He wears a white wedding favor, and carries a gun awkwardly.*] I'm a married woman, Alice! [*She turns and directs* ALICE'S *attention to* LEBANON, *on whom she gazes lovingly.*] Isn't he beautiful in his soldier clothes? [LEBANON *smiles, embarrassed but happy, and goes to shake hands with* ALICE.] Go on, you can kiss him, Alice. I won't be jealous, just this once on our wedding day!

Lebanon. [*To* ANGELICA.] No, really, thank you, Precious, but I'd rather not. [*To* ALICE.] You don't mind?

Alice. [*Smiling.*] Oh, no, pray don't put yourself out for me!

Angelica. [*Aside to* LEBANON.] You've hurt her feelings. [*She tries to take his arm, but it is his right in which he carries his gun. Aloud.*] Hold your gun in your other hand, I want to take your arm. [*He changes his gun awkwardly. They stand together, arm in arm, her head on his shoulder, and she gives a happy sigh.*] Alice, will you break it to mother, at once?

Alice. Mercy! I forgot about that. It's an elopement!

Angelica. Yes, and in the day time! I hated to do without a moon, but I could never get away evenings.

Alice. Does your mother suspect?

Angelica. Not a sign. She refused Ebenezer again this morning!

Mrs. Knowlton. [*Calls from off stage, left.*] Alice! [*All start.* ANGELICA *and* LEBANON *show abject terror, and, "grabbing" for each other, cling together.*]

Angelica. Oh, she's coming! Save us. Alice, save us!

Alice. Quick! Go back into the hall. [*Starts pushing them out.*]

Lebanon. Do it gently, Miss Alice.

Angelica. Yes, mother couldn't stand too great a shock. [*They go out, right.* ALICE *takes a ribbon out of the little bag she carries, and putting* COLONEL KNOWLTON'S *button on it, ties it around her neck, as* MRS. KNOWLTON *comes into the room.*]

Mrs. Knowlton. I heard voices. What did they want?

Alice. [*Embarrassed, but amused.*] They desired me to tell you, as gently as possible, that they—that she—that he—well, that *you* are a *mother-in-law!*

Mrs. Knowlton. What do you mean, child, by calling me names?

Alice. Angelica——

Mrs. Knowlton. Angelica!—Mother-in-law—Alice, don't tell me! Give me air! Give me air!

Alice. [*Fanning her.*] Air!

Mrs. Knowlton. No! no! I mean something to sit on. Angelica—my baby! hasn't made herself miserable for life? [*Sitting in a chair which Alice brings forward for her.*]

Alice. No. She's married.

Mrs. Knowlton. It's the same thing! Who was the wicked child's accomplice? [*She suddenly realizes, and rises.*] It wasn't—it wasn't—that— [*She chokes.*] that—*that!*——

Alice. Lebanon!

Mrs. Knowlton. No! [*Her legs give way, owing to her emotions, and she sits suddenly in the chair.*] I won't believe it! Those children! I'll spank them both and put them to bed! No! I won't do that either! Where are they?

Alice. In the hall.

Mrs. Knowlton. [*Rises and gestures tragically.*] Call them!

Alice. [*Going to the door, right.*] You won't be cruel to her— [MRS. KNOWLTON *breathes hard through her tightly com-*

pressed lips.] Angelica! [An-
gelica *and* Lebanon *enter
timidly.*

Angelica. Mother!

Mrs. Knowlton. Don't come
near me! I—you undutiful
child! [*She begins to break
down and tears threaten her;
—to* Lebanon,] As for you,
sir—words fail me—I [*She
breaks down completely, and
turns to* Angelica.] Oh, come
to my arms! [*The last is
meant for* Angelica *only, but*
Lebanon *takes it for himself
also. Both* Angelica *and*
Lebanon *go to* Mrs. Knowl-
ton's *arms, but she repulses* Lebanon.] Not you, sir! Not
you! [*And enfolds* Angelica.] My little girl! Why did you?
—— [*Crying.*]

Angelica. [*Herself a little tearful.*] He said he'd go fight
if I'd marry him! And I heard so much of our needing
soldiers; I did it, a little, for the sake of the country!

Mrs. Knowlton. Rubbish! Come to my room!——

Angelica. Look at him, mother! And I wouldn't marry him
till he put them all on! Gun and all!

Lebanon. [*Timidly.*] Mother!

Mrs. Knowlton. [*Turning.*] *What!!* How dare you, sir!

Lebanon. Please be a mother to me, just for a few minutes.
I'm going off to fight this evening.

Mrs. Knowlton. [*Witheringly.*] Fight! You?

Lebanon. Yes, I said to my wife— [*These words very
proudly.* Angelica *also straightens up at them, and* Mrs.
Knowlton *gasps angrily.*] Let's begin with your mother, and
if I'm not afraid before her, I'll be that much encouraged toward
facing the British. [Angelica, *seizing* Lebanon's *free hand, says*
"Come," *and the two kneel at* Mrs. Knowlton's *feet, in the
manner of old-fashioned story books.*]

Angelica. Forgive him, mother, for the sake of the country?

Mrs. Knowlton. Hm! We'll see— [*She goes out saying,*]
Come, Angelica! [Angelica *follows her out, beckoning to*

LEBANON *to follow, which he does, pushed forward by* ALICE. ALICE *is left alone.* JASPER *enters from the right.*]

Jasper. Has Colonel Knowlton gone out, Missy?

Alice. No, Jasper.

Jasper. 'Cause thah's a young Captain Hale hyah to pay his respecks.

Alice. Captain Hale!

Jasper. Yaas, Missy.

Alice. Then never you mind about Colonel Knowlton, Jasper; *I* will take all the respects that gentleman has to pay!

Jasper. La, Missy! Is you sweet on him? [*Opens door.*] This way, sah! Hyah's a young lady says as how she's been waiting up sence sunrise foa you!

Alice. Jasper! [HALE *enters.*]

Hale. [*Seeing her, is very much surprised.*] Alice! [*He rushes to her and takes her in his arms.*]

Jasper. [*By the door, right, with much feeling.*] Dat's right, kiss on, ma honeys! Smack each other straight from the heart. It does ole Jasper good to see you. Thah's a little yaller gal lying out in the graveyard, yonder, dat knows ole Jasper was fond of kissing, too! [ALICE *and* HALE *finish their embrace, and sit side by side on the sofa. They are unconscious of* JASPER'S *presence, who lingers to enjoy their love, unable to tear himself away. He speaks softly to himself.*] Don't stop, ma honeys, don't stop!

Hale. I had no hint I should find you here. [*Taking her hand.*]

Alice. Father brought me to-day.

Jasper. [*Taking a step nearer to them behind the sofa.*] Bress their little souls!

Hale. I have just come down from Connecticut—a lovely part of the country. [ALICE *draws her hand away.*]

Alice. Yes. I've heard of you there.

Jasper. [*Coming in earshot, disappointed.*] Oh, go on, ma honeys, don't stop! Kiss again, jes' for ole Jasper's sake!

Alice. Jasper!

Hale. What do you want, Jasper?

Jasper. Want to see you kiss again, Cappen. It warms ma ole heart, it does.

Hale. [*Laughing.*] I'll warm something else for you, if you don't get out!

Jasper. You don' mind ole Jasper, Cappen? Why, I done see the nobles' in the lan' kiss right yah in this very room!

Hale. Well, you go away now. You have kissing on the brain.

Jasper. Maybe I has, Cappen, but I'd a deal sight rather have it on the lips! You ain't the on'y sojer anyway, Cappen, what Missy's kissed. Take ole Jasper's word for dat, you ain't the on'y one this very day, you take ole Jasper's word for dat! [*Chuckling.*]

Alice. [*Leading* JASPER *on to make* HALE *jealous.*] Why, Jasper, where were you?

Jasper. I was jes' comin' in, Missy, and jes' goin' out. I shet my eyes tight, but they would squint, honey! Jasper's ears anyway are jes' as sartin as stealin' to hear kissin' goin' on any-where round these hyah parts. [*He goes out, right.*]

Hale. Is that true? [ALICE *looks at him, smiling provokingly, and playing with the military button on the ribbon around her neck, to call his attention to it. He sees the button.*] Whose —— [*He stops himself, resolved not to ask her about it; but he can't take his eyes off it.*]

Alice. *I* wish to ask a question or two! How many young ladies did you see in Connecticut?

Hale. [*Moodily.*] I don't know. What soldier's button is that you wear on your neck?

Alice. What young ladies have you made love to, since we've been separated?

Hale. Whom did you kiss to-day, before me?

Alice. Confess!

Hale. Whom?

Alice. [*Rises.*] Captain Hale, [*With a curtsey.*] I'm not your pupil any longer, to be catechised so!

Hale. [*Rises also.*] Very well! Please tell your uncle, Colo-nel Knowlton, I am here to see him.

Alice. Captain Hale, [*Another curtsey.*] I shan't do any such thing.

Hale. Then I'll go find him myself. [*Going toward the door, left.*]

Alice. [*Running before him.*] No, you won't—Captain Hale—— [*Going before the door and barring his way.*]

Hale. Give me that button. [*His eyes on it.*]

Alice. [*Leaning against the door-frame.*] Not for worlds! [*Kissing it.*]

Hale. [*Looking about the room.*] I'll climb out the window. [ALICE *runs to prevent him, and gets to the window first.*]

Alice. Do, if you like, but I shan't follow you *this time!*

Hale. Ah, you remember that day in the schoolhouse when you promised to be a soldier's sweetheart? I didn't know you meant a whole regiment's.

Alice. [*Coming away from the window, indignant.*] How dare you! Leave my house!

Hale. Whose house?

Alice. I mean—my uncle's house.

Hale. Which way may I go? The way I came?

Alice. [*Witheringly.*] Yes, back to your Connecticut young ladies!

Hale. Thank you! [*Bows, and steps out of the low window.* ALICE *stands listening a moment, then hurries to the window and leans out, calling.*]

Alice. Nathan! Nathan! Where are you going?

Hale. Where you sent me—to—ahem!—Connecticut!

Alice. Are there so many pretty girls there?

Hale. There isn't a petticoat in the State—at least there wasn't for my eyes!

Alice. Then come back! Come back! Quickly! [NATHAN *reappears outside the window.*]

Hale. Aren't you ashamed of yourself?

Alice. No!

Hale. [*Laughingly.*] Then I won't come back!

Alice. Very well, sir, don't!

Hale. What reward will you give me, if I do?

Alice. [*Thinks a second.*] This *button!*

Hale. Good! [*Putting his hands on window ledge, springs in. He holds out his hand for the button.*] Give it to me!

Alice. [*Teasing, pretends to be sad and repentant.*] First I must make a confession.

Hale. [*Depressed.*] Go on.

Alice. And tell you *whom* I kissed.

Hale. [*More depressed.*] Well?

Alice. You'll forgive me?

Hale. [*Desperate, between his teeth.*] Yes!

Alice. [*Looks up, smiling mischievously.*] It was *Uncle Knowlton!* [HALE *starts, looks at her a moment, comprehends, then laughs.*]

Hale. You little devil, you! To tease your true love out of his wits. But I will make you regret it—I have been very ill in Connecticut.

Alice. That's why you were there so long! [*All her teasing humor vanishes, and for the rest of the act* ALICE *is serious. From this moment in the play the woman in her slowly and finally usurps the girl.*]

Hale. Yes. As soon as I was able I came on here. I've been out of the fighting long enough.

Alice. Fighting! Is there to be another battle at once? Is that what this conference is for?

Hale. I don't know, but we must attack or we'll be driven entirely out of New York, as we were out of Boston.

Alice. General Washington has twenty thousand men!

Hale. Yes, with no arms for half of them, and two-thirds undrilled. Good Heavens, the patient courage of that man! Each defeat, he says, only trains his men the better, and fits them for winning victory in the end! But General Howe has crossed now to Long Island with thirty thousand British soldiers.

Alice. Oh, this dreadful war! When will it end?

Hale. Not till we've won our freedom, or every man among us is dead or jailed!

Alice. That's the horror that comes to me at night, Nathan. I see you starving, choking, in some black hole, with one of those brutes of a red coat over you, or worse,—lying on the battlefield, wounded, dying, and *away from me!* There's one horrible dream that comes to me often! It came again last week! I'm in an orchard, and the trees are pink and white with blossoms, and the birds are singing, and the air is sweet with spring; then great clouds of smoke drift through, and the little birds drop dead from their branches, and the pink petals fall blood-red on the white face of a soldier lying on the ground, and it's you— [*In a hysterical frenzy.*] you!! And—then I wake up. I'm afraid some day it will happen! Nathan! Nathan!

Hale. My darling, my darling! It's only a war dream, such

as comes to every one in times like these! [*Taking her in his arms and comforting her.*]

Alice. Yes, and how often they prove true! Oh, Nathan, must you go on fighting?

Hale. Alice!

Alice. Yes, yes, of course you must. I know we need every man we have and more! Ah, if only I were one, to fight by your side, or even a drummer-boy to lead you on! [*She adds with a slight smile, and a momentary return to her girlish humor, and quickly, in a confidential tone, as if she were telling a secret,*] I would be very *careful* where *I* led *you!* Not where the danger was greatest, I'll warrant! [*She returns to her former serious mood.*] Nathan, listen. Promise me one thing,—that when you do go back to the fighting, you won't expose yourself unnecessarily.

Hale. [*Smiling.*] My dear little woman, I don't know what you mean!

Alice. Yes, you do! You must! It *isn't* a foolish thing I'm asking! And I ask it for your love of me! You must fight, of course, and I want you to fight bravely—you couldn't do otherwise, that you've proved time and again! Well, let it be so! Fight bravely! But promise me you won't let yourself be carried away into leading some forlorn hope, that you won't risk your precious life just to encourage others! Remember, it's my life now! Don't volunteer to do more than your duty as a soldier demands,—not more, for my sake. Don't willingly place the life I claim for mine in any jeopardy your honor as a soldier does not make imperative. Will you promise me that?

Hale. Yes, dear, I will promise you that.

Alice. That you won't risk your life unnecessarily! Swear it to me!

Hale. [*Smiling.*] By what?

Alice. [*Very serious.*] By your love for me, and mine for you.

Hale. [*Serious.*] I swear it!

Alice. Ah, God bless you! [*In the greatest relief, and with joy, she goes to embrace him, but they stand apart, startled by a loud knocking of the iron knocker on the front door of the house.*]

Hale. The men, beginning to come for the conference!

Alice. Oh, I wish I could stay! Can't I stay?

Hale. No. No women can be present.

Alice. If I asked Uncle?

Hale. He hasn't the power!

[COLONEL KNOWLTON *and* CAPTAIN ADAMS *come into the room from upstairs.*]

Colonel Knowlton. Ah, Hale, you're in good time! [*Shakes his hand, and* HALE *passes on and shakes* CAPTAIN ADAMS'S *hand, as* JASPER *ushers in three other men in uniform, who are greeted cordially by* COLONEL KNOWLTON, *and who pass on in turn to* CAPTAIN ADAMS *and* HALE, *with whom each also shakes hands. Meanwhile,* ALICE, *seeing she is unobserved, steals to the big window recess, where she conceals herself behind the curtains. While the men are greeting each other with the ordinary phrases,* JASPER *speaks at the door, right.*]

Jasper. [*Shaking his head.*] What a pity Colonel Knowlton was down already! Ole Jasper was jes' a countin' on gittin' another kiss! [*Starts to go out, but stops to hold door open, saying,*] This way, gemmen, if you please. [HULL, *a handsome young officer,* HALE's *age, and another man in uniform enter. They greet, first* COLONEL KNOWLTON *and then the others.*]

Colonel Knowlton. Jasper, arrange the chairs and table for us.

Jasper. Yaas, sir. [*He goes about the room arranging chairs and talking aloud to himself. Places table for* COLONEL KNOWLTON *at right, with a chair behind it, and groups the other chairs in a semicircle on the left. Three more men come in together and two separately, each one shaking hands all around, and always with* COLONEL KNOWLTON *first.*] Lor' save us, ef I knows how to arrange chahs for dis hyah meetin'! It ain't exackly a gospel meetin', no yetwise a funeral. Mo' like a funeral n' anything else, I reckon! Funeral o' dat tha British Lion. [*Moving the table.*] Dat's the place for the corpse. [*Placing a chair behind.*] Dat's fo' the preacher, and these hyah other chahs— [*With a final arrangement of the chairs.*] is fo' de mourners! Guess dey's mighty glad to get red o' sech a pesky ole relation, seems as ef she want de mother country, but mo' like de mother-in-law country, to ole Jasper's mind. [*At this moment* COLONEL KNOWLTON, *looking up, sees that all is ready.*]

Colonel Knowlton. [*With a motion to the men, and to the chairs.*] Brother soldiers! [*They take their places in the chairs*

according to their military rank, HALE *in the last row behind all
the others.* COLONEL KNOWLTON *takes his chair behind the table.*
JASPER *draws the heavy brocade curtains in front of the window
recess, and in so doing discovers* ALICE. *He starts, but, with her
finger on her lips, she motions him to be silent. None of the
others know she is there.* TOM ADAMS *enters in Continental
soldier's uniform. He gives the military salute.*]

Tom. Uncle, may I be present?

Colonel Knowlton. Yes, my boy, if no one has any objection.
[*He looks at the other men, but they all murmur,* "Oh, no, no,"
and "Certainly not," *and* TOM *takes his place beside* HALE *at the
back.*] That is all, Jasper, and we are not to be interrupted.

Jasper. Yaas, sir.

Colonel Knowlton. Not on pain of imprisonment, Jasper.

Jasper. Nobody's not gwine to get into this hyah room, Colonel, with ole Jasper outside the door, not even King George
hisself, honey.

[*With a stolen look toward the window where* ALICE *is hiding,
he goes out, right. A moment's important silence. The men
are all composed, serious.*]

Colonel Knowlton. [*Who has taken a letter from his pocket.*]
Gentlemen, I will first read you portions of a letter from General Washington to General Heath, forwarded to me with the
request from headquarters that I should summon you here to-day.
[*He reads.*] "The fate of the whole war depends upon obtaining intelligence of the enemy's motions; I do most earnestly
entreat you and General Clinton to exert yourselves to accomplish this most desirable end. I was never more uneasy than
on account of my want of knowledge on this score. *It is vital.*"
[*He closes the letter, and places it in his breast pocket.*] Gentlemen, General Heath, General Clinton, and General Washington together have decided there is but one thing to be done.
[*A moment's pause.*] A competent person must be sent, in
disguise, into the British camp on Long Island to find out these
secrets on which depends *everything!* It must be a man with
some experience in military affairs, with some scientific knowledge, a man of education, one with a quick eye, a cool head, and
courage,—*unflinching courage!* He will need tact and caution,
and, above all, he must be one in whose judgment and fidelity
the American Nation may have implicit confidence! I have

summoned those men associated with me in the command of our army whom I personally think capable of meeting all these requirements. To the man who offers his services, in compensation for the risks he must run, is given the opportunity of serving his country supremely! Does any one of the men of this company now before me volunteer? [*He ends solemnly and most impressively. There is a long pause, the men do not move, and keep their faces set, staring before them. After waiting in vain for some one to speak,* KNOWLTON *continues.*] *Not one?* Have I pleaded so feebly in behalf of my country then? Or have I failed in placing her dire necessity before you? Surely you don't need me to tell you how our Continental Army is weak, wasted, unfed, unclothed, unsupplied with ammunition. We could not stand a long siege, nor can we stand a sudden combined attack. We must know beforehand and escape from both, should either be planned! After fighting bravely, as we have, are we to lose all we have gained, the *liberty* within our grasp, at this late day? No! One of you *will* come forward! What is it your country asks of you? Only to be a hero!

Hull. No! To be a spy! [*A murmur of assent from the men.*]

Captain Adams. There's not a man amongst us who wouldn't lead a handful of men against a regiment of the English! who wouldn't fight for liberty in the very mouth of the cannon! but this is a request not meant for men like us.

Hull. [*Looking at the other men.*] We are all true patriots here, I take it!

All. Aye! Aye! Patriots!

Hull. [*Appealing to the men.*] Are we the men to be called on to play a part which every nation looks upon with scorn and contumely?[7]

All. No! No!

Hull. [*Turning again to* KNOWLTON.] I would give my *life* for my country, but not my *honor!*

All. Hear! Hear!

Colonel Knowlton. But, do you understand? Do you realize all that's at stake?

All. Yes! Yes!

Colonel Knowlton. Then surely one of you *will* come forward

---

[7] CONTUMELY—A noun meaning contempt or disdain.

in response to this desperate appeal from your chief. In the name of Washington, I ask for a volunteer! [*He waits. Silence again. He rises.*] Men! Listen to me! Shall our fathers and brothers killed on the field of battle be sacrificed for nothing? Will you stand still beside their dead bodies and see our hero, George Washington, shot down before your eyes as a traitor? Will you accept oppression again and give up Liberty now you've won it? Or is there, in the name of God, one man among you to come forward with his *life and his honor* in his hands to lay down, if needs be, for his country? [*After a short pause,* HALE *rises, pale, but calm.*]

Hale. I will undertake it! [*General surprise not unmixed with consternation, and all murmur, questioningly,* "Hale!" *A short pause.*]

Colonel Knowlton. Captain Nathan Hale—— [HALE *comes forward.*]

Captain Adams. [*Interrupting, rises.*] I protest against allowing Captain Hale to go on this errand!

Hull. And I!

All. And I! And I!

Captain Adams. Captain Hale is too valuable a member of the army for us to risk losing. [*He turns to* HALE.] Hale, you can't do this! You haven't the right to sacrifice the brilliant prospects of your life! The hopes of your family, of your friends, of us, your fellow-soldiers! Let some one else volunteer; you must withdraw your offer. [*A second's pause. All look at* HALE *questioningly.*]

Hale. [*Quietly.*] Colonel Knowlton, I repeat my offer!

Captain Adams. [*Rising, excitedly.*] No! We are all op-posed to it! Surely we have some influence with you! It is to certain death that you are needlessly exposing yourself!

Hale. Needlessly?

Hull. [*Also rising, excitedly.*] It is to more than certain death, it is to an ignominious one! Captain Hale, as a member of your own regiment, I ask you not to undertake this! [HALE *shakes his head simply.*] We will find some one else! Some one who can be more easily spared. [*Here he loses his manner of soldier, and speaks impulsively as a boy.*] Nathan—dear old man!— We were schoolboys together, and for the love we bore each other then, and have ever since, for the love of all those who love you and whom you hold dear, I beg you to listen to me!

Hale. [*Looks at* HULL *with a smile of affection and gratitude, and turns to* KNOWLTON.] I understand, sir, there is no one else ready to perform this business?

Colonel Knowlton. I must confess there is no one, Captain.

Hale. Then I say again, I will go.

Tom. [*Hurrying forward.*] Mr. Hale!—Sir!—Captain! [*Seizes* HALE'S *hand.*] For the sake of my sis—— [*He is interrupted quickly and suddenly by* HALE, *who places his hand on his mouth to prevent his speaking the rest.* HALE *takes a long breath, sets his face, then gives* TOM'S *hand a mighty grip, and puts him behind him.*]

Hale. [*Who is much moved, but gradually controls himself.*] Gentlemen, I thank you all for the affection you have shown me, but I think I owe to my country the accomplishment of an object so important and so much desired by the commander of her armies. I am fully sensible of the consequences of discovery and capture in such a situation, but I hold that every kind of service necessary for the public good becomes *honorable* by being *necessary!* And my country's claims upon me are imperious!

[*Unnoticed by the men,* ALICE *draws aside the curtains and comes slowly forward during* COLONEL KNOWLTON'S *following speech.*]

Colonel Knowlton. [*Rises, and going to* HALE, *shakes his hand with deep feeling.*] Manly, wise, and patriotic words, sir, which I am sure your country will not forget! I—I will call for you this afternoon to appear before Washington. Gentlemen, this conference is finished. [*A general movement of the men is immediately arrested by* ALICE'S *voice.*]

Alice. No! It is not!

Captain Adams. Alice! [ALICE *is white, haggard, "beside herself." She is oblivious of all but* HALE. *She goes to him, and, seizing his wrist, holds it in a tight but trembling grasp.*]

Alice. [*In a low, hoarse whisper.*] Your promise to me! Your promise!

Hale. [*Surprised.*] Do you hold me to it?

Alice. Yes!

Hale. Then I must break it!

Alice. No! I refuse to free you. You have given two years

of your life to your country. It must give me the rest. It's
my share! It's my right! [*She holds out her two arms toward
him.*]

Hale. Still, I must do my duty.

Alice. [*Her hands drop to her side.*] And what about your
duty to me!

Hale. [*Takes one of her hands, and holds it in his own.*]
Could you love a coward?

Alice. Yes, if he were a coward for my sake.

Hale. I don't believe you!

Alice. It is true, and if you love me you'll stay!

Hale. If—*if* I love you!

Alice. Yes, *if* you love me! Choose! If you go on this
mission, it is the end of our love! Choose! [*She draws away
her hand.*]

Hale. There can be no such choice,—it would be an insult to
believe you.

Alice. [*In tearful, despairing entreaty.*] You heard them—
it's to *death* you're going.

Hale. Perhaps——

Alice. [*In a whisper.*] You *will* go?

Hale. I must!

Alice. [*A wild cry.*] Then I hate you!

Hale. And I *love you*, and always will so long as a heart
beats in my body. [*He wishes to embrace her.*]

Alice. No! [*She draws back her head, her eyes blazing, she
is momentarily insane with fear and grief and love.* HALE *bows
his head and slowly goes from the room.* ALICE, *with a faint,
heart-broken cry, sinks limply to the floor, her father hurrying to
her as the Curtain Falls.*]

ACT III

Scene I

September, 1776. Long Island, opposite Norwalk.[1] The WIDOW
CHICHESTER'S *Inn. Time: Night. A party of British
officers and soldiers, including* CUNNINGHAM, *and also some
men in civilian's dress are discovered drinking, the* WIDOW
serving them. At the curtain they are singing a jolly drink-

[1] NORWALK—In Connecticut.

参

ing song. As the WIDOW *refills each mug, each soldier takes some slight liberty with her, pinches her arm, or puts his arm about her waist, or kisses her wrist, or "nips" her cheek; she takes it all good-naturedly, laughing, and sometimes slapping them, or pushing them away, and joining them in their song. At the end of the song* FITZROY *swaggers in by the door on the right. He is greeted with shouts and cheers. The* WIDOW *has gone behind the bar.*

Cunningham. [*Seated on the corner of the table, which is at the left.*] Here's a man for a toast! A toast, Major!

All the Soldiers. [*Rapping the table with their mugs.*] A toast! A toast!

Fitzroy. Then give me stuff to drink it in! [*Leaning with his back against the bar.*] I've a wicked thirst in my throat. [*The* WIDOW *is ready, as he speaks, to fill his glass across the bar. As she is filling it he kisses her roughly, and she, to elude him, moves and thus spills half the liquor; he tries to seize her, but she pushes him off.*]

Widow. Enough of that! Kiss the liquor—it's your equal! [*The soldiers are laughing, singing, and filling their mugs.*]

Fitzroy. Ain't she coy, the Widow Chic! Well, boys,—here you are to our Royal Master! Long life to King George!

Widow and All. [*Holding up their glasses and rising.*] Long life to King George! Hip! Hip! [*All drink, and then sit down again, some of the men going on with the song.*]

Fitzroy. Here's another! [2]

Cunningham. Give us a wench this time!

All. Yes, a wench! Give us a wench's name!

First Soldier. Yes, if you can't give us the wench herself, give us her name!

Fitzroy. [*By their table.*] What's the matter with the Widow for a wench? [*All laugh, including* FITZROY, *who jeers derisively.*]

Widow. [*Coming to* FITZROY.] You're a gallant soldier to poke fun at the woman who supplies you with drink! I've been hugged many a time by *your* betters! [*A general murmur of approval from the soldiers,* "Right for the widdy!" *etc., etc.*]

Fitzroy. [*Bowing low, with mock courtesy, and taking his hat*

[2] ANOTHER—Another toast.

I'm a teacher, but the Americans drove me out of my school.

off as he bows.] I ask pardon of your Highness! [*All guffaw. She makes a mocking bob curtsey and goes back to the bar.*]

Cunningham. Go on with the toast, we're thirsty.

All. [*Shouting and pounding on the table.*] Your toast! Your toast! [*As they shout,* HALE *enters, from the right, very quietly and goes to the bar. He is dressed in a citizen's dress of brown cloth and a broad-brimmed hat. No notice is taken of him except by the* WIDOW, *who gives him a mug and a drink and watches him a little curiously through the scene.*]

Fitzroy. Here's death to George Washington!

All. Hurrah! Death to George Washington!

[HALE *has suddenly fixed his eyes on* FITZROY, *and shows that he finds something familiar in his voice and manner, and is trying to recall him.* HALE *has, at the giving of this toast, lost control of his muscles for a moment,—lost hold of his mug, it drops, and the liquor spills. As the others put their mugs down,* HALE *is stooping to pick up his. The noise when he dropped the mug and his following action bring him into notice. He comes forward as* FITZROY *goes up stage.*]

Cunningham. Hello! Who's this?

All. Hello! Hello! [FITZROY *doesn't pay much attention; he is talking with the* WIDOW *at the bar.*]

Hale. Gentlemen, I am an American, loyal to the King, but of very small account to His Majesty.

Cunningham. [*Tipping back his chair.*] What's your name?

Hale. Daniel Beacon.

First Soldier. What's your business here?

Hale. I'm a teacher, but the Americans drove me out of my school.

Cunningham. [*Crossing behind* HALE *to the bar, where he gets another drink.*] For your loyalty, eh?

Hale. Yes—for my loyalty.

First Soldier. [*Bringing his fist down hard on the table.*] The dirty rebels!

Hale. I am in hopes I can find a position of some sort over here.

Widow. [*Who has been half listening.*] Can't you teach these soldiers something? Lord knows they're ignorant enough. [*Comes out from behind the bar and places a big flagon of wine on the table. Takes away the empty flagon.*]

First Soldier. Widdy! Widdy! [*All laugh.* FITZROY *joins them again.*]

Widow. [*Behind the men at table.*] Well, have you heard what the Major here says—you drunken, lazy sots?

Cunningham. What's that?

Fitzroy. General Howe's new plans. [*The men lean over the table to hear.*]

Cunningham. Are we to make a move? [FITZROY *nods his head impressively several times. The men look at each other and nod their heads.*]

Widow. [*Poking* CUNNINGHAM *with her elbow.*] Bad news for you, lazy! Lord! How the fellow does love the rear rank.

Cunningham. Shut up! Let's hear the news!

Widow. You've a nice way of speaking to ladies!

Cunningham. [*Growls in disgust.*] Bah!

Fitzroy. It comes straight from headquarters! [*The men gather more closely about* FITZROY, HALE *with them, with calm, pale face, showing his suppressed excitement.* FITZROY *continues in lower tones.*] General Howe is going to force his way up the Hudson and get to the north of New York Island. [*An instantaneous expression of fear crosses* HALE's *face.*]

Cunningham. [*Grunts.*] Huh! What's that for?

Widow. Ninny!

Fitzroy. Use your brains!

Widow. [*Laughing.*] Use his *what?*

Fitzroy. Hush, Widow Chic! If we can get to the north of New York Island without their being warned, we'll catch Washington and cage what is practically the whole American army! They'll have to surrender or fight under odds they can never withstand.

First Soldier. Well! What's to prevent the scheme?

Fitzroy. Nothing, unless the Americans should be warned.

Cunningham. If they have an inkling of it they can prevent us getting up the Hudson, eh?

Fitzroy. Precisely. In any case if they're warned it won't be tried, because Washington wouldn't be trapped and after all Washington is the man we want to get hold of.

Cunningham. Wring Washington's neck, and we won't have any more of this crying for liberty!

Fitzroy. The expedition is planned for to-morrow night, and there's practically no chance for him to be warned before then.

First Soldier. Have you authority for this, sir?

Fitzroy. The orders are being issued now,—it's been an open secret among the men for two days. Down at the Ferry Station the betting is this business finishes the rebellion. [*The* WIDOW, *in answer to a signal from one of the men, comes out from behind the bar, with another flagon of wine.*] They're giving big odds.

Cunningham. Can't finish it too soon to please me. [*Rises unsteadily.*] Fighting's dangerous work!

Widow. [*Filling his cup.*] That's a brave soldier for ye!

Cunningham. Shut up!

Widow. I'll shut when I please.

Cunningham. You'll shut when I say! You old *hag!*

Widow. "Hag!" [*Slaps his face.*]

Cunningham. Enough! [*Throws the wine in his mug in her face.* HALE, *who has sprung up, knocks his mug out of his hand with a blow.*]

Hale. You coward! [*All the soldiers show excitement. Several rise.* WIDOW *goes to the bar, wiping the wine from her face; she is crying, but soon controls herself.*]

Cunningham. What business is it of yours?

Hale. It's every man's business to protect a woman from a brute!

Cunningham. Hear the pretty teaching gentleman quote from his reader!

Fitzroy. [*Rises. He has noticed* HALE *for the first time.*] Who is this?

Hale. Daniel Beacon.

Cunningham. A teacher the Rebs have driven out of New York.

Fitzroy. [*Who has looked at* HALE *curiously, turns to the* WIDOW.] Have you ever seen him before?

Widow. Not to my knowledge.

Fitzroy. [*At the bar with the* WIDOW.] There's a something about him mighty familiar to me. I'm suspicious! Here you, Beacon, how do we know you're not some Rebel sneak?

All. [*Rising.*] What's that?

Cunningham. That's true enough! What's your opinions?

All. Make him speak! Make him speak. [*A general movement among the soldiers.*]

Fitzroy. Yes, if you *are* a loyalist, give us a taste of your sentiments!

Cunningham. A toast will do! Give us a toast! [FITZROY *turns aside to the* WIDOW.]

All. [*In a general movement, seizing* HALE *they put him on top of table.*] Come on, give us a toast!

Fitzroy. [*To the* WIDOW.] I'm suspicious of this fellow! I've seen him somewhere before. [*He looks at* HALE *attentively, unable to recall him.*]

All. Give us a rouser! There you are! Now give us something hot!

Cunningham. A toast for the King, and then one with a wench in it.

Hale. Here's a health to King George! May right triumph and wrong suffer defeat!

All. Hip! Hip! To the King! [*All drink except* HALE, *who only pretends, which* FITZROY, *who is watching intently, notices.*]

Fitzroy. [*To the* WIDOW.] He didn't drink! I am sure of it!

Widow. No! *I* think he *did!*

Cunningham. Now for the wench!

Hale. To the Widow Chic—God bless her. [*All laugh except* CUNNINGHAM, *who says,* "Bah!" *and ostentatiously spills his liquor on the floor.*]

Hale and All. The Widow Chic! Hip! Hip! [*All drink, and then the soldiers take* HALE *down, and all talk together, slapping each other on the back, drinking, starting another song, etc.* HALE *sits by the table.*]

Fitzroy. [*To the* WIDOW, *suddenly.*] Ah! Now I know! [*In a voice of conviction and alarm.*]

Widow. [*Frightened by his voice and manner.*] What?

Fitzroy. Who he is! He's my girl's white-livered lover, one named Hale!

Widow. Are you sure?

Fitzroy. Almost,—and if I'm right, he's doing spy's work here! Get plenty of liquor; if we can drug him he may disclose himself! Anyway, we'll loosen his tongue! [WIDOW *exits at back, with an empty flagon.* FITZROY *joins* HALE *and the other soldiers; as he does so,* HALE *rises; he has grown uneasy under* FITZROY'S *scrutiny.*]

Hale. Well, gentlemen, I must retire for the night. I haven't a soldier's throat for wine.

Cunningham. Good! So much the better—the more for us! [HALE *goes toward the door at back;* FITZROY, *from the right, goes at same time to meet him. They meet at the door, back.*]

Fitzroy. Still, won't you stay and have a game with us?

Hale. I think you must excuse me.

Fitzroy. [*Angry.*] You're afraid to stay, you're afraid to drink, for fear we'll find out the truth as to who you are! [*The* WIDOW *comes in with more liquor, puts it on the table, and takes the empty flagon to the bar.*]

Hale. [*Laughs.*] Oh, that's it, is it! Very well, then I'll stay! [*He sits again at the table. The soldiers start up singing "The Three Grenadiers." They all sing and drink.*]

Fitzroy. [*Interrupts them.*] Stop singing a moment! Fill up, everybody! I have a bumper or two to give in honor of our guest here! [*He stands on a chair with one foot on the table, watching* HALE *closely.*] Here's to New London, Connecticut, and the schoolhouse there!

Cunningham. A silly toast!

Hale. Never you mind, it's an excuse for a drink! [*All repeat the first part of toast, but they are getting thick-tongued, and all come to grief over the word "Connecticut."* HALE *has answered* FITZROY's *look without flinching, but has managed to spill his liquor. All refill their glasses, singing.*]

Fitzroy. Here's another for you. The toast of a sly wench, and a prim one, who flaunts a Yankee lover in my face! But I've kissed her lips already, and before I'm through with her, I'll make her my wife. Drink to my success with the prettiest maid in the colonies!—Alice Adams!

All. To Alice Adams! Hip! Hip! [*All hold up their glasses with loud cries and then drink.* HALE *again manages to spill his liquor and pretends to drink.* FITZROY *jumps down from the chair and table to beside* HALE.]

Fitzroy. [*Loudly, fiercely to* HALE.] You didn't drink! I watched your throat and not a drop went down it! [*General movement of the soldiers. All rise; excitement.*]

All. Show us your cup! Show us your cup! [HALE, *with a sneering laugh, holds his glass above his head and turns it upside down; it is empty.*]

Cunningham. What's the matter with you? He knows good liquor when he tastes it! [*All laugh drunkenly; general movement again. All retake their seats, and continue singing.* HALE *looks defiantly in* FITZROY's *face, and throws his cup on the floor.*]

Hale. Good night, gentlemen!

All. [*Drunkenly.*] Good night, good night! [HALE *goes out by the door at back, shown by the* WIDOW, *who exits with him, taking a candle. One of the soldiers is asleep;* CUNNINGHAM *is on the floor; another under the table; they are singing in a sleepy, drunken way.* FITZROY *writes a letter rapidly on paper, which he finds on the corner of the bar. When he is finished,*]

Cunningham. [*On the floor, his head and arms on the chair, whining.*] I'm thirsty! Won't some kind person please give me a drink?

Fitzroy. [*Kicking him with his foot to make him get up.*] Get up! Get up, I say! I have an errand for you!

Cunningham. [*Rising, steadies himself against the chair.*] What is it?

Fitzroy. This man is a spy——

Cunningham. Hurrah! [*Waves the arm with which he was steadying himself, almost loses his balance.*] We'll hang him up to the first tree!

Fitzroy. Wait! We must prove it first, and I have thought of a plan. Take a horse and ride top speed to the Ferry Station. Cross to New York and give this letter to General Howe. He will see that you are conducted to a Colonel Knowlton's house, with a letter from him to a young lady who is staying there.

Cunningham. [*Who is a little drunk, throwing back his shoulders and swaggering a bit.*] A young lady! Ah, Major, you've hit on the right man for your business this time.

Fitzroy. Don't interrupt, you drunken fool! but listen to what I am telling you. The letter will say that Captain Nathan Hale is here wounded and wishes to see his sweetheart, Alice Adams, before he dies. If you are questioned, corroborate that, you understand! A young man named Hale is here wounded! That's who the fellow upstairs is, I'm very well nigh certain! The girl's in love with him, she'll come! and if it is Hale we've got here, we're likely to know it—if it isn't, well, no harm done!

Cunningham. Very pretty! Just the kind of business I like.

Fitzroy. Your password on this side will be "Love." Are you sober enough to remember that?

Cunningham. [*In a maudlin voice.*] "Love!" You do me an injustice, Major! [*With a half-tipsy effort at dignity.*]

Fitzroy. Mind you don't speak *my* name. You come at *General Howe's* orders.

Cunningham. Diplomacy was always my forte.[3] Fighting's much too common work!

Fitzroy. Go on now. There's no time to be lost! I want the girl here by daybreak, before the dog's up and off.

Cunningham. You guarantee, Major, that the girl's pretty?

Fitzroy. [*Turning on him.*] What! None of that! She's my property! You'd better not forget that. No poaching on my preserves!

Cunningham. [*Dogged.*] I understand, sir. [*Salutes and exits. All the soldiers are asleep. The* WIDOW *comes back.* FITZROY *turns a chair to face the fire.*]

Fitzroy. Bring more liquor. [*He throws himself into the chair.*]

Widow. More? at this hour?

Fitzroy. [*Loosening his neck gear.*] Yes, enough to last till morning. [*To himself.*] I warned her some day I would set to and drink myself mad for her! And the time's come! [*The stage darkens.*]

SCENE 2

Outside the WIDOW CHICHESTER'S. *Very early the next morning. The scene represents the front of the house, a low, rambling structure of gray stone, with a porch and a gabled roof, in which is the window of* FITZROY'S *bed-room. There is a well-sweep on the left, and a sign-post beside the road. There are trees and shrubs on each side. It is just at sunrise. As dawn begins a cock is heard crowing behind the house, answered by a second cock and by others. The sun rises and floods the scene.*

The WIDOW *is heard unbolting the door, and comes out on to the porch, carrying the mugs of the night before, which she has washed and which she places on a bench in the sun.*

---

[3] FORTE—Strong point.

A bugle call is heard, and while she is arranging the mugs, three soldiers come out from the house.

The Three Soldiers. [*On the porch, saluting with elaborate politeness.*]   Good morning, Widow Chic.

Widow. [*Imitating their salute.*]   God bless you and King George! [*The soldiers leave porch and start off, right.*] Where are you off to this early?

First Soldier. [*As he speaks, all three stop and turn.*]   On picket duty, between here and the Ferry Station. The Major's orders. [FITZROY *appears in the upstairs window, opening the shutters; he is without his coat; he is dishevelled and bloated; he looks as if he had not been to bed.*]

Fitzroy. Here you men! No loitering! You've no time to lose! Remember you're to pass no one but the girl, Alice Adams, with Cunningham. If she's brought any one with her, man, woman, or child, don't let 'em pass.

The Three Soldiers. [*Salute.*]   Yes, sir. [*They start to go.*]

Fitzroy. Burnham!

First Soldier. [*Salutes.*]   Yes, sir?

Fitzroy. Have you your bugle with you?

First Soldier. Yes, sir.

Fitzroy. Well, you change with Smith, then; take his position nearest to the Ferry, and sound a warning the moment they pass, that I may know *here* they're coming, and be ready.

First Soldier. [*Salutes.*]   Yes, sir.

Fitzroy. That's all. [*The three soldiers salute and go off down the road, right.* FITZROY *calls,*] Widow Chic!

Widow. [*Coming down from the porch, and looking up at* FITZROY.] Yes, Major.

Fitzroy. We're going to have some pretty sport presently.

Widow. I hope it's no harm to the young teacher who took my part last night, sir.

Fitzroy. So! You're sweet on him, too! He's quite a lady-killer. [*He laughs satirically and disappears from the window, leaving the shutters open.* HALE *opens the door and comes out on to the porch.*]

Hale. Good morning, madam.

Widow. [*With a curtsey.*]   Good morning, sir; the Lord bless you and King George.

Hale. Ahem! By the way, where is my horse? Has she had a good night?

Widow. She's tethered right there, sir. [*Pointing off, right.*] In the bushes. It's the best I could do, having no barn. I told the boy to feed her the first thing, sir. [HALE *goes to the right as she speaks. The* WIDOW *stands watching him.*]

Hale. [*Passes out of sight among the trees and bushes.*] Ah! Betsy, old girl! [*He is heard patting the horse.*] How is it, eh? Had a good night, my beauty? Hungry? Oh, no, you've had your breakfast, haven't you? [*He is heard patting her again.*] That's good! Be ready to start in a few minutes now. [*He comes back into sight.*] Will you kindly ask the boy to saddle her at once, madam?

[FITZROY *comes out on to the porch.*]

Widow. Certainly, sir. [*Goes into house.*]

Fitzroy. Good morning.

Hale. Good morning.

Fitzroy. [*Leaning against a pillar of the porch.*] I have a pleasant surprise for you.

Hale. [*Suspicious, walking slowly across the stage to hide his nervousness.*] That is a sufficient surprise in itself.

Fitzroy. I am expecting a visitor for you every moment now.

Hale. [*Involuntarily stops a second and turns.*] A visitor? [*He continues walking.*]

Fitzroy. For you.

Hale. [*More suspicious, but on his guard.*] Who?

Fitzroy. Alice Adams. [HALE *does not make any movement, but he cannot avoid an expression of mingled fear and surprise flashing across his face—it is so slight that though* FITZROY *does see it, he cannot be sure that it is anything.* HALE *continues to walk, returning from left to right.* FITZROY *comes down from the porch and meets* HALE *as he crosses.*] You change color.

Hale. [*Quietly, himself again completely.*] Do I? [*Walks on toward right.*]

Fitzroy. [*Looking after him.*] Yes—Nathan Hale!

Hale. [*Walks on with his back to* FITZROY.] Nathan what?

Fitzroy. Nathan Hale! And you are here stealing informa-tion of our movements for the rebel army! If I can only prove it—— [*He is interrupted.*]

Hale. [*Turning sharply.*] If!

Fitzroy. And I will prove it!

Hale. [*Walking towards* Fitzroy, *now from right.*] Indeed! How?

Fitzroy. If Cunningham has carried out my instructions, he has gone to Alice with a note from General Howe saying that Nathan Hale is wounded and dying here and wishes to see her! I think that will bring her readily enough—in which case we ought to hear them pass the sentinels any moment now! [*A short pause,* Fitzroy *watching for the effect on* Hale *of every word he speaks. They stand face to face.*]

Hale. And who is Nathan Hale?

Fitzroy. A rebel fool the girl's sweet on. If you *are* he, and she is brought face to face with you, alive, whom she fears to find dead, she's sure to make some sign of recognition, if I know women, and that sign will cost you your life!

Hale. It's a dastardly trick to make such use of a woman.

Fitzroy. All's fair in love and war, and this is a case of both, for I love the girl, too.

Hale. And if I'm not—[*Hesitates.*] what's his name—[Fitzroy *sneers.*] the man you think me?

Fitzroy. Oh, well then, no harm's done. Meanwhile you needn't try to get away before she comes. I've placed pickets all about with orders who's to pass and not. [*The* Widow *comes from the house carrying a horse's saddle.*]

Widow. That boy's gone to the village; I will have to saddle your horse myself, sir. [*Going toward the right.*]

Fitzroy. [*Passing behind* Hale *to the* Widow.] I'm hungry, Widow Chic! Is there a swallow of coffee and a bite of bread ready? I haven't time for more. [*With a meaning look toward* Hale.]

Widow. Yes, in the kitchen.

Fitzroy. [*Goes on to the porch, and there turns on the steps to say to* Hale,] Don't be alarmed, I won't miss your meeting; I shall be on hand. [*Goes into the house.*]

Hale. [*Quickly going after* Widow. *In half-lowered tones and showing suspense and suppressed excitement.*] Madam!

Widow. Yes, sir?

Hale. [*Taking her by the arm kindly.*] Dear madam, you thanked me last night for striking that dog of a soldier who had his cup raised against you——

Widow. Ah, sir, it's many a day since I've been protected by any man, let alone a handsome young beau like you, sir. [*With a curtsey.*]

Hale. [*Bows.*] Thank you, madam. Will you also do me a favor in return?

Widow. That I will, sir.

Hale. Then quick, leave the saddle by the horse to arrange on your return, and go a bit down the road toward the Ferry Station. Wait there! When you see Cunningham——

Widow. The brute who wanted to strike me!

Hale. Yes!—riding along with a girl, make some motion to her, wave your hand or kerchief or something. Do anything to attract her attention, if possible, without attracting his, and at the same time place your fingers on your lips—so! [*Showing her.*] You don't understand! and neither will she, perhaps. But a life is at stake, and it's a chance, and my only one——

Widow. Wave my hand, and do so?

Hale. Yes. She is the girl I love, madam, and I ask you to do this for me.

Widow. And sir, I will. [HALE *starts and listens as if he heard something.*]

Hale. Quick! Run, or you may be too late! [*The* WIDOW *hurries off, right. The saddle is heard falling in the bushes where she throws it.* HALE *shakes his head doubtfully as to the success of his plan; he goes to the right and speaks to the horse.*] Betsy! Ah! Bless your heart! Be ready, old girl. I may need you soon to race away from death with! Be ready, old girl. [*During the end of his speech* FITZROY *comes out on to the porch carrying a coffee bowl in his hand, from which he drinks. He doesn't hear* HALE's *words.*]

Fitzroy. That's a good horse of yours, Mr. Beacon. [*Drinks the coffee.* HALE *starts very slightly and turns, looks scornfully at* FITZROY, *and crosses stage slowly.*] Our friends are late! [*He starts to drink again, but just as the bowl touches his lips, a far-off bugle call of warning is heard. Both* HALE *and* FITZROY *start and stand still, except that very slowly the hand with the bowl sinks down from* FITZROY's *lips, as the head very slowly lifts, his eyes wide-open, a smile of expectant triumph on his face.* HALE *is at the left,* FITZROY *is on the porch steps, as the bugle stops.* FITZROY *hurls away the bowl, from which some coffee is spilled and which is broken as it strikes, while he cries out,*] They're coming! [*He comes down the steps.*]

Second Picket's Voice. [*Off stage, right, at a far distance.*] Who goes there?

Cunningham. [*Far off.*] Charles Cunningham, with Miss Alice Adams, on private business.

Second Picket. Your password?

Cunningham. "Love!" [*In a sneering voice.* FITZROY *listens till* CUNNINGHAM'S *reply is finished, then turns quickly to look at* HALE, *whose face shows nothing. The sound of the horse's hoofs is heard coming nearer and nearer. After a few seconds the third picket is heard.*]

Third Picket. [*Off stage at a distance.*] Who goes there?

Cunningham. [*Nearer.*] Charles Cunningham, with Miss Alice Adams, on private business.

Third Picket. Your password?

Cunningham. [*Again in a sneering voice.*] "Love!" [*The horse's hoofs are heard coming closer and then stop. There is the noise of dismounting in the bushes.*] Here! just tie these safe! Come along now, miss! [CUNNINGHAM *and* ALICE *come on, right.* ALICE'S *eyes fall first on* FITZROY.]

Alice. You here! [FITZROY *doesn't answer, but turning his face and eyes to* HALE *directs with his hand* ALICE'S *gaze in that direction, and then he quickly turns his eyes upon* ALICE, *to watch her face. She very slowly follows his glance to* HALE, *rests her eyes on his a full minute without making any recognition, and then turns to* CUNNINGHAM.]

Alice. Where is Captain Hale? Why don't you take me to him at once?

Fitzroy. [*In a rage.*] She's been warned! Who's spoiled my plot! [*Going menacingly to* CUNNINGHAM. *At this action there is one moment when unseen,* ALICE *and* NATHAN'S *eyes can seek each other, but only for a moment.*]

Cunningham. Not I! It has spoiled my fun, too.

Fitzroy. [*To* ALICE.] That's your lover, and you know it. I only saw him a few moments in his schoolhouse, but I can't have so bad a memory for a face as all that. [WIDOW *is heard singing "The Three Grenadiers" in the bushes at right, where she is tying the horses.*]

Alice. They told me Captain Hale was here and dying! Who

played this trick on me? [*Looking blankly at* HALE *and then at* CUNNINGHAM *and* FITZROY.]

Fitzroy. Well, *isn't* he here? [*Motioning to* HALE.]

Alice. [*To* FITZROY.] It was *you*, of course! You who have forced me to this ride through the night, half dead with fear, and all for a lie! Well, mark my word, you will lose your commission for this! Rebels or no rebels, we have our rights as human beings, and General Howe is a gentleman who will be the first to punish a trick like you have played on a woman!

Fitzroy. [*Going to* ALICE.] We'll see what General Howe will do when I give into his hands a man who has been stealing information of our movements for the rebel army, who has been working for the destruction of the King's men, and I will do this yet! You've been warned by some one! I'll question the pickets, and if I find one of them the traitor—[*To* HALE, *crossing before* ALICE.] he'll hang ahead of you to let the devil know you're coming. [*A look at* HALE, *then he recrosses before* ALICE *to* CUNNINGHAM.] There are men picketed all about—you need not hang around unless you want to. [*Aside to* CUNNINGHAM.] I shall steal back behind the house and watch them from inside —make some excuse to go in, too. I want you ready by the door. [*He goes off, right.*]

Alice. [*To* CUNNINGHAM, *going toward him.*] Aren't you going to take me back?

Cunningham. Well, not just this minute, Mistress. I've a hankering for some breakfast, when the Widow Chic comes back. [*He crosses behind her, strolls about in earshot and out, keeping an eye on them every other moment. He goes first to the old well, at the left.*]

Hale. [*To* ALICE.] You were brought here, Mistress——?

Alice. [*With a curtsey.*] Adams, sir.

Hale. Adams, to see Captain Hale? I used to know him; he taught the same school with me. [*He adds quickly in a low voice,* CUNNINGHAM *being out of hearing,*] A woman warned you?

Alice. [*Low, quickly.*] Yes! [*Then aloud, in a conventional voice, as* CUNNINGHAM *moves.*] I was his scholar once.

Hale. You were?

Alice. Yes, in many things, but most of all in—*love!* [*Added in an undertone. In their conversation they keep a constant lookout about them, and when they see themselves out of* CUN-

NINGHAM'S *hearing, they drop their voices a little and speak seriously. In* ALICE'S *speech just now, for instance, she adds the word "love" in a voice full of emotion and sentiment, seeing* CUNNINGHAM *is for the moment out of hearing.*]

Hale. [*Softly, lovingly.*] Alice! [CUNNINGHAM *approaches.*] You found him a good teacher? [CUNNINGHAM *goes on to the porch and opens the top part of the door; he leans on lower part, looking in; he is in earshot of the two, which they perceive.*]

Alice. Yes, in *love* only too proficient!

Hale. Oh, well—that was because of course he was enamoured desperately of you!

Alice. [*Coquettishly.*] He pretended so!

Hale. [*Seriously.*] And didn't you believe him?

Alice. Oh, I did, at first——

Hale. [*With difficulty keeping the anxiety out of his voice.*] Only at first! [CUNNINGHAM *passes on out of hearing.*] No—no—Alice, you didn't really doubt me! [ALICE *cannot answer, because the* WIDOW, *singing, enters at this moment, and* CUNNINGHAM *draws near again.*]

Widow. [*To* CUNNINGHAM.] Well, you brute, your horses are well pastured.

Cunningham. I give you curses for thanks! Have you food for a brave soldier in the house?

Widow. No, but I've scraps for a coward who strikes women. Come in and eat, if you wish. I don't let starve even dogs! [*Enters the house.*]

Cunningham. Seeing you press me! [*Laughing, follows her in. Since the* WID-ow's *entrance,* FITZROY *has appeared cautiously in the second story window, and leaning his arm out softly has caught hold of the shutters and bowed them shut. He watches behind them.* ALICE *sits on the porch steps, pretending to be bored, and* HALE *moves about with affected nonchalance. The moment they*

are apparently alone on the scene, they approach each other, but cautiously.]

Hale. [*Anxious.*] Did this Hale prove himself unworthy of you by some cowardly action? Had you any reason to doubt his passion?

Alice. He broke his word to me; that made me doubt his love.

Hale. But you are still betrothed to him?

Alice. Oh, no; when he broke faith, then I broke troth.

Hale. Yet you came this journey here to see him.

Alice. Out of pity—they told me he was dying.

Hale. [*Low voice.*] Are you in earnest! Was it pity, or was it love?

Alice. [*With a frightened look about her, ignores his question.*] I can't imagine how they took you for the other gentleman—Captain Hale is taller; you, I think, are short.

Hale. [*A little sensitive.*] Short?

Alice. I don't want to hurt your feelings, but it's only fair to you, sir, in this dilemma, to be frank. It may save your life.

Hale. [*Distressed, anxious, lest she loves him no longer.*] You came to Captain Hale then only out of pity?

Alice. Out of pity, yes! And now "out of pity" I hope this ruffian will take me back.

Hale. [*In a low voice, his passion threatening to overmaster him.*] No, no, say it isn't true! You love me still?

Alice. [*In a low voice.*] Be careful, the very trees have ears!

Hale. If they have hearts of wood they'll break to hear you! [*Leaning over her.*]

Alice. [*Loud voice, frightened, for fear they are being overheard.*] Let me pass, sir!

Hale. [*Desperate, in a low voice full of passionate love.*] No! Look! We're alone! They're at their breakfast—you drive me mad—only let me know the truth! You love me?

Alice. Yes!

Hale. [*His pent-up passion mastering him.*] My darling! For just one moment. [*Opening his arms, she goes into them, and as they embrace* FITZROY *throws open the shutters of his window and leaning out cries,*]

Fitzroy. I arrest you, *Nathan Hale*——

Alice. [*Cries out.*] No! No!

Fitzroy. —In the name of the King, for a spy! [*At the mo-*

ment that he has thown open the shutters with a bang, CUN-
NINGHAM *has thrown open the door below and stands on the
porch levelling his musket at* HALE.]

Alice. [*Cries out.*] Nathan!

Fitzroy. [*Calls down to* CUNNINGHAM.] If he attempts to
escape, fire. [*Climbing out of the window on to the roof of the
porch, and flinging himself off by one of the pillars.*] At last!
I've won! Before to-day's sun sets, you will be hanged to a
tree out yonder, Nathan Hale, and the birds can come and peck
out the love for her in your dead heart. For she'll be mine!
[ALICE *starts, frightened, with a low gasp.*]

Hale. Yours!

Fitzroy. Mine! [*To* ALICE.] You remember I told you once,
sometime I'd make up my mind I'd waited long enough for you?
Well, I made up my mind to that last night! [*To* HALE.] You
leave her behind! But you leave her in *my arms!* [*Seizing*
ALICE *in his arms and forcing her into an embrace.*]

Alice. You brute! [*Fighting in his arms.* CUNNINGHAM *has
put his hand on* HALE'S *shoulder to keep him from going to her
rescue.* HALE *has shown by the movement of his eyes that he
is taking in the situation, the places of every one, etc.*]

Fitzroy. Look! [*And he bends* ALICE'S *head back upon his
shoulder to kiss her on the lips.*]

Hale. Blackguard! [*With a blow of his right arm he knocks*
CUNNINGHAM *on the head, who, falling, hits his head against the
pillar of the porch and is stunned. Meanwhile, the moment he
has hit* CUNNINGHAM, HALE *has sprung upon* FITZROY, *and with
one hand over his mouth has bent his head back with the other
until he has released* ALICE. HALE *then throws* FITZROY *down,
and seizing* ALICE *about the waist dashes off with her to the right,
where his horse is.* FITZROY *rises and runs to* CUNNINGHAM,
kicks him to get his gun, which has fallen under him.]

Fitzroy. [*Beside himself with rage.*] Get up! Get up!
You fool! [*Horse's hoofs heard starting off.*]

Third Picket's Voice. [*Off stage.*] Who goes there?

Fitzroy. [*Stops, looks up, and gives a triumphant cry.*] Ah!
The picket! They're caught! They're caught!

Hale. Returning with Alice Adams on private business.

Picket. The password.

Hale. "Love!"

Fitzroy. Of course he heard! [*Runs off, right, yelling.*]
Fire on them! Fire!
[*A shot is heard, followed by a loud defiant laugh from* HALE,
*and an echoed "Love," as the clatter of horse's hoofs dies
away, and the Curtain Falls.*]

A Second Ending to the Act

*It was found on performing the Play that this ending of the
Act, in which* HALE's *pent-up passion overcame his control and
made him expose himself to* FITZROY, *did not, as the theatrical
phrase is, "carry over the footlights." In consequence a new
ending of the Act was devised, which proved to be more effective
theatrically. In this second ending* JASPER *follows his mistress,
and after* ALICE *has failed to recognize* NATHAN, FITZROY, *concealed upstairs, hears the servant being stopped and questioned
by the pickets. The Major orders* JASPER *brought into the presence of himself,* ALICE, *and* HALE, *and this time his scheme is
successful; for* JASPER, *unwarned, recognizes* HALE, *and from the
recognition the remainder of the Act is the same.*

ACT IV

SCENE I

*Saturday night, September 21, 1776. The tent of a British officer.
Above the tent is seen the deep blue sky full of stars, on
each side are trees and bushes. There is every little while
the noise of a company of soldiers encamped close by.* HALE
*is seated at a table inside the tent writing letters by candle-
light.* CUNNINGHAM *is outside the tent, on guard.* CUN-
NINGHAM's *head is plastered, where he struck it in falling
when* HALE *felled him.* CUNNINGHAM *paces slowly up and
down.*

Cunningham. Writing the history of your life?
Hale. [*Writing, without looking up.*] I am writing a letter
to my mother and sister.
Cunningham. Yankees, like yourself, I presume!
Hale. [*Still writing.*] Please God!
Cunningham. I suppose you're making a pretty story out of
your capture!

Hale. No, I'm only telling the truth—that I got the best of two pretty big men, yourself and Fitzroy. [*Half smiling. This is said not at all in the spirit of boasting, but only to ridicule* CUNNINGHAM.]

Cunningham. Yes, and don't forget to add how you were captured by the picket close to the Ferry Station.

Hale. [*Looks up.*] Yes, because, hearing Fitzroy's cries, the picket threatened if I didn't stop he'd shoot the girl with me.

Cunningham. It was a narrow escape for us!

Hale. [*With a half-smile.*] But too broad for me! [*Con. tinues his writing.*]

Cunningham. What else are you saying?

Hale. [*Writing.*] Oh, that I was taken before General Howe, who probably only does what he feels his duty, although he condemns me without a trial!

Cunningham. Yes, but with plenty of evidence against you, thanks to us witnesses and the papers found in your shoes, too!

Hale. [*Smiling a little.*] True, I walked on very slippery ground, didn't I? [*He comes out of the tent.*] However, you didn't find all the papers.

Cunningham. [*Surprised, changes his position.*] What do you mean?

Hale. Oh, the men were so taken up with me they didn't see my friend and confederate Hempstead, who was waiting by the Ferry Station! I don't mind telling you, now he is out of danger, the only paper that was of immediate importance—the plan of General Howe's attack on Washington and upper New York —wrapped nicely in a leather pouch, I dropped in the bushes by the roadside when I was arrested. [*He walks a few steps toward* CUNNINGHAM *and stops. He adds cunningly, trying to get information out of him,*] That's why the attempt to force the Hudson was a failure!

Cunningham. [*On his guard.*] Oh! was there such an attempt?

Hale. [*Goes nearer* CUNNINGHAM, *desperately anxious to know.*] Wasn't there?

Cunningham. [*Sneers.*] Don't you wish you knew! Go on —make haste with your scribbling! [*Crosses before* HALE *to the other side.*]

Hale. [*Reëntering the tent and taking up his letter.*] I

have finished. I do not find your presence inspiring. Have you a knife?

Cunningham. Yes.

Hale. Will you lend it me?

Cunningham. No! What do you want it for?

Hale. My mother—[*His voice breaks; he turns his back to* CUNNINGHAM.] poor little woman—wants a bit of my hair. [*He controls himself.*] Lend me your knife that I may send it to her.

Cunningham. [*Coming to* HALE]. Yes! That's a fine dodge! And have you cut your throat and cheat the gallows! [*Getting out his knife.*] I'll cut it off for you, shall I?

Hale. Thank you. [*Holding his head ready, and with his right hand choosing a lock.*]

Cunningham. [*Cuts it off roughly.*] There! [*Gives it to him.*]

Hale. [*Puts the hair in the letter; starts to fold it.*] May I have a chaplain attend me?

Cunningham. A what?

Hale. A minister—a preacher!

Cunningham. No! Give me your letter if it's finished. [HALE *comes out from the tent and hands him the letter.* CUNNINGHAM *opens the letter.*]

Hale. How dare you open that!

Cunningham. [*Sneeringly.*] How "dare" I?

Hale. You shall not read it!

Cunningham. Shan't I!

Hale. [*Coming nearer* CUNNINGHAM.] No! That letter is my good-bye to my mother, who for the sake of my country I have robbed of her "boy." It is sacred to her eyes only!

Cunningham. Is it! [*Spreads it open to read.*]

Hale. [*Springs toward him, his hand on the letter.*] Stop! There's the mark of one blow I've given you on your forehead now. Dare to read that letter, and I'll keep it company with another! I mean it! I'm not afraid, with death waiting for me outside in the orchard!

Cunningham. Either I read it, or it isn't sent. Take your choice. [HALE *looks at* CUNNINGHAM *a moment,—a look of disgust.*]

Hale. [*He drops* CUNNINGHAM's *wrist.*] Read it! [*He*

walks up and down as CUNNINGHAM *reads. He goes to right;
speaks to some one outside.*]   Sentinel!

Sentinel. [*Who speaks with a strong Irish accent, outside.*]
Yis surr! [*The* SENTINEL *comes on.*]

Hale. Ask the men to sing something, will you?

Sentinel. They haven't sung to-night purrposely, surr, fearing
it would disturb you.

Hale. Thank them for me, and say I'd like a song! Something gay! [*His voice breaks on the word "gay."*]

Sentinel. Yis, surr, but I'm afraid the soldiers haven't much
spirits to-night. They're regretting the woruk of sunrise, surr.

Hale. Well—let them sing anything, only beg them sing—
till sunrise!

Sentinel. Yis, surr. [HALE *turns.* CUNNINGHAM *has finished
reading letter; he has grown furious as he reads. The* SENTINEL
exits.]

Cunningham. Do you think I'll let these heroics be read by
the Americans! They shall never know through me they had
a rebel amongst them with such a spirit. [*He tears the letter
into pieces before* HALE. *The soldiers are heard singing, outside, "Drink to me only with thine eyes."*]

Hale. You cur! Not to send a dying man's love home!
[*Goes into the tent.*]

Cunningham. I'll make a coward of you yet!

Hale. You mean you'll do your best to make me seem one!
God knows the worst I have to suffer is to spend my last hours
with a brute like you. How can a man give his thoughts to
heaven with the devil standing by and spitting in his face!
[*The* SENTINEL *comes on and salutes.* CUNNINGHAM *speaks
with him.*]

Cunningham. Hale, you have visitors. Will you see them?

Hale. Who are they?

Cunningham. [*To* SENTINEL.] Say he refuses to see them.

Hale. That's a lie! I haven't refused! Who are they?

Cunningham. They come from General Howe!

Hale. Fitzroy! I refuse to receive him.

Cunningham. [*To the* SENTINEL.] Say he refuses to receive
them.

Sentinel. But it's not Major Fitzroy, surr; it's a lady.

Hale. What! [*On his guard now.*]

*He tears the letter into pieces
before Hale.*

Cunningham. [*To the* SENTINEL.] Hold your tongue!

Sentinel. I was told to ansurr all the prisoner's quistions, surr.

Hale. [*To* CUNNINGHAM, *coming out of the tent.*] You'd cheat me of every comfort, would you? [*To* SENTINEL.] Is the lady young or——

Sentinel. [*Interrupting.*] Young, surr.

Hale. [*Under his breath, scarcely daring to believe himself or the soldier, yet hoping.*] Alice! [*To the* SENTINEL.] Is she alone?

Sentinel. No, surr, a maid and a young man.

Hale. [*Again under his breath.*] Tom!

Sentinel. [*Continues.*] The young gintleman wishes to see you for a moment fust alone.

Hale. Quickly! Show him in!

Sentinel. Yis, surr. [*He exits.*]

Hale. [*To* CUNNINGHAM.] What a dog's heart you must have to wish to keep even this from me!

Cunningham. Say what you like, one thing is true: I'm here on guard, and any comfort that you have with your sweetheart must be in my presence. [*He chuckles.*] I shall be here to *share* your kisses with you. [*Goes to right and sits on the stump of a tree there. The soldiers sing "Barbara Allen." The* SENTINEL *shows in* TOM ADAMS.]

Tom. Nathan!

Hale. Tom! [*Taking his hand,* TOM *throws his arm about* NATHAN'S *shoulder, and burying his head sobs a boy's tears,* NATHAN *comforting him, for a moment, then.*]

Tom. Nathan, you *saved* the States!

Hale. [*Excited.*] What do you mean? Was there an attack made on Harlem Heights?

Tom. Yes!

Hale. And Washington?—Ah! Tom! don't tell me he was captured!

Tom. [*More excited.*] No, of course not—thanks to your information!

Hale. [*More excited.*] Hempstead got it, then?

Tom. Yes; after the men went off with you he searched the spot, thinking perhaps he might find something in the bushes, and he did! he came across your wallet!

Hale. [*With joy.*] Ah!

Tom. So, when the British tried to steal up the Hudson that night, they found us ready and waiting,—[*He takes off his hat with the manner of paying homage, of being bareheaded in* HALE'S *presence.*] your name on everybody's lips, your example in their hearts!

Hale. [*Stopping* TOM *modestly.*] And if you hadn't been warned? [*Putting his two hands on* TOM'S *shoulders.*]

Tom. It would have been the end of us, Nathan. Washington himself says so!

Hale. [*As if to himself, dropping his hands, half turning.*] I'm glad I shan't die for nothing.

Tom. Nothing? Oh! Even if your mission had been a failure your example has already worked wonders—your bravery has inspired the army with new courage!

Hale. [*Taking his arm and walking up and down with him.*] Sh! None of that. Talk to me about Alice. She is here?

Tom. General Howe has given her permission to see you, but only for five minutes. Can you bear it? Will you bear it for her sake? [*They stop.*]

Hale. Yes.

Tom. [*Looking at* CUNNINGHAM.] Is this the man Cunningham? [HALE *nods.*] Alice told me about him; we heard he was your guard, and she has General Howe's permission to choose any other soldier to take his place inside the tent. [HALE *looks at* CUNNINGHAM *with a smile.*]

Cunningham. [*Rising. To the* SENTINEL, *who is standing at one side.*] Have you such orders?

Sentinel. [*Stepping forward, salutes.*] Yis, surr.

Hale. [*To the* SENTINEL.] Very well, we'll ask *you* to stay in place of Cunningham.

Sentinel. Yis, surr.

Tom. [*To* CUNNINGHAM.] Then you can take me to my sister—now, at once. [CUNNINGHAM *crosses to* HALE *and speaks to him.*]

Cunningham. I'll be back on the minute when your time is finished. [*He goes out with* TOM, *right.*]

Sentinel. [*To* HALE.] I undershtand, surr. Don't think of me a minute. I must shtay in the tint, of course, but if iver a man could git away from his body, I'll promise you to git away from moine! [HALE *smiles his thanks and shakes the* SENTI-NEL'S *hand. The soldiers sing the air of what is now called*

"Believe Me if All Those Endearing Young Charms." HALE
stands listening for the sound of ALICE's *coming. The* SENTINEL
*retires to the farther corner of the tent and stands with arms
folded, his back toward* HALE. TOM *comes on first, bringing*
ALICE. *As they come into* HALE's *presence,* ALICE *glides from
out of* TOM's *keeping, and her brother leaves the two together.
They stand looking at each other a moment without moving, and
then both make a quick movement to meet. As their arms touch
in the commencement of their embrace, they remain in that position a few moments, looking into each other's eyes. Then they
embrace,* HALE *clasping her tight in his arms and pressing a long
kiss upon her lips. They remain a few moments in this position,
silent and immovable. Then they slowly loosen their arms—
though not altogether discontinuing the embrace—until they take
their first position and again gaze into each other's faces.* ALICE
*sways, about to fall, faint from the effort to control her emo-
tions, and* HALE *gently leads her to the tree stump at right. He
kneels beside her so that she can rest against him with her arms
about his neck. After a moment, keeping her arms still tight
about him,* ALICE *makes several ineffectual efforts to speak, but
her quivering lips refuse to form any words, and her breath comes
with difficulty.* HALE *shakes his head with a sad smile, as if to
say, "No, don't try to speak. There are no words for us." And
again they embrace. At this moment, while* ALICE *is clasped
again tight in* HALE's *arms, the* SENTINEL, *who has his watch in
his hand, slowly comes out from the tent.* TOM *also reënters,
but* HALE *and* ALICE *are oblivious.* TOM *goes softly to them and
touches* ALICE *very gently on the arm, resting his hand there.
She starts violently, with a hysterical drawing in of her breath,
an expression of fear and horror, as she knows this is the final
moment of parting.* HALE *also starts slightly, rising, and his
muscles grow rigid. He clasps and kisses her once more, but
only for a second. They both are unconscious of* TOM, *of everything but each other.* TOM *takes her firmly from* HALE *and leads
her out, her eyes fixed upon* HALE's *eyes, their arms outstretched
toward each other. After a few paces she breaks forcibly away
from* TOM, *and with a wild cry of "No! no!" locks her hands
about* HALE's *neck.* TOM *draws her away again and leads her
backward from the scene, her eyes dry now and her breath coming in short, loud, horror-stricken gasps.* HALE *holds in his hand
a red rose she wore on her breast, and thinking more of her than*

of himself, whispers, as she goes, "Be brave! be brave!" *The light is being slowly lowered, till, as* ALICE *disappears, the stage is in total darkness.*]

SCENE 2

COLONEL RUTGER'S *Orchard, the next morning. The scene is an orchard whose trees are heavy with red and yellow fruit. The centre tree has a heavy dark branch jutting out, which is the gallows; from this branch all the leaves and the little branches have been chopped off; a heavy coil of rope with a noose hangs from it, and against the trunk of the tree leans a ladder. It is the moment before dawn, and slowly at the back through the trees is seen a purple streak, which changes to crimson as the sun creeps up. A dim gray haze next fills the stage, and through this gradually breaks the rising sun. The birds begin to wake, and suddenly there is heard the loud, deep-toned, single toll of a bell, followed by a roll of muffled drums in the distance. Slowly the orchard fills with murmuring, whispering people; men and women coming up through the trees make a semicircle amongst them, about the gallows tree, but at a good distance. The bell tolls at intervals, and muffled drums are heard between the twittering and happy songs of birds. There is the sound of musketry, of drums beating a funeral march, which gets nearer, and finally a company of British soldiers marches in, led by* FITZROY, NATHAN HALE *in their midst, walking alone, his hands tied behind his back. As he comes forward the people are absolutely silent, and a girl in the front row of the spectators falls forward in a dead faint. She is quickly carried out by two bystanders.* HALE *is led to the foot of the tree before the ladder. The soldiers are in double lines on either side.*

Fitzroy. [*To* HALE.] Nathan Hale, have you anything to say? We are ready to hear your last dying speech and confession! [HALE *is standing, looking up, his lips moving slightly, as if in prayer. He remains in this position a moment, and then, with a sigh of relief and rest, looks upon the sympathetic faces of the people about him, with almost a smile on his face.*]

Hale. I only regret that I have but one life to lose for my country! [FITZROY *makes a couple of steps toward him;* HALE *turns and places one foot on the lower rung of the ladder, as the Curtain Falls.*]

THE END

Suggestions for Study: Read the play through rapidly for the story or main plot. Note how skillfully Fitch uses the historical and traditional accounts of Hale's life in working out the details of the story. Note the dates and locations of the various scenes. Do not memorize, but familiarize yourself with the cast of characters. Then re-read the play slowly, taking time to note the details of the author's stage directions (in italics), the cleverness of the speeches of the various characters, and the development of main incidents of the story.

Act I—Read the author's directions for the stage setting. What items would indicate to an audience the period of the play? Make a simple diagram of the stage indicating the placing of doors, windows, furniture, etc. What would you say to be the opening mood of the play (gay, sad, thoughtful, etc.)? How is this achieved?

What is your first impression of Lebanon? Does the remainder of the play change or confirm this impression? Why were Mrs. Knowlton and her daughter introduced so early in the play? What is the significance in the play of Tom's attitude toward the British national anthem? At what point did you guess the relationship between Hale and Alice? Show how the author prepares the audience all through this act for Hale's part in the drama. What sort of person are we led to expect in Fitzroy? Does his part in the scene confirm or change our idea? Does the scene between Fitzroy and Alice prepare us for later events in the play? Explain.

Act II—Make a simple stage diagram of the set for this act. What is the function of Jasper in the play? Illustrate. How are we prepared for Angelica's "news"? How does the conversation between Colonel Knowlton and Captain Adams prepare us for what follows? Recount the incident of the "soldier's button." Why is it in the play?

List the amusing elements of this act. Do they add to or detract from the play? What do we learn of the character of George Washington in this act? Can you defend Alice in her pleas to Hale? Be definite. Has the author prepared the reader for Hale's volunteering? How? Is the scene dramatic or weak? Criticize the closing scene.

Act III—Why has the author divided this act into two scenes? Draw a diagram and explain how the stage might be set for the first scene. How does the opening mood of this scene prepare us for later events? Trace the part played by "the widow" in this act. Show how Hale secures the information he desires. Trace the growing suspicion in Fitzroy's mind concerning Hale's identity. What scheme did he employ? Where did Hale make his mistake?

Try to find the original words of *The Three Grenadiers*. What is the effect of the Widow Chic's singing this through part of Scene 2? Trace the idea of the password as worked out in this act. Show how the author worked up the feeling of suspense at the close of Act III.

Act IV—What is the significance of the dialogue between Cunningham and Hale at the beginning of Scene 1? Show the author's development of the feeling of pathos in Scene 1. Is this effective or overdone? Explain. What element of victory does the author give to Hale? Discuss whether this victorious note makes the play a comedy or whether Hale's death makes it a tragedy. What does the attitude of the enemy guards show about the character of Hale? Explain. Is Scene 2 too unpleasant to be staged, or does the author hide the unpleasant note? Explain. What is the effect of the last line of the play? Does our familiarity with it make it less or more impressive?

The Play as A Whole—What do you consider the climax (moment of greatest interest) in the play? Outline briefly the main incidents leading up to this moment or incident. How has the author contrived to keep the element of suspense up to this moment? Are the incidents which follow the climax interesting or are they boresome? Do they satisfy the reader's curiosity about what happened to the main characters? Would you have handled this "falling action" differently?

Divide the cast of characters into two groups, main and subsidiary. What is the relationship among the main characters? Plan a character sketch of each of the main characters, showing definitely the evidence for each characteristic named. How did the author provide variety in the characters? In the incidents? In the settings? How many and which of the incidents are historically accurate?

Prepare to read to the class five speeches by various characters which you feel to be particularly dramatic. Select stage directions which you feel to be vital to the development of the play.

POOR AUBREY

George Kelly

CHARACTERS

AUBREY PIPER   MRS. FISHER (*Amy's Mother*)
AMY (*his wife*)   MRS. COLE (*A friend of Amy's*)

SCENE: AMY *enters briskly through the portieres at the right, carrying a fancy cushion, which she sets in the armchair at the back of the room; then continues on over to an arched doorway at the left and draws the curtains together. She is a dark-haired, trim-looking woman, in her late twenties, dressed in black—a very pretty dress, of black crepe, with a graceful side sash of the goods, piped with buff-colored silk. She has on black slippers and stockings, and wears a string of buff-colored beads—quite large. Her general manner suggests a quality of intelligent definiteness. While she is engaged at the curtains, the portieres over at the right are brushed aside, and her husband swings into the room, and stands preening himself near the table. He is painfully arrayed, even to the toupee; a feature that, as Dickens remarked of Sairey Gamp's transformation, could scarcely be called false, it is so very innocent of anything approaching to deception. And the quantities of brilliantine that have obviously been employed upon it only serve to heighten its artificiality. He is wearing a glistening white vest and a shiny gold watch chain, a necktie of living green, with a rather large horseshoe tie-pin of imitation diamonds, and a very high collar. He has a flashily bordered silk handkerchief set forth in the breast pocket of his coat, and there is a pair of heavy-rimmed nose glasses depending from his neck on a black tape.*

Aubrey. [*Touching his toupee.*] Does this look all right?
Amy. What?

Aubrey. This toupee. [*She glances over her right shoulder indifferently.*] I put some of that brilliantine on it.

Amy. [*Resuming her arrangement of the curtains.*] It's all right.

Aubrey. [*Turning to the little wall mirror just below the portieres at the right.*] You don't seem very enthusiastic about it.

Amy. [*Turning from the curtains and crossing quickly to the table—an oblong table, in the middle of the room, and towards the back.*] Because I don't think you need it. [*She picks up a small folded cover from the table, shakes it out, and tosses it across her left shoulder; then commences to gather up the scattered books and put them into the little table-rack.*]

Aubrey. [*Settling the toupee at the mirror.*] What do you want your friend to think, that you married an old man?

Amy. Why, a man doesn't look old simply because he hasn't a big head of hair.

Aubrey. Well, mine's pretty thin here on top.

Amy. Well, that's nothing; lots of young men haven't much.

Aubrey. [*Turning to her.*] Why, it was you that suggested my getting a toupee in the first place!

Amy. [*Stopping, and resting her hands on the table; and speaking directly to him.*] I know very well it was; because I knew I'd never have a minute's peace till you'd get one. All I heard morning, noon and night was something about your hair coming out. You might think nobody ever heard of anybody being baldheaded.

Aubrey. [*Turning back to the mirror.*] Well, a man's got to make the most of himself.

Amy. Well, if you think that thing's adding anything to *your* appearance, you've got another think. [*She starts towards the tabourette in front of the bay-window over at the left.*] Lift up this plant here for me, I want to put this cover on. [*She picks up a dead leaf or two from the floor and tosses them out the window. He remains standing at the mirror, looking at the toupee very critically from various angles.*] Aubrey!

Aubrey. [*Without moving, and with a touch of irritation.*] All right, all right!

Amy. Well, hurry up!—I want to change these covers. [*He withdraws lingeringly from the mirror.*] You'll keep fooling with that wig till there isn't a hair left on it.

Aubrey. [*Crossing to her.*] It isn't a wig, now, Amy! I've told you that half a dozen times!

Amy. [*Raising her hand quietly, to silence him.*] Well, a toupee then, dearie,—don't get excited.

Aubrey. I'm not getting excited at all!

Amy. [*Indicating the plant with an authoritative gesture.*] Lift up this plant and be quiet. [*He lifts up the plant and holds it, till she has changed the covers.*] There. [*He sets the plant down again, and she settles it more precisely.*]

Aubrey. [*Starting back across the room, in front of the sofa.*] You just call it a wig because you know it makes me mad!

Amy. [*Straightening up and looking after him, with one hand on her hip.*] I don't know why it should make you so mad, to have it called a wig.

Aubrey. [*Turning to her sharply.*] Because it *isn't* a wig! It's a toupee!

Amy. [*Turning to the plant again and giving it a final touch.*] Well, it's pretty, whatever it is.

Aubrey. It isn't even a toupee; it's just a patch!

Amy. [*Starting across to the back of the center table, carrying the soiled cover.*] It's a young *wig*, that's what it is. [*He turns and glares at her. She settles the scarf on the center table.*] And if it were only as big as it is, anybody that'd look at it a mile away'd know that it never grew on you. [*She goes quickly out through the portieres at the right, and he returns to the mirror and preens himself generally. Immediately she comes back into the room again, carrying a big, dark dust-cloth, with which she commences to dust the center table; while he struts across the room in front of the table, settling his cuffs and whistling the opening bars of the chorus of "I'm Forever Blowing Bubbles."*]

Aubrey. [*As he approaches the bay-window.*] What do you say about putting a couple of these plants out on the front porch?

Amy. What for?

Aubrey. I think it adds a lot to the appearance of the house as you come up the street.

Amy. Oh, don't be silly, Aubrey!

Aubrey. [*Wheeling around and looking at her in astonishment.*] What do you mean, don't be silly?

Amy. [*Pausing in her dusting.*] Why, who ever heard of anybody putting plants on a front porch in February!

Aubrey. I don't mean to leave them out there! We could bring them in again as soon as she goes.

Amy. [*Starting for the little corner table down at the right.*] Yes, and she'd go away thinking we were both crazy. [*She arranges the few magazines on the table, and then commences to dust it.*]

Aubrey. [*Sauntering back to the center table, where he proceeds to take the books which she has just arranged out of the little rack, and stand them on their ends.*] Oh, everybody's thinking you're crazy, with you!

Amy. [*Turning to him and speaking emphatically.*] Well, I know that's exactly what *I'd* think, if I were to come along and see plants on an open porch in the middle of winter.

Aubrey. [*Occupied with the book arrangement, and without looking up.*] Well, I've seen *lots* of plants on front porches in the winter.

Amy. [*Returning to her work of dusting the table.*] Well, if you did, they were *enclosed* porches. [*She finishes the dusting, and starts back towards the center table; but comes to a dead stop upon seeing the arrangement of the books, and her husband's intense absorption in it. There is a slight pause.*] What are you doing with those books?

Aubrey. [*Still busy.*] I'm just standing them up this way, so you can see what they are.

Amy. Can't you see what they are in the rack?

Aubrey. Certainly you can; but I think they show up better this way.

Amy. [*Stepping towards him and pushing him out of the way.*] Go away! and let them alone! [*She hurriedly commences to gather them up and restore them to the rack.*]

Aubrey. [*Wandering towards the arched doorway at the left.*] That's the way they have them in all the store windows. [*He proceeds to push the curtains back at the arched doorway.*]

Amy. Well, this isn't a store window. [*She glances at what he's doing, and starts towards him.*] And don't push those curtains back that way, Aubrey! I just fixed them. [*She pushes him towards the back of the room. He wanders around her and comes forward at the left.*]

Aubrey. They cover up the Victrola, that way.

Amy. [*Settling the curtains.*] That doesn't matter. These doors look too bare with the curtains pushed back. [*She starts back towards the center table to complete her rearrangement of the books.*] Now, let things alone, for heaven's sake! She can see the Victrola when she goes in there.

Aubrey. [*Sauntering a little towards the right, in front of the center table.*] She may not *go* in there.

Amy. [*Addressing him, as she crosses to the portieres at the right, taking the dust cloth with her.*] Well, I guess she's seen Victrolas before, even if she *doesn't* go in there. [*She goes out through the portieres. He stands for a second fixing himself, then breaks into "I'm Forever Blowing Bubbles" again. The detection of a speck of dust on his left shoe brings his whistling to a close; and, whipping out the eloquent handkerchief from his breast pocket, he leans over to flick it off. The effort dislodges the toupee, which drops to the floor in front of him. He snatches it up frantically, and claps it back upon his head; thrusts his handkerchief back into his pocket, and, with a panic-stricken glance over his right shoulder, in the direction of the portieres, bolts to the bay-window, at the left, holding the toupee in place with his left hand. Amy hurries in from the right carrying a small vase, which she takes to the little stand down at the right.*] Any sign of her?

Aubrey. [*Adjusting the toupee, and pretending to look out the window.*] I don't see any sign of her yet.

Amy. [*Turning from the little stand and moving towards the front of the center table.*] Maybe her train's late. [*She glances about the room, to see that everything is all right.*]

Aubrey. I don't know why it *should* be; there wasn't any hold-up along the line to-day that *I* heard of.

Amy. [*Settling her sash.*] She said in her telegram that she'd get into Broad Street at three o'clock sharp, and that she'd come right out here—Because she had to leave again on the Bridge train at four-fourteen.

Aubrey. [*Turning from the window and coming towards her.*] Too bad she didn't know, she could have gotten right off here at North Philadelphia—And then she could have gotten that Bridge train right there again at—a—four-twenty-seven.

[*He finishes his remarks with an explanatory gesture, and stands looking at his wife. She is still settling her sash. There is a fractional pause. Then she finishes and looks up*

*at him.   Then there is another pause, during which her eyes
shift to his toupee, which is on askew,—a bit over the left
eye.*]

Amy. [*With a kind of wearied impatience.*] Fix your toupee.

Aubrey. [*Putting his hand to it, and with a note of challenge
in his voice.*] What's the matter with it?

Amy. Why, it's all over the place.

Aubrey. Is that so!

Amy. Well, look at it!

Aubrey. Well, I fixed it that way! [*He emphasizes the remark
with a little bob of his head, and starts up around the center table
towards the mirror.*]

Amy. Well, it's pretty.

Aubrey. To let the air get to my scalp.

Amy. Well, for Heaven's sake, don't have it fixed that way
when Marion comes! [*Fixing the lace at her left cuff.*] You look
as though your head were lopsided. [*He turns from the mirror,
and gives her a withering look. But she is occupied with her cuff.*]

Aubrey. [*Turning back to the mirror.*] How is it you didn't
put on your other dress?

Amy. What other dress?

Aubrey. The one with all the beads.

Amy. [*Looking at him.*] Why, this is my good dress.

Aubrey. I think that other one's more of a flash.

Amy. [*Turning away again and settling the front of her dress.*]
Oh, don't be such a show-off, Aubrey.

Aubrey. [*Turning sharply and looking at her.*] Show-off!

Amy. That's what I said.

Aubrey. I don't know how you figure *that's* showing off!—Because I want you to *look* good.

Amy. [*Looking at him stonily, and speaking in a level key.*]
You want me to look good because I'm *your* wife. And you want
this friend of mine to *see* me looking good; just as you want her to
see that Victrola in there—[*She indicates the arched door on the
left with a slight nod.*] that isn't half paid for. [*She looks out.*]

Aubrey. [*Coming towards her a step or two.*] I suppose *you'd*
rather have her think you married some poor thing!

Amy. Listen, Aubrey—It won't make the least bit of difference
what we want her to think—She's a very smart girl; and all she'll
have to do is glance around this room, and she'll know *exactly*
what I married. [*She looks straight out again.*]

Aubrey. [*Mimicking her tone.*] Is that so! [*She simply emphasizes her remarks with a slow and very positive nod.*] Well, now, you listen to me for a minute, Amy! You know I can beat it right over to the barber shop [*She breaks into a rather tired little laugh.*] and stay there, till this friend of yours has gone, [*He moves over towards the little stand at the right.*] if you're so awfully afraid that I'm going to show up so badly in front of her!

Amy. [*Looking after him with a very knowing expression.*] No fear of your beating it over to the barber shop.

Aubrey. No?

Amy. You'll be strutting around here in front of her if she stays till midnight.

Aubrey. [*Very nettled, and securing his tie and tie-pin.*] All right.

Amy. [*Taking a step or two towards him.*] And, by the way, Aubrey—when Marion comes—I want you to do me a little favor; and don't be giving her a lot of big talk,—the way you were doing to that insurance man the other night; [*He turns and looks at her in astonished indignation.*] for I don't want her to think you're silly.

Aubrey. When was I doing any big talk to any insurance man?

Amy. The other night when you were talking to that man about the price of a fifty-thousand dollar policy.

Aubrey. Well, what about it?

Amy. Nothing; only that he was just laughing up his sleeve at you.

Aubrey. Is that so!

Amy. Well now, what else *could* he do, Aubrey? He knew you hadn't the slightest intention of taking any such policy.

Aubrey. How do you know he did?

Amy. Because he knows you're only a clerk. And that you don't get enough salary in six months to pay one year's premium on a policy like that. So when Marion comes, please don't be trying to impress her; [*She turns away and moves up at the right of the center table.*] for she's a very sensible woman.

Aubrey. [*Turning and going up to the mirror.*] I won't have anything to say to the woman at all.

Amy. [*Standing above the center table glancing through a magazine.*] Oh, yes, you will, dearie.

Aubrey. She's not coming to see me.

Amy. That doesn't make any difference to you.

Aubrey.   No reason why I should stand around *gabbing* to her.

Amy.   Well, you'll stand around gabbing, if you can get anybody to listen to you.

Aubrey.   Well, now, you watch me.

Amy.   I've been watching you; and listening to you too; for nearly four years.

Aubrey.   [*Turning to her from the mirror, very peevishly, and holding up his right hand.*] All right, I'll raise my hand,—if I want to say anything.   [*He moves forward at the right.*]

Amy.   I know what you'll do, if you get the chance; I've heard you before.   [*There is a slight pause, during which he frets a bit, down at the right.   Then his mood shifts and he breaks into whistling his familiar "I'm Forever Blowing Bubbles."   But this dies gradually as he becomes conscious of the little vase which* AMY *brought in for the stand at his right.   He tilts his head a bit to one side and looks at it with critical disapproval.*]

Aubrey.   You know, it's too bad we haven't got something flashier for this stand here.

Amy.   [*Just lifting her eyes over the top of the magazine.*] There's that vase up in mother's room.

Aubrey.   Is she up there now?

Amy.   She was when I came down.

Aubrey.   [*With a gesture of finality, and starting across in front of the center table.*] Well, *that's* out.

Amy.   Why, she wouldn't mind my taking it.

Aubrey.   [*Turning to his left and speaking emphatically.*] It isn't that!   But if she sees you taking anything out of her room, she'll get an idea there's something going on down here, and she'll be right down for the rest of the night and you won't be able to chase her!   [*He turns to his right and looks out the bay-window.*]

Amy.   Why, she knows that Marion Brill is coming here this afternoon.

Aubrey.   [*Turning to her sharply, with a distressed expression.*] Did you tell her?

Amy.   Certainly I told her.

Aubrey.   [*Despairingly, and crossing over again in front of the center table.*] Good night!

Amy.   Why, I want her to *meet* Marion!   She's never *met* her!

Aubrey.   Well, if your mother ever gets *talking*, this friend of yours'll know everything from *your* age to *my* salary!   [*He turns away to his right.*] Now, I'm telling you!

Amy. [*With a glance towards the portieres at the right, and speaking in an emphatic but subdued manner.*] I don't care whether she does or not.

Aubrey. Well, I do. [AMY *glances quickly towards the bay-window at the left; then, dropping the magazine, she steps eagerly towards it.*]

Amy. There's a taxi, now. [*She draws the curtain aside and looks keenly out.*]

Aubrey. [*Whirling round and striding towards the bay-window,—holding on to his toupee with his left hand.*] Is it stopping?

Amy. [*Suddenly, and in a tone of suppressed excitement.*] There she is! [*She runs to the door at the back of the room and vanishes into the hallway.*] She's looking for the number. [AU-BREY *peers eagerly through the bay-window, then steps quickly up to the door at the back.*]

Aubrey. Don't stand out there talking, now, Amy, without something around you! [*He rushes across at the back, still holding on to the toupee and, after a fleeting glance through the portieres at the right, reaches the mirror, where he gives himself a hasty and critical survey. Then the laughter and greetings of his wife and* MRS. COLE *reach him from the front door; so, with a glance in that direction, he struts forward at the right and strikes a pose,—swinging his nose-glasses carelessly back and forth, and looking away off.*]

Amy. [*Out at the left.*] I knew you through the window of the taxi!

Mrs. Cole. Well, you know, I was thinking all the way out, "Now, I wonder if Amy got my wire."

Amy. I got it yesterday morning.

Mrs. Cole and Amy. [*Together.*]

{ *Mrs. Cole.* Because, you know, I couldn't wait to hear from you.

{ *Amy.* But I said to Aubrey, "There's no use in my sending any word now, for she's already left Chicago by this time." [*The front door closes.*]

Mrs. Cole. Well, you see, dear, I didn't know *definitely*—

Mrs. Cole and Amy. [*Together.*]

{ *Mrs. Cole.* Up until Thursday night that I was coming.

{ *Amy.* [*Appearing in the hall door.*] Oh, well, it doesn't matter! [*Coming into the room.*] Just so long as I get to see you. [*She glances at her husband, then turns and faces the hall door.*]

There is a second's pause; then Mrs. Cole *enters the room; and,
glancing about, stops just inside the door. She is a bit older than*
Amy,—*probably three or four years, and considerably lighter in
coloring. And very smart.* Amy *said she was, and she is—extremely so. It's in the clearness of her eye, and the peculiarly deft
coördination of her general movement. Her clothes are smart too;
and by the looks of them, she must have married rather well; they
are quite gorgeous. A fine seal coat, full length, with a cape effect,
and an enormous muff made of black fox; rather large hat of black
lace over black satin, faced with pale coral, and black slippers
and stockings. She doesn't remove her coat, but when she opens
it, there is a glimpse of a light coral-colored dress, heavily trimmed
with steel beads, a long neck-scarf in steel silk, and a lovely-looking necklace of pale jade. She is wearing white kid gloves and
carries a fancy bag made of jade and coral beads on her left wrist.*]

Mrs. Cole. What an attractive house you have, Amy.

Amy. [*Smiling, and indicating her husband.*] There's the principal attraction, over there. [Aubrey *acknowledges the compliment by melting slightly.*]

Mrs. Cole. [*Smiling graciously and passing down at the left of
the center table, towards Aubrey.*] Is this *him?* [*He advances.*]

Amy. [*Coming forward at the left of the center table.*] That's
him.

Mrs. Cole. I'm *so* glad to meet you, Mr. Piper.

Aubrey. [*With a touch of condescension.*] How do you do.
[*They shake hands.*]

Mrs. Cole. You know, I've always been enormously *curious* to
see Amy's husband.

Aubrey. That so?

Amy. [*Looking straight out, and securing a hairpin in the
right side of her head.*] There he is.

Mrs. Cole. [*Tilting her head a bit to the left side and looking
at* Aubrey *with a smile.*] He's terribly good-looking.

Amy. [*Turning away.*] Oh! [Mrs. Cole *turns her head
sharply and looks at her, still smiling.*]

Aubrey. [*Addressing his wife.*] You hear *that?* [Mrs. Cole
turns again to* Aubrey.]

Amy. Please don't tell him that, Marion! he's bad enough as
it is.

Mrs. Cole. I don't know how you managed it, Amy. I could
never do it. You should see *my* husband, Mr. Piper. I don't sup-

pose he's any *older* than Mr. Piper, but, my dear, he *looks* old enough to be your father. [AMY *gives a little laugh of incredulity, and* MRS. COLE *turns suddenly to her.*] Really! [*Then she turns suddenly again to* AUBREY.] He's almost bald! [AUBREY'S *smile freezes.*]

Amy. Let me take your coat, Marion. [AUBREY *turns quietly around to the right, touching his toupee with his right hand, and moves up to the mirror, where he takes a reassuring peep at it, unobserved.*]

Mrs. Cole. I don't think I'll bother, dear, really; that taxicab's waiting out there for me. You see, I've got to get that Bridge train out of Broad Street at four-fourteen.

Aubrey. [*Coming forward at the right.*] I was just saying to Amy, it's too bad you didn't know, you could have gotten right off here at North Philadelphia, and wouldn't have had to go downtown at all.

Amy. You know, that Bridge train makes a stop here, Marion, at North Philadelphia, on the way to Atlantic City.

Mrs. Cole. Oh, does it!

Amy. Gets there at four-twenty-seven.

Mrs. Cole. Isn't it too bad I didn't know that?

Aubrey. Well, you won't have to go back downtown now, as it is, will you, Mrs. Cole?

Mrs. Cole. Yes, I've checked my grip at Broad Street.

Amy. Oh, isn't that too bad!

Mrs. Cole. Well, it doesn't matter! Just so long as I got to see you.

Amy. That's about all you'll be able to do.

Mrs. Cole. Well, sometime I'm going to invite myself to spend a few days with you, and then we'll have lots of time to talk.

Amy. I wish you could spend them now.

Mrs. Cole. So do I, dear child; but what can a poor woman do with a sick husband on her hands?

Amy. How is he, Marion?

Mrs. Cole. Why, he's pretty good, now.

Amy. Sit down. [*She picks up the cushion from the right end of the sofa to make a place for* MRS. COLE.]

Mrs. Cole. [*Stepping over to the sofa and unfastening her coat.*] I must unfasten this coat. [AMY *sits at the left end of the sofa; then* MRS. COLE *sits down.*] You know he had quite an attack of the flu last winter; and, I don't know, he never seemed to really get over it. [AUBREY *has assumed a position over at the right of the center table, and is listening with a general expression of heavy consequence.*]

Amy. So many people didn't.

Aubrey. One of the bookkeepers down at my office was telling me the other day that the flu has left him with a weak heart.

Mrs. Cole. Yes, I've heard of that, too. But with my husband, it all seems to be in his nerves. That's the reason he's at Atlantic City now.

Amy. How long has he been there, Marion?

Mrs. Cole. Since the week after New Year's.

Aubrey. They say Atlantic City's a great place for the nerves.

Mrs. Cole. Well, Ralph says he feels ever so much better. I had a letter from him on Tuesday, and he said he was only going to stay another week. So I thought I'd better just run down there myself and see how he is before he starts that long trip back to Chicago.

Amy. That flu was a dreadful thing, wasn't it?

Mrs. Cole. Dreadful! My dear, you've never seen anything change a person the way it has changed my husband. [*She turns suddenly to* AUBREY.] He's even lost his hair. [*She coughs a little, and uses her handkerchief; while* AUBREY *glides to the mirror again, touching his toupee discreetly.*]

Amy. [*Picking up the muff from* MRS. COLE's *lap.*] I love this muff, Marion.

Mrs. Cole. Do you know how long I've had that?

Amy. How long?

Mrs. Cole. Three years last Christmas.

Amy. Really!

Mrs. Cole. Ralph gave it to me the first Christmas we were married.

Amy. [*Holding it out on her left arm.*] It's beautiful! [AUBREY *comes forward again.*]

Aubrey. What kind of fur *is* that, Mrs. Cole?

Mrs. Cole. Fox.

Aubrey. Makes a nice looking fur.

Mrs. Cole. [*Turning and looking at it.*] It was pretty when I first got it. [*Turning again to* AUBREY.] But it's getting old now; [*Looking back to the muff.*] the hair's commencing to fall out. [*He turns and drifts to the back of the room.*] I was so sorry to hear about your father, Amy.

Amy. Yes, it was so sudden.

Mrs. Cole. How is your mother, Amy? [AUBREY *turns and looks towards his wife.*]

Amy. She keeps pretty well.

Mrs. Cole. That's good.

Amy. She's here with us, you know. [AUBREY *makes a despairing gesture.*]

Mrs. Cole. Oh, is she?

Amy. Yes.

Mrs. Cole. Living with you, you mean?

Amy. [*Getting up, and going round back of the sofa.*] Hum-hum. I must tell her you're here.

Mrs. Cole. Well, now, don't bother her, Amy, if she's doing anything.

Amy. [*Crossing to the portieres at the right.*] Not a thing—She's crazy to see you.

Mrs. Cole and Amy. [*Together.*]

⎰ *Mrs. Cole.* I don't want to bother her.
⎱ *Amy.* I told her I'd call her as soon as you came. [*Going out through the portieres.*] I'll be down in a second. [AUBREY, *standing up at the back of the room, glances after his wife, then turns and looks at* MRS. COLE. *She is settling her muff beside her on the sofa. He glances at himself in the mirror, and then comes forward at the right, rather grandly, flipping the nose-glasses back and forth.*]

Mrs. Cole. Isn't it nice that Amy can have her mother here with her?

Aubrey. Yes; I've had her here ever since Mr. Fisher died.

Mrs. Cole. She must be so much company for you.

Aubrey. Yes; a person'd never be lonesome.

Mrs. Cole. I often say to my husband, I wish there were some one like that with us; I get so lonesome sometimes in the house during the day.

Aubrey. Well, when my father-in-law died, I thought Amy's mother might just as well come here with us. She was alone; and we had plenty of room; so I said, "Come ahead! [*He makes a rather magnificent gesture.*] The more the merrier!"

Mrs. Cole. This is rather a large house, isn't it?

Aubrey. Yes, it is. Quite a wonderfully made house, too. They were put up by the McNeil people out here at Jenkintown. They're considered to build the best dwelling-house of anybody in the country. They just put up the twenty of them, as kind of sample houses—ten on that side, and ten on this. Of course, these on this side have the southern exposure; so a person's got to have quite a little pull to get hold of one of these. [*He catches his thumbs in the armholes of his vest, and, tilting his head a bit to the left side, looks away out and off, tapping his fingers on his chest.*] But I have a friend—that's one of the biggest real estate men here in town, and he was able to fix it for me.

Mrs. Cole. You were very lucky, weren't you?

Aubrey. Yes, I *was* pretty lucky in a way. Although I'd like to have gotten hold of one of the corner ones.

Mrs. Cole. Are they a much larger house than these?

Aubrey. They're fifteen-thousand-dollar houses; these are only ten. [*He moves across in front of her, with ever so slight a suggestion of strut.*]

Mrs. Cole. I see.

Aubrey. [*With a casual glance out of the bay-window.*] I'm very anxious to get hold of one of them. I told this friend of mine to keep his eye open, and if there's a chance, I'll go as high as twenty thousand. Then, of course, I could always rent this.

Mrs. Cole. It's an awfully nice street.

Aubrey. Nice in summer.

Mrs. Cole. I was so surprised when I saw it, because the taxi-cab driver didn't know where it was when I asked him. [AUBREY *looks at her, with a quick movement of his head.*]

Aubrey. Didn't know where Cresson Street was?

Mrs. Cole. He said not.

Aubrey. [*Shaking his head from side to side and smiling with heavy amusement.*] He must be an awful rube.

Mrs. Cole. He had to ask the traffic officer down on Broad Street.

Aubrey. Well, I'll tell you—I don't suppose they *have* many calls for taxis out this way. You see, most everybody in through here has his own car.

Mrs. Cole. Oh, I see.

Aubrey. Some of them have a half a dozen, for that matter. [*He laughs consequentially, and she reflects his amusement faintly*.] I was saying to Amy, when we got your wire yesterday, it was too bad my car was laid up, I could have picked you up at the station to-day.

Mrs. Cole. Oh, that didn't matter.

Aubrey. But I've been working it pretty hard lately, and I had to turn it in Thursday to have the valves ground.

Mrs. Cole. There's always something to be done to them, isn't there?

Aubrey. I should say so. Funny thing, too,—people have an idea if they get hold of a high-priced car their trouble's over. [*She smiles and shakes her head from side to side in appreciation of that illusion.*] I swear, I've had just as much trouble with my *Pierce Arrow* as I ever had with my *Buick.* [*They both laugh, and* AUBREY *looks out the window.*]

Amy. [*Coming in through the portieres at the right.*] Mother says she was just coming down to inquire how it was you hadn't come. [AUBREY *turns and looks at his wife, then turns around to his right and moves towards the back of the room.* MRS. FISHER *comes in through the portieres, and* MRS. COLE *rises.*] This is Mrs. Cole, Mother—Marion Brill that you've heard so much about.

Mrs. Fisher. [*Coming forward at the right of the center table.*] Well, indeed I have.

Mrs. Cole. [*Advancing.*] I'm so glad to meet you, Mrs. Fisher.

Mrs. Fisher. [*Shaking hands with her.*] How do you do. I'm certainly pleased to meet you, too.

Mrs. Cole. Thank you.

Mrs. Fisher. For I think I've heard your name more than any other girl's name I ever heard in this house.

Mrs. Cole. Well, Amy and I worked beside each other so long.

Mrs. Fisher. All I used to hear morning, noon and night was, "Marion Brill said so and so" [MRS. COLE *and* AMY *laugh.*] or, "Marion Brill is going to do so and so." [MRS. FISHER *laughs.*]

Amy. [*Standing at her mother's right.*] I'm afraid that's about all we did was talk, wasn't it, Marion? [*She laughs again.*]

Mrs. Cole. It's about all *I* used to do. [*She laughs.*]

Mrs. Fisher. [*Indicating the sofa.*] Won't you sit down, Mrs. Cole?

Mrs. Cole. [*Turning to her right, towards the sofa.*] Thanks.

Amy. [*Indicating the armchair at the right of the center table.*] Sit here, Mother.

Mrs. Fisher. [*Passing to the armchair, in front of* Amy.] Amy, why didn't you ask Mrs. Cole to take off her coat?

Mrs. Cole. [*Sitting on the sofa.*] She did, Mrs. Fisher. [Mrs. Fisher *sits down.*]

Amy. [*Sitting on the edge of the center table.*] Marion can't stay, Mother.

Mrs. Cole. I've got to go almost immediately, Mrs. Fisher.

Mrs. Fisher. It's too bad you can't stay for a cup of tea, anyway.

Mrs. Cole. I'd love it, Mrs. Fisher, but I really haven't time.

Mrs. Fisher. You're going to Atlantic City, aren't you?

Mrs. Cole. Yes.

Mrs. Fisher. [*As though admitting a weakness in herself.*] I wish I was going with you. [*She laughs shyly. And when she laughs she's pretty. She must have been a rather pretty girl; for there are traces of it yet; even after nearly thirty years as the wife of a poor man. Her husband was a wage-earner, always; and it was only by dint of vigilance and excessive scrimping that they were able to purchase and pay for the house in which she now lives. But the economic strain has told upon her, in many ways; perhaps, most obviously, in the developing of a certain plainness of personal quality,—a simplicity that is at once pathetic and, in a way, quaint. And her manner of dressing and the arrangement of her hair rather heighten this impression. She looks old-fashioned. But her hair is quite lovely; it's thick and silvery, with the loveliest wave in it; and she has it simply parted in the middle and drawn back over her ears. She must have been a decided blonde. Her dress, which looks as though she might have made it herself, a long time ago, has no particular pattern; simply a plain, brown poplin dress, without a bit of trimming except a little ruffle of the goods, about two inches deep, around the hem of the skirt. This skirt is one of the old-fashioned, full kind,—touching all the way round. She is wearing a deep lawn collar, probably to relieve the almost basque-like tightness of the body, and an enormous breast-pin, featuring a very vague likeness of a delicate-looking gentleman in a straw hat; presumably,* Mr. Fisher.]

Mrs. Cole. Do you like Atlantic City, Mrs. Fisher? [*She nods, still smiling.*]

Amy. Yes, mother's always been crazy about Atlantic City.

Mrs. Fisher. I like the bathing.

Mrs. Cole. Yes, wonderful, isn't it?

Mrs. Fisher. I used to go in sometimes twice a day. [*She laughs a little again.*]

Mrs. Cole. You must have liked it.

Mrs. Fisher. [*With an instant change to seriousness of expression and voice.*] Of course, that was before my operation. [AUBREY, *who has been standing at the back of the room watching her with an expression of contemptuous pity, makes an impatient gesture and turns to the bay-window.* AMY *feels the movement, and glances towards him.*]

Mrs. Cole. It certainly is a wonderful place.

Mrs. Fisher. I haven't been there now since my husband died.

Mrs. Cole. Is that so?

Mrs. Fisher. Yes; it'll be four years the seventeenth of next October. He died the day Amy was twenty-five. [AUBREY *turns from the bay-window and looks daggers at her.*] Died on her birthday. Didn't he, Amy?

Amy. Yes. [*She glances towards* AUBREY *again, and he says voicelessly to her, but with very eloquent gestures, "Didn't I tell you!" and goes towards the back of the room again.*]

Mrs. Cole. And you haven't been to Atlantic City *since* then?

Mrs. Fisher. No, not since then. But before that, we used to spend two days there every single summer. [AUBREY *turns at the back of the room and looks at her stonily.*] Go down on Saturday morning, and come up Sunday night. Of course, it didn't cost us anything, you know, 'cept our fares; because we used to carry our lunch with us. [AUBREY *begins to boil.*] And in those days, they used to allow the excursionists to sleep under the board walk, if you remember. [AUBREY *raises his hand in the hope of attracting her attention and silencing her; but she is oblivious of him. He's away up in the left-hand corner of the room, out of the range of* MRS. COLE'S *eye.*]

Mrs. Cole. Yes, I remember.

Mrs. Fisher. Dear me, I used to look forward to those two days the whole year round. [*She laughs a little.*] I was just saying to Amy the other day, that if I could see my way clear to do it, I believe I'd enjoy a day down there now, just as much as ever I did.

Mrs. Cole. Well, I don't see why you shouldn't, Mrs. Fisher.

Mrs. Fisher. [*With another instantaneous shift to seriousness.*] Well, of course, since my operation. [AUBREY *makes a movement of excessive irritation, and* AMY *gets it; and thinks it wise to interrupt her mother.*]

Mrs. Fisher and Amy. [*Together.*]

⎧ *Mrs. Fisher.* I've got to be more careful. I can't do the
⎨ things—that—I—
⎩ *Amy.* [*Turning suddenly to* Mrs. COLE.] You haven't been
in Atlantic City since you were married, have you, Marion?

Mrs. Cole. No, it's five years since I've been there.

Mrs. Fisher. Are you going to stay there for any length of
time, Mrs. Cole?

Mrs. Cole. No, I'm not, Mrs. Fisher; I just want to see how
my husband is.

Mrs. Fisher. Has he consumption? [AUBREY *snaps with irritation.*]

Mrs. Cole. No-o, he had the flu last winter; [Mrs. FISHER *folds
her lips in, shakes her head slowly from side to side, and looks at
the floor in front of her.*] and he's never been exactly himself since.

Mrs. Fisher. They never do much good after that flu. [AMY
rises and crosses towards the left, above the sofa.]

Amy. I suppose it depends upon how bad a person's had it,
Mother. [*As soon as she passes out of the range of* Mrs. COLE's
vision, AUBREY *appeals to her to know if there isn't something she
can do to shut her mother up. She simply dismisses him with a
deft gesture; and, with a sharp nod of her head, indicates the immediate presence of* Mrs. COLE.]

Mrs. Fisher. [*Unaware of the situation.*] Well, now, this
doctor that tended me during my operation [AUBREY *whirls round
and goes to the hall door, at the back, and* AMY *comes around and
sits down on the sofa, to* Mrs. COLE's *left.*] Doctor Stainthorpe—
she's a lady doctor—she was telling me that the flu is like scarlet
fever; if it don't leave you with one thing, it'll leave you with
something else.

Mrs. Cole. Well, Mr. Cole seems pretty good, most of the
time, but occasionally he has a spell of sort of—nervous exhaustion. [AUBREY *wanders over and stands resting his right hand on
the left end of the center table, listening to* Mrs. COLE.]

Mrs. Fisher. Maybe he works too hard.

Mrs. Cole. No, I don't think it's that; [*Speaking directly to*
AUBREY.] his work is easy enough. [*Shifting her eyes again to*
Mrs. FISHER.] He's just a wig-maker. [AUBREY *drifts towards
the mirror.*] Makes all kinds of hair goods, you know.

Mrs. Fisher. Oh, yes.

Amy. I don't think I ever knew your husband's business, Marion.

Mrs. Cole. Didn't I ever tell you?

Amy. You may have, but I've forgotten. [*With a glance at his toupee in the mirror,* AUBREY *glides down at the right of* MRS. FISHER.]

Mrs. Cole. That's what he does—Makes all these toupees that you see,—[AUBREY *turns quietly away to the right and glides up again towards the back of the room.*] and switches and—patches— all that kind of thing.

Mrs. Fisher. Did you have any trouble finding the house, Mrs. Cole?

Mrs. Cole. No, not very much.

Amy. Marion came out in a taxi.

Mrs. Fisher. [*As though coming out in a taxi were quite an experience.*] Oh, *did* you!

Mrs. Cole. [*Dropping her handkerchief at her left foot.*] Yes, I came right out Broad Street.

Amy. [*Handing her the handkerchief.*] Here's your handkerchief, Marion.

Mrs. Cole and Mrs. Fisher. [*Together.*]

{ *Mrs. Cole.* Oh, thanks. Did I drop that?
{ *Mrs. Fisher.* Have you any children, Mrs. Cole?

Mrs. Cole. No, I haven't, Mrs. Fisher.

Mrs. Fisher. Didn't you ever have any? [AUBREY *looks helplessly at his wife, then back to his mother-in-law.*]

Mrs. Cole. No.

Mrs. Fisher. Well, maybe you're just as well off.

Mrs. Cole. Yes, I suppose I am, in a way.

Mrs. Fisher. [*Looking at the floor in front of her, and shaking her head philosophically.*] If they never make you laugh, they'll never make you cry.

Mrs. Cole. That's true.

Mrs. Fisher. I buried a boy, when he was eight years old; and, dear me, it seemed as though I never in this world would get over it. But when I read in the newspapers now about all these bandits, and moving-picture people,—I'm kind of glad he went when he did. He might have gotten in with bad company and turned out just as bad as any of the others.

Mrs. Cole. It's hard to tell how they'll turn out.

Mrs. Fisher. Well, you see, this is such a terrible neighborhood in through here, to bring a boy *up* in. [AUBREY *makes a movement of controlled desperation towards the left.* AMY *glances at him, and he gives her a speaking look.*]

Mrs. Cole. Is that so?

Mrs. Fisher. Oh, it's just dreadful. [AUBREY *tries to signal her from the upper left-hand corner of the room, with divers shakes and waves of his hands. But it is utterly lost upon* MRS. FISHER. *She is all set for a good chat; and it will require more than the gesticulations of* MR. PIPER *to distract her. So she goes serenely on; never even casting a glance in his direction.*] A body'd be afraid to put their nose outside the door, after dark. Why, right across the street here [*She extends her arm and hand towards the right.*] in two-twenty-eight, there's a big foreign family; and I don't believe there's a soul in that house speaks a word of English. And there's a Bolshevik organization of some kind has just bought two-forty-nine—[AUBREY *has passed into a state of desperate unconsciousness, and stands glaring at his mother-in-law.*] that's the corner property on this side. [*She points to the right.*] Paid three thousand dollars cash for it, too. So you can see what the neighborhood's coming to.

Amy. [*Tactfully.*] Aubrey,—I wish you'd go down and close the heater; the house is getting cold again, I think. [*He starts for the portieres immediately, and* MRS. COLE *turns and says something to* AMY. *As* AUBREY *crosses the back of the room, he fixes* MRS. FISHER *with an icy glare, which he holds until he passes through the portieres. Not knowing wherein she has offended, she turns and looks over her right shoulder after him with an expression of puzzled resentment. Then she turns to* AMY.]

Mrs. Fisher. Amy, you'd better go down, too; he'll be locking those grates again, the way he did last week.

Amy. [*Rising and going around back of the sofa and over towards the portieres.*] He doesn't need to touch those grates; that fire's all right. [*Goes out.*]

Mrs. Fisher. We have one of those old-fashioned heaters; and when you're raking it, unless you turn it just a certain way, the grates'll lock. It's a perfect nuisance. I often say, I don't wonder people want to live in apartments; where they won't have to be bothered with all this heater business.

Mrs. Cole. It is a bother.

Mrs. Fisher. Oh, it's a pest.

Mrs. Cole. Although I had the hardest time getting used to an apartment when I was first married.

Mrs. Fisher. Oh, do you live in an apartment in Chicago, Mrs. Cole?

Mrs. Cole. Yes, I've lived in one ever since I've been out there.

Mrs. Fisher. Well, you ought to be glad of it.

Mrs. Cole. Well, really, it was the only place we could get—there have been so few houses go up in Chicago in the last few years.

Mrs. Fisher. That's just the way it's been here. Why, when Amy was married four years ago, she couldn't get a house for love or money. That is, I mean, one that she could afford the rent, you know.

Mrs. Cole. Yes, I know.

Mrs. Fisher. Of course, she could have gotten plenty at fancy rents; but as I said to her, "How are you going to pay it on his wages?" [*She turns carefully in her chair and glances over her right shoulder towards the portieres, for fear* AUBREY *might be within hearing distance. Then she turns back to* MRS. COLE, *and, leaning towards her a bit, speaks in a rather subdued tone.*] He's only a clerk, you know,—down here in the Pennsylvania Freight Office. But she couldn't get a thing. Of course, I'd have liked to have her stay here; because there was only Mr. Fisher and myself; but—a—[*She turns again and glances over her right shoulder, then back again to* MRS. COLE; *this time with even more confidence.*] my husband never liked *him.* [*She indicates* AUBREY *with a nod towards the portieres. Then to emphasize the fact, she looks straight at* MRS. COLE *and gives her head a little shake from side to side. But evidently she feels that she hasn't stated the circumstances sufficiently; or that, having mentioned it at all, it implies some measure of elucidation; for she rises gingerly, and, tiptoeing over to the center table, rests her left hand upon it and leans towards* MRS. COLE *in an attitude of extreme caution and confidence.*] Said he was kind of a blatherskite, you know—[*She tiptoes towards the portieres, but stops halfway and turns again.*] Very big ideas and very little brains. [*She continues on to the portieres and glances out; then returns to the table.*] So—a— finally, they had to take two little rooms over here on Lehigh Avenue. Nine dollars a month, so you can imagine what they were like. But you couldn't *tell* them anything. As I said to them, the night they first told me they were going to be married—

I said, "How do you two ever expect to make ends meet on thirty-two dollars a week?" "Oh," he says, "that's only temporary," he says,—"I'll *own* the Pennsylvania Railroad within the next five years." This is the way he's owning it. [*She looks towards the portieres; then turns back and says emphatically.*] He's never even gotten a raise. He's been getting thirty-two dollars a week for the last four years. [*She moves stealthily towards the portieres again; far enough over to enable her to glance through them; then comes back to the table.*] But—a—as soon as Mr. Fisher died, I told Amy she could come here, and I'd take my rent out in board. And then she makes me different things to wear; she's very handy, you know.

Mrs. Cole. Yes, she's a wonderful *girl*.

Mrs. Fisher. But, you know, you'd think *he* was doing me a favor to live here. [MRS. COLE *doesn't know exactly what to say, so she simply shakes her head from side to side and smiles.*] He doesn't like me, you know. Hardly ever speaks to me. I suppose you noticed it, didn't you?

Mrs. Cole. No, I didn't, Mrs. Fisher.

Mrs. Fisher. He's been *furious* ever since last spring. [*She turns away again and glances towards the portieres; then turns hurriedly back, as though she had a particularly incredible item of information to communicate.*] Wanted *me* to put a *mortgage* on this house to get him an automobile. Can you imagine that! He's *crazy* about automobiles. And, Mrs. Cole, I know just as well as I'm standing here, that if he *got* one, he'd only kill himself—for he has no more brains than a rabbit. So I told him. I sez— [AMY'S *voice, out at the right, interrupts her.*]

Amy. Be sure and close this cellar door, Aubrey; there's a draught here if you don't.

Mrs. Fisher. [*Tiptoeing back to her chair, with a significant gesture to* MRS. COLE.] Well, I hope you find your husband all right, Mrs. Cole. [*She sits down.*]

Mrs. Cole. I hope so, thanks, Mrs. Fisher. He *seems* pretty good, from his letters.

Amy. [*Coming through the portieres.*] I'm sorry, Marion, but I seem to be the only one around here that knows how to tend to that heater.

Mrs. Cole. [*Rising.*] Well, you know, you were always able to do everything, Amy. [*She moves a little towards the front of the center table, fastening her glove.*]

Amy. You don't have to go already, do you, Marion?

Mrs. Cole. I'm afraid so, dear; [MRS. FISHER *rises.*] it's getting on to four o'clock. [AUBREY *sways in through the portieres, flicking imaginary ashes from himself with the fancy handkerchief.*]

Mrs. Fisher. Couldn't you take a later train, Mrs. Cole? [AUBREY *comes forward at the right.*]

Mrs. Cole. Why, I suppose I could, Mrs. Fisher; but I've wired Mr. Cole that I'll be on *that* one.

Mrs. Fisher. Oh, I see.

Mrs. Cole. And he's so nervous and worrisome since he's been sick, that I'm afraid if I'm *not* on it, he'll be tearing his hair out. [*She turns, laughing a little, which* AMY *and her mother reflect, and goes back to the sofa for her muff.* AUBREY *is feigning a profound absorption in an examination of his finger nails.* AMY *crosses over after* MRS. COLE *and goes up back of the sofa towards the bay-window.*]

Mrs. Fisher. Are you going back to the station on the trolley, Mrs. Cole?

Mrs. Cole. No, I told the taxi to wait, Mrs. Fisher. I hope he's still out there. Is he, Amy?

Amy. [*At the window.*] Yes, he's still there.

Mrs. Fisher. [*Hurrying across in front of* MRS. COLE.] Oh, I must see it! Pardon me.

Mrs. Cole. Certainly. [*Turning around to her right and going up towards the hall door.*] Now, Amy, I do hope you're going to write to me occasionally.

Amy. [*Coming away from the window, towards her.*] You're the one who never writes.

Mrs. Cole. [*Laughing guiltily.*] I know, darling; but I'm going to reform, really.

Amy. Well, now, I'm going to wait and see.

Mrs. Cole. But, really, I've been so terribly busy since Mr. Cole's been ill, that I don't seem to be able to—[*She becomes confidential.*]

Mrs. Fisher. [*Turning, at the window, and addressing* AUBREY, *who is standing directly opposite her at the right, and who happens to be the first one her eye lights upon.*] Seems so funny to see an automobile in this street. [AUBREY *is paralyzed; and before he can recover the use of his arm sufficiently to try to silence her, she has turned again to the window; and he stands watching*

*her, frozen with the fear that she may turn again, and sustained
only by the hope that* Mrs. Cole *did not hear her. His agony is
very brief, however, for almost immediately,* Mrs. Fisher *turns
again and addresses him.*] I don't think I've, ever seen one in this
street before. [Aubrey *makes a frantic gesture to her, and, turning around to his left, strides up to the back of the room, pointing
vigorously at* Mrs. Cole. Mrs. Fisher *is bewildered—She simply
stares blankly at the goings-on of her son-in-law; and it is not
until he strides forward again at the right, glowering at her savagely, that it occurs to her to speak.*] Why, what's the matter
with you! [Aubrey *suddenly raises his left arm and hand as
though he'd like to sweep her from the earth, but the opportune
turning of* Mrs. Cole *to say good-by to* Mrs. Fisher, *restores
order.*]

Mrs. Cole. Good-by, Mrs. Fisher.

Mrs. Fisher. [*Shaking hands with her.*] Good-by, Mrs. Cole.

Mrs. Cole. I'm sorry to have to run away like this. [Amy
moves around to Mrs. Cole's *right.*]

Mrs. Fisher. Well, I know how you feel.

Mrs. Cole. [*Turning and chucking* Amy *under the chin.*] But
I *did* want to see my child here. And her husband—probably the
best-looking man I've seen in Philadelphia so far. [Amy *with an
exclamation of deprecation, turns to her left and goes laughing out
into the hallway.* Mrs. Fisher *laughs a little, out of courtesy.*]

Aubrey. [*Swaggering up at the right of the center table, ex-
cessively self-satisfied, and pointing after his wife.*] Tell *her* that!

Mrs. Fisher. I hope the next time you come this way you'll be
able to stay a little longer, Mrs. Cole.

Mrs. Cole. Thanks; I hope so, too, Mrs. Fisher. [*She turns
to the right to greet* Aubrey, *who has come across above the center
table.*] Good-by, Mr. Piper.

Aubrey. Good-by, Mrs. Cole. [*They shake hands.*]

Mrs. Cole. [*Dropping her glove at her right foot.*] I'm so
glad to have met you.—Oh!

Aubrey. [*Stooping.*] I'll get it. [*The toupee glides off and
falls on to the black, fur rug on which they're standing; but he
doesn't observe the circumstance, and restores the glove with a
touch of flourish.*]

Mrs. Cole. Thanks. [*She simply takes the glove, without the
slightest evidence of an appreciation of the situation. But old*

MRS. FISHER *is in a state of siege; and, taking advantage of her position behind* MRS. COLE, *endeavors to communicate to her son-in-law, by means of funny little pointings and movements with her head, some knowledge of his condition. But* AUBREY *is mercifully oblivious of everything, save that he is in the presence of a very attractive woman, who has admitted that she considers him probably the best-looking man she has seen in Philadelphia.*]

Aubrey. Sorry you have to go so soon.

Mrs. Cole. I'm sorry, too, Mr. Piper. But if I'm not on that train, [*She turns to* MRS. FISHER.] I'm afraid I'll get scalped. [*She goes out into the hallway.*]

Mrs. Fisher. [*Stepping to the hall door.*] Don't let her stand out there in the cold with nothing around her, Mrs. Cole.

Mrs. Cole. No, I'll send her right in, Mrs. Fisher.

Mrs. Fisher. Good-by.

Mrs. Cole. Good-by.

Aubrey. [*Standing immediately behind* MRS. FISHER, *looking out into the hallway.*] Good-by.

Mrs. Cole. Amy, your mother says you mustn't stand out here in the cold with nothing around you.

[MRS. FISHER *turns, and, with a glance at* AUBREY, *steps to the bay-window, to watch* MRS. COLE *get into the taxi.* AUBREY *follows her and takes up his position just back of her, looking out.*]

Mrs. Fisher. [*After a slight pause.*] Good-by. [*She waves to* MRS. COLE; *and so does* AUBREY,—*perhaps with a trifle more dignity than the occasion implies. Then the taxi moves away, and they watch it, smiling, down the street. Suddenly* MRS. FISHER *looks sharply in the opposite direction.*] There's the boy with the paper. [*Turning from the window, folding her arms tightly together.*] I've got to get my little woolen shawl, [*She crosses to the right, above the center table.*] this room's too chilly for me. [*She goes out through the portieres at the right. The front door, out at the left, closes; and* AUBREY *turns from the window to the hall door.*]

Amy. [*Entering briskly through the hall door, carrying the evening paper.*] Here's the *Ledger*.

Aubrey. You ought to have something around you.

Amy. [*Stepping to the bay-window.*] I'm not cold. Where's Mother?

Aubrey. [*Opening the paper, as he strolls across above the center table.*] She's gone up for her shawl. [*He sits in the armchair, down at the right, and* AMY *peers through the bay-window, as though trying to catch a last glimpse of the departing taxi.*]

Amy. [*Suddenly turning from the window and coming across to the right, above the center table.*] Isn't Marion nice?

Aubrey. Yes, she's very pleasant.

Amy. [*Looking at herself in the mirror.*] She's an awfully smart girl, too. She had charge of our entire department when I worked at the Bank. [*There is a slight pause.*]

Aubrey. [*Half-turning, and very significantly.*] Say, Amy.

Amy. What?

Aubrey. Listen. [*She turns her head sharply and looks at him. He beckons her to him with a rather mysterious nod, and she comes around to his left.*]

Amy. What?

Aubrey. [*In a subdued, level tone.*] Did you get your mother telling her your age?

Amy. That's nothing; Marion knows my age.

Aubrey. I *told* you what she'd do.

Amy. [*Starting towards the portieres.*] Well, now, it doesn't make the least bit of difference; so don't start anything. [*She glances through the portieres.*]

Aubrey. It's a good thing she didn't have any longer to stay.

Mrs. Fisher. [*Out at the right.*] You know, Amy,—

Amy. [*Turning suddenly to him with a deft gesture.*] Sh—sh—[*She steps to the mirror and pretends to be fixing her hair.*]

Aubrey. Or she'd have told her a whole lot more.

Mrs. Fisher. [*Coming through the portieres wearing a rather skimpy-looking white shoulder-shawl and carrying some pale-pink knitting.*] I always pictured that girl as a much bigger woman than she is, when you used to talk about her. [*She walks down between* AUBREY *and the center table and crosses over to the sofa. She appears to be having difficulty in disentangling her yarn.*]

Amy. Don't you think she's a big girl?

Mrs. Fisher. Well, *stouter*, I mean.

Amy. No, she never was stout.

Mrs. Fisher. [*Sitting on the sofa, and settling herself.*] I'd never know her in the world from that picture you have of her upstairs.

Amy. [*Turning from the mirror.*] Don't you think she's nice?

Mrs. Fisher. Very nice.

Amy. [*Standing at her husband's right.*] Give me a piece of that paper.

Mrs. Fisher. And very stylish, too.

Amy. Any part'll do. [*He detaches a section of the paper and gives it to her. She moves a step or two to the right and forward and commences to read.* AUBREY *resumes his reading; and* MRS. FISHER *knits.*]

Mrs. Fisher. [*After a pause.*] I'll bet there was five hundred dollars right on her back there to-day if there was a penny. And that's not counting her hat nor her shoes, either. [*There is another little pause.*] That wig business must be a very good business. [AUBREY *looks over at her stonily; but she's occupied with her knitting.*] I saw a piece in the *North American* the other morning, that a lot of people were wearing wigs now that don't need them at all. [*She looks over at* AMY, *to find* AUBREY *glaring at her.*] That's what it said. [*He snaps his head round and continues reading.*] She was telling me, Amy, that she lives in an apartment there in Chicago. Sez they couldn't *get* a house when they first went there. Sez there hasn't been a house go up in Chicago since before the war. [*She laughs faintly to herself.*] I was telling her about the time you and Aubrey had, when you were first married—[*He looks over at her, with a dangerous squint.*] trying to get even a couple of rooms somewhere. And the kind they were, when you *did* get them. [*She laughs a little more, at the recollection of them.*] But they had the nerve to charge you nine dollars a month for them, just the same. [*She smiles and looks at* AUBREY.]

Aubrey. [*Explosively.*] I suppose you told her *that*, too, didn't you! [AMY *is startled out of her interest in the newspaper.*]

Mrs. Fisher. [*After a second's amazement.*] Told her what?

Aubrey. When were you handing out all this information?

Amy. Now, Aubrey, don't start, please!

Aubrey. [*Jumping to his feet.*] It's enough to make [*He slams the piece of newspaper down on to the chair violently.*] a fellow start! [*He thrusts his hands into his trousers' pockets and strides*

towards the back of the room.] Trying to make me look like a
poor *sap!* [*He crosses to the hall door and right back again.*]

Mrs. Fisher. [*Looking in bewilderment at* Amy.] Why, what's
the matter with *him?*

Amy and Aubrey. [*Together.*]

{ *Amy.* Nothing at all, Mother.

{ *Aubrey.* [*At the upper right-hand corner of the center table.*]
You know very *well* what's the matter with me!

Mrs. Fisher. What?

Aubrey. Handing out a line of *gab* about my *business!* every
time you can get anybody to *listen* to you.

Mrs. Fisher. Who was handing out any line of gab about your
business?

Aubrey. *You* were!—and you're always doing it!

Mrs. Fisher. Why, you haven't got any line of business for
anybody to hand out any line of gab about—that I ever heard of.
[*She turns away.*]

Aubrey. It doesn't matter whether I have any line of business
or not! It isn't necessary for you to be gabbing to perfect
strangers about it.

Mrs. Fisher. What did you want me to do, sit there lookin' at
the woman, like a cow?

Amy. Mother, please.

Aubrey. You don't have to talk about my affairs!

Mrs. Fisher. [*With vast amusement.*] Your affairs—

Aubrey. That's what I said, my affairs! [Mrs. Fisher *laughs
derisively, and* Aubrey *turns to his wife, desperately.*] You hear
her!

Mrs. Fisher. That's funny.

Amy. She wasn't talking about you, Aubrey.

Aubrey. She *was* talking about me! That's all she ever *does*,
is talk about me! [Mrs. Fisher *whirls around.*]

Mrs. Fisher. I was talkin' about houses!—that ain't you, is it?

Aubrey. I know what you were talking about, you needn't tell
me.

Mrs. Fisher. I had to talk about something, didn't I?

Amy. Keep quiet, Aubrey.

Aubrey and Mrs. Fisher. [*Together.*]

{ *Aubrey.* [*Whirling around and going towards the hall door.*]
{ No, I won't keep quiet!

{ *Mrs. Fisher.* You two were down in the cellar fixing the fire!

And you can't sit there with your two hands as long as each other when a person's visiting in your house!

Aubrey. [*Stopping abruptly above the center table, on his way back towards the portieres.*] I suppose you mentioned *that,* too, didn't you!

Mrs. Fisher. [*Half-turning and listening narrowly.*] Mentioned what?

Aubrey. That it was *your* house! [MRS. FISHER *turns her whole body round to him in a literal bounce.*]

Mrs. Fisher. [*Shrilly.*] Well, whose house *would* I mention that it was!

Aubrey. [*Turning to* AMY *with a broad gesture of his right hand.*] You see! Didn't I tell you!

Amy and *Aubrey.* [*Together.*]

{ *Amy.* Well, what of it, Aubrey! What of it!

\ *Aubrey.* Every opportunity she gets she's trying to make me look like a poor thing! [*He brings his right hand down thunderously upon the center table. Then, thrusting his hands into his trousers' pockets again, strides over to the arched door and back again to the portieres.*]

Mrs. Fisher. [*After a strained pause.*] Why, what's the matter with the crazy Jack!

Amy. Pay no attention to him, Mother.

Mrs. Fisher. I suppose I won't be able to say this house *is* my own after a while.

Aubrey. [*Stopping above the center table and rapping his fist upon it.*] It isn't necessary for you to be gabbing to perfect strangers about *whose* house it is!

Mrs. Fisher. [*Keenly.*] I guess it'd have been all right if I'd told her it was yours, wouldn't it?

Aubrey. [*Repudiating her remark with a sharp gesture of his left hand.*] You don't have to tell anybody anything! [MRS. FISHER *springs to her feet.*]

Mrs. Fisher. I suppose that's what's the matter with you!

Aubrey and *Mrs. Fisher.* [*Together.*]

{ *Aubrey.* There's nothing at all the matter with me! [*He touches his handkerchief to his forehead.*]

\ *Mrs. Fisher.* [*Taking a few steps towards* AMY.] He's very likely been telling this friend of yours, Amy, that this is *his* house! And I guess with a lot of big talk about taking *me* in, and giving *me* a home! Trying to make *me* look like a poor thing!

Amy. [*Trying to pacify her mother.*] Now, he didn't tell her anything of the kind, Mother!

Mrs. Fisher. [*Shaking with wrath.*] He did if he got the chance! I know him.

Amy. Well, he didn't *get* the chance; I was only out of the room two minutes.

Mrs. Fisher. [*Returning to the sofa.*] Well, that's long enough for him! I've heard *him* before. [*She gathers up her knitting, preparatory to sitting down.*] Blowing his bubbles! [*She sits down, fuming.*] The big blatherskite! [*There is a pause.* AMY *and* AUBREY *look at each other, then at* MRS. FISHER, *who knits violently.*] I'm very glad now I *did* tell her this was my house!— [*She knits a little more.*] I'm glad I had sense enough! [*More knitting.*] For I know he'd very soon tell her it was *his*, if he got my back turned long enough! [*She draws some yarn from the ball.*] And it wouldn't be mine long, either, if I listened to all his silly blather about stocks, and bonds, and automobiles, and every other thing!—On his thirty-two dollars a week. [AUBREY *looks stonily at her for a second; then she turns sharply and leans on the arm of the sofa towards him.*] I told her *that*, too!

Aubrey. [*Turning to* AMY, *who is standing back of the armchair.*] You see! Didn't I tell you! [*He passes forward at the right of his wife.*]

Mrs. Fisher. [*Resuming her knitting.*] So she'd know how much brains you had!

Amy. It wasn't at all necessary, Mother, for you to tell Marion that.

Mrs. Fisher. [*Without looking up from her work.*] Well, I told her; whether it was necessary or not. [*She looks at* AMY *and speaks emphatically.*] It was the truth, anyway. And I guess that's more than can be said for a whole lot that *he* told her. [*She indicates* AUBREY *with a nod; then resumes her work. There is a pause.* AUBREY *is standing fuming down at the right.* AMY *picks up the piece of the paper that he threw on the chair, then extends the piece that she has been reading towards him.*]

Amy. Do you want this?

Aubrey. [*Half-turning, and with a shade of hauteur.*] What is it?

Amy. Why, it's the newspaper of course! what do you think it is? [*He deigns to take it. She gives him a long look, then opens the other half of the paper and reads.*]

Aubrey. [*Opening his part of the paper.*] A man'd certainly have a swell chance trying to make anything of himself around this *hut!*

Mrs. Fisher. I don't see that anybody's trying to *stop* you from making something of yourself.

Aubrey. No, and I don't see that anybody's trying to *help* me any, either. Only trying to make me look like a *pin-head* every chance they get.

Mrs. Fisher. Nobody'll have to try very hard to make *you* look like a pin-head. Your own silly talk'll do *that* for you, any time at all.

Aubrey. [*Turning to her sharply.*] I suppose it's silly talk to try to make a good impression.

Mrs. Fisher. [*Looking over at him, and inclining her head conclusively.*] Yes—it's silly to try to make an impression of *any* kind; for the only one that'll be made'll be the *right* one; and that'll make itself. [*She reverts to her work.*]

Aubrey. Well, if you were out in the world as much as I am, you'd very soon see how much easier it is for a fellow to get along if people think he's *got* something.

Mrs. Fisher. Well, anybody listening to you very long'd know you *couldn't* have very much.

Aubrey. Is that so.

Mrs. Fisher. [*Quietly.*] You heard me. [AUBREY *steps over to the armchair at his left and sits down, looking bitterly at his mother-in-law.*] People that are smart enough to be able to make it easier for anybody, are not interested in what you've *got*. [*Looking over at him.*] It's what you've got in your *brains* that they're interested in. And nobody has to tell them that, either. They'll know all about it, if you never opened your mouth.

Amy. Oh, stop talking about it, Mother. [*She turns, with a movement of wearied impatience, from the right end of the center table, and crosses over back of the armchair to the right, where she continues to read. There is a quiet pause; AMY and AUBREY reading, and MRS. FISHER knitting. Then AUBREY looks up from his paper, thinks for a second, and half turns to his wife.*]

Aubrey. Did you get that remark your friend made, as she was going out?

Amy. What remark? [MRS. FISHER *looks over.*]

Aubrey. [*With a self-satisfied smile.*] About the best-looking man in Philadelphia?

Mrs. Fisher. [*Rearranging her knitting.*] Oh, dear! [AUBREY *gives her a narrow look; then turns back to his wife.*]

Aubrey. She made it twice, too.

Amy. I suppose I'll never hear the end of that now.

Aubrey. No, but it made an awful hit with me, after all the talk you made about putting on the toupee.

Amy. Oh, it wasn't the toupee that made her say it; don't flatter yourself.

Aubrey. I don't think it hurt any.

Amy. No, and I don't think you're so crazy about the toupee yourself.

Aubrey. It's better than being baldheaded.

Amy. I notice you got rid of it very quickly, as soon as she went. [MRS. FISHER *listens.*]

Aubrey. What?

Amy. [*Without looking up from the paper.*] You heard me. [MRS. FISHER *can't resist a glance at* AUBREY; *but realizing that her expression might precipitate another row, she turns away quietly and continues with her knitting.* AUBREY *hasn't grasped the significance of his wife's remark. He turns and looks at her with a puzzled expression; but she is reading; so he turns back again and looks straight out, baffled. Then a thought occurs to him. He reaches up and touches his head. The toupee is off. His brows lift and his mouth falls open, and he sits staring straight ahead for a second. Then he glances furtively at his mother-in-law, but she is studiously avoiding the situation. He gets up, very quietly; and, with a little glance over his right shoulder at his wife, turns and gives a quick look on the armchair and under it. No sign of the toupee. He feels all over his head and around the back of his neck; puts his hand up under his coat, and looks on the floor back of the armchair. All very quietly, and with a pathetic attempt at nonchalance. But the toupee is not to be seen. He saunters up towards the back of the room, steps over and glances at himself in the mirror, then stands looking about the floor in a quandary. His wife observes him out of the corner of her eye, and turns to him.*] What are you looking for? [*He glances at* MRS. FISHER, *then goes very close to his wife and speaks in a confidential tone.*]

Aubrey. My toupee. Did you see anything of it?

Amy. Where'd you put it?

Aubrey. [*With a shade of impatience.*] I didn't put it any-where.

Amy. Well, where did you have it?

Aubrey. [*Becoming more impatient.*] I had it on my head, of course! where'd you think I had it!

Amy. I thought you took it off, when Marion went.

Aubrey. No, I didn't take it off!

Amy. Well, where is it?

Aubrey. [*Throwing discretion to the winds.*] I don't know *where* it is! That's why I'm asking *you!* [MRS. FISHER *can no longer contain herself, and bursts into unrestrained laughter. They both turn sharply and look at her,* AUBREY *glaring.*] Funny! isn't it! [AMY *crosses quickly to the center table, in front of her husband.*]

Amy. Did you see anything of it, Mother?

Mrs. Fisher. [*Bursting out afresh.*] I saw it *fall off,* that's all *I* know about it. [*They stand looking at her.*]

Aubrey. You see that! She'd let me walk around here all day with it off, and never tip me off that it was off!

Mrs. Fisher. What good was it to tip you off that it was off after it was off! [*Turning back to her knitting.*] The cat was out of the bag, then.

Amy. Where'd it fall off, Mother?

Mrs. Fisher. When he was picking that woman's glove up, up there at the hallway. [AMY *turns quickly towards the hall door, glancing about the floor; and* MRS. FISHER *turns to* AUBREY.] It isn't *my* fault if his old *wig* doesn't fit him. [*He is looking at her with murder in his eye; but she doesn't flinch. If anything, there is a glint of challenge in her look. And it's quite as steady as his own.* AMY *finds the toupee where it fell, and holds it up towards* AUBREY *by one hair.*]

Amy. Is this it? [*But the duel of eyes is still on between* AUBREY *and his mother-in-law; and he is oblivious of both his wife and her question. So the toupee, looking very much like a dead cat, depends from* AMY's *uplifted fingers. Then, suddenly,* AUBREY *snatches it, with a whirling movement to the left, and goes towards the mirror to adjust it.*]

Mrs. Fisher. [*Following him with her eyes.*] It just serves him right! That's what he gets for showing off!

Aubrey. [*Whirling at the mirror, and literally shouting at her.*

Stop it, will you! *The violence of his turning sends the toupee flying off his head on to the floor, and causes* MRS. FISHER *to start so that her ball of yarn flies four feet into the air.*]

Amy. [*Taking a step towards her husband and lifting her hand to enjoin silence.*] Sh—sh—sh—

Aubrey. [*Looking at her with an eye of fire.*] I won't stand much more of this Amy! now, I'm telling you!

Amy. Keep quiet, Aubrey! Marion probably never noticed it at all.

Mrs. Fisher. I don't know how she could *help* noticing it. *I* noticed it; and I don't think my eyesight's as good as hers.

Aubrey. Then, why didn't you say something!

Mrs. Fisher. Because I knew if I did I'd very likely get snatched baldheaded! [AUBREY *starts violently, and* MRS. FISHER *snaps back to her knitting.*]

Aubrey. [*Appealing to his wife.*] You hear that! Is it any wonder my nerves are the way they are!

Amy. Oh, keep quiet, Aubrey! for goodness' sake! [*Pointing to the toupee on the floor, as she steps forward at the right of the center table.*] And pick up your wig. [*This is too much for* AUBREY. *He literally sways against the portieres above the mirror.*]

Aubrey. [*Recovering himself.*] It isn't a wig, now, Amy! I've told you that a half a dozen times!

Amy. [*Looking up from the paper which she has commenced to read, and in an exhausted tone.*] Well, then, pick up your toupee! [*He picks it up and simply slaps it back on to his head. The effect is weird; for it is quite disheveled from its recent experiences, and, in his temper, he has put it on backwards. He swings forward at the right and sits in the armchair, very sulkily. * AMY *crosses over back of the armchair and stands down near the little table at the right, where she continues to read the evening paper.* MRS. FISHER *knits, and* AUBREY *sits sulking, looking straight ahead. There is a pause. Then, possibly at the recollection of certain of the remarks that his mother-in-law made earlier in the battle,* AUBREY *darts a sudden glare in her direction; only to find that she has been the victim of similar memories. So they sit and scowl at each other; then turn away. Then turn back again, and away again. Then* AUBREY *becomes conscious of his wife; and of the fact that she is reading the evening newspaper;*

and, by the association of ideas, his thought is diverted into more becoming channels. He half-turns to AMY, *with something of the self-importance that characterized his earlier manner, and, after a slight pause, addresses her.*]

Aubrey. Have you got the—a—financial page there? [AMY *hands it to him; and the curtain commences to descend very slowly.*]

Mrs. Fisher. Hum! [*He glares over at her, but she's knitting; so, withdrawing his eyes, he reaches into his vest pocket and brings forth the rimmed nose-glasses, which he settles rather authentically upon his nose. Then he takes a silver pencil from the other vest pocket, and, turning to his wife, accepts the newspaper. Then he crosses his knees, and, spreading the newspaper upon them, proceeds to figure profits in the margin.* AMY *stands looking at him, and* MRS. FISHER *knits.*]

The Curtain is Down

By Way of Appreciation: *Poor Aubrey* is the best of several one-act plays which George Kelly wrote, about twenty years ago, for his own performance on the vaudeville stage. So successful was the characterization of Aubrey Piper that later Kelly developed the sketch into the full-length play, *The Show-Off,* which Heywood Broun rated "the best comedy which has yet been written by an American." The plot of *Poor Aubrey* is negligible. It is the character of Aubrey that holds the center of the stage from beginning to end. Out of his shrewd observation of life the playwright has painted in Aubrey Piper so true and lively a picture of men that all of us know that we cannot possibly withhold our admiration and enjoyment of the portrayal.

Suggestions for Study: What is it in Aubrey's character that rouses our mirth? Are there men like him in your circle of acquaintances? How do the personalities of Amy and Mrs. Cole emphasize the comic character of Aubrey? What makes Mrs. Fisher, too, an amusing character?

The struggle of a human will against obstacles is essential to any drama. Against what obstacles must Aubrey struggle? Summarize the plot of the play. Do you find the ending of the play satisfactory?

Like a short story a one-act play must set to work at the very outset to produce the single effect it seeks to achieve. How early in this play does this effect begin to make itself felt? Are the playing directions effectively designed to contribute to this effect?

By all means read the longer play, *The Show-Off,* and compare the impression of Aubrey you then have with that you have of him after your reading of this shorter sketch.

MOONSHINE *

Arthur Hopkins

CHARACTERS

Luke Hazy, *moonshiner*
A Revenue Officer

Scene: *Hut of a moonshiner in the mountain wilds of North Carolina. Door back left. Window back right center. Old deal table right center. Kitchen chair at either side of table, not close to it. Old cupboard in left corner. Rude stone fireplace left side. On back wall near door is a rough pencil sketch of a man hanging from a tree.*
At rise of curtain a commotion is heard outside of hut.

Luke. [*Off stage.*] It's all right, boys. . . . Jist leave him to me. . . . Git in there, Mister Revenue.

[REVENUE, *a Northerner in city attire, without hat, clothes dusty, is pushed through doorway.* LUKE, *a lanky, ill-dressed Southerner, following, closes door.* REVENUE'S *hands are tied behind him.*]

Luke. You must excuse the boys for makin' a demonstration over you, Mister Revenue, but you see they don't come across you fellers very frequent, and they allus git excited.

Revenue. I appreciate that I'm welcome.

Luke. 'Deed you is, and I'm just agoin' to untie your hands long nuff fer you to take a sociable drink. [*Goes to stranger, feels in all pockets for weapons.*] Reckon yer travellin' peaceable. [*Unties hands.*] Won't yer sit down?

Revenue. [*Drawing over chair and sitting.*] Thank you. [*Rubs wrists to get back circulation.*]

Luke. [*Going over to cupboard and taking out jug.*] Yessa, Mister, the boys ain't seen one o' you fellers fer near two years. Began to think you wuz goin' to neglect us. I wuz hopin' you might be Jim Dunn. Have a drink?

Revenue. [*Starts slightly at mention of* JIM DUNN.] No, thank you, your make is too strong for me.

Luke. It hain't no luck to drink alone when you git company. Better have some.

Revenue. Very well, my friend, I suffer willingly. [*Drinks a little and chokes.*]

Luke. [*Draining cup.*] I reckon ye all don't like the flavor of liquor that hain't been stamped.

Revenue. It's not so bad.

Luke. The last Revenue that sit in that chair got drunk on my make.

Revenue. That wouldn't be difficult.

Luke. No, but it wuz awkward.

Revenue. Why?

Luke. I had to wait till he sobered up before I give him his ticker. I didn't feel like sendin' him to heaven drunk. He'd a found it awkward climbin' that golden ladder.

Revenue. Thoughtful executioner.

Luke. So you see mebbe you kin delay things a little by dallyin' with the licker.

Revenue. [*Picking up cup, getting it as far as his lips, slowly puts it down.*] The price is too great.

Luke. I'm mighty sorry you ain't Jim Dunn. But I reckon you ain't. You don't answer his likeness.

Revenue. Who's Jim Dunn?

Luke. You ought to know who Jim Dunn is. He's just about the worst one of your revenue critters that ever hit these parts. He's got four of the boys in jail. We got a little reception all ready for him. See that? [*Pointing to sketch on back wall.*]

Revenue. [*Looking at sketch.*] Yes.

Luke. That's Jim Dunn.

Revenue. [*Rising, examining picture.*] Doesn't look much like any one.

Luke. Well, that's what Jim Dunn'll look like when we git 'im. I'm mighty sorry you hain't Jim Dunn.

Revenue. I'm sorry to disappoint you.

Luke. [*Turning to cupboard and filling pipe.*] Oh, it's all right. I reckon one Revenue's about as good as another, after all.

Revenue. Are you sure I'm a revenue officer?

Luke. [*Rising.*] Well, since we ketched ye climbin' trees an' snoopin' round the stills, I reckon we won't take no chances that you hain't.

Revenue. Oh.

Luke. Say, mebbe you'd like a seggar. Here's one I been savin' fer quite a spell back, thinkin' mebbe I'd have company some day. [*Brings out dried-up cigar, hands it to him.*]

Revenue. No, thank you.

Luke. It hain't no luck to smoke alone when ye got company. [*Striking match and holding it to* Revenue.] Ye better smoke. [Revenue *bites off end and mouth is filled with dust, spits out dust.* Luke *holds match to cigar. With difficulty* Revenue *lights it.*] That's as good a five-cent cigar as ye can git in Henderson.

Revenue. [*After two puffs, makes wry face, throws cigar on table.*] You make death very easy, Mister.

Luke. Luke's my name. Yer kin call me Luke. Make you feel like you had a friend near you at the end—Luke Hazy.

Revenue. [*Starting as though interested, rising.*] Not the Luke Hazy that cleaned out the Crosby family?

Luke. [*Startled.*] How'd you hear about it?

Revenue. Hear about it? Why, your name's been in every newspaper in the United States. Every time you killed another

Crosby the whole feud was told all over again. Why, I've seen your picture in the papers twenty times.

Luke. Hain't never had one took.

Revenue. That don't stop them from printing it. Don't you ever read the newspapers?

Luke. Me read? I hain't read nothin' for thirty years. Reckon I couldn't read two lines in a hour.

Revenue. You've missed a lot of information about yourself.

Luke. How many Crosbys did they say I killed?

Revenue. I think the last report said you had just removed the twelfth.

Luke. It's a lie! I only killed six . . . that's all they wuz— growed up. I'm a-waitin' fer one now that's only thirteen.

Revenue. When'll he be ripe?

Luke. Jes as soon as he comes a-lookin' fer me.

Revenue. Will he come?

Luke. He'll come if he's a Crosby.

Revenue. A brave family?

Luke. They don't make 'em any braver—they'd be first-rate folks if they wuzn't Crosbys.

Revenue. If you feel that way why did you start fighting them?

Luke. I never started no fight. My grandad had some mis-understandin' with their grandad. I don't know jes what it wuz about, but I reckon my grandad wuz right, and I'll see it through.

Revenue. You must think a lot of your grandfather.

Luke. Never seen 'im, but it ain't no luck goin' agin yer own kin. Won't ye have a drink?

Revenue. No—no—thank you.

Luke. Well, Mr. Revenue, I reckon we might as well have this over.

Revenue. What?

Luke. Well, you won't get drunk, and I can't be put to the trouble o' havin' somebody guard you.

Revenue. That'll not be necessary.

Luke. Oh, I know yer like this yer place now, but this eve-nin' you might take it into yer head to walk out.

Revenue. I'll not walk out unless you make me.

Luke. Tain't like I'll let yer, but I wouldn't blame yer none if yu tried.

Revenue. But I'll not.

Luke. [*Rising.*] Say, Mistah Revenue, I wonder if you know what you're up against?

Revenue. What do you mean?

Luke. I mean I gotta kill you.

Revenue. [*Rising, pauses.*] Well, that lets me out.

Luke. What do yu mean?

Revenue. I mean that I've been trying to commit suicide for the last two months, but I haven't had the nerve.

Luke. [*Startled.*] Suicide?

Revenue. Yes. Now that you're willing to kill me, the problem is solved.

Luke. Why, what d'ye want to commit suicide fer?

Revenue. I just want to stop living, that's all.

Luke. Well, yu must have a reason.

Revenue. No special reason—I find life dull and I'd like to get out of it.

Luke. Dull?

Revenue. Yes—I hate to go to bed—I hate to get up—I don't care for food—I can't drink liquor—I find people either malicious or dull—I see by the fate of my acquaintances, both men and women, that love is a farce. I have seen fame and preference come to those who least deserved them, while the whole world kicked and cuffed the worthy ones. The craftier schemer gets the most money and glory, while the fair-minded dealer is humiliated in the bankruptcy court. In the name of the law every crime is committed; in the name of religion every vice is indulged; in the name of education greatest ignorance is rampant.

Luke. I don't git all of that, but I reckon you're some put out.

Revenue. I am. The world's a failure . . . what's more, it's a farce. I don't like it but I can't change it, so I'm just aching for a chance to get out of it. . . . [*Approaching* LUKE.] And you, my dear friend, are going to present me the opportunity.

Luke. Yes, I reckon you'll get your wish now.

Revenue. Good . . . if you only knew how I've tried to get killed.

Luke. Well, why didn't you kill yerself?

Revenue. I was afraid.

Luke. Afreed o' what—hurtin' yourself?

Revenue. No, afraid of the consequences.

Luke. Whad d'ye mean?

Revenue. Do you believe in another life after this one?

Luke. I kan't say ez I ever give it much thought.

Revenue. Well, don't—because if you do you'll never kill another Crosby . . . not even a revenue officer.

Luke. 'Tain't that bad, is it?

Revenue. Worse. Twenty times I've had a revolver to my head—crazy to die—and then as my finger pressed the trigger I'd get a terrible dread that I was plunging into worse terrors than this world ever knew. If killing were the end it would be easy, but what if it's only the beginning of something worse?

Luke. Well, you gotta take some chances.

Revenue. I'll not take that one. You know, Mr. Luke, life was given to us by some one who probably never intended that we should take it, and that some one has something ready for people who destroy his property. That's what frightens me.

Luke. You do too much worryin' to be a regular suicide.

Revenue. Yes, I do. That's why I changed my plan.

Luke. What plan?

Revenue. My plan for dying.

Luke. Oh, then you didn't give up the idea?

Revenue. No, indeed—I'm still determined to die, but I'm going to make some one else responsible.

Luke. Oh—so you hain't willing to pay fer yer own funeral music?

Revenue. No, sir. I'll furnish the passenger, but some one else must buy the ticket. You see, when I finally decided I'd be killed, I immediately exposed myself to every danger I knew.

Luke. How?

Revenue. In a thousand ways. . . . [*Pause.*] Did you ever see an automobile?

Luke. No.

Revenue. They go faster than steam engines, and they don't stay on tracks. Did you ever hear of Fifth Avenue, New York?

Luke. No.

Revenue. Fifth Avenue is jammed with automobiles, eight deep all day long. People being killed every day. I crossed Fifth Avenue a thousand times a day, every day for weeks, never once trying to get out of the way, and always praying I'd be hit.

Luke. And couldn't yu git hit?

Revenue. [*In disgust.*] No. Automobiles only hit people who try to get out of the way. [*Pause.*] When that failed, I frequented the lowest dives on the Bowery, flashing a roll of money and wearing diamonds, hoping they'd kill me for them. They stole the money and diamonds, but never touched me.

Luke. Couldn't you pick a fight?

Revenue. I'm coming to that. You know up North they believe that a man can be killed in the South for calling another man a liar.

Luke. That's right.

Revenue. It is, is it? Well, I've called men liars from Washington to Atlanta, and I'm here to tell you about it.

Luke. They must a took pity on ye.

Revenue. I don't know—I'm too disgusted to think about it. I wandered around until I thought of you moonshiners . . . scrambled around in the mountains until I found your still. I sat on it and waited until you boys showed up, and here I am, and you're going to kill me.

Luke. [*Pause.*] Ah, so ye want us to do yer killin' fer ye, do ye?

Revenue. You're my last hope. If I fail this time I may as well give it up.

Luke. [*Takes out revolver, turns sidewise and secretly removes cartridges from chamber. Rises.*] What wuz that noise?

[*Lays revolver on table and steps outside of door.* REVENUE *looks at revolver, apparently without interest.*

LUKE *cautiously enters doorway and expresses surprise at seeing* REVENUE *making no attempt to secure revolver. Feigning excitement, goes to table, picks up gun.*]

Luke. I reckon I'm gettin' careless, leavin' a gun layin' around here that-a-way. Didn't you see it?

Revenue. Yes.

Luke. Well, why didn't you grab it?

Revenue. What for?

Luke. To git the drop on me.

Revenue. Can't you understand what I've been telling you, mister? I don't want the drop on you.

Luke. Well, doggone if I don't believe yer tellin' me the truth. Thought I'd just see what ye'd do. Ye see, I emptied it first. [*Opens up gun.*]

Revenue. That wasn't necessary.

Luke. Well, I reckon ye better git along out o' here, mister.

Revenue. You don't mean you're weakening?

Luke. I ain't got no call to do your killin' fer you. If ye hain't sport enough to do it yerself, I reckon ye kin go on sufferin'.

Revenue. But I told you why I don't want to do it. One murder more or less means nothing to you. You don't care anything about the hereafter.

Luke. Mebbe I don't, but there ain't no use my takin' any more chances than I have to. And what's more, mister, from what you been tellin' me I reckon there's a charm on you, and I ain't goin' to take no chances goin' agin charms.

Revenue. So you're going to go back on me?

Luke. Yes, siree.

Revenue. Well, maybe some of the other boys will be willing. I'll wait till they come.

Luke. The other boys ain't goin' to see you. You're a leavin' this yer place right now—now! It won't do no good. You may as well go peaceable; ye ain't got no right to expect us to bear yer burdens.

Revenue. Hang it all! I've spoiled it again.

Luke. I reckon you better make up yer mind to go on livin'.

Revenue. That looks like the only way out.

Luke. Come on, I'll let you ride my horse to town. It's the only one we got, so yu can leave it at Two Gun Jake's, and one o' the boys'll go git it, or mebbe I'll be goin' over myself.

Revenue. I suppose it's no use arguing with you.

Luke. Not a bit. Come on, you.

Revenue. Well, I'd like to leave my address so if you ever come to New York you can look me up.

Luke. 'Tain't likely I'll ever come to New York.

Revenue. Well, I'll leave it, anyhow. Have you a piece of paper?

Luke. Paper what you write on? Never had none, mister.

Revenue. [*Looking about the room, sees* JIM DUNN's *picture on wall, goes to it, takes it down.*] If you don't mind, I'll put it on the back of Jim Dunn's picture. [*Placing picture on table, begins to print.*] I'll print it for you, so it'll be easy to read. My address is here, so if you change your mind you can send for me.

Luke. 'Tain't likely—come on. [*Both go to doorway—*LUKE

extends hand, REVENUE *takes it.*] Good-bye, mister—cheer up.
. . . There's the horse.

Revenue. Good-by. [*Shaking* LUKE's *hand.*]

Luke. Don't be so glum, mister. Lemme hear you laff jist
onct before yu go. [REVENUE *begins to laugh weakly.*] Aw,
come on, laff out with it hearty. [REVENUE *laughs louder.*]
Heartier yit.

[REVENUE *is now shouting his laughter, and is heard laughing
until hoof-beats of his horse die down in the distance.*

LUKE *watches for a moment, then returns to table—takes a
drink—picks up picture—turns it around several times before getting it right—then begins to study. In attempting
to make out the name he slowly traces in the air with his
index finger a capital "J"—then mutters "J-J-J," then describes a letter "I"—mutters "I-I-I," then a letter "M"—
muttering "M-M-M, J-I-M—J-I-M—JIM." In the same
way describes and mutters D-U-N-N.*]

Luke. Jim Dunn! [*He rushes to corner, grabs shot-gun,
runs to doorway, raises gun in direction stranger has gone—
looks intently—then slowly lets gun fall to his side, and scans
the distance with his hand shadowing his eyes—steps inside—
slowly puts gun in corner—seats himself at table.*] Jim Dunn!
—and he begged me to kill 'im!

Curtain

By Way of Appreciation: A game of wits with a man's life as the
stake, played against a background of primitive folk-ways, constitutes
the center of interest in this play. Here a single situation is exploited
with much technical skill. Suspense is built up and maintained until
very near the end of the play. The clash of character upon character
makes it something more than mere melodrama, however, and the
humorous touches add to its effectiveness with audiences. Mr. Hopkins'
own suggestion for its acting is summed up in the direction, "Be simple."

Suggestions for Study: Is the setting described with minute exactness? Does it need to be? What mountaineer customs and attitudes
are described in the course of the play? Are these faithful to reality?
Is the character of Luke exaggerated, or is it entirely plausible? Upon
what emotions did Revenue play in order to outwit his captor? Which
is the better drawn character, Luke or Revenue? Which would be the
more difficult to play? Why? Did you guess the outcome of this duel
of wits before the end of the play? If so, what sustained your interest?
Does the dialect add to the effectiveness of the play?

EXTENSIVE READING PROGRAM—THE DRAMA

The Colonial and Revolutionary Periods (1607–1800)

Thomas Godfrey
The Prince of Parthia
William Dunlap
André

Hugh Brackenridge
The Battle of Bunker's Hill
Royall Tyler
The Georgia Spec

The National Period (1800–1865)

Anna C. O. Mowatt
Fashion
Nathaniel P. Willis
The Kentucky Heiress

Steele Mackaye
Hazel Kirke
Richard Smith
The Triumph of Plattsburgh

The Transition Period (1865–1900)

William Gillette
Held by the Enemy
The Professor
Too Much Johnson
Bronson Howard
Saratoga
Shenandoah
Young Mrs. Winthrop

James A. Herne
Sag Harbor
Shore Acres
Dion Boucicalt
Rip Van Winkle
Langdon Mitchell
Becky Sharp
The New York Idea

The Twentieth Century (1900–   )

David Belasco
Lord Chumly
The Darling of the Gods
The Girl I Left Behind Me
The Return of Peter Grimm
The Boomerang
The Heart of Maryland
The Girl of the Golden West
Augustus Thomas
Alabama
Arizona
In Mizzoura
The Burglar
The Copperhead
The Witching Hour

Clyde Fitch
Beau Brummel
Captain Jinks of the Horse Marines
The Climbers
The Truth
Percy Mackaye
A Thousand Years Ago
The Scarecrow
Booth Tarkington
Clarence
Monsieur Beaucaire
Seventeen
The Country Cousin
The Man From Home

Emmet Lavery
  The First Legion
  Second Spring
Eugene O'Neill
  Anna Christie
  Marco Millions
George M. Cohan
  The Seven Keys to Baldpate
  The Talk of New York
George Ade
  Father and the Boys
  The College Widow
William Vaughan Moody
  The Great Divide
Edward Knoblock
  Kismet
  Milestones
  Grand Hotel
Edward Sheldon
  Romance
  The Boss
Daniel A. Lord
  Behold the Man
  Storm-Tossed
Marcus Bach
  Within These Walls
Charles Klein
  The Auctioneer
  The Music Master
  The Lion and the Mouse
Edna Ferber and George Kaufman
  Dinner at Eight
  The Royal Family

T. S. Eliot
  Murder in the Cathedral
Zona Gale
  Miss Lulu Bett
Rachel Crothers
  39 East
  Mary the Third
  Old Lady 31
  Once Upon a Time
  Ourselves
  The Three of Us
George Kaufman and Marc Connelly
  Dulcy
  Merton of the Movies
  To the Ladies
George Kelly
  Craig's Wife
  The Show-Off
  The Torchbearers
Elmer Rice
  Counsellor at Law
  On Trial
  The Adding Machine.
Philip Barry
  Holiday
  The Joyous Season
Paul Green
  In Abraham's Bosom
  The House of Connelly
Urban Nagle
  Barter
  Catherine the Valiant

A List of One-Act Plays

William Carson
  Tea
Alexander Dean
  Just Neighborly
Charles Divine
  Post Mortems
Hildegarde Flanner
  Mansions

Louise Driscoll
  The Poor House
Rachel Lyman Field
  The Cross-Stitch Heart
  The Patchwork Quilt
  Three Pills in a Bottle
Doris F. Halman
  Famine and the Ghost

Zona Gale
  The Clouds
  The Neighbors
Kenneth Sawyer Goodman
  Dust of the Road
Emmet Lavery
  Monsignor's Hour
Christopher Morley
  On the Shelf
Eugene O'Neill
  Where the Cross Is Made
  Ile
  Beyond the Horizon
  The Moon of the Caribbees
Oscar M. Wolff
  Where But in America?
George Kelly
  Finders Keepers
  The Flattering Word

Percy Mackaye
  Gettysburg
  Sam Average
George Middleton
  Tradition
Daniel A. Lord
  Mistress Castlemaine's Christmas Dinner
Booth Tarkington
  The Trysting Place
  Bimbo the Pirate
Franklin Tompkins
  Sham
Percival Wilde
  Confessional
  The Finger of Goa
  The Traitor

COLLECTIONS OF ONE-ACT PLAYS

S. A. Leonard
  Atlantic Book of Modern Plays
B. R. Lewis
  Contemporary One-Act Plays
R. W. Pence
  Dramas by Present-Day Writers
Phillips & Johnson
  Types of Modern Dramatic Composition
Clark & Cook
  One-Act Plays
H. L. Cohen
  One-Act Plays by Modern Authors
  The Junior Play Book
Francis X. Talbot
  Shining in Darkness

Webber & Webster
  One-Act Plays
G. A. Goldstone
  One-Act Plays
F. G. Barker
  Forty Minute Plays from Shakespeare
I. M. Gray
  Short Scenes from Shakespeare
E. B. Knickerbocker
  Plays for Classroom Interpretation
  Twelve Plays
S. M. Tucker
  Twelve One-Act Plays
Daniel A. Lord
  Six One-Act Plays

BOOKS ON PLAY PRODUCTION

Milton Smith
  The Book of Play Production

Clarence Stratton
  Producing in Little Theatres

John Dolman
  The Art of Play Production
Crafton & Royer
  The Process of Play Production
Barrett Clark
  How to Produce Amateur Plays
Halliam Bosworth
  Technique in Dramatic Art
Louis Calvert
  Problems of the Actor
A. E. Krows
  Equipment for Stage Production

Andre Smith
  The Scenewright
A. B. Young
  Stage Costuming
Grimball & Wells
  How to Costume a Play
Roy Mitchell
  Shakespeare for Community Players
Helena Chalmers
  The Art of Make-up
Theodore Fuchs
  Stage Lighting

THE NOVEL

THE NOVEL AS A TYPE OF LITERATURE

The Novel in Literature

The most conspicuous development in the literary history of the past century has been the rise of the novel as the favorite form of literature. "A novel is the name given to a sustained story which is not necessarily historically true, but might very easily be so. The novel has been made the vehicle for satire, for instruction, for political or religious exhortation, for technical information; but these are side issues. Its main purpose is to amuse by a succession of scenes painted from nature, and by a thread of emotional narrative." The novelist builds his characters and situations bit by bit, in a leisurely, unhurried manner. He develops not only leading characters but also minor characters; he constructs not only plots but also sub-plots; there may even be several different settings. In form, the novel may be one of plot, of character, or of setting. In subject matter, it may be one of almost innumerable classifications. Because of the great freedom which the novel offers in subject matter, style, and characterization, it is preferred above all other forms of literature by the reading public. It has assumed an unquestioned first place as the favorite literary form of the day.

THE HISTORY OF THE AMERICAN NOVEL

THE COLONIAL AND REVOLUTIONARY PERIODS (1607–1800)

General Characteristics

Although the great bulk of writing done during the Colonial and Revolutionary Periods was prose, it was not prose fiction. It consisted of pamphlets, speeches, addresses, letters, essays, and political documents rising out of the struggle for independence and the problems of organizing the new republic. There was neither time nor inclination for the fictional when the real was so absorbing and so vital to the lives of the colonists. Furthermore, religious scruples of the Puritans discouraged writings that did not point to a moral. To the strictest, fiction was a lie, it served no virtuous purpose, and it crowded out more useful and elevating writings. The name of only one fiction writer of this period stands out as important.

Charles Brockden Brown (1771–1810)

Brown, a Philadelphian, sometimes called "The Father of American Fiction," is the first professional man of letters in our literature. His decision to make literature his profession seems to have been a result of his continuous ill health. Although he was a contributor to magazines, the bulk of his work consisted of novels produced in rapid succession between 1798 and 1801. While Brown was deficient as a literary craftsman, especially in the development of character and in the construction of his plots, he produced a number of pages of vivid, realistic writing. His masterpiece is *Wieland*. He has a tendency to the melodramatic and the weird.

The National Period (1800–1865)

General Characteristics

Following the Revolution, and in keeping with the general enthusiasm and confidence, writings appeared which reflected the expanding life of the country. Novel reading increased and fiction which had been written in England thirty and forty years previously became suddenly popular. The natural outcome of this awakened interest in fiction was the appearance of native American novelists in considerable numbers. Between the years 1789 and 1819 were born four novelists who were to add luster to American letters.

James Fenimore Cooper (1789–1851)

In James Fenimore Cooper, born in 1789 at Burlington, New Jersey, and growing up as a boy in the frontier village of Cooperstown on Otsego Lake in New York, we find the first American novelist of note whose stories strike their roots deeply into the soil of the new land. The story of Cooper's first novel is interesting. As a result of his criticism of an English novel which he was reading, his wife challenged him to write a better one, and as a result he produced *Precaution,* the scene of which is laid in England. The book did not satisfy him for he was "ashamed to have fallen into the track of imitation." "I endeavored," he continued, "to repay the wrong done to my own views by producing a work which would be purely American, and of which love of country should be the theme." Next came *The Spy,* the success of which encouraged him to take up writing as a profession. This was followed by *The Pioneers* and one of his greatest books, *The Pilot,* a sea story which came out of his experience at sea in the navy. Cooper did a great deal of writing. His greatest accomplishment, however, consists of his novels of pioneer life, notably, *The Deer Slayer, The Last of the Mohicans, The Pathfinder,* and *The Pioneers,* collectively known as *The Leather Stocking Tales,* constituting a kind of prose epic of the American pioneer. These *Leather Stocking Tales,* together with *The Spy,* are as popular to-day as they were a hundred years ago.

Nathaniel Hawthorne (1804–1864)

Down a narrow street of Salem, Massachusetts, almost within the scuds of spray from Salem Harbor, Nathaniel Hawthorne was born July 4, 1804. The death of his father when Hawthorne was only four years old greatly affected his boyhood. His mother, grieving bitterly for her husband, became a recluse and refused to even eat her meals with her family. The house was darkened, the voices of the children were hushed, and gloom and solitude settled down over the house. In this unnatural atmosphere Hawthorne grew up, himself taking on the habits of solitude and quiet. The somber shadows of these early days were to reach far into the years to come.

In the summer of 1821 when he was seventeen, he set out by stagecoach for Brunswick, Maine, where he was to enter Bowdoin College. On the journey he met Franklin Pierce, then a sophomore at Bowdoin, afterwards President of the United States, who was ever afterward his friend. The poet Longfellow was a classmate also. Hawthorne's closest companion and confidant, however, was Horatio Bridge, who from first to last applauded Hawthorne's hesitant decision to choose authorship as his vocation. In the volume which he dedicated to Bridge, Hawthorne paid the tribute of grateful remembrance to this sturdy friend. "If anybody is responsible for my being at this day an author," he declares, "it is yourself. I know not whence your faith came, but it was your prognostic of your friend's destiny that he was to be a writer of fiction."

In the years to come Hawthorne was often to need the assurance of his friend's faith in his powers. After leaving college, he returned to his mother's home at Salem, and there for twelve years he lived virtually a recluse in a little room under the eaves, writing, reading, rarely going out except at night, and frequently not even meeting the members of his family. Mrs. Hawthorne had withdrawn more and more from the family circle, and the habit of solitude enveloped the household.

Hawthorne's first novel, *Fanshawe,* published anonymously and at his own expense, was a distinct failure. He later bought and destroyed all available copies. But it did bring him to the notice of the editor of a popular yearbook. To this and to other more obscure publications he contributed a number of sketches, fables, and tales, the best of which were later collected under the title, *Twice Told Tales,* published for the first time under Hawthorne's name, and favorably reviewed, among others, by Longfellow.

In replying to a kindly letter from the poet, Hawthorne describes his situation as follows: "By some witchcraft or other—for I really cannot assign any reasonable why and wherefore—I have been carried apart

C-AM

from the main current of life, and find it impossible to get back again. . . . I have secluded myself from society; and yet I never meant any such thing, nor dreamed what sort of life I was going to lead. . . . For the last ten years, I have not lived, but only dreamed of living."

This period of intense seclusion and solitary depression came to an end with his marriage to Sophia Peabody, youngest daughter of a neighboring family in Salem. This marriage, though a happy one, complicated Hawthorne's financial situation, which at best had never been prosperous, and he was on the edge of poverty. Unsuccessful attempts at employment brought him bitterness and discouragement but were fortunate for American literature for Hawthorne now set about the writing of *The Scarlet Letter*. When this novel was issued in the spring of 1850 it proved immediately popular and at once securely established Hawthorne's place in American literature.

Now began a happy family life, free from financial worries. In the visits from friends, and in the new acquaintances which he made, Hawthorne breathed at last the air of successful authorship. Five months were given to *The House of the Seven Gables*, preferred by the author himself to his earlier volumes. Then followed *The Wonder Book, Tanglewood Tales*, and *The Blithedale Romance*. After periods of residence in other places, the family settled in Concord, in a house which Hawthorne named "The Wayside." Here, except for a sojourn abroad, the rest of his days were spent. He died in 1864 while on a trip to the New Hampshire lakes with Franklin Pierce.

His life and background are reflected in his writings, most of which are somber and gloomy—the result, no doubt, of his solitary boyhood and the loneliness of his youth. From his Puritan ancestors he inherited a strong moral sense and a habit of self-analysis. He was deeply interested in character and in most of his stories there is a moral significance. One of his favorite themes is that of conscience, and the effects upon it of sin and guilt. He preferred romantic material of the supernatural and the ideal. His writings are not cheerful but they possess great beauty—they are like somber paintings on a canvas.

William Gilmore Simms (1806–1870)

Among our early novelists Simms is entitled to an important place. He was born at Charleston, South Carolina, where he grew up, a somewhat studious, scholarly boy. By profession he was a lawyer. His books, however, show him to have been a born story-teller. His chief works are *Martin Faber, Guy Rivers, The Yemassee*, a tale of the Yemassee War in 1715, and *The Cassique of Kiawah*. The circumstances of his life show him to have been an heroic character.

Herman Melville (1819–1891)

Herman Melville was born in New York, the grandson of Major Thomas Melville, the subject of Holmes's famous poem, *The Last Leaf*

After a short time at school in Albany, he shipped on a New Bedford whaler bound for the Pacific. Resenting the treatment accorded him aboard ship, he left ship at the Island of Nukuheva and wandered into the cannibal valley Typee. His experiences gave rise to the book *Typee* and to a sequel *Omoo*. His masterpiece is *Moby Dick*, the story of the pursuit of the white whale by the half mad ship-captain Ahab. It is one of the greatest of sea stories.

Minor Novelists of the National Period

Four contemporaries of Cooper, all born before 1800, deserve mention. The literary center of Baltimore produced John Neal (1793–1876) and a better novelist, John Pendleton Kennedy (1795–1870), whose novel, *Horse-Shoe Robinson,* is a tale of the Revolution in the Carolinas and whose *Rob of the Bowl* is laid in colonial Maryland. Virginia produced Nathaniel B. Tucker (1784–1851), who wrote two books of considerable merit, *The Partisan Leader* and *George Balcombe,* the last of which Poe thought the best American novel of his time. In New England, Daniel Pierce Thompson (1795–1868) wrote the Vermont classic, *The Green Mountain Boys,* which has for its hero the famous Ethan Allen.

Among other writers of fiction this period produced Richard Henry Dana (1815–1882), author of *Two Years Before the Mast;* Harriet Beecher Stowe (1811–1896), remembered for her *Uncle Tom's Cabin;* Edward Everett Hale (1822–1909), who wrote *The Man Without a Country;* and Donald Grant Mitchell (1829–1914), who under the pseudonym of Ik Marvel wrote *Reveries of a Bachelor.*

THE TRANSITION PERIOD (1865–1900)

General Characteristics

The dominant note of this period was realism—the presenting of real characters in an actual setting. The earlier novels had been romantic, many of them sentimental, and the new generation grew impatient with literature which did not conform to the changes which were taking place in American life and to the new conditions and problems which faced the country following the Civil War. There was a demand for fiction that would reflect the present in terms of the real and not the artificial.

William Dean Howells (1837–1920)

To William Dean Howells belongs the distinction of writing the first realistic American novel. Howells was born in Ohio, the son of a country printer and editor. His schooling was little. His father put him to work as a compositor and later as a reporter and assistant editor. Howells educated himself at his editorial desk and by diligent reading in English and classic literature. His first writing was in the form of poetry, published in 1860, followed by a campaign biography of Lincoln. From then on he published poems, travel sketches, literary criticism and plays, but he is best remembered for his novels. Chief among these are *A Modern Instance, The Minister's Charge,* and *The Rise of Silas Lapham.* They are all realistic in that they deal frankly with contemporary life. *The Rise of Silas Lapham* is said to be the first novel which had for its chief character a business man.

Samuel Langhorne Clemens (Mark Twain) (1835–1910)

Perhaps the most typical American author of the period is Mark Twain. He was born in the middle west at Florida, Missouri, in 1855 and grew up in the village of Hannibal. He had little formal education. His experience with life was gained as a printer in his home town and in larger cities, as a Mississippi pilot, and as a prospector in Nevada mining camps. Like Walt Whitman whom he resembles in having been quite free from the literary influences of the schools, he is an innovator whose literary independence is not disputed. He is remembered for his fun-making, but he was more than a humorist. He is the embodiment of what we might call the American "Comic Spirit," for much of his humor proceeds from his good-natured ridicule of institutions, conventions and manners which strangle humanity. He was a voluminous writer, and among his best novels are *The Adventures of Tom Sawyer, Huckleberry Finn, The Prince and the Pauper,* and *A Connecticut Yankee in King Arthur's Court.*

Henry James (1843–1916)

Although important as a novelist, James was not the typically American writer that we find in Howells and Mark Twain. He achieved his reputation from stories which narrated the experiences of Americans in Europe, and has been called the international novelist. Among his best novels are *Daisy Miller,* and *The Portrait of a Lady.* He is also well known as a short-story writer.

Other Novelists and Romancers of the Transition Period

During the years following the Civil War, particularly the decade between 1880 and 1890, there appeared a large number of novelists, some of whom were to continue writing into the twentieth century. Among those who are entitled to mention are: Louisa M. Alcott (1832–1888), well known for *Little Women;* Edward Eggleston (1837–1902), remembered for *The Hoosier Schoolmaster;* Francis Hopkinson Smith (1838–1915), creator of *Colonel Carter of Cartersville;* Frances Hodgson Burnett (1849–1924), best known probably for *The Secret Garden;* Margaret Deland (1857–   ), who wrote *The Awakening of Helena Ritchie* and *John Ward, Preacher;* Helen Hunt Jackson (1831–1885), author of *Ramona;* F. Marion Crawford (1854–1909), author of *Katherine Lauderdale* and *The Ralstons;* Lew Wallace (1827–1905), who wrote *Ben Hur;*

Edward Noyes Westcott (1847–1898), remembered for *David Harum;* and George W. Cable (1844–1925), author of *The Grandissimes.*

The last years of the nineteenth century saw the sudden rise in popularity of the historical romance. Among writers of historical novels are: S. Weir Mitchell (1829–1914), whose *Hugh Wynne* is a stirring tale of the Revolution; Thomas Nelson Page (1853–1922), author of *Red Rock,* a Civil War story; Winston Churchill (1871–   ), whose historical romances, *Richard Carvel* and *The Crisis,* together with his story of New England political life, *Coniston,* are among the most interesting books of the period; Paul Leicester Ford (1865–1902), author of *Janice Meredith* and *The Honorable Peter Stirling;* James Lane Allen (1849–1925), known for *The Reign of Law* and *The Choir Invisible;* Owen Wister (1860–   ), author of *The Virginian;* and Mary Johnston (1870–1936), known for *Prisoners of Hope* and *To Have and To Hold.*

The forerunners of the new realism to appear in the twentieth century were Frank Norris (1870–1902), author of *The Octopus* and *The Pit;* and Stephen Crane (1871–1900), best known for *The Red Badge of Courage.*

THE TWENTIETH CENTURY (1900–   )

General Characteristics

The contemporary novel shows a strong tendency toward romance on the one hand and toward stark realism on the other. The realism started by William Dean Howells and Henry James has projected itself into a more intense kind, and portrays not only the pleasant realities but the harsh and ugly side of life. On the other hand, there is a group of present-day novelists who lean definitely toward romance and adventure, although even they are touched with the realism of the times.

The Extreme Realists

Chief among these are Sinclair Lewis (1885–   ), a satirist and critic of the social order, who made a leap into fame with *Main Street,* and followed with such novels as *Babbitt, Arrowsmith,* and *Ann Vickers;* Theodore Dreiser (1871–   ), a realist with a somewhat mechanical and depressing philosophy of life, author of *An American Tragedy* and *Sister Carrie;* and Sherwood Anderson (1876–   ), author of *Winesburg, Ohio,* and *Marching Men.* The extreme realism by which these writers are dominated sometimes makes their books rather unpleasant reading.

The Social Realists

Most vehement of the novelists exposing political corruption and economic injustice is Upton Sinclair (1878–   ), who wrote *The Jungle* to bring public attention to the evils of the Chicago stockyards, and *King Coal* to expose the deplorable conditions in the Colorado mines. Other realists interested in portraying contemporary social life and problems, but in a less violent way, are Ernest Poole (1880–   ), whose best novel is *The Harbor,* a story of life on the New York docks; Willa Cather (1876–   ), whose characters are the farming pioneers of the Middle West, author of *O Pioneers!, My Antonia, The Professor's House,* and *One of Ours;* Edith Wharton (1862–1937), one of the best of our women novelists, whose masterpiece is *Ethan Frome;* Ellen Glasgow (1874–   ), most of whose stories are laid in Virginia, author of *Barren Ground,* and *The Miller of Old Church;* Zona Gale (1874–   ), better known as a writer of short stories and drama, but also famous for her novel *Miss Lulu Bett;* Dorothy Canfield Fisher (1879–   ), portrayer of family life in small communities, and author of *The Bent Twig* and *The Brimming Cup;* and Edna Ferber (1887–   ), author of *So Big* and *Cimarron.*

The Romancers

Among the romancers are James Branch Cabell (1879–   ), creator of imaginary characters in an imaginary land, author of *Jurgen* and *The Certain Hour;* William Stearns Davis (1877–   ), author of *A Friend of Caesar* and *Beauty of the Purple;* James Boyd (1888–   ), a writer of historical romance, best known for *Drums,* a story of the Revolution, and *Marching On,* which is a story of the Civil War; Gertrude Atherton (1857–   ), best known for *The Conqueror;* Anne Douglas Sedgwick (1873–1935), author of *The Little French Girl* and *Adrienne Toner;* Booth Tarkington (1869–   ), twice winner of the Pulitzer Prize, once with *The Magnificent Ambersons,* and again with *Alice Adams;* Christopher Morley (1890–   ), author of *Parnassus on Wheels* and *The Haunted Bookshop;* and Joseph Hergesheimer (1880–   ), whose *Linda Condon* has been called one of the greatest novels to be written in America since Hawthorne.

Writers of Adventure Novels

Among the writers of romantic fiction are a few who have definitely turned toward adventure and the out-of-doors. Chief among these are Jack London (1876–1916), best known for *The Call of the Wild* and *The Sea Wolf;* Stewart Edward White (1873–   ), whose best book is *The Blazed Trail;* Zane Grey (1875–   ), who has established himself as a popular writer of the Southwest with such stories as *The Last of the Plainsmen* and *Riders of the Purple Sage;* and James Oliver Curwood (1878–1927), who goes to the Canadian Northwest for his characters in such books as *Nomads of the North* and *The Country Beyond.*

The Younger Novelists

In addition to the novelists mentioned, there are many newer writers among whom are Thornton Wilder, author of the Pulitzer Prize novel, *The Bridge of San Luis Rey;* DuBose Heyward, author of *Porgy* and *Mamba's Daughters;* Ernest Hemingway, known for *A Farewell to Arms;* Anne Parrish, author of *The Perennial Bachelor;* and many others whom it is impossible to list in the brief space here.

THE HOUSE OF THE SEVEN GABLES

Nathaniel Hawthorne

Historical Background: By 1692, Salem, Massachusetts, had become a comfortable village, the center of a group of tiny hamlets and productive farms. The meetinghouse, severe in its unadorned simplicity, stood in the center of the town, symbol alike of Puritan piety and austerity. And there were also the stocks, the pillory, the whipping post and the gallows.

In such a community John Hathorne, ancestor of the man who was to write the story of Puritan New England, was a considerable figure. He occupied a seat in the Colonial Assembly; he held the rank of colonel in the military forces; he was a reputable and prosperous merchant. And he had lately been appointed a judge. His fitness for the position was soon to be tried.

A group of young girls and married women who had been amusing themselves with fortune telling were suddenly racked by violent contortions. The town physician expressed the opinion that they had been bewitched, an opinion finally concurred in by the ministers. The whole community now set about the task of ferreting out the witches.

Everyone was suspected. Among others, Rebecca Nurse, a grandmother of hitherto saintly life, was brought before Justice Hathorne for examination. One of her accusers was a twelve-year-old child. In court she was compelled to stand with arms outstretched, was denied the support of her husband, but stoutly protested her innocence. Though twice acquitted by a jury, she was tried a third time, found guilty, and sentenced to death by hanging.

After hearing the sentence of doom, she turned toward Justice Hathorne and, with eyes which were now tearless, she solemnly cursed him and his posterity to the last generation.

The witchcraft terror gradually subsided. But though Justice Hathorne was to receive further judicial honors, his fortune dwindled away in a series of unsuccessful ventures, two of his children died, and before his own death he had tasted the humiliation of being unable to repay the money he had borrowed. His disappointed heirs were further baffled by discovering that the deed to a vast tract of land in the northern forests, in what was later to become the state of Maine, had unaccountably disappeared. The witch's curse—what had not come of it! What would not come!

The legend of the witch's curse and its effect upon the family fortune—for now every reverse was ascribed to it—was but one of many which came to the ears of Nathaniel Hawthorne when, in the summer of 1825, he returned to his native Salem, a graduate of Bowdoin College, but without any definite plans for his future except the half-formed one of becoming an author. A distant cousin, Miss Susan Ingersoll, inhabited an old, many-gabled house not far from Hawthorne's home. In this dim, ancient mansion, surrounded by the relics of the past, and with little to sustain her but her family pride, his spinster cousin entertained the future romancer with her store of family legends and traditions. Although it was not written until considerably later, it is not difficult to trace the origin of *The House of the Seven Gables*.

I THE OLD PYNCHEON FAMILY

Wherein is shown old Matthew Maule pronouncing a curse upon Colonel Pyncheon, ancestor of the Pyncheon family, and builder of the House of Seven Gables; the house warming; murder comes to the house. Was it the curse revenged, or just the beginning of it?

HALFWAY down a by-street of one of our New England towns stands a rusty wooden house with seven acutely peaked gables, facing toward various points of the compass, and a huge, clustered chimney in the midst. The street is Pyncheon Street; the house is the old Pyncheon house; and an elm tree, of wide circumference, rooted before the door, is familiar to every townborn child by the title of the Pyncheon elm. On my occasional visits to the town aforesaid, I seldom failed to turn down Pyncheon Street, for the sake of passing through the shadow of these two antiquities—the great elm tree and the weather-beaten edifice.

The aspect of the venerable mansion has always affected me like a human countenance, bearing the traces not merely of outward storm and sunshine, but expressive, also, of the long lapse of mortal life, and accompanying vicissitudes that have passed within.

The House of the Seven Gables, antique as it now looks, was not the first habitation erected by civilized man on precisely the same spot of ground. Pyncheon Street formerly bore the humbler appellation of Maule's Lane, from the name of the original occupant of the soil, before whose cottage door it was a cow path. A natural spring of soft and pleasant water—a rare treasure on the seagirt peninsula,[1] where the Puritan settlement was made—had early induced Matthew Maule to build a hut, shaggy with thatch, at this point, although somewhat too remote from what was then the center of the village. In the growth of the town, however, after some thirty or forty years, the site covered by this rude hovel had become exceedingly desirable in the eyes of a prominent and powerful personage, who asserted plausible claims to the proprietorship of this, and a large adjacent tract of land, on the strength of a grant from the legislature. Colonel Pyncheon, the claimant, as we gather from whatever traits of him are preserved, was characterized by an iron energy of purpose. Matthew Maule, on the other hand, though an obscure man, was stubborn in the defense of what he considered his right; and, for several years, he succeeded in protecting the acre or two of earth, which, with his own toil, he had hewn out of the primeval forest, to be his garden ground and homestead. No written record of this dispute is known to be in existence. Our acquaintance with the whole subject is derived chiefly from tradition. It would be bold, therefore, and possibly unjust, to venture a decisive opinion as to its merits; although it appears to have been at least a matter of doubt, whether Colonel Pyncheon's claim were not unduly stretched, in order to make it cover the small metes and bounds of Matthew Maule. What greatly strengthens such a suspicion is the fact that this controversy between two ill-matched antagonists—at a period, moreover, laud it as we may, when personal influence had far more weight than

[1] SEAGIRT PENINSULA—See *The Historical Background* preceding the story.

now—remained for years undecided, and came to a close only with the death of the party occupying the disputed soil. The mode of his death, too, affects the mind differently, in our day, from what it did a century and a half ago. It was a death that blasted with strange horror the humble name of the dweller in the cottage, and made it seem almost a religious act to drive the plow over the little area of his habitation, and obliterate his place and memory from among men.

Old Matthew Maule, in a word, was executed for the crime of witchcraft.[2] He was one of the martyrs to that terrible delusion, which should teach us, among its other morals, that the influential classes, and those who take upon themselves to be leaders of the people, are fully liable to all the passionate error that has ever characterized the maddest mob.

Amid the disorder of such various ruin, it is not strange that a man of inconsiderable note, like Maule, should have trodden the martyr's path to the hill of execution almost unremarked in the throng of his fellow sufferers. But, in after days, when the frenzy of that hideous epoch had subsided, it was remembered how loudly Colonel Pyncheon had joined in the general cry, to purge the land from witchcraft; nor did it fail to be whispered, that there was an invidious acrimony[3] in the zeal with which he had sought the condemnation of Matthew Maule. It was well known that the victim had recognized the bitterness of personal enmity in his persecutor's conduct toward him, and that he declared himself hunted to death for his spoil. At the moment of execution—with the halter about his neck, and while Colonel Pyncheon sat on horseback, grimly gazing at the scene—Maule had addressed him from the scaffold, and uttered a prophecy, of which history, as well as fireside tradition, has preserved the very words. "God," said the dying man, pointing his finger, with a ghastly look, at the undismayed countenance of his enemy— "God will give him blood to drink!"

After the reputed wizard's death, his humble homestead had fallen an easy spoil into Colonel Pyncheon's grasp. When it was understood, however, that the Colonel intended to erect a family mansion—spacious, ponderously framed of oaken timber, and calculated to endure for many generations of his posterity

---

[2] WITCHCRAFT—See the *Historical Background*.
[3] INVIDIOUS ACRIMONY—Unjust bitterness.

—over the spot first covered by the log-built hut of Matthew Maule, there was much shaking of the head among the village gossips. Without absolutely expressing a doubt whether the stalwart Puritan had acted as a man of conscience and integrity throughout the proceedings which have been sketched, they, nevertheless, hinted that he was about to build his house over an unquiet grave. His home would include the home of the dead and buried wizard, and would thus afford the ghost of the latter a kind of privilege to haunt its new apartments, and the chambers into which future bridegrooms were to lead their brides, and where children of the Pyncheon blood were to be born. The terror and ugliness of Maule's crime, and the wretchedness of his punishment, would darken the freshly plastered walls, and infect them early with the scent of an old and melancholy house. Why, then—while so much of the soil around him was bestrewn with the virgin forest leaves—why should Colonel Pyncheon prefer a site that had already been accursed?

But the Puritan soldier and magistrate was not a man to be turned aside from his well considered scheme, either by dread of the wizard's ghost, or by flimsy sentimentalities of any kind, however specious. Had he been told of a bad air, it might have moved him somewhat; but he was ready to encounter an evil spirit on his own ground. Endowed with common sense, as massive and hard as blocks of granite, fastened together by stern rigidity of purpose, as with iron clamps, he followed out his original design, probably without so much as imagining an objection to it. On the score of delicacy, or any scrupulousness which a finer sensibility might have taught him, the Colonel, like most of his breed and generation, was impenetrable. He, therefore, dug his cellar, and laid the deep foundations of his mansion, on the square of earth whence Matthew Maule, forty years before, had first swept away the fallen leaves. It was a curious, and, as some people thought, an ominous fact, that, very soon after the workmen began their operations, the spring of water, above mentioned, entirely lost the deliciousness of its pristine quality. Whether its sources were disturbed by the depth of the new cellar, or whatever subtler cause might lurk at the bottom, it is certain that the water of Maule's Well, as it continued to be called, grew hard and brackish. Even such we find it now; and any old woman of the neighborhood will certify that it is pro-

ductive of intestinal mischief to those who quench their thirst
there.

The reader may deem it singular that the head carpenter of
the new edifice was no other than the son of the very man from
whose dead grip the property of the soil had been wrested. Not
improbably he was the best workman of his time; or, perhaps,
the Colonel thought it expedient, or was impelled by some better
feeling, thus openly to cast aside all animosity against the race
of his fallen antagonist. Nor was it out of keeping with the
general coarseness and matter-of-fact character of the age, that
the son should be willing to earn an honest penny, or, rather, a
weighty amount of sterling pounds from the purse of his father's
deadly enemy. At all events, Thomas Maule became the architect of the House of the Seven Gables, and performed his duty
so faithfully that the timber framework fastened by his hands
still holds together.

Thus the great house was built. Familiar as it stands in the
writer's recollection—for it has been an object of curiosity with
him from boyhood, both as a specimen of the best and stateliest
architecture of a long-past epoch, and as the scene of events more
full of human interest, perhaps, than those of a gray feudal
castle—familiar as it stands, in its rusty old age, it is therefore
only the more difficult to imagine the bright novelty with which
it first caught the sunshine. The impression of its actual state,
at this distance of a hundred and sixty years, darkens inevitably
through the picture which we would fain give of its appearance
on the morning when the Puritan magnate bade all the town
to be his guests. A ceremony of consecration, festive as well as
religious, was now to be performed. A prayer and discourse
from the Rev. Mr. Higginson, and the outpouring of a psalm
from the general throat of the community, was to be made acceptable to the grosser sense by ale, cider, wine, and brandy, in
copious effusion, and, as some authorities aver, by an ox, roasted
whole, or at least, by the weight and substance of an ox, in more
manageable joints and sirloins. The carcass of a deer, shot
within twenty miles, had supplied material for the vast circumference of a pasty. A codfish of sixty pounds, caught in the bay,
had been dissolved into the rich liquid of a chowder. The chimney of the new house, in short, belching forth its kitchen smoke,
impregnated the whole air with the scent of meats, fowls and

fishes, spicily concocted with odoriferous herbs and onions in abundance. The mere smell of such festivity, making its way to everybody's nostrils, was at once an invitation and an appetite.

Maule's Lane, or Pyncheon Street, as it were now more decorous to call it, was thronged, at the appointed hour, as with a congregation on its way to church. All, as they approached, looked upward at the imposing edifice, which was henceforth to assume its rank among the habitations of mankind. There it rose, a little withdrawn from the line of the street, but in pride, not modesty. Its whole visible exterior was ornamented with quaint figures, conceived in the grotesqueness of a Gothic fancy,[4] and drawn or stamped in the glittering plaster, composed of lime, pebbles, and bits of glass, with which the woodwork of the walls was overspread. On every side the seven gables pointed sharply toward the sky, and presented the aspect of a whole sisterhood of edifices, breathing through the spiracles of one great chimney. The many lattices, with their small, diamond-shaped panes, admitted the sunlight into hall and chamber, while, nevertheless, the second story, projecting far over the base, and itself retiring beneath the third, threw a shadowy and thoughtful gloom into the lower rooms. Carved globes of wood were affixed under the jutting stories. Little spiral rods of iron beautified each of the seven peaks. On the triangular portion of the gable, that fronted next the street, was a dial, put up that very morning, and on which the sun was still marking the passage of the first bright hour in a history that was not destined to be all so bright. All around were scattered shavings, chips, shingles, and broken halves of bricks; these, together with the lately turned earth, on which the grass had not begun to grow, contributed to the impression of strangeness and novelty proper to a house that had yet its place to make among men's daily interests.

The principal entrance, which had almost the breadth of a church door, was in the angle between the two front gables, and was covered by an open porch, with benches beneath its shelter. Under this arched doorway, scraping their feet on the unworn threshold, now trod the clergymen, the elders, the magistrates, the deacons, and whatever of aristocracy there was in town or county. Thither, too, thronged the plebeian classes as freely

---

[4] GOTHIC FANCY—A style of architecture which flourished between the twelfth and sixteenth centuries.

as their betters, and in larger number. Just within the entrance, however, stood two serving men, pointing some of the guests to the neighborhood of the kitchen, and ushering others into the statelier rooms—hospitable alike to all, but still with a scrutinizing regard to the high or low degree of each. Velvet garments, somber but rich, stiffly plaited ruffs and bands, embroidered gloves, venerable beards, the mien and countenance of authority, made it easy to distinguish the gentlemen of worship, at that period, from the tradesman, with his plodding air, or the laborer, in his leathern jerkin, stealing awe-stricken into the house which he had perhaps helped to build.

One inauspicious circumstance there was, which awakened a hardly concealed displeasure in the breasts of a few of the more punctilious visitors. The founder of this stately mansion—a gentleman noted for the square and ponderous courtesy of his demeanor—ought surely to have stood in his own hall, and to have offered the first welcome to so many eminent personages as here presented themselves in honor of his solemn festival. He was as yet invisible; the most favored of the guests had not beheld him. This sluggishness on Colonel Pyncheon's part became still more unaccountable, when the second dignitary of the province made his appearance, and found no more ceremonious a reception. The Lieutenant Governor, although his visit was one of the anticipated glories of the day, had alighted from his horse, and assisted his lady from her side saddle, and crossed the Colonel's threshold, without other greeting than that of the principal domestic.

This person—a gray-headed man, of quiet and most respectful deportment—found it necessary to explain that his master still remained in his study, or private apartment; on entering which, an hour before, he had expressed a wish on no account to be disturbed.

"Do not you see, fellow," said the high sheriff of the county taking the servant aside, "that this is no less a man than the Lieutenant Governor? Summon Colonel Pyncheon at once! I know that he received letters from England this morning; and, in the perusal and consideration of them, an hour may have passed away without his noticing it. But he will be ill pleased, I judge, if you suffer him to neglect the courtesy due to one of our chief rulers, and who may be said to represent King William,[5] in the absence of the Governor himself. Call your master instantly!"

"Nay, please your worship," answered the man, in much perplexity, but with a backwardness that strikingly indicated the hard and severe character of Colonel Pyncheon's domestic rule; "my master's orders were exceeding strict; and, as your worship knows, he permits of no discretion in the obedience of those who owe him service. Let who list open yonder door; I dare not, though the Governor's own voice should bid me do it!"

"Pooh, pooh, master high sheriff!" cried the Lieutenant Governor, who had overheard the foregoing discussion, and felt himself high enough in station to play a little with his dignity. "I will take the matter into my own hands. It is time that the good Colonel came forth to greet his friends; else we shall be apt to suspect that he has taken a sip too much of his Canary wine,[6] in his extreme deliberation which cask it were best to broach in honor of the day! But since he is so much behindhand, I will give him a remembrancer myself!"

Accordingly, with such a tramp of his ponderous riding boots as might of itself have been audible in the remotest of the seven gables, he advanced to the door, which the servant pointed out, and made its new panels reëcho with a loud, free knock. Then, looking around, with a smile, to the spectators, he awaited a response. As none came, however, he knocked again, but with the same unsatisfactory result as at first. And now, being a trifle choleric in his temperament, the Lieutenant Governor uplifted the heavy hilt of his sword, wherewith he so beat and banged upon the door, that, as some of the bystanders whispered, the racket might have disturbed the dead. Be that as it might, it seemed to produce no awakening effect on Colonel Pyncheon. When the sound subsided, the silence through the house was deep, dreary, and oppressive, notwithstanding that the tongues of many of the guests had already been loosened by a surreptitious cup or two of wine or spirits.

"Strange, forsooth!—very strange!" cried the Lieutenant Governor, whose smile was changed to a frown. "But seeing that our host sets us the good example of forgetting ceremony, I shall

---

[5] KING WILLIAM—William III, the then reigning King of England.
[6] CANARY WINE—Wine imported from the Canary Islands.

"*I will give him a remembrancer, myself!*"

likewise throw it aside, and make free to intrude on his privacy!"

He tried the door, which yielded to his hand, and was flung wide open by a sudden gust of wind that passed, as with a loud sigh, from the outermost portal through all the passages and apartments of the new house. It rustled the silken garments of the ladies, and waved the long curls of the gentlemen's wigs, and shook the window hangings and the curtains of the bed-chambers; causing everywhere a singular stir, which yet was more like a hush. A shadow of awe and half-fearful anticipation—nobody knew wherefore, nor of what—had all at once fallen over the company.

They thronged, however, to the now open door, pressing the Lieutenant Governor, in the eagerness of their curiosity, into the room in advance of them. At the first glimpse they beheld nothing extraordinary: a handsomely furnished room, of moderate size, somewhat darkened by curtains; books arranged on shelves; a large map on the wall, and likewise a portrait of Colonel Pyncheon, beneath which sat the original Colonel himself, in an oaken elbow chair, with a pen in his hand. Letters, parchments, and blank sheets of paper were on the table before him. He appeared to gaze at the curious crowd, in front of which stood the Lieutenant Governor; and there was a frown on his dark and massive countenance, as if sternly resentful of the boldness that had impelled them into his private retirement.

A little boy—the Colonel's grandchild, and the only human being that ever dared to be familiar with him—now made his way among the guests, and ran toward the seated figure; then pausing halfway, he began to shriek with terror. The company, tremulous as the leaves of a tree, when all are shaking together, drew nearer, and perceived that there was an unnatural distortion in the fixedness of Colonel Pyncheon's stare; that there was blood on his ruff, and that his hoary beard was saturated with it. It was too late to give assistance. The iron-hearted Puritan, the relentless persecutor, the grasping and strong-willed man, was dead! Dead, in his new house! There is a tradition, only worth alluding to as lending a tinge of superstitious awe to a scene perhaps gloomy enough without it, that a voice spoke loudly among the guests, the tones of which were like those of old Matthew Maule, the executed wizard—"God hath given him blood to drink!"

Thus early had that one guest—the only guest who is certain, at one time or another, to find his way into every human dwelling—thus early had Death stepped across the threshold of the House of the Seven Gables!

Colonel Pyncheon's sudden and mysterious end made a vast deal of noise [7] in its day. There were many rumors, some of which have vaguely drifted down to the present time, how that appearances indicated violence; that there were the marks of fingers on his throat, and the print of a bloody hand on his plaited ruff; and that his peaked beard was disheveled, as if it had been fiercely clutched and pulled. It was averred, likewise, that the lattice window, near the Colonel's chair, was open; and that, only a few minutes before the fatal occurrence, the figure of a man had been seen clambering over the garden fence, in the rear of the house. But it were folly to lay any stress on stories of this kind, which are sure to spring up around such an event as that now related, and which, as in the present case, sometimes prolong themselves for ages afterwards, like the toadstools that indicate where the fallen and buried trunk of a tree has long since moldered into the earth. For our own part, we allow them just as little credence as to that other fable of the skeleton hand which the Lieutenant Governor was said to have seen at the Colonel's throat, but which vanished away, as he advanced farther into the room. Certain it is, however, that there was a great consultation and dispute of doctors over the dead body. One—John Swinnerton by name—who appears to have been a man of eminence, upheld it, if we have rightly understood his terms of art, to be a case of apoplexy. His professional brethren, each for himself, adopted various hypotheses, more or less plausible, but all dressed out in a perplexing mystery of phrase, which, if it do not show a bewilderment of mind in these erudite physicians, certainly causes it in the unlearned peruser of their opinions. The coroner's jury sat upon the corpse,[8] and, like sensible men, returned an unassailable verdict of "Sudden Death!"

It is indeed difficult to imagine that there could have been a serious suspicion of murder, or the slightest grounds for implicating any particular individual as the perpetrator. The rank, wealth, and eminent character of the deceased must have insured

---

[7] VAST DEAL OF NOISE—Caused much comment.
[8] SAT UPON THE CORPSE—Held an investigation.

the strictest scrutiny into every ambiguous circumstance. As none such is on record, it is safe to assume that none existed.

The family of Colonel Pyncheon, at the epoch of his death, seemed destined to as fortunate a permanence as can anywise consist with the inherent instability of human affairs. It might fairly be anticipated that the progress of time would rather increase and ripen their prosperity, than wear away and destroy it. For, not only had his son and heir come into immediate enjoyment of a rich estate, but there was a claim through an Indian deed, confirmed by a subsequent grant of the General Court,[9] to a vast and as yet unexplored and unmeasured tract of eastern lands. These possessions—for as such they might almost certainly be reckoned—comprised the greater part of what is now known as Waldo County, in the State of Maine, and were more extensive than many a dukedom, or even a reigning prince's territory, on European soil. When the pathless forest that still covered this wild principality should give place—as it inevitably must, though perhaps not till ages hence—to the golden fertility of human culture, it would be the source of incalculable wealth to the Pyncheon blood. Had the Colonel survived only a few weeks longer, it is probable that his great political influence, and powerful connections at home and abroad, would have consummated all that was necessary to render the claim available. But, this appeared to be the one thing which Colonel Pyncheon, provident and sagacious as he was, had allowed to go at loose ends. So far as the prospective territory was concerned, he unquestionably died too soon. His son lacked not merely the father's eminent position, but the talent and force of character to achieve it: he could, therefore, effect nothing by dint of political interest; and the bare justice or legality of the claim was not so apparent, after the Colonel's decease, as it had been pronounced in his lifetime. Some connecting link had slipped out of the evidence, and could not anywhere be found.

Efforts, it is true, were made by the Pyncheons, not only then, but at various periods for nearly a hundred years afterwards, to obtain what they stubbornly persisted in deeming their right. But, in course of time, the territory was partly regranted to more favored individuals, and partly cleared and occupied by actual

---

[9] GENERAL COURT—The name of the legislature in Massachusetts and New Hampshire.

settlers. These last, if they ever heard of the Pyncheon title, would have laughed at the idea of any man's asserting a right— on the strength of moldy parchments, signed with the faded autographs of governors and legislators long dead and forgotten —to the lands which they or their fathers had wrested from the wild hand of nature by their own sturdy toil. This impalpable claim, therefore, resulted in nothing more solid than to cherish, from generation to generation, an absurd delusion of family importance, which all along characterized the Pyncheons. It caused the poorest member of the race to feel as if he inherited a kind of nobility, and might yet come into the possession of princely wealth to support it.

In almost every generation, nevertheless, there happened to be some one descendant of the family gifted with a portion of the hard, keen sense, and practical energy, that had so remarkably distinguished the original founder. His character, indeed, might be traced all the way down, as distinctly as if the Colonel himself, a little diluted, had been gifted with a sort of intermittent immortality on earth. At two or three epochs, when the fortunes of the family were low, this representative of hereditary qualities had made his appearance, and caused the traditionary gossips of the town to whisper among themselves, "Here is the old Pyncheon come again! Now the Seven Gables will be new-shingled!" From father to son, they clung to the ancestral house with singular tenacity of home attachment. For various reasons, however, and from impressions often too vaguely founded to be put on paper, the writer cherishes the belief that many, if not most, of the successive proprietors of this estate were troubled with doubts as to their moral right to hold it. Of their legal tenure there could be no question; but old Matthew Maule, it is to be feared, trod downward from his own age to a far later one, planting a heavy footstep, all the way, on the conscience of a Pyncheon. If so, we are left to dispose of the awful query, whether each inheritor of the property—conscious of wrong and failing to rectify it—did not commit anew the great guilt of his ancestor, and incur all its original responsibilities. And supposing such to be the case, would it not be a far truer mode of expression to say of the Pyncheon family, that they inherited a great misfortune, than the reverse?

The popular imagination, indeed, long kept itself busy with the affair of the old Puritan Pyncheon and the wizard Maule; the curse, which the latter flung from his scaffold, was remembered, with the very important addition, that it had become a part of the Pyncheon inheritance. If one of the family did but gurgle in his throat, a bystander would be likely enough to whisper, between jest and earnest, "He has Maule's blood to drink!" The sudden death of a Pyncheon, about a hundred years ago, with circumstances very similar to what have been related of the Colonel's exit, was held as giving additional probability to the received opinion on this topic. It was considered, moreover, an ugly and ominous circumstance that Colonel Pyncheon's picture—in obedience, it was said, to a provision of his will—remained affixed to the wall of the room in which he died. Those stern, immitigable features seemed to symbolize an evil influence, and so darkly to mingle the shadow of their presence with the sunshine of the passing hour, that no good thoughts or purposes could ever spring up and blossom there. To the thoughtful mind there will be no tinge of superstition in what we figuratively express, by affirming that the ghost of a dead progenitor —perhaps as a portion of his own punishment—is often doomed to become the Evil Genius of his family.

The Pyncheons, in brief, lived along, for the better part of two centuries, with perhaps less of outward vicissitude than has attended most other New England families during the same period of time. Possessing very distinctive traits of their own, they nevertheless took the general characteristics of the little community in which they dwelt; a town noted for its frugal, discreet, well-ordered, and home-loving inhabitants, as well as for the somewhat confined scope of its sympathies; but in which, be it said, there are odder individuals, and, now and then, stranger occurrences, than one meets with almost anywhere else. During the Revolution, the Pyncheon of that epoch, adopting the royal side, became a refugee; but repented, and made his reappearance, just at the point of time to preserve the House of the Seven Gables from confiscation. For the last seventy years the most noted event in the Pyncheon annals had been likewise the heaviest calamity that ever befell the race; no less than the violent death—for so it was adjudged—of one member of the family by the criminal act of another. Certain circumstances attending this fatal occurrence had brought the deed irresistibly home to a nephew of the deceased Pyncheon. The young man was tried and convicted of the crime; but either the circumstantial nature of the evidence, and possibly some lurking doubt in the breast of the executive, or lastly—an argument of greater weight in a republic than it could have been under a monarchy —the high respectability and political influence of the criminal's connections, had availed to mitigate his doom from death to perpetual imprisonment. This sad affair had chanced about thirty years before the action of our story commences. Lately, there were rumors (which few believed, and only one or two felt greatly interested in) that this long-buried man was likely, for some reason or other, to be summoned forth from his living tomb.

It is essential to say a few words respecting the victim of this now almost forgotten murder. He was an old bachelor, and possessed of great wealth, in addition to the house and real estate which constituted what remained of the ancient Pyncheon property. Being of an eccentric and melancholy turn of mind, and greatly given to rummaging old records and hearkening to old traditions, he had brought himself, it is averred, to the conclusion that Matthew Maule, the wizard, had been foully wronged out of his homestead, if not out of his life. Such being the case, and he, the old bachelor, in possession of the ill-gotten spoil—with the black stain of blood sunken deep into it, and still to be scented by conscientious nostrils—the question occurred, whether it were not imperative upon him, even at this late hour, to make restitution to Maule's posterity. To a man living so much in the past, and so little in the present, as the secluded and antiquarian old bachelor, a century and a half seemed not so vast a period as to obviate the propriety of substituting right for wrong. It was the belief of those who knew him best, that he would positively have taken the very singular step of giving up the House of the Seven Gables to the representative of Matthew Maule, but for the unspeakable tumult which a suspicion of the old gentleman's project awakened among his Pyncheon relatives. Their exertions had the effect of suspending his purpose; but it was feared that he would perform, after death, by the operation of his last will, what he had so hardly been prevented from doing in his proper lifetime. But there is no one thing which men so rarely do, whatever the provocation or inducement, as to bequeath patrimonial property away from their own blood. Accordingly, the mansion house, together with most of his other riches, passed into the possession of his next legal representative.

This was a nephew, the cousin of the miserable young man who had been convicted of the uncle's murder. The new heir, up to the period of his accession, was reckoned rather a dissipated youth, but had at once reformed, and made himself an exceedingly respectable member of society. In fact, he showed more of the Pyncheon quality, and had won higher eminence in the world than any of his race since the time of the original Puritan. Applying himself in earlier manhood to the study of the law, and having a natural tendency toward office, he had attained, many years ago, to a judicial situation in some inferior court, which gave him for life the very desirable and imposing title of judge. Later, he had engaged in politics, and served a part of two terms in Congress, besides making a considerable figure in both branches of the State legislature. Judge Pyncheon was unquestionably an honor to his race. He had built himself a countryseat within a few miles of his native town, and there spent such portions of his time as could be spared from public service in the display of every grace and virtue—as a newspaper phrased it, on the eve of an election—befitting the Christian, the good citizen, the horticulturist, and the gentleman.

There were few of the Pyncheons left to sun themselves in the glow of the judge's prosperity. In respect to natural increase, the breed had not thriven; it appeared rather to be dying out. The only members of the family known to be extant were, first, the judge himself, and a single surviving son, who was now traveling in Europe; next, the thirty years' prisoner, already alluded to, and a sister of the latter, who occupied, in an extremely retired manner, the House of the Seven Gables, in which she had a life estate by the will of the old bachelor. She was understood to be wretchedly poor, and seemed to make it her choice to remain so; inasmuch as her affluent cousin, the judge, had repeatedly offered her all the comforts of life, either in the old mansion or his own modern residence. The last and youngest Pyncheon was a little country girl of seventeen, the daughter of another of the judge's cousins, who had married a young woman of no family or property, and died early and in poor circumstances. His widow had recently taken another husband.

As for Matthew Maule's posterity, it was supposed now to be extinct. For a very long period after the witchcraft delusion, however, the Maules had continued to inhabit the town where their progenitor had suffered so unjust a death. To all appearances, they were a quiet, honest, well-meaning race of people, cherishing no malice against individuals or the public for the wrong which had been done them; or if, at their own fireside, they transmitted, from father to child, any hostile recollection of the wizard's fate and their lost patrimony, it was never acted upon, nor openly expressed.

The Maules, at all events, kept their resentments within their own breasts. They were generally poverty-stricken; always plebeian and obscure; working with unsuccessful diligence at handicrafts; laboring on the wharves, or following the sea, as sailors before the mast; living here and there about the town, in hired tenements, and coming finally to the almshouse as the natural home of their old age. For thirty years past, neither town record, nor gravestone, nor the directory, nor the knowledge or memory of man, bore any trace of Matthew Maule's descendants. His blood might possibly exist elsewhere; here, where its lowly current could be traced so far back, it had ceased to keep an outward course.

So long as any of the race were to be found, they had been marked out from other men—not strikingly, nor as with a sharp line, but with an effect that was felt rather than spoken of—by an hereditary character of reserve. Their companions, or those who endeavored to become such, grew conscious of a circle round about the Maules, within the sanctity or the spell of which, in spite of an exterior of sufficient frankness and good-fellowship, it was impossible for any man to step. It was this indefinable peculiarity, perhaps, that, by insulating them from human aid, kept them always so unfortunate in life. It certainly operated to prolong in their case, and to confirm to them as their only inheritance, those feelings of repugnance and superstitious terror with which the people of the town, even after awakening from their frenzy, continued to regard the memory of the reputed witches. The mantle, or rather the ragged cloak, of old Matthew Maule, had fallen upon his children. They were half believed to inherit mysterious attributes; the family eye was said to possess strange power. Among other good-for-nothing properties and privileges, one was especially assigned them—that of exercising an influence over people's dreams. The Pyncheons, if all stories were true, haughtily as they bore themselves in the noonday streets of their native town, were no better than bond servants to these plebeian Maules, on entering the topsy-turvy commonwealth of sleep. Modern psychology, it may be, will endeavor to reduce these alleged necromancies within a system, instead of rejecting them as altogether fabulous.

A descriptive paragraph or two, treating of the seven-gabled mansion in its more recent aspect, will bring this preliminary chapter to a close. The street in which it upreared its venerable peaks has long ceased to be a fashionable quarter of the town; so that, though the old edifice was surrounded by habitations of modern date, they were mostly small, built entirely of wood, and typical of the most plodding uniformity of common life. Doubtless, however, the whole story of human existence may be latent in each of them, but with no picturesqueness, externally, that can attract the imagination or sympathy to seek it there. But as for the old structure of our story, its white-oak frame, and its boards, shingles, and crumbling plaster, and even the huge, clustered chimney in the midst, seemed to constitute only the least and meanest part of its reality. So much of mankind's varied experience had passed there—so much had been suffered, and something, too, enjoyed—that the very timbers were oozy, as with the moisture of a heart. It was itself like a great human heart, with a life of its own, and full of rich and somber reminiscences.

The deep projection of the second story gave the house such a meditative look, that you could not pass it without the idea that it had secrets to keep, and an eventful history to moralize upon. In front, just on the edge of the unpaved sidewalk, grew the Pyncheon elm, which, in reference to such trees as one usually meets with, might well be termed gigantic. It had been planted by a great-grandson of the first Pyncheon, and, though now fourscore years of age, or perhaps nearer a hundred, was still in its strong and broad maturity, throwing its shadow from side to side of the street, overtopping the seven gables, and sweeping the whole black roof with its pendent foliage. It gave beauty to the old edifice, and seemed to make it a part of nature. The street having been widened about forty years ago, the front gable was now precisely on a line with it. On either side extended a ruinous wooden fence of open latticework, through which could be seen a grassy yard, and, especially in the angles of the building, an enormous fertility of burdocks, with leaves, it is hardly an exaggeration to say, two or three feet long. Behind the house there appeared to be a garden, which undoubtedly had once been extensive, but was now infringed upon by other inclosures, or shut in by habitations and outbuildings that stood on another street. It would be an omission, trifling, indeed, but unpardonable, were we to forget the green moss that had long since gathered over the projections of the windows, and on the slopes of the roof; nor must we fail to direct the reader's eye to a crop, not of weeds, but flower shrubs, which were growing aloft in the air, not a great way from the chimney, in the nook between two of the gables. They were called Alice's Posies. The tradition was, that a certain Alice Pyncheon had flung up the seeds, in sport, and that the dust of the street and the decay of the roof gradually formed a kind of soil for them, out of which they grew, when Alice had long been in her grave. However the flowers might have come there, it was both sad and sweet to observe how Nature adopted to herself this desolate, decaying, gusty, rusty old house of the Pyncheon family; and how the ever-returning summer did her best to gladden it with tender beauty, and grew melancholy in the effort.

There is one other feature, very essential to be noticed, but which, we greatly fear, may damage any picturesque and romantic impression which we have been willing to throw over our sketch of this respectable edifice. In the front gable, under the impending brow of the second story, and contiguous to the street, was a shop door, divided horizontally in the middle, and with a window for its upper segment, such as is often seen in dwellings of a somewhat ancient date. This same shop door had been a subject of no slight mortification to the present occupant of the august Pyncheon house, as well as to some of her predecessors. The matter is disagreeably delicate to handle; but, since the reader must needs be let into the secret, he will please to understand, that, about a century ago, the head of the Pyncheons found himself involved in serious financial difficulties.

The fellow (gentleman, as he styled himself) can hardly have been other than a spurious interloper; for, instead of seeking office from the king or the royal governor, or urging his hereditary claim to eastern lands, he bethought himself of no better avenue to wealth than by cutting a shop door through the side of his ancestral residence. It was the custom of the time, indeed, for merchants to store their goods and transact business in their own dwellings. But there was something pitifully small in this old Pyncheon's mode of setting about his commercial operations; it was whispered, that, with his own hands, all beruffled as they were, he used to give change for a shilling, and would turn a halfpenny twice over, to make sure that it was a good one. Beyond all question, he had the blood of a petty huckster in his veins, through whatever channel it may have found its way there.

Immediately on his death, the shop door had been locked, bolted, and barred, and, down to the period of our story, had probably never once been opened. The old counter, shelves, and other fixtures of the little shop remained just as he had left them. It used to be affirmed, that the dead shopkeeper, in a white wig, a faded velvet coat, an apron at his waist, and his ruffles carefully turned back from his wrists, might be seen through the chinks of the shutters, any night of the year, ransacking his till, or poring over the dingy pages of his daybook. From the look of unutterable woe upon his face, it appeared to be his doom to spend eternity in a vain effort to make his accounts balance.

And now—in a very humble way, as will be seen—we proceed to open our narrative.

II THE LITTLE SHOP WINDOW

Wherein Hepzibah Pyncheon makes preparations for an eventful day; the Malbone miniature; the interior of the old house; Miss Hepzibah opens a petty cent shop.

IT STILL lacked half an hour of sunrise, when Miss Hepzibah Pyncheon—we will not say awoke, it being doubtful whether the poor lady had so much as closed her eyes during the brief night of midsummer—but, at all events, arose from her solitary pillow, and began what it would be mockery to term the adorn-ment of her person. The Old Maid was alone in the old house. Alone, except for a certain respectable and orderly young man, an artist in the daguerreotype [1] line, who, for about three months back, had been a lodger in a remote gable—quite a house by itself, indeed—with locks, bolts, and oaken bars on all the inter-vening doors. Inaudible, consequently, were poor Miss Hepzi-bah's gusty sighs. Inaudible the creaking joints of her stiffened knees, as she knelt down by the bedside. And inaudible, too, by mortal ear, but heard with all-comprehending love and pity in the furthest heaven, that almost agony of prayer—now a whis-per, now a groan, now a struggling silence—wherewith she besought the Divine assistance through the day! Evidently, this is to be a day of more than ordinary trial to Miss Hepzibah, who, for above a quarter of a century gone by, has dwelt in strict seclusion, taking no part in the business of life, and just as little in its intercourse and pleasures.

The maiden lady's devotions are concluded. Will she now issue forth over the threshold of our story? Not yet, by many moments. First, every drawer in the tall, old-fashioned bureau is to be opened, with difficulty, and with a succession of spas-modic jerks; then, all must close again, with the same fidgety reluctance. There is a rustling of stiff silks; a tread of back-ward and forward footsteps to and fro across the chamber. We suspect Miss Hepzibah, moreover, of taking a step upward into a chair, in order to give heedful regard to her appearance on all sides and at full length, in the oval, dingy-framed toilet glass, that hangs above her table. Truly! well, indeed! who would have thought it! Is all this precious time to be lavished on the matutinal repair and beautifying of an elderly person, who never goes abroad, whom nobody ever visits, and from whom, when she shall have done her utmost, it were the best charity to turn one's eyes another way?

Now she is almost ready. Let us pardon her one other pause;

---

[1] DAGUERREOTYPE—An early kind of photograph, so named from Daguerre, the inventor of the process.

for it is given to the sole sentiment, or, we might better say—heightened and rendered intense, as it has been, by sorrow and seclusion—to the strong passion of her life. We heard the turning of a key in a small lock; she has opened a secret drawer of an escritoire,[2] and is probably looking at a certain miniature, done in Malbone's [3] most perfect style, and representing a face worthy of no less delicate a pencil. It was once our good fortune to see this picture. It is a likeness of a young man, in a silken dressing gown of an old fashion, countenance of reverie, with its full, tender lips, and the soft richness of which is well adapted to the beautiful eyes, that seem to indicate not so much capacity of thought, as gentle and voluptuous emotion. Of the possessor of such features we shall have a right to ask nothing, except that he would take the rude world easily, and make himself happy in it. Can it have been an early lover of Miss Hepzibah? No; she never had a lover! poor thing, how could she?—nor ever knew, by her own experience, what love technically means. And yet, her undying faith and trust, her fresh remembrance, and continual devotedness toward the original of that miniature, have been the only substance for her heart to feed upon.

She seems to have put aside the miniature, and is standing again before the toilet glass. There are tears to be wiped off. A few more footsteps to and fro; and here, at last—with another pitiful sigh, like a gust of chill, damp wind out of a long-closed vault, the door of which has accidentally been set ajar—here comes Miss Hepzibah Pyncheon! Forth she steps into the dusky, time-darkened passage; a tall figure, clad in black silk, with a long and shrunken waist, feeling her way toward the stairs like a nearsighted person, as in truth she is.

The room which Hepzibah entered, after descending the stairs, was a low-studded room, with a beam across the ceiling, paneled with dark wood, and having a large chimney piece, set round with pictured tiles, but now closed by an iron fireboard, through which ran the funnel of a modern stove. There was a carpet on the floor, originally of rich texture, but so worn and faded in these latter years that its once brilliant figure had quite vanished into one indistinguishable hue. In the way of furniture, there

[2] ESCRITOIRE—A writing desk.
[3] MALBONE—An eighteenth century American miniature painter.

were two tables: one, constructed with perplexing intricacy and exhibiting as many feet as a centipede; the other, most delicately wrought, with four long and slender legs, so apparently frail that it was almost incredible what a length of time the ancient tea table had stood upon them. Half a dozen chairs stood about the room, straight and stiff, and so ingeniously contrived for the discomfort of the human person that they were irksome even to sight, and conveyed the ugliest possible idea of the state of society to which they could have been adapted. One exception there was, however, in a very antique elbow chair, with a high back, carved elaborately in oak, and a roomy depth within its arms, that made up, by its spacious comprehensiveness, for the lack of any of those artistic curves which abound in a modern chair.

As for ornamental articles of furniture, we recollect but two, if such they may be called. One was a map of the Pyncheon territory at the eastward, not engraved, but the handiwork of some skillful old draftsman, and grotesquely illuminated with pictures of Indians and wild beasts, among which was seen a lion; the natural history of the region being as little known as its geography, which was put down most fantastically awry. The other adornment was the portrait of old Colonel Pyncheon, at two-thirds length, representing the stern features of a Puritanic-looking personage, in a skullcap, with a laced band and a grizzly beard; holding a Bible with one hand, and in the other uplifting an iron sword hilt. The latter object, being more successfully depicted by the artist, stood out in far greater prominence than the sacred volume. Face to face with this picture, on entering the apartment, Miss Hepzibah Pyncheon came to a pause; regarding it with a singular scowl, a strange contortion of the brow, which, by people who did not know her, would probably have been interpreted as an expression of bitter anger and ill will. But it was no such thing. She, in fact, felt a reverence for the pictured visage, of which only a far-descended and time-stricken virgin could be susceptible; and this forbidding scowl was the innocent result of her nearsightedness, and an effort so to concentrate her powers of vision as to substitute a firm outline of the object instead of a vague one.

We must linger a moment on this unfortunate expression of poor Hepzibah's brow. Her scowl—as the world, or such part of it as sometimes caught a transitory glimpse of her at the window, wickedly persisted in calling it—her scowl had done Miss Hepzibah a very ill office, in establishing her character as an ill-tempered old maid; nor does it appear improbable that, by often gazing at herself in a dim looking-glass, and perpetually encountering her own frown within its ghostly sphere, she had been led to interpret the expression almost as unjustly as the world did. "How miserably cross I look!" she must often have whispered to herself; and ultimately have fancied herself so, by a sense of inevitable doom. But her heart never frowned. It was naturally tender, sensitive, and full of little tremors and palpitations; all of which weaknesses it retained, while her visage was growing so perversely stern, and even fierce. Nor had Hepzibah ever any hardihood, except what came from the very warmest nook in her affections.

It has already been observed, that, in the basement story of the gable fronting on the street, an unworthy ancestor, nearly a century ago, had fitted up a shop. Ever since the old gentleman retired from trade, and fell asleep under his coffin lid, not only the shop door, but the inner arrangements, had been suffered to remain unchanged; while the dust of ages gathered inch-deep over the shelves and counter, and partly filled an old pair of scales, as if it were of value enough to be weighed. It treasured itself up, too, in the half-open till, where there still lingered a base sixpence, worth neither more nor less than the hereditary pride which had here been put to shame. Such had been the state and condition of the little shop in old Hepzibah's childhood, when she and her brother used to play at hide and seek in its forsaken precincts. So it had remained, until within a few days past.

But now, though the shop window was still closely curtained from the public gaze, a remarkable change had taken place in its interior. The rich and heavy festoons of cobwebs, which it had cost a long ancestral succession of spiders their life's labor to spin and weave, had been carefully brushed away from the ceiling. The counter, shelves, and floor had all been scoured, and the latter was overstrewn with fresh blue sand. The brown scales, too, had evidently undergone rigid discipline, in an unavailing effort to rub off the rust, which, alas! had eaten through and through their substance. Neither was the little old shop any longer empty of merchantable goods. A curious eye, privileged to take an account of stock, and investigate behind the counter, would have discovered a barrel—yea, two or three barrels and half ditto—one containing flour, another apples, and a third, perhaps, Indian meal. There was likewise a square box of pine wood, full of soap in bars; also, another of the same size, in which were tallow candles, ten to the pound. A small stock of brown sugar, some white beans and split peas, and a few other commodities of low price, and such as are constantly in demand, made up the bulkier portion of the merchandise. There was a glass pickle jar, filled with fragments of Gibraltar rock; not, indeed, splinters of the veritable stone foundation of the famous fortress, but bits of delectable candy, neatly done up in white paper. Jim Crow,[4] moreover, was seen executing his world-renowned dance, in gingerbread. A party of leaden dragoons were galloping along one of the shelves, in equipments and uniform of modern cut; and there were some sugar figures, with no strong resemblance to the humanity of any epoch, but less unsatisfactorily representing our own fashions than those of a hundred years ago. Another phenomenon, still more strikingly modern, was a package of lucifer matches, which, in old times, would have been thought actually to borrow their instantaneous flame from the nether fires of Tophet.[5]

In short, to bring the matter at once to a point, it was incontrovertibly evident that somebody had taken the shop and fixtures of the long-retired and forgotten Mr. Pyncheon, and was about to renew the enterprise of that departed worthy, with a different set of customers. Who could this bold adventurer be? And, of all places in the world, why had he chosen the House of the Seven Gables as the scene of his commercial speculations?

We return to the elderly maiden. She at length withdrew her eyes from the dark countenance of the Colonel's portrait, heaved a sigh—indeed, her breast was a very cave of Æolus[6] that morning—and stepped across the room on tiptoe, as is the customary gait of elderly women. Passing through an intervening passage, she opened a door that communicated with the shop, just now so elaborately described. Owing to the projection of the upper

---

[4] JIM CROW—Character in an early American minstrel troupe.
[5] TOPHET—Place of destruction, hell.
[6] CAVE OF ÆOLUS—In classic mythology, the abode of the god of the winds.

story—and still more to the thick shadow of the Pyncheon elm, which stood almost directly in front of the gable—the twilight, here, was still as much akin to night as morning. Another heavy sigh from Miss Hepzibah! After a moment's pause on the threshold, peering toward the window with her nearsighted scowl, as if frowning down some bitter enemy, she suddenly projected herself into the shop. The haste, and, as it were, the galvanic [7] impulse of the movement, were really quite startling.

Nervously—in a sort of frenzy, we might almost say—she began to busy herself in arranging some children's playthings, and other little wares, on the shelves and at the shop window. In the aspect of this dark-arrayed, pale-faced, lady-like old figure there was a deeply tragic character that contrasted irreconcilably with the ludicrous pettiness of her employment. It seemed a queer anomaly, that so gaunt and dismal a personage should take a toy in hand; a miracle, that the toy did not vanish in her grasp; a miserably absurd idea, that she should go on perplexing her stiff and somber intellect with the question how to tempt little boys into her premises. Yet such is undoubtedly her object. Now she places a gingerbread elephant against the window, but with so tremulous a touch that it tumbles upon the floor, with the dismemberment of three legs and its trunk; it has ceased to be an elephant, and has become a few bits of musty gingerbread. There, again, she has upset a tumbler of marbles, all of which roll different ways, and each individual marble, devil-directed, into the most difficult obscurity that it can find. Heaven help our poor old Hepzibah, and forgive us for taking a ludicrous view of her position! As her rigid and rusty frame goes down upon its hands and knees, in quest of the absconding marbles, we positively feel so much the more inclined to shed tears of sympathy, from the very fact that we must needs turn aside and laugh at her. For here—and if we fail to impress it suitably upon the reader, it is our own fault, not that of the theme—here is one of the truest points of melancholy interest that occur in ordinary life. It was the final throe of what called itself old gentility. A lady—who had fed herself from childhood with the shadowy food of aristocratic reminiscences, and whose religion it was that a lady's hand soils itself irremediably by doing aught for bread—this born lady, after

[7] GALVANIC—As caused by electrical shock or stimulus.

sixty years of narrowing means, is fain to step down from her pedestal of imaginary rank. Poverty, treading closely at her heels for a lifetime, has come up with her at last. She must earn her own food, or starve! And we have stolen upon Miss Hepzibah Pyncheon, too irreverently, at the instant of time when the patrician lady is to be transformed into the plebeian woman.

This business of setting up a petty shop is almost the only resource of women, in circumstances at all similar to those of our unfortunate recluse. With her nearsightedness, and those tremulous fingers of hers, at once inflexible and delicate, she could not be a seamstress; although her sampler of fifty years gone by, exhibited some of the most recondite specimens of ornamental needlework. A school for little children had been often in her thoughts; and, at one time, she had begun a review of her early studies in the New England Primer, with a view to prepare herself for the office of instructress. But the love of children had never been quickened in Hepzibah's heart, and was now torpid, if not extinct; she watched the little people of the neighborhood from her chamber window, and doubted whether she could tolerate a more intimate acquaintance with them. Besides, in our day, the very A B C has become a science greatly too abstruse to be any longer taught by pointing a pin from letter to letter. A modern child could teach old Hepzibah more than old Hepzibah could teach the child. So—with many a cold, deep heartquake at the idea of at last coming into sordid contact with the world, from which she had so long kept aloof, while every added day of seclusion had rolled another stone against the cavern door of her hermitage—the poor thing bethought herself of the ancient shop window, the rusty scales, and dusty till. She might have held back a little longer; but another circumstance, not yet hinted at, had somewhat hastened her decision. Her humble preparations, therefore, were duly made, and the enterprise was now to be commenced. Nor was she entitled to complain of any remarkable singularity in her fate; for, in the town of her nativity, we might point to several little shops of a similar description, some of them in houses as ancient as that of the Seven Gables; and one or two, it may be, where a decayed gentlewoman stands behind the counter, as grim an image of family pride as Miss Hepzibah Pyncheon herself.

It was overpoweringly ridiculous—we must honestly confess

it—the deportment of the maiden lady while setting her shop in order for the public eye. She stole on tiptoe to the window, as cautiously as if she conceived some bloody-minded villain to be watching behind the elm tree, with intent to take her life. Stretching out her long, lank arm, she put a paper of pearl buttons, a jew's-harp, or whatever the small article might be, in its destined place, and straightway vanished back into the dusk, as if the world need never hope for another glimpse of her. It might have been fancied, indeed, that she expected to minister to the wants of the community unseen, like a disembodied divinity or enchantress, holding forth her bargains to the reverential and awe-stricken purchaser in an invisible hand. But Hepzibah had no such flattering dream. She was well aware that she must ultimately come forward, and stand revealed in her proper individuality; but, like other sensitive persons, she could not bear to be observed in the gradual process, and chose rather to flash forth on the world's astonished gaze at once.

The inevitable moment was not much longer to be delayed. The sunshine might now be seen stealing down the front of the opposite house, from the windows of which came a reflected gleam, struggling through the boughs of the elm tree, and enlightening the interior of the shop more distinctly than heretofore. The town appeared to be waking up. A baker's cart had already rattled through the street, chasing away the latest vestige of night's sanctity with the jingle-jangle of its dissonant bells.

A milkman was distributing the contents of his cans from door to door; and the harsh peal of a fisherman's conch shell was heard far off, around the corner. None of these tokens escaped Hepzibah's notice. The moment had arrived. To delay longer would be only to lengthen out her misery. Nothing remained, except to take down the bar from the shop door, leaving the entrance free—more than free—welcome, as if all were household friends—to every passer-by, whose eyes might be attracted by the commodities at the window. This last act Hepzibah now performed, letting her bar fall with what smote upon her excited nerves as a most astounding clatter. Then—as if the only barrier betwixt herself and the world had been thrown down, and a flood of evil consequences would come tumbling through the gap—she fled into the inner parlor, threw herself into the ancestral elbow chair, and wept.

III THE FIRST CUSTOMER

Wherein the shop bell announces a customer; Hepzibah's generosity; comments of passers-by; a small urchin makes a purchase; other customers come, and the day proves to be a busy one.

MISS HEPZIBAH PYNCHEON sat in the oaken elbow chair, with her hands over her face, giving way to that heavy down sinking of the heart which most persons have experienced, when she was suddenly startled by the tinkling alarum— high, sharp, and irregular—of a little bell. The maiden lady arose upon her feet, as pale as a ghost at cockcrow; [1] for she was an enslaved spirit, and this the talisman to which she owed obedience. This little bell—to speak in plainer terms—being fastened over the shop door, was so contrived as to vibrate by means of a steel spring, and thus convey notice to the inner regions of the house when any customer should cross the threshold. Its ugly and spiteful little din (heard now for the first time, perhaps, since Hepzibah's periwigged predecessor had retired from trade) at once set every nerve of her body in responsive and tumultuous vibration. The crisis was upon her! Her first customer was at the door!

Without giving herself time for a second thought, she rushed into the shop, pale, wild, desperate in gesture and expression, scowling portentously, and looking far better qualified to do fierce battle with a housebreaker than to stand smiling behind the counter, bartering small wares for a copper recompense. Any ordinary customer, indeed, would have turned his back and fled. And yet there was nothing fierce in Hepzibah's poor old heart; nor had she, at the moment, a single bitter thought against the world at large, or one individual man or woman. She wished them all well, but wished, too, that she herself were done with them, and in her quiet grave.

The applicant, by this time, stood within the doorway. Com-

[1] PALE AS A GHOST AT COCKCROW—It was believed in olden times that ghosts faded away and disappeared at daybreak (cockcrow).

ing freshly, as he did, out of the morning light, he appeared to have brought some of its cheery influences into the shop along with him. It was a slender young man, not more than one or two and twenty years old, with rather a grave and thoughtful expression for his years, but likewise a springy alacrity and vigor. These qualities were not only perceptible, physically, in his make and motions, but made themselves felt almost immediately in his character. A brown beard, not too silken in its texture, fringed his chin, but as yet without completely hiding it; he wore a short mustache, too, and his dark, high-featured countenance looked all the better for these natural ornaments. As for his dress, it was of the simplest kind; a summer sack of cheap and ordinary material, thin checkered pantaloons, and a straw hat, by no means of the finest braid. Oak Hall [2] might have supplied his entire equipment. He was chiefly marked as a gentleman—if such, indeed, he made any claim to be—by the rather remarkable whiteness and nicety of his clean linen.

He met the scowl of old Hepzibah without apparent alarm, as having heretofore encountered it and found it harmless.

"So, my dear Miss Pyncheon," said the daguerreotypist—for it was that sole other occupant of the seven-gabled mansion— "I am glad to see that you have not shrunk from your good purpose. I merely look in to offer my best wishes, and to ask if I can assist you any further in your preparations."

People in difficulty and distress, or in any manner at odds with the world, can endure a vast amount of harsh treatment, and perhaps be only the stronger for it; whereas they give way at once before the simplest expression of what they perceive to be genuine sympathy. So it proved with poor Hepzibah; for, when she saw the young man's smile—looking so much the brighter on a thoughtful face—and heard his kindly tone, she broke first into a hysteric giggle and then began to sob.

"Ah, Mr. Holgrave," cried she, as soon as she could speak, "I never can go through with it! Never, never, never! I wish I were dead, and in the old family tomb, with all my forefathers! With my father, and my mother, and my sister! Yes, and with my brother, who had far better find me there than here! The world is too chill and hard—and I am too old, and too feeble, and too hopeless!"

---

[2] OAK HALL—A department store in Boston.

"Oh, believe me, Miss Hepzibah," said the young man, quietly, "these feelings will not trouble you any longer, after you are once fairly in the midst of your enterprise. They are unavoidable at this moment, standing, as you do, on the outer verge of your long seclusion, and peopling the world with ugly shapes, which you will soon find to be as unreal as the giants and ogres of a child's storybook. I find nothing so singular in life, as that everything appears to lose its substance the instant one actually grapples with it. So it will be with what you think so terrible."

"But I am a woman!" said Hepzibah, piteously. "I was going to say, a lady—but I consider that as past."

"Well; no matter if it be past!" answered the artist, a strange gleam of half-hidden sarcasm flashing through the kindliness of his manner. "Let it go! You are the better without it. I speak frankly, my dear Miss Pyncheon! for are we not friends? I look upon this as one of the fortunate days of your life. It ends an epoch and begins one. Hitherto, the lifeblood has been gradually chilling in your veins as you sat aloof, within your circle of gentility, while the rest of the world was fighting out its battle with one kind of necessity or another. Henceforth, you will at least have the sense of healthy and natural effort for a purpose, and of lending your strength—be it great or small—to the united struggle of mankind. This is success—all the success that anybody meets with!"

"It is natural enough, Mr. Holgrave, that you should have ideas like these," rejoined Hepzibah, drawing up her gaunt figure, with slightly offended dignity. "You are a man, a young man, and brought up, I suppose, as almost everybody is nowadays, with a view to seeking your fortune. But I was born a lady, and have always lived one; no matter in what narrowness of means, always a lady!"

"But I was not born a gentleman; neither have I lived like one," said Holgrave, slightly smiling; "so, my dear madam, you will hardly expect me to sympathize with sensibilities of this kind; though, unless I deceive myself, I have some imperfect comprehension of them. These names of gentleman and lady had a meaning, in the past history of the world, and conferred privileges, desirable or otherwise, on those entitled to bear them. In the present—and still more in the future condition of society —they imply, not privilege, but restriction!"

"These are new notions," said the old gentlewoman, shaking her head. "I shall never understand them; neither do I wish it."

"We will cease to speak of them, then," replied the artist, with a friendlier smile than his last one, "and I will leave you to feel whether it is not better to be a true woman than a lady. Do you really think, Miss Hepzibah, that any lady of your family has ever done a more heroic thing, since this house was built, than you are performing in it to-day? Never; and if the Pyncheons had always acted so nobly, I doubt whether an old wizard Maule's anathema, of which you told me once, would have had much weight, with Providence against them."

"Ah!—no, no!" said Hepzibah, not displeased at this allusion to the somber dignity of an inherited curse. "If old Maule's ghost, or a descendant of his, could see me behind the counter to-day, he would call it the fulfillment of his worst wishes. But I thank you for your kindness, Mr. Holgrave, and will do my utmost to be a good shopkeeper."

"Pray do," said Holgrave, "and let me have the pleasure of being your first customer. I am about taking a walk to the seashore, before going to my rooms, where I misuse Heaven's blessed sunshine by tracing out human features through its agency. A few of those biscuits, dipped in seawater, will be just what I need for breakfast. What is the price of half a dozen?"

"Let me be a lady a moment longer," replied Hepzibah, with a manner of antique stateliness to which a melancholy smile lent a kind of grace. She put the biscuits into his hand, but rejected the compensation. "A Pyncheon must not, at all events under her forefathers' roof, receive money for a morsel of bread from her only friend!"

Holgrave took his departure, leaving her, for the moment, with spirits not quite so much depressed. Soon, however, they had subsided nearly to their former dead level. With a beating heart, she listened to the footsteps of early passers-by, which now began to be frequent along the street. Once or twice they seemed to linger; these strangers, or neighbors, as the case might be, were looking at the display of toys and petty commodities in Hepzibah's shop window. She was doubly tortured; in part, with a sense of overwhelming shame that strange and unloving eyes should have the privilege of gazing, and partly because the idea occurred to her, with ridiculous importunity, that the window was not arranged so skillfully, nor nearly to so much advantage, as it might have been. It seemed as if the whole fortune or failure of her shop might depend on the display of a different set of articles, or substituting a fairer apple for one which appeared to be specked. So she made the change, and straightway fancied that everything was spoiled by it; not recognizing that it was the nervousness of the juncture, and her own native squeamishness as an old maid, that wrought all the seeming mischief.

Anon, there was an encounter, just at the doorstep, betwixt two laboring men, as their rough voices denoted them to be. After some slight talk about their own affairs, one of them chanced to notice the shop window, and directed the other's attention to it.

"See here!" cried he; "what do you think of this? Trade seems to be looking up in Pyncheon Street!"

"Well, well, this is a sight, to be sure!" exclaimed the other. "In the old Pyncheon house, and underneath the Pyncheon elm! Who would have thought it? Old Maid Pyncheon is setting up a cent shop!"

"Will she make it go, think you, Dixey?" said his friend. "I don't call it a very good stand. There's another shop just around the corner."

"Make it go!" cried Dixey, with a most contemptuous expression, as if the very idea were impossible to be conceived. "Not a bit of it! Why, her face—I've seen it, for I dug her garden for her one year—her face is enough to frighten the Old Nick himself, if he had ever so great a mind to trade with her. People can't stand it, I tell you! She scowls dreadfully, reason or none, out of pure ugliness of temper!"

"Well, that's not so much matter," remarked the other man. "These sour-tempered folks are mostly handy at business, and know pretty well what they are about. But, as you say, I don't think she'll do much. This business of keeping cent shops is overdone, like all other kinds of trade, handicraft, and bodily labor. I know it, to my cost! My wife kept a cent shop three months, and lost five dollars on her outlay!"

"Poor business!" responded Dixey, in a tone as if he were shaking his head, "poor business!"

For some reason or other, not very easy to analyze, there had hardly been so bitter a pang in all her previous misery about the matter as what thrilled Hepzibah's heart, on overhearing the above conversation. The testimony in regard to her scowl was frightfully important; it seemed to hold up her image wholly relieved from the false light of her self-partialities, and so hideous that she dared not look at it. She was absurdly hurt, moreover, by the slight and idle effect that her setting up shop—an event of such breathless interest to herself—appeared to have upon the public, of which these two men were the nearest representatives. A glance; a passing word or two; a coarse laugh; and she was doubtless forgotten before they turned the corner! They cared nothing for her dignity, and just as little for her degradation. Then, also, the augury of ill success, uttered from the sure wisdom of experience, fell upon her half-dead hope like a clod into a grave. The man's wife had already tried the same experiment, and failed! How could the born lady—the recluse of half a lifetime, utterly unpracticed in the world, at sixty years of age—how could she ever dream of succeeding, when the hard, vulgar, keen, busy, hackneyed New England woman had lost five dollars on her little outlay! Success presented itself as an impossibility, and the hope of it as a wild hallucination.

But, at this instant, the shop bell, right over her head, tinkled as if it were bewitched. The old gentlewoman's heart seemed to be attached to the same steel spring, for it went through a series of sharp jerks, in unison with the sound. The door was thrust open, although no human form was perceptible on the other side of the half window. Hepzibah, nevertheless, stood at a gaze, with her hands clasped, looking very much as if she had summoned up an evil spirit, and were afraid, yet resolved, to hazard the encounter.

"Heaven help me!" she groaned, mentally. "Now is my hour of need!"

The door, which moved with difficulty on its creaking and rusty hinges, being forced quite open, a square and sturdy little urchin became apparent, with cheeks as red as an apple. He was clad rather shabbily (but, as it seemed, more owing to his mother's carelessness than his father's poverty), in a blue apron, very wide and short trousers, shoes somewhat out at the toes, and a ship hat, with the frizzles of his curly hair sticking through its crevices. A book and a small slate, under his arm, indicated that he was on his way to school. He stared at Hepzibah a moment, as an elder customer than himself would have been likely enough to do, not knowing what to make of the tragic attitude and queer scowl wherewith she regarded him.

"Well, child," said she, taking heart at sight of a personage so little formidable, "well, my child, what did you wish for?"

"That Jim Crow there in the window," answered the urchin, holding out a cent, and pointing to the gingerbread figure that had attracted his notice, as he loitered along to school; "the one that has not a broken foot."

So Hepzibah put forth her lank arm, and, taking the effigy from the shop window, delivered it to her first customer.

"No matter for the money," said she, giving him a little push toward the door; for her old gentility was contumaciously squeamish at sight of the copper coin, and, besides, it seemed such pitiful meanness to take the child's pocket money in exchange for a bit of stale gingerbread. "No matter for the cent. You are welcome to Jim Crow."

The child, staring with round eyes at this instance of liberality, wholly unprecedented in his large experience of cent shops, took the man of gingerbread, and quitted the premises. No sooner had he reached the sidewalk (little cannibal that he was!) than Jim Crow's head was in his mouth. As he had not been careful to shut the door, Hepzibah was at the pains of closing it after him, with a pettish ejaculation or two about the troublesomeness of young people, and particularly of small boys. She had just placed another representative of the renowned Jim Crow at the window, when again the shop bell tinkled clamorously, and again the door being thrust open, with its characteristic jerk and jar, disclosed the same sturdy little urchin who, precisely two minutes ago, had made his exit. The crumbs and discoloration of the cannibal feast, as yet hardly consummated, were exceedingly visible about his mouth.

"What is it now, child?" asked the maiden lady, rather impatiently; "did you come back to shut the door?"

"No," answered the urchin, pointing to the figure that had just been put up; "I want that other Jim Crow."

"Well, here it is for you," said Hepzibah, reaching it down; but recognizing that this pertinacious customer would not quit her on any other terms, so long as she had a gingerbread figure in her shop, she partly drew back her extended hand, "Where is the cent?"

The little boy had the cent ready, but, like a true-born Yankee, would have preferred the better bargain to the worse. Looking somewhat chagrined, he put the coin into Hepzibah's hand, and departed, sending the second Jim Crow in quest of the former one. The new shopkeeper dropped the first solid result of her commercial enterprise into the till. It was done! The sordid stain of that copper coin could never be washed away from her palm. The little schoolboy, aided by the impish figure of the negro dancer, had wrought an irreparable ruin. The structure of ancient aristocracy had been demolished by him, even as if his childish gripe had torn down the seven-gabled mansion. Now let Hepzibah turn the old Pyncheon portraits with their faces to the wall, and take the map of her eastern territory to kindle the kitchen fire, and blow up the flame with the empty breath of her ancestral traditions! What had she to do with ancestry? Nothing; no more than with posterity! No lady, now, but simply Hepzibah Pyncheon, a forlorn old maid, and keeper of a cent shop!

Nevertheless, even while she paraded these ideas somewhat ostentatiously through her mind, it is altogether surprising what a calmness had come over her. The anxiety and misgivings which had tormented her, whether asleep or in melancholy day-dreams, ever since her project began to take an aspect of solidity, had now vanished quite away.

Her introductory day of shopkeeping did not run on, however, without many and serious interruptions of this mood of cheerful vigor. As a general rule, Providence seldom vouchsafes to mortals any more than just that degree of encouragement which suffices to keep them at a reasonably full exertion of their powers. In the case of our old gentlewoman, after the excitement of new effort had subsided, the despondency of her whole life threatened, ever and anon, to return. It was like the heavy mass of clouds which we may often see obscuring the sky, and making a gray twilight everywhere, until, toward nightfall, it yields temporarily to a glimpse of sunshine. But always, the envious cloud strives to gather again across the streak of celestial azure.

Customers came in, as the forenoon advanced, but rather

slowly; in some cases, too, it must be owned, with little satisfaction either to themselves or Miss Hepzibah; nor, on the whole, with an aggregate of very rich emolument to the till. A little girl, sent by her mother to match a skein of cotton thread, of a peculiar hue, took one that the nearsighted old lady pronounced extremely like, but soon came running back, with a blunt and cross message, that it would not do, and, besides, was very rotten! Then, there was a pale, care-wrinkled woman, not old but haggard, and already with streaks of gray among her hair, like silver ribbons; one of those women, naturally delicate, whom you at once recognize as worn to death by a brute—probably a drunken brute—of a husband, and at least nine children. She wanted a few pounds of flour, and offered the money, which the decayed gentlewoman silently rejected, and gave the poor soul better measure than if she had taken it. Shortly afterwards, a man in a blue cotton frock, much soiled, came in and bought a pipe, filling the whole shop, meanwhile, with the hot odor of strong drink, not only exhaled in the torrid atmosphere of his breath, but oozing out of his entire system, like an inflammable gas. It was impressed on Hepzibah's mind that this was the husband of the care-wrinkled woman. He asked for a paper of tobacco; and as she had neglected to provide herself with the article, her brutal customer dashed down his newly bought pipe and left the shop, muttering some unintelligible words, which had the tone and bitterness of a curse. Hereupon Hepzibah threw up her eyes, unintentionally scowling in the face of Providence!

No less than five persons, during the forenoon, inquired for ginger beer, or root beer, or any drink of a similar brewage, and, obtaining nothing of the kind, went off in an exceedingly bad humor. Three of them left the door open, and the other two pulled it so spitefully in going out that the little bell played the very deuce with Hepzibah's nerves. A round, bustling, fire-ruddy housewife of the neighborhood burst breathless into the shop, fiercely demanding yeast; and when the poor gentlewoman, with her cold shyness of manner, gave her hot customer to understand that she did not keep the article, this very capable housewife took upon herself to administer a regular rebuke.

"A cent shop, and no yeast!" quoth she, "that will never do! Who ever heard of such a thing? Your loaf will never rise, no more than mine to-day. You had better shut up shop at once."

"Well," said Hepzibah, heaving a deep sigh, "perhaps I had!"

Several times, moreover, besides the above instance, her lady-like sensibilities were seriously infringed upon by the familiar, if not rude, tone with which people addressed her. They evidently considered themselves not merely her equals, but her patrons and superiors. Now, Hepzibah had unconsciously flattered herself with the idea that there would be a gleam or halo, of some kind or other, about her person, which would insure an obeisance to her sterling gentility, or, at least, a tacit recognition of it. On the other hand, nothing tortured her more intolerably than when this recognition was too prominently expressed. To one or two rather officious offers of sympathy, her responses were little short of acrimonious; and, we regret to say, Hepzibah was thrown into a positively unchristian state of mind by the suspicion that one of her customers was drawn to the shop, not by any real need of the article which she pretended to seek, but by a wicked wish to stare at her. The vulgar creature was determined to see for herself what sort of a figure a mildewed piece of aristocracy, after wasting all the bloom and much of the decline of her life apart from the world, would cut behind a counter. In this particular case, however mechanical and innocuous it might be at other times, Hepzibah's contortion of brow served her in good stead.

"I never was so frightened in my life!" said the curious customer, in describing the incident to one of her acquaintances. "She's a real old vixen, take my word of it! She says little, to be sure; but if you could only see the mischief in her eyes!"

On the whole, therefore, her new experience led our decayed gentlewoman to very disagreeable conclusions as to the temper and manners of what she termed the lower classes, whom heretofore she had looked down upon with a gentle and pitying complaisance, as herself occupying a sphere of unquestionable superiority. But, unfortunately, she had likewise to struggle against a bitter emotion of a directly opposite kind: a sentiment of virulence, we mean, toward the idle aristocracy to which it had so recently been her pride to belong. When a lady, in a delicate and costly summer garb, with a floating veil and gracefully swaying gown, and, altogether, an ethereal lightness that made you look at her beautifully slippered feet, to see whether she trod on the dust or floated in the air—when such a vision happened to pass through this retired street, leaving it tenderly and delusively fragrant with her passage, as if a bouquet of tea roses had been borne along—then again, it is to be feared, old Hepzibah's scowl could no longer vindicate itself entirely on the plea of nearsightedness.

"For what end," thought she, giving vent to that feeling of hostility which is the only real abasement of the poor in presence of the rich—"for what good end, in the wisdom of Providence, does that woman live? Must the whole world toil, that the palms of her hands may be kept white and delicate?"

Then, ashamed and penitent, she hid her face.

"May God forgive me!" said she.

Doubtless, God did forgive her. But, taking the inward and outward history of the first half day into consideration, Hepzibah began to fear that the shop would prove her ruin in a moral and religious point of view, without contributing very essentially toward even her temporal welfare.

IV   A DAY BEHIND THE COUNTER

Wherein a portly, opulent gentleman with a gold-headed cane scrutinously inspects the House of Seven Gables and its elm; his countenance portrays now an acrid frown and now a benevolent smile; Cousin Jaffrey—how like the ancestral Pyncheon of old!— how unlike the original of Hepzibah's miniature! Uncle Venner, the patriarch and philosopher makes a call; he gives Hepzibah good advice, and asks a pertinent question. A very busy afternoon with customers nets the proprietor of the cent shop small returns. Little Phœbe comes.

TOWARD NOON, Hepzibah saw an elderly gentleman, large and portly, and of remarkably dignified demeanor, passing slowly along on the opposite side of the white and dusty street. On coming within the shadow of the Pyncheon elm, he stopped, and (taking off his hat, meanwhile, to wipe the perspiration from his brow) seemed to scrutinize, with especial interest, the dilapidated and rusty-visaged House of the Seven Gables. He himself, in a very different style, was as well worth looking at as the house. No better model need be sought, nor could have been found, of a very high order of respectability, which, by some indescribable magic, not merely expressed itself in his looks and gestures, but even governed the fashion of his garments, and rendered them all proper and essential to the man. Without appearing to differ, in any tangible way, from other people's clothes, there was yet a wide and rich gravity about them that must have been a characteristic of the wearer, since it could not be defined as pertaining either to the cut or material. His gold-headed cane, too—a serviceable staff, of dark polished wood—had similar traits, and, had it chosen to take a walk by itself, would have been recognized anywhere as a tolerably adequate representative of its master. This character—which showed itself so strikingly in everything about him, and the effect of which we seek to convey to the reader—went no deeper than his station, habits of life, and external circumstances. One perceived him to be a personage of marked influence and authority; and, especially, you could feel just as certain that he was opulent as if he had exhibited his bank account, or as if you had seen him touching the twigs of the Pyncheon elm, and, Midas-like,[1] transmuting them to gold.

In his youth, he had probably been considered a handsome man; at his present age, his brow was too heavy, his temples too bare, his remaining hair too gray, his eye too cold, his lips too closely compressed, to bear any relation to mere personal beauty. He would have made a good and massive portrait; better now, perhaps, than at any previous period of his life, although his look might grow positively harsh in the process of

[1] MIDAS—A legendary king whose touch transmuted everything into gold.

being fixed upon the canvas. The artist would have found it desirable to study his face, and prove its capacity for varied expression; to darken it with a frown—to kindle it up with a smile.

While the elderly gentleman stood looking at the Pyncheon house, both the frown and the smile passed successively over his countenance. His eye rested on the shop window, and putting up a pair of gold-bowed spectacles, which he held in his hand, he minutely surveyed Hepzibah's little arrangement of toys and commodities. At first it seemed not to please him—nay, to cause him exceeding displeasure—and yet, the very next moment, he smiled. While the latter expression was yet on his lips, he caught a glimpse of Hepzibah, who had involuntarily bent forward to the window; and then the smile changed from acrid and disagreeable to the sunniest complacency and benevolence. He bowed, with a happy mixture of dignity and courteous kindliness, and pursued his way.

"There he is!" said Hepzibah to herself, gulping down a very bitter emotion, and, since she could not rid herself of it, trying to drive it back into her heart. "What does he think of it, I wonder? Does it please him? Ah! he is looking back!"

The gentleman had paused in the street, and turned himself half about, still with his eyes fixed on the shop window. In fact, he wheeled wholly round, and commenced a step or two, as if designing to enter the shop; but, as it chanced, his purpose was anticipated by Hepzibah's first customer, the little cannibal of Jim Crow, who, staring up at the window, was irresistibly attracted by an elephant of gingerbread. What a grand appetite had this small urchin!—two Jim Crows immediately after breakfast!—and now an elephant, as a preliminary whet before dinner! By the time this latter purchase was completed, the elderly gentleman had resumed his way, and turned the street corner.

"Take it as you like, Cousin Jaffrey!" muttered the maiden lady, as she drew back, after cautiously thrusting out her head, and looking up and down the street—"take it as you like! You have seen my little shop window! Well!—what have you to say?—is not the Pyncheon house my own, while I'm alive?"

After this incident, Hepzibah retreated to the back parlor, where she at first caught up a half-finished stocking, and began knitting at it with nervous and irregular jerks; but quickly finding herself at odds with the stitches, she threw it aside, and walked hurriedly about the room. At length, she paused before the portrait of the stern old Puritan, her ancestor, and the founder of the house. In one sense, this picture had almost faded into the canvas, and hidden itself behind the duskiness of age; in another, she could not but fancy that it had been growing more prominent, and strikingly expressive, ever since her earliest familiarity with it as a child. For, while the physical outline and substance were darkening away from the beholder's eye, the bold, hard, and, at the same time, indirect character of the man seemed to be brought out in a kind of spiritual relief. Such an effect may occasionally be observed in pictures of antique date.

While gazing at the portrait, Hepzibah trembled under its eye. Her hereditary reverence made her afraid to judge the character of the original so harshly as a perception of the truth compelled her to do. But still she gazed, because the face of the picture enabled her—at least, she fancied so—to read more accurately, and to a greater depth, the face which she had just seen in the street.

"This is the very man!" murmured she to herself. "Let Jaffrey Pyncheon smile as he will, there is that look beneath! Put on him a skullcap, and a band, and a black cloak, and a Bible in one hand and a sword in the other—then let Jaffrey smile as he might—nobody would doubt that it was the old Pyncheon come again! He has proved himself the very man to build up a new house! Perhaps, too, to draw down a new curse!"

Thus did Hepzibah bewilder herself with these fantasies of the old time. She had dwelt too much alone—too long in the Pyncheon house—until her very brain was impregnated with the dry-rot of its timbers. She needed a walk along the noonday street to keep her sane.

By the spell of contrast, another portrait rose up before her, painted with more daring flattery than any artist would have ventured upon, but yet so delicately touched that the likeness remained perfect. Malbone's miniature, though from the same original, was far inferior to Hepzibah's air-drawn picture, at which affection and sorrowful remembrance wrought together. Soft, mildly, and cheerfully contemplative, with full, red lips, just on the verge of a smile, which the eyes seemed to herald by a gentle kindling up of their orbs! Feminine traits, molded inseparably with those of the other sex! The miniature, likewise, had this last peculiarity; so that you inevitably thought of the original as resembling his mother, and she a lovely and lovable woman, with perhaps some beautiful infirmity of character, that made it all the pleasanter to know and easier to love her.

"Yes," thought Hepzibah, with grief of which it was only the more tolerable portion that welled up from her heart to her eyelids, "they persecuted his mother in him! He never was a Pyncheon!"

But here the shop bell rang; it was like a sound from a remote distance—so far had Hepzibah descended into the sepulchral depths of her reminiscences. On entering the shop, she found an old man there, a humble resident of Pyncheon Street, and whom, for a great many years past, she had suffered to be a kind of familiar of the house. He was an immemorial personage, who seemed always to have had a white head and wrinkles, and never to have possessed but a single tooth, and that a half-decayed one, in the front of the upper jaw. Well advanced as Hepzibah was, she could not remember when Uncle Venner, as the neighborhood called him, had not gone up and down the street, stooping a little and drawing his feet heavily over the gravel or pavement. But still there was something tough and vigorous about him, that not only kept him in daily breath, but enabled him to fill a place which would else have been vacant in the apparently crowded world. To go of errands with his slow and shuffling gait, which made you doubt how he ever was to arrive anywhere; to saw a small household's foot or two of firewood, or knock to pieces an old barrel, or split up a pine board for kindling stuff; in summer, to dig a few yards of garden ground appertaining to a low-rented tenement, and share the produce of his labor at the halves; in winter, to shovel away the snow from the sidewalk, or open paths to the woodshed, or along the clothesline; such were some of the essential offices which Uncle Venner performed among at least a score of families. Within that circle, he claimed the same sort of privilege, and probably felt as much warmth of interest, as a clergyman does in the range of his parishioners. Not that he laid claim to the tithe pig; [2] but, as an analogous mode of reverence, he went his rounds, every morning, to gather up the crumbs of the table and

---

[2] TITHE PIG—A symbol of the Mosaic requirement that one-tenth of one's income or possessions be devoted to the maintenance of religion.

overflowings of the dinner pot, as food for a pig of his own.

In his younger days—for, after all, there was a dim tradition that he had been, not young, but younger—Uncle Venner was commonly regarded as rather deficient, than otherwise, in his wits. In truth, he had virtually pleaded guilty to the charge, by scarcely aiming at such success as other men seek, and by taking only that humble and modest part in the intercourse of life which belongs to the alleged deficiency. But now, in his extreme old age—whether it were that his long and hard experience had actually brightened him, or that his decaying judgment rendered him less capable of fairly measuring himself—the venerable man made pretensions to no little wisdom, and really enjoyed the credit of it. There was likewise, at times, a vein of something like poetry in him; it was the moss or wallflower of his mind in its small dilapidation, and gave a charm to what might have been vulgar and commonplace in his earlier and middle life. Hepzibah had a regard for him, because his name was ancient in the town and had formerly been respectable. It was a still better reason for awarding him a species of familiar reverence that Uncle Venner was himself the most ancient existence, whether of man or thing, in Pyncheon Street, except the House of the Seven Gables, and perhaps the elm that overshadowed it.

This patriarch now presented himself before Hepzibah, clad in an old blue coat, which had a fashionable air, and must have accrued to him from the cast-off wardrobe of some dashing clerk. As for his trousers, they were of tow cloth, very short in the legs, and bagging down strangely in the rear, but yet having a suitableness to his figure which his other garment entirely lacked. His hat had relation to no other part of his dress, and but very little to the head that wore it. Thus Uncle Venner was a miscellaneous old gentleman, partly himself, but, in good measure, somebody else; patched together, too, of different epochs; an epitome of times and fashions.

"So, you have really begun trade!" said he, "really begun trade! Well, I'm glad to see it. Young people should never live idle in the world, nor old ones neither, unless when the rheumatism gets hold of them. It has given me warning already; and in two or three years longer, I shall think of putting aside business and retiring to my farm. That's yonder—the great brick house, you know—the workhouse, most folks call it; but I mean to do my work first, and go there to be idle and enjoy myself. And I'm glad to see you beginning to do your work, Miss Hepzibah!"

"Thank you, Uncle Venner," said Hepzibah, smiling; for she always felt kindly toward the simple and talkative old man. Had he been an old woman, she might probably have repelled the freedom, which she now took in good part. "It is time for me to begin work, indeed! Or, to speak the truth, I have just begun when I ought to be giving it up."

"Oh, never say that, Miss Hepzibah!" answered the old man. "You are a young woman yet. Why, I hardly thought myself younger than I am now, it seems so little while ago since I used to see you playing about the door of the old house, quite a small child! Oftener, though, you used to be sitting at the threshold, and looking gravely into the street; for you had always a grave kind of way with you—a grown-up air—when you were only the height of my knee. It seems as if I saw you now: and your grandfather, with his red cloak, and his white wig, and his cocked hat, and his cane, coming out of the house, and stepping so grandly up the street! Those old gentlemen that grew up before the Revolution used to put on grand airs. In my young days, the great man of the town was commonly called King; and his wife, not Queen, to be sure, but Lady. Nowadays, a man would not dare to be called King; and if he feels himself a little above common folks, he only stoops so much the lower to them. I met your cousin, the Judge, ten minutes ago; and, in my old tow-cloth trousers, as you see, the Judge raised his hat to me, I do believe! At any rate, the Judge bowed and smiled!"

"Yes," said Hepzibah, with something bitter stealing unawares into her tone; "my cousin Jaffrey is thought to have a very pleasant smile!"

"And so he has!" replied Uncle Venner. "And that's rather remarkable in a Pyncheon; for, begging your pardon, Miss Hepzibah, they never had the name of being an easy and agreeable set of folks. There was no getting close to them. But now, Miss Hepzibah, if an old man may be bold to ask, why don't Judge Pyncheon, with his great means, step forward, and tell his cousin to shut up her little shop at once? It's for your credit to be doing something, but it's not for the Judge's credit to let you!"

"We won't talk of this, if you please, Uncle Venner," said

Hepzibah, coldly. "I ought to say, however, that, if I choose to earn bread for myself, it is not Judge Pyncheon's fault. Neither will he deserve the blame," added she, more kindly, remembering Uncle Venner's privileges of age and humble familiarity, "if I should, by and by, find it convenient to retire with you to your farm."

"And it's no bad place, either, that farm of mine!" cried the old man, cheerily, as if there were something positively delightful in the prospect. "No bad place is the great brick farmhouse, especially for them that will find a good many old cronies there, as will be my case. I quite long to be among them, sometimes, of the winter evenings; for it is but dull business for a lonesome elderly man, like me, to be nodding, by the hour together, with no company but his air-tight stove. Summer or winter, there's a great deal to be said in favor of my farm! And, take it in the autumn, what can be pleasanter than to spend a whole day on the sunny side of a barn or a woodpile, chatting with somebody as old as one's self; or, perhaps, idling away the time with a natural-born simpleton, who knows how to be idle, because even our busy Yankees never have found out how to put him to any use? Upon my word, Miss Hepzibah, I doubt whether I've ever been so comfortable as I mean to be at my farm, which most folks call the workhouse. But you—you're a young woman yet —you never need go there! Something still better will turn up for you. I'm sure of it!"

Hepzibah fancied that there was something peculiar in her venerable friend's look and tone; insomuch, that she gazed into his face with considerable earnestness, endeavoring to discover what secret meaning, if any, might be lurking there. Individuals whose affairs have reached an utterly desperate crisis almost invariably keep themselves alive with hopes, so much the more airily magnificent as they have the less of solid matter within their grasp whereof to mold any judicious and moderate expectation of good. Thus, all the while Hepzibah was perfecting the scheme of her little shop, she had cherished an unacknowledged idea that some harlequin trick of fortune would intervene in her favor. For example, an uncle—who had sailed for India fifty years before, and never been heard of since— might yet return, and adopt her to be the comfort of his very extreme and decrepit age, and adorn her with pearls, diamonds,

and Oriental shawls and turbans, and make her the ultimate
heiress of his unreckonable riches. Or the member of Parliament, now at the head of the English branch of the family—
with which the elder stock, on this side of the Atlantic, had held
little or no intercourse for the last two centuries—this eminent
gentleman might invite Hepzibah to quit the ruinous House of
the Seven Gables, and come over to dwell with her kindred at
Pyncheon Hall. But, for reasons the most imperative, she
could not yield to his request. It was more probable, therefore,
that the descendant of a Pyncheon who had emigrated to Virginia, in some past generation, and become a great planter there
—hearing of Hepzibah's destitution, and impelled by the splendid generosity of character with which their Virginian mixture
must have enriched the New England blood—would send her
a remittance of a thousand dollars, with a hint of repeating the
favor annually. Or—and, surely, anything so undeniably just
could not be beyond the limits of reasonable anticipation—the
great claim to the heritage of Waldo County might finally be
decided in favor of the Pyncheons; so that instead of keeping a
cent shop, Hepzibah would build a palace, and look down from
its highest tower on hill, dale, forest, field, and town, as her own
share of the ancestral territory.

These were some of the fantasies which she had long dreamed
about; and, aided by these, Uncle Venner's casual attempt at
encouragement kindled a strange festal glory in the poor, bare,
melancholy chambers of her brain, as if that inner world were
suddenly lighted up with gas. But either he knew nothing of her
castles in the air—as how should he?—or else her earnest scowl
disturbed his recollection, as it might a more courageous man's.
Instead of pursuing any weightier topic, Uncle Venner was
pleased to favor Hepzibah with some sage counsel in her shopkeeping capacity.

"Give no credit!"—these were some of his golden maxims—
"never take paper money! Look well to your change! Ring the
silver on the four-pound weight! Shove back all English half-
pence and base copper tokens, such as are very plenty about
town! At your leisure hours, knit children's woolen socks and
mittens! Brew your own yeast, and make your own ginger
beer!"

And while Hepzibah was doing her utmost to digest the hard

"Give no credit. Ring the silver on the four-pound weight!"

little pellets of his already uttered wisdom, he gave vent to his final, and what he declared to be his all-important advice, as follows:

"Put on a bright face for your customers, and smile pleasantly as you hand them what they ask for! A stale article, if you dip it in a good, warm, sunny smile, will go off better than a fresh one that you've scowled upon."

To this last apothegm, poor Hepzibah responded with a sigh so deep and heavy that it almost rustled Uncle Venner quite away, like a withered leaf—as he was—before an autumnal gale. Recovering himself, however, he bent forward, and, with a good deal of feeling in his ancient visage, beckoned her nearer to him.

"When do you expect him home?" whispered he.

"Whom do you mean?" asked Hepzibah, turning pale.

"Ah? you don't love to talk about it," said Uncle Venner. "Well, well! we'll say no more, though there's word of it all over town. I remember him, Miss Hepzibah, before he could run alone!"

During the remainder of the day poor Hepzibah acquitted herself even less creditably, as a shopkeeper, than in her earlier efforts. She appeared to be walking in a dream; or, more truly, the vivid life and reality assumed by her emotions made all outward occurrences unsubstantial, like the teasing phantasms of a half-conscious slumber. She still responded, mechanically, to the frequent summons of the shop bell, and, at the demand of her customers, when prying with vague eyes about the shop, proffering them one article after another, and thrusting aside— perversely, as most of them supposed—the identical thing they asked for. As the animosity of fate would have it, there was a great influx of custom in the course of the afternoon. Hepzibah blundered to and fro about her small place of business, committing the most unheard-of errors: now stringing up twelve, and now seven, tallow candles, instead of ten to the pound; selling ginger for Scotch snuff, pins for needles, and needles for pins; misreckoning her change, sometimes to the public detriment, and much oftener to her own; and thus she went on, doing her utmost to bring chaos back again, until, at the close of the day's labor, to her inexplicable astonishment, she found the money drawer almost destitute of coin. After all her painful traffic, the whole proceeds were perhaps half a dozen coppers, and a questionable ninepence which ultimately proved to be copper like-wise.

At this price, or at whatever price, she rejoiced that the day had reached its end. Never before had she had such a sense of the intolerable length of time that creeps between dawn and sunset, and of the miserable irksomeness of having aught to do, and of the better wisdom that it would be to lie down at once, in sullen resignation, and let life, and its toils and vexations, trample over one's prostrate body as they may! Hepzibah's final operation was with the little devourer of Jim Crow and the elephant, who now proposed to eat a camel. In her bewilder-ment, she offered him first a wooden dragoon, and next a handful of marbles; neither of which being adapted to his else omnivo-rous appetite, she hastily held out her whole remaining stock of natural history in gingerbread, and huddled the small cus-tomer out of the shop. She then muffled the bell in an unfinished stocking, and put up the oaken bar across the door.

During the latter process, an omnibus came to a standstill under the branches of the elm tree. Hepzibah's heart was in her mouth. Remote and dusky, and with no sunshine on all the intervening space, was that region of the Past whence her only guest might be expected to arrive! Was she to meet him now?

Somebody, at all events, was passing from the farthest interior of the omnibus toward its entrance. A gentleman alighted; but it was only to offer his hand to a young girl whose slender figure, nowise needing such assistance, now lightly descended the steps, and made an airy little jump from the final one to the sidewalk. She rewarded her cavalier with a smile, the cheery glow of which was seen reflected on his own face as he reëntered the vehicle. The girl then turned toward the House of the Seven Gables, to the door of which, meanwhile—not the shop door, but the an-tique portal—the omnibus man had carried a light trunk and a bandbox. First giving a sharp rap of the old iron knocker, he left his passenger and her luggage at the doorstep, and departed.

"Who can it be?" thought Hepzibah, who had been screwing her visual organs into the acutest focus of which they were capable. "The girl must have mistaken the house!"

She stole softly into the hall, and, herself invisible, gazed through the dusty side lights of the portal at the young, bloom-ing, and very cheerful face, which presented itself for admittance into the gloomy old mansion. It was a face to which almost any door would have opened of its own accord.

The young girl, so fresh, so unconventional, and yet so orderly and obedient to common rules, as you at once recognized her to be, was widely in contrast, at that moment, with everything about her. The sordid and ugly luxuriance of gigantic weeds that grew in the angle of the house, and the heavy projection that overshadowed her, and the time-worn framework of the door—none of these things belonged to her sphere. But, even as a ray of sunshine, fall into what dismal place it may, instantaneously creates for itself a propriety in being there, so did it seem altogether fit that the girl should be standing at the threshold. It was no less evidently proper that the door should swing open to admit her. The maiden lady, herself, sternly inhospitable in her first purposes, soon began to feel that the door ought to be shoved back, and the rusty key be turned in the reluctant lock.

"Can it be Phœbe?" questioned she within herself. "It must be little Phœbe; for it can be nobody else—and there is a look of her father about her, too! But what does she want here? And how like a country cousin, to come down upon a poor body in this way, without so much as a day's notice, or asking whether she would be welcome! Well, she must have a night's lodging, I suppose; and to-morrow the child shall go back to her mother!"

Phœbe, it must be understood, was that one little offshoot of the Pyncheon race to whom we have already referred, as a native of a rural part of New England, where the old fashions and feelings of relationship are still partially kept up. In her own circle, it was regarded as by no means improper for kinsfolk to visit one another without invitation, or preliminary and ceremonious warning. Yet, in consideration of Miss Hepzibah's recluse way of life, a letter had actually been written and dispatched, conveying information of Phœbe's projected visit. This epistle, for three or four days past, had been in the pocket of the penny postman, who, happening to have no other business in Pyncheon Street, had not yet made it convenient to call at the House of the Seven Gables.

"No!—she can stay only one night," said Hepzibah, unbolting the door. "If Clifford were to find her here, it might disturb him!"

PHŒBE PYNCHEON slept, on the night of her arrival, in a chamber that looked down on the garden of the old house. It fronted toward the east, so that at a very seasonable hour a glow of crimson light came flooding through the window, and bathed the dingy ceiling and paper hangings in its own hue. There were curtains to Phœbe's bed; a dark, antique canopy, and ponderous festoons of a stuff which had been rich, and even magnificent, in its time; but which now brooded over the girl like a cloud, making a night in that one corner, while elsewhere it was beginning to be day. The morning light, however, soon stole into the aperture at the foot of the bed, betwixt those faded curtains. Finding the new guest there—with a bloom on her cheeks like the morning's own, and a gentle stir of departing slumber in her limbs, as when an early breeze moves the foliage —the dawn kissed her brow.

At the touch of those lips of light, Phœbe quietly awoke, and, for a moment, did not recognize where she was, nor how those heavy curtains chanced to be festooned around her. Nothing, indeed, was absolutely plain to her, except that it was now early morning, and that, whatever might happen next, it was proper, first of all, to get up and say her prayers. She was the more inclined to devotion from the grim aspect of the chamber and its furniture, especially the tall, stiff chairs; one of which stood close by her bedside, and looked as if some old-fashioned personage had been sitting there all night, and had vanished only just in season to escape discovery.

When Phœbe was quite dressed, she peeped out of the window, and saw a rosebush in the garden. Being a very tall one, and of luxuriant growth, it had been propped up against the side of the house, and was literally covered with a rare and very beautiful species of white rose. A large portion of them, as the girl afterwards discovered, had blight or mildew at their hearts; but, viewed at a fair distance, the whole rosebush looked as if it had been brought from Eden that very summer, together with the mold in which it grew. The truth was, nevertheless, that it had been planted by Alice Pyncheon—she was Phœbe's great-great-grand-aunt—in soil which, reckoning only its cultivation as a garden plat, was now unctuous with nearly two hundred years of vegetable decay. Growing as they did, however, out of the old earth, the flowers still sent a fresh and sweet incense up to their Creator; nor could it have been the less pure and accept- able, because Phœbe's young breath mingled with it, as the fra- grance floated past the window. Hastening down the creaking and carpetless staircase, she found her way into the garden, gathered some of the most perfect of the roses, and brought them to her chamber.

Little Phœbe was one of those persons who possess, as their exclusive patrimony, the gift of practical arrangement. It is a kind of natural magic that enables these favored ones to bring out the hidden capabilities of things around them; and particu- larly to give a look of comfort and habitableness to any place which, for however brief a period, may happen to be their home. What was precisely Phœbe's process we find it impossible to say. She appeared to have no preliminary design, but gave a touch here and another there; brought some articles of furniture to light and dragged others into the shadow; looped up or let down a window curtain; and, in the course of half an hour, had fully succeeded in throwing a kindly and hospitable smile over the apartment.

After arranging matters to her satisfaction, Phœbe emerged from her chamber, with a purpose to descend again into the garden. Besides the rosebush, she had observed several other species of flowers growing there in a wilderness of neglect, and obstructing one another's development (as is often the parallel case in human society) by their uneducated entanglement and confusion. At the head of the stairs, however, she met Hepzi- bah, who, it being still early, invited her into a room which she would probably have called her boudoir, had her education em- braced any such French phrase. It was strewn about with a few old books, and a workbasket, and a dusty writing desk; and had, on one side, a large, black article of furniture, of very strange appearance, which the old gentlewoman told Phœbe was a harpsichord.[1] It looked more like a coffin than anything else; and, indeed—not having been played upon, or opened, for years —there must have been a vast deal of dead music in it, stifled for want of air. Human finger was hardly known to have touched its chords since the days of Alice Pyncheon, who had learned the sweet accomplishment of melody in Europe.

Hepzibah bade her young guest sit down, and, herself taking a chair near by, looked as earnestly at Phœbe's trim little figure as if she expected to see right into its springs and motive secrets.

"Cousin Phœbe," said she, at last, "I really can't see my way clear to keep you with me."

These words, however, had not the inhospitable bluntness with which they may strike the reader; for the two relatives, in a talk before bedtime, had arrived at a certain degree of mutual understanding. Hepzibah knew enough to enable her to appreciate the circumstances (resulting from the second marriage of the girl's mother) which made it desirable for Phœbe to establish herself in another home. Nor did she misinterpret Phœbe's character, and the genial activity pervading it—one of the most valuable traits of the true New England woman—which had impelled her forth, as might be said, to seek her fortune, but with a self-respecting purpose to confer as much benefit as she could anywise receive. As one of her nearest kindred, she had naturally betaken herself to Hepzibah, with no idea of forcing herself on her cousin's protection, but only for a visit of a week or two, which might be indefinitely extended, should it prove for the happiness of both.

To Hepzibah's blunt observation, therefore, Phœbe replied, as frankly, and more cheerfully.

"Dear cousin, I cannot tell how it will be," said she. "But I really think we may suit one another much better than you suppose."

"You are a nice girl—I see it plainly," continued Hepzibah; "and it is not any question as to that point which makes me hesitate. But, Phœbe, this house of mine is but a melancholy place for a young person to be in. It lets in the wind and rain, and the snow, too, in the garret, and upper chambers, in wintertime, but it never lets in the sunshine! And as for myself, you see what I am—a dismal and lonesome old woman (for I begin

---

[1] HARPSICHORD—An old-fashioned stringed instrument.

to call myself old, Phœbe), whose temper, I am afraid, is none of the best, and whose spirits are as bad as can be. I cannot make your life pleasant, Cousin Phœbe, neither can I so much as give you bread to eat."

"You will find me a cheerful little body," answered Phœbe, smiling, and yet with a kind of gentle dignity; "and I mean to earn my bread. You know I have not been brought up a Pyncheon. A girl learns many things in a New England village."

"Ah! Phœbe," said Hepzibah, sighing, "your knowledge would do but little for you here! And then it is a wretched thought that you should fling away your young days in a place like this. Those cheeks would not be so rosy after a month or two. Look at my face!"—and, indeed, the contrast was very striking—"you see how pale I am! It is my idea that the dust and continual decay of these old houses are unwholesome for the lungs."

"There is the garden—the flowers to be taken care of," observed Phœbe. "I should keep myself healthy with exercise in the open air."

"And, after all, child," exclaimed Hepzibah, suddenly arising, as if to dismiss the subject, "it is not for me to say who shall be a guest or inhabitant of the old Pyncheon house. Its master is coming."

"Do you mean Judge Pyncheon?" asked Phœbe, in surprise.

"Judge Pyncheon!" answered her cousin, angrily. "He will hardly cross the threshold while I live! No, no! But, Phœbe, you shall see the face of him I speak of."

She went in quest of the miniature already described, and returned with it in her hand. Giving it to Phœbe, she watched her features narrowly, and with a certain jealousy as to the mode in which the girl would show herself affected by the picture.

"How do you like the face?" asked Hepzibah.

"It is handsome!—it is very beautiful!" said Phœbe, admiringly. "It is as sweet a face as a man's can be, or ought to be. It has something of a child's expression—and yet not childish—only one feels so very kindly toward him! He ought never to suffer anything. One would bear much for the sake of sparing him toil or sorrow. Who is it, Cousin Hepzibah?"

"Did you never hear," whispered her cousin, bending toward her, "of Clifford Pyncheon?"

"Never! I thought there were no Pyncheons left, except

yourself and our cousin Jaffrey," answered Phœbe. "And yet I seem to have heard the name of Clifford Pyncheon. Yes!—from my father or my mother; but has he not been a long while dead?"

"Well, well, child, perhaps he has!" said Hepzibah, with a sad, hollow laugh; "but, in old houses like this, you know, dead people are very apt to come back again! We shall see. And Cousin Phœbe, since, after all that I have said, your courage does not fail you, we will not part so soon. You are welcome, my child, for the present, to such a home as your kinswoman can offer you."

With this measured, but not exactly cold assurance of a hospitable purpose, Hepzibah kissed her cheek.

They now went below stairs, where Phœbe—not so much assuming the office as attracting it to herself, by the magnetism of innate fitness—took the most active part in preparing breakfast. The mistress of the house, meanwhile, as is usual with persons of her stiff and unmalleable cast, stood mostly aside; willing to lend her aid, yet conscious that her natural inaptitude would be likely to impede the business in hand. Phœbe, and the fire that boiled the teakettle, were equally bright, cheerful, and efficient, in their respective offices. Hepzibah gazed forth from her habitual sluggishness, the necessary result of long solitude, as from another sphere. She could not help being interested, however, and even amused, at the readiness with which her new inmate adapted herself to the circumstances, and brought the house, moreover, and all its rusty old appliances, into a suitableness for her purposes. Whatever she did, too, was done without conscious effort, and with frequent outbreaks of song, which were exceedingly pleasant to the ear. This natural tunefulness made Phœbe seem like a bird in a shadowy tree; or conveyed the idea that the stream of life warbled through her heart as a brook sometimes warbles through a pleasant little dell. It betokened the cheeriness of an active temperament, finding joy in its activity, and, therefore, rendering it beautiful; it was a New England trait—the stern old stuff of Puritanism with a gold thread in the web.

Hepzibah brought out some old silver spoons with the family crest upon them, and a china tea set painted over with grotesque figures of man, bird, and beast, in as grotesque a landscape.

These pictured people were odd humorists, in a world of their own—a world of vivid brilliancy, so far as color went, and still unfaded, although the teapot and small cups were as ancient as the custom itself of tea drinking.

"Your great-great-great-great-grandmother had these cups, when she was married," said Hepzibah to Phœbe. "She was a Davenport, of a good family. They were almost the first teacups ever seen in the colony; and if one of them were to be broken, my heart would break with it. But it is nonsense to speak so about a brittle teacup, when I remember what my heart has gone through without breaking."

The cups—not having been used, perhaps, since Hepzibah's youth—had contracted no small burden of dust, which Phœbe washed away with so much care and delicacy as to satisfy even the proprietor of this invaluable china.

"What a nice little housewife you are!" exclaimed the latter, smiling, and, at the same time, frowning so prodigiously that the smile was sunshine under a thundercloud. "Do you do other things as well? Are you as good at your books as you are at washing teacups?"

"Not quite, I am afraid," said Phœbe, laughing at the form of Hepzibah's question. "But I was schoolmistress for the little children in our district last summer, and might have been so still."

"Ah! 'tis all very well!" observed the maiden lady, drawing herself up. "But these things must have come to you with your mother's blood. I never knew a Pyncheon that had any turn for them."

Before they left the breakfast table, the shop bell rang sharply, and Hepzibah set down the remnant of her final cup of tea, with a look of sallow despair that was truly piteous to behold. In cases of distasteful occupation, the second day is generally worse than the first; we return to the rack [2] with all the soreness of the preceding torture in our limbs. At all events, Hepzibah had fully satisfied herself of the impossibility of ever becoming wonted to this peevishly obstreperous little bell. Ring as often as it might, the sound always smote upon her nervous system rudely and suddenly. And especially now, while, with her crested teaspoons and antique china, she was flattering herself

---

[2] RACK—An instrument of torture for stretching the body.

with ideas of gentility, she felt an unspeakable disinclination to confront a customer.

"Do not trouble yourself, dear cousin!" cried Phœbe, starting lightly up. "I am shopkeeper to-day."

"You, child!" exclaimed Hepzibah. "What can a little country girl know of such matters?"

"Oh, I have done all the shopping for the family at our village store," said Phœbe. "And I have had a table at a fancy fair, and made better sales than anybody. These things are not to be learned; they depend upon a knack that comes, I suppose," added she, smiling, "with one's mother's blood. You shall see that I am as nice a little saleswoman as I am a housewife!"

The old gentlewoman stole behind Phœbe, and peeped from the passageway into the shop, to note how she would manage her undertaking. It was a case of some intricacy. A very ancient woman, in a white short gown and a green petticoat, with a string of gold beads about her neck, and what looked like a nightcap on her head, had brought a quantity of yarn to barter for the commodities of the shop. She was probably the very last person in town who still kept the time-honored spinning wheel in constant revolution. It was worth while to hear the croaking and hollow tones of the old lady, and the pleasant voice of Phœbe, mingling in one twisted thread of talk; and still better to contrast their figures—so light and bloomy—so decrepit and dusky—with only the counter betwixt them, in one sense, but more than threescore years, in another. As for the bargain, it was wrinkled slyness and craft pitted against native truth and sagacity.

"Was not that well done?" asked Phœbe, laughing, when the customer was gone.

"Nicely done, indeed, child!" answered Hepzibah. "I could

C-AM

not have gone through with it nearly so well. As you say, it must be a knack that belongs to you on your mother's side."

Thus, Hepzibah was well content to acknowledge Phœbe's vastly superior gifts as a shopkeeper; she listened, with compliant ear, to her suggestion of various methods whereby the influx of trade might be increased, and rendered profitable, without a hazardous outlay of capital. She consented that the village maiden should manufacture yeast, both liquid and in cakes; and should brew a certain kind of beer, nectareous to the palate, and of rare stomachic virtues; and, moreover, should bake and exhibit for sale some little spice cakes, which whosoever tasted would longingly desire to taste again. All such proofs of a ready mind and skillful handiwork were highly acceptable to the aristocratic huckstress, so long as she could murmur to herself with a grim smile, and a half-natural sigh, and a sentiment of mixed wonder, pity and growing affection:

"What a nice little body she is! If she could only be a lady, too!—but that's impossible! Phœbe is no Pyncheon. She takes everything from her mother."

As to Phœbe's not being a lady, or whether she were a lady or no, it was a point, perhaps, difficult to decide, but which could hardly have come up for judgment at all in any fair and healthy mind. Her figure, to be sure—so small as to be almost childlike, and so elastic that motion seemed as easy or easier to it than rest —would hardly have suited one's idea of a countess. Neither did her face—with the brown ringlets on either side, and the slightly piquant nose, and the wholesome bloom, and the clear shade of tan, and the half a dozen freckles, friendly remembrances of the April sun and breeze—precisely give us a right to call her beautiful. But there was both luster and depth in her eyes. She was very pretty; as graceful as a bird, and graceful much in the same way; as pleasant about the house as a gleam of sunshine falling on the floor through a shadow of twinkling leaves, or as a ray of firelight that dances on the wall while evening is drawing nigh. It should be woman's office to move in the midst of practical affairs, and to gild them all, the very homeliest—were it even the scouring of pots and kettles—with an atmosphere of loveliness and joy. Such was the sphere of Phœbe.

It really seemed as if the battered visage of the House of the Seven Gables, black and heavy-browed as it still certainly looked, must have shown a kind of cheerfulness glimmering through its dusky windows as Phœbe passed to and fro in the interior. Otherwise, it is impossible to explain how the people of the neighborhood so soon became aware of the girl's presence. There was a great run of custom, setting steadily in, from about ten o'clock until toward noon—relaxing, somewhat, at dinner time, but recommencing in the afternoon, and, finally, dying away a half an hour or so before the long day's sunset. One of the stanchest patrons was little Ned Higgins, the devourer of Jim Crow and the elephant, who to-day had signalized his omnivorous prowess by swallowing two dromedaries and a locomotive. Phœbe laughed, as she summed up her aggregate of sales upon the slate; while Hepzibah, first drawing on a pair of silk gloves, reckoned over the sordid accumulation of copper coin, not without silver intermixed, that had jingled into the till.

"We must renew our stock, Cousin Hepzibah!" cried the little saleswoman. "The gingerbread figures are all gone, and so are those Dutch wooden milkmaids, and most of our other playthings. There has been constant inquiry for cheap raisins, and a great cry for whistles, and trumpets, and jew's-harps; and at least a dozen little boys have asked for molasses candy. And we must contrive to get a peck of russet apples, late in the season as it is. But, dear cousin, what an enormous heap of copper! Positively a copper mountain!"

"Well done! well done! well done!" quoth Uncle Venner, who had taken occasion to shuffle in and out of the shop several times in the course of the day. "Here's a girl that will never end her days at my farm! Bless my eyes, what a brisk little soul!"

"Yes, Phœbe is a nice girl!" said Hepzibah, with a scowl of austere approbation. "But, Uncle Venner, you have known the family a great many years. Can you tell me whether there ever was a Pyncheon whom she takes after?"

"I don't believe there ever was," answered the venerable man. "At any rate, it never was my luck to see her like among them, nor, for that matter, anywhere else. I've seen a great deal of the world, not only in people's kitchens and backyards, but at the street corners, and on the wharves, and in other places where my business calls me; and I'm free to say, Miss Hepzibah, that I never knew a human creature do her work so much like one of God's angels as this child Phœbe does!"

The two relatives—the young maid and the old one—found time before nightfall, in the intervals of trade, to make rapid advances toward affection and confidence. A recluse, like Hepzibah, usually displays remarkable frankness, and at least temporary affability, on being absolutely cornered, and brought to the point of personal intercourse; like the angel whom Jacob wrestled [3] with, she is ready to bless you when once overcome.

The old gentlewoman took a dreary and proud satisfaction in leading Phœbe from room to room of the house, and recounting the traditions with which, as we may say, the walls were lugubriously frescoed. She showed the indentations made by the Lieutenant Governor's sword hilt in the door panels of the apartment where old Colonel Pyncheon, a dead host, had received his affrighted visitors with an awful frown. The dusky terror of that frown, Hepzibah observed, was thought to be lingering ever since in the passageway. She bade Phœbe step into one of the tall chairs, and inspect the ancient map of the Pyncheon territory at the eastward. In a tract of land on which she laid her finger, there existed a silver mine, the locality of which was precisely pointed out in some memoranda of Colonel Pyncheon himself, but only to be made known when the family claim should be recognized by government. Thus it was for the interest of all New England that the Pyncheons should have justice done them. She told, too, how that there was undoubtedly an immense treasure of English guineas hidden somewhere about the house, or in the cellar, or possibly in the garden.

"If you should happen to find it, Phœbe," said Hepzibah, glancing aside at her with a grim yet kindly smile, "we will tie up the shop bell for good and all!"

"Yes, dear cousin," answered Phœbe; "but, in the meantime, I hear somebody ringing it!"

When the customer was gone, Hepzibah talked rather vaguely, and at great length, about a certain Alice Pyncheon, who had been exceedingly beautiful and accomplished in her lifetime, a hundred years ago. The fragrance of her rich and delightful character still lingered about the place where she had lived, as a dried rosebud scents the drawer where it has withered and perished. This lovely Alice had met with some great and mysterious calamity, and had grown thin and white, and gradually

---

[3] JACOB WRESTLED—See *Genesis:* xxii.

faded out of the world. But, even now, she was supposed to haunt the House of the Seven Gables, and, a great many times—especially when one of the Pyncheons was to die—she had been heard playing sadly and beautifully on the harpsichord. One of these tunes, just as it had sounded from her spiritual touch, had been written down by an amateur of music; it was so exquisitely mournful that nobody, to this day, could bear to hear it played, unless when a great sorrow had made them know the still profounder sweetness of it.

"Was it the same harpsichord that you showed me?" inquired Phœbe.

"The very same," said Hepzibah. "It was Alice Pyncheon's harpsichord. When I was learning music, my father would never let me open it. So, as I could only play on my teacher's instrument, I have forgotten all my music long ago."

Leaving these antique themes, the old lady began to talk about the daguerreotypist, whom, as he seemed to be a well-meaning and orderly young man, and in narrow circumstances, she had permitted to take up his residence in one of the seven gables. But, on seeing more of Mr. Holgrave, she hardly knew what to make of him. He had the strangest companions imaginable; men with long beards, and dressed in linen blouses, and other such newfangled and ill-fitting garments; reformers, temperance lecturers, and all manner of cross-looking philanthropists; community men,[4] and come-outers,[5] as Hepzibah believed, who acknowledged no law, and ate no solid food, but lived on the scent of other people's cookery, and turned up their noses at the fare. As for the daguerreotypist, she had read a paragraph in a penny paper, the other day, accusing him of making a speech full of wild and disorganizing matter, at a meeting of his banditti-like associates. For her own part, she had reason to believe that he practiced animal magnetism, and, if such things were in fashion nowadays, should be apt to suspect him of studying the Black Art[6] up there in his lonesome chamber.

"But, dear cousin," said Phœbe, "if the young man is so dangerous, why do you let him stay? If he does nothing worse, he may set the house on fire!"

---

[4] COMMUNITY MEN—Those who believe in common ownership of property.
[5] COME-OUTERS—Those who withdraw from an organization because of dissatisfaction with it.   [6] BLACK ART—Magic.

"Why, sometimes," answered Hepzibah, "I have seriously made it a question, whether I ought not to send him away. But, with all his oddities, he is a quiet kind of a person, and has such a way of taking hold of one's mind, that, without exactly liking him (for I don't know enough of the young man), I should be sorry to lose sight of him entirely. A woman clings to slight acquaintances when she lives so much alone as I do."

"But if Mr. Holgrave is a lawless person!" remonstrated Phœbe, a part of whose essence it was to keep within the limits of law.

"Oh!" said Hepzibah, carelessly—for, formal as she was, still, in her life's experience, she had gnashed her teeth against human law—"I suppose he has a law of his own!"

VI   MAULE'S WELL

Wherein is shown the garden with its fallen leaves, rank weeds, vagrant plants, plebeian vegetables and antique flowers; the moss-covered well; Chanticleer and his family symbolize the diminished splendor of the aristocratic Pyncheons; Phœbe and Holgrave meet; a daguerreotype of a Pyncheon. Did the man of Hepzibah's minia-ture commit a crime? Holgrave warns Phœbe against drinking at Maule's well. The dusk of the evening shadows a person with Hepzibah.

AFTER an early tea, the little country girl strayed into the garden. The inclosure had formerly been very extensive, but was now contracted within small compass, and hemmed about, partly by high wooden fences, and partly by the outbuildings of houses that stood on another street. In its center was a grass plat, surrounding a ruinous little structure which showed just enough of its original design to indicate that it had once been a summer house. A hopvine, springing from last year's root, was beginning to clamber over it, but would be long in covering the roof with its green mantle. Three of the seven gables either fronted or looked sideways, with a dark solemnity of aspect, down into the garden.

The black, rich soil had fed itself with the decay of a long period of time; such as fallen leaves, the petals of flowers, and the stalks and seed vessels of vagrant and lawless plants, more useful after their death than ever while flaunting in the sun. The evil of these departed years would naturally have sprung up again, in such rank weeds (symbolic of the transmitted vices of society) as are always prone to root themselves about human dwellings. Phœbe saw, however, that their growth must have been checked by a degree of careful labor, bestowed daily and systematically on the garden. The white double rosebush had evidently been propped up anew against the house since the commencement of the season; and a pear tree and three damson trees, which, except a row of currant bushes, constituted the only varieties of fruit, bore marks of the recent amputation of several superfluous or defective limbs. There were also a few species of antique and hereditary flowers, in no very flourishing condition, but scrupulously weeded; as if some person, either out of love or curiosity, had been anxious to bring them to such perfection as they were capable of attaining. The remainder of the garden presented a well-selected assortment of esculent vegetables, in a praiseworthy state of advancement. Summer squashes, almost in their golden blossom; cucumbers, now evincing a tendency to spread away from the main stock, and ramble far and wide; two or three rows of string beans, and as many more that were about to festoon themselves on poles; tomatoes, occupying a site so sheltered and sunny that the plants were already gigantic, and promised an early and abundant harvest.

Phœbe wondered whose care and toil it could have been that had planted these vegetables, and kept the soil so clean and orderly. Not surely her cousin Hepzibah's, who had no taste nor spirits for the lady-like employment of cultivating flowers, and—with her recluse habits, and tendency to shelter herself within the dismal shadow of the house—would hardly have come forth under the speck of open sky to weed and hoe among the fraternity of beans and squashes.

It being her first day of complete estrangement from rural objects, Phœbe found an unexpected charm in this little nook of grass, and foliage, and aristocratic flowers, and plebeian vegetables. The eye of Heaven seemed to look down into it pleasantly, and with a peculiar smile, as if glad to perceive that nature, elsewhere overwhelmed, and driven out of the dusty town, had here been able to retain a breathing place. The spot acquired a somewhat wilder grace, and yet a very gentle one, from the fact that a pair of robins had built their nest in the pear tree, and were making themselves exceedingly busy and

happy in the dark intricacy of its boughs. Bees, too—strange
to say—had thought it worth their while to come hither, possibly
from the range of hives beside some farmhouse miles away.
How many aërial voyages might they have made, in quest of
honey, or honey-laden, betwixt dawn and sunset! Yet, late as
it now was, there still arose a pleasant hum out of one or two of
the squash blossoms, in the depths of which these bees were
plying their golden labor. There was one other object in the
garden which Nature might fairly claim as her inalienable property, in spite of whatever man could do to render it his own.
This was a fountain, set round with a rim of old mossy stones,
and paved, in its bed, with what appeared to be a sort of mosaic
work of variously colored pebbles. The play and slight agitation
of the water, in its upward gush, wrought magically with these
variegated pebbles, and made a continually shifting apparition
of quaint figures, vanishing too suddenly to be definable. Thence,
swelling over the rim of moss-grown stones, the water stole away
under the fence, through what we regret to call a gutter, rather
than a channel.

Nor must we forget to mention a hencoop of very reverend
antiquity that stood in the farther corner of the garden, not a
great way from the fountain. It now contained only Chanticleer, his two wives, and a solitary chicken. All of them were
pure specimens of a breed which had been transmitted down as
an heirloom in the Pyncheon family, and were said, while in
their prime, to have attained almost the size of turkeys, and,
on the score of delicate flesh, to be fit for a prince's table. In
proof of the authenticity of this legendary renown, Hepzibah
could have exhibited the shell of a great egg, which an ostrich
need hardly have been ashamed of. Be that as it might, the hens
were now scarcely larger than pigeons, and had a queer, rusty,
withered aspect, and a gouty kind of movement, and a sleepy
and melancholy tone throughout all the variations of their clucking and cackling. It was evident that the race had degenerated,
like many a noble race besides, in consequence of too strict a
watchfulness to keep it pure. These feathered people had existed too long in their distinct variety; a fact of which the present representatives, judging by their lugubrious deportment,
seemed to be aware. They kept themselves alive, unquestionably, and laid now and then an egg, and hatched a chicken; not

for any pleasure of their own, but that the world might not absolutely lose what had once been so admirable a breed of fowls. The distinguishing mark of the hens was a crest of lamentably scanty growth, in these latter days, but so oddly and wickedly analogous to Hepzibah's turban, that Phœbe—to the poignant distress of her conscience, but inevitably—was led to fancy a general resemblance betwixt these forlorn bipeds and her respectable relative.

The girl ran into the house to get some crumbs of bread, cold potatoes, and other such scraps as were suitable to the accommodating appetite of fowls. Returning, she gave a peculiar call, which they seemed to recognize. The chicken crept through the pales of the coop and ran, with some show of liveliness, to her feet; while Chanticleer and the ladies of his household regarded her with queer, sidelong glances, and then croaked one to another, as if communicating their sage opinions of her character. So wise, as well as antique, was their aspect, as to give color to the idea, not merely that they were descendants of a time-honored race, but that they had existed, in their individual capacity, ever since the House of the Seven Gables was founded, and were somehow mixed up with its destiny. They were a species of tutelary sprite, or Banshee,[1] although winged and feathered differently from most other guardian angels.

"Here, you odd little chicken!" said Phœbe; "here are some nice crumbs for you!"

The chicken, hereupon, though almost as venerable in appearance as its mother—possessing, indeed, the whole antiquity of its progenitors in miniature—mustered vivacity enough to flutter upward and alight on Phœbe's shoulder.

"That little fowl pays you a high compliment!" said a voice behind Phœbe.

[1] TUTELARY SPRITE, BANSHEE—Guardian spirits.

Turning quickly, she was surprised at sight of a young man, who had found access into the garden by a door opening out of another gable than that whence she had emerged. He held a hoe in his hand, and, while Phœbe was gone in quest of the crumbs, had begun to busy himself with drawing up fresh earth about the roots of the tomatoes.

"The chicken really treats you like an old acquaintance," continued he, in a quiet way, while a smile made his face pleasanter than Phœbe at first fancied it. "Those venerable personages in the coop, too, seem very affably disposed. You are lucky to be in their good graces so soon! They have known me much longer, but never honor me with any familiarity, though hardly a day passes without my bringing them food. Miss Hepzibah, I suppose, will interweave the fact with her other traditions, and set it down that the fowls know you to be a Pyncheon!"

"The secret is," said Phœbe, smiling, 'that I have learned how to talk with hens and chickens."

"Ah, but these hens," answered the young man, "these hens of aristocratic lineage would scorn to understand the vulgar language of a barnyard fowl. I prefer to think—and so would Miss Hepzibah—that they recognize the family tone. For you are a Pyncheon?"

"My name is Phœbe Pyncheon," said the girl, with a manner of some reserve; for she was aware that her new acquaintance could be no other than the daguerreotypist, of whose lawless propensities the old maid had given her a disagreeable idea. "I did not know that my cousin Hepzibah's garden was under another person's care."

"Yes," said Holgrave, "I dig, and hoe, and weed, in this black old earth, for the sake of refreshing myself with what little nature and simplicity may be left in it, after men have so long sown and reaped here. I turn up the earth by way of pastime. My sober occupation, so far as I have any, is with a lighter material. In short, I make pictures out of sunshine; and, not to be too much dazzled with my own trade, I have prevailed with Miss Hepzibah to let me lodge in one of these dusky gables. It is like a bandage over one's eyes, to come into it. But would you like to see a specimen of my productions?"

"A daguerreotype likeness, do you mean?" asked Phœbe, with less reserve; for, in spite of prejudice, her own youthfulness sprang forward to meet his. "I don't much like pictures of that sort—they are so hard and stern; besides dodging away from the eye, and trying to escape altogether. They are conscious of looking very unamiable, I suppose, and therefore hate to be seen."

"If you would permit me," said the artist, looking at Phœbe, "I should like to try whether the daguerreotype can bring out disagreeable traits on a perfectly amiable face. But there certainly is truth in what you have said. Most of my likenesses do look unamiable; but the very sufficient reason, I fancy, is, because the originals are so. There is a wonderful insight in Heaven's broad and simple sunshine. While we give it credit only for depicting the merest surface, it actually brings out the secret character with a truth that no painter would ever venture upon, even could he detect it. There is, at least, no flattery in my humble line of art. Now, here is a likeness which I have taken over and over again, and still with no better result. Yet the original wears, to common eyes, a very different expression. It would gratify me to have your judgment on this character."

He exhibited a daguerreotype miniature in a morocco case. Phœbe merely glanced at it, and gave it back.

"I know the face," she replied; "for its stern eye has been following me about all day. It is my Puritan ancestor, who hangs yonder in the parlor. To be sure, you have found some way of copying the portrait without its black velvet cap and gray beard, and have given him a modern coat and satin cravat, instead of his cloak and band. I don't think him improved by your alterations."

"You would have seen other differences had you looked a little longer," said Holgrave, laughing, yet apparently much struck. "I can assure you that this is a modern face, and one which you will very probably meet. Now, the remarkable point is, that the original wears, to the world's eye—and, for aught I know, to his most intimate friends—an exceedingly pleasant countenance, indicative of benevolence, openness of heart, sunny good humor, and other praiseworthy qualities of that cast. The sun, as you see, tells quite another story, and will not be coaxed out of it, after half a dozen patient attempts on my part. Here we have the man, sly, subtle, hard, imperious, and, withal, cold as ice. Look at that eye! Would you like to be at its mercy? At that

mouth! Could it ever smile? And yet, if you could only see
the benign smile of the original! It is so much the more unfortunate, as he is a public character of some eminence, and the
likeness was intended to be engraved."

"Well, I don't wish to see it any more," observed Phœbe, turning away her eyes. "It is certainly very like the old portrait.
But my cousin Hepzibah has another picture—a miniature. If
the original is still in the world, I think he might defy the sun
to make him look stern and hard."

"You have seen that picture, then!" exclaimed the artist, with
an expression of much interest. "I never did, but have a great
curiosity to do so. And you judge favorably of the face?"

"There never was a sweeter one," said Phœbe. "It is almost
too soft and gentle for a man's."

"Is there nothing wild in the eye?" continued Holgrave, so
earnestly that it embarrassed Phœbe, as did also the quiet freedom with which he presumed on their so recent acquaintance.
"Is there nothing dark or sinister anywhere? Could you not
conceive the original to have been guilty of a great crime?"

"It is nonsense," said Phœbe, a little impatiently, "for us to
talk about a picture which you have never seen. You mistake it
for some other. A crime, indeed! Since you are a friend of my
cousin Hepzibah's, you should ask her to show you the picture."

"It will suit my purpose still better to see the original," replied the daguerreotypist coolly. "As to his character, we need
not discuss its points; they have already been settled by a competent tribunal, or one which called itself competent. But, stay!
Do not go yet, if you please! I have a proposition to make you."

Phœbe was on the point of retreating, but turned back, with
some hesitation; for she did not exactly comprehend his manner,
although, on better observation, its feature seemed rather to be
lack of ceremony than any approach to offensive rudeness. There
was an odd kind of authority, too, in what he now proceeded to
say, rather as if the garden were his own than a place to which
he was admitted merely by Hepzibah's courtesy.

"If agreeable to you," he observed, "it would give me pleasure
to turn over these flowers, and those ancient and respectable
fowls, to your care. Coming fresh from country air and occupations, you will soon feel the need of some such out-of-door employment. My own sphere does not so much lie among flowers.

You can trim and tend them, therefore, as you please; and I will ask only the least trifle of a blossom, now and then, in exchange for all the good, honest kitchen vegetables with which I propose to enrich Miss Hepzibah's table. So we will be fellow laborers, somewhat on the community system."

Silently, and rather surprised at her own compliance, Phœbe accordingly betook herself to weeding a flower bed, but busied herself still more with cogitations respecting this young man, with whom she so unexpectedly found herself on terms approaching to familiarity. She did not altogether like him. His character perplexed the little country girl, as it might a more practiced observer; for, while the tone of his conversation had generally been playful, the impression left on her mind was that of gravity, and, except as his youth modified it, almost sternness. She rebelled, as it were, against a certain magnetic element in the artist's nature, which he exercised toward her possibly without being conscious of it.

After a little while, the twilight, deepened by the shadows of the fruit trees and the surrounding buildings, threw an obscurity over the garden.

"There," said Holgrave, "it is time to give over work! That last stroke of the hoe has cut off a bean stalk. Good night, Miss Phœbe Pyncheon! Any bright day, if you will put one of those rosebuds in your hair, and come to my rooms in Central Street, I will seize the purest ray of sunshine, and make a picture of the flower and its wearer."

He retired toward his own solitary gable, but turned his head, on reaching the door, and called to Phœbe, with a tone which certainly had laughter in it, yet which seemed to be more than half in earnest.

"Be careful not to drink at Maule's well!" said he. "Neither drink nor bathe your face in it!"

"Maule's well!" answered Phœbe. "Is that it with the rim of mossy stones? I have no thought of drinking there—but why not?"

"Oh," rejoined the daguerreotypist, "because, like an old lady's cup of tea, it is water bewitched!"

He vanished; and Phœbe, lingering a moment, saw a glimmering light, and then the steady beam of a lamp, in a chamber of the gable. On returning into Hepzibah's apartment of the house, she found the low-studded parlor so dim and dusky that her eyes could not penetrate the interior. She was indistinctly aware, however, that the gaunt figure of the old gentlewoman was sitting in one of the straight-backed chairs, a little withdrawn from the window, the faint gleam of which showed the blanched paleness of her cheek, turned sideway toward a corner.

"Shall I light a lamp, Cousin Hepzibah?" she asked.

"Do, if you please, my dear child," answered Hepzibah. "But put it on the table in the corner of the passage. My eyes are weak; and I can seldom bear the lamplight on them."

What an instrument is the human eye! How wonderfully responsive to every emotion of the human soul! In Hepzibah's tone, at that moment, there was a certain rich depth and moisture, as if the words, commonplace as they were, had been steeped in the warmth of her heart. Again, while lighting the lamp in the kitchen, Phœbe fancied that her cousin spoke to her.

"In a moment, cousin!" answered the girl. "These matches just glimmer, and go out."

But, instead of a response from Hepzibah, she seemed to hear the murmur of an unknown voice. It was strangely indistinct, however, and less like articulate words than an unshaped sound, such as would be the utterance of feeling and sympathy, rather than of the intellect. So vague was it, that its impression or echo in Phœbe's mind was that of unreality. She concluded that she must have mistaken some other sound for that of the human voice; or else that it was altogether in her fancy.

She set the lighted lamp in the passage, and again entered the parlor. Hepzibah's form, though its sable outline mingled with the dusk, was now less imperfectly visible. In the remoter parts of the room, however, its walls being so ill adapted to reflect light, there was nearly the same obscurity as before.

"Cousin," said Phœbe, "did you speak to me just now?"

"No, child!" replied Hepzibah.

Fewer words than before, but with the same mysterious music in them! Mellow, melancholy, yet not mournful, the tone seemed to gush up out of the deep well of Hepzibah's heart, all steeped in its profoundest emotion. There was a tremor in it, too, that —as all strong feeling is electric—partly communicated itself to Phœbe. The girl sat silently for a moment. But soon, her senses being very acute, she became conscious of an irregular respiration in an obscure corner of the room. Her physical organization, moreover, being at once delicate and healthy, gave her a perception, operating with almost the effect of a spiritual medium, that somebody was near at hand.

"My dear cousin," asked she, overcoming an indefinable reluctance, "is there not someone in the room with us?"

"Phœbe, my dear little girl," said Hepzibah, after a moment's pause, "you were up betimes, and have been busy all day. Pray go to bed; for I am sure you must need rest. I will sit in the parlor awhile, and collect my thoughts. It has been my custom for more years, child, than you have lived!"

While thus dismissing her, the maiden lady stepped forward, kissed Phœbe, and pressed her to her heart, which beat against the girl's bosom with a strong, high, and tumultuous swell. How came there to be so much love in this desolate old heart, that it could afford to well over thus abundantly?

"Good night, cousin," said Phœbe, strangely affected by Hepzibah's manner. "If you begin to love me, I am glad!"

She retired to her chamber, but did not soon fall asleep, nor then very profoundly. At some uncertain period in the depths of night, and, as it were, through the thin veil of a dream, she was conscious of a footstep mounting the stairs heavily, but not with force and decision. The voice of Hepzibah, with a hush through it, was going up along with the footsteps; and, again, responsive to her cousin's voice, Phœbe heard that strange, vague murmur, which might be likened to an indistinct shadow of human utterance.

VII THE GUEST

Wherein an elaborate breakfast is prepared, indicating a very special guest; Hepzibah betrays deep emotion; the forlorn stranger enters; his actions show long imprisonment; faint glimmers of life.

WHEN PHŒBE awoke—which she did with the early twittering of the conjugal couple of robins in the pear tree—she heard movements below stairs, and, hastening down, found Hepzibah already in the kitchen. She stood by a window, holding a book in close contiguity to her nose, as if with the hope of gaining an olfactory acquaintance with its contents, since her imperfect vision made it not very easy to read them. If any volume could have manifested its essential wisdom in the mode suggested, it would certainly have been the one now in Hepzibah's hand; and the kitchen, in such an event, would forthwith have steamed with the fragrance of venison, turkeys, capons, larded partridges, puddings, cakes, and Christmas pies, in all manner of elaborate mixture and concoction. It was a cookery book, full of innumerable old fashions of English dishes, and illustrated with engravings, which represented the arrangements of the table at such banquets as it might have befitted a nobleman to give in the great hall of his castle. And, amid these rich and potent devices of the culinary art (not one of which, probably, had been tested, within the memory of any man's grandfather), poor Hepzibah was seeking for some nimble little titbit, which, with what skill she had, and such materials as were at hand, she might toss up for breakfast.

Soon, with a deep sigh, she put aside the savory volume, and inquired of Phœbe whether old Speckle, as she called one of the hens, had laid an egg the preceding day. Phœbe ran to see, but returned without the expected treasure in her hand. At that instant, however, the blast of a fish-dealer's conch was heard, announcing his approach along the street. With energetic raps at the shop window, Hepzibah summoned the man in, and made purchase of what he warranted as the finest mackerel in his cart, and as fat a one as ever he felt with his finger so early in the season. Requesting Phœbe to roast some coffee—which she casually observed was the real Mocha, and so long kept that each of the small berries ought to be worth its weight in gold— the maiden lady heaped fuel into the vast receptacle of the ancient fireplace in such quantity as soon to drive the lingering dusk out of the kitchen. The country girl, willing to give her utmost assistance, proposed to make an Indian cake, after her mother's peculiar method, of easy manufacture, and which she could vouch for as possessing a richness, and, if rightly prepared, a delicacy, unequaled by any other mode of breakfast cake. Hepzibah gladly assenting, the kitchen was soon the scene of savory preparation.

Hepzibah had no natural turn for cookery, and, to say the truth, had fairly incurred her present meagerness by often choosing to go without her dinner rather than be attendant on the rotation of the spit, or ebullition of the pot. Her zeal over the fire, therefore, was quite an heroic test of sentiment. It was touching, and positively worthy of tears (if Phœbe had not been better employed than in shedding them), to see her rake out a bed of fresh and glowing coals, and proceed to broil the mackerel. Her usually pale cheeks were all ablaze with heat and hurry. She watched the fish with as much tender care and minuteness of attention as if—we know not how to express it otherwise—as if her own heart were on the gridiron, and her immortal happiness were involved in its being done precisely to a turn!

Hepzibah's small and ancient table, supported on its slender and graceful legs, and covered with a cloth of the richest damask, looked worthy to be the scene and center of one of the cheerfullest of parties. The quaint gorgeousness of the old china cups and saucers, and the crested spoons, and a silver cream jug (Hepzibah's only other article of plate, and shaped like the rudest porringer), set out a board at which the stateliest of old Colonel Pyncheon's guests need not have scorned to take his place.

By way of contributing what grace she could, Phœbe gathered some roses and a few other flowers, possessing either scent or beauty, and arranged them in a glass pitcher, which, having long ago lost its handle, was so much the fitter for a flower vase. The early sunshine—as fresh as that which peeped into Eve's bower while she and Adam sat at breakfast there—came twinkling through the branches of the pear tree, and fell quite across the table. All was now ready. There were chairs and plates for three. A chair and plate for Hepzibah—the same for Phœbe—but what other guest did her cousin look for?

Throughout this preparation there had been a constant tremor in Hepzibah's frame; an agitation so powerful that Phœbe could see the quivering of her gaunt shadow, as thrown by the firelight on the kitchen wall, or by the sunshine on the parlor floor. Its manifestations were so various, and agreed so little with one another, that the girl knew not what to make of it. Sometimes it seemed an ecstacy of delight and happiness. At such moments, Hepzibah would fling out her arms, and infold Phœbe in them, and kiss her cheek as tenderly as ever her mother had; she appeared to do so by an inevitable impulse, and as if her bosom were oppressed with tenderness, of which she must needs pour out a little, in order to gain breathing room. The next moment, without any visible cause for the change, her unwonted joy shrank back, appalled, as it were, and clothed itself in mourning; or it ran and hid itself, so to speak, in the dungeon of her heart, where it had long lain chained, while a cold, spectral sorrow took the place of the imprisoned joy, that was afraid to be enfranchised—a sorrow as black as that was bright. She often broke into a little, nervous, hysteric laugh, more touching than any tears could be; and forthwith, as if to try which was the most touching, a gush of tears would follow; or perhaps the laughter and tears came both at once, and surrounded our poor Hepzibah, in a moral sense, with a kind of pale, dim rainbow. Toward Phœbe, as we have said, she was affectionate—far tenderer than ever before, in their brief acquaintance, except for that one kiss on the preceding night—yet with a continually recurring pettishness and irritability. She would speak sharply to her; then, throwing aside all the starched reserve of her ordinary manner, ask pardon, and the next instant renew the just-forgiven injury.

At last, when their mutual labor was all finished, she took Phœbe's hand in her own trembling one.

"Bear with me, my dear child," she cried; "for truly my heart is full to the brim! Bear with me; for I love you, Phœbe, though I speak so roughly! Think nothing of it, dearest child! By and by, I shall be kind, and only kind!"

"My dearest cousin, cannot you tell me what has happened?" asked Phœbe, with a sunny and tearful sympathy. "What is it that moves you so?"

"Hush! hush! He is coming!" whispered Hepzibah, hastily wiping her eyes. "Let him see you first, Phœbe; for you are young and rosy, and cannot help letting a smile break out whether or no. He always liked bright faces! And mine is old now, and the tears are hardly dry on it. He never could abide tears. There; draw the curtain a little, so that the shadow may fall across his side of the table! But let there be a good deal of sunshine, too; for he never was fond of gloom, as some people are. He has had but little sunshine in his life—poor Clifford—and, oh, what a black shadow! Poor, poor Clifford!"

Thus murmuring in an undertone, as if speaking rather to her own heart than to Phœbe, the old gentlewoman stepped on tiptoe about the room, making such arrangements as suggested themselves at the crisis.

Meanwhile there was a step in the passageway, above stairs. Phœbe recognized it as the same which had passed upward, as through her dream, in the night time. The approaching guest, whoever it might be, appeared to pause at the head of the staircase; he paused twice or thrice in the descent; he paused again at the foot. Each time, the delay seemed to be without purpose, but rather from a forgetfulness of the purpose which had set him in motion, or as if the person's feet came involuntarily to a standstill because the motive power was too feeble to sustain his progress. Finally, he made a long pause at the threshold of the parlor. He took hold of the knob of the door; then loosened his grasp without opening it. Hepzibah, her hands convulsively clasped, stood gazing at the entrance.

"Dear Cousin Hepzibah, pray don't look so!" said Phœbe, trembling; for her cousin's emotion, and this mysteriously reluctant step, made her feel as if a ghost were coming into the room. "You really frighten me! Is something awful going to happen?"

"Hush!" whispered Hepzibah. "Be cheerful! whatever may happen, be nothing but cheerful!"

The final pause at the threshold proved so long, that Hepzibah, unable to endure the suspense, rushed forward, threw open the door, and led in the stranger by the hand. At the first glance, Phœbe saw an elderly personage, in an old-fashioned dressing gown of faded damask, and wearing his gray or almost white hair of an unusual length. It quite overshadowed his forehead, except when he thrust it back, and stared vaguely about the room. After a very brief inspection of his face, it was easy to conceive that his footstep must necessarily be such an one as that which, slowly, and with as indefinite an aim as a child's first journey across a floor, had just brought him hitherward. Yet there were no tokens that his physical strength might not have sufficed for a free and determined gait. It was the spirit of the man that could not walk. The expression of his countenance— while, notwithstanding, it had the light of reason in it—seemed to waver and glimmer, and nearly to die away, and feebly to recover itself again. It was like a flame which we see twinkling among half-extinguished embers; we gaze at it more intently than if it were a positive blaze, gushing vividly upward—more intently, but with a certain impatience, as if it ought either to kindle itself into satisfactory splendor, or be at once extinguished.

For an instant after entering the room, the guest stood still, retaining Hepzibah's hand, instinctively, as a child does that of the grown person who guides it. He saw Phœbe, however, and caught an illumination from her youthful and pleasant aspect, which, indeed, threw a cheerfulness about the parlor, like the circle of reflected brilliancy around the glass vase of flowers that was standing in the sunshine. He made a salutation, or, to speak nearer the truth, an ill-defined, abortive attempt at courtesy. Imperfect as it was, however, it conveyed an idea, or, at least, gave a hint, of indescribable grace, such as no practiced art of external manners could have attained. It was too slight to seize upon at the instant; yet, as recollected afterwards, seemed to transfigure the whole man.

"Dear Clifford," said Hepzibah, in the tone with which one soothes a wayward infant, "this is our cousin Phœbe—little Phœbe Pyncheon—Arthur's only child, you know. She has come from the country to stay with us awhile; for our old house has grown to be very lonely now."

"Phœbe?—Phœbe Pyncheon?—Phœbe?" repeated the guest, with a strange, sluggish, ill-defined utterance. "Arthur's child! Ah, I forget! No matter! She is very welcome!"

"Come, dear Clifford, take this chair," said Hepzibah, leading him to his place. "Pray, Phœbe, lower the curtain a very little more. Now let us begin breakfast."

The guest seated himself in the place assigned him, and looked strangely around. He was evidently trying to grapple with the present scene, and bring it home to his mind with a more satisfactory distinctness. He desired to be certain, at least, that he was here, in the low-studded, cross-beamed, oaken-paneled parlor, and not in some other spot, which had sterotyped itself into his senses. But the effort was too great to be sustained with more than a fragmentary success. Continually, as we may express it, he faded away out of his place; or, in other words, his mind and consciousness took their departure, leaving his wasted, gray, and melancholy figure—a substantial emptiness, a material ghost—to occupy his seat at table. Again, after a blank moment, there would be a flickering taper gleam in his eyeballs. It betokened that his spiritual part had returned, and was doing its best to kindle the heart's household fire, and light up intellectual lamps in the dark and ruinous mansion, where it was doomed to be a forlorn inhabitant.

At one of these moments of less torpid, yet still imperfect animation, Phœbe became convinced of what she had at first rejected as too extravagant and startling an idea. She saw that the person before her must have been the original of the beautiful miniature in her cousin Hepzibah's possession. Indeed, with a feminine eye for costume, she had at once identified the damask dressing gown, which enveloped him, as the same in figure, material, and fashion, with that so elaborately represented in the picture. This old, faded garment, with all its pristine brilliancy extinct, seemed, in some indescribable way, to translate the wearer's untold misfortune, and make it perceptible to the beholder's eye.

Hepzibah had now poured out a cup of deliciously fragrant coffee, and presented it to her guest. As his eyes met hers, he seemed bewildered and disquieted.

"Is this you, Hepzibah?" he murmured, sadly; then, more apart, and perhaps unconscious that he was overheard, "How changed, how changed! And is she angry with me? Why does she bend her brow so?"

Poor Hepzibah! It was that wretched scowl which time and her nearsightedness, and the fret of inward discomfort, had rendered so habitual that any vehemence of mood invariably evoked it. But at the indistinct murmur of his words her whole face grew tender, and even lovely, with sorrowful affection; the harshness of her features disappeared, as it were, behind the warm and misty glow.

"Angry!" she repeated; "angry with you, Clifford!"

Her tone, as she uttered the exclamation, had a plaintive and really exquisite melody trilling through it, yet, without subduing a certain something which an obtuse auditor might still have mistaken for asperity. It was as if some transcendent musician should draw a soul-thrilling sweetness out of a cracked instrument, which makes its physical imperfection heard in the midst of ethereal harmony—so deep was the sensibility that found an organ in Hepzibah's voice!

"There is nothing but love here, Clifford," she added, "nothing but love! You are at home!"

The guest responded to her tone by a smile, which did not half light up his face. Feeble as it was, however, and gone in a moment, it had a charm of wonderful beauty. It was followed by a coarser expression; or one that had the effect of coarseness on the fine mold and outline of his countenance, because there was nothing intellectual to temper it. It was a look of appetite. He ate food with what might almost be termed voracity; and seemed to forget himself, Hepzibah, the young girl, and everything else around him, in the sensual enjoyment which the bountifully spread table afforded. In his natural system, though high-wrought and delicately refined, a sensibility to the delights of the palate was probably inherent. It would have been kept in check, however, and even converted into an accomplishment, and one of the thousand modes of intellectual culture, had his more ethereal characteristics retained their vigor. But as it existed now, the effect was painful and made Phœbe droop her eyes.

In a little while the guest became sensible of the fragrance of the yet untasted coffee. He quaffed it eagerly. The subtle essence acted on him like a charmed draft, and caused the opaque substance of his animal being to grow transparent, or, at least, translucent; so that a spiritual gleam was transmitted through it, with a clearer luster than hitherto.

"More, more!" he cried, with nervous haste in his utterance, as if anxious to retain his grasp of what sought to escape him. "This is what I need! Give me more!"

Under this delicate and powerful influence he sat more erect, and looked out from his eyes with a glance that took note of what it rested on. It was not so much that his expression grew more intellectual; this, though it had its share, was not the most peculiar effect.

Not to speak it harshly or scornfully, it seemed Clifford's nature to be a Sybarite. It was perceptible, even there, in the dark old parlor, in the inevitable polarity with which his eyes were attracted toward the quivering play of sunbeams through the shadowy foliage. It was seen in his appreciating notice of the vase of flowers, the scent of which he inhaled with a zest almost peculiar to a physical organization so refined that spiritual ingredients are molded in with it. It was betrayed in the unconscious smile with which he regarded Phœbe, whose fresh and maidenly figure was both sunshine and flowers—their essence, in a prettier and more agreeable mode of manifestation. Not less evident was this love and necessity for the Beautiful, in the instinctive caution with which, even so soon, his eyes turned away from his hostess, and wandered to any quarter rather than come back. It was Hepzibah's misfortune—not Clifford's fault. How could he—so yellow as she was, so wrinkled, so sad of mien, with that odd uncouthness of a turban on her head, and that most perverse of scowls contorting her brow—how could he love to gaze at her?

The guest leaned back in his chair. Mingled in his countenance with a dreamy delight, there was a troubled look of effort and unrest. He was seeking to make himself more fully sensible of the scene around him; or, perhaps, dreading it to be a dream, or a play of imagination, was vexing the fair moment with a struggle for some added brilliancy and more durable illusion.

"How pleasant! How delightful!" he murmured, but not as if addressing anyone. "Will it last? How balmy the atmosphere through that open window! An open window! How beautiful that play of sunshine! Those flowers, how very fragrant! That young girl's face, how cheerful, how blooming!—a flower with the dew on it, and sunbeams in the dewdrops! Ah! this must be all a dream! A dream! A dream! But it has quite hidden the four stone walls!"

Then his face darkened, as if the shadow of a cavern or a dungeon had come over it; there was no more light in its expression than might have come through the iron grates of a prison window—still lessening too, as if he were sinking farther into the depths. Phœbe (being of that quickness and activity of temperament that she seldom long refrained from taking a part, and generally a good one, in what was going forward) now felt herself moved to address the stranger.

"Here is a new kind of rose, which I found this morning in the garden," said she, choosing a small crimson one from among the flowers in the vase. "There will be but five or six on the bush this season. This is the most perfect of them all; not a speck of blight or mildew in it. And how sweet it is!—sweet like no other rose! One can never forget that scent!"

"Ah!—let me see!—let me hold it!" cried the guest, eagerly seizing the flower, which, by the spell peculiar to remembered odors, brought innumerable associations along with the fragrance that it exhaled. "Thank you! This has done me good. I remember how I used to prize this flower—long ago, I suppose, very long ago!—or was it only yesterday? It makes me feel young again! Am I young? Either this remembrance is singularly distinct, or this consciousness strangely dim! But how kind of the fair young girl! Thank you! thank you!"

The favorable excitement derived from this little crimson rose afforded Clifford the brightest moment which he enjoyed at the breakfast table. It might have lasted longer, but that his eyes happened, soon afterwards, to rest on the face of the old Puritan, who, out of his dingy frame and lusterless canvas, was looking down on the scene like a ghost, and a most ill-tempered and ungenial one. The guest made an impatient gesture of the hand, and addressed Hepzibah with what might easily be recognized as the licensed irritability of a petted member of the family.

"Hepzibah!—Hepzibah!" cried he, with no little force and distinctness, "why do you keep that odious picture on the wall? Yes, yes!—that is precisely your taste! I have told you, a thousand times, that it was the evil genius of the house!—my evil genius particularly! Take it down, at once!"

"Dear Clifford," said Hepzibah, sadly, "you know it cannot be!"

"Then, at all events," continued he, still speaking with some energy, "pray cover it with a crimson curtain, broad enough to hang in folds, and with a golden border and tassels. I cannot bear it! It must not stare me in the face!"

"Yes, dear Clifford, the picture shall be covered," said Hepzibah, soothingly. "There is a crimson curtain in a trunk above-stairs—a little faded and moth-eaten, I'm afraid—but Phœbe and I will do wonders with it."

"This very day, remember!" said he; and then added, in a low, self-communing voice, "why should we live in this dismal house at all? Why not go to the south of France?—to Italy?—

Paris, Naples, Venice, Rome? Hepzibah will say we have not the means. A droll idea that!"

He smiled to himself, and threw a glance of fine sarcastic meaning toward Hepzibah.

But the several moods of feeling, faintly as they were marked, through which he had passed, occurring in so brief an interval of time, had evidently wearied the stranger. He was probably accustomed to a sad monotony of life, not so much flowing in a stream, however sluggish, as stagnating in a pool around his feet. A slumberous veil diffused itself over his countenance, and had an effect, morally speaking, on its naturally delicate and elegant outline, like that which a brooding mist, with no sunshine in it, throws over the features of a landscape. He appeared to become grosser—almost cloddish. If aught of interest or beauty—even ruined beauty—had heretofore been visible in this man, the beholder might now begin to doubt it, and to accuse his own imagination of deluding him with whatever grace had flickered over that visage, and whatever exquisite luster had gleamed in those filmy eyes.

Before he had quite sunken away, however, the sharp and peevish tinkle of the shop bell made itself audible. Striking most disagreeably on Clifford's auditory organs and the characteristic sensibility of his nerves, it caused him to start upright out of his chair.

"Good heavens, Hepzibah! what horrible disturbance have we now in the house?" cried he, wreaking his resentful impatience—as a matter of course, and a custom of old—on the one person in the world that loved him. "I have never heard such a hateful clamor! Why do you permit it? In the name of all dissonance, what can it be?"

"Dear Clifford, I wish I could keep the sound from your ears," said Hepzibah, patiently, but reddening with a painful suffusion of shame. "It is very disagreeable even to me. But, do you know, Clifford, I have something to tell you? This ugly noise—pray run, Phœbe, and see who is there!—this naughty little tinkle is nothing but our shop bell!"

"Shop bell!" repeated Clifford, with a bewildered stare.

"Yes, our shop bell," said Hepzibah, a certain natural dignity, mingled with deep emotion, now asserting itself in her manner. "For you must know, dearest Clifford, that we are very poor.

And there was no other resource, but either to accept assistance
from a hand that I would push aside (and so would you!) were
it to offer bread when we were dying for it—no help, save from
him, or else to earn our subsistence with my own hands! Alone,
I might have been content to starve. But you were to be given
back to me! Do you think, then, dear Clifford," added she, with
a wretched smile, "that I have brought an irretrievable disgrace
on the old house, by opening a little shop in the front gable?
Our great-great-grandfather did the same, when there was far
less need! Are you ashamed of me?"

"Shame! Disgrace! Do you speak these words to me, Hepzibah?" said Clifford, not angrily, however; for when a man's
spirit has been thoroughly crushed, he may be peevish at small
offenses, but never resentful of great ones. So he spoke with
only a grieved emotion. "It was not kind to say so, Hepzibah!
What shame can befall me now?"

And then the unnerved man—he that had been born for enjoyment, but had met a doom so very wretched—burst into a
woman's passion of tears. It was but of brief continuance, however; soon leaving him in a quiescent, and to judge by his
countenance, not an uncomfortable state. From this mood, too,
he partially rallied for an instant, and looked at Hepzibah with
a smile, the keen, half-derisory purport of which was a puzzle
to her.

"Are we so very poor, Hepzibah?" said he.

Finally, his chair being deep and softly cushioned, Clifford fell
asleep. Hearing the more regular rise and fall of his breath
(which, however, even then, instead of being strong and full, had
a feeble kind of tremor, corresponding with the lack of vigor
in his character)—hearing these tokens of settled slumber, Hepzibah seized the opportunity to peruse his face more attentively
than she had yet dared to do. Her heart melted away in tears;
her profoundest spirit sent forth a moaning voice, low, gentle,
but inexpressibly sad. In this depth of grief and pity she felt
that there was no irreverence in gazing at his altered, aged,
faded, ruined face. But no sooner was she a little relieved than
her conscience smote her for gazing curiously at him now that
he was so changed; and, turning hastily away, Hepzibah let
down the curtain over the sunny window, and left Clifford to
slumber there.

VIII THE PYNCHEON OF TO-DAY

*Wherein little Ned Higgins comes to the shop to make a purchase,
and to make an inquiry for his unduly inquisitive mother; he discloses Hepzibah's relationship to the guest, and indicates shame had
formerly befallen him. The Pyncheon of to-day comes to the shop;
Phœbe notices omens of the curse which hangs over the Pyncheon
family; Judge Pyncheon makes very solicitous offers, which are
repulsed.*

PHŒBE, on entering the shop, beheld there the already familiar
face of the little devourer—if we can reckon his mighty deeds
aright—of Jim Crow, the elephant, the camel, the dromedaries,
and the locomotive. Having expended his private fortune, on
the two preceding days, in the purchase of the above unheard-of
luxuries, the young gentleman's present errand was on the part
of his mother, in quest of three eggs and half a pound of raisins.
These articles Phœbe accordingly supplied, and, as a mark of
gratitude for his previous patronage, and a slight superadded
morsel after breakfast, put likewise into his hand a whale! The
great fish, reversing his experience with the prophet of Nineveh,[1]
immediately began his progress down the same red pathway of
fate whither so varied a caravan had preceded him.

After partly closing the door, the child turned back, and mumbled something to Phœbe, which, as the whale was but half disposed of, she could not perfectly understand.

"What did you say, my little fellow?" asked she.

"Mother wants to know," repeated Ned Higgins, more distinctly, "how Old Maid Pyncheon's brother does? Folks say he
has got home."

"My cousin Hepzibah's brother!" exclaimed Phœbe, surprised

[1] PROPHET OF NINEVEH—Jonah.

at this sudden explanation of the relationship between Hepzibah and her guest. "Her brother! And where can he have been?"

The little boy only put his thumb to his broad snub-nose, with that look of shrewdness which a child, spending much of his time in the street, so soon learns to throw over his features, however unintelligent in themselves. Then as Phœbe continued to gaze at him, without answering his mother's message, he took his departure.

As the child went down the steps, a gentleman ascended them, and made his entrance into the shop. It was the portly, and, had it possessed the advantage of a little more height, would have been the stately figure of a man considerably in the decline of life, dressed in a black suit of some thin stuff, resembling broadcloth as closely as possible. A gold-headed cane, of rare Oriental wood, added materially to the high respectability of his aspect, as did also a white neckcloth of the utmost snowy purity, and the conscientious polish of his boots. His dark, square countenance, with its almost shaggy depth of eyebrows, was naturally impressive, and would, perhaps, have been rather stern, had not the gentleman considerately taken upon himself to mitigate the harsh effect by a look of exceeding good humor and benevolence. Owing, however, to a somewhat massive accumulation of animal substance about the lower region of his face, the look was, perhaps, unctuous, rather than spiritual, and had, so to speak, a kind of fleshly effulgence, not altogether as satisfactory as he doubtless intended it to be. A susceptible observer, at any rate, might have regarded it as affording very little evidence of the genuine benignity of soul whereof it purported to be the outward reflection. And if the observer chanced to be ill-natured, as well as acute and susceptible, he would probably suspect that the smile on the gentleman's face was a good deal akin to the shine on his boots, and that each must have cost him and his bootblack, respectively, a good deal of hard labor to bring out and preserve them.

As the stranger entered the little shop, where the projection of the second story and the thick foliage of the elm tree, as well as the commodities at the window, created a sort of gray medium, his smile grew as intense as if he had set his heart on counteracting the whole gloom of the atmosphere (besides any moral gloom pertaining to Hepzibah and her inmates) by the

unassisted light of his countenance. On perceiving a young
rosebud of a girl, instead of the gaunt presence of the old maid,
a look of surprise was manifest. He at first knit his brows;
then smiled with more unctuous benignity than ever.

"Ah, I see how it is!" said he, in a deep voice—a voice which,
had it come from the throat of an uncultivated man, would have
been gruff, but, by dint of careful training, was now sufficiently
agréeable—"I was not aware that Miss Hepzibah Pyncheon had
commenced business under such favorable auspices. You are
her assistant, I suppose?"

"I certainly am," answered Phœbe, and added, with a little
air of lady-like assumption (for, civil as the gentleman was, he
evidently took her to be a young person serving for wages), "I
am a cousin of Miss Hepzibah, on a visit to her."

"Her cousin?—and from the country? Pray pardon me,
then," said the gentleman, bowing and smiling, as Phœbe never
had been bowed to nor smiled on before; "in that case, we must
be better acquainted; for, unless I am sadly mistaken, you are
my own little kinswoman likewise! Let me see—Mary?—
Dolly?—Phœbe?—yes, Phœbe is the name! Is it possible that
you are Phœbe Pyncheon, only child of my dear cousin and classmate, Arthur? Ah, I see your father now, about your mouth!
Yes, yes! we must be better acquainted! I am your kinsman,
my dear. Surely you must have heard of Judge Pyncheon?"

As Phœbe curtsied in reply, the judge bent forward, with the
pardonable and even praiseworthy purpose—considering the
nearness of blood, and the difference of age—of bestowing on
his young relative a kiss of acknowledged kindred and natural
affection. Unfortunately (without design, or only with such instinctive design as gives no account of itself to the intellect)
Phœbe, just at the critical moment, drew back; so that her
highly respectable kinsman, with his body bent over the counter,
and his lips protruded, was betrayed into the rather absurd
predicament of kissing the empty air. It was a modern parallel
to the case of Ixion [2] embracing a cloud, and was so much the
more ridiculous as the judge prided himself on eschewing all
airy matter, and never mistaking a shadow for a substance.

On raising her eyes, Phœbe was startled by the change in

_____

[2] Ixion—A mythological king of Thessaly who pursued a goddess only to
find her a cloud

Judge Pyncheon's face. It was quite as striking, allowing for the difference of scale, as that betwixt a landscape under a broad sunshine and just before a thunderstorm; not that it had the passionate intensity of the latter aspect, but was cold, hard, immitigable, like a day-long brooding cloud.

"Dear me! what is to be done now?" thought the country girl to herself. "He looks as if there were nothing softer in him than a rock, nor milder than the east wind! I meant no harm! Since he is really my cousin, I would have let him kiss me, if I could!"

Then, all at once, it struck Phœbe that this very Judge Pyncheon was the original of the miniature which the daguerrotypist had shown her in the garden, and that the hard, stern, relentless look, now on his face, was the same that the sun had so inflexibly persisted in bringing out. Was it, therefore, no momentary mood, but, however skillfully concealed, the settled temper of his life? And not merely so, but was it hereditary in him, and transmitted down, as a precious heirloom, from that bearded ancestor, in whose picture both the expression, and, to a singular degree, the features of the modern judge were shown as by a kind of prophecy? A deeper philosopher than Phœbe might have found something very terrible in this idea. It implied that the weaknesses and defects, the bad passions, the mean tendencies, and the moral diseases which lead to crime are handed down from one generation to another, by a far surer process of transmission than human law has been able to establish in respect to the riches and honors which it seeks to entail upon posterity.

But, as it happened, scarcely had Phœbe's eyes rested again on the judge's countenance than all its ugly sternness vanished; and she found herself quite overpowered by the sultry, dog-day heat, as it were, of benevolence, which this excellent man diffused out of his great heart into the surrounding atmosphere.

"I like that, Cousin Phœbe!" cried he, with an emphatic nod of approbation. "I like it much, my little cousin! You are a good child, and know how to take care of yourself. A young girl—especially if she be a very pretty one—can never be too chary of her lips."

"Indeed, sir," said Phœbe, trying to laugh the matter off, "I did not mean to be unkind."

Nevertheless, whether or no it were entirely owing to the inauspicious commencement of their acquaintance, she still acted under a certain reserve, which was by no means customary to her frank and genial nature. The fantasy would not quit her, that the original Puritan, of whom she had heard so many somber traditions—the progenitor of the whole race of New England Pyncheons, the founder of the House of the Seven Gables, and who had died so strangely in it—had now stepped into the shop. In these days of off-hand equipment, the matter was easily enough arranged. On his arrival from the other world, he had merely found it necessary to spend a quarter of an hour at a barber's, who had trimmed down the Puritan's full beard into a pair of grizzled whiskers, then, patronizing a ready-made clothing establishment, he had exchanged his velvet doublet and sable cloak, with the richly worked band under his chin, for a white collar and cravat, coat, vest, and pantaloons; and lastly, putting aside his steel-hilted broadsword to take up a gold-headed cane, the Colonel Pyncheon of two centuries ago steps forward as the judge of the passing moment!

Of course, Phœbe was far too sensible a girl to entertain this idea in any other way than as matter for a smile. Possibly, also, could the two personages have stood together before her eye, many points of difference would have been perceptible, and perhaps only a general resemblance.

The similarity, intellectual and moral, between the judge and his ancestor appears to have been at least as strong as the resemblance of mien and feature would afford reason to anticipate. For example: tradition affirmed that the Puritan had been greedy of wealth; the judge, too, with all the show of liberal expenditure, was said to be as closefisted as if his grip were of iron. The ancestor had clothed himself in a grim assumption of kindliness, a rough heartiness of word and manner, which most people took to be the genuine warmth of nature, making its way through the thick and inflexible hide of a manly character. His descendant, in compliance with the requirements of a nicer age, had etherealized this rude benevolence into that broad benignity of smile, wherewith he shone like a noonday sun along the streets, or glowed like a household fire in the drawing-rooms of his private acquaintance.

The Puritan—so, at least, says chimney-corner tradition,

which often preserves traits of character with marvellous fidelity —was bold, imperious, relentless, crafty; laying his purposes deep, and following them out with an inveteracy of pursuit that knew neither rest nor conscience; trampling on the weak, and, when essential to his ends, doing his utmost to beat down the strong. Whether the Judge in any degree resembled him the further progress of our narrative may show.

Scarcely any of the items in the above-drawn parallel occurred to Phœbe, whose country birth and residence, in truth, had left her pitifully ignorant of most of the family traditions, which lingered, like cobwebs and incrustations of smoke, about the rooms and chimney-corners of the House of the Seven Gables. Yet there was a circumstance, very trifling in itself, which impressed her with an odd degree of horror. She had heard of the anathemas flung by Maule, the executed wizard, against Colonel Pyncheon and his posterity—that God would give them blood to drink—and likewise of the popular notion, that this miraculous blood might now and then be heard gurgling in their throats. Thus it happened, that when Phœbe heard a certain noise in Judge Pyncheon's throat—rather habitual with him, not altogether voluntary, yet indicative of nothing unless it were a slight bronchial complaint, or, as some people hinted, an apoplectic symptom—when the girl heard this queer and awkward ingurgitation (which the writer never did hear, and therefore cannot describe), she, very foolishly, started, and clasped her hands.

Of course, it was exceedingly ridiculous in Phœbe to be discomposed by such a trifle, and still more unpardonable to show her discomposure to the individual most concerned in it. But the incident chimed in so oddly with her previous fancies about the Colonel and the Judge, that, for the moment, it seemed quite to mingle their identity.

"What is the matter with you, young woman?" said Judge Pyncheon, giving her one of his harsh looks. "Are you afraid of anything?"

"Oh, nothing, sir—nothing in the world!" answered Phœbe, with a little laugh of vexation at herself. "But perhaps you wish to speak with my Cousin Hepzibah. Shall I call her?"

"Stay a moment, if you please," said the judge, again beaming sunshine out of his face. "You seem to be a little nervous this

morning. The town air, Cousin Phœbe, does not agree with
your good, wholesome country habits. Or has anything happened to disturb you?—anything remarkable in Cousin Hepzibah's family? An arrival, eh? I thought so! No wonder you
are out of sorts, my little cousin. To be an inmate with such
a guest may well startle an innocent young girl!"

"You quite puzzle me, sir," replied Phœbe, gazing inquiringly
at the Judge. "There is no frightful guest in the house, but
only a poor, gentle, childlike man, whom I believe to be Cousin
Hepzibah's brother. I am afraid (but you, sir, will know better
than I) that he is not quite in his sound senses; but so mild
and quiet he seems to be, that a mother might trust her baby
with him; and I think he would play with the baby as if he
were only a few years older than itself. He startle me?—oh,
no, indeed!"

"I rejoice to hear so favorable and so ingenuous an account
of my Cousin Clifford," said the benevolent Judge. "Many years
ago, when we were boys and young men together, I had a great
affection for him, and still feel a tender interest in all his concerns. You say, Cousin Phœbe, he appears to be weak-minded.
Heaven grant him at least enough of intellect to repent of his
past sins!"

"Nobody, I fancy," observed Phœbe, "can have fewer to repent of."

"And is it possible, my dear," rejoined the Judge, with a com-
miserating look, "that you have never heard of Clifford Pyncheon
—that you know nothing of his history? Well, it is all right; and
your mother has shown a very proper regard for the good name
of the family with which she connected herself. Believe the
best you can of this unfortunate person, and hope the best! It
is a rule which Christians should always follow, in their judgments of one another; and especially is it right and wise among
near relatives, whose characters have necessarily a degree of
mutual dependence. But is Clifford in the parlor? I will just
step in and see."

"Perhaps, sir, I had better call my Cousin Hepzibah," said
Phœbe; hardly knowing, however, whether she ought to obstruct
the entrance of so affectionate a kinsman into the private regions
of the house. "Her brother seemed to be just falling asleep after
breakfast; and I am sure she would not like him to be disturbed.
Pray, sir, let me give her notice!"

But the Judge showed a singular determination to enter un-announced; and as Phœbe, with the vivacity of a person whose movements unconsciously answer to her thoughts, had stepped toward the door, he used little or no ceremony in putting her aside.

"No, no, Miss Phœbe!" said Judge Pyncheon, in a voice as deep as a thunder growl, and with a frown as black as the cloud whence it issues. "Stay you here! I know the house, and I know my cousin Hepzibah, and know her brother Clifford likewise!—nor need my little country cousin put herself to the trouble of announcing me!"—in these latter words, bye the bye, there were symptoms of a change from his sudden harshness into his previous benignity of manner. "I am at home here, Phœbe, you must recollect, and you are the stranger. I will just step in, therefore, and see for myself how Clifford is, and assure him and Hepzibah of my kindly feelings and best wishes. It is right, at this juncture, that they should both hear from my own lips how much I desire to serve them. Ha! here is Hepzi-bah herself!"

Such was the case. The vibrations of the Judge's voice had reached the old gentlewoman in the parlor, where she sat, with face averted, waiting on her brother's slumber. She now issued forth, as would appear, to defend the entrance, looking, we must needs say, amazingly like the dragon which, in fairy tales, is wont to be the guardian over an enchanted beauty. The habitual scowl of her brow was, undeniably, too fierce, at this moment, to pass itself off on the innocent score of nearsightedness; and it was bent on Judge Pyncheon in a way that seemed to confound, if not alarm him, so inadequately had he estimated the moral force of a deeply grounded antipathy. She made a repelling gesture with her hand, and stood a perfect picture of prohibition, at full length, in the dark frame of the doorway. But we must betray Hepzibah's secret, and confess that the native timorous-ness of her character even now developed itself in a quick tremor, which, to her own perception, set each of her joints at variance with its fellows.

Possibly, the Judge was aware how little true hardihood lay behind Hepzibah's formidable front. At any rate, being a gen-tleman of steady nerves, he soon recovered himself, and failed not to approach his cousin with outstretched hand; adopting the sensible precaution, however, to cover his advance with a smile so broad and sultry, that, had it been only half as warm as it looked, a trellis of grapes might at once have turned purple under its summer-like exposure. It may have been his purpose, indeed, to melt poor Hepzibah on the spot, as if she were a figure of yellow wax.

"Hepzibah, my beloved cousin, I am rejoiced!" exclaimed the Judge, most emphatically. "Now, at length, you have something to live for. Yes, and all of us, let me say, your friends and kindred, have more to live for than we had yesterday. I have lost no time in hastening to offer any assistance in my power toward making Clifford comfortable. He belongs to us all. I know how much he requires—how much he used to require—with his delicate taste, and his love of the beautiful. Anything in my house—pictures, books, wine, luxuries of the table—he may command them all! It would afford me most heartfelt gratification to see him! Shall I step in, this moment?"

"No," replied Hepzibah, her voice quivering too painfully to allow of many words. "He cannot see visitors!"

"A visitor, my dear cousin!—do you call me so?" cried the Judge, whose sensibility, it seems, was hurt by the coldness of the phrase. "Nay, then, let me be Clifford's host, and your own likewise. Come at once to my house. The country air, and all the conveniences—I may say luxuries—that I have gathered about me, will do wonder for him. And you and I, dear Hepzibah, will consult together, and watch together, and labor together, to make our dear Clifford happy. Come! why should we make more words about what is both a duty and a pleasure on my part? Come to me at once!"

On hearing these so hospitable offers, and such generous recognition of the claims of kindred, Phœbe felt very much in the mood of running up to Judge Pyncheon, and giving him, of her own accord, the kiss from which she had so recently shrunk away. It was quite otherwise with Hepzibah; the Judge's smile seemed to operate on her acerbity of heart like sunshine upon vinegar, making it ten times sourer than ever.

"Clifford," said she—still too agitated to utter more than an abrupt sentence—"Clifford has a home here!"

"May heaven forgive you, Hepzibah," said Judge Pyncheon —reverently lifting his eyes toward that high court of equity to which he appealed—"if you suffer any ancient prejudice or animosity to weigh with you in this matter! I stand here, with an open heart, willing and anxious to receive yourself and Clifford into it. Do not refuse my good offices—my earnest propositions for your welfare! They are such, in all respects, as it behooves your nearest kinsman to make. It will be a heavy responsibility, cousin, if you confine your brother to this dismal house and stifled air, when the delightful freedom of my countryseat is at his command."

"It would never suit Clifford," said Hepzibah, as briefly as before.

"Woman!" broke forth the judge, giving way to his resentment, "what is the meaning of all this? Have you other resources? Nay, I suspected as much! Take care, Hepzibah, take care! Clifford is on the brink of as black a ruin as ever befell him yet! But why do I talk with you, woman as you are? Make way!—I must see Clifford!"

Hepzibah spread out her gaunt figure across the door and seemed really to increase in bulk; looking the more terrible, also, because there was so much terror and agitation in her heart. But Judge Pyncheon's evident purpose of forcing a passage was interrupted by a voice from the inner room; a weak, tremulous, wailing voice, indicating helpless alarm, with no more energy for self-defense than belongs to a frightened infant.

"Hepzibah, Hepzibah!" cried the voice; "go down on your knees to him! Kiss his feet! Entreat him not to come in! Oh, let him have mercy on me! Mercy! mercy!"

For the instant, it appeared doubtful whether it were not the Judge's resolute purpose to set Hepzibah aside, and step across the threshold into the parlor, whence issued that broken and miserable murmur of entreaty. It was not pity that restrained him, for, at the first sound of the enfeebled voice, a red fire kindled his eyes, and he made a quick pace forward, with something inexpressibly fierce and grim darkening forth, as it were, out of the whole man. To know Judge Pyncheon, was to see him at that moment.

Yet, after all, are we not slandering an excellent and amiable man? Look at the Judge now! He is apparently conscious of having erred in too energetically pressing his deeds of loving-kindness on persons unable to appreciate them. He will await

"It would never suit Clifford,"
said Hepzibah.

their better mood, and hold himself as ready to assist them, then, as at this moment. As he draws back from the door, an all-comprehensive benignity blazes from his visage, indicating that he gathers Hepzibah, little Phœbe, and the invisible Clifford, all three, together with the whole world besides, into his immense heart, and gives them a warm bath in its flood of affection.

"You do me great wrong, dear cousin Hepzibah!" said he, first kindly offering her his hand, and then drawing on his glove preparatory to departure. "Very great wrong! But I forgive it, and will study to make you think better of me. Of course, our poor Clifford being in so unhappy a state of mind, I cannot think of urging an interview at present. But I shall watch over his welfare, as if he were my own beloved brother; nor do I at all despair, my dear cousin, of constraining both him and you to acknowledge your injustice. When that shall happen, I desire no other revenge than your acceptance of the best offices in my power to do you."

With a bow to Hepzibah, and a degree of paternal benevolence in his parting nod to Phœbe, the Judge left the shop, and went smiling along the street. As is customary with the rich when they aim at the honors of a republic, he apologized, as it were, to the people, for his wealth, prosperity, and elevated station, by a free and hearty manner toward those who knew him; putting off the more of his dignity, in due proportion with the humbleness of the man whom he saluted, and thereby proving a haughty consciousness of his advantages as irrefragably as if he had marched forth preceded by a troop of lackeys to clear the way.

No sooner had he disappeared than Hepzibah grew deadly white, and, staggering toward Phœbe, let her head fall on the young girl's shoulder.

"Oh, Phœbe!" murmured she, "that man has been the horror of my life! Shall I never, never have the courage—will my voice never cease from trembling long enough—to let me tell him what he is?"

"Is he so very wicked?" asked Phœbe. "Yet his offers were surely kind!"

"Do not speak of them—he has a heart of iron!" rejoined Hepzibah. "Go, now, and talk to Clifford! Amuse and keep him quiet! It would disturb him wretchedly to see me so agitated as I am. There go, dear child, and I will try to look after the shop."

Phœbe went, accordingly, but perplexed herself, meanwhile, with queries as to the purport of the scene which she had just witnessed, and also, whether judges, clergymen, and other characters of that eminent stamp and respectability, could really, in any single instance, be otherwise than just and upright men. But Phœbe, in order to keep the universe in its old place, was fain to smother, in some degree, her own intuitions as to Judge Pyncheon's character. And as for her cousin's testimony in disparagement of it, she concluded that Hepzibah's judgment was embittered by one of those family feuds which render hatred the more deadly, by the dead and corrupted love that they intermingle with its native poison.

IX   CLIFFORD AND PHŒBE

Wherein Hepzibah's great love and devotion to her brother are shown; Hepzibah fails in many respects to please him. Where Hepzibah falls short, Phœbe succeeds.

TRULY was there something high, generous, and noble in the native composition of our poor old Hepzibah! Or else—and it was quite as probably the case—she had been enriched by poverty, developed by sorrow, elevated by the strong and solitary affection of her life, and thus endowed with heroism which never could have characterized her in what are called happier circumstances. Through dreary years, Hepzibah had looked forward —for the most part despairingly, never with any confidence of hope, but always with the feeling that it was her brightest possibility—to the very position in which she had now found herself. In her own behalf, she had asked nothing of Providence, but the opportunity of devoting herself to this brother, whom she had so loved—so admired for what he was, or might have been—and to whom she had kept her faith, alone of all the world, wholly, unfalteringly, at every instant, and throughout life. And here, in his late decline, the lost one had come back out of his long and strange misfortune, and was thrown on her sympathy, as it seemed, not merely for the bread of his physical existence, but for everything that should keep him morally alive. She had responded to the call. She had come forward—our poor, gaunt Hepzibah, in her rusty silks, with her rigid joints, and the sad perversity of her scowl—ready to do her utmost; and with affection enough, if that were all, to do a hundred times as much! There could be few more tearful sights—and Heaven forgive us if a smile insists on mingling with our conception of it!—few sights with truer pathos in them, than Hepzibah presented, on that first afternoon.

How patiently did she endeavor to wrap Clifford up in her great, warm love, and make it all the world to him, so that he should retain no torturing sense of the coldness and dreariness without! Her little efforts to amuse him! How pitiful, yet magnanimous, they were!

Remembering his early love of poetry and fiction, she unlocked a bookcase, and took down several books that had been excellent reading in their day. There was a volume of Pope,[1] with *The Rape of the Lock* [2] in it, and another of the *Tatler*,[3] and an odd one of Dryden's *Miscellanies*,[4] all with tarnished gilding on their covers, and thoughts of tarnished brilliancy inside.

They had no success with Clifford. These, and all such writers of society, whose new works glow like the rich texture of a just-woven carpet, must be content to relinquish their charm, for every reader, after an age or two, and could hardly be supposed to retain any portion of it for a mind that had utterly lost its estimate of modes and manners. Hepzibah then took up *Rasselas* [5] and began to read of the Happy Valley, with a vague idea that some secret of a contented life had there been elaborated, which might at least serve Clifford and herself for this one day. But the Happy Valley had a cloud over it. Hepzibah troubled her auditor, moreover, by innumerable sins of emphasis, which he seemed to detect, without any reference to the meaning; nor, in fact, did he appear to take much note of the sense of what she read, but evidently felt the tedium of the lec-

[1] POPE—Alexander Pope (1688–1744), the foremost English poet of his time.

[2] *The Rape of the Lock*—A mock epic, based on the alleged theft of a maiden's lock of hair.

[3] The *Tatler*—A periodical published from 1709–11 by Richard Steele. It was succeeded by the more famous *Spectator*.

[4] DRYDEN's *Miscellanies*—Certain poems by John Dryden (1631–1700), celebrated English poet and critic.

[5] *Rasselas*—A romance by Dr. Samuel Johnson (1709–84), dealing with the adventures of a prince of Abyssinia in the Happy Valley.

ture, without harvesting its profits. His sister's voice, too, naturally harsh, had, in the course of her sorrowful lifetime, contracted a kind of croak, which, when it once gets into the human throat, is as ineradicable as sin.

Discerning that Clifford was not gladdened by her efforts, Hepzibah searched about the house for the means of more exhilarating pastime. At one time, her eyes chanced to rest on Alice Pyncheon's harpsichord. It was a moment of great peril; for—despite the traditionary awe that had gathered over this instrument of music, and the dirges which spiritual fingers were said to play on it—the devoted sister had solemn thoughts of thrumming on its chords for Clifford's benefit, and accompanying the performance with her voice. Poor Clifford! Poor Hepzibah! Poor harpsichord! All three would have been miserable together. By some good agency—possibly, by the unrecognized interposition of the long-buried Alice herself—the threatening calamity was averted.

But the worst of all—the hardest stroke of fate, for Hepzibah to endure, and perhaps for Clifford too—was his invincible distaste for her appearance. Her features, never the most agreeable, and now harsh with age and grief, and resentment against the world for his sake; her dress, and especially her turban; the queer and quaint manners, which had unconsciously grown upon her in solitude; such being the poor gentlewoman's outward characteristics, it is no great marvel, although the mournfullest of pities, that the instinctive lover of the Beautiful was fain to turn away his eyes. There was no help for it. It would be the latest impulse to die within him. In his last extremity, the expiring breath stealing faintly through Clifford's lips, he would doubtless press Hepzibah's hand, in fervent recognition of all her lavished love, and close his eyes—but not so much to die, as to be constrained to look no longer on her face! Poor Hepzibah! She took counsel with herself what might be done, and thought of putting ribbons on her turban; but, by the instant rush of several guardian angels, was withheld from an experiment that could hardly have proved less than fatal to the beloved object of her anxiety.

To be brief, besides Hepzibah's disadvantages of person, there was an uncouthness pervading all her deeds; a clumsy something, that could but ill adapt itself for use, and not at all for ornament. She was a grief to Clifford, and she knew it. She therefore turned to Phœbe, and resigned the task into the young girl's hands. The latter took it up cheerfully, as she did everything, but with no sense of a mission to perform, and succeeding all the better for that same simplicity.

By the involuntary effect of a genial temperament, Phœbe soon grew to be absolutely essential to the daily comfort, if not the daily life, of her two forlorn companions.

To the guest—to Hepzibah's brother—or Cousin Clifford, as Phœbe now began to call him—she was especially necessary. Not that he could ever be said to converse with her, or often manifest, in any other very definite mode, his sense of charm in her society. But, if she were a long while absent he became pettish and nervously restless, pacing the room to and fro, with the uncertainty that characterized all his movements; or else would sit broodingly in his great chair, resting his head on his hands, and evincing life only by an electric sparkle of ill humor, whenever Hepzibah endeavored to arouse him. Phœbe's presence, and the contiguity of her fresh life to his blighted one, was usually all that he required. Indeed, such was the native gush and play of her spirit, that she was seldom perfectly quiet and undemonstrative, any more than a fountain ever ceases to dimple and warble with its flow. She possessed the gift of song, and that, too, so naturally, that you would as little think of inquiring whence she had caught it, or what master had taught her, as of asking the same questions about a bird, in whose small strain of music we recognize the voice of the Creator as distinctly as in the loudest accents of his thunder. So long as Phœbe sang, she might stray at her own will about the house. Clifford was content, whether the sweet, airy homeliness of her tones came down from the upper chambers, or along the passageway from the shop, or was sprinkled through the foliage of the pear tree, inward from the garden, with the twinkling sunbeams. He would sit quietly, with a gentle pleasure gleaming over his face, brighter now, and now a little dimmer, as the song happened to float near him, or was more remotely heard. It pleased him best, however, when she sat on a low footstool at his knee.

Becoming habituated to her companionship, Clifford readily showed how capable of imbibing pleasant tints and gleams of cheerful light from all quarters his nature must originally have been. He grew youthful while she sat by him. A beauty—not precisely real, even in its utmost manifestation, and which a painter would have watched long to seize and fix upon his canvas, and, after all, in vain—beauty, nevertheless, that was not a mere dream, would sometimes play upon and illuminate his face. It did more than to illuminate; it transfigured him with an expression that could only be interpreted as the glow of an exquisite and happy spirit. That gray hair, and those furrows—with their record of infinite sorrow, so deeply written across his brow, and so compressed, as with a futile effort to crowd in all the tale, that the whole inscription was made illegible—these, for the moment, vanished. An eye, at once tender and acute, might have beheld in the man some shadow of what he was meant to be. Anon, as age came stealing, like a sad twilight, back over his figure, you would have felt tempted to hold an argument with Destiny, and affirm, that either this being should not have been made mortal, or mortal existence should have been tempered to his qualities. There seemed no necessity for his having drawn breath, at all—the world never wanted him—but, as he had breathed, it ought always to have been the balmiest of summer air.

Phœbe, it is probable, had but a very imperfect comprehension of the character over which she had thrown so beneficent a spell. Nor was it necessary. The fire upon the hearth can gladden a whole semicircle of faces round about it, but need not know the individuality of one among them all. Indeed, there was something too fine and delicate in Clifford's traits to be perfectly appreciated by one whose sphere lay so much in the Actual as Phœbe's did. For Clifford, however, the reality, and simplicity, and thorough homeliness, of the girl's nature, were as powerful a charm as any that she possessed. Beauty, it is true, and beauty almost perfect in its own style, was indispensable. Had Phœbe been coarse in feature, shaped clumsily, of a harsh voice, and uncouthly mannered, she might have been rich with all good gifts, beneath this unfortunate exterior, and still, so long as she wore the guise of woman, she would have shocked Clifford, and depressed him by her lack of beauty. But nothing more beautiful—nothing prettier, at least—was ever made than Phœbe. And, therefore, to this man—whose whole poor and impalpable enjoyment of existence, heretofore, and until both his heart and

fancy died within him, had been a dream—whose images of
women had more and more lost their warmth and substance,
and been frozen, like the pictures of secluded artists, into the
chilliest ideality—to him, this little figure of the cheeriest household life was just what he required to bring him back into the
breathing world.

There was something very beautiful in the relation that grew
up between this pair, so closely and constantly linked together,
yet with such a waste of gloomy and mysterious years from his
birthday to hers. On Clifford's part, it was the feeling of a
man naturally endowed with the liveliest sensibility to feminine
influence, but who had never quaffed the cup of passionate love,
and knew that it was now too late. He knew it, with the instinctive delicacy that had survived his intellectual decay. Thus,
his sentiment for Phœbe, without being paternal, was not less
chaste than if she had been his daughter. He was a man, it is
true, and recognized her as a woman. She was his only representative of womankind. All her little womanly ways, budding
out of her like blossoms on a young fruit tree, had their effect
on him, and sometimes caused his very heart to tingle with the
keenest thrills of pleasure. At such moments—for the effect was
seldom more than momentary—the half-torpid man would be
full of harmonious life, just as a long-silent harp is full of
sound when the musician's fingers sweep across it. But, after
all, it seemed rather a perception, or a sympathy, than a sentiment belonging to himself as an individual. He read Phœbe, as
he would a sweet and simple story; he listened to her, as if
she were a verse of household poetry, which God, in requital of
his bleak and dismal lot, had permitted some angel, that most
pitied him, to warble through the house. She was not an actual
fact for him, but the interpretation of all that he had lacked on
earth, brought warmly home to his conception; so that this
mere symbol, or lifelike picture, had almost the comfort of
reality.

And how did Phœbe regard Clifford? The girl's was not one
of those natures which are most attracted by what is strange and
exceptional in human character. The path which would best
have suited her was the well-worn track of ordinary life; the
companions in whom she would most have delighted were such
as one encounters at every turn. The mystery which enveloped

Clifford, so far as it affected her at all, was an annoyance, rather than the piquant charm which many women might have found in it. Still, her native kindliness was brought strongly into play, not by what was darkly picturesque in his situation, nor so much, even by the finer grace of his character, as by the simple appeal of a heart so forlorn as his to one so full of genuine sympathy as hers. She gave him an affectionate regard, because he needed so much love, and seemed to have received so little. With a ready tact, the result of ever-active and wholesome sensibility, she discerned what was good for him, and did it. Whatever was morbid in his mind and experience, she ignored; and thereby kept their intercourse healthy, by the incautious, but, as it were, Heaven-directed freedom of her whole conduct. Phœbe afforded her poor patient a supply of purer air. She impregnated it, too, not with a wild-flower scent—for wildness was no trait of hers—but with the perfume of garden roses, pinks, and other blossoms of much sweetness, which nature and man have consented together in making grow from summer to summer, and from century to century. Such a flower was Phœbe, in her relation with Clifford, and such the delight that he inhaled from her.

Yet, it must be said, her petals sometimes drooped a little in consequence of the heavy atmosphere about her. She grew more thoughtful than heretofore. Looking aside at Clifford's face, and seeing the dim, unsatisfactory elegance, and the intellect almost quenched, she would try to inquire what had been his life. Was he always thus? Had this veil been over him from his birth?—this veil, under which far more of his spirit was hidden than revealed, and through which he so imperfectly discerned the actual world—or was its gray texture woven of some dark calamity? Phœbe loved no riddles, and would have been glad to escape the perplexity of this one. Nevertheless, there was so far a good result of her meditations on Clifford's character, that, when her involuntary conjectures, together with the tendency of every strange circumstance to tell its own story, had gradually taught her the fact, it had no terrible effect upon her. Let the world have done him what vast wrong it might, she knew Cousin Clifford too well—or fancied so—ever to shudder at the touch of his thin, delicate fingers.

Within a few days after the appearance of this remarkable

inmate, the routine of life had established itself with a good deal of uniformity in the old house of our narrative. In the morning, very shortly after breakfast, it was Clifford's custom to fall asleep in his chair; nor, unless accidentally disturbed, would he emerge from a dense cloud of slumber, or the thinner mists that flitted to and fro, until well toward noonday. These hours of drowsy head were the season of the old gentlewoman's attendance on her brother, while Phœbe took charge of the shop; an arrangement which the public speedily understood, and evinced their decided preference of the younger shopwoman by the multiplicity of their calls during her administration of affairs. Dinner over, Hepzibah took her knitting work—a long stocking of gray yarn, for her brother's winter wear—and with a sigh, and a scowl of affectionate farewell to Clifford, and a gesture enjoining watchfulness on Phœbe, went to take her seat behind the counter. It was now the young girl's turn to be the nurse—the guardian, the playmate, or whatever is the fitter phrase—of the gray-haired man.

X   THE PYNCHEON GARDEN

Wherein Phœbe entertains Clifford in the garden with reading, conversation, flowers and humming birds; Chanticleer and the hens loosed at Clifford's request; activities in the garden; Sunday afternoon guests.

CLIFFORD, except for Phœbe's more active investigation, would ordinarily have yielded to the torpor which had crept through all his modes of being, and which sluggishly counseled him to sit in his morning chair till eventide. But the girl seldom failed to propose a removal to the garden, where Uncle Venner and the daguerreotypist had made such repairs on the roof of the ruinous arbor, or summerhouse, that it was now a sufficient shelter from sunshine and casual showers. The hopvine, too, had begun to grow luxuriantly over the sides of the little edifice, and made an interior of verdant seclusion, with innumerable peeps and glimpses into the wider solitude of the garden.

Here, sometimes, in the green play place of flickering light, Phœbe read to Clifford. Her acquaintance, the artist, who appeared to have a literary turn, had supplied her with works of fiction, in pamphlet form, and a few volumes of poetry, in alto-

gether a different style and taste from those which Hepzibah
selected for his amusement. Small thanks were due to the
books, however, if the girl's readings were in any degree more
successful than her elderly cousin's. Phœbe's voice had always
a pretty music in it, and could either enliven Clifford by its
sparkle and gayety of tone, or soothe him by a continued flow
of pebbly and brook-like cadences. But the fictions—in which
the country girl, unused to works of that nature, often became
deeply absorbed—interested her strange auditor very little, or
not at all. Pictures of life, scenes of passion or sentiment, wit,
humor, and pathos, were all thrown away, or worse than thrown
away, on Clifford; either because he lacked an experience by
which to test their truth, or because his own griefs were a touch-
stone of reality that few feigned emotions could withstand.
When Phœbe broke into a peal of merry laughter at what she
read, he would now and then laugh for sympathy, but oftener
respond with a troubled, questioning look. If a tear—a maiden's
sunshiny tear, over imaginary woe—dropped upon some melancholy page, Clifford either took it as a token of actual calamity,
or else grew peevish and angrily motioned her to close the
volume. And wisely, too! Is not the world sad enough, in
genuine earnest, without making a pastime of mock sorrows?

With poetry, it was rather better. He delighted in the swell
and subsidence of the rhythm, and the happily recurring rhyme.

Nor was Clifford incapable of feeling the sentiment of poetry—not, perhaps, where it was highest or deepest, but where it was most flitting and ethereal. It was impossible to foretell in what exquisite verse the awakening spell might lurk; but, on raising her eyes from the page to Clifford's face, Phœbe would be made aware, by the light breaking through it, that a more delicate intelligence than her own had caught a lambent flame from what she read. One glow of this kind, however, was often the precursor of gloom for many hours afterwards; because, when the glow left him, he seemed conscious of a missing sense and power, and groped about for them, as if a blind man should go seeking his lost eyesight.

It pleased him more, and was better for his inward welfare, that Phœbe should talk, and make passing occurrences vivid to his mind by her accompanying description and remarks. The life of the garden offered topics enough for such discourse as suited Clifford best. He never failed to inquire what flowers had bloomed since yesterday. His feeling for flowers was very exquisite, and seemed not so much a taste as an emotion; he was fond of sitting with one in his hand, intently observing it, and looking from its petals into Phœbe's face, as if the garden flower were the sister of the household maiden. Not merely was there a delight in the flower's perfume, or pleasure in its beautiful form, and the delicacy or brightness of its hue; but Clifford's enjoyment was accompanied with a perception of life, character, and individuality, that made him love these blossoms of the garden, as if they were endowed with sentiment and intelligence. This affection and sympathy for flowers is almost exclusively a woman's trait. Men, if endowed with it by nature, soon lose, forget, and learn to despise it, in their contact with coarser things than flowers. Clifford, too, had long forgotten it; but found it again, now, as he slowly revived from the chill torpor of his life.

When the bean vines began to flower on the poles, there was one particular variety which bore a vivid scarlet blossom. The daguerreotypist had found these beans in a garret, over one of the seven gables, treasured up in an old chest of drawers, by some horticultural Pyncheon of days gone by, who, doubtless, meant to sow them the next summer, but was himself first sown in Death's garden ground. By way of testing whether there was still a living germ in such ancient seeds, Holgrave had planted some of them; and the result of his experiment was a splendid row of bean vines, clambering, early, to the full height of the poles, and arraying them, from top to bottom, in a spiral profusion of red blossoms. And, ever since the unfolding the first bud, a multitude of humming birds had been attracted thither. At times, it seemed as if for every one of the hundred blossoms there was one of these tiniest fowls of the air; a thumb's bigness of burnished plumage, hovering and vibrating about the bean poles. It was with indescribable interest, and even more than childish delight, that Clifford watched the humming birds. He used to thrust his head softly out of the arbor, to see them the better; all the while, too, motioning Phœbe to be quiet, and snatching glimpses of the smile upon her face, so as to heap his enjoyment up the higher with her sympathy. He had not merely grown young; he was a child again.

Hepzibah, whenever she happened to witness one of these fits of miniature enthusiasm, would shake her head, with a strange mingling of the mother and sister, and of pleasure and sadness, in her aspect. She said that it had always been thus with Clifford, when the humming birds came—always, from his babyhood —and that his delight in them had been one of the earliest tokens by which he showed his love for beautiful things. And it was a wonderful coincidence, the good lady thought, that the artist should have planted these scarlet-flowering beans—which the humming birds sought far and wide, and which had not grown in the Pyncheon garden before for forty years—on the very summer of Clifford's return.

Then would the tears stand in poor Hepzibah's eyes, or overflow them with a too abundant gush, so that she was fain to betake herself into some corner, lest Clifford should espy her agitation. Indeed, all the enjoyments of this period were provocative of tears. Coming so late as it did, it was a kind of Indian summer, with a mist in its balmiest sunshine, and decay and death in its gaudiest delight. The more Clifford seemed to taste the happiness of a child, the sadder was the difference to be recognized. All his life long, he had been learning how to be wretched, as one learns a foreign tongue; and now, with the lesson thoroughly at heart, he could with difficulty comprehend his little airy happiness. Frequently there was a dim shadow of doubt in his eyes. "Take my hand, Phœbe," he would say, "and pinch it hard with your little fingers! Give me a rose, that I may press its thorns, and prove myself awake, by the sharp touch of pain!" Evidently, he desired this prick of a trifling anguish, in order to assure himself, by that quality which he best knew to be real, that the garden, and the seven weather-beaten gables, and Hepzibah's scowl and Phœbe's smile, were real, likewise. Without this signet in his flesh, he could have attributed no more substance to them than to the empty confusion of imaginary scenes with which he had fed his spirit until even that poor sustenance was exhausted.

One of the available means of amusement, of which Phœbe made the most, in Clifford's behalf, was that feathered society, the hens, a breed of whom, as we have already said, was an immemorial heirloom in the Pyncheon family. In compliance with a whim of Clifford, as it troubled him to see them in confinement, they had been set at liberty, and now roamed at will about the garden; doing some little mischief, but hindered from escape by buildings, on three sides, and the difficult peaks of a wooden fence, on the other. They spent much of their abundant leisure on the margin of Maule's well, which was haunted by a kind of snail, evidently a titbit of their palates; and the brackish water itself, however nauseous to the rest of the world, was so greatly esteemed by these fowls, that they might be seen tasting, turning up their heads, and smacking their bills, with precisely the air of wine bibbers round a probationary cask. Their generally quiet, yet often brisk, and constantly diversified talk, one to another, or sometimes in soliloquy—as they scratched worms out of the rich, black soil, or pecked at such plants as suited their taste—had such a domestic tone, that it was almost a wonder why you could not establish a regular interchange of ideas about household matters, human and gallinaceous. All hens are well worth studying, for the piquancy and rich variety of their manners; but by no possibility can there have been other fowls of such odd appearance and deportment as these ancestral ones. They probably embodied the traditionary peculiarities of their whole line of progenitors, derived through an unbroken succession of eggs; or else this individual Chanticleer and his two wives had grown to be humorists, and a little crack-brained withal, on account of their solitary way of life, and out of sympathy for Hepzibah, their lady patroness.

Queer, indeed, they looked! Chanticleer himself, though stalking on two stilt-like legs, with the dignity of interminable descent in all his gestures, was hardly bigger than an ordinary partridge; his two wives were about the size of quails; and as for the one chicken, it looked small enough to be still in the egg, and, at the same time, sufficiently old, withered, wizened, and experienced, to have been the founder of the antiquated race. Instead of being the youngest of the family, it rather seemed to have aggregated into itself the ages, not only of these living specimens of the breed, but of all its forefathers and foremothers, whose united excellencies and oddities were squeezed into its little body. Its mother evidently regarded it as the one chicken of the world, and as necessary, in fact, to the world's continuance, or, at any rate, to the equilibrium of the present system of affairs, whether in church or state. No lesser sense of the infant fowl's importance could have justified, even in a mother's eyes, the perseverance with which she watched over its safety, ruffling her small person to twice its proper size, and flying in everybody's face that so much as looked toward her hopeful progeny. No lower estimate could have vindicated the indefatigable zeal with which she scratched, and her unscrupulousness in digging up the choicest flower or vegetable, for the sake of the fat earthworm at its root. Her nervous cluck, when the chicken happened to be hidden in the long grass or under the squash leaves; her gentle croak of satisfaction, while sure of it beneath her wing; her note of ill-concealed fear and obstreperous defiance, when she saw her archenemy, a neighbor's cat, on the top of the high fence; one or other of these sounds was to be heard at almost every moment of the day. By degrees, the observer came to feel nearly as much interest in this chicken of illustrious race as the mother hen did.

Phœbe, after getting well acquainted with the old hen, was sometimes permitted to take the chicken in her hand, which was quite capable of grasping its cubic inch or two of body. While she curiously examined its hereditary marks—the peculiar speckle of its plumage, the funny tuft on its head, and a knob on each of its legs—the little biped, as she insisted, kept giving her a sagacious wink. The daguerreotypist once whispered her that these marks betokened the oddities of the Pyncheon family, and that the chicken itself was a symbol of the life of the old house, embodying its interpretation likewise, although an unintelligible one, as such clews generally are. It was a feathered riddle; a mystery hatched out of an egg, and just as mysterious as if the egg had been addle!

The second of Chanticleer's two wives, ever since Phœbe's arrival, had been in a state of heavy despondency, caused, as it afterwards appeared, by her inability to lay an egg. One day, however, by her self-important gait, the sideway turn of her head, and the cock of her eye, as she pried into one and another nook of the garden—croaking to herself, all the while, with inexpressible complacency—it was made evident that this identical hen, much as mankind undervalued her, carried something about her person, the worth of which was not to be estimated either in gold or precious stones. Shortly after, there was a prodigious cackling and gratulation of Chanticleer and all his family, including the wizened chicken, who appeared to understand the matter quite as well as did his sire, his mother, or his aunt. That afternoon Phœbe found a diminutive egg—not in the regular nest —it was far too precious to be trusted there—but cunningly hidden under the currant bushes, on some dry stalks of last year's grass. Hepzibah, on learning the fact, took possession of the egg and appropriated it to Clifford's breakfast, on account of a certain delicacy of flavor, for which, as she affirmed, these eggs had always been famous. Thus unscrupulously did the old gentlewoman sacrifice the continuance, perhaps, of an ancient feathered race, with no better end than to supply her brother with a dainty that hardly filled the bowl of a teaspoon! It must have been in reference to this outrage that Chanticleer, the next day, accompanied by the bereaved mother of the egg, took his post in front of Phœbe and Clifford, and delivered himself of a harangue that might have proved as long as his own pedigree, but for a fit of merriment on Phœbe's part. Hereupon, the offended fowl stalked away on his long stilts, and utterly withdrew his notice from Phœbe and the rest of human nature, until she made her peace with an offering of spice cake, which, next to snails, was the delicacy most in favor with his aristocratic taste.

We linger too long, no doubt, beside this paltry rivulet of life that flowed through the garden of the Pyncheon house. But we deem it pardonable to record these mean incidents and poor delights, because they proved so greatly to Clifford's benefit.

They had the earth smell in them, and contributed to give him health and substance. Some of his occupations wrought less desirably upon him. He had a singular propensity, for example, to hang over Maule's well, and look at the constantly shifting phantasmagoria of figures produced by the agitation of the water over the mosaic work of colored pebbles at the bottom. He said that faces looked upward to him there—beautiful faces, arrayed in bewitching smiles—each momentary face so fair and rosy, and every smile so sunny, that he felt wronged at its departure, until the same flitting witchcraft made a new one. But sometimes he would suddenly cry out, "The dark face gazes at me!" and be miserable the whole day afterwards. Phœbe, when she hung over the fountain by Clifford's side, could see nothing of all this—neither the beauty nor the ugliness—but only the colored pebbles, looking as if the gush of the water shook and disarranged them. And the dark face, that so troubled Clifford, was no more than the shadow thrown from a branch of one of the damson trees, and breaking the inner light of Maule's well. The truth was, however, that his fancy—reviving faster than his will and judgment, and always stronger than they—created shapes of loveliness that were symbolic of his native character, and now and then a stern and dreadful shape, that typified his fate.

On Sundays, after Phœbe had been at church—for the girl had a churchgoing conscience, and would hardly have been at ease had she missed either prayer, singing, sermon, or benediction—after church time, therefore, there was, ordinarily, a sober little festival in the garden. In addition to Clifford, Hepzibah, and Phœbe, two guests made up the company. One was the artist, Holgrave, who, in spite of his consociation with reformers, and his other queer and questionable traits, continued to hold an elevated place in Hepzibah's regard. The other, we are almost ashamed to say, was the venerable Uncle Venner, in a clean shirt, and a broadcloth coat, more respectable than his ordinary wear, inasmuch as it was neatly patched on each elbow, and might be called an entire garment, except for a slight inequality in the length of its skirts. Clifford, on several occasions, had seemed to enjoy the old man's intercourse, for the sake of his mellow, cheerful vein, which was like the sweet flavor of a frost-bitten apple, such as one picks up under the tree in December. A man at the very lowest point of the social scale was easier and more agreeable for the fallen gentleman to encounter than a person at any of the intermediate degrees; and, moreover, as Clifford's young manhood had been lost, he was fond of feeling himself comparatively youthful, now, in apposition with the patriarchal age of Uncle Venner. In fact, it was sometimes observable that Clifford half wilfully hid from himself the consciousness of being stricken in years, and cherished visions of an earthly future still before him; visions, however, too indistinctly drawn to be followed by disappointment—though, doubtless, by depression—when any casual incident or recollection made him sensible of the withered leaf.

So this oddly composed little social party used to assemble under the ruinous arbor. Hepzibah—stately as ever at heart, and yielding not an inch of her old gentility, but resting upon it so much the more, as justifying a princess-like condescension— exhibited a not ungraceful hospitality. She talked kindly to the vagrant artist, and took sage counsel—lady as she was—with the wood sawyer, the messenger of everybody's petty errands, the patched philosopher. And Uncle Venner, who had studied the world at street corners, and at other posts equally well adapted for just observations, was as ready to give out his wisdom as a town pump to give water.

"Miss Hepzibah, ma'am," said he once, after they had all been cheerful together, "I really enjoy these quiet little meetings of a Sabbath afternoon. They are very much like what I expect to have, after I retire to my farm!"

"Uncle Venner," observed Clifford, in a drowsy, inward tone, "is always talking about his farm. But I have a better scheme for him, by and by. We shall see!"

"Ah, Mr. Clifford Pyncheon!" said the man of patches, "you may scheme for me as much as you please; but I'm not going to give up this one scheme of my own, even if I never bring it really to pass. It does seem to me that men make a wonderful mistake in trying to heap up property upon property. If I had done so, I should feel as if Providence was not bound to take care of me; and, at all events, the city wouldn't be! I'm one of those people who think that infinity is big enough for us all —and eternity long enough!"

"Why, so they are, Uncle Venner," remarked Phœbe, after a

pause; for she had been trying to fathom the profundity and appositeness of this concluding apothegm. "But for this short life of ours, one would like a house and a moderate garden spot of one's own."

"It appears to me," said the daguerreotypist, smiling, "that Uncle Venner has the principles of Fourier [1] at the bottom of his wisdom; only they have not quite so much distinctness, in his mind, as in that of the systematizing Frenchman."

"Come, Phœbe," said Hepzibah, "it is time to bring the currants."

And then, while the yellow richness of the declining sunshine still fell into the open space of the garden, Phœbe brought out a loaf of bread, and a China bowl of currants, freshly gathered from the bushes, and crushed with sugar. These, with water—but not from the fountain of ill omen, close at hand—constituted all the entertainment. Meanwhile, Holgrave took some pains to establish an intercourse with Clifford, actuated, it might seem, entirely by an impulse of kindliness, in order that the present hour might be cheerfuller than most which the poor recluse had spent, or was destined yet to spend. Nevertheless, in the artist's deep, thoughtful, all-observant eyes, there was, now and then, an expression, not sinister, but questionable, as if he had some other interest in the scene than a stranger, a youthful and unconnected adventurer, might be supposed to have. With great mobility of outward mood, however, he applied himself to the task of enlivening the party; and with so much success, that even dark-hued Hepzibah threw off one tint of melancholy, and made what shift she could with the remaining portion. Phœbe said to herself, "How pleasant he can be!" As for Uncle Venner, as a mark of friendship and approbation, he readily consented to afford the young man his countenance in the way of his profession—not metaphorically, be it understood, but literally, by allowing a daguerreotype of his face, so familiar to the town, to be exhibited at the entrance of Holgrave's studio.

Clifford, as the company partook of their little banquet, grew to be the gayest of them all. Either it was one of those up-quivering flashes of the spirit, to which minds in an abnormal state are liable, or else the artist had subtly touched some chord that made musical vibration. Indeed, what with the pleasant

[1] FOURIER—A French socialist.

summer evening, and the sympathy of this little circle of not unkindly souls, it was perhaps natural that a character so susceptible as Clifford's should become animated, and show itself readily responsive to what was said around him. But he gave out his own thoughts, likewise, with an airy and fanciful glow; so that they glistened, as it were, through the arbor, and made their escape among the interstices of the foliage. He had been as cheerful, no doubt, while alone with Phœbe, but never with such tokens of acute, although partial intelligence.

But, as the sunlight left the peaks of the seven gables, so did the excitement fade out of Clifford's eyes. He gazed vaguely and mournfully about him, as if he missed something precious, and missed it the more drearily for not knowing precisely what it was.

"I want my happiness!" at last he murmured, hoarsely and indistinctly, hardly shaping out the words. "Many, many years have I waited for it! It is late! It is late! I want my happiness!"

XI   THE ARCHED WINDOW

Wherein Clifford's slow recovery is aided by viewing life in Pyncheon Street from the arched window; the new inventions puzzle and dismay Clifford; he is aroused by the organ grinder and political procession; Clifford yearns to join activities of the world again; a soap bubble brings an interesting reaction.

FROM the inertness, or what we may term the vegetative character, of this ordinary mood, Clifford would perhaps have been content to spend one day after another, interminably—or, at least, throughout the summertime—in just the kind of life described in the preceding pages. Fancying, however, that it might be for his benefit occasionally to diversify the scene, Phœbe sometimes suggested that he should look out upon the life of the street. For this purpose, they used to mount the staircase together, to the second story of the house, where, at the termination of a wide entry, there was an arched window of uncommonly large dimensions, shaded by a pair of curtains. It opened above the porch, where there had formerly been a balcony, the balustrade of which had long since gone to decay, and been removed. At this arched window, throwing it open, but keeping himself in comparative obscurity by means of the curtain, Clifford had an opportunity of witnessing such a portion of the great world's movement as might be supposed to roll through one of the retired streets of a not very populous city. But he and Phœbe made a sight as well worth seeing as any that the city could exhibit. The pale, gray, childish, aged, melancholy, yet often simply cheerful, and sometimes delicately intelligent aspect of Clifford, peering from behind the faded crimson of the curtain—watching the monotony of everyday occurrences with a kind of inconsequential interest and earnestness, and, at every petty throb of his sensibility, turning for sympathy to the eyes of the bright young girl!

If once he were fairly seated at the window, even Pyncheon Street would hardly be so dull and lonely but that, somewhere or other along its extent, Clifford might discover matter to occupy his eyes, and titillate, if not engross, his observation. Things familiar to the youngest child that had begun its outlook at existence seemed strange to him. A cab; an omnibus, with its populous interior, dropping here and there a passenger, and picking up another, and thus typifying that vast rolling vehicle, the world, the end of whose journey is everywhere and nowhere; these objects he followed eagerly with his eyes, but forgot them, before the dust raised by the horses and wheels had settled along their track. As regarded novelties (among which cabs and omnibuses were to be reckoned), his mind appeared to have lost its proper gripe and retentiveness. Twice or thrice, for example, during the sunny hours of the day, a water cart went along by the Pyncheon house, leaving a broad wake of moistened earth, instead of the white dust that had risen at a lady's lightest footfall; it was like a summer shower, which the city authorities had caught and tamed, and compelled it into the commonest routine of their convenience. With the water cart Clifford could never grow familiar; it always affected him with just the same surprise as at first. His mind took an apparently sharp impression from it, but lost the recollection of this perambulatory shower, before its next reappearance, as completely as did the street itself, along which the heat so quickly strewed white dust again. It was the same with the railroad. Clifford could hear the obstreperous howl of the steam whistle, and, by leaning a little way from the arched window, could catch a glimpse of the trains of cars, flashing a brief transit across the extremity of the street. The idea of terrible energy, thus forced upon him, was new at every recurrence, and seemed to affect him as disagreeably, and with almost as much surprise, the hundredth time as the first.

Clifford was indeed the most inveterate of conservatives. All the antique fashions of the street were dear to him; even such as were characterized by a rudeness that would naturally have annoyed his fastidious senses. He loved the old rumbling and jolting carts, the former track of which he still found in his long-buried remembrance, as the observer of to-day finds the wheel tracks of ancient vehicles in Herculaneum.[1] The butcher's cart, with its snowy canopy, was an acceptable object; so was the fish cart, heralded by its horn; so, likewise, was the countryman's cart of vegetables, plodding from door to door, with long pauses of the patient horse, while his owner drove a trade in turnips, carrots, summer squashes, string beans, green peas, and new potatoes with half the housewives of the neighborhood. The baker's cart, with the harsh music of its bells, had a pleasant effect on Clifford, because, as few things else did, it jingled the very dissonance of yore. One afternoon, a scissor grinder chanced to set his wheel a-going under the Pyncheon elm, and just in front of the arched window. Children came running with their mother's scissors, or the carving knife, or the paternal razor, or anything else that lacked an edge (except, indeed, poor Clifford's wits), that the grinder might apply the article to his magic wheel, and give it back as good as new. Round went the busily revolving machinery, kept in motion by the scissor grinder's foot, and wore away the hard steel against the hard stone. It was an ugly, little, venomous serpent of a noise, as ever did petty violence to human ears. But Clifford listened with rapturous delight. The sound, however disagreeable, had very brisk life in it, and, together with the circle of curious children watching the revolutions of the wheel, appeared to give him a more vivid sense of active, bustling, and sunshiny existence, than he had attained in almost any other way. Nevertheless, its charm lay chiefly in the past; for the scissor grinder's wheel had hissed in his childish ears.

He sometimes made doleful complaint that there were no stage coaches nowadays. And he asked, in an injured tone, what

---

[1] HERCULANEUM—City buried in 79 A.D. by an eruption of Mt. Vesuvius.

had become of all those old square-top chaises, with wings sticking out on either side, that used to be drawn by a plow horse,
and driven by a farmer's wife and daughter, peddling whortle-
berries and blackberries about the town. Their disappearance
made him doubt, he said, whether the berries had not left off
growing in the broad pastures and along the shady country lanes.

But anything that appealed to the sense of beauty, in however humble a way, did not require to be recommended by these
old associations. This was observable when one of the Italian
boys (who are rather a modern feature of our streets) came
along with his barrel organ, and stopped under the wide and
cool shadows of the elm. With his quick professional eye, he
took note of the two faces watching him from the arched window,
and, opening his instrument, began to scatter its melodies abroad.
He had a monkey on his shoulder, dressed in a Highland plaid;
and, to complete the sum of splendid attractions wherewith he
presented himself to the public, there was a company of little
figures, whose sphere and habitation was in the mahogany case
of his organ, and whose principle of life was the music which
the Italian made it his business to grind out. In all their variety
of occupation—the cobbler, the blacksmith, the soldier, the lady
with her fan, the milkmaid sitting by her cow—this fortunate
little society might truly be said to enjoy a harmonious existence,
and to make life literally a dance. The Italian turned a crank;
and behold! everyone of these small individuals started into the
most curious vivacity.

The monkey, meanwhile, with a thick tail curling out into
preposterous prolixity from beneath his tartans, took his station at the Italian's feet. He turned a wrinkled and abominable
little visage to every passer-by, and to the circle of children that
soon gathered round, and to Hepzibah's shop door, and upward
to the arched window, whence Phœbe and Clifford were looking
down. Every moment, also, he took off his Highland bonnet,
and performed a bow and scrape. Sometimes, moreover, he made
personal application to individuals, holding out his small black
palm, and otherwise plainly signifying his excessive desire for
whatever filthy lucre might happen to be in anybody's pocket.
The mean and low, yet strangely man-like expression of his
wilted countenance; the prying and crafty glance, that showed
him ready to gripe at every miserable advantage; his enormous

tail (too enormous to be decently concealed under his gabardine), and the deviltry of nature which it betokened—take this monkey just as he was, in short, and you could desire no better image of the Mammon of copper coin, symbolizing the grossest form of love of money. Neither was there any possibility of satisfying the covetous little fellow. Phœbe threw down a whole handful of cents, which he picked up with joyous eagerness, handed them over to the Italian for safe-keeping, and immediately recommenced a series of pantomimic petitions for more.

Clifford had taken childish delight in the music, and smiled, too, at the figures which it set in motion. But, after looking a while at the long-tailed imp, he was so shocked by his horrible ugliness, spiritual as well as physical, that he actually began to shed tears; a weakness which men of merely delicate endowments, and destitute of the fiercer, deeper, and more tragic power of laughter, can hardly avoid, when the worst and meanest aspect of life happens to be presented to them.

Pyncheon Street was sometimes enlivened by spectacles of more imposing pretensions than the above, and which brought the multitude along with them. With a shivering repugnance at the idea of personal contact with the world, a powerful impulse still seized on Clifford, whenever the rush and roar of the human tide grew strongly audible to him. This was made evident, one day, when a political procession, with hundreds of flaunting banners, and drums, fifes, clarions, and cymbals, reverberating between the rows of buildings, marched all through town, and trailed its length of trampling footsteps, and most infrequent uproar, past the ordinarily quiet House of the Seven Gables. As a mere object of sight, nothing is more deficient in picturesque features than a procession, seen in its passage through narrow streets. The spectator feels it to be fool's play, when he can distinguish the tedious commonplace of each man's visage, with the perspiration and weary self-importance on it, and the very cut of his pantaloons, and the stiffness or laxity of his shirt collar, and the dust on the back of his black coat. But, on the other hand, if an impressible person, standing alone over the brink of one of these processions, should behold it, not in its atoms, but in its aggregate—as a mighty river of life, massive in its tide, and black with mystery, and, out of its depths, calling to the kindred depth within him—then the contiguity would add to the effect. It might so fascinate him that he would hardly be restrained from plunging into the surging stream of human sympathies.

So it proved with Clifford. He shuddered; he grew pale; he threw an appealing look at Hepzibah and Phœbe, who were with him at the window. They comprehended nothing of his emotions, and supposed him merely disturbed by the unaccustomed tumult. At last, with tremulous limbs, he started up, set his foot on the window sill, and, in an instant more, would have been in the unguarded balcony. As it was, the whole procession might have seen him, a wild, haggard figure, his gray locks floating in the wind that waved their banners; a lonely being, estranged from his race, but now feeling himself man again, by virtue of the irrepressible instinct that possessed him. Had Clifford attained the balcony, he would probably have leaped into the street; but whether impelled by the species of terror that sometimes urges its victim over the very precipice which he shrinks from, or by a natural magnetism, tending toward the great center of humanity, it were not easy to decide. Both impulses might have wrought on him at once.

But his companions, affrighted by his gesture—which was that of a man hurried away, in spite of himself—seized Clifford's garment and held him back. Hepzibah shrieked. Phœbe, to whom all extravagance was a horror, burst into sobs and tears.

"Clifford, Clifford! are you crazy?" cried his sister.

"I hardly know, Hepzibah," said Clifford, drawing a long breath. "Fear nothing, it is over now, but had I taken that plunge, and survived it, methinks it would have made me another man!"

Possibly, in some sense, Clifford may have been right. He needed a shock; or perhaps he required to take a deep, deep plunge into the ocean of human life, and to sink down and be covered by its profoundness, and then to emerge, sobered, invigorated, restored to the world and to himself. Perhaps, again, he required nothing less than the great final remedy—death!

A similar yearning to renew the broken links of brotherhood with his kind sometimes showed itself in a milder form; and once it was made beautiful by the religion that lay even deeper than itself. In the incident now to be sketched, there was a touching recognition, on Clifford's part, of God's care and love toward him—toward this poor, forsaken man, who, if any mortal could, might have been pardoned for regarding himself as thrown aside, forgotten, and left to be the sport of some fiend, whose playfulness was an ecstasy of mischief.

It was the Sabbath morning; one of those bright, calm Sabbaths, with its own hallowed atmosphere, when heaven seems to diffuse itself over the earth's face, in a solemn smile, no less sweet than solemn. On such a Sabbath morn, were we pure enough to be its medium, we should be conscious of the earth's natural worship, ascending through our frames, on whatever spot of ground we stood. The church bells, with various tones, but all in harmony, were calling out, and responding to one an-. other, "It is the Sabbath!—the Sabbath!—yea; the Sabbath!" and over the whole city the bells scattered the blessed sounds, now slowly, now with livelier joy, now one bell alone, now all the bells together, crying earnestly, "It is the Sabbath!" and flinging their accents far off, to melt into the air, and pervade it with the holy word. The air, with God's sweetest and tenderest sunshine in it, was meet for mankind to breathe into their hearts, and send it forth again as the utterance of prayer.

Clifford sat at the window, with Hepzibah, watching the neighbors as they stepped into the street. All of them, however unspiritual on other days, were transfigured by the Sabbath influence; so that their very garments—whether it were an old man's decent coat, well brushed for the thousandth time, or a little boy's first sack and trousers, finished yesterday by his mother's needle—had somewhat of the quality of ascension robes. Forth, likewise, from the portal of the old house, stepped Phœbe, putting up her small green sunshade, and throwing upward a glance and smile of parting kindness to the faces at the arched window. In her aspect there was a familiar gladness, and a holiness that you could play with, and yet reverence it as much as ever. She was like a prayer, offered up in the homeliest beauty of one's mother tongue. Fresh was Phœbe, moreover, and airy and sweet in her apparel; as if nothing that she wore— neither her gown, nor her small straw bonnet, nor her little kerchief, any more than her snowy stockings—had ever been put on before; or, if worn, were all the fresher for it, and with a fragrance as if they had lain among the rosebuds.

The girl waved her hand to Hepzibah and Clifford, and went up the street; a religion in herself, warm, simple, true, with a substance that could walk on earth, and a spirit that was capable of heaven.

"Hepzibah," asked Clifford, after watching Phœbe to the corner, "do you never go to church?"

"No, Clifford!" she replied, "not these many, many years!"

"Were I to be there," he rejoined, "it seems to me that I could pray once more, when so many human souls were praying all around me!"

She looked into Clifford's face, and beheld there a soft, natural effusion; for his heart gushed out, as it were, and ran over at his eyes, in delightful reverence for God, and kindly affection for his human brethren. The emotion communicated itself to Hepzibah. She yearned to take him by the hand, and go and kneel down, they two together—both so long separate from the world, and, as she now recognized, scarcely friends with Him above—to kneel down among the people, and be reconciled to God and man at once.

"Dear brother," said she, earnestly, "let us go! We belong nowhere. We have not a foot of space in any church to kneel upon; but let us go to some place of worship, even if we stand in the broad aisle. Poor and forsaken as we are, some pew door will be opened to us!"

So Hepzibah and her brother made themselves ready—as ready as they could, in the best of their old-fashioned garments, which had hung on pegs, or been laid away in trunks, so long that the dampness and moldy smell of the past was on them—made themselves ready, in their faded bettermost, to go to church. They descended the staircase together—gaunt, sallow Hepzibah, and pale, emaciated, age-stricken Clifford! They pulled open the front door, and stepped across the threshold, and felt, both of them, as if they were standing in the presence of the whole world, and with mankind's great and terrible eye on them alone. The eye of their Father seemed to be withdrawn, and gave them no encouragement. The warm sunny air of the street made them shiver. Their hearts quaked within them, at the idea of taking one step further.

"It cannot be, Hepzibah!—it is too late," said Clifford, with deep sadness. "We are ghosts! We have no right among human beings—no right anywhere, but in this old house, which has a curse on it, and which therefore we are doomed to haunt! And, besides," he continued, with a fastidious sensibility, inalienably characteristic of the man, "it would not be fit nor beautiful to go! It is an ugly thought, that I should be frightful to my fellow beings, and that children would cling to their mothers' gowns at sight of me!"

They shrank back into the dusky passageway, and closed the door. But, going up the staircase again, they found the whole interior of the house tenfold more dismal, and the air closer and heavier, for the glimpse and breath of freedom which they had just snatched. They could not flee; their jailer had but left the door ajar, in mockery, and stood behind it, to watch them stealing out. At the threshold, they felt his pitiless gripe upon them. For, what other dungeon is so dark as one's own heart! What jailer so inexorable as one's self!

But it would be no fair picture of Clifford's state of mind, were we to represent him as continually or prevailingly wretched. On the contrary, there was no other man in the city, we are bold to affirm, of so much as half his years, who enjoyed so many lightsome and griefless moments as himself. He had no burden of care upon him; there were none of those questions and contingencies with the future to be settled, which wear away all other lives, and render them not worth having by the very process of providing for their support. In this respect, he was a child—a child for the whole term of his existence, be it long or short. Indeed, his life seemed to be standing still at a period little in advance of childhood, and to cluster all his reminiscences about that epoch; just as, after the torpor of a heavy blow, the sufferer's reviving consciousness goes back to a moment considerably behind the accident that stupefied him. He sometimes told Phœbe and Hepzibah his dreams, in which he invariably played the part of a child, or a very young man. So vivid were they, in his relation of them, that he once held a dispute with his sister as to the particular figure or print of a chintz morning dress, which he had seen their mother wear, in the dream of the preceding night. Hepzibah, piquing herself on a woman's accuracy in such matters, held it to be slightly different from what Clifford described; but producing the very gown from an old trunk, it proved to be identical with his remembrance of it.

Had Clifford, every time that he emerged out of dreams so life-like, undergone the torture of transformation from a boy into an old and broken man, the daily recurrence of the shock would have been too much to bear. It would have caused an acute agony to thrill, from the morning twilight, all the day through, until bedtime; and even then would have mingled a dull, in-scrutable pain, and pallid hue of misfortune, with the visionary bloom and adolescence of his slumber. But the nightly moon-shine interwove itself with the morning mist, and enveloped him as in a robe, which he hugged about his person, and seldom let realities pierce through; he was not often quite awake, but slept open-eyed, and perhaps fancied himself most dreaming then.

Thus, lingering always so near his childhood, he had sym-pathies with children, and kept his heart the fresher thereby, like a reservoir into which rivulets were pouring, not far from the fountain head. Though prevented, by a subtle sense of pro-priety, from desiring to associate with them, he loved few things better than to look out of the arched window, and see a little girl driving her hoop along the sidewalk, or schoolboys at a game of ball. Their voices, also, were very pleasant to him, heard at a distance, all swarming and in-termingling together, as flies do in a sunny room.

Clifford would, doubtless, have been glad to share their sports. One after-noon, he was seized with an irresistible desire to blow soap bubbles; an amuse-ment, as Hepzibah told Phœbe apart, that had been a favorite one with her brother, when they were both children. Behold him, therefore, at the arched window, with an earthen pipe in his mouth! Be-hold him, with his gray hair, and a wan, unreal smile over his countenance, where still hovered a beautiful grace, which his worst enemy must have acknowledged to be spiritual and immortal, since it had survived so long! Behold him, scattering airy spheres abroad, from the window into the street! Little impalpable worlds were those soap bubbles, with the big world depicted, in hues bright as imagination, on the nothing of their surface. It was curious to see how the passersby regarded these brilliant fantasies, as they came floating down, and made the dull atmosphere imaginative about them. Some stopped to gaze, and, perhaps, carried a pleasant recollection of the bubbles onward as far as the street corner; some looked angrily upward, as if poor Clifford wronged them, by setting an image of beauty afloat so near their dusty pathway. A great many put out their fingers or their walking sticks, to touch withal; and were perversely gratified, no doubt, when the bubble, with all its pictured earth and sky scene, vanished as if it had never been.

At length, just as an elderly gentleman of very dignified presence happened to be passing, a large bubble sailed majestically down, and burst right against his nose! He looked up—at first with a stern, keen glance, which penetrated at once into the obscurity behind the arched window—then with a smile, which might be conceived as diffusing a dog-day sultriness for the space of several yards about him.

"Aha, Cousin Clifford!" cried Judge Pyncheon. "What! still blowing soap bubbles!"

The tone seemed as if meant to be kind and soothing, but yet had a bitterness of sarcasm in it. As for Clifford, an absolute palsy of fear came over him. Apart from any definite cause of dread which his past experience might have given him, he felt that native and original horror of the excellent judge which is proper to a weak, delicate and apprehensive character, in the presence of massive strength. Strength is incomprehensible by weakness, and, therefore, the more terrible. There is no greater bugbear than a strong-willed relative, in the circle of his own connections.

XII THE DAGUERREOTYPIST

Wherein are related Phœbe's recreations away from her dreary surroundings and morbid relatives; Holgrave tells her of his own life —except of his family origin. His mystery still surrounds him; why was he living at the House of Seven Gables? Did he cherish more than an ordinary friendship for Phœbe? The discussion regarding the Pyncheon family seems to agitate Holgrave to a great degree.

It must not be supposed that the life of a personage naturally so active as Phœbe could be wholly confined within the precincts of the old Pyncheon house. Clifford's demands upon her time were usually satisfied, in those long days, considerably earlier than sunset. Quiet as his daily existence seemed, it nevertheless drained all the resources by which he lived. It was not physical exercise that overwearied him; for—except that he sometimes wrought a little with a hoe, or paced the garden walk, or, in rainy weather, traversed a large, unoccupied room—it was his tendency to remain only too quiescent, as regarded any toil of the limbs and muscles. But either there was a smoldering fire within him that consumed his vital energy, or the monotony that would have dragged itself with benumbing effect over a mind differently situated was no monotony to Clifford. Possibly, he was in a state of second growth and recovery, and was constantly assimilating nutriment for his spirit and intellect from sights, sounds, and events, which passed as a perfect void to persons more practiced with the world. As all is activity and vicissitude to the new mind of a child, so might it be, likewise, to a mind that had undergone a kind of new creation, after its long-suspended life.

Be the cause what it might, Clifford commonly retired to rest, thoroughly exhausted, while the sunbeams were still melting through his window curtains, or were thrown with late luster on the chamber wall. And while he thus slept early, as other children do, and dreamed of childhood, Phœbe was free to follow her own tastes for the remainder of the day and evening.

This was a freedom essential to the health even of a character so little susceptible of morbid influences as that of Phœbe. The old house, as we have already said, had both the dry-rot and the damp-rot in its walls; it was not good to breathe no other atmosphere than that. Hepzibah, though she had her valuable and redeeming traits, had grown to be a kind of lunatic, by imprisoning herself so long in one place, with no other company than a single series of ideas and but one affection, and one bitter sense of wrong. Clifford, the reader may perhaps imagine, was too inert to operate morally on his fellow creatures, however intimate and exclusive their relations with him. But the sympathy or magnetism among human beings is more subtle and universal than we think; it exists, indeed, among different classes of organized life, and vibrates from one to another. A flower, for instance, as Phœbe herself observed, always began to droop sooner in Clifford's hand, or Hepzibah's, than in her own; and by the same law, converting her whole daily life into a flower fragrance for these two sickly spirits, the blooming girl must inevitably droop and fade much sooner than if worn on a younger and happier breast. Unless she had now and then indulged her brisk impulses, and breathed rural air in a suburban walk, or ocean breezes along the shore—had occasionally obeyed the impulse of nature, in New England girls, by attending a metaphysical or philosophical lecture, or viewing a seven-mile panorama, or listening to a concert—had gone shopping about the city, ransacking entire depots of splendid merchandise, and bringing home a ribbon—had employed, likewise, a little time to read the Bible in her chamber, and had stolen a little more to think of her mother and her native place—unless for such moral medicines as the above, we should soon have beheld our poor Phœbe grow thin, and put on a bleached, unwholesome aspect, and assume strange, shy ways, prophetic of old maidenhood and a cheerless future.

Even as it was, a change grew visible; a change partly to be regretted, although whatever charm it infringed upon was repaired by another, perhaps more precious. She was not so constantly gay, but had her moods of thought, which Clifford, on the whole, liked better than her former phase of unmingled cheerfulness; because now she understood him better and more delicately, and sometimes even interpreted him to himself. Her eyes looked larger, and darker, and deeper; so deep, at some silent moments, that they seemed like artesian wells, down, down, into the infinite. She was less girlish than when we first beheld her, alighting from the omnibus; less girlish, but more a woman.

The only youthful mind with which Phœbe had an opportunity of frequent intercourse was that of the daguerreotypist. Inevitably, by the pressure of the seclusion about them, they had been brought into habits of some familiarity. Had they met under different circumstances, neither of these young persons would have been likely to bestow much thought upon the other; unless, indeed, their extreme dissimilarity should have proved a principle of mutual attraction. During the early part of their acquaintance, Phœbe had held back rather more than was customary with her frank and simple manners from Holgrave's not very marked advances. Nor was she yet satisfied that she knew him well, although they almost daily met and talked together in a kind, friendly, and what seemed to be a familiar way.

The artist, in a desultory manner, had imparted to Phœbe something of his history. Young as he was, and had his career terminated at the point already attained, there had been enough of incident to fill, very creditably, an autobiographic volume. Holgrave, as he told Phœbe, somewhat proudly, could not boast of his origin, unless as being exceedingly humble, nor of his education, except that it had been the scantiest possible, and obtained by a few winter months' attendance at a district school. Left early to his own guidance, he had begun to be self-dependent while yet a boy; and it was a condition aptly suited to his natural force of will. Though now but twenty-two years old (lacking some months, which are years in such a life), he had already been, first, a country schoolmaster; next, a salesman in a country store; and, either at the same time or afterwards, the political editor of a country newspaper. He had subsequently traveled New England and the Middle States, as a peddler, in the employment of a Connecticut manufactory of cologne water and other essences. In an episodical way, he had studied and practiced dentistry, and with very flattering success, especially in many of the factory towns along our inland streams. As a supernumerary official, of some kind or other, aboard a packet ship, he visited Europe, and found means, before his return, to see Italy, and part of France and Germany. At a later period, he had spent some months in a community of Fourierists.[1] Still more recently, he had been a public lecturer on Mesmerism, for which science (as he assured Phœbe, and, indeed, satisfactorily proved, by putting Chanticleer, who happened to be scratching near by, to sleep) he had very remarkable endowments.

His present phase, as a daguerreotypist, was of no more importance in his own view, nor likely to be more permanent, than any of the preceding ones. It had been taken up with the careless alacrity of an adventurer who had his bread to earn. It would be thrown aside as carelessly, whenever he should choose to earn his bread by some other equally digressive means. But

[1] FOURIERISTS—Disciples of Fourier, a French socialist.

what was most remarkable, and, perhaps, showed a more than common poise in the young man, was the fact, that amid all these personal vicissitudes, he had never lost his identity. Homeless as he had been—continually changing his whereabout, and, therefore, responsible neither to public opinion nor to individuals—putting off one exterior, and snatching up another, to be soon shifted for a third—he had never violated the innermost man, but had carried his conscience along with him. It was impossible to know Holgrave, without recognizing this to be the fact. Hepzibah had seen it. Phœbe soon saw it, likewise, and gave him the sort of confidence which such a certainty inspires. She was startled, however, and sometimes repelled,—not by any doubt of his integrity to whatever law he acknowledged—but by a sense that his law differed from her own. He made her uneasy, and seemed to unsettle everything around her, by his lack of reverence for what was fixed, unless, at a moment's warning, it could establish its right to hold its ground.

Then, moreover, she scarcely thought him affectionate in his nature. He was too calm and cool an observer. Phœbe felt his eye, often; his heart, seldom or never. He took a certain kind of interest in Hepzibah and her brother, and Phœbe herself. He studied them attentively, and allowed no slightest circumstance of their individualities to escape him. He was ready to do them whatever good he might; but, after all, he never exactly made common cause with them, nor gave any reliable evidence that he loved them better, in proportion as he knew them more. In his relations with them, he seemed to be in quest of mental food, not heart sustenance. Phœbe could not conceive what interested him so much in her friends and herself, intellectually, since he cared nothing for them, or, comparatively, so little, as objects of human affection.

Always, in his interviews with Phœbe, the artist made especial inquiry as to the welfare of Clifford, whom, except at the Sunday festival, he seldom saw.

"Does he still seem happy?" he asked, one day.

"As happy as a child," answered Phœbe; "but—like a child, too—very easily disturbed."

"How disturbed?" inquired Holgrave. "By things without, or by thoughts within?"

"I cannot see his thoughts! How should I?" replied Phœbe,

with simple piquancy. "Very often his humor changes without any reason that can be guessed at, just as a cloud comes over the sun. Latterly, since I have begun to know him better, I feel it to be not quite right to look closely into his moods. He has had such a great sorrow, that his heart is made all solemn and sacred by it. When he is cheerful—when the sun shines into his mind—then I venture to peep in, just as far as the light reaches, but no further. It is holy ground where the shadow falls!"

"How prettily you express this sentiment!" said the artist. "I can understand the feeling, without possessing it. Had I your opportunities, no scruples would prevent me from fathoming Clifford to the full depth of my plummet line!"

"How strange that you should wish it!" remarked Phœbe, involuntarily. "What is Cousin Clifford to you?"

"Oh, nothing—of course, nothing!" answered Holgrave, with a smile. "Only this is such an odd and incomprehensible world! The more I look at it the more it puzzles me; and I begin to suspect that a man's bewilderment is the measure of his wisdom. Men and women, and children, too, are such strange creatures, that one never can be certain that he really knows them; nor ever guess what they have been, from what he sees them to be now. Judge Pyncheon! Clifford! What a complex riddle—a complexity of complexities—do they present! It requires intuitive sympathy, like a young girl's, to solve it. A mere observer, like myself (who never have any intuitions, and am, at best, only subtle and acute), is pretty certain to go astray."

The artist now turned the conversation to themes less dark than that which they had touched upon. Phœbe and he were young together; nor had Holgrave, in his premature experience of life, wasted entirely that beautiful spirit of youth, which, gushing forth from one small heart and fancy, may diffuse itself over the universe, making it all as bright as on the first day of creation. It seemed to Holgrave—as doubtless it has seemed to the hopeful of every century, since the epoch of Adam's grandchildren—that in this age, more than ever before, the moss-grown and rotten Past is to be torn down, and lifeless institutions to be thrust out of the way, and their dead corpses buried, and everything to begin anew.

Holgrave had read very little, and that little in passing

through the thoroughfare of life, where the mystic language of his books was necessarily mixed up with the babble of the multitude, so that both one and the other were apt to lose any sense that might have been properly their own. Altogether, in his culture and want of culture—in his crude, wild, and misty philosophy, and the practical experience that counteracted some of its tendencies; in his magnanimous zeal for man's welfare, and his recklessness of whatever the ages had established in man's behalf; in his faith, and in his infidelity; in what he had, and in what he lacked—the artist might fitly enough stand forth as the representative of many compeers in his native land.

But our business is with Holgrave as we find him on this particular afternoon, and in the arbor of the Pyncheon garden. In that point of view, it was a pleasant sight to behold this young man, with so much faith in himself, and so fair in appearance of admirable powers—so little harmed, too, by the many tests that had tried his mettle—it was pleasant to see him in his kindly intercourse, with Phœbe. Her thought had scarcely done him justice, when it pronounced him cold; or, if so, he had grown warmer now. Without such purpose on her part, and unconsciously on his, she made the House of the Seven Gables like a home to him, and the garden a familiar precinct. With the insight on which he prided himself, he fancied that he could look through Phœbe, and all around her, and could read her off like a page of a child's storybook. But these transparent natures are often deceptive in their depth; those pebbles at the bottom of the fountain are farther from us than we think. Thus the artist, whatever he might judge of Phœbe's capacity, was beguiled, by some silent charm of hers, to talk freely of what he dreamed of doing in the world. He poured himself out as to another self. Very possibly, he forgot Phœbe while he talked to her, and was moved only by the inevitable tendency of thought, when rendered sympathetic by enthusiasm and emotion, to flow into the first safe reservoir which it finds. But, had you peeped at them through the chinks of the garden fence, the young man's earnestness and heightened color might have led you to suppose that he was making love to the young girl!

At length, something was said by Holgrave that made it apposite for Phœbe to inquire what had first brought him acquaintance with her cousin Hepzibah, and why he now chose to lodge in the desolate old Pyncheon house. Without directly answering her, he turned from the Future, which had heretofore been the theme of his discourse, and began to speak of the influences of the Past. One subject indeed is but the reverberation of the other.

"Shall we never, never get rid of this Past?" cried he, keeping up the earnest tone of his preceding conversation. "It lies upon the Present like a giant's dead body! In fact, the case is just as if a young giant were compelled to waste all his strength in carrying about the corpse of the old giant, his grandfather, who died a long while ago, and only needs to be decently buried. Just think a moment, and it will startle you to see what slaves we are to bygone times—to Death, if we give the matter the right word!"

"But I do not see it," observed Phœbe.

"For example, then," continued Holgrave, "a dead man, if he happen to have made a will, disposes of wealth no longer his own; or, if he die intestate, it is distributed in accordance with the notions of men much longer dead than he. A dead man sits on all our judgment seats; and living judges do but search out and repeat his decisions. We read in dead men's books! We laugh at dead men's jokes, and cry at dead men's pathos! We are sick of dead men's diseases, physical and moral, and die of the same remedies with which dead doctors killed their patients! We worship the living Deity according to dead men's forms and creeds. Whatever we seek to do, of our own free motion, a dead man's icy hand obstructs us! Turn our eyes to what point we may, a dead man's white, immitigable face encounters them, and freezes our very heart! And we must be dead ourselves, before we can begin to have our proper influence on our own world, which will then be no longer our world, but the world of another generation, with which we shall have no shadow of a right to interfere. I ought to have said, too, that we live in dead men's houses; as, for instance, in this of the seven gables!"

"And why not," said Phœbe, "so long as we can be comfortable in them?"

"But we shall live to see the day, I trust," went on the artist, "when no man shall build his house for posterity. Why should he? He might just as reasonably order a durable suit of clothes —leather, or gutta percha, or whatever else lasts longest—so that his great-grandchildren should have the benefit of them, and cut precisely the same figure in the world that he himself does. If each generation were allowed and expected to build its own houses, that single change, comparatively unimportant in itself, would imply almost every reform which society is now suffering for. I doubt whether even our public edifices—our capitols, statehouses, courthouses, city halls, and churches—ought to be built of such permanent materials as stone or brick. It were better that they should crumble to ruin, once in twenty years, or thereabouts, as a hint to the people to examine into and reform the institutions which they symbolize."

"How you hate everything old!" said Phœbe, in dismay. "It makes me dizzy to think of such a shifting world!"

"I certainly love nothing moldy," answered Holgrave. "Now, this old Pyncheon house! Is it a wholesome place to live in, with its black shingles, and the green moss that shows how damp they are?—its dark, low-studded rooms?—its grime and sordidness, which are the crystallization on its walls of the human breath that has been drawn and exhaled here, in discontent and anguish? The house ought to be purified with fire—purified till only its ashes remain!"

"Then why do you live in it?" asked Phœbe, a little piqued.

"Oh, I am pursuing my studies here; not in books, however," replied Holgrave. "The house, in my view, is expressive of that odious and abominable Past, with all its bad influences, against which I have just been declaiming. I dwell in it for a while, that I may know the better how to hate it. Bye the bye, did you ever hear the story of Maule, the wizard, and what happened between him and your immeasurably great-grandfather?"

"Yes, indeed!" said Phœbe; "I heard it long ago, from my father, and two or three times from my cousin Hepzibah, in the month that I have been here. She seems to think that the calamities of the Pyncheons began from that quarrel with the wizard, as you call him. And you, Mr. Holgrave, look as if you thought so too! How singular, that you should believe what is so very absurd, when you reject many things that are a great deal worthier of credit!"

"I do believe it," said the artist, seriously; "not as a superstition, however, but as proved by unquestionable facts, and as exemplifying a theory. Now, see—under those seven gables, at which we now look up, and which old Colonel Pyncheon meant to be the house of his descendants, in prosperity and happiness, down to an epoch far beyond the present—under that roof, through a portion of three centuries, there has been perpetual remorse of conscience, a constantly defeated hope, strife among kindred, various misery, a strange form of death, dark suspicion, unspeakable disgrace, all, or most of which calamity, I have the means of tracing to the old Puritan's inordinate desire to plant and endow a family. To plant a family! This idea is at the bottom of most of the wrong and mischief which men do. The truth is, that, once in every half century, at longest, a family should be merged into the great, obscure mass of humanity, and forget all about its ancestors. Human blood, in order to keep its freshness, should run in hidden streams, as the water of an aqueduct is conveyed in subterranean pipes. In the family existence of these Pyncheons, for instance—forgive me, Phœbe; but I cannot think of you as one of them—in their brief New England pedigree, there has been time enough to infect them all with one kind of lunacy or another!"

"You speak very unceremoniously of my kindred," said Phœbe, debating with herself whether she ought to take offense.

"I speak true thoughts to a true mind!" answered Holgrave, with a vehemence which Phœbe had not before witnessed in him. "The truth is as I say! Furthermore, the original perpetrator and father of this mischief appears to have perpetuated himself, and still walks the street—at least, his very image, in mind and body—with the fairest prospect of transmitting to posterity as rich and as wretched an inheritance as he has received! Do you remember the daguerreotype, and its resemblance to the old portrait?"

"How strangely in earnest you are!" exclaimed Phœbe, looking at him with surprise and perplexity, half alarmed and partly inclined to laugh. "You talk of the lunacy of the Pyncheons; is it contagious?"

"I understand you!" said the artist, coloring and laughing. "I believe I am a little mad. This subject has taken hold of my mind with the strangest tenacity of clutch, since I have lodged in yonder old gable. As one method of throwing it off, I have put an incident of the Pyncheon family history, with which I happen to be acquainted, into the form of a legend, and mean to publish it in a magazine."

"Do you write for the magazines?" inquired Phœbe.

"Is it possible you did not know it?" cried Holgrave. "Well, such is literary fame! Yes, Miss Phœbe Pyncheon, among the multitude of my marvelous gifts, I have that of writing stories; and my name has figured, I can assure you, on the covers of Graham and Godey,[2] making as respectable an appearance, for aught I could see, as any of the canonized beadroll [3] with which it was associated. In the humorous line, I am thought to have a very pretty way with me; and as for pathos, I am as provoca- tive of tears as an onion. But shall I read you my story?"

"Yes, if it is not very long," said Phœbe—and added laugh- ingly—"nor very dull."

As this latter point was one which the daguerreotypist could not decide for himself, he forthwith produced his roll of manu- script, and, while the late sunbeams gilded the seven gables, began to read.

[2] GRAHAM AND GODEY—Graham's Magazine and Godey's Lady's Book were popular magazines of the period.

[3] CANONIZED BEADROLL—A list of saints, here a list of prominent authors.

XIII   ALICE PYNCHEON

Wherein Holgrave reads his story about Alice Pyncheon—a Pyn- cheon again calls a Maule to do carpenter work; many insinuations exchanged; an agreement is made; Maule employs hypnotism; what Alice sees in her trance; Maule's influence over Alice; and what happened.

THERE was a message brought, one day, from the worshipful Gervayse Pyncheon to young Matthew Maule, the carpenter, de- siring his immediate presence at the House of the Seven Gables.

"And what does your master want with me?" said the car- penter to Mr. Pyncheon's black servant. "Does the house need any repair? Well it may, by this time; and no blame to my father who built it, neither! I was reading the old Colonel's tombstone, no longer ago than last Sabbath; and reckoning from that date, the house has stood seven-and-thirty years. No won- der if there should be a job to do on the roof."

"Don't know what massa wants," answered Scipio. "The house is a berry good house, and old Colonel Pyncheon think so too, I reckon; else why the old man haunt it so, and frighten ebbery body, as he does?"

"Well, well, friend Scipio; let your master know that I'm coming," said the carpenter, with a laugh. "For a fair, workman-like job, he'll find me his man. And so the house is haunted, is it? It will take a tighter workman than I am to keep the spirits out of the seven gables. Even if the Colonel would be quit," he added, muttering to himself, "my old grandfather, the wizard, will be pretty sure to stick to the Pyncheons, as long as their walls hold together."

"What's that you mutter to yourself, Matthew Maule?" asked Scipio. "And what for do you look so black at me?"

"No matter!" said the carpenter. "Do you think nobody is to look black but yourself? Go tell your master I'm coming; and if you happen to see Mistress Alice, his daughter, give Matthew Maule's humble respects to her. She has brought a fair face from Italy—fair, and gentle, and proud—has that same Alice Pyncheon!"

"He talk of Mistress Alice!" cried Scipio, as he returned from his errand. "The low carpenter man! He no business so much as to look at her a great way off!"

This young Matthew Maule, the carpenter, it must be observed, was a person little understood, and not very generally liked, in the town where he resided; not that anything could be alleged against his integrity, or his skill and diligence in the handicraft which he exercised. The aversion (as it might justly be called) with which many persons regarded him was partly the result of his own character and deportment, and partly an inheritance.

He was the grandson of a former Matthew Maule, one of the early settlers of the town, and who had been a famous and terrible wizard, in his day. This old reprobate was one of the sufferers when Cotton Mather,[1] and his brother ministers, and the learned judges, and other wise men, and Sir William Phipps,[2] the sagacious governor, made such laudable efforts to weaken the great enemy of souls, by sending a multitude of his adherents up the rocky pathway of Gallows Hill.[3] Since those days, no doubt, it had grown to be suspected, that, in consequence of an unfortunate overdoing of a work praiseworthy in itself, the proceedings against the witches had proved far less acceptable to the Beneficent Father than to that very Archenemy[4] whom they were intended to distress and utterly overwhelm. It is not the less certain, however, that awe and terror brooded over the memories of those who died for this horrible crime of witchcraft. Their graves, in the crevices of the rocks, were supposed to be incapable of retaining the occupants who had been so hastily thrust into them. Old Matthew Maule, especially, was known to have as little hesitation or difficulty in rising out of his grave as an ordinary man in getting out of bed, and was as often seen at midnight as living people at noonday. This pestilent wizard (in whom his just punishment seemed to have wrought no manner of amends) had an inveterate habit of haunting a certain mansion, styled the House of the Seven Gables, against the owner of which he pretended to hold an unsettled claim for ground rent. The ghost, it appears, with the pertinacity which was one of his distinguishing characteristics while alive, insisted that he was the rightful proprietor of the site upon which the house stood. His terms were, that either the aforesaid ground rent, from the day when the cellar began to be dug, should be paid down, or the mansion itself given up; else he, the ghostly creditor, would have his finger in all the affairs of the Pyncheons, and make everything go wrong with them, though it should be a thousand years after his death. It was a wild story, perhaps, but seemed not altogether so incredible, to those who could remember what an inflexibly obstinate old fellow this wizard Maule had been.

---

[1] COTTON MATHER—A celebrated American clergyman, author, and scholar who took an active part in the persecutions for witchcraft.

[2] SIR WILLIAM PHIPPS—Governor of Massachusetts from 1692–94.

[3] GALLOWS HILL—A hill near Salem which was the scene of the executions for witchcraft.

[4] ARCHENEMY—A synonym for Satan.

Now, the wizard's grandson, the young Matthew Maule of our story, was popularly supposed to have inherited some of his ancestor's questionable traits. It is wonderful how many absurdities were promulgated in reference to the young man. He was fabled, for example, to have a strange power of getting into people's dreams, and regulating matters there according to his own fancy, pretty much like the stage manager of a theater. There was a great deal of talk among the neighbors, particularly the petticoated ones, about what they called the witchcraft of Maule's eye. Some said that he could look into people's minds; others, that, by the marvelous power of this eye, he could draw people into his own mind, or send them, if he pleased, to do errands to his grandfather, in the spiritual world; others, again, that it was what is termed an Evil Eye, and possessed the valuable faculty of blighting corn, and drying children into mummies with the heartburn. But, after all, what worked most to the young carpenter's disadvantage was, first, the reserve and sternness of his natural disposition, and next, the fact of his not being a church communicant, and the suspicion of his holding heretical tenets in matters of religion and polity.

After receiving Mr. Pyncheon's message, the carpenter merely tarried to finish a small job, which he happened to have in hand, and then took his way toward the House of the Seven Gables. This noted edifice, though its style might be getting a little out of fashion, was still as respectable a family residence as that of any gentleman in town. The present owner, Gervayse Pyncheon, was said to have contracted a dislike to the house, in consequence of a shock to his sensibility, in early childhood, from the sudden death of his grandfather. In the very act of running to climb Colonel Pyncheon's knee, the boy had discovered the old Puritan to be a corpse! On arriving at manhood, Mr. Pyncheon had visited England, where he married a lady of fortune, and had subsequently spent many years, partly in the mother country, and partly in various cities on the continent of Europe. During this period the family mansion had been consigned to the charge of a kinsman, who was allowed to make it his home, for the time being, in consideration of keeping the premises in thorough repair. So faithfully had this contract been fulfilled, that now, as the carpenter approached the house, his practiced eye could detect nothing to criticize in its condition. The peaks of the seven gables rose up sharply; the shingled roof looked thoroughly water-tight; and the glittering plasterwork entirely covered the exterior walls, and sparkled in the October sun, as if it had been new only a week ago.

The house had that pleasant aspect of life which is like the cheery expression of comfortable activity in the human countenance. You could see, at once, that there was the stir of a large family within it. A huge load of oak wood was passing through the gateway, toward the outbuildings, in the rear; the fat cook—or probably it might be the housekeeper—stood at the side door, bargaining for some turkeys and poultry, which a countryman had brought for sale. Now and then a maidservant, neatly dressed, and now the shining sable face of a slave, might be seen bustling across the windows, in the lower part of the house. At an open window of a room in the second story, hanging over some pots of beautiful and delicate flowers—exotics, but which had never known a more genial sunshine than that of the New England autumn—was the figure of a young lady, an exotic, like the flowers, and beautiful and delicate as they. Her presence imparted an indescribable grace and faint witchery to the whole edifice. In other respects, it was a substantial, jolly-looking mansion, and seemed fit to be the residence of a patriarch, who might establish his own headquarters in the front gable, and assign one of the remainder to each of his six children; while the great chimney in the center should symbolize the old fellow's hospitable heart, which kept them all warm, and made a great whole of the seven smaller ones.

There was a vertical sundial on the front gable; and as the carpenter passed beneath it, he looked up and noted the hour. "Three o'clock!" said he to himself. "My father told me that dial was put up only an hour before the old Colonel's death. How truly it has kept time these seven-and-thirty years past! The shadow creeps and creeps, and is always looking over the shoulder of the sunshine!"

It might have befitted a craftsman, like Matthew Maule, on being sent for to a gentleman's house, to go to the back door, where servants and workpeople were usually admitted; or at least to the side entrance, where the better class of tradesmen made application. But the carpenter had a great deal of pride and stiffness in his nature; and, at this moment, moreover, his heart was bitter with the sense of hereditary wrong, because he considered the great Pyncheon house to be standing on soil which should have been his own. So young Maule went straight to the principal entrance, beneath a portal of carved oak, and gave such a peal of the iron knocker that you would have imagined the stern old wizard himself to be standing at the threshold.

Black Scipio answered the summons, in a prodigious hurry; but showed the whites of his eyes, in amazement, on beholding only the carpenter.

"Lord-a-mercy! what a great man he be, this carpenter fellow!" mumbled Scipio, down in his throat. "Anybody think he beat on the door with his biggest hammer!"

"Here I am!" said Maule, sternly. "Show me the way to your master's parlor!"

As he stepped into the house, a note of sweet and melancholy music thrilled and vibrated along the passageway, proceeding from one of the rooms abovestairs. It was the harpsichord which Alice Pyncheon had brought with her from beyond the sea. The fair Alice bestowed most of her maiden leisure between flowers and music, although the former were apt to droop, and the melodies were often sad. She was of foreign education, and could not take kindly to the New England modes of life, in which nothing beautiful had ever been developed.

As Mr. Pyncheon had been impatiently awaiting Maule's arrival, black Scipio, of course, lost no time in ushering the carpenter into his master's presence. The room in which this gentleman sat was a parlor of moderate size, looking out upon the garden of the house, and having its windows partly shadowed by the foliage of fruit trees. It was Mr. Pyncheon's peculiar apartment, and was provided with furniture, in an elegant and costly style, principally from Paris; the floor (which was unusual, at that day) being covered with a carpet, so skillfully and richly wrought, that it seemed to glow as with living flowers. In one corner stood a marble woman, to whom her own beauty was the sole and sufficient garment. Some pictures—that looked old, and had a mellow tinge diffused through all their artful splendor—hung on the walls. Near the fireplace was a large and very beautiful cabinet of ebony, inlaid with ivory; a piece of antique furniture, which Mr. Pyncheon had bought in Venice, and which he used as the treasure place for medals, ancient coins, and whatever small and valuable curiosities he had picked up on his travels. Through all this variety of decoration, however, the room showed its original characteristics; its low stud, its cross-beam, its chimney piece, with the old-fashioned Dutch tiles; so that it was the emblem of a mind industriously stored with foreign ideas, and elaborated into artificial refinement, but neither larger, nor, in its proper self, more elegant, than before.

There were two objects that appeared rather out of place in this very handsomely furnished room. One was a large map, or surveyor's plan, of a tract of land, which looked as if it had been drawn a good many years ago, and was now dingy with smoke, and soiled, here and there, with the touch of fingers. The other was a portrait of a stern old man, in a Puritan garb, painted roughly, but with a bold effect, and a remarkably strong expression of character.

At a small table, before a fire of English sea coal, sat Mr. Pyncheon, sipping coffee, which had grown to be a very favorite beverage with him in France. He was a middle-aged and really handsome man, with a wig flowing down upon his shoulders; his coat was of blue velvet, with lace on the borders and at the buttonholes; and the firelight glistened on the spacious breadth of his waistcoat, which was flowered all over with gold. On the entrance of Scipio, ushering in the carpenter, Mr. Pyncheon turned partly round, but resumed his former position, and proceeded deliberately to finish his cup of coffee, without immediate notice of the guest whom he had summoned to his presence. It was not that he intended any rudeness, or improper neglect, which, indeed, he would have blushed to be guilty of, but it never occurred to him that a person in Maule's station had a claim on his courtesy, or would trouble himself about it, one way or the other.

The carpenter, however, stepped at once to the hearth, and turned himself about, so as to look Mr. Pyncheon in the face.

"You sent for me," said he. "Be pleased to explain your business, that I may go back to my own affairs."

"Ah! excuse me," said Mr. Pyncheon, quietly. "I did not mean to tax your time without a recompense. Your name, I think, is Maule—Thomas or Matthew Maule—a son or grandson of the builder of this house?"

"Matthew Maule," replied the carpenter, "son of him who

built the house—grandson of the rightful proprietor of the soil."

"I know the dispute to which you allude," observed Mr. Pyncheon, with undisturbed equanimity. "I am well aware that my grandfather was compelled to resort to a suit at law, in order to establish his claim to the foundation site of this edifice. We will not, if you please, renew the discussion. The matter was settled at the time, and by the competent authorities—equitably, it is to be presumed—and at all events, irrevocably. Yet, singularly enough, there is an incidental reference to this very subject in what I am now about to say to you. And this same inveterate grudge—excuse me, I mean no offense—this irritability, which you have just shown, is not entirely aside from the matter."

"If you can find anything for your purpose, Mr. Pyncheon," said the carpenter, "in a man's natural resentment for the wrongs done to his blood, you are welcome to it!"

"I take you at your word, Goodman Maule," said the owner of the Seven Gables, with a smile, "and will proceed to suggest a mode in which your hereditary resentments—justifiable, or otherwise—may have had a bearing on my affairs. You have heard, I suppose, that the Pyncheon family, ever since my grandfather's days, have been prosecuting a still unsettled claim to a very large extent of territory at the eastward?"

"Often," replied Maule, and it is said that a smile came over his face, "very often—from my father!"

"This claim," continued Mr. Pyncheon, after pausing a moment, as if to consider what the carpenter's smile might mean, "appeared to be on the very verge of a settlement and full allowance, at the period of my grandfather's decease. It was well known, to those in his confidence, that he anticipated neither difficulty nor delay. Now, Colonel Pyncheon, I need hardly say, was a practical man, well acquainted with public and private business, and not at all the person to cherish ill-founded hopes, or to attempt the following out of an impracticable scheme. It is obvious to conclude, therefore, that he had grounds, not apparent to his heirs, for his confident anticipation of success in the matter of this eastern claim. In a word, I believe—and my legal advisers coincide in the belief, which, moreover, is authorized, to a certain extent, by the family traditions—that my grandfather was in possession of some deed, or other document, essential to this claim, but which has since disappeared."

"Very likely," said Matthew Maule, and again, it is said, there was a dark smile on his face, "but what can a poor carpenter have to do with the grand affairs of the Pyncheon family?"

"Perhaps nothing," returned Mr. Pyncheon, "possibly, much!"

Here ensued a great many words between Matthew Maule and the proprietor of the Seven Gables, on the subject which the latter had thus broached. It seems (although Mr. Pyncheon had some hesitation in referring to stories so exceedingly absurd in their aspect) that the popular belief pointed to some mysterious connection and dependence, existing between the family of the Maules and these vast, unrealized possessions of the Pyncheons. It was an ordinary saying, that the old wizard, hanged though he was, had obtained the best end of the bargain, in his contest with Colonel Pyncheon; inasmuch as he had got possession of the great eastern claim, in exchange for an acre or two of garden ground. A very aged woman, recently dead, had often used the metaphorical expression, in her fireside talk, that miles and miles of the Pyncheon lands had been shoveled into Maule's grave; which, bye the bye, was but a very shallow nook, between two rocks, near the summit of Gallows Hill. Again, when the lawyers were making inquiry for the missing document, it was a byword, that it would never be found, unless in the wizard's skeleton hand. So much weight had the shrewd lawyers assigned to the fables, that—(but Mr. Pyncheon did not see fit to inform the carpenter of the fact)—they had secretly caused the wizard's grave to be searched. Nothing was discovered, however, except that, unaccountably, the right hand of the skeleton was gone.

Now, what was unquestionably important, a portion of these popular rumors could be traced, though rather doubtfully and indistinctly, to chance words and obscure hints of the executed wizard's son, and the father of this present Matthew Maule. And here Mr. Pyncheon could bring an item of his own personal evidence into play. Though but a child at the time, he either remembered or fancied that Matthew's father had had some job to perform, on the day before, or possibly the very morning of the Colonel's decease, in the private room where he and the carpenter were at this moment talking. Certain papers belonging to Colonel Pyncheon, as his grandson distinctly recollected, had been spread out on the table.

Matthew Maule understood the insinuated suspicion.

"My father," he said, but still there was that dark smile, making a riddle of his countenance, "my father was an honester man than the bloody old Colonel! Not to get his rights back again would he have carried off one of those papers!"

"I shall not bandy words with you," observed the foreign-bred Mr. Pyncheon, with haughty composure. "Nor will it become me to resent any rudeness toward either my grandfather or myself. A gentleman, before seeking intercourse with a person of your station and habits, will first consider whether the urgency of the end may compensate for the disagreeableness of the means. It does so, in the present instance."

He then renewed the conversation, and made great pecuniary offers to the carpenter, in case the latter should give information leading to the discovery of the lost document, and the consequent success of the eastern claim. For a long time Matthew Maule is said to have turned a cold ear to these propositions. At last, however, with a strange kind of laugh, he inquired whether Mr. Pyncheon would make over to him the old wizard's homestead ground, together with the House of the Seven Gables, now standing on it, in requital of the documentary evidence so urgently required.

The wild, chimney-corner legend (which, without copying all its extravagances, my narrative essentially follows) here gives an account of some very strange behavior on the part of Colonel Pyncheon's portrait. This picture, it must be understood, was supposed to be so intimately connected with the fate of the house, and so magically built into its walls, that, if once it should be removed, that very instant the whole edifice would come thundering down in a heap of dusty ruin. All through the foregoing conversation between Mr. Pyncheon and the carpenter, the portrait had been frowning, clenching its fist, and giving many such proofs of excessive discomposure, but without attracting the notice of either of the two colloquists. And finally, at Matthew Maule's audacious suggestion of a transfer of the seven-gabled structure, the ghostly portrait is averred to have lost all patience, and to have shown itself on the point of descending bodily from its frame. But such incredible incidents are merely to be mentioned aside.

"Give up this house!" exclaimed Mr. Pyncheon, in amazement at the proposal. "Were I to do so, my grandfather would not rest quiet in his grave!"

"He never has, if all stories are true," remarked the carpenter, composedly. "But that matter concerns his grandson more than it does Matthew Maule. I have no other terms to propose."

Impossible as he at first thought it to comply with Maule's conditions, still, on a second glance, Mr. Pyncheon was of opinion that they might at least be made matter of discussion. He himself had no personal attachment for the house, nor any pleasant associations connected with his childish residence in it. On the contrary, after seven-and-thirty years, the presence of his dead grandfather seemed still to pervade. it, as on that morning when the affrighted boy had beheld him, with so ghastly an aspect, stiffening in his chair. His long abode in foreign parts, moreover, and familiarity with many of the castles and ancestral halls of England, and the marble palaces of Italy, had caused him to look contemptuously at the House of the Seven Gables, whether in point of splendor or convenience. It was a mansion exceedingly inadequate to the style of living which it would be incumbent on Mr. Pyncheon to support after realizing his territorial rights. His steward might deign to occupy it, but never, certainly, the great landed proprietor himself. In the event of success, indeed, it was his purpose to return to England; nor, to say the truth, would he recently have quitted that more congenial home, had not his own fortune, as well as his deceased wife's, begun to give symptoms of exhaustion. The eastern claim once fairly settled, and put upon the firm basis of actual possession, Mr. Pyncheon's property—to be measured by miles, not acres—would be worth an earldom, and would reasonably entitle him to solicit, or enable him to purchase, that elevated dignity from the British monarch. Lord Pyncheon!—or the Earl of Waldo! [5]—how could such a magnate be expected to contract his grandeur within the pitiful compass of seven shingled gables?

In short, on an enlarged view of the business, the carpenter's terms appeared so ridiculously easy, that Mr. Pyncheon could scarcely forbear laughing in his face. He was quite ashamed,

[5] EARL OF WALDO—A title Mr. Pyncheon believed he could get from the British king; Waldo being the eastern property in Maine.

after the foregoing reflections, to propose any diminution of so moderate a recompense for the immense service to be rendered. "I consent to your proposition, Maule," cried he. "Put me in possession of the document essential to establish my rights, and the House of the Seven Gables is your own!"

According to some versions of the story, a regular contract to the above effect was drawn up by a lawyer, and signed and sealed in the presence of witnesses. Others say that Matthew Maule was contented with a private written agreement, in which Mr. Pyncheon pledged his honor and integrity to the fulfillment of the terms concluded upon. The gentleman then ordered wine, which he and the carpenter drank together, in confirmation of their bargain. During the whole preceding discussion and subsequent formalities, the old Puritan's portrait seems to have persisted in its shadowy gestures of disapproval; but without effect, except that, as Mr. Pyncheon set down the emptied glass, he thought he beheld his grandfather frown.

"This sherry is too potent a wine for me; it has affected my brain already," he observed, after a somewhat startled look at the picture. "On returning to Europe, I shall confine myself to the more delicate vintages of Italy and France, the best of which will not bear transportation."

"My Lord Pyncheon may drink what wine he will, and wherever he pleases," replied the carpenter, as if he had been privy to Mr. Pyncheon's ambitious projects. "But first, sir, if you desire tidings of this lost document, I must crave the favor of a little talk with your fair daughter Alice."

"You are mad, Maule!" exclaimed Mr. Pyncheon, haughtily; and now, at last, there was anger mixed up with his pride. "What can my daughter have to do with a business like this?"

Indeed, at this new demand on the carpenter's part, the proprietor of the Seven Gables was even more thunderstruck than at the cool proposition to surrender his house. There was, at least, an assignable motive for the first stipulation; there appeared to be none whatever for the last. Nevertheless, Matthew Maule sturdily insisted on the young lady being summoned, and even gave her father to understand, in a mysterious kind of explanation, which made the matter considerably darker than it looked before, that the only chance of acquiring the requisite knowledge was through the clear, crystal medium of a pure and virgin intelligence, like that of the fair Alice. Not to encumber

"You are mad, Maule!" exclaimed Mr. Pyncheon.

our story with Mr. Pyncheon's scruples, whether of conscience, pride, or fatherly affection, he at length ordered his daughter to be called. He well knew that she was in her chamber, and engaged in no occupation that could not readily be laid aside; for, as it happened, ever since Alice's name had been spoken, both her father and the carpenter had heard the sad and sweet music of her harpsichord, and the airier melancholy of her accompanying voice.

So Alice Pyncheon was summoned, and appeared. If ever there was a lady born, and set apart from the world's vulgar mass by a certain gentle and cold stateliness, it was this very Alice Pyncheon. Yet there was the womanly mixture in her; the tenderness, or, at least, the tender capabilities. For the sake of that redeeming quality, a man of generous nature would have forgiven all her pride, and have been content, almost, to lie down in her path, and let Alice set her slender foot upon his heart. All that he would have required, was simply the acknowledgment that he was indeed a man, and a fellow being, molded of the same elements as she.

As Alice came into the room, her eyes fell upon the carpenter, who was standing near its center, clad in a green woolen jacket, a pair of loose breeches, open at the knees, and with a long pocket for his rule, the end of which protruded; it was as proper a mark of the artisan's calling, as Mr. Pyncheon's full dress sword of that gentleman's aristocratic pretensions. A glow of artistic approval brightened over Alice Pyncheon's face; she was struck with admiration—which she made no attempt to conceal —of the remarkable comeliness, strength, and energy of Maule's figure. But that admiring glance (which most other men, perhaps, would have cherished as a sweet recollection, all through life) the carpenter never forgave.

"Does the girl look at me as if I were a brute beast?" thought he, setting his teeth. "She shall know whether I have a human spirit; and the worse for her, if it prove stronger than her own!"

"My father, you sent for me," said Alice, in her sweet and harp-like voice. "But if you have business with this young man, pray let me go again. You know I do not love this room, in spite of that Claude,[6] with which you try to bring back sunny recollections."

[6] CLAUDE—Claude Gellee, a French artist of note.

"Stay a moment, young lady, if you please," said Matthew Maule. "My business with your father is over. With yourself, it is now to begin!"

Alice looked toward her father, in surprise and inquiry.

"Yes, Alice," said Mr. Pyncheon, with some disturbance and confusion. "This young man—his name is Matthew Maule—professes, so far as I can understand, to be able to discover, through your means, a certain paper or parchment, which was missing long before your birth. The importance of the document in question renders it advisable to neglect no possible, even if improbable, method of regaining it. You will therefore oblige me, my dear Alice, by answering this person's inquiries, and complying with his lawful and reasonable requests, so far as they may appear to have the aforesaid object in view. As I shall remain in the room, you need apprehend no rude nor unbecoming deportment, on the young man's part; and, at your slightest wish, of course, the investigation, or whatever we may call it, shall immediately be broken off."

"Mistress Alice Pyncheon," remarked Matthew Maule, with the utmost deference, but yet a half-hidden sarcasm in his look and tone, "will no doubt feel herself quite safe in her father's presence, and under his all-sufficient protection."

"I certainly shall entertain no manner of apprehension with my father at hand," said Alice, with maidenly dignity. "Neither do I conceive that a lady, while true to herself, can have aught to fear, from whomsoever, or in any circumstances!"

Poor Alice! By what unhappy impulse did she thus put herself at once on terms of defiance against a strength which she could not estimate?

"Then, Mistress Alice," said Matthew Maule, handing a chair, gracefully enough, for a craftsman, "will it please you only to sit down, and do me the favor (though altogether beyond a poor carpenter's deserts) to fix your eyes on mine!"

Alice complied. She was very proud. Setting aside all advantages of rank, this fair girl deemed herself conscious of a power —combined of beauty, high, unsullied purity, and the preservative force of womanhood—that could make her sphere impenetrable, unless betrayed by treachery within. She instinctively knew, it may be, that some sinister or evil potency was now striving to pass her barriers; nor would she decline the contest. So Alice put woman's might against man's might; a match not often equal, on the part of woman.

Her father, meanwhile, had turned away, and seemed absorbed in the contemplation of a landscape by Claude, where a shadowy and sun-streaked vista penetrated so remotely into an ancient wood, that it would have been no wonder if his fancy had lost itself in the picture's bewildering depths. But, in truth, the picture was no more to him, at that moment, than the blank wall against which it hung. His mind was haunted with the many and strange tales which he had heard, attributing mysterious if not supernatural endowments to these Maules, as well the grandson, here present, as his two immediate ancestors. Mr. Pyncheon's long residence abroad, and intercourse with men of wit and fashion—courtiers, worldlings, and freethinkers—had done much toward obliterating the grim Puritan superstitions, which no man of New England birth, at that early period, could entirely escape. But, on the other hand, had not the whole community believed Maule's grandfather to be a wizard? Had not the crime been proved? Had not the wizard died for it? Had he not bequeathed a legacy of hatred against the Pyncheons to this only grandson, who, as it appeared, was now about to exercise a subtle influence over the daughter of his enemy's house? Might not this influence be the same that was called witchcraft?

Turning half around, he caught a glimpse of Maule's figure in the looking-glass. At some paces from Alice, with his arms uplifted in the air, the carpenter made a gesture, as if directing downward a slow, ponderous, and invisible weight upon the maiden.

"Stay, Maule!" exclaimed Mr. Pyncheon, stepping forward. "I forbid your proceeding further!"

"Pray, my dear father, do not interrupt the young man," said Alice, without changing her position. "His efforts, I assure you, will prove very harmless."

Again Mr. Pyncheon turned his eyes toward the Claude. It was then his daughter's will, in opposition to his own, that the experiment should be fully tried. Henceforth, therefore, he did but consent, not urge it. And was it not for her sake, far more than his own, that he desired its success? That lost parchment once restored, the beautiful Alice Pyncheon, with the rich dowry which he could then bestow, might wed an English duke, or a German reigning prince, instead of some New England clergyman or lawyer! At the thought, the ambitious father almost consented, in his heart, that, if the devil's power were needed to the accomplishment of this great object, Maule might evoke him. Alice's own purity would be her safeguard.

With his mind full of imaginary magnificence, Mr. Pyncheon heard a half-uttered exclamation from his daughter. It was very faint and low; so indistinct that there seemed but half a will to shape out the words, and too undefined a purport to be intelligible. Yet it was a call for help!—his conscience never doubted it; and, little more than a whisper to his ear, it was a dismal shriek, and long reëchoed so, in the region round his heart! But, this time, the father did not turn.

After a further interval, Maule spoke.

"Behold your daughter!" said he.

Mr. Pyncheon came hastily forward. The carpenter was standing erect in front of Alice's chair, and pointing his finger toward the maiden with an expression of triumphant power, the limits of which could not be defined, as, indeed, its scope stretched vaguely toward the unseen and the infinite. Alice sat in an attitude of profound repose, with the long brown lashes drooping over her eyes.

"There she is!" said the carpenter. "Speak to her!"

"Alice! My daughter!" exclaimed Mr. Pyncheon. "My own Alice!"

She did not stir.

"Louder!" said Maule, smiling.

"Alice! Awake!" cried her father. "It troubles me to see you thus! Awake!"

He spoke loudly, with terror in his voice, and close to that delicate ear, which had always been so sensitive to every discord. But the sound evidently reached her not. It is indescribable what a sense of remote, dim, unattainable distance, betwixt himself and Alice, was impressed on the father by this impossibility of reaching her with his voice.

"Best touch her!" said Matthew Maule. "Shake the girl, and roughly too! My hands are hardened with too much use of ax, saw, and plane, else I might help you!"

Mr. Pyncheon took her hand, and pressed it with the earnestness of startled emotion. He kissed her, with so great a heartthrob in the kiss, that he thought she must needs feel it. Then, in a gust of anger at her insensibility, he shook her maiden form with a violence which, the next moment, it affrighted him to remember. He withdrew his encircling arms, and Alice—whose figure, though flexible, had been wholly impassive—relapsed into the same attitude as before these attempts to arouse her. Maule having shifted his position, her face was turned toward him, slightly, but with what seemed to be a reference of her very slumber to his guidance.

Then it was a strange sight to behold how the man of conventionalities shook the powder out of his periwig; how the reserved and stately gentleman forgot his dignity; how the gold-embroidered waistcoat flickered and glistened in the firelight, with the convulsion of rage, terror, and sorrow in the human heart that was beating under it.

"Villain!" cried Mr. Pyncheon, shaking his clenched fist at Maule. "You and the fiend together have robbed me of my daughter! Give her back, spawn of the old wizard, or you shall climb Gallows Hill in your grandfather's footsteps!"

"Softly, Mr. Pyncheon!" said the carpenter, with scornful composure. "Softly, an' it please your worship, else you will spoil those rich lace ruffles at your wrists! Is it my crime if you have sold your daughter for the mere hope of getting a sheet of yellow parchment into your clutch? There sits Mistress Alice, quietly asleep! Now let Matthew Maule try whether she be as proud as the carpenter found her a while since."

He spoke, and Alice responded, with a soft, subdued inward acquiescence, and a bending of her form toward him, like the flame of a torch when it indicates a gentle draft of air. He beckoned with his hand, and, rising from her chair—blindly, but undoubtingly, as tending to her sure and inevitable center—the proud Alice approached him. He waved her back, and, retreating, Alice sank again into her seat.

"She is mine!" said Matthew Maule. "Mine, by the right of the strongest spirit!"

In the further progress of the legend, there is a long, grotesque, and occasionally awe-striking account of the carpenter's incantations (if so they are to be called), with a view of discovering the lost document. It appears to have been his object to convert the mind of Alice into a kind of telescopic medium, through which Mr. Pyncheon and himself might obtain a glimpse into the spiritual world. He succeeded, accordingly, in holding an imperfect sort of intercourse, at one remove, with the departed personages, in whose custody the so much valued secret had been carried beyond the precincts of earth. During her trance, Alice described three figures as being present to her spiritualized perception. One was an aged, dignified, stern-looking gentleman, clad, as for a solemn festival, in grave and costly attire, but with a great bloodstain on his richly wrought band; the second, an aged man, meanly dressed, with a dark and malign countenance, and a broken halter about his neck; the third, a person not so advanced in life as the former two, but beyond the middle age, wearing a coarse woolen tunic and leather breeches, and with a carpenter's rule sticking out of his side pocket. These three visionary characters possessed a mutual knowledge of the missing document. One of them, in truth—it was he with the bloodstain on his band—seemed, unless his gestures were misunderstood, to hold the parchment in his immediate keeping, but was prevented, by his two partners in the mystery, from disburdening himself of the trust. Finally, when he showed a purpose of shouting forth the secret, loudly enough to be heard from his own sphere into that of mortals, his companions struggled with him, and pressed their hands over his mouth; and forthwith—whether that he were choked by it, or that the secret itself was of a crimson hue—there was a fresh flow of blood upon his band. Upon this, the two meanly dressed figures mocked and jeered at the much-abashed old dignitary, and pointed their fingers at the stain.

At this juncture, Maule turned to Mr. Pyncheon.

"It will never be allowed," said he. "The custody of this secret, that would so enrich his heirs, makes part of your grandfather's retribution. He must choke with it until it is no longer of any value. And keep you the House of the Seven Gables! It is too dear-bought an inheritance and too heavy with the curse upon it, to be shifted yet a while from the Colonel's posterity!"

Mr. Pyncheon tried to speak, but—what with fear and passion—could make only a gurgling murmur in his throat. The carpenter smiled.

"Aha, worshipful sir!—so, you have old Maule's blood to drink!" said he jeeringly.

"Fiend in man's shape! why dost thou keep dominion over my child?" cried Mr. Pyncheon, when his choked utterance could make way. "Give me back my daughter! Then go thy ways; and may we never meet again!"

"Your daughter!" said Matthew Maule. "Why, she is fairly mine! Nevertheless, not to be too hard with fair Mistress Alice, I will leave her in your keeping; but I do not warrant you that she shall never have occasion to remember Maule, the carpenter."

He waved his hands with an upward motion; and, after a few repetitions of similar gestures, the beautiful Alice Pyncheon awoke from her strange trance. She awoke, without the slightest recollection of her visionary experience; but as one losing herself in a momentary reverie, and returning to the consciousness of actual life, in almost as brief an interval as the down-sinking flame of the hearth should quiver again up the chimney. On recognizing Matthew Maule, she assumed an air of somewhat cold but gentle dignity, the rather as there was a certain peculiar smile on the carpenter's visage, that stirred the native pride of the fair Alice. So ended, for that time, the quest for the lost title deed of the Pyncheon territory at the eastward; nor, though often subsequently renewed, has it ever yet befallen a Pyncheon to set his eyes upon that parchment.

But, alas for the beautiful, the gentle, yet too haughty Alice! A power, that she little dreamed of, had laid its grasp upon her maiden soul. A will, most unlike her own, constrained her to do its grotesque and fantastic bidding. Her father, as it proved, had martyred his poor child to an inordinate desire for measuring his land by miles, instead of acres. And, therefore, while Alice Pyncheon lived, she was Maule's slave, in a bondage more humiliating, a thousandfold, than that which binds its chain around the body. Seated by his humble fireside, Maule had but to wave his hand; and, wherever the proud lady chanced to be, whether in her chamber, or entertaining her father's stately guests, or worshiping at church—whatever her place or occupation, her spirit passed from beneath her own control, and bowed itself to Maule. "Alice, laugh!"—the carpenter, beside his hearth, would say; or perhaps intensely will it, without a spoken word. And, even were it prayer time, or at a funeral, Alice must break into wild laughter. "Alice, be sad!"—and, at the instant, down would come her tears, quenching all the mirth of those around her, like sudden rain upon a bonfire. "Alice, dance!"—and dance she would, not in such court-like measures as she had learned abroad, but some high-paced jig, or hop-skip rigadoon, befitting the brisk lasses at a rustic merry-making. It seemed to be Maule's impulse not to ruin Alice, nor to visit her with any black or gigantic mischief, which would have crowned her sorrows with the grace of tragedy, but to wreak a low, ungenerous scorn upon her. Thus all the dignity of life was lost. She felt herself too much abased, and longed to change natures with some worm!

One evening, at a bridal party—(but not her own; for, so lost from self-control, she would have deemed it sin to marry)— poor Alice was beckoned forth by her unseen despot, and constrained, in her gossamer white dress and satin slippers, to hasten along the street to the mean dwelling of a laboring man. There was laughter and good cheer within; for Matthew Maule, that night, was to wed the laborer's daughter, and had summoned proud Alice Pyncheon to wait upon his bride. And so she did; and when the twain were one, Alice awoke out of her enchanted sleep. Yet, no longer proud—humbly, and with a smile all steeped in sadness—she kissed Maule's wife, and went her way. It was an inclement night; the southeast wind drove the mingled snow and rain into her thinly sheltered bosom; her satin slippers were wet through and through, as she trod the muddy sidewalks. The next day, a cold; soon, a settled cough; anon, a hectic cheek, a wasted form, that sat beside the harpsichord and filled the house with music! Music, in which a strain of the heavenly choristers was echoed! Oh, joy! For Alice had borne her last humiliation! Oh, greater joy! For Alice was penitent of her one earthly sin, and proud no more.

The Pyncheons made a great funeral for Alice. The kith and kin were there, and the whole respectability of the town besides. But, last in the procession, came Matthew Maule, gnashing his teeth, as if he would have bitten his own heart in twain —the darkest and woefullest man that ever walked behind a corpse! He meant to humble Alice—not to kill her; but he had taken a woman's delicate soul into his rude gripe, to play with—and she was dead!

XIV PHŒBE'S GOOD-BY

Wherein Holgrave and Phœbe come under the spell of moon-light; Holgrave feels that Destiny is arranging a fifth act in the Pyncheon tragedy; Phœbe leaves for her home in the country.

HOLGRAVE, plunging into his tale with the energy and absorption natural to a young author, had given a good deal of action to the parts capable of being developed and exemplified in that manner. He now observed that a certain remarkable drowsiness (wholly unlike that with which the reader possibly feels himself affected) had been flung over the senses of his auditress. It was the effect, unquestionably, of the mystic gesticulations by which he had sought to bring bodily before Phœbe's perception the figure of the mesmerizing carpenter. With the lids drooping over her eyes—now lifted, for an instant, and drawn down again, as with leaden weights—she leaned slightly toward him, and seemed almost to regulate her breath by his. Holgrave gazed at her, as he rolled up his manuscript, and recognized an incipient stage of that curious psychological condition, which, as he had himself told Phœbe, he possessed more than an ordinary faculty of producing. A veil was beginning to be muffled about her, in which she could behold only him, and live only in his thoughts and emotions. His glance, as he fastened it on the young girl, grew involuntarily more concentrated; in his attitude there was the consciousness of power, investing his hardly mature figure with a dignity that did not belong to its physical manifestation. It was evident, that, with but one wave of his hand and a corresponding effort of his will, he could complete his mastery over Phœbe's yet free and virgin spirit: he could establish an influence over this good, pure, and simple child, as dangerous, and perhaps as disastrous, as that which the carpenter of his legend had acquired and exercised over the ill-fated Alice.

To a disposition like Holgrave's, at once speculative and active, there is no temptation so great as the opportunity of acquiring empire over the human spirit; nor any idea more seductive to a young man than to become the arbiter of a young girl's destiny. Let us, therefore—whatever his defects of nature and education, and in spite of his scorn for creeds and institutions—concede to the daguerreotypist the rare and high quality of reverence for another's individuality. Let us allow him integrity, also, forever after to be confided in; since he forbade himself to twine that one link more which might have rendered his spell over Phœbe indissoluble.

He made a slight gesture upward with his hand.

"You really mortify me, my dear Miss Phœbe!" he exclaimed, smiling half sarcastically at her. "My poor story, it is but too evident, will never do for Godey or Graham! Only think of your falling asleep at what I hoped the newspaper critics would pronounce a most brilliant, powerful, imaginative, pathetic, and original winding up! Well, the manuscript must serve to light lamps with; if, indeed, being so imbued with my gentle dullness, it is any longer capable of flame!"

"Me asleep! How can you say so?" answered Phœbe, as unconscious of the crisis through which she had passed as an infant of the precipice to the verge of which it has rolled. "No, no! I consider myself as having been very attentive; and, though I don't remember the incidents quite distinctly, yet I have an impression of a vast deal of trouble and calamity—so, no doubt, the story will prove exceedingly attractive."

By this time the sun had gone down, and was tinting the clouds toward the zenith with those bright hues which are not seen there until some time after sunset, and when the horizon has quite lost its richer brilliancy.

So sweetly cool was the atmosphere, after all the feverish day, that the summer eve might be fancied as sprinkling dews and liquid moonlight, with a dash of icy temper in them, out of a silver vase. Here and there a few drops of this freshness were scattered on a human heart, and gave it youth again, and sympathy with the eternal youth of nature. The artist chanced to be one on whom the reviving influence fell. It made him feel—what he sometimes almost forgot, thrust so early as he had been into the rude struggle of man with man—how youthful he still was.

"It seems to me," he observed, "that I never watched the coming of so beautiful an eve, and never felt anything so very much like happiness as at this moment. After all, what a good world we live in! How good, and beautiful! How young it is, too, with nothing really rotten or age-worn in it! This old house, for example, which sometimes has positively oppressed my breath with its smell of decaying timber! And this garden, where the black mold always clings to my spade, as if I were a sexton, delving in a graveyard! Could I keep the feeling that now possesses me, the garden would every day be virgin soil, with the earth's first freshness in the flavor of its beans and squashes; and the house!—it would be like a bower in Eden, blossoming with the earliest roses that God ever made. Moonlight, and the sentiment in man's heart responsive to it, are the greatest of renovators and reformers. And all other reform and renovation, I suppose, will prove to be no better than moonshine!"

"I have been happier than I am now; at least, much gayer," said Phœbe, thoughtfully. "Yet I am sensible of a great charm in this brightening moonlight; and I love to watch how the day, tired as it is, lags away reluctantly, and hates to be called yesterday so soon. I never cared much about moonlight before. What is there, I wonder, so beautiful in it, to-night?"

"And you have never felt it before?" inquired the artist, looking earnestly at the girl, through the twilight.

"Never," answered Phœbe; "and life does not look the same, now that I have felt it so. It seems as if I had looked at everything, hitherto, in broad daylight, or else in the ruddy light of a cheerful fire, glimmering and dancing through a room. Ah, poor me!" she added, with a half-melancholy laugh. "I shall never be so merry as before I knew Cousin Hepzibah and poor Cousin Clifford. I have grown a great deal older, in this little time. Older, and, I hope, wiser, and—not exactly sadder—but, certainly, with not half so much lightness in my spirits! I have given them my sunshine, and have been glad to give it; but, of course, I cannot both give and keep it. They are welcome, notwithstanding."

"You have lost nothing, Phœbe, worth keeping, nor which it was possible to keep," said Holgrave, after a pause. "Our first youth is of no value; for we are never conscious of it, until after it is gone. But sometimes—always, I suspect, unless one is exceedingly unfortunate—there comes a sense of second youth, gushing out of the heart's joy at being in love; or, possibly, it may come to crown some other grand festival in life, if any other such there be."

"I hardly think I understand you," said Phœbe.

"No wonder," replied Holgrave, smiling; "for I have told

you a secret which I hardly began to know, before I found myself giving it utterance. Remember it, however; and when the truth becomes clear to you, then think of this moonlight scene!"

"It is entirely moonlight now, except only a little flush of faint crimson, upward from the west, between those buildings," remarked Phœbe. "I must go in. Cousin Hepzibah is not quick at figures, and will give herself a headache over the day's accounts, unless I help her."

But Holgrave detained her a little longer.

"Miss Hepzibah tells me," observed he, "that you return to the country in a few days."

"Yes, but only for a little while," answered Phœbe; "for I look upon this as my present home. I go to make a few arrangements, and to take a more deliberate leave of my mother and friends. It is pleasant to live where one is much desired, and very useful; and I think I may have the satisfaction of feeling myself so, here."

"You surely may, and more than you imagine," said the artist. "Whatever health, comfort, and natural life exists in the house, is embodied in your person. These blessings came along with you, and will vanish when you leave the threshold. Miss Hepzibah, by secluding herself from society, has lost all true relation with it, and is, in fact, dead; although she galvanizes herself into a semblance of life, and stands behind her counter, afflicting the world with a greatly-to-be-deprecated scowl. Your poor cousin Clifford is another dead and long-buried person, on whom the governor and council have wrought a necromantic miracle. I should not wonder if he were to crumble away, some morning, after you are gone, and nothing be seen of him more, except a heap of dust. Miss Hepzibah, at any rate, will lose what little flexibility she has. They both exist by you."

"I should be very sorry to think so," answered Phœbe, gravely. "But it is true that my small abilities were precisely what they needed; and I have a real interest in their welfare—an odd kind of motherly sentiment—which I wish you would not laugh at! And let me tell you frankly, Mr. Holgrave, I am sometimes puzzled to know whether you wish them well or ill."

"Undoubtedly," said the daguerreotypist, "I do feel an interest in this antiquated, poverty-stricken old maiden lady, and this degraded and shattered gentleman—this abortive lover of the beautiful. A kindly interest, too, helpless old children that they are! But you have no conception what a different kind of heart mine is from your own. It is not my impulse as regards these two individuals either to help or hinder; but to look on, to analyze, to explain matters to myself, and to comprehend the drama which, for almost two hundred years, has been dragging its slow length over the ground where you and I now tread. If permitted to witness the close, I doubt not to derive a moral satisfaction from it, go matters how they may. There is a conviction within me that the end draws nigh. But, though Providence sent you hither to help, and sends me only as a privileged and meet spectator, I pledge myself to lend these unfortunate beings whatever aid I can!"

"I wish you would speak more plainly," cried Phœbe, perplexed and displeased; "and, above all, that you would feel more like a Christian and a human being! How is it possible to see people in distress, without desiring, more than anything else, to help and comfort them? You talk as if this old house were a theater; and you seem to look at Hepzibah's and Clifford's misfortunes, and those of generations before them, as a tragedy, such as I have seen acted in the hall of a country hotel, only the present one appears to be played exclusively for your amusement. I do not like this. The play costs the performers too much, and the audience is too cold-hearted."

"You are severe," said Holgrave, compelled to recognize a degree of truth in this piquant sketch of his own mood.

"And then," continued Phœbe, "what can you mean by your conviction, which you tell me of, that the end is drawing near? Do you know of any new trouble hanging over my poor relatives? If so, tell me at once, and I will not leave them!"

"Forgive me, Phœbe!" said the daguerreotypist, holding out his hand, to which the girl was constrained to yield her own. "I am somewhat of a mystic, it must be confessed. The tendency is in my blood, together with the faculty of mesmerism, which might have brought me to Gallows Hill, in the good old times of witchcraft. Believe me, if I were really aware of any secret, the disclosure of which would benefit your friends, who are my own friends, likewise, you should learn it before we part. But I have no such knowledge."

"You hold something back!" said Phœbe.

"Nothing—no secrets but my own," answered Holgrave. "I can perceive, indeed, that Judge Pyncheon still keeps his eye on Clifford, in whose ruin he had so large a share. His motives and intentions, however, are a mystery to me. He is a determined and relentless man, with the genuine character of an inquisitor,[1] and had he any object to gain by putting Clifford to the rack, I verily believe that he would wrench his joints from their sockets, in order to accomplish it. But, so wealthy and eminent as he is—so powerful in his own strength, and in the support of society on all sides—what can Judge Pyncheon have to hope or fear from the imbecile, branded, half-torpid Clifford?"

"Yet," urged Phœbe, "you did speak as if misfortune were impending!"

"Oh, that was because I am morbid!" replied the artist. "My mind has a twist aside, like almost everybody's mind, except your own. Moreover, it is so strange to find myself an inmate of this old Pyncheon house, and sitting in this old garden— (hark, how Maule's well is murmuring!)—that, were it only for this one circumstance, I cannot help fancying that Destiny is arranging its fifth act for a catastrophe."

"There!" cried Phœbe, with renewed vexation; for she was by nature as hostile to mystery as the sunshine to a dark corner. "You puzzle me more than ever!"

"Then let us part friends!" said Holgrave, pressing her hand. "Or, if not friends, let us part before you entirely hate me. You, who love everybody else in the world!"

"Good-by, then," said Phœbe, frankly. "I do not mean to be angry a great while, and should be sorry to have you think so. There has Cousin Hepzibah been standing in the shadow of the doorway, this quarter of an hour past! She thinks I stay too long in the damp garden. So, good-night, and good-by!"

On the second morning thereafter, Phœbe might have been seen, in her straw bonnet, with a shawl on one arm and a little carpetbag on the other, bidding adieu to Hepzibah and Cousin

---

[1] INQUISITOR—Questioner, especially one associated with the Spanish Inquisition, noted for the severity of its dealings with heretics.

Clifford. She was to take a seat in the next train of cars, which would transport her to within half a dozen miles of her country village.

The tears were in Phœbe's eyes; a smile, dewy with affectionate regret, was glimmering around her pleasant mouth. She wondered how it came to pass, that her life of a few weeks, here in this heavy-hearted old mansion, had taken such hold of her, and so melted into her associations, as now to seem a more important center point of remembrance than all which had gone before. How had Hepzibah—grim, silent, and irresponsive to her overflow of cordial sentiment—contrived to win so much love? And Clifford—in his  abortive decay, with the mystery of fearful crime upon him, and the close prison atmosphere yet lurking in his breath—how had he transformed himself into the simplest child, whom Phœbe felt bound to watch over, and be, as it were, the providence of his unconsidered hours! Everything, at that instant of farewell, stood out prominently to her view. Look where she would, lay her hand on what she might, the object responded to her consciousness, as if a moist human heart were in it.

She peeped from the window into the garden, and felt herself more regretful at leaving this spot of black earth, vitiated with such an age-long growth of weeds, than joyful at the idea of again scenting her pine forests and fresh clover fields. She called Chanticleer, his two wives, and the venerable chicken, and threw them some crumbs of bread from the breakfast table. These being hastily gobbled up, the chicken spread its wings, and alighted close by Phœbe on the window sill, where it looked gravely into her face and vented its emotions in a croak. Phœbe bade it be a good old chicken during her absence, and promised to bring it a little bag of buckwheat.

"Ah, Phœbe!" remarked Hepzibah, "you do not smile so naturally as when you came to us! Then the smile chose to shine out; now, you choose it should. It is well that you are going back, for a little while, into your native air. There has been too much weight on your spirits. The house is too gloomy and lonesome; the shop is full of vexations; and as for me, I have no faculty of making things look brighter than they are. Dear Clifford has been your only comfort!"

"Come hither, Phœbe," suddenly cried her cousin Clifford, who had said very little all the morning. "Close!—close!—and look me in the face!"

Phœbe put one of her small hands on each elbow of his chair, and leaned her face toward him, so that he might peruse it as carefully as he would. It is probable that the latent emotions of this parting hour had revived, in some degree, his bedimmed and enfeebled faculties. At any rate, Phœbe soon felt that, if not the profound insight of a seer, yet a more than feminine delicacy of appreciation, was making her heart the subject of its regard. A moment before, she had known nothing which she would have sought to hide. Now, as if some secret were hinted to her own consciousness through the medium of another's perception, she was fain to let her eyelids droop beneath Clifford's gaze. A blush, too—the redder because she strove hard to keep it down—ascended, higher and higher, in a tide of fitful progress, until even her brow was all suffused with it.

"It is enough, Phœbe," said Clifford, with a melancholy smile. "When I first saw you, you were the prettiest little maiden in the world; and now you have deepened into beauty! Girlhood has passed into womanhood; the bud is a bloom! Go, now!—I feel lonelier than I did."

Phœbe took leave of the desolate couple, and passed through the shop, twinkling her eyelids to shake off a dewdrop; for—considering how brief her absence was to be, and therefore the folly of being cast down about it—she would not so far acknowledge her tears as to dry them with her handkerchief. On the doorstep, she met the little urchin whose marvelous feats of gastronomy have been recorded in the earlier pages of our narrative. She took from the window some specimen or other of natural history—her eyes being too dim with moisture to inform her accurately whether it was a rabbit or a hippopotamus—put it into the child's hand, as a parting gift, and went her way. Old Uncle Venner was just coming out of his door, with a woodhorse and saw on his shoulder; and, trudging along the street, he scrupled not to keep company with Phœbe, so far as their paths lay together; nor, in spite of his patched coat and rusty beaver, and the curious fashion of his tow-cloth trousers, could she find it in her heart to outwalk him.

"We shall miss you, next Sabbath afternoon," observed the street philosopher. "It is unaccountable how little time it takes some folks to grow just as natural to a man as his own breath; and, begging your pardon, Miss Phœbe (though there can be no offense in an old man's saying it), that's just what you've grown to me! My years have been a great many, and your life is but just beginning; and yet, you are somehow as familiar to me as if I had found you at my mother's door, and you had blossomed, like a running vine, all along my pathway since. Come back soon, or I shall be gone to my farm; for I begin to find these wood-sawing jobs a little too tough for my backache."

"Very soon, Uncle Venner," replied Phœbe.

"And let it be all the sooner, Phœbe, for the sake of those poor souls yonder," continued her companion. "They can never do without you now—never, Phœbe, never!—no more than if one of God's angels had been living with them, and making their dismal house pleasant and comfortable! Don't it seem to you they'd be in a sad case, if, some pleasant summer morning like this, the angel should spread his wings, and fly to the place he came from? Well, just so they feel, now that you're going home by the railroad! They can't bear it, Miss Phœbe; so be sure to come back!"

"I am no angel, Uncle Venner," said Phœbe, smiling, as she offered him her hand at the street corner. "But, I suppose, people never feel so much like angels as when they are doing what little good they may. So I shall certainly come back!"

Thus parted the old man and the rosy girl; and Phœbe took the wings of the morning, and was soon flitting almost as rapidly away as if endowed with the aërial locomotion of the angels to whom Uncle Venner had so graciously compared her.

XV THE SCOWL AND SMILE

Wherein Clifford is left alone with Hepzibah; the harpsichord awakens—Is it an omen of death? Judge Pyncheon comes to see Clifford; the Judge pleads to see Clifford, first in sympathy, then threatens force; Hepzibah relents; the Judge sits in a memorable chair, and waits.

SEVERAL days passed over the seven gables, heavily and drearily enough. In fact (not to attribute the whole gloom of sky and earth to the one inauspicious circumstance of Phœbe's departure), an easterly storm had set in, and indefatigably applied itself to the task of making the black roof and walls of the old house look more cheerless than ever before. Yet was the outside not half so cheerless as the interior. Poor Clifford was cut off, at once, from all his scanty resources of enjoyment. Phœbe was not there; nor did the sunshine fall upon the floor. The garden, with its muddy walks, and the chill, dripping foliage of its summerhouse, was an image to be shuddered at. Nothing flourished in the cold, moist, pitiless atmosphere, drifting with the brackish scud of sea breezes, except the moss along the joints of the shingle roof, and the great bunch of weeds, that had lately been suffering from drought, in the angle between the two front gables.

As for Hepzibah, she seemed not merely possessed with the east wind, but to be, in her very person, only another phase of this gray and sullen spell of weather; the east wind itself, grim and disconsolate, in a rusty black silk gown, and with a turban of cloud wreaths on its head. The custom of the shop fell off, because a story got abroad that she soured her small beer and other damageable commodities, by scowling on them. It is, perhaps, true that the public had something reasonably to complain of in her deportment; but toward Clifford she was neither ill-tempered nor unkind, nor felt less warmth of heart than always, had it been possible to make it reach him. The inutility of her best efforts, however, palsied the poor old gentlewoman. She could do little else than sit silently in a corner of the room, when the wet pear tree branches, sweeping across the small windows, created a noonday dusk, which Hepzibah unconsciously darkened with her woe-begone aspect. It was no fault of Hepzibah's. Everything—even the old chairs and tables, that had known what weather was for three or four such lifetimes as her own—looked as damp and chill as if the present were their worst experience. The picture of the Puritan colonel shivered on the wall. The house itself shivered, from every attic of its seven gables, down to the great kitchen fireplace, which served all the better as an emblem of the mansion's heart, because, though built for warmth, it was now so comfortless and empty.

Hepzibah attempted to enliven matters by a fire in the parlor. But the storm demon kept watch above, and, whenever a flame was kindled, drove the smoke back again, choking the chimney's sooty throat with its own breath. Nevertheless, during four days of this miserable storm, Clifford wrapped himself in an old cloak, and occupied his customary chair. On the morning of the fifth, when summoned to breakfast, he responded only by a broken-hearted murmur, expressive of a determination not to leave his bed. His sister made no attempt to change his purpose. In fact, entirely as she loved him, Hepzibah could hardly have borne any longer the wretched duty—so impracticable by her few and rigid faculties—of seeking pastime for a still sensitive, but ruined mind, critical and fastidious, without force or volition. It was, at least, something short of positive despair, that, to-day, she might sit shivering alone, and not suffer continually a new grief, and unreasonable pang of remorse, at every fitful sigh of her fellow sufferer.

But Clifford, it seemed, though he did not make his appearance below stairs, had, after all, bestirred himself in quest of amusement. In the course of the forenoon, Hepzibah heard a note of music, which (there being no other tuneful contrivance in the House of the Seven Gables) she knew must proceed from Alice Pyncheon's harpsichord. She was aware that Clifford, in his youth, possessed a cultivated taste for music, and a considerable degree of skill in its practice. It was difficult, however, to conceive of his retaining an accomplishment to which daily exercise is so essential, in the measure indicated by the sweet, airy, and delicate, though most melancholy strain, that now stole upon her ear. Nor was it less marvelous that the long-silent instrument should be capable of so much melody. Hepzibah involuntarily thought of the ghostly harmonies, prelusive of death in the family, which were attributed to the legendary Alice. But it was, perhaps, proof of the agency of other than spiritual fingers, that, after a few touches, the chords seemed to snap asunder with their own vibrations, and the music ceased.

But a harsher sound succeeded to the mysterious notes; nor was the easterly day fated to pass without an event sufficient in itself to poison, for Hepzibah and Clifford, the balmiest air that ever brought the humming birds along with it. The final

echoes of Alice Pyncheon's performance (or Clifford's, if his we
must consider it) were driven away by no less vulgar a dissonance than the ringing of the shop bell. A foot was heard
scraping itself on the threshold, and thence somewhat ponderously stepping on the floor. Hepzibah delayed a moment, while
muffling herself in a faded shawl, which had been her defensive
armor in a forty years' warfare against the east wind. A characteristic sound, however—neither a cough nor a hem, but a
kind of rumbling and reverberating spasm in somebody's capacious depth of chest—impelled her to hurry forward, with
that aspect of fierce faint-heartedness so common to women
in cases of perilous emergency. Few of her sex, on such occasions, have ever looked so terrible as our poor scowling Hepzibah. But the visitor quietly closed the shop door behind him,
stood up his umbrella against the counter, and turned a visage
of composed benignity, to meet the alarm and anger which his
appearance had excited.

Hepzibah's presentiment had not deceived her. It was no
other than Judge Pyncheon, who, after in vain trying the front
door, had now effected his entrance into the shop.

"How do you do, Cousin Hepzibah?—and how does this most
inclement weather affect our poor Clifford?" began the Judge;
and wonderful it seemed, indeed, that the easterly storm was
not put to shame, or, at any rate, a little mollified, by the genial
benevolence of his smile. "I could not rest without calling to
ask, once more, whether I can in any manner promote his comfort, or your own."

"You can do nothing," said Hepzibah, controlling her agitation as well as she could. "I devote myself to Clifford. He
has every comfort which his situation admits of."

"But allow me to suggest, dear cousin," rejoined the Judge,
"you err—in all affection and kindness, no doubt, and with the
very best intentions—but you do err, nevertheless, in keeping your brother so secluded. Why insulate him thus from all
sympathy and kindness? Clifford, alas! has had too much of
solitude. Now let him try society—the society, that is to say,
of kindred and old friends. Let me, for instance, but see Clifford, and I will answer for the good effect of the interview."

"You cannot see him," answered Hepzibah. "Clifford has
kept his bed since yesterday."

"What! How! Is he ill?" exclaimed Judge Pyncheon, starting with what seemed to be angry alarm; for the very frown of the old Puritan darkened through the room as he spoke. "Nay, then, I must and will see him! What if he should die?"

"He is in no danger of death," said Hepzibah, and added, with bitterness that she could repress no longer, "none; unless he shall be persecuted to death, now, by the same man who long ago attempted it!"

"Cousin Hepzibah," said the Judge, with an impressive earnestness of manner, which grew even to tearful pathos, as he proceeded, "is it possible that you do not perceive how unjust, how unkind, how unchristian, is this constant, this long-continued bitterness against me, for a part which I was constrained by duty and conscience, by the force of law, and at my own peril, to act? What did I do, in detriment to Clifford, which it was possible to leave undone? How could you, his sister—if for your never-ending sorrow, as it has been for mine, you had known what I did,—have shown greater tenderness? And do you think, cousin, that it has cost me no pang?—that it has left no anguish in my bosom, from that day to this, amidst all the prosperity with which Heaven has blessed me?—or that I do not now rejoice, when it is deemed consistent with the dues of public justice and the welfare of society that this dear kinsman, this early friend, this nature so delicately and beautifully constituted—so unfortunate, let us pronounce him, and forbear to say, so guilty—that our own Clifford, in fine, should be given back to life, and its possibilities of enjoyment? Ah, you little know me, Cousin Hepzibah! You little know this heart! It now throbs at the thought of meeting him! There lives not the human being (except yourself, and you not more than I) who has shed so many tears for Clifford's calamity! You behold some of them now. There is none who would so delight to promote his happiness! Try me, Hepzibah!—try me, cousin!— try the man whom you have treated as your enemy and Clifford's!—try Jaffrey Pyncheon, and you shall find him true, to the heart's core!"

"In the name of Heaven," cried Hepzibah, provoked only to intenser indignation by this outgush of the inestimable tenderness of a stern nature, "in God's name, whom you insult, and whose power I could almost question, since he hears you utter so many false words, without palsying your tongue, give over, I beseech you, this loathsome pretense of affection for your victim! You hate him! Say so, like a man! You cherish, at this moment, some black purpose against him, in your heart! Speak it out, at once!—or, if you hope so to promote it better, hide it till you can triumph in its success! But never speak again of your love for my poor brother! I cannot bear it! It will drive me beyond a woman's decency! It will drive me mad! Forbear! Not another word! It will make me spurn you!"

For once, Hepzibah's wrath had given her courage. She had spoken. But, after all, was this unconquerable distrust of Judge Pyncheon's integrity, and this utter denial, apparently, of his claim to stand in the ring of human sympathies, were they founded in any just perception of his character, or merely the offspring of a woman's unreasonable prejudice, deduced from nothing?

The Judge, beyond all question, was a man of eminent respectability. The church acknowledged it; the state acknowledged it. It was denied by nobody. In all the very extensive sphere of those who knew him, whether in his public or private capacities, there was not an individual—except Hepzibah, and some lawless mystic, like the daguerreotypist, and, possibly, a few political opponents—who would have dreamed of seriously disputing his claim to a high and honorable place in the world's regard. Nor (we must do him the further justice to say) did Judge Pyncheon himself, probably, entertain many or very frequent doubts, that his enviable reputation accorded with his deserts. His conscience, therefore, usually considered the surest witness to a man's integrity—his conscience, unless it might be for the little space of five minutes in the twenty-four hours, or, now and then, some black day in the whole year's circle—his conscience bore an accordant testimony with the world's laudatory voice. And yet, strong as this evidence may seem to be, we should hesitate to peril our own conscience on the assertion, that the Judge and the consenting world were right, and that poor Hepzibah, with her solitary prejudice, was wrong. Hidden from mankind—forgotten by himself, or buried so deeply under a sculptured and ornamented pile of ostentatious deeds that his daily life could take no note of it—there may have lurked

some evil and unsightly thing. Nay, we could almost venture
to say, further, that a daily guilt might have been acted by
him, continually renewed, and reddening forth afresh, like the
miraculous bloodstain of a murder, without his necessarily at
every moment being aware of it.

But our affair now is with Judge Pyncheon as he stood con-
fronting the fierce outbreak of Hepzibah's wrath. Without pre-
meditation, to her own surprise, and indeed terror, she had
given vent, for once, to the inveteracy of her resentment, cherished against this kinsman for thirty years.

Thus far, the Judge's countenance had expressed mild forbearance—grave and almost gentle deprecation of his cousin's unbecoming violence—free and Christian-like forgiveness of the
wrong inflicted by her words. But, when those words were
irrevocably spoken, his look assumed sternness, the sense of
power, and immitigable resolve; and this with so natural and
imperceptible a change, that it seemed as if the iron man had
stood there from the first, and the meek man not at all. The
effect was as when the light vapory clouds, with their soft coloring, suddenly vanish from the stony brow of a precipitous
mountain, and leave there the frown which you at once feel to
be eternal. Hepzibah almost adopted the insane belief that it
was her old Puritan ancestor, and not the modern judge, on
whom she had just been wreaking the bitterness of her heart.
Never did a man show stronger proof of the lineage attributed
to him than Judge Pyncheon, at this crisis, by his unmistakable
resemblance to the picture in the inner room.

"Cousin Hepzibah," said he, very calmly, "it is time to have
done with this."

"With all my heart!" answered she. "Then, why do you persecute us any longer? Leave poor Clifford and me in peace.
Neither of us desires anything better!"

"It is my purpose to see Clifford before I leave this house,"
continued the Judge. "Do not act like a madwoman, Hepzibah!
I am his only friend, and an all-powerful one. Has it never
occurred to you—are you so blind as not to have seen—that,
without not merely my consent, but my efforts, my representa-
tions, the exertion of my whole influence, political, official, personal, Clifford would never have been what you call free? Did
you think his release a triumph over me? Not so, my good

cousin; not so, by any means! The furthest possible from that! No; but it was the accomplishment of a purpose long entertained on my part. I set him free!"

"You!" answered Hepzibah. "I never will believe it! He owed his dungeon to you—his freedom to God's province!"

"I set him free!" reaffirmed Judge Pyncheon, with the calmest composure. "And I come hither now to decide whether he shall retain his freedom. It will depend upon himself. For this purpose, I must see him."

"Never!—it would drive him mad!" exclaimed Hepzibah, but with an irresoluteness sufficiently perceptible to the keen eye of the Judge; for, without the slightest faith in his good intentions, she knew not whether there was most to dread in yielding or resistance. "And why should you wish to see this wretched, broken man, who retains hardly a fraction of his intellect, and will hide even that from an eye which has no love in it?"

"He shall see love enough in mine, if that be all!" said the Judge, with well-grounded confidence in the benignity of his aspect. "But, Cousin Hepzibah, you confess a great deal, and very much to the purpose. Now, listen, and I will frankly explain my reasons for insisting on this interview. At the death, thirty years since, of our uncle Jaffrey, it was found—I know not whether the circumstance ever attracted much of your attention, among the sadder interests that clustered round that event —but it was found that his visible estate, of every kind, fell far short of any estimate ever made of it. He was supposed to be immensely rich. Nobody doubted that he stood among the weightiest men of his day. It was one of his eccentricities, however—and not altogether a folly, either—to conceal the amount of his property by making distant and foreign investments, perhaps under other names than his own, and by various means, familiar enough to capitalists, but unnecessary here to be specified. By Uncle Jaffrey's last will and testament, as you are aware, his entire property was bequeathed to me, with the single exception of a life interest to yourself in this old family mansion, and the strip of patrimonial estate remaining attached to it."

"And do you seek to deprive us of that?" asked Hepzibah, unable to restrain her bitter contempt. "Is this your price for ceasing to persecute poor Clifford?"

"Certainly not, my dear cousin!" answered the Judge, smiling benevolently. "On the contrary, as you must do me the justice to own, I have constantly expressed my readiness to double or treble your resources, whenever you should make up your mind to accept any kindness of that nature at the hands of your kinsman. No, no! But here lies the gist of the matter. Of my uncle's unquestionably great estate, as I have said, not the half— no, not one-third, as I am fully convinced—was apparent after his death. Now, I have the best possible reasons for believing that your brother Clifford can give me a clew to the recovery of the remainder."

"Clifford!—Clifford know of any hidden wealth?—Clifford have it in his power to make you rich?" cried the old gentlewoman, affected with a sense of something like ridicule, at the idea. "Impossible! You deceive yourself! It is really a thing to laugh at!"

"It is as certain as that I stand here!" said Judge Pyncheon, striking his gold-headed cane on the floor, and at the same time stamping his foot, as if to express his conviction the more forcibly by the whole emphasis of his substantial person. "Clifford told me so himself!"

"No, no!" exclaimed Hepzibah, incredulously. "You are dreaming, Cousin Jaffrey!"

"I do not belong to the dreaming class of men," said the Judge, quietly. "Some months before my uncle's death, Clifford boasted to me of the possession of the secret of incalculable wealth. His purpose was to taunt me, and excite my curiosity. I know it well. But, from a pretty distinct recollection of the particulars of our conversation, I am thoroughly convinced that there was truth in what he said. Clifford, at this moment, if he chooses—and choose he must!—can inform me where to find the schedule, the documents, the evidences, in whatever shape they exist, of the vast amount of Uncle Jaffrey's missing property. He has the secret. His boast was no idle word. It had a directness, an emphasis, a particularity, that showed a backbone of solid meaning within the mystery of his expression."

"And what if he should refuse?" inquired Hepzibah. "Or—as I steadfastly believe—what if he has no knowledge of this wealth?"

"My dear cousin," said Judge Pyncheon, with a quietude which he had the power of making more formidable than any violence, "since your brother's return, I have taken the precaution (a highly proper one in the near kinsman and natural guardian of an individual so situated) to have his deportment and habits constantly and carefully overlooked. Your neighbors have been eyewitnesses to whatever has passed in the garden. The butcher, the baker, the fishmonger, some of the customers of your shop, and many a prying old woman, have told me several of the secrets of your interior. A still larger circle—I myself, among the rest—can testify to his extravagances at the arched window. Thousands beheld him, a week or two ago, on the point of flinging himself thence into the street. From all this testimony, I am led to apprehend—reluctantly, and with deep grief—that Clifford's misfortunes have so affected his intellect, never very strong, that he cannot safely remain at large. The alternative, you must be aware—and its adoption will depend entirely on the decision which I am now about to make— the alternative is his confinement, probably for the remainder of his life, in a public asylum, for persons in his unfortunate state of mind."

"You cannot mean it!" shrieked Hepzibah.

"Should my cousin Clifford," continued Judge Pyncheon, wholly undisturbed, "from mere malice, and hatred of one whose interests ought naturally to be dear to him—a mode of passion that, as often as any other, indicates mental disease—should he refuse me the information so important to myself, and which he assuredly possesses, I shall consider it the one needed jot of evidence to satisfy my mind of his insanity. And, once sure of the course pointed out by conscience, you know me too well, Cousin Hepzibah, to entertain a doubt that I shall pursue it."

"Oh, Jaffrey—Cousin Jaffrey!" cried Hepzibah, mournfully, not passionately, "it is you that are diseased in mind, not Clifford! You have forgotten that a woman was your mother!— that you have had sisters, brothers, children of your own!—or that there ever was affection between man and man, or pity from one man to another, in this miserable world! Else, how could you have dreamed of this? You are not young, Cousin Jaffrey!—no, nor middle-aged—but already an old man! The hair is white upon your head! How many years have you to live? Are you not rich enough for that little time? Shall you be hungry—shall you lack clothes, or a roof to shelter you—between this point and the grave? No! but, with the half of what you now possess, you could revel in costly food and wines, and build a house twice as splendid as you now inhabit, and make a far greater show to the world, and yet leave riches to your only son, to make him bless the hour of your death! Then, why should you do this cruel, cruel thing?—so mad a thing, that I know not whether to call it wicked! Alas, Cousin Jaffrey, this hard and grasping spirit has run in our blood these two hundred years! You are but doing over again, in another shape, what your ancestor before you did, and sending down to your posterity the curse inherited from him!"

"Talk sense, Hepzibah, for Heaven's sake!" exclaimed the Judge, with the impatience natural to a reasonable man, on hearing anything so utterly absurd as the above, in a discussion about matters of business. "I have told you my determination. I am not apt to change. Clifford must give up his secret, or take the consequences. And let him decide quickly; for I have several affairs to attend to, this morning, and an important dinner engagement with some political friends."

"Clifford has no secret!" answered Hepzibah. "And God will not let you do the thing you meditate!"

"We shall see," said the unmoved Judge. "Meanwhile, choose whether you will summon Clifford, and allow this business to be amicably settled by an interview between two kinsmen, or drive me to harsher measures, which I should be most happy to feel myself justified in avoiding. The responsibility is altogether on your part."

"You are stronger than I," said Hepzibah, after a brief consideration; "and you have no pity in your strength! Clifford is not now insane; but the interview which you insist upon may go far to make him so. Nevertheless, knowing you as I do, I believe it to be my best course to allow you to judge for yourself as to the improbability of his possessing any valuable secret. I will call Clifford. Be merciful in your dealings with him!—be far more merciful than your heart bids you be!—for God is looking at you, Jaffrey Pyncheon!"

The Judge followed his cousin from the shop, where the foregoing conversation had passed, into the parlor, and flung himself heavily into the great ancestral chair. Many a former

Pyncheon had found repose in its capacious arms:—rosy children, after their sports; young men, dreamy with love; grown men, weary with cares; old men, burdened with winters—they had mused, and slumbered, and departed to a yet profounder sleep. It had been a long tradition, though a doubtful one, that this was the very chair, seated in which, the earliest of the Judge's New England forefathers—he whose picture still hung upon the wall—had given a dead man's silent and stern reception to the throng of distinguished guests. From that hour of evil omen until the present, it may be—though we know not the secret of his heart—but it may be that no wearier and sadder man had ever sunk into the chair than this same Judge Pyncheon, whom we have just beheld so immitigably hard and resolute. Surely, it must have been at no slight cost that he had thus fortified his soul with iron. Such calmness is a mightier effort than the violence of weaker men. And there was yet a heavy task for him to do. Was it a little matter—a trifle to be prepared for in a single moment, and to be rested from in another moment—that he must now, after thirty years, en-

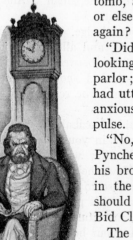

counter a kinsman risen from a living tomb, and wrench a secret from him, or else consign him to a living tomb again?

"Did you speak?" asked Hepzibah, looking in from the threshold of the parlor; for she imagined that the Judge had uttered some sound which she was anxious to interpret as a relenting impulse. "I thought you called me back."

"No, no!" gruffly answered Judge Pyncheon, with a harsh frown, while his brow grew almost a black purple, in the shadow of the room. "Why should I call you back? Time flies! Bid Clifford come to me!"

The Judge had taken his watch from his vest pocket, and now held it in his hand, measuring the interval which was to ensue before the appearance of Clifford.

XVI CLIFFORD'S CHAMBER

Wherein Hepzibah goes in search of Clifford; a surprise in Hol-
grave's room; Clifford cannot be found; Hepzibah meets Clifford
emerging from the parlor, but the Judge remains in the old chair;
Clifford and Hepzibah leave.

NEVER had the old house appeared so dismal to poor Hepzibah as when she departed on that wretched errand. There
was a strange aspect in it. As she trod along the foot-worn
passages, and opened one crazy door after another, and ascended the creaking staircase, she gazed wistfully and fearfully
around. It would have been no marvel, to her excited mind,
if, behind or beside her, there had been the rustle of dead
people's garments, or pale visages awaiting her on the landing
place above. Her nerves were set all ajar by the scene of
passion and terror through which she had just struggled. Her
colloquy with Judge Pyncheon, who so perfectly represented
the person and attributes of the founder of the family, had
called back the dreary past. It weighed upon her heart. Whatever she had heard, from legendary aunts and grandmothers,
concerning the good or evil fortunes of the Pyncheons—stories
which had heretofore been kept warm in her remembrance by
the chimney-corner glow that was associated with them—now
recurred to her, somber, ghastly, cold, like most passages of
family history, when brooded over in melancholy mood. The
whole seemed little else but a series of calamity, reproducing
itself in successive generations, with one general hue, and varying in little, save the outline. But Hepzibah now felt as if the
Judge, and Clifford, and herself—they three together—were on
the point of adding another incident to the annals of the house,
with a bolder relief of wrong and sorrow, which would cause it
to stand out from all the rest.

But Hepzibah could not rid herself of the sense of something
unprecedented at that instant passing, and soon to be accomplished. Her nerves were in a shake. Instinctively she paused
before the arched window, and looked out upon the street, in
order to seize its permanent objects with her mental grasp, and
thus to steady herself from the reel and vibration which affected her more immediate sphere. It brought her up, as we
may say, with a kind of shock, when she beheld everything

under the same appearance as the day before, and numberless preceding days, except for the difference between sunshine and sullen storm. Her eye traveled along the street, from doorstep to doorstep, noting the wet sidewalks, with here and there a puddle in hollows that had been imperceptible until filled with water. She screwed her dim optics to their acutest point, in the hope of making out, with greater distinctness, a certain window, where she half saw, half guessed, that a tailor's seamstress was sitting at her work. Hepzibah flung herself upon that unknown woman's companionship, even thus far off. Then she was attracted by a chaise rapidly passing, and watched its moist and glistening top, and its splashing wheels, until it had turned the corner, and refused to carry any further her idly trifling, because appalled and overburdened, mind. When the vehicle had disappeared, she allowed herself still another loitering moment; for the patched figure of good Uncle Venner was now visible, coming slowly from the head of the street downward, with a rheumatic limp, because the east wind had got into his joints. Hepzibah wished that he would pass yet more slowly, and befriend her shivering solitude a little longer. Anything that would take her out of the grievous present, and interpose human beings betwixt herself and what was nearest to her— whatever would defer, for an instant, the inevitable errand on which she was bound—all such impediments were welcome. Next to the lightest heart, the heaviest is apt to be most playful.

Hepzibah had little hardihood for her own proper pain, and far less for what she must inflict on Clifford. Of so slight a nature, and so shattered by his previous calamities, it would not well be short of utter ruin to bring him face to face with the hard, relentless man, who had been his evil destiny through life. It would be like flinging a porcelain vase, with already a crack in it, against a granite column. Never before had Hepzibah so adequately estimated the powerful character of her cousin Jaffrey—powerful by intellect, energy of will, the long habit of acting among men, and, as she believed, by his unscrupulous pursuit of selfish ends through evil means. It did but increase the difficulty, that Judge Pyncheon was under a delusion as to the secret which he supposed Clifford to possess. Thus, as the Judge required an impossibility of Clifford, the latter, as he could not perform it, must needs perish. For what, in the grasp of a man like this, was to become of Clifford's soft, poetic nature, that never should have had a task more stubborn than to set a life of beautiful enjoyment to the flow and rhythm of musical cadences! Indeed, what had become of it already? Broken! Blighted! All but annihilated! Soon to be wholly so!

For a moment, the thought crossed Hepzibah's mind, whether Clifford might not really have such knowledge of their deceased uncle's vanished estate as the Judge imputed to him. She remembered some vague intimations, on her brother's part, which —if the supposition were not essentially preposterous—might have been so interpreted. There had been schemes of travel and residence abroad, daydreams of brilliant life at home, and splendid castles in the air, which it would have required boundless wealth to build and realize. Had this wealth been in her power, how gladly would Hepzibah have bestowed it all upon her iron-hearted kinsman, to buy for Clifford the freedom and seclusion of the desolate old house! But she believed that her brother's schemes were as destitute of actual substance and purpose as a child's pictures of its future life, while sitting in a little chair by its mother's knee. Clifford had none but shadowy gold at his command; and it was not the stuff to satisfy Judge Pyncheon!

Was there no help, in their extremity? It seemed strange that there should be none, with a city round about her. It would be so easy to throw up the window, and send forth a shriek, at the strange agony of which everybody would come hastening to the rescue, well understanding it to be the cry of a human soul, at some dreadful crisis! But how wild, how almost laughable, the fatality, and yet how continually it comes to pass, thought Hepzibah, in this dull delirium of a world, that whosoever, and with however kindly a purpose, should come to help, they would be sure to help the strongest side!

Nevertheless, in spite of this perception that the Judge would draw all human aid to his own behalf, Hepzibah was so unaccustomed to act for herself, that the least word of counsel would have swayed her to any mode of action. Little Phœbe Pyncheon would at once have lighted up the whole scene, if not by any available suggestion, yet simply by the warm vivacity of her character. The idea of the artist occurred to Hepzibah. Young and unknown, mere vagrant adventurer as he was, she had been conscious of a force in Holgrave which might well adapt him to be the champion of a crisis. With this thought in her mind, she unbolted a door, cobwebbed and long disused, but which had served as a former medium of communication between her own part of the house and the gable where the wandering daguerreotypist had now established his temporary home. He was not there. A book, face downward, on the table, a roll of manuscript, a half-written sheet, a newspaper, some tools of his present occupation, and several rejected daguerreotypes, conveyed an impression as if he were close at hand. But, at this period of the day, as Hepzibah might have anticipated, the artist was at his public rooms. With an impulse of idle curiosity, that flickered among her heavy thoughts, she looked at one of the daguerreotypes, and beheld Judge Pyncheon frowning at her! Fate stared her in the face. She turned back from her fruitless quest, with a heart-sinking sense of disappointment. In all her years of seclusion, she had never felt, as now, what it was to be alone. It seemed as if the house stood in a desert, or, by some spell, was made invisible to those who dwelt around, or passed beside it; so that any mode of misfortune, miserable accident, or crime, might happen in it, without the possibility of aid. In her grief and wounded pride, Hepzibah had spent her life in divesting herself of friends—she had willfully cast off the support which God has ordained his creatures to need from one another—and it was now her punishment, that Clifford and herself would fall the easier victims to their kindred enemy.

Returning to the arched window, she lifted her eyes—scowling, poor, dim-sighted Hepzibah, in the face of Heaven!—and strove hard to send up a prayer through the dense gray pavement of clouds. Those mists had gathered, as if to symbolize a great, brooding mass of human trouble, doubt, confusion, and chill indifference, between earth and the better regions. Her faith was too weak; the prayer too heavy to be thus uplifted. It fell back, a lump of lead, upon her heart.

At last, finding no other pretext for deferring the torture that she was to inflict on Clifford—her reluctance to which was the true cause of her loitering at the window, her search for the artist, and even her abortive prayer—dreading, also, to hear the stern voice of Judge Pyncheon from below stairs, chiding her delay, she crept slowly, a pale, grief-stricken figure, a dismal shape of woman, with almost torpid limbs, slowly to her brother's door, and knocked!

There was no reply!

And how should there have been? Her hand, tremulous with the shrinking purpose which directed it, had smitten so feebly against the door that the sound could hardly have gone inward. She knocked again. Still, no response! Nor was it to be wondered at. She had struck with the entire force of her heart's vibration, communicating by some subtle magnetism, her own terror to the summons. Clifford would turn his face to the pillow, and cover his head beneath the bedclothes, like a startled child at midnight. She knocked a third time, three regular strokes, gentle, but perfectly distinct, and with meaning in them.

Clifford returned no answer.

"Clifford! dear brother!" said Hepzibah. "Shall I come in?"

A silence.

Two or three times, and more, Hepzibah repeated his name, without result; till, thinking her brother's sleep unwontedly profound, she undid the door, and entering, found the chamber vacant. How could he have come forth, and when, without her knowledge? Was it possible that, in spite of the stormy day, and worn out with the irksomeness within doors, he had betaken himself to his customary haunt in the garden, and was now shivering under the cheerless shelter of the summerhouse? She hastily threw up a window, thrust forth her turbaned head and the half of her gaunt figure, and searched the whole garden through, as completely as her dim vision would allow. She could see the interior of the summerhouse, and its circular seat, kept moist by the droppings of the roof. It had no occupant. Clifford was not thereabouts; unless, indeed, he had crept for concealment—(as, for a moment, Hepzibah fancied might be the case)—into a great wet mass of tangled and broad-leaved shadow, where the squash vines were clambering tumultuously upon an old wooden framework, set casually aslant the fence. This could not be, however; he was not there; for while Hepzibah was looking, a strange grimalkin stole forth from the very spot, and picked his way across the garden. Twice he paused to snuff the air, and then anew directed his course toward the parlor window. Whether it was only on account of the stealthy, prying manner common to the race, or that this cat seemed to have more than ordinary mischief in his thoughts, the old gentlewoman, in spite of her much perplexity, felt an impulse to drive the animal away, and accordingly flung down a window stick. The cat stared up at her, like a detected thief or murderer, and, the next instant, took to flight. No other living creature was visible in the garden. Chanticleer and his family had either not left their roost, disheartened by the interminable rain, or had done the next wisest thing, by seasonably returning to it. Hepzibah closed the window.

But where was Clifford? Could it be, that, aware of the presence of his Evil Destiny, he had crept silently down the staircase, while the Judge and Hepzibah stood talking in the shop, and had softly undone the fastenings of the outer door, and made his escape into the street? With that thought, she seemed to behold his gray, wrinkled, yet childlike aspect, in the old-fashioned garments which he wore about the house; a figure such as one sometimes imagines himself to be, with the world's eye upon him, in a troubled dream. This figure of her wretched brother would go wandering through the city, attracting all eyes, and everybody's wonder and repugnance, like a ghost, the more to be shuddered at because visible at noontide. To incur the ridicule of the younger crowd, that knew him not —the harsher scorn and indignation of a few old men, who might recall his once familiar features! To be the sport of boys, who, when old enough to run about the streets, have no more reverence for what is beautiful and holy, nor pity for what is sad—no more sense of sacred misery, sanctifying the human shape in which it embodies itself—than if Satan were the father of them all! Goaded by their taunts, their loud, shrill cries, and cruel laughter—insulted by the filth of the public ways, which they would fling upon him—or, as it might well be, distracted by the mere strangeness of his situation, though nobody should afflict him with so much as a thoughtless word, what wonder if Clifford were to break into some wild extravagance, which was certain to be interpreted as lunacy? Thus Judge Pyncheon's fiendish scheme would be ready accomplished to his hands!

Then Hepzibah reflected that the town was almost completely water girdled. The wharves stretched out toward the center of the harbor, and, in this inclement weather, were deserted by the ordinary throng of merchants, laborers, and sea-faring men; each wharf a solitude, with the vessels moored stem and stern, along its misty length. Should her brother's aimless footsteps stray thitherward, and he but bend, one moment, over the deep, black tide, would he not bethink himself that here was the sure refuge within his reach, and that, with a single step, or the slightest overbalance of his body, he might be forever beyond his kinsman's gripe? Oh, the temptation! To make of his ponderous sorrow a security! To sink, with its leaden weight upon him, and never rise again!

The horror of this last conception was too much for Hepzibah. Even Jaffrey Pyncheon must help her now! She hastened down the staircase, shrieking as she went.

"Clifford is gone!" she cried. "I cannot find my brother! Help, Jaffrey Pyncheon! Some harm will happen to him!"

She threw open the parlor door. But, what with the shade of branches across the windows, and the smoke-blackened ceiling, and the dark oak panelling of the walls, there was hardly so much daylight in the room that Hepzibah's imperfect sight could accurately distinguish the Judge's figure. She was certain, however, that she saw him sitting in the ancestral armchair, near the center of the floor, with his face somewhat averted, and looking toward a window. So firm and quiet is the nervous system of such men as Judge Pyncheon, that he had perhaps stirred not more than once since her departure, but, in the hard composure of his temperament, retained the position into which accident had thrown him.

"I tell you, Jaffrey," cried Hepzibah, impatiently, as she turned from the parlor door to search other rooms, "my brother is not in his chamber! You must help me seek him!"

But Judge Pyncheon was not the man to let himself be startled from an easy-chair with haste ill befitting either the dignity of his character or his broad personal basis, by the alarm of an hysteric woman. Yet, considering his own interest in the matter, he might have bestirred himself with a little more alacrity.

"Do you hear me, Jaffrey Pyncheon?" screamed Hepzibah, as she again approached the parlor door, after an ineffectual search elsewhere. "Clifford is gone!"

At this instant, on the threshold of the parlor, emerging from within, appeared Clifford himself! His face was preternaturally pale; so deadly white, indeed, that, through all the glimmering indistinctness of the passageway, Hepzibah could discern his features, as if a light fell on them alone. Their vivid and wild expression, seemed likewise sufficient to illuminate them; it was an expression of scorn and mockery, coinciding with the emotions indicated by his gesture. As Clifford stood on the threshold, partly turning back, he pointed his finger within the parlor, and shook it slowly as though he would have summoned, not Hepzibah alone, but the whole world, to gaze at some object inconceivably ridiculous. This action, so ill-timed and extravagant—accompanied, too, with a look that showed more like joy than any other kind of excitement—compelled Hepzibah to dread that her stern kinsman's ominous visit had driven her poor brother to absolutely insanity. Nor could she otherwise account for the Judge's quiescent mood than by supposing him craftily on the watch, while Clifford developed these symptoms of a distracted mind.

"Be quiet, Clifford!" whispered his sister, raising her hand, to impress caution. "Oh, for Heaven's sake, be quiet!"

"Let him be quiet! What can he do better?" answered Clifford, with a still wilder gesture, pointing into the room which he had just quitted. "As for us, Hepzibah, we can dance now! —we can sing, laugh, play, do what we will! The weight is gone, Hepzibah! it is gone off this weary old world, and we may be as light-hearted as little Phœbe herself!"

And, in accordance with his words, he began to laugh, still pointing his finger at the object, invisible to Hepzibah, within the parlor. She was seized with a sudden intuition of some horrible thing. She thrust herself past Clifford, and disappeared into the room; but almost immediately returned, with a cry choking in her throat. Gazing at her brother, with an affrighted glance of inquiry, she beheld him all in a tremor and a quake, from head to foot, while, amid these commoted elements of passion or alarm, still flickered his gusty mirth.

"My God! what is to become of us?" gasped Hepzibah.

"Come!" said Clifford, in a tone of brief decision, most unlike what was usual with him. "Let us leave the old house to our cousin Jaffrey! He will take good care of it!"

Hepzibah now noticed that Clifford had on a cloak—a garment of long ago—in which he had constantly muffled himself during these days of easterly storm. He beckoned with his hand, and intimated, so far as she could comprehend him, his purpose that they should go together from the house. Unaccustomed to action or responsibility—full of horror at what she had seen, and afraid to inquire, or almost to imagine, how it had come to pass—affrighted at the fatality which seemed to pursue her brother—stupefied by the dim, thick, stifling atmosphere of dread, which filled the house as with a death smell, and obliterated all definiteness of thought—Hepzibah yielded without a question, and on the instant, to the will which Clifford expressed. For herself, she was like a person in a dream, when the will always sleeps. Clifford, ordinarily so destitute of this faculty, had found it in the tension of the crisis.

"Why do you delay so?" cried he, sharply. "Put on your cloak and hood, or whatever it pleases you to wear! No matter what; you cannot look beautiful nor brilliant, my poor Hepzibah! Take your purse, with money in it, and come along!"

Hepzibah obeyed these instructions, as if nothing else were to be done or thought of. She began to wonder, it is true, why she did not wake up, and at what still more intolerable pitch of dizzy trouble her spirit would struggle out of the maze, and make her conscious that nothing of all this had actually happened. Of course, it was not real; no such black, easterly day as this had yet begun to be; Judge Pyncheon had not talked with her; Clifford had not laughed, pointed, beckoned her away with him; but she had merely been afflicted—as lonely sleepers often are—with a great deal of unreasonable misery, in a morning dream!

"Now—now—I shall certainly awake!" thought Hepzibah, as she went to and fro, making her little preparations. "I can bear it no longer! I must wake up now!"

But it came not, that awakening moment! It came not, even when, just before they left the house, Clifford stole to the parlor door, and made a parting obeisance to the sole occupant of the room.

"What an absurd figure the old fellow cuts now!" whispered he to Hepzibah. "Just when he fancied he had me completely under his thumb! Come, come; make haste! or he will start up, like Giant Despair in pursuit of Christian and Hopeful,[2] and catch us yet!"

As they passed into the street, Clifford directed Hepzibah's attention to something on one of the posts of the front door. It was merely the initials of his own name, which, with somewhat of his characteristic grace about the forms of the letters, he had cut there when a boy. The brother and sister departed, and left Judge Pyncheon sitting in the old home of his forefathers, all by himself.

[2] GIANT DESPAIR, CHRISTIAN, HOPEFUL—Characters in *Pilgrim's Progress* by John Bunyan.

XVII   THE FLIGHT OF TWO OWLS

Wherein Clifford and Hepzibah board a train; the interesting newness of the life within the car; Clifford relates to the conductor of a melancholy old house, of death and of life; they alight at a solitary way station.

SUMMER as it was, the east wind set poor Hepzibah's few remaining teeth chattering in her head, as she and Clifford faced it, on their way up Pyncheon Street, and toward the center of the town. Not merely was it the shiver which this pitiless blast brought to her frame (although her feet and hands, especially, had never seemed so death-a-cold as now), but there was a moral sensation, mingling itself with the physical chill, and causing her to shake more in spirit than in body. The world's broad, bleak atmosphere was all so comfortless! What, then, must it have been to Hepzibah and Clifford—so time stricken as they were, yet so like children in their inexperience—as they left the doorstep, and passed from beneath the wide shelter of the Pyncheon elm! They were wandering all abroad, on precisely such a pilgrimage as a child often meditates, to the world's end, with perhaps a sixpence and a biscuit in his pocket. In Hepzibah's mind, there was the wretched consciousness of being adrift. She had lost the faculty of self-guidance; but, in view of the difficulties around her, felt it hardly worth an effort to regain it, and was, moreover, incapable of making one.

As they proceeded on their strange expedition, she now and then cast a look sidelong at Clifford, and could not but observe that he was possessed and swayed by a powerful excitement.

It was this, indeed, that gave him the control which he had at once, and so irresistibly, established over his movements.

They met few people abroad, even on passing from the retired neighborhood of the House of the Seven Gables into what was ordinarily the more thronged and busier portion of the town. Glistening sidewalks, with little pools of rain, here and there, along their unequal surface; umbrellas displayed ostentatiously in the shop windows, as if the life of trade had concentrated itself in that one article; wet leaves of the horse chestnut or elm trees, torn off untimely by the blast, and scattered along the public way; an unsightly accumulation of mud in the middle of the street, which perversely grew the more unclean for its long and laborious washing; these were the more definable points of a very sombre picture. Had it been a sunny and cheerful day, Hepzibah and Clifford could hardly have gone through the streets without making themselves obnoxious to remark. Now, probably, they were felt to be in keeping with the dismal and bitter weather, and therefore did not stand out in strong relief, as if the sun were shining on them, but melted into the gray gloom, and were forgotten as soon as gone.

Poor Hepzibah! Could she have understood this fact, it would have brought her some little comfort; for, to all her other troubles—strange to say!—there was added the womanish and old-maiden-like misery arising from a sense of unseemliness in her attire. Thus, she was fain to shrink deeper into herself, as it were, as if in the hope of making people suppose that here was only a cloak and hood, threadbare and woefully faded, taking an airing in the midst of the storm, without any wearer!

As they went on, the feeling of indistinctness and unreality kept dimly hovering round about her, and so diffusing itself into her system that one of her hands was hardly palpable to the touch of the other. Any certainty would have been preferable to this. She whispered to herself, again and again, "Am I awake? Am I awake?"—and sometimes exposed her face to the chill spatter of the wind, for the sake of its rude assurance that she was. Whether it was Clifford's purpose, or only chance, had led them thither, they now found themselves passing beneath the arched entrance of a large structure of gray stone. Within, there was a spacious breadth, and an airy height from floor to roof, now partially filled with smoke and steam, which

*They were in keeping with the
dismal and bitter weather.*

eddied voluminously upward, and formed a mimic cloud region over their heads. A train of cars was just ready for a start; the locomotive was fretting and fuming, like a steed impatient for a headlong rush; and the bell rang out its hasty peal, so well expressing the brief summons which life vouchsafes to us in its hurried career.

Without question or delay—with the irresistible decision, if not rather to be called recklessness, which had so strangely taken possession of him, and through him of Hepzibah—Clifford impelled her toward the cars, and assisted her to enter. The signal was given; the engine puffed forth its short, quick breaths; the train began its movement; and, along with a hundred other passengers, these two unwonted travelers sped onward like the wind.

At last, therefore, and after so long estrangement from everything that the world acted or enjoyed, they had been drawn into the great current of human life, and were swept away with it, as by the suction of fate itself.

Still haunted with the idea that not one of the past incidents, inclusive of Judge Pyncheon's visit, could be real, the recluse of the Seven Gables murmured in her brother's ear:

"Clifford! Clifford! Is not this a dream?"

"A dream, Hepzibah!" repeated he, almost laughing in her face. "On the contrary, I have never been awake before!"

Meanwhile, looking from the window, they could see the world racing past them.

Within the car, there was the usual interior life of the railroad, offering little to the observation of other passengers, but full of novelty for this pair of strangely enfranchised prisoners. It was novelty enough, indeed, that there were fifty human beings in close relation with them, under one long and narrow roof, and drawn onward by the same mighty influence that had taken their two selves into its grasp. It seemed marvelous how all these people could remain so quietly in their seats, while so much noisy strength was at work in their behalf. Some, with tickets in their hats (long travelers these, before whom lay a hundred miles of railroad), had plunged into the English scenery and adventures of pamphlet novels, and were keeping company with dukes and earls. Others, whose briefer span forbade their devoting themselves to studies so abstruse, beguiled the little tedium of the way with penny papers. A party of girls, and one young man, on opposite sides of the car, found huge amusement in a game of ball. Boys, with apples, cakes, candy, and rolls of variously tinctured lozenges—merchandise that reminded Hepzibah of her deserted shop—appeared at each momentary stopping place, doing up their business in a hurry, or breaking it short off, lest the market should ravish them away with it. New people continually entered. Old acquaintances—for such they soon grew to be, in this rapid current of affairs—continually departed. Here and there, amid the rumble and the tumult, sat one asleep. Sleep; sport; business; graver or lighter study; and the common and inevitable movement onward! It was life itself!

Clifford's naturally poignant sympathies were all aroused. He caught the color of what was passing about him, and threw it back more vividly than he received it, but mixed, nevertheless, with a lurid and portentous hue. Hepzibah, on the other hand, felt herself more apart from humankind than even in the seclusion which she had just quitted.

"You are not happy, Hepzibah!" said Clifford, apart, in a tone of reproach. "You are thinking of that dismal old house, and of Cousin Jaffrey"—here came the quake through him—"and of Cousin Jaffrey sitting there, all by himself! Take my advice —follow my example—and let such things slip aside. Here we are, in the world, Hepzibah!—in the throng of our fellow beings! Let you and I be happy! As happy as that youth, and those pretty girls, at their game of ball!"

"Happy!" thought Hepzibah, bitterly conscious, at the word, of her dull and heavy heart, with the frozen pain in it. "Happy! He is mad already; and, if I could once feel myself broad awake, I should go mad too!"

If a fixed idea be madness, she was perhaps not remote from it. Fast and far as they had rattled and clattered along the iron track, they might just as well, as regarded Hepzibah's mental images, have been passing up and down Pyncheon Street. With miles and miles of varied scenery between, there was no scene for her, save the seven old gable peaks, with their moss, and the tuft of weeds in one of the angles, and the shop window, and a customer shaking the door, and compelling the little bell to jingle fiercely, but without disturbing Judge Pyncheon! This one old house was everywhere! It transported its great, lumbering bulk, with more than railroad speed, and set itself phlegmatically down on whatever spot she glanced at. The quality of Hepzibah's mind was too unmalleable to take new impressions so readily as Clifford's. He had a winged nature; she was rather of the vegetable kind, and could hardly be kept long alive, if drawn up by the roots. Thus it happened that the relation heretofore existing between her brother and herself was changed. At home, she was his guardian; here, Clifford had become hers, and seemed to comprehend whatever belonged to their new position with a singular rapidity of intelligence. He had been startled into manhood and intellectual vigor; or, at least, into a condition that resembled them, though it might be both diseased and transitory.

The conductor now applied for their tickets; and Clifford, who had made himself the purse bearer, put a bank note into his hand, as he had observed others do.

"For the lady and yourself?" asked the conductor. "And how far?"

"As far as that will carry us," said Clifford. "It is no great matter. We are riding for pleasure, merely!"

"You choose a strange day for it, sir," remarked a gimlet-eyed old gentleman, on the other side of the car, looking at Clifford and his companion, as if curious to make them out. "The best chance of pleasure, in an easterly rain, I take it, is in a man's own house, with a nice little fire in the chimney."

"I cannot precisely agree with you," said Clifford, courteously bowing to the old gentleman, and at once taking up the clew of conversation which the latter had proffered. "It had just occurred to me, on the contrary, that this admirable invention of the railroad—with the vast and inevitable improvements to be looked for, both as to speed and convenience—is destined to do away with those stale ideas of home and fireside, and substitute something better."

"In the name of common sense," asked the old gentleman, rather testily, "what can be better for a man than his own parlor and chimney corner?"

"These things have not the merit which many good people attribute to them," replied Clifford. "They may be said, in few and pithy words, to have ill served a poor purpose. My impression is, that our wonderfully increased and still increasing facilities of locomotion are destined to bring us round again to the nomadic state. These railroads—could but the whistle be made musical, and the rumble and the jar got rid of—are positively the greatest blessing that the ages have wrought out for us. They give us wings; they annihilate the toil and dust of pilgrimage; they spiritualize travel! Transition being so facile, what can be any man's inducement to tarry in one spot? Why, therefore, should he build a more cumbrous habitation than can readily be carried off with him? Why should he make himself a prisoner for life in brick, and stone, and old worm-eaten timber, when he may just as easily dwell, in one sense, nowhere—in a better sense, wherever the fit and beautiful shall offer him a home?"

Clifford's countenance glowed as he divulged this theory; a youthful character shone out from within, converting the wrinkles and pallid duskiness of age into an almost transparent mask. The merry girls let their ball drop upon the floor, and gazed at him. They said to themselves, perhaps, that, before his hair was gray and the crow's feet tracked his temples, this now decaying man must have stamped the impress of his features on many a woman's heart. But, alas! no woman's eye had seen his face while it was beautiful!

"I should scarcely call it an improved state of things," observed Clifford's new acquaintance, "to live everywhere and nowhere!"

"Would you not?" exclaimed Clifford, with singular energy. "It is as clear to me as sunshine—were there any in the sky—that the greatest possible stumblingblocks in the path of human happiness and improvement are those heaps of bricks and stones, consolidated with mortar, or hewn timber, fastened together with spike nails, which men painfully contrive for their own torment, and call them house and home! There is no such unwholesome atmosphere as that of an old home, rendered poisonous by one's defunct forefathers and relatives. I speak of what I know. There is a certain house within my familiar recollection—one of those peaked-gable (there are seven of them), projecting-storied edifices, such as you occasionally see in our elder towns —a rusty, crazy, creaky, dry-rotted, damp-rotted, dingy, dark, and miserable old dungeon, with an arched window over the porch, and a little shop door on one side, and a great, melancholy elm before it! Now, sir, whenever my thoughts recur to this seven-gabled mansion—(the fact is so very curious that I must needs mention it)—immediately I have a vision or image of an elderly man, of remarkably stern countenance, sitting in an oaken elbow chair, dead, stone dead, with an ugly flow of blood upon his shirt bosom! Dead, but with open eyes! He taints the whole house, as I remember it. I could never flourish there, nor be happy, nor do nor enjoy what God meant me to do and enjoy!"

His face darkened, and seemed to contract, and shrivel itself up, and wither into age.

"Never, sir!" he repeated. "I could never draw cheerful breath there!"

"I should think not," said the old gentleman, eyeing Clifford earnestly, and rather apprehensively. "I should conceive not, sir, with that notion in your head!"

"Surely not," continued Clifford; "and it were a relief to me if that house could be torn down, or burned up, and so the earth be rid of it, and grass be sown abundantly over its foundation. Not that I should ever visit its site again! for, sir, the farther I get away from it, the more does the joy, the lightsome freshness, the heart-leap, the intellectual dance, the youth, in short— yes, my youth, my youth!—the more does it come back to me. No longer ago than this morning, I was old. But now do I look old? If so, my aspect belies me strangely; for—a great weight being off my mind—I feel in the very heyday of my youth, with the world and my best days before me!"

"I trust you may find it so," said the old gentleman, who seemed rather embarrassed, and desirous of avoiding the observation which Clifford's wild talk drew on them both. "You have my best wishes for it."

"For Heaven's sake, dear Clifford, be quiet!" whispered his sister. "They think you mad."

"Be quiet yourself, Hepzibah!" returned her brother. "No matter what they think! I am not mad. For the first time in thirty years, my thoughts gush up and find words ready for them. I must talk, and I will!"

He turned again toward the old gentleman, and renewed the conversation.

"Yes, my dear sir," said he, "it is my firm belief and hope, that these terms of roof and hearthstone, which have so long been held to embody something sacred, are soon to pass out of men's daily use, and be forgotten. Just imagine, for a moment, how much of human evil will crumble away, with this one change! What we call real estate—the solid ground to build a house on—is the broad foundation on which nearly all the guilt of this world rests. A man will commit almost any wrong—he will heap up an immense pile of wickedness, as hard as granite, and which will weigh as heavily upon his soul, to eternal ages—only to build a great, gloomy, dark-chambered mansion, for himself to die in, and for his posterity to be miserable in. He lays his own dead corpse beneath the underpinning, as one may say, and hangs his frowning picture on the wall, and, after thus converting himself into an evil destiny, expects his remotest great-grandchildren to be happy there! I do not speak wildly. I have just such a house in my mind's eye!"

"Then, sir," said the old gentleman, getting anxious to drop the subject, "you are not to blame for leaving it."

"Within the lifetime of the child already born," Clifford went on, "all this will be done away. The world is growing too ethereal and spiritual to bear these enormities a great while longer. To me—though, for a considerable period of time, I have lived chiefly in retirement, and know less of such things than most men—even to me, the harbingers of a better era are unmistakable. Mesmerism now! Will that effect nothing, think you, toward purging away the grossness out of human life?"

"All a humbug!" growled the old gentleman.

"Then there is electricity!" exclaimed Clifford. "Is that a humbug, too? Is it a fact—or have I dreamed it—that, by means of electricity, the world of matter has become a great nerve, vibrating thousands of miles in a breathless point of time?"

"If you mean the telegraph," said the old gentleman, glancing his eye toward its wire, alongside the rail track, "it is an excellent thing. A great thing, indeed, sir; particularly as regards the detection of bank robbers and murderers."

"I don't quite like it, in that point of view," replied Clifford. "A bank robber, and what you call a murderer, likewise, has his rights. An almost spiritual medium, like the electric telegraph, should be consecrated to high, deep, joyful, and holy missions. But for these poor rogues, the bank robbers—who, after all, are about as honest as nine people in ten, except that they disregard certain formalities, and prefer to transact business at midnight, rather than 'Change hours—and for these murderers, as you phrase it, who are often excusable in the motives of their deed, and deserve to be ranked among public benefactors, if we consider only its result—for unfortunate individuals like these, I really cannot applaud the enlistment of an immaterial and miraculous power in the universal world hunt at their heels!"

"You can't, hey?" cried the old gentleman, with a hard look.

"Positively, no!" answered Clifford. "It puts them too miserably at disadvantage. For example, sir, in a dark, low, cross-beamed, paneled room of an old house, let us suppose a dead man, sitting in an armchair, with a bloodstain on his shirt bosom—and let us add to our hypothesis another man, issuing from the house, which he feels to be overfilled with the dead man's presence—and let us lastly imagine him fleeing, Heaven knows whither, at the speed of a hurricane, by railroad! Now, sir, if the fugitive alight in some distant town, and find all the people babbling about that self-same dead man, whom he has fled so far to avoid the sight and thought of, will you not allow that his natural rights have been infringed? He has been deprived of his city of refuge, and, in my humble opinion, has suffered infinite wrong!"

"You are a strange man, sir!" said the old gentleman, bringing his gimlet eye to a point on Clifford, as if determined to bore right into him. "I can't see through you!"

"No, I'll be bound you can't!" cried Clifford, laughing. "And yet, my dear sir, I am as transparent as the water of Maule's well! But come, Hepzibah! We have flown far enough for once. Let us alight, as the birds do, and perch ourselves on the nearest twig, and consult whither we shall fly next!"

Just then, as it happened, the train reached a solitary way station. Taking advantage of the brief pause, Clifford left the car, and drew Hepzibah along with him. A moment afterwards, the train—with all the life of its interior, amid which Clifford had made himself so conspicuous an object—was gliding away in the distance, and rapidly lessening to a point, which, in another moment vanished. The world had fled away from these two wanderers. They gazed drearily about them. At a little distance stood a wooden church, black with age, and in a dismal state of ruin and decay, with broken windows, a great rift through the main body of the edifice, and a rafter dangling from the top of the square tower. Farther off was a farmhouse, in the old style, as venerably black as the church, with a roof sloping downward from the three-story peak, to within a man's height of the ground. It seemed uninhabited. There were the relics of a woodpile, indeed, near the door, but with grass sprouting up among the chips and scattered logs. The small raindrops came down aslant; the wind was not turbulent, but sullen, and full of chilly moisture.

Clifford shivered from head to foot. The wild effervescence of his mood—which had so readily supplied thoughts, fantasies, and a strange aptitude of words, and impelled him to talk from the mere necessity of giving vent to this bubbling-up gush of ideas—had entirely subsided. A powerful excitement had given him energy and vivacity. Its operation over, he forthwith began to sink.

"You must take the lead now, Hepzibah!" murmured he, with a torpid and reluctant utterance. "Do with me as you will!"

She knelt down upon the platform where they were standing, and lifted her clasped hands to the sky. The dull, gray weight of clouds made it invisible; but it was no hour for disbelief—no juncture this, to question that there was a sky above, and an Almighty Father looking down from it!

"O God!"—ejaculated poor, gaunt Hepzibah, then paused a moment, to consider what her prayer should be—"O God—our Father—are we not thy children? Have mercy on us!"

XVIII GOVERNOR PYNCHEON

Wherein Judge Pyncheon still sits in his chair. Why does he not keep his appointments? Why does he not attend the important dinner toward which he has worked for so many years?

JUDGE PYNCHEON, while his two relatives have fled away with such ill-considered haste, still sits in the old parlor, keeping house, as the familiar phrase is, in the absence of its ordinary occupants. To him and to the venerable House of the Seven Gables, does our story now betake itself, like an owl, bewildered in the daylight, and hastening back to his hollow tree.

The Judge has not shifted his position for a long while now. He has not stirred hand or foot, nor withdrawn his eyes so much as a hair's breadth from their fixed gaze toward the corner of the room, since the footsteps of Hepzibah and Clifford creaked along the passage, and the outer door was closed cautiously behind their exit. He holds his watch in his left hand, but clutched in such a manner that you cannot see the dial plate. How profound a fit of meditation! You hear the ticking of his watch; his breath you do not hear. A most refreshing slumber, doubtless! And yet, the Judge cannot be asleep. His eyes are open! A cautious man is proverbially said to sleep with one eye open. That may be wisdom. But not with both; for this were heedlessness. No, no! Judge Pyncheon cannot be asleep.

It is odd, however, that a gentleman so burdened with engagements—and noted, too, for punctuality—should linger thus in an old lonely mansion, which he has never seemed very fond of visiting. The oaken chair, to be sure, may tempt him with its roominess. It is, indeed, a spacious, and, allowing for the rude age that fashioned it, moderately easy seat, with capacity enough, at all events, and offering no restraint to the judge's breadth of beam. Yes! in a score of drawing-rooms he would be more than welcome.

Still lingering in the old chair! If the Judge has a little time to throw away, why does not he visit the insurance office, as is his frequent custom, and sit a while in one of their leathern-cushioned armchairs, listening to the gossip of the day, and dropping some deeply designed chance word, which will be certain to become the gossip of to-morrow! And have not the bank directors a meeting, at which it was the Judge's purpose to be present, and his office to preside? Indeed they have; and the hour is noted on a card, which is, or ought to be, in Judge Pyncheon's right vest pocket. Let him go thither, and loll at ease upon his moneybags! He has lounged long enough in the old chair!

This was to have been such a busy day! In the first place, the interview with Clifford. Half an hour, by the Judge's reckoning, was to suffice for that; it would probably be less, but— taking into consideration that Hepzibah was first to be dealt with, and that these women are apt to make many words where a few would do much better—it might be safest to allow half an hour. Half an hour? Why, Judge, it is already two hours, by your own undeviatingly accurate chronometer! Glance your eye down at it, and see! Ah! he will not give himself the trouble either to bend his head, or elevate his hand, so as to bring the faithful timekeeper within his range of vision! Time, all at once, appears to have become a matter of no moment with the Judge!

And has he forgotten all the other items of his memoranda? Clifford's affair arranged, he was to meet a State Street broker, who has undertaken to procure a heavy percentage, and the best of paper, for a few loose thousands which the Judge happens to have by him, uninvested. The wrinkled note shaver will have taken his railroad trip in vain. Half an hour later, in the street next to this, there was to be an auction of real estate, including a portion of the old Pyncheon property, originally belonging to Maule's garden ground. It has been alienated from the Pyncheons these fourscore years; but the Judge had kept it in his eye, and had set his heart on reannexing it to the small demesne [1] still left around the Seven Gables; and now, during this odd fit of oblivion, the fatal hammer must have fallen, and transferred our ancient patrimony to some alien possessor! Possibly, indeed, the sale may have been postponed till fairer weather. If so, will the Judge make it convenient to be present, and favor the auctioneer with his bid, on the proximate occasion?

The next affair was to buy a horse for his own driving. The one heretofore his favorite stumbled, this very morning, on the road to town, and must be at once discarded. Judge Pyncheon's neck is too precious to be risked on such a contingency as a

---

[1] DEMESNE—Property, manor house and adjoining lands.

stumbling steed. Should all the above business be seasonably gotten through with, he might attend the meeting of a charitable society; the very name of which, however, in the multiplicity of his benevolence, is quite forgotten; so that this engagement may pass unfulfilled, and no great harm done. And if he have time, amid the press of more urgent matters, he must take measures for the renewal of Mrs. Pyncheon's tombstone, which, the sexton tells him, has fallen on its marble face, and is cracked quite in twain. She was a praiseworthy woman enough, thinks the Judge, and as she took her departure so seasonably, he will not grudge the second tombstone. It is better, at least, than if she had never needed any! The next item on his list was to give orders for some fruit trees, of a rare variety, to be deliverable at his countryseat, in the ensuing autumn. Yes, buy them, by all means; and may the peaches be luscious in your mouth, Judge Pyncheon! After this comes something more important. A committee of his political party has besought him for a hundred or two of dollars, in addition to his previous disbursements, toward carrying on the fall campaign. The Judge is a patriot; the fate of the country is staked on the November election; and besides, as will be shadowed forth in another paragraph, he has no trifling stake of his own in the same great game. He will do what the committee asks; nay, he will be liberal beyond their expectations; they shall have a check for five hundred dollars, and more anon, if it be needed. What next? A decayed widow, whose husband was Judge Pyncheon's early friend, has laid her case of destitution before him, in a very moving letter. She and her fair daughter have scarcely bread to eat. He partly intends to call on her to-day—perhaps so—perhaps not, accordingly as he may happen to have leisure, and a small bank note.

Another business, which, however, he puts no great weight on —(it is well, you know, to be heedful, but not overanxious, as respects one's personal health)—another business, then, was to consult his family physician. About what, for Heaven's sake? Why, it is rather difficult to describe the symptoms. A mere dimness of sight and dizziness of brain, was it?—or a disagreeable choking, or stifling, or gurgling, or bubbling, in the region of the thorax, as the anatomists say?—or was it a pretty severe throbbing and kicking of the heart, rather creditable to him than otherwise, as showing that the organ had not been left out of the Judge's physical contrivance? No matter what it was. The doctor, probably, would smile at the statement of such trifles to his professional ear; the Judge would smile, in his turn; and, meeting one another's eyes, they would enjoy a hearty laugh together! But a fig for medical advice! The Judge will never need it.

Pray, pray, Judge Pyncheon, look at your watch, now! What —not a glance! It is within ten minutes of the dinner hour! It surely cannot have slipped your memory that the dinner of to-day is to be the most important, in its consequences, of all the dinners you ever ate. Yes, precisely the most important; although, in the course of your somewhat eminent career, you have been placed high toward the head of the table, at the splendid banquets, and have poured out your festive eloquence to ears yet echoing with Webster's mighty organ tones.[2] No public dinner this, however. It is merely a gathering of some dozen or so of friends from several districts of the state; men of distinguished character and influence, assembling, almost casually, at the house of a common friend, likewise distinguished, who will make them welcome to a little better than his ordinary fare. The delicacies of the season, in short, and flavored by a brand of old Madeira[3] which has been the pride of many seasons. It is the Juno brand; a glorious wine, fragrant, and full of gentle might; a bottled-up happiness, put by for use; a golden liquid, worth more than liquid gold; so rare and admirable, that veteran wine bibbers count it among their epochs to have tasted it! It drives away the heartache, and substitutes no headache! Could the Judge but quaff a glass, it might enable him to shake off the unaccountable lethargy which—(for the ten intervening minutes, and five to boot, are already past)—has made him such a laggard at this momentous dinner. It would all but revive a dead man! Would you like to sip it now, Judge Pyncheon?

Alas, this dinner! Have you really forgotten its true object? Then let us whisper it, that you may start at once out of the oaken chair, which really seems to be enchanted, like the one

---

[2] WEBSTER'S MIGHTY ORGAN TONES—The resonant voice of Daniel Webster, one of America's greatest orators.

[3] MADEIRA—Wine made in the Madeira Islands off the coast of Africa.

in Comus,[4] or that in which Moll Pitcher[5] imprisoned your own grandfather. But ambition is a talisman more powerful than witchcraft. Start up, then, and, hurrying through the streets, burst in upon the company, that they may begin before the fish is spoiled! They wait for you; and it is little for your interest that they should wait. These gentlemen—need you be told it?—have assembled, not without purpose, from every quarter of the state. They are practiced politicians, every man of them, and skilled to adjust those preliminary measures which steal from the people, without its knowledge, the power of choosing its own rulers. The popular voice, at the next gubernatorial election, though loud as thunder, will be really but an echo of what these gentlemen shall speak, under their breath, at your friend's festive board. They meet to decide upon their candidate. This little knot of subtle schemers will control the convention, and, through it, dictate to the party. And what worthier candidate—more wise and learned, more noted for philanthropic liberality, truer to safe principles, tried oftener by public trusts, more spotless in private character, with a larger stake in the common welfare, and deeper grounded, by hereditary descent, in the faith and practice of the Puritans—what man can be presented for the suffrage of the people, so eminently combining all these claims to the chief rulership as Judge Pyncheon here before us?

Make haste, then! Do your part! The meed for which you have toiled, and fought, and climbed, and crept, is ready for your grasp! Be present at this dinner!—drink a glass or two of that noble wine!—make your pledges in as low a whisper as you will!—and you rise up from table virtually governor of the glorious old state! Governor Pyncheon, of Massachusetts!

Well! it is absolutely too late for dinner! Too late, we fear, even to join the party at their wine! The guests are warm and merry; they have given up the Judge; and, concluding that the free-soilers[6] have him, they will fix upon another candidate. Were our friend now to stalk in among them, with that wide-open stare, at once wild and stolid, his ungenial presence would

---

[4] COMUS—In the masque of *Comus* by John Milton the heroine is imprisoned in a chair by magic.

[5] MOLL PITCHER—A famous woman of the Revolutionary War days, about whom there are many legends.

[6] FREE-SOILERS—A political party opposed to the extension of slavery.

be apt to change their cheer. Neither would it be seemly in Judge Pyncheon, generally so scrupulous in his attire, to show himself at a dinner table with that crimson stain upon his shirt bosom. Bye the bye, how came it there? It is an ugly sight, at any rate; and the wisest way for the Judge is to button his coat closely over his breast, and, taking his horse and chaise from the livery stable, to make all speed to his own house. There, after a glass of brandy and water, and a mutton chop, a beefsteak, a broiled fowl, or some such hasty little dinner and supper all in one, he had better spend the evening by the fireside. He must toast his slippers a long while, in order to get rid of the chilliness which the air of this vile old house has sent curdling through his veins.

Up, therefore, Judge Pyncheon, up! You have lost a day. But to-morrow will be here anon. Will you rise, betimes, and make the most of it? To-morrow! To-morrow! To-morrow! We, that are alive, may rise betimes to-morrow. As for him that has died to-day, his morrow will be the resurrection morn.

XIX ALICE'S POSIES

Wherein the House of Seven Gables takes on a new aspect; Uncle Venner makes his morning rounds; many customers come to the shop, but find it locked; gossip on Pyncheon Street; Phœbe returns; mystery still pervades the house.

UNCLE VENNER, trundling a wheelbarrow, was the earliest person stirring in the neighborhood, the day after the storm.

Pyncheon Street, in front of the House of the Seven Gables, was a far pleasanter scene than a by-lane, confined by shabby fences, and bordered with wooden dwellings of the meaner class, could reasonably be expected to present. Nature made sweet amends, that morning, for the five unkindly days which had preceded it. The Pyncheon elm, throughout its great circumference, was all alive, and full of the morning sun and a sweetly-tempered little breeze, which lingered within this verdant sphere, and set a thousand leafy tongues a-whispering all at once. This aged tree appeared to have suffered nothing from the gale. It had kept its boughs unshattered, and its full complement of leaves; and the whole in perfect verdure, except a single branch, that, by the earlier change with which the elm tree sometimes prophesies the autumn, had been transmuted to bright gold.

A person of imaginative temperament, while passing by the house, would turn, once and again, and peruse it well—its many peaks, consenting together in the clustered chimney; the deep projection over its basement story; the arched window, imparting a look, if not of grandeur, yet of antique gentility, to the broken portal over which it opened; the luxuriance of gigantic burdocks, near the threshold—he would note all these characteristics, and be conscious of something deeper than he saw. He would conceive the mansion to have been the residence of the stubborn old Puritan, Integrity, who, dying in some forgotten generation, had left a blessing to all its rooms and chambers, the efficacy of which was to be seen in the religion, honesty, moderate competence, or upright poverty and solid happiness, of his descendants, to this day.

One object, above all others, would take root in the imaginative observer's memory. It was the great tuft of flowers—weeds, you would have called them, only a week ago—the tuft of crimson-spotted flowers, in the angle between two of the gables. The old people used to give them the name of Alice's Posies, in remembrance of fair Alice Pyncheon, who was believed to have brought their seeds from Italy. They were flaunting in rich beauty and full bloom to-day, and seemed, as it were a mystic expression that something within the house was consummated.

It was but little after sunrise, when Uncle Venner made his appearance, as aforesaid, impelling a wheelbarrow along the street. He was going his matutinal rounds to collect cabbage leaves, turnip tops, potato skins, and the miscellaneous refuse of the dinner pot, which the thrifty housewives of the neighborhood were accustomed to put aside, as fit only to feed a pig. Uncle Venner's pig was fed entirely, and kept in prime order, on these eleemosynary contributions; insomuch that the patched philosopher used to promise that, before retiring to his farm, he would make a feast of the portly grunter, and invite all his neighbors to partake of the joints and spareribs which they had helped to fatten. Miss Hepzibah Pyncheon's housekeeping had so greatly improved, since Clifford became a member of the family, that her share of the banquet would have been no lean one; and Uncle Venner, accordingly, was a good deal disappointed not to find the large earthen pan, full of fragmentary eatables, that ordinarily awaited his coming at the back door-step of the Seven Gables.

"I never knew Miss Hepzibah so forgetful before," said the patriarch to himself. "She must have had a dinner yesterday—no question of that! She always has one, nowadays. So where's the pot liquor and potato skins, I ask? Shall I knock, and see if she's stirring yet? No, no—'twon't do! If little Phœbe was about the house, I should not mind knocking; but Miss Hepzibah, likely as not, would scowl down at me out of the window, and look cross, even if she felt pleasantly. So I'll come back at noon."

With these reflections, the old man was shutting the gate of the little back yard. Creaking on its hinges, however, like every other gate and door about the premises, the sound reached the ears of the occupant of the northern gable, one of the windows of which had a side view toward the gate.

"Good morning, Uncle Venner!" said the daguerreotypist, leaning out the window. "Do you hear nobody stirring?"

"Not a soul," said the man of patches. "But that's no wonder. 'Tis barely half an hour past sunrise, yet. But I'm really glad to see you, Mr. Holgrave! There's a strange, lonesome look about this side of the house; so that my heart misgave me, somehow or other, and I felt as if there was nobody alive in it. The front of the house looks a good deal cheerier; and Alice's Posies are blooming there beautifully, and if I were a young man, Mr. Holgrave, my sweetheart should have one of those flowers in her bosom, though I risked my neck climbing for it! Well, and did the wind keep you awake last night?"

"It did, indeed!" answered the artist, smiling. "If I were a believer in ghosts—and I don't quite know whether I am or not —I should have concluded that all the old Pyncheons were running riot in the lower rooms, especially in Miss Hepzibah's part of the house. But it is very quiet now."

"Yes, Miss Hepzibah will be apt to oversleep herself, after being disturbed, all night, with the racket," said Uncle Venner. "But it would be odd, now, wouldn't it, if the Judge had taken both his cousins into the country along with him? I saw him go into the shop yesterday."

"At what hour?" inquired Holgrave.

"Oh, along in the forenoon," said the old man. "Well, well! I must go my rounds, and so must my wheelbarrow. But I'll be back here at dinner time; for my pig likes a dinner as well as a breakfast. No meal time, and no sort of victuals, ever seems to come amiss to my pig. Good morning to you! And, Mr. Holgrave, if I were a young man, like you, I'd get one of Alice's Posies, and keep it in water till Phœbe comes back."

"I have heard," said the daguerreotypist, as he drew in his head, "that the water of Maule's well suits those flowers best."

Here the conversation ceased, and Uncle Venner went on his way. For half an hour longer, nothing disturbed the repose of the Seven Gables; nor was there any visitor, except a carrier boy, who, as he passed the front doorstep, threw down one of his newspapers; for Hepzibah, of late, had regularly taken it in. After a while, there came a fat woman, making prodigious speed, and stumbling as she ran up the steps of the shop door. Her face glowed with fire heat, and, it being a pretty warm morning, she bubbled and hissed, as it were, as if all a-fry with chimney warmth, and summer warmth, and the warmth of her own corpulent velocity. She tried the shop door; it was fast. She tried it again, with so angry a jar that the bell tinkled angrily back at her.

"The deuce take Old Maid Pyncheon!" muttered the irascible housewife. "Think of her pretending to set up a cent shop, and then lying abed till noon! These are what she calls gentlefolk's airs, I suppose! But I'll either start her ladyship, or break the door down!"

She shook it accordingly, and the bell, having a spiteful little temper of its own, rang obstreperously, making its remonstrances heard—not, indeed, by the ears for which they were intended—but by a good lady on the opposite side of the street. She opened her window, and addressed the impatient applicant.

"You'll find nobody there, Mrs. Gubbins."

"But I must and will find somebody here!" cried Mrs. Gubbins, inflicting another outrage on the bell. "I want a half pound of pork, to fry some first-rate flounders, for Mr. Gubbins's breakfast; and, lady or not, Old Maid Pyncheon shall get up and serve me with it!"

"But do hear reason, Mrs. Gubbins!" responded the lady opposite. "She, and her brother, too, have both gone to their cousin, Judge Pyncheon's, at his countryseat. There's not a soul in the house, but that young daguerreotype man, that sleeps in the north gable. I saw old Hepzibah and Clifford go away yesterday; and a queer couple of ducks they were, paddling through the mud puddles! They're gone, I'll assure you."

"And how do you know they're gone to the Judge's?" asked Mrs. Gubbins. "He's a rich man; and there's been a quarrel between him and Hepzibah, this many a day, because he won't give her a living. That's the main reason of her setting up a cent shop."

"I know that well enough," said the neighbor. "But they're gone—that's one thing certain. And who but a blood relation, that couldn't help himself, I ask you, would take in that awful-tempered old maid and that dreadful Clifford? That's it, you may be sure."

Mrs. Gubbins took her departure, still brimming over with hot wrath against the absent Hepzibah. For another half hour, or, perhaps, considerably more, there was almost as much quiet on the outside of the house as within. The elm, however, made a pleasant, cheerful, sunny sigh, responsive to the breeze that was elsewhere imperceptible; a swarm of insects buzzed merrily under its drooping shadow and became specks of light whenever they darted into the sunshine; a locust sang, once or twice, in some inscrutable seclusion of the tree; and a solitary little bird, with plumage of pale gold, came and hovered about Alice's Posies.

At last our small acquaintance, Ned Higgins, trudged up the street, on his way to school; and happening, for the first time in a fortnight, to be the possessor of a cent, he could by no means get past the shop door of the Seven Gables. But it would not open. Again and again, however, and half a dozen other agains, with the inexorable pertinacity of a child intent upon some object important to itself, did he renew his efforts for admittance. He had, doubtless, set his heart upon an elephant; or, possibly, with Hamlet, he meant to eat a crocodile.[1] In response to his more violent attacks, the bell gave, now and then, a moderate tinkle, but could not be stirred into clamor by any exertion of the little fellow's childish and tiptoe strength. Hold-

---

[1] EAT A CROCODILE—Hamlet, in Shakespeare's play, proposes this to Laertes as a test of their love for the dead Ophelia.

ing by the door handle, he peeped through a crevice of the curtain, and saw that the inner door, communicating with the passage toward the parlor, was closed.

"Miss Pyncheon!" screamed the child, rapping on the window-pane, "I want an elephant!"

There being no answer to several repetitions of the summons, Ned began to grow impatient; and his little pot of passion quickly boiling over, he picked up a stone with a naughty purpose to fling it through the window; at the same time blubbering and sputtering with wrath. A man—one of the two who happened to be passing by—caught the urchin's arm.

"What's the trouble, old gentleman?" he asked.

"I want old Hepzibah, or Phœbe, or any of them!" answered Ned, sobbing. "They won't open the door; and I can't get my elephant!"

"Go to school, you little scamp!" said the man. "There's another cent shop round the corner. 'Tis very strange, Dixey," added he to his companion, "what's become of all these Pyncheons! Smith, the livery-stable keeper, tells me Judge Pyncheon put his horse up yesterday, to stand till after dinner, and has not taken him away yet. And one of the Judge's hired men has been in, this morning, to make inquiry about him. He's a kind of person, they say, that seldom breaks his habits, or stays out o' nights."

"Oh, he'll turn up safe enough!" said Dixey. "And as for Old Maid Pyncheon, take my word for it, she has run in debt, and gone off from her creditors. I foretold, you remember, the first morning she set up shop, that her devilish scowl would frighten away customers. They couldn't stand it!"

"I never thought she'd make it go," remarked his friend. "This business of cent shops is overdone among the womenfolks. My wife tried it, and lost five dollars on her outlay!"

"Poor business!" said Dixey, shaking his head. "Poor business!"

In the course of the morning, there were various other attempts to open a communication with the supposed inhabitants of this silent and impenetrable mansion. The man of root beer came, in his neatly painted wagon, with a couple of dozen full bottles, to be exchanged for empty ones; the baker, with a lot of crackers which Hepzibah had ordered for her retail custom;

the butcher, with a nice tidbit which he fancied she would be eager to secure for Clifford. Had any observer of these proceedings been aware of the fearful secret hidden within the house, it would have affected him with a singular shape and modification of horror, to see the current of human life making this small eddy hereabouts; whirling sticks, straws, and all such trifles, round and round, right over the black depth where a dead corpse lay unseen!

The butcher was so much in earnest with his sweetbread of lamb, or whatever the dainty might be, that he tried every accessible door of the Seven Gables, and at length came round again to the shop, where he ordinarily found admittance.

"It's a nice article, and I know the old lady would jump at it," said he to himself. "She can't be gone away! In fifteen years that I have driven my cart through Pyncheon Street, I've never known her to be away from home; though often enough, to be sure, a man might knock all day without bringing her to the door. But that was when she'd only herself to provide for."

Peeping through the same crevice of the curtain where, only a little while before, the urchin of elephantine appetite had peeped, the butcher beheld the inner door, not closed, as the child had seen it, but ajar, and almost wide open. However it might have happened, it was the fact. Through the passage-way there was a dark vista into the lighter but still obscure interior of the parlor. It appeared to the butcher that he could pretty clearly discern what seemed to be the stalwart legs, clad in black pantaloons, of a man sitting in a large oaken chair, the back of which concealed all the remainder of his figure. This contemptuous tranquillity on the part of an occupant of the house, in response to the butcher's indefatigable efforts to attract notice, so piqued the man of flesh that he determined to withdraw.

"So," thought he, "there sits Old Maid Pyncheon's bloody brother, while I've been giving myself all this trouble! I call it demeaning a man's business to trade with such people; and from this time forth, if they want a sausage or an ounce of liver, they shall run after the cart for it!"

He tossed the tidbit angrily into his cart, and drove off in a pet.[2]

---

[2] Pet—A fit of peevishness, ill-humor.

Not a great while afterwards, there was a sound of music turning the corner, and approaching down the street, with several intervals of silence, and then a renewed and nearer outbreak of brisk melody. A mob of children was seen moving onward, or stopping, in unison with the sound, which appeared to proceed from the center of the throng; so that they were loosely bound together by slender strains of harmony, and drawn along captive; with ever and anon an accession of some little fellow in an apron and straw hat, capering forth from door or gateway. Arriving under the shadow of the Pyncheon elm, it proved to be the Italian boy, who, with his monkey and show of puppets, had once before played his hurdy-gurdy beneath the arched window. The pleasant face of Phœbe—and doubtless, too, the liberal recompense which she had flung him—still dwelt in his remembrance. His expressive features kindled up, as he recognized the spot where this trifling incident of his erratic life had chanced. He entered the neglected yard (now wilder than ever, with its growth of hogweed and burdock), stationed himself on the doorstep of the main entrance, and, opening his show box, began to play. The throng of children stood near; some on the sidewalk; some within the yard; two or three establishing themselves on the very doorstep; and one squatting on the threshold. Meanwhile, the locust kept singing in the great old Pyncheon elm.

"I don't hear anybody in the house," said one of the children to another. "The monkey won't pick up anything here."

"There is somebody at home," affirmed the urchin on the threshold. "I heard a step!"

Still the young Italian's eye turned sidelong upward; and it really seemed as if the touch of genuine, though slight and almost playful emotion, communicated a juicier sweetness to the dry, mechanical process of his minstrelsy. He repeated all his music, over and over again, until his auditors were getting weary. So were the little wooden people in his show box, and the monkey most of all. There was no response, save the singing of the locust.

"No children live in this house," said a schoolboy, at last. "Nobody lives here but an old maid and an old man. You'll get nothing here! Why don't you go along?"

"You fool, you, why do you tell him?" whispered a shrewd

little Yankee, caring nothing for the music, but a good deal for the cheap rate at which it was had. "Let him play as long as he likes! If there's nobody to pay him, that's his own lookout!"

Before the conclusion of the Italian's performance, a couple of men happened to be passing, on their way to dinner.

"I say, you young French fellow!" called out one of them, "come away from that doorstep, and go somewhere else with your nonsense! The Pyncheon family live there; and they are in great trouble, just about this time. They don't feel musical to-day. It is reported, all over town, that Judge Pyncheon, who owns the house, has been murdered; and the city marshal is going to look into the matter. So be off with you, at once!"

As the Italian shouldered his hurdy-gurdy, he saw on the doorstep a card, which had been covered, all the morning by the newspaper that the carrier had flung upon it, but was now shuffled into sight. He picked it up, and, perceiving something written in pencil, gave it to the man to read. In fact, it was an engraved card of Judge Pyncheon's, with certain penciled memoranda on the back, referring to various businesses which it had been his purpose to transact during the preceding day. It formed a prospective epitome of the day's history; only that affairs had not turned out altogether in accordance with the program. The card must have been lost from the judge's vest pocket, in his preliminary attempt to gain access by the main entrance of the house. Though well soaked with rain, it was still partially legible.

"Look here, Dixey!" cried the man. "This has something to do with Judge Pyncheon. See!—here's his name printed on it; and here, I suppose, is some of his handwriting."

"Let's go to the city marshal with it!" said Dixey. "It may give him just the clew he wants. After all," whispered he in his companion's ear, "it would be no wonder if the Judge has gone into that door, and never come out again! A certain cousin of his may have been at his old tricks. And Old Maid Pyncheon having got herself in debt by the cent shop—and the Judge's pocketbook being well filled—and bad blood among them already! Put all these things together, and see what they make!"

"Hush, hush!" whispered the other. "It seems like a sin to

be the first to speak of such a thing. But I think, with you, that we had better go to the city marshal."

"Yes, yes!" said Dixey. "Well!—I always said there was something devilish in that woman's scowl!" The men wheeled about, accordingly, and retraced their steps up the street. The Italian, also, made the best of his way off, with a parting glance up at the arched window.

It could not have been more than half an hour after the disappearance of the Italian boy, with his unseasonable melodies, when a cab drove down the street. It stopped beneath the Pyncheon elm; the cabman took a trunk, a canvas bag, and a bandbox from the top of his vehicle, and deposited them on the doorstep of the old house; a straw bonnet, and then the pretty figure of a young girl, came into view from the interior of the cab. It was Phœbe! Though not altogether so blooming as when she first tripped into our story—for, in the few intervening weeks, her experiences had made her graver, more womanly, and deeper-eyed, in token of a heart that had begun to suspect its depths—still there was the quiet glow of natural sunshine over her.

Phœbe first tried the shop door. It did not yield to her hand; and the white curtain, drawn across the window which formed the upper section of the door, struck her quick perceptive faculty as something unusual. Without making another effort to enter here, she betook herself to the great portal, under the arched window. Finding it fastened, she knocked.

A reverberation came from the emptiness within. She knocked again, and a third time; and, listening intently, fancied that the floor creaked, as if Hepzibah were coming, with her ordinary tiptoe movement, to admit her. But so dead a silence ensued upon this imaginary sound, that she began to question whether she might not have mistaken the house, familiar as she thought herself with its exterior.

Her notice was now attracted by a child's voice, at some distance. It appeared to call her name. Looking in the direction whence it proceeded, Phœbe saw little Ned Higgins, a good way down the street, stamping, shaking his head violently, making deprecatory gestures with both hands, and shouting to her at mouth-wide screech.

"No, no, Phœbe!" he screamed. "Don't you go in! There's something wicked there! Don't—don't—don't go in!"

But, as the little personage could not be induced to approach near enough to explain himself, Phœbe concluded that he had been frightened, on some of his visits to the shop, by her cousin Hepzibah; for the good lady's manifestations, in truth, ran about an equal chance of scaring children out of their wits, or compelling them to unseemly laughter. Still, she felt the more, for this incident, how unaccountably silent and impenetrable the house had become. As her next resort, Phœbe made her way into the garden, where, on so warm and bright a day as the present, she had little doubt of finding Clifford, and perhaps Hepzibah also, idling away the noontide in the shadow of the arbor. Immediately on her entering the garden gate, the family of hens half ran, half flew, to meet her; while a strange grimalkin, which was prowling under the parlor window, took to his heels, clambered hastily over the fence, and vanished. The arbor was vacant, and its floor, table, and circular bench were still damp, and bestrewn with twigs, and the disarray of the past storm. The growth of the garden seemed to have got quite out of bounds; the weeds had taken advantage of Phœbe's absence, and the long-continued rain, to run rampant over the flowers and kitchen vegetables. Maule's well had overflowed its stone border, and made a pool of formidable breadth in that corner of the garden.

The impression of the whole scene was that of a spot where no human foot had left its print for many preceding days— probably not since Phœbe's departure—for she saw a side comb of her own under the table of the arbor, where it must have fallen on the last afternoon when she and Clifford sat there.

The girl knew that her two relatives were capable of far greater oddities than that of shutting themselves up in their old house, as they appeared now to have done. Nevertheless, with indistinct misgivings of something amiss, and apprehensions to which she could not give shape, she approached the door that formed the customary communication between the house and garden. It was secured within, like the two which she had already tried. She knocked, however; and immediately, as if the application had been expected, the door was drawn open, by a considerable exertion of some unseen person's strength, not widely, but far enough to afford her a sidelong entrance. As Hepzibah, in order not to expose herself to inspection from without, invariably opened a door in this manner, Phœbe necessarily concluded that it was her cousin who now admitted her.

Without hesitation, therefore, she stepped across the threshold, and had no sooner entered than the door closed behind her.

XX THE FLOWER OF EDEN

Wherein is shown Holgrave and Phœbe alone in the house; how death comes again in the Pyncheon family; Holgrave speaks his love to Phœbe; her answer; Clifford and Hepzibah return.

PHŒBE, coming so suddenly from the sunny daylight, was altogether bedimmed in such density of shadow as lurked in most of the passages of the old house. She was not at first aware by whom she had been admitted. Before her eyes had adapted themselves to the obscurity, a hand grasped her own, with a firm but gentle and warm pressure, thus imparting a welcome which caused her heart to leap and thrill with an indefinable shiver of enjoyment. She felt herself drawn along, not toward the parlor, but into a large and unoccupied apartment, which had formerly been the grand reception room of the Seven Gables. The sunshine came freely into all the uncurtained windows of this room, and fell upon the dusty floor; so that Phœbe now clearly saw —what, indeed, had been no secret, after the encounter of a warm hand with hers—that it was not Hepzibah nor Clifford, but Holgrave, to whom she owed her reception. The subtle, intuitive communication, or rather, the vague and formless impression of something to be told, had made her yield unresistingly to his impulse. Without taking away her hand, she looked eagerly in his face, not quick to forebode evil, but unavoidably conscious that the state of the family had changed since her departure, and therefore anxious for an explanation.

The artist looked paler than ordinary; there was a thoughtful and severe contraction of his forehead, tracing a deep vertical line between the eyebrows. His smile, however, was full of genuine warmth, and had in it a joy, by far the most vivid expression that Phœbe had ever witnessed, shining out of the New England reserve with which Holgrave habitually masked whatever lay near his heart.

"I ought not to rejoice that you have come, Phœbe," said he. "We meet at a strange moment!"

"What has happened?" she exclaimed. "Why is the house so deserted? Where are Hepzibah and Clifford?"

"Gone. I cannot imagine where they are!" answered Holgrave. "We are alone in the house!"

"Hepzibah and Clifford gone?" cried Phœbe. "It is not possible! And why have you brought me into this room, instead of the parlor? Ah, something terrible has happened! I must run and see!"

"No, no, Phœbe!" said Holgrave, holding her back. "It is as I have told you. They are gone, and I know not whither. A terrible event has, indeed, happened, but not to them, nor, as I undoubtingly believe, through any agency of theirs. If I read your character rightly, Phœbe," he continued, fixing his eyes on hers, with stern anxiety, intermixed with tenderness, "gentle as you are, and seeming to have your sphere among common things, you yet possess remarkable strength. You have wonderful poise, and a faculty which, when tested, will prove itself capable of dealing with matters that fall far out of the ordinary rule."

"Oh, no, I am very weak!" replied Phœbe, trembling. "But tell me what has happened!"

"You are strong!" persisted Holgrave. "You must be both strong and wise; for I am all astray, and need your counsel. It may be you can suggest the one right thing to do!"

"Tell me!—tell me!" said Phœbe, all in a tremble. "It oppresses—it terrifies me—this mystery! Anything else I can bear!"

The artist hesitated. Notwithstanding what he had just said, and most sincerely, in regard to the self-balancing power with which Phœbe impressed him, it still seemed almost wicked to bring the awful secret of yesterday to her knowledge.

"Phœbe," said he, "do you remember this?"

He put into her hand a daguerreotype; the same that

he had shown her at their first interview in the garden, and which so strikingly brought out the hard and relentless traits of the original.

"What has this to do with Hepzibah and Clifford?" asked Phœbe, with impatient surprise that Holgrave should so trifle with her, at such a moment. "It is Judge Pyncheon! You have shown it to me before!"

"But here is the same face, taken within this half hour," said the artist, presenting her with another miniature. "I had just finished it, when I heard you at the door."

"This is death!" shuddered Phœbe, turning very pale. "Judge Pyncheon dead!"

"Such as there represented," said Holgrave, "he sits in the next room. The Judge is dead, and Clifford and Hepzibah have vanished! I know no more. All beyond is conjecture. On returning to my solitary chamber, last evening, I noticed no light, either in the parlor, or Hepzibah's room, or Clifford's; no stir nor footsteps about the house. This morning there was the same death-like quiet. From my window, I overheard the testimony of a neighbor, that your relatives were seen leaving the house, in the midst of yesterday's storm. A rumor reached me, too, of Judge Pyncheon being missed. A feeling which I cannot describe—an indefinite sense of some catastrophe, or consummation—impelled me to make my way into this part of the house, where I discovered what you see. As a point of evidence that may be useful to Clifford, and also as a memorial valuable to myself—for, Phœbe, there are hereditary reasons that connect me strangely with that man's fate—I used the means at my disposal to preserve this pictorial record of Judge Pyncheon's death."

Even in her agitation, Phœbe could not help remarking the calmness of Holgrave's demeanor. He appeared, it is true, to feel the whole awfulness of the Judge's death, yet had received the fact into his mind without any mixture of surprise, but as an event preordained, happening inevitably, and so fitting itself into past occurrences that it could almost have been prophesied.

"Why have you not thrown open the doors, and called in witnesses?" inquired she, with a painful shudder. "It is terrible to be here alone!"

"But Clifford!" suggested the artist. "Clifford and Hepzibah!

We must consider what is best to be done in their behalf. It is a wretched fatality, that they should have disappeared! Their flight will throw the worst coloring over this event of which it is susceptible. Yet how easy is the explanation, to those who know them! Bewildered and terror-stricken by the similarity of this death to a former one, which was attended with such disastrous consequences to Clifford, they have had no idea but of removing themselves from the scene. How miserably unfortunate! Had Hepzibah but shrieked aloud—had Clifford flung wide the door, and proclaimed Judge Pyncheon's death—it would have been, however awful in itself, an event fruitful of good consequences to them. As I view it, it would have gone far toward obliterating the black stain on Clifford's character."

"And how," asked Phœbe, "could any good come from what is so very dreadful?"

"Because," said the artist, "if the matter can be fairly considered, and candidly interpreted, it must be evident that Judge Pyncheon could not have come unfairly to his end. This mode of death has been an idiosyncrasy with his family, for generations past; not often occurring, indeed, but, when it does occur, usually attacking individuals about the Judge's time of life, and generally in the tension of some mental crisis, or, perhaps, in an access of wrath. Old Maule's prophecy was probably founded on a knowledge of this physical predisposition in the Pyncheon race. Now, there is a minute and almost exact similarity in the appearances connected with the death that occurred yesterday and those recorded of the death of Clifford's uncle, thirty years ago. It is true, there was a certain arrangement of circumstances, unnecessary to be recounted, which made it possible—nay, as men look at these things, probable, or even certain—that old Jaffrey Pyncheon came to a violent death, and by Clifford's hands."

"Whence came those circumstances?" exclaimed Phœbe; "he being innocent, as we know him to be!"

"They were arranged," said Holgrave, "at least, such has long been my conviction, they were arranged after the uncle's death, and before it was made public, by the man who sits in yonder parlor. His own death, so like that former one, yet attended with none of those suspicious circumstances, seems the stroke of God upon him, at once a punishment for his wickedness, and making plain the innocence of Clifford. But this flight—it distorts everything! He may be in concealment, near at hand. Could we but bring him back before the discovery of the Judge's death, the evil might be rectified."

"We must not hide this thing a moment longer!" said Phœbe. "It is dreadful to keep it so closely in our hearts. Clifford is innocent. God will make it manifest! Let us throw open the doors, and call all the neighborhood to see the truth!"

"You are right, Phœbe," rejoined Holgrave. "Doubtless you are right."

Yet the artist did not feel the horror, which was proper to Phœbe's sweet and order-loving character, at thus finding herself at issue with society, and brought in contact with an event that transcended ordinary rules. Neither was he in haste, like her, to betake himself within the precincts of common life. On the contrary, he gathered a wild enjoyment—as it were, a flower of strange beauty, growing in a desolate spot, and blossoming in the wind—such a flower of momentary happiness he gathered from his present position. It separated Phœbe and himself from the world, and bound them to each other, by their exclusive knowledge of Judge Pyncheon's mysterious death, and the counsel which they were forced to hold respecting it. The secret, so long as it should continue such, kept them within the circle of a spell, a solitude in the midst of men, a remoteness as entire as that of an island in mid-ocean; once divulged, the ocean would flow betwixt them, standing on its widely sundered shores. Meanwhile, all the circumstances of their situation seemed to draw them together; they were like two children who go hand in hand, pressing closely to one another's side, through a shadow-haunted passage. The image of awful Death, which filled the house, held them united by his stiffened grasp.

These influences hastened the development of emotions that might not otherwise have flowered so soon. Possibly, indeed, it had been Holgrave's purpose to let them die in their undeveloped germs.

"Why do we delay so?" asked Phœbe. "This secret takes away my breath! Let us throw open the doors!"

"In all our lives, there can never come another moment like this!" said Holgrave. "Phœbe, is it all terror?—nothing but terror? Are you conscious of no joy, as I am, that has made this the only point of life worth living for?"

"It seems a sin," replied Phœbe, trembling, "to think of joy at such a time!"

"Could you but know, Phœbe, how it was with me the hour before you came!" exclaimed the artist. "A dark, cold, miserable hour! The presence of yonder dead man threw a great black shadow over everything; he made the universe, so far as my perception could reach, a scene of guilt, and of retribution more dreadful than the guilt. The sense of it took away my youth. I never hoped to feel young again! The world looked strange, wild, evil, hostile; my past life, so lonesome and dreary; my future, a shapeless gloom, which I must mold into gloomy shapes! But, Phœbe, you crossed the threshold; and hope, warmth, and joy came in with you! The black moment became at once a blissful one. It must not pass without the spoken word. I love you!"

"How can you love a simple girl like me?" asked Phœbe, compelled by his earnestness to speak. "You have many, many thoughts, with which I should try in vain to sympathize. And I,—I, too, have tendencies with which you would sympathize as little. That is less matter. But I have not scope enough to make you happy."

"You are my only possibility of happiness!" answered Holgrave. "I have no faith in it, except as you bestow it on me!"

"And then—I am afraid!" continued Phœbe, shrinking toward Holgrave, even while she told him so frankly the doubts with which he affected her. "You will lead me out of my own quiet path. You will make me strive to follow you, where it is pathless. I cannot do so. It is not my nature. I shall sink down and perish!"

"Ah, Phœbe!" exclaimed Holgrave, with almost a sigh, and a smile that was burdened with thought. "It will be far otherwise than as you forebode. The world owes all its onward impulses to men ill at ease. The happy man inevitably confines himself within ancient limits. I have a presentiment that, hereafter it will be my lot to set out trees, to make fences—perhaps, even, in due time, to build a house for another generation—in a word, to conform myself to laws, and the peaceful practice of society. Your poise will be more powerful than any oscillating tendency of mine."

"I would not have it so!" said Phœbe, earnestly.

"Do you love me?" asked Holgrave. "If we love one another, the moment has room for nothing more. Let us pause upon it, and be satisfied. Do you love me, Phœbe?"

"You look into my heart," said she, letting her eyes drop. "You know I love you!"

And it was in this hour, so full of doubt and awe, that the one miracle was wrought, without which every human existence is a blank. The bliss which makes all things true, beautiful, and holy, shone around this youth and maiden. They were conscious of nothing sad nor old. They transfigured the earth, and made it Eden again, and themselves the two first dwellers in it. The dead man, so close beside them, was forgotten. At such a crisis, there is no death; for immortality is revealed anew, and embraces everything in its hallowed atmosphere.

But how soon the heavy earth dream settled down again!

"Hark!" whispered Phœbe. "Somebody is at the street door!"

"Now let us meet the world!" said Holgrave. "No doubt, the rumor of Judge Pyncheon's visit to this house, and the flight of Hepzibah and Clifford, is about to lead to the investigation of the premises. We have no way but to meet it. Let us open the door at once."

But, to their surprise, before they could reach the street door —even before they quitted the room in which the foregoing interview had passed—they heard footsteps in the farther passage. The door, therefore, which they supposed to be securely locked —which Holgrave, indeed, had seen to be so, and at which Phœbe had vainly tried to enter—must have been opened from without. The sound of footsteps was not harsh, bold, decided, and intrusive, as the gait of strangers would naturally be, making authoritative entrance into a dwelling where they knew themselves unwelcome. It was feeble, as of persons either weak or weary; there was the mingled murmur of two voices, familiar to both the listeners.

"Can it be?" whispered Holgrave.

"It is they!" answered Phœbe. "Thank God!—thank God!"

And then, as if in sympathy with Phœbe's whispered ejaculation, they heard Hepzibah's voice, more distinctly.

"Thank God, my brother, we are at home!"

"Well!—Yes!—thank God!" responded Clifford. "A dreary home, Hepzibah! But you have done well to bring me hither!

Stay! That parlor door is open. I cannot pass by it! Let me go and rest me in the arbor, where I used—oh, very long ago, it seems to me, after what has befallen us—where I used to be so happy with little Phœbe!"

But the house was not altogether so dreary as Clifford imagined it. They had not made many steps—in truth, they were lingering in the entry, with the listlessness of an accomplished purpose, uncertain what to do next—when Phœbe ran to meet them. On beholding her, Hepzibah burst into tears. With all her might, she had staggered onward beneath the burden of grief and responsibility, until now that it was safe to fling it down. Indeed, she had not energy to fling it down, but had ceased to uphold it, and suffered it to press her to the earth. Clifford appeared the stronger of the two.

"It is our own little Phœbe! Ah! and Holgrave with her," exclaimed he, with a glance of keen and delicate insight, and a smile, beautiful, kind, but melancholy. "I thought of you both, as we came down the street, and beheld Alice's Posies in full bloom. And so the flower of Eden has bloomed, likewise, in this old, darksome house to-day."

XXI THE DEPARTURE

Wherein the murder of Jaffrey Pyncheon, thirty years ago, is explained; Clifford exonerated; the inheritance made known; Colonel Pyncheon's picture falls to the floor; the recess in the wall, and what it contained; Holgrave's identity revealed; they all depart for the countryseat.

THE sudden death of so prominent a member of the social world as the Honorable Judge Jaffrey Pyncheon created a sensation (at least, in the circles more immediately connected with the deceased) which had hardly quite subsided in a fortnight.

It may be remarked, however, that, of all the events which constitute a person's biography, there is scarcely one—none, certainly, of anything like a similar importance—to which the world so easily reconciles itself as to his death. As regarded Judge Pyncheon, it seemed probable, at first blush, that the mode of his final departure might give him a larger and longer posthumous vogue than ordinarily attends the memory of a distinguished man. But when it came to be understood, on the highest professional authority, that the event was a natural, and—except for some unimportant particulars, denoting a slight idiosyncrasy—by no means an unusual form of death, the public, with its customary alacrity, proceeded to forget that he had ever lived. In short, the honorable Judge was beginning to be a stale subject before half the country newspapers had found time to put their columns in mourning, and publish his exceedingly eulogistic obituary.

Nevertheless, creeping darkly through the places which this excellent person had haunted in his lifetime, there was a hidden stream of private talk, such as it would have shocked all decency to speak loudly at the street corners. The talk, or scandal, to which we now allude, had reference to matters of no less old a date than the supposed murder, thirty or forty years ago, of the late Judge Pyncheon's uncle. The medical opinion, with regard to his own recent and regretted decease, had almost entirely obviated the idea that a murder was committed in the former case. Yet, as the record showed, there were circumstances irrefragably indicating that some person had gained access to old Jaffrey Pyncheon's private apartments, at or near the moment of his death. His desk and private drawers, in a room contiguous to his bedchamber, had been ransacked; money and valuable articles were missing; there was a bloody hand print on the old man's linen; and, by a powerfully welded chain of deductive evidence, the guilt of the robbery and apparent murder had been fixed on Clifford, then residing with his uncle in the House of the Seven Gables.

Whencesoever originating, there now arose a theory that undertook so to account for these circumstances as to exclude the idea of Clifford's agency. Many persons affirmed that the history and elucidation of the facts, long so mysterious, had been obtained by the daguerreotypist from one of those mesmerical seers, who, nowadays, so strangely perplex the aspect of human affairs, and put everybody's natural vision to the blush, by the marvels which they see with their eyes shut.

According to this version of the story, Judge Pyncheon, exemplary as we have portrayed him in our narrative, was, in his youth, an apparently irreclaimable scapegrace. The brutish, the animal instincts, as is often the case, had been developed earlier than the intellectual qualities, and the force of character, for which he was afterwards remarkable. He had shown himself wild, dissipated, addicted to low pleasures, little short of ruffianly in his propensities, and recklessly expensive, with no other resources than the bounty of his uncle. This course of conduct had alienated the old bachelor's affection, once strongly fixed upon him. Now, it is averred—but whether on authority available in a court of justice, we do not pretend to have investigated—that the young man was tempted by the devil, one night, to search his uncle's private drawers, to which he had unsuspected means of access. While thus criminally occupied, he was startled by the opening of the chamber door. There stood old Jaffrey Pyncheon, in his night clothes! The surprise of such a discovery, his agitation, alarm, and horror, brought on the crisis of a disorder to which the old bachelor had an hereditary liability; he seemed to choke with blood, and fell upon the floor, striking his temple a heavy blow against the corner of a table. What was to be done? The old man was surely dead! Assistance would come too late! What a misfortune indeed, should it come too soon, since his reviving consciousness would bring the recollection of the ignominious offense which he had beheld his nephew in the very act of committing!

But he never did revive. With the cool hardihood that always pertained to him, the young man continued his search of the drawers, and found a will, of recent date, in favor of Clifford—which he destroyed—and an older one, in his own favor, which he suffered to remain. But, before retiring, Jaffrey bethought himself of the evidence, in these ransacked drawers, that someone had visited the chamber with sinister purposes. Suspicion, unless averted, might fix upon the real offender. In the very presence of the dead man, therefore, he laid a scheme that should free himself at the expense of Clifford, his rival, for whose character he had at once a contempt and a repugnance. It is not probable, be it said, that he acted with any set purpose of involving Clifford in a charge of murder. Knowing that his uncle did not die by violence, it may not have occurred to him, in the hurry of the crisis, that such an inference might be drawn. But, when the affair took this darker aspect, Jaffrey's previous steps had already pledged him to those which remained. So craftily had he arranged the circumstances, that, at Clifford's trial, his cousin hardly found it necessary to swear to anything false, but only to withhold the one decisive explanation, by refraining to state what he had himself done and witnessed.

Thus Jaffrey Pyncheon's inward criminality, as regarded Clifford, was, indeed, black and damnable; while its mere outward show and positive commission was the smallest that could possibly consist with so great a sin. This is just the sort of guilt that a man of eminent respectability finds it easiest to dispose of. It was suffered to fade out of sight, or be reckoned a venial matter, in the Honorable Judge Pyncheon's long subsequent survey of his own life. He shuffled it aside, among the forgotten and forgiven frailties of his youth, and seldom thought of it again.

We leave the Judge to his repose. He could not be styled fortunate, at the hour of death. Unknowingly, he was a childless man, while striving to add more wealth to his only child's inheritance. Hardly a week after his decease, one of the Cunard steamers brought intelligence of the death, by cholera, of Judge Pyncheon's son, just at the point of embarkation for his native land. By this misfortune, Clifford became rich; so did Hepzibah; so did our little village maiden, and, through her, that sworn foe of wealth and all manner of conservatism—the wild reformer—Holgrave!

It was now far too late in Clifford's life for the good opinion of society to be worth the trouble and anguish of a formal vindication. What he needed was the love of a very few; not the admiration, or even the respect, of the unknown many. The latter might probably have been won for him, had those on whom the guardianship of his welfare had fallen deemed it advisable to expose Clifford to a miserable resuscitation of past ideas, when the condition of whatever comfort he might expect lay in the calm of forgetfulness. After such wrong as he had suffered, there is no reparation.

The shock of Judge Pyncheon's death had a permanently invigorating and ultimately beneficial effect on Clifford. That strong and ponderous man had been Clifford's nightmare. There was no free breath to be drawn, within the sphere of so malevolent an influence. The first effect of freedom, as we have witnessed in Clifford's aimless flight, was a tremulous exhilaration.

Subsiding from it, he did not sink into his former intellectual apathy. He never, it is true, attained to nearly the full measure of what might have been his faculties. But he recovered enough of them partially to light up his character, to display some outline of the marvelous grace that was abortive in it, and to make him the object of no less deep, although less melancholy interest than heretofore. He was evidently happy. Could we pause to give another picture of his daily life, with all the appliances now at command to gratify his instinct for the Beautiful, the garden scenes, that seemed so sweet to him, would look mean and trivial in comparison.

Very soon after their change of fortune, Clifford, Hepzibah, and little Phœbe, with the approval of the artist, concluded to remove from the dismal old House of the Seven Gables, and take up their abode, for the present, at the elegant countryseat of the late Judge Pyncheon. Chanticleer and his family had already been transported thither, where the two hens had forthwith begun an indefatigable process of egg laying, with an evident design, as a matter of duty and conscience, to continue their illustrious breed under better auspices than for a century past. On the day set for their departure, the principal personages of our story, including good old Uncle Venner, were assembled in the parlor.

"The country house is certainly a very fine one, so far as the plan goes," observed Holgrave, as the party were discussing their future arrangements. "But I wonder that the late Judge —being so opulent, and with a reasonable prospect of transmitting his wealth to descendants of his own—should not have felt the propriety of embodying so excellent a piece of domestic architecture in stone, rather than in wood. Then, every generation of the family might have altered the interior, to suit its own taste and convenience; while the exterior, through the lapse of years, might have been adding venerableness to its original beauty, and thus giving that impression of permanence which I consider essential to the happiness of any one moment."

"Why," cried Phœbe, gazing into the artist's face with infinite amazement, "how wonderfully your ideas are changed! A house of stone, indeed! It is but two or three weeks ago, that you seemed to wish people to live in something as fragile and temporary as a bird's nest!"

"Ah, Phœbe, I told you how it would be!" said the artist, with a half-melancholy laugh. "You find me a conservative already! Little did I think ever to become one. It is especially unpardonable in this dwelling of so much hereditary misfortune, and under the eye of yonder portrait of a model conservative, who, in that very character, rendered himself so long the evil destiny of his race."

"That picture!" said Clifford, seeming to shrink from its stern glance. "Whenever I look at it, there is an old, dreamy recollection haunting me, but keeping just beyond the grasp of my mind. Wealth, it seems to say!—boundless wealth!—unimaginable wealth! I could fancy that, when I was a child, or a youth, that portrait had spoken, and told me a rich secret, or had held forth its hand, with the written record of hidden opulence. But those old matters are so dim with me, nowadays! What could this dream have been?"

"Perhaps I can recall it," answered Holgrave. "See! There are a hundred chances to one, that no person, unacquainted with the secret, would ever touch this spring."

"A secret spring!" cried Clifford. "Ah, I remember now! I did discover it, one summer afternoon, when I was idling and dreaming about the house, long, long ago. But the mystery escapes me."

The artist put his finger on the contrivance to which he had referred. In former days, the effect would probably have been to cause the picture to start forward. But, in so long a period of concealment, the machinery had been eaten through with rust; so that, at Holgrave's pressure, the portrait, frame and all, tumbled suddenly from its position, and lay face downward on the floor. A recess in the wall was thus brought to light, in which lay an object so covered with a century's dust, that it could not immediately be recognized as a folded sheet of parchment. Holgrave opened it, and displayed an ancient deed, signed with the hieroglyphics of several Indian sagamores,[1] and conveying to Colonel Pyncheon and his heirs, forever, a vast extent of territory at the eastward.

"This is the very parchment the attempt to recover which cost the beautiful Alice Pyncheon her happiness and life," said the artist, alluding to his legend. "It was what the Pyncheons

[1] SAGAMORES—Indian chiefs.

sought in vain, while it was valuable; and now that they find the treasure, it has long been worthless."

"Poor Cousin Jaffrey! This is what deceived him," exclaimed Hepzibah. "When they were young together, Clifford probably made a kind of fairy tale of this discovery. He was always dreaming hither and thither about the house, and lighting up its dark corners with beautiful stories. And poor Jaffrey, who took hold of everything as if it were real, thought my brother had found out his uncle's wealth. He died with this delusion in his mind!"

"But," said Phœbe, apart to Holgrave, "how came you to know the secret?"

"My dearest Phœbe," said Holgrave, "how will it please you to assume the name of Maule? As for the secret, it is the only inheritance that has come down to me from my ancestors. You should have known sooner (only that I was afraid of frightening you away) that, in this long drama of wrong and retribution, I represent the old wizard, and am probably as much of a wizard as ever he was. The son of the executed Matthew Maule, while building this house, took the opportunity to construct that recess, and hide away the Indian deed, on which depended the immense land claim of the Pyncheons. Thus they bartered their eastern territory for Maule's garden ground."

"And now," said Uncle Venner, "I suppose their whole claim is not worth one man's share in my farm yonder!"

"Uncle Venner," cried Phœbe, taking the patched philosopher's hand, "you must never talk any more about your farm! You shall never go there, as long as you live! There is a cottage in our new garden—the prettiest little yellowish-brown cottage you ever saw; and the sweetest looking place, for it looks just as if it were made of gingerbread—and we are going to fit it up and furnish it, on purpose for you. And you shall do nothing but what you choose, and shall be as happy as the day is long, and shall keep Cousin Clifford in spirits with the wisdom and pleasantness which is always dropping from your lips!"

"Ah! my dear child," quoth good Uncle Venner, quite overcome, "if you were to speak to a young man as you do to an old one, his chance of keeping his heart another minute would not be worth one of the buttons on my waistcoat! And—soul alive!—that great sigh, which you made me heave, has burst off

"Their whole claim is not worth one man's share in my farm."

the very last of them! But never mind! It was the happiest
sigh I ever did heave; and it seems as if I must have drawn in
a gulp of heavenly breath, to make it with. Well, well, Miss
Phœbe! They'll miss me in the gardens, hereabout, and around
by the back doors; and Pyncheon Street, I'm afraid, will hardly
look the same without old Venner, who remembers it with
a mowing field on one side, and the garden of the Seven Gables
on the other. But either I must go to your countryseat, or
you must come to my farm—that's one of two things certain;
and I leave you to choose which!"

"Oh, come with us, by all means, Uncle Venner!" said Clifford, who had a remarkable enjoyment of the old man's mellow,
quiet, and simple spirit. "I want you always to be within five
minutes' saunter of my chair. You are the only philosopher I
ever knew of whose wisdom has not a drop of bitter essence at
the bottom!"

"Dear me!" cried Uncle Venner, beginning partly to realize
what manner of man he was. "And yet folks used to set me
down among the simple ones, in my younger days! But I
suppose I am like a Roxbury russet [2]—a great deal the better,
the longer I can be kept. Yes; and my words of wisdom, that
you and Phœbe tell me of, are like the golden dandelions, which
never grow in the hot months, but may be seen glistening among
the withered grass, and under the dry leaves, sometimes as late
as December. And you are welcome, friends, to my mess of
dandelions, if there were twice as many!"

A plain, but handsome, dark-green barouche had now drawn
up in front of the ruinous portal of the old mansion house. The
party come forth, and (with the exception of good Uncle Venner, who was to follow in a few days) proceeded to take their
places. They were chatting and laughing very pleasantly together; and—as proves to be often the case, at moments when
we ought to palpitate with sensibility—Clifford and Hepzibah
bade a farewell to the abode of their forefathers, with hardly
more emotion than if they had made it their arrangement to
return thither at tea time. Several children were drawn to the
spot by so unusual a spectacle as the barouche and pair of gray
horses. Recognizing little Ned Higgins among them, Hepzibah

---

[2] ROXBURY RUSSET—An apple of excellent keeping qualities, formerly
grown at or near Roxbury, now a part of Boston.

put her hand into her pocket, and presented the urchin, her earliest and stanchest customer, with silver enough to buy all the animal cookies he might crave.

Two men were passing, just as the barouche drove off.

"Well, Dixey," said one of them, "what do you think of this? My wife kept a cent shop three months, and lost five dollars on her outlay. Old Maid Pyncheon has been in trade just as long, and rides off in her carriage with a couple of hundred thousand —reckoning her share, and Clifford's, and Phœbe's—and some say twice as much! If you choose to call it luck, it is all very well; but if we are to take it as the will of Providence, why, I can't exactly fathom it!"

"Pretty good business," quoth the sagacious Dixey. "Pretty good business!"

Maule's well, all this time, though left in solitude, was throwing up a succession of kaleidoscopic pictures in which a gifted eye might have seen foreshadowed the coming fortunes of Hepzibah and Clifford, and the descendant of the legendary wizard, and the village maiden, over whom he had thrown Love's web of sorcery. The Pyncheon elm, moreover, with what foliage the September gale had spared to it, whispered unintelligible prophecies. And wise Uncle Venner, passing slowly from the ruinous porch, seemed to hear a strain of music, and fancied that sweet Alice Pyncheon—after witnessing these deeds, this bygone woe, and this present happiness, of her kindred mortals—had given one farewell touch of a spirit's joy upon her harpsichord, as she floated heavenward from the HOUSE OF THE SEVEN GABLES.

HOW TO GET THE GREATEST ENJOYMENT FROM THIS STORY

For Appreciation, Read Slowly: While it is difficult to give any general advice to readers of varying tastes and habits, *The House of the Seven Gables* is very evidently the sort of book which does not demand to be read overnight, and which probably should not be read all at one sitting. Your teacher will be able to give you more specific suggestions, but it should be noted that the details with which the book is so completely furnished all contribute to the understanding of the novel, and should not be neglected. Many of them will appear in their true relation only after a second reading.

Try to Understand the Author's Purpose: Every piece of literature should be estimated first in terms of what the author has tried to do. While there is an element of mystery and suspense in *The House of the Seven Gables*, it is in no sense a "mystery story." Those who insist upon chills and thrills may be somewhat disappointed until they readjust their viewpoint so that the real issues of the novel are seen as those which depend on the nature and reactions of the various characters. Hawthorne is mainly interested in what is happening in the minds and hearts of his people. The large number of recent novels of this type demonstrates the fact that both authors and readers are coming to share this viewpoint.

Observe the Details of the Story: *Time and Place:* The early days of New England, following the period of the witchcraft delusion, provide the setting for the novel. What customs can you cite from the book to show the time the events took place? Why is a knowledge of New England witchcraft essential to an understanding of the setting? What influences, different from those of to-day, played upon the characters of the story? Do you clearly perceive the time of the story from the author's description?

The Characters Involved: What type of people are the characters in this novel? Have you ever before met any people like them, either in life or in other books? To what extent do they shape the circumstances at the end of the story? Do they grow and develop under the influences they meet? Prove your conclusion by citing one character. Would you say that the persons in the story respond naturally to the course of events, and to each other? Can you see, from their reactions, their essential attitudes, ideals, and innermost feelings? To sum up—has the author succeeded in portraying to you real people, with definite characteristics?

The Plot of the Story: Does the plot move rapidly or slowly? What is the author's purpose in thus regulating the tempo of the plot? What element or elements of suspense do you find in the story? What "big moments" of excitement hold your attention? To what is this excitement due—clash of characters, jealousies, unsolved mysteries, or accidents over which the characters have no control? What can you say of the writer's technique in keeping the outcome of the story secret, and at the same time bringing forth a reasonable conclusion which should have been expected?

The Novel as a Whole: Is this novel primarily one of character study, of setting, or of plot? What do you think inspired the author to write the story? What would you say he was most interested to put across to his readers? What was the theme of the whole story? Do you think the study of this story has been a worthwhile experience? Give your reasons. To what books would you compare this novel?

STUDY SUGGESTIONS

Chapter I: Study the artist's picture of the House of Seven Gables. In what respect does it reflect Hawthorne's description? Explain what New England witchcraft was. Tell how Colonel Pyncheon took advantage of this for his own personal gain. What curse did Maule pronounce? The water in Maule's well turned brackish. Do you think this was an omen? Who was the head carpenter in building the House of Seven Gables? Did Colonel Pyncheon have a motive in this? Describe a "house warming" of the old New England days. Give a description of Colonel Pyncheon's private study. Who discovered Colonel Pyncheon in his chair? What foundation was there for believing that the Colonel had been murdered? What possessions did the Pyncheons have? What is meant by "Now the Seven Gables will be new-shingled"? A nephew of some murdered Pyncheon was sent to prison. Relate the meager reference to the event. What members of the Pyncheons were now left? What Maules were left? Describe the House of Seven Gables, now more in detail.

Chapter II: Who were the present occupants of the house? Tell of Hepzibah's preparations for the day. If the miniature was not of a lover, could it be of a brother? Describe the interior of the house. Tell of Hepzibah's feelings toward opening a petty cent shop. Describe the shop.

Chapter III: What effect on Hepzibah did the first ring of the shop bell have? Describe the daguerreotypist. What did Hepzibah say to show her feelings? Did she suggest a brother coming back? What was Hepzibah's distinction between "lady" and "woman"? How was Hepzibah's generosity shown to her first customer? What comments did passers-by make of the cent shop and its proprietor? Why wouldn't Hepzibah take the little boy's cent for the gingerbread? On the return of the boy she did take it. What were her feelings then? How did she treat other customers who came? How was Hepzibah's dignity affected?

Chapter IV: Describe the portly gentleman who surveyed the Seven Gables and its elm so scrutinously. In what way did the cane represent its master? Describe "the frown and the smile" which seemed to govern his countenance. Was Hepzibah's surprise one of pleasure or repulsion? What was the effect of the little fellow breaking into the scene? Who was the portly gentleman? What resemblance to the ancestral Pyncheon who built the Seven Gables? What did Hepzibah say about him? Do you recognize in her monologue a possible prediction for the future? Why the contrast of again describing the original of the Malbone Miniature? Describe Uncle Venner and his various occupations. Do you know anyone in your own neighborhood like Uncle Venner? What was the farm to which Uncle Venner planned to retire? Give the bit of description of the Seven Gables during Revolutionary War times. Uncle Venner said that the opening of the cent shop was no credit to the Judge. Why? What advice did Uncle Venner give Hepzibah? Uncle Venner asked: "When do you expect him home?" Whom did he mean? —could it be that he referred to the original of the miniature? Hepzibah's busy afternoon with customers netted how much for her efforts? Why? Who was her last customer? Why was Hepzibah so excited when the omnibus stopped under the elm? Who alighted? Describe the thoughts which Hepzibah had. (Who was the girl? What was her relationship to Hepzibah? What man's name is mentioned at the end? Who might he be?)

Chapter V: Tell of Phœbe's awakening the next morning. In the story, what did the roses in the garden symbolize? What did Phœbe start doing about her room? What is the "parallel case in human society" when compared with the flowers in the garden? Describe the harpsichord. What conversation ensued? Why had Phœbe never heard of the master of Seven Gables? Tell of the preparations for breakfast. How did Hepzibah feel at the ring of the shop bell? Why did Hepzibah think Phœbe could never be a lady? How did Phœbe's success in keeping shop contrast with Hepzibah's experience? What did Uncle Venner say about Phœbe? What did Hepzibah tell Phœbe about Alice Pyncheon? Tell of the manners and actions of Holgrave. How would you characterize him? "May and November" is the chapter title. Is it appropriate?

Chapter VI: Describe the garden with its plants, trees, and well. What did the rank weeds symbolize? What signs of busy life were seen in the garden? Describe the well. Describe Chanticleer and his family. Tell of the meeting with Holgrave. How did Holgrave "make pictures out of sunshine"? How do these pictures "dodge away from the eye"? Whom did Phœbe think the daguerreotype resembled? Whom did it depict? What did Holgrave think of the man? What reference was made that the man of Hepzibah's miniature had committed a crime? What was Holgrave's warning about Maule's well? How do you think the two felt toward each other? Describe the gloominess in the parlor. Do you think there was another person in the room with Hepzibah? How do you account for the heavy footsteps which later ascended the stairs with Hepzibah?

Chapter VII: Tell how Hepzibah fumbled about trying to prepare breakfast. How did Phœbe help? What can you say of the suspense which the author employs in indicating the possibility of a guest, but not introducing him until later? Describe Hepzibah's emotions. Tell of Clifford's actions. What would lead you to the conclusion that he had been long imprisoned? Was Clifford the original of Hepzibah's miniature? Tell his reactions in adjusting himself to this first life situation. What part did the rose play? Did Clifford show any tendency toward an artistic nature and a love for the beautiful? What effect did seeing the picture have on Clifford? How did the ringing of the shop bell affect him?

Chapter VIII: Tell of Ned Higgins early visit to the shop. Do you think his mother desired merchandise or information? How did little Ned indicate that shame had befallen the guest? What was Hepzibah's relation to the guest? Describe fully and carefully the appearance and manners of the portly visitor with the gold-headed cane. Tell the relationship of Judge Pyncheon to the household. How did Phœbe elude his greeting? Where had Phœbe seen his likeness before? Describe the Judge's change of facial expression. Relate the traits of the first Colonel Pyncheon, founder of Seven Gables, as rehearsed here. Does the author indicate there may be a close resemblance between the present-day Judge Pyncheon, and the old Puritan, Colonel Pyncheon? What physical peculiarity did Phœbe notice in Judge Pyncheon which reminded her of the curse hanging over the family? How did the Judge insinuate that Clifford may have been a criminal? Tell of Hepzibah meeting the Judge in the doorway. How did the Judge indicate Clifford's artistic nature? Describe the Judge's all too solicitous invitation to come and live at his house. Why do you think the Judge offered this? How did Hepzibah react to him? How do you interpret the plaintive supplication from Clifford within the house? Describe the Judge's manner in leaving.

Chapter IX: Show Hepzibah's love and devotion to her brother. Again what evidences are given of Clifford's artistic nature? In what respects did Hepzibah fail to please Clifford? How did Phœbe affect Clifford's actions? What appreciation of beauty did Clifford show? What feeling of relationship did Clifford have toward Phœbe? How did Phœbe regard Clifford? What effect and change now began to appear in Phœbe?

Chapter X: Tell of Phœbe's reading to Clifford in the garden. What did he like? From whom did Phœbe get her books? Again, what evidence is there that Clifford loved the beautiful? Was Clifford "slowly reviving from the chill torpor of his life"? What part did the humming birds play in reviving Clifford? How long had been the lapse of years since Clifford was a young boy? What reflection on past years in Clifford's life is the fact that he could not bear to have the hens confined in their coop? Describe the chickens and tell in what way they reflected the oddities of the Pyncheon family. Tell the episode of the one egg.

How did these incidents of the chickens "prove so greatly to Clifford's benefit"? What did Clifford see reflected in Maule's well? What guests came Sunday afternoons? What effect did Uncle Venner have on Clifford? What did Clifford offer Uncle Venner? Does this show Clifford beginning to "come back to life"? What showed Holgrave to be acquainted with socialistic principles? Did Holgrave seem to be extraordinarily interested in Clifford? Why do you think so? What reaction came from Phœbe to Holgrave? How did Holgrave act in the group? What desires now began to come from Clifford? Do you think this is good?

Chapter XI: What did the life on Pyncheon Street reveal? Was this a step in Clifford's redemption to life? What was seen in life as it passed down Pyncheon Street? What sights seemed familiar and dear to him? Can you see where Clifford was recalling experiences of his childhood? What did he miss as he began to recall earlier days? Why did the organ-grinder please him? Show how a political procession passing by might represent a mighty river of life. How did this procession affect Clifford? Does this show Clifford making progress in his rehabilitation? Did Clifford intimate that he was "becoming another man"? What might be necessary to restore Clifford to the world and to himself? Do you suspect that this is a clue to the plot of the story? Tell the episode of Clifford and Hepzibah starting for church. What did this show regarding Clifford's mental recovery? What do his dreams of his childhood days reveal regarding his mental activity? Why did Clifford want to blow soap bubbles from the arched window? Was this also a step in his mental recovery? How did the bubbles bring out the various dispositions of the passers-by? Describe what one particular bubble did and the effect.

Chapter XII: Explain how Clifford might be "in a state of second growth and recovery." What were Phœbe's reactions? What changes are noticeable in Phœbe? What did Holgrave tell Phœbe about himself? Did you notice that Holgrave passed lightly over his family origin? Might there be any significance in such omission? Does Holgrave's occupation as a daguerreotypist satisfy you? Do you think the occasional reference to his being a Socialist dispels the mystery about him? Did he have any affection for any of the Pyncheon household? Then, can you answer why he was there? Can you imagine why? Do you think this has anything to do with the plot of the story? Do you feel that Holgrave is an important character in the story, or a very minor character? Why should Holgrave be so interested in Clifford? What "things without" might disturb Clifford? What "thoughts within" might disturb Clifford? Might these two things about Clifford bear on the plot of the story? Regarding Holgrave, tell "what he had" and "what he lacked." Do you perceive that Holgrave had any particularly personal interest in Phœbe? Would you say that their friendship was growing into love? How did Holgrave answer Phœbe as to why he took up his residence in the Seven Gables? Give Holgrave's argument that "we are slaves to bygone times." What did Holgrave propose to substitute for these antiquated ideas? Are these socialistic views? Do you hold these ideas in favor of or against Holgrave? How did Holgrave describe the House of Seven Gables? How did Holgrave refer to the living Judge Pyncheon? What was Holgrave's excuse for getting so excited as he talked of the Pyncheon family? Do you find in this extreme excitability any clue to the mystery of Holgrave's actions?

Chapter XIII: What connection have we had before between a Pyncheon and a Maule? Describe Alice Pyncheon. What happened to the first Matthew Maule? What stories were current about him? What peculiarities had this young Matthew Maule? What connection had this Gervayse Pyncheon with old Colonel Pyncheon? Tell about the sundial on the front gable. Explain Alice's relation to music and flowers. Describe the room, not omitting the wall decorations. Was the family feud shown in the conversation? Where had a secret search been made for the missing document? What had been found? Why did Gervayse Pyncheon think the document of the eastern lands was in the hands of a Maule? What is a "chimney corner legend"? What agreement was made, and why did Gervayse Pyncheon consent to such an agreement? Describe Alice Pyncheon. Explain Maule's actions toward Alice and the result. Why did the father consent to subjecting Alice to Maule's wizardly actions? Tell what Alice saw in her trance. Do you think Maule was sincere in doing what he did? Do you suspect any treachery? What indicated that the curse was on this Gervayse Pyncheon? Was the deed to the eastern lands found? Tell how Maule controlled Alice. Did this break her proud and haughty attitude? Where did she show true humility? Did Maule intentionally kill her? Did Maule repent his act?

Chapter XIV: What power did Holgrave have over Phœbe? What effect did the moonlight have on Holgrave? On Phœbe? What did Holgrave almost admit to Phœbe? How did Holgrave explain his interest in Clifford and Hepzibah? Do you feel, like Phœbe, that Holgrave is "holding something back"? What did Holgrave say Judge Pyncheon did to Clifford? Describe Phœbe's leave-taking. What did Clifford mean by "the bud is a bloom"? How did Uncle Venner regard Phœbe?

Chapter XV: Describe the situation in the house after Phœbe went away. What harsh sounds were heard within the shop? What was the purpose of the Judge's call? Why did the Judge become excited when he learned that Clifford had been ill? What method did the Judge use to force an interview with Clifford? What was Hepzibah's response? What was the Judge's real reason for wanting to see Clifford? Why does Hepzibah relent? What was the history of the chair in which the Judge sat?

Chapter XVI: How willingly did Hepzibah go in search of Clifford? What thoughts passed through her mind? What help did she seek? Tell of her consternation at not finding her brother. What ill omen appeared? Where did she imagine Clifford might have gone? Where did she find Clifford, and how did he act? Which one took the lead and did the planning?

Chapter XVII: Describe the interior life of a train coach. Tell the reactions of Clifford, and also of Hepzibah, to the new turn of affairs. What conversation did Clifford carry on? How did he relate what had happened to Judge Pyncheon? Was Clifford's state of mind natural under the circumstances? What uses of electricity did Clifford and his companion discuss? How did this argument fit Clifford's case? Did Clifford have grounds for his views? Why can Hepzibah pray now when she could not in the former instance? Is the chapter title appropriate?

Chapter XVIII: What appointments did the Judge have? To what other plans should he have attended? What charities were asked of him? What personal attention was he going to give himself? What important dinner was he missing? What was to occur at that dinner? Why did he not go?

Chapter XIX: Give the new description of the House of Seven Gables. What was Uncle Venner's morning custom? What did Uncle Venner find at the House of Seven Gables? Tell of his conversation with Holgrave. What exchange of news ensued between neighbor women? Tell of Ned Higgins' call at the shop. What remarks were made by passers-by? What response did the butcher get? Do you understand why the inner door was closed when little Ned looked in, and open when the butcher looked in? Tell of the return of the boy with the hurdy-gurdy. What gossip passed between Dixey and his friend? Tell about Phœbe's return. When Phœbe entered the garden, joy came to her and evil slipped away. What symbolizes this? How was Phœbe so mysteriously let into the house?

Chapter XX: Who let Phœbe into the house? What conversation ensued? What explanation of death did Holgrave give? How did he say that old Jaffrey Pyncheon came by his death? Why did the situation draw Holgrave and Phœbe so closely together? How did Holgrave tell Phœbe that he loved her? Did she return his love? What was the "Flower of Eden" which bloomed again?

Chapter XXI: Explain the circumstances of the murder thirty years ago. Tell the true character of Judge Pyncheon as a young man. How had he managed to cover this? How was Clifford's life now changed? What change came over Chanticleer and his family? What remarks did Clifford make about the future? How did the picture come to fall? What did it bring to light? Who was Holgrave? What place did Uncle Venner have in the new plans, and why? Tell of the departure. Do you like the concluding paragraph?

EXERCISES AND CREATIVE WORK

For Reports in Class
Salem in Witchcraft Days.
Witchcraft and Methods of Punishment.
Hypnotism.
Early Land Grants.
The House of the Seven Gables To-day.

Some Original Dialogues
The Neighbors Discuss the Flight of Clifford and Hepzibah.
Hepzibah and Phœbe Discuss the Latter's Visit to the House of the Seven Gables.
Hepzibah Talks with One of Her Customers in the Shop.
The Pyncheon Elm Talks Matters Over with Maule's Well.

A Letter
Phœbe Writes to Hepzibah Her Intention of Visiting the House of the Seven Gables.

A Newspaper Account
Extra! Extra! Judge Pyncheon Dies Mysteriously.

More or Less Imaginary
Hepzibah's "Periwigged Predecessor" Revisits His Shop.
Judge Pyncheon's Dinner Party.
Hepzibah Enters Business To-day.
An Incident in Holgrave's Past Life.
The Future of Holgrave and Phœbe.
Uncle Venner Visits His "Farm."
Clifford Takes a Journey To-day.

An Original Story
The Haunted House in Our Community.
The Witch's Curse.

For Exhibits
A miniature House of Seven Gables made from cardboard showing shape, position, gables, windows, etc., and not forgetting the arched window and Alice's posies. The artist's picture will help here. There are many ways of making a miniature elm for the front of the house.

A miniature garden could be made showing the flower beds, Maule's well, the hen coop, entrance to the house, the arbor, and even Chanticleer and his family, and a grimalkin slinking over the back fence.

A booklet of characters could be made showing original drawings giving the reader's conception of each character. A page of written description or characterization should accompany each drawing.

A collection of postcards showing The House of the Seven Gables as it stands today in Salem. This collection should include pictures of the Witch House, and other houses of Salem.

A collection of daguerreotypes.

EXTENSIVE READING REPORTS

The House of Seven Gables can be used as the key novel for the year's work, for reading in common. During the course of the year, several additional novels should be read by each individual member of the class. There are several methods of reporting on these novels.

Précis Method: In a précis, there should be included statements as to the time and place of the story, the characters involved, and the plot of the story—concisely given. As a conclusion, the opinion of the reader as to the worth of the book may be set forth, with reasons for the reaction.

Outline Method: The outline plan may be worked out topically, or in complete sentence form. The following order of topics is suggested:

I *The Time and Place of the Story:* Pertinent facts stated; interesting customs noted.

II *Characters Involved:* Types of people; reality of portrayal; reactions—normal or otherwise; dominant or subordinate to the plot; their merits, from readers' point of view.

III *The Plot of the Story:* Movement—rapid or slow; suspense or excitement; most exciting moment; material for dramatization; ability of author to conceal outcome.

IV *Classification as to Type:* Historical; adventure; mystery; psychological; love story; local color; character, etc. Also as to form: character, plot, setting.

V *Other Similar Novels*

VI *The Reader's Evaluation*

Book Review Method: Book reviews are found in many magazines, Sunday and daily papers. This form of report is probably the most effective, as well as efficient method. The review must be short, concise, conducive to interest in the book, and give pertinent information as to what the story contains. It is suggested that several book reviews be collected from various papers and studied for style of write-up. Then the style which appeals most to the student could be used for his individual reports.

A Card Filing System: Some students use a card file with 3″ x 5″ cards. For each book read, a card is filled out (using both sides) and filed with the teacher. The following form may be used.

Name of Reader   Date
    Title of Novel   Author
    Facts of Story: (Time, Setting, Characters.)
    Plot Movement: (Fast or Slow.)
    Classification: (Historical, Adventure, Mystery, etc.)
        Type as to Form: (Character Study, Local Color for Setting, or Predominately Plot.)
    Personal Evaluation: (To be recommended or not, and why. What the reader personally gained.)

The National Period (1800–1865)

James Fenimore Cooper
The Spy
The Pioneers
The Deerslayer
The Last of the Mohicans

Nathaniel Hawthorne
The Scarlet Letter
The Blithedale Romance
The Marble Faun

William Gilmore Simms
Martin Faber
Guy Rivers
The Yemassee

Herman Melville
Moby Dick

John Pendleton Kennedy
Horse-Shoe Robinson
Rob of the Bowl

Daniel Pierce Thompson
The Green Mountain Boys

Richard Henry Dana
Two Years Before the Mast

Harriet Beecher Stowe
Uncle Tom's Cabin

The Transition Period (1865–1900)

William Dean Howells
The Rise of Silas Lapham

Samuel Langhorne Clemens
(Mark Twain)
A Connecticut Yankee in King Arthur's Court
Personal Recollections of Joan of Arc
Pudd'nhead Wilson
The Adventures of Tom Sawyer
Huckleberry Finn

Louisa M. Alcott
Little Women

Frances Hodgson Burnett
The Secret Garden

Edward Eggleston
The Hoosier Schoolmaster

Francis Hopkinson Smith
Colonel Carter of Cartersville
Caleb West, Master Driver

Helen Hunt Jackson
Ramona

F. Marion Crawford
Saracinesca
Don Orsino
Via Crucis
In the Palace of the King

Edward Noyes Westcott
David Harum

Lew Wallace
Ben Hur

Henry James
Daisy Miller

S. Weir Mitchell
Hugh Wynne

Thomas Nelson Page
Red Rock
In Ole Virginia

Winston Churchill
Richard Carvel
The Crisis
Coniston

Paul Leicester Ford
Janice Meredith
The Honorable Peter Stirling

James Lane Allen
The Reign of Law
The Choir Invisible
A Kentucky Cardinal

Owen Wister
The Virginian

Mary Johnston
Prisoners of Hope
1492
To Have and to Hold

Richard Harding Davis
Captain Macklin
Soldiers of Fortune

Frank Norris
The Octopus
The Pit

Stephen Crane
The Red Badge of Courage

Robert W. Chambers
The Man They Hanged

Irving Bacheller
In the Days of Poor Richard
A Man for the Ages

THE TWENTIETH CENTURY (1900–   )

Bess Streeter Aldrich
Lantern in Her Hand
White Bird Flying

James B. Connolly
Steel Decks
Tide Rips

Gertrude Atherton
The Conqueror

Donn Byrne
Messer Marco Polo

James Boyd
Drums
Marching On

Willa Cather
O Pioneers!
My Antonia
Death Comes for the Archbishop
Shadows on the Rock
Song of the Lark

Myles Connolly
Mr. Blue

Louis Hemon
Maria Chapdelaine

Dorothy Canfield Fisher
The Brimming Cup
The Bent Twig

Zona Gale
Miss Lulu Bett
Friendship Village
Birth

Ellen Glasgow
Barren Ground
The Miller of Old Church
Romantic Comedians

Zane Grey
The Last of the Plainsmen
Riders of the Purple Sage

Jay William Hudson
Abbé Pierre
Abbé Pierre's People

James Oliver Curwood
Nomads of the North
The Country Beyond

William Stearns Davis
A Friend of Caesar
Beauty of the Purple
Whirlwind
Gilman of Redford

Doran Hurley
Herself
Monsignor

Richard A. Maher
Shepherd of the North

Emerson Hough
The Covered Wagon

Peter B. Kyne
Cappy Ricks

Sinclair Lewis
Main Street

Jack London
The Call of the Wild

Christopher Morley
Parnassus on Wheels
The Haunted Bookshop

Honoré Willsie Morrow
Forever Free
With Malice Toward None
We Must March

Anne Parrish
Perennial Bachelor

Edna Ferber
Fannie Herself
So Big
Cimarron

Isabel C. Clarke
By the Blue River
Prisoner's Years

Ethel Cook Eliot
Her Soul to Keep
Green Doors

Henrietta Skinner
Espiritu Santo

Elizabeth M. Roberts
Great Meadow

Francis Clement Kelley
Charred Wood

H. L. Barth
Flesh Is Not Life

Elizabeth Jordan
The Devil and the Deep Blue Sea
The Blue Circle

Sigrid Sweringen
As the Morning Rising

Hamlin Garland
Trail-Makers of the Middle Border

Kathleen Norris
Mother
Little Ships

James Stevens
Paul Bunyan

Booth Tarkington
The Magnificent Ambersons
Alice Adams
The Turmoil
Seventeen

Edith Wharton
Ethan Frome
New Year's Day
Spark

Stewart Edward White
The Blazed Trail
Gold
The Riverman

Mary Synon
Copper Country

Thornton Wilder
The Bridge of San Luis Rey

Anzia Yezierska
Hungry Hearts

Olive B. White
The King's Good Servant

Helen C. White
Not Built with Hands
A Watch in the Night

Frank A. Spearman
Man of Music Mountain
Robert Kimberley
Spanish Lover

Henry Harland
The Cardinal's Snuff-Box
Lady Paramount
My Friend Prospero

Lucille Papin Borden
Silver Trumpets Calling
White Hawthorne

LITERARY PERIODS

A SUMMARY AND REVIEW

A Cross Picture of the Literary Periods

The literature of America has been well represented in this volume of PROSE AND POETRY. Most of the great names and many of the great writings of our literature are to be found in its pages. All types of literature are represented. Each type has been developed historically through each of the literary periods and it now remains to give in brief form a cross picture which will present the various periods, types of literature, and authors in one unified impression of American literature as a whole.

The Colonial and Revolutionary Periods (Pages 1, 2)

What were the general characteristics of the Colonial Period which were unfavorable to a native literature? What were the leading types of writing? Why were these types important? What was the place of fiction in colonial writing? Why? What had been the purpose of the Puritans in coming to New England? How were their views and beliefs reflected in their literature? How does the literature of the Revolutionary Period differ from that of the Colonial Period? By illustration show how the crisis of the Revolution produced great writings.

Why is Franklin often called "the first American"? In what respects did he typify the times? What was his chief contribution to literature? Who was the "poet of the Revolution"? What was the character of most of the Revolutionary poetry? Name at least five great orators of the Revolutionary Period. Why were the short story and the novel so late in appearing? Were there any essays? What sort of prose writing other than patriotic was to be found in these early periods? What was the place of the theater?

The National Period (Page 2)

What was the effect of the new national consciousness on literature? What is meant by "romantic" literature? What types of literature are produced in a so-called "romantic" period? Why? What were the leading types of literature of the National Period? Where was the literary life of the period centered? Why?

Give an account of the rise of the short story. What was the place of biographical writing during the National Period? Can you account for this? Who were the New England poets? What were their characteristics? Show by examples how their lives were reflected in their writings. Who were the Southern poets? What was the difference between northern and southern poetry? Describe the emergence of the essay. Who were the great essayists of the period? What was the general characteristic of their writings? What was the place of oratory? Why have Lincoln's speeches lived as literature? By specific examples, show how a national crisis always produces great oratory. What was the place of the drama in the National Period? Describe the rise of the novel. Name at least four great novelists, giving the characteristics of each.

In what two types of literature did Irving take a leading place? In what two fields did Hawthorne excel? Name an author who took a leading place in the writing of both poetry and the short story. Name three authors who were both essayists and poets.

The Transition Period (Page 3)

Why is this period called the "transition" period? What changes took place in commercial and industrial fields? What were the advances in national area and population? What was the effect of the western movement on literature? Why did Southern literature now appear? What is meant by "local color" writing? How does regional literature contribute to an understanding of the various sections of the country? Give examples. What is meant by "realism" in literature? What kind of literature is the result of a realistic attitude?

What type of literature had unparalleled development in this period? Who was the first writer of the "local color" short story? By giving definite illustrations, show how his stories differ from those of Hawthorne and Poe. What southern names were important in the short story field? What eastern names? Who were some of the writers who further developed the technique and style of the short story? What was the place of biography in transition literature? Who was the outstanding poet of the period? How do his poems differ from those of the New England poets? Which poets wrote of western scenes? What was the place of the essay? Of the oration? Give an account of the increased writing in the field of the drama. Who were the leading playwrights? What was the importance of the novel?

Who was the most typically American figure of the period? In how many types of literature did he take a leading place? Name at least two titles illustrating each type.

The Twentieth Century (Page 4)

Why has the literature of the twentieth century been predominantly realistic? What are some of the outstanding characteristics of contemporary writing? Account for the present-day interest in world literature. Who was the leading short story writer of the early years of the century? What is meant by the "journalistic" story? Name at least ten contemporary short story writers. Discuss the "new biography." Give causes of the poetry revival. By example, show how present-day poetry differs from that of the National Period. Why has the essay taken such an important place in literature? What are some of the different types of the modern essay? Name at least two writers of each type. What was the effect of the World War on oratory? Discuss the radio as a factor in producing oratory. Discuss the importance of the drama in the present century. Who are some of the leading playwrights? What is the place of the novel?

INDEX